THE TECHNOLOGY OF WINE MAKING
FOURTH EDITION

THE TECHNOLOGY OF WINE MAKING

FOURTH EDITION

M.A. Amerine, Ph.D.
H.W. Berg, M.S.

Professors of Enology Emeritus
and Enologists Emeritus

R.E. Kunkee, Ph.D.

Professor of Enology, and Biochemist

C.S. Ough, M.S., D.Sc.

Professor of Enology, and Enologist

V.L. Singleton, Ph.D.
A.D. Webb, Ph.D.

Professors of Enology, and Chemists

Agricultural Experiment Station
University of California
Davis, California

AVI PUBLISHING COMPANY, INC.
Westport, Connecticut

Library of Congress Cataloging in Publication Data

Amerine, Maynard Andrew, 1911–
    The technology of wine making.

    Includes bibliographies and index.
    1. Wine and wine making. I. Berg, Harold W., joint
author. II. Title.
TP548.A47 1980   663'.2   79-15483
ISBN 0-87055-333-X

Printed in the United States of America by Eastern Graphics, Inc.

Preface to the Fourth Edition

Technological developments in the wine industry have continued unabated since 1971. Thus, much new material is available. The purpose of this edition has been three-fold: (1) to bring the technological development up-to-date, (2) to invite some of our colleagues to help us, and (3) to remove extraneous material and thus reduce the size as much as possible. We hope readers will let us know of our errors of judgement and of omission.

We are especially grateful to Mr. James Seff for answers to difficult legal questions and to Mr. Werner Allmendinger and Mr. James Crawford for statistical data, all of the Wine Institute.

M.A. AMERINE
H.W. BERG
R.E. KUNKEE
C.S. OUGH
V.L. SINGLETON
A.D. WEBB

August 1979

Preface to the Third Edition

We have taken the opportunity of correcting a number of errors in the second edition and also of eliminating some material and adding new. Because of the new classification of yeasts, Chapter 5 has been extensively revised. Recent changes in state and federal regulations required major alterations in Chapter 20.

We are indebted to Mr. Charles Crawford and Mr. Paul Frei of the California wine industry for their advice on the text. Mr. W. Allmendinger and Mr. James Seff of the Wine Institute have also been most generous in supplying statistical and legal information.

M.A. AMERINE
H.W. BERG

September 1, 1971

Preface to the Second Edition

Research in enology has been extensive in many countries since the first edition. This has been especially true in studies on the composition of grapes and wines, wine stability, yeasts and bacteria, and sparkling wines. We have taken advantage of the need of a new edition to make extensive changes in the text on these subjects. In Chapter 6, for example, more than 100 new references have been added. We have also minutely examined the whole book to correct errors, to reflect the latest information and to clarify the meaning.

Professor Cruess asked to be relieved of formal responsibility in this revision. Many parts of the text, however, reflect his extensive research and opinions so it is entirely proper that his authorship be continued.

We are grateful to Professor Ralph E. Kunkee who has read and corrected portions of the revised text. We also thank the Wine Institute, and especially Mr. J.R. Lazarus and Mr. W. Allmendinger for their assistance in supplying legal and statistical information. The errors that remain are the responsibility of the authors. We would be grateful to know of those found by our readers.

M.A. AMERINE
H.W. BERG
W.V. CRUESS

November 1, 1966

Preface to the First Edition

Pasteur's *Études sur le Vin* was first published in 1866.[1] The revolution in the fermentation industries that began with Pasteur over a hundred years ago continues still. The essence of this revolution was the application of scientific principles to the fermentation industries. Pasteur, himself a chemist, utilized his knowledge of chemistry. He became a microbiologist. His studies on heat are those of a chemical engineer. In the evaluation of his results by groups of tasters he approached recent techniques for the sensory evaluation of foods.

Today, no one can deny that fermentation industries, of which wine making is a part, have become to a high degree scientific. Applications of nearly all of the modern physical and biological scientific disciplines may be found in them and the results (in antibiotic production, for example) are ample proof of the value of the scientific approach.

However, we cannot explain wine making in a completely scientific manner. Neither the chemical composition of the grape nor of the wine is fully known. The influence of the biological and physical processes during fermentation and aging on each of these constituents has not been clearly elucidated. Finally, the subjective nature of the evaluation of wine makes the interpretation of these extremely complex interrelationships very difficult. Thus, there remains in wine making much that is empirical, for which we have, as yet, no complete explanation.

In this edition, we have attempted to apply scientific principles insofar as possible. We have included descriptive material of regions, varieties, and processes where it seems to us that these influence the quali-

---

[1] Actually Pasteur began his studies on wine in September, 1858, and the results finally incorporated in his text were largely published as scientific papers prior to 1866.

ty of the product, even though we are unable to delineate exactly the exact mechanism of their influence.

It may be pertinent here to point out that whereas processing is paramount for one type of wine—for example, California sherry—variety may be the critical factor for another—New York Delaware.

This is not a text in European wine making. However, nearly three-fourths of the world's wine is produced in that area and their experience can be of use to us. We hasten to add that this does not mean that California or American wines—the types primarily discussed—should be slavish imitations of European types. Both of the authors have previously noted that a new and better nomenclature for American wines, without European antecedents, would be of great utility. However, with some exceptions, which we shall note, there has been too little commercial interest in new type names. Some suggestions for others will be made in the text.

In many respects, this is the third edition of *The Principles and Practices of Wine Making* by W.V. Cruess which was published in 1947. However, we have concluded that the text has been changed so much that it would be better to give it a new title. This is still the principles and practices because we believe principles should and must precede practice.

We have received help from many of our colleagues within the University and the industry. We express here our thanks to all of them. Especially, thanks are due to Mr. Theodore Carl who prepared certain sections on wine making in Eastern United States and Canada, and to Professors H.W. Berg, J.F. Guymon, J.L. Ingraham, G.L. Marsh, H.J. Pfaff, R.H. Vaughn, and A.D. Webb of the College of Agriculture, and to our colleagues in the California and Mexican wine industry, R.C. Auerbach, J. H. Fessler, M. Ibarra, M. Nightingale, F.J. Pilone, and A. Pirrone.

M.A. AMERINE
W.V. CRUESS

September 1, 1960

Contents

1

Wines and Wine Regions of the World

Wine has been a part of the diet of man since he settled in the Tigris-Euphrates basin several thousand years before our era. From these regions the vine, *Vitis vinifera*, was carried to all the Mediterranean countries. According to Vogt (1977) grape culture for wine production was known to the Assyrians and Egyptians by 3500 B.C. and to the Greeks by about 1400 B.C. Greek traders brought grapes to Marseilles by 600 B.C. and grape culture had spread far down the Rhine by 200 A.D. and reached its widest extension in Europe by the 15th century.

Wine represented a safe and healthful beverage. It also provided calories and vitamins. At a time when food was not the best, wine was an important food adjunct. During periods when life was often strenuous it offered relaxation and surcease from pain. Wine thus became the normal table beverage of the Mediterranean countries, except for those where religion forbade its use. Even nonproducing countries, such as England, the Benelux and Scandinavian countries, imported large amounts of wine. Wherever Europeans have settled they have attemped the culture of the vine, or, failing this, they have imported wines for their needs.

History contains many references to the importance of wine, from Homer to Hemingway. The first miracle of the New Testament, Cana, has to do with wine. Roman historians and poets have left us eloquent testimony in praise of wine. The vine was cultivated and wines made throughout Europe during the post-Roman and pre-modern period. For general information on wines, see Allen (1961), Amerine and Singleton (1977), Debuigne (1976), Hyams (1965), Jeffs (1971), Lichine (1979), Marrison (1973), Schoonmaker (1973), and Younger (1966).

PRINCIPAL WINE REGIONS

Species of *Vitis*, the grape vine, are widely distributed throughout the world. The fruit of most of these species is unsuited to the production of wine because of deficiencies in composition or production or possibly to an undesirable flavor. The most important species, *Vitis vinifera*, is

1

believed to have been brought by man from southern Russia to Asia Minor. From there Phoenicians, Greeks, and later, Romans spread its culture. *V. vinifera* also followed European explorers to the temperate zones of the New World, South Africa, and Australia. Acreage and wine production are given in Table 1.1.

Europe is the most important wine-producing area with more than 70% of the acreage and wine production. If the Mediterranean regions of Africa are added the percentages are higher. Nearly all of the European production is from *V. vinifera*. Very little wine is now made from "direct producers," hybrids of *V. vinifera* and of a species of *Vitis* resistant to downy or powdery mildew, black rot, or phylloxera.

Regions where species other than *V. vinifera* are used extensively for wine making are Canada, Eastern United States and Brazil. Attempts to grow *V. vinifera* in Eastern United States have been made from Colonial times to the present. No extensive commercial success has resulted from these, although with better rootstocks more favorable results have been obtained. The warm humid growing period of this region (and of Brazil also) favors cryptogamic diseases, insect pests, and probably virus infection. Species other than *V. vinifera* have been domesticated for wine making and for table purposes. These include *V. labrusca, V. rotundifolia*, related species, and hybrids of these with each other. More recently, the hybrids of these with *V. vinifera*, the "direct producers" mentioned above, have also been planted.

Romanticists often claim that European wines are superior because the vineyards have low yields and the wineries use century-old methods. In fact, European vineyardists have been surprisingly fast in improving production and in changing production methods. At Schloss Johannisberg, according to Alleweldt (1965) from 1900 to 1927 production averaged only 146 gal. per acre! By the use of high-yielding clones this had been increased to 498 gal. per acre in 1964 without decreasing quality. Similar results have been obtained in Alsace. Replantings after the phylloxera invasion of 1870-1900 resulted in extensive changes in varieties. In recent years, many new varieties have been commercially planted throughout Europe. New equipment and processes are now widely employed.

France[1]

Climate is one of the critical factors influencing the cultivation of the

---

[1]In the discussion of regions which follows, no attempt has been made to give a comprehensive listing of all the wine types. Our objective has been rather to describe briefly the wine of the region and to evaluate the factors which contribute to its quality. For a more complete discussion of French regions see Amerine and Singleton (1977), Dion (1959), Jeffs (1971), Lichine (1977), Pestel (1959), Poulain and Jacquelin (1960), Ray (1976), Roger (1960), Schoonmaker and Marvel (1934), Shand (1960), Simon (1957), Thudichum and Dupré (1872), and Wildman (1972).

TABLE 1.1. WORLD ACREAGE, WINE PRODUCTION, AND PER CAPITA CONSUMPTION 1956, 1969 AND 1977

Country	Vineyards (Thousand Acres)			Production (Thousand Gallons)			Consumption (Gallons per Capita)		
	1956	1969	1977	1956	1969	1977	1956	1969	1977
Europe									
Albania	8.3[1]	30.2[1]	29.7	924[1]	810[5]	4,491[1]	—	—	—
Australia	85.5	112.5	123.6	10,306	59,803	68,528	3.7	8.8	9.5
Bulgaria	351.1	481.8	454.7	30,009[2]	125,645	75,397	1.9	5.8	5.3
Czechoslovakia	44.1[3]	78.9	103.8	10,824[1]	19,706	40,367	—	2.4	3.2[1]
France	3,500.0	3,220.9	3,125.9	1,331,923	1,314,720	1,382,850	38.3	29.6	26.7
Germany	164.9	205.0	249.6	24,517	157,010	274,457	2.4	4.2	6.2
Greece	552.0	530.0[5]	481.9	108,868	145,200[1]	136,925	12.4	7.4	10.5
Hungary	465.1	560.2	474.4	62,503	152,143	152,432	—	9.9	9.3
Italy	4,080.0	3,715.5	3,452.1	1,680,413	1,886,808	1,692,654	30.4	29.3	26.3[9]
Luxembourg	3.0	2.9	2.5	1,663	3,221	4,095	8.1	8.5	11.7
Malta	3.3[3]	2.9[1]	2.5	1,055[5]	528[1]	793[1]	—	—	—
Portugal	748.1	835.6	892.1	291,328	218,364	180,911	33.0	21.5	26.2
Rumania	569.9	819.1	741.3[9]	72,598	164,588	171,717[1]	4.1	6.1	7.9[1,9]
Spain	3,869.1	3,877.3	4,223.1	558,200	664,667	604,972	17.7	18.3	17.2
Switzerland	27.6	29.0	34.6	9,898	19,775	34,343	9.8	11.0	11.5
U.S.S.R.	1,200.0	2,597.0	3,163.0	115,944	650,865	845,376	—	1.8[7]	3.5[9]
Yugoslavia	655.9	651.3	607.9	84,954	186,375	166,354	7.4	6.9	7.6[9]
South America									
Argentina	536.1	706.0	877.2	351,666[2]	472,986	655,483	20.0	23.1	23.4
Bolivia	4.5[1]	4.6[6]	7.4	158[1]	158[1]	528[1]	—	—	—
Brazil	121.1	174.7	168.0	36,336[2]	44,230	69,744	—	0.5	0.7
Chile	264.5	274.0[5]	286.6	104,369	106,221	161,837	15.9	13.3	13.8
Peru	16.1[1]	20.0[6]	34.6	2,540	6,602[7]	2,113[1]	—	0.4[7]	0.3[9]
Uruguay	44.7	44.9[6]	54.4	23,074	22,090[1]	26,682	—	6.9[6]	6.6[9]
Africa									
Algeria	951.6	734.1	568.4[1]	491,855	230,610	126,806[1]	—	0.3	0.1
Egypt	19.2[1]	26.1[5]	44.5[1]	770[5]	1,347[8]	1,849[1]	—	—	—
Morocco	155.0	142.8	135.9	55,777	18,658	21,134	—	0.4	0.5
South Africa	153.6	238.0	271.8	85,511	129,418	127,388	4.5	2.7	2.4
Tunisia	113.5	110.5[5]	116.1[1]	33,542	13,562	26,418	—	—	1.1

TABLE 1.1 (Continued)

Country	Vineyards (Thousand Acres)			Production (Thousand Gallons)			Consumption (Gallons per Capita)		
	1956	1969	1977	1956	1969	1977	1956	1969	1977
North America									
Canada	20.8	20.2[1]	22.2	6,600[1]	11,383[8]	12,152[9]	0.5	0.7	1.9
Mexico	23.7[4]	40.8	111.2	1,584[1]	3,014[7]	3,170	—	0.1	0.1
United States	564.0[1]	463.9[5]	733.9[1]	153,648	224,400[1]	400,074	0.9	1.0	1.8[9]
Asia									
Afghanistan	—	—	271.8[1]	—	—	—	—	—	—
China	71.9[1]	92.6	74.1[1]	5,280[1]	30,571	29,060[9]	—	—	—
Cyprus	—	—	111.2[1]	—	—	—	—	3.0[8]	1.9[9]
India	180.0[1]	180.0[1]	215.0[1]	92[1]	95[1]	106[1]	—	—	—
Iran	—	—	395.4[1]	—	—	—	—	—	—
Iraq	24.4	22.1	47.0[1]	2,133			—	—	—
Israel	17.6[4]	55.9	22.2[1]	6,376	10,502	11,360[1,9]	1.0	1.1	1.0[9]
Japan	38.9	43.7[6]	74.1	633[1]	4,467	4,729[9]	0.1	0.1	0.1
Jordan	53.3	43.4[5]	17.3[1]	760	388[1]	396[1]	—	—	—
Lebanon	172.8[1]	206.4	42.0[1]	528[1]	1,003[1]	1,057[1]	—	0.7	—
Syria			197.7[1]		181[8]	185[1]	—	0.1	—
Turkey	1,747.5	2,011.2	1,897.8[9]	5,934	13,620	8,084	0.1	0.4	0.1
Oceania									
Australia	131.1	139.0	160.6	27,559	63,271	95,897[9]	1.3	2.2	3.0[9]
New Zealand	1.0[1]	2.5[5]	7.4	610	3,564[8]	9,194	—	1.0	2.3[9]
Total	21,755.3	23,547.5	25,276.8	5,793,262	7,182,569	7,635,383			

Source: Bulletin Office international vin. *31* (331), 37-44; (332), 37-62; (333), 10-49; *32* (337), 6-52; (348), 13-64; 349, 23-65; *34* (359), 49-83; *43* (477), 1190-97; *51* (573), 1958, 1959, 1960, 1961, 1970, 1978. La Journée Vinicole *33* (9725), 4, 6; (9726), 2, 4. 1959.

[1] Estimated.
[2] Includes wine for distilling.
[3] 1954.
[4] Total musts, only part fermented to wine.
[5] 1965.
[6] 1966.
[7] 1967.
[8] 1968.
[9] 1976.

vine. The heat summations of various regions of western Europe and California are given in Table 2.12, Chap. 2. See also Winkler *et al.* (1974).

The north of France is too cold for the vine. Even early-ripening varieties, such as Pinot noir, do not ripen sufficiently every year in Burgundy, for example, and sugar must often be added to make up the deficiency.

Soil temperature is not only a function of surface temperature but of soil drainage. This, in turn, depends partially on soil composition and texture. The successful culture of the vine on well-drained slopes in Alsace, Burgundy, and Champagne is partially related to soil temperature.

The nice adaptation of varieties to climatic and soil conditions is the second factor with a demonstrable influence on the quality of French wines. In some regions, Burgundy and Champagne, it is an early-ripening variety, such as Pinot noir, which is important. In others a *mélange* of varieties is necessary in order to secure the best balanced musts from year to year. Châteauneuf-du-Pape and Bordeaux (red and white) are examples of this. An excellent survey of the varieties used in the various regions of France is that of Galet (1957-1964). The standard treatise on French enology is Ribéreau-Gayon *et al.* (1977-1978).

Finally, the fermentation procedure, especially the low-temperature fermentation of white musts, and the method of aging influence quality. The aging of many Bordeaux red wines in new oak casks gives them a distinct character.

Government regulation of regional wine types, commonly known as *appellations contrôlées*, is of increasing importance to the French wine industry. As applied to quality wines they are administered by the Institut National des Appellations d'Origine des Vins et Eaux-de-Vie (1952). These regulations delimit the region, specify the varieties which may be employed, and limit the minimum percentage of alcohol and the maximum yield per hectare. For a discussion of these French laws and their interpretation see Capus in Lafforgue (1947). The history and philosophy of protected place names on French wines were reviewed by Quittanson (1965). Sensory examination of such wines is provided for. Quittanson makes the point that the right to a noble name carries obligations with respect to quality. For a description of the social and economic importance of wine *appellations d'origine* to France see Pestel (1959). A quality factor which we believe is particularly important in certain regions is that of the wine maker as an artist. This has been expressed by Pestel (1959) as follows:

Mais, et ceci est encore très particulier, dans les régions de vins fins le vigneron se transforme en artiste ... Esprit d'observation, patience, courage, discipline, sens artistique, ce ne sont pas des qualités à dédaigner chez les hommes, et la profession qui les fait naître ou les développe doit être considérée comme bien utile pour le pays tout entier.

Even given fine varieties and perfect soil and climate, the slovenly workman may make an ordinary rather than a great wine. The artist handles the wine in such a way as to develop and emphasize its individuality. If the treatment destroys the nuances of quality which the wine might have achieved, it loses quality. The artist may use modern tools but he has a clear picture in his mind of the kind of wine which he wishes to produce and then so handles the wine as to obtain the desired quality and character.

Burgundy.—The *vins de Bourgogne* have been famous for centuries. The region is approximately 35 miles long on a slope generally facing east and southeast, called the Côte d'Or. A smaller region to the northwest is called Chablis. South from the Côte d'Or is a third region which is popularly called Burgundy. Its wines are commonly sold as Beaujolais, Mâconnais, or Chalonnais. The soil is calcareous in the Côte d'Or, clay in Chablis, and granitic in the southern Burgundy regions.

Chablis is a greatly imitated name throughout the world. About 600 ha (1000 acres) are planted in the best locations. The variety is Chardon-

Courtesy of Institut National des Appellations d'Origine des Vins et Eaux-de-Vie

FIG. 1.1.   VINEYARD IN BEAUJOLAIS

nay. The wine is tart; the acidity usually exceeds 0.86% (as tartaric) often with a pH of no more than 3.1. It is light yellow in color. The alcohol content is seldom over 11% (by volume). Variety, climate, exposure and soil conditions have some importance to their quality, but the cool climate is critical. Sugar is added to the must in some years.

In the Côte d'Or both red and white wines are produced. For the whites the variety is Chardonnay but here the alcohol content is higher, up to 13% (or more) in the warm years, the acidity a little lower, the pH higher, the color more golden, and the flavor more pronounced. Their greatest whites are Montrachet, Puligny-Montrachet, Chassagne-Montrachet, Corton-Charlemagne, and Meursault.

The reds are mainly from Pinot noir. The northern, Côte de Nuits, wines are usually more flavorful and distinctive than the southern, Côte de Beaune, wines but with many exceptions. Famous vineyards in the former region are Chambertin, Clos de Vougeot, Eschézaux, Musigny, Nuits-Saint-Georges, Richebourg, etc., and in the latter Corton, Pommard, Volnay, Beaune, etc. Exposure, soil conditions and temperature differences explain some of the variations in character and quality. Low lying cooler areas produce lesser quality wines. Michel (1953) considers the most important problems in producing high quality Burgundy to be

Courtesy of Institut National des Appellations d'Origine
des Vins et Eaux-de-Vie

FIG. 1.2. PARTIAL CRUSHING OF THE GRAPES IN A BEAUJOLAIS VINEYARD

control of maturity and temperature of fermentation. He recommends frequent field sampling and different maturity standards for each variety and location to ensure proper harvesting. Too rapid a fermentation is the most important negative quality factor. The fermentation temperature should be near 25°C (77°F) for maximum quality. Harvesting during the coolest periods of the day and cooling or warming the musts, if necessary, are recommended.

A malo-lactic fermentation is employed to reduce excessive acidity. Occasionally a bottled wine may become gassy due to a delayed malo-lactic fermentation. Differences in production methods can be important. The variety, however, appears to be the most critical factor. Burgundy is first of all Pinot noir or Chardonnay. Where and when the temperature is favorable and the production practices carefully controlled, they produce great wines. Some of the differences in flavor are probably due to different clones. Aligoté and Gamay are grown but produce wines of less quality. Owing to the malo-lactic fermentation, the pH varies from 3.3 to 3.5 with titratable acidities usually about 0.65% (as tartaric).

In the southern Burgundy region, Pouilly-Fuissé is a famous white wine (from Chardonnay). Brouilly, Fleurie and Moulin-à-Vent are well-known reds (mainly from Gamay), sold as Beaujolais (Fig. 1.1 and 1.2). Throughout the region the seasonal influence is important. In many years, the grapes do not ripen sufficiently to produce a balanced wine and sugar is added. Recent years of high quality for reds include 1967, 1969, 1970, 1971 and 1975.[2] (The whites of 1972 and 1974 are also usually good.)

The custom of aging Burgundy 2 to 3 years before bottling in relatively small casks (60 to 300 gal.) in cool cellars may also be a factor in their character. Aeration is undesirable and filtration is avoided, if possible. White Burgundies age rapidly and should normally not be kept more than 4 or 5 years after bottling. Red Burgundies also age relatively rapidly and most should be drunk within 10 years. Beaujolais and other southern Burgundy wines are normally drunk within 2 years. Normally, shippers do not own the vineyards from which they sell wine. A few estate-bottled wines are shipped. The reputation and distinctiveness of these famous small vineyards are maintained by strict governmental controls and partially because their fame makes them profitable and the owners wish to maintain this profit by producing quality wines.

The best technical discussion of wines of Burgundy is to be found in Ferré's (1958) treatise. Arlott and Fielden (1976), Gadille (1967), Lichine (1979), Poupon and Forgeot (1972), Rodier (1948), and Yoxall (1970) are descriptive. Orizet (1959) on Beaujolais is authoritative.

----

[2]This does not mean that all wines of other years are inferior. Often very good wines may be made in "off" years by careful producers. This applies to other regions as well. Not all wines of "fine" vintage years are superior.

Bordeaux.—The region is large, producing both white and red wines. It lies along the Garonne, Dordogne, and Gironde rivers east and west of Bordeaux. Exposure and soil conditions are of relatively small importance. Grapes are grown on sandy, gravelly, loam, and clay soils and a calcareous subsoil is common. The exposure is generally to the northeast in the Médoc and to the southwest in St. Émilion, but this is unimportant.

The important quality factors are the climate, the mixtures of grapes, the method of aging, and, in the case of Sauternes, the mold *Botrytis cinerea*. Large vineyards, commonly called *"châteaux,"* have been preserved more or less intact for many centuries through the English law of inheritance. More than a hundred years ago, some of the better vineyards of the Médoc were officially classified into a series of five "growths" by the Bordeaux wine trade on the basis of price; see Cocks and Feret (1969) and Roger (1956). The wines of St. Émilion and Sauternes have also been officially classified. The owners of classified vineyards are, of course, proud of their wine and jealous in protecting its reputation. This classification and its emphasis on quality has had a salutary influence on maintaining the quality of all wines of the region. However, the 1855 classification of the Médoc is now often misleading as to relative quality of different *châteaux* and the *appellation d'origine* is for the commune *not* for the château.

The large export wine trade has also been an important factor in developing quality. Finally, bottling at the vineyard has been practiced at Bordeaux for more than a century. Château-bottling undoubtedly stimulated consumer interest. The château should not château-bottle wine of inferior years, but not all châteaux apply this high standard at present. The alcohol and color content of recent Bordeaux red wines is higher than earlier in the century while the acetic and malic acid contents are lower.

The most important vineyards producing red wines are in the Médoc, Graves, St. Émilion, and Pomerol, but large amounts entitled to the appellation Bordeaux are produced in adjacent regions. The varieties used vary. Cabernet Sauvignon is generally agreed to be the finest variety for red wines in the Médoc but its wines age slowly and varieties of similar flavors—Malbec, Cabernet franc, Carménère, Merlot, and Petit Verdot—are also planted. In St. Émilion and Pomerol, Merlot and Cabernet franc predominate.

This mixture of varieties helps to balance the acidity of the wine. The acidity of Cabernet Sauvignon is mainly tartaric. Malic acid predominates in Malbec. In warm years, malic acid tends to respire during ripening so Malbec musts are too low in acidity for a balanced wine. Little tartaric acid respires during ripening, thus Cabernet Sauvignon musts tend to maintain their acidity. A mixture of the two varieties thus gives a better balance. In cool years both the Malbec and Cabernet Sauvignon maintain their acidity but the wine maker depends on the malo-lactic fermentation (p. 291) to reduce the acidity of the wine. This fermentation is seldom employed to excess in Bordeaux.

The fermentation procedure is not unusual, although since 1950 there has been a tendency to remove the wine from the skins after only 4 to 6 days instead of 10 to 21. This shorter period produces wines of lower tannin and earlier maturity. Whether it gives wines of optimum keeping quality is doubtful.

The aging of Bordeaux red wines in oak barrels (about 60 gal.) for 1 or 3 years is considered to be an important factor in their character, particularly where new cooperage is employed. Aging in the bottle is also necessary for the finest red wines. The best wines may improve in quality in the bottle for 10 to 30 or more years.[3]

Climate has, finally, an overall control over the quality of the wines. In the colder years, the alcohol content is low and the wines tend to be thin and hard. In warmer years (1961, 1962, 1964, 1966, 1967, 1970, 1971, 1975 and 1976), the alcohol content is higher and the wines softer. The wine maker who gambles with the weather may harvest late and produce a good wine in a cold year while his neighbors are producing only ordinary wine. He may also be unfortunate and produce a poor wine from rain-damaged, moldy fruit. Some vineyards were harvested too late in 1964.

There are thousands of named vineyards producing red wines in the Bordeaux region and hundreds of them bottle their wine. It would be invidious to mention only a few. Generally, the wines of the classed growths are best, but with the increasing application of technology other vineyards can be expected to produce excellent wines. Bordeaux shippers blend district wines of communes (Pauillac, St. Julien, St. Estèphe) or of larger regions (Médoc, St. Émilion, Graves) and even of the whole region (Bordeaux) which can be good, or, at times, disappointing.

Dry or nearly dry white wines are produced in Graves and elsewhere; sweet white wines are produced in Sauternes and in neighboring regions. The white wines of Graves are produced from about ¾ Sauvignon blanc and ¼ Sémillon; the percentage varies among vineyards. The wines are aged 2 or 3 years in barrels before bottling. The wines are sometimes high in sulfur dioxide to the extent of reducing quality.

---

[3]Bottles of the same wine vary in their rate of aging depending on the level-of-fill of the bottle, the porosity of the cork, etc. When a case of wine has reached its normal maturity, some bottles in the case may be "over-the-hill" while others may still have years of goodness remaining. Wines stored under very even and low temperature conditions may last many years longer than wines of the same vintage which have been stored in cellars with variable or warm temperatures. Excessive vibration of the cellar will also hasten the rate of aging.

Sauternes has been a widely imitated wine. The imitations usually bear little resemblance to the Bordeaux product, since Sauternes is a difficult wine to produce. The varietal complement is about ⅔ Sémillon and ⅓ Sauvignon blanc. Little Muscadelle remains. As the Sémillon variety ripens it is attacked during periods of warm humid weather by the mold *Botrytis cinerea*. When conditions are unfavorable the attack is slow and covers only a few berries of each cluster. The effect of the mold is to loosen the skin so that moisture loss from the berry occurs rapidly. As the berry shrivels its sugar content increases proportionately. The botrytised fruit cannot be left on the vine indefinitely lest undesirable molds invade the fruit which is very susceptible to such attack. It is necessary, therefore, to harvest the botrytised berries by cutting them out from the cluster. If conditions are favorable more berries will become infected and further pickings are necessary. Depending on the rate of infection and drying and the wishes of the wine maker as to sugar content, two or more pickings are made.

The fermentation is slow, because of the high sugar content and because of the use of sulfur dioxide. The alcohol content may reach 14-15%. The finished wine is aged 2 to 4 years in barrels. Bottled wines may

Courtesy of Institut National des Appellations d'Origine des Vins et Eaux-de-Vie

FIG. 1.3. DELIVERY OF BOTRYTISED GRAPES AT CHÂTEAU D'YQUEM

improve in quality for many years. They contain 5 to 15% sugar. Obviously, the *Botrytis* attack raised the initial sugar content of the fruit to 30-40% sugar. Since the volume has been reduced proportionately the cost of production is high.

The *Botrytis* attack not only increases the sugar content but it reduces the skin-to-volume relationship so that there is an increase in aroma (Fig. 1.3 and 1.4). Furthermore, the *Botrytis* itself contributes a distinct aroma to the wine. The reduction in volume would increase the acidity unduly were it not that the mold preferentially utilizes acids in its metabolism. The increase in acidity is never so great as the increase in sugar. Glycerol is a by-product of the mold's metabolism but how important this is to the quality of wine is not known.

Courtesy of Institut National des Appellations d'Origine des Vins et Eaux-de-Vie

FIG. 1.4. CRUSHING OF BOTRYTISED GRAPES DIRECTLY INTO THE PRESS AT CHÂTEAU D'YQUEM

Obviously, climate is important to the quality of Sauternes wines. Château-bottling is practiced here and the vineyards of the region have been classified (Fig. 1.5). While Sauternes is the best known district, the appellation, Barsac, is a part of the general region of Sauternes.

Recent technical books on Bordeaux wines are those of Lafforgue (1947) and Peynaud (1971). See also Kressmann (1968), Laborde (1907), Penning-Rowsell (1973), Ribéreau-Gayon *et al.* (1977–1978), and Yoxall (1970).

Courtesy of Institut National des Appellations d'Origine
des Vins et Eaux-de-Vie

FIG. 1.5. CHÂTEAU LAFAURIE-PEYRAGUEY, SAUTERNES

Showing a typical Bordeaux Château in the midst of its vines. Note the nearly flat country.

Champagne.—There is no wine better known than Champagne—the sparkling wine from the region of the same name. The main quality factors are climate, soil, varietal components, pressing procedure, temperature of fermentation, blending, the bottle fermentation, aging, and the standards of the producers.

The soil is a modified chalk. Drainage is good and this is important in a cold region. Generally, the vineyards are on the slopes (Fig. 1.6) which also helps drainage and soil temperature (and probably protection from frosts). Vineyards extend into the plain if the proper chalk soil is present.

The climate is also important. In the coolest years, the grapes do not ripen sufficiently to produce a well-balanced base for a sparkling wine. This is the basic reason for nonvintage Champagne. It is simply low-alcohol, high-acid wine of a cold year to which wines of higher alcohol and lower acidity from a warmer year are added to secure a better balance. Well-balanced wines of the warmer years are also used for vintage Champagnes. Vintage Champagne may contain a small percentage of wines of a year other than that stated on the label.

Courtesy of Collection C.I.V.C.

FIG. 1.6. AERIAL VIEW OF CHAMPAGNE VINEYARDS AT BOUZY

The cold climate has also influenced the varieties planted. Normally, only white grapes are employed for making white wines. However, the Chardonnay does not ripen as well as is desired and the earlier-ripening red Pinot noir is used. Many clonal selections of Pinot noir are planted (Chappaz 1951). About ⅔ of the grapes are Pinot noir and ⅓ Chardonnay. Great care is needed in harvesting the Pinot noir so that all diseased fruit is removed, usually done by hand at the vineyard (Fig. 1.7). Rotten fruit has colored juice which is undesirable since the objective is to produce a white wine.

Usually, crushing is not done in order to reduce the time the juice is in contact with the skins. The whole fruit is placed in large, shallow, flat presses and pressed directly. Several pressings are made, of which the earlier ones are the best. Recently, various types of modern presses have been used. The fermentation is usually made at a temperature below

Courtesy of Collection C.I.V.C.

FIG. 1.7. CUTTING OUT MOLDY BERRIES OF PINOT NOIR FOR CHAMPAGNE MAKING

20°C (68°F). According to Chappaz (1951) a better quality in respect to bouquet is obtained at a fermentation temperature slightly below 15.7°C (60°F); low-temperature acclimatized yeasts are used. The musts are usually settled before fermentation.

Wines of Pinot noir and Chardonnay after two rackings and close filtration are blended in the spring. The Chardonnay adds tartness and finesse. Wines of various vineyards are also blended to secure the desired balance in composition and flavor. A clean, fresh wine of about 10.5-11% alcohol is required. Different firms secure a slightly different character to their wine by appropriate blending.

The secondary fermentation is always made in bottles. The fermentation is preferably made at a relatively low temperature, 10°-15°C (50° to 59°F).

Disgorging is legally delayed for at least nine months for nonvintage Champagne. Vintage Champagne should remain in the cellar for three years before disgorging. It is generally agreed by the Champagne trade that a delay of 2 or 3 years is desirable. In addition to Chappaz (1951), useful data on Champagne are given by Forbes (1967), Manceau (1929), Moreau-Berillon (1925), Pacottet and Guittonneau (1930), Rosa (1964), and Simon (1962). Recent vintage years are 1970, 1971, 1973 and 1975.

Many other sparkling wines are produced in France outside the Champagne region. They are not entitled to the appellation Champagne. Some of these are fermented in the bottle as for Champagne, while others are fermented in closed tanks (p. 469). These are sold as *mousseux*. Some carbonated wine, sold as such, is also made.

Other Districts.—Many other wines of above-average quality are produced in France and some have very distinctive factors influencing their quality.

In Alsace, variety is the most important quality factor; see Sittler (1956) and Hallgarten (1970). This is reflected in the varietal nomenclature of the wines. Climate and exposure are also important since the

Courtesy of Institut National des Appellations d'Origine
des Vins et Eaux-de-Vie

FIG. 1.8. PARTIAL CRUSHING OF WHITE GRAPES AT THE VINEYARD IN ALSACE

region is a cool one. Sylvaner, White Riesling, and Gewürztraminer make the best wines (Fig. 1.8). For a popular account see Layton (1970).

Along the Rhône from Lyon south many different wine types are made but the reds are the most interesting. Climate and exposure are less critical than in Burgundy, since the climate is warmer and sugaring is not necessary. The varietal complement does not appear to be a critical factor. More than one variety is used in Côte Rôtie and Châteauneuf-du-Pape. Hermitage is produced mainly from Petite Sirah. (It is doubtful if this is the variety of the same name in California.) These wines age relatively slowly, having a good color, tannin, and alcohol. In the bottle they may remain good and even improve in quality for 20 to 30 years. The few white wines are rather sturdy, full-bodied wines. A pink Rhône wine, Tavel, is produced mainly from the Grenache, a variety subject to oxidation. Hence, Tavels may contain noticeable sulfur dioxide.

The Loire has vines along much of its length (Fig. 1.9), mainly producing still and dry, or sweet, or sparkling white wines: from Sauvignon blanc at Pouilly-sur-Loire, Chenin blanc at Vouvray, and Angers-Saumur and Muscadet (Melon) near Nantes. The sweet table wines from Vou-

Courtesy of Institut National des Appellations d'Origine des Vins et Eaux-de-Vie

FIG. 1.9. CRUSHING IN THE VINEYARD AT VERNON, NEAR VOUVRAY

vray, Coteaux du Layon, and Angers-Saumur are produced only in the warmer years from botrytised grapes by procedures comparable to those of Sauternes (p. 11). Some of these wines are long-lived and of high quality. Two types of sparkling wines are produced. Musts in the Vouvray region may not ferment entirely dry. Later, after bottling, the wines may undergo a slight fermentation of the residual sugar and become gassy (*pétillant*). The process is tricky since deposits may form if too much yeast growth occurs. Bottle-fermented sparkling wines, *mousseux*, are produced by procedures comparable to those of Champagne. Generally, the sparkling wines are not so long-lived as Champagne.

A few red wines are produced from Cabernet franc in the vicinity of Bourgeuil and Chinon. They are pleasant but rather light wines, sometimes almost a rosé. For a good description of Loire wines, see Bréjoux (1956).

In the south of France a number of fortified wines are made—Banyuls, Muscat de Frontignan, etc. The grapes are left on the vines as long as possible to get the maximum sweetness. The fermentation is slow. The alcohol is brought to about 15-16%. Lesser wines are sold young for blending. Others are bottled after a few years' aging and reach the market as muscatels or red dessert wines. Some reds are aged for a number of years in the wood, or in glass in the sun, until they lose their red color and their aldehyde content increases. The particular *rancio* flavor of these wines is very distinctive.

Most of the wine produced in France is made in the Midi which produces more wine than any other region. It is low in alcohol, 7-10%. Aramon is widely planted, heavily-cropped and is responsible for many of the low-alcohol wines which are used primarily for blending or bulk sale, and is disappearing. The new vineyards are being planted to better varieties. The average worker in Paris and the northern departments drinks Midi wine (blended with other wine in many cases). Since the quality is moderate, little attention to positive quality factors is given except to soundness and alcohol content (which establishes the price). See Galtier (1961).

There are other French wines: rosés and reds from Provence, sweet whites of Monbazillac, Got (1949), and Jurançon (also dry), reds and whites of Gaillac, various Arbois types (including the rare film yeast wine of Château Chalon), the white Seyssel from Savoy, and many local sparkling wines, etc. Some of these owe their character to indigenous varieties and to unique methods of production.

Switzerland

The miracle is that Switzerland produces as much wine as it does in the very cool and limited areas available. In western Switzerland near Neu-châtel and Lausanne the early-ripening Chasselas doré is planted and rather neutral white wines are produced. In eastern Switzerland near Zürich the Pinot noir predominates and pleasant but light red wines are made. Some red, from Merlot, is produced in the Lugano region. The acidity of the new wines is often excessive and a malo-lactic fermentation is common. Following the primary fermentation the wines are lightly racked and the cellar temperature maintained. Yeast autolysis occurs, releasing amino acids, and *Lactobacillus* growth ensues. The total acidity is watched until it reaches the desired level (usually by January or February). The cellars are then opened up and the temperature allowed to drop to near freezing. Natural clarification occurs, the wines are filtered, and sulfur dioxide added. Many of the wines are sold immediately and few are aged more than 2 or 3 years. Some wines are bottled under carbon dioxide. The gas prevents oxygen absorption and helps avoid browning. It also gives the wines a slight but pleasant gassiness. Texts on the wines of Switzerland are those of Benvegnin *et al.* (1951), Duttweiler (1968), Peyer and Eggenberger (1965), Schellenberg (1962), and Schellenberg and Peyer (1951).

Germany

Germany has produced wines since Roman times. The climate is relatively poor for grapes and only on well-drained soils with favorable exposures can they be brought to maturity, and even there only in the warmer seasons. It is no accident that the slopes along the rivers are the favored areas for vines. Bocker (1959) presented evidence of a direct soil effect on the composition of German musts and wines. Grapes grown on more alkaline chalk (40 to 57% soluble calcium) soils were higher in potassium and magnesium than from neutral or slightly acid soils (5 to 17% soluble calcium). They also underwent a more complete malo-lactic fermentation. The German acreage in vineyards has nearly doubled in the last 30 years. This was made possible by increased exports (up from 0.5 million gallons in 1950 to 17.1 million in 1975), by a 25% increase in per capita consumption and by an increased total population. The best recent years are 1971, 1973, 1975 and 1976.

The Rhine.—From Switzerland nearly to Bonn, grapes are grown along this river and many of its tributaries. Three areas are particularly important for the production of quality wine: Rheinpfalz (Palatinate), Rheinhessen, and Rheingau. Many wines are produced in Baden and Württemberg but these are exported less and are mainly drunk locally. The tall brown bottle is used for all Rhine wines.

The vineyards in Pfalz and the Rheinhessen are on the west bank facing east so that they are warmed by the morning sun. In the Rheingau, the exposure is to the south. Thus, here the vines receive the sun's rays the maximum period and this is a most important and decisive factor differentiating this district from other Rhine vineyard areas. The vineyards with less favorable exposures produce lesser quality wines. Drainage, soil, temperature, and exposure are also important to the proper ripening of the grapes. White Riesling (about 78%), Müller-Thurgau (about 11%) and Sylvaner (about 6%) are the main varieties. The vinification is normal but sugaring is often necessary to secure the desired percentage of alcohol. Even in a year as warm as 1959 some musts required sugaring, but in 1976 few did.

Local variations in quality exist. These are due to use of various varieties, differences in climate and methods of production, and are protected by a unique system of nomenclature. The lesser wines are given regional or proprietary names but most of the wines are sold by the village name often associated with the vineyard name and that of the particular variety. The new German wine law (1971) permits labeling of the best wines as to bottling by the producer, year, etc. Wines with a vineyard appellation need only be ⅔ from the vineyard named. For example, a 1959er Geisenheimer Mäuerchen need contain only ⅔ wine of the Mäuerchen vineyard. The remainder may come from any of the other vineyards in the Geisenheim region. Vintage wines, likewise, need only be ¾ of the vintage.

Because of the cold climate and attack by *Botrytis*, the harvest may take place over a period of time to secure the maximum quality. These designations of times of harvest may also be placed on the label (often with the variety and always with the vintage). The grapes of the later pickings have considerable *Botrytis cinerea* infection (p. 11) and wines of more or less residual sugar can then be produced. For unsugared wines the order is *Kabinett, Spatlese, Auslese, Beerenauslese,* and *Trockenbeerenauslese.* A *Spatlese* means a wine made from late-picked grapes but it may or may not have a noticeable *Botrytis cinerea* infection. In any case, it is a natural wine—i.e., no sugar has been added to the must—and it is probably slightly sweet. An *Auslese* is always produced from selected grapes which are botrytised. If small botrytised parts of the cluster have been separately harvested, the wine may be even sweeter: a *Beerenauslese.* If the grapes have been allowed to shrivel (literally to dry up) on the vine, the wine may be labeled a *Trockenbeerenauslese.* This occurs only in exceptional years; the yield is always very small, and the price of the wines high.

Thus, a high quality Pfalz wine might be labeled Deidesheimer (village), Hohenmorgen (vineyard), Riesling (variety), 1976 (year), *Spätlese* (late harvesting), *Erzeugerabfüllung* or *Aus eigenem Lesegut* (bottled by the producer and not sugared). For a more complete explanation see Amerine and Singleton (1977), P.A. Hallgarten (1977), S. F. Hallgarten (1965,

1974), Langenbach (1962), Meinhard (1977), and Woschek (1970).

Because high quality German wines are often associated with residual sugar and because the sugar tends to mask the wines' high natural-acidity, there is a strong tendency for lesser quality German wines, such as district wines like Zeltinger (no vineyard name affixed) and wines of little geographical significance (such as Liebfraumilch), to be sold with residual sugar. This is achieved in two ways: by fermentation under pressure so that the fermentation "sticks" before all the sugar is fermented and by adding unfermented grape juice to the finished wine.

Sylvaner and Müller-Thurgau are the predominant varieties of the Rheinpfalz and Rheinhessen. Few vineyards are planted to White Riesling. The best years produce good wines. The negative quality factors are excessive sugaring and too high a sulfur dioxide content.

The Rheingau, one of the best vineyard areas, has a favorable exposure and well-drained, terraced, south-sloping sunny slopes. Vines not so favorably exposed fail to achieve such maturity and quality. The method of late harvesting of the predominant White Riesling variety is important. The practes of the producers are important. The soil-climate-producer-time-of-harvest factor differentiates the wines from each other. At their best, the wines have a distinctive aroma of the grape. The wines mature rapidly; the more alcoholic wines are kept in wood (Fig. 1.10).

Courtesy of Presse- und Informationsamt der Bundesregierung

FIG. 1.10. CELLARS AT SCHLOSS JOHANNISBERG ON THE RHINE

When they are sweet they are luscious and remain sound for many years. Famous villages in the Rheingau include Hattenheim, Rüdesheim, Geisenheim, and Hochheim (actually a few miles off on the Main). The word "hock" as a generic name for German wines may have originated here.

Joining the Rhine at Bingen is the Nahe river. The particular flavor of Nahe wines emphasizes that soil effect may be important, though it may be partially due to fermentation practices.

Moselle.—Even though the Moselle runs in a northeasterly direction, it twists so that some of the vineyards along its banks are exposed to the east and south. On well-drained slate soils these produce very distinctive wines in the best years. Some prefer the more grandiose Rheingau wines and others the rather sparse but often elegantly-odorous wines of the Moselle-Ruwer-Saar. The green or blue-green tall bottle is used for these

Courtesy of Prof. Kielhöfer

FIG. 1.11. THE VINEYARD OF BERNKASTELER DOKTOR ON THE MOSELLE RISING ABOVE THE TOWN OF BERNKASTEL

wines. Famous villages along the Moselle and Saar include Wehlen, Piesport, Trittenheim, Bernkastel (Fig. 1.11), Wiltingen, etc. (Loeb and Prittie 1972).

Franconia.—From Mainz the Main river turns east and finally south. Near Würzburg a number of distinctive wines are produced on its banks in finely terraced vineyards where the exposure is suitable (Fig. 1.12). The river bends so that favorable exposure is possible—usually south. The predominant variety is the Sylvaner. Red marl, limestone, or mixed soil types occur. There is less late harvesting. Early bottling constitutes a quality factor. The wines are bottled in the squat green *Bocksbeutel*. It is reputed to be a long-lived wine, but many post-World War II vintages have not borne this out. For descriptions see Kittel and Breider (1958) and Kraemer (1956).

One quality factor pervades the German wine industry: its high degree

Courtesy of Mainpost, Würzburg

FIG. 1.12. CASTLE AND INNERE LEISTE VINEYARD AT WURZBURG

of technical skill. German cellars are among the cleanest and most efficiently managed in the world. Germ-proof filtration which permits
safe bottling of sweet, low alcohol wines is regularly practiced. A commercial wine high in volatile acid is never encountered. There are more
enological stations and schools in Germany per acre of vineyard than in
any other country. The safe use of ferrocyanide for removal of copper
and iron and the careful adjustment of the total acidity are tributes to
their skill.

The negative quality factors in German wines are (1) the ubiquitous use
of sulfur dioxide and (2) thinness of wines made from unripe grapes and
sugar. There are a number of first rate technical books on German
enology. Among these are Geiss (1960), Goldschmidt (1951), Troost
(1972), and Vogt (1974, 1977). Of general interest are the books of
Ambrosi (1976), Cornelssen (1970), Hallgarten (1965), Langenbach
(1962), and Leonhardt (1963).

Italy

Italy produces over 1.5 billion gallons of wine per year, from low alcohol
table wines to sweet fortified dessert wines, from the Alps to Pantelleria
below Sicily. Vines are grown with every kind of soil, exposure, and elevation and along fences, in fields, or on trees. Most of the wine is a sound
beverage, much of no particular character.

The factors influencing quality are not so clear for Italy as for France or
Germany. With exceptions, the types are not so well standardized. The
failure to standardize types is due to complex political and economic
factors. For centuries Italy consisted of city states, Papal dominions, or
was under foreign control. It had only a small export trade to a nonwine
producing country (such as France possessed in England, Belgium, and
elsewhere) except for Marsala. The overpopulation of the country was
great. This results in polyculture—the cultivation of more than one crop
on the same plot of ground. Many of the grapes of Italy are grown in
conjunction with other crops. This leads to reduced production and
quality for all the crops, and especially for grapes, where pruning, disease,
and pest control, and proper timing of the harvest—all critical factors to
wine quality—may be interfered with by the culture and harvesting of
the other crops.

Also, the quality wine tradition, with exceptions, does not seem strong.
There was comparatively little shipment of bottled wine from one district to another in Italy, and even within a district only a few of the wines
are bottled (Bode 1956). Finally, the producers are often too small to care
about "commercial" quality, or so large that production of standard
wines is more important than of quality wines. There are relatively few
vineyard-bottled wines. Most of the attempts to differentiate regions

and limit varieties and production and to control quality under the corporative state came to naught. However, the European Common Market has stimulated classification and standardization of Italian wines. Nearly 200 Italian wines now have a *denominazione origine controllato* (D.O.C.). For each of these, the region is delimited, permitted varieties listed, and maximum production filed (Bruni 1970; Dallas 1974; Grossi 1973; Wasserman 1977). Still, the range of alcohol for each type is too great and not all D.O.C. wines are of merit. An even more impressive label, *denominazione origine controllato guarantie* (D.O.C.G.), is now to be granted. It will involve tasting standards. It will not be easy to administer considering the wide range of composition within each delimited district. Niederbacher (1978) has classified the D.O.C. wines according to quality for the years 1945 to 1977. In general, 1970 and 1971 wines were good in the main regions and 1972 poor. The other years were very variable in quality.

The warm climatic conditions often lead to high sugar (aggravated in many cases by late harvesting because of attention to other crops).[4] There is the lack of an export market and of a critical internal market. To summarize: there is a need for more critical standards for Italian wines. With so many uninteresting and unstandardized wines it is difficult to make any general summary of quality factors for Italian wines.

Mazzei (1959) has made an admirable summary of defects and how the Italian wine industry might be improved. He suggests wines of 10-13% alcohol (12 is recommended), 0.6-0.9% total acidity (as tartaric), and no more than 0.06% volatile acidity. The use of good varieties, clean fruit, and better wine making procedures (including cold fermentation and sulfur dioxide) is recommended. Central aging and bottling cellars are considered desirable. The sensory characteristics of each type should be kept as constant as possible. Cosmo and DeRosa (1960) make similar recommendations.

In Piedmont, where polyculture is the exception, a number of distinctive varietal types of wines are produced: Barbera, Freisa, Nebbiolo, Bonarda, Grignolino, etc. Barolo, Barbaresco, etc., are red wines produced from the Nebbiolo variety. While the variety and site are important, the care in vinification and aging is probably more important. A negative quality factor for many Piedmont red wines is their gassiness (*frizzante*), often due to a persistent malo-lactic fermentation. Sweet table wines produced from overripe Muscat blanc are very good in this

---

[4]In the Middle Ages and earlier, high alcohol wines were the only ones which could be kept without turning to vinegar. Late harvesting, addition of raisins or mixture with reduced must were some methods of achieving high sugar and hence high alcohol. The caramel flavors were excused as being better than half-vinegar low-alcohol products. Old customs die hard. Post-Pasteur technology makes such procedures unnecessary. Yet we still find, even in California, wine makers obsessed with the idea of picking so late that the wines will have 14% or more alcohol! These are dessert, not table, wines.

region. This is also the center of the *spumante* (sparkling and sparkling muscat) and vermouth industries. Thus, the quality factors of Piedmont are superior viticulture (Fig. 1.13), varietal selection, time of harvesting, and method of processing.

Courtesy of Prof. Cosmo

FIG. 1.13. SYSTEM OF TRAINING VINES IN NORTHERN ITALY

Some good varietal wines are produced north and east of Verona (Fig. 1.14). Here one finds labeled wines of Merlot, Sylvaner, Traminer, Pinot, and Riesling (not White Riesling but the Italian Riesling or Walschriesling). Variety, the cool climatic conditions, and thoroughness in the cellar are the dominant quality factors.

The red wines from near Verona—Valpolicella, Valtellina, and Bardolino—have a reputation as fresh, fruity, easy-to-drink beverages, and occasionally a nicely-aged one may be found. The wines of nearby Soave are standard white wines, pleasant but not normally memorable.

Chianti.—Although Chianti is probably the best-known Italian wine, there are certainly no general taste descriptions which will apply to all Chianti wines. Sangioveto is, indeed, the predominant variety but its aroma is not distinctive. The *governo* process (in which 10-20% of crushed semidried grapes is added to the newly-fermented wines) is used by

Courtesy of Prof. Cosmo

FIG. 1.14. HILLSIDE VINEYARDS IN NORTHERN ITALY

only a few of the producers. Some *governo* wines are slightly gassy (*frizzante*). This seems to be appreciated by consumers. It is a difficult process to control, however, and undesirable bacterial activity is not uncommon. Garino-Canina (1950) found that when the *governo* process was properly controlled it produced wines of better alcohol, color, and flavor. The *governo* wines had undergone considerable malo-lactic fermentation. Cantarelli (1958) showed that more alcohol is being produced per gram of sugar fermented. Individual producers do make and age wines of excellent quality.

Thousands of other wines are produced in Italy—Castelli Romani, Est! Est!! Est!!!, Lacryma Christi, Falerno, Orvieto, San Severo, etc. It is a rare village that does not have a wine named after it. Yet it is a rare wine which is worth a second taste. In our opinion, this is due to lack of quality standards.

Production techniques account for the other characteristic Italian wines. Many depend on very late harvesting of the grapes or on drying the grapes after harvesting in trays, in boxes or by tying on strings and hanging them up. Some of these are muscats of 15-16% alcohol. Others are the white alcoholic wines of Tuscany or Sardinia—Aleatico, *vino santo*, Malvasia, Vernaccia, Orvieto, etc. Similar types are produced on a small scale elsewhere, such as muscatels in Syracuse and Noto. Except for the *vino santo*, they are often fortified. For a description of Sicilian vines and wines see Rossi (1955) and Veronelli (1964).

Marsala.—Processing is responsible for the character of this type. The wines of Marsala were "created" during the 19th century by British wine merchants for export. Conditions in western Sicily were not favorable for the production of a quality table wine. The climate is warm, the grapes are white (Inzolia, Catarratto, and Grillo predominate), the vineyards are small and wine production crude. The quality-wise English merchants were able to create a unique type of wine from such unfavorable raw products. The process finally evolved consists of blending dry white wine, high-proof wine spirits, grape concentrate, *mute* and reduced must (boiled-down grape juice) to the desired flavor, sugar, and alcohol. The wines are then aged and a modified fractional blending system (p. 407) employed to standardize the types. Whether one appreciates the caramel-like flavor or not, Marsala represents a distinctive type of manufactured wine.

Vermouth.—The sweet Italian vermouth which originated in the Turin region is one of the world's classic wines and the type is produced in most of the wine-producing countries of the world. The custom of adding herbs to wine is a very ancient one. The presence of so many native herbs in northern Italy, particularly wormwood, probably helped its development. Essentially, Italian vermouth consists of a muscat base wine plus an infusion of herbs, sugar, caramel, and alcohol. Besides the regular amber-colored type, red and white vermouth are produced. The quality of the base wine, the skillfulness of the mixing of herbs (as well as the quality of the herbs), and the aging and finishing procedures are the primary quality factors.

The classical technical texts on Italian wines are those of Carpentieri (1948) and Garoglio (1965). Technical information is also given in the Atti of the Accademia Italiana della Vite e del Vino (1949-1976), Bruni (1964), Ferrarese (1951), Gianformaggio (1955), Marescalchi (1957), Montanari and Ceccarelli (1950), Paronetto and Dal Cin (1954), Tarantola (1954), Tarantola *et al.* (1954), and Verona and Florenzano (1956). Less technical but enthusiastic descriptions of Italian wines in English are those of Anon. (1957), Bode (1956), Dallas (1974), Dettori (1953), Layton (1961), Rau (1961), Ray (1966), and Veronelli (1964).

Spain

The third largest wine-producing country, but with the largest acreage, offers a wide variety of wines—from light table wines to some of the richest dessert wines. The quality factors, depending on the type of wine produced, include variety, climate, secondary fermentation, and process. Table wines are produced from La Mancha to the Pyrenees. Dessert wines are produced from New Castile to the south. Several wines are produced from delimited areas.

In the north in Rioja, the best table wines are produced. After the invasion of phylloxera in France, an influx of French vineyardists obviously had an influence. There has, however, been little change in the varietal complement: Grenache, Tempranilla and Graciano are the predominant varieties. The method of fermentation is variable, some crush and press normally while others use an old system where the whole grapes are placed in the fermentor (see p. 373). Others crush but keep the fermentors under a tight cover of carbon dioxide. The finished Rioja red wines are of normal red color. The French influence is obvious in their method of aging: small oak cooperage (Fig. 1.15), and bottle aging (Fig. 1.16). Fractional blending also appears in some of the northern Spanish wines (see p. 407). Vintage dates on Rioja wines should therefore be accepted with caution. Other table wines are produced throughout north-

Courtesy of Casa Codorniu

FIG. 1.15. BARREL AGING IN A BODEGA IN NORTHERN SPAIN

Courtesy of Casa Codorniu

FIG. 1.16. BOTTLE AGING IN A BODEGA IN NORTHERN SPAIN

ern Spain, especially in Navarre and near Barcelona. An important sparkling wine industry has developed in the latter region. Rather alcoholic red wines, suitable for blending, are produced near Valencia. The great variability of alcohol of wines from a given district should be noted. In Navarre, for example, wines of 11 to 15% are commonly provided.

Most of the La Mancha wines of central Spain are white, are sold young, and constitute the bulk of the wines drunk. The well-known Valdepeñas wine of La Mancha is seldom of more than ordinary quality.

Many table (and dessert) wineries are being modernized to permit greater economy of operation and better quality of product.

Dessert Wines.—The important Spanish wines are dessert wines. They owe their quality to the climate and to the method of production. Some of these wines are little changed in character from those produced in Roman times. For example, in Priorato, near Tarrogona, the Grenache is picked late at a high percentage of sugar. The wines are aged for a number of years in the cask and achieve a rancio (high-aldehyde) flavor similar to those of the south of France (p. 18).

At Málaga, the Muscat of Alexandria variety, partially dried as for raisins (Fig. 1.17), is used for producing wines. Málaga is, thus, one of the sweetest wines produced in the world. Fermentation is never complete. The high sugar and partial fortification stop the fermentation. The finished wines are 15-18% in alcohol, 12-20%, or more, in sugar content, of a dark amber color and have a strong caramel odor.

Courtesy of José Mata

FIG. 1.17. TRANSPORTATION OF MUSTS AND DRYING GRAPES BEFORE CRUSHING IN THE SOUTH OF SPAIN

In central and southern Spain (and in the Jura of France) the native yeast flora is such that if the new wines are left exposed the wine usually does not spoil but a film of yeast forms on the surface. The aldehyde content increases and the wines acquire a special flavor. The main centers in Spain for the commercial production of these wines are in Montilla (south of Cordoba) and near Jerez de la Frontera.

Montilla is one of the less well-known sherry-like wines of Spain. Several varieties are grown in this region of which Pedro Ximenez is the most important. Dry wines of 14-15% alcohol "flower" only a year or two to produce inexpensive aperitif wines. With longer aging under the *flor*, the intensity of odor (and the price) increase. The dry cellars also lead to the interesting phenomenon (also found in the Jerez area) of the alcohol content *increasing* with age.[5] Eventually, the alcohol content becomes high enough to inhibit yeast growth. Some of these wines have intense and complicated odors.

Sherry.—The wines of Jerez de la Frontera, and of the surrounding district as far as Puerta Santa Maria in one direction and Sanlúcar de Barrameda in another, are among the world's great wines. They form a family of related but diverse types. Their characteristic quality is due almost entirely to the method of production and aging.

FIG. 1.18.   METHOD OF TRANSPORTING GRAPES IN THE SHERRY DISTRICT

---

[5]The smaller water molecule moves more rapidly than the larger alcohol molecule through the wood. Evaporation of moisture from the surface is a function of the humidity of the air. In normal cellars, alcohol is lost more rapidly than water because of the high humidity of the air. In the dry, above-ground, dirt-floored, airy *bodegas* of southern Spain the humidity is very low and the opposite effect is observed.

The word "sherry" is undoubtedly derived from the name of the principal city in the sherry district, Jerez. According to Gonzalez (1972), Spanish sherry in Spain may be designated by any one of the following words: "Jerez," "Xerez," "Scheris" and "sherry."

Soil is considered an important quality factor but it is difficult to find objective evidence. The highly calcareous (*albariza*) soils produce the best wines. This *may* be related to degree of ripening. An important objective in sherry making is to produce a sound wine of 14-15% alcohol. Palomino grapes normally do not achieve sufficient sugar to produce this percentage of alcohol. Formerly, drying the fruit in the sun for a day or two (Fig. 1.17), was used to help shrivel the grapes slightly and thus raise the sugar content. Possibly the low production on the more highly calcareous soils and the unique method of pruning lead to higher sugar. The Pedro Ximenez and a number of other varieties are also grown.

Variety is, however, not the controlling factor in sherry quality. As a matter of fact, the highly-praised Palomino may be grown for its thick skin and disease-resistance more than for any real quality of its own. The need of high sugar favors late harvesting—a factor in favor of the Palomino. However, the musts are low in acid, high in pH, and have a tendency to darken.

The lack of acidity is the worst defect of this and of other varieties grown in this district. This was ameliorated by plastering—a practice where gypsum is added to the grape musts to lower their pH (p. 405). The gypsum treatment of the crushed grapes also gives higher yields of juice during pressing—important with the pulpy Palomino. Tartaric acid and sulfur dioxide are used. The old practice of "treading" of grapes also had for its purpose better disintegration of the grape and hence greater yield of juice. Nowadays, the grapes are crushed and pressed in Willmes or Vaslin presses. The fermentation is conducted in casks of about 130-gal. capacity. Following fermentation, the wines are racked once, or not at all, but are left in partially full containers. The wines are carefully tasted and classified (p. 406) into potential flor wines and into the *oloroso* type. The latter are fortified to 16%, or more, alcohol and do not undergo a secondary film yeast stage.

By early spring, a film stage of the yeast begins to develop on the unfortified wines rapidly covering the surface (Fig. 1.19). In the above-ground bodegas the film may "drop" during the summer, "flower" again in the fall, and "drop" a second time in the winter. Temperature control would be an advantage for maintaining continuous film growth and speeding up the process.

Sooner or later the wines, now classified into several types and grades, find their way into a fractional blending system of aging. For about one year the wines are held without blending. At that time a proportion is

Courtesy of Wine Institute

FIG. 1.19. FLOR FILM GROWING ON SURFACE OF WINE

transferred to older casks of the same type in order to replenish wine
which has been used to fill still older casks from which wine has been
taken. The "depth" or number of steps in the fractional blending system
varies from 3 to 6 or more. It is obvious that the wine withdrawn from
the bottom or *solera* cask is a very complicated blend of wines of varying
age. Baker *et al.* (1952) have shown that after a certain period of
operation the average age of the wine withdrawn from the oldest cask
reaches a constant. This is important because it clearly establishes
one of its functions—namely to supply uniform wine from a production
system which is notoriously fickle in producing wines of variable quality.

There are many *fino* and *oloroso* soleras in all sherry bodegas (Fig.
1.20). Generally, however, wine from a single solera is not used directly

Courtesy of Gonzalez, Byass

FIG. 1.20. SHERRY BODEGA

for bottling, but wines from several soleras may be employed to produce the commercial types. Much of the younger drier *fino*-type sold in Spain is only 14.5% in alcohol. The *manzanilla*, a *fino*-type wine produced at Sanlúcar de Barrameda, is often sold unfortified, even when shipped outside of Spain. For export, except for manzanillas, most sherry, *fino* or *oloroso* is raised to about 18% alcohol. Adjustments of color are made by adding very small amounts of *vino de color*—reduced must (boiled-down grape juice) which has been fortified and aged.

A sherry firm may produce several qualities of *finos*, one or more aged *finos* (called amontillados), several *olorosos*, and at least one dark *oloroso*. Basically, there are two types of sherry—one which owes its character to the effect of a film stage and the other which does not. The other quality factor is the aging system which yields wines of a consistent quality for both types. The soft oak casks employed may be a third quality factor and certainly the concentration effect produced by evaporation is important in the older wines. The flavor produced by autolysis in the deposit of yeasts has not been measured but is believed to be of some value.

The classic text on Spanish wines is that of Marcilla (1946). The books of Castillo and Hallett (1972), Larrea (1957, 1965) and Vega (1958) are also useful.

On sherry, González (1972) is the best. Marcilla *et al.* (1936) is indispensable. Bobadilla (1956), Bobadilla *et al.* (1954), and Bobadilla and Navarro (1949) should also be consulted. Descriptions in English of the production of sherry may be found in Allen (1933), Castello and Hallett (1972), Jeffs (1970), Joslyn and Amerine (1964), Rainbird (1966), and Read (1973).

Portugal

For its size, Portugal is an important viticultural area. Per capita consumption is about 95 liters (25 gal.) per year. In most districts, the Junta Nacional do Vinho (JNV) has functioned efficiently to (1) improve the quality of the product and (2) remove excess wines for distillation to hold the market price steady.

The main factors for quality improvement in the areas controlled by the JNV appear to be (1) planting of better varieties and (2) better methods of vinification. The JNV vigorously attacked both these problems, by competitions, awards of medals for quality of wine or cleanliness of cellar, extension activities, etc. The JNV constructed installations of its own where the enological discipline was exemplary. The quality of the grapes employed limits the quality of the wine. Its monumental study (1942) of the soils and composition of the grapes should be mentioned.

There are a number of local regions of quality wine production (aside from the Douro). In Sétubal, just south of Lisbon, the Muscat of Alexandria (or a close relative) is used to produce a luscious muscatel. The second region is that of the *vinho verde* wines of the Minho district, north of Opôrto. The quality factors here are different from those existing elsewhere. They may constitute a prime example of "making a virtue of a necessity." Vines are largely grown on pergolas or trees, as in parts of Italy, and hence usually overproduce. The fruit cannot reach full maturity. The musts therefore often attain no more than 16% sugar with more than 1% acidity. The resulting wines would be undrinkable were it not for the malo-lactic fermentation (p. 291).

The new wines are left unracked until yeast autolysis induces the malo-lactic fermentation. The wines are often bottled before or during this fermentation and the commercial wines are very gassy. The *frizzante* wines of northern Italy are similar, but seldom have such uniform degree of gassiness. Commercial wines exported to the United States are usually carbonated.

Two small delimited regions should be mentioned. Colares is a red wine produced near Lisbon on slopes facing the Atlantic. The high chloride content of the wine has an effect on the flavor of the wine. Dão is the best red table wine of Portugal. It is produced in a delimited district just south of the Douro.

Port.—The quality factors responsible for the red sweet wine called port are not entirely clear, in spite of the very important studies of Baron de Forrester (a 19th century British wine merchant), the Instituto do Vinho do Porto (IVP), the Casa do Douro, and, most important, the technological practices that the port wine shippers have developed over the past 100 years. The Douro wine region is a small delimited area mainly bordering the Douro river from Régua some distance eastward. No more unfavorable locale for vine growth can be imagined. Vines are grown on the terraced slopes on both sides of the river or its tributaries (Fig. 1.21 and 1.22). In spite of the rocky nature of the soil, vines flourish. The subsoil is a slate which is tilted up 90°. The vines' roots thus are believed to penetrate deeply and to find a source of moisture. Granted that this is correct, it can hardly constitute an important quality factor compared to vines which do not suffer moisture deficiency.

Courtesy of Instituto do Vinho do Pôrto

FIG. 1.21. FINE VIEW OF VINEYARDS ON BOTH SIDES OF THE DOURO AT PINHÃO

FIG. 1.22. CLOSE-UP OF TERRACED VINEYARD

Climate appears to have a critical importance. Some years are too warm, resulting in excessive sugar or deficient color for some varieties. However, because of the mixed plantings of varieties this may not be a necessarily critical factor. In a mixed planting, it is obviously impossible to pick each variety at its optimum maturity. Therefore, only in the most favorable (cool) years may the optimum maturity for all varieties be secured or over- and under-maturity be cancelled out.

Courtesy of Instituto do Vinho do Pôrto

FIG. 1.23. STONE LAGARES IN THE DOURO

The whole grapes are crushed into stone crushing vats (*lagares*, Fig. 1.23) and pumped over or punched down during the early stages of fermentation. The practice of treading, still used by a few producers, caused a thorough physical disintegration of the berries and aided color extraction—an important factor considering the limited period of fermentation on the skins. Cheap labor was surely the main factor in favor of treading. The fermenting juice is run directly into tanks containing the fortifying brandy. The spirits used have a proof not greater than 160°. Many ports thus have a noticeable fusel oil odor which the port shippers do not consider a negative quality factor. The initial fortification may be to only about 18%.

The new partially-fortified wines are transferred, usually within a year, to the lodges of the port shippers at Vila Nova de Gaia, opposite Opôrto. A little more spirits may be added before shipment. Storage conditions, even in the above-ground lodges (Fig. 1.24), are cooler than in Douro. The wines are aged in oak casks of about 477-liter (126-gal.) capacity. There

Courtesy of Guirmaraens

FIG. 1.24. PORT LODGE AT VILA NOVA DE GAIA

is a clear preference for casks of hard oak which contribute the least woody flavor to the wine. Further fortification can occur during aging.

The classification, aging, and blending system is a critical quality factor. The new wines are classified by color, sugar content, and quality. The lesser-colored wines are aged 3 to 6 years and blended to produce tawny ports. The moderately-colored wines are blended, bottled, or shipped earlier as ruby ports. The wines of highest color, flavor, and alcohol of a given vintage are bottled as vintage ports after two years, either at Vila Nova de Gaia or in Great Britain. Only a small percentage of the finest wine of the best years is so shipped.

Madeira.—The Portuguese island some 600 miles off the north coast of Africa produces a number of white dessert wines. Once an important wine type, it can no longer be considered a wine of outstanding quality. Prior to the introduction of oïdium, black rot, and phylloxera, grapes apparently ripened better. The higher alcohol permitted long aging, resulting in wines of superior quality. Following the invasion of the cryptogamic diseases, bunch rot and defective fermentations were common. Heating the new wines to 54.5° to 60°C (130° to 140°F) controlled spoilage, but has not resulted in wines of high quality. High volatile acidity is a common defect. Much of the Madeira is exported to Scandinavian countries where its high sugar content recommends it.

The present procedure is to ferment most of the wines dry, partially fortify and bake at not over 60°C (140°F) for 3 or 4 months in concrete tanks. The wine is then refortified. Some musts are fortified but are not heated. The producer blends the two types of wine to secure the desired sweetness. The wines are blended from a sort of fractional blending system to produce several types called Sercial, Boal (or Bual) and Malmsey in order of increasing sugar content. These types do not represent varietal types as they once did.

On Sétubal see Soares Franco (1938). Gahano's (1951) books on *vinhos verdes* is authentic. General texts on Portuguese table wines by Allen (1957, 1964) and Read (1973) are on the popular side. Articles of enological interest are found in the Anais of the Junta Nacional do Vinho (1949–1961). On port, there is a rich literature, much of which is not technical or critical. The treatise of Cockburn (undated) and the Anais of the Instituto do Vinho do Pôrto (1940-1972/73) are most important from the technical point of view. Simon (1934) and Valente-Perfeito (1948) give the contrasting English and Portuguese points of view. Allen (1957, 1964), Croft-Cooke (1957) and Read (1973) bring the popular side up to date. A generous view of Madeira is given by Croft-Cooke (1961).

OTHER EUROPEAN COUNTRIES

Austria

Schmidt (1965) reports wines were made from wild grapes in Austria before Roman times. He stresses the role of the church in viticulture during the Middle Ages. Austria has over 100,000 acres of vines. There has been a gradual increase in yield per acre. Over 80% of the wine is white.

The best vineyards are near bodies of water (the Danube or Neusiedler Sea) or on good hillside exposures. The most popular variety is Grüner Veltliner, followed by Walschriesling, Müller-Thurgau, Neuburger, Portuguese (white, gray and green cultivars), and Blau Franken. Other varieties are White Riesling, Sylvaner, Rotgipfler, Zierfahndler, and Ruländer). Consumption has increased since W.W. I to slightly over 35 liters per capita. A unique feature of the distribution of wine in Austria is that about ½ is sold in bulk directly by *Gaststube* (wine restaurants, etc.).

About ⅔ of the Austrian vines grow in the northern part along both sides of the Danube. Krems, Langenlois, Wachau, and Donauland are the most important production centers. Baden, Bad Vöslau, Pfaffstätten, Gumpoldskirchen, and Traiskirchen are well-known vineyards near Vienna. Burgenland, to the east, produces some red wines. The wines mature early. Many are drunk within a year in wine restaurants as an after-dinner beverage. Wines of late-harvested (botrytised) grapes are occasionally produced.

Both viticulture and enology are astutely practiced. Cool fermentations are favored. Other positive quality factors are the varietal and regional labeling, and the rapid distribution of white table wines in casks. Moser (1959) noted a trend toward mechanization of the vineyards and wines of better keeping qualities. He also believes wines with regional or company (producer) labels are more successful than those with varietal appellations. Arthold (1950) is the standard technical work on Austrian wines. Jeffs (1971), Jursa (1971), Leonhardt (1963), Lichine (1974), and Rau (1961) give popular discussions.

Hungary

Hungary is an important viticultural area in Europe with about 550,000 acres of grapes. The first vineyards were planted by the Romans[6] and exports have increased in recent years. Three hundred years ago Hungarian wines enjoyed a thriving export trade and, for Tokay, at least, a worldwide reputation for quality.

No fewer than 14 regions have been classified and produce wines of distinctive quality. Certain areas are too cold for grape culture. Quality is due primarily to temperature (climate, rainfall, exposure, soil conditions, drainage, etc.) and varietal complement. Leonhardt (1963), especially, emphasizes the extreme variation in temperature that may be expected. The varietal complement includes no fewer than 50 white and 15 red varieties. Western European varieties such as Sylvaner, Traminer, Müller-Thurgau, and Chardonnay are grown besides native varieties such as Furmint, Ezerjó, Hárslevelü, Kéknyelü, Zierfahndler (white), and Kadarka (red), Gamza (Bulgarian), etc. According to Halász (1962) the Furmint variety was introduced in the 13th century by Walloons and derived its name from its yellow-brown color which resembles that of ripe wheat (*froment*). Neubeller (1965), on the other hand, believes it was introduced from Italy and is derived from *fiori monti* (flowery mountains). Most of the wine is white (about 60%). Rosés constitute nearly ¼ of the production and red table wine, about 15%. Some sparkling and sweet dessert wines, and even vermouths, are produced. The best table wines are Móri, Badacsonyi, Debröi, Villányi-Pécsi, Egri,

---

[6]The Hungarian word for wine is *bor*. Thus, it is almost unique among European languages in not being derived from the Sankskrit *vena*. Perhaps the Hungarians got the word from the Turks?

and Somlyöi. Kobel (1947) particularly mentions the quality of Walschriesling, Ezerjó, Sylvaner, and other white Hungarian wines. He found the red wines less interesting, particularly those of the widely-planted Kadarka. Egri Bikavér, partially from Kadarka, is considered the best red.

The one exception to the lack of fame of Hungarian wines was Tokay (Tokaj in Hungarian). Tokay is one of the more expensive types of wines to produce and in a socialist state few are able to afford the price that its classic production demands. Attempts to collectivise the vineyards have also discouraged some growers.

About ½ of Tokay is the product of a temperamental grape, the Furmint. It ripens late, has a low acidity, and dries on the vine if allowed to hang until October or later. The other Tokay grape is Hárslevelu. The long, warm fall, early rains followed by dry weather, well-drained soils, the mixture of varieties and *Botrytis cinerea* are considered the major quality factors by Halász (1962). The best conditions—warm summer rains in early October followed by sunny days and cold nights—favor *Botrytis*. The vintage traditionally starts on October 28. In the best years, the juice of these shriveled grapes is used for the sweeter types— Aszu and essence. The finest grapes contain 40%, or more, sugar. Szamorodni is the lesser quality drier type of Tokay, up to 2.7% sugar according to Neubeller (1965). Aszus had 4.2 to 17.6% sugar and 9.9 to 15.9% alcohol.

The great fame of Tokay probably lies in the care with which the sweetest juice is added to ordinary juice (from 10 to 50% for Aszu). The traditional wines were strong in aroma without excessive caramel odor. Post-war Tokays with an amber color and a strong caramel odor may be suspected of containing concentrate.

The other Hungarian wines are sold with a district name plus, often, a varietal appellation. The standard text is that of Teleki (1937). Recent information on regions and varieties are given in Csepregi (1955), Gunyon (1971), Halász (1962), Lichine (1974), and Anon. (1958C). The post W.W. II problems were summarized by Kobel (1947). For technical data see Soós (1955), Rakcsányi (1963) and Neubeller (1965).

Czechoslovakia

The climate here is generally unfavorable and only early-ripening varieties, producing light wines, can be grown. Several vineyards with favorable exposures have achieved a good reputation by planting the best varieties and carefully vinifying them (Fig. 1.25) and acreage has increased. The wines are seldom exported since all are needed for local consumption. Melnik and Brno are centers of production. Hulač (1949) is

Courtesy of Prof. Blaha

FIG. 1.25. HILLSIDE AND VALLEY VINEYARDS IN CZECHOSLOVAKIA

Note modern equipment

a modern text on wine making and the treatise of Laho (1962) is admirable.

Rumania

This was a large viticultural country before W.W. II. About 40% of the area of prewar production is now in the Soviet Union but more than 500,000 acres remain. The best are white wines, indicating rather cool climatic conditions. Leonhardt (1963) reports that soil and climatic conditions are generally favorable. Native and western European varieties are often used: Fetească alba and neagră, Pinot gris, Aligoté, Walschriesling, Pinot noir, Cabernet Sauvignon, etc. A few wines are fortified to 18% alcohol: even Chardonnay, Cabernet Sauvignon, etc. A sweet table wine is produced from late-harvested, botrytised grapes in Grasa, and slightly sweet rosé wines are made at Nicoresti. Table-grape varieties are often used to prepare dessert wines. For further information on Rumanian wines see Bernaz (1962), Constantinescu (1958, 1959-1967), Gunyon (1971), Prisnea (1964), and Teodorescu (1968).

Bulgaria

There are over 400,000 acres of grapes in Bulgaria. Some are in high quality varieties: Cabernet Sauvignon, Saperavi, Rkatsiteli, Muscat blanc, Aligoté, White Riesling, etc. About 20% are in table grapes. Important native wine grape varieties are Pamid, Mavrud, Gamsa, and Sartschin. The climate of Bulgaria is very favorable for grape growing. The temperature summation for the period after the average temperature reaches 10°C (50°F) is 3700 to 4000 day degrees. Lack of a critical home or export market has been a handicap. They have developed an active table grape export market. According to Nedelchev (1959) they are trying to increase their wine exports and the industry is being modernized to accomplish this (Fig. 1.26). Vineyards have been consolidated and expanded into larger units, new and better varieties planted, and the wine types standardized. The following types of wine are now produced: red, pink, and white table wines, red and white dessert wines of 16-16.5% alcohol and an equal sugar content, or of 18-18.5% alcohol wth 10-11% sugar. The muscatels are especially appreciated. Bulgarian brandy (over 2½ million gal. per year) is called *rakia*. Leonhardt (1963) reports some wines of low acidity (due to the use of table grape varieties?). See also Georgiev (1949), Dalmasso (1958), Gunyon (1971), Kondarew (1965) and Lichine (1974).

Albania

According to Nasse and Zigori (1968) the best Albanian wine varieties are Debine (noir and blanche), Kallmet, Mereshnik, Mjaltez, Serine (rouge and blanche), Shesh blanc and Vlosh. Varieties such as Barbera and Merlot have recently been planted. Acreage is less than 30,000. The industry is being modernized. Mainly table wines are produced.

Courtesy of Prof. N. Nedeltchev

FIG. 1.26. ABOVE—VINTAGE SCENE IN BULGARIA. BELOW—INTERIOR
OF WINERY AT RAULIKENE, BULGARIA

Yugoslavia

Grapes—over 250,000 ha (600,000 acres) producing over 6 million hl
(160 million gal.)—are grown throughout the country. Most of the wines
are up to western standards. However, the dark red, high tannin, alcoholic wines of Dalmatia and elsewhere are almost undrinkable by
western standards. The predilection for high tannin wines may date to

the Slavic invasion from the fat-lamb-eating areas to the east. Some of the types of wine produced clearly reflect western European types or varieties—Burgundac, Traminac, Rizling, Refoško, Merlot, Sémillon, Veltlenac, Rulandec, etc., and some reflect Hungarian or local origin— Kadarka, Furmint, Smederevka, Žilavka, Plavina (called Slankamenka elsewhere), Prokupats, etc. The Walschriesling (Italian Riesling) is especially favored. The importance of varieties and their uses for standardizing types in Yugoslavia is fully explained by Bulič (1949) and Turcovič (1950A,B, 1952-1962).

Serbia produces Župa red wines and Prokupats (a variety) pink wines. The former is a wine of high color and tannin. Other Serbian wine regions are Krajina, Šumadija, Metohia, Vlasotinci, Venčac-Oplenac, and Smederevo (Smederevka is the vine).

Macedonian wines resemble those of Dalmatia—many are high in color and tannin. The Tikveš and Ohred are important regions and Vranats the native variety. Bosnia and Herzegovina produce few wines. A white Žilavka, mainly from the variety of the same name, and a red Blatina, of a deep red color and often high in tannin, may be noted.

Croatia includes Dalmatia, Istria, and Croatia proper. Dalmatian wines are often of relatively high alcohol and dry or sweet with a very high tannin content in the reds. Well-known types are Dingač (red), Prošek (white and sweet), Opol (pink, red, and dark red), Maraština (white table and dessert), Vugava (white table), and Benkovak (a region). Plavac mali is the important native variety. Istrian wines are lower in alcohol than those of Dalmatia. Western European varieties such as Refosco, Barbera, Cabernet Sauvignon, and Sémillon are widely planted. In Croatia, 75% of the wine is white. Besides western European varieties, a red Fruška Gora, Banat (Vršac is a well-known white and Merlot a high quality red), Subotica-Horgoš (a sandy region with dessert as well as table wines), and Graševina may be noted. Plješevac and Ilok (from a state vineyard) are also well known.

Slovenia is a northern region, usually of higher quality wines. Teran is a red wine with a pronounced lactic flavor. Ljutomer (formerly Luttenberger) has many wine types—mainly labeled under varietal appellations: Silvanac, Rizling, Sauvignon (also Sovinjon), Traminac, Merlot, etc., or vineyards.

While the climate is favorable for the growth of vines in Yugoslavia, it sometimes leads to excessive sugar and alcohol, and to slightly sweet wines. The high tannin content of some of the red wines is a negative quality factor by our standards. See also Cerletti (1958), Gunyon (1971), Lichine (1974), Pogrimilovic (1969) and Radenković (1962).

Soviet Union

The Soviet Union is expanding its grape area rapidly. See Dalmasso and Tyndalo (1957), Gerasimov (1957), Levy (1958), and Leonhardt (1963) for a fuller discussion in Italian, English, French, and German. The standard texts in Russian include Azarashvili (1959), Beridze (1965), Davitaya (1948), Egorov (1955), Agabal'yants (1972), Gerasimov (1964), Kalugina et al. (1957), Mogilyanskiĭ (1954), and Prostoserdov (1955). The technical publications of the Biochemical Institute of the Akademiya Nauk S.S.S.R. (1947-1964) should be consulted as well as the reports of the "Magarach" grape and wine experiment station at Yalta in the Crimea and of various other experiment stations. According to Amerine and Joslyn (1970) there are at least ten institutes devoted to the study of grapes and wine in Russia. The immediate postwar area of about 320,000 ha (800,000) acres has now (1977) reached 1.33 million ha (3.2 million acres) and plans have been announced for further expansion.

There are few unbiased appraisals of the quality of post W.W. II wines. These indicate that quality has been taken into account. The best indication of this is the retail price of wine which varies from 30¢ to $1.75 per bottle in Moscow, according to Levy (1958). The ampelography edited by Frolov-Bagreev (1946-1965) is a model of its kind. For a detailed evaluation of the Soviet industry and a slightly less optimistic view of the prospects for quality, see Amerine (1963, 1965).

Research is being developed with exemplary speed. This includes development of grapes for cold climates, new procedures for production of several types of wine, including continuous fermentation of sparkling wines (Amerine 1959B, 1963) and training of technologists capable of utilizing the most modern laboratory and control procedures. (See, for example, Durmishidze 1955.) The production of sparkling wines (Fig. 1.27) is especially favored.

There are some negative quality factors. Hot climatic conditions in some areas may lead to excessively alcoholic wines. The local traditional method of fermenting for long periods on the skins is certainly inimical to quality. Most important, perhaps, is the absence of a critical clientele capable of influencing the development of the wine industry.

The main areas for grape growing in the Soviet Union are in Moldavia, the Ukraine (including Crimea and the Transcarpathian region), R.S.F.R. (Rostov, Krasnodar, Daghestan), Georgia, Azerbaidzhan, Uzbekistan and Armenia. Georgia (over 200,000 acres) is one of the oldest, if not the oldest, viticultural region and has the best reputation (Beridze 1965).

As for brandy, Armenia, Moldavia and Georgia are the centers of the industry. Considerable attention has been given to standardizing a series of qualities of brandy based mainly on time of aging. The technical

Courtesy of S.S.S.R. Embassy

FIG. 1.27. SPARKLING WINE PLANT IN TBILISI

advance of the Russian wine and brandy industry is particularly noted in Agabal'yants (1969, 1972), Anon. (1958A), Kichovski (1975), Maltabar *et al.* (1959), Nilov and Skurikhin (1960), Popov (1970), and Valuiko (1973). The rapid rise in sparkling wine production is especially noticeable. Interesting advances are the draining tanks (for white musts), lined aluminum tanks, continuous sparkling wine production, and a central tasting commission.

Greece

Grapes were grown in Greece for centuries before our era, but the problems of producing good wines in a warm climate were no less in Homer's time than today. Thus, perfumes, spices, and honey were added to many ancient wines to mask or reduce the development of spoilage in wines stored in warm climates and to give the wines a special character. Less than 20% of the 125 million gallons of wine produced in Greece today contain 1% or more of sandarac resin. These wines, *retsinas*, have a distinct turpentine odor which is disagreeable to the uninitiated. Producers must keep separate equipment for handling them. Surprisingly, a taste for such wines can be achieved. The non-retsina wines are of only average interest. Fortified very sweet muscat wines for export occur from the island of Samos. Mavrodaphne is a sort of tawny port type, often with a distinct caramel flavor. The cooperative wineries and the development of trained enologists are hopeful signs for the future. Useful research in varieties and in developing regional standards is occurring. The lack of a critical local clientele and the unstandardized practices of the small producers are discouraging.

Other Countries

A number of European countries produce sizeable amounts of fruit wines in lieu of grape wines. These include the Netherlands, Norway, Denmark, Sweden and Poland. The wines are made from apples, pears, cherries and various other native fruits and berries. They are usually sweet. In Sweden, some are made sparkling.

Great Britain also produces fruit wines, primarily from apples, but they also make wines from imported grape juice or grape concentrate. These are sold as British vermouth, sherry or ruby (i.e., port). About 20% of the wine consumed in Great Britain is made thusly. A few grapes are also grown and made into wine.

ASIA

Few wines are made in Asia. The hot climate leads to high-sugar, low-acid grapes. The fermentations are often defective. Storage conditions are poor. Many of the resulting wines are sweet and acetic or dry and alcoholic. Islam religion prevents consumption of wines and many of the varieties of grapes available for wine are more suitable for eating or drying than for wine production.

Cyprus

There are 42,000 ha (100,000 acres) of grapes in Cyprus. Yield is very low—one ton per acre. Under the Ottoman Empire from 1571 until 1878 wine making was discouraged. The predominant grape (77%) is a red variety called Mavro. It is used for dry red, rosé, and sherry as well as for concentrate. Xinisteri (20%) is the main white variety. Both these grapes when dried to about 45° Brix are crushed together and slowly fermented to produce the sweet, tawny Commandaria wine. Improvement in varieties is considered to be one of the necessary steps for improving the wines. Since Cyprus is still free of phylloxera, this presents important quarantine problems for introduction of new varieties. Zivania is the native brandy, about 100° proof according to Kuchel (1959). It is often produced in small stills (less than 50 gal.).

Israel

In Israel, the wines show much improvement in recent years. The most important wineries are at Rishon-le-Zion and Zicron-Jacob where modern equipment has been installed. Israel, as a signatory to the Madrid pact, abandoned European-type names. This was a sacrifice and may constitute a step toward revision of wine nomenclature in other countries. Because of the warm climatic conditions, the best wines may be of the dessert types but some pleasant table wines, some dry, are now being produced. A text in grape growing in Israel is that of Hochberg (1954-1955). Concerning the problems of the Israeli wine industry see Ough (1965). According to Ough (1965), the 1964 acreages of wine grape varieties in Israel were 39% Carignane, 37% Grenache, 11% Muscat of Alexandria, 6% Sémillon, 5% Clairette (Boorbaulenc), and 2% other varieties. Since then, Carignane, French Colombard and Cabernet Sauvignon have been more widely planted.

Other Countries

The wines of Lebanon and Syria need little comment. They should receive a better vinification (cooling, etc.) and proper fortification of the dessert wines. There are about 760,000 ha (1,875,000 acres) of grapes in Turkey with an average yield of 2½ tons per acre. Grape culture certainly dates to 2000 B.C. Today 37% (Thompson Seedless) are used for raisins and another 37% for making *Pekmez*, a concentrated grape juice of 50-65% sugar. Only about 2-3% of the total grapes, 40,000 to 50,000 tons, go to wine production. A number of native wine grape varieties were listed by Alleweldt (1965): Dimrit (also used as a table grape), Misket Bornova, Papas Karasi, etc. Some European grapes are grown, i.e., Cinsaut. The wines are sold with type and district names, usually at a standard price through a governmental monopoly. Allweldt considered the following as quality red wines: Trakya, Buzbag (a blend of wines of the varieties Öküz Gözü and Buzbag), Horzkarasi, Kalecik and Kavaklideres. The best white wines were labeled Kalecik, Navince, Misket (or Musket or Bornova), Vinikol, Kavaklideres and Trakya. Other reds and whites include Cabuk, Güzelbag, Yeni Marmara, Mutuk and Taris. Turkey is an example of what can be done by technicians working for the government or a monopoly. The hot climate and lack of a critical clientele are handicaps.

Japan

There is a small but progressive and expanding wine industry in Japan. The high humidity makes growing of *V. vinifera* varieties difficult but some are produced plus a number of nonvinifera varieties and hybrids. The use of sugar is general and many of the wines are sweet and fortified with nonvinous alcohol. Wine production is about 11 million gallons in Japan. This was compared to sake production of about 100 million gallons. The two main Japanese grape growing regions are the Kofu and Osaka valleys. The native varieties in these districts, Koshu and Jaraku, respectively, appear to have been introduced from the continent. A number of *V. labrusca* varieties have been imported from the United States—Delaware and Campbell Early being widely grown. The unfavorable climatic conditions make some Japanese wines unbalanced, astringent, and of poor quality. Wine making procedures are primitive in some cases and very modern in others. For a more optimistic view see Amerine (1964). Grape concentrate is now imported for wine production.

AUSTRALIA AND NEW ZEALAND

Vines were first brought to Australia in 1788. Wine was shipped to England in 1822 where it received a silver medal. The dominant man in the industry after 1824 was James Busby. He wrote three books on grape culture and imported over 600 varieties from Europe into Australia (Laffer 1949). Several wineries in existence today started over 100 years ago. The pride which the older firms have in their product has been emphasized by Webb (1959). For further information see Evans (1973), James (1966), Murphy (1970, 1974), and Simon (1966).

The most important wine region today is in South Australia, followed by New South Wales and Victoria. There is a small but growing industry in Western Australia. There are nearly 65,000 ha (160,000 acres) in grapes and wine production is 3.4 million hl (90 million gal.). A limited number of varieties are planted, especially in South Australia which is free of phylloxera. Until recently it prohibited vine importations. Increasing attention is being given to planting of the best varieties and clones. The climate is warm and humid in the Hunter River valley though the district has a good reputation. Pirie (1978) found the heat summation of the viticultural districts to range from cool (at Coonawara) to hot (in Swan Valley). Rainfall during the ripening period is a problem. Research in viticulture and enology is excellent.

The wineries are generally large with modern equipment (Fig. 1.28). Adequate facilities for aging are available and there is much interest in producing high quality bottle-aged wines, particularly by certain firms. These include a variety of white and red table wines as well as flor sherries and red dessert wines of the port type. Table wine consumption has increased in recent years. There is also a thriving brandy industry.

Vines have been grown in New Zealand since Busby's time (Thorpy

FIG. 1.28. LARGE SOUTH AUSTRALIAN WINERY IN VINEYARD AREA

1971). The climate is moderate and the hectarage has increased rapidly in recent years. Several modern new wineries have been constructed. A number of varietal red and white table wines as well as some excellent flor sherries have been produced. The presence of labrusca type grapes and the use of sugar are negative quality factors.

AFRICA

The wine industry of this continent in the north is in Morocco, Algeria, Tunisia, and Egypt and in the far south in the Union of South Africa.

North Africa

The French developed Algeria to produce wines of 12% or more alcohol which would be suitable for blending with their thin Midi wines. They were successful. Red, rosé, and white table wines and some dessert wines are produced. The warm climatic conditions ensure good ripening and wines of 11-14% alcohol. Heavy-yielding varieties are employed—Carignane, Alicante Bouschet, Clairette blanche, etc. In the cooler, mountainous areas some wines of better quality are produced. The vinification follows pre-W.W. II methods—sulfur dioxide, concrete tanks, continuous systems of color extraction, etc. Most of the wine is exported in tank ships, for blending purposes. A study, with points of interest to California producers, is that of Brémond (1957). The future of the Algerian wine industry is in doubt since the independence of that country and the reduction in exports to France. Acreage is only about half a million acres.

Other Countries

Morocco has a very ancient wine history, going back to the Romans. Joppien (1960) notes that grapes are grown in many parts of Morocco, many of them native table grapes. With the French occupation of 1912, European wine grapes were planted and modern wineries constructed. Important vineyards were planted near Meknes, Marrakesh, Casablanca, Rabat, Kenitra, and Oujda. Varieties such as Clairette (blanche?), Maccabeo, (Pedro?) Ximenes, Grenache, Cinsaut, Carignane and Alicante Bouschet are planted. The vintage follows the Algerian pattern, starting in August during the hottest period. Joppien (1960) states that the fermentations are very rapid and that the new wines are cooled and centrifuged so that wine is ready to export in September! The vintage amounts to about 20 million gallons of which ⅔ is exported, most of it red of about 12% alcohol. Acreage and production have dropped in recent years.

Tunisia also produces wines, largely intended for export. The cellars may not be quite so modern as in Algeria and the local trade even less. It is not a very hopeful viticultural region for the future under present social conditions.

There is also a very small wine industry in Egypt, largely for export and tourists. The climate is too warm for table wine grapes.

South Africa

The vine was introduced at Capetown in 1655. A sweet muscatel, Constantia, achieved considerable fame in Europe in the 18th century. The climate is favorable (though rather warm in some areas) and 11,000 ha (270,000 acres) in vines. Wine production is 6 million hl (155 million gal.). In the Coastal Belt, Cinsaut, Steen (Chenin blanc), and Green Grape (Sémillon) are the important varieties. Newer plantings contain Riesling, French Colombard, Cabernet Sauvignon and Shiraz. In the Little Karroo region Cinsaut, Clairette blanche, Palomino, Muscat of Alexandria and other muscats, and Thompson Seedless, are planted (Fig. 1.29). Soil types are variable—from sandy to heavy loams of a range in fertility. The vinification is generally modern. About half the crush is distilled for high proof or brandy. Some (about 2%) of the wine is exported. These are of the dessert type: ports or muscatels or red table wine. The ports are tawny or ruby or a little bottle-aged vintage port. Aged flor sherry of 17-20% is a distinctive and high quality product.

Courtesy of K.W.V.

FIG. 1.29. SOUTH AFRICAN HARVEST SCENE

South Africa makes a distinction between the light-bodied claret type (12.6% alcohol) and the heavier-bodied burgundy types (13.2%). Besides Pinotage and Cinsaut, some Cabernet and Shiraz are used. Much attention has been given to cool fermentation of white table wines—particularly of the Riesling type. These are usually slightly sweet. Some of the white wines are estate (winery) bottled and have distinctive vineyard names (some of obvious German derivation).

Both bottle- and tank-fermented sparkling (Fonkelwyn) wines are produced. (They are not called champagne.) Perlwine (wines of about 0.6 atm pressure at 27°C (80.6°F) with not over 3.2 g per liter of carbon dioxide) are also made by the tank process.

South Africa produces a native liqueur called Van der Hum which has a wine alcohol base and a tangerine flavor. Brandy of several qualities and ages is also available. For brandy, pot stills are preferred and a special board controls the quality. Regulations on appellations of origin have been introduced.

For an account of Cape wines see De Bosdari (1966) and Ambrosi (1959).

The KWV (Ko-operative Wynbouwers Vereniging) stabilized the industry by establishing minimum prices, distilling surpluses, standardizing the types for export, and encouraging the production of flor sherry and port. The KWV maintains extensive storage cellars (Fig. 1.30). It has sponsored production of better brandy by introducing double distillation in pot stills, harvesting the grapes on the green side, and aging the brandy. South African red table wines are often praised, particularly those from the Cabernet Sauvignon but white table wines constitute more than half of the market.

Courtesy of K.W.V.

FIG. 1.30. WINERY OF K.W.V. AT PAARL, SOUTH AFRICA

Technical and historical information regarding the production of wine in South Africa has been given by Anon. (1977), Biermann (1971), De Bosdari (1966), Leipoldt (1952), and Theron and Niehaus (1948).

SOUTH AMERICA

There are vineyards in Peru, Chile, Argentina, Bolivia, Uruguay, Paraguay, Brazil, Venezuela and elsewhere. For a discussion of these wines see Marrison (1971), Amerine (1959C), and Alvarado Moore (1967).

Peru

Vines were planted here near Cuczo in the colonial period about 1550. In the 19th century wine and brandy were exported, particularly to California. About 12,000 ha (30,000 acres) are planted. Varieties similar to the Mission were planted and some are still grown there. They represent a negative quality factor because of their low acidity and color and relatively high sugar content. Wine grapes are also planted. The climate is warm and usually very dry so that vine growth is not good. Excessive rainfall at vintage time may reduce crop and quality. Marrison (1971) reports the methods of vinification are often crude though sulfur dioxide is employed in the better wineries. The wines, he says, are naturally high in alcohol and may be further fortified and then diluted with water. Pisco brandy was colorless. It achieved a certain fame in California, particularly as an ingredient of Pisco punch, in the pre-Prohibition period. It is still produced but the samples tasted have not been notable for quality.

Chile

Vines were introduced from Peru at a very early date—some of them worthless seedlings imilar to the Mission variety. The climate is quite favorable and vines were successfully cultivated. French influence on grape growing and wine making may be seen. French varieties were imported, starting in 1851, and varieties such as Sauvignon blanc, Sémillon, Malbec, Merlot, and Cabernet Sauvignon are planted (11,000 ha or 280,000 acres). The vinification is not yet the best. The whites are often fermented on the skins too long and kept in the wood past their prime. The reds are better.

Chilean viticulture is free of phylloxera and mildew. While most of the production is of table wines, some red sweet wine and brandy are produced. Chile has a modest export trade. The quality of selected wines is good, but some of the white wine is too dark and tannic. A description of Chilean wines is given by Léon (1947) and Dalmasso (1956). The best are labeled *Reservado* or *Gran Vino*.

Argentina

Grapes were introduced from Chile about 1557. It is the largest producer of wine in the New World, 240,000 hl (600 million gal.). The center of production is Mendoza. In the south near Neuquén some wines are produced. The climate and soil are favorable and the vineyards are well cared for. A few Criolla varieties from the colonial period remain. European varieties are widely planted—Malbec and Merlot for red wines and Pedro Ximenes, Trebbiano, Riesling, and Sauvignon blanc for whites. There are many large vineyards of high production. The wineries are also large and generally modern. The background of the producers is usually Italian. The wines are sound ordinary products. Argentina has the largest per capita consumption of wine in the Americas. Much of the wine (*chica*) is of low alcohol content (up to 8%). Vermouth and anise-flavored brandy are also made. Dalmasso (1956) gives a description of the industry, noting particularly the low cost of production (see also Lichine 1974). For technical information see Magistocchi (1955) and Oreglia (1964).

Brazil

Much of the country is too humid for grapes. In the state of Rio Grande do Sol there are 61,000 ha (150,000 acres). Besides the original Portuguese colonists, German vineyardists arrived in 1824 and Italians in 1875. American varieties, such as Isabella, Herbemont, Concord, and Niagara (68%), some direct producer hybrids (7%) are planted (Rui 1975). In the newer plantings, European varieties have been used. Demand is increasing: over 2.2 million hl (60 million gal.) are produced. Because of the prevalence of fungus diseases and the American varieties, the quality of the wines has not been high, but with the new vineyards with *V. vinifera* varieties and modern technology, much improvement is needed and can be expected.

Other Countries

Very few grapes can be grown successfully in the high plateau country of Bolivia. A little wine is produced for local consumption.

Near Montevideo in Uruguay there are extensive vineyards. The climate is not always favorable because of drought. A few wines of quality are produced but more are ordinary. Annual production amounts to over 760,000 hl (20 million gal.).

There have been vineyards in Paraguay since the earliest settlements at the missions. The climate is not favorable, the varieties are poor, and the production and quality are small. For a more complete description of these wines see Amerine (1959C) and Hyams (1965).

Venezuela makes a few wines from surplus locally-grown table grapes and from imported grape concentrate.

NORTH AMERICA

The vineyards of North America may be classified into four regions: Canada, eastern United States, California, and Mexico.

Canada

The Canadian industry is mainly on the Niagara peninsula where Lake Ontario protects it from the north winds and Lake Erie lies on the west and further moderates the temperature. About 70% of the grape acreage is planted to Concord, 15% to Niagara, and the remainder to native varieties such as Agawam, Delaware, and Catawba, plus considerable direct-producing hybrids and a small amount of V. vinifera (Rowe 1970). Prices vary according to the quality of the grapes. Water and sugar are used to reduce the total acidity and increase the alcohol—indicated by the statutory limitation of 250 gal. per ton. Since the Canadian tax on dessert wines is on the spirits used in fortification, syruped fermentation can be used (p. 439). Some wines of 17% alcohol are produced by fortification with high-proof spirits. Both baked (Tressler process) and flor sherry (submerged culture) are made.

There is a small grape industry in British Columbia (about 12,000 tons). The winter temperatures are low and grape growing difficult. Bowen et al. (1956) recommended direct producers. Sugar contents are low (11.4-19.5%) and the acidity high.

Mexico

Most of the Mexican vineyards are located in warm climatic regions. This, coupled with the low acidity and low color of the Mission fruit accounts for the lack of consumer acceptance of some of their wines. Recently, Mexican viticulture has begun to introduce new and better varieties and the acreage has increased rapidly (Anon. 1958B; Amerine 1959C). With suitable fermentation and aging controls, standard wines should be produced. Quality standards need to be established. The best Mexican wines currently produced may be dessert types—particularly of the muscatel and related types. Some of the brandies appear to be artificially flavored.

Eastern United States

During the Colonial period, numerous attempts were made to introduce the European grape along the Atlantic seaboard. Winter killing, high summer humidity, phylloxera, and perhaps virus diseases defeated all of these efforts. It was not until about the end of the 18th century that serious attention was turned to domesticating varieties of the local species. A number of varieties which were suited to cultivation were developed. These included Concord, Catawba, Niagara, Delaware, Ives Seedling, and a host of others.

These have a more or less strong and distinctive aroma, partially due to methyl anthranilate. This odor is commonly said to be "foxy" here and abroad. They are generally of insufficient sugar to produce a balanced table wine and sugaring is permitted. The industry is important in the Finger Lakes region of New York. The moderating influence of these deep lakes helps prevent winter killing and possibly late spring frosts. The vineyards are mainly on the slopes facing the lakes. There is a small wine industry in Ohio. Near Sandusky where Lake Erie exerts a moderating influence on the temperature, there are many vineyards. Other vineyards and wineries are found in Michigan, Pennsylvania, Illinois, Arkansas, Missouri, and elsewhere.

The native varieties are used to produce varietal types and also are often labeled with European appellations. Thus, we have New York Delaware, and New York Rhine. Considerable sparkling wine is also produced (p. 488). There is also an extensive shipment of wines from California to eastern producers for blending. Thus, eastern muscatels, ports, sherries and table wines may contain considerable California wine.

In Maryland and elsewhere, a wine industry, based on the direct producers, has developed. Small quantities of wines are produced in the South Atlantic states from varieties of *Vitis rotundifolia*—the so-called Scuppernong grapes. These have a different aroma from *V. labrusca* type grapes, due partially to phenethyl alcohol (p. 110).

While the summer temperatures of eastern United States are frequently very desirable for vine culture, extensive plantings of *V. vinifera* varieties have not been made there. However, in recent years using cold-resistant rootstocks, many vineyards (1 to 50 acres) have been established and some good wines produced. The eastern wines, because of their obvious and strong aromas, have an appeal for many consumers. Concord wines or Concord concentrate are blended with California red wines and sugar to produce sweet kosher-type wines. A large clientele for these wines has also developed. See Adams (1978) for general information on American wines. More detailed information on methods of production of eastern U.S. wines is given in Chap. 12.

Oregon and Washington

The vineyard hectarage in both states has increased rapidly in recent years, particularly in *V. vinifera*. Washington has important Concord vineyards, largely used for grape juice and concentrate. In both states a number of new wineries have been established. Fall frosts have been a problem in young *vinifera* vineyards in Washington. Fall rains have been of some concern in Oregon.

California

Many of the factors influencing the quality of California wines are considered elsewhere in the text—particularly climate (p. 113), varieties (p. 149–151), and production techniques. Since this book will probably be used most extensively in this state, the other quality factors will be considered in greater detail for this region than for others. Production of wines and brandy in California since 1909 is given in Table 1.2.

TABLE 1.2. PRODUCTION OF WINES AND BRANDIES IN CALIFORNIA, 1909-1976 AVERAGES

Calendar Years	Total All Wines[1]	Dessert and Appetizer Wines	Vermouth and Special Natural Wines	Table Wines	Beverage Brandy[2]
Thousands of Gallons					
1909-1913	43,950	19,161	—	24,434	—
1933-1937	54,081	38,199	—	16,482	1.854
1938-1942	81,721	56,455	—	25,266	3,971
1943-1947	113,878	78,204	1,242[3]	35,674	4,350
1948-1952	130,091	96,237	818	33,853	2,615
1953-1957	126,559	92,027	2,116[4]	34,532	3,650
1958-1962	148,704	96,343	14,210	52,361	5,380
1963-1967	172,582	94,900	18,835	77,682	12,865
1968-1972	211,428	68,429	36,502	142,999	10,944
1973	312,551	72,183	55,957	240,367	14,239
1974	291,092	52,316	53,339	238,776	16,406
1975	295,237	61,077	62,068	234,160	14,789
1976	334,589	—[5]	60,944	—[5]	15,363
1977	377,260	—[5]	48,169	—[5]	12,275

Source of data: Wine Institute Bulletins and 1st and 2nd Editions.
[1]The total is not obtained as a sum of the other entries since table and dessert wines are diverted to production of sparkling and flavored wines. For table, dessert and all wines the production is only for July to December.
[2]In proof gallons and on crop year basis. Estimates before 1963.
[3]1944-1947.
[4]Beginning of production of special natural wines.
[5]No longer available.

The historical influences are important for California. The original vineyards were planted at the Missions, primarily of the Mission grape from Baja California, in order to produce wines for religious and domestic use. It is a late-ripening grape of low color and acid and generally of high sugar. Its table wines are flat and spoil easily. The Mission grape is still grown to a limited extent in California. It was partially responsible for the generally low quality of California table wines in the pre-1880 period and when used for table wines is still a negative quality factor. It can be used for white dessert wines of above average quality.

There is one positive factor that remains from the Mission period—the development of the wine type angelica (Amerine and Winkler 1938). While the exact origin of this wine type remains in doubt it seems to have been made originally during the Mission period from musts of the Mission grape.

Another historical influence was the emphasis on varieties. This arose from three separate sources: the work of Agoston Haraszthy, the research of Eugene Waldemar Hilgard and the propaganda efforts of the State Board of Viticultural Commissioners.

Haraszthy's importation of varieties from Europe was of great potential importance. Regrettably, the political situation on his return was such that the vines could not be properly distributed and some misnaming of varieties probably occurred during their haphazard distribution; see Fredericksen (1947) and Adams (1978). Hilgard of the University of California published a series of masterful studies on the adaptation of grape varieties to California conditions between 1880 and 1892. He noted the critical importance of climate, variety, and time of harvesting in a region as warm as California. The State Board of Viticultural Commissioners was also interested in better varieties and provided useful propaganda in favor of planting better varieties (Amerine 1959A, 1960).

An important factor was, and is, the diversified European origin of California vineyardists and wine makers. From the start, French, German, Italian, British, Spanish, and other nationalities of grape growers and wine makers were active. They brought their several varieties, wine making procedures, and type nomenclature. The climatic conditions of California, however, were different from those of the European regions from which they came. Thus, the date of harvest in Europe was 2 to 6 weeks *too late* for California conditions. The temperature of fermentation and storage was also higher and this led to bacterial spoilage. The wonder is that so many sound wines were produced in the pre-1900 period.

Another negative influence was the free use of the only wine-type names which they knew—claret (for the British), champagne, chablis, and burgundy (for the French), chianti (for the Italians), etc. In some cases, this extended to use of private or local place names—Château d'Yquem, Johannisberg, etc. The ethics of the time and place should be considered. Their use helped distribution but it gave an imitative character to the industry. Often, attention was given to producing wines which resembled foreign types rather than to creation of unique native types. This continues today.

Since Repeal, the emphasis has been on rapid turnover and large-scale operations. This has changed normal aging.[7] The small producer found the competition too great and many left wine production. Only recently has this trend been reversed. Large, modern, well-equipped and -staffed wineries are obviously advantageous in the economical production of standard wines. It would be too bad for the future of the California wine industry if wineries produced only standard, sound, and alas, rather uninteresting wines. The "differences" among wines are a part of their aesthetic interest. The industry may underestimate the potential of the American market for wines of special character. The reputation of fine wines helps build the confidence of the public in all California wines. The large importations in foreign wines should convince us that there is a demand for special wines of distinctive quality, even though most imported wines are *not* of high quality.

The negative influence of using European names for native wines has often been noted in the new wine areas of the world. James (1966) stressed this for Australia. The use of foreign appellations for California wines is not in the best interest of the proper image of our wine industry. Furthermore, use of these names simply advertises the wines of the original region. The recent success of varietal wines in California is an indication of where the future may lie. One point may be important: If the varietal approach is made too "pure," progress may be hindered.

The continuing pattern of the California grape and wine industry until recently has been years of high production and low prices followed by years of lower production but higher prices. This has had a restraining influence on the industry. It encouraged, certainly, high production by the vineyardists and attitudes of short term profit by the wine makers. Under these circumstances the development of an acceptance of quality is difficult. As to which is the "egg and which is the chicken" we leave the decision to the agricultural economists. Certainly, the complex interrelation of the table, raisin, and wine industry has had a potent effect on the California industry and may have aided the up and down pattern. It has also tended to encourage the planting of dual- or triple-purpose grapes which in some cases are not suited to the production of high quality wines. The widespread planting of Thompson Seedless is a negative quality factor. Recent plantings of varietal grapes and higher prices should correct this (see also Anon. 1973).

One result of this uncertain economic status was the development of the California Wine Association (CWA) in the late 19th century (Pen-

---

[7]Aging in large containers, of course, reduced the rate of aging.

inou and Greenleaf 1954). It certainly stabilized the trade, and, what is more important, succeeded in standardizing types. The CWA blending and finishing cellar at Richmond plus the undoubted tasting ability of Henry Lachman resulted in the first large-scale standardization of California wine types. In the post-Prohibition period, this uncertain economic position gave birth to two other organizations—the Wine Institute and the Wine Advisory Board.

The Wine Institute is a nonprofit trade organization which includes most of the California producers. Its influences have been manifold. Trade and legal assistance to its members have been most important. It is also a sounding board for industry opinion. The industry has thus been able to speak singly in many important cases. The Wine Advisory Board (WAB) was a governmental agency whose revenue was derived from a tax on sales of wine and whose efforts were largely devoted to trade promotion. This, fortunately, was generously interpreted so that it included allotments for research. It ceased functioning in 1975.

Another historical factor was the development of vineyard-winery companies with an emphasis on quality. Their stature is certainly of considerable value to them commercially and to the industry as a whole.

Prohibition had other effects—the influence of which is difficult to evaluate. Sales of dessert wines were greatly stimulated by Prohibition. Whereas in the pre-W.W. I period (1900-1910) dessert wines accounted for about 40% of the production, it accounted for up to 75% of the production in the pre-W.W. II period. The reasons for this change in taste are not known. Recently, the percentage of dessert wine consumption has decreased to about 30%. Repeal of Prohibition brought a producer-wholesaler-retailer relationship which eventually did away with the retail sale of wine in bulk. While this may have increased the profits of the California producers it is by no means as certain that it favorably influenced per capita consumption since it markedly increased the cost of wine to the consumer. It surely improved the quality.

Prohibition brought the winery under close control of the government. In the post-Prohibition period many regulations were easily (possibly not all desirable) introduced. Analytical standards for volatile acidity, alcohol content, and even for sugar content for types were thus easily established. The effect continues with the continuing campaign to improve sanitary practices of the industry.

The impact of industrialization was gradually felt by the California wine industry in the post-Prohibition period. These various influences are too recent for complete evaluation but they have led to much centralization, a trend which will probably continue.

Gallo (1958) in an analysis of the future of the California wine industry predicted development of new wine types. He particularly noted the need for changes in laws and regulations to permit development of low-carbonation wines. Among the advances of the first 25 years after repeal he noted development of slightly sweet, red table wines, creation of the rosé market, cold fermentation, early bottling of white wines, sterile filtration, flor sherry, ion-exchange, better maturity standards, production of wine vinegar, a successful berry wine industry, introduction of special natural wines, etc.

The technological information provided by the College of Agricultural and Environmental Sciences of the University of California and its students was (and continues to be) of considerable value. The highest standards of viticulture and enology were emphasized. The importance of variety, an extension of Hilgard's work, was stressed. The importance of the newer techniques of food handling were brought to the attention of the industry and the responsible governmental agencies. Their recommendations have been promulgated by numerous conferences, circulars, bulletins and books, in addition to regular University classes and extension courses (Amerine 1959A). The wine judgings of the California State Fair and county fairs, and the meetings of the Technical Advisory Committee of the Wine Institute, and of the American Society of Enologists have been of importance in improving quality. The latter and the Wine Institute have provided scholarships for students.

REFERENCES[8]

ACCADEMIA ITALIANA DELLA VITE E DEL VINO. 1949-1976. Atti. Tipografia S.T.I.A.V., Siena. (28 Vols.)

ADAMS, L. D. 1978. The Wines of America, 2nd Edition. McGraw-Hill Book Co., New York.

AGABAL'IANTS, G. G. 1969. Khimiko tekhnologicheskii kontrol' vinodelia (Chemical-technological control of wine making). Pishchepromizdat, Moscow.

AGABAL'IANTS, G. G. 1972. Izbrannie Raboti po Khimii i Tekhnologii Vina, Shampanskogo i Koniaka, Pishchevaia Promishlennost, Moscow.

AKADEMIYA NAUK S.S.S.R., Institut Biokhimii. 1947-1964. Biokhimiya Vinodeliya. (Biochemistry of Wine Making.) Izdatel'stvo Akademii Nauk S.S.S.R., Moscow. (8 Vols.)

ALLEN, H. W. 1933. Sherry. Constable and Co., London.

ALLEN, H. W. 1957. Good Wine from Portugal. Sylvan Press, London.

ALLEN, H. W. 1961. A History of Wine: Great Vintage Wines from the Homeric Age to the Present Day. Faber and Faber, London.

ALLEN, H. W. 1964. The Wines of Portugal. McGraw-Hill Book Co., New York.

ALLEWELDT, G. 1965. Der Rebenanbau in der Turkei. Wein-Wissen. *20*, 109-126.

---

[8]Titles have been translated only for nonwestern European languages.

ALVARADO MOORE, R. 1967. Sinopsis de la Vitivinicultura Chilena. Asociación Nacional de Viticultores, Santiago de Chile.

AMBROSI, H. 1959. Die Weine Südafrikas. Deut. Wein-Ztg. *95*, 482, 484, 498, 500, 502.

AMBROSI, H. 1976. Where the Great German Wines Grow. Hastings House, New York.

AMERINE, M. A. 1959A. Chemists and the California wine industry. Am. J. Enol. Vitic. *10*, 124-129.

AMERINE, M.A. 1959B. Continuous flow production of still and sparkling wine. Wines Vines *40*, No. 6, 41-42.

AMERINE, M.A. 1959C. The romance of Pan-American wines. Pan American Medical Assoc., San Francisco Chapter, Ann. Bull. *1958*, 21-27.

AMERINE, M. A. 1960. Hilgard and California viticulture. Hilgardia *33*, 1-23.

AMERINE, M. A. 1963. Viticulture and enology in the Soviet Union. Wines Vines *44*, No. 10, 29-34, 36; No. 11, 57-62, 64; No. 12, 25-26, 28-30.

AMERINE, M. A. 1964. Der Weinbau in Japan. Wein-Wissen. *19*, 225-231.

AMERINE, M. A. 1965. Research on viticulture and enology in the Soviet Union. Food Technol. *19*, 179-182.

AMERINE, M. A. and DEMATTEI, W. 1940. Color in California wines. III. Methods of removing color from the skins. Food Res. *5*, 509-519.

AMERINE, M. A. and JOSLYN, M. A. 1970. Table Wines; the Technology of Their Production, 2nd Edition. University of California Press, Berkeley and Los Angeles.

AMERINE, M. A. and SINGLETON, V. L. 1977. Wine: An Introduction for Americans, 2nd Edition. University of California Press, Berkeley and Los Angeles.

AMERINE, M. A. and WINKLER, A. J. 1938. Angelica. Wines Vines *19*, No. 9, 5.

ANON. 1957. Wines of Italy. Instituto Nazionale per il Commercio Estero, Rome.

ANON. 1958A. The development of viticulture and wine making in Soviet Russia. Am. J. Enol. *9*, 86-91.

ANON. 1958B. Grape and wine industry of Mexico. Am. J. Enol. *9*, 92-93.

ANON. 1958C. Hungarian vineyards and wines. Am. J. Enol. Vitic. *10*, 142–146.

ANON. 1959. Wine grape varieties for new plantings. J. Agr. South Australia *62*, 428-435.

ANON. 1961. Wine-producing in Yugoslavia. Federal Chamber of Foreign Trade, Belgrade.

ANON. 1977. A Survey of Wine Growing in South Africa, 1976-1977. Public Relations Department of the KWV, Paarl.

ANON. 1973. California Wine. Edited by Bob Thompson. Lane Magazine, Menlo Park, California.

ARLOTT, J. and FIELDEN, C. 1976. Burgundy: Vines and Wines. Davis-Poynter, London.

ARTHOLD, M. 1950. Handbuch der Kellerwirtschaft, 5th Edition. Scholle-Verlag, Wien.

AZARASHVILI, P. B. 1959. Vinogradnye Vina i Kon'iaki Gruzii (Vineyards, Wines and Brandies of Georgia). Pishchepromizdat, Moscow.

BAKER, G. A., AMERINE, M. A. and ROESSLER, E. B. 1952. Theory and application of fractional blending systems. Hilgardia *21*, 383-409.

BENSON, C. T. 1959. The Canadian wine Industry. Wines Vines *40*, No. 9, 23.

BENVEGNIN, L., CAPT, E. and PIGUET, G. 1951. Traité de Vinification, 2nd Edition. Librairie Payot, Lausanne.

BERIDZE, G. I. 1965. Vino i Kon'iaki Gruzii; les Vins et les Cognacs de la Georgie. Izdatel'stvo "Sabchota Sakartvelo," Tbilisi.

BERNAZ, D. 1962. Tehnologia vinului. Editura Agro-Silvică, Bucharest.

BIERMANN, B. 1971. Red Wine in South Africa. Buren, Cape Town.

BOBADILLA, G. F. DE. 1965. Viniferas Jerezanas y de Andalucia Occidental. Instituto Nacional de Investigaciones Agronómicas, Madrid.

BOBADILLA, G. F. DE and NAVARRO, E. 1949. Vinos de Jerez. Estudios de sus Acidos, desde el Periódo de Madurez de la Uva Hasta el Envejecimiento del Vino. Instituto Nacional de Investigaciones Agronómicas, Madrid. Cuaderno No. 122, pp. 474-519.

BOBADILLA, G. F. DE, QUIROS, J. M. and SERRANO, J. J. 1954. Vinos de Jerez. El Enyesado de los Mostos. Instituto Nacional de Investigaciones Agronómicas, Madrid. Cuaderno No. 216, pp. 411-446.

BOCKER, H. 1959. Untersuchungen über den Einfluss von Mineralstoffen auf den bakteriellen Säurerückgang in Trauben- und Fruchtweinen. Zentr. Bakteriol. Parasitenk. Abt. II *112*, 337-350.

BODE, C. 1956. Wines of Italy. The McBride Co, New York.

BOWEN, J. F., FISHER, D. V. and MACGREGOR, D. R. 1965. Grape and wine production in British Columbia. Am. J. Enol. Vitic. *16*, 241-244.

BRÉJOUX, P. 1956. Les Vins de Loire. Compagnie Parisienne d'Éditions Techniques et Commerciales, Paris.

BRÉMOND, E. 1957. Techniques Modernes de Vinification et de Conservation des Vins dans les Pays Chauds. Librairie de la Maison Rustique, Paris.

BRUNI, B. 1970. Vini Italiani Portanti Una Denominazione di Origine, 2nd Edition. Edagricole, Bologna.

BULIČ, S. 1949. Dalmatinska Ampelografija (Dalmatian Ampelography). Poljoprovredni Nakladni Zavod, Zagreb.

CANTARELLI, C. 1958. The increase of the fermentation speed in wine making. Rev. Ferm. Indust. Aliment. *13*, 59-71.

CARPENTIERI, F. 1948. Enologia Teorico-Pratica, 14th Edition, 2 Vols. Editrice Fratelli Ottavi, Casale Monferrato.

CASTILLO, J. DEL. and HALLETT, D. R. 1972. The Wine of Spain. Proyección Editorial, Bilbao.

CERLETTI, B. 1958. Aspetti della enologia Jugoslava. Atti Accad. Ital. Vite Vino 10, 228-240.

CHAPPAZ, G. 1951. Le Vignoble et le Vin de Champagne. L. Larmat, Paris.

COCKBURN, E. (Undated) Port Wine and Oporto. Wine and Spirit Publications, London.

COCKS, C. and FÉRET, E. 1969. Bordeaux et Ses Vins, Classés par Ordre de Mérite, 12th Edition. Féret et Fils, Bordeaux.

CONSTANTINESCU, G. 1958. Raionarea Viticulturi. Editura Accademiei Republicii Populare Romîne, Bucharest.

CONSTANTINESCU, G. 1959-1967. Ampelografia Republicii Populare Romîne. 8 vol. Editura Academiei Republicii Populare Romîne, Bucharest.

CORNELSSEN, F. A. 1970. Die deutschen Weine. Seewald Verlag, Stuttgart.

COSMO, I. and DEROSA, T. 1960. Manuale di Enologia, Guida del Buon Cantiniere. Edizioni Agricole, Bologna.

CROFT-COOKE, R. 1957. Port. Putnam, London.

CROFT-COOKE, R. 1961. Madeira. Putnam, London.

CSEPREGI, P. 1955. Szölöfajtáink; Ampelográfia (Grape Growing, Ampelography). Mezögazdasági Kiadó, Budapest.

DALLAS, P. 1974. The Great Wines of Italy. Doubleday, Garden City, N.J.

DALMASSO, G. 1956. La viticoltura in Europa e nel Sud-America. Riv. Inter. Agr. 1, No. 5, 38-47.

DALMASSO, G. 1958. Viticoltura ed enologia nella Bulgaria d'oggi. Atti Accad. Ital. Vite Vino 10, 70-124.

DALMASSO, G. and TYNDALO, V. 1957. Viticoltura e ampelografia dell' U.R.S.S. Atti Accad. Ital. Vite Vino 9, 446-548.

DAVITAYA, F. F. 1948. Klimaticheskie Zony Vinograda SSSR (Grape Climatic Zones in the Soviet Union). Pishchepromizdat, Moscow.

DE BOSDARI, C. 1966. Wines of the Cape, 3rd Edition. A. A. Balkema, Cape Town, Amsterdam.

DEBUIGNE, G. 1976. Larousse Dictionary of Wines of the World. Hamlyn, London, New York.

DETTORI, R. G. 1953. Italian Wines and Liqueurs. Federazione Italiana Produttori ed Esportatori di Vini, Liquori ed Affini, Rome.

DION, R. 1959. Histoire de la Vigne et du Vin en France des Origines au XIXe Siècle. Paris.

DURMISHIDZE, S. V. 1955. Dubil'nie Veshchestva i Antots'yani Vinogradvoĭ Lozi i Vina. (Tannins and Anthocyanins of Grapes and Wine.) Izdatel'stvo Akademii Nauk SSSR, Moscow.

DUTTWEILER, G. 1968. Les Vins Suisses. Éditions Générales, Genève.

EGOROV, A. A. 1955. Voprosy Vinodeliya (Enological Principles). Pishchepromizdat, Moscow.

EVANS, L. 1973. Australian Complete Book of Wine. Hamlyn, Sydney.

FERRARESE, M. 1951. Enologia Pratica Moderna, 3rd Edition. Editore Ulrico Hoepli, Milan.

FERRÉ, L. 1958. Traité d'Oenologie Bourguignonne. Institut National des Appellations d'Origine des Vins et Eaux-de-Vie, Paris.

FLANZY, M. 1935. Nouvelle méthode de vinification. Rev. Viticult. *83*, 315-319, 325-329, 341-347.

FORBES, P. 1967. Champagne: The Wine, the Land and the People. Reynal & Company, New York.

FREDERICKSEN, P. 1947. The authentic Haraszthy story. Wines Vines *28*, No. 6, 25-26, 42; No. 7, 15-16, 30; No. 8, 17-18, 37-38; No. 9, 17-18, 34; No. 11, 21-22, 41-42.

FROLOV-BAGREEV, A. M. 1946-1965. Ampelografiya S.S.S.R., 8 Vols. (Russian Ampelography.) Gos. Pishchepromizdat, Moscow.

GADILLE, R. 1967. Le vignoble de la Côte Bourguignonne. Paris.

GAHANO, A. B. 1951. A Região dos Vinhos Verdes. Comissão de Viticultura da Região dos Vinhos Verdes, Porto. (Also published in French as Le Vin "Verde.")

GALET, P. 1957-1964. Cépages et Vignobles de France. I. Les Vignes Américaines. II. Les Cépages de Cuve. III. Les Cépages de Table. IV. Le Raisins de Table. La Production Viticole Française. Paul Déhan, Montpellier.

GALLO, E. 1958. Outlook for a mature industry. Wines Vines *39*, No. 6, 27-28, 30.

GALTIER, G. 1961. Le Vignoble du Languedoc Méditerranée et du Roussillon. Éditions Causse, Graille & Castelnau, Montpellier.

GARINO-CANINA, E. 1950. La Pratica Enologica del "Governo" nel Quadro delle Transformazion Chimico-Biologiche della Rifermentazione. Scuola Tipografica San Guiseppe, Asti. (*From* Atti VIII Congresso Internazionale Industria Agraria, Bruxelles. 1950).

GAROGLIO, P. G. 1965. La Nuova Enologia. Libreria LI. CO/SA, Florence.

GEISS, W. 1960. Lehrbuch für Weinbereitung und Kellerwirtschaft. Bad Kreuznach.

GEORGIEV, IV. 1949. Vinarstvo. (Wine Making.) Zemizdat, Sofia.

GERASIMOV, M. A. 1957. Viticulture and enology in Russia (translation by M.A.A.). Wines Vines *38*, No. 3, 26-27. (*From* Vignes & Vins No. 48, 14-16; No. 49, 12. 1956.)

GERASIMOV, M. A. 1964. Tekhnologiya Vinodeliya. (Technology of Wine Making.) Pishchepromizdat, Moscow.

GIANFORMAGGIO, F. 1955. Manuale Pratico di Enologia Moderna, 3rd Edition. U. Hoepli, Milan.

GOLD, A. H. 1968. Wines of the World. Virtue, London.

GOLDSCHMIDT, E. 1951. Deutschlands Weinbauorte and Weinbergslagen, 6th Edition. Verlag der Deutschen Wein-Zeitung, Mainz.

GONZÁLEZ GORDON, M. M. 1972: Sherry: The Noble Wine. Cassell, London.

GOT, A. 1949. Monbazillac. Éditions d'Aquitaine, Bordeaux.

GROSSI, S. 1973. Guida dei Vini d'Italia. Rietti, Milan.

GUNYON, R. E. H. 1971. The Wines of Central and South-Eastern Europe. Duckworth, London.

HALÁSZ, Z. 1962. Hungarian Wine Through the Ages. Corvina, Budapest.

HALLGARTEN, P. A. 1977. The Connoisseurs' Guide to the Good Wines of Germany. Wineographs, London.

HALLGARTEN, S. F. 1965. Rhineland; Wineland. Withy Grove Press, Manchester.

HALLGARTEN, S. F. 1970. Alsace and Its Wine Gardens, 2nd Edition. Wine and Spirit Publications, London.

HALLGARTEN, S. F. 1974. A guide to the Vineyards, Estates and Wines of Germany. Publivin, Dallas.

HEALY, M. 1963. Stay Me with Flagons. Michael Joseph, Ltd., London.

HOCHBERG, M. 1954-1955. Gidul Ha-Gefen. Grape Growing. 2 Vols. Tel-Aviv.

HOGG, A. 1976. Guide to Visiting Vineyards. M. Joseph, London.

HULAČ, V. 1949. Příručka Sklepniho Hospodárství (Manual of Cellar Management). Nákladem Ústredního Svazu Československých Vinařú, Brno.

HYAMS, E. S. 1965. Dionysus; a Social History of the Wine Vine. Macmillan, New York.

INSTITUT NATIONAL DES APPELLATIONS D'ORIGINE DES VINS ET EAUX-DE-VIE. 1952. L'Oeuvre de l'Institut National des Appellations d' Origine des Vins et Eaux-de-Vie. Paris.

INSTITUTO DO VINHO DO PORTO. 1940-1972/1973. Anais de Instituto do Porto. Porto. (25 Vols.)

JACQUELIN, L. and POULAIN, R. 1962. The Wines & Vineyards of France. G. P. Putnam's Sons, New York.

JAMES, W. 1966. Wine in Australia, 4th Edition. Georgian House, Melbourne.

JEFFS, J. 1970. Sherry, 2nd Edition. Faber and Faber, London.

JEFFS, J. 1971. The Wines of Europe. Taplinger Publishing Co., New York.

JOHNSON, H. 1968. Wine. Sphere, London.

JOHNSON, H. 1971. The World Atlas of Wine. Simon and Schuster, New York.

JOPPIEN, P. H. 1960. Zur Kenntnis der Weine Morokkos. Deut. Wein-Ztg. 96, 518, 520, 522, 524.

JOSLYN, M. A. and AMERINE, M. A. 1964. Dessert, Appetizer and Related Flavored Wines; The Technology of Their Production. University of California, Division of Agricultural Sciences, Berkeley.

JUNTA NACIONAL DO VINHO. 1942. Contribuicão para o Cadastro dos Vinhos Portugueses de Área de Influència da J. N. V. Tipografia Ramos, Lisbon.

JUNTA NACIONAL DO VINHO. 1949-1961. Anais da Junta Nacional do Vinho. Tip. Alcobacense, Lim., Lisbon. (13 Vols.)

JURSA, O. 1971. Wein aus Österreich. Kremayr & Scheriau, Wien.

KALUGINA, G. I., SAMARSKIĬ, A. T. and RUDNEV, N. M. 1957. Vinodelie i Vina Moldavii. (Wines and Vines of Moldavia.) Pishchepromizdat, Moscow.

KICHKOVSKI, Z. 1975. Sur l'oenologie de l'Union Soviétique. Atti Accad. Ital. Vite Vino 27, 139-149.

KITTEL, J. B. and BREIDER, H. 1958. Das Buch vom Frankenweine. Universitätsdruckerei H. Stürz AG, Würzburg.

KOBEL, F. 1947. Der Obst- und Weinbau in Ungarn. Schweiz. Z. Obst-Weinbau 56, 413-417, 429-436, 445-449.

KONDAREW, M. 1965. Die Entwicklung des Weinbaues in Bulgarien. Wein-Wissen. 20, 428-432.

KRAEMER, A. 1956. Im Lande des Bocksbeutels. Druck und Verlag Pius Halbig, Würzburg.

KRESSMANN, E. 1968. The Wonder of Wine. Hastings House, New York.

KUCHEL, R. H. 1959. Vine and wine industry of Cyprus. Australian Wine, Brew. Spirit Rev. 78, 72, 74, 78.

LABORDE, J. 1907. Cours d'Oenologie. Tome I. L. Mulo, Paris; Féret et Fils, Bordeaux.

LAFFER, H. E. 1949. The Wine Industry of Australia. Australian Wine Board, Adelaide.

LAFFORGUE, G. 1947. Le Vignoble Girondin. Louis Larmat, Paris.

LAHO, L. 1962. Vinohradnictvo. (Wine Making.) Slovenské Vydavatel'stvo Pôdohospodárskej Literatúry, Bratislava.

LANGENBACH, A. 1962. German Wines and Vines. Vista Books, London.

LARREA, A. 1965. Tratado Practico de Viticultura y Enologia; Manual para Capataces Bodegueros. Editorial Aedos, Barcelona.

LARREA, R. A. 1957. Arte y Ciencia de los Vinos Espanoles. Siler, Madrid.

LAYTON, T. A. 1961. Wines of Italy. Harper Trade Journals, London.

LAYTON, T. A. 1970. Wines and People of Alsace. Cassell, London.

LEIPOLDT, C. L. 1952. Three Hundred Years of Cape Wine. Stewart, Cape Town.

LÉON, V. F. 1947. Uvas y Vinos de Chile. Sindicato Nacional Vitivinícola, Santiago de Chile.

LEONHARDT, G. 1963. Das Weinbuch; Werden des Weines von der Rebe bis zum Glase. VEB Fachbuchverlag, Leipzig.

LEVY, J. F. 1958. Vignes et vins d'URSS. Vignes et Vins (65) 24-26; (66) 17-19; (67) 27-28; (68) 15-16. (Translation by M.A.A. In Wines Vines 40 (11) 45-46, 48; (12) 27-28, 1959.)

LICHINE, A. 1974. New Encyclopedia of Wines and Spirits, 2nd Edition. Knopf, New York.

LICHINE, A. 1979. Alexis Lichine's Guide to the Wines and Vineyards of France. Knopf, New York.

LOEB, O. W. and PRITTIE, T. 1972. Moselle. Faber and Faber, London.

MAGISTOCCHI, G. 1955. Tratado de Enología Adaptado a la República Argentina. Ed. El Ateneo, Buenos Aires.

MALTABAR, V. M., NUTOV, L. O. and FERTMAN, G. I. 1959. Tekhnologiia Kon'yaka. (Technology of brandy production.) Pishchepromizdat, Moscow.

MANCEAU, E. 1929. Vinification Champenoise. Chez l'Auteur, Épernay.

MARCILLA ARRAZOLA, J. 1946. Tratado Práctico de Viticultura y Enología Españoles, 2nd Edition. SAETA, Madrid. (2 Vols.)

MARCILLA ARRAZOLA, J., ALAS, G. and FEDUCHY, E. 1936 (i.e., 1939). Contribución al estudio de los levaduras que forman velo sobre ciertos vinos de elevado grado alcohólico. Anales Centro Invest. Vinícolas 1, 1-230.

MARESCALCHI, C. 1957. Manuale dell'Enologo, 12th Edition. Casa Editrice Fratelli Marescalchi, Casale Monferrato.

MARRISON, L. W. 1971. Wines for Everyone. St. Martin's Press, New York.

MARRISON, L. W. 1973. Wines and Spirits, 3rd Edition. Penguin, Harmondsworth.

MAXWELL, K. 1966. Fairest Vineyards. Keartland, Johannesburg.

MAZZEI, A. M. 1959. Buoni vini da pasto. Italia agricola 96, 757-788.

MEINHARD, H. 1977. The Wines of Germany. Stein and Day, New York.

MICHEL, A. 1953. Le problème de la qualité des grands vins de Bourgogne. Prog. Agric. Vitic. 140, 84-91, 116-121.

MOGILYANSKIĬ, N. K. 1954. Plodovoe i Yagodnoe Vinodelie. (Fruit and Berry Wine Making.) Pishchepromizdat, Moscow.

MONTANARI, V. and CECCARELLI, G. 1950. La Viticoltura e l'Enología nelle Tre Venezie. Arti Grafiche Longo e Zoppelli, Treviso. Supplemento Aggiornnato Sino all'Anno 1950. 1952.

MOREAU-BERILLON, C. 1925. Au Pays du Champagne. Le Vignoble-le Vin. Librairie L. Michaud, Reims.

MOSER, L. 1959. Die österreichischen Weine, ihre Art und die Absatzmöglichkeiten. Weinberg Keller 6, 342-343.

MURPHY, D. F. 1970. Australian Wine: The Complete Guide. Sun Books, Melbourne.

MURPHY, D. F. 1974. Murphy's Classification of Australian Wines. Sun Books, Melbourne.

NASSE, T. and ZIGORI, V. 1968. Disa të dhëna mbi karakteristikat e verërave të produhuara nga vinifikimi i varieteteve të rrushit të kiltivuar në vendin tonë. Bull. Univ. Shtet. Tiranës, Seria Shkencat Natypore 2, 95-105.

NEDELCHEV, N. 1959. The grapes and wines of Bulgaria. World Crops 11, 111-113.

NEUBELLER, J. 1965. Der Tokajerwein und seine Heimat. Mitt. Rebe Wein, Serie A (Klosterneuburg) *18*, 304-306.

NIEDERBACHER, A. 1978. Qualità dei vini Italiani secondo le annate. Enotria *23*, 12.

NILOV, V. I. and SKURIKHIN, I. M. 1960. Khimiya Vinodeliya i Kon'yachnogo Proizvodstva. (Chemistry of Wine and Brandy Production.) Pishchepromizdat, Moscow.

OREGLIA, F. 1964. Enología Téorico-Practica. Rodeo del Medio, Mendoza.

ORIZET, L. 1959. Mon Beaujolais. Jean Guillermet, Éditions du Cuvier, Villefranche-en-Beaujolais.

OUGH, C. S. 1965. Wine production and development of the research winery. Report to the government of Israel. FAO Rept. *2025*, 1-73.

PACOTTET, P. and GUITTONNEAU, L. 1930. Vins de Champagne et Vins Mousseux. Librairie J.-B. Baillière et Fils, Paris.

PARONETTO, L. and DAL CIN, G. 1954. I Prodotti Chimici nella Tecnica Enologíca. Scuola d'Arte Tipografia D. Bosco, Verona.

PENINOU, E. and GREENLEAF, S. 1954. Wine making in California. III. The California Wine Association. The Porpoise Bookshop, San Francisco.

PENNING-ROWSELL, E. 1973. The Wines of Bordeaux, 3rd Edition. Penguin, Harmondsworth.

PESTEL, H. 1959. Les Vins et Eaux-de-Vie à Appellations d'Origine Controlées en France. Imprimerie Buguet-Comptour, Mâcon.

PEYER, E. and EGGENBERGER, W. 1965. Weinbuch, 5th Edition. Verlag Schweizerischer Wirteverein, Zürich.

PEYNAUD, E. 1971. Connaissance et Travail du Vin. Dunod, Paris.

PIRIE, A. J. C. 1978. Comparison of the climates of selected Australian, French and Californian wine producing area. Australian Grapegrower Winemaker *15* (172) 74, 76, 78.

POGRIMILOVIC, B. 1969. Wines and Wine-growing Districts of Yugoslavia. "Zadruzna Stampa," Zagreb.

POPOV, K. S. 1970. Osnovy Proizvodstva Sovetskogo Shampanskogo i Igristykh Vin. (Production of Soviet Champagne and Sparkling Wines.) "Pishchevaya Prom-st," Moscow.

POULAIN, R. and JACQUELIN, L. 1960. Vignes et Vins de France. Flammarion, Paris.

POUPON, P. and FORGEOT, P. 1972. Les Vins de Bourgogne, 6th Edition. Presses Universitaires de France, Paris.

PRISNEA, C. 1964. Bacchus in Rumania. Meridiane Publishing House, Bucharest.

PROSTOSERDOV, N. N. 1955. Osnovy Vinodeliya. (Fundamentals of Enology). Pishchepromizdat, Moscow.

QUITTANSON, C. 1965. L'appellation d'origine, facteur permanent de recherche de la qualité. Rev. Ferm. Ind. Aliment. *20*, 49-61.

RADENKOVIĆ, D. G. 1962. Vino, Savremeni Problemi Vinarstva u Svetu i Kod Nas. (Wine, Current Problems of the World and National Wine Industry.) Belgrade.

RAINBIRD, G. M. 1966. Sherry and the Wines of Spain. McGraw-Hill, New York.

RAKCSÁNYI, L. 1963. Borászat. (Wine Making.) Verlag Mezögazdasági Kiadó, Budapest.

RANKOVIĆ, B. C. 1955. Vinarstvo. (Viticulture.) Zadruzhna Kniga, Belgrade.

RAU, K. 1961. Was Trinkt Man in Oesterreich? Albert Muller Verlag, Stuttgart.

RAY, C. 1966. The Wines of Italy. McGraw-Hill, New York.

RAY, C. 1976. The Wines of France. Allen Lane, London.

READ, J. 1973. The Wines of Spain and Portugal. Faber and Faber, London.

RIBÉREAU-GAYON, J., PEYNAUD, E., RIBÉREAU-GAYON, P., and SUDRAUD, P. 1977-1978. Traité d'oenologie. Dunod, Paris. (Sciences et Techniques du Vin) (4 vol)

RODIER, C. 1948. Le Vin de Bourgogne, 3rd Edition. Louis Damidot, Dijon.

ROGER, J. R. 1956. Les Vins de Bordeaux. Compagnie Parisienne d'Éditions Techniques et Commerciales, Paris.

ROGER, J. R. 1960. The Wines of Bordeaux. Dutton, New York.

ROSA, T. DE. 1964. Tecnica dei Vini Spumanti. Rivista di Viticoltura e di Enología, Conegliano.

ROSSI, A. 1955. La Viticoltura in Sicilia. Mori, Palermo.

ROWE, P. 1970. The Wines of Canada. McGraw-Hill Co. of Canada, Toronto.

RUI, D. 1975. Ragguagli sulla viticoltura brasiliana e sul recente "Simposio Italo-Sudamericano di Viticoltura et di Enología." Atti Accad. Ital. Vite Vino 27, 199-200.

SCHELLENBERG, A. 1962. Weinbau. Verlag Huber & Co., Frauenfeld.

SCHELLENBERG, A. and PEYER, E. 1951. Weinbuch für die Schweizer Wirte, 3rd Edition. Schweizerischer Wirteverein, Zurich.

SCHMIDT, H. C. 1965. Der Weinbau in Osterreich. Wein-Wissen. 20, 525-536.

SCHOONMAKER, F. 1973. Encyclopedia of Wine, 5th Edition. Hastings House, New York.

SCHOONMAKER, F. and MARBLE, T. 1934. The Complete Wine Book. Simon and Schuster, New York.

SHAND, P. M. 1960. A Book of French Wines, 2nd Edition. Alfred A. Knopf, New York.

SIMON, A. L. 1934. Port. Constable and Co., London.

SIMON, A. L. 1957. The Noble Grapes and the Great Wines of France. McGraw-Hill Book Company, New York.

SIMON, A. L. 1962. Champagne; with a Chapter on American Champagne by Robert J. Misch. McGraw-Hill Book Co., New York.

SIMON, A. L. 1966. The Wines, Vineyards and Vignerons of Australia. Lansdowne House, Melbourne.

SITTLER, L. 1956. La Viticulture et le Vin de Colmar à Travers les Siècles. Éditions Alsatia, Paris.

SOARES FRANCO, A. P. 1938. O Moscatel de Setúbal. Editorial Império, Lisboa.

SOÓS, I. A. B. 1955. Borászati Kémia. (Enological Chemistry.) Mezögazd. Kiádó, Budapest.

TARANTOLA, C. 1954. Enología. Unione Tipografico-Editrice Torinese, Torino.

TARANTOLA, C., CAMPISI, C., BOTTINI, E., and EMANUELE, F. 1954. Industrie Agrarie. Unione Tipografico-Editrice Torinese, Torino.

TELEKI, S. 1937. Weinbau und Weinwirtschaft in Ungarn. Payer and Co., Berlin.

TEODORESCU, I. C. 1968. Activités viticoles sur le territoire Dace. Ed. Rev. Redacția Revistelor Agricole, București.

THERON, C. J. and NIEHAUS, C. J. G. 1948. Wine Making, 3rd Edition. Union South Africa Dep. Agric. Bull. *191.*

THORPY, F. 1971. Wine in New Zealand. Collins, Auckland.

THUDICHUM, J. L. W. and DUPRÉ, A. 1872. A Treatise on the Origin, Nature and Varieties of Wine. Macmillan and Co., London.

TROOST, G. 1972. Die Technologie des Weines, 4th Edition. Eugen Ulmer, Stuttgart.

TURCOVIĆ, Z. 1950A. Gospodarska Vrijednost Sorata Vinove Loze. (Economic Value of Wine Grape Varieties.) Poljoprivredni Nakladni Zavod, Zagreb.

TURCOVIĆ, Z. 1950B. Savremeni Uzgoj Vinove Loze. (Modern Wine Grape Culture.) Poljoprivredni Nakladni Zavod, Zagreb.

TURCOVIĆ, Z. and TURCOVIĆ, G. 1952-1962. Ampelografski Atlas. (Ampelographical Atlas.) Poljoprivredni Nakladni Zavod, Zagreb. (2 Vols.)

VALENTE-PERFEITO, J. C. 1948. Let's Talk About Port. Instituto do Vinho do Porto, Porto.

VALUIKO, G. 1973. Biokhimia i Tekhnologie Stolovikh Vin (Biochemistry and Technology of Table Wines). Moscow, Pisthchevaia Promishlennost.

VEGA, L. A. DE. 1958. Guía Vinícola de España. Editora Nacional, Madrid.

VERONA, O. and FLORENZANO, G. 1956. Microbiologia Applicata all'Industria Enologíca. Edizione Agricole, Bologna.

VERONELLI, L. 1964. The Wines of Italy. McGraw-Hill Book Co., New York.

VOGT, E. 1974. Der Wein: Bereitung, Behandlung, Untersuchung, 5th Edition. Verlag Eugen Ulmer, Stuttgart.

VOGT, E. 1977. Weinbau, 5th Edition. Verlag Eugen Ulmer, Stuttgart.

WASSERMAN, S. 1977. The Wines of Italy. Stein and Day, New York.

WEBB, A. D. 1959. The Australian wine industry. Wines Vines *40* (7) 29-30.

WILDMAN, F. S., JR. 1972. A Wine Tour of France. Morrow, New York.

WINKLE, A. J., COOK, J. A., KLIEWER, M. M. and LIDER, L. A. 1974. General Viticulture, 2nd Edition. University of California Press, Berkeley and Los Angeles.

WOSCHEK, H. G. 1970. Der deutsche Weinführer. Das Deutschland-Weinbuch. Moderne Verlagsges., Mainz.

YOUNGER, W. 1966. Gods, Men and Wine. World Publishing Co., Cleveland.

YOXALL, H. W. 1970. The International Wine and Food Society's Guide to the Wines of Burgundy. Stein and Day, New York.

2

The Composition of Grapes

The character and quality of a wine are determined by (1) the composition of the raw material, (2) the fermentation process, and (3) the changes which occur naturally, or are made to occur, during the postfermentation period. This chapter considers the composition of grapes and the factors influencing it.

HOW GRAPES RIPEN

Physical and chemical changes occur during ripening. There is an intimate interrelationship between them.

Physical Changes

The grape berry in its early weeks is a tiny, green-colored, very acid pellet. Seed development, cell division and a very slow berry enlargement continue for some time. Cell division ceases about the time noticeable changes in berry size, color, and texture occur. This is the start of *véraison* (ripening).

The rate of increase in volume of the berry may show a slight decrease during the period of seed development (Fig. 2.1). Following this, a very rapid increase in berry size occurs and in a few weeks the tiny berry becomes a plump, sweet, colored fruit. The period of most rapid increase in volume does not exactly coincide with the start of ripening. The increase in soluble solids precedes this period by about two weeks, Fig. 2.1.

The fruit does not continue to increase in size. At normal maturity there is an abrupt cessation of cell enlargement and under warm conditions there may be a decrease in volume. Peynaud and Maurié (1956) suggest harvesting one week after the fruit reaches its maximum weight. The decrease in weight occurs mainly by withdrawal of water from the fruit—especially during periods of soil moisture deficiency. Poux (1950)

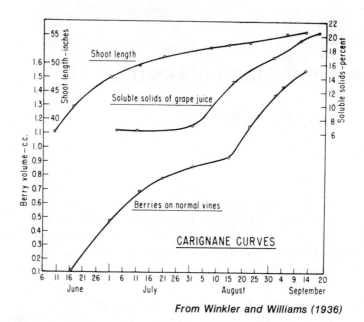

From Winkler and Williams (1936)

FIG. 2.1. BERRY SHOOT GROWTH AND RIPENING

also noted that increase in sugar content paralleled increase in berry weight.

There are changes in the relative amounts of skins, seeds, and pulp during maturation. On a percentage basis the pulp increases from about 73 to 89% of the weight while the percentage of seeds and skins decreases from about 13 to 4 and 8, respectively. On a per berry basis the increase in the weight of pulp is more striking and a slight increase in skin weight occurs. Separation of the pulp from the skin and seeds is difficult and subject to manipulative errors.

Unripe berries are hard and difficult to crush. As the fruit ripens there is an increase in turgidity. During overripening the fruit shrivels and there is a loss in turgidity—making the fruit again difficult to crush.

When the grape is attacked by *Botrytis cinerea* the attachment of the skin to the flesh is weakened and makes the fruit easier to crush (Nelson and Amerine 1957). For a summary of the physiology of *Botrytis cinerea* on grapes see Charpentié (1954). Besides the increase in glycerol and sugar, there is a net decrease in malic and tartaric acids, especially in tartaric. The effect on the acidity and the intensity of the infection depends on the climate following botrytis attack. Gluconic acid is a product of botrytis attack. Amounts of 0.50–2.50 g/liter were reported.

Recently, McCloskey (1974) found 1.3 to 5.9 g/liter. Normal wines had only about 0.29–0.92 g/liter. A minimum gluconic acid is suggested as a measure of the authenticity of botrytised wines. Galacturonic and glucuronic acids are present in musts and in larger amounts in musts or wines of grapes attacked by *Botrytis cinerea*. Rentschler and Tanner (1955) reported little glucuronic acid in normal or botrytised musts but considerable galacturonic acid. Dimotaki-Kourakou (1964) was unable to detect glucuronic. The presence of glucuronic and galacturonic acids in musts and wines helps to explain (Blouin and Peynaud 1963) the deficit of anions in the acid balance, the high dextro-rotatory condition of certain wines and the unknown compounds that combine with sulfur dioxide. For 100 mg of free sulfur dioxide, 1 milliequivalent of glucuronic acid will combine with 2 to 3 mg of sulfur dioxide and 1 milliequivalent of galacturonic acid will combine with 5 to 6 mg of sulfur dioxide. It is difficult to control field conditions to secure the optimum botrytis growth. Attack by other molds and rains may cause some sugar loss. Considerable net sugar is lost by respiration—up to 30%. Glucose is attacked more by the mold than fructose so the glucose/fructose ratio decreases.

Chemical Changes

The grape consists of seeds (except for a few varieties), surrounding pulp and an enclosing skin. The relative proportion of each of these changes during maturation (p. 78). The grape ripens from the exterior to the interior. The pulp near the skin is lower in acid and higher in sugar than that near the seed. Because of the increasing proportion of the fruit in the intermediate pulp zone, its composition increasingly dominates that of the total juice as the season advances. This is of importance in measuring ripening changes. In partially ripe or ripe fruit when the berries are turgid, the free-run juice is mainly from the pulp near the skin and will be higher in sugar and lower in acid than the juice from the press. In overripe fruit where both turgid and nonturgid fruit are present the free-run may be lower in sugar and higher in acids than the press juice. This is due to the lesser proportion of juice from near the skin—and from the nonturgid riper fruit—in the press juice.

When whole grapes are pressed, as in the Champagne region of France, the first juice is higher in sugar and lower in pH *and* in titratable acidity than that of later pressings (Table 2.1), apparently because more tartrate-buffered material is present. Few nonturgid berries are present so this represents the first case noted above. In California where shriveling is common the second case is more common.

The overall changes in sugar, total acidity, and pH are shown in Fig. 2.2

TABLE 2.1. COMPOSITION OF MUST AND RESULTING WINE OF EIGHT SUCCESSIVE
FRACTIONS (FROM THE SAME GRAPES IN A CHAMPAGNE PRESS)

Pressing No.	Amount (hl)	Alcohol, by Volume in Wine (%)	Titratable Acidity, as Tartaric (g/100 ml)[1]	pH Must	pH Wine
1	2	11.8	0.79	2.98	3.01
2	2	11.75	0.85	2.94	2.98
3	6	11.8	0.96	2.87	2.85
4	6	11.7	0.93	2.94	2.94
5	4	11.8	0.82	2.96	2.94
6	4	11.8	0.66	3.12	3.16
7	2.7	11.7	0.51	3.43	3.43
8	2	11.4	0.45	3.69	3.84

Source of data: Françot (1950).
[1]In original must.

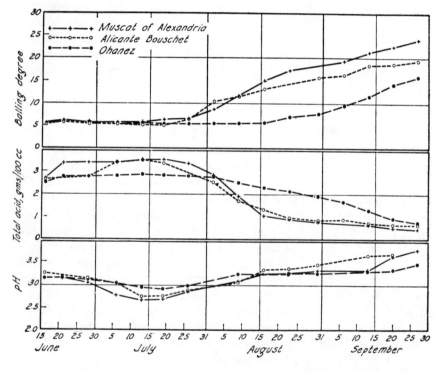

From Amerine and Joslyn (1970)

FIG. 2.2. RIPENING CHANGES IN THREE VARIETIES OF GRAPES

for two varieties which ripen in mid-season and one which ripens very
late (Ohanez). During the rapid stages of ripening in the warmer parts of
California the °Brix may increase 0.1 to 0.4 per day and for each increase
of a degree Brix the acidity may drop 0.05–0.15%. During ripening there

is a continuous increase in percentage of sugar. The two sugars present, glucose and fructose, do not increase at the same rate (Table 2.2). Glucose is the predominant sugar in unripe fruit while fructose is at least equal and often higher in ripe and overripe fruit (p. 93). Little sucrose is found in *V. vinifera*; more is found in *V. labrusca* and other native species.

TABLE 2.2. CHANGES IN TOTAL SUGAR, GLUCOSE, FRUCTOSE, AND THE FRUCTOSE-GLUCOSE RATIO DURING MATURATION

	Chasselas Doré				Furmint			
Date	Total Sugar (%)	Glu- cose (%)	Fruc- tose (%)	F/G	Total Sugar (%)	Glu- cose (%)	Fruc- tose (%)	F/G
August 22	11.3	6.1	5.2	0.85	–	–	–	–
August 27	12.9	7.3	5.6	0.77	2.7	1.8	0.9	0.50
September 11	18.1	9.0	9.1	1.01	14.4	7.2	7.2	1.00
September 24	15.2	7.5	7.7	1.03	15.2	7.4	7.8	1.05
October 9	19.2	9.2	10.0	1.09	19.5	9.3	10.2	1.10
October 29	22.7	10.4	12.3	1.18	22.3	9.9	12.4	1.25
November 22	20.0	8.8	11.2	1.27	20.3	8.9	11.4	1.28

Source of data: Szabó and Rakcsányi (1937).

The titratable acidity decreases during ripening, whether expressed on a per berry or on a percentage basis. Since the acids are translocated into the fruit from the leaves, the changes in acids occurring in the leaves during ripening are noteworthy. Amerine and Winkler (1958) and Peynaud and Maurié (1953B) both report a continuous increase in malates in the leaves. The tartrate content of the leaves decreases slightly during maturation. There are significant differences between varieties. On a percentage basis, malates and tartrates both decrease during ripening, but there are differences between varieties. On a per berry basis, the tartrate content generally remains relatively constant while the malate decreases, though less markedly than on a percentage basis.

The most rational explanation of these changes is that malates are respired during the later stages of ripening. Under very warm conditions tartrates also may be respired. The decreases on a percentage basis partially reflect the diluting effect of the continuous increase in volume of the fruit.

Important considerations are the changes in relative amounts of free acids, acid salts, and salts during ripening. These cause changes in pH. During ripening the pH increases continuously from about 2.8 to 3.1 or higher, depending on variety (p. 122) and season (p. 119). This means that the percentage of free acid decreases. The pK_1 of tartaric acid is 2.98 and of malic acid, 3.41. Thus, at a pH of 2.98, 50% of the tartrate is present as the free acid and at a pH of 3.41, 50% of the malate is present as the free acid. These changes are summarized for the Valdepeñas variety in

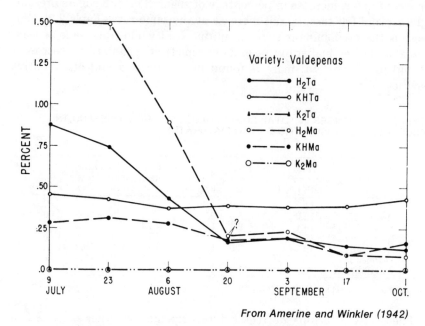

From Amerine and Winkler (1942)

FIG. 2.3. CHANGES IN ACID FRACTIONS DURING RIPENING

Fig. 2.3 (the percentage of potassium tartrate and potassium malate are essentially zero).

This change in pH is due to the translocation of potassium and other cations into the fruit. The alkalinity of the ash is a measure of cation content and this steadily increases during maturation. Table 2.3 also shows that the potassium and sodium contents increase. Calcium remains relatively constant on a percentage basis. On a per berry basis, all increase in an even more striking fashion. See Vitte and Guichard (1955), Peynaud (1947), Peynaud and Maurié (1956) and Amerine (1956). The method of expressing the results is particularly important.

The changes in nitrogen during ripening are important to the growth of yeasts and bacteria. The changes in the juice of one variety, on a w/v basis, are shown in Fig. 2.4. A slight decrease in total nitrogen, a more marked decrease in ammonia, no change in amine nitrogen, and an increase in polypeptide and protein nitrogen may be noted. On a per berry basis, the decreases are less and the increases greater. Again, there are differences among varieties. There is a significant increase in proline, serine, and threonine and a decrease in arginine, ammonia and amine nitrogen in musts of Cabernet Sauvignon and Merlot grapes (Lafon-Lafourcade and Guimberteau 1962). As grapes ripen there is an increase in the forms of nitrogen which are less easily utilized by yeasts.

TABLE 2.3. ALKALINITY OF THE ASH, CALCIUM, POTASSIUM AND SODIUM CHANGES DURING MATURATION OF SEMILLON

Date	Balling	Alkalinity of the Ash (ml 0.01 N)	Calcium (mg/liter)	Potassium (mg/liter)	Sodium (mg/liter)
August 26	18.1	23.4	26	825	34
September 1	18.7	29.7	18	1395	93
September 21	21.9	–	20	1400	158
October 12	24.3	38.9	20	1240	120

Source of data: Amerine (1956).

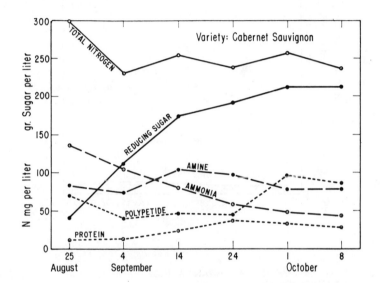

From Peynaud and Maurié (1953A)

FIG. 2.4. CHANGES IN NITROGEN FRACTIONS DURING RIPENING

This may partially explain why musts of overripe grapes sometimes ferment slowly.

The ease of separation of the juice from the solid matter is a function of the pectin content. The total pectic substances increase during maturation.

The amount of odorous materials increases during ripening. Thus, an unripe muscat berry has little of the muscat aroma. Lack of knowledge of the nature of the odorous substances of *V. vinifera* grapes has prevented the availability of quantitative data. For *V. labrusca* varieties, where methyl anthranilate is the most important odorous constituent, a marked increase during ripening has been noted for Concord (Fig. 2.5). Not all American varieties contain significant amounts of methyl anthranilate,

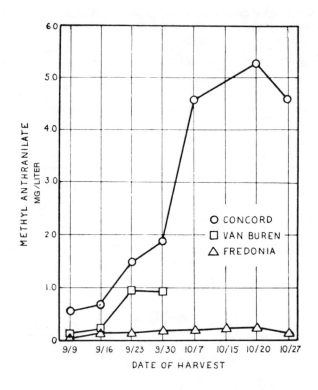

From Robinson et al. (1949)

FIG. 2.5.   METHYL ANTHRANILATE DEVELOPMENT
DURING RIPENING

however (Nelson *et al.* 1977).

Ethanol constitutes the most important part of the volatile material. There is an increase in oxidizable volatile materials (probably largely ethyl alcohol) until the sugar content reaches its maximum, and thereafter a decrease. Amount of oxidation by chromic acid is, therefore, not a good measure of amount of odorous material.

Qualitative changes in color during maturation are obvious. The chlorophyll content gradually decreases in both white and red varieties though some appears to remain. An increase in flavone pigments in white varieties and in anthocyanin pigments in red may also be observed. Ribéreau-Gayon (1958B) followed the formation of delphinidin, petunidin, malvidin, and peonidin during ripening of Merlot grapes. The increase in malvidin during ripening appeared to be greater than that of the other pigments but the differences were not great.

Durmishidze (1955) reported L-gallocatechin increased during ripening while D-catechin decreased. There is an overall decrease of tannins of over 50% in the fruit during ripening. For a detailed summary of the changes in polyphenolic compounds during ripening, see Singleton and Esau (1969).

Cantarelli and Peri (1964) showed that total phenolics and the leu-coanthocyanins decreased (weight per gram of fruit) during ripening of white grapes. There was considerable variation among varieties in the content of both. Singleton (1966) found that on a per berry basis a net increase in total phenols occurred to about 15° Brix and then either increased or decreased depending on weather and variety. Settling, centrifugation and filtration of musts are recommended as methods for reducing their amount.

The redox-potential decreases during ripening from about -500 mV to -350 mV. This may be related to the decrease in ascorbic acid (Vitamin C) which occurs during ripening.

Peynaud and Lafon-Lafourcade (1958) showed changes in B vitamins in Bordeaux grapes during ripening: decreases occurred in thiamin, biotin, and riboflavin. Inositol, nicotinamide and pantothenic acid increased.

MEASUREMENT OF MATURITY

Berries from the same cluster do not all have the same composition: those from the extremities (from the ends of the cluster or its subdivisions) are frequently greener in color, higher in acid and lower in sugar than are the berries from the main body of the cluster. Clusters from different parts of the vine are of varying composition. Some varieties have an appreciable second crop (Zinfandel, for example), which ripens later than the first crop. Grapes on vines in different parts of the same vineyard are sometimes of markedly different composition owing to differences in soil moisture, soil fertility or exposure. These variations are especially noticeable under cool climatic conditions (see p. 119). Maturity is also affected by vineyard practices. Poor control of leaf hoppers or red spider, resulting in loss of chlorophyll or foliage, will delay maturity. Grapes on vines of a single variety but of different ages will also mature at different times. Furthermore, maturation is not an even and regular process. Cold rainy weather may reduce the rate of ripening while very hot dry weather will increase it. Precise measurement of field maturity is not easy (Amerine 1956; Amerine and Roessler 1958A,B; Benvegnin and Capt 1955; Berg and Marsh 1954; and Roessler and Amerine 1958). For a recent report on characterizations of populations of grapes see Singleton et al. (1973).

Importance

The accurate determination of field maturity is important. Only when the grapes are harvested at their optimum maturity can wines of the greatest quality be produced. This is the basis for the vintage *bann* of Europe. The objective was to harvest at optimum maturity in order to achieve maximum quality. When the field determination of maturity is neglected, the wines are always of lesser and more variable quality. Closer control of harvesting would be advantageous in many regions. It is particularly important when governmental control of fruit sanitation is introduced, as is currently being done in California. It is then often of critical importance to pick the fruit before significant bunch rot develops.

Varieties do not ripen at the same time each year nor at the same time relative to each other. The sugar content (one measure of maturity) at the beginning of the ripening period is not always directly related to that at the time of harvest. Unverzagt (1954) measured the sugar maturity of three German varieties on September 1, October 1, and at harvest for the period 1943 to 1953. With White Riesling, Sylvaner, and Müller-Thurgau the results were generally similar: the date of harvest varied from year to year, often unrelated to the relative sugar content on September 1 or October 1.

How to Sample

In view of the variability of the fruit, some sort of statistically satisfactory system of field sampling is required. Amerine and Roessler (1958A,B) and Roessler and Amerine (1958, 1963) compared three methods of random sampling: lots of 100 berries, 10 clusters, or single vines.

They concluded that berry sampling was the simplest and most effective method of collecting maturity information. It is the least wasteful of fruit but is slower than cluster sampling. The advantages of berry sampling are summarized in Table 2.4.

This simply means that there is more variability in cluster and vine lots than there is in berry lots and, hence, for an equal standard error of the means, more 10-cluster lots or vine lots than 100-berry lots must be harvested. If one uses twice the standard error it will give the approximate deviation from the population mean that will be exceeded by the mean of a sample once in 20 times. If one wishes to be within 1° of the true Brix 95% of the time, 2 100-berry, 4 10-cluster, or 11 vine lots should be harvested. To reduce this to 0.5° Brix, 5 100-berry, 9-cluster, or 27 vine lots would have to be harvested. It would be impractical and wasteful to harvest 27 vine lots. These data indicate why direct field measurement with a hand refractometer is not likely to be popular. One

TABLE 2.4. APPROXIMATE EQUIVALENT NUMBERS OF LOTS FOR EQUAL
RELIABILITY

Standard Error of Means	No. of Lots of		
	100 Berries	10 Clusters	Vines
	Brix and Abbé		
0.39	2	4	11
0.32	3	5	17
0.28	4	7	22
0.25	5	9	27
	Total Acid		
0.028	2	4	8
0.023	3	6	10
0.020	4	8	14
0.018	5	10	18
	pH		
0.028	2	2	8
0.023	3	3	10
0.020	4	4	14
0.018	5	5	18

Source of data: Roessler and Amerine (1958).

would have to sample, record, and average 500 individual berry readings!

Field sampling should begin for each variety and each field about 3–4 weeks before the probable date of harvest. Samples should be taken weekly or, in the event of very warm weather, twice weekly. This will give the grower a picture of the relative degree of ripeness of each variety and, depending on the acreage of each, the probable size of the picking crew which will be necessary.

Preparation of Sample

A variety of methods is employed for crushing samples. The least desirable is the use of a piece of cheesecloth into which the grapes are placed and then macerated by pounding. Only the turgid fruit is thus crushed and the high sugar of the shriveled berries may not be adequately represented in the sample.

Small roller crushers (Fig. 2.6) do a fair job if the rollers are set close together and the fruit placed in the crusher in small portions (not as whole clusters). They are now in common use as the standard method. Blenders (or similar equipment) are not satisfactory because of pH changes caused when cells of skins and stems are broken.

Probably the best procedure to get the true °Brix is use of screw-type (or meat grinder) crushers (Fig. 2.7). These crush all the fruit and if not operated too tightly do not grind up the seeds. However, even with this equipment raisined fruit is only slightly broken up and little of its sugar

FIG. 2.6. ROLLER CRUSHER FOR SMALL SAMPLES OF GRAPES

has time to dissolve in the juice. The problem is an important one with varieties which ripen unevenly, such as Zinfandel. The true pH of the juice is altered and the problems involved in frequent screen clean-up preclude its use routinely. The stems must be separated prior to juicing. The alternatives of fermenting the sample or of extracting with water are slow and do not give the immediate results desired. See California Department of Agriculture (1955).

Whichever method of crushing is used the juice obtained will contain more or less suspended material, particularly with certain varieties and late in the season. The juice must be clarified if hydrometers are used to measure the °Brix but not if a refractometer is used. The pH and total acid measurements do not require cleared samples.

Methods of Measurement

The first, and often the only measure taken is that of the soluble solids. Hydrometers (p. 674–679), the Abbé refractometer (p. 679), or hand refractometers (p. 679) are used.

For determining the total acidity see p. 679–680. The pH meter is used to determine the pH of the must (p. 681). For wineries with many maturity samples per day automatic titrimeters will prove useful and economical.

FIG. 2.7.   SCREW-TYPE CRUSHER FOR SMALL SAMPLES OF GRAPES

Interpretation of Results

From the above measurements one will have a degree Brix, percentage of titratable acidity (as tartaric acid), and the pH. The recommended ranges for these in musts for making the various types of wine are as follows:

Type of Wine	°Brix	Titratable Acidity	pH
White table	19.5–23.0	>0.70	<3.3
Red table	20.5–23.5	>0.65	<3.4
Sweet table	22.0–25.0	>0.65	<3.4
Dessert	23.0–26.0	>0.50	<3.6

These recommendations have to be interpreted for special conditions. In a very warm, early-ripening season, especially if the crop is light, the acidity may be too low and harvesting should start at the lower end of the Brix range. The opposite will be true in cool, late-ripening years. For sparkling wine stock, the winery may want very tart wines of no more than 10–11% alcohol. This percentage of alcohol will be produced from grapes of approximately 18°−20° Brix.

No one of these measures of maturity alone is adequate. Amerine and Winkler (1940) studied the use of the Brix/acid ratio as a basis for determining the best date of harvest. They harvested grapes periodically during the ripening period. From these data a curve was drawn of degree Brix versus titratable acidity. The acidity at degree Brix of 20°, 22°, and 24° was read off the curve and the Brix/acid ratio at these Brixes for each variety calculated. If the standard is established that 0.65 is the minimum acceptable acidity for table wines, then a maximum Brix/acid ratio of 31 at 20°Brix, 34 at 22°, and 37 at 24° results. Varieties with Brix/acid ratios below these may be classified as true table wine varieties and those with ratios above as dessert wine varieties. A few varieties have a ratio below 31 at 20° but are above the limiting ratio at 22° or 24°. Such varieties require very careful harvesting if they are to be used for table wines. Amerine (1956) suggested maximum and minimum ratios be established for musts for dessert wines. Poulton (1970) recommended a ratio of 32 to 38 for table wines in South Africa. Ough and Alley (1970) found 30 to 32 best for Thompson Seedless.

Berg (1960) established minimum acid requirements in the various Brix ranges for each of four grades as a measure of grape quality. His tables are based on the analysis of nearly 47,000 loads of grapes delivered to wineries during the period 1950 to 1960. They may be used to measure the effect of seasonal variations and viticultural practices (such as over-cropping) on the Brix/acid ratio.

Amerine (1956) notes recommended Brix/acid ratios of 28 to 35 for varieties of the Burgundy district which compare favorably with the recommended ratios of 31, 34, and 37 mentioned above. Other measures of maturity may be used, such as maximum weight, etc.

Garino-Canina (1959) proposed a vinous index for wine grapes. This would include the following ratios: (a) sugar/acid (or some modification of it), (b) tartaric acid/malic acid, (c) tannin/nontannin polyphenol, and (d) amino acid/total nitrogen. Furthermore, a chemical determination of the unique aromatic constituents of each variety may be used. The finest table wines also seem to be made from varieties of small berries, and, for reds, of not too much color.

For region V conditions LaRosa (1955) and LaRosa and Nielsen (1956), recommended lower pH requirements for harvesting grapes, whether for table or dessert wines. While pH is not an adequate nor unique measure for harvesting grapes, it is an important variable in the warm grape-growing areas. We believe that, in addition to absolute sugar and total acidity, the variety of grape, and perhaps the season and relative time of the season, are all important. Doubtless, amount of crop is a crucial factor. Overcropping makes rational measures for harvesting meaningless. We can find no significant measures of maturity for Palomino grapes at Madera (V), cropped to 16 tons per acre and with 17° Brix on October 1. Such grapes had better be consigned to producing distilling material.

HARVESTING AND TRANSPORTATION

Grapes for winery use, if not mechanically harvested, are usually harvested with a curved knife in California (Fig. 2.8). However, picking shears, such as are used in table grape harvesting, would allow cutting out defective fruit. When botrytised fruit is being harvested separately, shears are useful.

A variety of containers is employed to receive the harvested fruit. In Europe, small baskets or buckets are used. The picker then dumps them into a larger container. In Alsace and Germany, the grapes may be dumped into a large wooden tank on a wagon at the edge of the vineyard (see Fig. 1.8). In Champagne, the grapes are placed in large baskets for sorting before being crushed (Fig. 1.7).

In California, grapes are usually picked into plastic or aluminum boxes and these dumped into low bed trailers. These are either hauled directly to the winery or the grapes transferred to over-the-road trucks for longer hauls.

The less the grapes are handled prior to crushing, the better. Therefore, systems where the pickers harvest into small gondolas which are moved directly to the crusher are probably best (Fig. 2.9). The shorter the delay from harvesting to crushing, the better. This is particularly true for mechanically-harvested fruit. On arrival at the winery the fruit is weighed and sampled for sugar, acidity, and defects.

A special sampling tube is used with gondola trucks. Grape quality inspection of grapes for winery use is probably a permanent part of the California industry. Introduction of mechanical harvesting has complicated grape quality inspection. Since mold count is difficult, a chemical procedure determining acetic acid, ethyl acetate and specific mold metabolites is being tested (Berg et al. 1977). For North Coast grapes where botrytis infection, which is normally not objectionable flavor-wise, may be prevalent in years of early rainfall, a somewhat higher maximum limitation may be desirable.

Gondola trucks should be washed after each load and picking containers should be washed daily when in use.

COMPOSITION OF MUSTS

Water

Ripe grapes contain 70–80% water.

Courtesy of Wine Institute

FIG. 2.8. PICKING KNIFE USED FOR PICKING CALIFORNIA WINE GRAPES

Courtesy of Wine Institute

FIG. 2.9. PICKING GONDOLA BEING LOADED ON TRUCK
FOR TRANSFER TO WINERY

Sugars and Related Compounds

As the source of ethanol, the sugars are of paramount importance. They are also, of course, important for their taste. Glucose and fructose are the primary sugars. While they normally are present at ful maturity in a 1:1 ratio, this ratio may fluctuate considerably. Thus, Amerine and Thoukis (1958) found fructose/glucose ratios of from 0.71 to 1.45 for 57 samples of the 1955 vintage. Kliewer (1965B) found that the glucose/fructose ratio varied from 0.85 to 1.04 for ripe fruit ranging from 20° Brix to 24° Brix. For overripe fruit from the same vines the ratio was from 0.53 to 0.76 and the °Brix from 23.0 to 26.9. In a wide variety of grapes, Sisakyan and Marutyan (1948) reported decreasing glucose/fructose ratios during ripening. Sucrose generally increased slightly.

These ratios may have some importance to the wine maker. Fructose is nearly twice as sweet as glucose. For making sweet table wines it would obviously be desirable to have high-fructose varieties available. Also, to retain residual sugar it would be desirable to use strains of yeast which ferment fructose as slowly as possible.

Little sucrose has been found in varieties of *V. vinifera*: 0.019 to 0.18%, Kliewer (1965A), 0.5 to 2.0%, Sisakyan and Marutyan (1948), 0.06 to 0.89%, Selvaraj *et al.* (1975), and 0.2 to 1.0%, Hawker *et al.* (1976). However, in non-*V. vinifera* grapes as much as 10% sucrose may be present. Most of this will be hydrolyzed during fermentation. Cordonnier *et al.* (1975) found the grape to contain a very active β-D-fructofuranoside-fructohydrolase which hydrolyzes sucrose. The enzyme is very resistant to heat and SO_2 but is sensitive to ethanol. The yeast, *S. cerevisiae,* also has a hydrolase which can rapidly invert sucrose. No sucrose remains in the wines even when sucrose is used for amelioration before fermentation. Tests for residual sucrose are, therefore, not reliable as indicators of amelioration. Kliewer also detected raffinose (0.01−0.32%), melibiose, stachyose and maltose but no pentoses in the musts of the varieties examined. Esau and Amerine (1966) and Esau (1967) reported small amounts of pentoses and 7-8 carbon sugars in wines and explained their origins. Small amounts of glycerol are found in musts of botrytised grapes (Holbach and Woller 1976).

Amerine and Bailey (1959) found that there is more sucrose and starch in the main stem compared to the lateral branches of the fruit cluster. There was more reducing sugar in the lateral branches, particularly in the brush. They reported 1−2 lb of fermentable sugar in the stems per ton of grapes. Later, in other varieties, Amerine and Root (1960) reported 2.3−4.8 lb of fermentable sugar per ton in the stems.

The pectin content of the ripe fruit varies from 0.02 to 0.6% (see Table 2.5). The pectin content of "eastern" grapes is generally higher than that of *V. vinifera* varieties. This includes alcohol-precipitable material and most of this is gums and arabans, according to Peynaud (1951), as the following data illustrate (gram/liter basis):

Variety	Total Pectin Material	Pectic Acid		Gums or Arabans
		Free	Esterified	
Merlot	1.77	0.07	0.19	1.51
Sémillon	4.43	0.02	0.14	4.27
Cabernet franc	1.22	0.08	0.37	0.77

These values are lower than those reported by Solms *et al.* (1952) but the percentage esterified is higher. They found an average of only 31.4% esterified in Swiss musts. Peynaud (1952) also reported that musts from grapes attacked by *Botrytis cinerea* were lower in pectic acid but nearly three times as high in gums. Also, high pectin results when heat is applied to musts to hasten color extraction. During fermentation, from 30 to 90% of the pectins are precipitated, apparently due to the pectolytic activity

TABLE 2.5. PECTIN CONTENT OF GRAPES

Species and Authority	Locality	Pectin Content, Percent Minimum	Maximum	Avg.
Vitis vinifera:				
von der Heide and Schmitthenner (1922)	Germany	0.11	0.33	—
Marsh and Pitman (1930)	California	0.03	0.17	0.12
Besone (1940)	Davis, Calif.	0.02 / 0.05	0.21 / 0.11	0.13 / 0.08
Ventre (1930)	France	0.14 / 0.03	0.39 / 0.07	0.26 / 0.05[1]
Françot and Geoffroy (1951)	France	0.05 / 0.04	0.08 / 0.53	0.06[2] / 0.20[3]
Garina-Canina (1938)	Italy	0.08	0.39	—
Vitis labrusca:				
Willaman and Kertez (1931)	New York	—	0.60	—
Besone (1940)	Davis, Calif.	0.11	0.29	0.18

Source of data: Amerine and Joslyn (1970).
[1]First press.
[2]Second press.
[3]Last press

of the yeasts and to precipitation at the alcohol content of the wine (see Usseglio-Tomasset 1959).

Marteau *et al.* (1961) showed that demethoxylation of pectins occurs rapidly in musts due to pectin enzymes and that the level of methanol depends on the level of pectinic acids in the must. Naturally-occurring pectin enzymes can affect the demethoxylation but added pectolytic enzymes act more rapidly. The final level of methanol is the same. This natural pectin enzyme activity explains the low pectin content of wines. Montedoro (1968) summarized the location and activity of the natural pectin methyl esterases in the grape.

The presence of colloidal materials in musts and wines has been known since Pasteur. Besides pectins, these have been attributed to gums, mucilaginous materials (dextrans), coloring matter, tannins, proteins and protein degradation products, and to certain inorganic salts. In some cases, an equilibrium between a compound in the colloidal and noncolloidal state appears to exist. Deibner *et al.* (1958) summarized data on the colloidal constituents of musts and wines. Usseglio-Tomasset and Castino (1975) measured the colloidal sugar-acid-pectin material in grapes and wines. They ranged from 280 to 1150 mg/liter. Galactose, mannose and arabinose were the most prevalent sugars. Galacturonic and glucuronic acids were the only acids found. The colloidal content is reduced by drying the grapes or by tannin fining, by pasteurization, by storage, and by oxidation of the musts.

The "hard" cuticular waxes from the surfaces of different varieties of grapes consist of ⅔ oleanolic acid (Radler 1965). There was less in grapes grown on unirrigated vineyards. The main (40−60%) constituents of the "soft" wax were free alcohols. In *V. vinifera* varieties only a small amount of hydrocarbon is present but in Isabella (*V. labrusca*) 23% of the "soft" wax was hydrocarbon. The chain length of the hydrocarbons varied from C_{18} to C_{35} with C_{25}, C_{27}, C_{29}, and C_{31} being most prevalent. The alcohol fractions varied in chain length from C_{20} to C_{34}, with C_{26} and C_{28} predominating. The results with the hydrocarbons of Isabella are similar to the earlier data of Markley *et al.* (1938) with Concord. They reported 30% C_{29} and 70% C_{31} compared to 27 and 50% in this paper. Oleanolic acid acts as a growth factor for wine yeast under anaerobic conditions, and can replace ergosterol or the essential steroids made by the yeast aerobically (Bréchot *et al.* 1971).

Acids

The principal acids of the grape are tartaric (L(+)-tartaric) and malic (L(−)-malic). Tartaric is a relatively strong acid. One of the reasons for the biological stability of wine is that it is buffered to a relatively low pH. The total acidity, calculated as tartaric acid, may vary from 0.3 to 1.5 g/100 ml or more. The amount varies with the season and variety. Tartaric acid appears to be a by-product of photosynthesis with carbon atoms 2 and 3 of tartaric acid being the same as atoms 3 and 4 of dextrose. Tartaric acid is not a part of the Krebs cycle. Ruffner and Rast (1974) have postulated two pathways of formation in the grape. It is respired more at higher temperatures (Takimoto *et al.* 1976).

The malate content, as malic acid, of ripe California grapes ranged from 0.08 to 0.84 g/100 ml (Amerine 1956). He suggested (1951), for California conditions, low-malate varieties, since the high-tartrate varieties were more likely to have a lower pH. He noted (1956) that a low potassium content was necessary if the pH was to be buffered to a low pH. The tartrate/malate ratio varies from 0.75 to 6.1. Lasko and Kliewer (1975) show probable losses of malic acid due to temperature instability of phosphoenolpyruvate carboxylase at 38°C (100.4°F) or higher.

Very little citric acid (L-citric) is found in mature grapes, about 0.01 to 0.03 g/100 ml. Musts of low total acidity are also likely to be lower in citric. Hennig and Lay (1965) reported 0.03 to 0.04 g/liter of oxalic acid in three German musts and 0.0 to 0.06 in 20 wines. Kliewer (1966) found small amounts of isocitric, *cis*-aconitic, glutaric, fumaric, pyrrolidone carboxylic and α-ketoglutaric acids in musts. In musts from moldy grapes, glucuronic and gluconic acids are found (Holbach and Woller

1976). A small amount of phosphoric acid, less than 0.05 g/100 ml as phosphate, is found in normal musts, up to 20% of this in the organic form. The significance of different forms of phosphate to fermentation rate and wine quality needs study.

pH and Buffer Coefficient

The pH of California musts at maturity varies from about 3.0 to 3.9 depending on the variety, region and season. Northern European musts may not reach 3.0 even in good seasons. The buffer capacity of grape musts (ΔpH/ΔNaOH, where ΔNaOH is the milliliters of 0.1 N sodium hydroxide added per liter) is very low, indicating a high buffer capacity, i.e., more dibasic acids (Amerine and Winkler 1958). Otsuka et $al.$ (1976) believe buffering by polyphenols (but not catechin) is important.

Nitrogenous Components

The total nitrogen contents of musts vary between 100 and 2000 mg/liter, the usual amount being about 600. Expressed as protein, pre-Prohibition data for California musts showed a range from 0.01 to 0.2 g/liter. The amount present varies with soil conditions. Musts from insect-injured grapes are high in total nitrogen. Ammonia nitrogen in musts varies from about 5 to 175 mg/liter. The amount and form of soil nitrogen will have an especially notable effect.

Only small amounts of amino nitrogen are found in musts—usually less than 100 mg/liter, though up to 400 have been reported. Polypeptide nitrogen, likewise, seldom exceeds 100 mg (as N)/liter in ripe fruit. Again, reports of up to 350 have been made. Protein nitrogen amounts to less than 50 mg/liter. The nitrogenous material (as mg/liter) in musts of the 1941 and 1942 German vintages was given by Hennig (1944) as:

Nitrogen Fraction (mg/liter)	1941	1942
Total	1075	748
Ammonia	112	15
Amino	408	319
Amide	34	16
Humin	20	17
Phospho-tungstic	349	231
Protein	40	18
Residue	112	132

The phospho-tungstic nitrogen fraction includes the tri- and tetra-peptides, diamino acids, such as arginine and lysine, and heterocyclic acids, such as histidine and proline, as well as purines. The amino fraction includes dipeptides; the humin nitrogen, tyrosine, and tryptophan; and the amides, asparagine, and glutamine. The residue is compounds of unknown composition. Lafon-Lafourcade and Peynaud (1959) reported the following average nitrogen content of Bordeaux musts and wines (mg/liter):

	Total	Ammonia	Amine[1]	Amine[2]
Musts	454	70.0	129	141
Red wines	320	11.5	96	90
White wines	184	6.3	36	95

[1]By formol titration.
[2]By microbiological assay.

The presence or absence of amino acids of musts and wines is given in Table 2.6. Hennig (1955) appears to be the only investigator who has reported citrulline in wines and Koch and Bretthauer (1957) first found ornithine. This was verified by Drawert et al. (1976). In addition, they reported sarcosine. A summary of the average values in musts and wines is given in Table 2.7.

Castor (1953) reported 265 to 1607 mg/liter of glutamic acid and 70 to

TABLE 2.6. FREE AMINO ACIDS OF MUSTS AND WINES

Amino Acid	Investigators 1	2	3	4	5	6	7	8	9	10	11	12
α-Alanine	+	+	−	−	+	+	+	+	+	+	+	+
β-Alanine	−	−	−	−	−	−	−	−	−	−	−	−
α-Aminobutyric acid	−	−	−	−	+	+	+	+	−	+	+	+
Arginine	−	−	−	+	+	+	+	+	−	−	+	+
Asparagine	−	−	+	−	−	+	−	−	−	+	+	+
Aspartic acid	+	+	−	+	+	+	+	+	+	−	+	+
Cysteine	−	−	−	−	−	−	−	−	−	−	+	+
Cystine	−	−	−	+	−	+	−	+	+	−	+	+
Glutamic acid	+	+	+	+	+	+	+	+	+	+	+	+
Glutamine	−	−	−			−	−	−	−	−	+	+
Glycine	+	+	−	+	+	+	+	+	+	+	+	+
Histidine	−	+	−	+	+	+	−	+	−	+	−	+
Hydroxyleucine	−	−	−	−	−	−	−	−	−	−	−	+
Hydroxypipecolic acid	−	−	−	−	−	−	−	−	−	−	−	+
Hydroxyproline	−	−	−	−	−	−	−	+	−	−	−	+
Isoleucine	+	−	−	+	+	+	+	−	−	−	−	+
Leucine	+	−	−	+	−	+	+	+	+	−	+	+
Lysine	−	−	−	+	+	+	+	+	−	+	−	+
Methionine	−	−	−	+	+	−	−	+	−	−	+	+
Methionine sulfone	−	−	−	−	−	−	−	−	−	−	−	+
Norvaline	−	−	−	−	−	−	−	+	−	−	−	−
Ornithine	−	−	−	−	−	+	−	−	−	−	−	+
2-Oxyproline	−	−	−	−	−	−	−	−	−	−	−	+
Phenylalanine	+	+	−	+	+	−	−	−	−	−	+	+
Pipecolic acid	−	−	−	−	−	−	−	−	−	−	−	+
Proline	+	+	+	+	−	+	+	+	+	+	+	+
Serine	+	+	+	+	+	+	+	+	+	+	+	+
Threonine	+	+	+	+	+	+	−	+	−	−	+	+
Tryptophan	−	−	+	+	−	−	−	+	−	−	−	+
Tyrosine	+	−	−	+	+	+	−	−	−	+	+	+
Valine	+	+	+	+	+	+	+	+	+	+	+	+

Source of data: Lafon-Lafourcade and Peynaud (1959).

1130 of arginine. The 14 other amino acids were usually below 100 mg. Lysine, methionine, glycine, and cystine were present at 20 mg/liter or less. He reported (1956) 3490 mg/liter of proline, 480 of serine and 210 of threonine. Flanzy and Poux (1965) found higher proline in musts of 1962, a warm year, compared to 1963, a cool year. Ough (1968) and Ough and Stashak (1974) showed varietal differences in proline content. The failure of yeast to metabolize proline generally was demonstrated; ½ to ¾ of the proline was shown to be located in the juice compared to 14 to 29% of the total nitrogen. Most of the other amino acids were present in larger amounts in 1963 compared to 1962. However, the total was greater in the 1962 musts. Bustos (1975) reported 53 to 2296 mg/liter in Chilean musts.

Koch and Sajak (1959) noted how complex the grape proteins are. The water-soluble nitrogenous constituents are low molecular-weight polypeptides and proteids. The complete list of amino acids involved and their peptide linkage is still unknown. Heating gives protein stability and bentonite treatment results in an essentially protein-free wine.

Koch (1963) finds soluble proteins in grapes differ among varieties. The amounts increase during ripening and more may be formed in warm seasons. In the varieties White Riesling and Müller-Thurgau, it appears to be a glucoprotein of 18 amino acids. The isoelectric point of the proteins of different varieties varies from 3.3 to 4.0.

Nucleosides and nucleotides of the following bases were identified in wine by Tercelj (1965): adenine, guanine, cytosine, hypoxanthine, uracil, and thymine. Feuillat *et al.* (1976) report the following amounts of nucleotides in a Chardonnay champagne stock:

Nucleotide	Amount mg/liter
Cytidine monophosphate	8.5
Adenosine monophosphate	1.8
Guanosine monophosphate + thymidine monophosphate	19.3
Uridine monophosphate	7.1
Di- and triphosphates	4.7

They attribute sensory importance to these compounds in wine.

Peynaud and Maurié (1953A) have observed a possible relationship between titratable acidity and amine nitrogen content which may indicate a parallelism in the formation of amino and other organic acids. Further work is needed.

The colloidal material of grape juice contains 10—13% protein according to Markh and Boneva (1952). Only 4 to 21% of the total colloids were irreversibly precipitated by heating and chilling.

TABLE 2.7. AVERAGE AMOUNTS OF FREE AMINO ACIDS IN MUSTS AND WINES (MG/LITER)

Amino Acid	Musts			Wines				
	Castor (1953)	Lafon-Lafourcade and Peynaud (1959)	Lüthi and Vetsch (1953)	Bourdet and Herard (1958) Red	White	Lafon-Lafourcade and Peynaud (1959) Red	White	Drawert et al. (1976)[1] White
Alanine			50–100	67	70			49
Aminobutyric				31	24			46
Arginine	403	327		84	91	47	46	263
Asparagine				56	41			2
Aspartic acid	52	2	6	76	72	31	38	20
Cystine	4	0		106	47	17	25	7
Glutamic acid	687	173	3–15	334	315	221	200	34
Glutamine				46	27			2
Glycine	7	22	5–8	12	16	28	26	16
Histidine	92	11		34	13	14	14	15
Isoleucine	66	7 ⎱		36	24	⎰ 26	29	16
Leucine	62	20 ⎰				⎱ 19	19	23
Lysine	16	16		43	37	47	40	18
Methionine	14	1		28	49	5	4	6
Phenylalanine	51	5		22	15	19	16	17
Proline		266		531	770	72	201	84
Serine		69	1–3	9	11	49	54	23
Threonine		258	20–25	27	32	187	111	20
Tryptophan	47	0.6		0	0	2.5	0	9
Tyrosine	20	0		32	37	11	13	17
Valine	60	6		19	16	45	36	19

Source of data: Lafon-Lafourcade and Peynaud (1959).
[1]In addition, the following were measured: pyroglutamic acid, 15 mg/liter; ornithine 8 mg/liter; cysteine, 8 mg/liter; citrullin, 8 mg/liter; hydroxyproline, 7 mg/liter; β-alanine, 7 mg/liter; and sarcosine, 1 mg/liter.

Variety	Titratable Acidity g/100 ml Tartaric	Amine Nitrogen mg/liter
Merlot	0.60	52
Cabernet Sauvignon	0.66	59
Sémillon	0.69	73
Malbec	0.72	82
Cabernet franc	0.78	92
Sauvignon blanc	0.84	98
Petit Verdot	0.87	104

Pigments

Little quantitative data on the amounts of the pigments of musts are available. Traces of chlorophyll, carotene, and xanthophyll are found in most musts. A summary of our knowledge of grape anthocyanins has been given by Webb (1964). Paper chromatographic techniques have been of great value. He notes that the isolated and purified pigment may differ from that actually present in the grape skin or the wine.

Quercetin (a flavonol) is relatively insoluble and present only in traces. Its glucoside, isoquercitrin, occurs in amounts of from 1 to 30 mg/liter. Genevois (1934) attributed the slight fluorescence of white wines to 0.04

to 0.1 mg/liter of flavine and lumiflavine. Hennig and Burkhardt (1957) found rutin in white wines. Filter pad clogging by a dry red wine was found to be due to quercetin (71%), kaempferol (24%) and myricetin (5%) (Ziemelis and Pickering 1969).

The main red pigment of *V. vinifera* varieties is the monoglucoside of malvidin (oenidin) (Ribéreau-Gayon and Sudraud 1957). In *V. labrusca*, delphinidin monoglucoside and monomethoxydelphinidin monoglucoside were reported by Brown (1940). Sastry and Tischer (1952) identified malvidin-3-monoglucoside in the skins of Concord grapes. In general, American species contain diglucosides and *V. vinifera* varieties do not. Interspecific hybrids may or may not contain diglucosides, but most do, since the gene is dominant.

No diglucosides of malvidin were found in the varieties of *V. vinifera* examined by Biol and Michel (1961, 1962). However, 29 of the 37 direct-producer hybrids tested contained the diglucoside. Biol and Foulonneau (1961) did find the diglucoside of peonidin in *V. vinifera* varieties and also some acylated diglucoside of malvidin. Cappelleri (1965) reported malvidin diglucoside in two varieties of *V. vinifera* (of 109 tested). Liuni *et al.* (1965) found diglucoside in Merlot, Cabernet franc and Raboso Piave (all *V. vinifera*). In most cases, the amounts present were small. In Merlot (*V. vinifera*), Zamorani and Pifferi (1964) reported 43% malvidin monoglucoside, 32% of delphinidin monoglucoside, 10% of petunidin monoglucoside, and 5% of peonidin monoglucoside. Traces of diglucosides were detected. More diglucoside was present when 100 mg/liter of sulfur dioxide was used for the fermentation.

Smith and Luh (1965) indicate that Rubired (a cross of Alicante Ganzin and Tinto Cão) has a predominant diglucoside pattern. Anderson *et al.* (1970) identified acetic acid as a major acylating acid in acylated anthocyanin-3-monoglucosides.

Precise determination of diglucosides is difficult. The official French procedure is that of Jaulmes and Ney (1960). See also Deibner and Bourzeix (1964) and Deibner *et al.* (1964). Bouschet hybrids have been shown to contain diglucosides by Deibner and Bourzeix (1960, 1964). A review of the problem has been given by Ribéreau-Gayon (1964). The presence of diglucosides of malvidin is now considered presumptive evidence of non-*V. vinifera* wine. Ribéreau-Gayon and Ribéreau-Gayon (1958) reported easy preparation of the paper chromatograms with young wines. With older wines little coloring material moves from the origin. This they attribute to transformation of some of the soluble anthocyans to a colloidal condition.

Grohmann and Gilbert (1959) have given a simple procedure for determining if non-*Vitis vinifera* wine is present in a sample. The test is based on the absence of diglucoside pigments that fluoresce in ultraviolet light. Hrazdina *et al.* (1970) determined the relative stability of the principal diglucoside pigments and found them most stable at pH 5.0 where they are rapidly converted to the colorless base form.

Table 2.8 gives some of the relationships between species. The important differences between species may be summarized as follows according to Ribéreau-Gayon (1958A): in *V. lincecumii, V. aestivalis* and *V. coriaceae* cyanidin and peonidin predominate (2 OH groups on the side ring); in *V. riparia* and *V. rupestris* diglucosides are the main pigments; and in other species, including *V. vinifera*, monoglucosides are present in the largest amounts (see Table 2.8). However, Ribéreau-Gayon (1958B) has also noted a regional variation. California-grown *V. vinifera* varieties contained a higher percentage of malvidin than did French-grown.

In *V. rotundifolia*, Brown (1940) reported the red pigment was probably a 3,5-diglucoside of 3',O-methyldelphinidin, which he named muscadine. In *V. hypoglauca* F.v.M., the Australian wild grape, Cornforth (1939) found malvidin monoglucoside but little or no delphinidin glucoside or its methyl esters.

The importance of leucoanthocyanin in red wines has been emphasized by Bate-Smith and Ribéreau-Gayon (1959). The principal source (up to ⅔) of the leucoanthocyanins is the seeds. These are desirable, up to a point, as a source of astringency. They also aid fining by organic fining agents. Ribéreau-Gayon (1957) reported leucocyanidin in a young red wine. He believed it important from the sensory point of view as well as for its possible vitamin-like activity. Four leucoanthocyanins were identified in Cabernet Sauvignon by Somaatmadja *et al.* (1965). Two were leucocyanidins, one was leucodelphinidin and one was not characterized. While they all had some inhibitory effects on growth of bacteria, they differed from each other in their effect on specific bacteria. This is similar to the report of Masquelier (1958) and of Powers *et al.* (1960). In Teinturier grapes and in some of their hybrids, such as Alicante Bouschet, Grand noir, etc., and in some direct-producer hybrids, the color pigments are present in the pulp.

Besides the pigments, grapes contain other polyphenolic compounds. In White Riesling grapes or young wines, Hennig and Burkhardt (1957, 1958, 1960) reported chlorogenic acid, isochlorogenic acid, caffeic acid (either the *cis* or *trans* form), a lactone of *p*-coumaric acid, quinic acid, and shikimic acid. The latter two acids are, of course, components of chlorogenic acid. Esculetin, umbelliferone, myricetrin and several unknown compounds were also noted. Egger *et al.* (1976) found the major amounts of flavonoids as 3-glucuronides. They also identified the usual glucoside and rhamnoglucosides of quercetin, kaempferol and myricetin and found two unidentified aglycones. Weurman and de Rooij (1958) did find chlorogenic acid isomers in grapes (possibly *neo*-chlorogenic and

TABLE 2.8. ANTHOCYANS OF THE SPECIES *VITIS*

Constituents	Ri-paria	Rupes-tris	Lince-cumii	Aesti-valis	Coria-cea	La-brusca	Arizo-nica	Berlan-dieri	Rubra	Monti-cola	Cordi-folia	Vini-fera
Total number of constituents	14	12	17	9	7	10	12	9	12	6	11	9
					Percentage of Each							
Cyanidin												
Monoglucoside	2	–	29	30	58	5	8	8	5	3	10	3
Diglucoside	5	2	2	3	4	–	1	–	1	–	–	–
Peonidin												
Monoglucoside	–	–	7	11	6	10	14	16	20	5	11	15
Diglucoside	2	8	3	4	4	1	10	2	1	–	2	–
Delphinidin												
Monoglucoside	14	9	17	30	20	21	13	23	30	36	15	12
Diglucoside	12	34	1	–	–	–	–	–	1	–	–	–
Petunidin												
Monoglucoside	10	3	8	10	4	15	10	20	20	26	18	12
Diglucoside	17	22	1	–	–	1	–	1	2	–	2	–
Malvidin												
Monoglucoside	6	2	4	6	–	33	29	26	16	27	30	35
Diglucoside	21	8	1	2	–	2	10	2	2	–	5	–
Constituents not identified	11	12	27	4	4	12	5	2	2	3	7	23

Source of data: Ribéreau-Gayon and Sudraud (1957). See also Ribéreau-Gayon (1958).

p-coumarylquinic acids). Tanner and Rentschler (1956) found *only* chlorogenic acid when the stems of Chasselas doré were crushed and fermented with the fruit. The stems of two other varieties, however, contained no chlorogenic acid. They, therefore, believe that this acid and caffeic and quinic acids are not present in grape juice or wine. Burkhardt (1965) reported *p*-coumarylquinic acid and its calcium salt in musts and wines.

Tannin

The tannins occur in the skins, stems and seeds. The free-run juice of white grapes usually contains less than 0.02% tannin. Benvegnin *et al.* (1951) report the following in a white and red variety:

| | Tannin | | | |
| | g/100 g | | kg/100 kg of Fruit | |
Part of Grape	Chasselas Doré	Pinot Noir	Chasselas Doré	Pinot Noir
Seed	5.2	6.4	0.17	0.26
Stem	3.2	3.1	0.12	0.11
Skin	0.6	1.7	0.05	0.10

The tannins of grapes are classified as hydrolyzable (those which are like esters in character and can be broken down by hydrolysis) and are condensed (where the nuclei are held together by carbon linkages). The tannins isolated by Durmishidze (1955) and Hennig and Burkhardt (1957, 1958) include D-catechin, L-epicatechin, L-epigallocatechin, DL-gallocatechin, and D-epicatechingallate. Except for the latter, these are condensed tannins. Su and Singleton (1969) have further clarified this problem. The skins are lower than the seeds in L-epigallocatechin. The Russian worker did not find free gallic acid. The Germans found both gallic and ellagic acids as well as protocatechuic acid. Gallic and ellagic acids are very bitter but are largely removed by gelatin fining. See Fig. 2.10 for the close relationships between tannins, flavanols, and anthocyanidins. Singleton and Noble (1976) report that flavonoids have large flavor effects in red wines. Typical young red table wines have, as gallic acid, about 120 mg/liter of anthocyanins, 50 mg/liter of flavanols, 5 mg/liter of flavanones, 250 mg/liter of catechins and 750 mg/liter of anthocyanogenic tannins. This tannin level, 5 to 10 times the threshold, contributes important flavors. For a complete review of the phenolic substances in grapes and wines and their significance see Singleton and Esau (1969).

Vitamins

The vitamins of grapes are primarily important as accessory growth factors for microorganisms, although some of them are present in suf-

Compounds Identified	Amount mg/liter Reds	Amount mg/liter Whites	Nature of Compounds
Benzoic acids R=R'=H p-hydroxybenzoic acid; R=OH, R'=H protocatechuic acid; R=OCH₃, R'=H vanillic acid; R=R'=OH gallic acid; R=R'=OCH₃ syringic acid	50–100	1–5	Esters
R=H salicylic acid; R=OH gentisic acid			
Cinnamic acids R=H p-coumaric acid; R=OH caffeic acid; R=OCH₃ ferulic acid	50–100	2–10	Esters with anthocyans and tartaric acid
Flavonols R=R'=H kaempferol; R=OH, R'=H quercetin; R=R'=OH myricetin	15	0	2 or 3 glucosides and 1 glucuronoside in musts; 3 aglycones in wines

Anthocyanidins

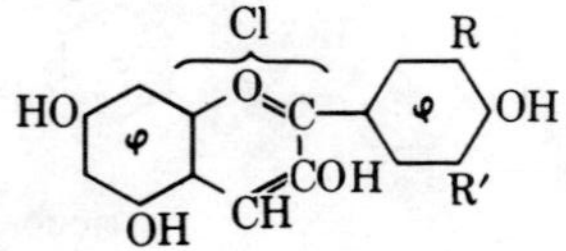

R=OH, R'=H cyanidin
R=OCH₃, R'=H peonidin
R=R'=OH delphinidin
R=OCH₃, R'=OH petunidin
R=R'=OCH₃ malvidin

20–500   0   Glucosides and acylated glucosides (to *p*-coumaric acid); varies for different species of *Vitis*

Tannins-flavan-3-ols

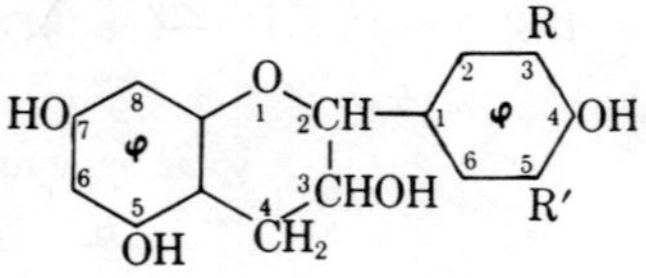

R=OH, R'=H catechin
R=R'=OH gallocatechin

1500–5000   0–100   X¹
50–100   0

Tannins-flavan-3,4-diols

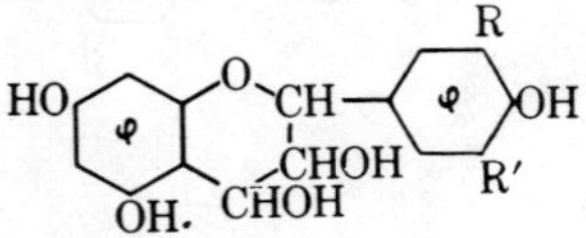

R=OH, R'=H leucocyanidin
R=R'=OH leucodelphinidin

Traces   0

Source of data: Ribéreau-Gayon (1964).
¹X = Polymers of flavans, principally of 3,4 flavan-diols: as monomers small amounts of the flavans are found in red wine.

FIG. 2.10. STRUCTURE OF POLYPHENOLIC COMPOUNDS

ficient amounts to be of possible value in human nutrition.

Ascorbic acid is present in *fresh* grapes in amounts of 1 to 18 mg/100 g with most values below 8 (Amerine and Joslyn 1970). Dehydroascorbic acid is also present. Little nutritive value is likely as the amounts are small and decrease rapidly after crushing. Zubeckis (1964) reported fresh grapes contained 1.1 to 11.7 mg/100 ml of juice of ascorbic acid, except for the Veerport variety which contained 18.5 to 33.8 mg/100 ml. Pasteurized grape juice retained about ⅓ the original ascorbic acid. When grapes are stored at 0°C (32°F) there is a slow decrease in ascorbic acid (Ournac 1958). Vitamin A is present in very small amounts in fresh grapes.

Thiamin is a normal constituent of grapes (Table 2.9). Fresh grapes usually contain less than 0.6 mg/kg. Sulfiting, pasteurization, or filtering grape juice through bentonite all markedly reduce the thiamin content. Schanderl (1959) found 0.12−0.13 mg/liter in fresh German grape juice and 0.03−0.13 in samples of commercial grape juice. Mathews (1958) reported traces to 0.25 mg/liter in 4 Swiss commercial grape juices. Riboflavin occurs in musts up to 1.45 mg/kg, (Table 2.9), but the usual amount is about 0.4 mg or less, especially in commercial grape juice, according to Mathews (1958). Riboflavin is easily destroyed by light. About 50% is lost by sulfiting or by fining with bentonite. If added to unsulfited grape juices in colored bottles, it is well retained.

TABLE 2.9. VITAMIN CONTENT OF VARIOUS MUSTS[1]

Vitamin	Minimum	Maximum	Source[2]
Thiamin (B_1)	0.1	1.2	1,5,8,10,11
Riboflavin (B_2)	T	1.5	1,4,5,6,7,8,10,11
Pyridoxine (B_6)	0.1	2.9	1,6,9,10,11
Pantothenic acid	0.25	10.5	1,2,3,6,7,8,9,10,11
Nicotinic acid	0.3	8.8	4,5,6,8,9
Biotin	0.001	0.06	3,6,9,10
Inositol	3.4	4.8	6,10
p-Aminobenzoic acid	0.00	0.04	6,10
Choline	0.5	4.01	6,10
Folic acid	T	0.05	8,10,11

[1]mg/liter except mg/100 ml for inositol.
[2]Source of data: (1) Perlman and Morgan (1945), (2) Peynaud and Lafon-Lafourcade (1955), (3) Peynaud and Lafon-Lafourcade (1956), (4) Cailleau and Chevillard (949), (5) Flanzy and Causeret (1954), (6) Castor (1953), (7) Smith and Olmo (1944), (8) Hall *et al.* (1956), (9) Radler (1957), (10) Mathews (1958), (11) Burger *et al.* (1956).

Pyridoxine is present up to 2.9 mg/kg in musts (Table 2.9). Added pyridoxine is retained well by grape juice. Pantothenic acid occurs in musts in amounts up to 15 mg/kg (Table 2.9). It is retained during storage. Smith and Olmo (1944) found significantly higher amounts of pantothenic acid in the juice of tetraploid compared to diploid varieties. *Labrusca* × *vinifera* interspecific hybrids were also higher in this vitamin than hybrids of *vinifera* varieties. Wines have up to 1.9 mg/liter as calcium pantothenate.

For musts, Lafon-Lafourcade and Peynaud (1958) showed a marked increase during maturation of p-aminobenzoic acid and a slight increase in pteroylglutamic acid and choline. Musts of Bordeaux grapes contained 0.015−0.09 mg/liter (average 0.05 of p-aminobenzoic acid), 0.001−0.015 mg of pteroylglutamic acid and 0.02−0.04 mg/liter of choline.

Nicotinic acid has been reported in amounts up to 2.8 mg/kg of Thompson Seedless grapes by Teply et al. (1942). Other vitamins present are B_6, biotin, p-aminobenzoic acid, and inositol, according to Castor (1953). Other data are given in Table 2.10. The "bioflavonoids," originally called vitamin P or blood-capillary fragility factors (Durmishidze 1955, 1958), include D-catechin and other flavonoids found in grapes and red wine in high amount. See also Lavollay and Sevestre (1944), DeEds (1949), and Singleton and Esau (1969).

TABLE 2.10. VITAMIN CONTENT OF MUSTS AND WINES[1,2]

Vitamin	Musts			White Wines			Red Wines		
	Mini-mum	Maxi-mum	Aver-age	Mini-mum	Maxi-mum	Aver-age	Mini-mum	Maxi-mum	Aver-age
Biotin	1.5	4.2	2.6	1.0	3.6	2.0	0.6	4.6	2.1
Choline	−	−	−	17	27	21	17	41	2
Inositol	380	710	500	220	730	497	290	510	334
Nicotinic acid	1650	4200	3260	990	2190	1570	1320	2180	1890
Pantothenic acid	500	1380	820	550	1240	810	470	1870	980
Pyridoxine	310	920	420	220	820	440	250	780	470
Riboflavin	3	60	21	8	133	32	103	245	177
Thiamin	160	450	333	2	58	10	−	−	7.5
Cobalamine (B₁₂)	0	0.13	0.05	0	0.16	0.07	0.04	0.10	0.06

[1]Source of data: Peynaud and Lafon-Lafourcade (1957).
[2]mg/liter for inositol and choline; μ/liter for the others.

Enzymes

A number of enzymes are found in musts. Bayer et al. (1957) studied the polyphenoloxidases of grapes and reported them to contain copper, as do all polyphenoloxidases. Their activity was rapidly and completely inhibited by sulfur dioxide. Centrifuging musts greatly reduced their enzyme activity, most of which is localized in or on the skins. Durmishidze (1955) also showed that peroxidase and polyphenoloxidase were observed in all phases of vegetative growth of vines. Olivieri (1975) studied the effect of temperature and pH on the action of the pectinases—methylesterase and polygalacturonase and on the oxydases. Grape peroxidase (Ournac and Poux 1974) was destroyed in grapevine by heat but was resistant to SO_2 and bentonite. Low pH aided in the inhibition. If juice is treated with polyvinylpyrrolidone, the peroxidase is very resistant to inhibition. Enzymatic oxidation is important for many wines, particularly when made from moldy grapes. Polyphenoloxidase is the enzyme responsible for the sensitivity of botrytis-free musts to oxidation, according to Dubernet and Ribéreau-Gayon (1973). Laccase, from *Botrytis cinerea* infections, is a phenoloxidase enzyme which consumes oxygen and results in browning of musts. Dubernet and Ribéreau-Gayon suggest the use of SO_2 and juice settling to minimize the effects. A concise review of the inhibitory effects of SO_2 on polyphenoloxidase is given by Haisman (1974).

Other enzymes noted by Amerine (1954) included: ascorbase, catalase, dehydratase, esterase, and a proteolytic enzyme.

Odorous Constituents

Many studies of the odor constituents have been made. Holley *et al.* (1955) confirmed that methyl anthranilate is the predominant aroma-producing constituent of Concord grapes (see also Nelson *et al.* 1977). They also found (mg/ml of essence): ethanol (35), methanol (1.5), ethyl acetate (3.5), methyl acetate (0.15), acetone (0.3), acetaldehyde (0.03), methyl anthranilate (0.033), and acetic acid. They note that, since about 90% of the volatile organic material is ethanol, procedures for testing juice quality based on the quantitative determination of volatile material by dichromate or permanganate oxidation do little more than determine the ethanol. The esters quantified in the recent study of Schreier *et al.* (1977) with five different German wines were (μg/liter): isobutyl acetate (30-82), ethyl 2-methylbutyrate (3-14), ethyl 3-methylbutyrate (2-24), ethyl 2-carboxyfuranoate (0.2-6.0), isopentyl octanoate (4-8), ethyl phenethyl acetate (4.9-9.1), ethyl laurate (4.7-14.1), 2-phenethyl acetate (252-708), diethyl malonate (3.7-15.6), diethyl glutarate (8.6-19.5), and isopentyl lactate (16.8-26.3). Also in the same study, the amounts of some terpineols and related compounds were determined (μg/liter): nerol oxide (3-67), linaloöl oxide (6-33), linaloöl (33-246), *cis*-linaloöl oxide (16-117), hotrienol (14-186), *trans*-linaloöl oxide (5-98), α-terpineol (31-339), crystallized linaloöl oxide (6-42), nerol (0.1-14), and geraniol (1.8-43).

Bayonove *et al.* (1975) identified 2-methoxy-3-isobutylpyrazine as the revealing aromatic compound in Cabernet Sauvignon.

Stevens *et al.* (1965) reported the higher boiling extract of Concord grapes was largely methyl anthranilate. The low-boiling constituents were ethyl acetate, *iso*-propyl acetate, ethanol, 2-propanol, ethyl propionate, propyl acetate, 1-propanol, 2-methyl-3-buten-2-ol, ethyl butyrate, 2-methyl-l-propanol, 1-butanol, 2-methyl-1-butanol, 3-methyl-1-butanol, and ethyl hexanoate.

Kepner and Webb (1956) reported the following composition of *V. rotundifolia:* ethyl, *n*-butyl, *n*-hexyl, β-phenethyl alcohols and acetate, laurate and isopropyl esters. Methanol, *n*-hexanal, 2-hexenal, and acetal were also probably present. No nitrogen or sulfur-containing compounds were found.

Haagen-Smit *et al.* (1949) used fresh Zinfandel grapes from the volatile oil of which they isolated (g/100 kg fruit in each case): ethanol (244), acetaldehyde (1.8), acetic acid (0.0053), n-butyric acid (0.003), n-caproic acid (0.0015), glyoxylic acid (0.118), n-butyl phthalate (2.25), leaf aldehyde (0.327), waxy substance (0.024), and a carbonyl compound (0.024).

In Muscat of Alexandria grapes Webb and Kepner (1957) isolated (mg/kg of fruit): methanol (3.7), ethanol (111.0), n-butanol (0.03), 3-methylbutanol (0.01), n-hexanol (0.49), cis-3-hexenol (0.26), acetaldehyde (0.85), n-hexanal (0.03), 2-butanone (0.01), 2-pentanone (0.01), 2-hexenal (0.05), methyl acetate (0.08), ethyl caproate (0.04), a butyrate ester, a valerate ester, another caproate ester, a caprylate ester, a caprate ester, a laurate ester, ethyl esters (all esters, 0.16), and acetals. They did not find any terpene alcohols. However, Cordonnier (1956) found about 2 mg/liter of geraniol, terpineol, limonene, and linaloöl in muscat essences. Bayonove and Cordonnier (1970) and others have confirmed that linaloöl is the main muscaty component of ripe grapes. Ribéreau-Gayon *et al.* (1975) showed linaloöl, geraniol, nerol, α-terpineol and four terpineol oxides to be the main muscat components and indicated percentages of each in several varieties. Threshold levels were also reported. Rodopulo *et al.* (1974) found the usual odor compounds in the muscat grapes of the Soviet Union. The varieties growing in the cooler northern areas had twice the amounts of volatiles as those grown in Crimea or Armenia.

Using paper chromatography, Cordonnier (1956) found four clear spots at R_f 0.48, 0.60, 0.74, and 0.94 for Muscat blanc (Muscat Canelli or Muscat Frontignan in California) and at 0.44, 0.58, 0.72, and 0.93 for Muscat of Alexandria. The intensity of the spots was positively correlated with the amount of muscat aroma. He suggested linaloöl or a compound containing linaloöl as the revealing aromatic constituent of these two muscat varieties. By simple chromatography, Cordonnier was not able to establish elder flowers as a sophisticant of non-muscat wines. Coriander gave a clear spot at R_f 0.75, so by his technique, wines sophisticated with coriander could not be differentiated from true muscat wines. To improve the extraction of the muscat aroma, Bayonove *et al.* (1976) recommend a short maceration of the skins and juice before pressing.

Rapp and Hastrich (1976) were able to differentiate and characterize four different varieties by the juice volatiles. Schreier *et al.* (1976A) identified 225 aroma compounds in grapes. Schreier *et al.* (1976B) also could differentiate some varieties based on volatile analysis.

Rapp *et al.* (1976) using Freon 11 extraction techniques and glass capillary columns found over 300 peaks in grape berry extracts.

Metals

For the metal content of musts, see Table 2.11 and Amerine (1958). According to Jaulmes *et al.* (1960), musts contain 0.025–0.4 mg/liter of lead with most samples with 0.1–0.25. In their studies there was gen-

TABLE 2.11. COMPOSITION OF MUSTS AND WINES[1]

	Must g/100 ml	Wine g/100 ml
1. Water	70-85	80-90
2. Carbohydrates	15-25	0.1-0.3
Glucose	8-13	0.5-0.1
Fructose	7-12	0.05-0.1
Pentoses	0.08-0.20	0.08-0.20
Arabinose	0.05-0.15	0.05-0.10
Rhamnose	0.02-0.04	0.02-0.04
Xylose	T	0.002
Pectin	0.01-0.10	T
Inositol	0.02-0.08	0.03-0.05
Galactose	–	0.013
Ribose	–	0.004
Mannose	–	0.004
Fucose	–	0.0005
3. Alcohols and related compounds		
Ethyl	T	8.0-15.0
Methyl	0.0	0.01-0.02
Higher	0.0	0.008-0.012
2,3-Butylene glycol	0.0	0.01-0.15
Acetoin	0.0	0.000-0.003
Glycerol[2]	0	0.30-1.40
Sorbitol	T	T
Diacetyl	0.0	T-0.0006
4. Aldehyde	T	0.001-0.050
5. Organic acids	0.3-1.5	0.3-1.1
Tartaric	0.2-1.0	0.1-0.6
Malic	0.1-0.8	0.0-0.6
Citric	0.01-0.05	0.0-0.05
Succinic	0	0.05-0.15
Lactic	0	0.1-0.5
Acetic	0.00-0.02	0.03-0.05
Formic	0	T
Propionic	0	In spoiled wines
Butyric	0	In spoiled wines
Gluconic		From botrytised grapes only
Glucuronic		From botrytised grapes only
Glyoxylic	?	0.00012
Mesoxalic	?	0.0001-0.0003
Glyceric	–	T
Saccharic	–	T
Amino	0.01-0.08	0.01-0.20
Pantothenic	–	T
Quinic	0	T
p-Coumaric	T	?
Shikimic	T	?
Sulfurous	0	0.00-0.05
Carbonic	T	Various
Glycolic	–	0.0012
α-Hydroxyisocaproic	–	0.0002
2-Methyl-2,3-dihydroxybutyric	–	0.009

TABLE 2.11. *(Continued)*

	Must g/100 ml	Wine g/100 ml
Oxalic	—	0.007
Malonic	—	0.001
Fumaric	—	0.008
Citramalic	—	0.002
α-Hydroxyglutaric	—	0.023
Aconic	—	0.002
Pyroracemic	°	0.001
α-Ketoglutaric	—	0.003
Galacturonic	°	0.019
6. Pigments and polyphenol	T	T
Anthocyans	0.05	0.05
Chlorophyll	T	0-T
Xanthophyl	T	?
Carotene	T	?
Flavonol		
Quercetin	T	T
Quercetrin	T	T
Rutin	?	?
Flavonoids and non-flavonoids	0.01-0.10	0.01-0.30
Catechin	T	T
Gallocatechin	T	T
Epicatechin gallate	T	T
Gallic acid	T	T
Ellagic acid	T	T
Caffeic acid	T	T
p-Coumaric acid	T	T
7. Nitrogenous compounds		
Total	0.03-0.17	0.01-0.09
Protein	0.001-0.01	0.001-0.003
Amino	0.017-0.110	0.010-0.200
Humin	0.001-0.002	0.001-0.002
Amide	0.001-0.004	0.001-0.008
Ammonia	0.001-0.012	0.00-0.071
Residual	0.01-0.02	0.005-0.020
8. Mineral compounds	0.3-0.5	0.15-0.40
Potassium	0.15-0.25	0.045-0.175
Magnesium	0.01-0.025	0.01-0.020
Calcium	0.004-0.025	0.001-0.021
Sodium	T-0.020	T-0.044
Iron	T-0.003	T-0.005
Aluminum	T-0.003	T-0.07
Manganese	T-0.0051	T-0.05
Copper	T-0.0003	T-0.0005
Boron	T-0.007	T-0.004
Rubidium	T-0.0001	T-0.0004
Phosphate	0.02-0.05	0.003-0.090
Sulfate	0.003-0.035	0.003-0.22
Silicic acid	0.0002-0.005	0.0002-0.005
Chloride	0.001-0.010	0.001-0.060
Fluoride	T	0.0001-0.001
Iodide	T	T-0.001
Carbon dioxide	0	0.01-0.05[3]
Oxygen	T	T-0.00006

[1]Source of data: Hennig (1958), Amerine (1954, 1958), Ribéreau-Gayon and Peynaud (1958), Eschnauer (1959).
[2]Except for botrytised grapes.
[3]In normal still wine. About 0.1 is the beginning of gassiness.

erally, but not always, a decrease in lead content during fermentation. The manganese content of Sicilian wines ranged from 0.25 to 2.20 mg/ liter, according to Corrao (1963).

Boron fertilization markedly delays grape maturity (in fact, prevented satisfactory ripening) according to Decau and Lamazou-Betbeder (1964). There are reports that potassium fertilization hastens maturity and increases sugar content. Dupuy *et al.* (1955) found that soils high in phosphorus often produced wines with higher iron contents. Much of the iron appeared to have been dissolved from soil adhering to the fruit. The enrichment was not due to simple dissolving of iron from the soil but to reductive biological processes during fermentation. This was confirmed by Flanzy and Deibner (1956). Iron pickup from crushers and presses is, of course, possible.

Table 2.11 summarizes data from a variety of sources for the composition of musts and table wines. Musts of raisined or botrytised fruit and their wines will not fit these limits.

ENVIRONMENTAL FACTORS

While the composition of most fruits reflects the environmental conditions under which they are grown, this appears to be more critical for the grape. The primary environmental factor is temperature (maximum, minimum, mean, and night versus day). Secondary factors are rainfall, sunshine versus cloudiness, humidity, hail, wind, soil (per se), and combinations of these.

Temperature

The primary environmental factors influencing the distribution of *V. vinifera* grapes within the various climatic regions in the temperate zones are the mean daily temperature and the minimum temperature. The rather narrow limits within which grapes are or can be grown are shown in Fig. 2.11. Outside of these limits the winter temperatures are so low that vines cannot survive (as in most of Canada, etc.); or, the summer temperatures are not warm enough to ripen grapes (as in England, etc.); or, late spring frosts may kill new growth (as in parts of Idaho or the Sierra Nevada foothills of California); or, high summer humidity may prevent growth of *V. vinifera* varieties owing to virus and other diseases, etc. (as in southern United States or Central America); or, summer temperatures may be too high (as in most desert regions, and especially under limited moisture supply).

Aside from these adverse conditions, it is the temperature received during the growing season which is most important. Vines normally start to grow in the spring when the average daily temperature reaches 10°C

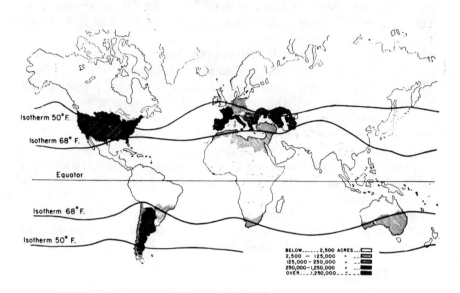

FIG. 2.11. DISTRIBUTION OF GRAPES IN THE WORLD

TABLE 2.12. TEMPERATURE SUMMATION DURING THE GROWING SEASON
IN ALGERIA, EUROPE, AND CALIFORNIA[1]

Place	Day Degrees Above 50°F	Winkler Region[2]
Algiers, Algeria	5200	V
Bakersfield	5030	V
Fresno	4680	V
Merced	4620	V
Palermo, Italy (Marsala)	4140	V
Naples, Italy (Lacrima Christi)	4010	V
Davis	3618	IV
Lodi-Stockton	3590	IV
Florence, Italy (Chianti)	3530	IV
Calistoga	3281	III
Livermore	3260	III
Asti, Italy (Barbera, etc.)	2980	II
Uiah	2970	II
St. Helena	2900	II
San Jose	2590	II
Bordeaux, France (Claret)	2519	II
Beaune, France (Burgundy)	2400	I
Sonoma	2360	I
Oakville	2300	I
Aptos	2110	I
Chalon-sur-Marne, France (Champagne)	2060	I
Auxerre, France (Chablis)	1850	I
Trier, Germany (Moselle)	1730	I
Geisenheim, Germany (Rheingau)	1709	I

[1]Source of data: Winkler (1936).
[2]I, 2500 day-degrees or less: II, 2501 to 3000: III, 3001 to 3500: IV, 3501 to 4000: and V, over 4000.

FIG. 2.12. WINE DISTRICTS OF CALIFORNIA

(50°F). The summation of temperature above 10°C (50°F) is then the effective temperature influencing vine growth and the composition of the fruit. Winkler (1936) has calculated the summation (as day-degrees) for the principal grape growing regions (Table 2.12 and Fig. 2.12). It may be seen that grapes are successfully grown when the summation of temperature is as low as 2000 day degrees and as high as 5000.

The effect of temperature on the growth of the vine is optimum at about 26.7°C (80°F) (Kliewer et al. 1972). Above this temperature growth and photosynthesis rapidly decrease. Below this temperature to 10°C (50°F) there is a decline in both growth and photosynthesis. The amount of light is also important. Areas which are temperature-modulated by nearness of large bodies of water or cooling winds may have consistently high heat summations but the vine and fruit response may be similar to that from a cooler region.

In the warmer regions, grapes mature earlier and at the same percentage of sugar have a lower titratable acidity, less color, and a higher pH. For example, in southern Spain the harvest normally begins in September, in southern France in late September or early October, and in

Germany in October or November. In California, grapes are picked for winery use in the south San Joaquin valley in August. The harvest at Lodi begins in September. The harvest at Napa (Fig. 2.13) peaks in early October. Grapes in the cool Santa Cruz mountains often ripen in late October. In the cool areas of Monterey county, grapes are harvested in November and in some years as late as December.

The main effects on total acidity and pH are shown in Table 2.13. In the cooler districts, even though the grapes were not harvested at the same stage of maturity, the acidity was usually higher and the pH lower. The effect of region on sugar content is not obvious from this table and, in practice, is often suppressed by the overcropping which occurs in the warmer regions (Winkler 1954). Overcropped vines show delayed maturity or may not ripen. Amerine (1956) has indicated possible differences in the tartrate/malate ratio due to temperature. This results from the fact that malic acid is respired at lower temperatures than tartaric acid. Therefore, one reason for the lower acidity of warm regions is their lower malic acid content. However, if the harvest is made very late in a cool region and very early in a warm region, this difference may not exist. Amerine (1956) also noted that exceptions to the rule would occur when (1) there is no very hot period during ripening in a warm region or (2) there is a very hot period during ripening in a cool region. See also Schrader *et al.* (1976) for the increase of potassium and decrease in

Courtesy of Wine Institute

FIG. 2.13. NAPA VALLEY WINERY WITH VINEYARD

TABLE 2.13. INFLUENCE OF REGION ON THE COMPOSITION OF GRAPES PICKED AT APPROXIMATELY THE SAME STATE OF MATURITY

Variety	Brix			Total Acid			pH		
	Fresno[1]	Davis[2]	Bonny Doon[3]	Fresno	Davis	Bonny Doon	Fresno	Davis	Bonny Doon
	Degrees	Degrees	Degrees	g/100 ml	g/100 ml	g/100ml	pH	pH	pH
Alicante Bouschet	–	18.8	18.9	–	0.78	1.20	–	3.47	3.10
Burger	–	17.8	17.6	0.55	0.81	–	–	3.46	3.15
Cabernet Sauvignon	22.9	22.4	20.7	0.65	0.67	1.10	3.48	3.63	3.41
Carignane	21.8	21.8	–	0.62	0.70	–	3.67	3.58	–
Sauvignon vert	23.3	–	20.3	0.50	–	0.67	3.81	–	3.24
Sémillon	–	19.0	18.0	–	0.67	0.97	–	3.45	3.10
Zinfandel	–	22.4	21.3	–	0.61	0.86	–	3.58	3.28

Source of data: Amerine and Joslyn (1970).
[1]Fresno—4680 day-degrees of temperature above 50°F during the growing season.
[2]Davis—3618 day-degrees of temperature above 50°F during the growing season.
[3]Bonny Doon—2400 day-degrees of temperature above 50°F during the growing season

calcium and magnesium during ripening under warm temperature conditions.

The effect of temperature on color is well known. The Tokay variety at Lodi (region IV) has an orange-red color. At Fresno and south (region V) it has no more than a pink blush. In the coast counties (region II) it may develop a slight purple-red color. Grenache in the cooler regions has a full red color. At Davis (region IV) it is barely suited for making a rosé. At Delano (region V) white free-run juice is easily obtained. Typical data are given in Table 2.14.

TABLE 2.14. INFLUENCE OF REGIONAL CONDITIONS ON COLOR OF GRAPES[1]

| | | | | Regions and Average Color Value[1] | |
Variety	Delano	Lodi, Guasti, Davis	Livermore Valley, Asti, Ukiah	Napa Valley, Santa Clara Valley	South Sonoma County, Santa Cruz Mts.
Alicante Bouschet	74	85	92	143	235
Carignane	45	49	57	83	100
Mataro	8	14	20	55	65
Petite Sirah	70	80	89	143	200
Zinfandel	27	44	52	62	200

[1]Source of data: Winkler and Amerine (1937).
[2]These figures represent the relative intensity of color expressed on an arbitrary scale; the higher the figure, the greater is the concentration of pigment.

The seasonal effect due to differences in temperature is well illustrated by the seasons of 1935 and 1936 in California. The 1935 season at St. Helena was cool (2276 day-degrees) and the harvest late. In 1936 very hot (2664 day-degrees) weather (plus a small crop) led to much earlier ripening, higher sugar content (and hence more alcohol), less color, and lower total acidity. For typical data see Table 2.15. Under winery conditions, the expected lower color in wines of warm seasons does not always develop. This is because fermentation of high sugar musts develops more alcohol and may extract a greater percentage of the color than the lower alcohol wines of cool years. The shriveling of the grapes in warm seasons may also decrease this difference between seasons.

Temperature differences as great as these are not common in California. They are common in Europe and eastern United States and Canada which may not receive enough heat to mature their grapes every year.

Favorable exposure results in very marked differences in maturity and in quality in cool regions.

TABLE 2.15. EFFECT OF SEASON AND VARIETY ON THE COMPOSITION OF MUST AND WINE[1]

Variety	Avg Date Collected 1935	Avg Date Collected 1936	Must — Brix Degrees 1935	Must — Brix Degrees 1936	Wine — Alcohol Per-cent[3] 1935	Wine — Alcohol Per-cent[3] 1936	Wine — Total Acid g/100 ml 1935	Wine — Total Acid g/100 ml 1936	Color Intensity[2] 1935	Color Intensity[2] 1936
Alicante Bouschet	Oct. 1	Sept. 23	21.7	22.9	10.9	12.3	0.61	0.57	64	63
Burger	Sept. 30	Sept. 19	19.8	19.5	9.6	11.0	0.66	0.55	–	–
Carignane	Sept. 30	Sept. 19	22.3	23.3	10.9	12.4	0.70	0.50	27	22
Palomino	Sept. 24	Sept. 30	21.5	22.9	11.0	12.5	0.38	0.36	–	–
Petite Sirah	Sept. 28	Sept. 22	23.2	25.6	11.3	13.9	0.67	0.56	77	59
Zinfandel	Oct. 1	Sept. 19	24.7	23.9	12.8	13.5	0.71	0.58	31	19
Average of 6 varieties	Sept. 29	Sept. 19	22.2	23.1	11.1	12.6	0.62	0.52	50	41
Average of 240 samples[4]	Sept. 30	Sept. 21	22.1	23.0	11.0	12.2	0.61	0.50	39	33

[1]Source of data; Winkler and Amerine (1938).
[2]These figures represent the relative intensity of color expressed on an arbitrary scale; the higher the figure, the greater is the consumption of pigment.
[3]Percentage by volume.
[4]Represents about 49 varieties from several districts of California.

Soil

It is believed in Europe that grapes grown on calcareous soils produce the best wines. This may be correct, but possibly not because of the calcium content of the soil per se. Calcareous soils are usually well drained. Well-drained soils are warmer,[1] hence there is better vine growth and better ripening. The slate soils of the Moselle are believed to retain the day-time heat and thus help warm the vine at night. The effect of soil structure on root growth in the Douro region has already been mentioned (p. 39). Also the high calcium sulfate content of some soils and its presence on the grapes constitute a sort of natural plastering in the sherry district of Spain (p. 33). One of the clearest bits of evidence on the importance of soil is the Cognac region of France where the more highly calcareous the zone the higher the price of the wines and their brandy. This may be a direct soil effect.

Rainfall

Vines require moisture. With sufficient moisture there is no evidence that moderate rainfall or irrigation has a deleterious effect. There is evidence that summer rainfall markedly increases the humidity and thus the susceptibility of the vine to fungus diseases. Control of the fungus diseases necessitates vineyard spraying with copper sulfate, etc. It also reduces sugar content according to Ferenczi (1955). Rainfall also may reduce the temperature. In Hungary, Ferenczi (1955) showed a high positive correlation ($r = +0.8459$) between titratable acidity and amount of precipitation for the period May through September. The correlation for the period July through September was less ($r = +0.6680$). Sunshine and temperature rather than the rainfall itself can account for these effects. For conditions in Czechoslovakia, Vereš and Polakovič (1975) found heat summation, heat summation plus cloud-free days plus precipitation, and a heat summation-rainfall index correlated best with grape ripening and wine quality. They stressed the importance of the microclimate around the vine as well as the macroclimate. This was, of course, for a cool-climate region. Nevertheless, their measures of vine growth, blooming, set, exposed leaf surface, etc., on the quantity and quality of the vintage are indicative of the more sophisticated climatic relations to quality that can be established.

Occasionally, the soil may become so dry that vine growth ceases and maturation is delayed or never attained. Where vines are overcropped, if a severe moisture deficiency occurs during the latter stages of ripening when the leaves are still functional, the leaves may withdraw water from

[1]The air above them is also warmer.

the fruit and cause severe fruit shriveling without full ripening. Such grapes produce poor wines.

Other Factors

Dehydrating winds off the Sahara early in the season prevent normal ripening of grapes in Madeira, Spain, and Sicily; later, the grapes may shrivel and raisin on the vine. Hail reduces or damages the crop and may defoliate the vine and thus delay or prevent maturity of the remaining fruit. Late spring frosts reduce the crop. If the season is otherwise good, this may result in better ripening and enhanced quality.

The rootstock may influence the composition (and hence the quality) of the fruit of the scion. Bénard et al. (1963) used nine stocks for Grenache. The analytical differences on the musts and wines were small. The statistical significance of the results is questionable.

Ough et al. (1968A, B) found large rootstock effects on grape and wine composition with a number of scions. The two rootstocks, St. George and 99R, were not heat-treated and did contain leaf roll and possibly other viruses. The results may well have been due to difference in vigor of the stocks due to these infections. Later work with St. George and A×R (both heat-treated) in the same vineyard and with essentially the same scions showed no pronounced differences in composition on the fourth and fifth leaf (Ough and Alley 1977).

VARIETY

There are perhaps 5000 named varieties of V. vinifera and 2000 of V. labrusca and other native species. There are also many hybrids between V. vinifera and American species—the so-called "direct producers" and resistant stocks.

Ripe grapes may be white, green, pink, red, or purple in color with small or large fruit clusters. The shape of their berries, clusters, and leaves vary. They may ripen early or late. The texture may be pulpy, solid, soft or liquid. The sugar content may be low or high and the titratable acidity can be small or large—even under favorable climatic conditions. The effect of temperature and other environmental factors on the composition of these many varieties is marked. They are, moreover, subject in varying degrees to insects and microbial diseases, and they respond differently to pruning. There are complex interrelations among these parameters.

Within each variety various clones exist—with various differences in growth and composition. Calo and Costacurta (1976) and Huglin (1976) have summarized the advantages of clonal selection not only for varietal character and production but also for disease and virus resistance.

The main varieties planted in the vineyard districts of the world have been mentioned elsewhere in the text. California grape acreages are given in Table 2.16.

The recommendations generally follow those of the California Agricultural Experiment Station with some modifications based on the authors' predilections. While these recommendations apply primarily to California conditions, they may have some validity for other regions of similar climatic conditions.

Estimating the grape acreage by varieties is not easy. Winkler (1964) estimated 879 bearing acres of Cabernet Sauvignon and 538 nonbearing in the central coast counties. The "official" figures of Henderson *et al.* (1965) showed 834 bearing acres of Cabernet Sauvignon in these and other counties of California.

Statewide, the largest increases in bearing wine grape varieties for the period 1952-1963 according to Winkler were for Chardonnay (1070%), Chenin blanc (258%), Emerald Riesling (190%), Pinot blanc (107%), Sylvaner (148%), Cabernet Sauvignon (133%), Gamay (244%), and Pinot noir (245%). These figures indicate increasing interest in the planting of fine wine grapes during this period. More recent planting in reds has been Cabernet Sauvignon, Barbera, Ruby Cabernet, Petite Sirah, and Merlot and in whites, White Riesling and Chardonnay (see also Table 2.18). The difficulty of prophesying is well illustrated by Olmo's Estimates of Future Plantings (1955). Burger and Sauvignon vert were predicted to increase in acreage. Neither has fulfilled this promise.

White Table Wines

In the selection of varieties for these types of wines, the first consideration is the varietal character. Distinctive varietal character is always needed for wines which are to be named after the variety. Neutral flavored wines may be needed for sparkling wine stock. The composition under the climatic conditions of the region is critical. Varieties which regularly ripen with sufficient titratable acidity and a fairly low pH are to be preferred; see p. 89. Resistance to sunburn and insects and disease is important. No variety which is incapable of high production should be grown in the regions where standard wines are produced (regions IV and V particularly) and, all other factors being equal, production is an important economic factor in the selection of a suitable variety for all regions.

Factors such as convenience of pruning and harvesting, ease of training, mechanical harvesting, and of separation of the juice from the skins, rootstock compatibility, resistance to darkening of color of the must and of the wine also need to be considered. Berg and Akiyoshi (1956) have noted undesirable darkening in a number of varieties, including, regret-

TABLE 2.16. CALIFORNIA GRAPE ACREAGE BY CLASSES AND VARIETIES
1944, 1959, 1969, AND 1976[1]

Class and Variety	Total Acreage			
	1944	1959	1969	1976
Raisin varieties	253,553	242,297	253,683	243,011
Thompson Seedless	182,194	215,054	235,543	228,477
Table varieties	82,619	86,565	75,867	65,640
Wine varieties	174,194	125,671	147,400	322,650
Alicante Bouschet	25,606	10,299	7,413	5,805
Barbera	–	–	2,112	20,838
Burger	2,987	2,992	2,310	1,680
Burgundy[2]	–	707	–	–
Cabernet Sauvignon	–	660	5,098	26,742
Carignane	32,051	25,257	26,963	27,623
Carmine	–	–	–	n.a.
Carnelian	–	–	–	2,797
Centurion	–	–	–	1,425
Chardonnay	–	–	2,457	11,410
Chenin blanc[3]	–	621	3,868	20,190
Colombar	1,480	617	–	–
Early Burgundy	–	–	801	800
Emerald Riesling	–	–	–	2,851
Flora	–	–	–	473
French Colombard	–	1,422	8,574	26,498
Gamay	–	757	1,640	6,049
Gamay Beaujolais	–	–	969	4,366
Gewürztraminer	–	–	591	2,543
Gray Riesling	–	–	754	1,900
Grenache	4,229	11,761	12,995	19,176
Mataro	7,692	3,777	2,003	1,503
Mission	10,906	8,388	6,991	5,061
Palomino	5,072	9,171	7,079	4,590
Pedro Ximenes	–	652	513	213
Petite Sirah	7,721	4,710	4,332	14,215
Pinot blanc	–	–	385	1,439
Pinot noir	–	–	2,715	10,134
Royalty	–	–	2,007	2,997
Rubired	–	–	2,033	11,303
Ruby Cabernet	–	–	1,656	18,266
St. Émilion	–	–	–	1,608
Salvador	–	2,177	2,002	3,002
Sauvignon blanc[4]	–	2,011	1,130	3,808
Sauvignon vert	–	–	1,120	833
Sémillon	–	1,272	1,224	3,020
Sylvaner[5]	574	1,331	1,195	1,374
Tinta Madeira	–	–	486	1,245
Valdepeñas	–	919	1,853	2,361
White Riesling	–	–	1,586	8,552
Zinfandel	50,349	25,572	21,704	30,588
Other whites	8,780	2,051	2,611	18,067
Other reds	16,747	7,016	5,737	

[1]Source: California Crop and Livestock Reporting Service (1945, 1960, 1970, and 1977).
[2]Includes Early Burgundy, Crabb's Black Burgundy, Mondeuse, Portuguese Blue and Refosco, except early Burgundy listed separately in 1969 and 1976.
[3]Includes Pinot blanc, White Pinot, Pinot de la Loire, White Zinfandel and Pinot vrai, except Pinot blanc listed separately in 1969 and 1976.
[4]Includes Sauvignon vert, except in 1969 and 1976.
[5]Includes White and other Rieslings, except White Rieslings listed separately in 1969 and 1976.

tably, some which have been widely planted.

The recommendations by region are given in Table 2.17. The production estimates are for good soil and climatic conditions but are only approximate. Lower production can be anticipated on shallow soils, particularly on hillside vineyards.

TABLE 2.17. RECOMMENDED VARIETIES FOR WHITE TABLE WINE PRODUCTION IN CALIFORNIA

Variety	Production[1] Tons/ Acre	Ripens[2]	Flavor[3]	Region[4] I and II	III and IV	V
Chardonnay	L	E	D	HR	NR	NR
Chenin blanc	M+	M−	N+	R	R	QR
Flora	M−	L	S	QR	NR	NR
Folle Blanche	M+	M	D−	QR	NR	NR
French Colombard	H	E+	D−	QR	R	HR
Gewürztraminer	L	E	D+	R	NR	NR
Red Veltliner	M	L	N	QR	NR	NR
Sauvignon blanc	M	M	D	HR	QR	NR
Sémillon	M+	M	D−	HR	QR	NR
Sylvaner	M	E	S	R	NR	NR
White Riesling	M−	M−	D−	HR	NR	NR

Source: Adapted from Amerine and Winkler (1963).
[1]L for 1 to 3, M for 4 to 6, H for over 6.
[2]E for early, M for mid-season, L for late.
[3]N for neutral, S for slightly distinctive, and D for distinctive.
[4]HR is highly recommended, R for recommended, QR for qualified recommendation, and NR for not recommended.

Red Table Wines

For these wines varietal character, composition and production are likewise important. The color should be adequate and stable. Salvador, Alicante Bouschet, and possibly Rubired and Royalty are examples of varieties of high but unstable color. Resistance to sunburn and mold is also important. Petite Sirah is an example of a variety which fails in some regions in hot years owing to excessive sunburn. It, Merlot, and Pinot St. George mold easily when the humidity is high owing to early rains.

The recommendations by region are given in Table 2.18. The production estimates are approximate.

Pink or Rosé Wines

Many of the varieties recommended for red table wines can also be used for pink wines if pressed off the skins soon enough. Cabernet Sauvignon and Pinot noir rosé wines have been produced. The early pressing reduces their varietal character. A strong varietal character may not be an important requirement for this type of wine. Zinfandel has been rec-

TABLE 2.18. RECOMMENDED VARIETIES FOR RED AND PINK TABLE WINE
PRODUCTION IN CALIFORNIA

Variety	Produc-tion[1] Tons/ Acre	Ripens[2]	Flavor[3]	Region[4] I and II	III and IV	V
Barbera	L+	E	S	NR	R	QR
Cabernet Sauvignon[5]	M−	L	D	HR	QR	NR
Carignane	H	L	S	NR	QR	QR
Gamay[6]	H	L	N+	QR	NR	NR
Grenache	M[7]	M	N+	QR	QR	NR
Merlot	M	M+	D	R	QR	NR
Petite Sirah	M+	M	S	R	QR	NR
Pinot noir	L	E	D	R	NR	NR
Ruby Cabernet	M[7]	M	D	NR	R	QR
Zinfandel	M	M	D	R	QR	NR

Source: Adapted from Amerine and Winkler (1963) and revised from Ough et al. (1973) and Kissler et al. (1973).
[1]L for 1 to 3, M for 4 to 6, H for over 6.
[2]E for early, M for mid-season, L for late.
[3]N for neutral, S for slightly distinctive, and D for distinctive.
[4]HR for highly recommended, R for recommended, QR for qualified recommendation, and NR for not recommended.
[5]In spite of statements of various amateurs there is an abundance of evidence that the Cabernet Sauvignon should be preferred to the Cabernet franc.
[6]The Gamay, of the Napa Valley; the Gamay Beaujolais now appears to us to be a Pinot as far as aroma is concerned.
[7]Production is variable (from M to H depending on region, season, clone, etc.).

ommended for rosé production in order to reduce its tendency to high alcohol (from its shrivelled berries). The most important rosé wines produced in the state are Grenache and Gamay. The Grenache rosé is very popular but some of its wines are too flat and others have a bitter aftertaste. The Gamay in the Napa Valley does very well in most years but may not ripen in the cooler seasons. It has a fruity flavor which is, above all, what a rosé should have.

Dessert Wines

The requirements listed on p. 89 should be considered in selecting varieties for dessert wines. The varietal flavor is essential for muscat-flavored wines. Production is critical for competitive standard wines. Freedom from mold will be more important as more stringent sanitation inspection systems are used. The selection of varieties with a higher natural acidity would do much to improve the quality of our California dessert wines.

Two new hybrids for dessert wines have been released by Olmo (1959). Rubired is a variety of high color, a good producer, is partially mildew tolerant and was recommended for blending. Royalty is a variety of good color and flavor and was suggested as a replacement for Souzão for dessert wines. The recommendations by region are given in Table 2.19. Further testing showed Rubired to be superior to Royalty in color, viticultural characteristics and wine quality (Ough et al. 1973).

TABLE 2.19. RECOMMENDED VARIETIES FOR DESSERT WINE PRODUCTION IN CALIFORNIA

Variety	Production Tons/ Acre	Ripens[2]	Flavor[3]	Region[4] I and II	III and IV	V
Carignane	H	L	S−	NR	QR	QR
Grenache	M[5]	M	S−	NR	QR	QR
Grillo	H	M−	N	NR	NR	R
Mission	H	L	N	NR	NR	R
Muscat blanc[5]	L+	E	D	QR	QR	QR
Muscat of Alexandria	M	L	D	NR	NR	R
Palomino	H−	L	N	NR	NR	QR
Rubired	H	M	S	NR	NR	QR
Souzão	M	M	S	NR	NR	R
Tinta Madeira	M	M−	D−	NR	QR	R

Source: Adapted from Amerine and Winkler (1963).
[1]L for 1 to 3, M for 4 to 6, H for over 6.
[2]E for early, M for mid-season, L for late.
[3]N for neutral, S for slightly distinctive, and D for distinctive.
[4]HR for highly recommended, R for recommended, QR for qualified recommendation, and NR for not recommended.
[5]Production variable (Depending on region, season, clone, etc.). Same as Muscat Canelli and Muscat Frontignan.

Table and raisin grapes, particularly the Thompson Seedless, are delivered to California wineries. Much is used for the production of distilling material. When used for table or light-colored flavored wines the fruit should be harvested early while the sugar-acid relationship is as favorable as possible. For dessert wines, later harvesting is permissible but the acidity should not be too low. Selection of varieties based on present and prospective types of sales is surely necessary. In California, demand for dessert wines has been slipping.

If urban development into rural vineyard areas continues in the coast counties future grape plantings will have to be made in new areas in the coast counties or in the central valley. Since these grapes are mainly varieties for table wines, this means that new varieties suitable for the production of such wines will have to be found or developed for central valley planting.

REFERENCES[2]

AMERINE, M.A. 1951. The acids of California grapes and wines. II. Malic acid. Food Technol. 5, 13-16.

AMERINE, M.A. 1954. Composition of wines. I. Organic constituents. Advan. Food Res. 5, 353-510.

AMERINE, M.A. 1956. The maturation of wine grapes. Wines Vines 37 (10) 27-30, 32, 34-36; (11) 53-55.

[2]Titles have been translated only for nonwestern European languages.

AMERINE, M.A. 1958. Composition of wines. II. Inorganic constituents. Advan. Food Res. *8*, 133-224.

AMERINE, M.A. and BAILEY, C.B. 1959. Carbohydrate content of various parts of the grape cluster. Am. J. Enol. Vitic. *10*, 196-198.

AMERINE, M.A. and JOSLYN, M.A. 1970. Table Wines. The Technology of Their Production, 2nd Edition. University of California Press, Berkeley and Los Angeles.

AMERINE, M.A. and ROESSLER, E.B. 1958A. Methods of determining field maturity of grapes. Am. J. Enol. Vitic. *9*, 37-40.

AMERINE, M.A. and ROESSLER, E.B. 1958B. Field testing of grape maturity. Hilgardia *28*, 93-114.

AMERINE, M.A. and ROOT, G.A. 1960. Carbohydrate content of various parts of the grape cluster. II. Am. J. Enol. Vitic. *11*, 137-139.

AMERINE, M.A. and THOUKIS, G. 1958. The glucose-fructose ratio of California grapes. Vitis *1*, 224-229.

AMERINE, M.A. and WINKLER, A.J. 1940. Maturity studies with California grapes. I. The Balling-acid ratio of wine grapes. Proc. Am. Soc. Hort. Sci. *38*, 379-387.

AMERINE, M.A. and WINKLER, A.J. 1942. Maturity studies with California grapes. II. The titratable acidity, pH, and organic acid content. Proc. Am. Soc. Hort. Sci. *40*, 313-324.

AMERINE, M.A. and WINKLER, A.J. 1958. Maturity studies with California grapes. III. The acid content of grapes, leaves and stems. Proc. Am. Soc. Hort. Sci. *71*, 199-206.

AMERINE, M.A. and WINKLER, A.J. 1963. California wine grapes; composition and quality of their musts and wines. Calif. Agric. Exp. Stn. Bull. *794*.

ANDERSON, D.W., GUEFFROY, D.E., WEBB, A.D. and KEPNER, R.E. 1970. Identification of acetic acid as an acylating agent of anthocyanin pigments in grapes. Phytochemistry *9*, 1579-1583.

BATE-SMITH, E.C. and RIBÉREAU-GAYON, P. 1959. Leuco-anthocyanins in seeds. Qual. Plant. Mat. Vég. *5*, 189-199.

BAYER, E., BORN, F. and REUTHER, K.H. 1957. Über die Polyphenoloxydase der Trauben. Z. Lebensm.-Untersuch.-Forsch. *105*, 77-81.

BAYONOVE, C. and CORDONNIER, R. 1970. Recherches sur l'arôme du muscat. I. II. Ann. Technol. Agric. *19*, 72-93, 95-105.

BAYONOVE, C., CORDONNIER, R., BÉNARD, P. and RATIER, R. 1976. L'extraction des composés de l'arôme du muscat dans la phase préfermentaire de la vinification. Compt. Rend. Acad. Agric. France *62*, 734-750.

BAYONOVE, C., CORDONNIER, R. and DUBOIS, P. 1975. Étude d'une fraction caractéristique de l'arôme du raisin de la variété Cabernet-Sauvignon; mise en évidence de la 2-méthoxy isobutylpyrazine. Comp. Rend. *281*, 75-78

(*Also* Rev. Franç. Oenol. *16* (61) 39-41, 1976).

BÉNARD, P., JOURET, C. and FLANZY, M. 1963. Influence des porte-greffes sur la composition minérale des vins. Ann. Technol. Agric. *12*, 277-285.

BENVEGNIN, L. and CAPT, E. 1955. L'échantillonnage à la vigne pour l'évaluation de la maturité du raisin sur cep. Rev. Romande Agric., Viticult. Arboricult. *11*, 13-14.

BENVEGNIN, L., CAPT, E. and PIGUET, G. 1951. Traité de Vinification. Librairie Payot, Lausanne.

BERG, H.W. 1960. Grape classification by total soluble solids and total acidity. Wine Institute, San Francisco. (Mimeo.)

BERG, H.W. and AKIYOSHI, M. 1956. Some factors involved in browning of white wines. Am. J. Enol. Vitic. *7*, 1-7.

BERG, H.W., KUNKEE, R.E., NELSON, K.E. and OUGH, C.S. 1977. Proposed research program on defect inspection methodology of harvested grapes delivered to wineries. Proc. Wine Institute, Grape and Wine Quality Meeting, Feb. 18, 1977.

BERG, H.W. and MARSH, G.L. 1954. Sampling deliveries of grapes on a representative basis. Food Technol. *8*, 104-108.

BIOL, H. and FOULONNEAU, C. 1961. Le paeonidol 3,5 diglucoside dans le genre *Vitis.* Ann. Technol. Agric. *10*, 345-350.

BIOL, H. and MICHEL, A. 1961. Étude chromatographique des vins rouges issus de cépages réglementés. Ann. Technol. Agric. *10*, 339-344.

BIOL, H. and MICHEL, A. 1962. Étude chromatographique des vins rouges issus de cépages réglementés. Ann. Technol. Agric. *11*, 245-247.

BLOUIN, J. and PEYNAUD, E. 1963. Présence constante des acides glucuronique et galacturonique dans les moûts de raisins et les vins. Comp. Rend. *256*, 4774-4775.

BOURDET, A. and HERARD, J. 1958. Influence de l'autolyse des levures sur la composition phosphorée et azotée des vins. Ann. Technol. Agric. *7*, 177-202.

BRÉCHOT, P., CHAUVET, J., DUPUY, P., CROSON, M. and RABATU, A. 1971. Acide oléanolique, facteur de croissance anaérobie de la levure de vin. Ann. Technol. Agric. *20*, 103-110.

BROWN, W.L. 1940. The anthocyanin pigment of the Hunt Muscadine grape. J. Am. Chem. Soc. *62*, 2808-2810.

BURGER, M., HEIN, L.W., TEPLY, L.J., DERSE, P.H. and DRIEGLER, C.H. 1956. Vitamin, mineral, and proximate composition of frozen fruits, juices, and vegetables. J. Agric. Food Chem. *4*, 418-425.

BURKHARDT, R. 1965. Nachweis der *p*-Cumarylchinasäure in Weinen und das Verhalten der Depside bei der Kellerbehandlung. Rebe Wein, Serie A (Klosterneuburg) *15*, 80-86.

BUSTOS, O. 1975. Ammonia nitrogen content, total (nitrogen) and proline in musts of ten grape varieties. (transl.) Invest. Agric. *1*, 35-38 (C.A. *85*, 121745k).

CAILLEAU, R. and CHEVILLARD, L. 1949. Teneur de quelques vins français en aneurin, riboflavin, acide nicotinique et acide pantothénique. Ann. Agron. N.S. *19*, 277-281.

CALIFORNIA CROP AND LIVESTOCK REPORTING SERVICE. 1945-1977. Acreage estimates California fruit and nut crops as of 1944-1976. Sacramento.

CALIFORNIA DEPARTMENT OF AGRICULTURE. 1955. Order adopting regulations of the Department of Agriculture pertaining to determining average soluble solids of grapes for by-products. Filed June 24, 1955. Sacramento.

CALO, A. and COSTACURTA, A. 1976. La selezione clonale della vite in Italia. Riv. Viticolt. Enol. *29*, 483-491.

CANTARELLI, C. and PERI, C. 1964. The leucoanthocyanins in white grapes: their distribution, amount, fate during fermentation. Am. J. Enol. Vitic. *15*, 146-153.

CAPPELLERI, G. 1965. Risultati di un'indiagine sulla ricerca della malvina in una serie di vini de *Vitis vinifera*. Atti Accad. Ital. Vite Vino *17*, 153-159.

CASTOR, J.G.B. 1953. The free amino acids of musts and wines. I and II. Food Res. *18*, 139-151.

CASTOR, J.G.B. 1956. Amino acids in musts and wines, proline, serine and threonine. Am. J. Enol. Vitic. 7, 19-25.

CHARPENTIÉ, Y. 1954. Contribution à l'Étude Biochimique des Facteurs de l'Acidité des Vins. Institut National de la Recherche Agronomique, Paris.

CORDONNIER, R. 1956. Recherches sur l'aromatisation et le parfum des vins doux naturels et des vins de liqueur. Ann. Technol. Agric. *5*, 75-110.

CORDONNIER, R., BIRON, C. and DUGAL, A. 1975. Les invertases du raisin et *Saccharomyces cerevisiae*. Leur participation respective á l'hydrolyse du saccharose ajouté à la vinification. Ann. Technol. Agric. *24*, 171-192.

CORNFORTH, J.W. 1939. The anthocyanin of *Vitis hypoglauca* F.v.M. J. Proc. Roy. Soc. N.S. Wales *72*, 325-328.

CORRAO, A. 1963. Sul contenuto in manganese dei vini siciliani. Riv. Viticolt. Enol. (Conegliano) *16*, 343-349.

DECAU, J. and LAMAZOU-BETBEDER, M. 1964. Étude des effets de la fertilisation boratée des vignes carencées en bore sur la vinification et sur la composition minérale des vins. Ann. Technol. Agric. *13*, 12-29.

DeEDS, F. 1949. Vitamin P properties in grapes and grape residue. Proc. Wine Technol. Conf., Davis 1949, 48-50.

DEIBNER, L. and BOURZEIX, M. 1960. Sur les incertitudes dans la différenciation des cépages *Vitis vinifera* et hybrides rouges par chromatographie sur papier de leurs substances colorantes. Comp. Rend. Acad. Agric.

France *46*, 968-971.

DEIBNER, L. and BOURZEIX, M. 1964. Recherches sur la détection des anthocyannes diglucosides dans les vins et les jus de raisin (par chromatographie sur papier et fluoriscopie de taches obtenues). Ann. Technol. Agric. *13*, 263-282.

DEIBNER, L., BOURZEIX, M. and CABIBEL-HUGUES, M. 1964. La séparation des anthocyannes diglucosides par chromatographie sur couche mince et leur dosage spectrophotométrique. Ann. Technol. Agric. *13*, 359-378.

DEIBNER, L., RIFAL, H. and FLANZY, M. 1958. Substances colloïdales des jus de raisin; influence des différents modes de conservation sur leur stabilité. Ann. Technol. Agric. *7*, 5-19.

DIMOTAKI-KOURAKOU, V. 1964. Absence d'acide glycuronique dans les vins. Ann. Technol. Agric. *13*, 301-308.

DRAWERT, F., LESSING, V. and LEUPOLD, G. 1976. Gruppentrennung von organischen Saüren, Kohlenhydraten und Aminosäuren mit Ionenaustauschern und quantitative gas-chromatographische Bestimmung der Einzelsubstanzen. Chromatographia *9*, 373-379.

DUBERNET, M. and RIBÉREAU-GAYON, P. 1973. Présence et signification dans les moûts et les vins de la tyrosinase du raisin. Connaiss. Vigne Vin *7*, 283-302.

DUPUY, P., NORTZ, M., and PUISAIS, J. 1955. Le vin et quelques causes de son enrichissement en fer. Ann. Technol. Agric. *4*, 101-112.

DURMISHIDZE, S.V. 1955. Tannin Compounds and Anthocyanins of Grape Vines and Wines (transl.). Izd. Akad. Nauk S.S.S.R., Moscow.

DURMISHIDZE, S.V. 1958. Vitamin P in grapes and wine (transl.). Vinodel. Vinograd. S.S.S.R. *18* (2) 15.

DURMISHIDZE, S.V. 1959. Tannins and anthocyans in the grape vine and wine. Am. J. Enol. Vitic. *10*, 20-28.

EGGER, K., REICHLING, J. and AMMANN-SCHWEIZER, R. 1976. Flavonol-Derivate in Formen der Gattung Vitis. Vitis *15*, 24-28.

ESAU, P. 1967. Pentoses in wine. I. Survey of possible sources. Am. J. Enol. Vitic. *18*, 210-216.

ESAU, P. and AMERINE, M.A. 1966. Quantitative estimation of residual sugars in wine. J. Enol. Vitic. *17*, 265-267.

ESCHNAUER, H. 1959. Spurenelemente im Wein. Angew. Chem. *71*, 667-671.

FERENCZI, S. 1955. Effect of the amount of summer rainfall on the titratable acidity of wines (transl.). Növénytermelés *4*, 323-332.

FEUILLAT, M., MORFAUX, J.N. and GENERT, J.P. 1976. Les nucléotides du vin séparation, concentration et analyse par chromatographie sur échangeur d'anions. Connaiss. Vigne Vin *10*, 33-49.

FLANZY, M. and CAUSERET, J. 1954. Les vitamines du vin. Office Intern. Vin. Bull. 27 (282) 20-24.

FLANZY, M. and DEIBNER, L. 1956. Sur la variation des teneurs en fer dans les vins, obtenus en présence ou en absence d'une terre ferrugineuse. Ann. Technol. Agric. 5, 69-73.

FLANZY, C. and POUX, C. 1965. Les levures alcooliques dans les vins. Protéolyse protéogénèse (III). Ann. Technol. Agric. 14, 35-48.

FRANÇOT, P. 1950. Champagne et qualité par le pressurage. Vigneron Champenois 71, 250-255, 273-283, 342-351, 371-382, 406-416.

GARINO-CANINA, E. 1959. Italie. Office Intern. Vin. Bull. 32 (344) 3-15.

GENEVOIS, L. 1934. Recherche de la flavine dans les vins blancs. Bull. Soc. Chim. France 1, 1503-1504.

GROHMANN, H. and GILBERT, E. 1959. Zum papierchromatographischen Nachweis von roten Hybridenfarbstoffen. Deut. Wein-Ztg. 95, 346, 348.

HAAGEN-SMIT, A.J., HIROSAWA, F.N. and WANG, T.H. 1949. Chemical studies on grapes and wines. I. Volatile constituents of Zinfandel grapes (Vitis vinifera). Food Res. 14, 472-480.

HAISMAN, D.R. 1974. The effect of sulphur dioxide on oxidizing enzyme systems in plant tissue. J. Sci. Food Agric. 25, 803-810.

HALL, A.P., BRINNER, L., AMERINE, M.A. and MORGAN, A.F. 1956. The B vitamin content of grapes, musts and wines. J. Sci. Food Agric. 21, 362-371.

HAWKER, J.S., RUFFNER, H.P. and WALKER, R.R. 1976. The sucrose content of some Australian grapes. Am. J. Enol. Vitic. 27, 125-129.

HENDERSON, W.W., KITTERMAN, J.M. and VANCE, F.H. 1965. California Grape Acreage by Varieties and Principal Counties as of 1964. Crop and Livestock Reporting Service, Sacramento.

HENNIG, K. 1944. Einige Fragen zur Bilanz der Sticksoffverbindungen im Most und Wein. Z. Lebensm.-Untersuch. -Forsch. 87, 40-48. (See also Bull. Office Intern. Vin 16 (159) 82-86, 1943.)

HENNIG, K. 1955. Der Einfluss der Eisweiss- und Stickstoffbestandteile auf Wein. Deut. Wein-Ztg. 91, 377-378, 380, 394, 396.

HENNIG, K. 1958. Das Chemische Bild des Mostes und Weines. Weinfach Kalender 1958, 194-209.

HENNIG, K. and BURKHARDT, R. 1957. Über die Farb- und Gerbstoffe, sowie Polyphenole und ihre Veränderungen im Wein. Weinberg Keller 4, 374-387.

HENNIG, K. and BURKHARDT, R. 1958. Der Nachweis phenolartiger Verbindungen und hydroaromatischer Oxycarbonsäuren in Traubenbestandteilen, Wein und weinähnlichen Getränken. Weinberg Keller 5, 542-552, 593-600.

HENNIG, K. and BURKHARDT, R. 1960. Vorkommen und Nachweis von

Quercitrin und Myricitrin in Trauben und Wein. Weinberg Keller 7, 1-3.

HENNIG, K. and LAY, A. 1965. Die gewichtsanalytische Bestimmung der Oxalsäure im Most und Wein. Weinberg Keller 12, 425-427.

HOLBACH, B. and WOLLER, R. 1976. Ueber den Zusammenhang zwischen Botrytisbefall von Trauben und dem Glycerin- sowei Gluconsäuregehalt von Wein. Wein-Wissen. 31, 202-214.

HOLLEY, R.W., STOYLA, B., and HOLLEY, A.D. 1955. The identification of some volatile constituents of Concord grape juice. Food Res. 20, 326-331.

HRAZDINA, G., BORZELL, A.J. and ROBINSON, W.B. 1970. Studies on the stability of the anthocyanidin-3,5-diglucosides. Am. J. Enol. Vitic. 21, 201-204.

HUGLIN, P. 1976. Critères de sélection clonale et méthodologie du jugement des clones. Vignes Vins 254, 30-38.

JAULMES, P., HAMELLE, G. and ROQUES, J. 1960. Le plomb dans les moûts et les vins. Ann. Technol. Agric. 9, 189-245.

JAULMES, P. and NEY, M. 1960. Recherche des vins d'hybrides producteurs directs par chromatographie. Ann. Fals. Fraudes 53, 180-192.

KEPNER, R.E. and WEBB, A.D. 1956. Volatile aroma constituents of Vitis rotundifolia grapes. Am. J. Enol. Vitic. 7, 8-18.

KISSLER, J.J., OUGH, C.S. and ALLEY, C.J. 1973. Evaluations of wine grape varieties for Lodi. Univ. California Agric. Exp. Stn. Bull. 865, 1-12.

KLIEWER, W.M. 1965A. The sugars of grapevines. II. Identification and seasonal changes in the concentration of several trace sugars in Vitis vinifera. Am. J. Enol. Vitic. 16, 168-178.

KLIEWER, W.M. 1965B. Changes in concentration of glucose, fructose, and total soluble solids in flowers and berries of Vitis vinifera. Am. J. Enol. Vitic. 16, 101-110.

KLIEWER, W.M. 1966. The sugars and the organic acids of Vitis vinifera. Plant Physiol. 41, 923-931.

KLIEWER, W.M., LIDER, L.A. and FERRARI, N. 1972. Effect of controlled temperature and light intensity on growth and carbohydrate levels of Thompson Seedless grape vines. J. Am. Soc. Hort. Sci. 97, 185-188.

KOCH, J. 1963. Protéines des vins blancs. Traitements des précipitations protéiques par chauffage et à l'aide de la bentonite. Ann. Technol. Agric. 12 (numéro hors série l) 297-311.

KOCH, J. and BRETTHAUER, J. 1957. Zur Kenntnis der Eiweissstoffe des Weines. I. Chemische Zusammensetzung des Wärmetrubes kurzzeiterhitzter Weissweine und seine Beziehung zur Eiweisstrübung und zum Weineiweiss. II. Einfluss der Mosterhitzung auf die Eiweissstabilität der Weissweine. Z. Lebensm.-Untersuch. -Forsch. 106, 272-280, 361-367.

KOCH, J. and SAJAK, E. 1959. A review and some studies on grape protein. Am. J. Enol. Vitic. *10*, 114-123.

LAFON-LAFOURCADE, S. and GUIMBERTEAU, G. 1962. Évolution des aminoacides au cours de la maturation des raisins. Vitis *3*, 130-135.

LAFON-LAFOURCADE, S. and PEYNAUD, E. 1958. L'acide p-aminoben-zoïque, l'acide ptérolglutamique et la choline (vitamines du groupe B) dans les vins. Ann. Technol. Agric. *7*, 303-309.

LAFON-LAFOURCADE, S. and PEYNAUD, E. 1959. Dosage microbiologique des acides aminés des moûts de raisins et des vins. Vitis *2*, 45-56.

LAROSA, W.V. 1955. Maturity of grapes as related to pH at harvest. Am. J. Enol. Vitic. *6*, 42-46.

LAROSA, W.V. and NIELSEN, U. 1956. Effect of delay in harvesting on the composition of grapes. Am. J. Enol. Vitic. *7*, 105-111.

LASKO, A.N. and KLIEWER, W.M. 1975. The influence of temperature on malic acid metabolism in grape berries. Plant Physiol. *56*, 370-372.

LAVOLLAY, J. and SEVESTRE, J. 1944. Le vin, considéré comme un aliment riche en vitamine P. Comp. Rend. Acad. Agric. France *30*, 259-261.

LIUNI, C.S., CALO, A. and CAPPELLERI, G. 1965. Contributo allo studio sui pigmenti antocianici de alcune specie del genere *Vitis* e di loro ibridi. Atti. Accad. Ital. Vite Vino *17*, 161-167.

LÜTHI, H. and VETSCH, U. 1953. Papierchromatographische Bestimmung von aminosäuren in Traubenmost und Wein. Deut. Weinbau, Wissensch. Beihefte *7* (1) 3-6; (2) 33-54.

MARKH, A.T. and BONEVA, L.A. 1952. Investigation of the colloids of grape juice (transl.). Vinodel. Vinograd. S.S.S.R. *12* (9) 14-17.

MARKLEY, K.S., SANDO, C.E. and HENDRICKS, S.B. 1938. Petroleum e-ther-soluble and ether-soluble constituents of grape pomace. J. Biol. Chem. *123*, 641-654.

MARTEAU, G., SCHEUR, J. and OLIVIERI, C. 1961. Cinétique de la libération enzymatique du méthanol au cours des transformations pectolytiques du raisin. Ann. Technol. Agric. *10*, 161-183.

MASQUELIER, J. 1958. The bactericidal action of certain phenolics of grapes and wine. *In* The Pharmacology of Plant Phenolics. J.W. Fairbairn (Editor). Academic Press, New York.

MATHEWS, J. 1958. The vitamin B complex content of bottled Swiss grape juices. Vitis *2*, 57-64.

MCCLOSKEY, L.P. 1974. Gluconic acid in California wines. Am. J. Enol. Vitic. *25*, 198-201.

MONTEDORO, G. 1968. L'attività pectolitica di uve di diverse cultivars distribuzione dell'enzima e sua caratterizzazione. Annal. Instit. Agrar. Univ. Perugia *23*, 1-30.

NELSON, K.E. and AMERINE, M.A. 1957. The use of *Botrytis cinerea* Pers. in the production of sweet table wines. Hilgardia *26*, 521-563.

NELSON, R.R., ACREE, T.E, LEE, C.Y. and BUTTS, R.M. 1977. Methyl anthranilate as a constituent of American wine. J. Food Sci. *42*, 57-59.

OLIVIERI, C. 1975. Considérations sur l'évolution des activités enzymatiques lors du traitement thermique de la vendange à différents pH. Prog. Agric. Vitic. *92*, 225-230.

OLMO, H.P. 1955. Our principal wine grape varieties present and future. Am. J. Enol. Vitic. *5*, 18-20.

OLMO, H.P. 1959. New University of California wine grape varieties released in 1958. Wines Vines *40* (2) 28-29.

OTSUKA, K., TOTSUKA, A., NOZU, S., HAGINO, T., ITO, M. and JIMURA, Y. 1976. Buffer capacity of red wine. I. II. Nippon Jozo Kyokai Zasshi *71*, 398-402, 545-548.

OUGH, C.S. 1968. Proline content of grapes and wines. Vitis *7*, 321-331.

OUGH, C.S. and ALLEY, C.J. 1970. Effect of Thompson Seedless grape maturity on wine composition and quality. Am. J. Enol. Vitic. *21*, 78-84.

OUGH, C.S. and ALLEY, C.J. 1977. Unpublished data.

OUGH, C.S., ALLEY, C.J., LUVISI, D. A., CHRISTENSEN, L.P., BARANEK, P. and JENSEN, F.L. 1973. Evaluations of wine grape varieties for Madera, Fresno, Tulare, and Kern counties. Univ. California Agric. Exp. Stn. Bull. *863*, 1-19.

OUGH, C.S., COOK, J.A. and LIDER, L.A. 1968A. Rootstock-scion interactions concerning winemaking. II. Wine compositional and sensory changes attributed to rootstock and fertilizer level differences. Am. J. Enol. Vitic. *19*, 254-265.

OUGH, C.S., LIDER, L.A. and COOK, J.A. 1968B. Rootstock-scion interactions concerning winemaking. I. Composition changes and effects on fermentation rate with St. George and 99-R rootstocks at two nitrogen fertilizer levels. Am. J. Enol. Vitic. *19*, 213-227.

OUGH, C.S. and STASHAK, R.M. 1974. Further studies on proline concentration in grapes and wines. Am. J. Enol. Vitic. *25*, 7-12.

OURNAC, A. 1958. Évolution de la vitamine C dans le raisin conservé en frigorifique. Ann. Technol. Agric. *7*, 167-175.

OURNAC, A., and POUX, C. 1974. La peroxydase du raisin. Étude de quelques propriétés. Ann. Technol. Agric. *23*, 17-37.

PERLMAN, L. and MORGAN, A.F. 1945. Stability of B vitamins in grape juices and wines. Food Res. *10*, 334-341.

PEYNAUD, E. 1947. Contribution à l'Étude Biochimique de la Maturation du Raisin et de la Composition des Vins. Imp. G. Sautai & Fils, Lille.

PEYNAUD, E. 1951. Sur les matières pectiques des fruits. Ind. Agric. Aliment. (Paris) *68*, 609-615.

PEYNAUD, E. 1952. Sur les matières pectiques des moûts de raisin et des vins. Ann. Fals. Fraudes *45*, 11-20.

PEYNAUD, E. and LAFON-LAFOURCADE, S. 1955. L'acide pantothénique dans les raisins et dans les vins de Bordeaux. Ind. Agric. Aliment. (Paris) *72*, 575-580, 665-670.

PEYNAUD, E. and LAFON-LAFOURCADE, S. 1956. Sur la teneur en biotine des raisins et des vins. Compt. Rend. *234*, 1800-1803.

PEYNAUD, E. and LAFON-LAFOURCADE, S. 1957. Les vitamines "B" dans le raisin et dans le vin. Congrès International Étude Scientifique Vin et Raisin, Bordeaux *1957*, 65-70.

PEYNAUD, E. and LAFON-LAFOURCADE, S. 1958. Évolution des vitamines B dans le raisin. Qual. Plant. Mater. Veg. *3/4*, 405-414.

PEYNAUD, E. and MAURIÉ, A. 1953A. Sur l'évolution d'azote dans les différentes parties du raisin au cours de la maturation. Ann. Technol. Agric. *2*, 15-25.

PEYNAUD, E. and MAURIÉ, A. 1953B. Évolution des acides organiques dans le grain de raisin au cours de la maturation en 1951. Ann. Technol. Agric. *2*, 83-94.

PEYNAUD, E. and MAURIÉ, A. 1956. Nouvelles recherches sur la maturation du raisin dans le Bordelais, années 1952, 1953, et 1954. Ann. Technol. Agric. *2*, 111-139.

POULTON, J. 1970. Harvesting grapes for maximum profit. Wynboer *38*, 22-26.

POUX, C. 1950. Relation entre le poids des sucres et le poids de matière fraîche dans les raisins de différentes variétés de *Vitis vinifera* au moment de la maturité. Compt. Rend. Acad. Agric. France *36*, 605-607.

POWERS, J.J., SOMAATMADJA, D., PRATT, D.E. and HAMDY, M.K. 1960. Anthocyanins. II. Action of anthocyanin pigments and related compounds on the growth of certain microorganisms. Food Technol. *14*, 626-632.

RADLER, F. 1957. Untersuchungen über den Gehalt der Moste einiger Rebensorten und -arten an den Vitaminen Pyridoxin, Pantothensäure, Nicotinsäure und Biotin. Vitis *1*, 96-108.

RADLER, F. 1965. The main constituents of the surface waxes of varieties and species of the genus *Vitis.* Am. J. Enol. Vitic. *16*, 159-167.

RAPP, A. and HASTRICH, H. 1976. Gaschromatographische Untersuchungen über die Aromastoffe von Weinbeeren. II. Möglichkeiten der Sortencharakterisiersung. Vitis *15*, 183-192.

RAPP, A., HASTRICH, H. and ENGEL, L. 1976. Gaschromatographische Untersuchungen über die Aromastoffe von Weinbeeren. I. Anreicherung und kapillarchromatographische Auftrennung. Vitis *15*, 29-36.

RENTSCHLER, H. and TANNER, H. 1955. Über den Nachweis von Glu-consäure in Weinen aus edelfaulen Trauben. Mitt. Gebiete Lebensm. Hyg. *46*, 200-208.

RIBÉREAU-GAYON, J. and PEYNAUD, E. 1958. Analyse et Contrôle des Vins, 2nd Edition. Béranger, Paris and Liège.

RIBÉREAU-GAYON, J. and RIBÉREAU-GAYON, P. 1958. The anthocyans and leucoanthocyans of grapes and wines. Am. J. Enol. Vitic. *9*, 1-9.

RIBÉREAU-GAYON, P. 1957. Le leucocyanidol dans les vins rouges. Compt. Rend. Acad. Agric. France *43*, 197-199, 596-598.

RIBÉREAU-GAYON, P. 1958A. Les anthocyannes des raisins. Qual. Plant. Mater. Vég. *3/4*, 491-499.

RIBÉREAU-GAYON, P. 1958B. Formation et évolution des anthocyannes au cours de la maturation du raisin. Compt. Rend. *246*, 1271-1273.

RIBÉREAU-GAYON, P. 1964. Les composés phénoliques du raisin et du vin. I. II. III. Ann. Physiol. Vég. *6*, 119-147, 211-242, 259-282.

RIBÉREAU-GAYON, P., BOIDRON, J.N. and TERRIER, A. 1975. Aroma of muscat grape varieties. J. Agric. Food Chem. *23*, 1042-1047.

RIBÉREAU-GAYON, P. and SUDRAUD, P. 1957. Les anthocyannes de la baie dans le genre *Vitis.* Compt. Rend. *244*, 233-235.

ROBINSON, W.B., SHAULIS, N.J. and PEDERSON, C.S. 1949. Ripening studies of grapes grown in 1948 for juice manufacture. Fruit Prod. J. *29*, (2) 36-37, 54, 62.

RODOPULO, A.K., EGOROV, I.A., BEZZUBOV, A.A. and SKUIN, K.P. 1974. Substances responsible for grape aroma and their contribution to the wine bouquet. Prikl. Biokhim. Mikrobiol. *10*, 280-287.

ROESSLER, E.B. and AMERINE, M.A. 1958. Studies on grape sampling. Am. J. Enol. Vitic. *9*, 139-145.

ROESSLER, E.B. and AMERINE, M.A. 1963. Further studies on field sampling of wine grapes. Am. J. Enol. Vitic. *14*, 144-147.

RUFFNER, H.P. and RUST, D. 1974. Die Biogenese von Tartrate in der Weinrebe. Z. Pflanzenphysiol. *73*, 45-55.

SASTRY, L.V.I. and TISCHER, R.G. 1952. Behavior of the anthocyanin pigments in Concord grapes during heat processing and storage. Food Technol. *6*, 82-86 (*See also Ibid. 6*, 264-268.)

SCHANDERL, H. 1959. Die Mikrobiologie des Mostes und Weines. Eugen Ulmer, Stuttgart.

SCHRADER, U., LEMPERLE, E., BECKER, N.J. and BERGNER, K.G. 1976. Der Aminosäure-, Zucker-, Säure- und Mineralstoffgehalt von Weinbeeren in Abhängigkeit von Kleinklima des Sandortes der Rebe. III. Säure- und Min-eralstoffgehalt. Wein-Wissen. *31*, 160-175.

SCHREIER, P., DRAWERT, F. and JUNKER, A. 1976A. Identification of volatile constituents from grapes. J. Agric. Food Chem. *24*, 331-336.

SCHREIER, P., DRAWERT, F. and JUNKER, A. 1976B. Gaschromatographische-massenspektrometrische Differenzierung der Traubenaromastoffe verscheidener Rebsorten von *Vitis vinifera*. Chem. Mikrobiol. Technol. Lebensm. *4*, 154-157.

SCHREIER, P., DRAWERT, F. and JUNKER, A. 1977. Gaschromatographische Bestimmung der Inhaltsstoffe von Garungsgetränken. X. Quantitative Bestimmung von Weinaromastoffen in myg/l-Bereich. Chem. Mikrobiol. Technol. Lebensm. *5*, 45-52.

SELVARAJ, Y., SURESH, E.R., DIVAKAR, N.G., RANDHAWA, C.S. and NEGI, S.S. 1975. Sugars, organic acids, amino acids and invertase activity of juices from 22 grape varieties. J. Food Sci. Technol. (India) *12*, 75-78.

SINGLETON, V.L. 1966. The total phenolic content of grape berries during the maturation of several varieties. Am. J. Enol. Vitic. *17*, 126-134.

SINGLETON, V.L., DE WET, P. and DU PLESSIS, C.S. 1973. Characterization of populations of grapes harvested for wine and compensation for population differences. Agroplantae *5*, 1-12

SINGLETON, V.L. and ESAU, P. 1969. Phenolic Substances in Grapes and Wine, and Their Significance. Supplement 1, Advan. Food Res. Academic Press, New York and London.

SINGLETON, V.L. and NOBLE, A.C. 1976. Phenolic, sulfur and nitrogen compounds in food flavors. Wine flavor and phenolic substances. ACS Symposium Series *26*, 47-70.

SISAKYAN, N.M. and MARUTYAN, S.A. 1948. Sakhara vinogradnoi yagody. (Sugars of grape berries.) Biokhemiya Vinodeliya *2*, 56-68.

SMITH, M.B. and OLMO, H.P. 1944. The pantothenic acid and riboflavin in the fresh juice of diploid and tetraploid grapes. Am. J. Bot. *31*, 240-241.

SMITH, R. M. and LUH, B.S. 1965. Anthocyanin pigments of the hybrid grape variety Rubired. J. Food Sci. *30*, 995-1005.

SOLMS, J., BÜCKI, W. and DEUEL, H. 1952. Untersuchungen über den Pektingehalt einiger Traubenmoste. Mitt. Gebiete Lebensm. Hyg. *43*, 303-307.

SOMAATMADJA, D., POWERS, J.J. and WHEELER, R. 1965. Action of leucoanthocyanins of Cabernet grapes on reproduction and respiration of certain bacteria. Am. J. Enol. Vitic. *16*, 54-61.

STEVENS, K.L., LEE, A., MCFADDEN, W.H. and TERANISHI, R. 1965. Volatiles from grapes. I. Some volatiles from Concord grapes. J. Food Sci. *30*, 1006-1007.

SU, C.T. and SINGLETON, V.L. 1969. Identification of three flavan-3-ols from grapes. Phytochemistry *8*, 1553-1558.

SZABÓ, J. and RAKCSÁNYI, L. 1937. Das Mengenverhältnis der Dextrose und der Lävulose in Weintrauben, im Mosten und im Wein. 5th Cong. Intern. Tech. Chem. Agric. *1*, 936-939 (*See also* Magyar Ampelol. Evkonyv. *9*, 346-361, 1935.)

TAKIMOTO, K., SAITO, K. and KASAI, Z. 1976. Diurnal change of tartrate dissimilation during the ripening of grapes. Phytochemistry *15*, 927-930.

TANNER, H. and RENTSCHLER, A.H. 1956. Über Polyphenole der Kernobst- und Traubensäfte. Fruchtsaft-Ind. *1*, 231-245.

TEPLY, L.J., STRONG, F.M. and ELVEHJEM, C.A. 1942. Distribution of nicotinic acid in foods. J. Nutr. *32*, 417-423.

TERCELJ, F. 1965. Étude des composés azotés du vin. Ann. Technol. Agric. *14*, 307-319.

UNVERZAGT. 1954. Reifemessungen bei verschiedenen Traubenmosten. Deut. Wein-Ztg. *90*, 374-376.

USSEGLIO-TOMASSET, L. 1959. L'evoluzione delle sostanze colloidali dal mosto al vino. Ann. Sper. Agrar. (Rome) *13*, 375-404.

USSEGLIO-TOMASSET, L. and CASTINO, M. 1975. I colloidi solubili di natura glucidica dei mosti e dei vini. Riv. Viticolt. Enol. (Conegliano) *28*, 328-339, 374-391, 401-412.

VEREŠ, A. and POLAKOVIČ, F. 1975. Influence du climat et du microclimat sur la vignoble. Progrès. Res. Viti-vinicole *7*, 51-70.

VITTE, G. and GUICHARD, G. 1955. Évolution des acides organiques de la vigne. Rev. Gen. Bot. *62*, 622-628.

WEBB, A.D. 1964. Anthocyanins of grapes. *In* Phenolics in Normal and Diseased Fruits and Vegetables. V.C. Runeckles (Editor). Plant Phenolics Group of North America, Montreal.

WEBB, A.D. and KEPNER, R.E. 1957. Some volatile aroma constituents of *Vitis vinifera* var. Muscat of Alexandria. Food Res. *22*, 384-395.

WEURMAN, C. and de ROOIJ, C. 1958. Chlorogenic acid isomers in "Black Alicante" grapes. Chem. Ind. *1958*, 72.

WINKLER, A.J. 1936. Temperature and varietal interrelations in Central Western Europe and Algeria. Wines Vines *17* (2) 4-5.

WINKLER, A.J. 1954. Effects of overcropping. Am. J. Enol. Vitic. *5*, 4-12.

WINKLER, A.J. 1964. Varietal wine grapes in the Central Coast Counties of California. Am. J. Enol. Vitic. *15*, 204-205.

WINKLER, A.J. and AMERINE, M.A. 1937. What climate does. Wine Rev. *5* (6) 9-11; (7) 9-11, 16.

WINKLER, A.J. and AMERINE, M.A. 1938. Color in California wines. I and II. Food Res. *3*, 429-447.

WINKLER, A.J. and WILLLIAMS, W.O. 1936. The effect of seed development on the growth of grapes. Proc. Am. Soc. Hort. Sci. *33*, 430-434.

ZAMORANI, A. and PIFFERI, P.G. 1964. Contributo alla conoscenza della sostanza colorante dei vini. Riv. Viticolt. Enol. (Conegliano) *17*, 85-93.

ZIEMELIS, G. and PICKERING, J. 1969. Precipitation of flavanols in dry red table wine. Chem. Ind. *1969*, 1781-1782.

ZUBECKIS, E. 1964. Ascorbic acid in Veerport grape during ripening and processing. Rept. Hort. Exp. Stn. Prod. Lab. Ontario *1964*, 114-116.

3

American Wine Types
and Their Composition

The nomenclature of American wine types is far from standardized. This is not surprising. The industry is comparatively young. Traditional European wine type names were adopted early as a guide for consumers. In the pre-Prohibition era, type names such as Margaux were used. The U.S. Bureau of Alcohol, Tobacco and Firearms (1976A, 1978) defines four types of wines which may be produced in this country for interstate commerce: grape types (i.e., varietal), generic (sake and vermouth), semi-generic (see p. 141), and nongeneric (i.e., geographic) (see pp. 147–148). "Special natural" wines probably fall in the generic class.

GENERIC TYPES

Only sake and vermouth have been so classed. Sake is defined as a product "produced from rice in accordance with the commonly accepted method of manufacture of such product." Little is produced in this country.

Vermouth

Vermouth production is described in Chap. 13. It is defined as a "type of aperitif wine compounded from grape wine, having the taste, aroma, and characteristics generally attributed to vermouth." Three types are commonly produced in this country: dry, light dry, and sweet. California dry vermouth is described by the recommended specifications of the Wine Institute (1978) as an herb-flavored, straw-to-light-golden colored wine of less than 4% sugar and with an alcohol content of over 15%. No single herb odor should be recognizable and excessive bitterness is objec-

140

tionable. There was a tendency to reduce the vermouth character in American dry vermouths. This was undoubtedly due to the use of dry vermouth as an ingredient of the martini cocktail. Bartenders demanded a product with little color so that as much as possible of the cheaper vermouth could be used. The type was often barely recognizable as vermouth and lost its desirability as a "straight" drink. Would it be better to keep "dry" vermouth as a beverage type with adequate vermouth character and a light amber color? The light, dry, low-color, low-flavor type would fill cocktail needs.

Sweet vermouth is defined by the Wine Institute (1978) as an appetizer wine. In spite of its high sugar content sweet vermouth is used as an appetizer in Europe. It should be amber to dark amber in color (many have a slightly reddish hue) and a muscat aroma is desirable, but an excessive baked character is not. The recommended °Brix is 8 to 14. This indicates a sugar content of about 12 to 18%. The herb character must be pronounced but the characteristics of no herb should predominate.

A variety of "special natural" (flavored) wines are also produced (U.S. Bureau of Alcohol, Tobacco and Firearms 1976B). They seem to be "generic."

SEMIGENERIC TYPES

These include 16 specific examples given in federal regulations. These can be classified as white, rosé or red table, sparkling, or dessert types.

White Table

Chablis, moselle, rhine (syn. hock), sauterne and white chianti[1] are geographical names that are now considered semigeneric types in this country. They must, however, be used on the label only in conjunction with an appropriate appellation of origin disclosing the actual place of production of the wine. Thus, in practice these wines must be labeled "American" chablis, "California" moselle, "Napa Valley" sauterne, as appropriate.

The Wine Institute (1978) recommendations are that California chablis be light- to medium-straw in color, light-to-medium in body, of medium acidity, fruity, well-balanced, and have a good bottle bouquet.[2] These specifications cover a wide range of wine types and do not describe a type which can be distinguished from California sauterne, rhine, or white chianti. This could be rectified by abandoning all three type names and

---

[1]The regulations list only chianti but this may, presumably, mean white or red.
[2]Very wishful thinking.

selling the wines as California dry white table wine. The industry is obviously economically fearful of such a development. After all, the producers say there is a demand for California "sauterne." If California chablis is to be different from the other dry white semigeneric types, we would recommend that the industry consider keeping it low in pH (below 3.3), high in acidity (0.65% minimum), very dry (below 0.2% sugar), light in color, and fresh and fruity, with not over 11.5% ethanol. A maximum free sulfur dioxide content should be set at a low figure—perhaps 25 mg/liter. The crux of this suggestion is the low maximum ethanol content. This is partially to ensure that the wine would be fresh and fruity but also to make a distinguishable difference between one type and another.

California rhine or Riesling is defined (Wine Institute 1978) as a pale-to medium-straw colored wine of medium body and medium-to-tart acidity. It should be fresh and fruity and have good bottle age. Again, the recommendations cover a wide range and overlap those of other types. Frankly, we believe rhine should replace the varietal appellation Riesling unless Riesling clearly represents a varietal type. We see no nonvarietal type between California chablis and California rhine. California rhine could be similar to chablis in color, acidity and pH but be in a more reduced condition (minimum free sulfur dioxide of 25 mg/liter). It might also be slightly sweet (0.5−2.5% sugar as against not more than 0.2% for chablis).

Sauterne and medium sauterne are defined in the Wine Institute (1978) specifications. The Federal Alcohol Administration Act specifies only sauterne and haut sauterne (a miserable appellation with no legal status in France; fortunately, it has been little used here). California sauterne is defined as a straw to light-golden colored wine of full body and without noticeable high acidity. It should have balance and softness on the palate and a good bottle bouquet. Again, there is a considerable area of overlapping with other semigeneric types. We would recommend that color, acidity, and alcohol content be used to differentiate the type from California chablis and rhine. The color should be a full yellow, the acidity moderate (maximum 0.65%), the alcohol not *less* than 11.5% and the sugar above 2.5%.

The Wine Institute recommendation for California medium sauterne is the same as for dry sauterne except that the sugar content must be between 0.5 and 3% and a slight muscat aroma is permitted. If the above modifications of color, acidity and alcohol content were employed for California chablis, rhine and sauterne, there would appear to be no need for other semigeneric names. In fact, California white chianti is no longer defined in the Wine Institute (1978) recommendations and certainly there is little justification for the type.

Rosé

American and California rosé now covers a wide range of composition, color, and flavor. Variety in color and flavor is commercially desirable. The consumer, however, may be confused by the lack of distinction between those which are dry and sweet. Some label distinction at about 1.5% sugar would be useful.

Red Table

Burgundy and chianti are geographical names that are considered semigeneric in this country. As sold on the American market, the eastern "burgundy" wines usually have a pronounced labrusca character which is foreign to the original European wine types. We have no suggestions, therefore, for defining these semigeneric types when they have a labrusca character.

It is no secret that California claret, burgundy, and chianti as sold on the American market are not easily distinguishable as types of wines. For a given firm there may be a distinction. Between wineries, one person's claret may be another person's burgundy. This is immediately obvious from the recommendations of the Wine Institute (1978). California claret is a tart, light- to medium-red colored wine of light or medium body. California burgundy is a full-bodied, medium- to deep-red colored wine of balance and softness on the palate derived from proper aging. California chianti is a full-bodied, medium-red colored wine of medium tartness, fruity flavor and a moderately aged, well-balanced character. Certainly the prescribed body, color, or tartness is not sufficiently different for the average or even expert consumer to differentiate among the types.

Suggestions have been made for distinguishing among these types. The most rational one of having them conform to some varietal origin has not been accepted by the industry. Among the varietal suggestions have been those to include some Cabernet in claret and some Pinot noir in the burgundy. Lack of these varieties in the past led to rejection of this proposal. The alternative suggestion that California claret contain some Zinfandel character and burgundy some Petite Sirah has likewise been rejected, although individual producers have followed this concept. Pre-Prohibition practice apparently was to include Zinfandel in clarets but not in burgundy.

A color, alcohol, and acidity differentiation appears practicable. California claret would then have a light-red color and contain at least 0.65% acidity and *not over* 11.5% alcohol. California burgundy would be a medium- to dark-red colored wine of less than 0.65% acidity and *over* 11.5% alcohol. We see no need for California chianti. Fortunately, it is seldom employed. The concept of chianti as a rough high-tannin wine has long since disappeared here and in Italy. We have seen no indication since the first edition of this book that these suggestions have met with any favor!

Sparkling

Champagne is the only sparkling type recognized as being a semigeneric appellation of geographical region. Owing to the production of sparkling wines by two procedures (see Chap. 11), two specifications are given by the Wine Institute (1978). California champagne (bottle-fermented) is defined as a pale- to straw-colored sparkling wine of good acidity and body with a fresh, fruity, well-balanced flavor and a distinctive bottle bouquet. We suggest a minimum acidity of 0.75% to ensure the fresh fruity flavor.

There are no generally accepted industry standards for sugar content. To fill this need we recommend that finished *brut* or *nature* champagnes contain less than 1.5% sugar, that *extra dry* or *extra sec* wines have 1.5 to 3.5% sugar, that *dry* or *sec* wines have 3.5 to 5.0%, and *sweet* or *doux* wines over 5%. The same limits would apply to tank-fermented sparkling wines. For judgings, the Wine Institute (1971) classifies wines as group 1 (less than 1.5% sugar), group 2 (1.5−2.5%), and group 3 (over 2.5%).

The requirement that bottle-fermented sparkling wines have a distinctive bottle bouquet is a good one. With the introduction of the transfer system (p. 464) it will be difficult to attain. The requirement that bottle-fermented wines be kept in the bottle for at least 9 months to 1 year *before* disgorging is a plausible restriction. To improve these types some limitation in maximum sulfur dioxide content could be imposed. Bottle-fermented wines must be very low in free sulfur dioxide and tank-fermented should not contain over 10 mg/liter free. The federal requirement that American (or California) champagne should possess the taste, aroma, and other characteristics attributed to Champagne as made in the Champagne district of France is interesting as it would imply some sort of varietal limitation on the grapes to be used for champagne in this country. When applied to labrusca-flavored eastern United States sparkling wines, the requirement is less rational.

Pink champagne is not mentioned in the semigeneric terms of the federal regulations but presumably is approved with use of the word champagne. California pink champagne is defined as a wine of "true" pink color, fruity, fresh, tart, well-balanced, and light-bodied and with over 1.5% reducing sugar. How a wine of over 1.5% reducing sugar can be light-bodied is not clear to us. The "tart" requirement might be strengthened by setting a minimum percentage of total acidity, perhaps as high as 0.75%. The "true" pink color is apparently designed to prevent blending of red and white wines which may give a purplish pink color. It eliminates, however, Petite Sirah, Pinot noir and Grenache rosé wines—all of which may have an orange hue. This, we think, is undesirable. A color specification which would include orange-pink (p. 694) might prove useful.

Sparkling burgundy (synonym: champagne rouge) legally includes both bottle- and tank-fermented wine. The Wine Institute (1978) recommendation is that these shall include both light- and heavy-bodied and light- and dark-colored wines. They should have a good acidity and be fruity, smooth, well-balanced, and have a distinctive bottle bouquet and over 1.5% sugar. The requirement that tank-fermented wines have a distinctive bottle bouquet is probably wishful thinking. Cold Duck may or may not have a "labrusca" flavor. It is produced by blending sparkling burgundy and champagne.

Dessert

Geographical appellations which are considered to be semigeneric in this country include angelica, malaga, marsala, madeira, port, sherry, and tokay.

If angelica is a wine of geographical origin, it apparently originated in California and hence should have been classified as a wine entitled to an appellation of origin. The California wine industry has not acted to protect this appellation—the only typical American generic appellation for a wine of consumer acceptance. It should be a smooth, fruity-flavored wine of full body[3] and light to dark amber. A minimum °Brix of 7 is prescribed by the Wine Institute (1978). California regulations set the minimum fixed total acidity at 0.25% and an alcohol content in the range of 18.0 to 21.0%. Muscat aroma or a baked character are considered undesirable. In sum, this should be a very sweet, unbaked nonmuscat dessert wine, hopefully aged in wood.

Malaga, madeira, and marsala are seldom produced in this country and there are no Wine Institute specifications for them. Should distinctive types resembling these be produced it would be desirable to develop unique California or American type names for them.

California port is defined as a medium to deep ruby-colored red wine with a rich, fruity,[3] and full-bodied[2] taste. The minimum °Brix is 6. It should have moderate acidity (0.25% fixed in the minimum legal limit, but this is far too low). The intention, apparently, is that California port should be a younger wine than California tawny port.

---

[3]The meaning of "fruity" in dessert wines is not clear in the Wine Institute specifications.

California tawny port should have a reddish-brown or tawny color and should show considerable aging. Since a baked character is undesirable this means that hydroxymethylfurfural (p. 226) should not be present in more than traces. A legal minimum for this compound would prevent baked sherry-like ports being sold as tawny port. Tawny port has the same sugar and acid limitations as port. Neither should contain a recognizable muscat character.

California white port is described as a neutral-flavored, light-straw to pale-gold colored wine which is smooth and medium- to full-bodied and with a °Brix of 6 or more. It should also be fresh[4] and mellow. This conglomeration of requirements may be meaningful for a specific wine but many California white ports are not fresh and, as previously noted, medium- and full-bodied have little meaning for wines of 6° Brix. Fortunately, water-white charcoaled wines are now seldom sold as white port. With the advent of lined steel tanks, by fermenting light-colored musts out of contact with the air, a very light-colored wine can be produced without the use of charcoal. We would be in favor of keeping angelica as a very sweet nonmuscat white wine and allowing white port to develop into a less sweet, nonbaked appetizer type. A maximum °Brix of about 2 would differentiate between the types. This may not develop and some overlapping of the two types is inevitable.

California sherry is the type produced by baking (p. 391) whereas California flor sherry is a type produced by the use of an aldehyde-producing yeast (p. 412). The former must have a baked character while Wine Institute (1978) specifications state that a baked character must be absent from the latter. This should prevent blending of the first into the second but not the reverse. Neither type may have a recognizable muscat aroma. An alcohol content of 17.0—21.0% is prescribed.

California dry or cocktail sherry should be golden to a pale amber color, have a nutty,[5] well-developed "sherry" character without any burnt taste and should be light in body[2] but mellow. A maximum reducing sugar content of 2.5% is provided. This is too high for a genuinely "dry" type and 1.0 would be a better maximum. A minimum total acidity of perhaps 0.5% or more could be established to prevent flat-tasting wines from reaching the market.

California medium sherry (usually sold simply as California sherry) should be medium amber in color, full-bodied, rich, nutty with a well-developed "sherry" character. There are further requirements that it be well-balanced, smooth, without any burnt taste, and have 2.5—4.0% sugar. This is too small a range and if dry sherry had a maximum sugar of

---

[4]The meaning of "fresh" in a dessert wine is not clear.
[5]"Nutty" is a nebulous term. Does it refer to woodiness or to a baked caramel-like odor?

1.0 the range 1.5 to 3.5 would be more easily differentiated.

California sweet sherry (often called cream or mellow sherry) is defined as a medium to dark amber-colored wine of full body and a rich and nutty[5] flavor with well-developed "sherry" (i.e., baked) character. It must be well-balanced and smooth without any burnt taste. A sugar range of 4.0 to 12.0% is provided and this should certainly be adequate. The rather dark color limitation may be too stringent. Light-colored cream sherry can be produced by baking in the absence of air.

For California dry flor, medium flor, and sweet flor sherry the same general characteristics and sugar limitations apply as to the above three types, except, of course, the baked character must be absent and a flor (aldehyde) character be present. Medium flor sherry may be light- to medium-amber in color rather than medium- to dark-amber as with California medium sherry. A genuine dry flor sherry will usually be lighter than golden in color. The "light" body[2] requirement for both dry types does not seem meaningful. The restriction of the dry type to 1.0% maximum sugar could also apply here.

California tokay is defined by the Wine Institute (1978) as a blended wine, meaning that port, sherry, and angelica are used (p. 447). It must be an amber-colored wine with a pinkish tinge though light red wines with an amber hue are permitted. This latter requirement is not likely to be confused with tawny port since California tokay must have a slight nutty[5] sherry (i.e., baked) "taste" (sic) and tawny port may not have such an odor. A "light fruitiness" is said to be desirable but we are unable to define this desideratum. The wine type must be mellow and well-balanced and have a °Brix of 4−6. This is a rather narrow range and might better be 3°−7°. The California type does not in any way resemble its Hungarian prototype.

GEOGRAPHICAL TYPES

The only American geographical *type* specifically mentioned in regulations is "Central Coast Counties Dry Wine" but this has not been used so far as we are aware. San Joaquin (Fig. 3.1), Napa Valley Wine, Alameda County Wine, and the like are *not* adequate descriptions by themselves since they do not represent recognizable types. American geographical type names can be used if 75% of the grapes came from the region named. This is then combined with some generic, semigeneric, or grape type name, e.g., "American" vermouth, "California" port, or "Napa Valley" Sémillon. Most newly-developed viticultural regions do not use geographical names as a type name. Note that Alsace has not developed regional names since its liberation in 1918 although it appears to be moving in this direction. For recent U.S. regulations see U.S. Bureau of Alcohol, Tobacco and Firearms (1978).

Courtesy of Wine Institute

FIG. 3.1. SAN JOAQUIN VALLEY VINEYARD

Geographical appellations of origin have advantages from the consumer's point of view. They identify the wine with something he/she already knows—a region. They also differentiate the wine from all other wines since they are obviously not imitations. This may give the consumer confidence and add to his/her appreciation. The French, Italians and Germans have been most active in delimiting regions and using geographical appellations (pp. 5 and 25).

At present, "dry red table" and "dry white table" are available for developing into regional appellations, such as "Livermore" dry white table wine, etc. However, if every producer made his/her Livermore dry white table wine from different varieties, harvested them at different degrees of maturity, and vinified and aged them by varying procedures, the wines would have little resemblance to each other. They would, therefore, not represent a unique type. Further controls appear necessary other than the "75% from the region" requirement if geographical names are to be used as type names. If the vintage date is stated the regional requirement is 95%.

GRAPE (VARIETAL) TYPES

When a wine is produced from at least 75% by volume of a given variety of grape *and* derives its predominant taste, aroma and characteristics from this variety it is entitled to be so labeled. Varietal names are used in Alsace, Australia, Austria, Germany, Israel, northern Italy, South Africa, Switzerland and Yugoslavia as well as in the United States. Most of the premium wines of California carry varietal names. For suggestions on description of varietal aromas see Amerine and Singleton (1977).

White Table

The following types are in production in California: Chenin blanc, Flora, Folle blanche, French Colombard, Gewürztraminer, Gray Riesling, light muscat, light sweet muscat, Pinot blanc,[6] Pinot Chardonnay (better just Chardonnay), Sauvignon blanc (sometimes Fumé blanc or Blanc fumé), Sémillon, Sylvaner (rarely Franken Riesling), and White (Johannisberg) Riesling. These are not all that may be produced in the future.

They must have a distinguishable varietal aroma. Except for muscat it is difficult to describe in words this varietal aroma. Some attempts in this direction are given in Table 3.1.

TABLE 3.1. RECOMMENDED DEFINITIONS OF CALIFORNIA VARIETAL WHITE TABLE WINES

Type	Sugar (%)	Total Acidity (%)	Color	Aroma
Sauvignon blanc	<1.5	>0.6	L-M yellow[1]	Spicy, aromatic
Sweet Sauvignon blanc	>1.5	>0.6	L gold	Spicy, aromatic
Sémillon	<1.5	>0.6	L-M gold	Aromatic, fig-like
Sweet Sémillon	>1.5	>0.6	L gold	Aromatic, fig-like
Light Sweet Muscat	>6.0	>0.5	L gold	Muscat
Gray Riesling	<0.2	>0.5	L yellow	Slightly aromatic
White Riesling	<0.2	>0.7	L yellow	Slightly aromatic, yeast-like
Sylvaner	<0.2	>0.6	L yellow	Slightly aromatic, yeast-like
Gewürztraminer	<0.2	>0.6	L yellow	Spicy, very aromatic
Chardonnay	<0.2	>0.6	L-M yellow	Aromatic, ripe-grape
Pinot blanc	<0.2	>0.6	L yellow	Slightly aromatic
Chenin blanc	<0.2	>0.7	L yellow	Very slightly aromatic
Flora	<0.2	>0.7	L yellow	Slightly aromatic
Folle blanche	<0.2	>0.7	VL yellow	Fruit-like
French Colombard	<0.2	>0.7	VL yellow	Very slightly aromatic, pungent

[1]L for low, M for medium, VL for very low.

[6]This is considered synonymous with White Pinot but is not necessarily so. Most California White Pinot comes from Chenin blanc (Pineau de la Loire). There is, however, a true Pinot blanc which is produced by a few growers. The name White Pinot, if used, should be reserved for wines of this variety and the rest sold as Chenin blanc.

Malaga and Tokay have been approved as "varietal" types but they have very bland flavor. Furthermore, these appellations are already used for dessert wine types.

Red Table

Barbera, Cabernet Sauvignon, Concord, Gamay, Grignolino, Pinot noir, Red or Black Pinot,[7] and Zinfandel are listed in the Wine Institute (1978) specifications. Cabernet franc, Merlot, Petite Sirah, and Ruby Cabernet are also produced. Each must have a distinguishable varietal aroma. Some suggested definitions are given in Table 3.2. We confess that distinctive definitions between varietal types are not yet possible. However, this does not mean that such definitions will not be devised.

TABLE 3.2. RECOMMENDED DEFINITIONS OF CALIFORNIA VARIETAL RED TABLE WINES

Type	Total Acidity (%)	Color[1]	Aroma
Barbera	>0.75	M red	Slightly aromatic
Cabernet Sauvignon	>0.55	M red	Musty, aromatic
Concord[2]	>0.65	M red	Methyl anthranilate (foxy)
Gamay	>0.65	L-M red	Fruit-like
Grignolino	>0.60	Orange red to M red	Aged to reduce astringency
Merlot	>0.60	M red	Cabernet-type
Petite Sirah	>0.60	M red	Slightly distinctive
Pinot noir	>0.60	L-M red	Ripe grape, aromatic
Red Pinot	>0.60	L-M red	Moderately aromatic
Ruby Cabernet	>0.65	M red	Cabernet-type
Zinfandel	>0.65	M red	Berry-like

[1]M for medium, L for low.
[2]In California 12° to 14° Brix, but elsewhere in this country may be a dry or nearly dry wine.

Sparkling Types

The only California varietal sparkling type presently defined is sparkling muscat. This should be pale to straw in color, "have a good acidity and body. It should be fresh, fruity, well-balanced, have the unmistakable flavor and aroma of muscat grapes, and a reducing sugar above 4%" (Wine Institute 1978). A minimum total acidity of at least 0.6% would be helpful.

---

[7]This is the so-called Pinot St. George and does not appear, at least from its pigment complex, to be a Pinot variety. See Rankine *et al.* (1958) and Albach *et al.* (1959).

Dessert Types

Several varietal dessert types are in production and more may be produced in the future. These include muscatel, Muscat de Frontignan (or Muscat Canelli), Tinta Madeira port, and black (or red) muscatel.

Muscatel should, according to industry recommendations, be rich (in muscat aroma?), fruity,[3] and full-bodied with the unmistakable aroma of muscat grapes. It may range in color from straw (light yellow) to amber. A moderate acidity and a minimum °Brix of 6 is prescribed. The intention of the regulations is apparently that Muscat of Alexandria grapes should be used. A baked character is specifically considered undesirable. The present California minimum fixed acidity of 0.25% is certainly too low to be considered "moderate" in acidity—0.50 would be better. Muscat de Frontignan, Muscat Frontignan and Muscat Canelli are dessert types produced from a variety correctly known as Muscat blanc. It is the predominant variety in the regions of Frontignan and of Canelli. The geographical implications of "de Frontignan" and "Canelli" may prove confusing to the consumer. Whether White Muscat or Muscat blanc would differentiate this wine from the muscatel from Muscat of Alexandria is questionable. The wine must possess an unmistakable muscat character.

Black or red muscatel should be medium- to deep-red in color. A rich, fruity[3] and full-bodied wine with a pronounced muscat aroma is required. The specific notice that the muscat aroma be derived from Muscat Hamburg or Aleatico grapes rules out blends of Muscat of Alexandria (51%) and some red dessert wine. The minimum °Brix is again 6. The requirements that the wine be fruity and show balance (of what?) and be derived from proper aging (how long?) are at least confusing. Tinta Madeira port does not have a strong varietal aroma but does have a characteristic flavor.

Other Types

Not defined so far are several miscellaneous types—rosé, sweet rosé, dry red table wine, red table wine, sweet red table wine, dry white table wine, sweet white table wine, and aperitif wines.

California rosé is a wine of a fruity, light, and tart flavor. The color is specified as "pink with or without an orange modifying tint and should not have an amber tint." The color specifications appear to be sufficiently broad but the type should be qualified to limit the sugar content. Certainly "dry" rosés should not have over 0.5% sugar. The fruity tart flavor might be qualified by a minimum total acidity of at least 0.60%.

California sweet rosé is a relatively recent type which has been added to provide a rosé wine of over 0.5% sugar. The other requirements are as for California rosé and the same qualifications are applicable.

California red table and sweet red table wines provide for nonvarietal, nongeneric, or semigeneric wines. The sugar limits are respectively <1.5 and >1.5%. A variety of proprietary types is included in these classes. For example, most kosher-type wines would presumably be classified in the sweet, red, table-wine class.

Only two white table wine classes are presently defined: dry white table wine and sweet white table wine. The first has a maximum of 0.5% sugar and the latter must be of more than 0.5% sugar.

No explicit specifications for the "special natural" wines or for various flavored dessert wines have yet been devised. In many respects, these are flavored wines which resemble vermouth or fruit-flavored wines. Since they are all, so far, proprietary wines the specifications of the individual producers must suffice for their identification. The main limitation is that they cannot be made to resemble a natural fruit wine. However, since no natural lemon wine exists lemons can be used to flavor grape wine to make a "special natural" wine. This is produced with <14 and >14% alcohol.

For more information on California wine types see Adams (1964, 1978), Balzer (1970, 1978), Blumberg and Hannum (1976), Cook (1966), Melville (1972), Morgan (1971), and Thompson and Johnson (1976).

REFERENCES[1]

ADAMS, L.D. 1964. The Commonsense Book of Wine. David McKay Company, New York.

ADAMS, L.D. 1978. The Wines of America, 2nd Edition. Houghton Mifflin, Boston.

ALBACH, R., KEPNER, R.E. and WEBB, A.D. 1959. Comparison of anthocyan pigments of vinifera grapes. II. Am. J. Enol. Vitic. 10, 164-172.

AMERINE, M.A. and SINGLETON, V.L 1977. Wines, an Introduction. University of California Press, Berkeley and Los Angeles.

ANON. 1973. California Wine. Bob Thompson (Editor). Lane Magazine, Menlo Park, Calif.

BALZER, R.L. 1970. This Uncommon Heritage. The Ward Ritchie Press, Los Angeles.

BLUMBERG, R.S. and HANNUM, H. 1976. The Fine Wines of California, 2nd Edition. Doubleday & Co., Garden City, N.Y.

COOK, F.S. 1966. The Wines and Wineries of California. Mother Lode Publishing Co., Jackson, Calif.

---

[1]Titles have been translated only for nonwestern European countries.

MELVILLE, J. 1972. Guide to California Wines, 4th Edition. (Revised by J. Morgan.) Nourse Publishing Co., San Carlos, Calif.

MORGAN, J. 1971. Adventures in the Wine Country. Chronicle Books, San Francisco.

RANKINE, B., KEPNER, R.E. and WEBB, A.D. 1958. Comparison of anthocyan pigments of vinifera grapes. Am. J. Enol. Vitic. 9, 105-110.

THOMPSON, B. and JOHNSON, H. 1976. The California Wine Book. William Morrow & Co., New York.

U.S. BUREAU OF ALCOHOL, TOBACCO AND FIREARMS. 1976A. Labeling and Advertising of Wine. Part 4 of Title 27, Code of Federal Regulations. Govt. Print. Off., Washington, D.C. Amended in the Federal Register of May 9, 1978 regarding standards of fill.

U.S. BUREAU OF ALCOHOL, TOBACCO AND FIREARMS. 1976B. Wine. Part 240 of Title 27, Code of Federal Regulations. Govt. Print. Off., Washington, D.C. [This is the most important U.S. document on wines.]

U.S. BUREAU OF ALCOHOL, TOBACCO AND FIREARMS. 1978. Labeling and Advertising of Wine. Appellation of origin, grape type designations, etc. Federal Register 43, 37672-37678. Aug. 23, 1978.

WINE INSTITUTE. 1978. California wine type specifications, recommended as desirable for California wine and brandy types for guidance of judges at fairs. Wine Institute, San Francisco. June 12

4

The Molds and Yeasts of Grapes and Wine

Molds are of importance in wine making because of the damage they may do to the grapes before or after picking and because they can grow in empty wooden cooperage and subsequently impart a moldy odor and flavor to the wine. They do not grow in wine because of the inhibitory effect of the ethanol and the generally anaerobic conditions.

Yeast strains of the genus *Saccharomyces* are necessary in the fermentation of the must, but they and other yeasts may cause the clouding of bottled table wines. The flor yeasts, which represent a special group, are used in the making of Spanish sherries and certain Jura French wines (*vins jaunes*). Wild yeasts, such as the apiculate yeasts and others, may be harmful to wine quality when they develop during fermentation, although it is possible that they may sometimes produce flavors which give a distinct or unique character to the wines. Microbiological instability or spoilage of wine by yeasts may be of two types: spoilage of dry wine, in storage or bottles; and spoilage of bottled table wines containing residual sugar. The former conditions are discussed in this chapter in the descriptions of the individual yeast genera, and the latter conditions in Chap. 6 (pp. 308−309). See the end of Chap. 16 and Table 16.1 (p. 573) for further techniques for identification of microorganisms causing wine spoilages.

GENERAL CLASSIFICATION

The present chapter considers only yeasts and molds; the bacteria that are of concern to the enologist are discussed in Chap. 16. The complete classification and description of the molds and yeasts of interest to the wine maker are beyond the scope of this book, but a brief discussion of the more important forms will be given. See Lodder (1970), Kunkee and Amerine (1970), Reed and Peppler (1973), Hewitt (1974) and Kunkee and Goswell (1977) for further information.

Molds have been described as microfungi having well-marked mycelia or spore mass—especially the economic saprobes (Ainsworth 1971). Although some of the fungi are saprophytes and can utilize only nonliving substances for growth, others are parasitic and can attack living tissues. Examples of the former are *Penicillium* mold and wine yeast strains of *Saccharomyces cerevisiae*. Typical fungal parasites are *Botrytis cinerea* ("noble mold") and *Oïdium* (powdery mildew).

Fungi may be unicellular or multicellular. Yeasts are higher fungi whose dominant form of growth is unicellular. Certain other fungi are always multicellular in growth. Still others may under certain conditions grow as one-celled organisms and later on under changed conditions become multicellular.

This chapter deals with the occurrence, morphology, and some other general properties of the yeasts and molds of importance in wine production. The chemistry of fermentation and certain other chemical aspects of yeast activity are presented in Chap. 5.

MOLDS

Molds differ from each other principally in their methods of producing spores and conidia, but there are also easily recognizable differences in the appearance of the mycelium and in the nature of the chemical changes which they induce in media suited to their growth. Variations in external and microscopical appearance, however, are not reliable for identification and classification as the appearance is often affected profoundly by conditions of growth. Some molds form yeast-like cells under certain conditions and may even induce a weak alcoholic fermentation, as do some of the *Monilia* and *Mucor* molds. Molds are usually aerobic, although they have been encountered as a feeble growth in bottled juices which have not been pasteurized. They are usually not troublesome in wine, not only because of anaerobic conditions, but also because of the inhibitory effect of ethanol. When molds are a problem for the winemaker it is generally because of the secondary effects of premature alcoholic fermentation (by indigenous yeasts) of the juice of the broken moldy berries before the load reaches the winery, and because of the further detrimental effect of the action of acetic acid bacteria (see Chap. 16) on the ethanol thus formed. The susceptibility of the fruit to this deterioration depends upon weather, especially at the time of ripening, and upon the pruning and thinning practices in the vineyard which may result in overcropping. This is further discussed in Chap. 2 and 6. In many California wineries, a voluntary inspection system has been instigated with the cooperation of the State, as a check on the extent of the acceptance of moldy material. Aside from the unesthetic aspect, a major reason for rejection of moldy material is the extent of volatile acids and esters formed by bacteria. But in some cases, the mold may also contribute unpleasant off-flavors. These cases are mentioned specifically below.

In recent years, attention has been placed on the discoveries of the formation of mycotoxins by some molds, the most notable being the carcinogenic aflatoxins produced by *Aspergillus flavus*. This species has not been reported as a spoilage agent of grapes; Drawert and Barton (1974) were unable to detect aflatoxin, even in wine made from "moldy" (*Botrytis* infected) grapes. However, another mycotoxin, patulin, has been shown to be formed by *Penicillium expansum*, a well-known grape infectious agent. Indeed, patulin has been reported in juice from grapes infected with this organism, but not in wine made from them (Scott *et al.* 1977). The authors were careful before the fermentation to avoid the addition of sulfur dioxide, which is known at high levels to inactivate this toxin (Burroughs 1977). The disappearance of patulin is apparently due to some aspect of the fermentation process (Burroughs 1977), or possibly due to the action of sulfur dioxide formed by the yeast during fermentation. Of course, sulfur dioxide is used ubiquitously in grape fermentation. Another mycotoxin, ceramide, has been found to be produced by the mold *Aspergillus niger*, but this compound has not been reported in grapes.

Penicillium

Molds of the penicillium group are sometimes troublesome to the California wine maker. In the initial stages of growth *Penicillium* is white in appearance. Later, spores or conidia are formed in enormous numbers and give a powdery appearance to the growth, which is blue, green, or pink according to the color and age of the conidia and the age of the culture. See Raper and Thom (1949) for a comprehensive discussion.

P. expansum.—This species (formerly *P. glaucum*) is the best known of the penicillium molds and the one responsible for great losses to fresh fruit shippers and fruit product manufacturers. The asexual spores of conidia are spherical in shape and are formed in great abundance upon upright hyphae or conidiophores. The conidia are light and are carried by air currents. They are universally distributed on surfaces and in the air.

This mold will grow on practically all food materials exposed to the air, if the conditions of moisture content and freedom from antiseptics permit the growth of any microorganism. It prefers sugar-containing substances such as fruits, fruit juices, jams, etc., but will also develop on such material as moist leather or the moist inner surface of empty wooden barrels or tanks. Any acid material affords a more favorable medium for growth than does an alkaline or neutral medium. After early fall rains it often grows in great abundance on cracked grapes rendering them unfit for wine making. The taste of these wines is very unpleasant; and on the basis of our experience, very little is required to taint the wine. "Corked" wines may also have *Penicillium* sp. in the cork. Growth is more abundant at temperatures ranging from 15° to 24°C (59° to 75°F), but will occur at temperatures near freezing and slowly at temperatures as high as 37°C (98°F). It is known as a "cold weather" mold.

Aspergillus

The members of this group are recognized by their peculiar method of conidia formation. The conidia are borne upon upright conidiophores which terminate in abrupt enlargements or "knobs." From these enlargements, known as "vesicles," spring numerous spike-like projections—the sterigmata—bearing chains of conidia (Fig. 4.1). For a key to the aspergillus molds see Raper (1945).

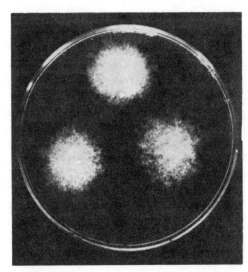

FIG. 4.1. YOUNG COLONIES OF ASPERGILLUS MOLD FROM GRAPES

A. niger.—This species is also common in California vineyards and orchards. Growth at first resembles that of the *Penicillium* molds, being white and cottony. After conidia are formed in abundance, the growth becomes black in color. Unlike *P. expansum* it produces only a little moldy flavor or odor in grapes but may lead to secondary infection by yeasts and bacteria. It often grows abundantly on grapes damaged by rain, particularly in the San Joaquin Valley. It is recognized by its black, dustlike conidia. It is sometimes termed a hot weather mold (Fig. 4.2).

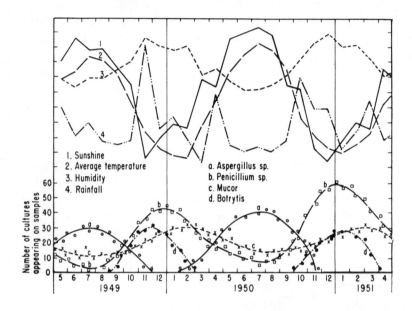

FIG. 4.2. CHANGES IN MOLD COUNT IN VINEYARD DURING YEAR

Mucor and Rhizopus.—The *Mucor* and *Rhizopus* molds are widely distributed. A general characteristic is the possession of a unicellular mycelium in which hyphae are not divided by cross walls or septa. The conidia or spores are borne in spherical sacs known as sporangia, which are usually visible to the unaided eye. Each is carried upon an upright fruiting thread or sporangiophore, hence the name "pin molds."

The *Mucor* molds (Fig. 4.3) occur frequently upon fresh fruit, especially during shipment. Grapes often develop a hairy, grayish cottony growth of this mold which prevents their fresh sale. Most members of this group are capable of converting starch into sugar. In sugary liquids under anaerobic conditions, yeast-like cells are formed which convert the sugar into ethanol and carbon dioxide. The species *Rhizopus* is closely related to *Mucor*, *R. nigricans* being encountered frequently on damaged grapes. Again it is the secondary infection which follows the mold attack which may seriously reduce the value of the grapes.

Rhizopus sp., *Aspergillus* sp., and *Acetobacter* sp. are the main organisms involved in summer bunch rot in grapes grown in the southern San Joaquin Valley. Hewitt *et al.* (1962) showed that the fungus *Diplodia*

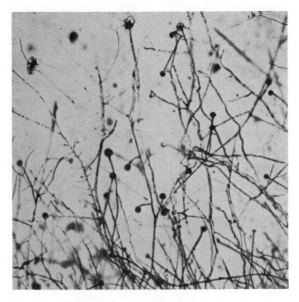

FIG. 4.3. MUCOR MOLD FROM GRAPES (×80)

viticola was responsible for initiation of summer bunch rot.

Botrytis.—This mold develops upon grapes in rainy and foggy weather as a short, grayish, hair-like growth. The mycelial threads penetrate the grape skin. Under the microscope the wall structure of the mycelia are especially notable and the conidia appear as micro grape clusters or handgrenades. The infection causes rapid evaporation of the water from the fruit, which results in a marked concentration of sugar. As much as 2% glycerol may be found in musts of botrytised grapes. Botrytis also metabolizes organic acids in the fruit. The Sauternes wines of France and the especially picked late-harvested German wines owe their quality to these facts (pp. 10–12). Nelson (1951) and Nelson and Amerine (1956, 1957) have used this mold successfully on grapes after picking for the production of natural sweet table wines, and attempts have been made to infect artificially the grapes in some California and Washington vineyards. Botrytis seldom grows abundantly on grapes on the vine except in years of early rainfall and high humidity.

The question of whether botrytis is beneficial or not under field conditions depends entirely on the weather after its first attack. If it is fortuitously dry and warm, the botrytised grapes will lose water and produce high sugar musts of superior quality. However, if cold humid conditions ensue after the initial attack, *Botrytis cinerea* is not a beneficial mold. When this occurs, the skin cracks, secondary yeast, bacterial and mold infections occur and the grapes lose sugar and quality. Under these conditions, rapid and immediate harvesting is advisable. In some climates this mold can attack the grapevine well before harvest, causing weakening of the cluster stem and dropping of the clusters to the ground. In these regions, the mold has been best controlled by the applications of the fungicide Benomyl (Benlate) or diethyl carbamate.

The favorable and unfavorable effects of *Botrytis cinerea* on the quality of musts have been emphasized by Charpentié (1954). Malic and tartaric acids are attacked about equally at low pH's by the fungus. Bertrand *et al.* (1976) found little change in the higher alcohols or esters in wine produced from fruit infected by botrytis to varying extents. Acetic acid was somewhat raised, while propionic acid was lowered. Generally, polyalcohols were also increased. The experiments of Dittrich (1964) do not substantiate the claim that botrytised musts ferment slowly because of the presence of an antibiotic, botryticin. The slow fermentation of botrytised musts appeared to be due to their higher sugar contents.

Brown Rot.—*Sclerotinia fructigena* causes brown rot of various fruits and attacks fruit on the tree (or in boxes). It is one of the most widely distributed and destructive of the fungus parasites, and although of minor importance in grape or grape wine production it may greatly damage other fruits used for making wines.

Oïdium (Acrosporium).—The "powdery mildew" is a very destructive fungus on California grapes and grape vines. It is controlled by dusting the vines with sulfur. When it attacks grapes early in the season it causes the grapes to crack and in severe cases prevents ripening. *Oïdium* forms a pure white, felt-like mycelium on culture media. Under the microscope, mycelial threads as well as the characteristic barrel-shaped oïdia will be found.

Downy Mildew (Plasmopara).—This mildew, a *Phycomyces*, almost destroyed the grape industry of Europe in the 1870's. It became controlled by use of Bordeaux spray. It is still a serious disease of grapes in Europe and eastern United States, but seldom occurs in California because of the usual dry weather and low humidity during the ripening period.

Alternaria and Dematium.—*Alternaria* species and *Dematium pullulans* are frequently found on fruits, especially on grapes that have been left on the vine until after the fall rains. *Alternaria* appears as a brownish-green or often black growth similar in appearance to *Penicillium*.

Under the microscope the conidia resemble Indian clubs divided by walls.

Actinomyces.—So far as the authors know, growth of *Actinomyces* does not occur in normal wines. However, it may grow in empty casks or on equipment. It is reported to produce an earthy odor. Since earthiness is found in some wines, *Actinomyces* have been suggested as a source. We know of no proof. For data on these microorganisms see Nonomura and Ohara (1959).

YEASTS

Yeasts are not taxon, *per se*, but are distinguished from the other fungi in that they usually maintain a unicellular growth, although many of them may form mycelia or pseudomycelia under special conditions.

Classification of Yeast

Yeasts have been classified (Lodder and Kreger-van Rij 1952) by their relationship to the corresponding fungal groups: thus, single-celled Ascomycetes are the ascosporogenous (forming sexual spores) yeast; those of the Basidiomycetes are the ballistosporogenous yeast; and the remainder, the single-celled Fungi Imperfecti, are the yeasts which form neither sexual spores nor ballistospores. The ballistosporogenous yeasts are not of general interest to the enologist and will not be discussed here further. The most recent accepted taxonomy of yeasts (Lodder 1970) uses the mode of cell-division rather than sporulation properties for the initial step in the identification of the genera.

Identification of Enologically Important Yeast Genera

The cells which divide by fission are separated from those which divide by budding. The latter are further divided into those genera which divide by multilateral budding, as compared to those by bipolar budding only. Further classification (Lodder 1970) depends upon the ability of the culture to form ascospores or not. This determination is not always easy to make (see p. 163).

If we use Lodder's (1970) classification and if we confine ourselves to those yeasts only which have been found associated with grapes, must, wine or wineries (Kunkee and Amerine 1970; Kunkee and Goswell 1977), we find only the genus *Schizosaccharomyces* in the fission group, and only *Saccharomycodes, Hanseniaspora* and *Kloeckera* in the bipolar-budding group. In the bipolar group, the first two are distinguished from the third by being ascospore formers. [*Hanseniaspora* is considered to be the perfect form of *Kloeckera* (Lodder 1970).]

Further classification of yeast genera of enological importance depends also upon physiological characteristics. Thus, of the multilaterally budding yeasts, those which will grow on 10 to 100 mg/liter cycloheximide ("Actidione") are *Dekkera* (spore-forming) and *Brettanomyces* (nonspore-forming) genera. These identifications are confirmed by the presence of many ogive-shaped cells in the culture; by intensive acid production, enough to bring about self-destruction of *Dekkera* or *Brettanomyces* on solid medium; and by production of a characteristic pungent odor.

A next step in the classification is the characterization of the spore-forming yeasts which are capable of utilizing nitrate as a nitrogen source. These are the *Hansenula*. The remaining spore-forming yeasts of importance to the wine microbiologist cannot assimilate nitrate. Of these, *Metschnikowia* can be identified by its needle-shaped spores, but there is an overlapping of the morphological and physiological characteristics of the other four: *Saccharomyces* (which includes the wine yeast, see pp. 170–171), *Debaryomyces*, *Pichia* and *Kluyveromyces*. The criteria for their identifications (Lodder 1970) include the time of conjugation before ascus formation, the ease of rupture of the ascus, shape of spores formed, ability to form a pellicle or film, and the vigor of the fermentation (anaerobic production of carbon dioxide from carbohydrate).

The remaining yeast of interest to us are nonsporogenous: *Candida, Torulopsis* and *Cryptococcus*. These are characterized by colony color (pigmentation), fermentation capability, ability to assimilate inositol, and the formation on solid medium of mycelium or pseudomycelium. The latter is a filamentous structure, but arises by budding rather than by septum formation, as in the true mycelia. Both *Candida* and *Torulopsis* genera are heterogenous collections of asporogenous yeast, and some species of *Saccharomyces* (including *Sacch. cerevisiae*) may be considered as some of their perfect forms. The cryptococci are all oxidative yeasts; that is, they do not grow anaerobically (and will not form carbon dioxide anaerobically, of course). *Rhodotorula*, a red-pigmented, nonsporulating, oxidative yeast should be included in our list because it often appears as a laboratory contaminant.

Identification of Yeast Cultures

For classification of yeast at the species level, further physiological tests are required. The species identification of the *Saccharomyces* is given on pp. 170–172. These include the types of carbon sources which can be fermented or assimilated. For details of the procedures for genus and species identification, see Guilliermond and Tanner (1920), Henrici (1930), Stelling-Dekker (1931), Tanner (1944), Mrak and Phaff (1948),

Lodder and Kreger-van Rij (1952), Roman *et al.* (1957), Cook (1958), Lodder (1970), and Barnett and Pankhurst (1974).

Procedures for practical identification of yeast strains at the subspecies level are not available. The differences between yeast strains are of a general qualitative nature. The best that can be done for their identification, perhaps, is to group the strains in relation to the formation, under specified conditions, of certain end products such as sulfur dioxide, hydrogen sulfide, or *n*-propanol. Qualitative grouping of yeast on the basis of fermentation vigor has been done for beer yeast strains (Thorne 1961) and might be applicable to wine strains. Flocculation capability, response to temperature, or sensitivity to sulfur dioxide, ethanol, or sugar are other possibilities.

Spore Formation.—Under favorable conditions of temperature and moisture supply, the sporogenous yeasts form ascospores. The spores vary in number per cell and in shape according to the species concerned. Those of wine yeast are spherical, and usually 2, 3, or 4 spores are formed per ascus. Sporulation in yeasts should not be equated to bacterial sporulation which results in cells which are resistant to heat and other adverse environmental conditions. In yeast, sporulation is the beginning of the sexual stage of reproduction. The isolation of the individual spores, and the culturing of the haploid clones which develop from them, is used by yeast geneticists to obtain mutants of wild-type yeasts. This is easiest in strains of *Sacch. cerevisiae* which are heterothallic. In these strains, single-spore clones remain haploid for many generations (Mortimer and Hawthorne 1969). Development of mutants of these strains might be one method for improvement of wine yeasts. However, many wine strains of *Sacch. cerevisiae* are homothallic (Thornton and Eschenbruch 1976). In these, sporulation produces ascospores which when isolated give rise predominantly to diploid cultures. In such strains, soon after ascospore germination, a change to the opposite mating type occurs in one of the buds which then fuses with a cell of the original unchanged mating type, thereby very quickly restoring the diploid condition. Thus, it is far more difficult to obtain mutants of these strains and this is one of the obstacles in the attempts to improve wine strains by genetic manipulation.

The classical medium for demonstrating spore formation is the moist gypsum block. Other spore media are sterilized carrot slices, potato slices, acetate medium, Gorodkowa's medium, and V-8 juice agar (see Mrak and Phaff 1948). See Tanner (1944) or other books on yeast for details. The sporulating cells may be fixed on the microscope slide by heating in the usual manner and staining; however, the authors find staining usually unnecessary for wine yeasts.

Isolation and Purification of Yeast

Yeasts may be isolated from natural sources by cultivation on solid medium. Grape juice, diluted three times with water; 10% malt or wort; or commercial yeast-mold medium may be used as media to which 2% agar is added before the material is sterilized by being autoclaved and poured into sterile Petri dishes. Cultivation of yeast cultures is made by streaking the juice or other source material on the solidified agar, incubating, usually at room temperature, and picking isolated colonies with sterile inoculating wire. Before taxonomical classifications are made, it is important that the cultures be purified by being restreaked, one or two times, and that the yeasts be identified as yeasts, not bacteria (see Table 16.1, p. 573, Chap. 16). For detailed instructions see Tanner (1944), Guilliermond and Tanner (1920), Rose and Harrison (1968-1970), and Guiraud and Galzy (1977). The latter reference includes instructions for conservation of yeast, and for study of growth, genetics, cytology, physiology and biochemistry of yeast.

Yeasts of Grapes and Wine

Many extensive studies have been made of the yeasts naturally occurring on grapes in vineyards all over the world. We will give some examples of these and references to others. As Amerine and Joslyn (1970) have stated, these investigations often have been incomplete because they have not included the role of the yeasts in wine making. In some cases, however, careful studies have been made on succession of kinds of yeast present throughout the fermentation and some examples will be given below. See Kunkee and Amerine (1970) and Kunkee and Goswell (1977) for lists of yeasts reported on grapes and in wine, and for references to other such listings. For the remainder of this discussion we will endeavor to use accepted yeast species (and generic abbreviations) given by Lodder (1970).

On the grapes, the yeasts are not evenly distributed on the skin, but are found near the pedicels or near the stomata—or near points of skin damage. This has been shown clearly by Belin (1972) and Belin and Henry (1972, 1973) by use of electron scanning microscopy. Generally, the cells shown have the appearance of being in a dormant state.

At the time of harvest, the most common organisms present on the grapes are apiculate yeast and species of *Saccharomyces*. For example, Domercq (1957) showed in musts of Bordeaux that *Kl. apiculata* and *Sacch. cerevisiae* were the predominant yeasts, with the following species of *Saccharomyces* also represented: *bayanus, chevalieri, uvarum, italicus* and *rosei*. She also found varieties of *Sacch. bailii*, in white musts, and *T. stellata* on white grapes infected with *Botrytis cinerea*. In the Beaujolais region, the same general ecological picture was reported by Bréchot *et al.* (1962), except they found fewer numbers of *Sacch. bayanus* and more species of other genera such as *Hansenula, Brettanomyces, Candida* and *Torulopsis*. Variations on this theme were found in warmer climates, such as parts of Spain, southern Italy, Sicily, Malta and Israel, where more nonspore-forming yeasts were found in comparison to those found in the cooler regions (Castelli 1952, 1965; Castelli and Iñigo Leal 1958; Iñigo Leal *et al.* 1961, 1969). For other studies of yeasts of grapes and musts of wine growing regions, see: Germany (Benda 1962), Czechoslavakia (Minárik 1964), the Soviet Union (Mavlani 1969), South Africa (van Kerken 1963; van der Walt and van Kerken 1958B; van Zyl and du Plessis 1961), Greece (Melás-Joannidis *et al.* 1958; Picca *et al.* 1959), New Zealand (Parle and Di Menna 1965), Brazil (Toledo *et al.* 1959) and Japan (Ohara *et al.* 1959).

In California, many of the studies of the ecology of yeasts on grapes and musts were made in areas which had not yet been established as the intensive viticultural regions which they later became. Thus, Cruess (1918) isolated and studied 19 different organisms occurring on California grapes grown in five districts. In all cases, the undesirable organisms greatly outnumbered the desirable wine yeasts. Grape samples from vines grown in three districts in which wine had never been made commercially contained no *Sacch. cerevisiae* (Fig. 4.4), indicating that wine yeasts are apt to be rare in regions where wine making is not carried on. In these cases, mainly molds were found on green grapes. As the grapes ripened, nonwine-yeasts appeared. The wine yeasts were the last to appear, but in all cases they were greatly outnumbered by undesirable microorganisms. There was a great increase in all types of microorganisms when the grapes were allowed to stand in the boxes after picking.

Holm (1908) isolated several yeasts from grapes grown in regions in California remote from wineries. No wine yeasts were found. Mrak and McClung (1940) made an extensive study of the yeasts naturally occurring on grapes and in grape products from the principal grape-growing regions of California. Of the 241 pure cultures studied, 159 formed spores and included *Sacch. cerevisiae, Sacch. bayanus* (perhaps a flor yeast), two species of haploid species of *Saccharomyces*, and a few species each of *Pichia, Debaryomyces, Hansenula* and *Hanseniaspora*. The 82 cultures of imperfect, nonspore forming yeasts included *Torulopsis, Candida, Kloeckera, Schizoblastosporion, Rhodotorula* and several species of *Candida*.

The above California studies were made before the practice of inoculation of musts with yeast starter cultures was as common as it is there today. More recent studies from our laboratories of yeasts isolated from

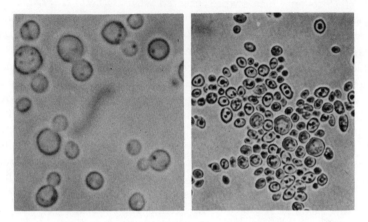

FIG. 4.4. YOUNG AND OLD CELLS OF *SACCHAROMYCES CEREVISIAE*

musts of red grapes of a rather isolated winery in Amador county (California)—a winery which up to the present time had not utilized starter cultures of yeast—gave an ecological picture of yeast very similar to that found in the European vineyards already described (Carisetti and Kunkee 1975).

In summary, the types of yeasts found in grapes and wines throughout the world are remarkably similar. There are, however, distinct differences in the proportion of each yeast in different regions. The predominant yeasts found under almost all conditions are *Sacch. cerevisiae* and *Kl. apiculata*.

However, concerning natural fermentations (i.e., those which are not intentionally inoculated with a starter culture), not only would the yeast complement of the must be of special importance, but also the predominances of the various yeast types throughout the fermentation. Again, Domercq's (1957) study of Bordelaise fermentation of red wine serves as a good example. Although apiculate yeast such as *Kl. apiculata* were found in the greatest amount at first and initiated the fermentation, they were relatively quickly overcome by the more ethanol-tolerant *Saccharomyces* species, especially *Sacch. cerevisiae*. But other kinds of yeast also were found at the end of the fermentation. These included other species of *Saccharomyces* such as *bayanus, chevalieri, florentinus* and *uvarum*, and *Hansenula anomala* and *Pichia fermentans*. During the fermentation, *Pichia membranaefaciens* and *Brettanomyces* also appeared. Much the same succession of yeasts were found in studies from other parts of the world (for references, see those cited previously for yeasts found on grapes and in musts, p. 165).

In California, in the recent study mentioned previously (pp. 165–166), the fermentation of red must commenced with *Kl. apiculata, Hanseniaspora uvarum, Sacch. cerevisiae, Sacch. italicus* and *Hansenula anomala*. As the fermentation progressed, only *Sacch. cerevisiae* was found.

One can see why the natural fermentations, or "spontaneous fermentations," might also be described as being mixed fermentations or sequential fermentations. Before discussing the relative merits of the mixed or successive fermentations as compared with inoculations with starter cultures, usually of a single strain, it should be noted that the microbiology of natural fermentations may be influenced, not only by the organisms found on the grapes, but also by the microflora of the winery itself. For example, Peynaud and Domercq (1959) found the following isolates (the number is given in the parentheses). Outside of tanks: *Sacch. bayanus* (6), *Sacch. cerevisiae* (3), *C. vini* or *C. valida* (13), *Pichia* (1). At bungs: *Sacch. bailii* (7), *C. vini* or *C. valida* (2). Bottling equipment: *Sacch. bayanus* (4), *Sacch. bailii* (4), *C. vini* or *C. valida* (10), *Brettanomyces* sp. (5). Floors of cellars: *Sacch. cerevisiae* (1), *Pichia* sp. (7), and *C. vini* or *C. valida* (7). For other studies see Ciferri and Verona (1941), Castelli (1941, 1948, 1954, 1955, 1960), Capriotti (1954) and Florenzano (1949).

Single Strains Versus Mixed Cultures

See Chap. 6 (pp. 268–270) for discussion on use of pure yeast starter cultures.

There is a difference of opinion among enologists concerning the use of a single strain of yeast in the fermentation of must. Some believe that better flavor and bouquet are obtained by the use of natural mixed cultures. Florenzano (1949) found several species other than *Sacch. cerevisiae* in the refermentation of new wine by the "governo" technique (pp. 26–27) used in Tuscany. He concluded that they are of importance in the development of the quality of these wines. Mestre and Mestre (1946) found that selected pure cultures of *Sacch. cerevisiae* produced more ethanol and gave a faster fermentation than the native yeasts, but that they did not convey the characteristic flavor of their region of origin.

Malan and Lovisolo (1958) found that in botrytised musts of high sugar content the initial fermentation is carried out by *Kl. apiculata*. Tarantola (1946) reported that his strains of *Kl. apiculata* were objectionable because of their low alcohol-forming power and production of excessive amounts of acetic acid and aldehyde. Bioletti and Cruess (1912) and Cruess (1918) had come to a similar conclusion.

Castelli (1955, 1960) reviewed the past research conducted on this problem at the University of Perugia giving the results of 1301 cultures. He stated that the effects produced by yeasts other than *Sacch. cerevisiae* in the natural fermentation of Italian musts cannot be neglected. In this regard, he listed six genera and species including *Kl. apiculata*, two species of *Torulopsis, Sacch. bayanus* and *uvarum*.

Rankine (1955) in Australia compared 98 strains of wine yeast from various sources. The final ethanol content of the fermented musts varied from 8 to 15%. The production of aldehyde was investigated for 11 strains, two of which produced exceptionally large amounts. Castor and Amerine (1942) used 32 different strains of wine yeast in the fermentation of Trebbiano musts and observed minor differences, particularly in bouquet. Castor (1954) compared the products of fermentation and flavors produced by different yeasts. He found considerable variation, particularly in the flavor.

A large (8-fold) influence of yeast strain on hydrogen sulfide formation was emphasized by Rankine (1963). Not only do strains of yeast differ remarkably in their ability to produce hydrogen sulfide, but Zambonelli (1964) was able to show that hybridization of positive and negative strains was possible. The F_1 progeny were positive producers.

Mestre and Mestre (1946), in studies on spontaneous fermentations and those conducted with pure cultures of *Sacch. cerevisiae* from various regions, found that the wine yeasts did not differ greatly in their effect on the character of the wine. The pure cultures gave more consistent and more satisfactory results than did the spontaneous fermentations with natural mixed cultures.

Saller (1957) concludes from his investigations that wines of better quality are obtained by use of fermentations with pure cultures of *Sacch. cerevisiae* than by spontaneous fermentation with the natural, mixed yeast flora of grapes. He found that, in addition to elimination or inhibition of the undesirable yeasts by pasteurization or sulfur dioxide, low temperature during fermentation was successful in securing a dominant fermentation by the true wine yeast. However, there is a rather marked belief among wine makers of certain European countries that the mixed cultures of spontaneous fermentation often give wines of superior flavor and bouquet. We found this belief held especially by some wine producers of the Bordeaux district in France. While the investigations of Peynaud and Domercq (1953, 1955) do not verify this belief, nevertheless, they state that it is difficult to say whether or not certain yeasts impart special characteristics to the wine. See also Peynaud and Ribéreau-Gayon (1947), Marcus Gomes (1969), Renaud (1939-1940), and Rankine (1968).

Wahab *et al.* (1949) found that wines of different flavors and bouquets could be made by fermenting sterilized musts with pure cultures of ester-forming yeasts and completing the fermentations with *Sacch. cerevisiae.* Their observations tend to confirm those of Castelli (1955) and of other Italian investigators, that the effects of yeasts other than *Sacch. cerevisiae* cannot be disregarded.

Toledo and Gonzalves-Teixiera (1955), in experiments on the effect of kind of yeast starter on production of volatile acidity, obtained the best results when the must was inoculated initially with *Sacch. rosei* and 48 to 96 hours later with *Sacch. cerevisiae.* They also (1957) compared 25 strains of *Sacch. cerevisiae* isolated from Brazilian grape musts and found that these gave similar results except in production of volatile acidity. They concluded that the strains that produced the least volatile acidity should be used in making wine in Brazil.

Schulle (1953A) found that the addition of a *Saccharomyces (rouxii?)* culture with *Sacch. cerevisiae* to a must rich in sugar resulted in an increased yield of ethanol in comparison with fermentation of the same must with a culture of the latter yeast alone. He also (1953B) obtained similar results by use of *Hanseniaspora* sp. with *Sacch. cerevisiae.*

We think too much is made of advocating the use of natural or sequential fermentations. In most regions where the practice is held to be important, either relatively high concentrations of sulfur dioxide are used in the must to inhibit effectively the development of the mixed culture of nonwine yeast, or natural fermentations are allowed to proceed in early harvested musts which are then later used as a source of natural yeast to be added to the regularly picked harvest. This source of "natural" yeast would be, in fact, a starter culture of one kind of yeast—the fastest growing one. It is possible that wines of distinctive flavor and bouquet can be made with mixed cultures under carefully controlled conditions, but because of the difficulty in selecting and securing the special microflora required and because of the danger of spoilage in uncontrolled natural fermentations, it is recommended, for the present at least, that only selected, proven strains of wine yeast be used in the commercial production of wine. See also Jorgensen (1936).

The question of which yeast strain to use has been reviewed (Rankine 1955, 1968; Kunkee and Amerine 1970), but has not been completely answered. We have mentioned (p. 163) some ways the wine yeast strains may differ, one from another. The selection of strains may be based primarily on fermentation technology, depending upon temperature and duration of fermentation, and the yield of ethanol. With regard to sensory characteristics of the wine produced, it has been our experience that marked differences at the end of the fermentation often become diminished with time. In some special cases, however, the difference might be striking and lasting, as with the formation of hydrogen sulfide, for example (Rankine 1963). Wine yeast strains have also been classified by their ability to produce high or low levels of sulfur dioxide (sulfite) (Dittrich and Staudenmayer 1970; Minárik 1975; Dott *et al.* 1977; Eschenbruch and Bonish 1976A), which may also bring about lasting effects on the quality of the wine, including the malo-lactic fermentation (Fornachon 1963). The sulfite-producing capability of the yeast strain may also be reflected (inversely) in its capacity to produce hydrogen sulfide (Minárik and Navara 1974). The formation of these sulfur containing compounds in some cases has been shown to be influenced by the medium, especially with respect to amounts of the vitamin, pyridoxine, and the sulfur-containing amino acids, cysteine and methionine (see the above references and Eschenbruch and Bonish 1976B, and a review by Eschenbruch 1974).

Rose (1977) points out that over the centuries fermentation yeasts seem to have a remarkable stability with respect to their fermentation characteristics, and thus improvement of strains may be difficult. We have mentioned one difficulty in attempts to improve strains by genetic manipulation (p. 163), and Rose (1977) discusses others. Even so, Alikhanyan and Nalbandyan (1971) have reported the production of a mutant wine yeast strain with increased ability to accumulate ethanol. An element which may have contributed to the stabilization of wine and other industrial fermentative yeast strains is the "killer factor," by which sensitive strains are killed by the excretion of a complex protein material from the killer strain yeast (Woods and Bevan 1968; Bussey 1972). Killer strains have been isolated from wine, saké, beer and refinery yeast (Young and Phillipskirk 1975).

The Genus Saccharomyces

The species of this genus are typified in part by their efficient capacity to convert sugar to ethanol (Rose 1977). The genus is divided into four subdivisions, but we are mainly concerned with only one which includes *Sacch. cerevisiae* and its close relatives.

Saccharomyces cerevisiae.—Hansen is credited with the first description of the species (Lodder 1970). It embraces most of the wine yeasts, but also nonwine yeasts as well, including bakers' yeasts. The species was first isolated from beer, but the main brewing strains are now included in the species which became classified as *Sacch. carlsbergensis*— but which is now correctly named *Sacch. uvarum*; although, as Rose (1977) points out, this later designation has been "unenthusiastically received by . . . the brewing fraternity." Wine strains of *Sacch. cerevisiae* were formerly classified as the variety *ellipsoideus* of the species, or as the species *Sacch. ellipsoideus*. Original descriptions of these species can be found in Lodder and Kreger-van Rij (1952). Other obsolete names are *Sacch. willianus*, and *Sacch. vini*, which now are included with *Sacch. cerevisiae*.

Sacch. cerevisiae is used for the fermentation of grape juice and other fruit juices. The shape of the cells varies from almost spherical to plump sausage shape, but the typical outline under the high power of the microscope is short ellipsoidal. The usual size of the cells is about 6×12 μm. Spores are usually formed in abundance on moist gypsum blocks, or on acetate medium (Lodder 1970).

A vinous or wine-like flavor is produced in fruit juices. Different strains do not differ greatly in their effect on flavor. One should not expect a strain of this yeast to impart a Pinot noir or Chardonnay or Sémillon flavor when isolated from these varieties of grapes because the principal flavor in these cases is that of the grape. Some vendors of yeasts have made extravagant claims in this regard.

Many strains of *Sacch. cerevisiae* form high amounts of ethanol in suitable media containing an excess of fermentable sugar, 16% ethanol by volume by unsyruped fermentation being fairly common and 18% or more by syruped fermentation (p. 439).

In grape must or other fermentable liquid, the first evidence of growth is a slight haziness. As growth proceeds, gas is formed, rises through the liquid, and, during active fermentation, froth or foam forms on the surface. The gas carries the yeast cells through the liquid causing it to be cloudy. At the same time a strong odor of alcoholic fermentation develops. When the grape juice is fermented to a very low sugar content, 0.2% or less, it is spoken of as being dry. After fermentation ceases, the yeast cells sink and form a sediment called lees or yeast lees. Most juices at a favorable temperature become completely fermented within 2 to 3 weeks.

Sacch. cerevisiae yeasts are used in the Orient in the fermentation of rice wort for saké. The starch of the rice is converted to sugar by *Aspergillus oryzae*. The mixed culture of yeast and mold is known as *koji*. Although *saké* yeasts are classified as *Sacch. cerevisiae*, they can be differentiated from other strains of the species by additional characteristics such as adaptability to dominate growth of the *koji* mold (Kodama and Yoshizawa 1977). Possibly because of the gradual furnishing of sugar to the yeast by slow hydrolysis of the starch by the mold, conditions are similar to those in syruped fermentation. Very high amounts of ethanol are formed, 17% by volume or more, according to Roman *et al.* (1957).

Distillery yeasts are classified as *Sacch. cerevisiae* strains and produce rapid fermentation and high ethanol content in suitable media.

Other Saccharomyces Species.—Closely related species, at least as evidenced by the pattern of assimilation or fermentation of carbohydrates, are *Sacch. bayanus* and *Sacch. fermentati*, which cannot ferment galactose; *Sacch. diastaticus*, which can ferment starch; *Sacch. uvarum*, which can ferment melibiose; *Sacch. montanus*, which can assimilate cellobiose; and *Sacch. pretoriensis*, which has the same fermentation pattern as *Sacch. cerevisiae*, but has a different sexual cycle. *Sacch. bayanus* (which includes the wine strains of the now obsolete species name, *Sacch. oviformis*) has already been mentioned as being found in musts and as sometimes the predominant yeast at the end of a natural vinification (see p. 166), which probably accounts for the belief that these strains are generally more ethanol-tolerant (Kunkee and Amerine 1970). Generally, yeasts used for sparkling wine production are strains of *Sacch. bayanus*.

Flor yeasts, used for traditional sherry production, are usually of the species *Sacch. bayanus, Sacch. capensis* or *Sacch. fermentati* (Kunkee and Amerine 1970; Rose 1977; Goswell and Kunkee 1977).

The flor yeast of Spain was classified by Prostoserdov and Afrikian (1933) as *Sacch. cheresiensis*, but Mrak and Phaff (1948) point out that Marcilla Arrazola *et al.* (1936) in Spain had given it the name *Sacch. beticus*, a term also used by Castor (1957), by Amerine (1958), by Joslyn and Amerine (1964), and Barnett and Pankhurst (1974). Both these species terms are now obsolete and are classified by Lodder (1970) as *Sacch. capensis* or *Sacch. bayanus*. We have found that the flor yeast strain widely used in California was apparently originally misclassified (as *Sacch. beticus*) and should now be called *Sacch. fermentati*. A flor strain differs from typical strains of wine yeast, *Sacch. cerevisiae*, by its ability to form a pellicle on wines of 12—16% ethanol. For use of flor strains in wine production see p. 406. A similar yeast is used in France in the Château Chalon area in the production of the well-known *vin jaune* of the Arbois district. It resembles *Sacch. cerevisiae* in its fermentation characteristics and general morphology. Scheffer and Mrak (1951) called a flor yeast isolated from California wines *Sacch. chevalieri*. It closely resembles the Spanish flor yeasts used experimentally in California by Cruess (1948) (p. 412). See also Feduchy Marino (1956) and Yokotsuka (1954) for further information on these yeasts.

The beer yeast cultures that we have encountered form larger cells than wine yeast, and the cells are usually spherical or egg shaped. In grape must, they form less ethanol than does wine yeast. Bread yeasts that we have used experimentally have been characterized by rapid fermentation of grape must and the formation of amounts of ethanol that compare favorably with those produced by wine yeast.

Other Genera

Fission Yeasts.—These yeasts multiply in the same manner as bacteria by formation of a transverse wall or septum in the cell and the splitting of the cell into two new cells along the line of the septum. A species of this genus was described in 1893 by Lindner, who was the first to use the term *Schizosaccharomyces*. The yeast described by him was isolated from African beer. Lodder (1970) states that the genus contains four species, namely *Schiz. japonicus, Schiz. malidevorans, Schiz. pombe* and *Schiz. octosporus*.

Dittrich (1963A,B) and Peynaud and Sudraud (1964) made early attempts to utilize the ability of *Schiz. pombe* to ferment malic acid to ethanol and other compounds, but not to lactic acid, as a means to deacidify musts with high acidity. Both found it a slow fermenter and showed that it was difficult to prevent other yeasts from overgrowing it. Since then there have been other attempts to overcome the difficulties of utilization of this genus for wine (Kunkee and Amerine 1970). These difficulties include high optimal temperature, and the poor flavor of the product. Benda and Schmitt (1966) surveyed many strains found in various yeast collections and found some which showed promise for wine-making. Some American workers in cold regions, where deacidification can be a major problem, have also experimented with a few of these *Schizosaccharomyces* strains (Yang 1973, 1975; Gallander 1977; Munyon and Nagel 1977). Some strains were found to be more sulfur dioxide-resistant, and it was suggested (Yang 1975) that these yeasts be used in a mixed culture with the regular *Saccharomyces* wine yeast in musts with somewhat elevated levels of sulfur dioxide—thus allowing the *Schizosaccharomyces* strain to begin the fermentation and catabolize the malic acid and let the regular yeast finish the fermentation with a minimal production of off-flavors. It should be noted that in musts with very high concentrations of malic acid, deacidification by this method might bring about an overall loss in too much acidity.

Hansenula.—This genus is quite widely distributed and is common in natural fermentations (see p. 165). Cruess (1918) described a pure culture isolated from wine grapes. Mrak and McClung (1940) reported on four cultures of *Hansenula* from grapes. Lodder (1970) lists 25 species.

Most species of *Hansenula* form films on liquid culture media and on wines of low ethanol content such as distilling material. They differ from most other yeasts, especially the film-forming *Pichia*, in their ability to use nitrate as a source of nitrogen, and in the shape of their spores, usually hat-shaped or "saturn"-shaped. Also, in grape must they form large amounts of esters, chiefly ethyl acetate. Wahab *et al.* (1949) conducted experimental fermentations of grape must and orange juice with ten cultures of *Hansenula* in comparison with eight other yeasts including champagne "Ay" yeast, a *Kloeckera*, a *Nadsonia*, two *Hanseniaspora*, *Saccharomycodes ludwigii* and one of *Schizosaccharomyces octosporus*. In most cases the wines fermented with *Hansenula* possessed too much odor of ethyl acetate to be palatable but after aging ten weeks, several of the wines had developed pleasing flavors and bouquets which were more pronounced and more aromatic than those of wines made with champagne "Ay" yeast alone. Surprisingly, several of the strains were quite resistant to sulfur dioxide. It is possible that one or more strains of *Hansenula* might be useful for increasing the ester content, flavor, and bouquet of wines. (See also the discussion of mixed cultures pp. 168– 169). For a study of *H. uvarum* and its rapid disappearance during fermentation, except in continuous procedures, see Sapis-Domercq (1969).

Candida.—*Candida vini* and *C. valida* are non-sporulating film yeasts that grow on wines of low ethanol content. They form a chalky-white film. They are frequently found on distilling material and on pickle brines. They were first described by Persoon in 1822. His description, according to Lodder and Kreger-van Rij (1952), was very inadequate. *Mycoderma* is a name that has been used in connection with yeasts, molds, and bacteria. Thus, in the early French literature one finds the terms *"Mycoderma aceti"* for vinegar bacteria and *"Mycoderma vini"* for the yeast film occurring on wines. Lodder and Kreger-van Rij (1952) classified *Mycoderma vini* as *C. mycoderma*, and Lodder (1970) split the species into *C. vini* and *C. valida*. The term "wine flowers" is often used to designate the yeast film that develops on wines of low ethanol content, but this is a loose term that could include several genera. These species of *Candida* can utilize ethanol as a source of carbon and form films on synthetic media containing ethanol as the only carbon source. They are strongly oxidative; they produce little or no fermentation in glucose media. An extensive mycelium is formed on slide cultures. *C. tropicalis* is frequently found on fruits, forms a pellicle on fruit juice and ferments glucose, fructose, maltose, and sucrose.

Brettanomyces.—Spoilage by *Brettanomyces*, or its sporulating forms *Dekkera*, are rare, but Kunkee and Goswell (1977) describe a recent outbreak in some wineries in California. They reported that the focal points of the infections were corrected by centrifugation or filtration and sulfur dioxide treatment of the affected wine, followed by good sanitation or sterilization of equipment and vessels. Previous workers (Van der Walt and Van Kerken 1958A, 1961; van Zyl 1962) have suggested that these infections can commence from lack of attention to thorough cleansing and sanitation of crushing equipment during the busy times of the vintage. Descriptions and diagnoses of these genera are given on p. 162. It is thought that these yeasts can grow on ethanol as a carbon source (even in bottled wine, depending upon the redox potential) and also on malic acid; and that the spoilage imparts either a metallic or a "horsey" tone to the wine.

Apiculate Yeasts.—These small yeasts (Fig. 4.5), often lemon-shaped, occur in abundance during the early stages of natural fermentation of grape must and apple juice. The term *Hanseniaspora* is used for spore-forming apiculate yeasts, and *Kloeckera* for the non-sporulating species (Lodder 1970). The species *Kl. apiculata* is one most frequently encountered in the natural fermentation of grape must and apple juice. A comparative study of the apiculate yeasts was made by Miller and Phaff (1958).

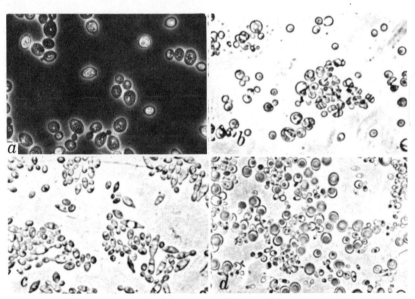

(A) Courtesy of Prof. Lemperle; (B), (C), (D) Courtesy of Prof. Castelli

FIG. 4.5. *SACCHAROMYCES (A), HANSENULA (B), KLOECKERA (C)* AND *CANDIDA (D)*

Variation in Yeast Sedimentation

Some wine yeasts give a "powdery" or fine-grained sediment after fermentation. This sediment is easily disturbed during racking and on that account it is difficult to draw off the new wine close to the lees. Other varieties, notably some champagne yeast strains, give a very coarse or granular and heavy sediment. The yeast settles quickly after fermentation, and in racking there is little tendency for the yeast lees to rise and mix with the wine. Consequently, the racked wine is apt to be clearer and less of it is lost in the lees. The physiology of flocculation is not at all well understood but seems to involve calcium ions in salt bridges formed at the cell wall (Rose 1977). Some information on the genetics of flocculation capability has been obtained (Stewart and Russell 1977).

The clouding of bottled wines by various yeasts is a very important problem and is discussed in Chap. 16. (See also Van der Walt and Van Kerken 1958A.)

Exogenous Vitamin Requirements

It was once thought that yeast strains might be classified by their "bios factor" number, based on their response to vitamins (Cook 1958, p. 286), but the responses were generally found so qualitative to be impractical for this use. It is now recognized that yeasts have an absolute requirement for hardly any vitamins, biotin being the usual exception, and they give invariable response to vitamins only under special conditions of deprivation, conditions not found in grape juice (Suomalainen and Oura 1971). For example, Wikén and Richard (1951) found that the wine yeasts known as Fendant, Herrliberg, and Salenegg used in commercial wine making in Switzerland showed excellent growth in synthetic media devoid of vitamins, whereas the Dezaley strain required at least three vitamins for normal growth. See Joslyn (1951), Thorne (1946) and Suomalainen and Oura (1971) for further information.

Growth at Low Temperatures

Strains of *Sacch. cerevisiae* vary considerably in their ability to carry on fermentation at low temperatures. For example, Castelli (1941) in fermentation at six different temperatures by ten strains of wine yeast isolated from Italian musts and wines found that one strain gave about 12% of ethanol of 6°C (43°F) while another gave only 6%. At 11°C (52°F) and 16°C (61°F) all cultures gave high yields of ethanol; but at 25°C (77°F) the yeast that gave the highest ethanol yields at the low temperature produced only 9% of ethanol. Porchet (1938) in Switzerland isolated two varieties of wine yeast that fermented must at temperatures below 0°C (32°F). Osterwalder (1934A, B) presented evidence that wine yeast can be acclimatized to low temperatures. The research of Porchet and Osterwalder is of considerable importance in Switzerland where the temperature often becomes low during the vintage season.

Tchelistcheff (1948) found that white musts fermented at low temperatures (say, 10°C or 50°F) with a finishing temperature of 20°C (68°F) gave wines of greater freshness of flavor and fruitiness, low volatile acidity, higher glycerol and less lees than musts fermented at higher temperatures. Fermentation of white musts at low temperature, 16°C (61°F) or lower, is now common practice in the production of dry table wines of high quality in California. Hohl and Cruess (1936), using syruped fermentations of must with champagne yeast, obtained about 16% ethanol at 7°C (45°F) to 22°C (72°F), but less at higher temperatures: 6% at 37°C (100°F). Pederson *et al.* (1959) found that grape juice stored commercially below −2°C (28°F) in tanks occasionally developed large numbers of yeast cells. It was found that several species were represented, although strains of *Saccharomyces, Torulopsis, Hanseniaspora,* and *Candida* predominated.

Thermal Death Time

Using specially-designed capillary tubes, Jacob *et al.* (1964) reported thermal death times of *Saccharomyces cerevisiae* of 1 min at 58°C (136.4°F) and 0.1 min at 62°C (143.6°F) for one strain and about 1° lower for another. Synergistic effects were noted due to alcohol but the yeast death time was not lowered sufficiently to account for the results of Yang *et al.* (1947).

REFERENCES[1]

AINSWORTH, G.C. 1971. Ainsworth & Bisby's Dictionary of the Fungi, 6th Edition. Commonwealth Mycological Institute, Kew, Surrey, England.

ALIKHANYAN, S.I. and NALBANDYAN, G.M. 1971. Selection of wine yeasts using mutagens. Communication I. Production of strains of *Saccharomyces vini* for the preparation of natural, strong table wines from high-sugar varieties of the grape. Sov. Genet. *2*, 1200-1205.

AMERINE, M.A. 1958. Personal communication.

AMERINE, M.A. and JOSLYN, M.A. 1970. Table Wines: the Technology of Their Production, 2nd Edition. University of California Press, Berkeley and Los Angeles.

BARNETT, J.A. and PANKHURST, R.J. 1974. A New Key to the Yeasts. North-Holland Publishing Co., Amsterdam.

BELIN, J.-M. 1972. Recherches sur la répartition des levures à la surface de la grappe de raisin. Vitis *11*, 135-145.

---

[1]Titles have been translated only for nonwestern European languages.

BELIN, J.-M. and HENRY, P. 1972. Contribution à l'étude écologique des levures dans le vignoble. Répartition des levures à la surface du pédicelle et de la baie de raisin. Compt. Rend. Acad. Sci. Paris 274D, 2318-2320.

BELIN, J.-M. and HENRY, P. 1973. Répartition de levures à la surface de la tige de vigne. Compt. Rend. Acad. Sci. Paris 277D, 1885-1887.

BENDA, I. 1962. Ökologische Untersuchungen über die Hefeflora in frankischen Weinbaugebiet. Bayer. Landwirtsch. Jahrb. 39, 595-613.

BENDA, I. and SCHMITT, A. 1966. Önologische Untersuchungen zum biologisches Säureabbau im Most durch Schizosaccharomyces pombe. Weinberg Keller 13, 239-255.

BERTRAND, A., PISSARD, R., SARRE, C. and SAPIS, J.C. 1976. Étude de l'influence de la pourriture grise des raisins (Botrytis cinerea) sur le comportement et la qualité des vins. Connaiss. Vigne Vin 10, 427-446.

BIOLETTI, F.T. and CRUESS, W.V. 1912. Enological investigations. Calif. Agric. Exp. Stn. Bull. 230, 23-118.

BRÉCHOT, P., CHAUVET, J. and GIRARD, H. 1962. Identification des levures d'un moût de Beaujolais au cours de sa fermentation. Ann. Technol. Agric. 11, 235-244.

BURROUGHS, L.F. 1977. Stability of patulin to sulfur dioxide and to yeast fermentation. J. Assoc. Off. Anal. Chem. 60, 100-103.

BUSSEY, H. 1972. Effects of yeast killer factor on sensitive cells. Nature (London) New Biol. 235, 73-75.

CAPRIOTTI, A. 1954. Recherches sur les levures de la fermentation vinaire en Italie. Antonie van Leeuwenhoek J. Microbiol. Serol. 20, 374-384.

CARISETTI, D. and KUNKEE, R.E. 1975. Personal communication.

CASTELLI, T. 1941. Temperatura e chimismo dei blastomiceti. Ann. Microbiol. 2, 8-22.

CASTELLI, T. 1948. I lieveti della fermentazione vinaria nelle regione Pugliese. Ric. Sci. 18, 66-94.

CASTELLI, T. 1952. Considérations sur les relations entre climat et agents de la fermentation vinaire. Rev. Ferm. Ind. Alim. 7, 35-42.

CASTELLI, T. 1954. Fermentazione e rifermentazione nei paesi caldi. Xe Congrès Inter. Ind. Agric. 2, 1891-1909.

CASTELLI, T. 1955. Yeasts of wine fermentations from various regions in Italy. Am. J. Enol. Vitic. 6, 18-20. [See also Riv. Vitic. Enol. (Conegliano) 1, 258-264, 1948.]

CASTELLI, T. 1960. Lieviti e Fermentazioni. In Enologia. Luigi Scialpi Editore, Rome.

CASTELLI, T. 1965. La collezione dei lieviti vinari dell'Instituto di Microbiologia Agriria e Technica (I.M.A.T.) dell'Univ. Perugia, Ann. Fac. Agric. Univ. Perugia 20, 251-283.

CASTELLI, T. and IÑIGO LEAL, B. 1958. Los agentes de la fermentación vinica en la región machega y zonas limitrofes. Ann. Fac. Agric. Univ. Perugia *13*, 3-20, 186-203.

CASTOR, J.G.B. 1954. Fermentation products and flavor profiles of yeasts. Wines Vines *35* (8) 29-31.

CASTOR, J.G.B. 1957. Nutrient requirements for growth of sherry flor yeast, *Saccharomyces beticus*. Appl. Microbiol. *6*, 51-60.

CASTOR, J.G.B. and AMERINE, M.A. 1942. Unpublished data. Dept. of Viticulture and Enology, Univ. Calif., Davis.

CHARPENTIÉ, Y. 1954. Contribution à l'étude biochimique des facteurs de l'acidité des vins. Ann. Technol. Agric. *3*, 89-167.

CIFERRI, R. and VERONA, O. 1941. Descrizione dei lieviti della uve, dei mosti e dei vini. In: Garoglio, P. G. Trattato di Enologia. *2*, 275-309. Il Progresso Vinicolo ed Oleario, Florence, 1941.

COOK, A.H. 1958. The Chemistry and Biology of Yeasts. Academic Press, New York.

CRUESS, W.V. 1918. The fermentation organisms from California grapes. Univ. Calif. Publ. Agric. Sci. *4* (1) 1-66.

CRUESS, W.V. 1948. Investigations of the flor sherry process. Calif. Agric. Exp. Stn. Bull. *710*.

DITTRICH, H H. 1963A. Versuche zum Apfelsäureabbau mit einer Hefe der Gattung *Schizosaccharomyces*. Wein-Wissen. *18*, 392-405.

DITTRICH, H.H. 1963B. Zum Chemismus des Apfelsäureabbaues mit einer Hefe der Gattung *Schizosaccharomyces*. Ibid. *18*, 406-410.

DITTRICH, H.H. 1964. Über die Glycerinbildung von *Botrytis cinerea* auf Traubenbeeren und Traubenmosten sowie über der Glyceringehalt von Beeren- und Trockenbeerenausleseweinen. Ibid. *19*, 12-20.

DITTRICH, H.H. and STAUDENMAYER, T. 1970. Über die Zusammelhänge zwischen der Sulfit-Bildung und der Schwefelwasserstoff-Bildung bei *Saccharomyces cerevisiae*. Zentr. Bakteriol. Parastenk. Abt. II *124*, 113-118.

DOMERCQ, S. 1957. Étude et classification des levures de vin de la Gironde. Ann. Technol. Agric. *6*, 5-58, 139-183.

DOTT, W., HEINZEL, M. and TRÜPER, H.G. 1977. Sulfite formation by wine yeasts. IV. Active uptake of sulfate by "low" and "high" sulfite producing wine yeasts. Arch. Microbiol. *112*, 283-285.

DRAWERT, F. and BARTON, H. 1974. Zum Nachweis von Aflatoxinen in Wein. Z. Lebens.-Untersuch. Forsch. *154*, 223.

ESCHENBRUCH, R. 1974. Sulfite and sulfide formation during winemaking —a review. Am. J. Enol. Vitic. *25*, 157-161.

ESCHENBRUCH, R. and BONISH, P. 1976A. The influence of pH on sulfite formation by yeasts. Arch. Microbiol. *107*, 229-231.

180   TECHNOLOGY OF WINE MAKING

ESCHENBRUCH, R. and BONISH, P. 1976B. Production of sulfite and sulphide by low- and high-sulfite forming wine yeasts. Arch. Microbiol. *107*, 299-302.

FEDUCHY MARINO, E. 1956. Contribución al estudio y relación de la "Flor" española de levadura perteneciente a las principales regiones vinícolas. Bol. Inst. Nac. Invest. Agron. (Madrid) *35*, 211-237.

FLORENZANO, G. 1949. La microflora blastomiceta dei mosti e dei vini di alcune zona Toscane. Ann. Sper. Agrar. (Rome) [N.S.] *3* (4) 887-918.

FORNACHON, J.C.M. 1963. Inhibition of certain lactic acid bacteria by free and bound sulfur dioxide. J. Sci. Bd. Agric. *14*, 857-862.

GALLANDER, J.F. 1977. Deacidification of eastern table wines with *Schizosaccharomyces pombe*. Am. J. Enol. Vitic. *28*, 65-68.

GOSWELL, R.W. and KUNKEE, R.E. 1977. Fortified wines. *In* Economic Microbiology, Vol. 1. A. H. Rose (Editor). Academic Press, London.

GUILLIERMOND, A. and TANNER, F. 1920. The Yeasts. John Wiley & Sons, New York.

GUIRAUD, J. and GALZY, P. 1977. Techniques d'études des champignons levurifermes. Bios *8*, 25-80.

HENRICI, A.T. 1930. The Yeasts, Molds and Actinomycetes. John Wiley & Sons, New York.

HEWITT, W.B. 1974. Rots and bunch rots of grapes. Calif. Agric. Exp. Stn. Bull. *868*, Univ. Calif. Div. Agric. Sci., Richmond, Calif.

HEWITT, W.B., GOODING, G.V., JR., CHIARAPPA, L. and BUTLER, E. E. 1962. Etiology of summer bunch rot of grapes in California. (Abstr.) Phytopathology *52*, 13.

HOHL, L.A. and CRUESS, W.V. 1936. Effect of temperature, variety of juice and method of increasing sugar content on maximum alcohol production by *Saccharomyces ellipsoideus*. Food Res. *1*, 405-411.

HOLM, H.C. 1908. A study of yeasts from California grapes. California Agric. Exp. Stn. Bull. *197*, 169-175.

IÑIGO LEAL, B., ARROYO VARELA, V., BRAVO ABAD, F. and LLAGUNO, C. 1961. Diferencias metabólicas de interés industrial entre especies de levaduras vínicas. Rev. Agroquím. Tecnol. Aliment. *1* (2) 11-17.

IÑIGO LEAL, B., TOMEO, M. and HEGARDT, F.G. 1969. Los agents de la fermentatión vínica en la zone de Aragón. *Ibid. 9*, 437.

JACOB, F.S., ARCHER, T.E. and CASTOR, J.G.B. 1964. Thermal death time of yeast. Am. J. Enol. Vitic. *15*, 69-74.

JORGENSEN, A. 1936. Practical Management of Pure Yeast, 3rd Edition. Rev. by A. Hansen. Lippincott Co., Philadelphia.

JOSLYN, M.A. 1951. Nutrient requirements of yeast. Mycopath. Mycol. Appl. *5*, 260-276.

JOSLYN, M.A. and AMERINE, M.A. 1964. Dessert, Appetizer and Related Flavored Wines. University of California, Div. Agric. Sci., Berkeley.

KODAMA, K. and YOSHIZAWA, K. 1977. Saké. *In* Economic Microbiology, Vol. 1. A. H. Rose (Editor). Academic Press, London.

KUNKEE, R.E. and AMERINE, M.A. 1970. Yeasts in winemaking. *In* The Yeasts, Vol. 3. A. H. Rose and J. S. Harrison (Editors). Academic Press, New York.

KUNKEE, R.E. and GOSWELL, R.W. 1977. Table Wines. *In* Economic Microbiology, Vol. 1. A. H. Rose (Editor). Academic Press, London.

LODDER, J. 1970. The Yeasts—A Taxonomic Study. North-Holland Publishing Co., Amsterdam, London.

LODDER, J. and KREGER-VAN RIJ, N.J.W. 1952. The Yeasts—A Taxonomic Study. North Holland Publishing Co., Amsterdam, and Interscience Publishers, New York.

MALAN, C.E. and LOVISOLO, R. 1958. I lieviti della fermentazione vinaria in Piedmont. Atti Accad. Ital. Vite Vino *10*, 124-146.

MARCILLA ARRAZOLA, J., ALAS, G. and FEDUCHY, E. 1936. Contribución al estudio de las levaduras que forman velo sobre ciertos vinos de elevado grado alcohólico. An. Centro Invest. Vinícolas *1*, 1-230.

MARCUS GOMES, J.V. 1969. Emprego de levaduras seleccionadas em vinificacão. Anais Inst. Vinho Porto *23*, 41-70.

MAVLANI, M.I. 1969. Yeast micro flora of wine-making districts of Uzbekistan. Antonie van Leeuwenhoek *35* Supplement, Ycast Symposium, D3.

MELÁS-JOANNIDIS, Z., CARNI-CATSADIMAS, I., VERONA, O. and PICCI, G. 1958. Ricerche microbiologische sopri i mosti d'uva in fermentazione. Ann. Microbiol. Enzimol. *8*, 118-137.

MESTRE ARTIGAS, C. and MESTRE JANE, A. 1946. Fermentaciones comparativos con diferentes levaduras. Min. agric. inst. nac. invest. agron, Estación Vitíc. y Enol., Villafranca del Panadés, Cuaderno *68*, 1-28.

MILLER, M.W. and PHAFF, H.J. 1958. A comparative study of the apiculate yeasts. Mycopath. Mycol. Appl. *10*, 113-141.

MINÁRIK, E. 1964. Die Hefeflora von Jungweinen in der Tschechoslowakei. Mitt. Rebe Wein, Serie A (Klosterneuburg) *14*, 306-315.

MINÁRIK, E. 1975. Réduction du sulfate en sulfite et sa signification taxonomique pour la classification des levures. Prog. Tech. Viti Vinicole (Bratislava) *7*, 279-298.

MINÁRIK, E. and NAVARA, A. 1974. Effect of sulphate and sulphur amino acid levels on sulphite and sulphide formation by wine yeasts. Ann. Microbiol. Enzimol. *24*, 21.

MORTIMER, R.K., and HAWTHORNE, D.C. 1969. Yeast genetics. *In* The Yeasts, Vol. 1. A. H. Rose and J. S. Harrison (Editors). Academic Press, New York.

MRAK, E.M. and MCCLUNG, L.S. 1940. Yeasts occurring on grapes and grape products in California. J. Bacteriol. *40*, 395-407.

MRAK, E.M. and PHAFF, H.J. 1948. Yeasts. Ann. Rev. Microbiol. *17*, 1-46.

MUNYON, J.R. and NAGEL, C.W. 1977. Comparison of methods of deacid- ification of musts and wines. Am. J. Enol. Vitic. *28*, 79-89.

NELSON, K.E. 1951. Factors influencing the infection of table grapes by *Botrytis cinerea*. Phytopathology *41*, 319-326.

NELSON, K.E. and AMERINE, M.A. 1956. Use of *Botrytis cinerea* for the production of sweet table wines. Am. J. Enol. *7*, 131-136.

NELSON, K.E. and AMERINE, M.A. 1957. Further studies on the production of natural, sweet wines from botrytised grapes. Am. J. Enol. *8*, 127-134.

NONOMURA, H. and OHARA, Y. 1959. Distribution of *Actinomycetes* in the soil. Bull. Res. Inst. Fermentation, Yamanashi Univ., 77-78.

OHARA, Y., NONOMURA, H. and YUNOME, H. 1959. Dynamic aspect of yeast flora during vinous fermentation. Bull. Res. Inst. Fermentation, Yamanashi Univ., 7-12, 13-18.

OSTERWALDER, A. 1934A. Die verkannten Kaltgärhefen. Schweiz. Z. Obst- Weinbau *50*, 487-490.

OSTERWALDER, A. 1934B. Von Kaltgärhefen und Kaltgärung. Z. Bakteriol. Parasitenk. Abt II. *90*, 226-249.

PARLE, N.J., and DI MENNA, E.M. 1965. The source of yeasts in New Zealand wines. New Zealand J. Agric. Res. *9*, 98-108.

PEDERSON, C.S., ALBURY, M.N., WILSON, D.C. and LAWRENCE, N.L. 1959. The growth of yeasts in grape juice at low temperatures. Appl. Microbiol. *7*, 1-16.

PEYNAUD, E. and DOMERCQ, S. 1953. Étude des levures de la Gironde. Ann. Technol. Agric. *4*, 265-300.

PEYNAUD, E. and DOMERCQ, S. 1955. Étude de la microflore des moûts et des vins de Bordeaux. Compt. Rend. Acad. Agric. France *41*, 103-106.

PEYNAUD, E. and DOMERCQ, S. 1959. A review of microbiological problems in wine-making in France. Am. J. Enol. Vitic. *10*, 69-77.

PEYNAUD, E. and RIBÉREAU-GAYON, J. 1947. Sur les divers de fermentation alcoolique déterminés par diverses races de levures elliptiques. Compt. Rend. Acad. Sci. Paris *224*, 1388-1390.

PEYNAUD, E. and SUDRAUD, P. 1964. Utilisation de l'effet désacidifiant des *Schizosaccharomyces* en vinification de raisins acides. Ann. Technol. Agric. *13*, 309-328.

PICCA, G., MÉLAS-JOANNIDIS, Z., CARNIS, A., and VASSILATOS, G. 1959. Ancora spora la microflora presente nei mosti d'uva del peloponneso (Nota III). Ann. Fac. Agraria, Univ. Pisa *20*, 9-33.

PORCHET, B. 1938. Biologie des levures provoquant la fermentation alcoolique à basse température. Ann. Ferment. *4*, 578-600.

PROSTOSERDOV, N.N. and AFRIKIAN, R. 1933. Jerezwein in Armenien. Das Weinland *5*, 389-391.

RANKINE, B.C. 1955. Quantitative differences in products of fermentation by different strains of wine yeasts. Am. J. Enol. Vitic. *6*, 1-10.

RANKINE, B.C. 1963. Nature, origin, and prevention of hydrogen sulfide aroma in wine. J. Sci. Food Agric. *14*, 79-91.

RANKINE, B.C. 1968. The importance of yeasts in determining the composition and quality of wines. Vitis 7, 22-49.

RAPER, K.B. 1945. A Manual of the Aspergilli. Williams and Wilkins, Baltimore.

RAPER, K.B. and THOM, C.C. 1949. A Manual of the Penicillia. Williams and Wilkins, Baltimore.

REED, G. and PEPPLER, H.J. 1973. Yeast Technology. AVI Publishing Co., Westport, Conn.

RENAUD, J. 1939-1940. La microflore des levures du vin. Son role dans la vinification. Ann. Ferment. *5*, 410-417.

ROMAN, W., ARIMA, I.T., NICKERSON, W.J., PYKE, M., SCHANDERL, H., SCHULTZ, A.S., THAYSEN, A.C. and THORNE, R.S. 1957. Yeasts. Academic Press, New York.

ROSE, A.H. 1977. Scientific basis of alcoholic beverage production. *In* Economic Microbiology, Vol. 1. A.H. Rose (Editor). Academic Press, London.

ROSE, A.H. and HARRISON, J.S. 1968-1970. The Yeasts, 3 Vols. Academic Press, New York.

SALLER, W. 1957. Die Spontane-Sprosspilzflora frisch gepresster Traubensäfte und die Reinhefegärung. Mitt. Rebe Wein, Serie A (Klosterneuburg), 7, 130-138.

SAPIS-DOMERCQ, S. 1969. Comportement des levures apiculées au cours de la vinification. Connaiss. Vigne Vin *4*, 379-392.

SCHEFFER, W.R. and MRAK, E.M. 1951. Characteristics of yeast causing clouding of dry white wines. Mycopath. Mycol. Appl. *5*, 236-249.

SCHULLE, H. 1953A. Die Bedeutung der Apiculatus-Hefen für die Gartatigkeit der echten Weinhefen in zuckerreichen Mosten. Archiv. Mikrobiol. *18*, 342-348.

SCHULLE, H. 1953B. Über das Zusammenwirken von Hefen der Gattung *Saccharomyces* und der Untergattung *Zygosaccharomyces* bei der Vergärung von zuckerreichen Mosten. Archiv. Mikrobiol. *18*, 133-148.

SCOTT, P.M., FULEKI, T. and HARWIG, J. 1977. Patulin content of juice and wine produced from moldy grapes. J. Agric. Food Chem. *25*, 434-437.

STELLING-DEKKER, N.M. 1931. Die Sporogenen Hefen. Die Hefesammlung des "Central-bureau voor Schimmelcultures," I Teil, Amsterdam.

STEWART, G.G. and RUSSELL, I. 1977. The identification, characterization and mapping of a gene for flocculation in *Saccharomyces* sp. Can. J. Microbiol. *23*, 441-447.

SUOMALAINEN, H. and OURA, E. 1971. Yeast nutrition and solute uptake. *In* The Yeasts, Vol. 2. A.H. Rose, and J.S. Harrison (Editors). Academic Press, New York.

TANNER, F.W. 1944. The Microbiology of Foods. Garrard Press, Champaign, Illinois.

TARANTOLA, C. 1946. Nuovo contributo allo studio dei lieviti apiculati. Ann. Accad. Agric. Turino 88, 115-133. (See also Bull. Off. Intern. Vin 21 (208) 70-72. 1948).

TCHELISTCHEFF, A. 1948. Comments on cold fermentation. Univ. California College Agric. Wine. Technol. Conf., Davis, 98-101.

THORNE, R.S. 1946 The nitrogen nutrition of yeast. Wallerstein Lab. Commun. 9, 97-114.

THORNE, R.S.W. 1961. Fermentation velocity of brewery yeasts. Brewer's Dig. 36, 38-40, 43 (July).

THORNTON, R.J. and ESCHENBRUCH, R. 1976. Homothallism in wine yeasts. Antonie van Leeuwenhoek J. Microbiol. Serol. 42, 503-509.

TOLEDO, O. and GONZALVES-TEIXIERA, C. 1955. Vantaggi della associazone di lieviti nella fermentazione vinaria: riduzione dell' acidita volatile nei vini. Agric. Itali. 55, 155-164.

TOLEDO, O. and GONZALVES-TEIXIERA, C. 1957. O emprego de levaduras selecionadas na fermentação do vinho. Bol. Tecnico Instituto Agronomico Estado São-Paulo 16, 251-260.

TOLEDO, O., GONZALVES-TEIXIERA, C. and VERONA, O. 1959. Prime ricerche sopra i lieviti presenti sulle reve e nei mosti della regione viticola di S. Pãolo (Brazil). Ann. Microbiol. Enzim. 9, 22-34.

VAN DER WALT, J.P. and VAN KERKEN, A.E. 1958A. Survey of yeasts causing turbidity in South African wines. Bull. Wine Industry Research Group. Stellenbosch.

VAN DER WALT, J.P. and VAN KERKEN, A.E. 1958B. The wine yeasts of the Cape. Part I. Antonie van Leeuwenhoek J. Microbiol. Serol. 24, 239-252.

VAN DER WALT, J.P. and VAN KERKEN, A.E. 1961. The wine yeasts of the Cape. Part V. Studies on the occurence of Brettanomyces intermedius and Brettanomyces schanderlii, Antonie van Leeuwenhoek J. Microbiol. Serol. 27, 81-90.

VAN KERKEN, A.E. 1963. Contribution to the ecology of yeasts occurring in Wine. University of the Orange Free State, Pretoria. Mimeo.

VAN ZYL, J.A. 1962. Turbidity of South Africa Dry Wines Caused by the Development of Brettanomyces Yeast. Sci. Bull. 381, Dept. Agric. Tech. Serv., Pretoria.

VAN ZYL, J.A. and DU PLESSIS, W. DE L. 1961. The microbiology of South African winemaking. I. The yeast occurring in vineyards, musts and wines. S. Afr. J. Agric. Sci. 4, 393-403.

WAHAB, A., WITZKE, W. and CRUESS, W.V. 1949. Experiments with ester forming yeasts. Fruit Prod. J. 28, 198-200, 202-219.

WIKÉN, T. and RICHARD, O. 1951. Untersuchungen über die Physiologie der Weinhefen I. Mitteilung zur Kenntnis der Wachstumsbedingungen einer auxoautotrophen schweizerischen Kulturweinhefe. Antonie van Leeuwenhoek J. Microbiol. Serol. 17, 209-226; 18, 31-34, 293-315.

WOODS, D.R. and BEVAN, G.A. 1968. Studies on the nature of the killer factor produced by *Saccharomyces cerevisiae*. J. Gen. Microbiol. *51*, 115-126.

YANG, H.Y. 1973. Deacidification of grape musts with *Schizosaccharomyces pombe*. Am. J. Enol. Vitic. *24*, 1-4.

YANG, H.Y. 1975. Effect of sulfur dioxide activity on *Schizosaccharomyces pombe*. Am. J. Enol. Vitic. *26*, 1-4.

YANG, H.Y., JOHNSON, J.H., and WEIGAND, E.H. 1947. Electronic pasteurization of wine. Fruit Prod. J. *26*, 295-299.

YOKOTSUKA, I. 1954. Studies on Japanese Wine Yeasts. Research Institute of Fermentation, Yamanashi University, Kofu.

YOUNG, T.W. and PHILLIPSKIRK, G. 1975. The occurrence of killer character in yeasts of various genera. Antonie van Leeuwenhoek J. Microbiol. Serol. *41*, 147-151.

ZAMBONELLI, C. 1964. Richerche genetiche sulla produzione di idrogeno solforato in *Saccharomyces cerevisiae* var. *ellipsoideus*. Ann. Microbiol. *14*, 143-153.

5

Chemistry of Fermentation and Composition of Wines

Ethanol and many components of lesser content in wine are produced during fermentation by yeast. The solvent power of ethanol and the fermentation process also influence grape constituents that enter the wine, especially if pomace (grape skins and seeds) is present during fermentation. Other microbial actions and processing may modify wines. Further discussion is required, although grape composition has been discussed in Chap. 2 and gross wine composition by type (alcohol, acid, sugar, color) in Chap. 3.

FERMENTATION

Fermentations are metabolic processes bringing about chemical changes in organic substrates through the action of enzymes of microorganisms or other cells. The term "fermentation" originally applied only to anaerobic conditions such as wine production. Fermentation (Pasteur's "life without air") was seen as quite distinct from respiration (aerobic metabolism). Today, however, alcoholic and other anaerobic fermentations such as acetone-butyl alcohol production and lactic acid pickling fermentations have been joined by aerobic industrial fermentations of importance for production of antibiotics, citric acid, acetic acid (vinegar), etc. Yeasts can ferment either way, being facultative anaerobes, but if they grow fully aerobically no ethanol and many more yeast cells are produced.

History

Enologists rightly can be proud not only of the ancient origins of the craft of winemaking, but also of the major contributions of wine study to the emergence of science including microbiology, organic chemistry, and biochemistry. Small wonder that the violently seething, magical conversion of perishable, sweet grape juice into preservable alcoholic wine

186

was a fascinating subject for early study. Ideas drawn from fermentation permeated alchemy and made the possibility of transmitting base metals into gold seem plausible.

Separation of alcohol, tartrates (named tartarum by Paracelsus about 1500), and sugars from wine and grapes were among the first purifications of organic chemicals from nature. In 1789, Lavoisier made quantitative studies on alcoholic fermentation, one of the first such studies of a natural phenomenon. By 1815, Gay-Lussac correctly reported the overall equation for alcoholic fermentation of sugar which, converted later in molecular terms, is:

$$C_6H_{12}O_6 \rightarrow 2C_2H_5OH + 2CO_2$$

Pasteur, in his classic 1848 experiments, separated racemic (from the Latin raceme, grape cluster) tartaric acid into its *dextro-* and *levo*-rotatory optical isomers, thus making the first important advance in the understanding of stereoisomerism. About 1837, Cagniard-Latour, Schwann, and Kützing independently showed that yeast was not a chemical substance as previously thought but a living member of the vegetable kingdom. Yeasts, however, were thought to be incidental associates not the cause of alcoholic fermentation. Pasteur reasoned that, since optically active compounds were believed only produced by living systems and optically active amyl alcohol and lactic acid were produced in alcoholic and lactic fermentations, the metabolism of living microorganisms in fact caused fermentation. His publications, beginning in 1857, proved this and verified the essential validity of the Gay-Lussac equation for alcoholic fermentation by yeasts. He also found a variety of by-products, among them glycerol, acetaldehyde and acetic acid, were produced and not accounted for by the theoretical equation.

The Buchner brothers in 1897 produced zymase, a cell-free extract of yeast which would ferment sugar but was destroyed by heating. Thus, "organized ferments" (cells) produced their reactions via "unorganized ferments" or enzymes (enzyme means "in yeast"), a concept formulated by Traube in 1858. Harden and Young showed in 1905 that phosphate was essential for alcoholic fermentation. The fermentation system was gradually shown to be more complex with heat-labile enzymes and heat-stable cofactors. Neuberg and co-workers by 1918 knew that during fermentation pyruvic acid was decarboxylated to acetaldehyde and that, by prevention of the reduction of acetaldehyde to ethanol, glycerol could be made to accumulate in amounts equivalent to the acetaldehyde. This was used to make glycerol for explosives in World War I.

Further details of early history of alcoholic fermentation are given by Harden (1932). By about 1940, essentially all the basic reactions were known and found to be identical except for the last steps with the

Embden-Meyerhof glycolysis scheme whereby glucose of glycogen is converted to lactic acid by animal muscle. Elucidation of these enzymatic pathways was the first important advance in modern metabolic biochemistry and involved many of the best researchers of the period. Research continues on specific mechanisms, physical chemistry, and interactions of the various steps even though most of the enzymes have been crystallized and the sequence of reactions is clear.

Biochemistry

The reactions of alcoholic fermentation are depicted in Fig. 5.1. The hexose (6-carbon) sugars being fermented are isomerized if necessary and phosphorylated to fructose-1,6-diphosphate which is split into two triose units. The triose units are converted to pyruvic acid and this is decarboxylated to acetaldehyde. The decarboxylation step is irreversible, as is hexokinase and, although the other steps theoretically are reversible, in practice the energy input necessary is too high for significant reversal of the phosphofructokinase or phosphopyruvic transphosphorylase steps. Sugar synthesis in the grape vine does use some of the same enzymes in the reverse direction, but avoids those reactions excessively endergonic by alternative routes.

The acetaldehyde is reduced to ethanol by accepting hydrogen from reduced nicotinamide adenine dinucleotide (NADH), the heat-stabile coenzyme with alcohol dehydrogenase. During the initial induction phase of alcoholic fermentation no acetaldehyde is present and 3-phosphoglycerate is converted to glycerol. This is one example of the diversion of sugar to products other than ethanol that explains why the Gay-Lussac equation represents only the theoretical maximum yield. As acetaldehyde accumulates it becomes the hydrogen acceptor (in place of dihydroxyacetone phosphate) and reacts with NADH to produce ethyl alcohol. During the rest of a normal fermentation this process predominates and little glycerol is formed. If acetaldehyde is not available (when bound with excess sulfite, for example) glycerol is produced instead of ethanol.

In the presence of a high concentration of sulfur dioxide in acid solution, acetaldehyde, carbon dioxide, and glycerol are the primary products and alcohol a by-product. If the sulfite solution is alkaline, acetaldehyde, glycerol, alcohol, and carbon dioxide are all produced. Other types of fermentation have been reported. See Amerine (1965). The glycolytic sequence clearly shows the complexity of the system. It also shows how glycerol and acetaldehyde may accumulate as by-products.

Wine fermentations ordinarily occur in a more or less complicated mixture of many different microorganisms. Certain lactic acid bacteria,

1. Glucose $\xrightarrow[(Mg^{++}, ATP \to ADP)]{(hexokinase, EC\ 2.7.1.1)}$ glucose-6-phosphate

1a. Fructose $\xrightarrow[(Mg^{++}, ATP \to ADP)]{(hexokinase, EC\ 2.7.1.1)}$ fructose-6-phosphate

2. Glucose-6-phosphate $\xrightleftharpoons{(phosphoglucoisomerase,\ EC\ 5.3.1.9)}$ fructose-6-phosphate

3. Fructose-6-phosphate $\xrightarrow[(Mg^{++}, ATP \to ADP)]{(phosphofructokinase,\ EC\ 2.7.1.11)}$ fructose-1,6-diphosphate

4. Fructose-1,6-diphosphate $\xrightleftharpoons[(Zn^{++}, Co^{++}, Fe^{++}, Ca^{++}, or\ K^+)]{(fructose\ diphosphate\ aldolase,\ EC\ 4.1.2.13)}$ D-glyceraldehyde-3-phosphate + dihydroxyacetone phosphate

5. D-Glyceraldehyde-3-phosphate $\xrightleftharpoons{(triosephosphate\ isomerase,\ EC\ 5.3.1.1.)}$ dihydroxyacetone phosphate

5a. Dihydroxyacetone phosphate $\xrightleftharpoons[(H^+ + NADH \to NAD^+)]{(glycerolphosphate\ dehydrogenase,\ EC\ 1.1.1.8)}$ glycerol-3-phosphate

5b. Glycerol phosphate $\xrightarrow{(phosphatase)}$ glycerol + H_3PO_4

6. D-Glyceraldehyde-3-phosphate + H_3PO_4 $\xrightleftharpoons[(NAD^+ \to NADH + H^+)]{(3\text{-}phosphoglyceraldehyde\ dehydrogenase,\ EC\ 1.2.1.12)}$
   1,3-diphosphoryl-D-glycerate

7. 1,3-Diphosphoryl-D-glycerate $\xrightleftharpoons[(Mg^{++}, ADP \to ATP)]{(phosphorylglycerate\ kinase,\ EC\ 2.7.2.3)}$ 3-phosphoryl-D-glycerate

8. 3-Phosphoryl-D-glycerate $\xrightleftharpoons[(2,3\text{-}diphosphoryl\text{-}D\text{-}glycerate)]{(phosphorylglyceromutase,\ EC\ 2.7.5.3)}$ 2-phosphoryl-D-glycerate

9. 2-Phosphoryl-D-glycerate $\xrightleftharpoons[(Mg^{++})]{(enolase, EC\ 4.2.1.11)}$ phosphorylenolpyruvate

10. Phosphorylenolpyruvate $\xrightarrow[(Mg^{++}, K^+, ADP \to ATP)]{(pyruvate\ kinase, EC\ 2.7.1.40)}$ pyruvate

11. Pyruvate $\xrightarrow[TPP]{(pyruvate\ decarboxylase, EC\ 4.1.1.1)}$ acetaldehyde + CO_2

11a. Pyruvate $\xrightleftharpoons[(Zn^{++}, NADH + H^+ \to NAD^+)]{(lactic\ dehydrogenase, EC\ 1.1.1.27)}$ lactic acid

12. Acetaldehyde $\xrightleftharpoons[(NADH + H^+ \to NAD^+)]{(alcohol\ dehydrogenase, EC\ 1.1.1.1)}$ ethanol

ADP, ATP. Di- and triphosphates of adenosine.
NAD$^+$, NADH. Oxidized and reduced nicotinamide adenine dinucleotide. (NAD$^+$ was also called coenzyme I or DPN).
TPP. Thiamin pyrophosphate.

FIG. 5.1. CHEMICAL REACTIONS IN ALCOHOLIC FERMENTATION

for example, by the same Embden-Meyerhof pathway, can divert some of the sugar to lactic acid production (reaction 11a, Fig. 5.1). The Krebs tricarboxylic acid cycle enzymes also exist in yeasts and are responsible for the conversion of pyruvate completely to carbon dioxide and water in aerobic conditions. This system can explain other by-products of fermentation occurring in wine such as succinic acid. Other enzymatic systems also exist which divert sugar into amino acids, nucleosides, and other building blocks for yeast cells and by-products which appear in wine, thus also lowering the conversion to ethanol from the theoretical.

For conversion of glucose or fructose to ethanol, note that no fewer than 12 enzymes are required, at least 3 sets of cofactors (ADP-ATP, NAD$^+$-NADH, TPP) and several inorganic ions. The overall reaction becomes:

$$C_6H_{12}O_6+2ADP+4H^++2HPO_4{}^{-2} \rightarrow$$
$$2C_2H_5OH+2CO_2+2ATP+2H_2O+heat$$

For more details of sugar metabolism by yeasts see Barnett (1976).

Energy Conversion and Temperature Rise

The adenosine triphosphate (ATP) generated by fermentation serves the yeast as its source of useful energy. The overall standard free energy change of fermentation of one mole of glucose gives 234 joules (56 kcal) energy released.

If one mole of glucose is metabolized aerobically to carbon dioxide and water 2876 J (688 kcal) of energy are freed. By difference, the ethanol from the glucose could be oxidized to yield 2642 J (632 kcal). Thus, if yeast used the same proportion of energy liberated, about 2876 ÷ 234 = 12.8 times as many yeast cells would be produced from a certain amount of sugar by yeast growing aerobically instead of by anaerobic fermentation.

The net gain of two ATP units per mole of glucose fermented, based upon standard free energy of ATP hydrolysis to ADP, represents about 61 J (14.6 kcal) of energy captured by the yeast to enable it to do the work of living and multiplying. Owing to effects related to pH, existing concentrations, etc., the actual value is considerably higher, about 105 J (24 kcal). We, therefore, expect about 234 − 105 = 129 J (31 kcal) of waste heat to be liberated by the fermentation of a mole of glucose. Experimental calorimetry with wine fermentations has given values of the order of 100 J (24 kcal) per mole of glucose fermented (Bouffard 1895; Genevois 1936). The lower experimental yield of waste heat than expected from theory is again at least partly because not all of the glucose consumed is converted to ethanol and CO_2 but some to yeast cell substance and other products.

The heat generated by alcoholic fermentation and not trapped in usable form appears as an increase in temperature of the fermenting must. In very small containers the heat radiated to the environment and lost by such effects as water evaporation into the escaping carbon dioxide may prevent significant temperature rise. However, in very large or insulated fermentors the temperature rise can be large and make the fermentation difficult to control or complete and can lower wine quality. Particularly in warm climates and hot vintages, refrigeration becomes essential for good quality in commercial wines and avoidance of sticking fermentations. Owing to the variable effects of tank size, heat loss, temperature gradients, etc., in any specific winemaking situation it does not seem very useful here to discuss further the heat load and planning for its control (see Chap. 6).

The temperature rise expected if 10 g of sugar per liter is fermented would be about 1.3°C (2.3°F) from the 100 J (24 kcal) experimental value for released heat. This is, in fact, the value used as a "rule of thumb," i.e., in a fermentor with no heat loss (large or insulated) expect about 1.3°C (2.3°F) temperature rise per degree Brix drop during fermentation. This value plus the initial temperature and details of tank volume, etc., can estimate whether the fermentation will stick and how much cooling is necessary. With increased size, standardization, and sophistication of modern wineries, updated study and increased application of these principles for economy and quality are foreseen.

Yield

The yield of alcohol is of obvious practical importance to the wine maker. According to the Gay-Lussac equation, theoretical yields of 51.1% alcohol and 48.9% carbon dioxide by weight of the glucose fermented are possible. This is biologically unobtainable and in practice will depend on a variety of factors—amount of by-products, amount of sugar used by yeasts, sugars used by other microorganisms, alcohol lost by evaporation or entrainment (which in turn partially depends on the temperature and the rate of fermentation), presence of air, stirring or other movement of fermenting mass, and other factors. The best practical yardstick for yield is therefore empirical studies made under carefully controlled conditions. The following experiments are suggestive.

Various practical experiments in Europe indicate that 1% alcohol by volume can be obtained from 16—17 g of sugar whereas the stoichiometric yield is 1% from 15.65 g. Gvaladze (1936) found yields of alcohol varying from 47.86 to 48.12% and of carbon dioxide of from 47.02 to 47.68% of the weight of sugar fermented. In other words, in practice, yields are about 90—95% of the theoretical.

Warkentin and Nury (1963) evaluated literature reports of alcohol losses during fermentation. The high losses reported by Banolas (1948) they attribute to using the vapor pressures of pure compounds in his calculations. The low results of Stradelli (1951) they believe due to the assumption that the alcohol-water-sugar system follows Raoult's law. Marsh (1958) has summarized estimation of the sugar content of musts and alcohol yields as shown in Table 5.1.

TABLE 5.1. YIELD OF ALCOHOL FROM MUST

Must		Brix −3.0			g/liter −30	
Brix	sp gr $\frac{}{20°/20°}$	sp gr $\frac{}{20°/20°}$	Sugar[1] g/100 ml	Alcohol[2] %/vol	Sugar[3] g/100 ml	Alcohol[2] %/vol
15	1.061	1.048	12.56	7.4	12.89	7.6
20	1.083	1.070	18.15	10.7	18.62	11.0
25	1.106	1.092	23.98	14.1	24.59	14.5
30	1.126	1.115	30.05	17.8	30.81	18.2

[1](°Brix − 3.0) × sp gr = g/100 ml of sugar. The 3.0 is an average; it may be as low as 2.5 or as high as 3.5.
[2]G/100 ml of sugar × 0.59 = %/vol of alcohol.
[3](°Brix of must × sp gr of must) − 3.0 = g/100 ml of sugar.

Marsh (1951) notes that a rough approximation of proof gallons per ton of grapes is obtained from the formula (Brix minus 3.0) × 284.5 × (100 minus % pomace). The number of proof gallons of alcohol in dry table wines is simply the percentage of alcohol × 2 × volume of wine at 15.6°C (60°F). For dessert and sweet wines the proof gallon equivalent of the alcohol plus the remaining sugar may be obtained from Table 5.2 which has been abbreviated from the original. These values enable estimation of the overall fermentation efficiency and pinpointing of losses in wineries. The percentage of unfermentable material varies from variety to variety. For the same variety, it varies during the season depending on the degree of dehydration of the stems, ratio of skins to pulp (which also varies with the size of the fruit), the percentage of raisins present, and on other factors. For grapes of about 21° to 23° Brix, yields of 20−25 gal. of alcohol per ton of grapes may be expected. The wine makers, of course, want to get the maximum yield but so many variables affect it that except for very large operations no single factor is likely to prove controlling. This is particularly true when there are marked differences in the composition of grapes between seasons. It should be particularly emphasized that delivery or tank Brix is very unreliable for establishing yield. It seldom includes a proportionate amount of juice from shriveled or raisined berries. During fermentation the sugar of such fruit is dissolved and markedly increases the fermentable sugar. Deceptively high alcohol yields, based on the original load or tank Brix, are then obtained.

Berti (1951) and Marsh (1958) have both studied this for California conditions. Berti's results on the theoretical yields of wine for different must Brix and losses are shown in Table 5.3.

TABLE 5.2. PROOF GALLON EQUIVALENTS PER GALLON OF WINE

Brix of Wine	Percentage Alcohol by Volume											
	14.0	15.0	16.0	17.0	18.0	18.5	19.0	19.5	20.0	20.5	21.0	21.5
−4.0	—	—	—	—	—	—	0.38166	0.39315	0.40464	0.41623	0.42782	0.43938
−3.5	—	—	—	—	0.36418	0.37573	0.38730	0.39887	0.41044	0.42205	0.43366	0.44526
−3.0	—	—	0.3234	0.34072	0.36974	0.38128	0.39282	0.40439	0.41586	0.42750	0.43916	0.45077
−2.5	0.28804	0.30574	0.32910	0.34648	0.37552	0.38709	0.39866	0.41023	0.42180	0.43338	0.44496	0.45657
−2.0	0.29392	0.31140	0.33472	0.35232	0.38116	0.39271	0.40426	0.41583	0.42740	0.43898	0.45056	0.46217
−1.5	0.29964	0.31724	0.34054	0.35802	0.38700	0.39855	0.41010	0.42166	0.43322	0.44481	0.45640	0.46800
−1.0	0.30542	0.32298	0.34624	0.36380	0.39272	0.40426	0.41580	0.42734	0.43892	0.45052	0.46212	0.47372
−0.5	0.31132	0.32882	0.35214	0.36952	0.39856	0.41010	0.42164	0.43320	0.44476	0.45635	0.46794	0.47954
0.0	0.31720	0.33464	0.35796	0.37536	0.40440	0.41593	0.42746	0.43902	0.45058	0.46216	0.47374	0.48534
0.5	0.32314	0.34050	0.36372	0.38120	0.41020	0.42177	0.43334	0.44488	0.45642	0.46800	0.47958	0.49117
1.0	0.32904	0.34644	0.36974	0.38704	0.41612	0.42767	0.43922	0.45077	0.46232	0.47390	0.48548	0.49706
1.5	0.33494	0.35234	0.37564	0.39296	0.42202	0.43356	0.44510	0.45664	0.46818	0.47976	0.49134	0.50293
2.0	0.34090	0.35824	0.38154	0.39886	0.42790	0.43945	0.45100	0.46254	0.47408	0.48566	0.49722	0.50880
2.5	0.34686	0.36420	0.38748	0.40472	0.43380	0.44536	0.45692	0.46846	0.48000	0.49158	0.50316	0.51475
3.0	0.35286	0.37016	0.39344	0.41070	0.43976	0.45130	0.46286	0.47439	0.48594	0.49750	0.50906	0.52064
3.5	0.35886	0.37614	0.39942	0.41670	0.44578	0.45730	0.46882	0.48037	0.49192	0.50349	0.51506	0.52663
4.0	0.36490	0.38214	0.40544	0.42262	0.45178	0.46330	0.47482	0.48636	0.49790	0.50946	0.52102	0.53262
4.5	0.37098	0.38820	0.41148	0.42862	0.45778	0.46931	0.48084	0.49238	0.50390	0.51547	0.52704	0.53861
5.0	0.37702	0.39426	0.41752	0.43464	0.46384	0.47537	0.48690	0.49843	0.50996	0.52152	0.53308	0.54466
5.5	0.38313	0.40034	0.42360	0.44070	0.46992	0.48143	0.49294	0.50448	0.51602	0.52757	0.53912	0.55070
6.0	0.38932	0.40644	0.42972	0.44678	0.47600	0.48752	0.49904	0.51057	0.52208	0.53365	0.54522	0.55679
6.5	0.39548	0.41258	0.43584	0.45286	0.48206	0.49361	0.50516	0.51669	0.52822	0.53977	0.55132	0.56289
7.0	0.40166	0.41872	0.44198	0.45900	0.48826	0.49977	0.51128	0.52280	0.53432	0.54588	0.55744	0.56901
7.5	0.40786	0.42490	0.44816	0.46512	0.49442	0.50593	0.51744	0.52897	0.54050	0.55204	0.56358	0.57515
8.0	0.41412	0.43112	0.45438	0.47130	0.50062	0.51212	0.52362	0.53514	0.54666	0.55823	0.56978	0.58133
8.5	0.42038	0.43736	0.46058	0.47750	0.50684	0.51837	0.52990	0.54139	0.55288	0.56444	0.57600	0.58755
9.0	0.42664	0.44360	0.46684	0.48372	0.51308	0.52458	0.53608	0.54760	0.55912	0.57066	0.58220	0.59376

Source of data: Marsh (1951).

TABLE 5.3. THEORETICAL ALCOHOL YIELD

Alcohol (%)	Sugar (°Brix)	Must Brix					
		18°	20°	20°	20°	22°	24°
		Percentage Loss					
		10	8	10	12	10	10
		Gallons per Ton					
20	No sugar	98	112	110	108	123	136
20	6	76	87	86	83	96	105
20	7	74	85	83	81	93	103
21	6	72	83	81	79	91	101

The effect of strain of yeast on alcohol yield has been extensively studied. The problem is complicated, as Amerine (1954) has noted, by the fact that total soluble solids, not fermentable sugar, has been measured in most studies. Unless actual reducing sugar is measured it appears useless to try to establish an exact relationship between sugar and alcohol yield. Possibly under conditions of a given region and a limited number of grape varieties a useful factor can be found, but such a factor varies from season to season (Amerine 1954).

FACTORS INFLUENCING FERMENTATION

Only the most important factors which affect the process of alcoholic fermentation of grapes will be considered here. For more details see books on the physiology of yeasts such as Cook (1958), Rose and Harrison (1969–1971), and Schanderl (1959). Most wine yeasts (strains of S. cerevisiae) can grow on a medium which provides utilizable sources of energy and carbon, nitrogen and certain inorganic salts. Wine grape musts are normally very good culture media for wine yeasts and require no supplementation for fermentation to wine. With juices of other fruit and sometimes with refermentation, especially of mishandled grape musts or wines, this may not be true.

Carbon and Energy Sources

Certain sugars, particularly glucose, fructose, sucrose, and maltose (Barnett 1976) are the normal substrate for wine yeasts, but they do not ferment lactose, pentose, dextrins, or starch. They also can grow on a variety of other carbon sources especially aerobically. Acetic acid, for example, can be utilized by yeasts and during the early stages of fermentation appreciable amounts of acetic acid can disappear. Wine yeasts also oxidize ethyl alcohol but only certain strains will grow on it. Most wine yeasts ferment glucose more rapidly than fructose even though fructofuranose has an affinity for hexokinase twice that of any form of glucose. The Sauternes' strain S. bailii ferments fructose more rapidly.

Gottschalk (1946) believes this is because the cell walls of this strain are more permeable to fructose. Szabó and Rakcsányi (1937) found glucose to ferment more rapidly when the musts contained 17−20% reducing sugar. Between 20 and 25% both sugars fermented at the same rate, while at higher concentrations fructose fermented more rapidly.

Fructose is much sweeter than glucose. According to Koch and Bretthauer (1960), the glucose/fructose ratio can be increased by sugaring with partially-fermented wine, sucrose, or grape juice. This gives the wine a less sweet taste for a given total sugar content. Use of yeasts preferring glucose could result in sweeter wines at the same total sugar content.

Above about 25%, sugar retards fermentation and at even higher levels (about 70%) most wine yeasts will not ferment. This is partially owing to the osmotic effect. The fermentation of German *Trockenbeerenauslese* musts of 40 to 67% sugar is very slow according to Schanderl (1959) with a final alcohol content of only 5 to 9%. He notes also that alcohol-tolerant yeasts have been known to ferment *Auslese* wines up to 16% alcohol. At higher sugar content there is also an increase in volatile acid production (Fig. 5.2).

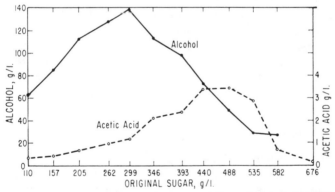

From Schanderl (1959)

FIG. 5.2. EFFECT OF SUGAR CONCENTRATION ON ALCOHOL AND VOLATILE ACID PRODUCTION

The optimum sugar concentration for maximum speed of fermentation is fairly low, perhaps only 1−2%. For maximum yield of alcohol per gram of sugar fermented the optimum sugar concentration is higher but has not been established for grape musts. It certainly varies depending on the other constituents of the must, the temperature, the strain of yeast (p. 209). Gray (1945) for distillers' yeast reported diminished yields of alcohol per gram of sugar fermented at above 5% glucose. The maximum alcohol content obtainable in normal winery practice is from musts of 25 to 35% sugar and is up to about 18%. However, this varies with strain of yeast (p. 168), temperature, conditions of aeration, and the method of conducting the fermentation. For syruped fermentations it is higher (see p. 439). Yeasts acclimatized to ferment at higher sugar concentrations may be reduced in alcohol tolerance.

According to Delle (1911), 4.8% sugar has the same repressing influence on alcohol fermentation as 1% by volume of alcohol. Amerine and Kunkee (1965) show that the repressing influence of sugar is greater when the fortification is made in the early stages of fermentation compared to later stages. There was a small effect of variety and yeast strain. The practical implication is that wines of lower alcohol could be safely marketed at high sugar contents.

Alcohol

Alcohol itself has an inhibiting effect on fermentation which increases with temperature. This effect is, of course, related to the maximum yield of alcohol which can be expected from various sugar concentrations. The direct effect of alcohol and its dependence on temperature has been demonstrated in this simple experiment by Schanderl (1959). A wine was dealcoholized to various percentages of alcohol, yeasts were introduced, and the samples held at 50°C (122°F) for 1 to 5 min. The percentage of the yeast surviving was 15% in 1 min, and 0.22% at 5 min with 0% alcohol, but 1.5% and 0.04% with 3% alcohol, and 0.20% and 0.002% with 9% alcohol.

Carbon Dioxide and Pressure

The effect of carbon dioxide in alcoholic fermentation is too often neglected. Schmitthenner (1950) showed that a carbon dioxide content of 15 g per liter (about 7.2 atm) essentially stopped yeast growth. The carbon dioxide effect on yeast growth did not prevent alcoholic fermentation. A much higher carbon dioxide pressure, up to 30 atm, was necessary to halt alcoholic fermentation. Especially important is his observation that *Lactobacillus* can grow at high carbon dioxide pressures. This may explain some of the differences in pressure fermentation by various experimenters according to the amount and nature of microflora present and their varying effects on the character and quality of the product. Schanderl (1959) reports *Lactobacillus* and *Mucor racemosus* in pressure tanks. Also present were *Torulopsis* sp. and *Kloeckera* sp., both of which produced acetic acid under carbon dioxide pressure. Carbon dioxide pressure is especially inhibitory to yeasts at low pH or high alcohol levels (Kunkee and Ough 1966).

Pressure tanks for controlling the rate of fermentation have been employed in Germany, South Africa, Australia and elsewhere. The basic text of the process of pressure fermentation is that of Geiss (1952). The fermentations are conducted in pressure tanks in which the fermentation is allowed to build up to 2 to 4 atm depending on the stage of fermentation in order to keep the rate of fermentation essentially constant. The main advantage of the procedure is that there is a greater yield of alcohol per gram of sugar fermented (owing to less growth of yeast). Moreover, pressure fermentations often do not go to completion and this is considered an advantage for the high acid German musts. Higher ester contents are also reported. While the process appears to be useful for sugared German musts the results have not all been favorable and Amerine and Ough (1957) could not recommend it for California conditions on the basis of the higher volatile acid production. The practice has been largely abandoned presumably because of higher costs and questionable benefit compared to control by lowering temperature. A large Australian installation of 10,000-gal. pressure tanks is shown in Fig. 5.3.

Acids

Little attention has been paid to the effects of fixed organic acids on the alcoholic fermentation of musts. If the pH is very low, 3.0 or lower, fermentation is somewhat reduced. Yeasts are, however, not very sensitive to the amounts of fixed organic acids present in normal musts. There may be some effect of organic acids on the by-products of alcoholic fermentation. The acids, are, however, important in maintaining the pH low enough so as to inhibit the growth of many undesirable bacteria, thus giving a growth advantage to wine yeasts.

Fatty acids such as acetic, butyric, and propionic, do have a decided inhibitory effect on yeasts. Fortunately, the amounts present in normal fermenting musts are far below the critical concentration. However, sticking of acetified musts has been noted and there they may be important (pp. 275 and 558).

Nitrogen

Normal wine yeasts can synthesize their own needed amino acids from ammonium ions or certain other simple nitrogen sources and sugar carbon. Although they have no absolute requirements for amino acids, the amino acids of musts are important as nitrogen sources and do stimulate the rate of yeast growth. Most grape musts contain adequate nitrogen

Courtesy of G. Gramp and Sons, Ltd.

FIG. 5.3. REFRIGERATED PRESSURE TANKS (10,000 GALLONS) IN AUSTRALIA

for 4 or 5 fermentations. Except in very unusual cases, nitrogen addition to fermenting grape musts is not necessary. Sparkling wines for the secondary fermentation can profit by nitrogen addition in particular circumstances according to Schanderl (1959). He recommended addition of ammonium salts in such cases. Fruit musts are often deficient in nitrogen and urea or ammonium phosphate must be added. Yeasts also utilize the small amounts of ammonia present in musts and the relative amount present is an important factor in fermentation rate (Ough 1964).

The familiar decrease in nitrogen in the must and increase in the yeast are shown in Fig. 5.4. Nilov and Valuĭko (1958) reported less nitrogen loss from the solution (and incorporation into the yeasts) in the absence of air, as expected from the increased cell production in air. This was reported to be true for total nitrogen, amino nitrogen, and protein nitrogen. Aeration seemed to cause more nitrogen incorporation at lower temperatures. True proteins, however, cannot be readily hydrolyzed nor taken in by wine yeast cells as shown by survival of grape proteins in white wine.

Since each generation of yeasts reduces the nitrogen content of the must, stable sweet table wines might be produced by growing successive generations of yeasts in musts and filtering off the yeasts early in the alcoholic fermentation. This is actually practiced in Italy for the production of very sweet, low alcohol, sparkling *moscato spumante*. According to Schanderl (1959), the total nitrogen content is reduced to 30 to 50 mg/liter with no ammonia and the wine is stable as far as further alcoholic fermentation is concerned. However, in California the desired stability has not been reached when this has been tried. A more rational approach would be to develop mutant yeast strains which had an absolute demand for critical amino acids. Upon depletion of these required amino acids yeast growth would be greatly inhibited.

Growth Factors

Yeasts may respond to accessory growth factors. Among those found desirable or necessary with certain yeasts are biotin, inositol, nicotinic acid, pantothenic acid, *p*-aminobenzoic acid, pyridoxine, and thiamin. However, under winery conditions conclusive results as to the value of adding growth factors to musts have not been obtained. This is undoubtedly due to the fact that several of these are present in appreciable quantities in musts (pp. 107−108) and also to the fact that yeasts can themselves produce some in sufficient quantities.

Biotin is an absolute requirement of most strains of *Saccharomyces* including the wine yeasts, yet doubling the amount of biotin and several other growth factors present in grape musts did not increase the fermentation rate (Ough and Kunkee 1968). Additions of thiamin have given marginal improvements in alcohol yield in some trials, but not in others including some of large scale.

Although sulfur dioxide destroys thiamin, addition of this vitamin to desulfited grape juice did not activate fermentation in the experiments of Flanzy and Ournac (1963). Lafon-Lafourcade and Peynaud (1965) believe that the liberation of pyruvic acid indicates that alcoholic fermentations progress with deficiency of thiamin.

Generally, grape musts are adequate in growth factors. Ough and Kunkee (1968) found that the natural biotin content correlated with fermentation rate but only as an indicator of a must's micronutrient content in general. Even though lactic acid bacteria generally have higher requirements than yeasts for biotin and several other growth factors, malo-lactic fermentations generally proceed well at the end of alcoholic fermentation.

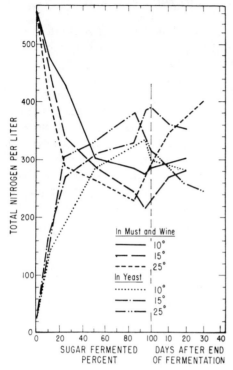

FIG. 5.4. CHANGES IN TOTAL NITROGEN DURING AND AFTER FERMENTATION IN MUSTS AND IN YEASTS FERMENTING THEM

From Nilov and Valuĭko (1958)

Joslyn (1951) has summarized the studies on the nutrilite requirements of yeast, noting especially that yeasts during a long incubation period may grow in the absence of most nutrilites, whereas to give rapid growth several may be required.

Minerals

The normal course of alcoholic fermentation requires magnesium, potassium, zinc, cobalt, iodine, iron, calcium, copper, and anions of phosphorus and sulfur. For growth alone, yeasts require copper, iron, magnesium, potassium, phosphorus, and sulfur. Adequate amounts are supplied by grape juices and, with the occasional exception of phosphate, most other fruit juices.

The presence of excessive iron (over 6 mg/liter) and copper as factors in hindering the fermentation of sparkling wines have been noted by

Schanderl (1959). The amounts of copper noted as inhibitory were far above those normally encountered in practice, at least in this state. Aluminum is also an inhibitor of fermentation, if 25 or more mg/liter are present.

Yeasts are able to reduce sulfate ions to sulfite and on to sulfide and incorporate the sulfide into its essential sulfur-containing constituents, notably cysteine and methionine. The biochemical scheme is outlined in Fig. 5.5. Eschenbruch (1974) has reviewed the complex problem of high and low production of sulfite and of hydrogen sulfide in wines by different yeasts under different conditions. Most wine yeasts produce 10 to 30 mg/liter of sulfite from sulfate during fermentation, but some strains produce below 10 and others over 100 mg/liter. With added sulfate ions more than 500 mg/liter of sulfite has been produced by some high-sulfite strains of wine yeast. The production of high sulfite is yeast-strain specific and parallels fermentation and cell production (Dott *et al.* 1976). It appears that the highest producing strains can produce sufficient sulfite to be even self-inhibitory, and sulfite production is seen as a natural competitive advantage for the yeast over bisulfite-sensitive microorganisms.

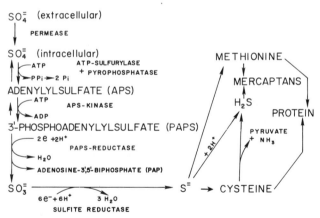

FIG. 5.5. SULFUR METABOLISM IN WINE FERMENTATION

The high sulfite-producing strains appear to have, compared to the more normal strains, enzymes with a higher saturation level for sulfate and ATP and to have escaped feedback inhibition from sulfide and certain other intermediates (Heinzel and Trüper 1976). The production of hydrogen sulfide by yeasts appears to be only partially strain-dependent and the relation to high sulfite production appears complex. Low sulfite producers tend to produce more hydrogen sulfide than do high-producing yeasts unless cysteine is added to the medium (Eschenbruch and Bonish 1976). Addition of methionine tends to suppress sulfate reduction and hydrogen sulfide production, but other undesirable products can form (Eschenbruch 1974). Pantothenate deficiency, excess copper content, and other factors can increase hydrogen sulfide production in wine yeast fermentations. Selection of a wine yeast producing low sulfite, low hydrogen sulfide, and capable of synthesizing adequate pantothenate is recommended.

Yeasts can reduce elemental sulfur occurring in musts because of application to vines as a fungicide. This is ordinarily the main source of hydrogen sulfide in wine, and since cell-free yeast extracts can reduce sulfur to H_2S, production of high levels of H_2S in wines appears mainly the result of the content of reducing agents (NADH?) and the accessibility of the sulfur particles (fine dispersion, etc.) (Schütz and Kunkee 1977). Hydrogen sulfide formation in white wines ordinarily can be eliminated by settling or centrifuging to remove high density solids and with them the hydrogen sulfide precursor, presumably dusting sulfur (Singleton et al. 1975). Oxidation of any hydrogen sulfide formed to elemental sulfur followed by clarification may serve the same purpose in red wines. Prevention or very early removal of H_2S is recommended because with time mercaptan derivatives are produced with even more intractable odors.

Antiseptics

The value of addition of sulfur dioxide to wines was probably known to the early Egyptians and Romans. Since about 1911, it has been universally employed to protect containers as well as wine. Since sulfur dioxide or sulfite is a product of normal yeast fermentation, it is present in young wine whether or not it is added. When sulfur dioxide is dissolved in an aqueous solution an equilibrium between various forms is set up:

$$SO_2 \text{ (gas)} \rightleftharpoons SO_2 \text{ (aq.)}$$
$$SO_2 \text{ (aq.)} + H_2O \rightleftharpoons H_2SO_3$$
$$H_2SO_3 \rightleftharpoons H^+ + HSO_3^- \qquad K_1 = 1.7 \times 10^{-2}$$
$$HSO_3^- \rightleftharpoons H^+ + SO_3^= \qquad K_2 = 5 \times 10^{-6}$$
$$2HSO_3^- \rightleftharpoons S_2O_5^= + H_2O$$

All forms of sulfur dioxide in this equilibrium are known as free sulfur dioxide.

Sulfurous acid (H_2SO_3) apparently does not exist and the hydrated dissolved gas dissociates directly, but it is often written as H_2SO_3. The effect of pH on the relative amounts of the various forms of sulfur dioxide is shown in Fig. 5.6. Not only is the antiseptic property of sulfur dioxide due mainly to the free and unbound forms, but specifically to the undissociated dissolved SO_2. Thus, it will take considerably more "free SO_2" at pH 3.8 than it would at pH 3.2 to provide the same inhibitory level of hydrated SO_2 (Fig. 5.6).

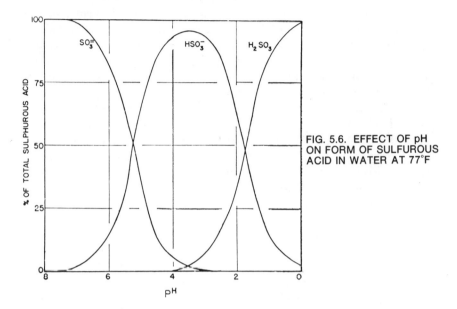

FIG. 5.6. EFFECT OF pH ON FORM OF SULFUROUS ACID IN WATER AT 77°F

The bisulfite ion $(HSO_3{}^-)$ can react with aldehydes, dextrins, pectic substances, proteins, ketones and certain sugars to form bisulfite addition compounds:

$$\underset{O}{\overset{H}{R\overset{|}{C}O}} + HOSO^- \rightarrow HO\overset{H}{\underset{R}{C}}-\overset{O}{\underset{O}{S}}O^-$$

These are the forms known as fixed or bound sulfur dioxide. Acetaldehyde reacts preferentially with the bisulfite but as more sulfur dioxide is added, or in musts, some will react with glucose. It is rare to find a wine with sufficient sulfurous acid in excess of acetaldehyde to combine with sugars, and sulfur dioxide only combines with sugars with a free aldehyde group (Gehman and Osman 1954; Joslyn and Braverman 1954). The amount fixed and the speed of binding are lower and slower the lower the pH.

The ratio of free to bound in a given wine depends on the temperature, the amounts and kinds of binding agents, and the pH. The percentage of sulfur dioxide fixed at 20°C (68°F) at pH 3−4 with 50 mg/liter of free sulfur dioxide in cider was determined for various compounds by Burroughs and Whiting (1960) as follows: acetaldehyde 100, pyruvic acid 66, α-ketoglutaric acid 47, L-xylosone 27, monogalacturonic acid 2.5, trigalacturonic acid 2.1, xylose 1.1, and glucose 0.12. Burroughs and Sparks (1973) were able to chromatographically separate the bound forms and by use of equilibrium constants account completely for the SO_2-binding capacity of a wine from rotten grapes and slightly less completely for the much lower binding capacity of a sound wine. The extra binding capacity of the wine from grapes seriously affected by molds and bacteria was from microbially-produced carbonyl compounds, particularly the dicarbonyls 2,5-diketogluconic acid, D-*threo*-2,5-hexodiulose,and L-xylosone. In the botrytized white sweet table wines of Bordeaux such components appear to account for 40 to 80% of the total sulfur dioxide (Blouin 1963).

Although the antiseptic property of sulfur dioxide is due mainly to the free form, Fornachon (1963) indicated that the level of sulfur dioxide bound to acetaldehyde was important in determining whether lactic acid bacteria will grow in wines. He reported that this varied with the strain of bacteria. Finally, when sulfur dioxide and excess acetaldehyde were present, certain strains of lactic acid bacteria rapidly attacked the aldehyde and liberated sufficient sulfur dioxide to prevent further growth. After fermentation, sulfur dioxide should be added in sufficient quantities to completely combine with acetaldehyde. Sulfur dioxide gives lasting protection against enzymatic oxidation but little against nonenzymatic oxidation due to slow exposure to air during aging.

Acetaldehyde bound by sulfur dioxide is not reducible to ethanol by the yeast's enzymes, as active fermentation soon binds the available free bisulfite. Extra glycerol as well as more bound acetaldehyde is produced, as discussed earlier, with high levels of sulfur dioxide. However, up to 200 mg/liter of SO_2 added to musts did not significantly change the glycerol content of wines in experiments by Ough *et al.* (1972).

Not only does the antiseptic power of sulfur dioxide depend on the forms present but on the kind and activity of the microorganisms. Yeasts can be acclimated to grow and ferment in the presence of high amounts of sulfur dioxide. Schanderl (1959) has shown, moreover, that a sulfite-tolerant yeast is more sensitive to sulfur dioxide at high concentrations than a nonacclimatized strain of the same yeast. He reported yeasts which fermented in the presence of 1000 mg/liter of sulfur dioxide at pH 3.18. Yeasts are also more sensitive to sulfur dioxide in the presence of alcohol, at the same pH, than in its absence. Since sulfur dioxide reduces the oxidation-reduction potential of musts Schanderl believes this may have an effect in slowing down fermentation—aside from any antiseptic property. Musts with an rH value of 20.2 ferment more rapidly than those at rH 18.2.

Some bacteria are sensitive to very small amounts of sulfur dioxide. Molds and many yeasts are very sensitive to sulfur dioxide and most microorganisms are repressed with no more than 100 mg/liter of sulfur dioxide at normally acidic pH. Some effects of sulfur dioxide in preventing volatile acid formation by bacteria are shown in Table 5.4.

TABLE 5.4. EFFECT OF SULFUR DIOXIDE IN PREVENTING HIGH VOLATILE ACIDITY IN WINES[1]

	Method of Fermentation			Num-ber of Sam-ples	Percentage of Samples Containing Viable Lactic Acid Bacteria	Composition of Wine, Percent			
Year	Metabi-sulfite Added	Cool-ing	Pure Yeast			Alco-hol	Vola-tile Acid	Total Acid	Sugar
1913	No	No	No	101	100	11.5	0.118	0.66	0.49
	Yes	No	No	6	0	12.6	0.048	0.50	0.42
	Yes	No	Yes	67	0	12.1	0.066	0.57	0.21
1934	No	No	No	81	81	12.7	0.173	0.80	0.52
	Yes	No	No	64	20	11.6	0.064	0.71	0.21
	Yes	No	Yes	21	80	13.4	0.087	0.62	0.36
	Yes	Yes	Yes	69	14	12.4	0.060	0.50	0.17

[1]Sources of data: Cruess (1935A, B).

Schanderl (1959) believes that the fungicidal action of sulfur dioxide on wild yeasts has been exaggerated. The concentration of free sulfur dioxide is small in must and its effect better explained on the basis of antioxidative action—wine yeasts growing better under anaerobic conditions.

Sulfur dioxide is less effective when the yeasts are in full fermentation, no doubt because the sulfur dioxide is fixed by the acetaldehyde as it is produced. This is one reason why a single addition of sulfur dioxide is more effective than the same total amount added in smaller doses during fermentation. The latter procedure also results in a high fixed sulfur dioxide content. There are also losses by entrainment.

Sulfur dioxide helps prevent the malo-lactic fermentation, which is desirable in some cases but not in others. For other properties of sulfur dioxide see pp. 264–267. There is a long controversy as to the animal toxicity of sulfites. Causert et al. (1964) reported no anatomical or physiological problems due to ingestion of sulfite but there was a marked and significant decrease in excretion of thiamin and an increase in urinary excretion of calcium when sulfites were ingested. They recommend caution in consumption of wines approaching 450 mg/liter of sulfur dioxide. The data of DeEds (1961) and Lanteaume et al. (1969) also indicated little danger of toxicity. The sulfur of cysteine and methionine is catabolized via sulfite to sulfate by a person's sulfite oxidase and added sulfur dioxide apparently can be metabolized the same way (Anon. 1975).

Substitutes for Sulfur Dioxide and Yeast Inhibitors

While sulfur dioxide is universally used for its antiseptic and antioxidative properties there is general agreement that the odor of free sulfur dioxide is undesirable. There has been, therefore, a long search for a substitute. Owing to the multiple effects of sulfur dioxide, a single substitute remains unlikely.

Because of their toxicity, salicylic acid, monobromoacetic and monochloroacetic acids, ethylene oxide and numerous other antiseptics have been prohibited. Benzoic acid has not been used because of its low yeast toxicity and also because public health regulations frequently require a statement in the label of the amount used. Heptyl p-hydroxybenzoate was found by Chan et al. (1975) to be a potent inhibitor of malo-lactic bacteria in wine and in combination with the analogous 6- and 8-carbon alcohol esters, each at about 10 mg/liter, also inhibited yeast.

Ascorbic acid has been widely used in Germany as an antioxidant. The most detailed study of its effectiveness is that of Kielhöfer (1959). He found that small amounts of free sulfur dioxide could not be replaced completely by ascorbic acid because ascorbic acid does not bind acetaldehyde as sulfur dioxide does. For most white table wines there is presently no substitute for free sulfur dioxide.

Sulfur dioxide alone is not effective for inhibition of wine yeast regrowth in slightly sweetened table wines.

Applications of fungicides which remain in the grapes can cause inhibition of alcoholic fermentation. Captan has been found by Castor et al. (1957) to interfere with yeast growth, but, of course, is not suitable for wine treatment.

Sorbic acid can be an effective inhibitor of yeasts (see Auerbach 1959 and p. 267). Most countries permit addition of a maximum of 200 to 300 mg/liter to wine (Würdig 1976). The United States presently permits 1000 mg/liter, but this level yields flavor and is not used in practice. The minimum effective dose in inhibiting wine yeasts in slightly sweet, low alcohol wines is variable, with low acid, high pH, and lower alcohol requiring more. The amount generally added is 180 to 220 mg/liter and, because of solubility, potassium sorbate is used. Sorbic acid is not very effective against some wine bacteria and therefore should be used along with sufficient sulfur dioxide to prevent malo-lactic fermentation. Whether sorbate should be used in wines high in sulfur dioxide has not been established.

There are two potential flavor problems with the use of sorbic acid. The sensory threshold for sorbic acid in wine is about 135 mg/liter with some persons sensitive to 50 mg/liter (Ough and Ingraham 1960). Although oxidation may lead to an extra "oxidized fat" note there is a somewhat butter-like off-odor arising in well-stored wine after addition of sufficient sorbic acid. It has generally been satisfactory to reduce the sulfur dioxide by heat treatments required for stability of sweet table wines for current consumption but use of sorbate in high-quality or long-stored wines is contraindicated.

The second flavor problem which occurs in wine or in stored juice involves development by lactic bacterial action of a geranium-like off-odor. This involves conversion of sorbic acid to the very potent odorant 2-ethoxyhexa-3,5-diene (Crowell and Guymon 1975). This has led to considerable financial losses in some instances, especially when affected sorbic-treated juice has been used to sweeten additional wine, notably in the 1971 vintage in Germany (Laubenheimer 1974).

Diethylpyrocarbonate (DEPC) was first used as an antiseptic and yeast sterilant in wine by Hennig (1960). It appeared nearly ideal: it could kill yeasts and other microorganisms in wine, it was needed only at low dosage (about 100 mg/liter), it was unstable and did not persist in wine, and it decomposed largely to ethanol and carbon dioxide. It rapidly gained commercial acceptance after a few problems, notably satisfactorily rapid and complete dispersion in wine, were solved. Since it was a sterilant but short-lived, sterile bottles, corks and faultless technique were necessary.

A sensory difference was produced with 280 mg/liter of DEPC or more (Cooke *et al.* 1964). This appeared to be from a small amount of ethyl carbonate produced in the decomposition of DEPC in wine. A report that addition of DEPC to food produced urethane, known to be carcinogenic under some circumstances, caused rapid abandonment of DEPC usage and prohibition in the United States in 1972. Subsequently, more careful and detailed studies have shown the original report to be greatly in error in the amount of urethane generated (Ough 1976A,B).

All nonfermented beverages and foods appear to be free of natural urethane, while all fermented foods, including bread, beer, soy sauce sake, yogurt and wine have natural amounts at a few parts per billion level. The addition of DEPC to wines changes the amounts of urethane only slightly if the ammonia content is low (less than 10 mg/liter) and the pH is less than 3.5. The methyl analog of DEPC—dimethyl dicarbonate (DMDC)—appears to be a potential substitute incapable of yielding urethane although it is not yet legal or fully tested.

Antibiotics

Antibiotics have been recommended for the beer industry and may find a place in wine making. The public health aspects of their use require, however, careful consideration. While antibiotics appear attractive there are definite limitations to their use. Gillissen (1954) has summarized these as follows: must not be toxic in large amounts in a short period, man must not be sensitive to them, they should not cause the resistance of microorganisms to increase, the normal bacterial flora of man should not be harmed, they must not be toxic to man when used in small amounts over a long period, they should be specific for undesirable microorganisms in wines, in wine they should be odorless and tasteless, and the constituents of wine should not affect their activity. To these requirements we would add that any antiseptic added to wine should be easy to detect and to determine quantitatively.

Actidione, mycosubtilin and other antibiotics have been tested by Ribéreau-Gayon et al. (1952A), by Kielhöfer (1953), and others. Vitamin K_5 has been tested by Yang et al. (1958). Yang and Orser (1962) used 10 mg/liter plus 100 mg/liter of sulfur dioxide to stabilize sweet table wines. The odor threshold is 50 mg/liter. Some darkening of white wines was noted. Many antibiotics are effective for short periods of time, but none is presently permitted by federal regulations. An antibiotic naturally present in musts infected with *Botrytis cinerea* was reported by Ribéreau-Gayon et al. (1952B). This may be partially responsible for the slow fermentation of botrytised grapes. (See, however, p. 160.)

Tannins

Singleton and Esau (1969) reviewed the evidence and concluded that the natural phenols of grapes or wine including the tannins and tannin-pigment polymers are definitely inhibitory to yeasts and bacteria. However, the inhibitory effect is of such a low order that it rarely has practical significance and only in cases of combinations of inhibitory factors. Some difficulties in sparkling wine fermentations appear related to phenol content. Certainly, table wines too astringent for consumption undergo alcoholic and malo-lactic fermentation generally without problems from tannin. There is some evidence for effects ranging from stimulation to inhibition of yeasts by different specific phenols. Adsorption of tannin to the cell surface is one source of inhibitory effect.

Temperature

The optimum temperature for fermentation by most wine yeasts is between 22°C (71.6°F) and 27°C (80.6°F) according to Schanderl (1959). However, temperature has many other effects besides its direct effect on yeast growth and activity. These are due to losses of alcohol and aromatic constituents at higher temperatures and to the by-products formed as well as to direct effects on the efficiency of fermentation. For a more complete discussion see Amerine and Joslyn (1951), Rose and Harrison (1969–1971, Vol. 2) and Chap. 4.

European enologists generally believe that considerable evaporation and entrainment of alcohol by carbon dioxide occurs at the higher fermentation temperatures. Saller (1955) showed losses of about 0.65% of the alcohol occurred with a fermentation temperature of 20°C (68°F). The loss was only 0.18% at 5°C (41°F). It is believed that the loss amounts to less than 1.5% of the alcohol produced at 32°C (90°F) in California and probably to much less under optimum conditions. Dietrich (1954) reported loss of 1.4% of the alcohol produced in fermentations at 25°C (77°F). In fruit wine fermentations to 18% alcohol the loss was 1.7%.

The loss of alcohol by entrainment during laboratory-scale fermentations was demonstrated by Zimmermann *et al.* (1964) to increase with the temperature of fermentation, alcohol level of the wine being fermented, agitation of the fermenting liquid, and the presence of the pomace cap. The evaporation and entrainment losses were 0.65% at 26.5°C (79.7°F) for grape juice with an initial Brix of 21° and 0.84% for crushed grapes. The losses in plant operations were 0.7% for a juice of 16° Brix at 25.5°C (77.9°F). This result is not in conflict with the 0.83% loss reported by Warkentin and Nury (1963) with a higher Brix juice.

Castelli (1941), also using small fermentors, found that the optimum temperature for alcoholic fermentation was about 15.6°C (60°F). At the higher temperatures the yield was not only less but greater amounts of volatile acidity were produced. Acetoin was also always present in the wines fermented at the higher temperatures.

Yeasts can be acclimated to ferment at rather low temperatures. Some of the differences in results obtained are undoubtedly due to this. Beraud and Millet (1949), for example, found that yeasts grown at 7°C (44.6°F) produced more alcohol per cell than those grown at 25°C (77°F). They reported that increased alcohol production of low temperature-acclimatized yeasts lasted through several fermentations. See also p. 176.

Schanderl (1959) indicates another disadvantage of high fermentation temperature—the slowing down of the fermentation and the invasion of undesirable thermophilic organisms. Table 5.5 shows that yeasts are much more sensitive to heat at 12 and 15% alcohol.

In practice, temperatures above 26.7°C (80°F) for white table wine fermentations give lesser quality wines. For California conditions, Jordan's (1911) results were clear and still timely. Milder wines of greater aroma and keeping qualities resulted from cool fermentations. Saller (1955) recommended cold-resistant yeasts and temperatures of not over 10°C (50°F). An example of such a cooled fermentation is given in Fig. 5.7. He reported enhanced quality in the cooled fermentation wines. Similar results were obtained by Tchelistcheff (1948) in the Napa Valley of

TABLE 5.5. EFFECT OF TEMPERATURE AND ALCOHOL ON YEAST SURVIVAL[1]

Duration of Heating at 50°C (122°F) (Min)	Ethanol Content, Percent					
	0	3	6	9	12	15
	Yeast Cells Remaining After Four Days (Cells per 0.5 ml)					
0	50,000	50,000	50,000	50,000	10,900	4,200
1	7,500	755	140	100	1	2
2	2,640	140	150	14	0	0
3	520	100	70	14	0	0
4	120	147	47	11	0	0
5	110	19	10	1	0	0

[1]Source of data: Schanderl (1959).

California using cellar temperatures of 7.2°–15.6°C (45°–60°F) and a finishing temperature of not over 68°F. His observation that cold-fermented wines are cloudy and yeasty at the end of fermentation is a general one. He noted particularly the greater freshness and fruitness of flavor, together with a lower volatile acidity. The amount of alcohol loss was also less, the alcohol yield higher and the tartrate content lower. Cold fermentation of clarified white musts well protected from air gave Singleton *et al.* (1975) greatly improved quality.

Low fermentation temperatures for white table wines are now in wide use in California, South Africa, and elsewhere. Various explanations for the enhanced quality of low temperature fermentations have been given. There appears to be a retention of aromatic constituents of the grape and from the fermentation.

Some investigators have found more glycerol (Tchelistcheff 1948; Hickinbotham and Ryan 1948; and Brockmann and Stier 1948; etc.) while others have found less (Uchimoto and Cruess 1952; etc.). The results of

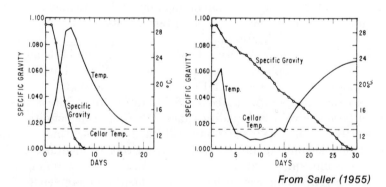

From Saller (1955)

FIG. 5.7. EFFECT OF COOLING ON THE RATE OF FERMENTATION

Hickinbotham and Ryan (1948) may help to explain some of the divergent results. They found less glycerol in laboratory-scale fermentations and suggest that carbon dioxide content may have an effect. The lower acidity and extract content of cold-fermented wines do not appear to be important quality factors. Their lower volatile acidity is, of course, desirable.

The advantages of cool fermentations for white table wine may be summarized as follows: less activity of bacteria and wild yeasts, less loss of volatile aromatic principles, greater alcohol yield, more residual carbon dioxide, and less residual bitartrate.

For red wines warmer temperatures are desirable partly because color extraction is necessary. Warmer temperatures give increasingly higher glycerol (Ough et al. 1972). Amerine and Ough (1957) found better flavor and color for Pinot noir fermentations at 24°−26.7°C (75°−80°F) than at 10°−15.6°C (50°−60°F) and this is true for most red grape fermentations with, generally, quality increasing up to 26°−29°C (80°− 85°F). For more detail on temperature effects with both red and white wine see Ough and Amerine (1966).

Alcoholic fermentation takes place best in the absence of air. Less of the sugar is used by the yeast in respiration and there is no oxygen to interfere with enzyme activity. Aeration also involves losses in alcohol by entrainment and evaporation. Many wine makers have noted that aeration during normal fermentation results in wines with higher aldehyde and darker color.

Nevertheless, it is possible that some fermentations may be slow to start because there is inadequate oxygen to stimulate yeast growth. Jordan (1911) recommended aeration during fermentation more often than modern enologists would think desirable. Schanderl (1959) has shown that yeasts from aerated cultures generally produce more alcohol than those from nonaerated cultures but the effect varies according to strain of yeast.

Surface Effect and Particulate Matter

The naturally cloudy must or one which has been made cloudy ferments much more rapidly than the same must which has been clarified or fined. This is demonstrated in Fig. 5.8. Settling or centrifuging musts has this effect and whether settling is desirable or not must be determined in each case. Musts made water-clear by pectinase treatment are particularly likely to be difficult to ferment. The presence of bentonite during fermentation often helps the fermentation proceed to completion (Groat and Ough 1978).

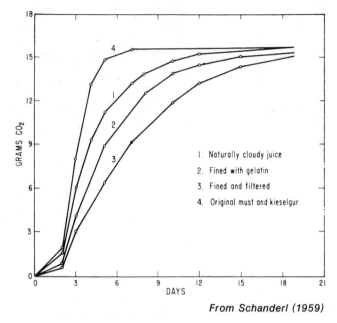

From Schanderl (1959)

FIG. 5.8. EFFECT OF SURFACE ON RATE OF FERMENTATION

Fermentation Rate

Though temperature has the greatest influence on fermentation rate, Ough and Amerine (1961) showed that musts of different varieties had different fermentation rates at the same fermentation temperature. Ough (1964) found the principal variables (outside of temperature) to be degree Brix, pH and ammonia content of the juice. From these he was able to calculate rate prediction equations at 21.1°C (70°F), which give both maximum and average rates of fermentation over the range of 20°–0° Brix.

COMPOSITION OF WINE

The information given in Chap. 2 and previously in this chapter is pertinent to a discussion of the composition of wines. Mainly, points of legal, biochemical, and sensory importance will be summarized here.

Wine is a very complex mixture of organic and inorganic compounds. For a discussion of wine composition see von der Heide and Schmitt-henner (1922), Ribéreau-Gayon *et al.* (1972-1977), Amerine (1954, 1958B), Vogt (1958), and Webb and Muller (1972).

Ethanol

The biochemical aspects of ethanol have been considered in other sections. The importance of ethanol to the sensory quality of the wine has not been adequately studied. At low concentrations ethanol has only a slight odor, but it is an excellent solvent for odorous materials. It has a slight sweet taste and moderates the taste of acids. A dealcoholized wine is much more tart than the same wine with its alcohol. The odor threshold, according to Berg *et al.* (1955B) is 0.004 to 0.0052 g/100 ml. Hinreiner *et al.* (1955B) have demonstrated that sugar increases the threshold for alcohol and also the minimum-detectable-difference concentration, the effects increasing with sugar and alcohol concentration. The following data are typical:

Ethanol %	Sucrose			
	0%	5%	10%	15%
0	0.005	0.15	0.35	0.45
10	2.0	3.0	4.0	4.0
15	3.0	4.0	4.2	4.2

These were with sugar-water-alcohol solutions. With wine Hinreiner *et al.* (1955A) did not find that addition of sugar increased the difference threshold.

The legal limits for ethanol vary markedly for different countries and are usually related to the tax structure. See p. 739 for the taxes on wines in the United States. In some countries higher alcohol wines are not only subject to higher tax but also to much closer governmental supervision.

Methanol

It is generally agreed that methanol is not produced by alcoholic fermentation, from glycine as a fusel alcohol for example, but is primarily derived from hydrolysis of naturally-occurring pectins. Thus, higher methanol has been reported when pectolytic enzymes were added to musts or pomace. More is also produced when must is fermented on the skins; hence, there is generally more in red wines than rosé or white. Fruit wines are especially high in methanol. Flanzy and Loisel (1958) noted higher methanol in wines from macerated grapes than from non-macerated fruit. Flanzy and Bouziques (1959) found no change in the methanol content during the fermentation of a white must. There was an increase with a red must during fermentation. The higher content in the red must they attributed to the higher methyl esterase content of the solid part of the fruit. They concluded that the methanol content was not related to the pectin content and that fermentation did not change the methanol content. They also reported that distillation did not produce methanol, nor did heating *per se*. Even addition of formic acid did not produce methanol. See Bertrand and Silberstein (1950) for a different view.

The amount of methanol in wines (Amerine 1954) ranges from traces to 0.635 g/liter, average about 0.1. Ribéreau-Gayon and Peynaud (1958) give a range of 0.036 to 0.350 g/liter. Feduchy *et al.* (1964) reported 0.039 to 0.624 g/liter in 220 Spanish wines. Flanzy (1934) discusses concentrations of methanol in *V. vinifera* vs French-American hybrids. The sensory importance of methanol has not been studied.

Higher Alcohols

Formation of higher alcohols during fermentation of alcoholic beverages has been reviewed by Castor and Guymon (1952), Thoukis (1959), Webb and Ingraham (1963), Moutonet (1969), Äyräpää (1971), and Harvalia (1976) among others. Compounds always present in fusel oils and related to naturally-occurring amino acids are 1-propanol, 2-methyl-1-propanol, 2-methyl-1-butanol, 3-methyl-1-butanol, and 2-phenylethanol. Many other alcohols, as well as other classes of organic compounds are found in fusel oils (see Chap. 16). The carbon skeleton of the higher alcohol can come from the amino acid of one more carbon atom or from hexoses through pyruvate of the glycolytic pathway (see Chen 1978; Konavalona *et al.* 1977; Kunkee *et al.* 1972).

It is not generally recognized that the higher alcohols of wines are of sensory importance as Guymon and Heitz (1952) noted. The amounts in table wines varied from about 0.14 to 0.42 g/liter and in dessert wines from about 0.16 to 0.90—the higher amount undoubtedly arising from the use of fortifying spirits of high fusel oil content.

At very low concentrations the higher alcohols may play a desirable role in sensory quality. Even at rather high concentrations, the port industry of Portugal seems to accept and appreciate their odor. In this country, dessert wines of high fusel oil are considered undesirable. Filipello (1951) found a negative correlation between higher alcohol content and sensory quality in rather neutral California dessert wines.

Guymon and Heitz (1952) and Villforth and Schmidt (1953–1954) showed that red wines contain slightly more higher alcohols than white. The latter also demonstrated that wines of some varieties contained more than others and that less was produced in pressure-tank fermentations and more in wines of sugared musts. Guymon *et al.* (1961) showed that oxidative conditions during fermentation favor production of higher alcohols. The presence of pomace, as in red wine production, aerates the wine and this leads to greater amounts of higher alcohols. Even yeasts which are very poor fermenters (*Hansenula anomala* and

Debaryomyces hansenii) produce high amounts of higher alcohols. Crowell and Guymon (1963) demonstrated that vigorous aeration during fermentation greatly increased formation of higher alcohols (up to sevenfold) and of 3-oxobutan-2-ol and 2,3-butandione. They also show that naturally-occurring suspended materials also resulted in larger production of higher alcohols, particularly of isobutyl and isoamyl alcohols. The amounts of 1-propanol and 2-methyl-1-butanol were little changed by the presence of suspended solids. The wide difference in ability of yeast to produce higher alcohols was also noted by Webb and Kepner (1961) (data in weight percentage based on these four alcohols only):

Yeast	1-Propanol	2-Methyl-1-propanol (Isobutanol)	2-Methyl-1-butanol (Act.-amyl)	3-Methyl-1-butanol
Burgundy	18.2	12.4	12.0	57.4
Jerez	20.2	8.4	4.5	66.9
Montrachet	2.6	2.7	16.5	78.2

Amerine *et al.* (1959) suggested that the higher alcohols may not only be important because of their own odor but because of their solvent action towards other odorous substances and the volatility of these in such mixtures.

Polyols and Related Compounds

Pasteur reported glycerol as a by-product of alcoholic fermentation. No constant ratio of alcohol to glycerol has been established. Castino and Stefano (1975) have studied the effect of variety on 2,3-butandiol concentration in wine, and Švejcar and Papcun (1976) have determined effects of yeast type and temperature on glycerol content. There are a variety of reasons for this. According to Gentilini and Cappelleri (1959) glycerol production is favored by lower temperatures, higher tartaric acid content, and by additions of sulfur dioxide (see p. 266). Increase in sugar content decreases glycerol yield relative to ethanol. Vitamins and other growth factors did not change the glycerol content. Most of the glycerol develops in the early stages of fermentation. Yeasts differ markedly in their glycerol yield. Finally, moldy grapes, particularly from *Botrytis cinerea*, contain glycerol and, hence, wines made from such fruit are higher in glycerol, and in mucic acid (Würdig 1976).

Amerine (1954) has summarized a large number of glycerol analyses. Enologists have considered that glycerol is of considerable sensory importance because of its sweet taste and its oiliness. A threshold of 0.38–0.44% in water was established by Berg *et al.* (1955A). Hinreiner *et al.* (1955B) reported acidifying to pH 3.4 raised the threshold to 1.5 g per 100 ml, and that a 10% alcohol solution had a threshold of 1.0 g/100 ml.

Hinreiner *et al.* (1955A) found a difference threshold of 0.9 g/100 ml in a dry white table wine (of 0.3 g/100 ml of glycerol) and 1.3 for a red table wine (of 0.8 g/100 ml of glycerol). These results do not indicate that glycerol is of importance in the quality of wines, and certainly not in the case of sweet wines.

Ribéreau-Gayon *et al.* (1959) have shown that arginine and ammonia increase the production of 2,3-butandiol and that cysteine and a full complement of amino acids resulted in higher succinic acid production. High amino acid content and ammonia also increase acetic acid production. Application of these studies to practical conditions would be interesting, since California musts are generally high in nitrogen but acetic acid formation is low. There is little interest in the determination of glycerol or 2,3-butandiol except in research work. In Europe where sugaring is used, it has been suggested by Rebelein (1957B, 1958) that the K value (the ratio of glycerol $\times$ 2,3-butandiol divided by (alcohol)^3) might give an indication of sugaring, fortification, or use of green grapes if the value fell below 7×10^{-6}. Hennig (1959) did not find this to be so using wines of known origin. He did report that the analytical methods used by Rebelein (1957A, 1958) were accurate.

The origin of 2,3-butandiol, 3-oxobutan-2-ol (acetoin) and 2,3-butandione (diacetyl) during alcoholic fermentation has not been clearly established. Some biochemists believe that certain yeasts form only the glycol and other yeasts only ketols. Others find both produced during active fermentation. Lafon (1956), on the basis that the amount of ketol formed was independent of the degree of respiratory intensity, considers that it is not produced by oxidation of the diol. Amerine (1954) suggested that the varying results may be due to differences in experimental technique—age of cultures, oxidation-reduction potential, etc. He has also summarized the data on the amounts present in various wines. For 2,3-butandiol this ranges from about 0.1 to 1.6 g/liter, with the average generally being in the range 0.4 to 0.9. The amounts present do not appear to be related to quality (it has practically no odor and a slight bitter-sweet taste which would be masked by the 10- to 20-times greater amounts of glycerol present). There is more in wines which have fermented more sugar. This is the basis for suggestions that the alcohol to 2,3-butandiol relationship be used to establish if a wine has been fortified or not. It is curious that Armagnac brandy should have eight times as much as Cognac. Peynaud and Lafon (1951A,B) suggested that this might be useful in distinguishing different brandies.

3-Oxobutan-2-ol does have an odor but the amounts present are small: 2 to 84 mg/liter, 3 to 32 in normal German wines according to Dittrich and Kerner (1964). During alcoholic fermentation there is an increase up to the middle of fermentation to a maximum of 25 to 100 mg/liter after which it almost disappears, according to Guymon and Crowell (1965). This accounts for the higher amounts in fortified dessert wines where the fermentation is stopped about midway. In submerged-culture flor sherries very high amounts are reported. Its apparent source in this case is ethanol via acetaldehyde. 2,3-Butandione is present in normal amounts in these sherries. (This is in contrast with a previous report but the method then used did not distinguish diones from ketols.) More ketol is reported in wines fermented with added acetaldehyde and in wines attacked by *Acetobacter.*

2,3-Butandione has a pronounced buttery odor and in a few cases may be of sensory importance. Normal wines average about 0.2 mg/liter according to Dittrich and Kerner (1964). Above 0.89 wines have a sour milk odor. It is curious that Cognac brandy contains more dione than pomace brandy. For typical analysis see Table 5.6.

TABLE 5.6. 2,3-BUTANDIOL, 3-OXOBUTAN-2-OL AND 2,3-BUTANDIONE IN WINES[1]

Diol mg/liter	Ketol mg/liter	Dione mg/liter
492	2.0	0.4
513	9.6	0.7
535	7.6	0.4
612	7.8	0.5
628	4.6	0.1
653	3.0	0.6
720	10.7	0.3
750	5.4	0.1
763	14.8	0.3
783	3.6	0.3
828	5.2	0.1
1260	15.2	1.6
1298	30.3	1.6
1485	84.0	1.8

[1]Source of data: Ribéreau-Gayon and Peynaud (1958).

Inositol, $(CHOH)_6$ (or better, *myo*-inositol), is another alcohol found in wines. It is present in musts. Mannitol, $CH_2OH(CHOH)_4CH_2OH$, is always a bacterial spoilage product (p. 572), from the reduction of fructose. Sorbitol is an indication of addition of fruits, particularly of apples.

Acetaldehyde

Acetaldehyde is a normal by-product of alcoholic fermentation (p. 188). Kielhöfer and Würdig (1960B) have also shown that aldehyde retention is much greater when sulfur dioxide is added before the fermentation, and especially high when sulfur dioxide is added during fermentation. They also confirmed the high production of aldehyde when incompletely fermented wines were aerated in the presence of actively-growing yeast cells. Nonenzymatic production of acetaldehyde in white wines is very small, especially in the absence of iron, according to Kielhöfer and Würdig (1960A). They did report nonenzymatic aldehyde formation in the light was greater than in the dark. They conclude that the primary source of aldehydes is from enzymatic processes.

In the amounts found in newly-fermented wines, below about 75 mg/ liter, it has little sensory importance, especially so since most wines have sulfur dioxide added or produced during fermentation which fixes most of the aldehyde. However, it has a pronounced odor and Berg et al. (1955A) reported a threshold of only 1.3 to 1.5 mg/liter in water. But in table wines Hinreiner et al. (1955A) found difference thresholds of 100 to 125 mg/liter.

During aging, owing to oxidation of ethanol or to the activity of film yeast, the amount present in wines is greatly increased. Thus, Spanish sherries may have up to 500 mg/liter and average over 200. Amerine (1958A) and Ough and Amerine (1958) have reported accumulations of up to 1000 mg/liter when the flor yeast, Saccharomyces fermentati, is grown under aerobic conditions with a slight pressure and occasional stirring (see pp. 416–417). The "faded" odor of newly bottled, low sulfur dioxide wines is apparently due to temporary accumulation of acetaldehyde.

While an aldehyde tone is desirable in sherry, the quality of sherry cannot be entirely attributable to acetaldehyde. Other aldehydes occur and are important (see p. 424).

Acetal

Acetaldehyde reacts with ethanol to form acetal, a substance with a strong aldehyde-like odor. Very little is found in wines, usually less than 5 mg/liter because of unfavorable equilibrium constants. The reaction is catalyzed by low pH. Soviet investigators believe a high acetal to acetaldehyde ratio to be an important measure of quality in flor sherry.

All of the acetals possible by reacting acetaldehyde with ethanol, 2-methylbutanol, 3-methylbutanol and 2-phenylethanol were found in submerged-culture flor sherry by Galetto et al. (1966). The cyclic acetals of acetaldehyde with 2,3-butanediol and with glycerol have also been found in sherries, Webb et al. (1967) and Muller et al. (1978).

Hydroxymethylfurfural

When fructose is heated in acid solutions, it is dehydrated to produce hydroxymethylfurfural as follows:

$$
\begin{array}{c}
\text{H} \qquad\quad \text{H} \\
\text{HOC}\!-\!\!-\!\!-\!\!-\!\!-\!\text{COH} \\
\text{HOH}_2\text{C}\!-\!\text{CH} \quad \text{HOC}\!-\!\text{CH}_2\text{OH} \\
\diagdown\;\text{O}\;\diagup
\end{array}
\;\rightarrow\;
\begin{array}{c}
\text{HC}\!-\!\text{CH} \\
\|\quad\| \\
\text{HOH}_2\text{C}\!-\!\text{C}\quad\text{CCHO} + 3\text{H}_2\text{O} \\
\diagdown\;\text{O}\;\diagup
\end{array}
$$

Its presence in wines is a good indication that they have been heated during processing. Since heating of port to give it a tawny character is prohibited in Portugal, a low legal limit has been placed on the presence of hydroxymethylfurfural. It has a caramel-like odor. Amerine (1954) found ⅔ of the 154 California dessert wines which he tested showed its presence, indicating rather general heating of these wines during processing. California sweet sherrys, tokays and Madeiras can, of course, be expected to have a large concentration of this substance—up to 300 mg/liter. Malaga, which is made partly from raisined fruit, also contains hydroxymethylfurfural.

Esters and Lactones

The esters in wines arise from enzymatic production within yeast or bacterial cells, from catalysis by esterases in very young wine and from slower hydrogen ion-catalyzed esterifications and transesterifications in the wine after loss of the enzymes. Given these processes and the relatively high concentrations of ethanol and acetic acid, it is not surprising to find that esters of these predominate and that ethyl acetate is present in highest concentrations.

Both neutral and acid esters are found in wine. The total esters in various wines as summarized by Amerine (1954) varied between about 200 and 400 mg/liter (as ethyl acetate). Ports and sherries were higher. The volatile neutral esters averaged 70 to 200 (344 for sherry) mg/liter as ethyl acetate.

Peynaud (1937) showed that as wines age they may approach the theoretical equilibrium concentrations of esters.

. As to the mechanism of ester formation, equilibrium is seldom attained even for very old wines as the following data of Peynaud (1937) indicate:

Year	Age	Ratio[1]		
		Minimum	Maximum	Average
1893–1914	22–43	0.73	0.79	0.75
1926–1930	6–10	0.57	0.71	0.66
1931–1932	4–5	0.59	0.73	0.64
1933	3	0.49	0.67	0.62
1934	2	0.50	0.65	0.56
1935	0.75	0.28	0.38	0.34

[1]Actual/theoretical (from Berthelot formula).

Esters of hydroxycinnamic acids and tartaric acid (*p*-coumaroyltartaric, caffeoyltartaric and feruloyltartaric acids) have been isolated from grapé leaves and wines (Ribéreau-Gayon 1965; Singleton *et al.* 1978).

Peynaud (1937) suggested amount of ethyl acetate rather than percentage acetic acid as the legal limit, because: (1) addition of *pure* acetic acid to a wine does not give it a spoiled character, (2) applying a vacuum to a moderately spoiled wine improves its odor but only ethyl acetate is removed, (3) adding pure ethyl acetate to a wine gives it a spoiled character, and (4) heating a clean wine with acetic acid in a sealed tube will give it a spoiled character. New wines of high spoiled character and a low volatile acidity and wines of high volatile acidity and low spoiled character are occasionally observed. Peynaud suggested a maximum volatile neutral ester content of 220 mg/liter (as ethyl acetate) in lieu of a limit on volatile acidity. However, in most cases ethyl acetate ánd acetic acid are present in proportionate amounts so that if one is high so is the other. Furthermore, with time, the esterification equilibrium should bring them into a predictable relation to each other. The slightly more laborious procedure for determining the volatile neutral ester content probably prevents adoption of Peynaud's suggestion.

The lactones in wines are principally gamma-lactones, intramolecular cyclic esters of 4-OH-carboxylic acids according to Muller *et al.* (1973). The simplest lactone, gamma-butyrolactone, has a very mild odor, but the related ethyl 4-hydroxybutanoate is fruity smelling. Substituents on the fourth carbon atom generally lower the sensory thresholds of gamma-lactones of wines.

Volatile Acidity

Chemists distinguish a group of short chain-length acids which are volatile with steam as *volatile acids*. Enologists delete from this group lactic, succinic, carbonic and sulfurous, and recognize the rest (acetic with traces of formic, propionic, butyric and possibly others) as indicators of spoilage when present in more than trace concentrations.

The amounts of acetic acid produced during alcoholic fermentation are small—usually less than 0.030 g/100 ml. Bacterial action before, during, and after fermentation may lead to much higher quantities by oxidation of alcohol or occasionally to bacterial attack on citric acid, sugars, tartrates, glycerol, etc. The spoiled vinegary character of such wines is the reason for the adoption of legal standards.

Reduction of a high volatile acidity by neutralization is not practicable because the fixed acids are also diminished. Film yeasts will reduce the volatile acidity as will addition of the high volatile acid wine to a must in vigorous fermentation. However, the legal aspects of converting a food product that is over the legal limits to one which is below the limits needs to be considered. Furthermore, the addition of high volatile acid wines to sound fermenting musts does run the risk of contaminating the whole product (see Amerine 1954).

Little formic acid is present in normal wines—possibly more in raisin wines than other wines (Vogt 1958). Whether or not a high pH and formic acid are associated with the mousy flavor in wines has not been clearly established. Butyric acid is present in very small amounts in normal wines (10 to 20 mg/liter) but much more is found in wine vinegar (290 mg/liter) and in wine to which St. John's bread, *Ceratonia silqua*, has been added (80 to 250 mg/liter). It is rare in wines in this country. Propionic acid is probably not found in unspoiled wine.

The amount of volatile acidity in commerical wines naturally varies very markedly with their source and condition of fermentation. Experience indicates that careful wine makers can produce wine with less than 0.030 mg/100 ml of volatile acidity (as acetic) and that during aging this should not exceed 0.100. No detailed studies of volatile acidity-ester relationships in old dessert wines appear to have been made but the amounts in Madeira and other aged dessert wines seem to indicate that a high volatile acidity is less objectionable when desirable volatile products of aging are present. The legal limits in this country are given in Chap 19. According to Jaulmes (1951) the French limit for wines at wholesale is 0.15 g/100 ml (as acetic) and 0.187 for wines at retail.

Fixed Acids

Acids of grapes and wines which are not volatile with steam are designated *fixed acids*. Tartaric and malic acids and their half-neutralized anions constitute the majority of the fixed acids. The Krebs cycle acids plus a number of others are found in grapes in smaller amounts. Several acids, of which succinic, lactic, and pyruvic are probably the most important, are formed during fermentation. Acids are of importance in wines for their acid taste, and for their effects on spoilage organisms, color, and hydrogen ion catalysis. Tartaric and malic, because of their relatively high concentrations and their dissociation constants, buffer wines at pH levels between 3 and 4.

The acid taste is due to the hydrogen ion concentration and undissociated acid, hence there is no direct relationship between pH and acid taste. The thresholds for the various acids tested by Berg *et al.* (1955A) were as follows:

Acid	pKa$_1$	pKa$_3$	Threshold g/100 ml	Difference Threshold[1] g/100 ml
Citric	3.09	4.39[2]	0.0023–0.0025	0.07
Lactic	3.81	—	0.0038–0.0040	—
Malic	3.46	5.05	0.0026–0.0030	0.05
Succinic	4.18	5.23	0.0034–0.0035	—
Sulfurous	1.77	7.00	0.0011	—
Tartaric	3.01	4.05	0.0024–0.0027	0.05
Bitartrate[3]	—	—	0.0075–0.0090	0.10

[1]At 0.25% for d-tartaric, at 0.30% for potassium acid tartrate, at 0.21% for malic, and at 0.23% for l-malic.
[2]pKa$_3$ 5.74.
[3]Potassium acid tartrate.

Münz (1963) notes that the acid taste of wines is primarily due to the acid salts since most of the acids are partially neutralized. Soluble salts appear to reduce the acid taste. Amerine et al. (1965) reported that, at the same titratable acidity, the order of decreasing sourness was malic, tartaric, citric, and lactic. At the same pH, the decreasing order was malic, lactic, citric, and tartaric. A noteworthy feature of this report was the relatively small differences in pH (0.05 pH unit) and titratable acidity (0.02–0.05%) which could be detected by the panel. They concluded that both pH and titratable acidity were important in determining sensory response to sourness.

Hinreiner et al. (1955B) did not find up to 10% sucrose to influence the acid threshold. Ethanol, however, did increase the acid threshold and the effect was greater if sucrose was present. Tannin also seemed to increase the minimum detectable difference for acid in the absence of sugar. Sugar in the absence of tannin did not have this effect. However, the presence of sugar tends to minimize the effect of tannin on the minimum detectable-difference concentration of acid. Hinreiner et al. (1955A) also reported a difference threshold of 0.15 g/100 ml in a white table wine. One percent sucrose did not change the difference threshold. Ough (1963) and Pangborn et al. (1964) also studied difference thresholds of acids in wines.

Potassium acid tartrate occurs in grapes as a supersaturated solution. Since it is less soluble in alcoholic solution, it precipitates during and after fermentation. Cambitzi (1947) found optically inactive racemic calcium tartrate in old wine deposits. Since grapes contain only dextrotartaric acid this indicates autoracemization. The calcium salt of racemic tartaric acid is only about ⅛ as soluble as the dextro salt. Calcium tartrate is less soluble at higher pHs. DeSoto and Warkentin (1955) recommended that the pH of California dessert wines be kept below 3.70.

Genevois (1951) considers that tartaric acid catalyzed by ferrous ion yields dihydroxymaleic, and by oxidation-reduction and decarboxylation finally results in glyoxal. Baraud (1953) was unable to find dihydroxymaleic acid. Rodopulo (1951) also studied possible iron-catalyzed changes in tartaric acid. He reported glyoxylic and oxalic acids to be oxidation products. During bottle storage diketosuccinic and dihydroxymaleic acids were believed to be formed. Dihydroxymaleic acid accelerated the oxidation of tartaric acid. The exact mechanism is not clear and some enologists question the presence and importance of dihydroxymaleic acid.

Tartaric acid appears to give rise to oxalic via dihydroxyfumaric and diketosuccinic acids. Little dihydroxyfumaric or diketosuccinic acid accumulates, according to Dupuy (1960). Another possible source of oxalic acid is L-ascorbic acid. Ascorbic acid is oxidized to dehydroascorbic acid which is degraded by further oxidation to oxalic and L-threonic acids. Both copper and iron act as catalysts. The oxidation is greater at low pH. Polyphenoloxidase catalyses oxidative degradation of ascorbic acid indirectly.

Malic acid disappears during alcoholic fermentation to the extent of 10 to 30%. Peynaud (1947) considers this due to splitting off of two hydrogen atoms and decarboxylation of the resulting oxaloacetic acid to acetaldehyde which in turn acts as a hydrogen acceptor and is reduced to ethanol. The influence of the malo-lactic fermentation on malic acid has been discussed elsewhere (pp. 565–570).

Citric acid from the grapes is attacked by various bacteria (there is less in reds than in whites) to produce acetic acid. Citric acid complexes with iron so it is frequently added as preventative against iron casse (p. 536). A number of countries limit the amount of citric acid which can be added (usually to 0.05 g/100 ml). However, as Ribéreau-Gayon and Peynaud (1958) note, Sauternes have far more than this so that it is impossible to say that a wine of over 0.08 g/100 ml has had more than 0.05 g added or not. Amerine (1954) indicates averages for various types of wines of 0.01 to 0.03.

Citric acid is slowly decarboxylated during aging. Citramalic (or α-methylmalic) acid is one product. Carles (1959) did not find citramalic acid in musts and believes its presence in wines is from decarboxylation of citric acid. However, Dimotaki-Kourakou (1962) believed citramalic acid was only a product of alcoholic fermentation.

Succinic acid is a product of alcoholic fermentation. As a general rule, in table wines about 1% as much succinic acid is present as alcohol by volume, but the range of succinic acid as percentage of the weight of alcohol produced varies from 0.68 to 2.25. More is formed at the beginning of fermentation than later and the amount formed per gram of sugar fermented varies with the must and yeast. Relatively high concentrations of ethyl acid succinate are also found in young wines. Succinic acid is very resistant to bacterial attack. It has a salt-bitter-acid taste which is vinous in character.

Lactic acid has a slight odor and is a weak acid. It is a constant by-product of alcoholic fermentation, 0.04 to 0.75 g/liter. Its relation to the malo-lactic fermentation and spoilage organisms has been mentioned elsewhere (p. 561). In flor sherry aging there is a slow increase, with a parallel increase in the concentration of the ethyl ester. It is increased by a malo-lactic fermentation and moreso by excessive bacterial activity. More is produced in red wines than white.

The other fixed acids are of less importance. Glyoxylic acid is found in wines and in grapes. In diseased grapes up to 0.13% glucuronic and 1.0% gluconic may be formed whereas normal fruit contained only 0.03% of the former. Botrytised grapes in Peynaud and Charpentié's (1953) study had 0.29 to 2.46 g/liter, average 1.02, of gluconic acid.

Würdig et al. (1969) reported an average of 68 mg/liter 2- and 3-methyl-2,3-dihydroxybutyric acids and 2-hydroxyglutaric acid (and its lactone). Möhler and Pires (1969A,B,C) also found 2-methyl-2,3-dihydroxybutyric acid in wines (20 to 525 mg/liter, average 220). Castino (1969) found 52 to 144 mg/liter (average 92).

Carbonic acid constitutes a very special case for both still and sparkling wines. It has no odor and little taste, but it does have a feel, and disengagement of the bubbles from the wine probably brings out more odor. Table wines with some residual carbon dioxide are rated as better. It also plays a protective role by keeping oxygen away from the surface of wines.

New wines are saturated with carbon dioxide. Thereafter carbon dioxide is gradually lost. The state of carbon dioxide in wine has been investigated by Lonvaud-Funel and Ribéreau-Gayon (1977). It is not the same as in a water-alcohol solution of the same composition. Wine retains carbon dioxide much longer than water-alcohol solutions. The time the wine is kept under pressure influences the rate at which carbon dioxide is given off.

For beer, Anderson (1959) states that carbon dioxide is dissolved and in equilibrium with carbonic acid, small amounts form basic salts and carbamino compounds, and some may be fixed by colloids. From the fact that carbon dioxide is easily lost from beer he rejects chemical forces and believes that the carbon dioxide-protein relationship is one of electrostatic attraction, the negative pole of the carbonic acid being adsorbed to the positively charged beer proteins. This was supported by electrolysis experiments. Carbon dioxide may be present in a supersaturated condition in new wines, according to the data summarized in Amerine (1955B). The data of Ettienne and Mathers (1956) are given in Table 11.1 (Chap. 11) for low carbon dioxide pressures. For the relation of pressure, carbon dioxide and temperature, see Chap. 11.

Miller (1959) finds that deaerating the wine before carbonation gives a better impregnation and a slower evolution of gas when the bottle is opened.

The forms in which carbon dioxide is present have stimulated much Russian work which has been summarized by Amerine (1954, 1958B). A physical adsorption or an esterification reaction is indicated. Diethyl-pyrocarbonate, $(C_2H_5OOC)_2O$, is not normally present.

Sugars

The importance of glucose and fructose in alcoholic fermentation has been discussed (p. 194). Their importance to taste should be emphasized. Glycerol and 2,3-butandiol are also sweet. Berg et al. (1955A) reported thresholds in water of 0.13 to 0.15 g/100 ml for fructose, 0.40 to 0.44 for glucose and 0.38 to 0.44 for glycerol. For glucose in water the difference concentrations were: at 1%, 0.4 to 0.7 g/100 ml; at 5%, 0.6 to 0.8; at 10%, 0.8; and at 15% 1.0 to 1.1. The influence of ethanol, acids and tannins on sucrose thresholds was also studied by Berg et al. (1955B). Ethanol enhances the sweetness of sugar solutions over a range of 1 to 15% sucrose as determined by sugar threshold or by minimum detectable difference. In the range 2.55 to 3.40, pH had a negligible effect on sugar thresholds. Tannin increased the threshold level for sugar detection and the minimum detectable difference.

Hinreiner et al. (1955A) reported the following thresholds:

Sucrose Level g/100 ml	Minimum Detectable Sucrose Increment In	
	White Wine g/100 ml	Red Wine g/100 ml
0	0.9	0.8
1	0.8	0.7
5	1.1	1.0
10	1.7	1.6

These differences are greater than for aqueous solutions but are similar to those for water-alcohol-acid solutions. During aging there may be a slight increasing in reducing sugar due to hydrolysis of glucosides.

Esau and Amerine (1964) identified altro-heptulose, D-glycero-D-manno-octulose, and manno-heptulose in wine.

Little sucrose is found in wines. A sensitive procedure for sucrose is given by Guimberteau and Peynaud (1965). However, sucrose is rapidly hydrolyzed in wines and the test must be carried out a few days after addition of the sucrose. Amerine (1954) summarized various data showing an average sucrose in wines of 0.01 to 0.06 g/100 ml.

Caramel may not be added to California wines. Its detection in wines is therefore of some importance. Amerine (1954) indicates several tests should be used before stating that caramel has been added. Wucherpfennig and Lay (1965) found a slow increase in hydroxymethylfurfural (hmf) when wines of 0.4 to 3.4% sugar were heated at 50°C (122°F) for 120 hours and more at 60°C (158°F). Reducing the pH increased the hmf produced; adding amino acids had little effect. Old German white wines had higher amounts than young. The sensory threshold is 100 to 200 mg/liter.

The nonfermentable residual reducing material of wines is largely pentoses and amounts to from 0.01 to 0.20 g/100 ml. From 0.04 to 0.13 g/100 ml of arabinose is found. It is one possible source of furfural during distillation or pasteurization of wines and it is attacked by some lactobacilli. Rhamnose is reported at less than 0.05 mg/100 ml. Xylose is absent from most wines, less than 0.005 g/100 ml according to Guichard (quoted by Ribéreau-Gayon and Peynaud 1958). Pentosans are slowly hydrolyzed during aging.

Pectins

If a clear must is slightly acidified and 4 or 5 volumes of alcohol are added, a haze will develop and eventually settle as a gelatinous deposit. This is pectin. This precipitation occurs naturally during alcoholic fermentation so that the amount of pectin material, 0.3−0.5 g/100 ml, in finished wines is only 10 to 70% that of the musts. The gums of wines are generally arabans and galactans, anhydrates of arabinose and galactose. The mucilaginous materials are classified as glucosans, anhydrides of glucose. Wines with oily disease (*graisse*) contain considerable mucilaginous material. Grapes attacked by *Botrytis cinerea* also have considerable glucosans, which act as protective colloids in wines and thus hinder clarification. They also make filtration difficult. Wines have from 14 to 30% of the colloid content of musts according to Tarantola and Usseglio-Tomasset (1963). For 3 varieties, the total colloids in the wine were composed of (in percentages):

Variety	Araban	Galactan	Pectin	Protein
Dolcetto	22.1	28.1	43.5	6.6
Cortese	35.6	47.4	5.8	10.3
Barbera	35.4	29.6	23.6	11.7

To remove pectins, pectolytic enzymes are frequently used—either before or after fermentation. They do aid filtration and reduce the pectin content. They also raise the galacturonic acid content and slightly increase the methyl alcohol content.

Nitrogen

Nitrogen-containing compounds of grapes and wines are of importance to growth of yeast and bacteria and, hence, to fermentation rate and extent and to aroma compound production. Clarification and stability are affected by the nature and concentrations of these substances, as well.

Paparelli and Colby (1890) reported total nitrogen of 0.011 to 0.090% (average 0.041) and of proteins of 0.071 to 0.560% (average 0.262) in 16 young Californian wines. European data summarized by Amerine (1954) gave averages of 0.10 to 0.77 g/liter for total nitrogen.

There are many different kinds of nitrogenous material in wine: proteins, peptones, polypeptides, amides, amino acids, and ammonia. Only very small amounts of ammonia are found in wine—it is nearly or completely utilized in alcoholic fermentation. Finished wines summarized by Amerine (1954) had none to 0.071 g/liter (averages for various types of wine 0.01 to 0.027). Diemair and Maier (1962) reported protein contents of white German wines to range from 60 to 411 mg/liter.

Lafon-Lafourcade and Peynaud (1961) found threonine, lysine, glutamic acid, and serine next abundant after proline; then—alanine, glutamic acid, aspartic acid, histidine, leucine, etc. In general, proline and threonine constituted about 70% of the total amino acid content.

The malo-lactic fermentation of white wines generally resulted in slight variations in the amino acid content of wines; for red wines there were slight decreases in arginine, alanine, phenylalanine and serine, and increase in glutamic acid, methionine, threonine (sometimes) and tryptophan.

Tarantola (1954) found marked increases in valine, leucine, and tyrosine in wines stored on the lees. This was not observed by Bidan and André (1958). Bourdet and Hérard (1958) showed large increases in aspartic acid, glutamic acid, lysine, α-alanine, glycine, serine, threonine, valine, leucine, isoleucine, γ-aminobutyric acid, phenylalanine, tyrosine, asparagine, and glutamine in red wines stored seven days on the lees (in small containers, stirred once each day), compared to new wine separated before the seven days' storage. There was, however, a decrease in arginine, proline, histidine, and cystine and little change in methionine and α-aminobutyric acid. In contrast, in a flor yeast wine there were spectacular increases in arginine, lysine, histidine and methionine compared to those present in a white wine of another source. In two young wines 90—91% of the nitrogen was present as free amino acids, 6—9% as amides and only 0.4—3.3% as ammonia and nonprotein nitrogen.

The wide variation in qualitative and quantitative data on the amino acid contents of musts and wines is attributed by Bidan and André (1958) to differences in the methods employed, to the heterogeneity of samples (particularly as to the age and treatment of wines), to the differences in methods of fermenting the wines, and to the presence or absence of malo-lactic fermentation.

The amino acids present in musts and wines have been given in Tables 2.6 and 2.7. There have been reports that there was a relation between amino acid content and the bouquet of the wine. Bidan and André (1958) did not find any such correlation with eight French white wines.

Flanzy et al. (1964) confirmed that new wines have less total nitrogen than the musts from which they were derived. They also showed that when the wine was left in contact with the lees for 1 to 3 months that the nitrogen content of the wine increased, reaching a maximum in about 2 months. Most (87%) of the increase was in amine nitrogen and the rest in amide and protein nitrogen. During this period obviously yeast autolysis is occurring. They classified the amino acids in four groups: 1. used during fermentation and not restored by autolysis: arginine, phenylalanine and histidine; 2. partially used during fermentation and restored by autolysis: proline; 3. used during fermentation and present in increased quantities after autolysis: glutamic acid, aspartic acid, leucine, isoleucine, valine, serine, lysine, tyrosine and tryptophan; and 4. increased by fermentation and by autolysis; cystine, methionine and glycine.

When ammonia was added to musts there was a notable increase (10 to 30 times) in certain amino acids in the resulting wines according to Flanzy et al. (1964). This was especially marked for arginine, histidine, lysine, valine, tyrosine, isoleucine, methionine, aspartic acid, and alanine, and less marked for glutamic acid, tryptophan, cystine, serine and proline. There were, however, marked differences in the increases for certain amino acids between the musts of the two varieties studied and with those of a later study (Flanzy and Poux 1965.) Aeration during fermentation influenced these changes differently for various amino acids— naturally being less favorable for the amino acids such as glutamic acid and aspartic acid which are involved in the respiratory cycle. In general, addition of ammonia improved the quality and Flanzy and Poux (1965) confirmed this for wines of another season.

Tyrosol, 15 to 45 mg/liter, was reported in Bordeaux red and white wines by Ribéreau-Gayon and Sapis (1965). They also found 0 to 0.8 mg/liter of tryptophol but rarely in white wines. Ough (1971) reported an average of 1.8 mg/liter of histamine in 253 California table wines and slightly more in dessert wines and less in fruit wines.

Amide nitrogen is present in very small amounts—0.001 to 0.008 g/ liter. Asparagine and glutamine are examples. The polypeptides—usually determined by precipitation with phosphomolybdic acid—represent the most important part of the organic nitrogen of wines, from 60 to 90% according to Ribéreau-Gayon and Peynaud (1958).

In 41 white Spanish wines, Cabezudo *et al.* (1963) reported 2 to 13 $\mu g/$ liter of biotin compared to 2 to 18 in 46 red wines. The averages tended to be higher in red wines aged in the wood. According to Peynaud and Lafourcade (1957) the free pyridoxine content of 31 Bordeaux white wines was 0.12 to 0.67 mg/liter (average 0.31) and the total 0.22 to 0.82 (average 0.44); for 58 reds the free ranged from 0.13 to 0.68 (average 0.35) and the total from 0.25 to 0.78 (average 0.47).

In 15 Bordeaux white wines, Lafon-Lafourcade and Peynaud (1958) reported 15 to 133 $\mu g/$liter (average 69) of *p*-aminobenzoic acid, 0.4 to 4.5 μg (average 2.4) of pteroylglutamic acid and 19 to 27 $\mu g/$liter (average 21) of choline (12 wines). The averages of the first two were similar in red wines but choline was higher (29). Wines are as high or higher in these three vitamins as their musts. See Chap. 2 for additional data.

Phenols

The natural phenolic substances of wines include small to medium-sized colorless compounds, flavonoids and pigments, and larger tannins. The unfortunate tendency to call the entire group "tannins" or "tannins plus pigments" persists in some wine literature. Most of these phenols originate directly from the grape (see Chap. 2), but they may appear, be removed, or change in wine depending on the circumstances of fermentation, processing, or aging. Such changes are usually at least partially selective among the various classes of phenols.

The phenols of grapes and wine and their significance were reviewed in critical detail by Singleton and Esau (1969). Recent general reviews covering wine phenols include those by Bourzeix (1976A,B), Rapp *et al.* (1977), and Amerine and Ough (1972). Durmishidze (1971) reviewed recent research in Russia especially on degradative changes of phenols in wine. Anthocyanins and red wine phenols were reviewed by Webb (1970), Bourzeix and Saquet (1975), and Ribéreau-Gayon(1974). Singleton and Esau (1969) considered that a complete "balance sheet" of the different phenols in wines and changes in them with aging or processing was an important goal. Considerable progress has been made and research continues to be active in this area.

Singleton and Noble (1976) estimated typical concentrations of each class of phenols in wines and their probable flavor consequences. Most of the following comments are drawn from their summary.

The total of extractable phenols in the whole grape berry calculated as gallic acid is, depending on the grape variety and growing conditions, about 2000–6000 mg/kg. Prolonged fermentation of the whole grape mass may thus give wines approaching 2000–6000 mg/liter, but actual wines are invariably lower than the indicated maximum owing to incomplete extraction, precipitation of some of the tannins by grape protein, adsorption by yeast cells, etc. Of course, wines made with high extraction from grape solids after earlier partial removal of fluid, press wines for example, may be very high in total phenol content.

White wines made from rapidly separated and clarified juice from grapes in good condition have minimal total phenol contents averaging about 250 mg/liter. Flavonoids are low or absent in such wines and increase in others in proportion to additional extraction or breakdown of the firmer tissues of the grapes (skins, seeds, possibly stems) by such factors as higher ethanol, higher temperature, longer contact, etc. The level of nonflavonoid phenols is relatively constant in white or red wines because these substances are present mainly in the easily expressed juice or are produced (tyrosol) by yeast fermentation of juice components. Nonflavonoid phenols thus represent nearly the total of phenols in light white wines with minimal pomace contact. The nonflavonoid phenols of wines include a large proportion of hydroxycinnamate derivatives. Ribéreau-Gayon (1965) by paper chromatography identified these wine components as p-coumaroyl, caffeoyl, and feruloyl tartaric acid. Other workers before and since had identified these wine components as the similar chlorogenic acid analogs containing quinic acid rather than tartaric acid. The controversy appears to have been resolved in favor of the tartaric acid series (Castino and Di Stefano 1976; Singleton et al. 1978).

The total of the hydroxycinnamates is estimated to be equivalent to about 150 mg/liter of gallic acid with the more important part caffeic acid derivatives. About 30 mg/liter reportedly would be various benzoic acid derivatives including 4-hydroxybenzoic, protocatechuic, vanillic, syringic, gallic, salicylic, and gentisic acids. Tyrosol averages about 25 mg/liter in wine. Various volatile phenols together range from about 1 to 50 mg/liter depending on the total phenol content and aging since a number of these substances arise from degradation of other phenols in wine or from wood cooperage. Identified substances include o-cresol, m-cresol, p-cresol, guaiacol, vanillin, 4-ethylphenol, 4-vinylphenol, 4-ethylguaiacol, 4-vinylguaiacol, isoeugenol, eugenol, 2,6-dimethoxyphenol, acetovanillone, and 1-naphthol (Singleton and Noble 1976; Schreier and Drawert 1977). Most of these substances are individually present below their indicated sensory thresholds in wines, but by additive effects are believed to contribute as a group to bitterness and perhaps to spiciness or odor in wines.

Except for unusual grape varieties with anthocyanins or other flavonoids in their easily expressed juice, the flavonoid content is initially very low during fermentation of wine, but is augmented in proportion to continued pomace contact. Initially, the true tannins are precipitated by grape protein or yeast and do not remain in the wine so that the flavonoid increase is mostly from monomeric flavonoids including the anthocyanins. Once this precipitation capacity is exceeded, much of further increase in wine flavonoids during fermentation with the pomace is dimeric and larger condensed flavonoid tannins. A typical young red table wine with 1400 mg/liter of phenols as gallic acid is expected to have at least 200 mg/liter as nonflavonoid, about 150 mg/liter as anthocyanins (gallic acid equivalents or 350 mg/liter as malvidin-3-glucoside), perhaps 50 mg/liter as flavonols (quercetin, kaempferol, and traces of myricetin derivatives), about 250 mg/liter of other flavonoids (mainly (+)-catechin, (−)-epicatechin with smaller amounts of (+)-gallocatechin, (−)-epigallocatechin, and (−)-epicatechin gallate), and by difference about 750 mg/liter of dimeric and larger anthocyanogenic condensed tannins. As the wine ages the anthocyanins are nearly all incorporated into polymeric tannins, some polymers precipitate, and both polymerization and depolymerization affect the portion of the flavonoid oligomers which can be precipitated with agents such as methylcellulose or cinchonine.

The anthocyanins as a group are estimated to have a mild and approximately threshold effect on the richness of young red wine flavor. The catechin group and the phlobaphene group (large tannin-like products especially partially oxidized and poorly mobile in chromatography) are bitter with no or moderate astringency, respectively. The smallest oligomers are bitter but also appreciably astringent and the intermediate tannins, tetramers or so, are highly astringent and less noticeably bitter. The threshold for sensory effect when added to white wine was 200 mg/liter for combined catechins, 120 mg/liter for small oligmeric anthocyanogen, and 12 mg/liter for the intermediate plus large tannins. Studies of the amount of increase in total phenol by fermentation contact with pomace to give a threshold increase in astringency indicate about 100 mg/liter in white wine with 200−400 mg/liter total as gallic acid and about 250 mg/liter in red wine at 1200 to 1500 mg/liter total phenol.

Aging not only modifies wine phenols by oxidation, polymerization, precipitation, etc., but aging in wooden cooperage adds more or fewer phenols by extraction from the wood depending on the time, size, and previous use of the container. The phenols extractable from oak are all or nearly all nonflavonoid with the macromolecules being hydrolyzable tannins and lignin fragments. The amount of oak wood producing a threshold effect on wine flavor by extraction is about 200 to 500 mg of dry wood per liter of wine (Singleton 1974) depending on the cooperage source (American or European oak) and wine type. The amount of extractable phenol represented by this amount of wood is about 7 to 15 mg, but substances other than phenols are also involved. One year of storage in a new oak barrel can contribute at least 250 mg/liter of nonflavonoid phenols to wine and it is estimated that a threshold sensory difference could be contributed to wine representing 100 times the barrel's contents based on typical wine penetration into the staves and optimum distribution.

The color of white wines appears to be primarily the result of their flavonoid content as affected by limited oxidation (Rossi and Singleton 1966). Browning of wines at moderate temperature is prevented if oxygen is completely excluded and the phenols are the substrate for color formation by oxidation (Singleton and Kramling 1977). The anthocyanins of very young wines are the same as those of the grapes, cyanidin, peonidin, delphinidin, petunidin, and malvidin present as the 3-glucosides in *Vitis vinifera*, also as 3,5-diglucosides in most other species and partially acylated on the glucose with *p*-coumaric, caffeic or acetic acids (Webb 1970; Fong *et al.* 1971).

The measurement of visible color in red wines in relation to anthocyanin content has been reviewed by Francis and Clydesdale (1971). Van Buren *et al.* (1974) found the apparent color was affected not only by the pH [lower pH gives higher intensity owing to higher percentage flavylium ion, the colored form in red wine; see Brouillard and Delaporte (1977)], but also by the concentration and the thickness viewed. The presence of catechin and acetaldehyde at wine pH augments anthocyanin color (Timberlake and Bridle 1977) and shifts the hue toward violet. The incorporation of wine anthocyanins into complexes or polymers as wine ages results in making the pigment less pH responsive and shifts the color to more tile-red hues. This phenomenon and the polymerization reactions in wine are currently the subject of considerable study (Berg and Akiyoshi 1975; Glories and Augustin 1976; and Margheri and Tonon 1977).

Somers and Evans (1974), in a study of wines from a single warm area, found that red wine quality ratings correlated with the percentage of the anthocyanin in the ionized form. The correlation appears to be an indirect index rather than a direct flavor effect and in wines from widely different climates or processing procedures the correlation may not hold (Timberlake and Bridle 1976). Nevertheless, detailed spectral evaluation of red wines taking into consideration the effects of anthocyanin equilibria, pH, total phenolic content, and the decolorization effects of sulfur dioxide and its free and total content in the wine can give valuable correlations with wine color, quality, and relative age (Somers and Evans 1977).

Effects of Oxygen

The oxygen content of wines, the factors which influence its absorption, and the exact sequence of reactions which it produces are only poorly understood. The first potentiometric curves on the variation in oxidation-reduction potential in wines appear to be those of Geloso (1931). Done at pH 9, their application to normal wine aging is doubtful. Changes in the oxidation-reduction potential during fermentation and processing have been given by Deibner (1957A). See also Garino-Canina (1935), Joslyn (1938, 1949), Joslyn and Dunn (1938), and Schanderl (1948). The studies of Ribéreau-Gayon and Gardrat (1957) were done at the normal pH of wines. Ascorbic acid does not appear to be a factor in determining the oxidation or reduction titration curves of wines. The minimum potential found by reduction was lower in old than in young wines. The polyphenolic constituents begin to be reduced at relatively high potentials. However, if the polyphenols are first reduced they begin to be oxidized at relatively low potentials. The polyphenolic compounds thus appear to be important in the oxidation and reduction of wines. The inflection point for the curve for the reduction of red wines is 0.26 mv at pH 3. For malvidin the normal potential at pH 2.4 is 0.3 mv. Ribéreau-Gayon and Gardrat were careful not to claim that the polyphenolic compounds, the anthocyans in particular, constitute the oxidation-reduction system of wine. But they do state that they may have an influence on such a system. Condensation of anthocyans during aging is an oxidation and, particularly for bottled wines, must be balanced by an equivalent reduction of other compounds in the wine. It is important to distinguish reactions due to rapidly reversible thermodynamic systems from others. Ribéreau-Gayon (1963) emphasized the complicated nature of the redox system of wines. Copper complexes are much more active as catalyzers of oxidation than iron or iron complexes but traces of sulfhydryl derivatives (glutathione, for example) inhibit their activity. Wine is not a poised system; the oxidation-reduction potential is primarily dependent upon the ratios of oxidized to reduced copper and iron present. These, in turn, react slowly to the $SO_4^=$ /$SO_3^=$; perhaps the NAD/ NADH, and other complexes.

During fermentation, there is a rapid decrease in potential from about +0.4 to 0.1 v. Following fermentation, wines stored in wood and racked frequently show a rapid increase in potential but in the absence of oxygen the potential may decrease. Wines stored in the bottle several years also show a decrease in potential. Joslyn (1949) showed that California red table wines generally had a lower potential while aging in the wood than white wines. Garino-Canina (1935) and Schanderl (1950–51) reported marked decrease in potential of wines exposed to direct sunlight. Deibner (1957B) noted potentials of up to 0.5 v when wines were aerated. But as Joslyn (1949) stated, the relation does not seem to be direct. Lower potentials occur in wines stored several weeks in the bottle and likely are essential for development of bottle bouquet, but simply lowering the potential will not produce bottle bouquet (Singleton and Draper 1963).

The simple and rapid potentiometric procedure of Ough and Amerine (1960) should facilitate more accurate data on O_2 content. According to Ribéreau-Gayon et al. (1972–1977) the maximum oxygen which table wines can absorb is 5.6 to 6 ml per liter at 20°C (68°F). However, wine can absorb a relatively large amount of oxygen over a period of time. Frolov-Bagreev and Agabal'yants (1951) demonstrated that wines in small casks (250-liter) absorbed 40 ml of oxygen the first year—20 by diffusion, 4 from around the bung and 16 during four rackings. The second year, about 30 ml were absorbed per liter of wine.

Inorganic Compounds

The inorganic constituents of wines are of considerable biochemical, technological and physiological importance. Traces of many are needed in alcoholic fermentation. Some are a part of the oxidation-reduction system. Others affect the clarity and flavor. Many are significant in human nutrition. Except for the most recent publications, references to original papers will be found in Amerine (1958B).

Boric acid (H_3BO_3) concentration in wines is usually less than 50 mg/liter, usually 15 to 30 (Bionda and Ciurlo 1959; Jaulmes et al. 1961A). Film yeasts are believed to grow better in wines of higher boron content.

Bromide occurs in very small amounts (Jaulmes et al. 1961B; Bergner and Lang 1970). The recommended maximum is 1 mg/liter. Higher amounts probably indicate use of monobromacetic acid as an antiseptic—illegal in the United States and many other countries.

Chloride is present in appreciable quantities—up to 0.4 g/liter. The French and Swiss limit is 0.607 g/liter (as chloride). The limit is of some importance because of the possible contamination of wines from improperly cleaned ion-exchangers and also to detect use of monochloracetic acid as an antiseptic. Cabanis (1962) reported that when the chloride content was less than 60 mg/liter, the bromide content was less than 0.6 mg/liter. When the chloride content was 60 to 80 mg/liter, the bromide could be as high as 1 mg/liter; for more than 80 mg/liter of chloride, bromides up to 3 mg/liter were found.

Normal musts and wines contain less than 5 mg/liter of fluoride, and most wines contain considerably less than this—below one. Wines with more than five may have gotten it from late applications of fluosilicate insecticides or from illicit use of fluoride antiseptics. Sudraud and Cassignard (1959) also report that concrete tanks lined with magnesium fluosilicate are a potential source. Not only were the wines high, up to 50 mg/liter, in fluorine but the musts fermented more slowly. Fluorine concentrations above 25 mg/liter delay and above 50 mg/liter prevent fermentations. Iodide is present only in traces in wines, seldom over 0.3 mg/liter.

Phosphates are very important in alcoholic fermentation (p. 188). Ferric phosphate casse, before the use of stainless steel, was a troublesome problem of wines. Fermentation on the skins increases the phosphate content of the resulting wine. Archer and Castor (1956) reported a phosphate uptake of 0.00128 to 0.00167 mg/10^6 cells. In new wines, there are about 50 to 900 mg/liter of which only a small amount, about 10 to 20%, is present as organic phosphate (glycerophosphates, etc.). Many of the older enology texts claim a relationship between phosphate content and sensory quality, but there is very little critical data which would substantiate this claim.

Silicate is found in very small amounts—20 to 60 mg/liter.

Sulfate is of technological, sensory and legal importance. Sulfates have a slight salty-bitter taste. The plastering (p. 405) of musts leads to very high sulfate values. Furthermore, the oxidation of sulfurous acid may lead to high wine-sulfate contents. Finally, there are legal limits on the maximum sulfate content of wines in various countries, usually 2 or 3 g/liter (as potassium sulfate). Schanderl (1959) reported that sulfate could be reduced to sulfurous acid during alcoholic fermentation. Zang (1963) and Zang and Franze (1966) showed that sulfur dioxide was produced in fermenting musts that had not been treated with sulfur dioxide. See also pp. 201–202.

Hydrogen sulfide and methyl (and possibly ethyl) mercaptan are occasionally found in young wines. The former usually arises from reduction of elemental sulfur (remaining in the grapes from mildew control) (Thoukis and Stern 1962; Schütz and Kunkee 1977). Therefore, late sulfuring for mildew should be avoided. There are differences in the hydrogen-sulfide producing tendency of different yeasts (Ricketts and Coutts 1951; Macher 1952; Rankine 1963; Schütz and Kunkee 1977). Methyl mercaptan could arise from reduction of cysteine, which is formed from cystine by reduction with sulfites.

The detection threshold for hydrogen sulfide in wines is given as 1 mg/liter by Rankine (1963). Free sulfur dioxide removed 97% of 10 mg per liter of hydrogen sulfide in 5 days. Prompt removal of hydrogen sulfide from young wines is recommended. Tanner and Rentschler (1965) noted that ethyl mercaptan has a relatively low boiling point and can be removed by aeration.

Cations.—Aluminum is a normal constituent of wines. While Jaulmes (1951) has proposed a maximum limit of 50 mg/liter the amounts found in normal wines do not exceed about 15 and most wines have no more than 1 to 3 mg/liter. Aluminum containers and pipes and fining agents are the usual source of higher amounts. Red wines are higher in aluminum than whites.

Arsenic is present in wines in amounts of no more than 0.01 to 0.02 mg/liter. The recommended maximum is 0.02. Arsenical insecticides are the source of higher amounts but these are not used in California and seldom elsewhere. Most of the arsenical which reaches the fermentor is removed during fermentation. Lead arsenate is nearly insoluble at the alcoholic concentration of wine.

Cadmium is slightly soluble in wine hence cadmium-lined containers should not be used for storage of wines.

The calcium present in wines is derived from the fruit, from soil or plastering, calcium-containing filter-aids, and fining agents, concrete tanks, filter pads and possibly from the careless use of calcium hypochlorite. Concrete tanks should be treated to avoid calcium pick-up so far as possible. Filter pads, as presently produced, contain little calcium. They should, however, occasionally be checked and properly washed (p. 308). The amount of calcium pick-up from filter aids and fining agents such as bentonite is not known. The insidious nature of excess calcium tartrate is the long delay in its deposition.

Copper is important in musts and wines for fermentation, as a part of the oxidation-reduction system (particularly as leading to copper casse, p. 537), and as a factor in taste. Very small amounts of copper are normally present in new wines. The data of Amerine and Joslyn (1951) for newly fermented California wines are pertinent in this regard (mg/liter):

Source of Wine	No. of Samples	Minimum	Maximum	Average
Commercial	46	0.16	0.39	0.25
Experimental white	39	0.04	0.43	0.12
Experimental red	33	0.04	0.28	0.09

Vasconcellos (1947) reported that only 3.1% of the must copper remained in the new wine. Amerine and Thoukis (1956) found in small scale fermentations that 41 to 89% was lost during fermentation. Benvegnin and Capt (1934) also showed that 90% of the must copper was removed with the pomace and lees. Françot and Geoffroy (1956) reported that 25 to 83% of the must copper was lost during fermentation.

For information on the theories of copper clouding of wines see p. 537. Flavor may be affected by as little as 5 mg/liter. Wines seldom contain over 0.5 to 1 mg/liter unless (a), the must had a very high copper content or (b), the wine had been in contact with copper. The recommended legal maximum is 1 mg/liter. Excessive copper in wine is primarily due to contamination. For this reason, modern wineries have eliminated copper equipment which might come in contact with must or wine. For methods of removal of copper, see pp. 539—541.

Iron is of interest to enologists for the same reasons as copper—cloud formation, oxidation-reduction reactions, effect on yeast, and flavor impairment. Surface iron on grapes exceeds that from the interior of the fruit. Must iron is lost during fermentation, the percentage depending on the oxidation-reduction conditions during and after fermentation and on the length of time the new wine remains on the skins. The data of Schanderl (1959), which were obtained under winery conditions, suggest that from $\frac{1}{3}$ to $\frac{1}{2}$ is lost during fermentation and that essentially all of this is in or on yeast cells (see p. 537).

The primary source of excessive iron in wine appears to be from contact with iron equipment. For methods of removal of excessive iron see p. 539. The importance of iron in an oxidation-reduction system is recognized by most enologists. Whether or not some minimum amount is necessary for normal aging has not been established, but adequate aging occurs with wines very low in iron. While iron content can be 50 mg/liter, most California wines contain less than 10 mg/liter.

Little or no lead is found in normal musts. Even where lead sprays are used, little is reported in wine, and this rapidly decreases during racking and storage as lead tartrate is very insoluble. Settling the must also helps eliminate lead. The legal limit varies from 0.2 mg/liter in Great Britain, to 0.35 in Germany, to 3.5 in Switzerland. Jaulmes *et al.* (1960) reported that for French wines 29% exceeded the 0.2 limit and 0.6 would be a more practical maximum. The sources are lead capsules, unlined cement tanks, lead-based paints, rubber hoses, lead-containing metals in pumps, filters, fillers, faucets, gaskets, etc., and even lead in filter pads, bentonite, and glass. See Rankine (1957), Gentilini (1961), and Edwards and Amerine (1977). Amati and Rastelli (1967) found 1 to 92 mg/liter of lithium in 112 Italian wines with most samples between 5 and 60.

Magnesium is found in very small quantities in wines, 50 to 165 mg/liter. There is more in the musts than in the wine. The magnesium/calcium ratio increases during fermentation from about one to two to four.

Manganese is found in all wines in very small amounts—more in wines made of grapes grown in high manganese soils. There is more in red than white wines. The range reported in various wines is from 0.5 to 15 mg/liter but wines of over about 2.5 mg are believed to be sophisticated—either from potassium permanganate (added to reduce excessive sulfur dioxide?) or from manganese-containing charcoal. Würziger (1954) found 0.5 to 3.2 mg/liter in 70 wines. In 66 German musts, Gärtel (1956) reported 0.29—2.30 mg/liter (average 0.70). Wines of hybrids (direct producers) are slightly higher in manganese according to Tuzson (1964). In 842 Hungarian wines, the average was about 1.5 mg/liter. Deibner and Bénard (1956) found additions of 5 to 15 mg/liter of manganese plus heating improved the sensory quality of sweet wines. They believed that 1 to 5 mg/liter of molybdenum, with or without manganese, enhanced quality. Gärtel (1960) reported 0.001 to 0.0358 mg/liter in 41 wines. Russian enologists reported wines high in manganese, molybdenum, vanadium, titanium, and boron of better sensory quality. Amerine (1955B) found these claims difficult to evaluate. The amounts of trace elements were summarized by Eschnauer (1961).

Potassium constitutes about ¾ of the total cation content of wines, which, when added to the fact that wines are also normally low in sodium, makes them extremely valuable for those on medically restricted diets. Its importance in alcoholic fermentation and in bitartrate stability may be noted. Reports that it favorably affects sensory quality have not been documented adequately. Possibly the effect is mainly one of reducing the acidity. Amerine (1958B) reported potassium values from 0.1 to 1.76 g/liter with the average varying from 0.36 to 1.1. Use of tartrate-potassium solubility-product calculations to predict tartrate stability have been proposed by Nègre (1954) and Wiseman (1955). The actual values of the latter varied from 8.2 to 21.8×10^{-5} compared to calculated values of 1.40 to 2.85×10^{-5}. Berg and Keefer (1958–1959) have made similar calculations which are a useful guide and Bertrand et al. (1978) have discussed complexing of the potassium ion (see pp. 544–546).

Rubidium is present in amounts of 0.2 to 4.2 mg/liter, average about 0.5. More rubidium in the skins and stems make red wines higher than whites.

Sodium is of particular concern to wine makers today because of the use of ion exchangers for tartrate stability. Other sources of high sodium are from ocean spray (for vineyards near the sea), sodium bisulfite or metabisulfite, and possibly from fining agents. There may be undesirable flavor effects from high sodium. The amounts in wines vary very widely. From 5 to 443 mg/liter were noted by Amerine (1958B) but most wines had less than 100. Jouret and Poux (1961) reported about 4 times as much sodium and 5 to 6 times as much chloride in wines produced from vines grown on saline soils compared to those on nonsaline soils. Surprisingly, there is also more potassium but a lower alkalinity of the ash. Jouret and Bénard (1965) have demonstrated wide variations in chloride/sodium and potassium/sodium ratios in wines from different rootstocks. Cultural and climatic conditions were also important. It has been suggested that the sodium content (as sodium chloride) not be higher than 50 mg/liter. Tamborini and Magro (1970) recommended for Italian wines that the potassium/sodium ratio not be under 10.

Tin is seldom found in wines—usually from contact with tin utensils. Small amounts of tin result in cloudiness and hydrogen sulfide formation. Tin-plated equipment is reported by Eschnauer (1963) to be the source of tin in wines (0.1 to 0.9 mg/liter). Tin pickup should be avoided since at about 1 mg/liter it may lead to tin-albumin cloudiness.

Zinc has been determined more often because of the use of zinc-containing insecticides and fungicides. Normal wines usually contain less than 5 mg/liter though reports as high as 19 have been made. The recommended limit is 5–6 mg/liter (Vogel and Deshusses 1962; Tanner 1963). As much as half of the tin in musts is lost during fermentation. The use of zinc to prevent over-blue fining is illegal. More than about 5 mg/liter of zinc gives a slight metallic taste to wines. In German musts, Gärtel (1957) reported 0.5 to 2.0 mg/liter.

The cation and anion balance of wines has successfully been made on a number of wines. Ribéreau-Gayon and Peynaud (1958) have summarized much of these data. The following is the balance of 47 Bordeaux red wines (average pH 3.40) by Peynaud (1947) (in milliequivalents):

Cations	
Titratable acidity	75.00
Alkalinity of the ash	23.50
Ammonia	1.20
Sum of Cations	99.70
Anions (acids)	
Tartaric	26.9
Malic	2.8
Citric	1.4
Acetic	17.4
Succinic	15.5
Lactic	25.5
Acid esters	3.1
Phosphoric	4.5
Sulfurous	0.8
Sum of Anions	97.9

More data are needed using improved methods of analyses.

REFERENCES[1]

AMATI, A. and RASTELLI, R. 1967. Sul contenuto in litio di vini italiani. Ind. Agr. 5, 233-237.

---

[1]Titles have been translated only for nonwestern European languages.

AMERINE, M.A. 1954. Composition of wines. I. Organic constituents. Adv. Food Res. 5, 353-510.

AMERINE, M.A. 1958A. Acetaldehyde formation in submerged cultures of *Saccharomyces beticus.* App. Microbiol. 6, 160-168.

AMERINE, M.A. 1958B. Composition of wines. II. Inorganic constituents. Adv. Food Res. 8, 133-224.

AMERINE, M.A. 1965. The fermentation industries after Pasteur. Food Technol. 19, 75-80, 82.

AMERINE, M.A. and JOSLYN, M.A. 1951. Table Wines. The Technology of Their Production in California. Univ. Calif. Press, Berkeley and Los Angeles.

AMERINE, M.A. and KUNKEE, R.E. 1965. Yeast stability tests on dessert wines. Vitis 5, 187-194.

AMERINE, M.A. and OUGH, C.S. 1957. Studies on controlled fermentation. III. Am. J. Enol. 8, 18-30.

AMERINE, M.A. and OUGH, C.S. 1972. Recent advances in enology. Critical Rev. Food Technol. 2, 407-415.

AMERINE, M.A., ROESSLER, E.B. and FILIPELLO, F. 1959. Modern sensory methods of evaluating wine. Hilgardia 28, 477-567.

AMERINE, M.A., ROESSLER, E.B. and OUGH, C.S. 1965. Acids and the acid taste. I. The effect of pH and titratable acidity. Am. J. Enol. Vitic. 16, 29-37.

AMERINE, M.A. and THOUKIS, G. 1956. The fate of copper and iron during fermentation of grape musts. Am. J. Enol. 7, 45-52.

ANDERSON, J.H. 1959. CO_2 retention and an academic theory. Comm. Master Brewers Assoc. America 20 (1-2) 3-7, 15; (3-4) 6-12; (5-6) 12-14.

ANON. 1975. Sulfites as food additives. Food Technol. 29, 117-120.

ARCHER, T.E. and CASTOR, J.G.B. 1956. Phosphate changes in fermenting must in relation to yeast growth and ethanol production. Am. J. Enol. 7, 45-52.

AUERBACH, R.C. 1959. Sorbic acid as a preservative agent in wine. Wines Vines 40 (8) 26-28.

ÄYRÄPÄÄ, T. 1971. On the formation of higher alcohols by yeast and its dependence on nitrogenous nutrients. Svensk Kemish Tridskrift 83, 1-12.

BANOLAS, E. 1948. On the new apparatus for the rational equipment of wine making cellars. Inter. Inst. Refrig. Bull. Annex. 2, 9-23.

BARAUD, J. 1953. La réaction de la tartrazine appliquée à l'étude des vins. Bull. Soc. Chim. France 20, 525-527.

BARNETT, J.A. 1976. The utilization of sugars by yeasts. Adv. Carbohydrate Chem. Biochem. 32, 125-234. Academic Press, New York.

BENVEGNIN, L. and CAPT, E. 1934. Contribution à l'étude du cuivre dans les moûts et vins. Mitt. Gebiete Lebensm. Hyg. 25, 124-138.

BERAUD, P. and MILLET, J. 1949. Observations sur le pouvoir alcoogène des levures cultivées à basse température. Ann. Inst. Pasteur 77, 581-587.

BERG, H.W. and AKIYOSHI, M. 1975. On the nature of reactions responsible for color behavior in red wine: a hypothesis. Am. J. Enol. Vitic. 26, 134-143.

BERG, H.W. and KEEFER, R.M. 1958–1959. Analytical determination of tartrate stability in wine. Am. J. Enol. 9, 180-193; 10, 105-109.

BERG, H.W., FILIPELLO, F., HINREINER, E. and WEBB, A.D. 1955A. Evaluation of thresholds and minimum differences concentrations for various constituents of wines. I. Water solutions of pure substances. Food Technol. 9, 23-26.

BERG, H.W., FILIPELLO, F., HINREINER, E. and WEBB, A.D. 1955B. Evaluation of thresholds and minimum difference concentrations for various constituents of wines. II. Sweetness: the effect of ethyl alcohol, organic acids and tannin. Food Technol. 9, 138-140.

BERGNER, K.G. and LANG, B. 1970. Zum Bromgehalt deutscher Wein. Mitt. Rebe Wein, Obstbau. Früchteverw. (Klosterneuburg) 20, 189-201.

BERTI, L.A. 1951. Production factors. Proc. Am. Soc. Enol. 1951, 186-190.

BERTRAND, G.L., CARROLL, W.R. and FOLTYN, E.M. 1978. Tartrate stability of wines. I. Potassium complexes with pigments. Am. J. Enol. Vitic. 29, 25-29.

BERTRAND, G. and SILBERSTEIN, L. 1950. La fermentation du sucre par la levure produit-elle normalement du méthanol? Compt. Rend. 230, 800-803. See also Ibid. 229, 1281-1284, 1949; 234, 491-494, 1952.

BIDAN, P. and ANDRÉ, L. 1958. Sur la composition en acides aminés de quelques vins. Ann. Technol. Agric. 7, 403-432.

BIONDA, G. and CIURLO, R. 1959. Sur la teneur en bore de quelques vins de la Ligurie. Ann. Fals. Fraudes 52, 369-372.

BLOUIN, J. 1963. Constituants du vin combinant de l'acide sulfureux. Ann. Technol. Agric. 12 (numéro hors série 1), 97-98.

BOUFFARD, A. 1895. Détermination de la chaleur dégagée dans la fermentation alcoolique. Prog. Agric. Vit. 24, 345-347.

BOURDET, A. and HÉRARD, J. 1958. Influence de l'autolyse des levures sur la composition phosphorée et azotée des vins. Ann. Technol. Agric. 7, 177-202.

BOURZEIX, M. 1976A. Les composés phénoliques du raisin et du vin. Leurs transformations au cours de l'élaboration des vins et leurs effets sur la qualité (vins rouges). Bull. Offic. Intern. Vin 49 (550), 986-1004.

BOURZEIX, M. 1976B. Les composés phénoliques du raisin et du vin. Leurs effets sur la qualité. Rev. Franç. Oenol. 15 (63) 53-69.

BOURZEIX, M. and SAQUET, N. 1975. Les anthocyanes du raisin et du vin. Vignes Vins, Spec. No., 1-86.

BROCKMANN, M.C. and STIER, T.J.B. 1948. Influence of temperature on the production of glycerol during alcoholic fermentation. J. Am. Chem. Soc. 70, 413-414.

BROUILLARD, R. and DELAPORTE, B. 1977. Chemistry of anthocyanin pigments. 2. Kinetic and thermodynamic study of proton transfer, hydration, and tautomeric reactions of malvidin-3-glucoside. J. Am. Chem. Soc. 99, 8461-8468.

BURROUGHS, L. and SPARKS, A.H. 1973. Sulphite binding power of wines and ciders. III. Determination of carbonyl compounds in a wine and calculation of its sulphite-binding power. J. Sci. Food Agric. 24, 207-217.

BURROUGHS, L. and WHITING, G. 1960. The sulphur dioxide combining power of cider. Ann. Rept. Agric. Hort. Exp. Stn., Long Ashton 1960, 144-147.

CABANIS, J.E. 1962. Le brome dans les vins. Montpellier.

CABEZUDO, D., LLAGUNO, C. and GARRIDO, J.M. 1963. Contentido en biotina y otros componentes fundamentales en vinos de las principales zonas vinícolas de España. Agroquim. Technol. Alim. 3, 369-375.

CAMBITZI, A. 1947. Formation of racemic calcium tartrate in wines. Analyst 72, 542-543.

CARLES, J. 1959. Sur les décarboxylations dans les vins et l'apparition de l'acide citramalique. Rev. Esp. Fisiol. 15, 193-200.

CASTELLI, T. 1941. Temperatura e chimismo dei blastomiceti. Ann. Microbiol. 2 (1) 8-22.

CASTINO, M. 1969. Gli acidi 2-metilmalico, 2,3-diidrossilisovalerianico e 2,3-diidrossi-2-metilbutirico nei vini. Riv. Viticolt. Enol. (Conegliano) 22, 197-207.

CASTINO, M. and DI STEFANO, R. 1975. Correlation between the vine varieties of a viticultural region and their 2,3-butanediol content. Vini d'Italia 17, 233-238.

CASTINO, M. and DI STEFANO, R. 1976. Frazionamento degli acidi fenolici dei vini fianchi per gel filtrazione. Riv. Viticolt. Enol. (Conegliano) 29, 290-305.

CASTOR, J.G.B. and GUYMON, J.F. 1952. On the mechanism of formation of higher alcohols during alcoholic fermentation. Science 115, 147-149.

CASTOR, J.G.B., NELSON, K.E. and HARVEY, J.M. 1957. Effect of captan residues on fermentation of grapes. Am. J. Enol. 8, 50-57.

CAUSERT, J., HUGOT, D., THUISSIER, M., BIETTE, E. and LECLERC, J. 1964. L'utilisation des sulfites en technologie alimentaire: quelques aspects toxicologiques et nutritionnels. IV Congrès d'Expertise Chimique, Athens, Spec. No., 215-224.

CHAN, L., WEAVER, R. and OUGH, C.S. 1975. Microbial inhibition caused by p-hydroxybenzoate esters in wine. Am. J. Enol. Vitic 26, 201-207.

CHEN, E.C.H. 1978. The relative contribution of Ehrlich and biosynthetic pathways to the formation of fusel alcohols. J. Am. Soc. Brew. Chem. 36, 39-43.

COOK, A.H. 1958. The Chemistry and Biology of Yeasts. Academic Press, New York.

COOKE, G.M., KUNKEE, R.E. and OUGH, C.S. 1964. Continuous addition of diethylpyrocarbonate into wine. Wine Institute, Tech. Advis. Committee, Dec. 11, 1964.

CROWELL, E.A. and GUYMON, J.F. 1963. Influence of aeration and suspended material on higher alcohol, acetoin, and diacetyl during fermentation. Am. J. Enol. Vitic. 14, 214-222.

CROWELL, E.A. and GUYMON, J.F. 1975. Wine constituents arising from sorbic acid addition, and identification of 2-ethoxyhexa-3,5-diene as source of geranium-like off-odor. Am. J. Enol. Vitic 26, 97-102.

DeEDS, F. 1961. Summary of toxicity data on sulfur dioxide. Food Technol. 15, 28, 33.

DEIBNER, L. 1957A. Modifications du potentiel oxydoreducteur au cours de l'élaboration des vins de différents types. Ann. Technol. Agric. 6, 313-345.

DEIBNER, L. 1957B. Effet de différents traitements sur le potentiel oxydo-réducteur des vins au cours de leur conservation. Ibid. 6, 363-372.

DEIBNER, L. and BÉNARD, P. 1956. Recherches sur la maturation des vins doux naturels. II. Essai de catalyseurs métalliques. Ibid. 5, 377-397.

DELLE, P.N. 1911. The influence of must concentration on the fermentation and composition of wine and its stability. Odessa, Otchet-vinodeiel'-cheskoi stantsii russkikh" vinogradarei i vinodielov" za 1908 i 1909g, 118-160. (Russian)

DESOTO, R. and WARKENTIN, H. 1955. Influence of pH and total acidity on calcium tolerance of sherry wine. Food Res. 20, 301-309. (Also in Am. J. Enol. 7, 91-97. 1956.)

DIEMAIR, W. and MAIER, G. 1962. Bestimmung des Eiweissgehaltes. Z. Lebensm.-Untersuch. -Forsch. 118, 148-152.

DIETRICH, K.R. 1954. Die Vermeidung von Schwundverlusten an Alkohol bei der Gärung. Deut. Wein-Ztg. 90, 448.

DIMOTAKI-KOURAKOU, V. 1962. Le présence de l'acide α-methyl-malique dans le vins. Ann. Fals. Expert. Chim. 55, 149-158.

DITTRICH, H. H. and KERNER, E. 1964. Diacetyl als Weinfehler; Ursache und Beseitigung des "Milchsäuretones." Wein-Wissen. 19, 528-538.

DOTT, W., HEINZEL, M. and TRÜPER, H.G. 1976. Sulfite formation by wine yeasts. I. Relationships between growth, fermentation and sulfite formation. Arch. Microbiol. 107, 289-292.

DUPUY, P. 1960. Le métabolisme de l'acide tartrique. Ann. Technol. Agric. 9, 139-184.

DURMISHIDZE, S.V. 1971. Les polyphénols du raisin et du vin. Bull. Offic. Intern. Vin 44 (480) 132-135.

EDWARDS, M.A. and AMERINE, M.A. 1977. The lead content of wines by atomic absorption spectrophotometry using flameless atomization. Am. J. Enol. Vitic. 28, 239-240.

ESAU, P. and AMERINE, M.A. 1964. Residual sugars in wine. Am. J. Enol. Vitic. 15, 187-189.

ESCHENBRUCH, R. 1974. Sulfite and sulfide formation during winemaking—a review. Am. J. Enol. Vitic. 25, 157-161.

ESCHENBRUCH, R. and BONISH, P. 1976. Production of sulphite and sulphide by low- and high-sulphite forming yeasts. Arch. Microbiol. 107, 299-302.

ESCHNAUER, H. 1961. Spurenelemente im Wein und im Weinbau. Mitt. Rebe Wein, Serie A (Klosterneuburg) 11, 123-130.

ESCHNAUER, H. 1963. Zinntrübungen im Wein. Weinberg Keller *10*, 523-528.

ETTIENNE, A.D. and MATHERS, A.P. 1956. Laboratory carbonation of wine. J. Assoc. Offic. Agric. Chem. *39*, 844-848.

FEDUCHY MARIÑO, E., SANDOVAL PUERTA, J.A., HIDALGO ZABALLOS, T., RODRÍGUEZ MATÍA, E. and HORCHE DÍEZ, T. 1964. Contribución al estudio analítico des las dosis de metanol existentes en productos procedentes de la fermentatión vínica. Bol. Inst. Nac. Invest. Agron. *51*, 453-484.

FILIPELLO, F. 1951. Correlation of fortifying brandy with wine quality. Proc. Am. Soc. Enol. *1951*, 154-156.

FLANZY, C. and POUX, C. 1965. Les levures alcooliques dans les vins. Protéolyse, protéogenèse. (III). Ann. Technol. Agric. *14*, 35-48.

FLANZY, C., POUX, C. and FLANZY, M. 1964. Les levures alcooliques dans les vins. Protéolyse et protéogenèse. *Ibid. 13*, 283-300.

FLANZY, M. 1934. L'Alcool Méthylique dans les Liquides Alcooliques Naturels. Imprimerie Regionale, Toulouse.

FLANZY, M. and BOUZIGUES, L. 1959. Pectines et méthanol dans les moûts de raisin et les vins. Ann. Technol. Agric. *8*, 59-68.

FLANZY, M. and LOISEL, Y. 1958. Evolution des pectines dans les boissons et production de méthanol. *Ibid. 7*, 311-321.

FLANZY, M. and OURNAC, A. 1963. Fermentation des jus de raisins frais et désulfités. Influence d'additions de levures et de thiamine. *Ibid. 12*, 65-84.

FONG, R.A., KEPNER, R.E. and WEBB, A.D. 1971. Acetic-acid-acylated anthocyanin pigments in the grape skins of a number of varieties of *Vitis vinifera*. Am. J. Enol. Vitic. *22*, 150-155.

FORNACHON, J.C.M. 1963. Inhibition of certain lactic acid bacteria by free and bound sulphur dioxide. J. Sci. Food Agric. *12*, 857-862.

FRANCIS, F.J. and CLYDESDALE, F.M. 1971. Color measurement of foods. 24. Wine. Food Prod. Dev. *5* (1) 34-35, 38, 40, 42, 97.

FRANÇOT, P. and GEOFFROY, P. 1956. Réparition du cuivre dans les moûts et vins au cours du pressurage Champenois. Vigneron Champenois *77*, 451-459.

FROLOV-BAGREEV, A.M. and AGABAL'YANTS, G.G. 1951. Khimiya Vina. (Chemistry of Wine). Pishchepromizdat, Moscow.

GALETTO, W.G., WEBB, A.D. and KEPNER, R.E. 1966. Identification of some acetals in an extract of submerged-culture flor sherry. Am. J. Enol. Vitic. *17*, 11-19.

GÄRTEL, W. 1956. Untersuchungen über den Mangangehalt von Rebteilen und Most. Weinberg Keller *3*, 554-560.

GÄRTEL, W. 1957. Untersuchungen über den Zinkgehalt von Rebteilen und Most. *Ibid. 4*, 419-424.

GÄRTEL, W. 1960. Molybdänbestimmung in Most und Wein. *Ibid. 7*, 373-379.

GARINO-CANINA, E. 1935. Il potenziale di ossidoriduzione e la tecnica enologica. Ann. Chim. Appl. 25, 209-217.

GEHMAN, H. and OSMAN, E.M. 1954. The chemistry of the sugar sulfite-reaction and its relationship to food problems. Adv. Food Res. 5, 53-96.

GEISS, W. 1952. Gezügelte Gärung. Sigurd Horn Verlag, Frankfurt.

GELOSO, J. 1931. Relation entre le vieillissement des vins et leur potentiel d'oxydo-réduction. Ann. Brass. Distil. 29, 177-181, 193-197, 257-261, 273-279.

GENEVOIS, L. 1936. L'energétique des fermentations. Ann. Ferment. 2, 65-78.

GENEVOIS, L. 1951. Les produits secondaries de la fermentation; acids organiques des vins; matiéres colorantes et vieillissement des vins. Rev. Ferment. Ind. Aliment. 6, 18-25, 43-47, 88-96, 111-115.

GENTILINI, L. 1961. Il piombo in enologia. Riv. Viticolt. Enol. (Conegliano) 14, 307-311.

GENTILINI, L. and CAPPELLERI, G. 1959. Variazioni del contenuto in glicerina del vino in funzione di fattori che influenzano il decorso dell'atto fermentativo. Ann. Sper. Agrar. (Rome) [N.S.] 13, 289-306.

GILLISSEN, G. 1954. Über die Verwendung antibiotischer Stoffe anstelle von schwefliger Säure in der Oenologie. Deut. Wein-Ztg. 90, 195-196.

GLORIES, Y. and AUGUSTIN, M. 1976. Recherches sur la structure et les propriétés des composés phénoliques polymérines des vins rouges. Connaiss. Vigne Vin 10, 51-71.

GOTTSCHALK, A. 1946. Mechanism of selective fermentation of d-fructose from invert sugar by Sauternes yeast. Biochem. J. 40, 621-626.

GRAY, W.D. 1945. The sugar tolerance of four strains of distillers' yeast. J. Bacteriol. 49, 445-452.

GROAT, M.L. and OUGH, C.S. 1978. Effect of particulate matter on fermentation rates and wine quality. Am. J. Enol. Vitic. 29, 112-119.

GUIMBERTEAU, G. and PEYNAUD, E. 1965. Recherche et estimation du saccharose ajouté aux moûts et aux vins á l'aide de la chromatographie sur papier. Ann. Fals. Expert Chim. 58, 32-38.

GUYMON, J.F. and CROWELL, E.A. 1965. The formation of acetoin and diacetyl during fermentation, and the levels found in wines. Am. J. Enol. Vitic. 16, 85-91.

GUYMON, J.F. and HEITZ, J.E. 1952. The fusel oil content of California wines. Food Technol. 6, 359-362.

GUYMON, J.F., INGRAHAM, J.L. and CROWELL, E.A. 1961. Influence of aeration upon the formation of higher alcohols by yeasts. Am. J. Enol. Vitic. 12, 60-66.

GVALADZE, V. 1936. Relation Between the Products in Alcoholic Fermentation (transl.) Lenin Agric. Acad. U.S.S.R., Moscow.

HARDEN, A. 1932. Alcoholic Fermentation, 4th Edition. Longmans, Green and Co., London.

HARVALIA, A. 1976. Relation entre la teneur des vins en alcools supérieurs et la teneur des moûts en substances azotées en particulier en acides aminés. Bull. Off. Intern. Vin Vigne *49* (541) 222-233.

HEIDE, C. VON DER and SCHMITTHENNER, F. 1922. Der Wein. F. Vieweg und Sohn, Braunschweig, Germany.

HEINZEL, M. and TRÜPER, H.G. 1976. Sulfite formation by wine yeasts. II. Properties of ATP-sulfurylase. Arch. Microbiol. *107*, 293-297.

HENNIG, K. 1959. Erfahrungen beim Nachweis gezuckerter und gespriteter Wein nach Rebelein. Bericht Hessische Lehr.-u. Forch. Wein-, Obst- Gartenbau, Geisenheim *1957/58*, 28-29.

HENNIG, K. 1960. Der Pyrokohlensäurediäthylester, ein neues, rückstandloses, gärhemmendes Mittel. Weinberg Keller *7*, 351-360.

HICKENBOTHAM, A.R. and RYAN, V.J. 1948. Glycerol in wine. Austral. Chem. Inst. J. Proc. *15*, 89-100.

HINREINER, E., FILIPELLO, F., BERG, H.W. and WEBB, A.D. 1955A. Evaluation of thresholds and minimum difference concentrations for various constituents of wines. IV. Detectable differences in wines. Food Technol. *9*, 489-490.

HINREINER, E., FILIPELLO, F., WEBB, A.D. and BERG, H.W. 1955B. Evaluation of thresholds and minimum difference concentrations for various constituents of wines. III. Ethyl alcohol, glycerol and acidity in aqueous solutions. *Ibid.* *9*, 351-353.

JAULMES, P. 1951. Analyse des Vins, 2nd Edition. Librarie Coulet, Dubois et Poulain, Montpellier.

JAULMES, P., BRUN-CORDIER, S. and BASCOU, P. 1961A. La teneur naturelle des vins en acide borique. Ann. Fals. Expert. Chim. *53*, 70-82.

JAULMES, P., BRUN-CORDIER, S. and CABANIS, J.E. 1961B. Teneur naturelle des vins en brome. Trav. Soc. Pharm. Montpellier *20*, 84-92.

JAULMES, P., HAMELLE, G. and ROQUES, J. 1960. Le plomb dans les moûts et les vins. Ann. Technol. Agric. *9*, 189-245.

JORDAN, J.R. 1911. Quality in Dry Wines Through Adequate Fermentations. San Francisco.

JOSLYN, M.A. 1938. Electrolytic production of rancid flavor in sherries. Ind. Eng. Chem. *30*, 568-577.

JOSLYN, M.A. 1949. California wines. Oxidation-reduction potentials at various stages of production and aging. Ind. Eng. Chem. *41*, 587-592.

JOSLYN, M.A. 1951. Nutrient requirements of yeast. Mycopath. Mycol. Appl. *5*, 260-276.

JOSLYN, M.A. and BRAVERMAN, J.B.S. 1954. The chemistry and technology of the pretreatment and preservation of fruit and vegetable products with sulfur dioxide and sulfites. Adv. Food Res. *5*, 97-160.

JOSLYN, M.A. and DUNN, R. 1938. Acid metabolism of wine yeast. I. The relation of volatile acid formation to alcoholic fermentation. J. Am. Chem. Soc. *60*, 1137-1141.

JOURET, C. and BÉNARD, P. 1965. Influence des porte-greffes sur la composition minérale des vins des vignes de terrains salés. Ann. Technol. Agric. 14, 349-355.

JOURET, C. and POUX, C. 1961. Note sur les teneurs en potassium, sodium et chlore des vignes des terrains salés. Ibid. 10, 369-374.

KIELHÖFER, E. 1953. Die Wirkung antibiotischen Stoffe auf die Weingärung. Deut. Wein-Ztg. 89, 638, 640, 642. (For translation see Am. J. Enol. 5, 13-17, 1954.)

KIELHÖFER, E. 1959. Neue Erkenntnisse über die Wirkung der Schwefligen Säure in Wein und die Möglichkeit ihres Ersatzes durch Ascorbinsäure. Verlag Sigurd Horn, Frankfurt.

KIELHÖFER, E. and WÜRDIG, G. 1960A. Die an Aldehyd gebundene schweflige Säure im Wein. I. Acetaldehydbildung durch enzymatische und nicht enzymatische Alkohol-Oxydation. Weinberg Keller 7, 16-22.

KIELHÖFER, E. and WÜRDIG, G. 1960B. Ibid. II. Acetaldehydbildung bei der Gärung. Ibid. 7, 50-61.

KOCH, J. and BRETTHAUER, G. 1960. Das Glucose-Fructose Verhältnis der Konsumweine in Abhängigkeit von verschiedenen kellertechnischen Massnahmen. Z. Lebensm.-Untersuch. -Forsch. 112, 97-105.

KONOVALOVA, L.A., DZHURIKYANTS, N.G. and GORYAEV, M.I. 1977. Formation of higher alcohols in wine. (transl.) Vinodel. Vinograd. SSSR (2) 14-16.

KUNKEE, R.E., GUYMON, J.F. and CROWELL, E.A. 1971. Studies on control of higher alcohol formation by yeasts through metabolic inhibition. Yeasts: Models. Sci. Tech., Proc. Spec. Intern. Symp., 1st, 531-542.

KUNKEE, R.E. and OUGH, C.S. 1966. Multiplication and fermentation of Saccharomyces cerevisiae under carbon dioxide pressure in wine. Appl. Microbiol. 14, 643-648.

LAFON, M. 1956. Sur quelques caractères physiologiques et biochimiques des levures de vin. Ann. Inst. Pasteur 91, 91-99.

LAFON-LAFOURCADE, S. and PEYNAUD, E. 1958. L'acide p-aminobenzoïque, l'acide ptéroylglutamique et la choline (vitamines du groupe B) dans les vins. Ann. Technol. Agric. 7, 303-309.

LAFON-LAFOURCADE, S. and PEYNAUD, E. 1961. Composition azotée des vins en fonction des conditions de vinification. Ibid. 10, 143-160.

LAFON-LAFOURCADE, S. and PEYNAUD, E. 1965. Sur l'évolution des acides pyruvique et α-cétoglutamique au cours de la fermentation alcoolique. Compt. Rend. 261, 1778-1780.

LANTEAUME, M.T., RAMEL, P., GIRARD, P., JAULMES, P., GASQ, M. and RANNAUD, J. 1969. Détermination et comparaison des DL 50 du métabisulfite de potassium, de l'éthanal et de leur combinaison (hydroxy-éthanesulfonate de potassium) par voie orale sur le rat de souche Wistar. Ann. Fals. Expert. Chim. 62, 231-241.

LAUBENHEIMER, 1974. Löst die Sorbinsäure das Süssreservproblem? Deut. Weinbau 29 (14) 467-468.

LONVAUD-FUNEL, A. and RIBÉREAU-GAYON, P. 1977. Le gaz carbonique des vins. II. Aspect technologique. Connaiss. Vigne Vin 11, 165-182.

MACHER, L. 1952. Hefegärung und Schwefelwassertoffbildung. Deut. Lebensm.-Rdsch. 48, 183-189.

MARGHERI, G. and TONON, D. 1977. Evoluzione de colore dei vini rossi nel corso della loro conservazione e del loro invecchiamento. Vini Ital. 19, 264-270.

MARSH, G.L. 1951. Calculation of Proof Gallon Equivalent Per Ton of Grapes. Wine Institute, Tech. Advis. Committee, July 20, 1951.

MARSH, G.L. 1958. Alcohol yield: factors and methods. Am J. Enol. 9, 53-58.

MILLER, F.J. 1959. Carbon dioxide in wine. Wines Vines 40 (8) 32. See also Carbon Dioxide in Water, in Wine, in Beer and in Other Beverages. Oakland, California. 1958.

MÖHLER, K. and PIRES, R. 1969A. Verteilungschromatographie organischer Säuren, Z. Lebensm.-Untersuch. -Forsch. 139, 337-345.

MÖHLER, K. and PIRES, R. 1969B. Bestimmung von organischer Säuren in Wein durch Verteilungschromatographie. Ibid. 140, 3-12.

MÖHLER, K. and PIRES, R. 1969C. Nachweis und Bestimmung von Anglicerinsäure (2-Methyl-2,3-dihydroxybuttersäure) in Wein. Ibid. 140, 88-93.

MOUTONET, M. 1969. Biosynthèse des alcools supérieurs des boissons fermentées. Ann. Technol. Agric. 18, 249-261.

MULLER, C.J., KEPNER, R.E. and WEBB, A.D. 1973. Lactones in wines—a review. Am. J. Enol. Vitic. 24, 5-9.

MULLER, C.J., KEPNER, R.E. and WEBB, A.D. 1978. 1,3-Dioxanes and 1, 3-dioxolanes as constituents of the acetal fraction of Spanish fino sherry. Am. J. Enol. Vitic. 29, 207-212.

MÜNZ, T. 1963. Die Kalium-Pufferung im Most und Wein. Wein-Wissen. 18, 496-502.

NEGRE, E. 1954. Les facteurs de solubilité, de l'acide tartrique en présence de potassium. Application au cas du vin. Compt. Rend. Acad. Agric. France 40, 705-709.

NILOV, V. I. and VALUĬKO, G.G. 1958. Izmenenie soderzhaniya azotistykh veshchestvo pri brozhenii vinogradnogo susla (Changes in nitrogen during fermentation). Vinodel. Vinograd. S.S.S.R. 18 (8) 4-7.

OUGH, C.S. 1963. Sensory examination of four organic acids added to wine. J. Food Sci. 28, 101-106.

OUGH, C.S. 1964. Fermentation rates of grape juice. I. Effects of temperature and composition on white juice fermentation rates. Am. J. Enol. Vitic. 15, 167-177.

OUGH, C.S. 1971. Measurement of histamine in California wines. J. Agric. Food Chem. 19, 241-244.

OUGH, C.S. 1976A. Ethyl carbamate in fermented beverages and foods. I. Naturally occurring ethyl carbamate. J. Agric. Food Chem. 24, 323-328.

OUGH C.S. 1976B. Ethyl carbamate in fermented beverages and foods. II. Possible formation of ethyl carbamate from diethyl dicarbonate addition to wine. J. Agric. Food Chem. *24*, 328-331.

OUGH, C.S. and AMERINE, M.A. 1958. Studies on aldehyde production under pressure, oxygen, and agitation. Am. J. Enol. *9*, 111-122.

OUGH, C.S. and AMERINE, M.A. 1960. Dissolved oxygen determination in wine. Food Res. *24*, 744-748.

OUGH, C. S. and AMERINE, M.A. 1961. Studies with controlled fermentation. IV. Effects of temperature and handling on rates, composition and quality of wines. Am. J. Enol. Vitic. *12*, 117-128.

OUGH, C.S. and AMERINE, M.A. 1966. Effects of temperature on wine making. Calif. Agric. Exp. Stn. Bull. *827*, 1-36.

OUGH, C.S. FONG, D., and AMERINE, M.A. 1972. Glycerol in wine: determination and some factors affecting. Am. J. Enol. Vitic. *23*, 1-5.

OUGH, C.S. and INGRAHAM, J.L. 1960. Use of sorbic acid and sulfur dioxide in sweet table wines. Am. J. Enol. Vitic. *11*, 117-122.

OUGH, C.S. and KUNKEE, R.E. 1968. Fermentation rates of grape juice. V. Biotin content of juice and its effect on alcoholic fermentation rate. Appl. Microbiol. *16*, 572-576.

PANGBORN, R.M., OUGH, C.S. and CHRISP, R.B. 1964. Taste interrelationship of sucrose, tartaric acid, and caffeine in white table wine. Am. J. Enol. Vitic. *15*, 154-161.

PAPARELLI, L. and COLBY, G.E. 1890. On the quantities of nitrogenous matters contained in California wines. Soc. Prom. Agric. Sci. 7 p. *See also* Univ. California. Report of the Vitic. Work. 1887−1893, part II, 422-446.

PEYNAUD, E. 1937. Études sur les phénomènes d'estérification. Rev. Viticult. *86*, 209-215, 227-231, 248-253, 299-301, 394-396, 420-423, 440-444; *87*, 49-52, 113-116, 185-188, 242-249, 278-295, 297-301, 344-350, 362-364, 383-385. *See also* Ann. Ferment. *3*, 242-252. 1937.

PEYNAUD, E. 1947. Contribution à l'étude biochimique de la maturation du raisin et de la composition des vins. Inds. Agric. Aliment. *64*, 87-95, 167-188, 301-317, 399-414. Printed as a book by Imprimerie G. Santai et Fils, Lille. 1948. *Summarized in* Rev. Viticult. *92*, 177-180, 271-272. 1946. and Bull. Office Intern. Vin *20* (191) 34-51. 1947.

PEYNAUD, E. and CHARPENTIÉ, Y. 1953. Dosage de l'acide gluconique dans les moûts et les vins provenant de raisins attaques par le *Botrytis cinerea*. Ann. Fals. Fraudes *46*, 14-21.

PEYNAUD, E. and LAFON, M. 1951A. Note complémentaire sur les corps acétoïniques des eaux-de-vie. *Ibid. 44*, 399-402.

PEYNAUD, E. and LAFON, M. 1951B. Présence et signification du diacétyle, de l'acétoine et du 2,3-butanediol dans les eaux-de-vie. *Ibid. 44*, 264-283.

PEYNAUD, E. and LAFOURCADE, S. 1957. Teneurs en pyridoxine des vins de Bordeaux. Ann. Technol. Agric. *6*, 301-312.

RANKINE, B.C. 1957. Factors influencing the lead content of wine. *Ibid. 8*, 458-466.

RANKINE, B.C. 1963. Nature, origin and prevention of hydrogen sulphide aroma in wines. *Ibid. 14,* 79-91.

RAPP, A., BACHMANN, O and STEFFAN, H. 1977. Les composés phénoliques du raisin et du vin. Leurs transformations au cours de l'élaboration des vins et leurs effets sur la qualité (vins blancs). Bull. Offic. Intern. Vin *50* (553) 167-196.

REBELEIN, H. 1957A. Unterscheidung naturreiner von gezuckerten Weinen und Bestimmung des natürlichen Alkoholgehaltes. Z. Lebensm.-Untersuch. -Forsch. *106,* 403-420.

REBELEIN, H. 1957B. Vereinfachtes Verfahren zur Bestimmung des Glycerins und Butylenglykols in Wein. *Ibid. 105,* 296-311.

REBELEIN, H. 1958. Zur Erkennung naturreiner Weine mittels des K-Werts. Deut. Lebensm. Rdsch. *54,* 297-307.

RIBÉREAU-GAYON, J. 1963. Phenomena of oxidation and reduction in wines and applications. Am. J. Enol. Vitic. *14,* 139-143.

RIBÉREAU-GAYON, J. and GARDRAT, J. 1957. Application du titrage potentiométrique à l'étude du vin. Ann. Technol. Agric. *6,* 185-216.

RIBÉREAU-GAYON, J. and PEYNAUD, E. 1958. Analyses et Contrôle des Vins, 2nd Edition. Librairie Polytechnique Ch. Béranger. Paris and Liège.

RIBÉREAU-GAYON, J., PEYNAUD, E. and GUIMBERTEAU, G. 1959. Formation des produits secondaires de la fermentation alcoolique en fonction de l'alimentation azotées des levures. Compt. Rend. *248,* 749-751.

RIBÉREAU-GAYON, J., PEYNAUD, E. and LAFOURCADE, S. 1952A. Action inhibitrice sur les levures de la vitamine K_5 et de quelques antibiotiques. Compt. Rend. Acad. Agric. France *39,* 479-481. (*See also* Compt. Rend. *235,* 1163-1165.)

RIBÉREAU-GAYON, J., PEYNAUD, E. and LAFOURCADE. S. 1952B. Sur la formation de substances inhibitrices de la fermentation par *Botrytis cinerea.* Compt. Rend. *234,* 478-480.

RIBÉREAU-GAYON, J., PEYNAUD, E., SUDRAUD, P. and RIBÉREAU-GAYON, P. 1972–77. Traité d'Oenologie, 4 Vol. Dunod, Paris.

RIBÉREAU-GAYON, P. 1965. Identification d'esters des acides cinnamiques et de l'acide tartrique dans les limbes et les baies de *V. vinifera.* Compt. Rend. *260,* 341-343.

RIBÉREAU-GAYON, P. 1974. The chemistry of red wine color. *In* Chemistry of Winemaking. A.D. Webb (Editor). Advances in Chemistry, Vol. 137. American Chemical Society, Washington, D.C.

RIBÉREAU-GAYON, P. and SAPIS, J.C. 1965. Sur la présence dans le vin de tyrosol, de tryptophol, d'alcool phényléthylique et de γ-butyrolactone, produits secondaires de la fermentation alcoolique. Compt. Rend. *261,* 1915-1916.

RIBÉREAU-GAYON, P. and STONESTREET, E. 1964. La constitution des tanins du raisin et du vin. Compt. Rend. Acad. Agric. France *50,* 662-670.

RICKETTS, J. and COUTTS, M.W. 1951. Hydrogen sulfide in fermentation gas. Am. Brewer *84* (8) 27-30; (9) 27-30, 74-75; (10) 33-36, 100-101.

RODOPULO, A.K. 1951. Okislenie vinnoĭ kisloty v vine v prisutsvii soleĭ tyaz-helykh metallov (aktivirovanie kisloroda zhelezom) (Oxidation of tartaric acid in wine in the presence of salts of heavy metals, (activation by iron). Izvest. Akad. Nauk. S.S.S.R., Ser. Biol. *1951* (3) 115-128.

ROSE, A.H. and HARRISON, J.S. 1969–1971. The Yeasts. 1969: Vol. 1, Biology of Yeasts. 1970: Vol. 2, Physiology and Biochemistry of Yeasts. 1971: Vol. 3, Yeast Technology. Academic Press, New York.

ROSSI, J.A., JR., and SINGLETON, V.L. 1966. Contributions of grape phenols to oxygen absorption and browning of wines. Am. J. Enol. Vitic. *17*, 231-239.

SALLER, W. 1955. Die Qualitätsverbesserung der Weine und Süssmoste durch Kälte. Sigurd Horn Verlag, Frankfurt.

SCHANDERL, H. 1948. Die Reduktions-Oxydations-Potentiale während der Entwicklungsphasen des Weines. Weinbau Wiss. Beih. *2*, 191-198, 209-229. (*See also* Wines Vines *29* (10) 27-28. 1948.)

SCHANDERL, H. 1950–51. Über den Einfluss des Entsäuerns verschiedener Schönungen und des Lichtes auf das rH and pH der Weine. Wein Rebe *1950– 1951*, 118-128.

SCHANDERL, H. 1959. Die Mikrobiologie des Mostes und Weines, 2nd Edition. Eugen Ulmer, Stuttgart. (Revised by H.H. Dittrich, 1977.)

SCHMITTHENNER, F. 1950. Die Wirkung der Kohlensäure auf Hefen und Bakterien. Seitz Werke, Bad Kreuznach.

SCHREIER, P. and DRAWERT, F. 1977. Gaschromatographisch-Massen-spektrometrische Identifizierung flüchtiger Säuren and Phenole im Trauben- und Weinaroma. Appl. Spectrom. Masse (SM) Reson. Magn. Nucl. (RMN) Ind. Aliment. (Symp. Intern. Comm. Int. Ind. Agric. Aliment. 15th, 1975), 151-150.

SCHÜTZ, M. and KUNKEE, R.E. 1977. Formation of hydrogen sulfide during fermentation by wine yeast. Am. J. Enol. Vitic. *28*, 137-144.

SINGLETON, V.L. 1974. Some aspects of the wooden container as a factor in wine maturation. *In* Chemistry of Winemaking. A.D. Webb (Editor). Advances in Chemistry, Vol. 137. American Chemical Society, Washington, D.C.

SINGLETON, V.L. and DRAPER, D.E. 1963. Ultrasonic treatment with gas purging as a quick aging treatment for wine. Am. J. Enol. Vitic. *14*, 23-25.

SINGLETON, V.L. and ESAU, P. 1969. Phenolic substances in grapes and wine and their significance. Adv. Food Res., Suppl. *1*, 1-282. Academic Press, New York.

SINGLETON, V.L. and KRAMLING, T.E. 1977. Browning of white wines and an accelerated test for browning capacity. Am. J. Enol. Vitic. *27*, 157-160.

SINGLETON, V.L. and NOBLE, A.C. 1976. Wine flavor and phenolic substances. *In* Phenolic, Sulfur, and Nitrogen Compounds in Food Flavors. G. Charalambous and A. Katz (Editors). Am. Chem. Soc. Symp. Ser. *26*, 47-70.

SINGLETON, V.L., SIEBERHAGEN, H.A., DEWET, P. and VAN WYK, C.J. 1975. Composition and sensory qualities of wines prepared from white grapes by fermentation with and without grape solids. Am. J. Enol. Vitic. *26*, 62-69.

SINGLETON, V.L., TIMBERLAKE, C.F. and LEA, A.G.H. 1978. The phenolic cinnamates of white grapes and wine. J. Sci. Food Agric. *29*, 403-410.

SOMERS, T.C. and EVANS, M.E. 1974. Wine quality: correlations with colour density and anthocyanin equilibria in a group of young red wines. J. Sci. Food Agric. *25*, 1369-1379.

SOMERS, T.C. and EVANS, M.E. 1977. Spectral evaluation of young red wines: anthocyanin equilibria, total phenolics, free and molecular SO_2, "Chemical Age." J. Sci. Food Agric. *28*, 279-287.

STRADELLI, A. 1951. Evaporazione di alcool durante la fermentazione dei mosti. Riv. Viticolt. Enol. (Conegliano) *4*, 50-53.

SUDRAUD, P. and CASSIGNARD, R. 1959. Enrichessement des vins en fluor par les enduits de cuves à base de fluosilicates. Vignes Vins *77* (Feuillets Techniques), 2-4.

ŠVEJCAR, V. and PAPCUN, M. 1976. Faktoren, die den Glyceringehalt im Wein beeinflussen. Kvasny Prumysl (Prague) *22*, 254-256.

SZABO, J. and RAKCSÁNYI, L. 1937. Das Mengenverhältnis der Dextrose und der Lävulose in Weintrauben, im Mosten und im Wein. 5th Congr. Intern. Tech. Chim. Agric. *1*, 936-949. (*See also* Magyar Ampelol. Evkonyv. *9*, 346-361, 1935.)

TAMBORINI, A. and MAGRO, A. 1970. Il trattamento dei vini con resine scambiatrici e il rapporto potassio:sodio. Riv. Viticolt. Enol. (Conegliano) *23*, 87-94.

TANNER, H. 1963. Der Zinkgehalt von Weinen und Obstweinen. Mitt. Rebe Wein, Serie A (Klosterneuburg) *13*, 120-123.

TANNER, H. and RENTSCHLER, H. 1965. Weine mit Böckser; Ursachen das Böcksers und Weiderherstellung davon befallener Weine. Schweiz Z. Obst. Weinbau *74* (1) 11-14.

TARANTOLA, C. 1954. Separazione e identificazione cromatografia degli amino acidi nei vini. Att. Accad. Ital. Vite Vino *6*, 146-157.

TARANTOLA, C. and USSEGLIO-TOMASSET, L. 1963. I colloidi delle uve nei vini. Riv. Viticolt. Enol. (Conegliano) *16*, 449-463.

TCHELISTCHEFF, A. 1948. Comments on cold fermentation. Univ. Calif. Wine Technol. Conf., Aug. 11–13, 1948, Davis.

THOUKIS, G. 1959. The mechanism of isoamyl alcohol formation using tracer techniques. Am. J. Enol. *9*, 161-167.

THOUKIS, G. and STERN, L.A. 1962. A review and some studies of the effect of sulfur on the formation of off-odors in wine. Am. J. Enol. Vitic. *13*, 133-140.

TIMBERLAKE, C.F. and BRIDLE, P. 1976. The effect of processing and other factors on the colour characteristics of some red wines. Vitis *15*, 37-49.

TIMBERLAKE, C.F. and BRIDLE, P. 1977. Anthocyanins: colour augmentation with catechin and acetaldehyde. J. Sci. Food Agric. *28*, 539-544.

TUZSON, I. 1964. Mangangehalt ungarischer Weine. Mitt. Rebe Wein, Serie A (Klosterneuburg) *14*, 299-305.

UCHIMOTO, D. and CRUESS, W.V. 1952. Effect of temperature on certain products of vinous fermentation. Food Res. *17*, 361-366.

VAN BUREN, J.P., HRAZDINA, G. and ROBINSON, W.B. 1974. Color of anthocyanin solutions expressed in lightness and chromaticity terms. Effect of pH and type of anthocyanin. J. Food Sci. *39*, 325-328.

VASCONCELLOS A LANCASTRE, A. DE Q. 1947. O cobre no vinho do Pôrto. Anais Inst. Vinho Pôrto *8*, 55-103.

VILLFORTH, F. and SCHMIDT, W. 1953—1954. Über höhere Alkohole im Wein. Deut. Weinbau, Wissen. Beih. *7*, 161-170; *8*, 107-121.

VOGEL, J. and DESHUSSES, J. 1962. Sur la teneur des vins en zinc. Mitt. Gebiete Lebensm. Hyg. *53*, 269-271.

VOGT, E. 1958. Weinchemie und Weinanalyse, 2nd Edition. E. Ulmer, Stuttgart.

WARKENTIN, H. and NURY, M.S. 1963. Alcohol losses during fermentation of grape juice in closed containers. Am. J. Enol. Vitic. *14*, 68-74.

WEBB, A.D. 1970. Anthocyanin pigments in grapes and wines. Suom. Kemistilehti A *43*, 67-74.

WEBB, A.D. and INGRAHAM, J.L. 1963. Fusel oil. *In* Advances in Applied Microbiology, Vol. 5. Academic Press, New York, London.

WEBB, A.D. and KEPNER, R.E. 1961. Fusel oil analysis by means of gas-liquid partition chromatography. Am. J. Enol. Vitic. *12*, 51-59.

WEBB, A.D., KEPNER, R.E. and MAGGIORA, L. 1967. Sherry aroma. VI. Some volatile compounds of flor sherry of Spanish origin. Neutral substances. Am. J. Enol. Vitic. *18*, 190-199.

WEBB, A.D. and MULLER, C.J. 1972. Volatile aroma components of wines and other fermented beverages. *In* Advances in Applied Microbiology, Vol. 15. Academic Press, New York, London.

WIKÉN, T. and RICHARD, O. 1951—1952. Untersuchungen über die Physiologie der Weinhefen. Antonie van Leeuwenhoek J. Microbiol. Serol. *17*, 209-226; *18*, 31-44.

WISEMAN, W.A. 1955. Potassium and cream of tartar in wines. Chem. Ind. (London) *1955*, 612-617.

WUCHERPFENNIG, K. and BRETTHAUER, G. 1962. Versuche zur Stabilisierung von Wein gegen oxydative Einflusse durch Behandlung mit Polyamidpulver. Weinberg Keller *9*, 37-55. (*See also* Fruchtsaft-Ind. 7, 40-54, 1962.)

WUCHERPFENNIG, K. and LAY, A. 1965. Zur Bildung und zum Vorkommen von Hydroxymethylfurfurol in Weinen. Weinberg Keller *12*, 209-216.

WÜRDIG, G. 1976. Schleimsäure—ein Inhaltsstoff von Weinen aus botrytisfaulem Lesegut. Weinwirtschaft, R.F.A. *1/2*, 16-17.

WÜRDIG, G., SCHLOTTER, H.A. and BEDESSEM, G. 1969. Vorkommen, Nachweis und Bestimmung von 2- und 3-Methyl-2,3-dihydroxybuttersäure und 2-Hydroxyglutarsäure im Wein. Vitis *8*, 216-230.

WÜRZIGER, J. 1954. Beitrag zur Kenntnis des Mangangehaltes im Wein. Deut. Lebensm.-Rdsch. *50*, 49-51. (*See also* Wein Rebe *21*, 364-368. 1954.)

YANG, H.Y. and ORSER, R.E. 1962. Preservative effect of vitamin K_5 and sulfur dioxide on sweet table wines. Am. J. Enol. Vitic. *13*, 152-158.

YANG, H.Y., STEELE, W.F., STEIN, R.W., CAIN, R.F. and SINNHUBER, R.O. 1958. Vitamin K_5 as a food preservative. Food Technol. *12*, 501-504. (*See also Ibid. 11*, 536-540. 1957.)

ZANG, K. 1963. Schweflige Säure im ungeschwefelten Most. Deut. Wein-Ztg. *99*, 214.

ZANG, K. and FRANZE, K. 1966. Schweflige-Säure-Bildung im Verlauf der Traubenmost-Gärung. *Ibid. 102*, 128, 130.

ZIMMERMANN, H.W., ROSSI, E.A. JR. and WICK, E. 1964. Alcohol losses from entrainment in carbon dioxide evolved during fermentation. Am. J. Enol. Vitic. *15*, 63-68.

6

Winery Design, Equipment, Operation, and Sanitation

The equipment used in winery operations, the principles of their operation, and the overall operation of the winery from crushing to bottling are considered in this chapter. However, since the crushing and fermentation aspects differ so much from one type to another, some will be considered only briefly here and in more detail in the appropriate succeeding chapters. The finishing operations, which are somewhat similar for all types, will be considered more fully.

FACTORS INFLUENCING LOCATION

In selecting a location, the size of winery should be a major consideration. With large wineries, the aging and finishing operations can be concentrated in a central plant while the crushing and fermenting processes can be located near the sources of the grapes. This arrangement permits crushing of the grapes soon after harvest thus assuring minimum deterioration in quality.

It is also obvious that finishing operations for standard wines can be conducted on a large scale. Since highly skilled technicians are required, it is desirable that these operations be on a scale which justifies their employment. This has long been practiced in France and has become the practice in the Soviet Union, Yugoslavia, the United States and other countries.

The problems of operating large wineries in the hot interior valley of California, particularly for the production of table wines, have been emphasized by La Rosa (1963). He noted the critical importance of control of harvesting and fermentation (especially cooling), development of new and simpler methods for achieving stability, reduction of sugar and pigment losses, purity of water, waste disposal, and quality control.

Close proximity of vineyard and crusher facilitates operations and reduces costs of transportation. Among the other factors which should be considered are drainage and sewage facilities. This has become one of the most critical problems of California wineries and will be considered in greater detail later, p. 341. Because of the problem of waste disposal, wineries should not normally be located near cities. However, since some cities provide sewage facilities this may prove advantageous. Large wineries with many employees may find it easier to secure labor when located in or near cities. Also, if the winery has a public relations program for visitors, cities or a location on a main highway may be desirable. Wineries with retail departments should consider ease of access and parking for the motorist.

The location should be such that the prevailing wind is away from the populated area. For fruit fly control it is desirable that the winery not be near orchards or vineyards or food processors with exposed wastes.

DESIGN

Few California wineries have been functionally and artistically designed. This is unfortunate because winery operation is more expensive when the functions are not properly considered. Also, by proper architectural design the winery can be a credit to the community and a tourist attraction.

By functional design, we mean that each department of the winery should be designed with its particular operation clearly in mind. This means that the architect and the technical staff should study each operation together so that there is a clear understanding of what the essential operations are and how each should be carried out. Many wineries could profitably examine their operations for more rational arrangements. See Peterson (1975) and Webb (1976) for detailed discussion on planning wineries.

Departments

The crushing operations are normally separated from the winery proper, yet they should be arranged for easy transfer of the must to the fermenting room or pressing area with a minimum of piping. The aging or storage area should be air-conditioned. A centralized and well arranged processing department will be necessary. This should be convenient to the control laboratory. Adjacent bottling and shipping departments are desirable. The machinery room must be well separated from the wine storage because of possible undesirable odor arising from it. The distillery department is, for underwriter reasons and U.S. Bureau of Alcohol, Tobacco and Firearms regulations, separated from the winery—usually outdoors. Brandy storage is usually placed in a separate building. The sparkling wine, vermouth, and other specialized departments logically require separate storage facilities, though near the aging, processing, and bottling departments.

A well-designed winery will not only be functionally arranged with respect to different departments, but each department will be designed for efficient operation and ease of cleaning. This means waterproof concrete-surfaced floors with adequate drainage and sufficient high pressure hot and cold water and steam throughout the plant. Adequate lighting and electrical outlets for equipment must be installed. Special protection for electrical fixtures near sherry heaters, in brandy dumping areas and near stills is required.

CRUSHING

This department is now usually located outside the winery for two reasons: to facilitate delivery of the grapes and for ease of cleaning. Also, by keeping the crusher outside the winery, fruit flies are not introduced into the winery. The crushing area should be carefully designed for ease of unloading (hoists, conveyors, etc.) and for ease of cleaning (well-drained concrete pavement, water supply, etc.) (Fig. 6.1). The must pump should be adequate to handle the capacity of the crusher. The must line should be corrosion-resistant.

Two types of crushers are in use—namely, the roller type and the Garolla type. The latter predominates in California. Machinery producers offer improved crusher-stemmers.

The roller crusher consists of two fluted, horizontal rolls of rubber-coated steel or stainless steel, operated by gears and turning toward each other during operation. The rolls are adjustable, and should be set so that the berries are thoroughly crushed without breaking the seeds or grinding the stems. The crushed grapes and stems fall through the rolls into the stemmer, consisting of a stationary horizontal cylinder perforated with holes large enough to allow the crushed grapes to fall through and small enough to retain most of the stems. Rapidly revolving metal paddles hammer the grapes through the holes and the stems are carried out of the end of the cylinder. Both stems and leaves should be removed as they contain undesirable compounds. Crushers that operate at variable speeds for different varieties are needed. After removal of the stems, the

Courtesy of Wine Institute

FIG. 6.1. UNLOADING GRAPES FROM GONDOLA

crushed grapes are pumped by must pumps to the fermentor. Another type of roller-crusher stems first, then crushes.

The Garolla crusher (Fig. 6.2) was introduced from Italy to California after repeal and is now made by machinery manufacturers in California. It consists of a large, horizontal, coarsely perforated cylinder. Revolving blades inside the cylinder move the stems toward the exit and hammer the bunches of grapes. The combined effects of the moving parts do a thorough job of crushing and stemming. One objection to this type of crusher-stemmer is the excessive quantity of stems left in the must, particularly if the paddles are operated at high speed as they usually are. This may be corrected by adjusting the pitch of the blades. The Garolla crusher should be made of stainless steel, although mild steel has been used.

The stems should be washed or ground for fermenting and distilling. Other wineries remove them to the fields daily. Centrifugal crushers have, so far, not been used in the United States, but they are widely employed in Europe.

THE FERMENTING ROOM

The fermenting room includes fermentors, juice separators, presses, pomace conveyors, sumps, yeast propagators, and cooling equipment.

Courtesy of Valley Foundry and Machine Works, Inc.

FIG. 6.2. LARGE CRUSHER STEMMER

Left, covered, right, open. Rated capacity 25 tons per hour

Fermentors

Lined iron and stainless steel tanks (Fig. 6.3) predominate in California. Some smaller wineries still use oak or redwood fermentors. The metal tanks are usually closed so they can also be used for storage. The size of the fermentors depends on the number of varieties and the amount of each handled, the qualities of fruit, etc.

Drag screens, horizontal rotating cylinders, and flat rotating screens are used to separate liquid from pomace prior to pressing. The latter are preferred because they release less solids to the liquid.

Pressing

The amount of free-run juice from white grapes varies somewhat from variety to variety and with degree of maturity. From 60 to 70% of the extractable juice is usually obtained as free-run; with pressing an additional 30−40% is obtained.

A number of different systems of juice separation are used in California. One of the best, from the standpoint of labor requirements, juice yield and suspended solids content of the juice, combines a tank with a cylindrical perforated core for juice draining, an inclined screw dejuicer, and a Coq press. Average respective yields in gallons per ton and suspended solids content in percent are: 110−≤2, 50−≤4, and 20. In a second system the must is pumped into an inclined screw dejuicer followed by pressing.

Courtesy of Wine Institute

FIG. 6.3. STAINLESS STEEL FERMENTING TANKS

Note their location outdoors

And in a third system the must is pumped directly into a press.

The effect of pressing on the composition of musts and of their resulting wines is very complex. For example, Carles *et al.* (1963) reported a decrease in tartrate but an increase in malate in musts during pressing. The potassium and phosphate contents increased during pressing. Those of calcium, magnesium, iron and copper at first decreased and then increased; so did the pH. These results were obtained with one variety with two types of hydraulic presses in one region.

Two types of batch presses, the Willmes bladder (Fig. 6.4) and the Willmes and Vaslin horizontal basket-type, are commonly used in California. "Tapered" screw presses such as the Coq work well on unfermented musts and produce less cloudy juice than "straight" screw presses (Fig. 6.5), which are used mainly to press the pomace from distilling

FIG. 6.4. WILLMES PRESSES IN NEW YORK WINERY

material.

Recovery of alcohol from fermented pomace is a major problem of California wineries. Various procedures are used: grinding the pomace in a hammer mill or disintegrator and distilling in a special still, passing through a Metzner-type still, and water extraction. In washing, the single-contact batch operation is the simplest. It produces a relatively dilute wash solution.

Berg and Guymon (1951) studied countercurrent extraction as a means of improving recovery and increasing the sugar or alcohol content of the wash. They concluded that reasonable recoveries cannot be obtained with fewer than three stages. Coffelt *et al.* (1965) devised a 3-stage countercurrent system that provided good sugar levels in the product. A 4-stage system, constructed by L & A Engineering and Equipment Co., Turlock, Calif., is now in use at a number of wineries.

Pomace Conveyors

Where it is desired to recover as much wine as possible, the pomace may be discharged through the gate either into a conveyor or a pomace pump. Alternatively, it may be sluiced out with press wine (113 liters/910 kg or 30 gal./2000 lb of grapes) into a 20-cm (8-in.), double-action piston pump

Courtesy of Valley Foundry and Machine Works, Inc.
FIG. 6.5.   LARGE DOUBLE CONTINUOUS PRESS

attached to the bottom tank valve. Where distilling material is desired the pomace is usually sluiced out with water into the pomace conveyor. Continuous chain conveyors and screw conveyors are commonly used.

Fermentation of Uncrushed Grapes

There have been many reports of placing uncrushed grapes in tanks and allowing them to ferment. The theory appears to be that the fermentation of the free-run juice will produce carbon dioxide in sufficient quantities to asphyxiate the cells of the uncrushed grapes—resulting in greater color and flavor release. An example of this type of research is that of Bénard and Jouret (1963). Peynaud and Guimberteau (1962) showed that three types of reactions occur when grapes are placed under carbon dioxide or nitrogen for several days: (1) alcoholic fermentation, (2) reduction in malic acid, and (3) internal movement of constituents into solution, particularly of nitrogenous compounds, polyphenols and aroma materials. Hydrolysis of pectins with liberation of methanol and some increase in free amino acids also occurs.

USE OF SULFUR DIOXIDE

The forms present and the antiseptic value of sulfur dioxide have already been considered (p. 205). The practical aspects of its use will be considered here.

Sources

Sulfur dioxide is most conveniently and cheaply available to the wine maker in cylinders as the liquid under a pressure of about 9 kg/cm^2 (50 lb/in.^{2}) The specific gravity is about 1.4. For large operations this may be metered directly into the must lines. It can also be weighed out of tanks; or, volumetric dispensers are available. Many smaller wineries use liquid sulfur dioxide to prepare a water solution. The gas is slowly added to ice cold water. It can be weighed in from the cylinder so as to prepare an approximately 6% solution. See Borodin (1976) for description of an apparatus for continuous addition of a water solution of sulfur dioxide to must.

The exact concentration of sulfur dioxide in the solution can be determined by titration of an aliquot as follows: pipette 10 ml into a 100 ml volumetric flask. Fill to the mark with distilled water and mix. Pipette 10 ml of this solution into 50 ml of distilled water. Titrate at once with 0.1 N iodine solution to near the end point. Add 0.5 ml of 1% starch solution and titrate to a light blue end point. From the normality of the iodine and the amount of iodine used one can calculate the sulfur dioxide content. If a solution of bisulfite or metabisulfite is to be titrated, acidify the final diluted aliquot with 5 ml of 10% sulfuric acid before titration.

The sulfur dioxide content can also be determined from the specific gravity of the solution. The following table from Willson *et al.* (1943) is useful in this connection:

Concentration of Sulfur Dioxide %	Specific Gravity at		
	59°F	68°F	86°F
1.0	1.004	1.003	1.000
2.0	1.009	1.008	1.005
3.0	1.014	1.013	1.010
4.0	1.020	1.018	1.014
5.0	1.025	1.023	1.019
6.0	1.030	1.028	1.024
7.0	1.035	1.032	1.028
8.0	1.040	1.037	—

These solutions lose strength in storage so their concentration should be redetermined frequently. They should be stored in glass.

Some use potassium metabisulfite. The sodium salt, though cheaper, is not recommended. Both have slightly more than 50% available sulfur dioxide when dissolved in musts or wines but the 50% value is used in practice. The salts lose strength in storage. They may also be used to prepare a 6% solution—this also loses strength in storage.

Sulfur wicks are employed by small wineries. These are easy to use and have the advantage of exhausting the oxygen in the container in which they are burned. Unless the sulfur dioxide is removed by repeated rinsings, wine subsequently placed in the cask will pick up sulfur dioxide—up to 60 mg/liter from small barrels. Sulfur wicks are a simple method of disinfecting casks during storage. The disadvantage of sulfur wicks is that sulfur may sublime into the walls of the container or pieces of elemental sulfur from the wick may fall to the bottom of the cask. If the container is used for fermentation, this elemental sulfur will be reduced to hydrogen sulfide.

Whatever form is employed, it must be distributed evenly throughout the must or wine. Even when the sulfur dioxide is added continuously during the filling of the tank it is wise to pump the liquid over to mix it thoroughly. Much of the effectiveness of sulfur dioxide is lost in many cases because it is unevenly distributed.

Amounts to Add

Very little sulfur dioxide is needed for musts when the grapes are in perfect condition, cool, and have a large microflora of desirable wine yeast. In practice 100 to 200 mg/liter of sulfur dioxide are added. The amount to be used depends on the condition of the musts as indicated in Table 6.1.

The amounts to add to wines differ with the type of wine, its composition and condition, size of container, and temperature of storage and other factors (see pp. 264, 384, 392 and 434).

Effects of Sulfur Dioxide

Besides its effective antiseptic action (p. 202), sulfur dioxide has a number of other desirable properties in musts and wines.

Its clarifying action in musts is due to the fact that it neutralizes the negatively charged colloids and thus aids in their settling. By preventing fermentation, sulfur dioxide allows natural settling to take place. This effect is particularly used for settling white musts (p. 385).

Sulfurous acid is a strong acid and thus has an acidifying action of its own. It also prevents growth of the malo-lactic organisms and thus helps to maintain the acidity.

Sulfur dioxide (70 mg/liter) in the presence of an excess of acetaldehyde

TABLE 6.1. AMOUNT OF SULFUR DIOXIDE TO ADD TO MUSTS

Maturity	Condition	Temp	Concentration (mg/liter)	Liquid Sulfur Dioxide		Sulfurous Acid 6%		Potassium Metabisulfite	
				per 910 kg (g)	per ton (oz)	per 910 kg (liter)	per ton (pt)	per 910 kg (g)	per ton (oz)
Underripe	Clean, sound	Cool	75	57	2	1	2	99	3.5
Mature	Clean, sound	Cool	112	71	2.5	1.5	3	141	5
Overripe	Moldy, low acid	Hot	270	170	6	2	4.25	254	9

Source of data: Amerine and Joslyn (1970). Table modified to show values in metric units as well as English.

does not inhibit growth of the homofermentative *Lactobacillus plantarum* but completely inhibits the heterofermentative *L. hilgardii* and *Leuconostoc mesenteroides*. In the latter cases the bacteria reduce the aldehyde content so that the resulting wine contains sufficient free sulfur dioxide to inhibit growth. Finally, there is its dissolving activity as a strong acid, because of its solvent effect on potassium acid tartrate. Sulfur dioxide also has a solvent effect on anthocyan pigments. Berg and Akiyoshi (1962) also showed that treated wines retained their color better than untreated.

The antioxidative property of sulfur dioxide prevents direct effects of oxygen on musts and wines and inhibits some enzyme systems. The antioxidative effect of a given amount of sulfur dioxide varies markedly from one must or wine to another. White and Ough (1973) reported that the amounts of sulfur dioxide required to inhibit enzymatic oxidase activity varied from 25 to 100 mg/liter. And Schanderl (1959) has shown that the rH value is markedly reduced with a small amount of sulfur dioxide in some wines and very little in others. See Burroughs and Sparks (1973) for the effect of wine composition on the sulfur dioxide required, and Meidinger (1976) for a review on the chemistry of sulfur dioxide in wine.

Wines made from sulfited musts are of higher alkalinity of ash, fixed acidity, glycerol and extract and of lower volatile acidity. The hue of red wines is also better. The wines also keep better in storage.

If too much sulfur dioxide is added to musts, fermentation will be delayed, may be incomplete, and the resulting wines will have a high fixed sulfur dioxide content. If too much is added to wines the color will be bleached, the odor will be objectionable and the consumer may reject the wine.

Fessler (1961) noted that ascorbic acid (or erythorbic acid, an isomer) should not be used on wines of high sulfur dioxide content. His observations would seem to indicate that if 60 to 180 mg/liter (0.5 to 1.5 lb/1000 gal.) of ascorbic or erythorbic acid are to be added then the sulfur dioxide content should not be greater than about 100 mg/liter. Addition of 908 gm (2 lb) of either acid raised the free sulfur dioxide from 18 to about 90 mg/liter.

Trial bottlings with different amounts of sulfur dioxide and ascorbic or erythorbic acid should be made on each wine. Kielhöfer (1960) showed that ascorbic acid does not function as an antioxidant but rather as a catalyst for the oxidation of certain constituents of the wine, particularly of sulfur dioxide. For example, without ascorbic acid the sulfur dioxide content of a wine decreased from 128 to 106 mg/liter in 15 days; with ascorbic acid it decreased in the same time to 29 mg/liter. The redox potential attains very low values in the presence of ascorbic acid, sufficient to dissolve, at least partially, precipitated ferric complexes. For best results, ascorbic acid should be added to wines just before they are to undergo aeration, as in racking or filtration. In some cases wines treated with ascorbic acid undergo greater oxidation than untreated wines, probably because ascorbic acid catalyzes the oxidation of certain constituents that are not oxidized in its absence.

Chapon and Urion (1960) in their work on beer have provided the probable explanation for the action of ascorbic acid in wine. By following the rate of disappearance of added ascorbic acid, they found that the oxidation of ascorbic acid was accompanied by the oxidation of an equivalent amount of various organic substances. Wildenradt and Singleton (1974) extended this finding by showing that oxidation of ethanol to acetaldehyde by direct chemical reaction with air occurs in wine only by a coupled autoxidation of certain phenolic substances occurring in wine. They postulated a mechanism which appears to be general for autoxidation of phenols, ascorbic acid, melanoidins, reductones, enediols, and related compounds. This involves the oxidation of the phenol to a quinone (or ascorbic to dehydroascorbic, etc.) coproducing a strong oxidant which then can oxidize other substances in the wine such as ethanol.

As long as free sulfur dioxide is present the reaction is markedly inhibited, but in its absence is greatly accelerated.

OTHER ANTISEPTICS

Sorbic acid or its potassium or sodium salts have been approved for use in wines providing that not more than 0.1% remains in the wine. A number of wineries experimented with it particularly for preventing yeast activity in sweet table wines, but the undesirable odor which develops during storage has reduced interest. Crowell and Guymon (1975) found the geranium-like off-odor associated with spoilage in sorbate-containing wines was due to the formation of 2-ethoxyhexa-3,5-diene by lactic bacteria. Baerwald (1976) reported addition of 5 mg/liter (0.7 oz/1000 gal.) of pimaricin plus 25 mg/liter (3.5 oz/1000 gal.) of free sulfur dioxide completely inhibited yeast growth in must. And Ough (1975B) in studies on dimethyldicarbonate, as a possible replacement for diethylpyrocarbonate, found it extremely effective in sterilizing white wines against yeast growth, and somewhat less effective with red wines. Also see Chap. 5.

With the increasing use of new antiseptics it is desirable to determine whether a wine contains an unknown antiseptic. Various procedures have been proposed. Most of these are necessarily biological methods involving inhibition of growth of a standard organism. The procedures of Carafa (1959) and Lüthi and Bezzegh (1963) appear useful. Use of gas-liquid chromatography should also facilitate their detection.

DEACIDIFICATION OF MUSTS AND WINES

Musts and wines from grapes grown in cool climatic regions frequently require acid adjustment for sensory purposes. Nagel *et al.* (1975) compared different methods of acid and pH adjustment and their effect on the sensory qualities. They recommended a treatment method according to must or wine composition. A comparative study of deacidification methods by Munyon and Nagel (1977) included neutralization of wines with K_2CO_3 and $CaCO_3$, calcium double-salt deacidification of musts, and malic acid fermentation with *Schizosaccharomyces pombe* in musts and *Leuconostoc oenos* ML-34 in wines (red only). Sensory analysis indicated that the double-salt method was preferred in red wines and was equal to or better than other methods in white wines.

PURE YEAST STARTERS

In some small wineries it is customary to allow the crushed grapes or the juice to ferment spontaneously, that is, without the addition of a starter of yeast. However, the true wine yeasts (p. 170) are greatly outnumbered on the skins and stems of sound grapes by the wild yeasts. The latter may interfere with the fermentation. Grapes that arrive at the winery in partially crushed condition or badly molded, as is often the case after early fall rains, may also have large numbers of acetic bacteria. On the other hand, grapes early in the season may have on their surface very few yeast cells of any kind and molds will predominate. At this time of the season also, the crusher, pumps, pipe lines, vats, and tanks are probably relatively free of yeasts. Hence, early in the crushing season, it is desirable to inoculate the crushed grapes or juice with a pure yeast starter.

In midseason, and from that period to the end of the season, true wine yeasts are very abundant. Open fermentation vats, after one successful fermentation has been conducted in them, are heavily impregnated with yeast cells. Under such a condition fermentation begins promptly after the vats are filled and, if other conditions are favorable, satisfactory fermentations generally ensue. However, certain wild yeasts may also get a foothold in the fermentation vats and contaminate succeeding vats of crushed grapes. For this reason we recommend use of yeast starters throughout the season. Uznadze *et al.* (1971) found the most efficient ethanol formation was obtained with an inoculum of about 18 g/liter of dry yeast. For a general discussion of yeast starters see pp. 167–170, Fornachon (1950), Lüthi (1955), Rankine (1955), and Schulle (1954).

Sources

Since the time of Pasteur, microbiologists have given much attention to

the naturally-occurring yeasts of grapes. Among these earlier investigators shoud be mentioned Pacottet (1926), Guilliermond (1912), and
Kayser (1924) of France; Wortmann (1892) of Germany; and Müller-
Thurgau (1889) of Switzerland. Pure cultures of many different strains
of wine yeast have been studied as to their suitability for wine making.

Among the most desirable strains are those of Pacottet, among them
the well-known burgundy and champagne wine yeasts in the University
of California's collection. These two yeasts have been supplied to wineries
for the past 60 years. They, and several other yeasts, form a heavy
granular and compact sediment at the end of the fermentation period.
They are known as agglomerating, or agglutinating yeasts (pp. 175–176).
Wines made with these yeasts clear rapidly after fermentation is complete.[1] The volume of the lees or yeast sediment is small and, being compact and granular, the yeast does not tend to rise in the wine during racking. The usual California wine yeast naturally occurring on our grapes is
fine grained, and during fermentation forms a finely divided cloud
throughout the fermenting liquid. When the fermentation period is complete and the yeast has settled, it is easily disturbed, causing cloudiness.
However, the granular and the fine-grained type of yeast do not appear
to differ materially in respect to rate of fermentation, alcohol-forming
power, and effect on flavor of the wine.

Commercially used wine yeasts in California, in addition to burgundy
and champagne, are Montrachet,[2] Tokay,[3] and Steinberg.[4] In European
wine making countries many other strains of wine yeasts are utilized by
wine makers. A number of these are in the collections of the University of
California at Davis; others can be secured from fermentation laboratories, such as those in the American Type Culture Collection, Rockville,
Maryland; the Institut National Agronomique or the Institut Pasteur of
Paris; the Botanische Institut at Geisenheim, Germany; the Versuch-
sanstalt für Obst-, Wein- und Gartenbau at Wädenswil, Switzerland;
the Centraalbureau voor Schimmelcultures, Delft, Holland; or the Northern Regional Research Laboratory, U. S. Dept. of Agriculture, Peoria,
Illinois.

The University of California's cultures were at one time carried in 10%
sucrose solution in Steinberg flasks and in some cases yeasts have remained alive in this solution for more than 30 years. At present, the pure
cultures are carried on agar slants under sterile oil. The cultures should
be obtained well in advance of the vintage season as it usually requires

---

[1] The "champagne" and "burgundy" yeasts were brought to California by Professor F.T.
Bioletti, who introduced their use in California wineries and who encouraged the application of pure yeast in wine making for many years.
[2] A burgundy strain introduced by Professor J.G.B. Castor.
[3] Introduced by Fruit Industries Ltd.
[4] A popular wine yeast of Germany.

about 2 to 4 weeks to revive and increase them sufficiently for use in the winery.

Pure wine yeast in compressed cake and in dry granular form is now widely used in California. Thoukis *et al.* (1963) described the large-scale commercial production of *Saccharomyces cerevisiae*. By means of mass pitching, little grape sugar is used for growth of yeast. The rapid establishment of anaerobic conditions permits lower levels of sulfur dioxide in the musts. The yeast cakes are also much simpler to use than the traditional winery procedures and are less expensive since the sugars of grapes are not used for yeast multiplication. Goldman (1963) recommended the use of wet compressed yeast cake for sparkling wine production because the yeast population for the tirage bottling could be more accurately calculated and controlled.

Brémond (1957) reports that lyophilized yeasts were successfully used in Algeria in 1954. The Institut Pasteur in Paris prepares these by freezing at the temperature of solid carbon dioxide and alcohol, then evaporating at a low temperature under vacuum. A dry powder of yeast cells was produced and on being placed in the proper media rapidly remultiplied. Fell (1961) was able to freeze-dry (lyophilize) mixtures of yeast and lactic acid bacteria. He used the samples to successfully ferment grape musts with a simultaneous malo-lactic fermentation. However, in plant experiments even wines which had no added bacteria underwent a malo-lactic fermentation. This is not surprising since the winery equipment probably contained many lactic acid bacteria. At present, most of the yeast used in the larger California wineries is obtained as dry pressed yeast. It is added in large amounts to reduce use of sugar for yeast multiplication.

For fermentation at low temperatures, yeasts especially acclimated to cold should be used; see Osterwalder (1934).

Propagating Equipment

Pure wine yeast propagating installations are of several types. Such equipment may consist of two or more covered tanks. One is placed above the other. The upper tank is fitted with a steam coil of stainless steel. The juice in this tank can be sterilized by heating it with the steam coil and can then be cooled by passing cold water through the coil. The lower tank is fitted with a small coil or cross of stainless steel pipe with small holes in it to permit passage of compressed air through the juice to aerate it. Such aeration increases the rate of yeast growth. The compressed air should be filtered by passage through cotton or several layers of cloth in the air supply line to remove dust, oil droplets, and other materials that might contaminate the juice.

Propagating Procedure.—The following directions may be followed for increasing the pure yeast culture for use in the winery:

(1) Purchase a 0.94 liter (1 qt) bottle of grape juice, or heat a quart of fresh juice to boiling and scald a quart bottle in boiling water. Pour the boiling hot juice into the scalded bottle. Plug the bottle with clean, sterile, absorbent cotton. Set bottle aside to cool overnight.

(2) Take a test tube slant of pure yeast and fill it about ¾ full with the sterile grape juice, and replace the cotton plug. Set aside overnight. Transfer to the bottle of juice. Set aside in a warm place, between 21.1° and 26.7°C (70.0° and 80.0°F). Shake bottle occasionally to aerate the juice.

(3) In the meantime prepare a 19-liter (5-gal.) bottle of sterile juice. This is done by boiling 17 liters (4.5 gal.) of juice in a large aluminum or agate ware pot, and pouring it into a 19-liter (5-gal.) bottle. Or sterilize the 5-gal. bottle containing 17 liters (4.5 gal.) of juice in an autoclave or in live steam in an enclosed space (steamer) until the juice is about 74°C (165°F). Plug it with sterile absorbent cotton. Allow the juice to cool 24 hr or until a thermometer sterilized in alcohol or 180 proof brandy shows that the temperature is below 32.2°C (90.0°F).

(4) When the quart bottle of yeast is in active fermentation, 3 to 4 days, pour into the 5-gal. container. Shake or roll the 5-gal. container several times a day to aerate the juice. Keep the mouth of the bottle well plugged with sterile cotton. In about 4 or 5 days this juice should be actively fermenting.

(5) After the 5-gal. bottle of juice is in fermentation, sterilize fresh juice in the upper pure yeast tank by heating it to 71.1°C (160.0°F) and cooling to below 32.2°C (90.0°F). Sterilize the lower tank of the pure yeast apparatus with live steam and allow it to cool.

Draw off the cooled, sterile juice from the upper tank into the lower, but do not fill it more than ¾ full. About 3 or 4 hours before adding the fermenting juice from the 5-gal. bottle, add 100 to 125 mg/liter (13 to 17 oz/1000 gal.) of sulfur dioxide in the form of bisulfite or metabisulfite to the sterile juice in the tank. The purpose is to acclimate the yeast to sulfur dioxide. Then pour the fermenting contents of the 5-gal. bottle into the tank of sterile juice. Aerate the juice by passing filtered compressed air through it for a few minutes.

(6) In 3 or 4 days the juice in the lower tank should be fermenting vigorously. About ⅔ to ¾ of its liquid may be drawn off and used to inoculate a vat of crushed red grapes or tank of white must. About 7.6 to 11.4 liters (2 to 3 gal.) of the yeast culture are used to inoculate each 100 gal. of crushed grapes or must.

(7) More juice is then sterilized and cooled in the upper tank to replace that used in the winery. The lower tank should be equipped with a large

fermentation bung to allow escape of carbon dioxide gas and to protect the juice against contamination from the surrounding air. The upper tank is protected against contamination by the cotton bung or an air filter. Filtered air is used for aeration of the culture in the lower tank.

In other wineries, the juice in the two upper tanks is treated with about 150 mg/liter of sulfur dioxide and allowed to settle overnight. The settled juice is drawn off the sediment into two lower tanks where it is heavily inoculated with a pure yeast culture. When actively fermenting, this juice is used in the winery, leaving ¼ to ⅓ of the culture in the lower vats to inoculate the next lot of settled juice. In practice, the cultures in the two lower vats are generally used on alternate days, so that each culture when used in the plant is 48 hr old and at maximum vigor. The propagation and use of pure yeasts in a large California winery have been described by De Soto (1955). Other useful publications are given in the list of references at the end of thid chapter. After one or more tanks of juice or vats of crushed grapes have been heavily inoculated with pure yeast and are in full fermentation their contents may be used to inoculate other tanks, though pure yeast cultres are preferred.

Caution.—If at any time in either method of propagating the yeast starter for winery use in the pure yeast apparatus, there is reason to believe that the culture is no longer reasonably pure, empty and sterilize the apparatus and begin all over again with a pure culture from a yeast laboratory. Do not run the risk of spoiling a large proportion of your vintage with contaminated yeast.

FERMENTATION

The specific fermentation requirements for each type of wine are considered in the succeeding chapters.

Continuous Fermentation

Systems in which the raw material is continuously introduced into the fermentor and removed continuously from the same or another fermentor are now in wide use by the fermentation industries. See Kunkee and Goswell (1977) for details, especially in France and Italy.

Such systems make possible considerable saving in space and labor. The process can be instrumented for automatic control. The product is thus of uniform composition. The primary problem is in sterilizing the raw material and in preventing contamination during operation. There may also be occasional problems with development of mutant yeasts. Amerine (1959) has reviewed the problem and noted especially the successful use of a continuous process for production of sparkling wines in the Soviet Union. Konovalov (1958) showed that in continuous fermentation at 7.6% alcohol, yeast cells continue to grow and to fix P^{32}, while in the batch process the yeast cells stop dividing or fixing phosphorus at an early stage of the fermentation. Kunkee and Ough (1966) found that lack of yeast multiplication was a problem in continuous fermentations under pressure. See also Willig (1950).

Riddell and Nury (1958) describe a semicontinuous fermentation system. It operated on a ten-day cycle. The wine in the main fermentor fermented at about 3° Brix and the feed was about 5% per hr. Wick *et al.* (1974), in comparative fermentations, found 31 hr were required to ferment all of the sugar in a continuous fermentation, whereas about 140 hr were required in batch fermentation.

Cooling

For the theory of this operation, see pp. 208—211. Alcoholic fermentation liberates much heat. In a small container, such as a gallon jug, most of the heat is lost by radiation to the surroundings, but in a fermentation vat or tank considerable is retained with consequent rise in temperature in the tank. Even in a cool cellar, the temperature of the fermenting grapes may rise to the danger point unless artificial cooling is used. At 35°C (95°F) wine yeast is greatly weakened, and at 37.8° to 40.6°C (100.0° to 105.0°F) most of it dies or loses its fermenting power with consequent stopping ("sticking") of the fermentation. This is a common occurrence if cooling is not applied. For the best results, the fermentation should not be allowed to rise above 29.4°C (85.0°F) in a red wine fermentation; at 32.2°C (90.0°F) the yeast may be injured and the flavor and bouquet of the wine damaged.

Another disadvantage of very high fermentation temperature lies in the fact that heat-tolerant spoilage bacteria may grow, producing volatile acids, mannitol, and off-flavors. They may completely spoil the wine. While Ough and Amerine (1961) reported fermentation of Pinot noir at 21.1° or 26.7°C (70.0° or 80.0°F) gave better wines than at 11.7°C (53.0°F), with Cabernet Sauvignon they found 21.1°C (70.0°F) was better than 26.7° or 11.7°C (80.0° or 53.0°F). Prehoda (1963) reported similar results.

Consequently, as the temperature approaches 29.4°C (85.0°F) during fermentation, cooling should be instituted and the fermenting must cooled some 5.5°C (10.0°F) or more. Proportionally, there is less loss of heat by radiation from a large than from a small vat. However, for average conditions it is possible, by means of empirical formulas, to calculate in advance about how much cooling will be needed for a given set of conditions. For example, Bioletti (1906) gave the following formula: $C = 1.17S + T - M$, in which S is the Brix degree, T the temperature of contents of the vat, M, the maximum temperature desired, and C, the number of degrees F to be removed by cooling. For example, if S = 24, T, 26.7°C (80.0°F), and M, 29.4°C (85.0°F), then C = (1.17 × 24) + 80 − 85 = 12.8°C (23.0°F). This means that at some time during the fermentation the must will have to be cooled at least 12.8°C (23.0°F) in order to prevent the temperature rising about 29.4°C (85.0°F). This assumes that about 50% of the heat produced is lost from the fermentor.

According to Marsh (1959), the loss of heat during the first half of the fermentation is no more than 33%. Thus, the minimum cooling required under average conditions is 158,000 × 10^3 J (150,000 Btu) per 3780 liters (1000 gal.) of must. For grapes received in a warm condition or with a high sugar content, 264,000 × 10^3 J/3780 liters (250,000 Btu/ 1000 gal.) or 53,000 × 10^3 J/910 kg (50,000 Btu/ton) should be used in cooling calculations.

For dessert wines, with their limited fermentation period, about half the above requirements can be used. Should constant temperature be needed during fermentation of table wines the Btu requirements will be about ⅓ greater than those indicated. Barrillon et al. (1970) calculated that for 4000-hl (106,000-gal.) continuous fermentors, 40% of the heat produced had to be removed by cooling.

The three main systems employed for cooling musts in California are internal cooling coils in the fermentors, external shell-and-multitube coolers, and jacketed tanks. In the first two cases 15.6°C (60.0°F) water (or cooler) is often used—usually with a cooling tower. However, mechanically refrigerated water coolers may be required to supplement the cooling tower. In the third case, refrigerated glycol is the usual cooling medium. Marsh estimates that if cooling operations are conducted on a 12-hr basis, 61,000 W (208,000 Btu) per hour of refrigeration will be required per 45.5 metric (50 English) tons of grapes crushed for table wine. This means 85 hl (2500 gal.) of water per hour rising 5.5°C (10.0°F) will be needed for cooling.

In actual plant studies, Marsh (1959) reported the mean overall coefficient of heat transfer was 1390 W/m·K (Btu/hr ft²°F) of heat transfer area. The range was 625 to 2220 W/m·K (Btu/hr ft²°F). The most economical use of cooling water results when wine and water flow through the unit at approximately the same rates.

When red musts have been heated to facilitate color extraction a much greater cooling capacity is required. To reduce the temperature from 48.9° to 21.1°C (120.0° to 70.0°F) requires the removal of nearly 105,500 × 10^3 J/910 kg (99,500 Btu/ton).

One may do all of the needed cooling in one cooling operation, or may prefer to apply cooling 2 or 3 times during the fermentation, in order not to have to reduce the temperature so low in a single cooling that fermentation is slowed unduly. In most cases, cooling is begun at about 26.7° to 29.4°C (80.0° to 85.0°F), and the must is cooled to 21.1° to 23.9°C (70.0° to 75.0°F), and, if it again rises to 29.4°C (85.0°F), is cooled a second time. However, at the end of fermentation, cooling must not be so low that the fermentation is arrested. Where stainless steel fermentors are used water may be run over them to cool by exchange and evaporation.

Stuck Wines

When the fermentation stops before all of the desired sugar is fermented, the wines are said to have "stuck." Sticking occurs due to overheating, to infection by various bacteria, to too cold a temperature, and in a few cases because of unbalanced musts. The first is the only type observed nowadays and it is rare. One peculiarity of wines which cease fermentation at a high temperature is the difficulty with which they are refermented and their susceptibility to bacterial spoilage. When a wine sticks the wine maker should immediately determine the cause of the difficulty.

If sticking is due to a high temperature, cool the must at once to about 21.1°C (70.0°F). Another fermentor of the same type of must should be brought to vigorous fermentation and about 10% of the stuck wine added each day. If another tank is not available, pump a small amount of the cooled stuck wine to another fermentor and add 10 to 20% of an actively fermenting pure yeast starter. When the wine is in fermentation proceed as above by adding portions of the stuck wine. Following fermentation, the wine should be carefully checked for composition and condition, the acidity corrected, and sulfur dioxide added as necessary. Addition of ammonium phosphate, 900 mg/liter (7.5 lb/1000 gal.), has proven useful in stimulating stuck fermentation in some cases.

When the sticking is due to low temperatures, warming is usually sufficient, but addition of a large starter of actively-fermenting pure yeast culture is recommended. Sticking due to excessive growth of microorganisms is now very rare in California. The best use of such wines is to dilute and sulfite them, and gradually add them to an actively-fermenting tank of distilling material. The sooner they are disposed of the better.

FORTIFICATION

Since about ⅓ of the wine made in America is of the dessert type fortification is an important winery operation. Many sherries are not fortified until the fermentation is completed. Some muscatel and angelica are fortified after only a very limited period of fermentation. In order to produce a wine of a given final sugar content, the time of fortification will vary depending on the initial sugar content of the grapes. Figure 6.6 is very useful in predicting when the fortification should be made. Note that the data in this figure are based on fortifying to 18.0% alcohol, and that the degree Brix is determined by hydrometer. Singleton and Guymon (1963) found some enhancement of the quality of white port which was fractionally fortified during fermentation. They attribute this to reduction of the aldehyde content during the continuing fermentation. With red port, the quality improvement was less apparent. However, there was an increase in the color of red ports fortified with spirits of higher aldehyde content. This result was confirmed by Singleton *et al.* (1964).

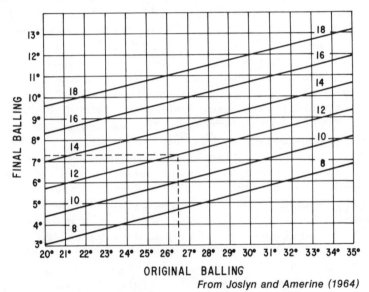

ORIGINAL BALLING

From Joslyn and Amerine (1964)

FIG. 6.6. WHEN TO FORTIFY MUSTS OF VARYING ORIGINAL BRIX TO PRODUCE WINES OF 18.0% ALCOHOL AND A GIVEN BRIX

In the example: to produce wine with 7.3° Balling and 18.0% alcohol from a must whose original Balling was 26.5°, it is necessary to add the fortifying spirits at 12°. This assumes immediate cessation of fermentation after fortification which may not be strictly correct.

To distinguish between fermented dessert wines and fortified grape juice (*mistelle*) Dimotaki-Kourakou (1964) suggested paper chromatographic detection of citramalic acid. This acid is formed during fermentation, 60 to 180 mg/liter (0.5 to 1.5 lb/1000 gal.), and its absence would indicate a beverage prepared from unfermented grape juice. Again confirmation is needed.

Procedure

The actual fortification is under the supervision of a gauger of the Bureau of Alcohol, Tobacco and Firearms. In theory he measures the volume of wine, determines its alcohol content, and supervises the addition of the necessary volume of high proof spirits, and its mixing (usually by compressed air). In practice, the wine maker determines the alcohol concentration, verifies the volume, and carries out the fortification.

The calculation of the volume of fortifying brandy to add can be made by reference to Table 6.2 or by calculation from the formula $X = [V(C-A)]/(B-C)$ where X is the wine gallons of fortifying brandy of B percent, V the gallons of wine of A percent alcohol, and C, the desired alcohol content of the final wine (usually 18.0 in California). Since there is a contraction when alcohol and water are mixed (of 0.6 to 1.5% depending on the original alcohol and sugar contents) this will not be exact. There are also discrepancies owing to the alcohol's continuing to increase during fermentation and, if the fortifying brandy is not rapidly and thoroughly mixed, after the fortification. This can lead to low sugar and high alcohol. It is therefore customary to pump the wine to the fortifying tanks at a Brix 2° to 3° above that shown in Fig. 6.6. Furthermore, the wine maker soon acquires experience with his equipment to judge the correct time of fortification. One method of preventing errors is to always fortify the same volume of wine. Following mixing, the gauger is required to take samples to verify the actual alcohol content.

A sample calculation of the volume of spirits is as follows: 25,000 gal. (945 hl) of wine of 5.5% alcohol are to be fortified to 20.5% alcohol using high proof of 189°. How many gallons of high proof spirits are required? $X = [25,000 (20.5 - 5.5)]/(94.5 - 20.5) = 5067.57$ wine gal. (192 hl). Regulations require the calculation to the second decimal place though this has little significance in practice.

Quality of Spirits

Neutral spirits are preferred by most California producers. Low fusel oil content is especially desired. This appears to be best for early-maturing dessert wines which are not to be aged in wood. However, there are no extensive commercial experiments showing the quality to be expected when spirits of lower proof and a higher content of congenerics are used and the wine aged.

Flanzy (1959) preferred high proof spirits to commercial neutral alcohol for fortification but the differences only developed during aging. Bénard et al. (1958) reported high proof spirits better than Armagnac or Cognac.

TABLE 6.2. NUMBER OF GALLONS OF WINE SPIRIT TO BE ADDED TO 100 GALLONS OF WINE CONTAINING VARIOUS PERCENTAGES OF ALCOHOL TO PRODUCE A FORTIFIED WINE CONTAINING 18 PERCENT ALCOHOL

Alcohol in Initial Wine (Volume Percent)	Percent of Alcohol in Wine Spirits									
	82	84	86	88	90	91	92	93	94	95
	Gallons of Wine Spirits to Be Added to 100 Gallons									
0	28.13	27.27	26.47	25.71	25.00	24.66	24.32	24.00	23.68	23.38
1	26.56	25.76	25.00	24.29	23.61	23.29	22.97	22.67	22.37	22.08
2	25.00	24.24	23.53	22.86	22.22	21.92	21.62	21.33	21.05	20.78
3	23.44	22.73	22.06	21.43	20.83	20.55	20.27	20.00	19.74	19.48
4	21.88	21.21	20.59	20.00	19.44	19.18	18.92	18.67	18.42	18.18
5	20.31	19.70	19.12	18.57	18.06	17.81	17.57	17.33	17.11	16.88
6	18.75	18.18	17.65	17.14	16.67	16.44	16.22	16.00	15.79	15.58
7	17.19	16.67	16.18	15.71	15.28	15.07	14.86	14.67	14.47	14.29
8	15.63	15.15	14.71	14.29	13.89	13.70	13.51	13.33	13.18	12.99
9	14.06	13.64	13.24	12.86	12.50	12.33	12.16	12.00	11.84	11.69
10	12.50	12.12	11.76	11.43	11.11	10.96	10.81	10.67	10.53	10.39
11	10.94	10.61	10.29	10.00	9.72	9.59	9.46	9.33	9.21	9.09
12	9.38	9.09	8.82	8.57	8.33	8.22	8.11	8.00	7.89	7.79
13	7.81	7.58	7.35	7.14	6.94	6.85	6.76	6.67	6.58	6.49
14	6.25	6.06	5.88	5.71	5.56	5.48	5.41	5.33	5.26	5.19
15	4.69	4.55	4.41	4.29	4.17	4.11	4.05	4.00	3.95	3.90

Source: U.S. Internal Revenue Service (1962).

Only a few samples were used and no statistical analyses of the sensory results given. Costa (1938), on the other hand, preferred spirits of only 150° to 160° proof for port in Portugal. Observation of Portuguese ports indicates that many are high in fusel oil and that this is not considered a negative quality factor. (See also p. 40.) Unless a demand for aged, highly flavored dessert wines is developed it is doubtful if California producers should or will change their present practice.

STORAGE

Wines are stored in oak (Fig. 6.7), concrete (Fig. 6.8), redwood (Fig. 6.9), lined iron or steel (Fig. 6.10), stainless steel and polyester containers. All storage areas should be air-conditioned, and if wood is employed, humidity control is also needed. Caves provide temperature and humidity control. If the tanks are outdoors they should be insulated.

The storage room (except for a very small one) should be arranged with permanent pipes (stainless steel, glass or fiberglass) for transfer of wines. Hoses should be used only for temporary transfer. It is, of course, hardly necessary to add that all equipment must be installed for ease of cleaning.

Courtesy of Wine Institute

FIG. 6.7. OAK OVALS, TANKS AND LINED STEEL TANKS IN CALIFORNIA WINERY

Courtesy of Wine Institute

FIG. 6.8. LARGE CONCRETE TANKS FOR STORING WINE IN CALIFORNIA WINERY

Containers

The type and size of container used will depend on the quality of wines and the purpose of the aging program. Wineries with a quality wine program may profitably and necessarily use oak cooperage, particularly for their red wines. Lined iron, or stainless steel, containers minimize aging but they offer permanent storage with a minimum of loss or aeration. They can be lagged for better temperature control. Wines stored in smooth lined tanks do not clarify as well as those in smaller tanks with a rough interior.

For fine red table wines and for quality dessert wines oak is the preferred material for storage. Not only do the wines clarify better in small containers but they acquire a slight woody character and the necessary air for aging. Very large oak tanks, however, are probably little better than redwood, lined-iron or concrete for storage. The preferable size of oak for wine storage is from 190 to 1900 liters (50 to 500 gal.). Sizes of 190 liters (50 gal.) or smaller are known as barrels. Larger sizes are called ovals, puncheons (round), pipes (for port), butts (for sherry), or

Courtesy of Wine Institute

FIG. 6.9. REDWOOD STORAGE TANKS IN CALIFORNIA WINERY

simply casks. When properly cared for, the thicker staved will last for centuries. See Graff (1970) for a practical discussion of the use of barrels in aging wines of different styles with emphasis on the calculation of space-capacity relationships and methods of operation with different methods of stacking.

Data on the extraction of material from wood meal and wood chips was given by Singleton and Draper (1961). The composition of the extracts was surprisingly constant. Sensory tests indicated that an extract equiv-

Courtesy of Gallo Wine Co.

FIG. 6.10. LINED STEEL WINE STORAGE TANKS

alent to 454 g (1 lb) of wood would give a detectably woody character to 755 liters (200 gal.) of port. Singleton (1974) compares oak from different sources, their relative flavor contribution, and cask size during aging.

Redwood and concrete were commonly used for tank construction in the California industry through the 1940's. Beginning in the 1950's lined steel tanks, because of their many advantages, including lower costs in the larger sizes, largely replaced concrete. The satisfactory maintenance of concrete tanks has proven difficult in California.

The annual losses from different type tanks in percent were as follows: concrete (2250 hl-60,000 gal.) 0.70, redwood (2250 hl-60,000 gal.) 0.33, steel (2250 hl-60,000 gal.) 0.08, and steel (7600 hl-200,000 gal.) 0.03.

Due to improvements in fabricating techniques, the cost of stainless steel tanks has been reduced materially. Peters (1977) estimated their costs as follows (cents per gallon), including tank erection and fittings:

Tank Capacity	Total Cost	Tank Capacity	Total Cost
6,000	68	110,000	26
12,000	44	170,000	22
18,000	36	225,000	21
48,000	32	350,000	19
60,000	30		

Connolly (1971) states that if free sulfur dioxide content of the wine is always below 75 mg/liter and if the containers are invariably full, type 304 stainless steel is satisfactory. If sulfur dioxide content is high, pitting and corrosion by condensation droplets on the steel in the vapor space are a problem unless 316 SS is used. Duplex construction with 304 SS bottom and 316 SS top portions can also be used.

Moiroud and Berger (1977) advise purchasers of polyester resin casks to obtain a written contract from the manufacturer guaranteeing the storage of wine for five years without sensory alteration. They also state that commercial casks are not adapted to a long storage unless a coating of epoxy resin is applied (without solvent) on the inside of the cask.

Care of Cooperage.—Alkaline solutions are most effective in removing tannins from new barrels. Soaking with 1% sodium carbonate is the usual treatment. Combined with superheated steam (2 or 3 atm pressure) and several rinsings with water they will produce a container with little extractable tannin. However, most wineries now only treat the barrels with warm water in order to leave the tannin for extraction by the wine.

New redwood tanks should be soaked with a warm dilute solution, about 1%, of soda ash for several days, followed by soaking with water for several days with two or more changes. Storage of clean distilling material before using the tank is also desirable. New oak containers are preferably treated only with warm water.

Berg (1948) recommends the following cleaning procedure for used cooperage: wash the interior with water and then spray with a hot, about 49°C (120°F) 20% solution of "Winery Special," which consists of 90% soda ash and 10% caustic soda; then wash thoroughly with hot water and spray with a solution of chlorine compound containing about 440 mg/liter of available chlorine. Again wash thoroughly with cold water, drain, and mop dry. Burn sulfur in the tank (700 mg/hl, 2 oz/1000 gal.). Rewash and inspect visually and by smell before use.

To remove cream of tartar deposits, argols, most wineries use a hot alkaline solution. Berg (1948) suggests a solution containing 950 g/hl (80 lb/1000 gal.) each of soda ash and sodium hydroxide. About 1.4 kg (3 lb) of Oronite D-40 may be included. This solution is used until it contains 12 to 15% tartrates. For recovery of the tartrates see Chap. 18. A jet of steam is sometimes used to remove tartrate deposits from concrete tanks.

Barrels are best cleaned and sanitized by soaking with a warm 5% soda ash solution for 24 hr, washed well, stored with 5% citric acid solution for 24 hr, washed well, filled with 85°C (185°F) water for a few hours, washed well and drained. Burning a sulfur wick in the barrel is advisable if it is not to be used immediately.

Connolly (1971) recommends cleaning stainless steel tanks with low chloride solutions to avoid pitting. Sterilization with hypochlorite can be used if contact is limited to a few minutes with not over 200 mg/liter of free chlorine, pH 8−9, and removal by rinsing is complete. Care in introducing sulfur dioxide into wine is essential if corrosion is to be avoided.

Molding of the *outside* of storage tanks occurs under humid conditions. Amerine and Joslyn (1970) state that washing with a solution of a quaternary ammonium compound may be effective in removing the mold and the residual disinfectant may retard future mold growth. Paints containing copper-8-quinolinolate appear to be the most promising for control of mold growth.

Berg (1948) recommends V.E.X. (trade designation of a proprietary preparation) 30 to 90 g/liter (4 to 12 oz/gal.) at 71.1° to 82.2°C (160.0° to 180.0°F) to remove mold, grime, varnish, and linseed oil from the outside of containers when such drastic treatment is necessary.

Tank trucks and railroad cars are often returned in unsatisfactory condition and require special treatment. The interior surfaces should first be examined for defects. Chlorinated solutions are usually best for disinfection. Ample supplies of hot and cold water, under good pressure, are especially useful in such cases.

Where casks or tanks leak because of cracked staves they should be recoopered. The staves of redwood sherry cooking tanks (not recommended) often become soft and leaky and require recoopering. This includes scraping of the staves and replacing leaky or moldy staves. It may be necessary in some cases to replace the head also. A single moldy stave may contaminate and damage the flavor of a whole tank of wine. The inside of the tank or cask should be examined carefully for mold, cracks, and other defects. Mold should be scraped off as it cannot be removed by washing. The walls are then washed with hot alkaline solution such as a strong solution of a mixture of soda ash and caustic. This should be followed by rinsing with water and spraying with a hypochlorite solution containing 500 to 1000 mg/liter of available chlorine. This treatment should be followed by several washings with hot water.

Steaming may be necessary in severe cases. All of the free chlorine must be removed by thorough washing. Inert and impervious plastic or wax have been used to temporarily repair old or badly leaking tanks. (See also Berg 1948.)

Concrete fermentation tanks are left open and dry when not in use. They should be thoroughly cleaned before being left open in order to prevent mold growth. Spraying detergents and cleaners, using automatic equipment, over the interior surfaces is useful for all kinds of containers. All the residual detergent must be washed out with water before reuse.

Storing empty barrels and tanks during the hot, dry summer months is a serious problem. Amerine and Joslyn (1970) recommend that stored empty barrels be sulfured by sulfur wick or by introducing sulfur dioxide from a cylinder of gas. The inside of the barrels should be kept wet, and the barrels should be stored indoors or in the shade. Sulfuring is repeated as needed; but oversulfuring should be avoided.

Open wooden tanks should be thoroughly cleaned and then may be filled with saturated lime water, which is made by mixing about 1.8 g/liter (15 lb/1000 gal.) of lime. This solution will usually keep the tank sweet. If storage is prolonged, it is usually necessary to drain out the lime solution periodically and replace it with freshly prepared solution, particularly during the first months of storage.

Dilute hypochlorite solution (250 mg/liter of active chlorine) has been used to fill storage tanks but soon loses its strength because of reaction with the wood and other organic matter. Sodium bisulfite in dilute sulfuric acid, 60 mg/liter (0.5 lb/1000 gal.) of concentrated sulfuric acid and 120 mg/liter (1 lb/1000 gal.) of bisulfite, will usually keep tanks or barrels in good condition. It is advisable to inspect the containers occasionally to prevent drying-out of the top. Painting lime on the interior surfaces of open tanks is not recommended.

Filling Up

Tanks of table wine must be kept completely filled and sealed, in order to prevent acetification. This requires that smaller containers of like wine be on hand from which to fill the larger tanks and casks. This is particularly true of vintage wines which must be "topped" by wine of the same vintage. The smaller the container the more frequent the filling up—particularly in warmer cellars and during the warmer periods of the year. For very large containers, 37,800 liters (10,000 gal.) and up, "topping" may be needed every month or six weeks and in the warmer part of the year there may be sufficient expansion in volume that some wine must be removed.

Racking

This simple operation is often neglected as an aid to clarification. Racking, first of all, removes a considerable amount of carbon dioxide. It also raises the redox potential. One of the dangers in leaving the new wine in contact with its yeast sediment is that it may lead to yeast autolysis[5] and, at the low redox potential, formation of hydrogen sulfide. Of course, if residual sugar remains some delay in racking may be desirable to allow the wine to ferment dry. Also, if a malo-lactic fermentation is desired to reduce the total acidity this racking may be delayed. Great care and frequent analyses are suggested in this latter case.

Normally, however, wines should be racked within a month of the end of the fermentation, and sooner is advisable under warm cellar conditions, with small containers, and with low acid table wines.

AGING[6]

Aging is one of the most interesting and important, yet one of the most complex processes in wine making. Newly-fermented wine is cloudy, harsh in taste, yeasty in odor, and without the pleasing bouquet that develops later in its history. As it ages properly, the harsh taste and yeasty odor diminish and a smooth, mellow flavor and clean odor are produced. The bouquet also develops during aging in the wood and the bottle. The wine maker's task is to free the wine from its suspended material and yeasty odor and to prepare it for bottling by proper aging practices.

The process of clarification involves reducing the temperature, storage in various types of containers, racking, filtration, fining, centrifugation, pasteurization (or other heat treatments), refrigeration, passage through ion exchange resins, and other processes.

The objectives of must and wine treatment have been summarized by Mayer-Oberplan (1956) as follows: (1) removal of suspended material, (2) removal of off-tastes and -odors, (3) removal of off-color, (4) removal of substances which would later cloud the wine, (5) removal of foreign or toxic materials, (6) removal of residual fining agents, (7) hydrolysis of pectins and proteins, (8) to make musts and wines filterable, or (9) as a preventive measure against future undesirable changes.

Red table wines may improve in bouquet in the wood (Fig. 6.11) at

---

[5] Yeast autolysis is defined by Joslyn (1955) as "an enzymatic self-destruction of the yeast cell and essentially involves hydrolysis of the protoplasmic constituents and their excretion into the surrounding medium."

[6] The Soviet practice of designating changes that occur in the wines before bottling as "maturation" and those that occur in the bottle later as "aging" seems a rational one.

FIG. 6.11. OAK CASKS FOR TABLE WINE STORAGE IN CALIFORNIA

optimum storage temperatures and in moderate-sized containers for about 1 to 4 years, depending upon the composition of the wines. A light, white wine, such as a Riesling, will age more rapidly than a heavy red wine. Most California dry red wines improve in the wood for 3 to 4 years whereas white wines require little, if any, wood aging and are ready for bottling in only a year or two. Singleton *et al.* (1971) point out that assay for nonflavonoid phenols can serve to monitor the progress of aging in wooden cooperage.

When a table wine has attained its optimum quality in the tank (when it has become bottling ripe) it then begins to decrease in quality. New table wines, particularly reds, when placed in completely filled bottles and sealed tightly remain new and harsh in flavor and age very slowly. Properly aged wines placed in bottles (Fig. 6.12) continue to improve for several years after bottling. This is notably true of red table wines where maximum quality may not be attained for ten or more years, as for our best California Cabernet wines.

Dessert wines continue to improve for many years in wood. However, these fortified wines also undergo a rather rapid initial aging and, within a few months after the vintage, are generally sufficiently aged to be passably pleasing in flavor. However, ports, especially tawny ports, require several years of wood aging and some ports improve with bottle aging. Madeira and California sherry are "cooked" for several months at a relatively high temperature in order to hasten aging and develop the desired flavor and color.

Courtesy of Wine Institute

FIG. 6.12. TABLE WINE BOTTLE AGING CELLAR IN CALIFORNIA WINERY

Theory

The principal changes in flavor and bouquet during aging in the wood are generally believed to be due to slow oxidation. Wood extractives also have an effect on flavor. For information see Amerine (1950), and Singleton (1959, 1976, 1978). Oxidation may be beneficial or injurious to the quality of the wine. Every wine maker knows that to leave a tank or cask of dry wine exposed to the air, or to leave it partly filled, will result in the rapid accumulation of acetaldehyde and possibly of ethyl acetate and acetic acid. On the other hand, oxygen does play an important role in aging of several types of wines. The average oak cask or redwood wine tank is not air-tight but is rather porous. Air can, and does, enter slowly; the oxygen is absorbed by the wine and brings about a series of oxidation reactions that may change the character of the wine in many respects. Oxygen also enters the wine during pumping, filtering, and racking as well as from the head space in the tank or cask. These sources of oxygen are probably much more important than entry of air by diffusion through the wood.

Pasteur showed that normal aging of certain red wines cannot take place without oxidation. He also proved that the amount of oxygen required is small and that when this amount is exceeded the wine becomes flat and may take on a "madeirized" odor. He also believed that table wines in hermetically-sealed bottles failed to age. There is no doubt that this last conclusion is incorrect, particularly for white table and red wines of low tannin content.

Table wines exposed to the air rapidly absorb oxygen. In a bottle filled about four-fifths full and sealed, the wine absorbs all the oxygen from the air in 24 hr. The first effect of the oxygen is to make the wine flat in flavor due to formation of aldehyde. This change occurs when a wine is fully exposed to the air for a short time. If the bottle is filled and sealed it will gradually improve in flavor, provided the oxidation has not been too severe.

Oxidation of tannin and coloring matter and precipitation of the oxidation by-product may occur. The reddish brown layer of coloring matter in the bottom or on the sides of bottles of old red wines is well known. In this case, the action of the oxygen is evidently slow.

It is well known that exposing partly-filled bottles to sunlight very greatly increases the rate of aging. In fact, Pasteur secured a patent on this process of rapid aging more than 80 years ago. Wildenradt and Singleton's (1974) finding that air contact with wine produces a strong oxidant points to the need to reconsider some beliefs about aging reactions. The old idea that rapid oxidation gives different products and less desirable aging than slow diffusion seems doubtful. Since air contact leads immediately to the production of a strong oxidant, the effects of "strong" oxidation should be the same as limited oxidation provided the wine was kept well mixed and the same final amount of oxidation occurred. Thus, quick aging by metered amounts of air in stirred stainless steel tanks appears possible.

Aldehydes and acetals are said to be responsible for much of the "new" taste of immature table wines. There is some evidence that these are desirable for some dessert wines. Some of the higher alcohols of the wine may be converted to acids and these in turn may form esters with the ethyl and other alcohols to give part of the flavor and bouquet of aged wines.

Oxygen is absorbed, not only during storage from the air that penetrates the pores, but also, as stated above, during racking, pumping, filtration, and filling up. Water (and to a lesser extent alcohol) is lost by evaporation through the pores of the wood, resulting in a head space beneath the bung. Air diffuses in to fill this space and the wine then absorbs the oxygen from this air. Once in every 20 to 30 days the cellarman must open the tank or cask and fill this space with wine. In so doing he unavoidably aerates the added wine thus introducing more oxygen. Peterson (1976) noted that oxygen pickup may vary widely from barrel to barrel during aging, and that the taste of the wines can also vary widely from barrel to barrel. This observation led him to studies of barrels which were not topped for many months or years, in which he found intermittent evidence of vacuum inside the barrels. From this, it appears that the prevalent practice of topping barrels in order to prevent or reduce oxidation may, in fact, do more harm than good.

The saturation level of oxygen in wine is generally considered to be 6 to 7 ml/liter. Cant (1960) showed that wines being removed from cold stabilization approached oxygen saturation. He used a nitrogen stripping column which on a single pass reduced oxygen to 2 ml. An in-line nitrogen sparger was less effective for high oxygen wines and equally effective to the column for low oxygen wines. Carbon dioxide was less effective. The cost of stripping was about 50¢ per 1000 gal.

The presence of sulfur dioxide in wines materially retards aging since much of the oxygen is consumed in oxidizing the sulfurous acid. Aldehydes, formed by oxidation of the various alcohols in the wine, affect the flavor and bouquet and may also form insoluble compounds with the tannin and coloring matter or with other aldehydes.

According to the observations of most cellar men, different wines require different amounts of oxygen. Thus, a light white table wine requires less than heavy red wine or sherry. Controlled oxidation and reduction of table and dessert wines offer many opportunities for improvement of U.S. wines. Ough and Amerine (1959) have described electrodes for measuring the oxygen content. Continuous control of the redox potential during aging is the next step.

There are a number of alcohols and acids in the wine that may unite to form esters. First, there are fixed acids, namely, tartaric acid, malic acid, succinic acid, and lactic acid (the first two present in the juice, the latter two formed during fermentation). Acetic acid, propionic acid, formic acid, and probably traces of other more or less volatile acids are formed during fermentation. Acetic acid is much the most abundant. The important volatile esters, largely those of acetic acid, are important in spoilage but in small amounts undoubtedly contribute to the fragrance of the wine. The contribution of the nonvolatile esters to the odor of a wine has not been established but it must be small when one considers the small quantities present and their relatively indistinctive odors. Further evidence is necessary to establish this. Methyl esters, particularly, may play a part and ethyl laurate and related esters seem to have some role in wine odor (p. 219).

Some varieties of grapes, such as the Muscat, Sémillon, Cabernet, Concord, and Catawba, have pronounced characteristic aromas and flavors (see pp. 109–110). These are carried over to a large degree in the wine and form an important part of the aroma of the aged wine. Aging tends to cause these natural grape aromas and flavors to become less obvious.

Microorganisms

An acid-reducing fermentation is common in California wines. It is a capricious fermentation, not occurring with some wines, being a dangerous fermentation if allowed to reduce the acidity too much, which is common with the high pH California wines. See also Chap. 4 and 16 for a fuller discussion of microorganisms.

Sudraud and Cassignard (1959) report that addition of 100 mg/liter of sulfur dioxide before fermentation delayed the start of the malo-lactic fermentation in the wine for up to 60 days. It was also delayed considerably by storage at 15°C (59°F) compared to 25°C (77°F). Pilone et al. (1974) reported the addition of fumaric acid proved bactericidal to added wine leuconostocs, and Ough and Kunkee (1974) found routine addition of fumaric acid at the time of the first racking will, in general, significantly improve quality of wine made from grapes from warm areas by inhibiting malo-lactic fermentation.

Marques Gomes et al. (1954) and Peynaud and Domercq (1959, 1961) believed it practical to supply wine makers with pure cultures of malo-lactic bacteria for winery use—cultures which do not form volatile acidity and which can be rapidly increased to the desired amounts. These they proposed to use on nonsulfited musts or on sulfited musts several days after the fermentation is under way.

Similar results were reported by Webb and Ingraham (1960). Webb (1962) described the original isolation of pure strains. In some cases there was an undue rise in volatile acidity. He noted that it was difficult to induce the malo-lactic fermentation in old wines. Several yeast types also appeared to inhibit a malo-lactic fermentation. Webb felt that some of his strains contributed desirable odors to Pinot noir wines. Kunkee *et al.* (1964) were able to induce a malo-lactic fermentation at any state of alcoholic fermentation. This was much more rapid with a strain of *Leuconostoc* than with one of *Lactobacillus*. Although there was a slight increase in volatile acidity in the treated wines, it did not adversely affect quality. Ingraham *et al.* (1960) identified three rods, *L. hilgardii* (15 isolates), *L. brevis* (1), *L. delbrueckii* (2), and two cocci, *Leuconostoc* sp. (10) and *Pediococcus* (12) from California wines. Fornachon (1957) reported *L. hilgardii* and *L. brevis* in Australian wines undergoing the malo-lactic fermentation. Later (1964) he identified *Leuconostoc mesenteroides*. In general, this strain tolerated a low pH better than species of *Lactobacillus*. Since these are the wines that most need a malo-lactic fermentation the importance of this bacterium is emphasized. Fornachon (1963) stated that for Australian conditions species of *Leuconostoc* were the most suitable organisms. Lafon-Lafourcade (1970) induced very rapid (<8 hr) degradation of malic acid using massive (1 to 5 g/liter) amounts of bacterial cells, or more slowly (<12 days) with 100 mg/liter.

Every wine constitutes a different problem as to the desirability or nondesirability of a malo-lactic fermentation. See also Chap. 16.

In Yugoslavia, Milisavljević (1958) has shown that the malo-lactic fermentation is very general—occurring first in wines of low alcohol, low acid, and little free sulfur dioxide, especially when stored at warmer temperatures. Thus, a wine of 13% alcohol started the malo-lactic fermentation with 50 mg/liter of total sulfur dioxide at pH 3.22; 75 mg was the limit at pH 3.46 and 100 did not prevent it at a pH of 3.85. At 10% alcohol a malo-lactic fermentation can occur at a pH of 2.93. He believed the effect of the malo-lactic fermentation to be generally very desirable in Yugoslavian wines. Later (1964) he reported some strains of yeast inhibited the malo-lactic fermentation more than others.

In 144 California commercial wines, Ingraham and Cooke (1960) reported over half had undergone a malo-lactic fermentation as evidenced by the disappearance of malic acid. The malo-lactic fermentation was much more common in red table wines (75%) compared to white table (32.1%), and rosé (12.5%). They believed there was a causal relationship between the malo-lactic fermentation and the quality of red table wines. However, most of the high quality wines were from the cooler coastal districts and other quality factors were present.

The amino acid requirements of the malo-lactic bacteria have been studied by Radler (1958). Of 22 amino acids studied ten were absolutely essential. They also require nicotinic, folic and pantothenic acids, riboflavin, and possibly thiamin. Silva Babo (1963) found the vitamin B complex especially favorable to the growth of lactic acid bacteria and believes the favorable effects of adding lactic acid bacteria during the alcoholic fermentation were due to the better nutrition provided by the presence of yeasts. More data would be useful. The changes in amino acids in an enriched culture by *Leuconostoc* sp. or *Lactobacillus* sp. appear to be more different than in musts and wines. Peynaud and Domercq (1961) reported marked decreases in all of the amino acids except alanine. They also noted much less meso-inositol in wines which had undergone a malo-lactic fermentation. It has long been known that diacetyl and acetoin are by-products of the malo-lactic fermentation. In 41 white wines which had not undergone a malo-lactic fermentation, Radler (1962) reported an average value of acetoin plus diacetyl of 4.3 mg/liter compared to an average of 9.3 in 101 white wines which had undergone a malo-lactic fermentation. However, the malo-lactic fermentation does not always result in higher acetoin and diacetyl contents. Radler believed that in some red wines small amounts of diacetyl (detection threshold 1 mg/liter) gave the wine a desirable odor. Kielhöfer and Würdig (1960) also showed that these two compounds are produced during alcoholic fermentations.

Peynaud (1955), Lüthi (1957), Radler (1957), Carr (1958), and Tarantola (1959), reviewing the whole problem of the malo-lactic fermentation, believed its rational control is now possible. See Chap. 16.

In the sherry district of Jerez de la Frontera, film yeasts are active in bringing about the aging of the famous wines of southern Spain. In Japan, it has been found by Takahashi and others that aging of sake can be hastened by the use of certain film yeasts. See Chap. 4 and 9 for a discussion of film yeasts, and Chap. 16 for malo-lactic fermentation.

Temperature

A temperature of about 11.1° to 15.6°C (52.0° to 60.0°F) is best for the aging of table wines. For dessert wines the range may be somewhat higher. It is desirable to have the storage room, for table wines especially, well insulated against fluctuations in temperature. For dessert wines some fluctuation in storage temperature may be desirable because of the improved absorption of oxygen which this aids but so far no critical experiments seem to have been made. In hot climates it appears necessary to artificially refrigerate the storage room, certainly for table wines, to prevent a harmful rise in temperature. While aging of dessert wines is a function of the temperature and such wines will age much more rapidly at 32.2°C (90.0°F) than at 15.6° to 21.1°C (60.0° to 70.0°F) it appears that quality is best preserved and enhanced when the wine is aged in the temperature range of not over 21.1°C (70.0°F). After the wine is aged it will keep best at low temperatures as further chemical changes are then retarded. For a fuller discussion of the effect of temperature, see Ough and Amerine (1966).

Accelerated Maturation

When repeal of prohibition reopened the wine market, almost all conceivable treatments for aging wine rapidly were attempted in various wineries. Some treatments were never accepted, some were abandoned as soon as traditionally aged wines became available, but some remained in use.

Several treatments, once part of aging, are no longer thought of as aging, e.g., early clarification, tartrate stabilization, and malo-lactic fermentation. Racking as soon as fermentation and subsequent settling are complete followed at once by filtration gives clarity without requiring appreciable time. Cooling table wines to −5.0° to −3.3°C (23.0° to 26.0°F) and dessert wines to about −7.8°C (18.0°F) to crystallize cream of tartar followed by filtration achieves tartrate stability quicker and more reliably than winter aging. Malo-lactic fermentation can be encouraged by inoculation toward the end of alcoholic fermentation, by yeast autolysate, low SO_2, and slightly warmer storage. Some types of wine, notably Madeiras and California baked sherries, are regularly aged by accelerated methods.

Most procedures now in general use for standard quality wines in California and elsewhere which result in early maturation involve heating or oxidation or both. They do not often produce high quality in the finished wine, but this is to be expected because the initial quality often is not high and even traditional aging would not result in a premium quality wine.

Baked sherry and Madeira are heated in the presence of air or oxygen. The favorable effect of heating other dessert wines in the absence of air has been claimed by many investigators, particularly in the Soviet Union. See, for example, Deibner and Bénard (1957). Singleton et al. (1964) found that heating flor sherry in the absence of air changed it to a white port-like wine. Heating of selected table wines in the complete absence of air for 30 days at 53°C (128°F) produced bottle bouquet and increased complexity, but decreased grapey aromas. A blend of fresh grapey varietal wine with a portion of a selected heat-treated wine can often produce a better wine than either alone.

Part of the benefits of aging is the result of increasing complexity of flavor which leads to increased sensory quality (Singleton and Ough 1962). Treatments to accelerate aging can be easily overdone destroying complexity rather than increasing it, and causing serious damage to the wine. Each wine behaves differently; a given treatment may improve one and spoil another. Therefore, rapid aging cannot be applied by rule of thumb, but must be used with intelligence, skill, and care, adapting the severity of the various treatments to the product at hand. Much further progress can be expected in this area (Singleton 1976).

Most of the older treatments for accelerated aging involve some induced oxidation: exposure to sunlight or ultraviolet light, aeration at low temperature to allow easier oxygen absorption followed by raising the temperature to induce oxidation, use of ozone, hydrogen peroxide, catalysts, etc. Many of the treated wines have a "faded" or "over-aged" character which is unpleasant. Addition of oak shavings or chips or extracts therefrom can, if carefully controlled, hasten the development of the component of barrel aging involving the flavor effects of oak extractables especially in dessert wines, but also in appropriate table wines.

Singleton (1962) has reviewed physical methods of accelerated aging. Claims of success have been variable; overtreatments are invariably bad. Working with a variety of types of wine, Singleton and Draper (1963) found ultrasonic treatment in combination with various gases (air, oxygen, nitrogen, carbon dioxide, and hydrogen) tended to give a "scorched" flavor and undesirable results. Similarly, using ionizing radiation (Singleton 1963; Paunovic 1963) at sterilizing dosage produced color bleaching and off-flavors. Such exotic treatments appear to have little future unless the new flavors are considered attractive in their own right or are so restrained as to be an unidentifiable contributor to complexity. More promise is held for "dissecting" traditional aging into its component reactions and managing each for optimum results.

PROCESSING

A central area, temperature-controlled for comfort of workmen, should be provided outside the storage area. This will include pumps, heat exchangers, filters, pasteurizers, fining tanks, centrifuges, ion exchange columns, blending devices, flow meters, in-line strippers to remove oxygen, and other equipment used in the modern winery. These should be arranged with a central control panel so that wine from any part of the winery can be processed without contamination with other wine. For the smaller winery, rubber hoses may be used for transfer of wine from one container to another or to and from the processing equipment.

Special rooms for vermouth or flavored wine production may be needed in the larger wineries. The sparkling wine department may require a variety of facilities: bottling room, fermenting room for tanks or bottles, aging room, riddling area, disgorging area, and labeling, storage and shipping rooms. Low temperature rooms, refrigeration equipment, special filters, and other equipment may be needed.

Pumps

A variety of pumps are available for special uses in the winery. All should be made of stainless steel.

Piston pumps are the oldest pumping principle. They need little care, last a long time and are little affected by foreign matter in the wine. They have a good suction and efficiency and can be buffered against irregular operation by an air regulator. They can be used for all kinds of work, especially where there is a considerable difference in height. Both single- and double-action piston pumps are manufactured. Lees are often pumped with single cylinder double-acting reciprocating piston-type pumps.

Centrifugal pumps are the most used pumps and are especially good where a nonpulsating pressure is required. These are made with a number of modifications—self-priming and nonself-priming and these can be single speed or variable speed. They can be mounted on wheeled trucks or permanently installed, as at sumps. They can be controlled by valves at the inlet or at the outlet by means of a by-pass. They are especially used as must pumps.

Gear and rotary pumps are similar in outward appearance to centrifugal pumps and depend on revolving gears or impellers to force the wine through the line. These have found wide use in modern wineries.

For maintaining a vacuum on a concentrator used in concentrating grape must, various types of vacuum pumps are used. Probably the most satisfactory is the steam jet vacuum pump which develops and maintains a high vacuum by the passage of high pressure steam past an orifice connecting to the vacuum line. Modern vacuum pans are equipped with a barometric condenser to handle the condenser water and condensate from the pan; while the steam jet handles only the noncondensable gases, air chiefly, from the must and air leakage.

Rotary vacuum pumps are similar in principle and design to the familiar laboratory vacuum pump used for laboratory filtrations, operation of vacuum drying ovens, etc. Special vanes, revolving rapidly in oil in a closely fitting cylindrical housing, maintain a high vacuum although this pump will not handle much water or condensable vapors without excessive wear and loss of vacuum. They are intended to handle dry gases.

All pumps should be operated at the pressure and speed suggested by the manufacturer, or as determined by trial, for best efficiency. Positive-displacement pumps are used in vacuum-type automatic bottling machines. The stainless steel impeller bump type or the rubber impeller type such as are used in canneries are also used in wineries.

Transfer Lines

Musts and wines are transported about the winery through metal pipes, rubber hoses, glass tubes, or fiberglass lines.

The best metal for pipes is stainless steel. It is expensive and hence is used more for wines than for musts. Glass pipes are practicable and permanent though somewhat expensive. Fiberglass pipes are much less costly than stainless steel and equally satisfactory for both must and wine lines. All lines should be installed so they can be easily drained.

Aluminum pipes have been used satisfactorily with musts. Rubber hoses are standard equipment in California wineries. They are made in a wide variety of sizes. Only those lined with odorless rubber should be used for wine. Rubber hoses become stained with wine after use and should be cleaned occasionally. A dilute warm solution of citric acid or a mild hot detergent can be used. Trial is sometimes needed to find the proper agent. When not in use rubber hoses should always be placed in racks at an angle so that they will drain dry.

Refrigeration

New wines are supersaturated with respect to potassium acid tartrate. As Marsh and Joslyn (1935) have shown, the excess tartrate will usually precipitate if enough time is allowed, or if the temperature is reduced sufficiently for shorter periods of time.

In most northern European countries, the cold winters chill the wines sufficiently to cause satisfactory separation of excess cream of tartar; but under Mediterranean or Californian conditions, detartration is so slow, especially in the very large tanks in the warm interior valley wineries, that it is customary to resort to artificial refrigeration of the wine to near its freezing point (see Skofis 1953). The temperatures employed are $-5.5°$ to $-3.9°C$ ($22.0°$ to $25.0°F$) for table wines and $-9.4°$ to $-7.2°C$ ($15.0°$ to $19.0°F$) or slightly lower for fortified dessert wines.

However, at low temperatures, the wine dissolves oxygen to a greater degree than at room temperature, resulting in rapid aging through oxidation when the wine is returned to the warm cellar temperatures. This is a disadvantage for many table wines but may not be harmful for certain dessert wines, and may even be somewhat beneficial for many dessert wines.

Some wineries store the refrigerated wine in tanks located in a cold room. This is the most expensive system. However, if a longer storage period is possible the minimum temperature need not be so low. Others refrigerate the wine to near the freezing point by pumping it from a large tank through a tubular refrigerator, usually direct-cooled with Freon or ammonia, and returning it to the tank until the desired low temperature is attained. The temperature then rises slowly and, when it reaches about 0°C (32°F) it is refrigerated again. Some wineries use auxiliary brine-cooled coils in the tanks to maintain the desired temperature after attaining it by an outside refrigerating unit. The refrigerating tubes and coils should be of stainless steel. Storage periods of about two weeks at −3.9°C (25.0°F) are usually employed for table wines and slightly lower temperatures for dessert wines, though Berg and Keefer (1958−1959) have shown that this is often inadequate. By using a swept surface, ultra-cooler to just form ice crystals in table wines, about −5.5°C (22.0°F), and then storing in insulated tanks a 5-day holding period is sufficient to achieve tartrate stability instead of 10 to 15 days required when crystals are not formed.

Marsh and Guymon (1959) have given an excellent presentation of the behavior of tartrates in wine and of methods of stabilization of wine against deposition of tartrates after bottling. The two common methods in use for this purpose are refrigeration and the use of ion exchange resins. Three methods are in use for applying refrigeration, namely, (a) the method in which the cooling apparatus is mounted in the chilling tank, (b) that in which it is mounted externally to the tank, and (c) that in which the tanks are located in a refrigerated room. In method (c) the wine is usually refrigerated by external cooler as it flows from storage to the chilling room. The freezing point of table wines is usually between −6.7° and −5.5°C (20.0° and 22.0°F) and of dessert wines between −11.1° and −8.3°C (12.0° and 17.0°F). Marsh and Guymon (1959) point out that while a period of 15 days storage of the wine at within one degree of its congealing temperature may often be adequate, a rise of only a few degrees markedly prolongs the required time of storage. This is one of the chief disadvantages of the first two. They state also that in these two methods uniform temperature throughout the contents of the tank is seldom attained because of the often large difference in temperatures of the wine near the top of the tank and that near the bottom.

Pipes or hollow plates are used in the coolers. There is a tendency for water to separate on the cooling pipes or plates, especially if the difference in temperature between the refrigerant and wine is great, thus reducing their efficiency.

The solubility of cream of tartar not only decreases with decrease in temperature but also with increase in alcohol content. Perin (1977) gives the following formula to calculate the temperature required to tartrate-stabilize:

$$\text{Temperature } (-\ {}^\circ C) = (\%\text{ alcohol content}/2) - 1$$

As an example, a wine with an alcoholic content of 10.6%,

$$(10.6/2) - 1 = -4.3{}^\circ C\ (24.3{}^\circ F)$$

However, as Marsh and Guymon (1959) point out, the rate of separation of cream of tartar at low temperatures is more rapid in table than in dessert wines and more rapid in white than in red wines. Storage time can also be shortened by seeding the wine with clean crystals of potassium bitartrate and by mild agitation. Chilling is not as effective in removing excess calcium tartrate as potassium bitartrate.

The response of wines to refrigeration varies greatly not only between types but even between wines of the same type. Berg *et al.* (1968) point out that only with periodic sampling and laboratory analysis is it possible to ascertain the rate of potassium bitartrate deposition and the total amount removable within a given period of refrigeration. Therefore, they suggest that the wine be analyzed for potassium and tartrate content before and after 4 and 6 days of refrigeration, and the decrease in values be used to determine whether it is worthwhile to continue refrigerating for potassium bitartrate removal.

The external refrigerating units are usually of the single pass shell-and-multitube type (Fig. 6.13), the wine flowing through the tubes (or plates) and the refrigerant expanding into the shell. The wine is circulated through the refrigerating unit until it reaches the desired temperature. Marsh and Guymon (1959) state that wine in tanks (not in a refrigerated room) warms more rapidly than usually believed. Therefore, they suggest that the refrigeration load be carried by two units instead of one; one to rapidly cool the wine to refrigeration temperature and a second, smaller unit to maintain that temperature. Approximately 10 tons of mechanical refrigeration capacity is required to hold 1140 hl (30,000 gal.) of wine at $-8.9{}^\circ C\ (16.0{}^\circ F)$.

A refrigerant should be used that will not damage the wine in case of a leak in the refrigerating unit. The unit should be made of metal that is not attacked by the wine. The surface of the plates or pipes of the unit may become coated with tartrates, a condition that reduces efficiency, but the coating is easily removed with dilute alkaline solution.

Schreffler (1952) has emphasized the importance of efficient use of mechanical refrigeration equipment in the winery as a means of reducing costs. Under average winery conditions 1 ton of refrigeration, 3520 W (12,000 Btu/hr), should require 1.0 to 1.3 horsepower applied to the compressor. The actual overall operating efficiency of a unit can be determined by measuring the temperature drop and the volume of wine being cooled and then calculating the number of Btu being removed per hour. This is checked against the ammeter reading of the motor to find

Courtesy of Valley Foundry & Machine Works, Inc.

FIG. 6.13. MODERN REFRIGERATION EQUIPMENT IN A CALIFORNIA WINERY

the relative amount of work being done by the compressor. The efficiency of heat exchangers is greatly reduced by deposits of tartrates or other material. Passing wine through the cooler at high velocity reduces the tendency to deposit tartrates. Schreffler also notes that if the velocity in some tubes is less than that in others they may become completely clogged, thus reducing the effective capacity of the unit.

Efficient oil separators with baffles and regular draining of the separators are also recommended for ammonia systems to increase efficiency. For water-cooled heat exchangers, removal of algae and scale is necessary to prevent reduced capacity. Expansion valves should be sufficiently large so no back pressure is built up. Finally, Schreffler recommends that insulated storage tanks be used to hold the wine being cooled so that when the wine reaches the desired temperature it may be held constant at this temperature by the use of a small refrigerating unit with cooling coils in the tank. The larger unit can then be used for another lot of wine. This procedure obviously increases the processing capacity of the plant.

Plate-type heat exchangers recover some of the refrigeration from wine being removed from cold storage, as much as 50–60%. This is usually done by passing the cold wine through the heat exchanger directly from the filter. This, however, may cause back pressure and slow down flow through the filter. In this case, a pump may be connected to the discharge side of the heat exchanger to increase flow. Plate-type heat exchangers should be cleaned carefully at frequent intervals to prevent accumulation of deposits on the plates.

The use of a refrigerated room is the most satisfactory and most expensive system. In order to avoid undue fluctuation of temperature in the room the wine is usually passed through a shell-and-tube cooler on entering the room.

When brandy aged at above 101° proof is reduced to 84° proof with water a precipitation of some alcohol-soluble water-insoluble wood extractives occurs. Usually, therefore, the brandies are held at −9.4° to −3.9°C (15.0° to 25.0°F) for 1 to 14 days. The insoluble materials are much more soluble at higher temperatures so the precipitate must be filtered off at a low temperature. According to Marsh and Guymon (1959) the only advantage for chilling more than 1 or 2 days is to allow the sediment to settle and thus facilitate filtration. The high viscosities of water-alcohol mixtures at low temperatures also makes them difficult to filter.

Ion Exchange

At present, ion exchange resins are used in California for two purposes: (1) to exchange hydrogen ions for potassium and calcium ions in order to improve the sensory qualities by lowering the pH of high pH wines, and (2) following refrigeration to remove remaining excess potassium and calcium ions, replacing them with either sodium or hydrogen ions as sensory considerations dictate.

High capacity cation exchange resins can be prepared as sulfonic acid resins. Dorfer (1970) gives practical directions.

If a cation resin is regenerated by treatment with strong sodium chloride solution, the resin is then in the sodium form and will exchange sodium for the potassium, magnesium, and calcium of the wine; if regenerated with an acid, it will be in the hydrogen form and will exchange hydrogen ions for the calcium, magnesium, potassium, and certain other positive ions. The sodium cation resins have little effect on the pH value of the wine, whereas acid resins (hydrogen resins) lower the pH value appreciably.

The chemical reactions for the action of the sodium-exchange resin are as follows where Z represents the resin:

$$CaSO_4 + Na_2Z \rightarrow CaZ + Na_2SO_4$$
$$2KH(C_4H_4O_6) + Na_2Z \rightarrow K_2Z + 2NaH(C_4H_4O_6)$$

In regenerating the resin, the scheme is as follows:

$$K_2Z + 2NaCl \rightarrow 2KCl + Na_2Z$$

The potassium chloride is leached out and discarded in the sodium chloride brine. The reactions for the cation resin in acid form are similar, with hydrogen replacing the sodium. The use of ion-exchange resins is now permitted by state and federal wine regulatory agencies.

The resin is generally used in a column (a tall, narrow tank) (Fig. 6.14) and the wine is usually allowed to flow downward through the resin. However, the resin may also be added directly to the wine. Only about 30% of the capacity of the resin is realized in this case, according to McGarvey *et al.* (1958), and the resin is used but once. With the column method the resin is regenerated after use and lasts indefinitely. Thus, it

Courtesy of Valley Foundry and Machine Works, Inc.

FIG. 6.14. TWO RESIN AND ONE BRINE SOLUTION ION EXCHANGE TANKS IN A CALIFORNIA WINERY

is much more economical in its use of resin than is the batch method. The latter is primarily for use in smaller wineries in which the cost of a permanent installation of stainless steel columns and connections might not be justified. With a column, the uppermost portions are continuously receiving fresh wine and on that account the procedure results in a fully exhausted exchanger, starting from the top downward.

Percival *et al.* (1958), Dickinson and Stoneman (1958), Moser (1956), Rankine and Bond (1955), Ribéreau-Gayon *et al.* (1956), and McGarvey *et al.* (1958) have presented the basic principles for the treatment of wines with ion-exchange resins and their practical use in the winery. They generally recommend the columnar method for the reasons previously given. The tall stainless steel tank is filled with an appropriate cation resin. Water covers the resin in the column and must be displaced by wine. Each $0.028 \ m^3$ (1 ft^3) of resin will introduce about 2.6 liters (0.7 gal.) of water. This displacement of the water is done by upward flow of the wine to be treated, the flow being at the rate of about 20 liters/m^2 (0.5 gal./ft^2) of cross section area per minute.

After the wine has been introduced in the above manner to displace the water and air in the interstices between the resin beads, the direction of wine flow is reversed, i.e., wine is introduced into the top of the column and flows downward at the rate of 270 to 340 liters/m^3 (2.0 to 2.5 gal./ft^3) per minute. This is continued until the resin no longer removes potassium from the wine satisfactorily (as determined by chemical analysis).

At this point the wine remaining in the column is drained off; the amount remaining in the bed, chiefly in the spaces between the beads, will be about 2.6 liters/$0.028 \ m^3$ (0.7 gal./ft^3) of resin. This wine is displaced by a volume of water equal to the volume of resin, the wine being diluted somewhat in this process. The diluted wine may be returned to process or used for distilling material.

As the beads act as a filter, considerable solids may accumulate during a run. Therefore, the bed should be backwashed with water at a flow rate of 15 to 23 liters (4 to 6 gal.) per minute until the effluent is quite clear. The time required is usually about 30 min. The bed is allowed to settle and is then regenerated.

A regenerant solution of 10% NaCl, 2 to 4% H_2SO_4, or 2 to 10% HCl is prepared. A flow rate of about 2 liters (0.5 gal.) per minute per cubic foot of resin is recommended by the manufacturer. After regeneration the bed should be rinsed with water to displace all the brine remaining in the column. About 52 hl/m^3 (40 gal./ft^3) of water will be required. Rinsing is continued until a negative test is obtained for regenerant in the effluent.

The water remaining in the column is displaced with wine in the manner previously described and the cycle started again. If the column is not to be used again at once, the resin should be left in water and sufficient sulfur dioxide added to prevent growth of microorganisms.

The removal of potassium ions by the exchange resin is instantaneous, according to Percival *et al.* (1958). Almost complete removal of the potassium from the resin is attained during regeneration and calcium and magnesium are completely removed. The content of sodium or hydrogen in the treated wine is increased approximately equivalent to the potassium, calcium and magnesium removed by the resin.

Du Plessis (1964) treated two South African musts (pH 3.6 and 3.7) with ion exchange resins in the hydrogen cycle, reducing the pH to 3.2, 3.0 and 2.8. However, the quality was decreased by the treatment probably because of the high tartaric acid in the wine (especially for Riesling). Gerasimov and Kuleshova (1965) and others have observed near or complete removal of thiamin by either sodium or hydrogen form cation exchangers or by bentonite fining. From 12 to 40% of the pantothenic acid was removed by the ion exchangers, 17 to 35% of the pyridoxine and 48 to 84% of the nicotinic acid but the inositol and biotin were not affected. Bentonite removed 70% of the pyridoxine and nicotinic acid but did not affect pantothenic acid.

Fessler (1958) believed the sodium form of exchange resins would be of definite value in reducing the iron content of wines, but agrees with Joslyn and Lukton (1953) that their value for reducing the copper content is doubtful. A specific resin for copper removal is now available.

With a sodium-cycle ion exchanger, Permutit Q, Mindler *et al.* (1958) found no change in alcohol, total acidity, fixed acidity, or pH. They also claimed that treated wines resisted oxidation better than nontreated. The claim that there was sufficient reduction in copper, iron and calcium to avoid metal cloudiness is not borne out by commercial practice as usually only a small portion of the iron and copper are removed. Also, in practice, the pH goes up. Anion resins are available that will remove excess oxidized color from wine (see McGarvey *et al.* 1958).

Continuous column exchangers are less expensive than the batch process. Not all the wine is run through the ion exchanger—only enough so that when blended back to the main lot the average potassium content will be below some critical value. Berg and Akiyoshi (1971) have given data on this level (Chap. 15). Cation exchangers must be used judiciously so as not to unduly reduce the potassium content and increase the sodium.

Ion exchange is also used in the processing of fruit juices. One of the problems is the regenerant cost. Popper and Nury (1964) used calcium tartrate as the recoverable regenerant. There was little change in pH or flavor. Ion-exchange treated wines frequently fine poorly with bentonite according to Rankine and Emerson (1963). They recommend fining with sodium bentonite prior to ion-exchange treatment. If this is not possible, the bentonite fining should be accompanied by addition of gelatin.

Electrodialysis and Reverse Osmosis

The Germans are leading investigators of the use of electrodialysis for tartrate-stabilizing wines. The effect of electrodialysis on wine stability by reducing the concentration of potassium and associated anions was investigated by Wucherpfennig and Millies (1976). They reported removal of 100 mg of K/liter was sufficient to confer practically absolute stability on a number of wines of different quality. Wucherpfennig and Badior (1976) compared the effect of electrodialysis stabilization with that of refrigeration on the sensory qualities of eight wines. In three cases the refrigerated wines were judged slightly better, in one case the refrigerated wine was designated as being significantly the best of all, and in four cases the electrodialysis treated wines were judged superior. For a general review of electrodialysis treatment see Pierrard (1976).

Rhein (1976) has patented the use of reverse osmosis to accelerate the crystallization and removal of tartrate from wine.

Comparison of Tartrate Stabilization Procedures

Wucherpfennig *et al.* (1976) compared the following tartrate stabilization processes: metataric acid treatment, cooling, treatment with calcium salts, ion exchange, electrodialysis, and reverse osmosis. They recommended electrodialysis or ion exchange for wine stabilization.

Filtration

With the introduction of large filter presses, filtration has become the predominant method of clarifying wines after racking in California. Filtration is a physical process, that is, it mechanically removes suspended material by passage of the wine through a filter medium of smaller pore size than the particles to be removed. In addition to the screening action, adsorption on the filter aid is also a factor in most filtrations. If nothing is done to keep the pores open, pressure builds up and the volume passing through diminishes. This is prevented by continuously adding a filter aid to the wine. Most filter aids are diatomaceous earths which, because of their irregularly shaped particles, are effective in increasing the period of efficient filter operation. For a general discussion of wine filtration see Geiss (1952, 1957) and Muller-Spath (1975).

The factors governing filtration rate are size of pores, number of pores, percentage and type of solids (crystalline or amorphous), rate of deposition of solids, flow characteristics of the liquid, filter area, and pressure difference.

Filters can be operated at constant pressure or constant volume of flow. The latter is preferable, but to achieve a constant flow a flow-measuring device to regulate a variable speed drive pump is necessary. For adding diatomaceous earth slurry as a filter aid, proportionating pumps or injection systems can be used.

Filters should be made of stainless steel or other inert material. The plates are often made of plastic or other light material to facilitate handling.

In order to reduce filtration costs, attention should be paid to pre-clarification. Bentonite fining, centrifuging, and reducing the temperature are means to this end. Schloder and Boch (1977) reported that the best results were obtained with white wines which had undergone a clarification with kieselsol-gelatin. Dubourdieu et al. (1976) found ultra-dispersion particularly effective in improving the filtration of wines rich in protective colloids.

Also, one should never filter from the bottom of the tank but the clear wine should be filtered first and the cloudy wine last. To determine if a wine would benefit from preclarification, Descout et al. (1976) developed an index of filterability, and Peleg and Brown (1976) and Peleg et al. (1979) devised a method for evaluating the filterability of wine.

Bulk Filtration.—Filter presses consist of hollow metal frames and fluted plates attached to a metal frame (Fig. 6.15). The metal used must

Courtesy of Valley Foundry and Machine Works, Inc.

FIG. 6.15. MODERN FILTER PRESS WITH FILTER–AID MIXING TANK (LEFT)

be corrosion-resistant so that it does not affect the wine. Aluminum, or an aluminum alloy, is often used as it is light and resistant but some aluminum pickup occurs. Special canvas sheets usually protected by a paper sheet are placed between the frames and plates. On its way to the filter press the wine is mixed continuously with infusorial earth filter aid such as Hyflo Super-Cel or Filter-Cel. Too much filter aid should not be used. The amount will vary with the type and cloudiness of the wine. The wine is forced through the filter by a variable speed, positive displacement pump of the same capacity as the filter. Filter presses have a great filtering capacity, will handle cloudy to brilliant wines, and use an inexpensive filter medium. However, the filter cloths become torn and must be laundered, the presses are difficult to automate and they tend to leak. See Fig. 6.15 for illustration of a typical filter press.

Leaf filters consist of several hollow screens inside a metal cylinder. The screens are supported by an inner metal frame. All metal used in the filter is stainless steel or other corrosion-resistant metal or alloy. A precoat of filter aid is deposited on the screens by pumping wine or water heavily charged with filter aid through the filter. Then the wine to be filtered is mixed continuously with a little filter aid and is pumped through the filtering layer of filter aid on the screens. These, like filter presses, have a high filtration capacity and will handle cloudy to brilliant wines. They are easily automated and do not leak. However, the screens are expensive and easily damaged. They also become partially plugged with resultant uneven coating and poor filtration.

Rotary vacuum filters consist of a large, horizontal, perforated cylinder rotating with the base in the liquid to be filtered. The cylinder is covered with a cloth to which a precoat of diatomaceous earth 75 to 100 mm (3 to 4 in.) in thickness is applied. During filtration a knife running the length of the cylinder continuously removes a thin strip of the precoat, thus exposing a fresh, unplugged surface for filtration. A vacuum inside the cylinder forces the liquid through the precoat. These filters can handle juices or wines with a high percentage of solids, or with the type of solids that would seal off a pressure filter in a short time. However, they involve very high capital costs, have a low filtration rate, high powder consumption, and aerate and strip the filtrate.

Polishing Filtration.—Wine to be bottled should be brilliantly clear. It is essential in conducting a polishing filtration to avoid undue aeration as it may cause clouding or injure flavor, bouquet, or color. The metal parts of the filter should be made of stainless steel or other corrosion-resistant alloy.

The usual polishing filter consists of a series of hollow metal plates mounted on a frame, with thin filter pads placed between the metal plates. The pads may be made of cellulose fiber, asbestos fiber, or a mixture of the two. The pads may become a source of contamination of the wine with calcium salts, with subsequent clouding of the wine or deposition of calcium tartrate crystals. Therefore, in case of doubt, a dilute solution (1%) of citric acid should be passed through the pads after the filter is set up, in order to remove calcium and earthy flavors. This is followed by circulating water and draining. The pads are available in various porosities, i.e., degrees of tightness or density. The coarser the texture or density, the more rapid the filtration rate and the less brilliant the appearance of the wine. The wine is pumped through the filter pads by nonpulsating centrifugal pumps. Asbestos pads are not recommended.

Hyperfiltration is a new process which, according to Staude *et al.* (1976), may be used to tartrate-stabilize wine. The process concentrates the liquid to the point where potassium bitartrate crystallizes and is removed by subsequent filtration.

Sterilization Filtration.—The Seitz Co., of Bad Kreuznach, Germany, demonstrated a number of years ago that wine and fruit juices can be rendered sterile, germ- or yeast-free, by filtration through sterile, very tight filter pads such as that company's special EK pads. The most recent Seitz process of sterile filtration includes three stages: sterilization, filling, and corking (Fig. 6.16 and 6.17).

Courtesy of Seitz-Werke, Kreuznach

FIG. 6.16. FULLY AUTOMATIC STERILE BOTTLING ROOM

From left to right, sterilizing, filling, and corking. The sterilizing is done with sulfur dioxide gas

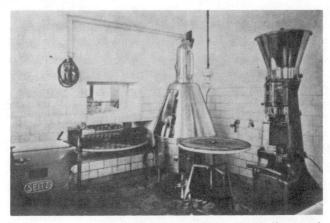

Courtesy of Seitz-Werke, Kreuznach

FIG. 6.17. STERILE BOTTLING ROOM FOR HAND OPERATION

Note rotary table in wall for introduction of bottles. The machine in the background is a semi-automatic rotary filter and on the right is a semi-automatic corking machine, capacity 1400 bottles per hour

Whenever sterile filtration is to be used the following precautions must be taken: (1) the filter and all the lines, bottling equipment and corks and bottles must be sterile and (2) sterilizing agent should not remain in the bottles or filter to contaminate the wine. The filter, pump, bottling machine and lines can be sterilized with steam or hot water at least for 20 minutes. The corks are usually supplied presterilized and new bottles are also sterile. In the best installations the entire filtration, bottling and corking are done in a small room which can be sterilized. One secret of success is to operate at a low, even filtration pressure. This means that the wine should be as nearly brilliant as possible before sterile filtration. Also see p. 337.

Membrane filters are now widely used in sterile filtration. The filters are porous membranes composed of inert cellulose esters or of polycarbonate.

Because of the uniformity of pore size, absolute sterility can be achieved by choosing a filter of the correct pore size. Since pore volume occupies approximately 80% of the total filter volume, extremely large flow rates are obtained provided the wine is prefiltered.

Centrifugation

California was slow to adopt centrifugation because the early centrifuges unduly aerated the wine. However, the development in recent years of centrifuges fitted with inert gas devices has led to the widespread use of centrifuges to clear both juice and wine. They are used to clear white juice prior to fermentation and both white and red wines immediately following fermentation. They are particularly useful for quickly clearing red press wines thus preventing the quality deterioration resulting from the usual settling and racking procedure. In a number of cases centrifuging can replace filtration, eliminating its stripping action.

Pasteurization

Both bulk pasteurization and the hot bottling of wine are being less and less used by wine makers throughout the world, and especially in the United States. Improved filtration and fining techniques and the rational use of antiseptic agents have made heating normally unnecessary. Fine table wines, particularly, should not be pasteurized. Furthermore, the early-maturing table wines being produced today are relatively free of potentially harmful microorganisms and pasteurization is not only unnecessary but often is harmful to the quality of the wine, particularly the color.

Pasteurization is applied in one of three ways, namely, (a) by flash pasteurizing and returning to the storage tanks; (b) flash pasteurizing into the final bottle; and (c) pasteurization by heating the filled and sealed bottle. There is also some bulk pasteurization and hot holding at a temperature of 48.9°C (120.0°F) for several days to stabilize wines—usually dessert types; see Holden (1955).

Bulk pasteurization is used for three purposes; first, to stabilize the wine chemically and physically by coagulating certain heat-coagulable colloids; second, to stabilize it microbiologically by destroying bacteria and yeasts; and third, to hasten aging, particularly of ordinary dessert wines.

Pasteurizers should be constructed of stainless steel and so designed that they can be easily disassembled and cleaned. Two designs are in use in California wineries. The first consists of a tubular heat interchanger made up of several horizontal metal tubes encased in another tube, in which incoming wine is heated nearly to pasteurizing temperature by the outgoing hot pasteurized wine; and of a similar set of tubes heated by steam. They are the least efficient, heating not as likely to be uniform, and difficult to clean. However, when these are used for bulk pasteurization for bringing the contents of a tank of wine up to a given temperature, they give satisfactory results. They are often used, for example, to bring the wines in the sherry baking tank up to the desired baking temperature.

A more recent development is the plate heat exchanger which is definitely superior to the tubular exchanger. The heating section consists of a series of hollow plates that are clamped together in a metal frame. Steam or hot water is on one side of each plate to act as a heating medium, and the liquid to be heated is on the other side. A similar set of plates forms the heat interchanger. Heating and cooling are rapid and efficient, and the plates are easily removed for cleaning. One advantage of the plate pasteurizer is that the temperature of the wine can be raised to the desired figure very quickly and held there for a short but determined time. The two forms of wine pasteurizers (plate and tubular) are shown in Fig. 6.18 and 6.19. While the tubular heat exchanger has been used for pasteurizing at the time of bottling the plate pasteurizer is preferred for this purpose.

Courtesy of Wine Institute

FIG. 6.18. PLATE–TYPE HEAT EXCHANGER AND HOLDING TANKS

In the best method of flash pasteurizing wine in bulk, it is heated for about 1 min to 82.2°−85.0°C (180.0°−185.0°F) and is then cooled continuously against the incoming wine and water or refrigerant cooled pipes.

The time × temperature relationship for pasteurization of wines was considered by Sudraud (1963). Vegetative yeast cells are killed at 45°−

Courtesy of Valley Foundry and Machine Works, Inc.

FIG. 6.19. HEAT EXCHANGER AND PASTEURIZER

50°C (113°−122°F) while yeast spores are only killed at 55°−60°C (131°−140°F). (See also p. 177.)

To stabilize ordinary white dry table and dessert wines, a common method consists of adding about 100 mg/liter of sulfur dioxide, heating to about 60.0°−62.8°C (140.0°−145.0°F), adding bentonite, holding at 54.4°−48.9°C (130.0°−120.0°F) for 1 to 3 days, racking, cooling, and filtering. It is often very effective for removing heat-sensitive proteins.

Most fruit wine produced in the Pacific Coast states is pasteurized to 62.8°C (145.0°F) (or higher) and bottled hot. Usually, but not always, the bottled wine is cooled rapidly by water sprays to room temperature. At least one large California winery pasteurizes all table wine on its way to the bottling machine. For a discussion of the principles of pasteurization and its application to wine see Glemann (1976).

Fining

Fining is the clarification of a wine or other liquid by adding a substance or substances in solution or suspension which, when added to the wine, react with the tannin, acid, protein or with some added substance to give heavy, quick-settling coagula. In most cases, the fining agent also adsorbs suspended material. All fining agents also exert some clarifying action mechanically as the precipitated material settles. The usual fining agents for wine are tannin, gelatin, casein, bentonite, isinglass, egg albumen, pectic enzymes, carbon, metal removal materials, and polyvinylpyrrolidone.

For best fining, wines should be low in carbon dioxide. The fining agent (or the fining agent plus constituents from the wine with which it combines) should be more dense than the wine. High acid and high tannin wines are easier to fine than low acid and low tannin, and dry than sweet.

Since the normal suspended materials in wine are negatively charged, a positively charged fining agent is preferred. The smallest possible amount of fining agent should be used. The fining agent should be quickly and thoroughly mixed with the wine. A low and especially a constant temperature is important for successful fining. The fining agent should remain in contact with the wine the shortest possible period. Fining is used to effect a rapid clearing of the wine, to clear wines which will not clear naturally, to remove substances which would render the wine unstable after bottling, and to effect changes in the sensory properties.

In choosing a fining agent the following considerations should be paramount: specific effect to be achieved, effect on sensory properties, effect on ultimate stability, amount of lees produced, and cost of fining material.

Laboratory Fining Tests.—In order to determine how much of any given fining agent or agents is required for a given wine, small-scale fining tests should be made.

For example, it is desired to know how much tannin and gelatin are needed for a certain wine. Have on hand in the laboratory a 1% solution of tannin dissolved in 100° proof (50% alcohol) brandy, and 1% solution of gelatin in water made by warming 1 g of gelatin in water until dissolved, adding 0.5 g of citric acid and 0.1 g of sodium benzoate as preservative. Then to 100 ml portions of the wine in 4 oz bottles add 0.5, 1.0, 1.5, 2.0, 2.5, and 3.0 ml of tannin, with shaking, and then the same volumes of the gelatin solution. The samples are shaken and allowed to stand several hours. The one showing brilliancy at the lowest concentration of fining agents is, naturally, chosen. If none is clear, try a larger volume of tannin in relation to gelatin, also larger amounts of both until the proper ratio and amounts are found; normally, one part of gelatin reacts with one of tannin, but for white wines deficient in tannin it may be necessary to use more of tannin than gelatin.

Suppose 1.5 ml of tannin and 1.5 ml of gelatin solutions were found best. This represents 0.015 g of each per 100 ml; or 0.15 g of each per liter. Since 1 gal. equals 3785.4 ml, the amount of each per gallon is 3.8 × 0.15=0.57 g and for 100 gal., 100 × 0.57 or 57 g. Since an ounce is 29.8 g, this is roughly 2 oz.

Similar calculations and laboratory solutions are used for casein, bentonite, and other fining solutions.

Sycher *et al.* (1976) determined wine clarity with a laser ray of 15 to 20 mv and wavelength of 6328Å. They claimed the laser technique permitted the determination of required amounts of clarifying substances in 15 sec.

Tannin and Gelatin Fining.—In the pre-Prohibition era in California the most common fining agents were tannin and gelatin. Gelatin itself has a positive charge in wine and hence precipitates with the negatively charged tannin. Tannin need not be added to pink and red wines. Certain fruit wines of high tannin content fine very well with gelatin alone.

One of the best tannins is that extracted from grape seeds and skins and known commercially as "oenotannin." Its use is not permitted in the United States. So-called tannic acid is used here.

The tannin should be free of off-flavor and -odor and should impart as little color as possible to the wine. In addition to its use as a fining agent, tannin is also added to wines occasionally to impart a slight astringency, and should be of high purity, such as is USP tannin and tannic acid.

Gelatin is a collagen fraction which is a submember of the albuminoid proteins. It is found in skin, tendons and bones, and is converted into the water-soluble protein, gelatin, by boiling with water. For use in the fining of wines it should be of high purity and free of undesirable odors and flavors.

As gelatin micelles are positively charged and haze particles in wine usually negatively charged, neutralization occurs resulting in rapid precipitation. Factors affecting its action are temperature, pH, metals, aeration, dextran, previous treatment and amount of gelatin added. Usually, lowering the temperature below 25°C (77°F) as far down as 16.0°C (50.8°F) aids, lower pH (within limits) aids, ferric iron is required, and dextrans act as protective colloids, hindering the reaction. Previous heating can form protective colloids. And overfining can result in the haze particles in wine acquiring a positive charge and forming a stable colloidal cloud.

In fining a white wine, the tannin is added first, followed 24 hr later by the gelatin as a 6 to 10% solution in water. The wine is allowed to settle until clear, usually 2 or 3 weeks. It is then racked and given a polish filtration. Because of the danger of overfining and the persistent cloudiness which results, white wines are now seldom fined with gelatin. When used, about 15 to 120 mg/liter (⅛ to 1 lb) each of tannin and gelatin per

1000 gal. are sufficient.

Red wines are sometimes fined with this agent, especially where the wine is excessively high in tannin. Addition of gelatin will, however, lighten the color; consequently it should be used cautiously. From 30 to 300 mg/liter (¼ to 2½ lb/1000 gal.) may be required.

Casein.—Casein is the principal protein of milk. It is prepared from milk by precipitating with acid. Normal casein is insoluble in water, but a water-soluble modified casein (sodium or potassium caseinate) is available. According to the usual theory, when the casein solution is added to wine, the acidity of the latter neutralizes the alkali of the caseinate and precipitates the casein as a flocculent curd. This precipitate adsorbs and mechanically removes material from the wine as it settles. Sodium and potassium caseinate can be used directly.

Factors affecting its action are concentration of the casein solution, tannin, temperature, and previous treatment of the wine. A 2% water solution is maximum, previous addition of tannin aided, higher temperatures hindered (cellar temperature best), and previously heated wines are often difficult to fine. It is used principally to remove color from white wines. For further information on casein fining see O'Neal *et al.* (1951).

Bentonite.—Bentonite should be referred to as montmorillonite which is an all-embracing term for aluminum silicate clays with a defined expanding crystal-lattice structure. The Wyoming bentonites are particularly suitable for wine clarification as they carry sodium as the dominant cation instead of calcium. For the fining of dessert wines and most table wines of average quality, bentonite has replaced other fining agents in California. See Mayer-Oberplan (1956) concerning bentonite fining of various wine types.

While Ough and Amerine (1960) reported 1500 mg/liter (12.5 lb/1000 gal.) of bentonite in must did increase clarity and filter speed and lightened the color of the new wines, they did not recommend its use in fermenting musts. Their recomendation was backed by Somers and Ziemelis (1973) who reported that fining after fermentation gave much more efficient removal of residual wine proteins than fining during fermentation.

Bentonite exists as exceedingly small plates about 1 nm units thick by about 500 nm wide. These plates are negatively charged due to having more negatively-charged atoms on the flat side of the plate than positively-charged atoms on the edges. When bentonite is soaked in water, the plates separate more or less completely to form a homogeneous colloidal suspension, which presents an enormous surface area of the order of 750 sq m per gram for sodium bentonite. In the calcium form, the plates tend to clump together in groups of up to 20, with consequent reduction in surface area and fining effectiveness.

There are basically two actions involved in protein adsorption: (1) Electrostatic precipitation by neutralizing positively-charged particles either by proton transfer or cation exchange, e.g., adsorption of proteins by binding them through their amino groups. (2) Adsorption of uncharged molecules by hydrogen bonding. Proteins in wine are normally positively charged and are adsorbed by charge neutralization. When they are present uncharged they are adsorbed by hydrogen bonding. When present as negatively-charged particles they are bound by the positive charges on the edges of the plate.

Factors influencing protein removal are: (1) Method of preparing the bentonite suspension—preswelling in warm water is most effective. (2) Acidity of the wine—the more acid the wine the more effective is the removal of protein due to the increased positive charge of the protein at low pH values. Usually ¼ as much bentonite is required at pH 3.0 as at pH 3.6. (3) Tannin content—tannin lowers the efficiency of protein removal. (4) Wine composition—wines ion exchanged with resin in the sodium form frequently fine poorly. This is due to removal of divalent cations as flocculation only occurs when the divalent cation concentration is above about 4 meq/liter. This condition may be remedied by adding a small amount of magnesium chloride. (5) Alcohol content—high alcohol content increases effectiveness. (6) Temperature—warm wines fine better than cold. (7) Protective colloids—greatly hinder fining. They are negatively charged; therefore, it is logical to fine with a positively-charged protein, followed by bentonite to remove any excess protein.

The advantages of bentonite fining are protein removal, prevention of copper cloudiness, adsorption of growth factors, oxidases and other materials, and mechanical clarification. The disadvantages are adsorption of red colors, removal of vitamins and amino acids, and excessive lees. Bentonite is also very useful in case of overfining with an organic fining agent; it will usually clarify the most recalcitrant wine.

The recommended method of preparing the bentonite suspension is to sift about 100 g/liter (0.8 lb/gal.) of bentonite into water while mechanically stirring and agitating with steam. Agitate with steam to about 50°C (120°F) after 24 hr, and repeat after another 24 hr. Use on the third day.

The range of bentonite required is about 240 to 1200 mg/liter (2 to 10 lb/1000 gal.). According to Weger (1965) bentonite can be used as needed in Italy but German law limits it to 1.5 g/liter (about 12 lb/1000 gal.) and Austria to 2.0 g/liter (about 17 lb/1000 gal.).

When properly used, bentonite has little or no effect on the flavor and bouquet of table or dessert wines. However, it should be used with caution for the best wines. The recommendation of the Bordeaux school of enologists that some activated charcoal should be added to remove the off-odor of bentonite suggests that it can give a flavor to the wine. Bentonite may be added with a tannin and gelatin or casein fining, where it greatly hastens settling of the other finings.

In fining red and rosé wines with gelatin or bentonite, Bergeret (1963) found that the preferred agent depends on the type and age of the wine. Bentonite removes more color from young wines than gelatin; the opposite is true for old wines. Bergeret considers this to be due to the relatively greater activity of bentonite on the colloidal colored material of young wines. Bentonite is also especially effective (often too much so) in removing color from rosé wines. Generally, tannins are better removed by gelatin fining.

Isinglass.—This fining agent is a protein made from the bladder of the sturgeon. It reacts with the tannin in the wine, though it does not require as much as gelatin. The factors affecting its action are previous treatment of the wine, tannin, and iron. Heating of the wine may form protective colloids which will hinder the reaction; tannin and presence of ferric iron are beneficial. This should be used only in fine wines to achieve brilliance prior to bottling, thus eliminating the need for filtration. It is prepared for use by soaking overnight in water containing sulfur dioxide, Waring blended, then diluted with wine to about 1%. Amounts used range from about 15 to 40 mg/liter (⅛ to ⅓ lb/1000 gal.).

Egg Albumen.—Fresh or frozen egg albumen is the clarifying agent of choice for reducing the astringency of red table wines. About 1 to 2 egg whites/hl (40 to 80/1000 gal.) of wine are recommended. They are beaten to a froth and mixed with about 10 volumes of wine before being added to the main volume of wine.

Use of Pectic Enzymes.—Commercial preparations of pectin-hydrolyzing enzymes contain the enzymes polygalacturonase and pectin methyl esterase. They split the pectin into galacturonic acid and methanol. The main factor affecting their action is temperature. The activity increases from 0° to 48.9°C (32.0° to 120.0°F) with complete inactivation at 60°C (140°F). They are added to crushed grapes to facilitate pressing and to musts and wines to facilitate clearing (see Ough and Berg 1974).

Carbon.—Activated carbon is a more or less pure form of carbon of vegetable origin. It acts by adsorption which consists of several factors including surface action, electrical charges, and chemical activity. The factors affecting its action are the method of preparation, pH, solubility and temperature. According to the method of preparation, carbon is most selective for color removal or odor removal. Lowering the pH usually increases adsorption as does raising the temperature. And less soluble materials are more easily removed. Carbon is used to de-colorize wine and to remove objectionable odors. As it can impart off-tastes, it should be used with caution. From 120 to 2400 mg/liter (1 to 20 lb/1000 gal.) of carbon are added directly to wine, usually followed by the addition of 240 mg/liter (2 lb/1000 gal.) of bentonite. As much additional carbon is required to remove the last 10% of color as was required for the first 90%. In evaluating efficiency of carbons for removal of red or brown colored pigments from wine, Singleton and Draper (1962) found that there was a general positive correlation of efficiency and ability of the carbon to catalyze the air-oxidation of ascorbic acid. The oxidizing property of carbon can be reduced by adding ascorbic acid, without influencing the decolorizing effect.

Metal Removal.—While use of potassium ferrocyanide (blue fining) is not legal in the United States, it is widely, successfully, and legally used in Germany and many other countries. It reacts with copper and iron and also removes protein. In blue fining the ferrous iron combines rapidly with ferrocyanide, while ferric iron is partly complexed with organic acids and reacts slowly with ferrocyanide. For this reason wines should be blue-fined in the absence of oxygen. It is added to the wine as a water solution followed by the addition of 240 mg/liter (2 lb/1000 gal.) of bentonite. Small amounts of cyanide can form in wine as a result of the addition of excess potassium ferrocyanide. However, even with a great excess of potassium ferrocyanide, the amount of cyanide formed is only 1/60 to 1/120 the lethal dose.

Cufex, a compounded ferrocyanide preparation which does not leave cyanide residues in wine, is legal for metal removal in the United States. Its properties and use are described in Chap. 15.

PVPP and Other Agents.—Polyvinyl-polypyrrolidone is a polymeric resin with polyamide linkages similar to protein. It reacts principally with tannins and is used to reduce browning in white wines because of its great affinity for catechin, the main substrate for browning reactions. It is added directly to must or wine and removed by racking or filtration. In a comparative test between PVPP and gelatin, Ough (1960) reported PVPP removed more color and tannin than gelatin. Tannin adsorption by PVPP proceeds efficiently at 6.1°C (43.0°F) according to Mennett and Nakayama (1970).

Yeast fining has not been used in this country but it offers certain advantages for new wines of excessive color or off-flavor. About 10% of fresh yeast is added to the wine. After about 1 or 2 weeks the wine is centrifuged or filtered. The yeasts not only reduce the rH of the wine but absorb appreciable color and off-odors such as those of molds or frost, etc. Simultaneous use of charcoal and bentonite is often useful.

Sparkolloid, a proprietary fining agent, is approved for use in this country. It appears to be most useful for pre-bottling clarification. Aferrin, mainly magnesium phytate, is approved for removal of iron. Martini (1965) has proposed using racemic tartaric acid before refrigerating wines as a method of removing excess calcium. A number of substances have been suggested to reduce browning (see Chap. 15). Glucose oxidase has been recommended by Ough (1975A) as an agent for removal of oxygen from dry white table wines. Shpritsman *et al.* (1976B) on treating wine with 1% methylcellulose found not only that the wine contained significantly decreased amounts of phenolic compounds but was also cold stable.

Shpritsman *et al.* (1976A) found the addition of 3 g/liter (25 lb/1000 gal.) of silica gel decreased the protein content 25% and produced a stable wine. They concluded that silicon dioxide polymers are more selective and more advantageous than bentonite for wine stabilization. Hahn and Possman (1977) compared 25 different formulations of "kieselsol," a generic name for an aqueous colloidal suspension of silicon dioxide. Baykisol 30, a 30% silicon dioxide preparation, was selected as the most effective. It is available both negatively (−) and positively (+) charged; (+), (−) kieselsol-gelatin (1:1:0.25) was found superior to tannin-gelatin in the amount of gelatin required, volume of lees, clarity achieved, and speed of sedimentation (24 hr instead of 1 to 2 weeks). Kieselsol and gelatin are also useful in other fining operations. They are added after Cufex fining to ensure rapid and total precipitation of the complex and to make the sediment immobile during racking. They are also used to reduce the volume of bentonite lees formed.

At present kieselsol is being used to a very limited extent in the United States. More widespread use seems warranted.

Blending

The blending of wines is one of the more important cellar operations, for upon its proper conduct depends the uniformity of quality and character of each of the cellar's principal brands of wine. The proper function of blending is often misunderstood by the public and even by winery personnel. The primary purposes of blending are to (a) develop specific types and (b) to maintain the character and quality of these types. Mixing of the wine of several casks to equalize the vintage is not considered blending in the sense used here.

Blending is normally not employed where the character and type of the wine are established by the regional origin of the wine and its vintage. Thus, most of the products of specific vineyards in Germany, Burgundy, and Bordeaux are not blended but represent solely the product of the vineyards or regions named. Moreover, since the quality varies from year to year the vintages are kept separate from each other. To a lesser extent this is true for varietal type wines, but many are blended and not vintaged, particularly in California.

However, in Spain, Portugal, and many other regions the type depends on judicious blending of wines produced by various production and aging techniques. Obviously, wine of a single vintage is impossible under these circumstances. Furthermore, the vintage is often of little importance, as for wines of moderate or standard quality. This applies to many California wines where the ultimate bottler does his own blending from a variety of sources. For a discussion and demonstration of the values of blending see Singleton and Ough (1962).

All of the wines in the cellar should be analyzed regularly before blending. The usual determinations are alcohol, volatile acidity, total acidity, extract, sugar, and tannin (see Chap. 19). Careful sensory evaluation should also be done on each of the wines which are to be employed in the blend to establish the characteristic sensory qualities of each.

A sample of the previous blend that is to be matched should be available. This sample must be held in a tightly sealed bottle at a cool temperature. The standard is tasted carefully to fix its qualities in mind. There should also be on hand an analysis of this older blend. Then, with the notes and analyses of previous blends before him, the taster makes up several small blends in the laboratory; taking perhaps 50 ml of one wine, 40 of another, and 70 of another in order to approximate the quality and composition of the standard. After mixing without undue aeration, the blend is tasted and analyzed carefully and compared with the flavor and composition of the standard blend. By several blends of this sort, one can usually closely approximate the old blend provided, of course, the wines are of the proper types.

From the laboratory blends, one decides how much of each of the wines to be blended will be needed. A trial blend of a gallon or two is then made and after a week or two retasted for conformity to the standard. This is followed by preparation of the cellar blend. As an aid in blending, Little and Wei-Yi Liew (1974) propose a method of blending wines to the desired color, based on the construction of blending diagrams.

Triangular taste tests (p. 670) are very useful for establishing the success of the new blend. Success in this case is inability to distinguish the quality and character of the standard from that of the new blend.

Blending is often neglected as a means of producing standard wines. It is generally agreed that for mass distribution, wines of uniform quality are most important. Careless blending and failure to maintain such uniform quality and type are reprehensible. Attention is also called to the advantages of fractional blending as a means of maintaining a standard quality and type (p. 407).

Blending should not be practiced indiscriminately. The reputation of a winery can be enhanced by keeping especially fine tanks separate and aging and bottling them under premium labels. The public has demonstrated, in many cases, its willingness to pay for such wines if they are truly of exceptional quality.

BOTTLING

Bottling, labeling, and casing are the final operations that the wine receives at the cellar. At present, most of the larger California wineries bottle their wines at the cellar, although much of the state's wine is shipped in tank cars to bottling plants throughout the United States. World War II price ceilings and scarcity of wine tank cars combined to increase greatly the bottling of wines at the cellar. This change is generally beneficial to both the industry and the consumer, as it protects both against unscrupulous, inexperienced, and careless bottlers or bulk suppliers. However, it may have increased the price of wine to the consumer and it is in almost complete contrast to French, Italian, and Spanish practice where much of the wine is sold in bulk directly to the consumer. Even in these countries, sales in bulk are decreasing.

The principal objects of bottling are to protect the wine against spoilage or deterioration by microorganisms and oxygen, to present the winery's customers with dependable wines, and to provide bottle-aged wines to critical consumers.

Good wine can be, and often is, spoiled or damaged by extreme aeration during bottling, or by infection with spoilage organisms, or by improper corking or sealing. Cleanliness and sanitation are extremely important in these operations. Corks should be sterilized and the bottles should be scrupulously clean. In the United States new bottles are almost always used.

Bottles

Wine bottles are of many forms and sizes, ranging in size from the 5-gal. demijohn to the small "split," holding only enough wine for an individual serving. They vary in form from the Italian balloon-shaped "fiasco" to the elongated, narrow Rhine wine bottle. The bottle should be carefully selected for size, strength, shape, and for freedom from defects. Strength is very important to prevent breakage by present high speed bottling, corking, and capping machines.

The glass should be clear white, greenish, greenish-brown or brown for white wines; and dark green or greenish-brown for red or pink wines. It should be free of flaws, strains, and bubbles, and uniform in thickness. Abnormalities in the glass can be readily detected by examining the bottle before a lighted surface through spectacles fitted with polarizing lenses. This is especially important with bottles which must withstand heavy pressures, such as those used for sparkling wines. As shown in Fig. 6.20, greenish-brown or amber colored bottles filter out more light of the wavelengths of the ultraviolet portion of the spectrum that are responsible for the undesirable photochemical reactions in wines.

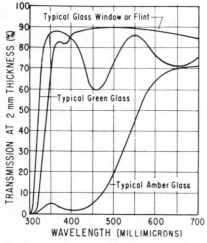

FIG. 6.20. EFFECT OF COLOR OF GLASS ON LIGHT TRANSMISSION AT DIFFERENT WAVELENGTHS

From Dillon (1958)

The necks of the bottles to be corked should be properly blown to take the corks, that is, properly tapered and smooth. The necks of those to be sealed with screw caps should be so threaded that the inner disc of the cap fits tightly on the top of the bottle and the side of the cap is flush with the side of the bottle. Data from our laboratories indicate that screw caps do permit greater access of oxygen and therefore more rapid deterioration of oxygen-sensitive wines, but the harmful effects on color and odor develop slowly.

Riesling wines are bottled in tall, narrow, long-necked, light brown bottles, commonly spoken of as Rhine wine bottles. In Germany, Moselle wines are bottled in similarly shaped bottles but are of green or blue-green color. Franconia wines are bottled in squat, broad bottomed flagons (*Bocksbeutel*) of green glass. This bottle is also used in Chile for certain white and even red wines.

The red burgundies of France and California come in greenish bottles similar in outline but less heavy than champagne bottles. However, many French Burgundies are bottled in distinctly brownish-green bottles, which for the reasons previously given, offer the best protection against adverse light effects. These bottles are also used for French Chablis.

The clarets of Bordeaux reach the consumer in straight sided bottles of light to very dark green glass. The shoulder is rather flat and the neck, like the body, is cylindrical rather than tapering. This bottle is used in California for claret, Zinfandel, and some other red wines. The bottle used for French Sauternes and Graves, and for California Sauterne is similar in shape to the Bordeaux claret bottle but is made of clear white or light green glass. The color of the glass is less important for these types of wines because of their generally high sulfur dioxide content which reduces the effect of adverse light-induced reactions in the wine.

Sparkling wines are usually sold in green bottles of very heavy walls and deeply indented bottoms. The tops carry a rather wide flange to hold the wire used in tying down the cork or to catch the crown cap.

One of the most famous of wine bottles is the straw-covered chianti flask or *fiasco* of Tuscany. The fiasco is round-bottomed and, if the woven straw covering is removed, it will not stand up. Some California red wines as well as white are bottled in modifications of these picturesque fiaschi. However, the finest chianti wines of Tuscany are often packed in bottles of conventional Bordeaux shape; nevertheless, American wine consumers have long associated the *fiasco* with chianti or chianti-type wines. Because of cost, straw-covered *fiaschi* are now rare.

California dessert wines sometimes are packed in bottles similar in outline to whisky bottles, and usually sealed with screw caps. Spanish sherries and Portuguese ports come in dark green or brown glass bottles of straight sides and are somewhat similar to the Bordeaux red wine bottles in outline. They are usually, but not always, sealed with cork rather than screw tops. These, and various special mold bottles, are also employed for California dessert wines. While most are closed with screw caps some have taper corks with wood or plastic tops.

Vermouths are usually marketed in green-colored bottles with a shape somewhat between that of the Bordeaux- and burgundy-type bottle. Many producers have special shaped bottles for their wines.

Second-hand bottles require soaking and washing in hot alkaline solution to thoroughly cleanse the interior. A thorough final rinsing in water is essential. Continuous automatic washers are available for this purpose. No trace of chemical or dirt should remain in the bottle. The bottles should be allowed to drain and dry before use but not to become contaminated with dust. Most European wineries employ used bottles, especially for ordinary wines. Their sterilization is difficult. Halter (1960) showed that even with a 15-18 min period in an antiseptic solution, many yeasts and molds remained in the bottle. Used bottles are seldom employed in the United States at present. New bottles usually require only thorough rinsing with water. The rinse water should be potable water completely above suspicion of contamination. However, Castor (1956), Schanderl (1957), and Halter (1959, 1960) have shown that one should not assume the new bottles are free of undesirable microorganisms unless specially closed at the factory. While some wineries have used forced air drafts to clean new bottles, a better procedure is to rinse and drain the bottles before filling in automatic bottling machines.

Filling

Four types of fillers are commonly used: siphon, vacuum, gravity and pressure. The fillers (Fig. 6.21) must be kept scrupulously clean and are best sterilized with steam prior to use. It is fairly common practice in the United States to remove oxygen from white table wines just prior to filling by sparging with nitrogen. This, coupled with the practice of bottle sparging with carbon dioxide, ensures bottled wines of low oxygen content. Membrane filtration and hot bottling are two of the methods

FIG. 6.21. FILLER FOR QUART BOTTLES (LEFT) AND GALLON JUGS

commonly used to achieve a sterile bottled product. The latter process is potentially damaging to wine quality. In the study of Haushofer and Rethaller (1964), they found that bottles filled at 60°C (140°F) and stored at 17.8°C (64.0°F) did not reach room temperature for 24 hr. And Wucherpfennig and Kleinknecht (1965) reported much less color in cold-filled white wines compared to those bottled and stored for 24 hr at 80°C (176°F).

Corks and Corking

Many of those accustomed to use of dry wines on the table prefer that the bottles be closed with straight, untapered corks, in the conventional manner. The corks should be at least 38 mm (1.5 in.) long for choice wines which may remain in the bottle several years and 50 mm (2 in.) or longer corks are preferred for red wines which may remain even longer. They should be fine-grained, smooth, and free of serious defects. The necks of the bottles should have the proper straight taper, and be free of bumps, grooves, and other imperfections so that the cork will be sealed throughout its length against the neck of the bottle.

Freshly cut corks contain dust in the pores and substances that may impart a disagreeable taste to the wine. They may also be infected with mold spores, yeasts, etc. Therefore, they should be cleaned and sterilized, and also slightly softened before use. One method consists of soaking for an hour or longer in a dilute (1%) sulfur dioxide solution containing a little glycerol, and then rinsing in water. The corks are then drained or centrifuged prior to use. The corks should not be soaked too long so that when they are compressed into the neck of the bottle excessive moisture and water-soluble material are pressed out.

Presterilized corks packed in plastic bags are now available. They should be periodically checked for molds. Rankine and Pilone (1972) suggest a procedure for checking sterility of wine corks, and Marias and Kruger (1975) give a method for determining viable mold spores in corks. They recommend that corks be gamma-radiation sterilized to prevent off-odors occurring because of mold growth.

Amerine and Joslyn (1970) describe the operation of the corking machine as follows. The corking machine operates in two stages: first, the cork is compressed to a small cylinder by the operation of horizontal movable jaws, or stationary jaws and plunger; and next, the compressed cork is driven into the bottle by a vertical plunger. The best type of corker is one that compresses the cork from all sides by jaws closing uniformly like the iris of a camera lens, although machines in which the cork is rolled as it is compressed from three sides by movable jaws are also satisfactory. Stationary-jaw, horizontal-plunger type compression is less desirable because of the danger of pinching or irregularly compressing the cork. As the cork is compressed, if it is not dry, drops of moisture ooze out from the bottom; these must be wiped off or blown off by an air stream to prevent contamination of the wine.

To minimize compression of the gas in the head space, most corkers are now fitted with a device which pulls a vacuum just prior to insertion of the cork.

The laminated cork (two or more pieces glued together) dates from at least 1895, according to Sharf and Lyon (1958). They are especially useful for making sparkling wine corks. They attribute the "corked" odor to the presence of *Aspergillus glaucus* in the cork.

Stephan (1964) has shown that cork stoppers permit passage of about 0.01 ml of oxygen per month while polyethylene stoppers allowed 0.16 ml per month. Even specially treated polyethylene stoppers permitted 0.01 to 0.03 ml per month to pass. For this reason, we do not recommend use of polyethylene stoppers for sparkling or still wines that are to be aged in the bottle for more than a short period of time (less than a year).

Screw caps are now used as regular-type closures for most ordinary table wines, and for nearly all dessert wines. These are available in a variety of types and patterns. When screw caps are used, particular attention should be paid to the finish on the neck of the bottle. The cap should seat properly on an inert material and seal the bottle completely. Capping machines which form a screw as they screw an aluminum cap onto the bottle are widely employed. Some liners are permeable to oxygen. Pilfer-proof closures are satisfactory and commonly used.

To prevent insect infestation of the top of the exposed cork and to make the seal more air-tight, it was once customary to seal off the top with beeswax. This practice is not common at present. Imported or domestic metal foil caps are placed over the neck of the bottle and crimped into place in a special machine in some wineries but plastic capsules are now used by most. These are placed in a moist condition on the neck of the bottle and are then dried so that they form a tight seal over the closure. Crown caps are used for the bottle fermentation of sparkling wines and for fruit wines. Small bottles of sparkling wines are sometimes distributed with crown caps.

Inspection and Storage Tests

It is good practice to take samples from the 1st and 8th case and check them immediately for clarity and fill point. One of these samples should be given the usual heat and cold stability tests. It is also good practice to take samples periodically and count the viable yeast. Witness samples should be taken from about the 25th case and kept for at least one year in a dark room, temperature controlled to about 12.8° to 15.6°C (55.0° to 60.0°F).

Labeling

The labeling requirements of the federal government and the various states are very complicated and frequently require legal interpretation. The general requirements for wines bottled in the United States are given in Chap. 20. Wines imported into the United States now generally require certificates that they conform to the labeling requirements of the region of origin.

In general, the source and type of wine must be stated in a similar size of type. Place of production and of bottling are also given on the label. The percentage of alcohol must be stated, but in practice need only approximately state the true percentage of alcohol. The size of the bottle must, however, be accurately given.

Hand labeling is messy and expensive. Semiautomatic labelers are better but each bottle must be handled individually. They can take up to 2000 or more bottles per hour. Automatic labelers which will handle 24,000 or more bottles per hour are manufactured and widely used (Fig. 6.22).

Courtesy of Wine Institute

FIG. 6.22. MODERN BOTTLING LINE WITH AUTOMATIC CORKING AND LABELING EQUIPMENT

Note small number of employees

Casing

For large wineries, automatic casing is necessary. These are constructed so that the bottles are inserted automatically. If a stamp is required it is automatically placed on the case at the same time as the lid is being glued and sealed shut.

Sources of Information.—The California magazine *Wines and Vines* each year in September publishes an issue which includes lists of suppliers of all kinds of winery equipment. A useful reference work on German equipment is Weinfach-Kalender (1977).

OTHER DEPARTMENTS

Quality Control

Modern quality control involves interaction among the laboratory, sensory testing and plant operations. An odor-free area for critical sensory evaluation is needed (p. 667 *et seq.*). Quality control charts or permissible limits of variation from the norm can be constructed from these data. See Kramer and Twigg (1970) for use of quality control charts.

Machinery

Refrigerating compressors, boilers, hot water tanks and air-conditioning equipment should all be centralized in a single area separated from the other departments. Adequate fire protection equipment should be installed. An adjacent shop area is desirable.

Distillery

The still tower is separated from the winery, often outdoors, to obtain lower insurance rates. Adjacent rooms for receiving the spirits, for fortification and for an office for the government agent are needed. Metal receiving tanks are commonly used. The fortification tanks should be as close to the fermenting room as possible. They should be equipped with compressed air for rapid mixing. The brandy warehouse is usually equipped with wooden or metal racks or pallets for holding 190-liter (50-gal.) barrels in which brandy is stored. Scales for weighing are necessary. If brandy is to be bottled, a dumping area, tanks for mixing and diluting, refrigeration equipment and a special bottling line in a separate room are necessary. The industry prefers "wine spirits addition" to fortification. For a review article discussing the properties of the various materials which can be used for constructing vessels for use in distilleries, see Van Pieper (1976).

Other Facilities

The office may be a single room for the small winery and may serve as a tasting room for visitors. In a large winery a whole complex of offices will be needed. The public relations department may require various types of tasting rooms for visitors with off-sale facilities. Several wineries are arranged with a special raised walkway through the winery for conducted tours of visitors. This keeps the visitors from interfering with winery operations.

Employees' dressing room and lockers, and sanitary facilities for the public and employees are required. Large wineries provide a dining room for their employees—with or without a cafeteria.

SANITATION

The modern winery must be kept impeccably clean at all times. Truax (1950) emphasized that sanitary measures are not necessarily introduced for public health reasons but also to increase plant efficiency, protection of equipment, avoidance of off-flavors, satisfaction of consumers' aesthetic values, meeting legal requirements, and improvement of employee working conditions. This was also noted by Amerine and Joslyn (1970) and Doyle (1951, 1952). For the same reasons, the new construction which has accompanied the great expansion of the California wine industry in the 1970's has generally brought with it facilities which are capable of being easily sanitized.

Davison (1961) summarized the accomplishments of the sanitation program of the California wine industry as follows: voluntary grape inspection, better harvesting and handling of grapes, better in-plant sanitation and better trained personnel. Wine Institute recommendations (Davison 1971) are periodically updated, last in 1971. Wine Institute now has an Environmental Studies committee to study methods of preventing pollution.

Effective sanitation is required by state and federal Food and Drug agencies. In recent years these agencies have become increasingly vigilant and active with respect to sanitary conditions in wineries and the enforcement of legal sanitation regulations. An important provision of these regulations is the famous "may have" clause, which provides that food shall be deemed to be adulterated "if it has been prepared, packed, or held under insanitary conditions whereby it *may have* become contaminated with filth, or whereby it *may have* been rendered injurious to health." This provision permits action to be taken against a product, including wine, solely on the basis of insanitary conditions during production.

The disposal of stillage, pomace, stems, and other winery wastes is an important part of a winery sanitation program. Certain aspects of this problem have been discussed in Chap. 18.

Surveys

The California Department of Public Health, Food and Drug Section, has conducted sanitary surveys and has made recommendations in writing to each winery. These inspections have been continued until the present (1979). Enforcement action is contemplated where conditions warrant.

The policy of the Department is one of education rather than drastic police action; the wine producer is given ample time to conform to the recommendations. The Federal Food and Drug officials also take an active interest in the wine industry's sanitation problems.

The wine industry through the Wine Institute has hired a sanitarian whose duties include assistance to wineries in setting up sanitation programs; furnishing information and training to sanitarians employed by wineries; evaluating equipment, materials and production procedures; making surveys upon request of wineries; and establishment of research projects in cooperation with scientists of the University of California and other research agencies on such subjects as picking practices, picking containers for grapes, gondolas, grape loading devices, lug box washing, insect control, etc.

Every winery should have a sanitation program with some competent individual responsible for this very important aspect of production. The winery that is too small to afford a full-time sanitarian can make use of the industry's sanitarian and can also delegate responsibility for sanitation to a key member of the plant's personnel as a part-time duty. Where a state or federal inspection or survey is made, a responsible member of the winery's staff should accompany the one making the survey and seek his advice and recommendations. The same applies to surveys conducted by the industry's sanitarian.

The National Food Processors Association has an outline for a sanitary survey (available in mimeographed form at the National Food Processors Association, Washington, D. C., or from their Western Laboratory at University Avenue and 6th Street in Berkeley, California). It includes such points as sanitary hazards from adjacent property, plant grounds, buildings, steam and moisture removal, water supply, drainage, floors, waste disposal, clean-up procedures, preparation department, warehousing, packaging department, insect infestation and control, rodent infestation and control, storage of unused equipment and containers, basement, drinking fountains, toilets, washing facilities for plant personnel, dressing rooms and lockers, employee sanitation, first-aid facilities, laboratory, lunch room, and general housekeeping. While the outline is specifically designed for canneries, it contains many very useful suggestions for sanitary surveys of wineries. See also Food Engineering (1954) and Pearson et al. (1955).

The Vinegar Fly Problem

In recent years the vinegar or fruit fly, *Drosophila melanogaster* Meigen, has been recognized as a pest of certain crops, particularly tomatoes, figs, and grapes. In California a great many of laboratory and field investigations have been conducted on control of the fly in and on tomatoes and on grapes used for wine making. It is a field and vineyard problem and control must include measures which will reduce infestation of the raw product before it is harvested. Furthermore, the flies are especially attracted to fermenting musts which creates an important sanitation problem for the wine industry. The problem is complicated where there is a huge buildup of the fly population, such as in the Central Valley grape regions of California prior to grape ripening. Figs, peaches, melons, and tomatoes are particularly notorious breeders of fruit flies. Since whole or parts of drosophila flies are considered filth by federal and state agencies, it is essential that means be developed to prevent fly and egg contamination.

Much of the fly population in wineries is brought to the wineries from the vineyard. In California, Berg et al. (1958) found the fruit fly content to be greatest in the Fresno area, less in the Lodi-Modesto area, and rather small in the Napa-Sonoma region. Field control measures presently considered desirable include discing in all dropped and cull fruit immediately after harvest, disposing of all organic wastes, use of repellent insecticides in the orchard or vineyard and attractant insecticides on dumps, use of poison baits in and downwind from orchards before and during harvest, and generally following good sanitation practices. These recommendations (Anon. 1958) will also help control dried fruit beetle which is also a problem with grapes.

The fact that female fruit flies can retain eggs in their bodies, lacking suitable sites for oviposition, means that a new life cycle can be started very soon after a female fly arrives. The summer life cycle varies from 5 to 8 days but is much longer in the winter months; in fact, there is little fly activity at temperatures below about 12.8°C (55.0°F). Maximum fly activity occurs in the range of 23.9° to 26.7°C (75.0° to 80.0°F) in low light intensity and with low wind velocity.

In studies of many loads of grapes delivered to wineries over a two-year period, it was established (Berg et al. 1958; Berg 1959) that (1) delay in harvesting, overcropping, and late irrigation increases the amount of rot in the fruit; (2) wine grapes are more susceptible to rot than table or raisin grapes; (3) rain during the picking season increases rot; (4) the degree of insect infestation varies among areas, seasons, and varieties; and (5) although insect infestation increases with increasing amounts of rot up to a maximum there is not sufficient correlation between the two to use one as a predictor of the other.

In these studies, the forms of the fly present in the bunches of uncrushed grapes were the larvae and eggs: the winged insects, of course, had flown before counts were made. There was an increase in flies in the majority of loads allowed to stand overnight. Berg et al. (1958), Middlekauff (1957), and Duffy (1958), therefore, recommend that picking and crushing be controlled so that grapes are crushed promptly after picking and loading. Most grapes in the interior valley wine districts are delivered in gondola trucks. Various forms of loaders are used. It was found that cleated conveyor type loaders crushed many of the grapes with the result that vinegar flies swarmed in great numbers around and above such loads. Growers should not be allowed to "tramp" the loads as it crushes many grapes with consequent increase in vinegar flies.

In cases where loads had to be held overnight, spraying with 0.1% or stronger solution of pyrethrin or with a mixture of 0.1% pyrethrin and 1% piperonyl butoxide repelled the insects but did not kill them. Deposition of eggs on the grapes was prevented temporarily by these treatments. In the vineyard Ebeling (1958) and others have stated that more powerful insecticides can be used, provided dangerous residues do not remain on the grapes. For example, malathion disappears from the plant and fruit within a few days after application. Malathion has been used successfully on apples and its use approved for grapes, provided it is applied at least three days prior to harvest.

Influencing Factors.—Middlekauff (1957) states that most eggs are deposited at temperatures above 12.8°C (55.0°F) and when the light intensity is low. There is little activity when the sun is bright or when a strong breeze is blowing. The insect becomes objectionable about mid-August and increases until cold weather occurs. Michelbacher and Middlekauff (1954) state that the average time required for drosophila eggs to hatch is 24 hr and that one female can lay about 2000 eggs in her lifetime. Middlekauff (1957) has observed hatching of the eggs within 2 hr after laying. These facts account for the sudden appearance of great numbers of the fly. See also Michelbacher et al. (1953) and Yerington (1958).

Berg et al. (1958) found that varieties with tight bunches such as Zinfandel, Grenache, Carignane, and Alicante Bouschet showed more molding and vinegar fly infestation than did the Muscat of Alexandria and the Emperor. The Tokay, in spite of its thick skin, also showed heavy molding and vinegar fly infestation after the 1957 rains, perhaps because it develops large tight clusters subject to berry rupture. Overcropping not only results in tight clusters but also in late-maturing, weak berries which are subject to rupture following rain, or late irrigation, with consequent increase in mold and drosophila infestation.

Successful attempts to control flies in wineries with aerosols of pyrethrins and synergists were made by Yerington (1971), although the fly problem was not eliminated by these means.

Recommendations.—There is no doubt that elimination of waste fruit would do much to reduce the fly problem. Such control would be expensive and would have to be done on a community-wide basis. To alleviate the problem vineyard practices which reduce incidence of rot are a first line of control. These include proper pruning so as to prevent overcropping, withholding irrigation water during ripening, harvesting as soon as the grapes reach maturity, harvesting and transporting the grapes to the winery rapidly and with a minimum of injury. Insecticides that kill fruit flies are available but with the tremendous fly population of adjacent unsprayed areas their value is doubtful. In using insecticides the latest Food and Drug tolerances must be very carefully and strictly adhered to and it is advisable to consult the latest annual "Pest and Disease Control Program for Grapes" of the California Agricultural Experiment Station, Berkeley, Calif., published in 1973. Write for latest information.

Protection of the interior of wineries from drosophila is also an important problem. The first requirement is that no interior breeding spots be available such as leaking tanks, a favorite breeding spot. The second requirement is that no flies be permitted to enter the storage and bottling areas of the plant. Considerable information on fruit fly control is given in Anon. (1958) and California Agricultural Experiment Station (1959). DeCamargo and Phaff (1957) give information on the yeasts carried by drosophila.

The Bureau of Food and Drug Inspection of the California State Department of Public Health, has made the following recommendations to the wine industry:

(1) Remove pomace from the winery premises before it becomes a breeding place for vinegar flies and other insects such as dried fruit beetles. Most wineries now remove the pomace daily.

(2) Remove stems, as vinegar flies multiply in stem piles. If not removed, spray the stem piles with a powerful insecticide.

(3) Spread pomace and stems in a thin layer in the field or vineyard in order that they will dry quickly. Stems may be burned when dry.

(4) Eliminate all conditions under which vinegar flies can multiply; such as unclean gutters or hoses, pumps, conveyors, crushers and stemmers, and leakage under storage or sherry baking tanks. Vinegar flies may breed in small pools of wine caused by leakage, after alcohol evaporates.

(5) Wash gondola delivery trucks thoroughly after each delivery. Washing and sterilizing lug boxes frequently is another desirable practice.

(6) Do not allow grapes to accumulate in cracks and crevices around the crushing department or elsewhere.

(7) Use concrete instead of dirt or gravel floors as the latter may become a breeding place for the flies if they become and remain wet with wine.

(8) Replace wooden chutes, conveyor flumes, bins, etc., at the crushing station with metal, preferably stainless steel. Many wineries have already replaced wood with stainless steel at crushing stations.

(9) Exclude, insofar as possible, vinegar flies from the winery. A fan placed in the doorway to create a strong outward flow of air is desirable. Many wineries have now installed such fans. Screening of doorways, windows, and other openings of the bottling room is recommended. The screen should be of 20 or finer mesh.

(10) In using insecticide sprays in the plant, only those that are not toxic to humans are permitted. These are the pyrethrins, rotenone, and piperonyl butoxide. Do not use the sprays in locations where the dead flies may drop into the must or wine, as dead flies in the wine are just as objectionable as living ones flying over the wine.

(11) Cooperate in control and research with other industries; such as, those of tomato canning, dried fruit production, and fresh fruit packing.

(12) Arrange daily deliveries so that loads of grapes will be crushed promptly and none allowed to stand overnight.

Other Insects and Rodent Control

The housefly (*Musca domestica*) can become a pest in and around the winery. It breeds in manure piles, garbage, human excrement, and other refuse. Elimination of such breeding places is the best means of control.

Cockroaches, of which there are five common species, are frequent pests. Like rats they are omniverous in their food habits. They are very prolific and live for two or three years. They live in cracks, crevices, under moist boards and similar spots and come out at night. Pyrethrin, sodium fluoride, or chlordane applied to cracks, floors near baseboards, and other likely spots will kill them. Care must be taken to prevent contamination of grapes, must, or wine with the insecticide.

Crickets sometimes invade wineries during late summer or early fall. Spraying or dusting the floor or ground area in front of doorways or the other entrances and dusting the floor near the baseboards with 4–5% malathion dust will kill most of the crickets.

Ants may enter the bottling room or other area. Poisonous ant pastes and malathion placed in runways are commonly used for control. Destruction of colonies, usually located outside the plant, is an effective control measure. Carbon bisulfide, kerosene, chlordane, and malathion are lethal to ant colonies. Wasps and bees sometimes become numerous at the crush station, but there is no very safe and satisfactory program of control.

The presence of rats or mice in the winery is highly undesirable. Rats are carriers of filth and spread their droppings, hair, and urine about the plant and in this manner may cause contamination of equipment and stored supplies such as fining materials, filter aid, etc. They are always more numerous than the few that are seen in the plant. There are, according to Doyle (1954), 20 hidden rats for each that is seen. All new construction should be rodent-proof and old buildings made as rodent-proof as possible. Supplies should be stored in a rodent-proof enclosure. Rats may enter through doorways left open at night, through skylights, partly closed windows and through the space beneath the eaves. Great ingenuity and care are required in order to make any exclusion program effective. Mice are even more difficult to exclude. Holsendorff (1937) and Storer (1948) have given methods of rodent-proofing buildings. The bottling room, above all others, should be screened and otherwise made rat proof. Harborages should be eliminated. Rats are wary of traps, although the setting of traps in runways may catch a fair number. Cats and dogs should not be permitted in the winery even for such a desirable objective as rodent control.

Birds and bats are also possible pests. Their droppings may contaminate equipment, tanks, vats, etc.

Poisoning has proven an effective rodent control measure, although in the winery itself poisons that are toxic to humans cannot be used. The rodenticide, Warfarin, is now used extensively in food establishments for the control of rats and mice. It acts slowly and kills by internal bleeding. It is used in a dry, granular bait or in a cereal such as barley or wheat or in water. The bait should be put out daily in order to maintain a fresh and fairly constant supply. Red squill, a plant product harmless to humans, is also used as a rodenticide. It is a powerful emetic and is therefore soon eliminated by domestic animals but the rat cannot vomit, and hence retains the poison.

In certain locations outside the winery other poisons such as "1080," strychnine, "Antu," zinc phosphide, and others may be used, if proper care is taken to prevent their entry into the winery or the poisoning of humans or domestic animals. See Sampson (1943), Kalmbach (1945),

Parker (1948), and Anon. (1952) for further information on rodent control.

General Sanitation

Very small accumulations of organic material such as partially crushed grapes, wine seepage, must, etc., will support a large population of insects, particularly vinegar flies. Therefore, frequent cleaning of floors, conveyors, floor gutters, flumes, hoses, crushers and crushing stations, pumps, and other equipment is essential. Corners and crevices that cannot be reached easily add greatly to the difficulty of effective clean-up operations. Floors should be of concrete, properly sloped and drained, and should be scrubbed and washed down with ample water. It is desirable to wash them occasionally with dilute hypochlorite to disinfect the surface and cracks. Excessive concentrations or too frequent use should, of course, be avoided. Industrial vacuum cleaners have proven effective for dry cleaning.

Wine spilled on the floor should be washed away immediately. If the spilled wine has stood on the floor for a considerable time, it is advisable to follow washing by applying lime or strong hypochlorite solution. In general, it is best to keep the floors dry between washings.

The tops of tanks, overhead walks, and ramps should be swept and kept clean. Washing may be necessary occasionally, but care must be taken to keep water and washings out of the wine. Skofis (1957) states that plastic bunghole extensions for the openings in the tops of tanks have proven very useful.

When it is necessary, a pyrethrin or other permissible spray may be "fogged" into a room or load of grapes. Fogs of oil-based insecticides, although effective for a longer period than water-based, are apt to be inflammable. Unless the fogging is complete some insects will escape (Stafford 1958).

Yerington (1964) reports vapor dispensers of Vapora (also dichlorvos or DDVP which is 0,0-dimethyl 0,2,2-dichlorovinyl phosphate), used in the form of pellets placed in a heating chamber, can assure effective control in a cellar for a full season with one loading.

Again, receiving bins, chutes, conveyors, and other parts of the crushing station should be made of stainless steel, and crevices in which grapes or stems may lodge and spoil should be eliminated. The crushers and all equipment, including must lines, must be kept clean. They should be washed and flushed with water frequently, at least twice a day, and should not be allowed to stand with crushed grapes in them for more than an hour or two. *Brettanomyces* spoilage of wine has been attributed by van der Walt and van Kerken (1961) to poor cleaning practices of crushing equipment during the vintage. Stemmers and crushers should be carefully inspected before the crushing season and any badly worn or defective parts replaced. A breakdown during the season may prove very costly and inconvenient.

It is also customary to wash out gondolas thoroughly with a powerful stream of water after each delivery.

Equipment after use should be dismantled, thoroughly washed in water, and with a detergent if necessary. It should then be sterilized with hot water or live steam or sanitized with disinfectants, such as hypochlorite solution, rinsed thoroughly with water, and drained. Filter cloths should be thoroughly washed, rinsed, and dried. Hoses should be placed on sloping racks to drain and dry after washing. Special precautions should be taken to clean and sterilize equipment after contact with spoiled or contaminated wine. This includes hoses, pumps, filters, pipes, fillers, pasteurizers, etc.

As the bottling room is the final possible source of contamination with bacteria or metal, its care and cleanliness must be very thorough. It should be well lighted, well ventilated, and its floors and walls easily cleaned. Ample space between machines is highly desirable to permit easy cleaning. Equipment should be dismantleable in order to permit thorough cleaning.

Special attention needs to be given where it is necessary to bottle wine free of microbes, such as semidry wines without wine yeast contamination, or young wines before malo-lactic fermentation without malo-lactic bacteria. For this, it is best for the bottling room to contain only the filling and stoppering machines, and a bottle sterilizer, if one is used. The room should be well separated from the fermentation area and ideally be enclosed to prevent easy access by winery personnel traffic. The requirements for ease of cleaning, given above, must be especially met in this case. Bottles can often be considered germ-free as removed from the manufacturers cartons needing only sparging of lint by germ-free air obtained by sterile filtration. Otherwise the bottles can be sterilized by hot water of at least 72.0°C (161.6°F), or with 2% sulfurous acid, or with sulfur dioxide gas. For the latter, care must be taken to remove sulfur dioxide from the escaping gases. The filling machine can be sterilized with hot water or live steam provided all parts of the equipment are above 72.0°C (161.6°F) for at least 15 min. Corks sterilized with sulfur dioxide gas can be purchased and should be added directly from their container to the sterilized hopper of the corking machine. The hopper and the passageways for the corks and the jaws holding the corks can be sterilized with sulfurous acid or with heat. The wine itself should be rendered germ-free by use of depth filters or membrane filters, or, as commonly done in California, by both. The filters and filter holders also need to be sterilized by heat, hot water, or steam treatment. Further information concerning the requirements for sterile bottling can be obtained from depth and membrane filter manufacturers and from producers of bottling equipment. Also see pp. 308–309.

Toilets and urinals must be adequate, kept in sanitary condition, and located at a reasonable distance from the bottling department or other operation where the wine or must is handled. Washing of the hands after use of the toilet facilities should be required. Drinking fountains with proper guards to prevent contact of the mouth or nose with the metal of the water outlet should be provided.

Workers should not be permitted to enter recently emptied tanks unaccompanied, because carbon dioxide or alcohol vapors may be present in dangerous amounts. In the past, workers have been killed by carbon dioxide gas in a covered tank, and violent explosions of alcohol vapors have occurred. If a person enters an empty tank, a second person should remain outside to render aid if necessary. The emptied tank should be thoroughly drained by leaving the bottom and top manholes open for several hours before a worker enters, or forced air ventilation employed.

Detergents and Cleaners

Increasingly, wineries are installing cleaning-in-place systems to replace manual cleaning. Cleaning-in-place procedures are highly recommended for permanent installations, such as large tanks. However, for wooden barrels of about 2 hl (50 gal.) capacity, such as used for aging, manual cleaning, including inversion and draining, is the only recommended procedure.

Hot water is itself a good cleaning medium and an adequate supply is needed for good winery sanitation. Nevertheless, chemical detergents and cleaners are indispensable.

A balanced detergent must have the ability to dissolve organic matter, adequate tendency to keep undissolved matter in suspension, and good wetting and rinsing properties. Furthermore, it must have sufficient sequestering ability to prevent the formation of insoluble calcium salts which would otherwise deposit on cleaned surfaces. Since no one compound possesses all of these properties, mixtures of a basic cleaner, a dispersing agent, a wetting compound and a sequestering chemical are recommended.

Basic Cleaning Agents.—Alkalis and alkaline salts are now used, caustic soda (sodium hydroxide) being the most common. It dissolves proteins but has poor dispersing, wetting, and rinsing properties. Sodium metasilicate has good dispersing and wetting properties and is a fair protein dissolver. Moreover, it can be used on aluminum which caustic soda cannot. The alkaline phosphates are the agents of choice for lined tanks. They have poor organic matter-dissolving ability but have excellent dispersing properties.

Dispersing and Wetting Agents.—The purposes of these are to secure an intimate contact of the liquid with the surface being cleaned and to aid rinsing. The alkaline phosphates and sodium metasilicate are satisfactory. Highly surface-active compounds, usually nonionic organic compounds containing a long polyethylene glycol chain, are very effective at low concentrations (0.2 to 0.5%). For cleaning-in-place systems formulations which do not foam are preferred.

Sequestering Agents.—These agents are used to complex dissolved calcium and magnesium, thus preventing formation of insoluble salts and buildup of surface deposits. At present, EDTA (ethylenediaminetetraacetic acid) is used. Its complexing properties are good in the pH range 8 to 13 and it is thermally stable. It is also effective in dissolving calcium salt deposits. Use of 0.1% EDTA will prevent deposits with water containing 260 mg/liter of hardness (expressed as calcium carbonate). When large calcium deposits must be removed, up to 5% EDTA in caustic soda can be sprayed on the surface and recirculated.

Upperton (1965) recommended a mixture of 1.5% caustic soda, 0.25% of a wetting agent, and 0.1% EDTA for general use in the brewery, either for hot soaking or cold recirculation. With a high-pressure system 0.75% caustic soda should be adequate.

Sterilizing Agents.—Chemical agents can be considered sterilizing agents only when it is assured that all parts of the equipment being treated are readily accessible to the agent. This is generally not the case, and thus, for assurance of sterility, heat is usually necessary. What are commonly called sterilizing agents, in practice, might better be referred to as sanitizing agents.

Hypochlorites are widely used for cold sterilization in wineries; see Griffin (1946), Harris (1947), Mercer and Somers (1957), and Somers (1951). They tend to corrode stainless steel. Quaternary ammonium compounds have been used to sterilize filters, etc. Thorough rinsing is necessary.

It is possible to combine the detergent and the sterilizer according to Upperton (1965). Quaternaries, with proper precautions, can be mixed with caustic soda. EDTA is usually added. One problem is that the sterilant may be exhausted before the detergent because of contact with contaminated surfaces. Such combinations are, therefore, more economical when used after a prerinsing (see also Somers 1948, 1949). A good general cleanser is a mixture of sodium hydroxide and a silicate; it is less caustic than hydroxide and is more easily removed by rinsing. "TSP," trisodium phosphate, is a popular cleansing agent; although alkaline it is less caustic than sodium hydroxide, rinses readily, softens water, and prevents calcium deposits in hard waters.

So-called cationic detergents work only in acid solutions and are therefore inactivated by soaps. Roccal and Emulsol are trade preparations of this type and act not only as cleaners but also as germicides. The anionic detergents (such as Dreft, Vel, Drene, etc.) work only in alkaline solutions; soap also belongs in this group. Non-ionic detergents also exist. One should make certain that the detergent used does not impart an odor or taste to equipment surfaces. See Anon. (1952) and Lawrence and Block (1968) for further information on the proper use of detergents and disinfectants.

Amerine and Joslyn (1970) have given three lists of materials used for cleaning and disinfecting: one for surfaces in contact with grapes, must or wine; one for walls, floors, and outside surfaces of equipment, and one for outdoor purposes. The lists have been prepared from "Winery Sanitation Guide," Wine Institute (see Davison 1971). With permission of the authors, the three lists are reproduced here.

LIST NO. 1. FOR SURFACES IN CONTACT WITH GRAPES, MUSTS, OR
WINE

For cleaning wooden or concrete containers:
    1. Materials containing sodium carbonate, silicates, and phosphates usually sold under trade names.
    2. Trisodium phosphate and other phosphates.
    3. Soda ash or sal soda.
For cleaning metal equipment:
    4. Any one of the three above.
    5. Caustic soda (injures wood and concrete).
    6. Carbon abrasive.
    7. Citric acid (to remove scale and oxides).
For neutralizing, in the form of a solution or spray:
    8. Lime (slaked).
    9. Soda ash or sal soda.
For sterilizing:
    10. Sodium or calcium hypochlorite.
    11. Combinations of sodium or calcium hypochlorite and alkaline materials, sold under trade names.
    12. Chloramines.
    13. Combinations of chloramines and alkaline materials, sold under trade names.
    14. Sulfur dioxide in the form of liquid sulfur dioxide or metabisulfite. Sodium bisulfite is also used.
    15. Sulfur wicks or sulfur pots, burned inside of closed wooden cooperage.

LIST NO. 2. FOR WALLS, FLOORS, AND OUTSIDE SURFACES OF EQUIPMENT

For cleaning:
  16. Same as No. 1 to 3.
For sterilizing:
  17. Chlorine compounds mentioned under No. 10 and 11.
  18. Sulfur dioxide.
  19. Quaternary ammonium compounds, sold under trade names: but must be used so that no trace of the compounds can get into the wine.

LIST NO. 3. FOR OUTDOOR PURPOSES

For cleaning and disinfecting wood or concrete platforms or crushing equipment, or for spraying on grounds and pomace piles:
  20. Lime (unslaked).
  21. Chloride of lime.
  22. Sodium bisulfite.
For disinfecting and insect control, usually in the form of spray:
  23. Chlorinated benzenes (do not use near processing equipment or cooperage or anywhere inside the winery).
  24. Dichlorvos (DDVP) (do not use near processing equipment, above open tanks or anywhere it could come into contact with wine).
  25. Sulfur dioxide.
  26. Pyrethrin.
These four materials (No. 23, 24, 25, 26), alone or in combinations, are also sold under various trade names.

Chlorination.—In most canneries the entire water supply for the plant is chlorinated and this may often be a desirable practice for wineries. In some cases in California wineries, wine spoilage has been attributed to lack of chlorination of the water supply. Chlorination beyond the "break point" is termed "in-plant chlorination." Usually 0.5 to 1.0 mg/liter of free chlorine in the chlorinated water is sufficient. Stronger solutions are used in floor and equipment clean-up operations. The chlorine kills bacteria, yeasts and molds on floors and equipment and thus prevents bacterial slime formation on floors, conveyors, etc.

WASTE DISPOSAL

Pomace and stems, as previously mentioned, are now removed daily by most plants. The recovery of tartrates from pomace and the drying of pomace are discussed in Chap. 18. The cream of tartar separating in rather important quantities during the refrigeration of wine for stabilization is usually recovered.

The disposal of stillage (still slops), the waste dealcoholized liquid from brandy stills, presents a difficult problem. If it is run into artificial basins or settling ponds to disappear by percolation and evaporation, anaerobic putrefaction with production of very offensive odors may occur. Complaints of nearby residents have forced remedial measures. This method is still in use by some wineries. If the stillage is run into a stream it may kill the fish and make the water unsuitable for other use. In 1946 and 1947, extensive pilot plant and industrial scale investigations were conducted on disposal of grape stillage by the Coast Laboratories of Fresno in cooperation with Marsh and Vaughn of the University of California. The principal finding was that by running the stillage on to prepared plots of land to a fairly shallow depth and then allowing each plot to dry thoroughly before using it again, offensive odors and the breeding of mosquitoes were prevented (Fig. 6.23). Such a system of stillage disposal is known as "intermittent irrigation." For each 3800 hl (100,000 gal.) of conventional stillage produced per day, 2.8 hectares (7 acres) of suitable land should be available. The stillage during a 24-hr period is run on to one of the 7 plots for 24 hr and then is allowed to percolate into the soil

FIG. 6.23. STILL SLOPS ON INTERMITTENT IRRIGATION PLOT (UPPER). DRIED STILL SLOPS SHOWING CURLING

and dry. Usually, if the stillage is not more than 10 cm (4 in.) deep on the plot, it will seep into the soil within 48 hr leaving a cake of solids on the surface. In a few days the cake will dry and break up into small pieces that curl up around the edges and expose the soil for an additional run of stillage. Each plot is used once in seven days. If the soil is heavy, a longer drying period and hence more land will be required. If the stillage is from pomace stills, twice as long a drying period is needed (see Marsh and Vaughn 1944; Mercer 1955; O'Connell and Fitch 1950; Rudolfs and Heukelekian 1954; Vaughn and Marsh 1945, 1953, 1956; and Vaughn *et al.* 1950).

Another approach to the problem of stillage disposal is that of Matteoli *et al.* (1973) who report that the addition of commercial polyelectrolyte preparations followed by centrifugation results in sludge volumes of approximately 1/10 of the original liquid volume.

In the present method of heating distilling material in the still by direct steam, the volume of the distilling material (DM) is increased about 15% by condensation of steam. For example, 3800 hl (100,000 gal.) of DM will give about 4350 hl (115,000 gal.) of stillage.

The "clean" waste water, such as that from cooling fermenting must and for condensing the alcoholic distillate from the still, should be kept separate from the stillage in order not to increase greatly the total volume. It can be disposed of by running into a stream after gaining permission from the proper authorities, or by intermittent irrigation of a vineyard or orchard.

The investigators have recommended that the volume of stillage be held to a minimum by so operating the plant that the DM has at least 8% of alcohol. Use of countercurrent extraction contributes materially to the maintenance of a satisfactory level of alcohol in the DM (Table 6.3).

The effect of the volume of water added to the pomace in extracting it for DM is shown in Table 6.3.

If settling tanks are installed for pomace stillage much of the suspended solids can be removed and dried on land plots separately from the stillage. About 190 hl (5000 gal.) of sludge per 3800 hl (100,000 gal.) of pomace stillage will settle out. At least seven sludge drying beds, one for each day's operation, will be required, according to Coast Laboratories (1947). As soon as it is dry the sludge should be removed from the plot before fresh sludge is put on the plot again. For each acre of land used for disposal of the main volume of stillage, about 1/10 of an acre is required for the sludge. Another method consists of passing the drained pomace through a disintegrator and, then, over a fine screen. The skins and other coarse material that pass over the screen are pressed. Only the fines that pass through the screen go to the still.

By liming conventional stillage to pH 11, suspended materials and colloids coagulate and settle, giving 20 to 30% by volume of sludge and 50 to 70% clear amber colored liquid. The dried cake from conventional and

TABLE 6.3. RELATION OF VOLUME OF STILLAGE TO ALCOHOL CONTENT
OF DISTILLING MATERIAL[1]

Volume of Water Added		Percent Alcohol in Final DM	Volume of Stillage Produced[2]	
hl	gal.		hl	gal.
0	0	12	4,350	115,000
760	20,000	10	5,230	138,000
1,900	50,000	8	6,500	172,500
3,800	100,000	6	8,700	230,000
7,600	200,000	4	13,500	345,000
19,000	500,000	2	26,600	690,000

Source of data: Coast Laboratories (1947). Table modified to show volumes in hectoliters as well as gallons.
[1] Based on 3,800 hl (100,000 gal.) of original 12% DM producing 910 hl (24,000 gal.) of 50% alcohol.
[2] Because of steam condensate from the still, the stillage volume is approximately 15% greater than the DM volume.

from pomace stillage, as well as the dried sludge from DM settling tanks, has considerable fertilizing value, equal to 2 to 4 times the fertilizing value of barnyard manure.

Municipalities object to the disposal of stillage in their sewage disposal systems because of its high BOD (biological oxygen demand—a measure of the difficulty of converting the organic matter into nonobjectionable compounds), the low pH value of the stillage, which interferes seriously with bacterial decomposition of the organic matter, and the seasonal rather than year round operation of the stills.

In one plant, according to Marsh and Vaughn (1959), stillage is neutralized with lime to the point of color change, about pH 5, and is then diluted with wash water and other waste water as much as possible. If the DM is lees from racking and from refrigeration, it is centrifuged to remove most of the tartrates before neutralization, as they would cause plugging of the pipe line from the winery to the city sewage line and greatly increase the BOD of the stillage. By neutralizing the stillage to about pH 5 its buffering power on the sewage is also greatly reduced. The treated stillage adds a great deal of bacterial food to the sewage; consequently, decomposition in the sewage plant is very rapid with evolution of much gas, largely combustible methane and hydrogen which could be collected from covered digestion tanks and burned under boilers to produce steam. This would also conserve on energy use.

According to Marsh and Vaughn (1959), at least two wineries use the stillage for vineyard irrigation by the furrow method. Great care must be taken, however, to use it rather sparingly for it is toxic to plants if applied too generously. It is recommended that small-scale tests first be made to establish safe practice. Proebsting and Jacob (1938) made a study of the use of stillage for irrigation and found that plants were killed when it was used in amounts equivalent to the water normally used in irrigation. In time, the soil poisoned by the stillage recovered. They also pointed out the danger of contaminating the underground water supply.

Disposal of winery waste waters also poses a problem, though not to the same extent as does stillage. For a thorough discussion of waste characteristics and treatment methods for wine and grape waste waters see Tofflemire (1972). Ryder (1973) describes the full-scale testing of aerated lagoons processing table wine winery waste water and discusses the economic considerations.

HEALTH OF WORKERS

It is recommended that all prospective employees be given a physical examination and, if later employed, they be placed in work for which they are physically fitted (Russell *et al.* 1939).

Sufficient light and ventilation must be provided. In addition to adequate sanitary facilities, the importance of good personal hygiene should be emphasized.

Use of waterproof boots and clothing is essential for certain workers. First aid cabinets should be placed at convenient locations and properly maintained. Gas masks should be provided for ammonia fumes in case of leakage of ammonia equipment or pipelines of the refrigeration department where ammonia is used as the refrigerant. Freon because of its nontoxicity is a safer refrigerant than ammonia. Large wineries will provide in-plant facilities for treatment of sick or injured personnel.

It is strongly recommended that a safety-minded member of the staff be placed in charge of an active safety education program. Wiring should be of the four wire grounded type, and extension cord lights should be adequately protected. Motors should be splash-proof. Electrical outlets for pumps and other equipment operated by electric motors should be covered. The federal Occupational Safety and Health Administration (OSHA) provides stringent guidelines for plant, laboratory and office safety.

Rankine (1976) points out the danger of carbon dioxide, and Amerine and Joslyn (1970) also call attention to the toxicity of sulfur dioxide gas and state that its concentration in the air in the plant should not exceed 10 mg/liter. At higher concentrations, the employee should wear eye protectors and an approved respirator. The American Petroleum Institute (1948) has a useful report on its toxicity and on precautionary measures.

For a thorough discussion of the "do's" and "do nots" of winery safety see Anon. (1974).

REFERENCES[7]

AMERICAN PETROLEUM INSTITUTE. 1948. API Toxicological Review: Sulfur Dioxide. American Petroleum Institute, New York.

AMERINE, M.A. 1950. The response of wine to aging. Wines Vines *31* (3) 19-22; (4) 71-74; (5) 28-31.

AMERINE, M.A. 1959. Continuous flow production of still and sparkling wine. Wines Vines *40* (6) 41-42.

AMERINE, M.A. and JOSLYN, M.A. 1970. Table Wines; the Technology of Their Production, 2nd Edition. University of California Press, Berkeley, Los Angeles.

ANON. 1952. Sanitation for the Food Preservation Industries. McGraw-Hill Book Co., New York.

ANON. 1958. Drosophila Conference, Western Regional Research Laboratory, Mimeo. U.S. Dept. Agric., Albany, Calif.

ANON. 1974. Wine Institute Safety Handbook for Winery Employees. Wine Institute, San Francisco, Calif.

BAERWALD, G. 1976. Die Kaltsterilisation bei Wein und Süssreserve mit Pimaracin. Weinwirtschaft (Mainz) *112* (40) 1084-1085.

BARRILLON, D., GAC, A., PIERSON, G. and POUX, C. 1970. Étude du bilan thermique d'un vinificateur continu. Ann. Technol. Agric. *19*, 155-175.

BÉNARD, P. and JOURET, C. 1963. Essais comparitifs de vinification en rouge. *Ibid. 12*, 85-102.

BÉNARD, P., ANDRÉ, P. and DEIBNER, L. 1958. Influence du mode d'alcoolisation et de la nature des alcools sur la qualité des vins doux naturels. *Ibid. 7*, 111-125.

BERG, H.W. 1948. Cooperage handling. Univ. Calif., Wine Technol. Conf. *1948*, 38-45.

BERG, H.W. 1959. Investigation of defects in grapes delivered to California wineries: 1958. Am. J. Enol. Vitic. *10*, 61-69.

BERG, H.W. and AKIYOSHI, M. 1962. Color behavior during fermentation and aging of wines. *Ibid. 13*, 126-132.

BERG, H.W. and AKIYOSHI, M. 1971. The utility of potassium bitartrate concentration-product values in wine processing. *Ibid. 22*, 127-134.

BERG, H.W., ALLEY, C.J. and WINKLER, A.J. 1958. Investigation of defects in grapes delivered to California wineries, 1957. *Ibid. 9*, 24-31.

BERG, H.W., DE SOTO, R. and AKIYOSHI, M. 1968. The effect of refrigeration, bentonite clarification and ion exchange on potassium behavior in wines. *Ibid. 19*, 208-212.

BERG, H.W. and GUYMON, J.F. 1951. Countercurrent water extraction of alcohol from grape pomace. Wines Vines *32* (10) 27-31.

[7]Titles have been translated only for nonwestern European languages.

BERG, H.W. and KEEFER, R.M. 1958-1959. Analytical determination of tartrate stability in wine. Am. J. Enol. 9, 180-193; 10, 105-109.

BERGERET, J. 1963. Action de la gélatine et de la bentonite sur la couleur et l'astringence de quelques vins. Ann. Technol. Agric. 12, 15-25.

BIOLETTI, F.T. 1906. A new wine-cooling machine. California Agric. Exp. Stn. Bull. 174, 1-27.

BORODIN, A.I. 1976. Apparat dlya sul'fitatsii sulsa i vinomaterialor v potoke. (Apparatus for continuous sulfiting of must and wine). Vinodel. Vinograd. SSSR (7) 36-37.

BRANDS, E.R. 1956. Steel tank coatings. Wine Institute Tech. Advis. Comm. Feb. 20, 1956.

BRÉMOND, E. 1957. Techniques Modernes de Vinification et de Conservation des Vins dans les Pays Chauds. Librairie de la Maison Rustique, Paris.

BURROUGHS, L.F. and SPARKS, A.H. 1973. Sulphite-binding power of wines and ciders. J. Sci. Food Agric. 24, 187-217.

CALIFORNIA AGRICULTURAL EXPERIMENT STATION. 1959. Research on drosophila flies in fruits and vegetables. Mimeo. Berkeley, Calif.

CANT, R.R. 1960. The effect of nitrogen and carbon dioxide treatment of wines on dissolved oxygen levels. Am. J. Enol. Vitic. 11, 164-169.

CARAFA, P. 1959. La ricerca aspecifica per via biologica degli antifermentativi nei mosti e nei vini mediante impiego di substrato solidificabile. Riv. Viticolt. Enol. (Conegliano) 12, 277-287.

CARLES, J., ALQUIER-BOUFFARD, A. and MAGNY, J. 1963. De quelques variations apparaissant dans le jus de raisin au cours du pressurage. Compt. Rend. Acad. Agric. France 48, 773-780.

CARR, J. 1958. The vitamin requirements of lactic acid bacteria from ciders. Antonie van Leeuwenhoek J. Microbiol. Serol. 24, 63-68.

CASTOR, J.G.B. 1956. Bacteriological test of the sterility of factory-closed, new wine bottles. Am. J. Enol. 7, 137-141.

CHAPON, L. and URION, E. 1960. Ascorbic acid and beer. Wallerstein Lab. Comm. 23, 38-44.

COAST LABORATORIES. 1947. Grape stillage disposal by intermittent irrigation. Mimeo. Wine Institute, San Francisco.

COAST LABORATORIES. 1948. Improved distilling material production methods as an aid in stillage disposal. Ibid.

COFFELT, R.J., BERG, H.W., FREI, P. and ROSSI, E.A., JR. 1965. Sugar extraction from grape pomace with a 3-stage countercurrent system. Am. J. Enol. Vitic. 16, 14-20.

CONNOLLY, B.J. 1971. Stainless steel for wine storage and treatment installations. Rev. Vin. Intern. 92 (180) 49-56.

COSTA, L.C. DA. 1938. O problema das aguardentes e dos alcoóis. Influência de sua origem e grau na beneficiacão de vinhos. Anais Inst. Super. Agron., Univ. Téc. Lisboa 9, 67-76.

CROWELL, E.A., and GUYMON, J.F. 1975. Wine constituents arising from sorbic acid addition, and identification of 2-ethoxyhexa-3,5-diene as source of geranium-like off-odor. Am. J. Enol. Vitic. *26*, 97-102.

DAVISON, A.D. 1961. Review of wine industries' sanitation program. *Ibid.* *12*, 31-36.

DAVISON, A.D. 1971. Wine Institute Sanitation Guide for Wineries. Wine Institute, San Francisco. (Last version edited by M. H. Cook.)

DECAMARGO, R. and PHAFF, H.J. 1957. Yeasts occurring in drosophila flies and in fermenting tomato fruits in northern California. Food Res. *22*, 367-372.

DEIBNER, L. and BÉNARD, P. 1957. Effets de traitements thermiques, a l'abri de l'air, sur les qualités des vins doux naturels. Ann. Technol. Agric. *6*, 421-427.

DESCOUT, J., BORDIER, J., LAURENTY, J.L. and GUIMBERTEAU, J. 1976. Contribution á l'étude des phénomènes de colmatage lors de la filtration des vins sur filtre écran. Connaiss. Vigne Vin. (1) 93-123.

DE SOTO, R.T. 1955. Integrating yeast propagation with winery operation. Am. J. Enol. *6*, 26-30.

DICKINSON, B.N. and STONEMAN, G.F. 1958. Stabilization of wines by ion exchange. Wines Vines *39* (6) 33, 35.

DILLON, C.L. 1958. Current trends in glass technology. Am. J. Enol. *9*, 59-63.

DIMOTAKI-KOURAKOU, V. 1964. Differenciation des mistelles d'avec les vins doux. IV Congrès d'Expertise Chimique, Athenes, Spec. No., 355-359.

DOON, H.R. 1958. Closed steel fermentors. Wine Institute, Tech. Advis. Committee, May 26, 1958.

DORFER, K. 1970. Ionenaustauscher, 3rd Edition. Verlag Walter de Gruyter, Berlin.

DOYLE, E.S. 1951. The role of sanitation in production and quality control. Mod. Sanit. *3* (9) 30-32.

DOYLE, E.S. 1952. Preventive sanitation. Canner *115* (9) 11-12.

DOYLE, E.S. 1954. Plant sanitation. *In* Fruit and Vegetable Juices. D. K. Tressler and M. A. Joslyn (Editors). AVI Publishing Co., Westport, Conn.

DUBOURDIEU, D., LEFEBVRE, A. and RIBÉREAU-GAYON, P. 1976. Influence d'un traitement physique d'ultra-dispersion sur la filtration des vins. Connaiss. Vigne Vin. (1) 73-92.

DUFFY, M.P. 1958. Sanitation and better housekeeping in the production of wine in California. Wine Institute, Tech. Advis. Committee, May 26, 1958.

DU PLESSIS, C.S. 1964. The ion exchange treatment (H cycle) of white grape juice prior to fermentation. II. The effect upon quality. S. Afr. J. Agric. Sci. *7*, 3-16.

EBELING, W. 1958. Vinegar fly control treatments. Calif. Agric. *12*, 12-15.

FELL, G. 1961. Étude sur la fermentation malolactique du vin et les possibilités de la provoquer par ensemencement. Land. Jahr. Schweiz. *75*, 249-264.

FESSLER, J.H. 1958. Ion exchange resins for tartrate stabilization. Wine Institute, Tech. Advis. Committee, May 26, 1958.

FESSLER, J.H. 1961. Erythorbic acid and ascorbic acid as antioxidants in bottled wines. Am. J. Enol. Vitic. *12*, 20-24.

FLANZY, M. 1959. Élaboration des vins spiritueux doux (vins doux naturels); réglementation et alcoolisation. Ann. Technol. Agric. *8*, 81-100.

FOOD ENGINEERING. 1954. Food Plant Sanitation and Maintenance. Mc-Graw-Hill Book Co., New York.

FORNACHON, J.C.M. 1950. Yeast cultures. Aust. Brewing Wine J. *69* (3) 32.

FORNACHON, J.C.M. 1957. The occurrence of malo-lactic fermentation in Australian wines. Aust. J. Appl. Sci. *8*, 120-129.

FORNACHON, J.C.M. 1963. Travaux récents sur la fermentation malo-lactique. Ann. Technol. Agric. *12* (numéro hors série 1) 45-53.

FORNACHON, J.C.M. 1964. A *Leuconostoc* causing malo-lactic fermentation in Australian wines. Am. J. Enol. Vitic. *15*, 184-186.

GEISS, W. 1952. Die Filtration von Wein, Süssmost, Schaumwein und Spirituosen. Joh. Wagner and Söhne K. G., Frankfurt.

GEISS, W. 1957. Kaltsterile Abfüllung von Wein. J. Diemer Verlag der Deutschen Wein-Zeitung, Mainz.

GERASIMOV, M.A., and KULESHOVA, E.S. 1965. Deĭstvie ionitov na vitaminy vin (Effect of ion exchange on the vitamins of wines). Vinodel. Vinograd. S.S.S.R. *25* (8) 4-8.

GLEMANN, C. 1976. Technische Möglichkeiten der Pasteurisation von Most und Wein. Dtsch. Weinbau. (11) 387-390.

GOLDMAN, M. 1963. Rate of carbon dioxide formation at low temperatures in bottle-fermented champagne. Am. J. Enol. Vitic. *14*, 155-160.

GRAFF, R.H. 1970. Small cooperage, some practical aspects. Wines Vines. *51* (1) 27-30.

GRIFFIN, A.E. 1946. Break point chlorination practices. Wallace and Tiernan Co., Tech. Bull. *213*, Belleville, N. J.

GUILLIERMOND, A. 1912. Les Levures. Doin et Fils, Paris. *See also* The Yeasts by Guilliermond, A., translated and revised by F. W. Tanner. John Wiley & Sons, New York, 1920.

HAHN, G.D. and POSSMAN, P. 1977. Colloidal silicon dioxide as a fining agent for wine. Am. J. Enol. Vitic. *28*, 108-112.

HALTER, P. 1959. Biologische Untersuchungen fabrikneuer Weinflaschen. Schweiz Z. Obst- Weinbau *68*, 211-213, 241-245.

HALTER, P. 1960. Biological investigations of new wine bottles. Am. J. Enol. Vitic. *11*, 15-18.

HARRIS, J.J. 1947. Chlorination in the food plant. Continental Can Co., Res. Dept. Bull. *13*.

HAUSHOFER, H. and RETHALLER, A. 1964. Die Heissabfüllung von Wein unter besonderer Berücksichtigung des Kohlensäuregehaltes und der Reduktionsmittel. Mitt. Rebe Wein, Serie A (Klosterneuburg) *14*, 1-20.

HOLDEN, C. 1955. Combined method for heat and cold stabilization of wine. Am. J. Enol. *6*, 47-49. (*Also* Food Technol. *8*, 565-566. 1954.)

HOLSENDORFF, R. 1937. The rat and rat-proof construction. U.S. Public Health Serv. Suppl. *131*.

INGRAHAM, J.L. and COOKE, G.M. 1960. A survey of the incidence of the malo-lactic fermentation in California table wines. Am. J. Enol. Vitic. *11*, 160-163.

INGRAHAM, J.L., VAUGHN, R.G. and COOKE, G.M. 1960. Studies on the malo-lactic organisms isolated from California wines. *Ibid. 11*, 1-4.

JOSLYN, M.A. 1955. Yeast autolysis. I. Wallerstein Lab. Commun. *18*, 107-122.

JOSLYN, M.A. and AMERINE, M.A. 1964. Dessert, Appetizer and Related Flavored Wines. Univ. Calif., Division of Agricultural Sciences, Berkeley.

JOSLYN, M.A. and LUKTON, A. 1953. Prevention of copper and iron turbidities in wine. Hilgardia *22*, 451-533.

KALMBACH, E.R. 1945. "Ten-eighty"; a war-produced rodenticide. Science *102*, 232-233.

KAYSER, E. 1924. Les races des levures et leur influence sur le bouquet des vins. Chim. Ind., Sp. No. May, 619-625.

KIELHÖFER, E. 1960. Neue Erkenntnisse über die schweflige Säure im Wein und ihren Ersatz durch Ascorbinsäure. Deut. Wein-Ztg. *96*, 14, 16, 18, 20, 22, 24.

KIELHÖFER, E. and WURDIG, G. 1960. Die Bestimmung von Acetoin und Diacetyl im Wein und der Gehalt deutscher Weine an diesen Substanzen. Wein-Wissen. *15*, 135-146.

KONOVALOV, S.A. 1958. Osobennosti zhiznedeyatel'nosti drozhzhei pri nepreryvnom sposobe brozheniya (Characteristics of yeast activity in the continuous method of fermentation). Mikrobiologiya *27*, 120-126.

KRAMER, A. and TWIGG, B.A. 1970. Quality Control for the Food Industry, 3rd Edition, Vol. 1. AVI Publishing Co., Westport, Conn.

KUNKEE, R.E. and GOSWELL, R.W. 1977. Table wines. *In* Economic Microbiology, Vol. 1. A.H. Rose (Editor). Academic Press, London.

KUNKEE, R.E. and OUGH, C.S. 1966. Multiplication and fermentation of *Saccharomyces cerevisiae* under carbon dioxide pressure in wine. Appl. Microbiol. *14*, 643-648.

KUNKEE, R.E., OUGH, C.S. and AMERINE, M.A. 1964. Induction of malo-lactic fermentation by inoculation of must and wine with bacteria. Am. J. Enol. Vitic. *15*, 178-183.

LAFON-LAFOURCADE, S. 1970. Étude de la dégradation de l'acide L-malique par les bactéries lactiques non proliférantes isolées des vins. Ann. Technol. Agric. *19*, 141-154.

LA ROSA, W.V. 1963. Enological problems of large-scale wine production in the San Joaquin Valley. Am. J. Enol. Vitic. 14, 75-79.

LAWRENCE, C.A. and BLOCK, S.S. 1968. Disinfection, Sterilization, and Preservation. Lea & Febiger, Philadelphia.

LITTLE, A.C. and WEI-YI LIAW, M. 1974. Blending wines to color. Am. J. Enol. Vitic. 25, 79-83.

LÜTHI, H. 1955. Reinhefe Anwendung und Qualitäts-Produktion. Schweiz. Weinzeitung 63, 722-725.

LÜTHI, H. 1957. La rétrogradation malolactique dans les vins et les cidres. Rev. Ferm. Ind. Alim. 12, 15-21.

LÜTHI, H. and BEZZEGH, T. 1963. A microbiological method for qualitative determination of a chemical preservative in wines. Am. J. Enol. Vitic. 14, 61-67.

MARIAS, P.G. and KRUGER, M.M. 1975. Fungus contamination of corks responsible for unpleasant odors in wine. Phytophylactica 7, 115-116.

MARQUES GOMES, J.V., SILVA BABO, J.V. DA and GUIMARAIS, A.F. 1954. L'emploi des bactéries sélectionnées dans la fermentation malolactique du vin. Bull. Off. Intern. Vin. 29 (299) 349-357.

MARSH, G.L. 1959. Personal communication. Davis, Calif.

MARSH, G.L. and GUYMON, J.F. 1959. Refrigeration in wine making. Am. Soc. Refrig. Eng. Data Book, Vol. I, Chap. 10. (Periodically updated.)

MARSH, G.L. and JOSLYN, M.A. 1935. Precipitation rate of cream of tartar from wine. Ind. Eng. Chem. 27, 1252-56.

MARSH, G.L. and VAUGHN, R.H. 1944. Slop disposal system based on tartrate recovery. Wines Vines 25 (6) 15, 17, 28-30, 35.

MARSH, G.L. and VAUGHN, R.H. 1959. Personal communication. Davis, Calif.

MARTINI, M. 1965. L'acido tartarico racemico come decalcificante nei vini. Riv. Viticolt. Enol. (Conegliano) 17, 379-386.

MATTEOLI, R., SCHROEDER, E.E., JACKMAN, A.P. and TCHOBAN-OGLOUS, G. 1973. Physical treatment of winery stillage. Eng. Ext. Serv., Purdue Univ. 142, 792-801.

MAYER-OBERPLAN, M. 1956. Das Schönen und Stabilisieren von Wein, Schaumwein und Süssmost. Verlag Sigurd Horn, Frankfurt.

MCGARVEY, F.S., PERCIVAL, R.W. and SMITH, A.J. 1958. Ion exchange develops as a process in the wine industry. Am. J. Enol. 9, 168-179.

MEIDINGER, F. 1976. Gedanken zum Oxydationsschutz im Hinblick auf die SO_2-Einsparung bei der Weinbereitung. Weinwirtschaft 112 (14) 332-334, 336-338.

MENNETT, R.H. and NAKAYAMA, T.O.M. 1970. Temperature dependence of tannin adsorption by poly-N-vinyl pyrrolidone. Am. J. Enol. Vitic. 21, 162-167.

MERCER, W.A. 1955. Cannery waste disposal and its problems. I and II. Canning Trade 77 (40) 6-7; (41) 6-7.

MERCER, W.A. and SOMERS, I.I. 1957. Chlorine in food plant sanitation. Adv. Food Res. 7, 120-171.

MICHELBACHER, A.E. and MIDDLEKAUFF, W.W. 1954. Vinegar fly investigations in Northern California. J. Econ. Entomol. 47, 917-922.

MICHELBACHER, A.E., BACON, D.G. and MIDDLEKAUFF, N.W. 1953. Vinegar fly in tomato fields. Calif. Agric. 7, 19.

MIDDLEKAUFF, W.W. 1957. Biological and control observations on drosophila. Wine Institute, Tech. Advis. Committee, May 13, 1957.

MILISAVLJEVIĆ, D. 1958. Mlečno vrenje jabučne kiseline u vinu (The malolactic fermentation in wines). Arhiv Poljopriv. Nauke Tehniku 11, 67-81.

MILISAVLJEVIĆ, D. 1964. Méthodes d'isolement de culture et de classification des bactéries malolactiques. Bull. Office Intern. Vin. 37, 374-384.

MINDLER, A.B., GRUNDNER, W.T. and SELTZ, P. 1958. Ion exchange in wine treatment. Wines Vines 39 (9) 27-28, 30.

MOIROUD, A. and BERGER, J.L. 1977. La conservation du vin en cures de plastique. Vignes Vins 258, 33-37.

MOSER, J. 1956. The ion exchanger in modern cellar practice. Am. J. Enol. Vitic. 7, 157-161.

MÜLLER-SPATH, H. 1975. Evolution de la technique de filtration. Rev. Fr. Oen. 15 (59) 4-9.

MÜLLER-THURGAU, H. 1889. Über den Ursprung der Weinhefe- und hieran sich knüpsende praktische Folgerungen. Weinbau Weinhandel 7, 427-428, 438-440.

MUNYON, J.R. and NAGEL, C.W. 1977. Comparison of methods of deacidification of musts and wines. Am. J. Enol. Vitic. 28, 79-87.

NAGEL, C.W., TAMIS, L.J. and CARTER, G.H. 1975. Investigation of methods for adjusting the acidity of wines. Ibid. 26, 12-17.

O'CONNELL, W.J., JR. and FITCH, K.A. 1950. Waste disposal. Food Ind. 22, 71-78.

O'NEAL, R., WEIS, L. and CRUESS, W.V. 1951. Observations on the fining of wine with casein. Food Technol. 5, 64-68.

OSTERWALDER, A. 1934. Die verkannten Kaltgärhefen. Schweiz. Z. Obst-Weinbau 50, 487-490.

OUGH, C.S. 1960. Gelatin and polyvinylpyrrolidone compared for fining red wines. Am. J. Enol. Vitic. 11, 170-173.

OUGH, C.S. 1975A. Further investigations with glucose oxidase-catalase enzyme systems for use with wine. Ibid. 26, 30-36.

OUGH, C.S. 1975B. Dimethyldicarbonate as a wine sterilant. Ibid. 26, 130-133.

OUGH, C.S. and AMERINE, M.A. 1959. Dissolved oxygen determination in wine. Food Res. 24, 744-748.

OUGH, C.S. and AMERINE, M.A. 1960. Experiments with controlled fermentation. IV. Am. J. Enol. Vitic. 11, 5-14.

OUGH, C.S. and AMERINE, M.A. 1961. Studies with controlled fermentation. VI. Effects of temperature and handling on rates, composition, and quality of wines. *Ibid. 12*, 117-128.

OUGH, C.S. and AMERINE, M.A. 1966. Effects of Temperature on Wine Making. Calif. Agric. Exp. Stn. Bull. *827*.

OUGH, C.S. and BERG, H.W. 1974. The effect of two commercial pectic enzymes on grape musts and wines. Am. J. Enol. Vitic. *25*, 208-211.

OUGH, C.S. and KUNKEE, R.E. 1974. The effect of fumaric acid on malolactic fermentation in wines from warm areas. *Ibid. 25*, 188-190.

PACOTTET, P. 1926. Vinification. Librairie J.-B. Baillière et Fils, Paris.

PARKER, M. 1948. Food Plant Sanitation. McGraw-Hill Book Co., New York.

PAUNOVIC, R. 1963. Possibilité d'utilisation des radiations dans la conservation des vins. Ann. Technol. Agric. *12* (numéro hors série 1) 143-153.

PEARSON, E.A., FEUERSTEIN, H. and ONODEAN, B. 1955. Treatment and utilization of winery wastes. Univ. Calif. Sanitary Engineering Lab., Berkeley.

PELEG, Y. and BROWN, R.C. 1976. Method of evaluating the filterability of wine and similar fluids. J. Food Sci. *41*, 805-808.

PELEG, Y., BROWN, R.C., STARCEVICH, P.W. and ASHER, R. 1979. Method for evaluating the filterability of wine and similar fluids. Am. J. Enol. Vitic. *30*, 174-178.

PERCIVAL, R.W., MCGARVEY, F.X., and SONNEMAN, H.O. 1958. Wine stabilization by columnar ion exchange. J. Assoc. Offic. Agric. Chemists *38*, 144-151.

PERIN, J. 1977. Compte rendu de quelques essais de réfrigération des vins. Le Vigneron Champenois *98* (3) 97-101.

PETERS, P. 1977. Personal communication. Fresno, Calif.

PETERSON, R.G. 1975. An expert plans the premium winery. Wines Vines *56* (10, 11, 12) 32-38, 40-42.

PETERSON, R.G. 1976. Formation of reduced pressure in barrels during wine aging. Am. J. Enol. Vitic. *27*, 80-81.

PEYNAUD, E. 1955. Neue Gegebenheiten bezüglich des biologischen Säureabbaues. Mitt. Rebe Wein, Serie A (Klosterneuburg) *5*, 183-191.

PEYNAUD, E. and DOMERCQ, S. 1959. Possibilité de provoquer la fermentation malolactique en vinification à l'acide de bactéries cultivées. Compt. Rend. Acad. Agric. France *45*, 355-358.

PEYNAUD, E. and DOMERCQ, S. 1961. Études sur les bactéries lactiques des vins. Ann. Technol. Agric. *10*, 43-60.

PEYNAUD, E. and GUIMBERTEAU, G. 1962. Sur la formation des alcools supérieurs pars les levures de vinification. *Ibid. 11*, 85-105.

PIERRARD, P. 1976. Récents progrès en electrodialyse. Ind. Aliment. Agric. *93* (5) 569-581.

PILONE, G.J., RANKINE, B.C. and PILONE, D.A. 1974. Inhibiting malolactic fermentation in Australian dry red wines by adding fumaric acid. Am. J. Enol. Vitic. 25, 99-107.

POPPER, K. and NURY, F.S. 1964. Recoverable static regenerant ion exchange treatment of Thompson Seedless grape juice. Ibid. 15, 82-86.

PREHODA, J. 1963. Hömérsékletszabályozás a vörös borok erjesztésénél. (Temperature regulation of the fermentation of red wines.) Borgazdaság 11, 15-23.

PROEBSTING, E.L. and JACOB, H.E. 1938. Some effects of winery distillery waste on soil and plants. Proc. Am. Soc. Hort. Sci. 36, 69-73.

RADLER, F. 1957. Untersuchungen über die experimentelle Durchführung des biologischen Säureabbaues. Vitis 1, 42-52.

RADLER, R. 1958. Der Nähr- und Wuchsstoffbedarf der Apfelsäure-abbauenden Bakterien. Arch. Mikrobiol. 32, 1-15.

RADLER, F. 1962. Die Bildung von Acetoin und Diacetyl durch die Bakterien des biologischen Säureabbaus. Vitis 3, 136-143.

RANKINE, B.C. 1955. Yeast cultures in Australian wine making. Am. J. Enol. 6, 11-15.

RANKINE, B.C. 1976. Danger of carbon dioxide in wineries. Aust. Grapegrower Winemaker 148, 72-74.

RANKINE, B.C. and BOND, R.D. 1955. Prevention of potassium bitartrate deposition in wine by cation exchange resins. Aust. J. Appl. Sci. 6 (4) 541-549. (Abstract in Am. J. Enol. 7, 124.)

RANKINE, B.C. and EMERSON, W.W. 1963. Wine clarification and protein removal by bentonite. J. Sci. Food Agric. 14, 685-689.

RANKINE, B.C. and PILONE, D.A. 1972. Procedure for checking sterility of wine corks. Aust. Grapegrower Winemaker 107, 10.

RHEIN, O.H. 1976. Method for accelerating the crystallization and removal of tartar from a tartarous beverage. U.S. Pat. 3,988,486, Oct. 26. (Assigned to Henkell & Co.)

RIBÉREAU-GAYON, J., PEYNAUD, E., PORTAL, E., BONASTRE, J. and SUDRAUD, P. 1956. La stabilisation des vins par les exchangeurs d'ions métalliques. Ind. Agric. Aliment. (Paris) 7, 157-161.

RIDDELL, J.L. and NURY, M.S. 1958. Continuous fermentation of wine at Vie-Del. Wines Vines 39 (5) 35.

RUDOLFS, W. and HEUKELEKIAN, H. 1954. Sure methods of disposing of food wastes. In Food Engineering, "Food Plant Sanitation and Maintenance," 2nd Edition. McGraw-Hill Book Co., New York.

RUSSELL, J.P., INGRAM, F.R. and DAKAN, E.W. 1939. Industrial hygiene survey of California wineries. Calif. Dept. Public Health, Indus. Hyg. Invest. Rept. 2, 1-36.

RYDER, R.A. 1973. Winery waste water treatment and reclamation. Eng. Ext. Serv., Purdue Univ. 142, 564-587.

SAMPSON, W.W. 1943. Annotated outline of the principles of control of rodents affecting man. Sanitarian 5, 271-274, 299-302; 6, 327-332, 359-361, 379-381.

SCHANDERL, H. 1957. Über den Keimgehalt direkt am Kühlkanal der Glashütte verpackter neuer Weinflaschen. Deut. Wein-Ztg. 93, 155-160.

SCHANDERL, H. 1959. Die Mikrobiologie des Mostes und Weines. Eugen Ulmer, Stuttgart. (Revised by H.H. Dittrich 1977)

SCHLODER, F.R. and BACH, H.P. 1977. Einfluss von Behandlungsmassnahmen. Dtsch. Weinbau. 1, 29-31.

SCHREFFLER, C. 1952. Heat transfer in winery refrigeration. Proc. Am. Soc. Enol. 1952, 211-217.

SCHULLE, H. 1954. Reinhefezusatz und Gärverlauf. Deut. Wein-Ztg. 90, 736-739.

SHARF, J.M. and LYON, C.A. 1958. Historical development of stoppers for sparkling wines. Am. J. Enol. 9, 74-78.

SHPRITSMAN, E.M., ARONINA, I.V. and PARASKA, P.I. 1976A. Neorganicheeskie polimery kremnezema-stabilizatory vin. (Inorganic silicon dioxide polymers as wine stabilizers.) Vinodel. Vinograd. SSSR. (4) 14-17.

SHPRITSMAN, E.M., LUK'YANETS, T.S., PROKOF'EVA, M.V. and SIDOROVA, S.A. 1976B. Ispol'zovanie metiltsellyulozy dlya stabilizatsii vin ot obratimykh kolloidnykh pomutnenii. (Use of methylcellulose for the stabilization of wines.) Sadovod. Vinograd. Vinodel. Mold. 31 (5) 25-27.

SILVA BABO, M. 1963. Essais d'application des bactéries malolactiques aux vins verts. Ann. Technol. Agric. 12 (numéro hors série 1) 57-58.

SINGLETON, V.L. 1959. Some possibilities of rapid aging. Wines Vines 40 (7) 26.

SINGLETON, V.L. 1962. Aging of wines and other spiritous products, acceleration by physical treatments. Hilgardia 32 (7) 319-392.

SINGLETON, V.L. 1963. Changes in quality and composition produced in wine by cobalt-60 gamma irradiation. Food Technol. 17, 112-115.

SINGLETON, V.L. 1974. Some aspects of the wooden container as a factor in wine maturation. Advan. Chem. Ser. 137, American Chemical Society.

SINGLETON, V.L. 1976. Wine aging and its future. Walter and Carew Reynell Memorial Lecture 1, 1-30. Roseworthy Agricultural College, Roseworthy, Australia.

SINGLETON, V.L. 1978. Recent developments in wine aging. Proc. 5th Wine Industry Seminar, 31-37.

SINGLETON, V.L., BERG, H.W. and GUYMON, J.F. 1964. Anthocyanin color level in port-type wines as affected by the use of wine spirits containing aldehydes. Am. J. Enol. Vitic. 15, 75-81.

SINGLETON, V.L. and DRAPER, D.E. 1961. Wood chips and wine treatment; the nature of aqueous alcohol extracts. Ibid. 12, 152-158.

SINGLETON, V.L. and DRAPER, D.E. 1962. Adsorbents and wines. I. Selection of activated charcoals for treatment of wine. Ibid. 13, 114-125.

SINGLETON, V.L. and DRAPER, D.E. 1963. Ultrasonic treatment with gas purging as a quick aging treatment of wine. *Ibid. 14*, 23-35.

SINGLETON, V.L. and GUYMON, J.F. 1963. A test of fractional addition of wine spirits to red and white port wines. *Ibid. 14*, 129-136.

SINGLETON, V.L. and OUGH, C.S. 1962. Complexity of flavor and blending of wines. J. Food Sci. *27*, 189-196.

SINGLETON, V.L., OUGH, C.S. and AMERINE, M.A. 1964. Chemical and sensory effects of heating wines under different gases. Am. J. Enol. Vitic. *15*, 134-145.

SINGLETON, V.L., SULLIVAN, A.R. and KRAMER, C. 1971. Analysis of wine to indicate aging in wood or treatment with wood chips or tannic acid. *Ibid. 22*, 161-166.

SKOFIS, E. 1953. The role of refrigeration in the stabilization and clarification of wines. Proc. Am. Soc. Enol. *1953*, 69-77.

SKOFIS, E.C. 1957. Sanitary progress at Roma. Wine Institute, Tech. Advis. Comm., Dec. 6, 1957.

SKOFIS, E.C. 1966. Personal communication.

SOMERS, I.I. 1948. How to establish a plant cleaning program. Food Ind. *20*, 8-12, 166, 199-204, 328-330.

SOMERS, I.I. 1949. How to select detergents for food plant cleaning. *Ibid. 21*, 295-296, 429-431.

SOMERS, I.I. 1951. In-plant chlorination. Food Technol. *5*, 1-7.

SOMERS, T.C. and ZIEMELIS, G. 1973. The use of gel column analysis in evaluation of bentonite fining procedures. Am. J. Enol. Vitic. *24*, 51-54.

STAFFORD, E.M. 1958. Spray program for drosophila in wineries. Wine Institute, Tech. Advis. Committee, May 26, 1958.

STAUDE, E., STENGER, K. and WILDHARDT, J. 1976. Die Weinsteinkristallisierung durch konzentrierung weinsteinhaltiger Lösungen mit Hilf der Hyperfiltration. Dtsch. Lebensm.-Rundsch. *72* (6) 189-193.

STEPHAN, E. 1964. Polyäthylenstopfen für Wein- und Sektflaschen. Weinberg Keller *11*, 447-450.

STORER, T.I. 1948. Control of rats and mice. Calif. Agric. Exp. Stn. Circ. *142*.

SUDRAUD, P. 1963. Stabilisation biologique des vins par chauffage. Ann. Technol. Agric. *12* (numéro hors série 1) 131-140.

SUDRAUD, P. and CASSIGNARD, R. 1959. Travaux récents sur la fermentation malolactique en Bordelais. Vignes Vins *80*, 10-13. (This issue contains other articles on the importance of the malo-lactic fermentation.)

SYCHER, A. YA., PONOMARCHENKO, V.B., ZEMSHMAN, A. YA. and POSTNAYA, A.N. 1976. Primenenie opticheskikh krantovykh generatorov (pazerov) dlya opredeleniya prozrachnosti vin. (Use of lasers for determining the clarity of wines.) Sadovod. Vinograd. Vinodel. Mold. *31* (10) 27-29.

TARANTOLA, C. 1959. Attuali vedute sulla fermentazione malolattica. Riv. Viticolt. Enol. (Conegliano) *12*, 191-205.

THOUKIS, G., REED, G. and BOUTHILET, R.J. 1963. Production and use of compressed yeast for winery fermentation. Am. J. Enol. Vitic. *14*, 148-154. (*See also* Wines Vines *44* (1) 25-26.)

TOFFLEMIRE, T.J. 1972. Survey of methods of treating wine and grape waste water. *Ibid. 23*, 165-172.

TRUAX, D.L. 1950. Why sanitation in the food industry. Proc. Am. Soc. Enol. *1950*, 124-128. (*See also Ibid. 1950*, 129-137.)

UPPERTON, A.M. 1965. Some observations on detergents and sterilizing agents in British breweries. Wallerstein Lab. Comm. *28*, 137-142.

U.S. INTERNAL REVENUE SERVICE. 1962. Gauging Manual Embracing Instructions and Tables for Determining the Quantity of Distilled Spirits by Proof and Weight. U.S. Govt. Print. Office, Washington (IRS Publ. *455*).

UZNADZE, E.I., KOSSOBUDSKAYA, N.S. and VESLOV, A.I. 1971. Effect of yeast inoculum on the composition of wine. Appl. Biochem. Microbiol. 7, 694-702.

VAN PIEPER, H.J. 1976. Maische- Gär- und Lagerbehälter in der Obstbrennerei. Kleinbrennerei *28* (3) 21-23; (4) 33-35; (5) 43-45.

VAN DER WALT, J.P. and VAN KERKEN, A.E. 1961. The wine yeasts of the Cape. Antonie van Leeuwenhoek, J. Microbiol. Serol. 27, 81-90.

VAUGHN, R.H. and MARSH, G.L. 1945. The disposal of dessert winery waste. Wine Rev. *13* (11) 8-11.

VAUGHN, R.H. and MARSH, G.L. 1953. Disposal of California winery wastes. Ind. Eng. Chem. *45*, 2686-2688.

VAUGHN, R.H. and MARSH, G.L. 1956. Problems in disposal of California winery wastes. Am. J. Enol. 7, 26-34.

VAUGHN, R.H., NIGHTINGALE, M.S., PRIDMORE, J.A., BROWN, E.M. and MARSH, G.L. 1950. Disposal of wastes from brandy stills by biological treatment. Wines Vines *31* (2) 24-25.

WEBB, A.D. 1976. Building a small commercial winery. Vinifera Wine Growers J. *3* (3) 207-215.

WEBB, R.B. 1962. Laboratory studies of the malo-lactic fermentation. Am. J. Enol. Vitic. *13*, 189-195.

WEBB, R.B. and INGRAHAM, J.L. 1960. Induced malo-lactic fermentations. *Ibid. 11*, 59-63.

WEGER, B. 1965. Calcium- und Natriumbentonite. Wein-Wissen. *20*, 545-559.

WEINFACH-KALENDER. 1977 Weinfach-Kalender 1977/78. 88 Jahrgang. Verlag Diemer & Meininger, Mainz.

WHITE, B.B. and OUGH, C.S. 1973. Oxygen uptake studies on grape juice. Am. J. Enol. Vitic. *24*, 148-152.

WICK, E., POPPER, K. and GRAHAM, R.P. 1974. Performance characteristics of continuous yeast-alcohol fermentors with no mechanical stirring. Biotechnol. Bioeng. *XVI*, 1611-1631.

WILDENRADT, H.L. and SINGLETON, V.L. 1974. The production of aldehydes as a result of oxidation of polyphenolic compounds and its relation to wine aging. Am. J. Enol. Vitic. *25*, 119-126.

WILLIG, R. 1950. Continuous fermentation of wine. Wynboer *19*, 14-15.

WILLSON, K.S., WALKER, W.O., MARS, C.V. and RINELLI, W.R. 1943. Liquid sulfur dioxide in the fruit industries. Fruit Prod. J. *23*, 72-82. (*See also* Chem. Ind. *53*, 176-186.)

WORTMANN, J. 1892. Untersuchungen über reine Hefen. I. Landwirt. Jahrb. *21*, 901-936.

WUCHERPFENNIG, K., and BADIOR, S. 1976. Vergleichende sensorische Beurteilung von Weinen die mit Hilfe verscheidener Verfahren gegen Weinsteinausfall stabilisiert wurden. Weinberg Keller *10*, 407-418.

WUCHERPFENNIG, K., BRETTHAUER, G. and NEUBERT, S. 1976. Veränderungen von Weinen durch verschiedene Verfahren zur Weinsteinstabilisierung unter besonderer Berücksichtigung der von Rebelein Vorgeschlagenen kennzahlen RE-, Rez-, Vf- und H-wert. Weinwirtschaft. *112* (10) 222-230.

WUCHERPFENNIG, K. and KLEINKNECHT, E.M. 1965. Beitrag zur Veränderung der Farbe und der Polyphenole bei Abfüllung von Weisswein durch Einwirkung von Säuerstoff und Wärme. Wein-Wissen. *20*, 489-514.

WUCHERPFENNIG, K. and MILLIES, K.D. 1976. Über den Einfluss der Electrodialysebehandlung zum Zwecke der Weinsteinstabilisierung auf die Konzentration der Aminosauren in Wein. Mitt. Rebe Wein, Obstbau Früchteverw. (Klosterneuburg) *26* (1) 13-26.

YERINGTON, A.P. 1958. What wineries can do about drosophila. Wine Institute, Tech. Advis. Committee, May 26, 1958.

YERINGTON, A.P. 1964. The use of dichlorvos (DDVP) in wineries for drosophila control. *Ibid.*, Dec. 11, 1964.

YERINGTON, A.P. 1971. Evaluation of pyrethrin thermal aerosols for control of vinegar flies and dried fruit beetles in wine cellars. J. Econ. Entomol. *64*, 986.

7

Red Table Wine Production

OUTLINE OF RED WINE MAKING

The pigments of most red grapes are localized in the skins. Therefore, in the making of red table wines the juice is fermented on the skins in order to extract this color.

In the making of white wine, on the other hand, the juice is fermented free of the skins, in order to extract as little color and tannin as possible. As the cellar operations differ somewhat in other respects the two wine types will be considered in separate chapters. For general information see Amerine and Joslyn (1970), Brémond (1965), Geiss (1952), and Ribéreau-Gayon *et al.* (1976).

VARIETIES

The recommended varieties for red table wine production in the various regions of California have been listed on p. 115. The comments here are on their special wine-making characteristics.

There does not seem to be any doubt that Cabernet Sauvignon produces the highest quality red table wines yet made in California. The grapes normally arrive at the winery in excellent condition and ferment well. If fermented on the skins more than 4 or 5 days, the tannin content may be high and the wines will require longer aging. In both California and Bordeaux, there has been a tendency to press early. This results in wines of less tannin and color but earlier maturity. The best Cabernets may not mature until they have had 10 or more years of bottle aging.

Pinot noir presents special problems in California because it ripens very early in the season. Also, it appears to favor a warm fermentation and in some cases, a malo-lactic fermentation. We believe the highest possible quality has not yet been achieved from Pinot noir in California. Both cask and bottle aging are recommended.

Zinfandel ripens unevenly and great care in harvesting must be exercised. The best wines appear to come from the vineyards on the slopes of hills in regions II and III (see Table 2.12, Chap. 2). In regions IV and V bunch rot is a problem. Contrary to pre-Prohibition opinion the best Zinfandels profit by cask and bottle aging. We have tasted excellent Zinfandels of 10 to 15 years of age.

Petite Sirah is highly subject to bunch rot and sunburn. Grapes from regions II and III are most likely to produce the best wines. The same is true of Refosco and Carignane. Grenache produces its best red wines when grown in region I. Elsewhere it should be used for producing rosé wines.

Ruby Cabernet, because of its high total acidity, should be used for red table wines only when grown in regions IV and V. Barbera, also because of its high total acidity, is recommended for planting only in regions IV and V.

TESTING THE GRAPES

As grapes approach maturity, they should be tested frequently in order that they may be picked at the proper stage of ripeness (see pp. 89–90).

As the grapes are received, each load should be tested for °Brix. If the grapes are found to be excessively high in sugar they should be used for making port wine or for distilling material. The addition of acid is often indicated for table wines. Tartaric acid is preferred in cases of low acidity (below 0.6%).

For this reason, Brix tests on the grapes should always be accompanied by titration of the samples for total acidity. There is some evidence to indicate that acidification (if required) before fermentation results in better development of bouquet and flavor than if it is delayed until fermentation is complete. It is also desirable to follow the pH during ripening as musts of high pH are unsuitable for making high quality table wines.

PICKING

In California, harvesting is usually done, often by contract, by crews of pickers who pick several vineyards in succession. Short, curved knives or short-bladed shears are used in cutting the bunches from the vines but picking shears, such as used for table-grape harvesting, are preferable, as they slash the fruit less and also permit easier cutting out of rotten berries. The grapes, after picking into buckets, are usually dumped into small gondolas which are taken directly to the winery (Fig. 7.1 and 7.2). Transportation over long distances in bulk is objectionable from the

FIG. 7.1. PICKING BY BUCKET AND TRANSPORTATION BY
GONDOLA

standpoint of sanitation and microbiology. Inevitably many of the grapes
are crushed, with consequent fermentation and contamination with fruit
flies (*Drosophila melanogaster*). Fermentation, bacterial growth, and
volatile acid formation have often been noted in gondola trucks where
crushing was delayed. Mechanical harvesting is now common and will
undoubtedly be generally used in the future. Ough *et al.* (1971) found
holding times prior to start of winery processing to be critical with
mechanically harvested grapes and recommended field crushing and
stemming. Petrucci and Siegfried (1976) recommended certain operating

Courtesy of Wine Institute
FIG. 7.2. GONDOLA TRUCKS BEING DUMPED INTO
CONTINUOUS CONVEYOR

procedures to reduce extraneous matter in the harvested grapes.

Only sound (not moldy) grapes should be harvested. Some varieties develop a considerable quantity of second crop bunches that ripen 2 or 3 weeks later than the main crop. If the main crop is overripe, it is often desirable to pick the second crop along with the first in order that the second crop will furnish much needed acidity. On the other hand, if the first crop grapes are not overripe, it is better that the second crop be left on the vine to ripen. The Zinfandel usually sets a good second crop which if picked with the first crop in a cool region will make the must unduly acid.

TRANSPORTATION

Many wineries, particularly in the coastal counties of California and in the wine districts of European countries, are located in or adjacent to the vineyards. In such cases, transportation to the winery is quick and convenient. However, some grapes are shipped 100 miles or more in large gondola trucks. This is not recommended for the reasons previously given. A much better plan is to make the grapes into wine in a winery near the vineyards, and then ship the new wine. If this is not possible, an alternative procedure is to crush the grapes at the vineyard into closed tanks and add sulfur dioxide prior to transporting.

CRUSHING

For a discussion of crushers, see pp. 257–258.

Beneath the crusher is a sump of metal or concrete into which the crushed grapes fall. From this sump the crushed grapes are pumped through pipes of large diameter to the fermentation tanks. These pipes are of steel, aluminum, or fiberglass. Pyrex glass, stainless steel and fiberglass piping are recommended for transfer of wines. Aluminum and steel are not recommended for wines.

Pumps and must lines should be flushed out with water, an antiseptic, and water again after the day's crushing is over and again before use the next morning since, in the presence of air, the juice attacks the metal. Alkaline detergents should never be used on aluminum must lines. Must lines, after considerable use, often accumulate a coating of tartrate which protects the must against metallic contamination. If the must lines are steel it is desirable to leave the coating of tartrate undisturbed.

MUST TREATMENT

In some regions, and with certain varieties of grapes, the acidity of the grapes is too high and the sugar content too low for production of palatable wine. In such cases, the addition of both water and sugar may be essential. In Switzerland, where this condition prevails, sugar only is added and no water. After the wine is made, certain bacteria, discussed later, destroy the excess acidity. In Canada and eastern United States, both sugar and water are used by some producers, sugar only by others. In some regions of France, sugar is used in cold years. In Germany, sugar is also employed in many seasons. (See pp. 20 and 485.)

Addition of Enzymes

Enzymes are being more generally used in the production of red wines. Ough and Berg (1974) found pectic enzyme treatment of musts of red grapes increased wine yield 3.5% and color about 12%. Montedoro and Bertuccioli (1976), in trials with polygalacturonase, cellulase, hemicellulase, protease, and xylanase, reported that all increased the yield and color intensity of the wines, while the wines obtained by treatment with cellulase, protease and pectinase showed an increase in aroma.

Amelioration

In California, grapes ripen very rapidly during hot weather and often become too ripe for the making of wine of normal composition. Diluting slightly with water is permissible within certain limits prescribed in the regulations but, at best, it is a poor and unnecessary practice which the better wine makers avoid by picking at the proper stage of maturity. If the °Brix exceeds 25°, it is considered that the grapes are not suitable for dry wine production, even if both acid and water could be added.

In California, a state law forbids the addition of sugar to crushed grapes or must. However, grape concentrate may be used for amelioration.

Addition of Sulfur Dioxide

As previously stated in Chap. 6, it is essential that a small amount of sulfur dioxide, or one of its salts, be added to the crushed grapes in red wine making in order that wild yeasts and spoilage bacteria be held in check.

For sound grapes, about 75 mg/liter of sulfur dioxide is needed; for moldy or soured grapes, about twice this amount. Preferably, sulfur dioxide is automatically added at the crusher. If added in the vat, pumping over should follow the addition to ensure even distribution. For general principles on the use of sulfur dioxide see pp. 202–206 and 263–267.

Warming

At the end of the season, when the weather has turned cold, it may be necessary to warm the crushed grapes by drawing off the free-run, heating to about 60°C (140°F) and returning it to the vat, continuing until the mass is heated to about 21.1°C (70.0°F) in order that the yeast will initiate fermentation promptly. In the Burgundy region of France, such heating is fairly common. There is evidence also that color and flavor extraction are better at 21.1° to 29.4°C (70.0° to 85.0°F).

Addition of Starter

The preparation of a starter of pure wine yeast has been described in Chap. 6. We shall assume that enough starter has been prepared, that is, must fermenting with a pure culture of a desirable strain of wine yeast, such as champagne Ay, burgundy, Montrachet, or other proven strain.

Within about 2 hr after addition of the sulfurous acid or bisulfite, add to each 3785 liters (1000 gal.) of crushed grapes about 76 liters (20 gal.) of the pure yeast starter. This period of waiting before addition of the yeast allows time for the sulfur dioxide to lose some of its germicidal value through formation of combined sulfur dioxide and also allows time for it to act upon the wild yeasts and spoilage bacteria. After the first fermentations of the season when the fermentors are filled with active yeast, a lesser amount of starter may be used. Several hours after addition of the starter, when the yeasts have had a chance to multiply, the crushed grapes are pumped over to mix the yeast with the entire contents of the vat.

When this vat of grapes is fermenting rapidly, the wine maker may take some of the fermenting must to inoculate another vat of crushed grapes. When it is in fermentation, it may be used to start one or more other vats of crushed grapes, and so on through the season. However, it is preferable to have a fresh starter of pure yeast available throughout the season and to inoculate from one vat to the next only when no pure starter is available. This is particularly true at the end of the season when the grapes may be of less desirable quality. If too large a starter is used the fermentation may become violent too early in the fermentation, making extra cooling necessary.

FERMENTATION

Fermentation converts grape sugars to alcohol and carbon dioxide with the liberation of considerable heat (pp. 190–191).

The carbon dioxide gas escapes from the vat. The sugar in the must is converted to alcohol which is lower in density than water. Hence, the specific gravity (or the °Brix) of the must decreases in proportion to the progress of the fermentation; and the decrease in °Brix is an approximate measure of the amount of sugar that has been fermented.

Brix and Temperature Records

Most wine makers keep a record of °Brix and temperature of the fermenting grapes against time. For example, they will usually take the Brix and temperature 2 or 3 times daily and record the data.

In making a temperature reading, a long-stemmed, metal-cased thermometer, several feet long, is inserted through the cap and readings taken immediately below the cap and also at 310 or 620 mm (12 to 24 in.) below the cap (Fig. 7.3). These thermometers are equipped with a dial scale that is very easily and quickly read. The thermometer should be checked before each season against an accurate chemical thermometer. The practice of scooping out a pailful, or dipper, of the fermenting juice and pomace, and taking its temperature with a small mercury thermometer, is likely to give very erroneous results, as much as 5.5°C (10°F) too low. Larger tanks may have recording thermometers installed at various places in the tank.

FIG. 7.3. TAKING TEMPERATURE OF RED WINE FERMENTATION WITH LONG STEM
THERMOMETER

Temperature observations will indicate when it is necessary to cool the fermenting must. The Brix readings also show the progress of the fermentation, as well as indicating the approximate time to draw the free-run off the pomace and to press the pomace.

Punching and Pumping Over

The skins, pulp, and seeds (at least some of the seeds) are brought to the surface during fermentation by the buoyant effect of the carbon dioxide gas, and form a thick layer or cap, from one to several feet in thickness. This cap becomes very dense during the height of the fermentation (in large fermentors it is so dense that it will almost hold the weight of a man). Fermentation is extremely rapid in the cap, and the temperature therein may be several degrees above that of the must beneath the cap. Consequently, thermophilic (heat-loving) bacteria may grow in the cap and in some cases cause a rapid rise in volatile acid; or the temperature may rise so high that the yeast in the cap are killed or greatly weakened. Ough and Amerine (1960, 1961) have presented data showing cap temperatures 5.6° to 8.3°C (10.0° to 15.0°F) higher than that of the main volume of must below the cap. Guymon and Crowell (1977) found the large temperature differences between cap and liquid were caused by a faster fermentation of the sugar in the liquid adhering to the cap than in the bulk liquid.

For these reasons, and also to promote extraction of the color and tannin from the skins and seeds, the pomace of the cap and the fermenting must should be thoroughly mixed several times a day. Mixing is attained by drawing the must from the bottom and pumping it back over the cap, spraying or spreading it over the entire surface of the cap. This is done from 1 to 10 times a day with 10−100% of the tank contents pumped over each time (Cooke and Berg 1969, 1973).

The progress of the fermentations, the physical movement of the skins against each other, and enzyme action result in disintegration of the pulp. Extraction of color and tannin from the skins is primarily due to the solvent action of the alcohol produced by the fermentation. Pectic enzymes apparently hydrolyze the pectic substances and hence destroy the slimy nature of freshly crushed grapes. The alcohol produced by fermentation also precipitates pectins and other organic matter. Thus, after fermentation the skins are no longer slippery to the touch and hence may be pressed easily, whereas freshly crushed grapes are difficult to press.

STUCK WINES

If the fermentation is arrested by too high temperature, with considerable remaining unfermented sugar, the yeast will be so weakened in most cases that it will be unable to complete the fermentation. The wine may contain 1 to 6% of unfermented sugar, and is very liable to spoilage by bacteria. To avoid this the wine must be refermented at once to dryness (see p. 275).

DRAWING OFF

When the fermenting must has attained the desired amount of color and tannin, it is drawn off the pomace. In California, this is at 0° to 12° Brix after 2 to 5 days on the skins. In northern Italy, the wine may be allowed to remain with the skins and seeds for a week or more after fermentation is complete, in order to secure wines of very high tannin content. Such practice is not advisable under American conditions and is dangerous because acetification may occur.

Berg and Akiyoshi (1957) showed that color extraction from Carignane and Zinfandel grapes reaches a maximum with only 3 to 6% alcohol. Ough and Amerine (1962) reported color extraction from Cabernet Sauvignon and from Cabernet Sauvignon-Grenache blends was not complete until about 12% alcohol. In order to extract the maximum color from heavily pigmented grapes, such as Cabernet Sauvignon, they recommended pre-fermentation blending. This recommendation is only when blending is considered desirable. In spite of blending, only about 41% of the color available at the start of the fermentation was present 4 months after fermentation. For varieties such as Cabernet Sauvignon, the rate of color extraction is relatively independent of the concentration of extracted color or of the amount of pigment present.

The total amount of color extracted is dependent on the amount of pigment present.

In drawing off, the wine will be aerated and thus invigorate the yeast, so that fermentation will run smoothly to completion in the storage tank. It is very desirable to strain out the seeds and particles of pulp that accompany the free-run. The screen used for the purpose should be of stainless steel.

The free-run wine is less astringent, smoother, and of somewhat lower color content than the press wine and, in making fine wines, should be kept separate from the press wine.

Singleton and Draper (1964) indicate that grape seeds contribute significantly to the tannin content of red wines. Complete extraction of the tannins of the seed could contribute 0.2 to 0.4% tannin to the wine. Half or less actually appears in red wines in normal fermentation. Ribéreau-Gayon and Milhé (1970) found 35 to 50% of the tannin of red wines from skins, 15 to 20% from seeds and 20 to 40% from stems. The stems reduced the color intensity of the wine. At higher fermentation temperatures the proportion of tannin from the skins increases.

Pressing

In the pressing of red wine pomace, a press which does not grind the pomace (or only minimally) should be used. Cooke and Berg (1969, 1973) indicated this principle is being observed with bag, horizontal basket, or minimally grinding screw presses most commonly used.

Some wineries combine the press wine with the free-run immediately after pressing. Others ferment them separately and later either blend according to taste or consign the press wine to a generic blend.

For Bordeaux red wines, Sudraud and Cassignard (1958) find that low fermentation temperatures decrease color and tannin extraction. Acidifying the musts increases the color but not the tannin and retards the start of the malo-lactic fermentation. Sulfiting delays the malo-lactic fermentation. For early-maturing red wines under Bordeaux conditions they recommend no correction of acidity, *no* sulfur dioxide, complete removal of the stems, and a pumping over, with aeration, on the second day of the fermentation. The free-run and press wines are combined. Ribéreau-Gayon *et al.* (1970) obtain maximum color extraction with Bordeaux grapes with 8 to 9 days of fermentation on the skins. Color decreases with longer periods but tannin content continues to increase.

Berg and Akiyoshi (1957, 1958, 1960, 1962) have shown that in nonsulfited musts alcohol is the factor of major importance in color and tannin extraction. Sulfur dioxide increased color extraction but with Zinfandel decreased color stability. On aging, sulfur dioxide increased color stability. Fermentation was responsible for a 35% decrease in spectral color.

THE AFTER FERMENTATION

Although the wine from the fermentation vat may show $0°$ Brix or even a reading of less than $0°$, it may still contain unfermented sugar. The alcohol causes a low Brix reading as it is of lower density than sugar and water. Therefore, it is highly essential that the fermentation run to completion in the storage tank; that is, to 0.20% sugar or lower by chemical analysis. Conduct of this secondary or after fermentation requires close attention, because dropping temperature may result in sticking. Supplying oxygen may result in renewed yeast growth and fermentation.

For this reason, the wines in the storage tanks during this period should be sampled every 2 or 3 days and the degree Brix measured. At this stage a −5° to +5° Brix hydrometer can be usefully employed. Temperature corrections should be made. When the degree Brix remains constant for two samplings then the wine should be analyzed chemically for sugar content as described in Chap. 19.

Also the temperature should be observed occasionally and, if fermentation is arrested by too low a temperature, the wine may require warming by passage through a heat exchanger to bring the contents of the tank up to about 21.1° C (70.0°F). If fermentation ceases, and the temperature is still sufficiently high, the wine should be aerated by pumping over vigorously or allowing it to splash into a sump. Or air may be pumped into the bottom of the tank to rise vigorously through the wine. The sediment should be well stirred to resuspend the yeast to encourage growth of yeast.

In obstinate cases, it may be necessary to add yeast food; that is, ammonium phosphate or urea. Ammonium phosphate is better as it furnishes both nitrogen and phosphorus. If only nitrogen is needed urea is adequate. The legality of such additions should be checked.

The tank of wine during this period should be protected against oxygen and vinegar bacteria by means of a fermentation bung. This may be made by boring a small hole in a cellar bung and inserting through it a U-shaped tube. The bung is inserted in the bunghole of the tank and one arm of the U tube is inserted in a jar or bottle of dilute metabisulfite solution. This fermentation bung builds up a slight pressure of carbon dioxide gas in the tank, which prevents the aerobic growth of vinegar bacteria or of yeast films. The U tube may be made of block tin or copper or, for that matter, of glass tubing. Winery supply houses usually carry the bungs and tubes in stock. For very large tanks, simply loosely covering the manhole of the tank is usually sufficient to maintain an atmosphere of carbon dioxide over the surface of the wine.

After bubbling in the fermentation bung practically ceases, indicating that fermentation is nearly complete, the fermentation bung is replaced by a plain, solid, cellar bung. However, some fermentation is still going on and gas pressure will develop in the tank. Therefore, workmen must loosen the bungs every day or two at first and less frequently later to release the gas pressure. They then insert the bung fairly tightly. Also, toward the end of fermentation new wine of the same lot is added to fill the tank completely and, as needed, this addition is repeated to keep the tank full. It is possible to dispense with a fermentation bung by merely inserting a cellar bung loosely in the top of the storage tank during the secondary fermentation, but vinegar flies may be a problem.

FIRST RACKING, FILLING UP, ETC.

Usually within six weeks after crushing, the wine has been completely fermented and it is perfectly dry; that is, chemical analysis shows that it contains less than 0.20% of the fermentable sugar. Keep the tank completely full by regular (weekly at first and later at intervals not exceeding a month) filling up with new wine of like variety or character from smaller containers and keep the tank tightly bunged.

When a sample drawn from near the bottom of the tank shows that the wine is well settled, it is ready for the first racking. Usually this will be within 4 to 6 weeks after drawing off from the fermentation vat. The first racking in many wineries is made during the month of November or December and, at the latest, in early January in the Northern Hemisphere. Sulfur dioxide should be added to give about 75 to 100 mg/liter total. Wines should be tasted at this time and, when necessary, appropriate blends made.

The lees, namely the sediment of yeast, pulp, tartrates, etc., left in the bottom of the tank after racking, contain considerable wine and tartrates. The lees from several tanks may be combined and allowed to settle for recovery of additional clear wine, or the wine recovered by passing through a lees press. Or, the lees may be sold "as is" for brandy production. In racking, great care must be taken not to stir up the lees.

In European countries and to a lesser extent in California, the primary fermentation is followed by the malo-lactic fermentation. This fermentation is due to lactic acid bacteria and converts malic to lactic acid with the release of carbon dioxide. This release of carbon dioxide is why many wine makers have confused the malo-lactic fermentation with a continuation of the primary fermentation. The advantage of this fermentation is that it reduces the titratable acidity and raises the pH. This is desirable for high acid wines and probably useful in the cooler regions of California in certain seasons and with some varieties. However, often the acidity is already too low and the pH too high in California and such a fermentation may lead to actual spoilage of the wine. The greatest use of the fermentation appears to be in eastern United States wines which have not been unduly ameliorated with water and in certain red wine producing areas of Europe. The malo-lactic fermentation may be induced to occur simultaneously with the alcoholic fermentation. Ough and Amerine (1961) preferred a delayed malo-lactic fermentation.

The malo-lactic fermentation can be facilitated by leaving the wine on the lees to facilitate yeast autolysis and release of amino acids, etc., for growth of the bacteria. High temperature storage also favors the autolysis. To prevent the malo-lactic fermentation, early racking, cool storage and maintaining 100 mg/liter or more sulfur dioxide are usually sufficient.

Loss of color during the secondary fermentation of red wines is commonly observed. Vetsch and Lüthi (1964) demonstrated that in some cases this was related to the degradation of citric acid by *Leuconostoc* types of bacteria. The dehydrogenation of citric acid apparently supplies the hydrogen to reduce the anthocyanin pigments.

OTHER METHODS OF RED WINE FERMENTATION

At one time during the pre-Prohibition era in California, the California Wine Association made much of its dry red wine as follows: the grapes were crushed into a vat in the usual manner. The juice was drawn off from the bottom of the vat and heated in a continuous pasteurizer to about 60°C (140°F) and pumped back into the vat. The heating was continued until the crushed grapes and must had attained a temperature of about 54.4°C (130.0°F). They were allowed to stand, with pumping over occasionally, until sufficient color and tannin were extracted. The free-run was then drawn off and the drained grapes pressed. The two juices were combined, cooled to 26.7°C (80.0°F), sulfited, and fermented with a starter of pure yeast. Heating destroys the slipperiness of freshly crushed grapes and renders pressing fairly simple. It also sterilizes the juice. Wines made in this manner were mellow and smooth in character and it was said that they aged more rapidly than wines made without heating. Modern procedures are described by Berg (1950), Berg and Marsh (1950), Marsh and Guymon (1959), Frank and Trogus (1975), and Lowe et al. (1976). While heat-extraction of color has many attractive features, the wines often have a purplish tint and usually are difficult to clarify. A procedure for rapid extraction of color without its accompanying disadvantages would be very useful.

Coffelt and Berg (1965) treated whole grapes with steam under pressure. The objective of their study was to produce wines of good color and quality without fermentation on the skins. They reported grapes from region IV to respond better to the heat treatment than those from I. The most favorable results for dry red wines were obtained with a 4-sec heating period in 1961, and, with less favorable results in 1962 and 1963, with heating times of 27 and 10–15 sec. Rankine (1964) showed that there was little measurable difference between wine made from grapes dipped in boiling water for 30 sec and then held at 40°–50°C (104°–122°F) for about 1 hr and pressed compared to those that were fermented for 5 days on the skins and then pressed. There was, however, a slight reduction in quality in the wine from the heated grapes. Colagrande et al. (1976) heated the pomace of Barbera grapes to 50°–60°C (122°–140°F) for 15 min, pressed, combined the juice with the juice from the first pressing, and fermented. After six months the wine had a smoother and fruitier flavor. Amati and Carnacini (1976) held crushed grapes at 5°C (41°F) for 48 hr, pressed, and fermented the juice. The wine was of good color stability but with an enhanced and more delicate flavor.

Another method is the Algerian lessivage system in which a special concrete vat is used. The cap is submerged and the rising gas appears to cause the liquid to circulate up through the cap. Actually little circulation occurs and in essence the system is a submerged cap type of fermentation. Control of temperature is difficult.

Other systems, in which an intermittent automatic flow of liquid over the surface is controlled by the pressure of the carbon dioxide produced by fermentation, are employed. When combined with temperature control such systems do give adequate color extraction but they are complicated in design, difficult to clean, and it is questionable if they result in any saving in cost or improvement in quality.

Procedures by which the crushed grapes are introduced under the cap have been recommended by Cremaschi (1951) and Maveroff (1955). The cap is then pushed to the top from which it is continuously scraped off. The theory is that the low percentage of alcohol solution into which the freshly crushed grapes are introduced acts as an antiseptic and ensures a clean fermentation. In essence, this is a modification of the Sémichon *superquatre* procedure (Quaccia 1935). In practice it depends on having a continuously clean fermentation. This may occur under ideal conditions but it has proven difficult to control in practice. Certainly it has not been tested for the production of premium-quality wines.

The ancient practice of filling the fermentation tank with intact grapes and allowing the anaerobic fermentation to proceed spontaneously (*macération carbonique*) is still used in many regions, in the Rioja district of Spain, in Italy, Switzerland, the south of France, on the Rhône, and particularly in Beaujolais, according to Chauvet et al. (1963). The persistence of the practice is apparently due to favorable effects on the quality of the resulting wines: a special bouquet, earlier maturity, slightly more alcohol, and a softer taste. Two processes appear to take place in this procedure: an intracellular fermentation of malic acid (and possibly of some tartaric) and production of small amounts of ethanol and aroma materials. Flanzy (1973) reports that a high ratio of diethyl succinate to γ-butyro-lactone distinguishes macération carbonique wines from normally fermented wines. The process is not more generally used because of the longer period of fermentation, the high amount of press wine, and the danger of contamination. For previous studies see Garino-Canina (1948), Peynaud and Guimberteau (1962), Bénard and Jouret (1963), Fantozzi and Rossini (1975), and Pallotta et al. (1976). See also p. 262.

Metal pressure tanks were introduced into the German wine industry after World War II. Klenk (1958) has reviewed this trend. He considers them to have been particularly valuable for red table wines. The main advantages of the pressure tanks are their ease of control of temperature, reduced danger of bacterial contamination, and simplicity of cleaning. In California, Ough and Amerine (1961) found pressure fermentation of Pinot noir gave less satisfactory wines than by standard procedures.

Rotating, horizontally-mounted tanks (ROTO tanks) are a recent development. Weger (1975) reported from 27 to 69% more color obtained with the ROTO tank than with the stationary tank. Also the ROTO tanks produced wines with a fuller and more intense red wine character. However, commercial trials in a California premium winery have been discontinued in favor of more traditional processing.

CARE OF WINE

Laboratory Examination

At the time of the first racking the composition of all new red wines should be determined by analysis for volatile acid, total acid, pH, sugar, alcohol and tannin. The sulfur dioxide content should also be determined and raised to about 100 mg/liter.

At regular intervals thereafter during aging, certain of these analyses should be repeated. Also, it is advisable to examine the wines once or twice a year under the high power of a microscope to make certain that spoilage bacteria do not gain a foothold.

On the basis of laboratory examination, measures should be taken to halt any deleterious changes that may be indicated. The total sulfur dioxide content should be maintained at or about 75 mg/liter after any desired malo-lactic fermentation has been accomplished. See Chap. 16 for methods of controlling wine contamination. It should be emphasized that routine sulfuring of empty casks and subsequent filling with wine results in appreciable pick-up of the sulfur dioxide by the wines placed in them. Thorough washing of sulfured casks is recommended.

Fining and Racking

In the Bordeaux district of France, it is customary to fine the new wine with gelatin some time during the first year of aging, not only to clear it but also to remove excess tannin. In California wineries, it is customary to fine the new wine after the first racking with bentonite as described in Chap. 6. For common wines this is the desirable procedure and hastens development of the wine. Fine red wines may be fined with gelatin after the second or third racking. Use of fresh egg white is also recommended. During aging the wine should be racked at least twice a year to rid it of sediment and aerate it, thus promoting normal aging.

Aging

The larger the storage container the slower is the aging. Thus, in 1130 to 2260 hl (30,000 to 60,000 gal.) tanks the aging of dry red wine is very slow unless rackings and aerations are frequent. Aging is hastened by aerating and pasteurizing. In some wineries bulk common wines are subjected to such a cycle several times early in their life in order to hasten aging. Such quick aging may be justifiable for common wines but can be ruinous for fine wines. Development of a fine bouquet and flavor is—so far—attained only by slow aging.

If large tanks are used for storage and aging of high quality wines, it is desirable that final aging be done in much smaller containers such as ovals, puncheons, or other small oak cooperage. Many successful producers of premium quality red table wines age the wine finally for about 6 months in 190 liter (50 gal.) oak barrels. However, it is possible to mature a common California red wine sufficiently in one year or less for the standard wine trade. But for a fine Cabernet, one should age for about 2 to 3 years in wood. After bottling, such wines should be held at least a year before sale. They will improve for 5 to 15 years in the bottle.

A red wine of light body and tannin content requires less aging than does a heavy bodied and high tannin Cabernet. It may be at its best after one year in the wood and one year in the bottle. In Italy and France, it is customary to drink most of the common red wines within a year after crushing. Many drinkers of common wines prefer their "raw" flavor to the mellow flavor of aged wine. Wines of low alcohol are probably best drunk young. Due to the demand for white wines, early-maturing, low-tannin, light red wines are being produced. They are served cool.

Other Cellar Operations

During aging it will be necessary to filter the wine or fine it at least once and to give it a finishing filtration before bottling. Also, in most California wineries it is customary to refrigerate table wines to near the freezing point, $-3.9°$ to $-5.0°C$ ($25.0°$ to $23.0°F$), for about 3 weeks to rid them of excess cream of tartar. Cation exchange resins are also being used (see p. 301). Stabilizing ordinary wines by heating to $60°C$ ($140°F$) and allowing to cool slowly for 3 to 4 days, followed by racking and fining and filtration has been used but may actually contribute to instability.

Many California red wines are benefited by the addition of citric or tartaric acid as they are often deficient in total acidity. This should be done early in the aging of the wine in order to permit the wine to come to equilibrium before finishing. For details of these and other operations see Chap. 6 and Cooke and Berg (1969, 1973).

In Europe, where the alcohol is frequently very low, equipment to freeze out water and thus increase the alcohol has been used. The disadvantages of increasing the alcohol content by freezing wines are well known: changing the tartrate/malate ratio, increase in titratable acidity, and browning of white wines. In California, the process is unnecessary. In the occasional year when musts are low in sugar, California wine makers should add grape concentrate to the musts or should blend the wines. Use of grape spirits to raise the alcohol is not advisable.

Blending

Usually, the wines of a given vintage are blended and the earlier this is done the better. If the wine is to be aged as a "vintage wine" then it is not permitted to blend the wines of two different seasons. Common wines that are not to be labeled "vintage wines" are not restricted as to blending; consequently, their blending should be designed to give the best possible wines.

Also, blending should be used to maintain similarity of character of a given brand of wine from year to year in order that the customer will find the wines of that brand reasonably constant in flavor, color, and bouquet. For details see Chap. 6.

Rosé

Pink or rosé wines are produced either by fermenting pink varieties of grapes on the skins or by using red grapes and separating the juice from the skins early in the fermentation—usually in 24 to 36 hr.

Amati *et al.* (1976) have developed a new technology involving decolorization of a base wine by adding carbon during fermentation, then refermenting this wine with given quantities of juice obtained from grapes conditioned in a carbonic gas atmosphere. The Sangioveto and Barbera rosé wines produced by this new technique showed better physical-chemical and sensory characteristics than those of other rosé wines. Low-color, low-tannin red wines destined to be served chilled are now being widely produced.

COLOR REACTIONS

Observations on color behavior in red wines has led in recent years to a number of studies designed to develop an explanation for the observed behavior. It was felt that if the reactions involved and the factors responsible could be elucidated, then technology could be developed for controlling color behavior.

Berg (1963) advanced the concept of two pigment forms in wine: one responsive to pH changes and the other nonresponsive. He also proposed the degree of pigment association as one of the major factors responsible for varying color behavior in wines.

Somers (1971) found that polymeric pigments are resistant to color change caused by pH shifts and decolorization by bisulfite. The contribution of polymeric pigments to red wine color increased with wine age averaging about 40% at 1 year and 85% at 10 years. He also hypothesized that the polymeric anthocyanin pigments contain quinoid anhydrobase chromophores stabilized by substitution with reactive flavans.

Timberlake and Bridle (1976A) studied the effect of processing on the color characteristics of some red wines. They reported that wine made by thermovinification had nearly twice the color of that fermented on the skins, and though it contained less anthocyanin it had more polymeric pigment. The wine made by carbonic maceration was the least colored, though it contained anthocyanins equal in amount to those in the thermovinified wine. The wine made by thermovinification contained an excess of acetaldehyde over bisulfite, which was probably a factor in increasing its color.

Timberlake and Bridle (1976B) also studied the interactions of pure anthocyanins, various phenolic compounds, and acetaldehyde in model solutions. Anthocyanins and phenolic compounds reacted very slowly, with eventual formation of yellow xanthylium salts. Little reaction occurred between the anthocyanins and acetaldehyde. However, adding acetaldehyde to mixtures of phenolics and anthocyanins caused rapid and spectacular color increase with shifts toward the violet. Color increase was due to formation of highly colored new compounds believed to consist of anthocyanins and phenolics linked by CH_3CH bridges. The presence of free sulfur dioxide prevents these reactions from occurring.

Berg and Akiyoshi (1975) found that either alcohol or sugar had a greater effect than acetaldehyde in increasing color. This was believed to be due to polymerization as their addition was always accompanied by a decrease in pH-responsive anthocyanin. It is hypothesized that increases in spectral color occur whenever more colored pH-responsive anthocyanin than uncolored is fixed in the polymer. This requires the equilibrium shift of a proportionate amount (depending on wine pH) of the uncolored pH-responsive to the colored pH-responsive form.

REFERENCES[1]

AMATI, A. and CARNACINI, A.B. 1976. Vinificazione di uve "Albania di Romagna" per macerazione delle vinacce a bassa temperatura. Vignevini *3*, 9-14.

---

[1]Titles have been translated only for nonwestern European languages.

AMATI, A., GALASSI, S., TOSSANI, NATALI, N. and PALLOTTA, U. 1976. Sulla produzione dei vini rosati. I. Confronto fra diverse techniche di vinificazione. Vignevini 6, 17-23.

AMERINE, M.A. and JOSLYN, M.A. 1970. Table Wines: The Technology of Their Production, 2nd Edition. University of California Press, Berkeley, Los Angeles.

BÉNARD, P. and JOURET, C. 1963. Essais comparatifs de vinification en rouge. Ann. Technol. Agric. 12, 85-102.

BERG, H.W. 1950. Heat treatment of musts. Wines Vines 31 (6) 24-26.

BERG, H.W. 1963. Stabilisation des anthocyannes comportement de la couleur dans les vins rouges. Ann. Technol. Agric. 12 (No. hors-série 1) 247-261.

BERG, H.W. and AKIYOSHI, M. 1957. The effect of various must treatments on the color and tannin content of red grape juices. Food Res. 22, 373-383.

BERG, H.W. and AKIYOSHI, M. 1958. Further studies of the factors affecting the extraction of color and tannin from red grapes. Ibid. 23, 511-517.

BERG, H.W. and AKIYOSHI, M. 1960. The effect of sulfur dioxide and fermentation on color extraction from red grapes. Ibid. 25, 183-189.

BERG, H.W. and AKIYOSHI, M. 1962. Color behavior during fermentation and aging of wines. Am. J. Enol. Vitic. 13, 126-132.

BERG, H.W. and AKIYOSHI, M. 1975. On the nature of reactions responsible for color behavior in red wines. A hypothesis. Ibid. 26, 134-143.

BERG, H.W. and MARSH, G.L. 1950. Heat treatment of musts. Wines Vines 31 (7) 23-24; (8) 29-30.

BREMOND, E. 1965. Techniques Modernes de Vinification et de Conservation des Vins en Pays Méditerranéens. La Maison Rustique, Paris.

CHAUVET, J., BRÉCHOT, P., DUPUY, P., CROSON, M. and IRRMANN, R. 1963. Évolution des acides malique et lactique dans la vinification par macération carbonique de la vendange. Ann. Technol. Agric. 12, 237-246.

COFFELT, R.J. and BERG, H.W. 1965. Color extraction by heating whole grapes. Am. J. Enol. Vitic. 16, 117-128.

COLAGRANDE, O., RATTOTTI, M.T. and MAZZOLENI, V. 1976. Osservazione sperimentali sull'impiego della macerazione a caldo nella vinificazione di uve rosse. Riv. Vitic. Enol. 29, 331-340.

COOKE, G.M. and BERG, H.W. 1969. Varietal table wine processing practices in California. I. Varieties, grape and juice handling and fermentation. Am. J. Enol. Vitic. 20, 1-6.

COOKE, G.M. and BERG, H.W. 1973. Table wine processing practices in the San Joaquin Valley. Ibid. 24, 153-158.

CREMASCHI, V.W. 1951. Continuous fermentation process. U.S. Pat. 2,536,993. June 2.

FANTOZZI, P. and ROSSINI, G. 1975. Application de la macération carbonique au cours de la vinification du Rosso Piceno. Aspects technologiques d'une série d'essais de deux. Vini d'Italia 17, 415-423.

FRANK, J. and TROGUS, H. 1975. Farbaufbesserung und Farbgewinnung bei der Rotwein Bereitung. Deut. Weinbau *30*, 660-661.

FLANZY, M. 1973. La Vinification par Macération Carbonique. Étude 56. INRA, Éditions S.E.I., Versailles.

GARINO-CANINA, E. 1948. Fermentation "vinaire" avec des détails biochimiques du processus de la fermentation. Bull. Off. Intern. Vin. *21* (204) 55-61.

GEISS, W. 1952. Gezügelte Gärung. Joh. Wagner & Söhne K.G., Frankfurt.

GUYMON, J.F. and CROWELL, E.A. 1977. The nature and cause of cap-liquid temperature differences during wine fermentation. Am. J. Enol. Vitic. *28*, 74-78.

KLENK, E. 1958. Erfahrungen mit Anwendung von Metalltanks zur Rot- und Weissweinbereitung. Deut. Wein-Ztg. *94*, 398-406.

LOWE, E.J., OEY, A. and TURNER, T.M. 1976. Gasquet thermovinification system perspective after two years operation. Am. J. Enol. Vitic. *27*, 130-133.

MARSH, G.L. and GUYMON, J.F. 1959. Refrigeration in wine making. Am. Soc. Refrig. Eng. Data Book, Chap. 10. (This is periodically updated.)

MAVEROFF, A. 1955. Vinificación continua sistéma Cremaschi. Bol. Tec. Fac. Cien. Agric. Univ. Nac. Cuyo *12*, 1-32.

MONTEDORO, G. and BERTUCCIOLI, M. 1976. Essai de vinification en rouge avec l'emploi de différentes préparations enzymatiques. Lebensm.-Wiss. Technol. *9*, 225-231.

OUGH, C.S. and AMERINE, M.A. 1960. Experiments with controlled fermentation. IV. Am. J. Enol. Vitic. *11*, 5-14.

OUGH, C.S. and AMERINE, M.A. 1961. Studies on controlled fermentation. V. Effects on color, composition, and quality of red wines. *Ibid. 12*, 9-19.

OUGH, C.S. and AMERINE, M.A. 1962. Studies with controlled fermentation. VII. Effect of ante-fermentation blending of red must and white juice on color, tannins, and quality of Cabernet Sauvignon wine. *Ibid. 13*, 181-188.

OUGH, C.S. and BERG, H.W. 1974. The effect of two commercial pectic enzymes on grape musts and wines. *Ibid. 25*, 208-211.

OUGH, C.S., BERG, H.W., COFFELT, R.J. and COOKE, G.M. 1971. The effect on wine quality of simulated mechanical harvest and gondola transport of grapes. *Ibid. 22*, 65-70.

PALLOTTA, V. *et al.* 1976. Risultati di alcune esperienzi su moderne techniche di vinificazione in rosso. Riv. Sci. Tecn. Alim. Nutr. Um. *6*, 223-229.

PETRUCCI, V.E. and SIEGFRIED, R. 1976. The extraneous matter in mechanically harvested wine grapes. Am. J. Enol. Vitic. *27*, 40-41.

PEYNAUD, E. and GUIMBERTEAU, G. 1962. Modification de la composition des raisins au cours de leur fermentation propre en anaérobiose. Ann. Physiol. Veget. *4*, 161-167.

QUACCIA, L. 1935. The Sémichon process of fermentation. Fruit Prod. J. *14*, 169.

RANKINE, B.C. 1964. Heat extraction of colour from red grapes for wine making. Aust. Wine, Brewing Spirit Rev. *82* (6) 40-42.

RIBÉREAU-GAYON, P. and MILHÉ, J.C. 1970. Recherches technologiques sur les composés phénoliques des vins rouges. I. Influence des différentes parties de la grappe. Connaiss. Vigne Vin *4*, 63-74.

RIBÉREAU-GAYON, J., PEYNAUD, E., RIBÉREAU-GAYON, P. and SU-DRAUD, P. 1976. Traité d'Oenologie, Sciences et Techniques du Vin. Vol. III. Vinifications. Transformations du Vin. Dunod, Paris.

RIBÉREAU-GAYON, P., SUDRAUD, P., MILHÉ, J.C. and CANABAS, A. 1970. Recherches technologiques sur les composés phénoliques des vins rouges. II. Les facteurs de dissolution des composés phénoliques. Connaiss. Vigne Vin *4*, 133-144.

SINGLETON, V.L. and DRAPER, D.E. 1964. The transfer of polyphenolic compoundsrom grape seeds into wines. Am. J. Enol. Vitic. *15*, 34-40.

SOMERS,T.C. 1971. The polymeric nature of wine pigments. Phytochemistry *10*, 2175-2186.

SUDRAUD, P. and CASSIGNARD, R. 1958. Influence de certaines conditions dans la vinification en rouge. Ann. Technol. Agric. 7, 209-216.

TIMBERLAKE, C.F. and BRIDLE, P. 1976A. The effect of pressing and other factors on the color characteristics of some red wines. Vitis *15*, 37-49.

TIMBERLAKE, C.F. and BRIDLE, P. 1976B. Interactions between antho-cyanins, phenolic compounds, and acetaldehyde and their significance in red wines. Am. J. Enol. Vitic. *27*, 97-105.

VETSCH, U. and LÜTHI, H. 1964. Farbstoffverluste während des biolog-ischen Säureabbaues. Schweiz. Z. Obst-Weinbau *73*, 124-126.

WEGER, B. 1975. Versuche zur Rotweinbereitung mit dem System "ROTO." Mitt. Rebe Wein, Obstbau Früchteverw. (Klosterneuburg) *25*, 347-356.

8

Production of White Table Wine

White wines differ from red wines in production, composition, and sensory quality. Since they are not produced by fermentation on the skins the tannin and extract contents are lower. White table wines may be dry or nearly so or they may be very sweet, as with French Sauternes, the *Auslese* wines of Germany, or with a number of California types.

PROCESS

White wines are usually more delicate in flavor owing to low amounts of tannin and coloring matter. Defects in taste and appearance are easily apparent in them.

White juice is preferably fermented for dry wine in tanks or casks. The fermentation is usually allowed to go to completion. The casks or tanks are racked as soon as the gross yeasts settle out. Clarification and bottling may take place in 3 to 24 months—the lighter (lower-alcohol) types being processed first. The fermentation of white juice in closed tanks helps prevent the loss of bouquet and flavor. For general information, see Amerine and Joslyn (1970). Benvegnin *et al.* (1951), Ribéreau-Gayon *et al.* (1976), Saller (1955), and Troost (1972).

Varieties

The recommended varieties for planting in California have been listed (pp. 124–125). Further comments regarding their enological characteristics follow.

White Riesling is *the* variety for Riesling wine. It is a shy producer, sunburns easily, and requires a low fermentation temperature. In California, it is often erroneously named Johannisberg (or Johannisberger or Johannisburg) Riesling but White Riesling is correct. Sylvaner (Franken Riesling) and the so-called Grey Riesling have little Riesling character, either in this country or abroad. The Walschriesling (Italian Riesling) is not grown commercially in the United States and only produces pleasant nonvarietal wines in Italy and Yugoslavia. Emerald Riesling has a tendency to darken, as noted by Berg and Akiyoshi (1956). Its high acidity is a debatable compensating factor. The Sylvaner and Grey Riesling, if vinified separately and properly cared for, have a place in the United States wine industry if planted in the correct region. Because of their tendency to darken, musts of Grey Riesling should be well settled or centrifuged before fermentation.

Chardonnay produces excellent wines but is a low producer. The grapes should be fully matured, 23° Brix, before harvesting for the characteristic ripe grape aroma to develop. Another low producer is the distinctive Gewürztraminer. Very careful harvesting is necessary to secure sufficient maturity for flavor and still avoid low acidity and excessive sugar by too late harvesting. The choice of the correct region is essential.

Sémillon is a good all-purpose variety if picked in mid-season at a Brix of 22.5° to 23.5°. At a slightly higher Brix, even under California conditions, it can produce sweet table wines. In years of early rainfall it rots quickly.

Sauvignon blanc is excellent but the fruit must be mature if its wine is to have a characteristic aroma. This means harvesting at a Brix of at least 22.5°. When grown in very cool areas this variety has an aroma that is often characterized as too intense. Some of the best white table wines of California have been made from this variety.

For standard white wines, French Colombard and Chenin blanc are useful. Rot may develop in Chenin blanc clusters in rainy years.

Not recommended for general planting for white table wines are Trebbiano (Ugni blanc or St. Emilion), Palomino (darkens), Sauvignon vert (low acidity), Green Hungarian (thin, neutral wines), and Burger (thin and neutral but possibly useful as a sparkling wine stock), or any of the table grape varieties.

Generic types, such as California dry sauterne, chablis and rhine, are produced from available white varieties and by blending.

PICKING AND TRANSPORTING

The proper time of harvest varies from variety to variety, region, season, amount of crop, and the prospective use of the fruit. To fix the time accurately, determine the maturity of the grapes in the vineyard as outlined on p. 85 et seq. For early-maturing, fruity, white table wines, harvesting can begin at 20° to 21° Brix. For richer, more flavorful, slower-maturing wines, harvesting may be delayed to a Brix of 22° to 23°. Wines of better flavor and keeping quality and easier clarification are produced from musts from properly cropped vines with an acidity of over 0.70 g/100 ml (as tartaric) and pH of 3.3 or lower.

In California, the white grapes are commonly picked into clean plastic or aluminum tubs; dumped into or conveyed into small or large metal containers for transport to the winery (Fig. 8.1). Where the transfer is carefully made, the gondolas clean, excessive crushing of the grapes avoided, and the movement to the winery rapid, the system works well. It is difficult to transfer the delicate white grapes long distances in gondola trucks without considerable crushing. Harvesting directly into large metal containers which can be unloaded by power lifts is also common. Mechanical harvesting is now being widely used. Night harvest, vineyards free of mold and rot, proper use of sulfur dioxide, and rapid transport of the fruit to the winery are essential.

Courtesy of Valley Foundry and Machine Works, Inc.

FIG. 8.1. GRAPE HARVESTING DUMP TRAILER

Care should be exercised to avoid unclean fruit or "materials other than grape" (MOG). Many wineries limit these and have economic penalties in their harvesting contracts.

PROCESSING

Crushing

The Garolla-type crusher is satisfactorily used in California for crushing white grapes. Crushing equipment is described in Chap. 6.

White grapes should be thoroughly crushed to facilitate pressing.

Most of the copper and iron dissolved from crushers, stemmers, pumps, and must lines is lost in the lees after fermentation. Nevertheless, it is good practice to avoid as much metallic contamination as possible by using stainless steel or other inert equipment.

Juice Separation

From 75 to 150 mg/ liter of sulfur dioxide, or its equivalent as potassium-bisulfite or metabisulfite, should be adequately mixed into the must line or the crushed grapes to prevent browning of color and growth of wild yeasts. See pp. 202–205 and 255–258.

Crushed grapes are put into various types of tanks and the juice drained. The most efficient types are those with internal screens and which are self-emptying. The juices drain reasonably clear. The drained skins and seeds are put either through pre-presses (Fig. 8.2) or directly into continuous presses.

Courtesy of Valley Foundry and Machine Works, Inc.

FIG. 8.2. A SCREW-TYPE DEJUICER OR PRE-PRESS
USED AFTER DRAINING AND PRIOR TO PRESSING

The style of wine can be modified by the duration of skin-juice contact time. Ough (1969) and Ough *et al.* (1969) show increased phenol and other composition changes due to contact of the crushed grapes and juice.

Wineries with needs for distilling material may use only the free-run juice and add water to the remaining pomace to produce distilling material (see p. 261).

In some wineries the crushed grapes may be allowed to stand in the vat overnight to extract a small amount of tannin and to lose some of their sliminess. This treatment can easily be overdone, resulting in browning of the color and extraction of too much tannin and skin flavor. Pectic enzymes can effectively reduce the sliminess and allow for more rapid and increased juice yields (Ough and Berg 1974).

There are several different qualities of press juices from a continuous press. The final or "hard" press juice should be kept separate for lower quality wines. Willmes and Vaslin presses (p. 260) are widely used for pressing white musts. Basket presses are used by few wineries. Rack-and-cloth presses are often used in eastern United States for the native grapes which are very slippery and hence difficult to press in basket presses (p. 484).

Juice Clarification

At this stage of the process, the must should contain about 75 to 150 mg/liter of sulfur dioxide. This will prevent fermentation of sound grapes for 8 to 24 hr, depending on the temperature. A good practice is to keep the juice at $10°-13°C$ ($50°-55.4°F$), allow it to settle and then draw the clear juice off the sediment. This removes most of the suspended material including colloidal sulfur, thus avoiding major hydrogen sulfide problems. Centrifugation serves the same purpose. Wines made from clarified juices are easier to clarify. Musts of moldy grapes should always be clarified prior to fermentation. Some wineries use vacuum filters to recover juice from the settlings or from the centrifuge sediment. The quality of wines made from the clarified juices is superior (Singleton 1969; Bayly 1974; Ribéreau-Gayon et al. 1975) to those made from unsettled juice.

Amelioration

Addition of acid before fermentation promotes cleaner fermentations and gives better wines than if added later during aging. Losses of acid in the lees are greater if the acid is added before fermentation. Fumaric acid can be added to wine up to 0.05% to inhibit malolactic fermentation. If added to juice it is metabolized by the yeast during fermentation.

Addition of Starter

A starter of pure yeast to the extent of 2–3% is advisable. The yeast should be of an agglomerating and rapid settling type, i.e., granular type of *Saccharomyces cerevisiae*, such as Montrachet or burgundy strains. The choice of yeast strain is to some extent responsible for the style of wine that will result. Use of fermenting musts as starters is not recommended (see pp. 164–167).

FERMENTATION

White wines should be fermented at lower temperatures for the best results. The most desirable temperature range under California conditions is about 7.2° to 12.8°C (45° to 55°F). Above 21.1° C (70°F), bouquet, aroma and flavor are damaged. Fermentation is conducted in lined steel or stainless steel tanks for the least flavor and oxidation problems (see Fig. 8.3). Chardonnay is occasionally fermented in oak barrels or casks.

Courtesy of Valley Foundry and Machine Works, Inc.

FIG. 8.3. A MODERN WHITE WINE FERMENTING FACILITY AT WENTE BROS. WINERY, LIVERMORE, CALIFORNIA

Fermentation cooling will almost always be necessary. Some wineries ferment in special cold rooms 10°C (50°F) or lower. In such rooms, carbon dioxide accumulates at the floor level and appropriate safety measures should be taken. Temperatures are usually allowed to rise slightly after reaching 5° Brix to allow the fermentations to finish without undue delays.

Small containers should be protected with fermentation bungs throughout the fermentation. During the final stages it is also advisable to equip tanks or casks with fermentation bungs to prevent acetification. During the last slow stages of fermentation, the containers should be kept full.

Must treated with bentonite or other suitable nonsoluble material will allow for a smooth fermentation with little chance of sticking at lower temperatures (Ough and Groat 1978).

Geiss (1952) has advocated controlling the rate of fermentation of white table wines by pressure. The results of Amerine and Ough (1957) and of Ough and Amerine (1960) in California have not been favorable—the pressure-fermented wines being higher in volatile acidity and more subject to bacterial spoilage. Control of temperature as a means of maintaining a slow rate of fermentation is more rational (see Saller 1955).

Ribéreau-Gayon *et al.* (1963) have shown increased quality of white wines prepared from musts heated to 65° to 75°C (149° to 167°F) before fermentation. This may be true of musts infected with *Botrytis* only. This result should be accepted with caution for California conditions.

AGING AND FINISHING

Racking should be done as soon as fermentation is complete, usually in early December or *sooner* in warm cellars. The free sulfur dioxide content should be maintained at 20−25 mg/liter in California white table wines to prevent darkening of the color, though high acid wines require less. The reducing sugar content of *dry* white wines should not be above 0.12 g/100 ml. Spoilage of wines with residual sugar may occur unless special attention is given to their keeping. Rapid clarification by chilling, fining, centrifugation, and close-filtration is employed. Storage under constant low temperature conditions is also helpful. Prevention of oxygen contact with wine is desirable. Tanks should be kept full or blanketed with CO_2. When wine treatment causes oxygen pickup, sparging with nitrogen may be appropriate. A slight residual CO_2 in the wine can improve the flavor.

A problem results from the near complete exclusion of air from a white wine. Phenols, high molecular weight anthocyanins with aryl substitution at the 4 position, tend to oxidize to colored species. Normally, this occurs early in the life of the wine; however, if the wine is kept anaerobic, then it can occur during or after final stabilization and bottling. Simpson (1977) suggests addition of hydrogen peroxide to the sample to determine if a treatment is required. Polyvinylpolypyrrolidone (PVPP) is the usual prevention or cure.

The addition of high grade tannin is occasionally advisable early in the aging process in order to stabilize the wine. It should be white USP tannin. The amount required is usually less than 0.05 g/100 ml. Any excess can be removed later by fining with gelatin. Use of approved procedures to remove excess iron and copper is often advisable (see pp. 318 and 539−541).

Aging and cellar operations such as fining, racking, centrifugation, filtration, refrigeration to remove excess tartrates, and other operations are similar to those previously described for red wines. Stabilization by heating to 60°−61.1°C (140°−142°F) with bentonite may be useful in clarifying wines of high nitrogen content (pp. 315−317). White wines are seldom marketed with detectable bottle bouquet. The desideratum today is that they be fresh and fruity.

SWEET TABLE WINES

Sweet sauterne requires additional treatment. This type may be made from very sweet grapes and the fermentation arrested by racking before fermentation is complete and adding a dose of sulfur dioxide (250 mg/liter or more) and chilling, racking or centrifuging, and rough filtration.

Dry wines may be sweetened after fermentation and aging by adding sweet reserve. Adding muté results in wines with higher levels of sulfur dioxide. White dessert wines can be used for sweeteners but a dessert wine character can result. High quality grape juice concentrate made from "wiped film" or "falling film" concentrators also can be used to sweeten the dry wines to a desirable level of sugar.

Microbiological stability is achieved by membrane filtration and less desirably by use of sorbic acid for wines with low sugar levels. For the more viscous sweet sauterne types, cellulose filters are more appropriate. Asbestos pad filtration (not recommended) should be followed by a membrane filtration.

Non-grape sugars cannot be used for sweetening California table wines.

Recommendations for commercial production of wines from botrytised grapes in California have been given by Nelson and Nightingale (1959) (see p. 159 for the process). See Dormontal (1930) for the French process. Nelson *et al.* (1963) developed a technique for the large-scale production of spores of *Botrytis cinerea* Pers. The spores could be stored for at least ten months without appreciable reduction in viability.

Mucic acid is a by-product of botrytis mold. It reacts with calcium to form insoluble precipitates which deposit slowly. Calcium carbonate treatment is the suggested method of stabilization (Würdig 1977).

The use of special yeasts in the production of sweet table wines has not yet been brought to commercial perfection. The results of Peynaud (1956–1957) for Bordeaux musts would indicate preferential use of *Saccharomyces bayanus* for dry wines and its avoidance (or that of *S. bailii*) for sweet table wines. What is true for one area may not be true for another.

California dry sauterne should contain less than 1% of sugar; California sauterne, less than 3% and more than 2%; and California chateau type, more than 6%. French Sauternes usually have more than 10% reducing sugar.

STABILIZATION

Dry, white table wines in California should become permanently clear, i.e., stable, during the first year's aging. For sweet types it may be necessary to stabilize them by flash pasteurization to about 61.1°C

(142°F). This may be followed by holding them at about 54.4°C (130°F) for 24 to 48 hr, accompanied by about 100 mg/liter of sulfur dioxide. A bentonite fining is followed in 48 hr by racking, cooling, and filtering. Or, the wine is stabilized by flash pasteurization to 71.1° to 85°C (160° to 185°F) followed by cooling, refrigeration for several days to remove tartrates and colloids (or by ion-exchange treatment), fining, and filtration. These procedures are more desirable from the clarity than the quality point of view.

The first of the two methods removes colloids and some metals, particularly copper. Check the stability of white wines as directed in Chap. 15.

In stubborn cases, it may be necessary to fine with Cufex or other permissible procedures as described in Chap. 6 and 15, to remove heavy metals and certain unstable colloids; in fact, both pasteurization and treatment for metal removal may be be necessary with some wines, particularly those of certain years. However, only necessary processing should be done.

REFERENCES[1]

AMERINE, M.A. and JOSLYN, M.A. 1970. Table Wines: The Technology of Their Production, 2nd Edition. University of California Press, Berkeley, Los Angeles.

AMERINE, M.A. and OUGH, C.S. 1957. Studies on controlled fermentations. III. Am. J. Enol. Vitic. 8, 18-30.

BAYLY, F.C. 1974. Treatment of white juice prior to fermentation. Wynboer 509, 18-19.

BENVEGNIN, L., CAPT, E. and PIGUET, G. 1951. Traité de Vinification, 2nd Edition. Librairie Payot, Lausanne.

BERG, H.W. and AKIYOSHI, M. 1956. Some factors involved in browning of white wines. Am. J. Enol. Vitic. 7, 1-7.

DORMONTAL, C. 1930. Sauternes. J. Bière, Bordeaux.

GEISS, W. 1952. Gezügelte Gärung. Joh. Wagner und Söhne, Frankfurt.

NELSON, K.E. and NIGHTINGALE, M.S. 1959. Studies in the commercial production of natural sweet wines from botrytised grapes. Am. J. Enol. Vitic. 10, 135-141.

NELSON, K.E., KOSUGE, T. and NIGHTINGALE, A. 1963. Large-scale production of spores to botrytise grapes for commercial natural sweet wine production. Ibid. 14, 118-128.

OUGH, C.S. 1969. Substances extracted during skin contact with white musts. I. General wine composition and quality changes with contact time. Ibid. 20, 93-100.

---

[1]Titles have been translated only for nonwestern European languages.

OUGH, C.S. and AMERINE, M.A. 1960. Studies on controlled fermentations. IV. *Ibid. 11,* 5-14.

OUGH, C.S. and BERG, H.W. 1974. The effect of two commercial pectic enzymes on grape musts and wines. *Ibid. 25,* 308-311.

OUGH, C.S., BERG, H.W. and AMERINE, M.A. 1969. Substances extracted during skin contact with white musts. II. Effect of bentonite additions during and after fermentation on wine composition and quality. *Ibid. 20,* 101-107.

OUGH, C.S. and GROAT, M.L. 1978. Particle nature, yeast strain, and fermentation temperature interactions on fermentation rates in grape juice. Appl. Envir. Microbiol. *35,* 881-885.

PEYNAUD, E. 1956-1957. Les problèmes microbiologiques de la vinification et de la conservation des vins blancs doux. Vignes Vins *51,* 5-7; *52,* 11-13; *54,* 8-12; *55,* 13-15.

RIBÉREAU-GAYON, J., CASSIGNARD, R., SUDRAUD, P., BLOUIN, J. and BARTHE, J.C. 1963. Sur la vinification en blanc sec. Compt. Rend. Acad. Agric. France *49,* 509-512.

RIBÉREAU-GAYON, J., PEYNAUD, E. and SUDRAUD, P. 1976. Traité d'Oenologie. Sciences et Techniques du Vin. Vol. III. Vinifications. Transformations du Vin. Dunod, Paris.

RIBÉREAU-GAYON, P., LAFON-LAFOURCADE, S. and BERTRAND, A. 1975. Le bourbage des moûts de vendange blanche. Connaiss. Vigne Vin *9,* 117-139.

SALLER, W. 1955. Die Qualitätsverbesserung der Weine und Süssmoste durch Kälte. Verlag Sigurd Horn, Frankfurt.

SIMPSON, R.F. 1977. Oxidative pinking of white wines. Vitis *16,* 286-294.

SINGLETON, V.L. 1969. Browning of wines. Wynboer *455,* 13-14.

TROOST, G. 1972. Die Technologie des Weines, 4th Edition. E. Ulmer, Stuttgart.

WÜRDIG, G. 1977. Apparition de l'acide mucique dans le moût provenant de raisins attaqués de Botrytis. Bull. OIV *50* (551) 50-56.

9

Production of Sherry

Sherry is one of the more important California wine types. White wines of low acidity containing unfermented sugar readily develop on exposure to air a characteristic rancio flavor. The excessive caramelized odor of some baked sherries is different (Joslyn and Amerine 1964).

California has three types of sherry. The first is flor sherry similar to that of Jerez de la Frontera in Spain which owes its characteristic flavor and bouquet to the growth and action of flor yeasts either on the wine's surface or submerged in the wine. Similar types are produced in Australia, California, Canada, the Jura region of France, the Soviet Union, and South Africa. The second type owes its flavor and bouquet to baking. This type resembles the wine of the island of Madeira. The third type is that which is aged in small cooperage for several years without flor yeast or baking. The aged, nonflor sherries of Australia and California are of this type, as are the olorosos of Jerez and some of the wines of Banyuls in the south of France and the Prioratos of northern Spain.

Dry sherries are used traditionally as appetizers while the sweeter types are more suited to accompany desserts.

BAKED SHERRY

The origin of the baked sherry process is not definitely known. Amerine and Twight (1938), Marquis (1936) and Twight (1936) suggest that it may have been an unsuccessful attempt by a California wine maker to produce wines similar in flavor and bouquet to certain kinds of Spanish sherry. It is known that some California sherry in the last century was baked in glass hot houses in barrels or puncheons, heat being furnished by the sun. Later, artificially-produced heat was employed.

The principal sherry-producing areas in California are in the San Joaquin Valley and the Lodi district.

Grapes

The Palomino is grown in California as in Spain for sherry production. It is low in acidity but the sugar content is acceptable for sherry, when well ripened. It is neutral in flavor and aroma and browns easily, according to Berg and Akiyoshi (1956). Also used in California are other white varieties available in abundance such as Thompson Seedless, grown extensively in the San Joaquin Valley for raisin production and for fresh shipment for table use; Malaga, an important white table and shipping variety; Emperor, a shipping grape of light red skin color and white juice; and Tokay (Flame Tokay), a red grape of white juice grown extensively in the Lodi area. In New York and other eastern states, labrusca varieties characterized by their pronounced varietal flavor are used. By the Tressler method the foxy flavor is partially eliminated (p. 489).

The grape variety is probably of less importance in the making of baked sherry than in the making of any other California wine, because the flavor and bouquet of the final product depend chiefly on the baking process. Muscat of Alexandria should not be used, however, because sherry should not possess a muscat varietal flavor.

Picking and Delivery

The grapes for sherry making should be well ripened, as the final acid taste should not be as high as for table wines. Berg (1956) made sherries with pH values adjusted to 4.0, 3.8, 3.6, 3.4, and 3.2. Experienced tasters rated the sherry of pH 3.2 highest and those of 3.4 and 3.6 and 4.0 successively lower. One defect of the Palomino variety is its relatively high pH.

Grapes for sherry are harvested by hand into large pans or lug boxes and transferred to gondola trucks for delivery to the winery, or are harvested by machine. In the latter case, it is desirable to destem and crush on the machine moving through the vineyard or at a field installation. Sulfur dioxide should be added immediately to control bacteria and oxidation.

Crushing

Sherry making in California is usually a large-scale operation. Grapes are crushed and stemmed at the winery in the same manner as for other wines (p. 257). Garolla-type crushers and stemmers are usually employed.

It is important that sulfur dioxide be added as soon as possible after crushing to control bacteria and oxidation.

Draining

The maximum amount of juice is separated from the skins in a draining operation as described in the making of white table wines (p. 384). The juice is transferred to fermentors and the skins are usually watered and fermented into distilling material.

Fermentation

The juice, contained in a large, jacketed, stainless steel fermentor, is inoculated with starter and fermented at temperatures of 25°–30°C (77°–86°F).

Usually, the must is fermented dry or to a low sugar content. A small amount of sugar is considered desirable during baking, but is often added later in the form of angelica or fortified sherry material of high sugar content. In a survey of Martini and Cruess (1956), 11 of the 16 cellars fortified at −1° or lower Brix, one at 0° Brix, and two "when dry."

Settling and Racking Before Fortification

It is desirable to allow the wine to settle for a few days after fermentation in order to rid it of the yeast lees before fortification to avoid loss of fortifying spirit in the lees. However, it is not always practicable to allow time for settling, so in many cases the wine is pumped directly from the fermentor to the fortifying room.

Fortification

The new wine is pumped from the fermentor or settling tank into a special tank approved for fortifications, where it is measured and its alcohol content determined by ebullioscope. The Federal gauger, in theory, supervises the actual addition of high proof spirits. He calculates the gallons of high proof spirits to bring the sherry material to the desired alcohol content, usually 17–18% by volume. See Chap. 6 for methods of calculating the amount of high proof spirits needed for fortification.

It is difficult to secure uniform mixing of high proof spirits and wine. The spirits are of lower density than the wine and tend to float. In some wineries the wine is pumped over vigorously during and after addition of the spirits until it is found by analysis that the fortified wine is of a uniform alcohol content throughout the fortifying tank. In most plants, compressed air is used to agitate the mixture vigorously; in some plants, mixing is done by propeller or by a combination of propeller and compressed air. Aeration has the advantages, in addition to its speed, of removing excess carbon dioxide from the wine and of aiding subsequent maturation. Before the Prohibition era, Joslyn and Amerine (1964) state, some wine makers preferred to add the spirits to the fortifying tank before the wine and permit natural mixing of the two. Although there is a slight decrease in total volume when wine and spirits are mixed, the heat of mixing causes a volume increase which, temporarily, nearly cancels the decrease.

After thoroughly mixing, a sample of the fortified wine is carefully analyzed to see if the actual final alcohol content corresponds to the estimated, and a sealed one pint sample set aside. Two such samples, representing fortifications at different periods of the month, are forwarded to the nearest laboratory of the Bureau of Alcohol, Tobacco and Firearms, Department of the Treasury. There are many variations in the details of fortification, such as the type and size of the fortifying tank, the method of adding the spirits, the method of mixing and the period of time the fortified wine is left in the fortifying tank. See Chap. 6 for further information on fortification.

Typical fortification data, after Joslyn and Amerine (1964), are given in Table 9.1. Of interest are the higher Brix degrees of the Sanger pre-Prohibition wines and their low alcohol content before fortification. The newly fortified wine destined to become sherry is known as shermat.

TABLE 9.1. ALCOHOL AND BRIX BEFORE AND AFTER FORTIFICATION OF SHERRY MATERIAL[1]

	Location of Winery, and Years		
	Sanger, 1906−1913	Lodi, 1938−1940	Fresno, 1938−1940
Number of samples	27	53	32
Initial alcohol content			
Range, percent	6.2−13.4	9.8−15.5	10.8−14.2
Average, percent	9.1	12.5	12.2
Initial Brix			
Range, degree	4.0−20.0	....−4.6	−1.7−3.4
Average, degree	11.5	—	1.1
Final Brix			
Range, degree	—	−4.8 to 1.4[2]	−4.3 to −0.5
Average, degree	—	−3.3[2]	−2.3
Final alcohol content			
Range, percent	18.2−23.6	20.1−23.9	20.4−21.2
Average, percent	21.1	20.8	20.7

[1]Source of data: Joslyn and Amerine (1964).
[2]Average and range for 22 samples only.

Settling

During fortification there is rapid flocculation of the yeast and colloids. Therefore, it is desirable to leave the newly fortified wine in the fortification tank for about 24 hr before it is racked and pumped to storage.

However, this is frequently not practicable and the new sherry material is transferred to the storage cellar before settling. In any event, the sooner the newly fortified sherry material is separated from the crude lees (yeast, coagulated colloids, seeds, skins, and other solids) after settling, the better its flavor is and the more rapidly it will mellow during storage. Fornachon *et al.* (1949) point out that, if left on the lees too long yeast autolysis occurs, resulting in an increase in bacterial nutrients and thus making the wine much more susceptible to spoilage by *Lactobacillus trichodes.*

Treatment Before Baking

Usually, the shermat is not aged before baking. Most producers would prefer to age it for at least one year before baking, but economic factors prevent this for competitive sherries.

Only one of the plants in the Martini and Cruess (1956) survey refrigerated the sherry material before baking. Such treatment is usually applied to the baked product. None pasteurized the sherry material before baking. About half of the plants surveyed adjust the sulfur dioxide content before baking. Eleven of the 16 plants did not adjust the pH or total acidity of the wine before baking; one added acid to lower the pH to 3.7, one added acid to give a total acidity of 0.4 g/100 ml, one to give 0.45−0.50% and one to give 0.5% total acidity.

The majority of the plants surveyed, 11, clarified the sherry material with bentonite and filtered the wine before baking. See Chap. 6 for a discussion of fining operations. Where filtration is employed at this stage it is a rough rather than a polishing filtration. The sugar content of the sherry material during baking is important. The presence of a small amount of reducing sugar is generally considered necessary for satisfactory baking, as it shortens the time required, and caramelization of the sugar improves the flavor. The reducing sugar content actually used in the industry varies from 1.0 to 2.2% for dry sherry, 2.7 to 3.5% for medium, and 7.5 to 10% for sweet (cream sherry). The majority of California sherry producers surveyed bake their sherry material at about 2% reducing sugar, as determined chemically, and add sweeter sherry or angelica after baking to obtain the desired reducing sugar content. (Note that a Brix degree of −1.0 usually indicates in shermat a wine about 2% in reducing sugar.)

Baking

In California, the usual baking practice consists of heating the wine under conditions which result in slight caramelization of the sugar and a certain degree of oxidation, although the importance of oxidation is not known. It is probably of minor importance in view of the fact that very large, relatively impervious concrete and metal tanks are now used for baking. On the other hand, in baking by the Tressler process in eastern states, very extensive oxidation probably occurs. The time necessary for the desired changes is dependent upon the temperature of baking and access of air. Contact with iron or copper during baking should be avoided, because they may impart metallic tastes and cause stability problems. Baking also brings about a blending of the brandy used in the fortification and the wine.

Formerly, a few wineries baked some of their sherry material in 190 to 760 liter (50 to 200 gal.) oak containers stored in a heated room, usually 48.9°C (120.0°F) for 4 to 6 months. Evaporation loss is heavy in this method, one cellar reporting a loss of 5.7 to 6.6% per year. Because of the high cost of handling small wooden containers, most California wineries use large lined steel, stainless steel, concrete, or wood tanks of capacities up to 7550 hl (200,000 gal.) for baking. Evaporative and other losses are small for these large containers. Lined steel tanks are now used by several wineries for baking. A heat-resistant lining is necessary.

The methods of heating the wine vary considerably but fall into two classes, namely internal (in the tank) heaters and outside heaters. Usually the in-tank heaters consist of steam- or hot water-heated stainless steel coils. To avoid excessive scorching and sticking of baked-on wine solids to the coils, their temperatures should not exceed 85°C (185°F). The coils are usually placed near the bottom of the tank and about one foot from the walls. Convection currents are set up by the rising heated wine; but slow circulation of the wine by pump helps to minimize local overheating. An automatic temperature recorder-regulator should be placed on each large tank.

On completion of baking, the hot sherry is passed through a regenerative heat exchanger where it is cooled by a stream of unheated sherry material on its way to a baking tank. In some plants, the wine is heated continuously in a heat interchanger outside the tank and returned to the tank. Temperature is maintained automatically. In a few plants, the maximum cooking temperature is not maintained continuously, the wine being brought to that temperature and heating discontinued until the wine drops during a period of several days to 50°C (122°F) when it is again heated. In a few plants the sherry cooking tanks are located in a heated room.

The length of baking required varies more or less indirectly with the temperature, that is, the higher the baking temperature the shorter the time of baking. For example, in the survey made by Berg (1951), 22 cellars using concrete tanks baked at 54.4° to 60.0°C (130.0° to 140.0°F) for 9 to 20 weeks. The longer periods were used at 54.4°C (130.0°F) and the shorter at 60°C (140°F). In the survey by Martini and Cruess (1956), the length of baking ranged from 45 to 120 days. Sherry producers interviewed in 1965, stated then that baking was less severe than in former years; probably because of the growing consumer preference for sherries of light color and mild flavor.

The character of sherry is usually improved by contact with oak. Six of 16 cellars in the sherry survey used oak chips at the rate of 0.6 to 1.2 g/liter (5.0 to 10.0 lb/1000 gal.) and 2 cellars aged the sherry in oak barrels. The others used no oak. One large plant in 1958 used about 1.2 g/liter (10.0 lb/1000 gal.) of oak chips in $\frac{2}{7}$ of its sherry during the last 30 days of baking. Each 2 tanks of oak-treated sherry are blended with 5 tanks of untreated sherry.

Typical analyses before and after baking as reported in the survey previously mentioned showed that a slight loss in alcohol content and practically no loss in volatile acid and total acid content occurred. However, a sharp decrease in sulfur dioxide content was observed. Joslyn and Amerine (1964) state that during baking aldehydes increase initially but decrease as baking is continued, and rise as the sherry cools. Color increases during baking. Mattick and Robinson (1960) noted an especially high amount of formic acid in wines heated in the presence of oxygen (160 mg/liter). Acetic acid was also comparatively high in the treated wines (at or above the legal limit). Preobrazhenskii (1963) reported the highest temperature used in the Soviet Union was 77.2°C (171.0°F). The typical raw material was a wine of 19% or more alcohol and 4 to 6% sugar. The aldehyde content of the finished product was 120 to 160 mg/liter.

Fremenko et al. (1963) simultaneously heated and aerated shermat to produce what we would call baked sherry but which in the Soviet Union is called "Madera." The quality was considered better than that produced without aeration. Heitz et al. (1951) reported baking in the absence of oxygen resulted in wines with a special low-aldehyde flavor.

Warkentin (1970) patented a process of baking wine to which had been added ascorbic, isoascorbic or other reductive acids. These compounds could function as reducing agents under anaerobic conditions or as autocatalytic agents for oxidation under aeration conditions.

Usually, taste is the principal criterion of judging when baking is adequate, although color comparison is also used in some plants. In a few wineries, baking is done at a certain temperature for a definite period for all sherries. One plant tests the sherry qualitatively for hydroxymethylfurfural as a check on the taste of the baked product (p. 226).

Cooling and Stabilization

Of 16 plants surveyed in 1956, 10 allowed the sherry to cool naturally after baking; 4 cooled rapidly by heat interchanger, generally using the ingoing sherry material to cool the outgoing baked sherry. Most sherry producers rely on the baking to stabilize the finished product against hazing or clouding in the bottle by colloids precipitated by heat, although a few plants flash pasteurize the baked sherry at 82.2° to 85.0°C (180.0° to 185.0°F). Theoretically, the long heating at baking temperature should precipitate all of the heat-coagulable colloids.

The customary clarification of the new sherry with bentonite has a very definite stabilizing effect as it removes most of the protein, according to Kean and Marsh (1956). In a typical case, the total protein content of a wine was reduced from an original of 78 to 2 mg/liter by addition of 600 mg/liter of bentonite.

Koch (1957) has reported that all wines heated to 75°C (167°F) in his experiments were practically heat stable. All commercial wines treated with bentonite and examined by him were protein-free. Heat-treated wines were also stable, but contained some protein and were fuller bodied to the taste than the same wines clarified with bentonite. Kielhöfer (1951) found that clarification with bentonite reduced the total nitrogen content of the wine 9 to 59 mg/liter. Holden (1955) states that bentonited dessert wines remain as stable as those that have been heat treated. The general experience of commercial producers of California sherries is that clarification of new sherries with bentonite stabilizes them against clouding by heat-degraded substances.

Clarification

The cooled sherry is racked from any sediment that forms during heating and subsequent settling. The amount of bentonite required varies with the cloudiness of the wine from about 240 mg/liter (2 lb/1000 gal.) for fairly clear wine to 600 or more mg/liter (5 or more lb/1000 gal.) for very cloudy wine. Bentonite is also useful in case of failure of attempted clarification with gelatin and tannin or with casein. See Chap. 6 for further information on bentonite.

After clarification, the sherry is racked and filtered as described in Chap. 6. Of 16 plants reporting in the survey previously mentioned, 8 filtered twice, 6 three times, and 2 only once. When carbon is used, it is customary to filter the treated wine twice in order to completely remove all carbon particles. In addition, the sherry is usually given a polishing filtration before bottling.

Aging

Most California sherry is bottled or shipped in bulk after aging for a relatively short time. The majority of the plants in the survey previously mentioned age their competitive sherries less than 6 months and premium quality sherries for 2 to 3 years or longer.

Cooperage for aging in these wineries ranged from 190-liter (50-gal.) oak barrels to concrete, lined metal, or stainless steel tanks of large capacity.

Although sherry is greatly improved by aging in oak, care in the use of new oak containers is required to avoid over "oakiness."

In order to stabilize the wine against deposition of cream of tartar and hazing or clouding on chilling, it is customary to hold it near the freezing point, about $-8.9°$ to $-7.8°C$ ($16.0°$ to $18.0°F$) for 2 to 3 weeks and to filter while cold. The equipment and procedure are discussed in Chap. 6. Treatment of wines, including sherry, with ion exchange resins to replace much of the potassium with sodium or hydrogen ions is practiced by some wineries. See pp. 301–305.

Color Adjustment

Some of the competitive sherries produced in California are partially decolorized with activated carbon. The taste and color of sherries that have undergone treatment with activated carbon are less desirable than those of wines not so treated. The decolorizing carbon is usually added during refrigeration, although in some plants it is added after and in some before refrigeration. The carbon powder is usually added as a slurry in wine. However, in at least one large plant it is added dry. It is left in the wine from 24 hr to as long as 30 days; in most plants 24 hr only. Filter aid is added before or during filtration; the amount reported varies from 240 to 1080 mg/liter (2 to 9 lb/1000 gal.), depending upon the condition of the wine. If filter aid is not added, fine particles of carbon are likely to pass through the filter. The amount of carbon used in the various plants varies greatly and, in a given plant, according to the result desired. As little as 30 mg/liter (0.25 lb/1000 gal.) has been used by one producer largely for reduction of off-flavor, although 240 mg/liter (2 lb or more/1000 gal.) is more often employed, if color reduction is also desired. Another plant adds 120 to 180 mg/liter (1.0 to 1.5 lb/1000 gal.) toward the end, and another uses 120 to 240 mg/liter (1 to 2 lb/1000 gal.) 1 to 3 days before the end of the refrigeration period. Another plant uses 240 mg/liter (2 lb/1000 gal.) as a routine addition and an additional 0.96 to 1.8 g/liter (8.0 to 15.0 lb) later if severe reduction in color is required.

The legal aspects of excessive reduction in color should be considered (p.

559). In one plant, a preliminary clarification with caseinate and bentonite, or gelatin and bentonite is given. In this case the clarified wine is racked and filtered before treatment with carbon, and the carbon is used after refrigeration. Usually one filtration is given to remove the carbon and a polishing filtration is applied before bottling or before bulk shipment.

Blending

After the sherry has been baked, stabilized, and cleared, various lots are blended in order to produce final products that will be as uniform in appearance, flavor, and bouquet as possible from year to year. Uniformity is a well-known characteristic of Spanish sherries, attained by use of the solera fractional blending system.

A reasonable continuity of character of the final wine in California is secured by following a fairly rigid program of processing and blending. The wines going into the blend are accurately analyzed and any necessary adjustment made with respect to acidity or other component.

Careful attention should be given to tasting of all major lots of sherry. By careful comparison with samples of previous blends an attempt is made to match the flavor, bouquet, and color by blending. It is advantageous to make up small blends in the laboratory to determine in advance as accurately as possible how much of each wine is required in the final blend. Color may be judged by eye, although use of a colorimeter may be helpful. Composition of the two wines can be matched on the basis of chemical analysis. Taste and bouquet, however, must be matched as nearly as possible by sensory tests made by experienced persons. The plant should not rely entirely upon the judgment of a single person. See p. 672, Amerine et al. (1959), and Amerine and Roessler (1976).

Mixing of the wines in the blend is usually accomplished by pumping over or by mechanical stirrers. The blend should be tested for cold and heat stability and analyzed for copper and iron content. In case too much of either metal is present the wine should be treated to remove the excess. See Chap. 6 and 15. Calcium should be determined also if the plant has had difficulty with calcium tartrate deposition.

A fractional blending system is used in a few instances. In this method the sherry is aged in oak puncheons or small tanks and only part of the contents of several different containers is removed for use in a blend. The wine removed is replaced with newer wine of the same type. Usually not more than 50% of the contents of each container should be removed and not more than twice a year. Continuity of character is thereby maintained. A few cellars do follow this practice, particularly in the production of blends of flor sherry. See Amerine et al. (1959) and Baker *et al.* (1952) for further discussion of blending and evaluating wines.

Citric acid is the usual acid employed for adjusting the acidity. It also prevents clouding due to iron if sufficient acid is added.

Addition of Sulfur Dioxide

As sherry is very susceptible to spoilage by *Lactobacillus trichodes* the sulfur dioxide content of the final blend should be brought to 100 mg/liter.

Excess Metals

It is believed by some that sherry will tolerate a much higher content of copper than will other wines and that much of the copper gained during processing is lost in the lees formed during refrigeration. However, Fessler (1952) recommends that no copper be permitted in finished wines. Of the 16 plants reporting in the 1956 survey, three set the desired limit for copper content of sherry at 0 mg/liter; one at 0.1 mg/liter; five at 0.2 mg/liter; two 0.3 mg/liter; one 0.4 mg/liter; two 0.5 mg/liter; and one 1.0 mg/liter. The limits suggested for iron content were: one plant, 1.5; two, 2.5−4.0; two, 4.0; one, 4.5; three, 5.0; one, 7; one, 8; two, 10; and one, less than 3.0 mg/liter.

Copper is usually removed by Cufex. If the iron content is excessive, citric acid is added in sufficient amount to prevent iron casse. One plant uses 360 mg/liter (3 lb/1000 gal.) for this purpose.

Those reporting in the survey set the limit for calcium content of sherry within the range of 60 to 100 mg/liter. Its concentration is reduced during refrigeration or can be brought to any desired level by use of ion exchange resin in the sodium or hydrogen form. For further discussion of calcium instability and removal of excess calcium see pp. 541−543 and Warkentin (1955).

It is of interest that 3 of the plants in the 1956 survey stabilized sherry for metals just before refrigeration; 11 just before bottling; 1 before baking and 2 did not treat the wine for metal stabilization.

The baked and stabilized sherry should be aged at least one year in small cooperage, preferably in oak ovals, puncheons, sherry butts, or barrels to develop flavor and smoothness. If aging is conducted in large tanks, three years' aging is none too much. However, most California sherry is bottled and marketed soon after baking and finishing.

Finishing

The sherry is given a polishing filtration before bottling or shipment in bulk. Care should be taken to use only filter pads that do not contribute calcium or asbestos to the wine. In the survey previously mentioned, the majority of the wineries reporting filtered their sherry directly into a bottling tank.

Sherry is commonly shipped from one winery to another in California or out of state by tank car or by tank truck.

Bottling

Most California sherry is bottled at the winery today, a situation much different from the case early in the postrepeal period. Bottling equipment and bottling have been discussed in Chap. 6. The bottles are usually closed with screw caps. In some cases, such as for premium sherries, special corks that may be removed without a cork puller and readily used for reclosure are employed.

Owing to fortification and oxidation, sherry, unlike table wines, is not damaged by moderate exposure to air, and therefore may be left in a partly filled bottle for several weeks, as is often customary in the home.

A considerable amount of sherry is made in New York and other states in the eastern United States. See Chap. 12.

AUSTRALIA AND SOUTH AFRICA

The production of nonflor sherries in Australia according to Fornachon (1959) of Adelaide, South Australia is as follows:

1. A fortified dry or sweet wine is made in the usual way with fortification to between 19 and 20% of alcohol by volume. The sugar content of these wines varies from less than 1% to over 5% depending on the type of sherry being made. The titratable acidity is normally between 0.4 and 0.55 g/100 ml (as tartaric) and the pH is between 3.4 and 3.9.
2. After the gross lees have settled, the wine is racked and is again racked once or twice during the first year and clarified by fining with bentonite if necessary.
3. After clarification, the wine is racked into oak "hogsheads" (casks of about 65 imperial gallons, i.e., about 290 liters (78 U.S. gal.) which are stored in the warmest part of the winery until the wine is considered sufficiently aged. Sometimes a special building of corrugated iron is kept for use as a sherry house, but artificial heating is not used and the temperature is not controlled. Maturation of the wine may take from 1 or 2 up to 4 or 5 years or more according to the quality of the wine, the conditions of storage and the opinion of the wine maker. During this period the wine is usually racked once a year and in some cases the casks are allowed to become slightly ullaged (not completely full).

4. Sulfur dioxide is used during fermentation and usually again at the first or second racking. Some wine makers continue to determine and adjust the sulfur dioxide content of the wine during maturation while others do not.
5. The matured sherry is racked and blended if necessary to adjust the sugar content and fined or filtered. It is usually refrigerated, racked and filtered cold some time before bottling.

The making of the "brown sherry" in South Africa is similar to that of producing nonflor sherry in Australia except that gypsum is added to the must before fermentation. Theron and Niehaus (1947−48) state that brown or South African oloroso-type sherry is made about as follows:

Must for brown sherry is drawn off the skins after fermentation has begun and a cap formed. Gypsum is added at the rate of 2 to 4 lb per leaguer, about 1.9 to 3.8 g/liter (15.75 to 31.50 lb/1000 gal.). The lower amount is used with musts of higher acidity. The gypsum causes a more rapid clarification of the young wine, lowers the pH value by increasing the free, fixed acidity and according to Theron and Niehaus promotes the real sherry flavor. Although a flor yeast is used for fermenting the must, the new wine for brown sherry is not aged under flor yeast film. Small casks are preferred and proper attention is given to control of temperature during fermentation. Sulfur dioxide is used in the customary manner, though not to excess. The must is usually fermented completely dry but it may also be fortified with sugar remaining. The fortification is made at the first racking with neutral high proof to 30° to 32° "proof spirit" (17.1 to 18.3% alcohol by volume). It is then matured in a solera, but of course, without the growth of a flor film. Final finishing of the sherry is done in the large cellars of the co-operative "KWV" or other wine merchants. A very sweet wine, Jeripico, is made by fortifying the unfermented, or only slightly fermented, must and aging in the same manner as "brown sherry." It is generally used for blending with drier sherries and appears to be similar to California angelica, at least in composition.

SPANISH SHERRY

Sherry can be produced in Spain in only a delimited area near Cadiz (p. 32). Other information on the sherry industry of Spain is given in Chap. 1.

The sherries of Spain are made in and around Jerez de la Frontera, which lies near the Guadalquivir River between Seville and Cadiz and about ten miles from the ocean. The climate is warm and favorable to the production of well ripened grapes of fairly high sugar content. The word sherry is undoubtedly derived from the name of the principal city in the sherry district, Jerez de la Frontera. According to Gonzalez (1972) Spanish sherry in Spain may be designated by any one of the following words:

"Jerez," "Xerez," "Scheris," and "sherry." The Spanish government has defined and given the limits of the area in which wines that are permitted to bear the name of Jerez de la Frontera are produced. Quoting from the Act, the following statement is of interest: "Article 8. Pursuant to Article 30 of the Statute of Wine, the zone with the right to use the designation 'Jerez-Xerez-Sherry,' shall be within the municipal limits of Jerez de la Frontera, Puerto de Santa Maria and Sanlúcar de Barrameda." See also Anon. (1941, 1950), Berg (1977), Goswell (1968), and Joslyn and Amerine (1964).

The two main varieties grown are the Palomino and the Pedro Ximinez. Only the Palomino can be used for the production of sherry. The Pedro Ximinez is used for the production of P.X., a very sweet wine used to sweeten shipping blends.

The best soil for growing Palomino grapes on the low rolling hills of the Jerez district is a white, gypsiferous one known as *albariza*. It is very high in calcium content. Vines grown on it give a low yield but produce grapes of high quality for sherry production. *Barros* soils are more extensive and are a mixture of limestone soil and clay. They are said to produce much heavier crops than do the *albariza* soils. *Arenas* soils are very sandy, and prevalent in the Sanlúcar district, where the grapes are used in making *manzanilla* wines.

Vines are planted close together, pruned very low, and are grown without irrigation.

Harvesting

According to Castella (1909, 1926) the harvest (Fig. 9.1) usually begins in the Sanlúcar area earlier than in the Jerez de la Frontera district. The soils of Sanlúcar are sandy and the wines usually are lower in body and alcohol content than those of Jerez. The harvest begins in September at Jerez and continues to mid-October. The grapes are cut at the desired maturity (after the main stems have become brown) with short-bladed knives, rather than with clippers. The vineyard is picked over more than once if the grapes are not all of the desired maturity. The former practice of drying the Palomino grapes in the sun for 24 hr has been discontinued because of the labor required.

Grape Processing

Formerly, the grapes were crushed by treading in a shallow rectangular

Courtesy of Pedro Domecq

FIG. 9.1. HARVESTING GRAPES IN SHERRY DISTRICT
Note white soil

vat, lagar, the crushed grapes plastered by sprinkling with yeso, a crude $CaSO_4$, to lower the pH, the juice drained from the lagar into a butt, and the grapes pressed by a hand-operated screw and plate.

Present practice is to crush and stem, partially dejuice in a rotating-screw dejuicer, press in a horizontal, ram-type press, screen the juice by passing through horizontal, rotating, screens, raise the acidity if needed by adding tartaric acid, and add sulfur dioxide.

Fermentation

The juice is settled overnight in tanks and then racked into either butts of about 500 liters (130 gal.) capacity or tanks not exceeding about 110 hl (2900 gal.) for fermentation. Temperature control is not practiced nor is the use of pure cultures of yeast.

During the fermentation of Jerez de la Frontera must, Iñigo *et al.*

(1963), found 13 yeast species but *S. cerevisiae, S. italicus* and *S. chevalieri* were the yeasts primarily responsible for alcoholic fermentation, *S. fermentati* was found in only 1 of 20 musts compared to its appearance in half the musts from Montilla. *Saccharomycodes ludwigii* and *S. delbrueckii* were reported for the first time in Spanish musts. *Candida utilis* also appeared frequently. It is especially notable that flor films appeared within 10 to 12 days of the completion of alcoholic fermentation. Film formation under aerobic conditions is a characteristic of a number of yeasts (see. p. 172).

At the time of the first racking each butt of new wine is carefully tasted, analyzed, and classified into one of three general groups, namely, one, two, and three *rayas*, and the butts marked /, / /, and / / /. Later, the wines are classified again, this time as *palmas, cortados*, and *rayas*. There are several subclasses in each of these major groups. This rather complex system of classification will be described only briefly here.

The *palma* wines possess the composition, flavor, bouquet, and color desired for producing *fino* and *amontillado* sherries. They are pale in color, completely dry, delicate in flavor and bouquet and resemble a young dry white table wine, although of lower acidity. They should contain 14.5−15.5% alcohol and be free of any suggestion of coarseness of flavor and bacterial spoilage. If the alcohol content of the *palma* wine is below 14.5%, neutral high-proof brandy is added to bring it to 14.5−15.5% at the time of the first racking.

Next are the *cortado* wines. These are more generous or bigger wines than the *palmas* and are of higher alcohol content, often of darker color, but free of coarseness of flavor and bouquet. They are the wines from which *oloroso* sherries are made. If one of these wines is still fermenting in late November or early December, racking may be delayed until mid-winter. They are usually of 16% or higher alcohol content, or if below 16% and distinctly of *cortado* type may be fortified to 16% or above. Bobadilla (1947) states that all *cortado* wines were fortified to about 18% alcohol. A wine between a *palma* and a *cortado* may be classed as a *palo cortado*, which may develop into a *fino* during aging, and hence is not fortified.

The *raya* wines constitute a group of lower grade. At time of classification they are often not as far advanced as the *palmas* and *cortados*, and it is not certain whether or not they may develop into something better. Thus, a good, or *una raya* wine may become a *fino* or *oloroso*, although it has not progressed far enough for a *fino* at the time of first classification. A *dos rayas* wine is of lower quality and may be coarse in character, but may develop into an *oloroso* in time. A *tres rayas* wine is of still poorer quality, and may eventually have to be used as distilling material. As with the *palmas* and *cortados,* alcohol may be added to the *rayas* that are too low in this constituent.

After racking, the new wines are usually held several months and examined again before being placed in a solera, and some changes may be made in the previous classification, depending on the development of the wine. During this preliminary storage, flor film develops on wine in many of the butts. Wines in this preliminary storage stage are known as *añada* wines.

The Solera System

Strictly speaking, the term solera means only the final stage in the Jerez aging system. In most Spanish literature all other stages of the system are called *criaderas*, and Bobadilla (1947) calls the entire system a *criaderas-soleras* system. Castella (1909) and Gonzalez (1972) have suggested that solera is derived from the word *suelo*, meaning ground, or floor of the *bodega*, since the butts of the last stage (solera) rest on the floor of the cellar, or on skids a few inches above the floor. However, members of the Spanish sherry trade generally use the term solera to mean the entire system, including all stages, and we so use it in this book.

The following is Castella's (1926) description of a solera:

A solera is a series of butts of sherry in process of maturation or rearing, so arranged as to provide for progressive, fractional blending. It is divided into a varying number of stages; from the final stage is withdrawn the finished wine, whilst young wine is introduced into the earliest stage. Let us suppose for the sake of illustration a solera of 50 butts divided into five stages each containing ten butts is being operated. The butts are of 490 liters (130 gal.) capacity but as they are a little ullaged their net content would be about 430 liters (113 gal.). This solera has been functioning for many years; when first established each stage probably represented a single vintage, but with continual replenishing these have long since lost their original significance.

Stage I contains the oldest wine; from it the finished wine is withdrawn, but in doing so the butts are only partially emptied, not more than one-half being removed in any one year. Withdrawal is usually made twice a year, 94 liters (25 gal.) being removed on each occasion. Butts of stage I are immediately replenished from stage II, which, in turn, is replenished from stage III and so on. Stage V is replenished with young wine or with wine kept as an *añada* for a year or even longer. The usual age is a few months.

The wine thus moves steadily forward through the different stages until its final withdrawal, when it is a complex blend, none of it being less than 5½ years old, but containing in varying proportion still older wine, including very small quantities of every wine that has reached stage I since its establishment.

A solera on the above lines would yield only 19 hectoliters (500 gal.) of finished wine each year, from a stock of 190 hectoliters (5000 gal.). Interest and loss by evaporation[1] render it impossible for a solera wine to be reared at a low price. Nor

---

[1]Gonzalez (1972) reports that the loss in volume by evaporation is about 15 liters (4 gal.) per year for each 380 liters (100 gal.) of wine in the butts, but that it will vary considerably according to ratio of surface exposed to volume, location in the cellar, temperature, and other factors.

is the above an extreme sample. Soleras differ in the number of their stages. For the rapidly developing *manzanillas* of Sanlúcar 3 or 4 stages is the rule. Five or 6 stages are frequent in *fino* soleras at Jerez, although some consist of 8 or 9, turning out as might be expected very expensive wines.

Though it (the solera system) finds its greatest utility in connection with *fino* wines, it is now generally applied to all types [Fig. 9.2]. *Oloroso* and the final stage of *amontillado* soleras, owing to their strength, have no flor on the surface of the wine. With these, the merit lies in the automatic blending and uniformity of product the system assures. In addition to the above, composite soleras are to be met with, destined for the production of special wines of very high price. One of these might be termed a solera of soleras, the youngest stage being replenished with a blend of finished wines from other soleras; such complex soleras comprise very few stages.

Courtesy of Wisdom and Warter

FIG. 9.2. SHERRY BODEGA SHOWING OLOROSO SOLERA

In replenishing one stage from the preceding, the Spanish do not merely add 95 liters (25 gal.) from one butt to another butt in the next stage. A part of each butt in a given stage goes into every butt of the next stage. The amount taken from a butt in stage II, for example, will be divided among all the butts in stage I, in order to ensure uniformity throughout the solera. Each butt of stage III will be divided among all butts of stage II, and so on.

To accomplish the transfer, wine is drawn off by syphon and special pitchers or directly into pitchers from a small bunghole near the bottom of the butt. It is poured into the butts of the following stage by means of a funnel and a copper tube, with perforations near the bottom, which is inserted into the bunghole. Wine poured through this tube flows out sidewise through the perforations, thus disturbing neither the lees nor the flor film. In large operations the wine is pumped from the butts into a tank, mixed, and then returned to the next stage by pump.

The wine is rather freely exposed to the air in the butts, the bungholes being loosely fitted with large corks, according to both Gonzalez (1972) and Castella (1922). This is done in the belief that too abundant an air supply results in flatness of flavor rather than in development of the pungent bouquet and flavor of a *fino*.

Marcilla *et al.* (1936) give the following analysis of a Spanish *fino* wine of high quality before final fortification (per 100 ml): alcohol 16.5% by volume; glycerol, 0.41 g; aldehydes, 0.0294 g; volatile esters, 0.051 g; total acid as tartaric, 0.59 g; volatile acid as acetic, 0.022 g; total sugars 0.095 g, total ash 0.584 g, potassium sulfate 0.478 g, total extract, 2.57 g; and total sulfur dioxide, 0.0058 g. They found the composition of five wines of a typical solera to be as follows:

Stage	Alcohol %	Glycerol g/100 ml	Aldehydes g/liter
New wine	15.70	0.76	0.020
Third criadera	15.80	0.64	0.048
Second criadera	15.45	0.63	0.038
First criadera	15.60	0.45	0.189
Solera (oldest)	16.30	0.34	0.310

Bobadilla (1943) states that the following conditions should be observed in establishing and operating a *fino* solera: (1) there should be abundant surface of wine exposed to air in each butt, i.e., the head space should be not less than 20%; (2) the temperature should not exceed 25°C (77°F) nor be below 15.6°C (60.0°F), the optimum being about 20°C (68°F); (3) the alcohol content should not be above 15.5% nor below 14.5 %, since above 15.5%, flor film growth may be slow or absent and below 14.5%, acetification is apt to occur; (4) the sulfur dioxide content should not exceed 180 mg/liter; above this level growth of the film is difficult; (5) the tannin content must be very low (not above 0.01%), else the color is apt to be dark and the flavor coarse; (6) the iron content should be low as there are indications that excessive amounts interfere with film growth (and may cause clouding); and (7) the pH value should be between 2.8 and 3.5; below pH 2.8 film formation is difficult; above 3.5

there is grave danger of bacterial spoilage. In Spain, plastering or addition of tartaric acid usually ensures a pH within this range.

Wines destined for flor sherry should not contain over 110 mg/liter of total sulfur dioxide nor more than 6 or 7 free, according to Abramov and Potyaka (1965).

The Flor Film

Flor yeasts form a film over the wine in the butts usually within a few weeks after completion of fermentation. It is composed of cells of the same yeast that fermented the must. If the film is slow to develop, transfer is made from a butt of wine covered with a vigorous film. Bobadilla (1943) advises such transfer as regular practice.

At first, islands of film form. These grow and coalesce to form a smooth, thin, continuous film. Within a few weeks it thickens and becomes wrinkled. With abundant air supply the young film is nearly white in color. Old film is apt to be gray and with scanty air supply may become light brown. As the film thickens and becomes wrinkled, portions break away and sink to the bottom of the container, to be replaced by growth of new film. The yeast sediment slowly autolyzes, a process that undoubtedly affects the flavor and bouquet of the wine.

The primary products of the film yeasts from ethyl alcohol are acetaldehyde, 2,3-butylene glycol and acetoin, according to Saavedra and Garrido (1963).

Once a flor solera is established, the film is allowed to grow relatively undisturbed on the wines in all stages of the solera. The butts are seldom emptied; hence the sediment, formed of film that has settled to the bottom of the butts, is allowed to accumulate. Amerine (1948) states that butts may be emptied and cleaned after many years' sediment has been allowed to collect.

Blending and Finishing

The usual sherry exported from Jerez is a blend, often a rather complex one. The producers of well-known, established brands of sherry attempt to make wines that are uniform in color, bouquet, flavor, and composition regardless of the year of bottling. In addition to the exported brands, a considerable amount of sherry is blended on order. No wine is sold as it comes from the solera. Blending is the art of making sherry. Many different soleras, besides blending wines, may be used.

There are four main shipping classifications: *fino, amontillado, oloroso* and *brown* sherries. They all may be of varying sweetness and color though usually the *finos* are the driest and the *browns* the sweetest.

Color usually increases the same way. In making a *fino* shipping blend, wine may be drawn from a number of *fino* soleras. In an *amontillado* blend, a sweet wine such as *Pedro Ximinez* and *color wine* are usually used; while with *olorosos* and *browns*, it is customary to use *amontillado*, *oloroso*, *Pedro Ximinez* and *color wine*. *Mitad y mitad*, an aged 50-50 blend of high proof brandy and *fino*, is added to all types to boost the alcohol content to the shipping strength of 16 to 21%.

Requisite amounts of the various wines to be used in the blends are usually drawn from the last stage (often termed the first stage in Spain) of the soleras and blended in a tank of suitable size. If needed, the total acidity is raised by the addition of either citric or tartaric acid.

The blend is usually clarified and filtered. Common clarifying agents are gelatin, isinglass, Spanish clay and bentonite; Gonzalez and others state that egg whites are also used.

A smaller shipping solera for the more popular types is maintained by the larger firms. From this solera the final blend may be given a polishing filtration. Before bottling or transferring to shipping containers the sulfur dioxide content is usually brought to 75 mg/liter to prevent the growth of *Lactobacillus trichodes*.

Stabilizing

Refrigeration of the wines to stabilize them against deposition of tartrates and clouding of bottled wine is commonly employed for Spanish sherry. Either refrigeration alone or a combination of refrigeration and ion exchange (in either the sodium or magnesium form) is used to tartrate stabilize. For tartrate stabilization studies on Spanish sherries see Berg (1960).

Spoilage

If the alcohol content is too low acetification may occur. Bobadilla (1947) and Cruess (1948) recommended that the alcohol content be at least 15% by volume. Occasionally, lactic bacteria develop, as 15—15.5% alcohol is not sufficient to prevent their activity. Fornachon (1943) found that lactic bacteria cannot grow in wine of pH 3.4 or lower. Sulfur dioxide can also be used as a preventive; however, this reduces the free acetaldehyde content.

Characterization of Spanish Sherries

The usual classes of Spanish sherry in commerce are the following: *fino*, a very pale, very dry sherry, light in body and of characteristic, slightly pungent bouquet and flavor; *vino de pasto*, similar to *fino* and made from *palma* wine, usually somewhat milder than *fino*; *amontillado*, a *fino* that has aged for a long period in wood and lost much of its original *fino* character, darker than a *fino*, very dry to slightly sweet; *manzanilla*, a dry *fino* wine of light color and delicate flavor, produced near Sanlúcar de Barrameda, often not fortified; *oloroso*, wine of deeper color than *fino*, usually fairly sweet, not aged under flor yeast film, sometimes called "golden" or "East India" sherry in commerce; and *amoroso*, a wine which is similar to the *oloroso*, often quite dark in color, and not aged under flor film.

INVESTIGATIONS AND PRACTICE IN CALIFORNIA

The following investigations have been conducted in the former laboratories of the Food Technology Department at Berkeley, the laboratories of the Viticulture and Enology Department at Davis, and in several California wineries. See especially Cruess (1943, 1948), Cruess *et al.* (1938), Joslyn and Amerine (1964), Martini (1950), and Strud (1953).

The Yeasts

Hohl and Cruess (1939, 1940) studied 15 distinct strains from more than 50 pure cultures isolated from Spanish sherry and from Château Châlon wine (an Arbois *vin jaune*).

French flor yeasts were included, because in the Arbois district, near Dijon and Beaune in France, they are used in making an unfortified white wine similar to Spanish *fino*. The yeasts have been fully described by Hohl and Cruess (1939, 1940) and a condensed description is given by Cruess (1948): Six spore formers were classified as strains of *Saccharomyces cerevisiae* and four non-sporulating cultures were classified, temporarily at least, as *Torulopsis*. However, these yeasts closely resembled the spore-forming strains of *S. cerevisiae* in other respects. Four of the yeasts produced no to very little fermentation, although they formed films on wine of less than 13% alcohol. Marcilla *et al.* (1936) have given the species names of *Saccharomyces beticus* to the Jerez film yeasts. Fornachon (1953B) and Ough and Amerine (1958) have used Marcilla's designation, *S. beticus*. Iñigo and Bravo (1963) reported that *S. cheriensis* differed from *S. beticus* in rate of formation and utilization of volatile acids during fermentation. Lodder (1970) classifies *S. beticus, S. cheriensis* and *S. oviformis* as *S. bayanus* or *S. capensis* on taxonomic grounds. See also p. 172.

Both the Jerez and the Arbois flor yeasts imparted the characteristic flor flavor and bouquet to wine, although the Arbois yeasts appeared to be somewhat more active than the Jerez yeasts in this respect. In 30°

Brix must, the Jerez yeasts formed from 16.0 to 18.0% alcohol by volume and the Arbois yeasts from 15.9 to 17.4%. For comparison, champagne Ay yeast formed 15.6% alcohol. By syruped fermentation, the Jerez flor yeasts formed from 17.6 to 19.1% and the Arbois flor yeasts 18.2 to 18.8%. The Jerez yeasts generally showed slightly higher average alcohol tolerance than the Arbois yeasts and developed films somewhat more rapidly.

At 20.0° to 22.0°C (68.0° to 71.6°F) all yeasts formed films on white wine. At 27.0° to 30.0°C (80.6° to 86.0°F) film formation was very scant and was absent at 32.0°C (89.6°F). In winery experiments, the films in 190-liter (50-gal.) barrels dropped during the warm summer months and reappeared during the cool fall months, confirming the observations of Gonzalez (1972), Fornachon (1953B) and of many others. Fornachon states that film growth is seldom satisfactory above 22.2°C (72.0°F) under cellar conditions. He states that 20°C (68°F) is optimum for film growth, but that production of flor flavor is often more satisfactory at 15°C (59°F).

Saenko and Sacharova (1959) and Saenko (1964) have recommended a continuous film process in which the temperature is maintained at 18.0° to 20.0°C (64.4° to 68.0°F). Small amounts of new wine are introduced daily under the film to replace that which is removed.

Sulfur Dioxide Tolerance

Hohl and Cruess (1939, 1940) found that the fermentative strains studied by them possessed the usual tolerance of *S. cerevisiae* yeasts to sulfur dioxide in wine and must. Marcilla *et al.* (1936) and Fornachon (1953B) recommend that the sulfur dioxide content not be above 100 mg/liter total because it interferes with development of the flor flavor and bouquet. Williams (1943) opposed the use of any sulfur dioxide as he believed that it lessens the development of flor character.

Effect of Film on Acids

The observations of Schanderl (1936), Marcilla *et al.* (1936), Marcilla (1946), Baker (1945), Saenko (1945), Fornachon (1953B), and Bobadilla (1943) that the film stage of flor yeasts rapidly reduces the volatile acidity (acetic acid content) of wines was confirmed by Cruess and Podgorny (1937). Fixed acidity decreased in laboratory and winery scale experiments as shown in the data given in Table 9.2, for lots of wine in 50-gal. barrels or in butts.

With small lots of wine in flasks, the rate of destruction of fixed acid is much more rapid than in 190-liter (50-gal.) barrels. It is also rapid in tanks when the depth of wine is shallow. The rate is a function of area to

TABLE 9.2. EFFECT OF JEREZ FLOR YEAST FILM ON TOTAL ACIDITY[1]

Winery	Months Under Film	Original Total Acidity as Tartaric g/100 ml	Final Total Acidity as Tartaric g/100 ml
Inglenook	18	0.60	0.38
Italian Swiss Colony	24	0.43	0.37
Solano	23	0.48	0.26

[1]Source of data: Cruess (1948).

volume ratio: the greater the ratio of area exposed to film to volume, the more rapid is the oxidation of fixed acid.

In laboratory scale experiments with small lots of wine, the alcohol content decreased during the film stage but in winery experiments with 50-gal. barrels the alcohol content gradually increased as shown in Table 9.3.

TABLE 9.3. CHANGES IN ALCOHOL CONTENT OF WINE UNDER FLOR FILM IN WINERY EXPERIMENTS[1]

Winery	Months Under Film	Original Alcohol %	Final Alcohol %
Italian Swiss Colony	11	15.80	16.30
Novitiate	20	14.80	15.45
Cresta Blanca	22	14.22	14.70
Cribari	13	15.50	15.90

[1]Source of data: Cruess (1948).

Effect of Sugars and Yeast Nutrients

Fornachon (1953B) states that added sugar is soon fermented by the flor yeast and that such addition is inadvisable as it may delay development of flor character. He recommends that wine to be made into flor sherry have less than 0.20 g/100 ml. See Allen (1939) and Chaffey (1940) for a contrary view which still needs to be checked.

Addition of ammonium phosphate stimulated film formation in Hohl and Cruess' experiments (1939, 1940). Grape concentrate stimulated growth moderately and glucose had very little effect. The effects of various other substances were studied by Freiberg and Cruess (1955). Film formation was satisfactory at pH values of 3.1 to 4.0.

Effect of Yeast Lees on Flavor

In laboratory experiments, relatively large volumes of flor film sediment were added to unfortified and to fortified wine that had been well aged under flor film. The treated wines were stored in well-filled, tightly sealed glass containers for a year. The effect on flavor was favorable and very pronounced. The treated wines possessed much of the characteristic aftertaste of imported Spanish sherries.

At the surface of wines under flor film, the condition is strongly oxidative; but in the wine under the film, a reducing condition exists as evidenced by the bleaching of the color of the wine and measurement of the redox potential (Nielson 1952).

Winery Experiments

Flor sherries were made experimentally in 15 different wineries in 150- to 75,500-liter (40- to 20,000-gal.) lots using 190-liter (50-gal.) barrels of sherry butts in most cases, but tanks or ovals of 5650 to 11,300 liter (1500 to 3000 gal.) capacity were also employed. At least 2 years, and usually 3, were necessary to develop sufficient flor character. Aged wine required less time under flor than new wine. In most experiments the entire contents of the container were fortified when sufficient flor flavor and bouquet had developed.

Acetification occurred in one experiment in which the wine under experiment contained 15% alcohol; but did not occur at 15.5%.

Baking destroyed the flor flavor and bouquet. Aging was found most satisfactory in completely filled, tightly-sealed, oak containers. Excess color was removed in some experimental flor sherries by fining with casein. Bentonite proved very effective for fining flor wines of satisfactory color.

Tank and Barrel Process.—In one plant in which flor sherry was produced on a commercial scale for several years, redwood tanks were used. These were filled with dry Palomino wine to within about two feet of the top and inoculated with flor film. Growth of the film was heavy and development of flor character was rapid. The tanks were equipped with the usual covers fitted with bungholes of customary diameter. The wine was over 15% in alcohol. When the wine had attained sufficient flor character, about ½ the wine in each tank was removed and fortified. New dry Palomino wine replaced that drawn off. Drawing off and replacement were repeated at about four-month intervals; in this manner a modified solera was maintained. The cellar temperature was held artificially within the optimum range for growth of the flor film. The fortified wine was aged in well-filled sherry butts and later used for blending with pale dry baked sherry of mild flavor.

In another plant, the wine under flor was in sherry butts and a portion drawn off at regular intervals for fortification, aging, and blending with unbaked sherry. The portion drawn off was replaced with new wine of similar composition. Several California wineries have made flor sherry in

190-liter (50-gal.) barrels or sherry butts and fortified portions with-drawn at intervals.

Another winery used tanks in a room in which the temperature was controlled. Only a portion of the wine in each tank was withdrawn for fortification at regular intervals and replaced by dry wine of similar composition. The depth of wine in the tanks is such that development of flor character is rapid, as it was found that at too great a depth, de-velopment of flor bouquet was very slow. In all of these cases a modified solera system was used.

SUBMERGED FLOR PROCESS

Experiments have been made in Canada, Australia, and California on production of flor-type sherry without the customary film stage.

Australia and Canada

Fornachon (1953A) obtained very rapid production of aldehyde by shaking suspensions of active cells of *S. bayanus* (flor yeast) in a 14% alcohol solution. In pure nitrogen (that is, under anaerobic conditions) no aldehyde was formed. In a water-alcohol solution of 14% alcohol, equi-librium was reached at about 1200 mg/liter of acetaldehyde. In wine of similar alcohol content, 630 mg/liter of acetaldehyde was attained at equilibrium. These values are above those reached in wines under films.

Fornachon, according to Rankine (1955), also packed a column with oak chips on which he grew flor yeast. This procedure is similar to the process used for impregnating beechwood chips or coke with vinegar bacteria in a vinegar generator. Wine was passed slowly through the column and acquired considerable flor wine character. The column was difficult to operate and the product was not entirely satisfactory.

Crowther and Truscott (1955–56, 1957) in Canada found that by con-tinuously pumping over new wine fermented with flor yeast the wine developed flor wine flavor and bouquet. In later experiments they ob-tained maximum flor character in three weeks and a rise in aldehyde content to 250 mg/liter.

In California

Amerine (1958) and Ough and Amerine (1958) have reported on the rapid production of acetaldehyde in wine by flor yeast under air pressure. The apparatus used was that described by Amerine (1953). It consists of two 90-liter (approximately 23-gal.) stainless steel tanks, capable of withstanding over 689.5×10^3 Pa (100 lb/in.²) internal pressure. It is equipped with temperature control equipment which can maintain 18.3°C (65.0°F) within 0.6°C (1.0°F), stirrers, a source of compressed air,

air filters, air regulatory system, and lines also able to stand a pressure of 689.5 × 10³ Pa (100 lb/in.²).

In one experiment grape concentrate was diluted to 22.5° Brix and fermented to dryness with *S. fermentati* (flor yeast). The new wine was fortified to 14.5% alcohol and maintained at 689.5 × 10³ Pa (100 lb/in.²) air pressure with the yeast in one of the pressure tanks for 3 days and then at 103 × 10³ Pa (15 lb/in.²). The wine was stirred mechanically for 5 min each hour. When the wine reached the desired level of acetaldehyde content about ½ of it was removed and replaced with dry white wine of 14.5% alcohol, and the above process was repeated. During the run, air was allowed to escape from the tank at the rate of 100 ml per min continuously. The wine was fortified to 17.5% alcohol content at the end of each experiment.

A culture of the film stage of *S. fermentati* was used very successfully in another experiment. Also air pressures of 34.5 × 10³, 51.6 × 10³, 69.0 × 10³, 103.0 × 10³, and 138.0 × 10³ Pa (5.0, 7.5, 10.0, 15.0 and 20.0 lb/in.²) were compared. The rate of aldehyde production was greatest at 103 × 10³ Pa (15 lb/in.²) (143 mg/liter per day) and least rapid at 34.5 × 10³ Pa (5.0 lb/in.²) (58 mg/liter per day). In some runs the malic acid decreased and the lactic acid increased, indicating the growth and activity of malolactic bacteria.

There was very little change in pH value, volatile acidity, and total acidity during other runs and only a slight decrease in alcohol. Aldehyde content, however, increased rapidly. An interesting observation was that aldehyde production increased as the number of active yeast cells increased. After 11 more days no further increase in aldehyde was observed. In a typical experiment aldehyde production was at the rate of 77 mg/liter per day; at 1100 to 1200 mg/liter aldehyde production ceased, confirming Guymon and Nakagiri's observation (1955) that at this range of aldehyde content wine yeast cease to ferment.

The intimate and direct relation between yeast count and aldehyde formation is indicated in Fig. 9.3. These data clearly indicate that continuous submerged culture fermentations are possible. Crowell and Guymon (1963) showed such sherries to be very high in diacetyl and acetoin (1.8 to 160 mg/liter of diacetyl and 4.3 to 450 mg/liter of acetoin).

The 1957 experimental wines of Amerine and Ough were aged in 38-liter (10-gal.) oak barrels. After nine months' aging the wines were analyzed. There was very little change in the composition including the aldehyde content and there was no clouding during aging, while flavor and bouquet improved. The experimental wines possessed a marked flor flavor and bouquet. Sugar content was adjusted to a considerable range after fortification; the preferred concentration being 0.5 to 1.5%. Also, the flor wine was blended in various proportions with good quality baked

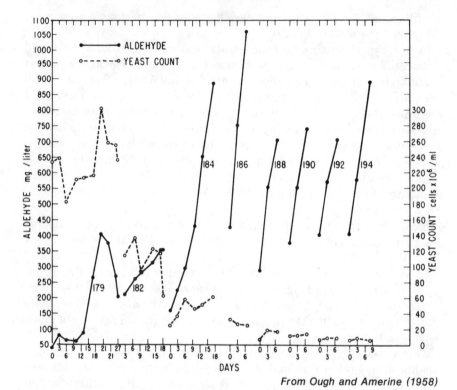

From Ough and Amerine (1958)

FIG. 9.3. CHANGES IN YEAST COUNT AND ALDEHYDE CONTENT DURING SUB-
MERGED CULTURE FERMENTATION

sherry. A blend of 75% of the experimental with 25% of baked sherry
was considered best by an experienced taste panel. High aldehyde content was preferred to low by the taste panel. In this case blends of
experimental flor sherries of 276, 637, and 1002 mg/liter with 25% of
baked sherry were used, although Ough and Amerine (1958) point out
that this observation may have no special practical significance.

Their (1958) recommendations are given below.

1. The process, if used, should be arranged as a continuous system; tanks, lines,
   and other accessories must be constructed to stand 103×10^3 Pa (15 lb/in.²)
   pressure plus a safety factor.
2. A culture from an active flor yeast of good quality can be used to start a
   submerged culture.
3. Alcohol level must be kept between 14 and 15% during aldehyde formation.
4. The wine used should have a pH between 3.2 and 3.4. Slightly lower pH will
   yield a better product.

5. Operating pressure should be kept between 69 × 10³ and 103 × 10³ Pa (10 and 15 lb/in.²).
6. For high quality, aging in oak barrels is probably necessary.
7. Blending will vary according to the wine used, but indications are that a very good product can result from 25% of baked pale dry sherry blended with a high-aldehyde flor sherry with a final sugar level of 0.5 to 1.5%.

In a more recent study, Ough and Amerine (1972) found that the rate of acetaldehyde formation is superior in the range of 3.20 to 3.50 pH.

At present, several California wineries produce wines of high aldehyde content by the discontinuous submerged technique. De Soto (1961) reported on the successful commercial application of the submerged flor culture process. Both a 37-hl (990-gal.) Charmat tank and a 190-hl (5000-gal.) glass lined, steel tank were successfully used. Approximately 6 to 7 weeks were required in both cases to raise the aldehyde level to about 650 mg/liter. DeSoto indicated that they were quite satisfied with the process as to simplicity, feasibility, and quality of the product. We have heard that tanks of from 750 to 3800 hl (20,000 to 100,000 gal.) capacity have been used. The submerged culture process was successfully used under plant conditions by Farafontoff (1964). In contrast to the results of Ough and Amerine (1958) they did not use pressure and aldehyde content peaked at the same time as maximum yeast cell count and decreased thereafter. One reason for the pressure in the Ough and Amerine work was to prevent contamination during long continuous fermentation. Singleton et al. (1964) heated submerged culture flor sherry of high aldehyde content in the hopes of inducing acetal formation and greater odor complexity. The experiment was unsuccessful.

FLOR SHERRY PROCESS IN AUSTRALIA

According to Rankine (1958), the Spanish methods have been adapted to Australia. The first flor cultures were introduced in 1908 by Castella, but the first Australian flor sherry was not marketed until 1930. See Williams (1936) for an early report. The output of this type of wine has steadily increased until about 10% of the fortified wine production is made annually as flor sherry. The full-bodied medium dry flor sherry is more popular than the drier *finos*.

Grapes and Yeasts

The varieties of grapes normally used are Pedro Ximenez, Doradillo, and Palomino (also known as Sweetwater). The Sémillon is often used to soften the higher acidity of the Pedro Ximenez. The amount of Palomino is limited although it was considered the best variety for making *fino*-type sherries.

The sherry is made with a selected strain of flor yeast, usually obtained from the Australian Wine Research Institute. In some of the grape growing areas, flor yeast has become indigenous and causes trouble by its unwanted growth on and in unfortified table wine.

Methods of Production

Rankine (1958) has described the Australian method of making flor sherry about as follows: The base wine is made in the same manner as white table wine with use of sulfur dioxide and a selected wine yeast (not flor yeast). The wine is fined and its alcohol content increased to about 15% by light fortification. The wine is put on flor in hogsheads or puncheons or waxed concrete tanks, the latter with wooden covers slanted to prevent dripping of condensate into the wine with consequent breaking of the film. The wine is under flor about 2 years in casks and 3 to 6 months in tanks. If film formation is delayed because of lack of nitrogenous yeast nutrient, a small amount of an ammonium salt is added. A moderate film growth rather than a heavy film is desired because yeastiness of flavor and slow development of flor character result from the latter.

The wine is fortified to 18–19% alcohol and the sulfur dioxide content adjusted to about 100 mg/liter when it has developed the desired amount of flor character. It is then aged for about two years in wood. A few wineries employ a modified solera system during aging of the fortified wine. Some of the flor sherry is blended with nonflor sherry to improve the flavor and bouquet of the latter.

Fornachon's Investigations

On the basis of his research, Fornachon (1953B) recommended that the alcohol content of the wine for flor yeast growth be 14.5–15.2%; sugar content less than 1500 mg/liter; tannin less than 200 mg/liter; pH, 3.1 to 3.4; sulfur dioxide concentration about 100 mg/liter; depth of wine in tanks used for flor growth about 610 mm (24 in.); cotton "bungs" for casks of wine under flor to provide ventilation and exclude vinegar flies; inoculation by spraying the surface of the wine with a culture of flor yeast in wine; and that the wine be filtered or fined immediately after separation from the flor. He found that the yeast destroyed acetaldehyde under anaerobic conditions with increase in volatile acid, the reaction probably being:

$$2CH_3CHO + H_2O \rightarrow C_2H_5OH + CH_3COOH$$

The higher the oxygen content of the headspace the more rapid was the production of acetaldehyde, although as much as 20% of carbon dioxide in the headspace did not retard aldehyde production. The mineral requirements of the flor yeast were found to be adequate in all Australian wines tested. The flor wine was very susceptible to oxidation and he recommended, therefore, that containers be well filled and sealed during aging. Aldehyde production was more rapid and the redox potential was higher at 14.5% alcohol than at higher alcohol concentrations. He suggested that the oxidation of alcohol to acetaldehyde near the surface of the wine under flor and conversion of aldehyde to acetic acid and ethyl alcohol in the depths of the wine go on simultaneously. He particularly emphasized the value of using high quality wines as a base for the flor.

FLOR SHERRY PROCESS IN SOUTH AFRICA

Niehaus (1958) describes flor sherry production in South Africa. He states that flor yeasts occur naturally on the grapes of that region and that it is unnecessary to use cultures from Spain. He recommends the procedure outlined below.

The grapes, preferably of the Palomino variety, are harvested at 22°– 23° Brix, crushed and immediately pressed. Gypsum is added to the must at the rate of 1.8 kg (4.0 lb) per leaguer, 580 liters (153.7 gal.), and the must is inoculated with an active culture of flor yeast, 7.6 to 11.3 liters (2.0 to 3.0 gal.) of starter per leaguer. The fermentation is controlled by cooling and by addition of small amounts of potassium metabisulfite from time to time. The must is fermented dry, being completed in closed tanks fitted with fermentation bungs. The young wine is stored for about 2 weeks and is then drawn off the lees and fortified to 16–16.5% alcohol with sound, clean, neutral fortifying brandy. Pipes or sherry butts are thoroughly steamed. Two gallons of thick lees from recently fermented wine are placed in the cask and the entire inner surface coated by rolling the cask. The fortified wine is then introduced. Some of the yeast floats and an active film of flor soon develops.

Great care is taken not to raise the alcohol content beyond 16.5% and to use only sound lees. The oak containers are then stored in a cool well-ventilated cellar. The bungholes are stoppered with a special ventilated bung. The wines are then allowed to remain under the flor film for 15 to 18 months, after which the wine is fortified to almost 18% and entered into a solera for fractional blending. See also Theron and Niehaus (1947–48) and Niehaus (1937).

FLOR PROCESS IN FRANCE AND THE SOVIET UNION

For the flor-type (Château Châlon) wines of the Jura, Bidan and André (1958) found very little lees after 6 years' aging, 1 to 1.5 liters for 400 to 600 liters. They report cellar foremen to say that these wines "mangent leur lie." Neither the high aldehyde nor acetoin contents of these wines would account for their bitter aftertaste. They were unable to relate the odor or taste of flor wines with their amino acid content. In commerce the wines are very dry, low in alcohol, and high in total acidity. Production is very small. According to Bidan and André, the yeasts are *Saccharomyces fermentati* and *S. bisporus*, var. *bisporus*.

Native flor-type wines have been produced in Armenia and Georgia in the Soviet Union for many years according to Prostoserdov and Afrikian (1933) and Saenko (1964). During the period under the film, Saenko (1948) showed that the oxidation-reduction potential decreased rapidly as the acetaldehyde and acetal contents increased. In recent years, the process has been industrialized and flor-type sherries are commercially available in the Soviet Union (Saenko *et al.* 1976). Experiments on continuous production of flor-type wines are also underway (Averbukh *et al.* 1976).

Saenko (1964) analyzed 26 Soviet flor-type sherries. The alcohol content varied from 13.9 to 20.5%, sugar from 2.7 to 3.5%, aldehyde from 106 to 656 mg/liter and acetal from 142 to 555 mg/liter. Her analysis of 21 Spanish sherries showed 17.3 to 21.6% alcohol, 0.0 to 8.2% sugar, 90 to 233 mg/liter of aldehyde and 83 to 437 mg/liter of acetal. The sensory scores for the Soviet wines ranged from 8.17 to 9.50, average 8.51, while those of the Spanish wines ranged from 8.61 to 9.48, average 9.22.

Slight decreases or increases in amino acids occurred in sherry wines under a film, according to Saenko and Sakharova (1963). No changes or only slight changes in organic acids occurred under the film up to 180 days. Kozub *et al.* (1976) correlated absorbance between 270 and 280 nm with sherry composition.

COMPOSITION OF COMMERCIAL SHERRIES

Valaer (1945, 1947, 1950) has made many analyses of Spanish sherries and of California sherries (Table 9.4).

The foreign and the California sherries were of similar alcohol content which is not surprising, owing to the federal regulations with respect to alcohol content of fortified wines. The ash of the foreign sherries was higher than the California owing to the use of gypsum (plastering) in the production of Spanish sherries; for the same reason, the alkalinity of the ash of the Spanish sherries was lower than of the California. (With the

TABLE 9.4. COMPOSITION OF VARIOUS SHERRIES

Type and Source	No. of Samples	Alcohol %	Total Solids (at 212°F) g/100 ml	Ash g/100 ml	Total Acid as Tartaric g/100 ml	Volatile Acid g/100 ml	Alkalinity of H_2O-soluble Ash as ml 0.1-$N H_2SO_4$ to Neutralize Ash
California dry, maximum	16	20.64	4.88	0.400	0.497	0.079	18.8
California dry, average	16	20.10	3.80	0.295	0.416	0.063	14.1
California dry, minimum	16	19.56	1.58	0.228	0.332	0.042	10.6
Spanish, fino or amontillado, maximum	38	20.72	4.92	0.490	0.536	0.124	7.6
Spanish, fino or amontillado, average	38	19.88	3.43	0.421	0.454	0.080	5.7
Spanish, fino or amontillado, minimum	38	17.74	1.45	0.374	0.364	0.048	3.4
Spanish, oloroso and amoroso, maximum	23	20.52	12.72	0.520	0.578	0.120	14.9
Spanish, oloroso and amoroso, average	23	19.72	7.82	0.434	0.477	0.102	7.7
Spanish, oloroso and amoroso, minimum	23	18.78	5.32	0.370	0.420	0.073	5.0
Eastern U.S.A., sherry, maximum	10	20.04	7.52	0.305	0.480	0.110	17.0
Eastern U.S.A., sherry, average	10	18.90	4.03	0.245	0.406	0.071	12.4
Eastern U.S.A., sherry, minimum	10	15.66	2.05	0.175	0.315	0.046	8.0

Source of data: Valaer (1947).

use of gypsum largely replaced by organic acids, the ash and alkalinity of the ash is now similar to that of the domestic sherries.) The Spanish sherries analyzed by Valaer seemed to be somewhat higher in volatile acidity than those made in the U.S. In total acidity, the sherries from the three regions represented were similar, although the lowest total acidity was that of an eastern U.S. sherry (0.315 g/100 ml) and the highest was that of a Spanish sherry (0.578 g/100 ml). The total solids content of the dry sherries, as would be expected, was lower than that of the medium sweet to sweet sherries.

Valaer also gave the aldehyde content of 27 typical sherries, some of which were foreign and some American. The average aldehyde content of the Spanish sherries was 141.1 mg/liter, the maximum was 198 mg and the minimum was 66 mg. For the California sherries the average, maximum, and minimum values were 29.1, 41.8, and 13.2 mg/liter. For the eastern U.S. samples, the values were 66.2, 127.6, and 9.4 mg/liter. It is of interest that sherries made in the eastern U.S. were of higher aldehyde content than the California sherries. This may be due to use of oxygen during baking by the Tressler process. The Spanish sherries were higher than the American sherries in aldehyde content, owing to the use of flor yeast in the production of many of the imported samples analyzed by Valaer. See also Amerine (1947).

The importance of aldehydes in flor sherry was re-emphasized by later studies. Nilov and Furman (1964) reported acetaldehyde, propionaldehyde, iso-butyraldehyde (2-methyl-propanal), iso-valeraldehyde (2-methyl-butanal) and furfural. Rodopulo et al. (1965) and Rodopulo and Egorov (1965) also found formaldehyde, caprylaldehyde, and enanthaldehyde. During aging under the flor film, the esters (especially ethyl acetate) and some alcohols (3-methyl-1-butanol and 1-hexanol) increased markedly. Thus, aldehydes, acetals, esters and higher alcohols are all involved in the flor sherry bouquet.

Using gas chromatographic techniques on flor sherries, Webb and Kepner (1962) found relatively large amounts of 2-phenethyl alcohol and diethyl succinate, moderate quantities of 3-methyl-1-butanol, diethyl malate, and 2-phenethyl acetate, small amounts of 2-methyl-1-butanol, 1-hexanol, ethyl isobutyrate, ethyl caproate, ethyl caprylate, ethyl lactate, isoamyl acetate, isoamyl caproate, isoamyl caprylate, γ-butyrolactone, and 2-phenethyl caproate and only traces of 2-methyl-1-propanol, ethyl acetate, isobutyl isobutyrate, isobutyl caproate, isoamyl isovalerate, and hexyl acetate. Several unidentified components were found. Webb (1965) later identified act.-amyl lactate as one of these. Probably present were act.-amyl isovalerate, act.-amyl caproate, act.-amyl caprylate, and isoamyl 2-methylbutyrate. Webb and Kepner suggested that 2-phenethyl alcohol and its acetate and caproate esters contribute significantly to the overall odor of flor sherry. Diethyl succinate and diethyl malate have much less distinctive odors but likely contribute to tactile impressions. The ethyl esters of isobutyric, caproic, and caprylic acids do appear to be important to flor sherry odor. Ethyl lactate, they suggest, is responsible for the cheese-like odor of certain flor sherries. The esters of the higher molecular weight acids and alcohols also contribute to the overall odor. See also Suomalainen and Nykänen (1966).

The nature of the aroma components of the methylene chloride extracts of flor, baked and submerged culture sherries was compared by Webb et al. (1964). Since furfural was the only component unique to a single type (baked), they concluded that the differences in odor were due to differences in the ratios of components. They particularly noted the large quantity of ethyl acid succinate in all types of sherry. However, in the flor sherries a number of unidentified components were noted. They held out the hope that it might be possible to define the different types by correlation of subjective and objective results. In a flor sherry wine, Bourdet and Hérard (1958) reported 57% of the nitrogen was present as free amino acids and 35% as peptides. They also noted marked enrichment of wines in inorganic and organic phosphorus in wines stored on the lees. This was especially true of a film yeast wine.

Brajnikoff and Cruess (1948) give the analysis of several California and imported sherries as shown in Table 9.5. As was the case for the samples analyzed by Valaer, the Spanish sherries were higher in ash than the domestic. They were also higher in sulfates owing to plastering. All of the California sherries were dry or medium dry and therefore of low or medium low sugar content. Samples 6, 7, and 9 of the Spanish were dry and samples 5 and 8, sweet. The aldehyde contents of three experimental flor sherries were found by Brajnikoff and Cruess to be 127.2, 130.9, and 153.0 mg/liter. These values are much lower than obtained by Ough and

TABLE 9.5. COMPOSITION OF SEVERAL CALIFORNIA AND SPANISH SHERRIES

Sample	Total Acidity as Tartaric g/100 ml	Volatile Acidity as Acetic g/100 ml	Alcohol %	pH	Total Sugars g/100 ml	Total Ash g/100 ml	Sulfates as SO$_4$ g/100 ml
California Sherries							
Solano, dry	0.39	0.064	18.85	3.65	1.40	0.236	0.064
Cresta Blanca, dry	0.42	0.048	19.20	3.58	2.14	0.289	0.082
Concannon, dry	0.58	0.067	18.70	3.55	2.42	0.374	0.144
Calif. Growers, dry	0.45	0.050	18.80	3.45	2.42	0.308	0.107
Spanish Sherries							
Amoroso	0.48	0.085	20.7	3.47	4.93	0.401	0.158
Pinta brand (fino)	0.46	0.054	21.0	3.40	1.84	0.462	0.221
Amontillado	0.48	0.066	19.6	3.30	2.38	0.428	0.252
Oloroso	0.53	0.085	20.0	3.40	6.95	0.408	0.202
Apitiv (fino)	0.33	0.048	19.3	3.75	1.08	0.371	0.182

Source of data: Brajnikoff and Cruess (1948).

Amerine by their submerged-oxidation-under-pressure procedure, but comparable to the aldehyde content of imported Spanish sherries as reported by Valaer. A list of volatile compounds of sherries has been compiled by Webb and Noble (1976).

REFERENCES[2]

ABRAMOV, S.A. and POTYAKA, P.K. 1965. Vliyanie sernistoĭ kislosty na razvitie kheresnykh drozhzhie. (Influence of sulfur dioxide on the development of the flor yeast.) Vinodel. Vinograd. S.S.S.R. 25 (5) 14-17.

ALLEN, H.M. 1939. A study of sherry flor. Aust. Brewing Wine J. 58 (10) 31-33; (11) 70-71.

AMERINE, M.A. 1947. The composition of wines of California at expositions. Wines Vines 28 (1) 21-23, 42-43, 45; (2) 24-26; (3) 23-25, 42-46.

AMERINE, M.A. 1948. Personal communication. Davis, Calif.

AMERINE, M.A. 1953. New controlled fermentation equipment at Davis. Wines Vines 34 (9) 27-30.

AMERINE, M.A. 1958. Aldehyde formation in submerged cultures of Saccharomyces beticus. Appl. Microbiol. 6, 160-168.

AMERINE, M.A. and ROESSLER, E.B. 1976. Wines: Their Sensory Evaluation. W. H. Freeman & Co., San Francisco.

AMERINE, M.A., ROESSLER, E.B. and FILIPELLO, F. 1959. Sensory evaluation of wine. Hilgardia 28, 477-567.

AMERINE, M.A. and TWIGHT, E.H. 1938. Sherry. Wines Vines 19 (5) 3-4.

ANON. 1941. Designation of origin of Jerez, Xerez, Sherry. Order of Dept. of Agric., Madrid, Spain, Oct. 20, 1941. Translation by D.B. Mattimore, Wine Institute, San Francisco.

ANON. 1950. Jerez, Xerez, Sherry. Bull. Off. Intern. Vin. 23 (233) 22-33.

AVERBUKH, B.Y., KOZUB, G.I., KOREISHA, M.A. and BARANOVA, E.A. 1976. Kislorodnyi rezhim pri potochnom kheresovanii vinomaterialor. (Oxygen conditions in the continuous production of sherry from wines.) Sadovod. Vinograd. Vinodel. Mold. 31 (8) 35-37.

BAKER, G.A., AMERINE, M.A. and ROESSLER, E.B. 1952. Theory and application of fractional blending systems. Hilgardia 21, 383-409.

BAKER, R. 1945. A study of base wines for flor sherries. Thesis, Roseworthy College, Australia.

BERG, H.W. 1951. Stabilization practices in California wineries. Proc. Am. Soc. Enol. 1951, 90-147.

BERG, H.W. 1956. Personal communication. Davis, Calif.

BERG, H.W. 1960. Stabilization studies on Spanish sherry and on factors influencing KHT precipitation. Am. J. Enol. Vitic. 11, 123-128.

---

[2]Titles have been translated only for nonwestern European languages.

BERG, H.W. 1977. Personal communication on visit to Jerez de la Frontera, Spain.

BERG, H.W. and AKIYOSHI, M. 1956. Some factors involved in the browning of white wines. Am. J. Enol. 7, 1-8.

BIDAN, P. and ANDRÉ, L. 1958. Sur la composition en acides aminés de quelques vins. Ann. Technol. Agric. 7, 403-432.

BOBADILLA, G.F. DE. 1943. Aplicaciones industriales de las levaduras de flor. Agricultura (Revista Agropecuaria) 12 (133) 203-207.

BOBADILLA, G.F. DE. 1947. Graduaciones alcoholica de los vinos en las soleras. Typed Rept. Estación de Viticultura y Enologia, Jerez de la Frontera.

BOURDET, A. and HÉRARD, J. 1958. Influence de l'autolyse des levures sur la composition phosphorée et azotée des vins. Ann. Technol. Agric. 7, 177-202.

BRAJNIKOFF, I. and CRUESS, W.V. 1948. Observations on Spanish sherry process. Food Res. 13, 128-135.

CASTELLA, F. DE. 1909, 1926. Sherry, its making and rearing. Victoria Dept. Agric. J. 7, 442-446, 515-528, 577-583, 621-630,724-727; Ibid. 24, 690-698.

CASTELLA, F. DE. 1922. Maturation of sherry. Aust. Brewing Wine J. 41, 37.

CHAFFEY, W.B. 1940. Some factors influencing the development and the effect of flor yeasts. Ibid. 58 (9) 33-34; (10) 31-34; (11) 31-32.

CROWELL, E.A. and GUYMON, J.F. 1963. Influence of aeration and suspended material on higher alcohol, acetoin, and diacetyl during fermentation. Am. J. Enol. Vitic. 14, 214-222.

CROWTHER, R.F. and TRUSCOTT, J.H.L. 1955-56. Flor type Canadian sherry wine. Hort. Exp. Stn. Prod. Lab. Rept., Vineland, Ontario, Canada 1955-56, 75-83.

CROWTHER, R.F. and TRUSCOTT, J.H.L. 1957. The use of agitation in making of flor sherry. Am. J. Enol. 7, 11-12.

CRUESS, W.V. 1943. Notes on Spanish sherry experiments. Wine Rev. 11 (9) 8-9.

CRUESS, W.V. 1948. Investigations of the flor sherry process. Calif. Agric. Exp. Stn. Bull. 710.

CRUESS, W.V. and PODGORNY, A. 1937. Destruction of volatile acidity of wine by film yeasts. Fruit Prod. J. 17, 4-6.

CRUESS, W.V., WEAST, C.A. and GILILAND, R. 1938. Summary of practical investigations on film yeast. Ibid. 17, 229-231, 251.

DE SOTO, R.T. 1961. Commercial production of flor sherry by the submerged method. Wine Inst. Tech. Advis. Committee, Aug. 11, 1961.

FARAFONTOFF, A. 1964. Studies to determine the feasibility of flor sherry production in California. Am. J. Enol. Vitic. 15, 130-134.

FESSLER, J.H. 1952. Development of the Fessler compound. Wines Vines 33 (7) 15-16.

FORNACHON, J.C.M. 1943. Bacterial Spoilage of Fortified Wines. Aust. Wine Board, Adelaide.

FORNACHON, J.C.M. 1953A. The accumulation of acetaldehyde by suspensions of yeast. Aust. J. Biol. Sci. 6, 222-233.

FORNACHON, J.C.M. 1953B. Studies on the Sherry Flor. Aust. Wine Board, Adelaide. (Reprinted 1972.)

FORNACHON, J.C.M. 1959. Personal communication.

FORNACHON, J.C.M., DOUGLAS, H.C. and VAUGHN, R.H. 1949. *Lactobacillus trichodes* nov. spec., a bacterium causing spoilage in appetizer and dessert wine. Hilgardia 19, 129-132.

FREIBERG, K.J. and CRUESS, W.V. 1955. A study of certain factors affecting the growth of flor yeast. Appl. Microbiol. 3, 208-213.

FREMENKO, G.G., BOL'SHOI, V.A. and BELOGUROV, D.M. 1963. Noyvi metod prigotovleniya madery (A new method of making madeira.) Vinodel. Vinograd. S.S.S.R. 23 (5) 21-27.

FREYRE NIETO, E. 1954. Applicación de fitato de calcio a la clarificación y establización de vinos de Jerez. Bol. Inst. Nac. Invest. Agron. (Madrid) 14 (31) 395-409.

GONZALEZ, G.M.M. 1972. Sherry: The Noble Wine. Cassell, London.

GOSWELL, R.W. 1968. Sherry manufacture. Process Biochem. 3 (2) 47-49.

GUYMON, J.F. and NAKAGIRI, J.A. 1955. Utilization of heads by addition to alcoholic fermentation. Am. J. Enol. 6, 12-25.

HEITZ, J.E., ROESSLER, E.B., AMERINE, M.A. and BAKER, G.A. 1951. A study of certain factors influencing the composition of California-style sherry during baking. Food Res. 16, 192-200.

HOHL, L.A. and CRUESS. W.V. 1939, 1940. Observations on certain film forming yeasts. Zentr. Bakteriol. Parasitenk. Abt. II 101, 65-78. (Also Fruit Prod. J. 20, 72-75, 108-111, 1940.)

HOLDEN, C. 1955. Combined method for heat and cold stabilization. Am. J. Enol. 6, 47-49.

IÑIGO LEAL, B. and BRAVO ABAD, F. 1963. Acidez y levaduras vínicas. III. Curso cinético de la acidez volátil en fermentados de mosto originados por distintas especies de levaduras vínicas. Rev. Cienc. Apl. 17, 132-135.

IÑIGO LEAL, B., VÁZQUES MARTÍNEZ, D. and ARROYO VARELA, V. 1963. Los agentes de fermentación vínica en la zona de Jerez. Ibid. 17, 296-305.

JOSLYN, M.A. 1948. Personal communication. Berkeley, Calif.

JOSLYN, M.A. and AMERINE, M.A. 1964. Dessert, Appetizer and Related Flavored Wines. Univ. Calif. Div. Agric. Sci., Berkeley.

KEAN, C.E. and MARSH, G.L. 1956. Investigation of copper complexes causing cloudiness in wines. II. Bentonite treatment of wines. Food Technol. 10, 355-359.

KIELHÖFER, E. 1951. Die Eiweisstrübung des weines. IV. Z. Lebensm.-Unters. -Forsch. 92, 1-9.

KOCH, J. 1957. Die Eiweisstoffe des Weines und ihre Veränderungen bei verschiedenden kellerischen Behandlungsmethoden. Weinberg Keller 4, 521-526.

KOZUB, G.I., AVERBUKH, B.YA., and KHARKOVER, M.Z. 1976. Issledovanie kheresnykh vin spectrophotometricheskim metodom. (Spectrophotometric study of sherry wines.) Sadovod. Vinograd. Vinodel. Mold. 31 (5) 20-22.

LODDER, J. 1970. The Yeasts; A Taxonomic Study. North Holland Publishing Co., Amsterdam.

MARCILLA ARRAZOLA, J. 1946. Tratado die Viticultura y Enologia Españolas. Vol. II. Sociedad Anónima Española de Traductores y Autores, Madrid.

MARCILLA, J., ALAS, G. and FEDUCHY, E. 1936. Contribución al estudio de las levaduras que forman velo sobre ciertos vinos de elevado grado alcoholico. Anales Centro Invest. Vinícolas 1, 1-230.

MARQUIS, H.H. 1936. California sherry production. Wine Rev. 4 (6) 6-7, 22.

MARTINI, L.P. 1950. Flor sherry experiments. Proc. Am. Soc. Enol. 1950, 113-118.

MARTINI, L.P. and CRUESS, W.V. 1956. Sherry production practices survey. Wine Inst. Tech. Advis. Committee, Feb. 20, 1956, San Francisco.

MATTICK, L.R. and ROBINSON, W.B. 1960. Changes in the volatile acids during the baking of sherry wine by the Tressler baking process. Am. J. Enol. Vitic. 11, 113-116.

NIEHAUS, C.J.G. 1937. South African sherries. Farming in South Africa 12, 82, 85.

NIEHAUS, C.J.G. 1958. Personal communication.

NIELSON, N.E. 1952. The effect of oxygen on growth and carbon metabolism of flor and related yeasts. Ph.D. Thesis. Dept. Food Technol., Univ. Calif., Berkeley.

NILOV, V.I. and FURMAN, D.B. 1964. Oveshchestvakh, obuslovlivayuschikh buket vina tipa kheres (Substances causing the bouquet of a wine of the sherry type.) Sadovod. Vinograd. Vinodel. Mold. 1964 (11) 32-34.

OUGH, C.S. and AMERINE, M.A. 1958. Studies on aldehyde production under pressure, oxygen and agitation. Am. J. Enol. 9, 111-123.

OUGH, C.S. and AMERINE, M.A. 1972. Further studies with submerged flor sherry. Am. J. Enol. Vitic. 23, 128-131.

PREOBRAZHENSKIĬ, A.A. 1963. Osobennosti maderizatsii v germetizirovannykh reservuarakh. (Heating wines in closed tanks.) Vinodel. Vinograd. S.S.S.R. 23 (6) 4-9.

PROSTOSERDOV, N.N. and AFRIKIAN, R. 1933. Jerez Wein in Armenien. Das Weinland 5, 389-391.

RANKINE, B.C. 1955. Yeast cultures in Australian wine making. Am. J. Enol. 6, 11-15.

RANKINE, B.C. 1958. An outline of flor sherry making in Australia. Mimeo. Rept.

RODOPULO, A.K. and EGOROV, I.A. 1965. Karbonil'nye soedineniya kheresa. (The carbonyls of sherry.) Vinodel. Vinograd. S.S.S.R. 25 (1) 6-9.

RODOPULO, A.K., EGOROV, I.A. and LASHINA, V.E. 1965. O buketistykh veshchestvakh keresa. (Bouquet properties of sherry.) Prikl. Biokh. Mikrobiol. 1, 95-101.

SAAVEDRA, I.J. and GARRIDO, J.M. 1963. La levadura de "flor" en la crianza del vino; el etanol en el metabolismo en fase de velo. Rev. Cienc. Apl. 17 (95) 497-501.

SAENKO, N.F. 1945. Improving sick and defective wines by means of a sherry film (transl.). Vinodel. Vinograd. S.S.S.R. 5 (4) 4-10.

SAENKO, N.F. 1948. Ismenenie okislitel'no-vosstanovitel'nogo potentsiala i sostava vina pri vydershke ego pod kheresnoi plenkoi. (Modification of the oxidation-reduction potential and of the composition of sherry wine during aging under a film.) Biokhim. Vinodeliya 2, 86-100.

SAENKO, N.F. 1964. Kheres (Sherry). Izdatel'stvo "Pishchevaya Promyshlennost" Moscow.

SAENKO, N.F. and SAKHAROVA, T.A. 1959. Vliyanie uslovii kul'tivirovaniya kheresnykh drozhzhei na ikh rost i biokhimicheskuyu aktivost'. (Influence of cultural conditions of sherry yeasts on their development and biochemical activity.) Vinodel. Vinograd. S.S.S.R. 19 (2) 19-23.

SAENKO, N.F. and SAKHAROVA, T.A. 1963. Prevrashchenie organicheskikh kislot i aminokislot v protsesse vyderzhki vina pod kheresnoi plenkoi. (Changes in the organic and amino acids in sherries under a film.) Ibid. 23 (3) 3-6.

SAENKO, N.F., SCHOUR, I.M. and VOLOSCHINA, A.I. 1976. Intensifikatsia protessa kheresovania vina plenochnym metodom. (Intensification of the processes of producing film sherry.) Vinodel. Vinograd. U.R.S.S. No. 4 (323) 17-21.

SCHANDERL, H. 1936. Untersuchungen über sogenannte Jerez-Hefen. Wein Rebe 18, 16-25.

SINGLETON, V.L., OUGH, C.S. and AMERINE, M.A. 1964. Chemical and sensory effects of heating wines under different gases. Am. J. Enol. Vitic. 15, 134-145.

STRUD, S. 1953. Flor sherry production. Wine Inst., Tech. Advis. Committee, July 24, 1953.

SUOMALAINEN, H. and NYKÄNEN, L. 1966. The aroma compounds produced by sherry yeast in grape and berry wines. Suom. Kemist. B 39, 252-256.

THERON, C.J. and NIEHAUS, C.J.G. 1947-48. Wine making. Union of South Africa Dept. Agric. Bull. 191.

TWIGHT, E.H. 1936. California sherry making. Wines Vines 17 (4) 5, 15.

VALAER. P. 1945. Composition of domestic and imported sherries. Alcohol and Tobacco Tax Unit, Internal Revenue Service, Washington, D.C. Mimeo.

VALAER, P. 1947. Sherry wine, methods of its production and the analyses of Spanish and American sherry wine. Alcohol and Tobacco Tax Unit, Internal Revenue Service, Washington, D.C.

VALAER, P. 1950. Wines of the World. Abelard Press, New York.

WARKENTIN, H. 1955. Influence of pH and total acidity on calcium tolerance of sherry wine. Food Res. *20*, 301-310.

WARKENTIN, H. 1970. Process for making sherry wine. U.S. Patent 3,518,089; (appl. May 15, 1967) June 30, 1970.

WEBB, A.D. 1965. Personal communication. Davis, Calif.

WEBB, A.D. and KEPNER, R.E. 1962. The aroma of flor sherry. Am. J. Enol. Vitic. *13*, 1-14.

WEBB, A.D., KEPNER, R.E. and GALETTO, W.E. 1964. Comparison of aromas of flor sherry, baked sherry, and submerged-culture sherry. *Ibid. 15*, 1-10.

WEBB, A.D. and NOBLE, A.C. 1976. Aroma of sherry wines. Biotech. Bioeng. *18*, 939-952.

WILLIAMS, J.L. 1936. The manufacture of flor sherry. Aust. Brewing Wine J. *55*, 64. *(See also* S. Aust. Dept. Agric. Bull. *46*, 267-274, 322-325.)

WILLIAMS, J.L. 1943. The manufacture of flor sherry. J. Dept. Agric. S. Aust. *46*, 267-274, 322-325.

10

Port and Other Dessert Wines

Port, angelica, Málaga, Madeira, Marsala, California tokay, muscatel, sherry and similar types produced in many countries are the principal wines made by adding wine spirits. With the exception of some sherries already discussed (Chap. 9) these are all traditionally sweet dessert wines. Fortified wines of these types have declined drastically in percentage of the total U.S. wine market, although the total gallonage marketed has become fairly constant, 261 to 231 million liters (69 to 61 million gal.) per year for 1973 to 1976 and 16—20% of all wine versus nearly 378 million liters (100 million gal.) and 85% in 1950. Similar trends of increasing popularity of table wines and static or decreasing interest in traditional dessert wines have been worldwide.

Part of this decline in interest in dessert wines may represent consumer fad, but it has persisted since 1950. Sweet wines face antagonism by the calorie-conscious consumer, and by those favoring wines of lighter alcohol content. Lowering the minimum (and typical) alcohol level of Californian dessert wines from 20 to 18% in 1971 has not yet produced the anticipated upturn in dessert wine consumption. Interestingly, however, the decline in sweet dessert wine consumpton has coincided with booming consumption of sweeter table wines.

Both American and foreign labels with reputations for quality have resisted or reversed the decline in dessert wine consumption and the most decline has been in lower priced wines. It is believed the strong shift to table wines has caused emphasis on their technology and sales at the expense of attention to dessert wines. This is substantiated by the relative dearth of recent research reports on dessert wine technology. This chapter will be short owing to the relative lack of new technology specific for dessert wines (of course, many developments discussed with table wines or sherry are applicable), the relative decline in dessert wine production, the publication of Joslyn and Amerine's monograph on dessert wines in 1964, and Goswell and Kunkee's 1977 review. Nevertheless, these wines represent a large and valuable segment of the total diversity of wines and deserve to remain important. Hopeful signs for their future are renewed interest in high quality examples of these wines by consumer and producer, increases in hectarage (acreage) of selected dessert wine grape varieties (acreage of Tinta Madeira has doubled and Rubired quadrupled in California from 1971 to 1976), and possibly increased consumer appeal, especially in winter or cold climates as a result of lowered thermostats and fuel shortages.

PORT

Sweet red wines of Portugal have been one of that country's most important exports for two and a half centuries. Red sweet wines, often called port, or port-type, are also produced in Australia, Argentina, California, Chile, South Africa, and the Soviet Union. California is the principal producing region in the United States. See Chap. 1 and Allen (1963), Castella (1908), Fletcher (1978), Ottavi and Garino-Canina (1930), Robertson (1978), and Simon (1934) for general discussions and Lachman (1903) and Twight (1934) for historical data on the California industry.

At present, California wine makers must use such red wine varieties as are available. Probably the Alicante Bouschet is the poorest of these, owing to its low sugar musts, the tendency of its wines to lose color, and to its slightly unpleasant aroma. Carignane, Zinfandel, and Petite Sirah are satisfactory when picked before raisining occurs. Mataro is deficient in color. The Mission and Grenache, grown in the same area, are lacking in acid and color but are of pleasing flavor. Touriga has low color, but otherwise good quality. Blends often have to be employed in order to bring up the color. Increased acreages of more suitable grape varieties have been planted in the Fresno area, such as Tinta Madeira, Souzão, and Rubired. The latter and Royalty are two hybrids created by Prof. H. P. Olmo of the University of California specifically for red sweet wine and concentrate production. In the hot interior valleys of California, where most of the sweet dessert wines are made, many varieties of red wine grapes fail to develop sufficient color for production of port of satisfactory tint, unless special methods of vinification are used. There is great need for the planting of varieties of maximum red color in these areas to bring up to a desirable depth the color of ports made from the varieties grown at present. The Salvador is widely used for this purpose but its flavor is poor. The Souzão, Rubired and Royalty should help supply this deficiency without the undesirable flavor. Color stability is often a problem with wines from red juice (teinturier) grapes which include Alicante Bouschet, Royalty, Rubired, and Salvador.

Normal Vinification of Port

The principal problem in making port is extraction of sufficient color from grapes grown in warm areas, and therefore relatively low in anthocyanins, during a period of fermentation restricted by the need to retain residual grape sugar.

The grapes should be well ripened, 23° to 26° Brix, picked to eliminate moldy or minimize raisined fruit and handled with care to avoid bruising. They should be crushed as soon as possible after picking. Shipping loose in bulk in gondolas with long delays in crushing is not conducive to quality. Rain-damaged grapes that have molded on the vines give wines of poor flavor and unstable color. Crushing and stemming are conducted as for grapes for dry red wine (p. 257). The crushed grapes are pumped into large fermentation vats usually holding 38,000 liters (10,000 gal.) or more. Some sulfur dioxide should be added during crushing to give about 100 mg/liter in the must. This will ensure a cleaner fermentation, help stabilize the color, and assist in extraction of the color.

Early in the season a 1–5% starter of pure yeast or the equivalent of activated dry yeast is added to the crushed grapes. Later in the season, a similar quantity of fermenting must from a vat in active fermentation will serve the purpose but it is better to continue to use a pure yeast inoculum. Flanzy (1959) reported better quality dessert wines when the must was fermented at 15°–20°C (59°–68°F) compared to 30°C (86°F). He believed sulfur dioxide reduced the quality of the dessert wines. Both these results need confirmation; 30°C is certainly too warm, but 20°C may not be optimum.

Frequent pumping over of must in large vats is essential to extraction of the color. In Portugal, color extraction was accomplished by intermittent treading of the fermenting grapes, an effective but not very aesthetic procedure (p. 39) now largely replaced by small crushers and pumping over even when the lagares are retained. Perhaps 70% of the port is now made in centralized wineries with modern equipment and management and only 30% in the smaller estate or farm wineries (*quintas*). The *quinta* in contract to a port shipper is supervised by frequent visits by a representative of the shipper during the vintage and until transfer of the wine.

If the grapes have good color, and the wine maker has been diligent, his must will have attained fair color when it has fermented to the point at which it is ready for fortification to give a standard port of 18 × 6 composition (18% alcohol and 6° Brix) after fortification. Thus, if the original grapes tested 24° Brix and were fermented and fortified at 12.5° to 18% alcohol, the resulting wine should be about 6°. As a matter of fact, in this case, the fermenting must would be drawn from the vat at about

14.5° Brix, since there may be nearly 2° drop during drawing off, pumping to the fortifying tank, measuring, and wine spirits addition. In warm regions the 14.5° Brix will be reached 24 to 48 hours after crushing. A continuous press is generally used because of its convenience and economy of operation. The press wine is often fortified and is of deeper color. One can readily see the difficulty in extracting sufficient color in such a short period of fermentation, especially with grapes grown in hot localities. Hence, "normal vinification" of port is usually modified in the United States. Other methods are discussed in the next sections.

Most wineries of California's central valley draw the free-run, colored, fermenting must off at the proper stage and pump it to the fortifying tanks. The pomace is then watered and fermented for distilling material. The fermented mixture may be ground and passed directly to a pomace still or pressed in a continuous screw press and the solution distilled. Pomace dealcoholizers which steamed the alcohol from the moist pomace on movable trays have been displaced. Recently, to save water and energy even though losing some alcohol, pomace may be merely pressed very dry (45–50% moisture) and discarded. Alternatively a "scalping" apparatus (sprays of water over a conveyor) or countercurrent extractor systems (discussed in Chap. 6) may recover the sugar or alcohol from the pomace before or after final fermentation.

The relation between initial Brix degree of the grapes, Brix of the must, and final Brix after fortification to 18% alcohol is shown in Fig. 6.6 in Chap. 6. Wine makers commonly pay too little attention to fortification at the proper sugar content. The result is that some lots are fortified too soon and more too late. Closer attention to this table would reduce this problem.

The character of the fortifying alcohol has a great deal to do with the quality achieved and aging required by the wine. Fortification has been discussed in Chap. 6 and production of wine spirits in Chap. 17. A few additional comments are pertinent here. In Portugal, port was formerly fortified with wine spirit pot-distilled at fairly low proof. The resultant recognizable pot-distillate flavor and rather high fusel oil content when coupled with proper aging and judicious blending can give exceptional products. Higher fusel alcohol content is considered part of the distinguishing quality of Portugese port compared to port-type wines from elsewhere (Ramos 1974).

The fortifying spirit used in Portugal is obtained from a government monopoly. Various lots of spirit are offered and the winemaker selects the ones he purchases, but he has no control over its origin and ordinarily no information other than an analysis of the sample and his sensory judgment. Most of the spirit used has not come from the Duoro but from areas with less costly grapes, and not all of it from grapes! A few years ago certain batches of ethanol supplied by the government monopoly to port makers were later found to have been synthesized from petroleum. This illustrates not only the importance of full knowledge and considerable control by the winemaker of his raw materials, but also suggests that nearly congener-free pure alcohol was being used so that the lack of fruit or fermentation character was not obvious.

By American law, the fortifying spirit must come from grapes (or the specific fruit for wines from fruits other than grapes) and is ordinarily distilled at about 189–192 proof in continuous stills. The resultant grape wine spirit is relatively low in congeners and fortified wine made with it is less heavy, relatively smooth and quickly aged to an acceptable degree, although perhaps not to as high or interesting ultimate quality as with a suitable lower-proof, congener-rich fortifying brandy and longer aging. For obvious economic reasons, the world trend has been toward high-proof distillate and minimum aging for dessert wines. A few of the best ports of California are made from very ripe grapes, 25°–28° Brix, and about 170° proof spirit so that rich wines with extra character from the brandy result.

In Portugal, some shippers "refresh" the wine with small additions of wine spirit at intervals during barrel (pipe) aging of port. This is considered to add fruitiness and, at least in part, acts by adding a slight fieriness from the fresh spirit. This is quite different from stopping the fermentation by fortification in two or more portions (rather than all at once) which, according to several European reports, results in a higher quality product. Singleton and Guymon (1963) made a test of this with California white and ruby ports. The multiple addition did seem to result in better quality, particularly with white port. They showed that this was probably due to the reduction in aldehydes by fermentation at the relatively low alcohol following the initial partial fortification. Commercial use of multiple additions of wine spirits would seem to be indicated if high aldehyde spirits are used, as they apparently often are in European countries. There may be additional effects. Higher amino acid content leading to greater flavor in the wine and in distillate is said to be the result of minimizing the early logarithmic yeast fermentation phase in favor of fermentation at higher alcohol with minimal yeast multiplication (Abdurazakova et al. 1974).

Singleton et al. (1964) reported better color in young ruby ports fortified with high aldehyde wine spirits. They suggested this was due to reaction of acetaldehyde with anthocyanins via an acid-catalyzed Baeyer reaction to produce polymers. See also Costa (1938) and Egorov et al. (1951).

Fermenting Dry Before Wine Spirits Addition

A few wine makers ferment much of the must for port on the skins to about 0° Brix, that is, as if they were going to make claret or burgundy. Then, this more or less dry wine is fortified to give a wine of good color. Pressing of the drained pomace gives a press wine of deep color, which may also be fortified. Another must is fortified after a very short fermentation period to give a wine of high sugar content but of pale color. The dry and sweet ports are later blended to give standard port of 18 × 6 composition. Instead of using a fortified must, red concentrate has been used to give the desired sugar. If only high quality red concentrate is used, the latter procedure is preferable.

Extraction of Color by Heat

In early versions of this procedure the must was drawn off, pumped through a pasteurizer, and returned to the vat of crushed grapes until the temperature reached about 50°C (122°F), at which temperature it was held for perhaps 24 hours. Joslyn and Amerine (1964) suggested heating to 60°C (140°F) or higher for a shorter time. At 60°C (140°F) the color "flows" (is extracted) rapidly. The must is drawn off and the grapes pressed; when color extraction is sufficient at the time of drawing off, pressing may be omitted. If still hot, the juice should be cooled. A small amount of wine may be added to bring the alcohol to above the legal minimum of 0.5 to 1.0% and the must fortified to 18% alcohol. Or it may be cooled, fermented to the proper sugar content, and fortified. In the former case it can be blended later with fortified dry port to give a wine of standard alcohol and Brix.

The present tendency is to heat the crushed grapes to 80°C (176°F), hold at this temperature for 2−3 min, and pump through a cooler to a fermentor. The free-run, colored juice is drawn off, cooled, yeasted, fermented and fortified. The pomace is cooled, diluted with water, yeasted, and fermented for distilling material. Unfortunately, the red color of wines made from heated musts is often too blue and of poor stability. It is also common experience that wines from heated musts are difficult to clarify. For further details see Berg (1940), Berg and Marsh (1950), Berg and Akiyoshi (1958), Joslyn and Amerine (1964), and Nury (1957).

Amerine and De Mattei (1940) have shown that good color extraction can be attained immediately by dipping the grapes in boiling water for 1 min before crushing. Color can be released from the skin without the heat penetrating through the berry.

Coffelt and Berg (1965) developed equipment for heat treating whole grapes with steam under pressure. Because of the high temperatures obtainable, heating times of only a few seconds were required to give juices which after partial fermentation and fortification produced ports of superior color and equal or better quality than those produced by more conventional procedures. Various equipment for "thermovinification" is in use or under trial for red wines in France, Italy, the United States, Australia, South Africa, and elsewhere. Although table wines have been emphasized they are applicable to port (see, for example, Lowe *et al.* 1976). They generally operate by removal of a portion of the juice, heating the pomace under controlled conditions (e.g., 73°C or 163°F, for 30 min) pressing, and cooling prior to fermentation. The unheated portion of the juice is added back at different stages depending on the objectives (unchanged pectic enzyme content, to aid cooling, to aid extraction of pigment, to retain fruitiness, etc.).

Color extraction by heat or by fermenting on the skins should not be too long, or the wine may be too high in tannin. Port should be smooth, not astringent. Heating of must, concentrate, or sweet wine converts portions of the sugars to furfural or hydroxymethylfurfural. These are low or absent in young sweet wines made without heating but occur at similar levels in old ports apparently made without heating (Ramos and Gomes 1969).

Addition of alcohol to the fermenting pomace in order to extract more color has been recommended by Berg and Akiyoshi (1960) and by Nedeltchev (1959). Nedeltchev also tried heating the crushed grapes and the pomace only. The best results were obtained by preheating whole grapes in boiling water for 3—4 min. He reported particularly that heating of the whole grapes avoids the cooked taste. Finally, Nedeltchev reported that addition of tartaric was superior to use of concentrate as a method of increasing the acidity of low acid musts. This result should be checked.

Balancing the Port Cellar

The port to be bottled should be of standard composition, often, about 18 × 6—about 18% alcohol and 6° Brix (about 12% extract). Obviously then, if the entire season's ports are all blended into one uniform blend, the composition of the components should be such that the average will be about 18 × 6.

If some of the ports are dry, others must be very sweet, in order to even out when the blends are made. The same is true of color and other components to be standardized such as total "tannins" (phenols) or acidity. Therefore, careful check must be kept on the volume of all lots of port as made during the season. It may be necessary to make up extra gallonage of sweet or dry port, as the case requires, near the end of the season in order that the final blend will be about 18 × 6. It should be re-emphasized that closer control of the time of harvesting and of fortification to produce standard ports is the best practice.

Use of Concentrate

Some of the larger California wineries operate vacuum pans during the grape season in the production of concentrated musts to be used in sweetening fortified wines, including port. In making red concentrate the crushed grapes are heated to 60°C (140°F) or higher by drawing off the free-run juice, heating it, and returning it to the vat until the color is extracted. The free-run is drawn off and the grapes pressed in a horizontal basket or continuous press. The press and free-run are combined, clarified, and sent to the vacuum pan.

Or, the similar method described by Nury (1957) may be used. In making white concentrate, the grapes are not heated and only the free-run is used. The juice is usually concentrated to 70°−72° Brix. Formerly, some wine makers have fortified the concentrate to 20−21% alcohol in order not to reduce the alcohol content of wine to which it was added later. The concentrate may be added to the wine at any time before it is refrigerated and finally filtered.

It has been observed that grape concentrate often develops very resistant cultures of lactic bacteria that can infect and spoil or damage the wine to which the concentrate is added. Use of freshly prepared concentrate of high quality and 75−100 mg/liter of sulfur dioxide should reduce this hazard. Condensation of evaporated moisture in the top of the tank can lead to dilution and microorganism growth. Refrigeration helps retain fruitiness, but leads to excessive precipitation of tartrates.

Syruped Fermentations

Cruess et al. (1916), Hohl and Cruess (1936), Cruess and Hohl (1937), and Hohl (1938) found it possible to reach high alcohol levels by periodically adding concentrate during fermentation. The legal and tax incentives for such production no longer exist and it has largely disappeared in the United States. In Great Britain, both white and red dessert wines are so made from imported concentrate.

Clarification

In most wineries, the newly fortified port is allowed to settle for 3 to 4 weeks, or longer, to undergo natural clarification. Like other fortified wines, port usually clears rather rapidly. When the color has been extracted with heat, the addition of a pectic enzyme is essential and clarification may remain difficult.

The wine is drawn off the sediment and fined with about 3 to 5 lb of bentonite per 1000 gal. in the form of a slurry in wine or water as outlined elsewhere for sherry. It is then allowed to settle about three weeks or until the fining agent settles.

Usually, the fined wine settles clear or brilliantly clear, but it will contain a few small flocks of bentonite or pulp, etc. Also, if insufficient bentonite has been used the wine may be more or less hazy. In either event it must be filtered. Therefore, it is racked from the sediment, diatomaceous earth filter-aid is added continuously, and the wine filtered in a filter press or metal screen filter. The earlier a dessert wine is fined and filtered, usually the more stable it will be.

The filtered wines are then blended to give a standard port of the desired sugar content. Attention should also be paid to balancing the color and standardizing the flavor and quality. Ribeiro (1968) has studied the visual, analytical, and processing relationships in port color.

Stabilization

Ports seldom need to be heat-stabilized either before or after refrigeration, even if intended for early shipment. However, a major problem in the stabilization of port wine is to prevent deposits in the bottle. In one experiment, Azevedo (1963) reported storage at $-9°C$ (16°F) for 6 to 7 days, filtration and flash pasteurization at 104°C (219°F) for 7 sec gave the best results. Pasteurization before chilling was unsuccessful. Fining with bentonite (0.6 g per liter) and then with 0.1 g per liter of gelatin gave wines with less cloudiness after aging, irrespective of the treatment.

The filtered blended wine is refrigerated to $-9°$ to $-8°C$ (18° to 16°F) and either held at that temperature for about 3 weeks or longer to rid the wine of excess cream of tartar and certain colloids or it is cooled to that temperature and allowed to rise to about 0°C (32°F), when it is again chilled to $-8°C$; this cycle being repeated 3 to 4 times over a 30-day period. Some wine makers store the refrigerated wine in tanks in a cold room maintained at about $-3°C$ (26°F); others maintain $-8°C$ by auxiliary cooling coils in the tank, which is at cellar temperature. Cream of tartar collects on the walls and in the sediment in the refrigerating tank. After crystallization or separation of cream of tartar is complete, the wine is drawn off and filtered. If the original stabilization is done at a low enough temperature for a long enough period and no subsequent tartrate pick-up occurs (from inadequately *cold* filtration or tartrate-lined tanks) re-refrigeration is unnecessary and costly. Ion-exchange treatment (p. 301) is also used for tartrate stabilization.

Cooling from cellar temperature to −9° to −8°C (18° to 16°F) is accomplished by passing the wine through tubular coolers refrigerated with Freon or ammonia. Needless to say, the tubes must be intact in order that the refrigerant not contaminate the wine. Ammonia can quickly ruin the wine; pure Freon may do little harm if it comes in contact with wine, but refrigeration reduces the Brix degree slightly, possibly 0.1° to 0.15°, owing chiefly to loss of cream of tartar. But compressor oil must not get into the wine.

Aging

The previous operations of fining, filtering, and refrigerating, coupled with pasteurizing, bring about marked aging of the wine. In fact, this cycle may be repeated several times to rapidly age the wine, particularly when the demand is very brisk. Occasional aeration between or during these operations still further speeds up aging, of a kind. As stated elsewhere, aging is a very complex process involving oxidative changes, esterification, etc. Quick aging of this type intensifies oxidative changes but not all of the other normal aging processes. Hence, quickly aged wines are usually slightly oxidized and may be low in color owing to losses during treatment. However, the oxidation-reduction potential of bottled dessert wines falls to a low rest potential even for port-type wine stored in the bottle for 15 to 45 years (Deibner 1957).

Some ports are baked for a few days at 49° to 60°C (120° to 140°F). It may also be aerated by pumping over after or before baking. This often gives the port an amber color and oxidized odor. Some demand has developed for this rapid-aged tawny port. However, much better quality, from the point of view of many port drinkers, is secured by aging the clarified and stabilized wine 1 to 2 years in small oak casks at cellar temperature, racking occasionally. In Portugal, aging is preferred in well-seasoned, low-extractive oak pipes of about 600 liters (158 gal.). Economics dictate a maximum of about 2½ years in wood for the standard quality tawny or ruby ports.

Oak shavings produce the flavor extraction effect of aging in oak. The threshold level for flavor is about 0.5 g of dry oak per liter of port (Singleton 1974). Port improves for several years in wood. However, some consumers prefer a newer wine of a bright red color and a fruity flavor. Well-aged port is, however, smoother, possesses a fine odor and a beautiful tawny color. At present, the prevailing custom is to market most California port rather young—at 1 to 2 years, or even at less than 1 year. Addition of sweet sherry has also been employed to impart "age" to new port; but it is also likely to give it a caramelized flavor and an undesirable nutty sherry character.

Finishing

Like other dessert wines, port is subject to attack by certain bacteria—particularly by *L. trichodes* (p. 571). As this organism is very sensitive to sulfur dioxide it may be held in check by maintaining a total of 75 to 100 mg/liter. This is particularly important just before bottling or shipping as the infection is most likely to develop in the bottle. The wine is given a polishing filtration before bottling or shipping. Hot bottling is still sometimes practiced to ensure microbial stability, but quality is safer with sterile filtration.

RED MUSCATEL

There are several varieties of red or purple muscat grapes that do well in California—Muscat Hamburg and Aleatico being the most common. A Los Gatos, California, winery makes an excellent red (or "black") muscatel. The muscat flavor is pronounced but pleasing; the acidity is somewhat higher than typical for ordinary muscatel, and the general flavor and bouquet smooth. Regular port technique is used in making this wine, including aging in small cooperage.

The Aleatico is an orange-red variety of muscat flavor extensively grown in Italy (particularly in Tuscany) and, to some extent, in the San Joaquin Valley in California. It can be made into a dessert wine of light or of medium tawny color by port wine techniques. It has also been made into an unfortified sweet wine preserved with a high concentration of sulfur dioxide.

WHITE PORT

In Portugal, a relatively small amount of white port is made by fortifying the partially-fermented juice of white grapes and aging in the same manner as red port. Some is made nearly dry and initial fermentation with the skins is usual. In California, white port was made after Repeal by decolorizing angelica with activated carbon and filtering to give a water-white fortified sweet wine of neutral flavor. A wine now may be decolorized to not less than the equivalent of 0.6 Lovibond in a ½-in. cell, although a wine produced below this color level without decolorization is permitted. Precise measurement of such a small amount of color is not difficult with modern spectrophotometers, although the Lovibond scale is difficult to match exactly (Little 1971). Present practice is to fortify light colored free-run musts and keep the wine in metal tanks out of contact with the air to prevent darkening. Charcoal is thus much less used than formerly. Most California white ports today are light colored, fresh, grapey, sweet wines with no wood age and intended for early consumption or use as a base for vermouth or other flavored wines. Although separate statistics are not available, more white port probably is produced than port in California.

ANGELICA

This is a product unique to California although mistelles or fortified musts are produced elsewhere. The origin of the name is not definitely known. Perhaps early California wine makers derived the name from Los Angeles (see Amerine and Winkler 1938).

The process of manufacture is very simple. White grapes are crushed, stemmed, pumped into a vat, and about 100 mg/liter of sulfur dioxide added as the vat is filled. The free-run juice is drawn off and fermented slightly; or is allowed to ferment on the skins slightly to give at least 0.5% alcohol before fortification (a legal requirement). Or, a little dry white wine may be added to the drawn-off juice. Use of low-color red grapes, such as Mission and Grenache, is also possible. Only the free-run juice is used and settling of the musts is recommended. The juice (essentially unfermented) is then fortified to 18–20% alcohol. Most wine makers allow the fermentation to proceed to several percent alcohol if the must is very sweet; but the preferred practice may be to fortify the slightly fermented juice. Settling of the fortified wine 1 to 30 days, racking, fining with bentonite, settling, filtering, refrigeration, aging, pasteurization and finishing are conducted essentially as described for port.

MUSCATEL

This is one of California's best dessert types (see Twight and Amerine 1938). Since W.W. II, sales have decreased. Famous muscatels from elsewhere include those from Frontignan and Lunel in France, Setúbal in Portugal, from Rutherglen in Australia, Hanepoot and Muscadel in South Africa, and Samos in Greece.

Some wine connoisseurs disdain the muscat as plebeian and of obvious flavor. Its flavor is a highly distinctive one. Cordonnier (1956) showed that the odorants making muscat grapes distinctive include linaloöl and related terpene derivatives (see also Chap. 2). These very pleasantly odorous substances have thresholds of the order of a few mg/liter and are also part of the varietal character, but lower in amount, in Gewürztraminer, White Riesling and similar prestigious grapes (Van Wyk et al. 1967). It is not unknown for a small portion of muscat wine to be used to enhance fruitiness of other wines. One defect of some of California's muscatel is its low content of well-ripened muscat juice or wine. The law formerly allowed a wine containing as little as 51% of muscat to be labeled muscatel. This ruling was often a mistake. There is a considerable supply (about 5600 ha or 14,000 acres) of muscat grapes in California; more could be grown if needed. Much more luscious muscatel can be made of 100% muscat grapes, including muscat brandy for fortifying! Some muscatel has been made so as to minimize the potential flavor. Its taste was often so nondescript that one could scarcely detect any muscat flavor. The recent elevation of the minimum varietal content to 75% should be a major improvement. Winemakers should insist on properly cropped grapes with good muscat flavor.

Varieties

In California, the Muscat of Alexandria, the well-known seeded raisin grape of Spain, Australia, and California, is used in making most of the muscatel. The berries are large and grow in loosely filled bunches. The flavor and aroma are very pronounced if the vines are not overcropped. The Muscat blanc (called Muscat Frontignan in California and Muscat Canelli in Italy) is grown in small quantities only, as the vines are poor producers and the grapes sunburn easily. However, its wine is of better flavor and aroma than that of the Muscat of Alexandria. The Malvasia bianca is another white variety of muscat flavor suitable for making muscatel, and Orange Muscat has also been recommended.

Most of the muscat grapes of California are produced in the San Joaquin Valley in the Fresno and Kings County area. They are grown in sandy loam soil in most cases and always under irrigation. A small quantity is grown in southern California in the Cucamonga region and a few near Escondido. The muscat attains high sugar content and is usually of 23° to 25° Brix or higher when picked. One of its defects is the tendency for raisining of some of the grapes on the vine. The raisined grapes are difficult to crush and, if crushed, may darken the color of the wine and impart a raisin flavor.

The muscat is grown in California and Australia principally for drying for raisins. Often in the past, its use for wine making has served as a balance wheel for the raisin industry, absorbing the surplus grapes in years of poor prices for raisins. Muscat grapes are consumed in the fresh condition in California but do not ship well, and, hence, are not very plentiful in the fruit markets.

Fermentation

The muscat grapes are crushed and stemmed as described for other varieties and are pumped into open vats. About 100 mg/liter of sulfur dioxide, or its equivalent of sodium or potassium metabisulfite, should be added at crushing in order to prevent bacterial spoilage. If some of the grapes are moldy, more sulfur dioxide should be used. A starter of yeast should be added; preferably 2—3% of a pure yeast culture, or, less desirably, a similar quantity of fermenting must from another vat.

It is customary to ferment crushed muscat grapes 24 hr or longer before drawing off the fermenting juice or pressing, in order to extract more flavor from the skins and also to get more fluid from the pulpy muscat berry. If the must has not dropped to the degree Brix desired for fortification at the time of pressing, fermentation is continued in another tank. Another procedure used for extracting as much muscat flavor as possible has been to heat the crushed grapes for 2—3 min at 82°C (180°F). Others draw off the free-run, heat to about 70°C (160°F) and pump back over the pomace. While heating processes do increase the amount of muscat aroma extracted, as well as the yield, they may lead to dark-colored wines which are difficult to clarify and are of lesser quality. Skin fermentation and heating may give extra coarseness and bitterness and may prolong aging.

Fortification

The fermenting must is fortified to give a finished wine of about 18% alcohol and 7° Brix. This is over 10% sugar as determined chemically. For a must originally 25° Brix, fortification would be made at about 14°. As in the case with port, it may not be feasible to make every fortification at the proper sugar content. Some wines will be below 7° after fortification. Therefore, it will be necessary to fortify some wines at higher sugar content in order that the Brix of wines of too low degree can be brought to 7° by blending.

The alternative is the sweetening of the wines with muscat grape concentrate. Most wine makers prefer to avoid the expense and trouble of making, storing, and using concentrate. However, without the use of concentrate, the wine maker must see to it that the average degree Brix of his muscatels is close to 7°, and the alcohol about 18%. Greater care in timing the fortification is the proper solution of this problem.

For dessert wines, particularly those of the muscatel type, Flanzy (1959) counsels slow fermentation to better preserve the varietal aroma. He also recommends the fermenting must be of high original sugar. Contributing factors for the production of quality dessert wines in the south of France are the limitation on varieties planted and on their yield per acre to ensure high sugar musts. He also stresses the critical importance of fortifying at the right time. Flanzy distinguishes two types of fortified wines in France. First, *vins doux naturels*, which have not less than 5% and not more than 10% of 90% (or over) alcohol added. The second category is *vins de liqueur* where there is no limit on how much fortification takes place, with alcohol as low as 46% being used. It is not usual to fortify with muscat brandy, but it can be used to enhance the muscat aroma.

Spoilage During Fermentation

During the 1935 vintage, considerable muscat must was lost by acetification during fermentation. Vaughn (1938) showed that this spoilage could be induced by certain strains of rapidly growing acetic bacteria that developed even during yeast fermentation. Cruess (1937) also reported that lactic bacteria as well were responsible in experimental fermentations. The musts that were lost by acetification in the wineries had not been sulfited. As little as 70 mg/liter of sulfur dioxide prevented the spoilage by either acetic or lactic bacteria during fermentation.

Finishing

The subsequent operations for muscatel are approximately as described for port; namely, settling after fortification, fining with bentonite, filtration, refrigeration, cold filtration, pasteurization, and a polishing filtration before bottling. Some wine makers hasten aging by giving the wine a short baking at 50° to 60°C (122° to 140°F) as described for sherry, but such treatment may seriously damage the muscat flavor. Aeration by pumping over, refrigeration, and pasteurization are all aging operations and tend to lessen the rough character of the newly fortified wine but may give it an undersirable oxidized character. Every precaution should be used to keep the color light golden and the flavor fruity during processing and aging.

Proper Aging

Muscatel greatly improves in quality through sufficient aging, that is, aging for 2 to 4 years. This allows the harsh flavor of the added brandy to ameliorate and the new-wine flavor and the yeastiness to completely disappear. The wine becomes mellow and smooth. As Joslyn and Amerine (1964) point out, aeration during several years aging should not be excessive, i.e., the puncheons or casks or tanks should, after the first few months, be kept well filled at least once each 3 to 6 months. Part of the aging period should be in oak, but usually no more than a hint of oakiness is preferred and the cooperage used is often large and well-seasoned. Use of fractional blending systems for aging muscatels appears rational and practicable.

CALIFORNIA TOKAY

California tokay wine is usually a blend of about ⅓ each of port, sherry, and angelica. It must not be too red nor have too strong a baked flavor. The sherry imparts the baked flavor and the port the red color. It has *no* relation in character to Hungarian Tokay, which is not fortified wine, nor to the Flame Tokay table grape variety. Sometimes muscatel is included in the blend to add fruitiness.

CALIFORNIA MALAGA, MADEIRA, AND MARSALA

Only small quantities of these are produced and the standards vary markedly from winery to winery. It is doubtful if they would continue to be produced if there were not a small local demand for them in various parts of the country. Spanish Malaga is a wine from raisined muscat grapes. Portugese Madeiras are baked wines and Italian Marsala is produced with the aid of boiled down must (Chap. 1). California generic wines of the same names have somewhat similar characteristics.

California malaga is made by baking a very sweet sherry material or by sweetening a sherry with grape concentrate (see Bioletti 1934). In eastern United States kosher-type wines, a raisin flavor is usually present but muscat may not be; they have sometimes been labeled as malaga even though more a red sweet table type than a dessert wine.

In California, very little wine called madeira is made. It may be a baked angelica, or sweet sherry, or a blend of angelica and sherry. California sherry is much nearer true Madeira than Spanish sherry, both in character and method of production. It is particularly unfortunate that baked white dessert wine was not called American madeira or some other more appropriate name in the United States rather than sherry now that the flor and aged but not baked sherries are becoming a more important part of U.S. production.

In California, a marsala type is occasionally made by baking sweet fortified sherry material. Joslyn and Amerine (1964) state that black grapes, such as the Mission and Carignane, are sometimes used in California, the grapes being pressed before fermentation. It may be necessary to remove the color by aeration of the must although most of it disappears in baking if some aeration is given. One wine maker formerly concentrated must by boiling it down in an open copper kettle until well caramelized. This was added to the marsala after baking. This wine did resemble Italian Marsala since a burnt flavor is a characteristic feature of this wine (see p. 28). The process is legal in this country.

REFERENCES[1]

ABDURAZAKOVA, S.KH., SALMOV, KH.T. and BABAKHANOV, B.A. 1974. Sposob proizvodstva kreplenykh vin i ikh biokhimicheskaya kharakteristika. (Production of fortified wines and their biochemical characteristics.) Vinodel. Vinograd. S.S.S.R. 5, 21-24.

ALLEN, H.W. 1963. The Wines of Portugal. McGraw-Hill Book Co., New York.

AMERINE, M.A. and DE MATTEI, W. 1940. Color in California wines. III. Methods of removing color from the skins. Food Res. 5, 509-519.

AMERINE, M.A. and WINKLER, A.J. 1938. Angelica. Wines Vines 19 (9) 5, 24.

AZEVEDO, M. PACHECO DE. 1963. Problèmes de la stabilisation du vin de Porto. Ann. Technol. Agric. 12 (numéro hors série 1) 379-389.

BERG, H.W. 1940. Color extraction for port-wine manufacture. Wine Rev. 8 (1) 12-14.

BERG, H.W. and AKIYOSHI, M. 1958. Further studies of the factors affecting the extraction of color and tannin from red grapes. Food Res. 23, 511-517.

BERG, H.W. and AKIYOSHI, M. 1960. The effect of sulfur dioxide and fermentation on color extraction from red grapes. Ibid. 25, 183-189.

BERG, H.W. and MARSH, G.L. 1950. Heat treatment of musts. Ibid. 31 (7) 23-24; (8) 29-30.

BIOLETTI, F.T. 1934. How Marsala is made. Calif. Grape Grower 15 (12) 5, 17.

CASTELLA, F. DE. 1908. Port. Victoria Dept. Agric. J. 6, 176-191.

COFFELT, R.J. and BERG, H.W. 1965. Color extraction by heating whole grapes. Am J. Enol. Vitic. 16, 117-128.

CORDONNIER, R. 1956. Recherches sur l'aromatisation et le parfum des vins doux naturels et des vins de liqueur. Ann. Technol. Agric. 5, 75-110.

COSTA, L.C. DA. 1938. O problema das aguardentes e dos alcoóis. Influência da sua origem e grau na beneficiação de vinho. Anais Inst. Super. Agron., Univ. Téc. Lisboa 9, 67-76.

CRUESS, W.V. 1937. Observations on volatile acid formation in muscat fermentations. Fruit Prod. J. 16, 198-200, 219.

CRUESS, W.V., BROWN, E.M. and FLOSSFEDER, F.C. 1916. Unfortified sweet wines of high alcohol content. Ind. Eng. Chem. 8, 1124-1126.

CRUESS, W.V. and HOHL, L.A. 1937. Syruped fermentation of sweet wines. Wine Rev. 5 (11) 12, 24-25.

DEIBNER, L. 1957. Évolution du potentiel oxydoréducteur au cours de la maturation des vins. Ann. Technol. Agric. 6, 347-362.

---

[1]Titles have been translated only for nonwestern European languages.

EGOROV, A.A., KOTLIARÉNKO, M.R. and PREOBRAZHENSKIĬ, A.A. 1951. U lushenie kachestva spirtovannykh vinogradnykh vin. (Improvement in wine quality from fortifying spirits.) Vinodel. Vinograd. S.S.S.R. *11* (8) 6-8.

FLANZY, M. 1959. Élaboration des vins spiritueux doux. Ann. Technol. Agric. *8*, 81-100.

FLETCHER, W. 1978. Port, an Introduction to Its History and Delights. Sotheby Parke-Bernet, London.

GOSWELL, R.W. and KUNKEE, R.E. 1977. Fortified wines. *In* Economic Microbiology, Vol. 1. A.H. Rose (Editor). Academic Press, London.

HOHL, L.A. 1938. Further observations on production of alcohol by *Saccharomyces ellipsoideus* in syruped fermentations. Food Res. *3*, 453-465.

HOHL, L.A. and CRUESS, W.V. 1936. Effect of temperature, variety of juice and method of increasing sugar content on maximum alcohol production by *Saccharomyces ellipsoideus. Iid 1*, 405-411.

JOSLYN, M.A. and AMERINE, M.A. 1964. Dessert, Appetizer and Related Flavored Wines. University of California, Division of Agricultural Sciences, Berkeley.

LACHMAN, H. 1903. A monograph on the manufacture of wines in California. U.S. Dept. Agric. Bur. Chem. Bull. *72*, 25-40.

LITTLE, A.C. 1971. The color of white wine. I. A review and critical analysis of the Lovibond unit specification. Am. J. Enol. Vitic. *22*, 138-143.

LOWE, E.J., OEY, A. and TURNER, T.M. 1976. Gasquet thermovinification system perspective after two years' operation. Am. J. Enol. Vitic. *27*, 130-133.

NEDELTCHEV, N.J. 1959. Research on basic technology of dessert wines of the Shiróka Melnishka Loza variety (transl.) Nauch. Trud. Tekh. Inst. Vina Vino. Promishlenost. *3*, 1-37.

NURY, M.S. 1957. Continuous color and juice extraction of grapes. Wine Inst. Tech. Advis. Committee, Dec. 6, 1957, San Francisco.

OTTAVI, O. and GARINO-CANINA, E. 1930. Vini di Lusso, Aceti di Lusso. 8 ed. Casa Editrice Fratelli Ottavi, Casale Monferrato.

RAMOS, M. DA C. and GOMES, L.G. 1969. Determinação espectrafotometrica do furfural e do *p*-hidroximetilfurfural. An. Inst. Vinho Porto *1967-68* (22) 48-70.

RAMOS, M. DA C. and GOMES, L.G. 1974. Os álcoóis superiores no vinho do Porto. An. Inst. Vinho Porto *1972-73* (25) 97-115.

RIBEIRO, M.B. 1968. Apreciação da cor no vinho do Porto, avaliação e interpretação das suas caracteristicas aromaticas. An. Inst. Vinho Porto *1965-66* (21) 133-186.

ROBERTSON, R. 1978. Port. Faber and Faber, London and Boston.

SIMON, A.L. 1934. Port. Constable and Co., London.

SINGLETON, V.L. 1974. Some aspects of the wooden container as a factor in wine maturation. *In* Chemistry of Winemaking. A.D. Webb (Editor). Advan. Chem. *137*, 254-277. Amer. Chem. Soc., Washington, D.C.

SINGLETON, V.L. and GUYMON, J.F. 1963. A test of fractional addition of wine spirits to red and white port wines. Am. J. Enol. Vitic. *14*, 129-136.

SINGLETON, V.L., BERG, H.W. and GUYMON, J.F. 1964. Anthocyanin color level in port-type wines as affected by the use of wine spirits containing aldehydes. *Ibid. 15*, 75-81.

TWIGHT, E.H. 1934. Sweet wine making in California. Calif. Grape Grower *15* (10) 4-5; (11) 4-5, 7.

TWIGHT, E.H. and AMERINE, M.A. 1938. Wines made from Muscat grapes. Wines Vines *19* (7) 3-4.

VAN WYK, C.J., KEPNER, R.E. and WEBB, A.D. 1967. Some volatile components of *Vitis vinifera* variety White Riesling. 3. Neutral components extracted from wine. J. Food Sci. *32*, 669-674.

VAUGHN, R.H. 1938. Some effects of association and competition on *Acetobacter*. J. Bacteriol. *36*, 357-367.

11

Sparkling Wine Production

Sparkling wines, those which contain a visible excess of carbon dioxide, are difficult to define precisely. The present United States maximum for still wines is 0.392 g/100 ml of carbon dioxide at 15.6°C (60°F) (U.S. Internal Revenue Service 1961). This is equivalent to 1.10 bars (15.9 lb/sq in.) pressure. Protin (1960) notes most countries now distinguish (at least unofficially) between slightly gassy wine, *crémant*, pearl, *perlant*, *perlé*, or *pétillant*, from those with full pressure as shown below:

Country	Type	Pressure lb/sq in., bars	Tem-perature	
			°C	°F
Australia	*Pétillant*	1.1 Max, 0.0758	20	68
	Sparkling	10.0 Min, 0.689	20	68
Chile	Sparkling	10.0 Min, 0.689	15	59
France	*Pétillant*	3.3 Max, 0.227	15	59
	Sparkling	10.0 Min, 0.689	15	59
Germany	*Pétillant*	1.1 Max, 0.0758	20	68
	Sparkling	6.6 Min, 0.455	20	68
Spain	*Pétillant*	2.2 Max, 0.197	?	?
	Sparkling	7.7 Min, 0.530	?	?
Switzerland	*Pétillant*	1.1 Max, 0.0758	15	59
	Sparkling	8.8[1] Min, 0.606	15	59

[1]Also the minimum is reported as 4 g/liter which does not check with the data in Table 11.1.

The problem is complicated in this country because of the higher taxes on sparkling compared to still wines. Postel (1970) gives 1.8–2.0 g of carbon dioxide per liter as the limit above which the wine may no longer be considered "still." Jaulmes (1973) should be consulted for data on pressure and carbon dioxide content.

DEFINITION

Methods of production are inadequate to define types of sparkling wine.

TABLE 11.1. RELATIONSHIP OF PRESSURE AT 15.56°C (60°F) TO AMOUNT OF CARBON DIOXIDE IN WINE[1]

Pounds Pressure per sq in.	Volume of CO_2	CO_2 Dissolved g/100 ml
0	0.95	0.1866
1	1.00	0.1964
2	1.08	0.2121
3	1.15	0.2259
4	1.23	0.2416
5	1.30	0.2560
6	1.35	0.2652
7	1.40	0.2750
8	1.45	0.2848
9	1.52	0.2986
10	1.65	0.3241

[1]Source of data: U.S. Internal Revenue Service (1961).

The consumer is not interested in the method of production as much as in the recognizability of the various types. Here, we arbitrarily define as sparkling wines those which have more than 1.5 atm pressure at 10°C (50°F). The amount of dissolved carbon dioxide at this pressure and temperature is approximately 0.39 g/100 ml. If the carbon dioxide is kept at this figure, the pressure at 15.7°C (60°F) will be about 1.8 atm; at 21.1°C (70°F), 2.1 atm; and at 26.7°C (80°F), 2.4 atm (see Fig. 11.1). This is about half the minimum suggested by the Office International de la Vigne et du Vin for sparkling wines: 4 atm at 20°C (68°F) (Protin 1960).

The enologist, tax expert, and connoisseur need a detailed classification of the types on the market. In the classification which follows there are some overlappings in carbon dioxide content. The *source* of the carbon dioxide is the basis of this subdivision. There may be no sensory test which will consistently distinguish between types!

Type   I. Excess carbon dioxide produced by fermentation of residual sugar from the primary fermentation. This includes many Alsatian, German, Loire, and Italian wines as well as the muscato amabile in California.

Type   II. Excess carbon dioxide from a malo-lactic fermentation. The Vinho Verde wines of northern Portugal are representative of this type, but there are examples in Italy and elsewhere in Europe.

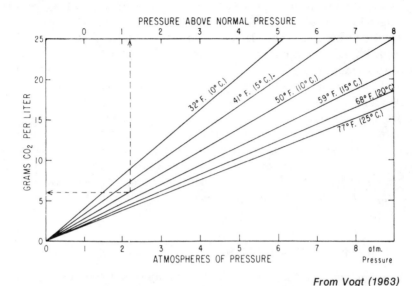

FIG. 11.1. EFFECT OF PRESSURE AND TEMPERATURE ON CARBON DIOXIDE CONTENT

Type III. Excess carbon dioxide from fermentation of sugar added after the process of fermentation. Most of the sparkling wines of the world are produced by this procedure.

Type IV. Excess carbon dioxide added. This includes the carbonated wines and many "crackling" wines.

Carpenè (1959) distinguished four types of fermented sparkling wines: (1) slow bottle fermentation, long aging on yeast, disgorging, (2) same but transferred and filtered, (3) rapid bottle fermentation, no aging on lees, transferred and filtered, and (4) tank fermented. He stresses the importance of aging on the yeast. He agrees with Schanderl (1943, 1959) that while the fermentation is the same in tanks or bottles the products of methods (1) and (3) or (4) are different. See also Amerine and Monaghan (1950).

TYPE I SPARKLING WINES

Almost any wine can be made sparkling by stopping the fermentation before all of the must sugar has fermented and then, later, bottling the wine. If a few viable yeasts are in the wine at the time of bottling, and the sulfur dioxide content is not excessive, the sugar will most likely ferment later and the wine will become gassy. If the fermentation is slow at a low even temperature, the amount of yeast cells produced may be surprisingly low. In some cases, when the yeast deposit is excessive, the wines are treated as Type III sparkling wines and clarified in the usual way (p. 305 *et seq.*). Sparkling wines probably originated in this manner. It is no accident that the first centers of sparkling wine production were in northern France. It is in such cold regions that the initial fermentation is slow and incomplete. When the temperature increased the following spring the fermentations restarted and gassy wines resulted.[1]

More wines of this type are not produced because it is difficult to stop the fermentation with the desired residual sugar content. However, with technological control of fermentation (temperature, pressure, depletion of amino acids, etc.) it should not be difficult to produce such wines. The addition of *high quality* grape concentrate before fermentation also offers interesting possibilities.

TYPE II SPARKLING WINES

Sparkling wines of this type are not normally produced in this country. Italian red wines are found which are gassy and in some cases this is owing to the growth of lactic acid bacteria. It is unlikely that regular production of such types can be expected. To secure an adequate malo-lactic fermentation, the wines must be of relatively low alcohol content and contain malic acid. Overcropped vines produce grapes of low sugar and high malic acid. These yield wines with the desired composition—low alcohol and high acid. Such conditions exist in the Minho district of northern Portugal and in parts of Italy. Often a malo-lactic fermentation takes place, naturally or induced, after bottling and gassy wines result.

The process is unlikely to be a popular one for two reasons: the wines are of low alcohol and thin; and the process is difficult to control as the growth of the bacteria is not easy to predict or even to induce.

TYPE III SPARKLING WINES

In the early 19th century when sugar became easily available and a more scientific concept of the process of alcoholic fermentation began to develop, this type of wine began to be produced on a commercial scale. The tradition that it originated in the 18th century with the Benedictine monk, Dom Pérignon, in the Champagne region of France is a

[1]This is as good a place as any to lay to rest the romantic idea that wine is *per se* a living thing which moves in sympathy, i.e., ferments and becomes gassy, with the vines in the spring and fall. Wine is a living thing because of the microorganisms and enzyme systems which it contains and it does move "in sympathy" with the vine for precisely the same reasons that the vine shows seasonal growth—changes in temperature. If the wine is kept at a constant temperature such activity is not restricted to the spring and fall.

pretty one and is nicely demolished by Chappaz (1951). Chappaz pays tribute to Dom Pérignon, as well as a number of others, for perfecting the culture of the vine and the production of wine in such a northern region. Possibly he was responsible for introduction of the heavy tied-in cork. Chappaz (1951) believes his blending of wines from different areas of the Champagne region was his great contribution to the Champagne industry. It was not until the sugar tables of François were published in 1829 that the *sparkling* wine trade of this district began to be commercially successful.

Champagne

The old province of Champagne in northern France has given its name to the most famous sparkling wine in the world. It is one of the most imitated types of wine. We have discussed elsewhere (pp. 13−16) the primary factors influencing the quality of this wine type: mixing of white wines from red and white grapes to achieve the necessary balance of alcohol and fruitiness;[2] skilled blending of wines of different parts of the district and even of different years; slow cool fermentations; relatively long aging in the bottle and control of the sugar content of the finished product. Even before the Champagne riots of 1910−1911, the district had been delimited (on January 4, 1909, for example) and only wines produced from grapes grown in this district may now be sold as Champagne in France and the European Common Market. For production details, see Françot (1945, 1950), Françot and Geoffroy (1951), and Weinmann and Telle (1929).

Sparkling wines from other parts of France are legally know as *vins mousseux*, even though they may be fermented in the bottle and otherwise handled by the same procedures as Champagne. Some tank-fermented sparkling wines are produced in France where they are also sold as *mousseux* (Pacottet and Guittonneau 1930).

Other Regions

German sparkling wine (*Schaumwein*) is commonly sold as *Sekt*, a coined name which does not refer to sugar content. Tank and bottle processes are used (Herzog 1954; Koch 1923; Schanderl 1938; Vogt 1977). In Italy non-muscat sparkling wines are usually sold as *spumante* or *gran spumante* and muscat sparkling wines as *moscato spumante*. Both the tank and bottle processes are used in Italy. The muscat-flavored Asti *spumante* is usually produced by a filtration system (Tarantola 1937). Kichkovshiĭ (1963) showed the resulting wine to be low in total ni-

[2]This truly brilliant idea is also credited to Dom Pérignon.

trogen and in most, but not all, amino acids. Spain and Portugal produce *espumante*.[3]

In Australia and the United States, tank and bottle-fermented wines are sold as champagne. South Africa sells its sparkling wines as such, i.e., not under the name champagne. There is a large sparkling wine industry in the Soviet Union where the wine is called *shampanskii* (Brusilovskiï *et al.* 1977) and in Argentina, where it is labeled *champaña*.

The sparkling wine industry in the Finger Lakes region of New York dates back to 1860. Light white wine of the area when properly blended produced a good sparkling product. Delaware, Catawba, Dutchess and other varieties have been used. For sparkling burgundy, varieties such as Ives Seedling, Fredonia, Clinton, and Concord make an acceptable base. Cold Duck is a red sparkling wine, with or without labrusca flavor, made in various states. It must be a blend of red and white wine, not less than 60 to 40 either way.

California

One of the first sparkling wines produced in California was that of Arpad Haraszthy in 1860's. It was made by the traditional bottle-fermentation process; Haraszthy received his training in France. Prior to Prohibition a number of California producers had sparkling wines on the market, all produced by the bottle-fermentation process except a few carbonated types. Following repeal, bottle and tank sparkling wine production increased slowly until after World War II. Since then, production has increased more sharply as shown in Table 11.2. Both bottle- and tank-fermented production have increased. Since 1958, much of the bottle production has been handled by the transfer system (p. 464).

TYPE IV SPARKLING WINES

The production of carbonated wines is decreasing in this country. At least two reasons are probably responsible. Following repeal, some over-aged and high sulfur dioxide wines were carbonated in the mistaken belief that the American public would buy any sparkling wine. Secondly, producers, distributors, and retailers often overpriced carbonated wines so they had little price differential from other sparkling wines. This was partially due to the discriminatory and excessive taxes which the federal government places on all sparkling wines.

However, carbonated wines have a place on the American market,

---

[3]A Spanish sparkling wine imported into Great Britain as Spanish champagne was granted the right to use this name, much to the annoyance of the French Champagne industry. Court action reversed this decision. See Simon (1962) for an illuminating history of the incident.

TABLE 11.2. SPARKLING WINE ENTERING DISTRIBUTION CHANNELS IN THE UNITED STATES ACCORDING TO ORIGIN, 1949 TO 1976 INCLUSIVE (IN 1000 GAL.)

Year[1]	United States Produced			Foreign Produced[2]	Total
	California	Other States	Total		
1949−1950	382	699	1,081	512	1,593
1951−1955	532	847	1,379	627	2,006
1956−1960	1,311	1,331	2,642	821	3,463
1961−1965	2,326	2,322	4,828	1,131	5,794
1966−1970	7,461	4,626	12,087	1,996	14,083
1971−1975	15,117	4,425	19,542	1,921	21,463
1976−1978[3]	17,058	3,577	20,635	3,267	23,902

Source: Compiled by Wine Institute from reports of the U.S. Treasury Department, Internal Revenue Service, U.S. Department of Commerce, Bureau of the Census and California State Board of Equalization.
[1]Calendar year.
[2]Imports for consumption.
[3]Preliminary for 1978.

especially if the tax structure and type definition become more realistic. The odious "carbonated" might be avoided by the use of special names. The popularity of some of the imported carbonated "crackling" wines is evidence that this can be accomplished.

PRODUCTION OF THE CUVÉE

The ideal wine for bottle fermentation is also quite appropriate for the tank process.

Varieties

The grapes should not be allowed to become too ripe, since the wine to be used for a sparkling wine should be of good acidity and not too high in alcohol content. In California, grapes suitable for making the highest quality sparkling wines have been grown successfully in regions I to III. In regions IV and V, if the grapes are picked early in the season when they have just reached 19°−20° Brix, wines of acceptable, though neutral, quality may be produced.

The best variety for California sparkling wine is still not established. Amerine and Monaghan (1950) found White Riesling suitable, if the grapes are not too ripe. Its low productivity makes it expensive to produce. Folle Blanche and Burger have produced a number of pleasant sparkling wines but little is available. French Colombard is suitably high in acid but has a rather too-pronounced aroma. Chenin blanc produces wines which may be useful. Chardonnay and Pinot noir are recommended but must be harvested early in California. The importance of the cuvée has been emphasized by Rossi (1965): "a sparkling wine can be no better than the base wine used and the base wine, in turn, can be no better than the grapes originally crushed." He emphasized that not only good varieties but harvesting at the optimum maturity and "cold" fermentations were desirable.

Processing

Only the free-run should be used since a light color is desired. Sulfur dioxide may be necessary to permit settling of the musts. Cold storage and centrifugation are also used. The fermentation should be carried to completion. It is a mistake to leave fermentable sugar in the wine although in pre-Prohibition days it was customary to do so. Champagne yeast, a culture or pressed, and a cool fermenting temperature (15.6°C, 60°F or less) are desirable practices.

The fermented wine should contain no more than 10−11.5% alcohol. If the alcohol content is higher, it will be difficult to secure satisfactory fermentation in the bottle or tank. If too low, the wine will not keep well and the addition of brandy may be necessary to attain the proper alcohol content in the finished product. As little as possible should be used.

When fermentation is complete and the lees have settled, the wine is racked and filtered.

Pure, light-colored tannin was formerly added (0.01−0.03%) but this is seldom required. Nowadays, the wine is fined with bentonite, or less often with gelatin or isinglass, as described in Chap. 6. Gelatin fining will remove most of the residual tannin but must be used with care. A further racking and close filtration are also needed.

Tartrate stabilization is essential in sparkling wine production. The procedures previously given (p. 305) may be employed. Rossi (1965) found no adverse effect on fermentation when a portion of the wine was ion-exchanged. Schanderl (1965B) found cuvées made with cation-exchange wine fermented slowly in the bottle.

Blending

The four critical stages in the preparation of sparkling wines are (1) the preparation of a well-balanced cuvée, (2) the proper conduct of the fermentation, (3) the aging on the lees (for bottle-fermentation), and (4) the clarification.

It is rare that a single wine having all the desired characteristics for the cuvée is available in sufficient quantity. It is necessary, therefore, to blend several lots of wine to secure the desired quality and quantity.

The cuvée should first be prepared in the laboratory based on analysis and sensory examination. The primary requisites are a good total acidity (0.70 g/100 ml or more), a low volatile acidity (below 0.040 g/100 ml), a moderate alcohol content (between 10 and 11.5%), a light yellow color, a fresh and impeccably clean flavor, a relatively low pH (below 3.3), a balanced aroma in which no single varietal characteristic predominates, and low aldehyde content. Citric acid may be added to increase the acidity and to inhibit ferric phosphate. Producers also balance the acidity by judicious blending of wines of suitable acidity. The policy of the individual producer and the demands of his clientele will determine the proper level of acidity.

The wines should be low in sulfur dioxide to secure the maximum quality. A total sulfur dioxide limit of 60 mg/liter was suggested by Manceau (1929) and we see no reason to raise this limit. Sulfur dioxide may reduce the rate of fermentation and it may give a foreign odor to sparkling wines. Paul (1960) analyzed sparkling Austrian wines that had been awarded gold, silver and bronze medals. The total sulfur dioxide content of the 6 gold medal wines ranged from 53 to 92 mg/liter (average 70), in the 12 silver medal wines from 18 to 220 (average 112), and in the 5 bronze medal wines 51 to 201 (average 145). In 7 French Champagnes, the total varied from 23 to 72 mg/liter (average 55). Only one of the gold medal wines had any free sulfur dioxide and none of the Champagnes had any. Paul recommends as small an amount of sulfur dioxide as possible both in the fermentation of the musts and in the preparation of the cuvée. Paul also analyzed the wines for the other constituents, none of which appeared to be significantly related to quality. The best sparkling wines had a pH of 3−3.2 and a titratable acidity of 0.65−0.75 g $H_2Ta/100$ ml.

When a suitable laboratory blend is selected, a blend of a few gallons is prepared and a trial bottling made. The cuvée will have to be cold-stabilized and filtered.

United States regulations require that wines with a vintage label be at least 95% of the year given. French regulations require that no more than 80% of a given vintage can be used for producing vintage-labeled sparkling wines. This is a recognition of the difficulty of securing a perfectly balanced wine of a single vintage. California producers no longer must ferment wines intended for vintage dating, thus preventing them from buying wines, even of the same vintage, to balance their own stocks. The pertinent law was recently repealed. We see less need in California for permitting blending in a certain portion of wines of another vintage to balance vintage wines.

Sugaring

The wine maker will now have a brilliant wine of the proper aroma, flavor, and alcohol content. The pressure desired in sparkling wines at the end of the closed fermentation is about 5 to 6 atm at 10°C (50°F); that is, about 75 to 90 lb pressure per square inch. For each atmosphere of pressure approximately 0.4% of sugar (4 g/liter) is required. Thus, to produce 6 atm pressure would require 6 × 0.4 or 2.4%, or 24 g/liter sugar, or about 20 lb/100 gal. of wine. The wine must be analyzed for its reducing sugar content and allowed for in calculating the amount to be added. Thus, if the wine contains 0.5% sugar, that is, 5 g/liter, then there would be required 24–(5–1) or 20 g/liter to give 6 atm pressure. (About 1 g does not ferment.) Unless this allowance is made, too much sugar may be added, resulting in excessive loss through bursting of the bottles during fermentation.

The sugar is dissolved in a brilliant stable wine to give a solution of 500 g/liter of sugar, that is, a 50% solution of sugar in wine. There is also added 1.0–1.5% citric acid, which, if the wine is allowed to stand several weeks before use, will invert much of the cane sugar. Or, if the wine to be bottled has a rather high alcohol content, the sugar may be dissolved in water and the solution heated with the acid to hasten inversion. Invert syrup may be purchased and diluted with wine to 50% sugar content. The syrup must be free of iron, or it may cause the wine to cloud in the bottle because of ferric phosphate casse. For wine maker's use, it should be delivered in tanks or drums, as are corn syrup and molasses. The diluted syrup should be filtered to remove pieces of lint, etc.

After addition of one of the above to the wine to be bottle- or tank-fermented, the wine should be thoroughly mixed because the syrup tends to settle to the bottom of the mixing tank. A glass-lined tank with mechanical agitator is very useful for mixing the syrup and the wine. If the syrup contains exactly 50% sugar, the amount to be added to the wine is easily calculated. A laboratory test of the reducing sugar content is a useful precaution.

Yeasting

Well in advance of making up the sweetened wine for bottling, a pure culture of fermenting yeast should be prepared in sufficient quantity. This should be of the champagne yeast type; that is, a granulating or agglomerating yeast that forms a coarse, heavy sediment in the bottle and that can be completely and easily removed after fermentation in the bottle is complete.

To prepare a starter of yeast, use wine from the same lot that is to be bottled later. Begin about 8 days in advance of bottling with a room temperature of about 21.1°C (70°F). The yeast is received from the supplier in a small bottle or test tube in which the yeast is growing on the surface of agar. To some of the wine to be used in preparing the starter, add enough of the wine syrup (containing 50% sugar) to give about 5% sugar. Add to the test tube of yeast culture. Shake gently to aerate. Store in a warm place (21.1°−29.4°C, 70°−85°F) until fermenting. Then prepare about ⅔ of a gallon of wine by adding enough of the syrup to give 5% sugar. Shake the test tube of fermenting yeast culture, and add the liquid to the wine in the gallon bottle. Plug with cotton and shake well. When in fermentation it may be used to start the fermentation of 5 gal. or more of wine of 5% sugar content. When this has fermented to 1 or 2% sugar, it may be used to inoculate the lot of wine. Enough pure yeast starter is required to allow the addition of 2 or 3% starter to the wine to be bottle- or tank-fermented. Large sparkling wine producers should maintain a vigorous starter in wine continuously. Dried yeast starters are available. Sulfur dioxide acclimated and alcohol-tolerant strains are preferred. Stainless steel tanks are useful for this purpose.

The starter is added to the sugared wine and the wine stirred to distribute the yeast evenly throughout the wine; during bottling, gentle agitation is required to prevent the yeast from settling to the bottom, thus giving too little yeast in some bottles and too much in others. Occasionally ammonium phosphate (or urea) is a desirable addition to provide yeast food; the amount required will probably lie between 0.5 and 1.0 g/liter. Tannin or charcoal is seldom desirable or necessary. A number of wineries add bentonite. During bottling the wine must be well aerated since air is necessary for growth of the yeast.

Bottling

Bottles for sparkling wines must withstand relatively high pressure and therefore are of special design and of thick glass. Careful annealing is necessary to give bottles of sufficient strength. Inspection under polarized light of a certain number of bottles of each lot for defects is good practice. The 0.1-gal. (375-ml), 0.2-gal. (now 750-ml) and 0.4-gal.(magnum, 1500-ml) bottles are normally used. Larger sizes are filled from smaller bottles. The wine is placed in clean, dry bottles and closed with crown caps or corked with large "champagne" corks. It is recommended that these corks be softened by placing them in a basket and moistening them several times a day until soft enough to be used, often 2 to 3 days. They should not be softened by soaking in hot water. The cork is held in place by an iron clamp (*agrafe*). The clamp is applied easily and rapidly by a special machine and may be used repeatedly. Most wineries now use crown caps. They are cheaper, give fewer "leakers," and are easier to remove for disgorging or transfer.

The Second Fermentation

Some wineries neglect the heat produced by the secondary fermentation and the temperature of the fermentation room may rise too high, resulting in poorer carbon dioxide absorption and greater bottle breakage. About 15.6°C (60°F) should be the maximum for the bottle fermentation if quality sparkling wine is to be produced. Two considerations apparently cause producers to use a higher temperature for this fermentation. First is the desire for a very rapid turnover. Second is the fear that at too cool a temperature some of the bottles may not ferment to dryness. The bottles must be placed horizontally, not upright, in order that the corks be kept wet with the wine (Fig. 11.2). During the sec-

Courtesy of Wine Institute

FIG. 11.2. CHAMPAGNE BOTTLES AWAITING CLARI-FICATION

ondary fermentation the producer should periodically examine bottles from the pile to determine the completeness of the fermentation.

The wine should be left in contact with the yeast at least a year before disgorging, in order that fermentation will be complete, to allow the yeast cells to die, and to permit development of the "champagne" bouquet. The importance of this aging on the yeast cannot be overemphasized if bottle-fermented sparkling wines are to be distinctively different from tank-fermented wines. If the fermentation is not uniform or appears unusually slow, then the stack should be torn down, the contents shaken up, and the bottles restacked in their original position—easily done by placing a chalk mark on the bottom of the bottle to indicate the original position of the sediment in the bottle.

Finishing

The yeast sediment must be removed from the bottles, or the wine from the yeast in the case of the tank process.

From Bottles.—In order to get the yeast onto the cork, the bottles are placed *sur point* (or *en masse*, or *sur latte*, or *sur pupître*), that is, upside down in racks with the bottles nearly vertical, necks downward (Fig. 11.3). The bottles are turned frequently to the right and to the left while they are in this position to loosen the yeast and cause it to settle (called riddling); the bottle is at the same time "jolted" by dropping it back into the rack to dislodge the yeast (Fig. 11.4). Eventually, the yeast and other sediment rest on the cork. There is an art to getting the light and heavy deposits down onto the cork at the same time. A white mark is made on the bottom of the bottle to guide the "turner" as to how much distance to the right or left the bottle should be turned each day. Wineries also "spin" the bottles to dislodge the sediment before riddling.

Usually, the bottles are turned ⅛ of a turn per day. The shaking is accomplished by letting the bottles drop back onto the racks after the twirling. At the start, the bottles are kept at a less acute angle. Later, the angle of the bottles in the racks is increased. A skilled turner can handle up to 30,000 bottles per day unless the clarification is slow. Wines differ greatly in their rate of clarification. A coarse granular sediment may move onto the cork within a week; others need a month or more.

Masking is the term used when some of the solids stick to the sides of the bottle during and after fermentation. These deposits are difficult to remove. They are not caused by a malo-lactic fermentation but appear to result from interactions of fatty acids, albumin fining agents and the glass surface (Maujean *et al.* 1978).

FIG. 11.3. CHAMPAGNE BOTTLES ON RACKS

The bottles may be stacked in cages or boxes and mechanically tilted or subjected to vibration to simulate the riddling process.

Transfer System.—Because of the labor and other problems inherent in clearing a bottle of its deposit, the "transfer" system was developed in Germany. The fermentation in the bottles takes place as above. However, the bottles are not placed in racks but are chilled and emptied into a tank under nitrogen or carbon dioxide pressure. A special emptying apparatus permits this with a minimum loss of wine or pressure (Fig. 11.5). From the tank, the dosaged wine is then filtered, under pressure, to bottles. The bottles are washed and reused to receive the filtered wine. As Geiss (1959) points out, the transfer system is not new—patents were issued as early as 1903, one to Karl Kiefer of Cincinnati. The main objections to individual disgorging of bottles are the unaesthetic use of the finger to remove yeast in the neck of the bottle, the loss of wine and pressure, and the high labor cost.

Wines produced by the transfer system have a considerable economic advantage over those produced entirely by the bottle process. The costly riddling step is eliminated. The cost and loss of wine during disgorging are also eliminated. They also enjoy an advantage over the tank system since they can be labeled "champagne" without the *déclassé* statement that they are "bulk-fermented," "fermented in bulk," "Charmat" pro-

Courtesy of Gold Seal Vineyards

FIG. 11.4. RIDDLING BOTTLE-FERMENTED NEW YORK SPARK-LING WINE

cess, etc. It is also possible to disgorge wines of different ages into the transfer tank and thus create blends.

If wineries using the transfer system aged the wine in the bottles for at least a year before transferring, there would be less to criticize in the practice. However, the transfer system is often used on wines which have barely completed their fermentation. Many viable yeast cells are present. Since it is difficult to germ-proof filter a wine under pressure, viable yeast cells may get into the bottle. When these wines contain an appreciable percentage of reducing sugar they may referment unless considerable sulfur dioxide is added. The same problem arises with the tank system as we shall presently point out (p. 474).

Disgorging.—The next operation in the normal bottle process is that of disgorging (Fig. 11.6). This is accomplished by freezing a small "plug" of wine in the neck of the bottle next to the cork. The wine in the bottles

FIG. 11.5. CHAMPAGNE BOTTLES BEING PLACED IN TRANSFER MACHINE

also should first be cooled to about 7.2°C (45°F) to reduce the pressure. The freezing mixture can be an ice and calcium chloride mixture or various proprietary products. The operation is mechanized so that bottles enter the cold bath, neck down, at a constant rate and are removed when the neck is properly frozen.

Disgorging is the removal of the yeast and other deposits which have been so carefully collected on the cork, with hopefully, minimum loss of pressure. The bottle is held at a 45° upward angle pointing into an opening cut in the side of a barrel or similar receiver (Fig. 11.7). The clamp is then removed and the pressure in the bottle allowed to force out the cork and ice plug. If a crown cap is used it is easily pried off.

Occasionally, when a bottle under pressure is opened the wine will gush out. Gushing is caused by dirty bottles, from bottles with rough interiors, from particles in the wine, when air is used as a counterpressure during bottling, from excess carbon dioxide, insufficient chilling, etc.

The bottle is now quickly returned to a vertical position. Any yeast adhering to the neck of the bottle is removed with the finger or a special rubber covered stick. The careful disgorger will also smell the froth from a bottle to be sure that no hydrogen sulfide has developed. Automatic disgorging machines are now available.

Courtesy of Irroy

FIG. 11.6. CHAMPAGNE DISGORGING

The bottles can then be placed in a rack which seals the mouth of the bottle until it can be filled and corked. Or the bottle is passed on directly in the bottling line for dosage and filling. Enough wine or liqueur must be added to replace that lost in disgorging. The wine at this stage is "dry," that is, very low in sugar content. Many consumers prefer that the champagne contain some to considerable sugar—markets vary in their requirements.

A syrup is prepared of cane sugar, fine brandy (Cognac has been used by some American producers, California brandy by others), and high quality, well-aged, white wine. Some use a wine of about 20% alcohol to which sugar is added until the wine is about 50% sugar. To prevent refermentation, up to 150 mg/liter of sulfur dioxide are added. The usual syrup contains 60 g/100 ml of sugar and about 10 to 15% as much brandy as wine. If a very sweet champagne is desired, the syrup is not diluted; if a "dry" champagne is to be made, the syrup may be diluted with wine to the necessary extent before addition to the bottle. In either

FIG. 11.7. DISGORGING SPARKLING WINE IN NEW YORK CELLAR

Note freezing unit on left and dosage machine in rear

case, a measured amount is added, and, if the bottle is then not sufficiently full, sufficient champagne from another bottle is added. Machines that add the syrup automatically in measured amounts are available. In adding the syrup, the liquid must be poured in gently and allowed to flow down the side of the bottle to avoid frothing. The bottle is then corked and the cork wired down in the characteristic manner with a machine designed for the purpose.

Single, double, and up to 5-piece corks are found on the market. Corks are being replaced by polyethylene closures for the final bottling in many areas. These appear to be satisfactory for short storage periods and are less costly than cork. However, they are more porous to air than cork stoppers. Consumers generally like polyethylene stoppers for sparkling wines because of their ease of removal and their cleanness; however, Stephan (1964) reported an appreciable number of consumers thought them "untraditional."

The usual significance of the marks on the labels for sparkling wines is *brut* or *nature* (for the driest), *sec* and *demi-sec* (for the medium sweet) and *doux* (for the sweetest). Because of the prestige value of *brut* some producers make their *brut* very sweet—up to 2 or even 2.5% sugar. Doubtless, this appeals to people and is good for sales. However, the producer who is trying to make a high quality really dry *brut* will find it hard to compete since a dry *brut* demands a higher quality (and more expensive) raw material than a "sweet" *brut*.

Bruts should be restricted to less than 1.5% reducing sugar, *secs* to about 2 to 4%, and *demi-secs* to about 5%. Should a *doux* be produced, a sugar content of 6% or more is indicated. Similar levels for Austria were given by Paul (1960).

There may be breakage during fermentation in bottles. There is considerable danger also to the operator during disgorging and handling of the sealed bottles. This danger is reduced if the bottles are refrigerated before handling. *Whenever undisgorged or warm sparkling wine bottles are handled the operator's face should be protected by a face mask.*

Sparkling burgundy can be prepared by the bottle or tank process. Red wine may be somewhat more difficult to referment than white. The difference appears to be due to the tannins and their usually higher alcohol content.

Hemphill (1965) noted that bottle-fermented sparkling wines constituted a decreasing percentage of the total American sparkling wine production. This is due, he states, to increasing labor costs rather than to any claimed quality advantage of tank-fermented or transfer system wines. To reduce costs, Hemphill recommends plywood bins holding about 500 bottles, use of a forklift, and automated riddling. He believes that an electric vibrator largely eliminated riddling. He used portable electric vibrators with permanently mounted air vibrators connected to solenoid valves and timed to work at night. No manual riddling was necessary. By combinations of vibration time and frequency the clarification time was reduced. Bidan (1975) also notes the increasing costs.

From Tanks.—In California, the Soviet Union, and elsewhere, much of the sparkling wine is made by the tank or Charmat process (Tschenn 1934). The preparation of the cuvée is exactly the same for tank- and bottle-fermented wines. The economic advantage of the tank process is rapid fermentation and less labor cost. Care must be considered in selecting the temperature of fermentation. Various wineries ferment at temperatures as low as 10°C (50°F) and as high as 23.9°C (75°F). Certainly at the higher temperature there is a less satisfactory absorption of the carbon dioxide in the wine and when the bottled wine is opened the wine may rapidly go "flat" in the glass. Cold-acclimatized yeasts should always be used with low-temperature fermentations.

Carpenè (1959) in Italy and Rossi (1965) in California reported tank fermentations at about 13°C (50°F) were completed in about two weeks but the yeast must be carefully selected. Following the necessary fermentation, the wine is cooled to about 2.2°C (36°F) to precipitate tartrates, sometimes centrifuged and filtered, and then bottled.

Rossi (1965) reported that some producers of tank-fermented wines added all of the sugar at the start and manipulated the temperature to retain the required sugar concentration in the finished wines. Others ferment "dry" and then sweeten. Biologically, the first probably makes "sense" but the second seems to be more practical.

Sparkling wine tanks are normally insulated with cork or, more recently, with urethane foam (which can be sprayed on and provides a seamless finish). A thin vaporproof outer coat is applied to prevent water absorption.

Tank fermentations have several advantages. Excess pressure can be allowed to escape by the use of safety valves. The rate of fermentation can be controlled by controlling the temperature. The labor cost is only a fraction of the bottle process. They also have disadvantages. The thick yeast sediment in the bottom of the tank must be removed from contact with the wine since, because of its depth, reducing conditions are extreme and hydrogen sulfide production may occur. It is difficult to remove all viable yeast cells from a young wine at 5−6 atm of pressure and there is some oxygen pick-up during filtration and bottling; hence more sulfur dioxide is needed.

To increase the amino acid content of tank-fermented wines, Schanderl (1959) recommended high speed stirrers in the tank. When used for even a short period of time after the yeast is added, he noted a striking increase in the amino acid content of the wine and claimed a decrease in the amount of aging required to produce the "champagne" nose. This is the practice for some German tank producers. However, Schanderl (1965A) reports formation of fatty substances in yeast cells when free sulfur or sulfites are present. Excessive shaking of bottles or stirring of tank-fermented wines can result in release of the fat and accumulation of fat particles on the surface. These are not removed by disgorging or filtration.

Continuous sparkling wine production is used in Russia (Amerine 1959; Anon. 1963). Brusilovskiĭ (1959) and Brusilovskiĭ et al. (1977) stressed the importance of conducting continuous tank fermentations in the absence of air, often fining the cuvées with fresh yeast. They claim an enrichment of the wine in amino acids during oxygen-free fermentations. With continuous fermentations the tanks had to be cleaned every 2 or 3 years because of accumulation of yeasts in the tanks. The continous fermentations were found to produce less diacetyl than the discontinous tank procedure. Kunkee and Ough (1966) were not successful in getting adequate yeast growth in continuous fermentations under pressure.

As originally conceived by Charmat, the tank process involved a pretreatment by heating in a closed tank to a temperature of about 60°C
(140°F) under a pressure of 9.65 to 11.0 bars (140 to 160 lb/sq in.)
pressure. Charmat also envisaged heating the wine with various amounts
of air, presumably to improve quality by esterification. Russian work
indicates this probably did not actually improve the quality of the
finished product. The heating period recommended was 8 to 10 hr and
internal heaters were used, as indicated in Fig. 11.8, in the maturation
tank. Following the heating, the wine was cooled by circulating brine
through the jacket of the maturation tank. The cooled wine was then
transferred to the fermentation tank by connecting valve 1 to valve 3,
leaving valve 4 open during the transfer. The requisite amounts of yeast
starter and sugar were added to the fermentation tank at the same time.
The recommended fermentation temperature in the original studies was
about 23.9°C (75°F). The fermentation lasted no more than 10 to 15
days. A better quality product is obtained with a longer fermentation

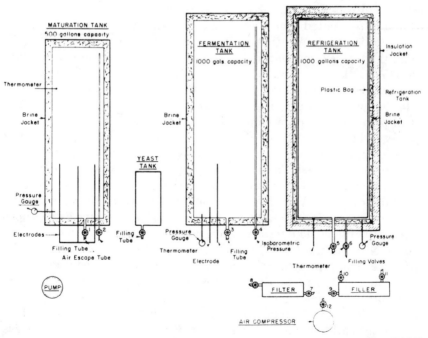

From Amerine and Joslyn (1970)

FIG. 11.8. THREE-TANK SPARKLING WINE SYSTEM

Note plastic bag in third tank

period at a lower temperature. While the amount of sugar added is usually calculated to produce 5 or 6 atm of pressure, should too much sugar be added the excess pressure can be allowed to escape through a safety valve. The interesting feature of the original Charmat process was the refrigeration tank arrangement. This tank contained an inner, leak-proof plastic bag. The fermented wine plus sweetening desired was transferred from the fermentation tank to the refrigeration tank by connecting valve 3 to valve 6. It is necessary in transfers of this type that a counter pressure be established in the receiving tank prior to the transfer in order to prevent unnecessary loss of carbon dioxide. The wine entering through valve 6 goes outside the plastic bag which collapses against the wall of the tank. Refrigeration is then applied to reduce the temperature of the wine to about −5.5°C (22°F). The wine is left at this temperature for several days and is then filtered under isobarometric pressure by connecting valve 6 through a pump to valve 7 of the filter and from valve 8 of the filter to valve 5 of the refrigeration tank, i.e., to the *inside* of the plastic bag. Theoretically, the plastic bag lining permits carbon dioxide to diffuse through. The filled bag finally fills the tank and thus does not come into contact with air. When it is desired to bottle wine, a new charge of fermented wine is pumped from the fermentation tank into the refrigeration tank into the space outside the plastic bag. As it fills the tank the filtered and clarified wine inside the plastic bag is forced out into the bottling machine by connecting valve 5 to 9, valve 10 of the filler to valve 4, and valve 11 to valve 12 of the air compressor.

In the two-tank procedure (Fig.11.9) used in this country, two stainless steel pressure tanks are employed. These are usually of 1000-gal. capacity although 15,000- to 25,000-gal. tanks are used. An active yeast culture or pressed yeast is added, usually 1 to 5% of the volume of the wine to be fermented. The wine itself is sweetened so as to produce 6 atm pressure and the desired final residual sugar. The contents should be stirred (or pumped over) to ensure a uniform mixture. The yeast culture and wine are pumped to tank No. 1 through valve 1, leaving valve 3 open during the filling. The fermentation takes place at 10° to 15.6°C (50° to 60°F). No more than 2 or 3 weeks are required to produce the requisite pressure. The wine is analyzed and additional sugar added if necessary. The tank is then promptly cooled to about −4.4°C (24°F) to stop the fermentation. Some wineries adjust the sulfur dioxide content to 150−200 mg/liter. This certainly reduces the quality of the finished product. The wine is held at the low temperature for about a week. Tank No. 2 is then cooled and its pressure adjusted with compressed air or preferably with nitrogen to a pressure slightly greater than that of tank No. 1, by using valve 5. Wine from tank No. 1 is then filtered into tank No. 2 by

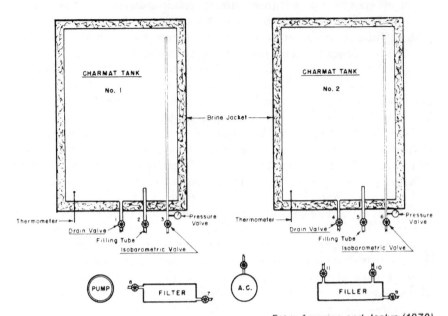

From Amerine and Joslyn (1970)

FIG. 11.9. CALIFORNIA TWO-TANK SYSTEM OF SPARKLING WINE PRODUCTION

connecting valves 3 and 6, the pump to valve 2 and to valve 7 of the
filter. Valve 8 of the filter is connected to valve 5. When the wine level in
tank No. 1 reaches that of the tube attached to valve 2, valves 2, 5, 7,
and 8 are closed. The pump is then connected to valve 1, and valves 5, 7,
and 8 are opened as before. This gives the maximum filter efficiency by
filtering the clear wine before the cloudy. The clarified cold wine in tank
No. 2 is now ready to bottle. To do this, the air compressor (or nitrogen
source) is connected to valve 10 of the filler. Valves 11 and 6 and 5 and 9
are connected. The pressure on valve 10 of the filler is adjusted to be
slightly greater than that in tank No. 2. At this time valves 10, 6, 11, and
5 are opened in this order and the bottling is started. When the wine level
reaches that of the tube attached to valve 5, valve 9 is then connected to
valve 4 and the remainder of the wine bottled.

It is filtered cold under pressure of compressed air, carbon dioxide or
nitrogen. Using a counterpressure of carbon dioxide is not now prohibited
by federal regulations. Compressed air is objectionable because some of
the air will be dissolved in the wine and may cause undue oxidative
darkening of the wine. To prevent this, and also to inhibit the growth of

viable yeasts which pass through the filter, sulfur dioxide must be added. This is objectionable from the point of view of quality since as much as 200 mg/liter may be required. For isobarometric transfer, Carpenè (1959) finds compressed air the worst, carbon dioxide is legally wrong in Italy and he recommends nitrogen. He recommends that sparkling wine plants be air conditioned—to avoid day-to-day temperature variations and the differences in pressure which this would cause.

In both tank and transfer systems, settling of the wine to allow the major part of the sediment to settle before filtration is recommended. Filtration under pressure is a special problem. The large "surface" of the filter pads offers a large area for release of gas. Geiss (1959) recommends a higher pressure in the receiving tank in order to prevent release of carbon dioxide. Figure 11.10 shows a filtration with and without such a counterpressure. The wine is bottled (evacuation of the air with nitrogen has been recommended) and corked under pressure. The pressure is low at this temperature and there is little loss of pressure in bottling. All operations by the tank system can be completed in a month or less. Labor cost is greatly reduced and the process is placed on a factory basis.

Drboglav (1940) and others have shown that the low quality of many tank-fermented sparkling wines is due to the introduction of oxygen during finishing, increasing the aldehyde content and darkening the color. Much better wines are produced when the wine is handled under carbon dioxide and the best under carbon dioxide and with a small amount of sulfur dioxide. Kielhöfer and Würdig (1963) found 5 to 20 mg/liter of oxygen in newly-bottled, tank-fermented wines, but none in bottle-fermented wines. To reduce the oxygen content in the first case, they recommend sulfur dioxide and ascorbic acid. Transfer system wines must be treated the same as tank-fermented. In German tank-fermented sparkling wines, acetaldehyde is produced in considerable amounts during the fermentation. It is thus necessary to add more sulfur dioxide. Schanderl and Staudenmayer (1964) recommend adding fresh yeast to the wine and agitating. This reduces the acetaldehyde content and may remove some metals and tannins by adsorption. Some reduction of the redox potential is obtained by adding ascorbic acid at the time of the triage bottling. During aging in the bottle, there was usually a decrease in potential.

Turbulent-flow transfer of sparkling wines in nonwettable or rough pipes results in large losses of carbon dioxide compared to transfer in smooth wettable pipes, according to Merzhanian (1963). He also reported 20% loss during filtration.

Rossi (1965) reported that in California tank-fermented wines the brandy dosage is infrequently used. He believes this reflects industry satisfaction with "natural grape flavors as developed with sound fermentation and aging techniques." Excessive use of brandy dosage is, of

Courtesy of Seitz Werke

FIG. 11.10. EFFECTS OF FILTERING WITH AND WITHOUT COUNTERPRES-
SURE
Left, with counterpressure, cross section of pad below filter. Right, without
counterpressure

course, to be deplored. However, discreet use of a dosage may be useful,
especially for neutral-flavored sparkling wines. Following tank fermentation, Filippov (1963) added 2–3% of enzyme concentrate to the wine
at the time of bottling. The enzyme concentrate was prepared by storing
wine and yeast (1 to 1) for 3 months at 5° to 10°C (41° to 50°F) stirring
twice monthly with carbon dioxide. Only the clear supernatant material
was used.

One of the persistent problems of tank-fermentation production of
sparkling wine is the "sweating" following bottling and preceding labeling. Rossi (1965) used infrared lamps in the far infrared region. Automatic timer control and various arrangements of the circuits helped to
standardize the process and prevent overheating of the bottles.

Comparison of Tank and Bottle Process.—The differences between bottle-
fermented and tank-fermented wines were studied by Janke and Röhr
(1960A). They developed two objective tests: (1) carbon dioxide release
ratio, i.e., ratio of the amount of carbon dioxide released at 14.4° and

35°C (58° and 95°F) expressed as percentage; and (2) the amount of nitrogen separated from one liter of wine by ultrafiltration. The first test gives a measure of the relative stability of carbon dioxide in wines and the second may measure the colloidal nitrogen released by yeast autolysis. In 53 commercial wines, the carbon dioxide release ratio was 21 to 31 (average 27.8) for 24 bottle-fermented wines and 30 to 46 (average 35.5) for 29 tank-fermented wines. Obviously tank-fermented wines lose their carbon dioxide more rapidly than bottle-fermented wines. The nitrogen content of wine was 9.6 mg/liter for the bottle-fermented and 6.2 for the tank-fermented.

When the same cuvée was used for tank and bottle fermentation (Janke and Röhr 1960B), there was a significant difference between the wines after 42 days as measured by the carbon dioxide release test, 29 to 45, average 34, for 28 tank-fermented bottles and 23 to 35, average 30.6, for 34 bottle-fermented bottles. The average carbon dioxide release test value for tank-fermented bottles stored for 18 months decreased to 31.0, while that for bottle-fermented bottles disgorged after 18 months was 26.0. After 250 to 380 days, the nitrogen by the ultrafiltration test was 6.2 mg/liter for the tank-fermented wine and 8.2 for the bottle-fermented. Janke and Röhr concluded that the difference between tank- and bottle-fermented wines lay in the influence of yeast autolysis. They asked the question of whether an improvement in quality of the tank-fermented wines could be obtained by influencing yeast autolysis.

The decrease and then increase in total nitrogen and in the amounts of the amino acids are illustrated by the data of Bergner and Wagner (1965)—all in mg/liter:

	Cuvée	\multicolumn{6}{c}{Days from Addition of Yeast}
		1[1]	3[1]	21[1]	21[2]	180[3]	395[3]
Total N	855.2	785.9	766.3	768.3	792.2	805.5	837.7
Alanine	27.8	9.7	7.6	7.6	12.8	14.0	21.6
Arginine	38.2	24.3	23.5	23.7	27.2	30.4	33.6
Aspartic acid	28.2	4.8	3.4	3.8	4.6	8.0	18.8
Cystine	6.6	5.9	5.5	6.0	5.9	5.1	5.5
Glutamic acid	65.6	15.5	10.3	10.9	11.3	16.0	25.7
Glycine	23.0	11.3	11.5	11.6	14.1	19.4	21.9
Histidine	19.4	18.1	17.1	18.9	20.4	22.6	25.4
Leucine + iso-leucine	23.2	6.7	4.8	4.9	6.6	10.9	14.4
Lysine	6.0	5.3	4.3	4.8	5.2	10.3	40.5
Phenylalanine	11.8	5.3	4.8	5.1	5.8	9.0	9.7
Proline	296.0	286.0	282.0	280.0	306.0	350.0	420.0
Serine	15.0	3.1	3.4	3.7	4.0	6.5	9.8
Threonine	7.4	5.4	6.0	6.2	5.6	5.6	5.7
Tryptophan	14.6	12.8	14.1	16.5	14.0	14.4	14.8
Valine	31.2	5.9	4.5	4.8	6.6	8.3	14.2

[1]Tank fermentation.
[2]Bottled tank wine after fining, filtering, and liqueuring.
[3]Bottle fermented and aged on the yeast.

The increases in proline, lysine, glutamic acid, leucine and isoleucine, phenylalanine, serine and valine are especially notable in the bottle-aged wine. Addition of lysed yeast cells improved the quality of disgorged sparkling wines according to Shakarova and Avakiants (1974).

It is probably not the fermentation in the bottle which differentiates tank- and bottle-fermented wines, but the period of time the bottle-fermented wine remains in contact with the yeast. The oxygen introduced in bottling tank-fermented and in handling and bottling transfer wines may introduce a difference. Colagrande and Mazzoleni (1977) distinguish the types by use of discriminant functions applied to analytical data. The minimum amounts of ethyl linoleate, etc., may also be useful (Rodopulo et al. 1978).

CARBONATION

Carbonated wines are those charged with carbon dioxide artificially instead of by fermentation. Several different methods of carbonating are in use. Probably the best method is that of carbonating in bulk at low temperature. In this system the wine is cooled in a brine-jacketed tank to near the freezing point and is charged at about −4.4°C (24°F). It is allowed to stand to come to equilibrium with the gas and is then bottled cold. It is advisable to pass the charged wine through a filter and bottle under pressure of the gas. The wine should have a pressure of about 5.17 bars (75 lb/sq in.) at 10°C (50°F). The product should be served cold.

One French-made carbonator consists of four heavy bottles covered with strong wire netting. The wine is chilled and filled into these charging bottles and impregnated with carbon dioxide. These charging bottles are then connected to champagne bottles; these are filled by the pressure of the gas and corked at once. Two bottles are charged and filled at a time, while the other two are absorbing the gas.

Various high-pressure water carbonators of the types used for soda water can be used if made of stainless steel or other completely corrosion-resistant metal, but unless the wine is chilled to near the freezing point, loss by frothing will be very severe and corking difficult. At low temperatures, the solubility of the gas in the wine greatly increases, and its pressure is correspondingly less. Miller (1958, 1959) has shown that if the wine is first placed under a slight vacuum to deaerate it and then slowly carbonated, that the carbon dioxide will not be rapidly lost when the bottle is opened, i.e., will discharge carbon dioxide for a longer period of time. His process is patented (see Miller 1964, 1966). For a discussion of carbon dioxide in wine, see Anon. (1969) and Jaulmes (1973).

Carbonated wines are much less costly to prepare than are wines fermented in the tank or bottle. They can be pleasing in character if made of wine of good quality. Most wines should be acidified with citric acid before carbonating, as consumer preference seems to be for carbonated wines of rather high acidity. Also some sugar should be added. On this account, the wines used should be of relatively high (12%) alcohol content to minimize danger of fermentation in the bottle.

The practical problems of low level carbonation of wines were considered by Rossi and Thoukis (1960). They observed that a wine carbonated to a given pressure at a high temperatures contained less carbon dioxide than if carbonated at low temperatures. For this type of carbonation they also showed higher carbon dioxide at low soluble solids content (0.236 g/100 ml) at 3.5° Brix versus 0.219 at 11.2°, 0.208 at 16.9°, 0.192 at 22.7° and 0.179 at 27.80°). Ethanol had only a small effect with a decreasing solubility from 11.9% alcohol to 19.5 (0.257 g/100 ml versus 0.241). They recommended use of gauge pressure as a means of controlling the carbon dioxide content of the wine. One must make allowances for the influence of various factors on carbon dioxide solubility. Nevertheless, they found it possible to carbonate two wines to contain the same amount of carbon dioxide even though their gauge pressure was slightly different.

The data of Etienne and Mathers (1956) give the equilibrium head pressures at 15.6°C (60°F) containing the indicated amounts of carbon dioxide. Their data differ from those of Rossi and Thoukis (1960) because the latter's carbonator gave less than 100% efficiency of carbon dioxide dispersion at the carbonator pressures used.

The work of Deinhardt (1961) indicates that accurate data on the solubility of carbon dioxide in wine are not available. Subtraction of about 1.5 atm from the solubility of carbon dioxide in 10% alcohol gives an approximately correct value. (See also Fig. 11.1.) No general solubility coefficient for carbon dioxide is possible because of the number of variables. The carbon dioxide content at various pressures and temperatures in Deinhardt (1965) are lower than those usually reported. The chart of Rentschler (1965) at 10% alcohol gives a lower pressure for the same amount of dissolved carbon dioxide than Deinhardt's values.

The problem of distinguishing between carbonated wines and those produced by tank- or bottle-fermentation was studied by Liotta (1956). He opened the bottles and left them open for 7 days at 4.4°C (40°F). At this time, carbonated wines contained less than 0.23 g/100 ml of carbon dioxide (0.15 to 0.22 in 8 samples) while those fermented in the bottle had over that amount (0.27 to 0.54 g in 13 examples). Further data would be desirable.

REFERENCES[4]

AGABAL'YANTS, G.G. 1954. Khimiko-Tekhologicheskii Kontrol' Proizvodstva Sovetskogo Shampanskogo. (Chemical and Technological Control of Soviet

Champagne Production.) Pishchepromizdat, Moscow.

AMERINE, M.A. 1959. Continuous flow production of still and sparkling wine. Wines Vines *40* (6) 41-42.

AMERINE, M.A. and JOSLYN, M.A. 1971. Table Wines. The Technology of Their Production, 2nd Edition. University of California Press, Berkeley and Los Angeles.

AMERINE, M.A. and MONAGHAN, M. 1950. California sparkling wines. Wines Vines *31* (8) 25-27; (9) 52-54.

AMERINE, M.A. and OUGH, C.S. 1979. Must and Wine Analyses, 2nd Edition. John Wiley & Sons, New York.

ANON. 1963. Continuous champagne production method patented. Wines Vines *44* (6) 49-50.

ANON. 1969. Die Bedeutung der Kohlensäure in der Kellerwirtschaft. Seitz Informationen Nr. *32*, 3-13.

BERGNER, K.G. and WAGNER, H. 1965. Die freien Aminosäuren während der Flaschen- und Tankgärung von Sekt. Mitt. Rebe Wein, Ser. A (Klosterneuburg) *15*, 181-198.

BIDAN, P. 1975. Les Vins Mousseux. Centre Document. Intern. Ind. Utilisat. Prod. Agric. Ser. Synth. Bibliog. 7, Paris.

BRUSILOVSKIĬ, S.A. 1959. Modification of the continuous sparkling wine process. (transl.) Vinodel. Vinograd. S.S.S.R. *19* (3) 12-26.

BRUSILOVSKIĬ, S.A., MEL'NIKOV, A.I., MERZHANIAN, A.A., and SARISHVILI, N.G. 1977. Proizvodstvo Sovetskogo Shampanskogo Nepreryvnym Sposobom. (Production of Soviet Champagne in a Continuous Procedure.) Pishchevia Promy'shlennost', Moscow. (Best text on tank fermentation.)

CARPENÈ, A. 1959. Della tecnica dei vini spumanti. Riv. Viticolt. Enol. (Conegliano) *12*, 179-189.

CHAPPAZ, G. 1951. Le Vignoble et le Vin de Champagne. Louis Larmat, Paris.

COLAGRANDE, O. and MAZZOLENI, V. 1977. Analytical characteristics of Italian sparkling wines. Ann. Fac. Agric., Univ. Cattol. Sacro Cuore, Milan *17*, 159-184.

DEINHARDT, H. 1961. Löslichkeit von Kohlensäure im Wein. Deut. Wein-Ztg. *97*, 68, 70, 72.

DEINHARDT, H. 1965. Die Löslichkeit von Kohlensäure im Wein und Sekt. Weinberg Keller *12*, 428-434.

DE ROSA, T. 1964. Tecnica dei Vini Spumanti. Tipografia Editrice F. Scarpis. Conegliano, Italy.

DRBOGLAV, U. 1940. Variation of dissolved oxygen and of the oxidation-reduction potential in the course of fermentation by the Chaussepied procedure. (transl.) Vinodel. Vinograd. S.S.S.R. *2*, 3.

---

⁴Titles have been translated only for nonwestern European languages.

ETIENNE, A.D. and MATHERS, A.P. 1956. Laboratory carbonation of wine. J. Assoc. Off. Agric. Chem. *39*, 844-848.

FILIPPOV, B.A. 1963. Poluchenie fermentnykh kontsentratov i ikh primeneni. (Production of enzyme concentrates and their use.) Vinodel. Vinograd. S.S.S.R. *23* (2) 11-14.

FRANÇOT, P. 1945. Acide total et acidité fixe réelle des moûts et des vins de Champagne. Bull. Office Intern. Vin *18* (167/170) 114-118.

FRANÇOT, P. 1950. Champagne et qualité par le pressurage. Vigneron Champenois *71*, 250-255, 273-283, 342-351, 371-382, 406-416.

FRANÇOT, P. and GEOFFROY, P. 1951. Les pectines et les gommes dans les moûts et les vins de Champagne. Vigneron Champenois *72*, 54-59.

GEISS, W. 1959. Technische Fortschritte bei der Sektherstellung. Deut. Wein-Ztg. *95*, 616, 618, 620, 622, 624.

HEMPHILL, A.J. 1965. The traditional method of champagne production. Wine Inst. Tech. Advis. Committee, June 7.

HERZOG, G. 1954. Die deutschen Sektkellereien, ihre Entwicklung und ihre Bedeutung für den Deutschen Weinbau. Daniel Meininger, Neustadt a.d. Weinstrasse.

JANKE, A. and RÖHR, M. 1960A. Über Schaumweine und deren Untersuchung. I. Objektive Teste zur Beurteilung von Schaumweinen. Mitt. Rebe Wein, Ser. A (Klosterneuburg) *10*, 111-123.

JANKE, A. and RÖHR, M. 1960B. *Ibid.* II. Über einem kontrollierten Vergleichsversuch Tankgärverfahren/Flaschengärverfahren. *Ibid. 10*, 210-217.

JAULMES, P. 1973. Relation entre la pression et la quantité d'anhydride carbonique contenu dans les vins mousseux. Ann. Fals. Expert. Chim. *66*, 96-109.

KIELHÖFER, E. and WÜRDIG, G. 1963. Die Oxydationsvorgänge im Wein. 6. Die Sauerstoffaufnahme durch den Sekt bei der Sektbereitung nach dem Grossraumgärverfahren. *Ibid. 13*, 18-35.

KICHKOVSKIĬ, Z.N. 1963. Aminokislotynyĭ sostav nekotorykh vin. (Amino acid compounds in various wines.) Vinodel. Vinograd. S.S.S.R. *23* (1) 13-15.

KOCH, K. 1923. Deutsche Sektindustrie. Zabern, G.m.b.H., Mainz.

KUNKEE, R.E. and OUGH, C.S. 1966. Multiplication and fermentation of *Saccharomyces cerevisiae* under carbon dioxide pressure in wine. Appl. Microbiol. *14*, 643-648.

LIOTTA, C. 1956. Interim report concerning experiments on naturally fermented and artificially carbonated wines. Internal Revenue Service, Washington, D.C.

MANCEAU, E. 1929. Vinification Champenoise. Chez l'Auteur, Epernay.

MAUJEAN, A., HAYE, B., and BUREAU, G. 1978. Etude sur un phenomene de masque observe en Champagne. Vigneron Champenois *99*, 308-313.

MERZHANIAN, A.A. 1963. Nekotorye fizicheskie usloviia rozliva shampanskogo. (Some physical conditions in transfer of sparkling wines.) Vinodel.

Vinograd. S.S.S.R. *23* (8) 3-8.

MILLER, F.J. 1958. Carbon Dioxide in Water, in Wine, in Beer and in Other Beverages. Oakland, Calif.

MILLER, F.J. 1959. Carbon dioxide in wine. Wines Vines *40* (8) 32.

MILLER, F.J. 1964. Carbon dioxide stability in beverages. Food Technol. *18*, 60-63.

MILLER, F.J. 1966. Viewpoint: quality carbonation of wine. Wines Vines *47* (6) 49-50.

PACOTTET, P. and GUITTONNEAU, L. 1930. Vins de Champagne et Vins Mousseux. J.-B. Baillière et Fils, Paris.

PAUL, F. 1960. Chemische Untersuchungen an Schaumweinen I. II. Der Gehalt an schwefeliger Säure. Mitt. Rebe Wein, Ser. A (Klosterneuburg) *10*, 138-155, 238-247.

POSTEL, W. 1970. Kohlensäurebestimmung und Kohlensäuregehalt in Wein, Perlwein und Schaumwein. Deut. Lebensm.-Rundsch. 66, 185-190.

PROTIN, R. 1960. Personal communication. Office International du Vin, Paris.

RENTSCHLER, H. 1965. Die Löslichkeit von Kohlensäure in Wein in Abhängigkeit von Temperatur und Druck. Schweiz. Z. Obst- Weinbau 74, 662-663.

RODOPULO, A.K. 1966. Biokhimiya Shampanskogo Proizvodstvo. (Biochemistry of Champagne Production.) "Pishchevaya Promyshlennost," Moscow.

RODOPULO, A.K., EGOROV, I.A., KORMAKOVA, G.A. and BEZZOUBOV, A.A. 1978. Gasokhromatograficheskiĭ metod opredeleniia kachestva shampanskogo i igristykh vin (Gas chromatographic method of evaluating the quality of champagnes and sparkling wines). Vinodel. Vinograd. S.S.S.R. (8) 24-26.

ROSSI, E.A., JR. 1965. Sparkling wine production by Charmat process. Wine Inst. Tech. Advis. Committee, June 7.

ROSSI, E.A., JR. and THOUKIS, G. 1960. Low-level carbonation of still wines. Am. J. Enol. Vitic. *11*, 35-45.

SCHANDERL, H. 1938. Kellerwirtschaftliche Fragen zur Schaumweinbereitung. Wein Rebe *20*, 1-8.

SCHANDERL, H. 1943. Eine vergleichende Studie über Champagner- und Schaumweinbereitung. *Ibid. 25*, 74-82.

SCHANDERL, H. 1959. Die Mikrobiologie des Mostes und Weines. Eugen Ulmer, Stuttgart.

SCHANDERL, H. 1965A. Über die Entstehung von Hefefett bei der Schaumweingärung. Mitt. Rebe Wein, Ser. A (Klosterneuburg) *15*, 13-20.

SCHANDERL, H. 1965B. Der Einfluss von Kationenaustausch des Grundweines auf Sektgärungen. Jahresbericht Hessiche Lehr- Forschungsanstalt Wein-, Obst- Gartenbau, Geisenheim 1965, 18-19.

SCHANDERL, H. and STAUDENMAYER, T. 1964. Über den Einfluss der schwefligen Säure auf die Acetaldehydebildung verschiedenen Schaumweingärungen. Mitt. Rebe Wein, Ser. A (Klosterneuburg) *14*, 267-281.

SHAKAROVA, F.I. and AVAKIANTS, S.P. 1974. Biochemical processes during the aging of disgorged champagne using lysed yeasts (transl.). Biol. Zh. Arm. *27* (7) 72-79.

SIMON, A.L. 1962. Champagne: with a Chapter on American Champagne by Robert J. Misch. McGraw-Hill Book Co., New York.

STEPHAN, E. 1964. Polyäthylenstopfen für Wein- und Sektflaschen. Weinberg Keller *11*, 447-450.

TARANTOLA, C. 1937. La preparazione dell' "Asti Spumante" con fermentazione a bassa temperatura. Ann. Staz. Enol. Sper. Asti Ser. 2, *2*, 315-321.

TSCHENN, C. 1934. Champagnization by the Charmat Process. Fruit Prod. J. *13*, 334-336.

U.S. INTERNAL REVENUE SERVICE. 1961. The determination of carbon dioxide in wine. Washington , D.C., *IRS-14791*.

U.S. TREASURY DEPARTMENT. 1976. Wine. Part 240.531 of Title 27, Code of Federal Regulations. U.S. Govt. Print. Office, Washington, D.C.

VOGT, E. 1977. Der Wein, seine Bereitung, Behandlung und Untersuchung, 7th Edition. Verlag Eugen Ulmer, Stuttgart.

WEINMANN, J. and TELLE, L.F. 1929. Manuel du Travail des Vins Mousseux. Hirt et Cie., Reims.

12

Wine Making in Eastern United States

The most important grape growing areas east of the Rocky Mountains are the Finger Lakes region of New York State, the western area of New York bordering on Lake Erie, and the Niagara River and the southern shores of Lake Ontario. This latter region extends into Canada on the Niagara Peninsula between Lake Ontario and Lake Erie and around the western end of Lake Ontario. Also to be included in the grape belt are parts of southern Michigan, northern Ohio, and a section of northern Pennsylvania bordering on Lake Erie. There are grape producing areas in the Hudson Valley, in south central New Jersey, Maryland, Arkansas, Missouri, Texas, Virginia, and to a very limited extent in many other states. Adams (1978) documents the rebirth of interest in grape growing from 1960 to 1970.

VARIETIES

The grapes grown in these areas are mainly varieties of the *labrusca* species, inter-specific hybrids (crosses of *vinifera* with American species) and, in the southeast, varieties of *rotundifolia*. The most common varieties are Elvira, Delaware, Concord, Niagara, Ives Seedling, and Catawba. These grapes are generally winter-hardy, productive, and resistant to the attacks of fungus diseases and phylloxera. The pulp of the berry is not firmly attached to the skin (thus the origin of the term "slip skin"), and the seeds are rather difficult to separate from the pulp. The juice of these grapes is lower in sugar content and of higher acidity than the *Vitis vinifera* grapes grown in California. For further information on the varieties, see Hedrick (1908, 1945), Munson (1909), Wagner (1956, 1965, 1976).

Attempts have been made to grow *Vitis vinifera* grapes in the eastern parts of the United States since colonial times. Severely low winter temperatures and fungus-inducing summer heat and rainfall have made these attempts unsuccessful in the past. Today, vineyard management to encourage early dormancy in the vines and use of modern fungicides has made growing of *vinifera* possible, if still expensive and difficult. Several small vineyards of the varieties successful in Northern Europe exist and yield wines of great interest.

In the New York Finger Lakes area and other grape growing areas of the state, the different varieties reach maturity during a 6 to 8 week period, starting usually about the middle of September and lasting until the last week in October or early November.

Thus, Delaware, Elvira, and Fredonia ripen early; followed by Niagara, Dutchess, Concord, and Ives Seedling; Catawba reaching maturity last. Earlier harvest of the labrusca-flavored varieties tends to minimize the flavor intensity (Rice 1974). Many wineries own vineyards but few grow enough fruit to meet their annual requirements. Close cooperation is maintained between the wineries and the independent grower throughout the year.

WINE PRODUCTION

At the approach of the harvesting season field tests of the grapes to ascertain the degree of ripeness of the various varieties are made. When it is determined that the grapes are ready for harvesting, a picking and delivery schedule is set.

Prior to the start of the crushing and pressing operation, all winery equipment is thoroughly cleaned and operationally checked so that the work will proceed smoothly and efficiently when the grapes begin to arrive at the weighing platform.

Ninety to 95% of the grapes are harvested mechanically. At the winery, grapes are inspected, weighed and then stemmed and crushed.

There are several types of presses used in the eastern wineries. Earlier, the hydraulic rack and cloth press were used. Today, however, wineries use cylindrical presses, such as the Willmes and the Vaslin types and continuous presses such as the Coq. They report highly satisfactory results both in cold pressing and hot pressing of all varieties of labrusca-type grapes. Although this type of press can be loaded fairly fast (3–4 min), the best results are obtained by loading at a slower rate of about 12 min. Even though upward of 5 tons can be used, best results are obtained with a load of approximately 3.75 tons. The pressing cycle in this type of press averages about 50 min. It is important to use filter aid such as paper pulp and pectic-splitting enzymes to obtain best results. The chief advantage of these cylindrical types of presses is the saving of labor.

Pretreatment

There are several methods for preparing the grapes for the fermentation tubs and casks. For white wines, the varietal grapes used are cold pressed as they come from the stemmer and crusher.

For red wines, two methods are used. In the more popular hot pressing method, the stemmed and crushed grapes are heated either in kettles or through heat exchangers to a temperature of 60° to 65.5°C (140° to 150°F) prior to loading of the press.

Juice from the presses flows into an accurately metered series of press tanks, usually glass lined containers, from which uniform samples of the juice are obtained. These are tested immediately for degree Brix and total acidity so that the necessary amelioration can be calculated and directions given into which fermentors the juice is to be pumped.

The other method is known as fermenting on the skin. In this procedure, the bottom of each fermentor is equipped with an inverted perforated box, around which is piled clean straw. The straw is weighted down with bricks. The grapes are crushed but not stemmed and deposited in the previously prepared fermentors. Each 1000-gal. capacity of the fermentor will accommodate about 2¼ tons of crushed grapes. Samples of free-run juice are drawn off at intervals to get the average degree Brix of the juice in order to calculate amelioration prior to fermentation. The grapes are pressed toward the latter stages of fermentation.

Amelioration

The matter of degree of amelioration of respective juices is a decision the wine maker must make (within legal restrictions) and is dependent on the type of wine for which the particular juice is destined to be used. For practically all varieties of grapes grown in eastern United States, the total acid of the juice is sufficiently high to permit full amelioration of 35% of the resulting product. However, judgment must be used in determining the degree of amelioration the individual wine maker uses. Some of the more delicately flavored grapes, such as the Delaware and Dutchess, should receive little or no amelioration, especially when they are to be used for champagne production. Other juices, if they are destined for eventual use in dessert wines, may advantageously be ameliorated close to the permissible limits.

In cold pressing of grapes, the average yield will approximate 170–175 gal. per ton. In hot pressing a yield close to 190 gal. of juice per ton is attained. The degree Brix of juices obtained from eastern labrusca grapes varies from approximately 14 to 21. Thus, we see that amelioration is necessary in most cases to produce wines of the desired alcoholic content. For those wines which are to be used for champagne and sparkling wines, a fermented wine of 11% alcohol is needed. For tables wines, an alcoholic content of 12.5% is desired and for dessert wines not over 13% alcohol prior to fortification with wine spirits, plus the desired sugar, is the aim.

Dividing the alcohol percentage wanted by the factor 0.55 gives the degree Brix the ameliorated juice should have prior to fermentation. Thus, if a wine of 12.5% alcohol is desired the ameliorated juice should have a degree Brix of approximately 22.

Calculation of amelioration can best be done following tables in ATF P 5120.2 (12/74) Wine (Part 240 of Title 27-CFR) Department of the Treasury.

An old rule of thumb states that 1 lb of cane sugar dissolved in enough water to make 1 gal. results in a Brix reading of 12°. When glucose sugar is used instead of sucrose, allowance must be made for the 8% water of crystallization in the glucose sugar, unless anhydrous glucose is used. In recent years the use of liquid sugar has become increasingly popular. This form of invert sugar is a syrup of about 76.5° Brix, weighs about 11.5 lb to the gallon, and each gallon contains the equivalent of approximately 9 lb of sucrose, calculated on dry basis. The use of liquid sugar results in a considerable saving in time and labor.

Water and sugar may be added to juice of newly fermented wine provided the acid content is not reduced below 5 g/liter as tartaric and provided the final volume contains not more than 35% of ameliorating water and sugar. Following fermentation, more sugar for sweetening and brandy may be added provided specified conditions are met.

Containers

White oak casks, redwood, and cypress fermentors are in quite general use in the eastern wineries. Coated steel and stainless steel tanks are also used. These containers are used both as fermentors and storage tanks. To the juices as they come from the presses is added about 75 mg/liter, of sulfur dioxide to retard the action of the undesirable yeasts and other microorganisms. After the necessary amount of amelioration (sugar or sugar and water solution) is added, a pure culture yeast is pumped in to initiate fermentation. Fermentors are filled to about 75% of capacity to prevent overflowing from effects of the initial violent fermentation.

Temperature Control

In the eastern United States the temperatures prevalent during the harvesting season are relatively cool. Hence, the juice being processed will have a temperature of from 4.4° to 15.5°C (40° to 60°F). When fermentation is conducted in casks of under 5000 gal. capacity, there is little danger of fermentation temperatures rising above 29.4°C (85°F). However, where larger fermentors are employed, it is necessary to remove heat to keep the fermentation temperatures below the critical point. This may be accomplished by passing the fermenting wine through heat exchangers using water as the cooling medium.

When hot pressing is used for extraction of color, it is necessary to cool the juice to 15.5° to 18.3°C (60° to 65°F) before the fermentation starts.

Post-fermentation Care

After the initial very active fermentation quiets down, the fermentors are filled almost to capacity. Fermentation is allowed to continue to completion in tanks protected from air by water seals. In 2 to 3 weeks, the various fermentations should be completed and racking or filtering may be started. The sooner the fermented juice is separated from the lees or sediment the better the quality of the new wine. Delayed racking encourages a malo-lactic fermentation. Rice (1965, 1974) demonstrated malo-lactic fermentation in 28 of 41 New York red wines and in 15 of 55 white wines. There was a marked difference between wineries in the incidence of the malo-lactic fermentation. He isolated three types of bacteria: a heterofermentative rod, a homofermentative rod, and a homofermentative coccus.

Rackings separate the new wine from the heavy lees. The wines are held according to variety after racking or filtering for later selection in preparing blends. Those to be used in dessert wines for fortification with grape brandy to the desired alcoholic content may also be sweetened to the desired level of market acceptability.

At present no eastern winery produces its own grape brandy for fortification. Wine spirits come from California. The spirits are usually 189°–192° proof and are transported in metal drums or in tank cars. Only grape or raisin brandy is permitted by the government for the fortification of grape wine. Calculations given in Chap. 6 should be noted.

FINISHING

After fermentation is completed and the wines have been either filtered or racked, the wine makers decide upon the blends. Each winery has its particular blends. White table wines frequently are blends of Delaware, Catawba, Dutchess, and Elvira. Other white varieties may also be utilized. In red table wines, hot-pressed Concord, Fredonia and Ives Seedling are used for burgundies and claret, and these may be supplemented with wines of the inter-specific hybrids. For dessert wines various varieties are used. In reds such as port, Concord and Ives may be employed. As the acidity of eastern wines is quite high, it is a general practice to blend in up to 25% of California wines to obtain wines of the desired acidity. No more than 25% California wines may be used for blending if it is desired to maintain the geographical identity for labeling purposes.

Clarification

Fining agents used are tannin and gelatin, bentonite, casein, or proprietary products. Some wineries flash-pasteurize their blends in a closed system while others do not. All wineries make a general practice of refrigerating their blends at −4°C (26°F) for table wines and at −7°C (19°F) for dessert wines. They are held at these colder temperatures for 10 days to 2 weeks after which they are filtered to remove the excess cream of tartar. Use of ion exchange columns for removal of excess cream of tartar is also practiced. It is the aim of most wineries to hold finishing blends several months in casks or tanks prior to bottling. These wines are examined periodically and tested for stability.

At the time of the polishing filtration for bottling, some wine makers make a practice of adding small amounts of sulfur dioxide to retard any oxidation that may occur due to the oxygen in the headspace of the bottle. Each day's bottling is generally coded with the date of bottling and samples of each bottling are kept for about a year for reference purposes.

TYPES

Some eastern wineries make a practice of marketing varietal wines. A highly sweetened Concord wine, both fortified and unfortified, has proven quite popular and has been produced and sold very successfully. Other varietal eastern wines, usually of the table wine type, have been produced and successfully marketed. These include Aurore, De Chaunac, Maréchal Foch, Chelois, Baco noir, Cascade, Rosette, Delaware, Elvira, Niagara, and others.

Only a few vintage wines are produced by eastern wineries. This is probably because most wineries try to keep on hand varietal wines of several years' vintages to blend together in order to maintain uniformity. A number of New York wineries specialize in sparkling wine production—some blended to a low anthranilate odor (p. 109) while others are distinctively "eastern."

The success of New York and other "eastern" sparkling wines is attributed by Goldman (1965) to their "eastern" or labrusca flavor. He also claims low yield, rocky well-drained soils, cool climate, and low pH, high acid, high extract musts, and use of sucrose as positive factors.

Most eastern sherry wines are produced by a method, or modification of the method, patented by Tressler (1939A,B) which consists of heating a fortified labrusca wine such as Concord, Niagara, Elvira, Catawba, or blends of these for 4 to 6 weeks at approximately 60°C (140°F). Oxygen or air is diffused into the wine. Since the pores of the diffusers are very small, the oxygen entering the wine is in the form of extremely fine bubbles which give a relatively large surface in constant contact with the wine and greatly increase the rate of oxidation. The oxygen leaving the top of the tank carries in it, in the form of vapor, some alcohol and esters. Hence, a trap containing cold wine is provided at the top of the tank to recover these volatile materials and return them to the wine. Various methods may be employed in maintaining the temperature of the wine under process. Hot water coils, thermostatically controlled, have proven very satisfactory. It is believed essential that the acidity of the sherry baking stock be 0.5% or lower calculated as tartaric acid, as higher acidity seems to mask the sherry flavor being developed by baking. Calcium carbonate can be used to reduce the acidity to the desired level. The wine being baked is examined daily and sensory testing is at present the criterion upon which the completion of treatment is based. Upon completion of baking, the wine is cooled, fined, and filtered and held for several months or longer before being used in preparing finished blends.

In a study of the Tressler Process, Mattick and Robinson (1960) reported that the volatile carbonyl, volatile and total acidity and esters increased during the baking process. The pH decreased from 3.52 to 3.22 in one case. No such decrease is noted in the baking of California sherries. They attributed this increase in the total acidity and decrease in pH to the effect of a nonenzymatic browning system which releases a carboxyl group.

A modification of the aforementioned process is being successfully used in preparing a tawny port. Port stock of bright ruby red color is heated to 49°C (120°F) for a period of 10 days while bubbling oxygen through the wine. It is necessary to regulate the time and temperature so that the oxygen treatment is terminated before a sherry flavor is developed. The oxygen treatment reduces the labrusca (foxy) flavor of the wine.

Another method of producing eastern sherries is by what is known as the weathering process. The sherry stock, made with labrusca grapes, is produced by fermentation and fortification. After clarification and filtering, oak sherry barrels are filled with this stock and exposed to the weather for four years. One large eastern winery conducts this process on the roof of the winery. The buildings on the roofs of which the method is used are specially constructed to carry the extra load of the full barrels, four high.

The barrels are completely filled, then ½ gal. drawn out to allow for expansion and the barrels sealed with long bungs. Normally, the shrinkage and losses during the 4 year aging period do not exceed 18%. As the sherry stock is taken off the roofs, it is blended, clarified, refrigerated, and filtered, and then this 4 year-old sherry is blended with older sherries removed in previous years.

While this is not the traditional solera system (p. 407), this winery maintains a constant blend of stock taken from the barrels after four years with the older sherry. The average life of the barrels so exposed is about 12 years, in some instances 16 to 20 years. The iron hoops of the barrels are painted before filling to extend the life of the barrels. While this sherry method is time-consuming and costly it does produce an excellent product.

REFERENCES

ADAMS, L.D. 1978. The Wines of America, 2nd Edition. McGraw-Hill Book Co., New York.

GOLDMAN, M. 1965. Sparkling wine production in New York. Wine Inst. Tech. Advis. Committee, June 7.

HEDRICK, U.P. 1908. The Grapes of New York. J. B. Lyon Co., Albany. (New York Department of Agriculture.)

HEDRICK, U.P. 1945. Grapes and Wines from Home Vineyards. Oxford University Press, New York.

MATTICK, L.R. and ROBINSON, W.B. 1960. Changes in volatile constituents during the making of sherry wine by the Tressler process. Food Technol. 14, 30-33.

MUNSON, T.V. 1909. Foundations of American Grape Culture. Denison, Texas.

RICE, A.C. 1965. The malo-lactic fermentation in New York State wines. Am. J. Enol. Vitic. 16, 62-68.

RICE, A.C. 1974. Chemistry of winemaking from native American grape varieties. In Chemistry of Winemaking. A. D. Webb (Editor). American Chemical Society, Advances in Chemistry, Ser. 137, Washington, D.C.

TRESSLER, D.K. 1939A. Wine process. U.S. Pat. 2,181,838. Nov. 22.

TRESSLER, D.K. 1939B. Wine process. U.S. Pat. 2,181,839. Nov. 28.

U.S. DEPARTMENT OF THE TREASURY. Bureau of Alcohol, Tobacco and Firearms. Wine (Part 240 of Title 27-CFR) ATF P 5120.2 (12/74).

WAGNER, P.M. 1956. American Wines and Wine-Making. Alfred A. Knopf, New York.

WAGNER, P.M. 1965. A Wine-Grower's Guide, 2nd Edition. Alfred A. Knopf, New York.

WAGNER, P.M. 1976. Grapes Into Wine. Alfred A. Knopf, New York.

13

Special Natural Wines: Vermouth and Flavored Wines

Vermouth is a 15 to 21% alcohol wine flavored with a characteristic mixture of herbs and spices, some of which impart an aromatic flavor and odor and others a bitter flavor. Two classes are recognized in the trade, the sweet or Italian-type vermouth and the dry or French type. Italian, or sweet, vermouth contains from 15 to 17% alcohol by volume and 12 to 16% reducing sugar. French or dry vermouth usually contains about 18% alcohol and about 4% reducing sugar (Joslyn and Amerine 1964). The quantity of herbs and spices used for dry vermouth is less per unit volume than for the sweet. Vermouth is served principally "straight" in European countries. In America it is used principally in mixed drinks such as Martini and Manhattan cocktails. Some is served with sherry as a "sherry cocktail."

Dubonnet, Byrrh, Bonal, and Cap Corse are flavored wines that are usually classed with vermouth and will also be discussed in this chapter. In addition, there are several wines that are lightly flavored with certain herbs, spices, fruit juices, essences, aromatics, and other natural flavorings, such as sangria-types (citrus-flavored), Thunderbird, Silver Satin, etc. Many formulas for the preparation of these exist.

Flavored wines, euphemistically and legally called "Special Natural[1] Wines," have come on the market in the past 20 years in considerable quantities. These are not vermouths and they do not resemble the usual aperitif wines very closely, although classed as such. They represent a new type of wine. They may contain the same amount of alcohol as dessert wines, 18–19% by volume or more often like table wines, about 12%. Some are sweeter than dry vermouth but not so sweet as Italian-style sweet vermouth. The natural flavors used for flavoring these wines must be approved by the U.S. Bureau of Alcohol, Tobacco and Firearms.

---

[1] "Natural" should not be confused with below-14% wines made without addition of sugar or alcohol which are sometimes called natural wines.

The flavoring is often mild. These products sell at prices similar to dessert wines. They are served usually "straight," often with ice ("on the rocks"), rather than as an ingredient of mixed drinks, in that respect differing from vermouth in use. Many special natural wines have less than 14% alcohol, a few with noticeable carbonation.

The regular types often contain citrus or tropical-fruit flavors. Analysis of three brands in 1959 were as follows (the alcohol contents would now be lower):

Sample	Alcohol % by Vol	Total Acid as Tartaric g/100 ml	°Brix	Color
1	20.4	0.66	5.2	Very light
2	20.5	0.65	5.6	Very light
3	20.1	0.66	5.1	Amber

ORIGIN OF VERMOUTH

The name is probably derived from "Wermut," the German word for wormwood, a frequent ingredient of vermouth. The word is probably based on the alleged beneficial properties of wines containing wormwood. The addition of wormwood to wine dates from the Roman and probably the early Greeks. Modern vermouths were first produced in Italy in the 18th century. The type and quality of vermouth depend upon the quality and nature of the base wine and on the kind, quality, and amounts of the various herbs used. According to Valaer (1950), the formulas for the European-made vermouths are closely guarded secrets. There is less secrecy among the American producers. However, few producers are willing to divulge their vermouth formulas.

Before passage of the 18th Amendment, only a limited amount of vermouth was produced in the United States; most of that on the market came from Italy and France. After repeal, demand increased and production in America rose. According to Valaer (1950), California produced about 2,000,000 gal. of vermouth in 1945. New York state is also an important producer of vermouth. Table 13.1 gives the production for the United States from 1948 to 1976.

In 1976, California produced 4,116,066 gal. and New York state produced 745,774. The imports of vermouth totaled 4,016,929 of which Italy supplied 3,288,029 and France, 707,974 gal. Other countries supplied only small amounts. South America, principally Argentina, was of importance during World War II, owing to lack of imports from Italy and France. South American vermouth often is made by European producers or according to their formulas.

TABLE 13.1. PRODUCTION STATISTICS FOR VERMOUTH AND FLAVORED
WINES IN THE UNITED STATES

Fiscal Year	Vermouth Number of Producers	Production	Flavored Wines Number of Producers	Production
1948–1952	181	2,332,100	13[1]	219,440
1953–1957	144	3,345,480	16	451,755
1958–1962	137	4,223,738	53	11,354,169
1963–1967	121	4,996,735	65	16,234,986
1968–1972	90	5,403,391	62	31,298,801
1973	80	5,281,698	54	59,370,790
1974	67	5,410,080	63	56,899,662
1975	72	5,200,324	53	54,762,513
1976	—	5,963,067	—	58,833,127

[1]Source: Annual reports of U.S. Treasury Department.
[1]Average of 1949–1952.

LEGAL REQUIREMENTS

Before June, 1963, vermouth made in the United States paid three taxes and production of vermouth in wineries was illegal. Vermouth now pays only the withdrawal tax, provided it is made by a bonded winery from fortified wine without addition of additional alcohol during manufacture. The product must have the taste, aroma, and other characteristics generally attributed to vermouth. If vermouth is used in making a cordial it must pay an additional rectification tax. Distilled spirits may not be added to previously fortified dessert wine or to vermouth without payment of a rectifier's tax. However, the producer may add an essence made with tax-paid brandy (Valaer 1950). Such essence (brandy extract of herbs) may be made by the vermouth producer or obtained from a manufacturer; but it must be made with tax-paid spirits (usually high proof brandy) or spirits withdrawn tax free. If essence is used it must be declared in the formula. The base wine may be sweetened with grape concentrate or sucrose. See also Jacoby (1948) and Fessler and Jacoby (1949).

Vermouth may be made in any tank on bonded winery premises, and, after manufacture, be transferred to and stored in any department of the winery. A formula showing the ingredients used, details of manufacture, and the alcohol content of the finished product must be filed with the Assistant Regional Commissioner of the Bureau of Alcohol, Tobacco and Firearms. The producer must obtain approval before manufacture is undertaken. A natural wine must be used in making vermouth or the flavored special natural wines, but such wine may be made with the usual permitted cellar practices. Regulations of the U.S. Treasury Department contain the various legal requirements that apply in the production of vermouth (see also p. 721).

A number of botanicals, flavoring substances and natural substances formerly used are now forbidden. Calamus may no longer be used (U.S.

Food and Drug Administration 1970). For wine containing wormwood (*Artemisia* spp.), white cedar (*Thuja occidentalis*), oak moss (*Evernia prunastri*), tansy (*Tanacetum vulgare*), and yarrow (*Achillea millefolium*) the finished product must be thujone-free. The thujone content is to be determined by an analytical method sensitive to at least 10 mg/ liter. The method of the Association of Official Analytical Chemists (1975) or equivalent must be used, e.g., the gas chromatography one of Usseglio-Tomasset (1966) or possibly that of Mérat *et al.* (1976). The former found 0 to 0.36 and 1 to 0.12 mg/liter of α- and β-thujone in vermouths. Wines to which St. John's wort (*Hypericum perforatum*) has been added must be hypericum-free in the alcoholic distillate.

HERBS AND SPICES

The herbs and spices used in vermouth are furnished in dry form and represent parts of various plants such as the seeds, wood, leaves, bark, or roots (see Table 13.2). Until World War II practically all of the herbs used for vermouth production in the United States were imported. During the war, successful attempts were made to cultivate some of the herbs by harvesting plants growing wild. Considerable quantities are now locally produced. Most of the herbs and spices now used are still imported. They are obtained from the tropics, the Near East, and mostly from European countries such as Italy, France, and Belgium.

Bitter-tasting plants include aloe, angelica, blessed thistle, cinchona, European centaury, germander, lungwort, lungmoss, quassia, and rhubarb. Aromatic plants are anise, bitter almond, cardamom, cinnamon, clove, coriander, dittany of Crete, galingale, marjoram, nutmeg, Roman camomile, rosemary, summer savory, thyme, tonka bean, and vanilla bean. The bitter-aromatic plants include allspice, elder, elecampane, gentian, juniper, bitter orange, sweet orange, saffron, sage, sweet flag, speedwell, wormwood (common), wormwood (gentile), wormwood (Roman), and yarrow.

The major flavoring constituents of the herbs and spices used in vermouth manufacture (Brevans 1920) are: hydrocarbons (such as styrol, cymene, pinene, and other terpenes), aldehydes (such as citral, citronellal, furfural, benzoic aldehyde, vanillin, and cinnamaldehyde), ketones (such as methyl heptenone, carvone, luparone, and thujone), lactones (such as alantolactone), oxides (such as cineole or eucalyptol), phenols and phenol derivatives (such as luparol, thymol, cadinone, and caryophyllene), alcohols, particularly terpenic alcohols (such as calamenol, citronellol, borneol, anethol, eugenol, terpineol, and safrol), alkaloids (such as quinine, cusparine, and absotin), glucosides (such as absinthin, gratiolin, quassin, and aloin), saccharides (such as gentinose), tannins, coloring matters,

TABLE 13.2. SCIENTIFIC, ENGLISH, ITALIAN, AND FRENCH NAMES AND THE PLANT PART USED, OF THE HERBS REQUIRED IN THE MAKING OF VERMOUTH AND RELATED WINES[1]

Common Commercial[2]	Scientific Name	Italian[2]	French[2]	Portion of Plant Commonly Used
Alkanet	*Anchusa tinctoria*	Ancusa	Orcanète	Plant
Allspice	*Pimenta dioica* or *P. officinalis*	Pépe garofanato	Piment, toute-épice	Berry
Aloe (socotrine)	*Aloë perryi*[3]	Aloè ordinario	Aloès lucide socotrin	Plant
Angelica	*Angelica archangelica*	Angelica	Angélique	Root (occasionally seed)
Angola weed	*Rocella fuciformis*			
Angostura	*Cusparia febrifuga* or *Galipea cusparia*	Fave tonke, angustura	Angusture	Bark
Anise	*Pimpinella anisum*	Anice	Anis, anis vert	Seed
Benzoin, benzoin resin	*Styrax benzoin*[10]	Benzoino	Benzoin	Gum
Bitter almond	*Prunus amygdalus* var. *amara*	Mandorla amara	Amande amère	Seed
Bitter orange[9]	*Citrus aurantium* var. *amara*	Arancio amaro	Orange amer, bigaradier	Peel of fruit
Blessed thistle	*Cnicus benedictus*	Cardo santo	Chardon bénit	Aerial portion + seeds
Boldo, boldus	*Peumus boldus*			Leaf
Bryony, briony	*Bryonia alba* or *B. dioica*		Bryone	Root, etc.
Buckbean	*Menyanthes trifoliata*	Trifoglio fibrino	Ménianthe trifolié	Leaves

TABLE 13.2. (Continued)

Common Commercial[2]	Scientific Name	Italian[2]	French[2]	Portion of Plant Commonly Used
Calamus, sweet flag	*Acorus calamus*	Calamo aromatico	Acore aromatique	Root
Calumba[7]	*Jateorhiza palmata*	Calombo	Colombo	Root
Cascarilla	*Croton eleuteria*	Cascarilla	Cascarille	Bark
Chirata	*Suertia chyrayita*	Chiretta	Chirette indien	
Cinchona	*Cinchona calisaya*[11]	China	Quinquina	Bark
Cinnamon	*Cinnamomum zeylanicum*	Cannella	Cannellier de Ceylon	Bark
Clammy sage, common clary	*Salvia sclarea*	Salvia sclarea	Sauge sclarée	Flowers and leaves
Clove	*Syzygium aromaticum*	Garofano	Girofle des moluques[4]	Flower
Coca	*Erythroxylon coca*	Coca	Coca	Leaves
Common horehound	*Marrubium vulgare*	Marrobio	Marrube	Aerial portion
Common hyssop	*Hyssopus officinalis*	Issopo	Hyssope	Flowering plant
Coriander	*Coriandrum sativum*	Coriandolo	Coriandre	Seed
Costmary	*Chrysanthemum balsamita*	Balsamite odorosa	Balsamite	Plant
Dittany of Crete	*Amaracus dictamnus*	Dittamo cretico, origano di Creta	Dictane de Crète	Aerial portion + flowers
Elder	*Sambucus nigra*	Sambuco	Sureau	Flowers (also leaves)
Elecampane, common inula	*Inula helenium*	Enula campana	Aunée	Root

TABLE 13.2. (Continued)

Common Commercial[2]	Scientific Name	Italian[2]	French[2]	Portion of Plant Commonly Used
European centaury	Erythraea centaurium[1,2]	Centaurea minore	Petite centaurée	Plant
European meadowsweet[5]	Filipendula ulmaria	Ulmaria	Reine des prés	Root
Fennel	Foeniculum vulgare	Finocchio	Fenouil	Seed
Fenugreek	Trigonella foenum-graecum	Fieno greco	Fénugrec	Seed
Fraxinella, gas plant	Dictamnus albus	Dittamo bianco, frassinella	Dictame	Root
Galangal, galingale	Alpinia officinarum or A. galanga	Galanga minore	Galanga mineur	Root
Gentian	Gentiana lutea	Genziana maggiore	Grand gentiane	Root and rhizome
Germander, chamaedrys	Teucrium chamaedrys	Camendrio	Germandrée, petite chêne	Plant
Ginger	Zingiber officinale	Zenzero	Gingembre	Root
Golden germander	Teucrium polium	Polio	Germandrée polium	Plant
Hart's tongue	Phyllitis scolopendrium	Lingua cervina, scolopendria	Scolopendre	Plant
Hop	Humulus lupulus	Luppolo	Houblon	Aerial portion + flowers
Iceland moss	Cetraria islandica			
Lemon balm, common balm	Melissa officinalis	Melissa, cedronella	Mélisse	Flowering plant
Lemon verbena	Lippia citriodora			Leaves
Lesser cardamom	Elettaria cardamomum	Cardamomo	Cardamome mineur[4]	Dried fruit, leaves

TABLE 13.2. (Continued)

Common Commercial[2]	Scientific Name	Italian[2]	French[2]	Portion of Plant Commonly Used
Linden	Tilia spp.	Tiglio	Tilleul	
Lungwort, sage of Bethlehem	Pulmonaria officinalis or P. saccharata	Polmonaria officinale	Pulmonaire	Aerial portion + flowers
Lungwort lichen, lungmoss	Stycta polmonacea	Lichene pulmonare	Lichen pulmonaire	Plant (a lichen)
Maidenhair fern	Adiantum capillus-veneris			
Marjoram	Origanum vulgare	Origano	Origan	Aerial portion of plant + flowers
Masterwort, hog's fennel[13]	Peucedanum ostruthium	Imperatoria	Impératoire	Root, leaves
Mullein	Verbascum phlomoidus, V. thapsiforma			Leaves
Myrtle	Myrtus communis	Mirto	Myrte	Leaves
Nutmeg and mace	Myristica fragrans	Noce moscata, macias	Muscadier, noix muscade	Seed
Orris, Florentine iris	Iris germanica var. florentina	Iride fiorentina, giaggiolo	Iris de Florence	Root
Pansy	Viola tricolor	Viola de pensiero	Pensée	
Peach	Prunus persica	Pesca	Pêche	Leaves
Pomegranate	Punica granatum	Melegrano	Grenadier	Bark of root
Quassia	Quassia amara	Quassio, legnuo quassio	Quassia	Wood

TABLE 13.2. (Continued)

Common Commercial[2]	Scientific Name	Italian[2]	French[2]	Portion of Plant Commonly Used
Quinine fungus	*Fomes officinalis*	Agarico bianco	Agaric blanc	Plant
Rhubarb	*Rheum rhaponticum*	Rabarbaro	Rhubarbe	Root
Roman camomile	*Anthemis nobilis*	Camomilla romana	Camomille romaine	Flowers
Roman wormwood	*Artemisia pontica*	Assenzio gentile[6]	Absinthe pontique, petite absinthe	Plant
Rosemary, old man	*Rosmarinus officinalis*	Rosmarino	Rosmarin	Flowering plant
Saffron, crocus	*Crocus sativus*	Zafferano	Safran	Portion of flower
Sage	*Salvia officinalis*	Salvia	Sauge	Aerial portion + flowers
Sandalwood (white, yellow or East Indian)	*Santalum album*	Legno sandalo	Santal	
Sandarac	*Tetraclinis articulata*			Resin
Savory (summer)	*Satureja hortensis*	Santoreggio	Sarriette	Aerial portion of plant
Serpentaria, Virginia snakeroot	*Aristolochia serpentaria*		Serpentère	Root
Speedwell	*Veronica officinalis*	Veronica	Véronique mâle thé d'Europe	Plant?
Star anise	*Illicium verum*	Anice stellato	Anis étiole, badiane	Seed
Sweet marjoram	*Marjorana hortensis*	Maggiorana	Marjolaine, amaracus	Aerial portion+ flowers
Thyme, garden thyme[8]	*Thymus vulgaris*	Timo setpillo	Thym	Leaf

TABLE 13.2. (Continued)

Common Commercial[2]	Scientific Name	Italian[2]	French[2]	Portion of Plant Commonly Used
Valerian	*Valeriana officinalis*	Valeriana officinale	Valériane, herbe aux chats	Root
Vanilla	*Vanilla planifolia*	Vaniglia	Vanillier légume[4]	Bean
Vervain	*Verbena officinalis*	Verbena officinale	Verveine	
Woodruff (sweet)	*Asperula odorata*	Asperula	Aspérule odorante	
Wormwood	*Artemesia absinthium*	Assenzio maggiore	Grande absinthe, absinthe amère	Plant
Yarrow	*Achillea millefolium*	Achillea	Achillée	Plant
Zedoary, setwell, curcum	*Curcuma zedoaria*	Zeodaria	Zedoaire	Root

[1]Source of data: Joslyn and Amerine (1964) and Amerine (1973).
[2]Many local synonyms and divergent spellings have been omitted; for additional names in each language see: Bedevain, A. Illustrated polyglottic dictionary of plant names. Argus and Papazian Presses, Cairo, Egypt (1936); Hoare, A. An Italian dictionary. Cambridge University Press, Cambridge, England (1925); Amerine, M.A. A multi-language dictionary of vermouth ingredients. Rivital essen. prof. piante offic. aromicosmet. aerosoi (1973).
[3]*Aloë barbadensis* and *A. feros* and *A. feros* × *A. africana* and *A. feros* × *A. spicata* hybrids also approved.
[4]Preferred.
[5]Possibly same as the commercial "Queen of the Meadows" (*Eupatoreum pur-*

pureum).
[6]*Artemesia vallesiaca* (assenzio gentile alpino) is usually confused with *A. pontica*. For a discussion of the various wormwoods and their uses see: Mattirolo (1915) and Balzac (1915).
[7]Also spelled colombo, columbo, and calumbo.
[8]*Thymus serpyllum* (timo serpillo, Italian) also used.
[9]The peel of sweet oranges is also used.
[10]*S. paralleloneurus*, *S. tonkinensis*, etc., also approved.
[11]Or *C. ledgeriana* or hybrids.
[12]Or *Centaurium umbellatum*.
[13]Or imperatorica.

gums and pectins, resins (such as humulon), esters (such as amyl valeriate), simple acids (such as citric), and complex acids (such as angelic and alantolic).

For comprehensive lists of the plants used in vermouth production and their scientific, English, Italian, and French names, see Table 13.2 and Joslyn and Amerine (1964), Lazarus (1965), and Amerine (1973). In some cases, the scientific names on the lists differ from those in Table 13.2. These differences arise from changing taxonomic classifications rather than from different herbs. See also Morini (1955), Ottavio and Garina-Canina (1930), Valvassori (1954) and Amerine (1973, 1974).

The herbs and spices are usually purchased in dried form. Their quality is affected by the care given them in harvesting and storage. They should be purchased only from a reliable supplier. The same variety grown under different climatic or cultural conditions may differ markedly in character and quality. The longer the dried products are stored before use, the poorer will be their flavor and aroma, as these depend to a great extent on volatile compounds that slowly evaporate during storage. Cold dry storage is recommended. Furthermore, staling of the flavor through oxidation and other chemical reactions occurs during storage. Thus, the dried herbs and spices should be as fresh as possible. During prolonged storage, insects may infest the dried products and render them unfit for use. If the moisture content of the storage room or of the dried products during storage is too high, molding with more or less damage to quality may occur. Fumigation at suitable intervals with methyl bromide, or other effective fumigant, is advisable to control insects if the products are to be stored for an appreciable period. If they are in tightly sealed containers, such as friction top cans, jars, or moistureproof plastic bags, observe occasionally to make certain that moisture has not distilled from the product and condensed on the walls of the package or on the product causing a local rise in moisture content with resultant mold spoilage. Inspection before purchase is recommended.

Dried plant materials in the whole form can be examined more satisfactorily than if powdered or in granular form. Also, the storage life of the powdered and granular products is shorter than that of the whole materials because volatilization of flavor and aroma is more rapid from the ground material. Furthermore, in ground or powdered form the amount of stems, etc., is difficult to determine.

Fluid and solid extracts, concretes, absolutes, oils, gums, balms, resins, oleóresins, waxes, and distillates may be used, but in amounts not to exceed the amount reasonably required to accomplish their intended effect. Microscopic detection of impurities in or falsification of *Artemesia absinthium* with other *Artemesia* or with *Achillea* is described by Griebel (1955).

Methods of Flavoring Base Wine

A variety of procedures for extraction of flavors and their addition to the wine has been employed.

Direct Extraction.—The simplest method of flavoring is by placing weighed amounts of the herbs and spices in the base wine and leaving them until the wine has absorbed the desired flavors and aromas. The plant materials may be finely ground or in granular form to hasten extraction. Some producers believe that undesirable flavoring and odorous constituents are more likely to be taken up by the wine if the herbs and spices are in powdered form. During extraction the wine is usually circulated or stirred daily. The wine may be heated to 60°C (140°F) or applied at room temperature, extraction being more rapid at the higher temperature. The extraction period is about two weeks if the wine is not heated. The extraction tank should be covered to minimize excessive loss of volatile flavors and aromas. The herbs and spices are placed in cloth bags and suspended in the wine. After the first extraction, fresh base wine may be used for a second (less desirable) extraction. The spent materials should not be pressed to secure the residual flavoring and aromatic substances because this may extract objectionable bitter compounds.

Concentrates.—Instead of directly flavoring a large lot of wine in the above manner, it is more common to prepare a smaller volume of more concentrated extract. This is done by placing the herbs and spices in a special vessel and circulating the wine by pump from a tank through the herbs in the extraction vessel until most of the desired substances have been extracted. The wine is usually heated during extraction (Pilone 1954). This extract may then be used to flavor a relatively large volume of base wine.

For sweet (Italian style) vermouth, according to Joslyn and Amerine (1964), 0.5 to 1 oz of mixed dry flavoring materials per gallon of base wine is sufficient to give an adequate flavor. These amounts are for each gallon of the final vermouth, regardless of the method of flavoring (direct or by addition of extract). For dry (French style) vermouth the amount is less, about 0.5 oz of the herb and spice mixture per gallon of wine (Valaer 1950). [One kilogram per hectoliter (100 liters) is equivalent to 1.27 oz per gal.]

Hot water has also been used to prepare a concentrated extract. Water extracts different substances from the herbs and spices than does alcohol or wine. If the herbs and spices are softened by a short immersion in hot water, they may then be more readily extracted with wine or brandy.

Jacoby (1948) has suggested that a "library" be made up by placing a weighed amount of each herb and spice in a bottle and filling with wine. After standing for a month with frequent shaking, measured portions of these extracts can be used to flavor a measured small volume of base wine (such as 1000 ml). By varying the amounts of each extract a vermouth of the desired flavor and aroma can theoretically be approximated.

Other Extraction Methods.—Brandy or alcohol extracts are available from reputable manufacturers of essences and flavoring materials, especially since World War II (Valaer 1950). These may be used alone to flavor a commercial lot of base wine for vermouth, or they are more often used in small amounts to balance or "round out" the flavor of a lot of base wine previously flavored by the addition of concentrated wine extract. Theoretically, vermouths produced at different times can be matched fairly closely. In practice it is not so simple.

Kasakova (1958) recommended that the herbs be extracted first with a wine and brandy mixture of 50% alcohol content for 10 days, then with wine for 5 days with a moderate amount of heating.

A method used by a large American producer for preparing an extract (Valaer 1950) consisted in macerating a mixture of herbs in sherry material at 60°C (140°F), cooling and allowing to stand for 3 to 6 weeks. The wine was then removed, the herbs covered with hot wine, and allowed to stand ten days. This wine was blended with the first extract. The blend was used to flavor base wine. The use of a baked sherry as a base does not, we believe, produce vermouth of highest quality.

The amount of material extracted from the herbs and spices is small and only slightly affects the basic composition of the wine.

Bo and Filice (1948) preferred preliminary laboratory experiments to determine the proper amounts of each herb. The herbs and spices are then weighed and mixed. About 5% of the base wine is heated to 60°C (140°F) and pumped into the extraction tank and the dry flavoring materials are added and the tank closed. After 24 hr, the rest of the wine is added at cellar temperature and left, with circulation once daily for 7 days. The wine is then separated from the herbs and spices and filtered. The sugar content is increased to the desired level by addition of sucrose.

It is doubtful if manufacturers have discovered how to extract the optimum flavor from herbs and spices. Otherwise, so many systems of extraction would not be employed. Different herbs and spices may require different extraction systems. Systematic studies are lacking.

ITALIAN TYPE (SWEET) VERMOUTH

Sweet vermouth is produced in Italy, Spain, Argentina, the United

States, and other countries. Since 1959, the volume of sweet vermouth produced in this country has been greater than that of the imported. For a description of the Italian industry see Cotone (1922). Typical analyses are given in Table 13.3.

Italian Methods

A best-known Italian vermouth is that of Martini and Rossi. It is dark tawny-amber in color, with a light muscat, sweet nutty flavor and a well-developed and pleasing fragrance. It has a warming taste, and a slightly bitter but agreeable aftertaste. Vermouth made in Italy must contain at least 15.5% alcohol and 13% or more of reducing sugar (Rizzo 1957; Walter 1956). American sweet vermouths are higher in alcohol.

A fortified wine with a muscat flavor, such as that of the Muscat blanc produced in northern Italy, was formerly preferred. Dry white Italian wines are also used. The vermouth from dry wines ages more quickly and is easier to clarify. In Turin, the wine is usually flavored with an alcohol extract of various herbs and spices. Those most commonly used are wormwood, coriander, bitter orange peel, Roman wormwood, cinchona, European centaury, calamus, elder flowers, angelica, orris, gentian, cinnamon, cloves, nutmeg, and cardamom. See Table 13.2 for the Italian, French, English, and botanical names. Sweetening is done with sucrose or liquid invert sugar of over 60° Brix. Caramel may be added to give or reinforce the customary dark color of sweet vermouths.

In France, the base wine is usually flavored by direct maceration of the herbs and spices. About 0.5 to 1 oz of the mixed herbs per gallon are allowed to macerate in the wine for 1 or 2 weeks, with stirring or pumping over once a day. The wine is tasted periodically during extraction and at the first sign of any excessive bitterness or "herbaceous" character the wine is drawn off and filtered. Now, essences and extracts are more often used than direct extraction of the herbs in wine.

California Methods

The base wine for sweet vermouth in California is a fortified sweet wine of light color such as a new angelica or white port. It should have a recognizable muscat flavor, but this is not general industry practice. Tawny port or port-angelica-muscatel blends are also used as a base wine.

The base wine should be analyzed for copper and iron and excess of either metal removed by fining with Cufex or other permissible treatment. Copper may cause clouding of the bottled product. If the wine is too low

TABLE 13.3. COMPOSITION OF DRY AND SWEET VERMOUTH[1]

Source	No. of Samples	Alcohol %			Extract g/100 ml			Total Acid g/100 ml			Tannin g/100 ml		
		Min	Max	Avg	Min	Max	Avg	Min	Max	Avg	Min	Max	Avg
Dry													
France (a)	6	17.4	19.3	18.3	3.7	6.1	4.8	0.55	0.66	0.61	0.05	0.08	0.07
United States (a)	77	15.0	22.0	17.7	1.4	7.9	3.8	0.31	0.66	0.50	0.03	0.07	0.04
Sweet													
Italy (a)	20	15.5	17.1	16.1	14.9	20.7	18.6	0.36	0.52	0.28	0.058	0.110	—
Italy (b)	10	13.7	16.9	15.7	14.0	17.2	15.6	0.36	0.52	0.45	0.05	0.11	0.08
United States (a)	100	14.0	21.0	17.1	10.0	19.0	13.8	0.26	0.63	0.45	0.03	0.10	0.06

[1]Source of data: (a) Valaer (1950) and (b) Rizzo (1957).

in sugar, pure dry sugar, liquid sugar, or invert sugar syrup, etc., may be added. The total volume of ameliorating material may not exceed 20%, i.e., the vermouth must consist of 80% natural wine. Citric acid is used if the total acidity is too low. The alcohol content must be high enough to allow for dilution when low-alcohol extracts are employed for flavoring. The final alcohol content of sweet vermouth is about 17%, the total extract (total soluble solids) 13−14%, total acidity (expressed as tartaric) about 0.45−0.5%, and tannin about 0.03−0.04%. Caramel syrup is added to improve color. Jacoby (1948) recommended that grape concentrate darkened by heating in the open to a boiling point of 114° to 116°C (238° to 240°F) be used instead of caramel to darken the color. American consumers apparently do not demand as deep a color in sweet vermouth as formerly. Tannic acid may be added if the tannin content is too low. Pectin materials may cause slow filtration but can be removed by treatment with a pectic enzyme (Jacoby 1948). Laboratory tests are needed in each case (see p. 317).

Pasteurization, refrigeration, and filtration are usually sufficient to stabilize the vermouth. Persistent cloudiness may develop (Luckow 1937) on refrigeration if licorice or catechu is used. They should be extracted separately, the extract diluted, cooled, allowed to settle, and then filtered before addition to the wine base. Prolonged aging is not desirable because of possible loss of odor by volatilization and oxidation. Jacoby (1948) recommended the vermouth be aged about three months before filtration. Experiments in this country are not known to the authors as to the quality of vermouth after various aging periods. Economic demands more than quality considerations may dictate practice.

Formulas.—One of the formulas given in Tables 13.4 or 13.5 can be used as a starting point and the dry or sweet vermouth then balanced or adjusted to the desired flavor and odor by addition of a small amount of a commercial essence or extract or by modifying the amounts of the ingredients. The amounts of various additional herbs and spices required for each formula are given in these tables. None of the formulas gives products that closely approach the imported vermouths in flavor and odor. However, according to Fessler (1959) and others familiar with American methods, producers no longer attempt to duplicate the imported vermouths, but aim to manufacture dry vermouth that is uniform in character from year to year and that possesses a pleasing and moderately distinctive flavor and odor. Sweet vermouth should be well flavored.

Aging and Finishing

In Italy and France the wine used for manufacture of vermouth was

TABLE 13.4. HERB MIXTURES IN SWEET VERMOUTH FORMULAS[1]

Herbs	Amount Used per Hectoliter (100 Liters) of Wine Base							
	No. 1 Grams	No. 2 Grams	No. 3 Grams	No. 4 Grams	No. 5 Grams	No. 6 Grams	No. 7 Grams	No. 8 Grams
Angelica	—	60	6	44	30	—	36	—
Bitter orange peel	—	250	50	—	58	60	—	50
Blessed thistle	—	135	—	—	—	60	100	—
Calamus	22	150	40	86	—	60	96	80
Cinchona	—	150	30	—	—	500	80	80
Cinnamon	22	100	15	—	72	—	—	50
Clammy sage	33	—	—	60	60	100	—	—
Clove	22	50	2	36	24	—	20	20
Coriander	112	500	100	76	84	25	76	70
Elder	—	200	—	90	90	100	—	—
Elecampane	—	125	50	80	70	500	—	50
European centaury	—	135	12	—	—	60	—	40
Galingale	—	50	—	—	—	100	—	40
Gentian	—	—	50	—	—	100	—	—
Germander	—	125	—	—	—	100	—	—
Lesser cardamom	—	—	12	—	—	—	—	80
Mace	—	—	6	—	56	—	—	—
Marjoram	—	—	—	70	70	—	84	—
Nutmeg	17	50	—	—	80	25	70	—
Orris	—	250	—	60	—	—	—	—
Quassia	—	30	—	—	—	—	—	50
Roman wormwood	50	—	—	—	—	60	—	—
Saffron	—	—	—	10	10	—	2	2
Wormwood	56	124	—	200	240	—	180	180

Additional constituents:
No. 1, 56 grams of thyme; 167 grams sweet marjoram; 50 grams angostura; 67 grams savory.
No. 3, 6 grams allspice.
No. 4, 16 grams anise; 50 grams lemon balm; 60 grams sweet marjoram; 76 grams masterwort; 50 grams zedoary.
No. 5, 12 grams Roman camomile; 64 grams masterwort; 80 grams hops.
No. 6, 25 grams angostura; 25 grams yarrow.
No. 7, 66 grams sage; 70 grams hop flowers.
No. 8, 70 grams zedoary; 40 grams quinine fungus; 30 grams each benzoin and sage; 70 grams common hyssop; 16 grams star anise.
[1]Source of data: Bennet (1935), Cotone (1922), Dober (1927), Hopkins (1921), Marescalchi (1943), Rizzo (1957), and Sebastian (1909).

formerly at least one year of age. After flavoring, the vermouth was aged up to five years or longer, according to Valaer (1950). In both France and Italy, he states, the time between infusion of the herbs and spices and final bottling was usually 3 to 5 years. The vermouth was refrigerated to cold stabilize it, filtered and aged. It was again filtered before bottling. Preference is now for a younger base wine and less aging of the product.

Pilone (1954) recommended the pH be adjusted to a sufficiently low level to prevent spoilage and that the sulfur dioxide content be sufficiently high for the same reason. Sweet vermouth can be spoiled by *Lactobacillus trichodes* ("the hair bacillus") (p. 562). It is easily controlled by maintaining a total sulfur dioxide content of above 100 mg/liter.

FRENCH-TYPE (DRY) VERMOUTH

Dry vermouths are not only much lower in sugar content and lighter in color than the sweet, but also higher in alcohol content and in France, but

TABLE 13.5. HERB MIXTURES IN DRY VERMOUTH FORMULAS[1]

Herbs	Amount Used per Hectoliter (100 Liters) of Wine Base				
	No. 1 Grams	No. 2 Grams	No. 3 Grams	No. 4 Grams	No. 5 Grams
Angelica	—	60	—	75	—
Bitter orange peel	1000	350	200	75	400
Blessed thistle	300	125	200	150	500
Calamus	—	150	—	150	—
Cinchona	—	—	200	—	750
Cinnamon	10	—	—	—	—
Clammy sage	—	—	—	—	—
Elder	—	—	50	200	—
Elecampane	—	—	—	150	—
European centaury	800	150	50	150	—
Gentian	—	—	—	75	—
Germander	—	50	50	150	—
Lesser cardamom	100	—	—	—	—
Marjoram	—	—	100	—	—
Nutmeg	10	—	—	75	—
Orris	100	—	160	—	400
Quassia	—	15	—	—	—
Roman wormwood	—	—	200	—	—
Wormwood	1000	35	200	150	1000

Additional constitutents:
   No. 1, 250 grams Roman camomile; 5 grams socotrine aloe; 40 ml of an infusion of raspberries; some muscat wine or elder flowers.
   No. 2, 25 grams vanilla extract; 125 grams speedwell; 50 grams rosemary; 25 grams Chinese rhubarb.
   No. 3, 200 grams each of speedwell and lungwort; 24 grams Chinese rhubarb.
   No. 4, 200 grams of peach pits.
   No. 5, 450 grams lungwort; 300 grams elder flowers.
[1]Source of data: Same as for sweet vermouth formulas (see Table 13.4).

not in this country, more bitter in flavor. A popular French dry vermouth, that of Noilly Prat, contains alcohol, 18% by volume; reducing sugar, 4%; total acidity, as tartaric, 0.65 g/100 ml; and volatile acidity as acetic, 0.053 g/ml. It is more difficult to produce a dry vermouth that closely resembles the imported than to produce a sweet vermouth that approximates the imported (see also Valaer's analyses given in Table 13.3).

European Methods

The formulas for dry vermouth in Table 13.5 call for larger amounts of wormwood and bitter orange peel than those for sweet vermouth. Lack of coriander, cinnamon, and clove should be noted. In France, according to Sichel (1945), a sound white wine of light color and moderate acidity is preferred. It is fortified with good quality high proof brandy to about 18%.

One method in use in France is to place the herbs in the extraction tank and cover with fortified wine of about 18% alcohol and leave for 30 to 40 days. The wine is drawn off and the extraction repeated several times with fresh wine. The extracts are combined and base wine is added in sufficient amount to dilute the flavor to the desired amount. The blended vermouth is then refrigerated and filtered. *Mistelle*, grape juice preserved with alcohol, or *muté*, grape juice preserved with sulfur dioxide, is added to give the desired reducing sugar.

One of the formulas given in Table 13.5 may be used as a starting point and modified by changing the proportions of the ingredients or by the addition of small amounts of essence until the desired flavor is obtained.

California Methods

Most California wine makers prefer to use a neutral shermat or sauterne-type as the base for dry vermouth. It is usually made by fortifying wine, low in sulfur dioxide, to 24% alcohol and then mixing the fortified wine with one of a 12–14% alcohol content to give a blend containing about 18% alcohol. American dry vermouths are pale in color and lightly flavored. If the color is too dark, it is treated with decolorizing carbon. However, the federal regulations require that the color not be reduced below a certain level (p. 737). By careful production practices, it is possible to produce a sufficiently light-colored wine. Carbon should not be used in vermouth but only in the base wine, because carbon absorbs herb flavoring and aromatic compounds. Casein fining will reduce the color of vermouth without removing an appreciable amount of flavor or aroma. Gelatin fining can be employed to remove excess tannin.

Maintaining a light color of dry vermouth is essential for the American market. Wright (1960) recommended: as little herbs as possible without adversely affecting the flavor, storage at 1.6°C (35°F), bottling at or above 15.6°C (60°F) to reduce oxygen solubility, and a sulfur dioxide level of 100 mg/liter or greater. Vermouth stored for 4 months at 20°C (68°F) or 30°C (86°F) were inferior to those held at 1.6°C (35°F).

The base wine should be made from grapes that are well balanced in acidity and sugar content and that produce wines that are not subject to oxidative deterioration in color and flavor. Better American dry vermouth would be produced if a wine of higher natural acidity were used. The wine should be fortified with neutral, high proof brandy. Pilone (1954) recommends that a sherry not be used in the base wine as its cooked taste masks the flavor of the vermouth. Uniformity of the final product is essential. A young wine is used, as aging darkens the color and develops an aged flavor. This may tend to mask the flavor of a high quality dry vermouth. Pilone (1954) states that sucrose "brings out" and does not mask the flavor and aroma of vermouth as much as does grape concentrate or *mistelle*.

Caramel is usually not needed in dry vermouth as the color of the wine is usually deep enough, and, in fact, often too deep. Dry vermouth for the present market should not be aged very long, but finished and bottled

young. This is in contrast with traditional French practice, in which the
dry vermouth is aged before bottling. Dry vermouth should not be low in
total acidity. It is usually higher in total acidity than sweet vermouth.
Dry vermouth may be made according to one of the formulas given in
Table 13.5 and balanced by the addition of the required amount of a
commercial extract or essence to the desired flavor and aroma. However,
the use of such extract or essence must appear in the approved formula.
As with the sweet vermouth the pH value and sulfur dioxide content
should be at such levels that spoilage by *L. trichodes* is prevented (see
Chap. 16).

Composition of Vermouth

Analyses of imported and domestic vermouths are given in Table 13.3.

NON-VERMOUTH TYPES

Federal regulations state that aperitif wine is a grape wine containing
grape spirit or added alcohol, having an alcohol content of not less than
15% by volume, flavored with herbs, spices, fruit juices, natural aromatic
flavoring materials, natural essences or other natural materials, and
processed in such manner that the final product possesses a distinctive
flavor, which is distinquished from natural wine not so treated. Retsina
wine produced by the addition of resin was similar under the regulations
to aperitif wines and like the latter may be made on bonded wine
premises.

Dubonnet is now made in the United States by the French formula.
Others made in Europe and imported are Byrrh, Campari, Bonal, Amer
Picon and Cap Corse, all made with red wine, and St. Raphaël, made
with white. Aperitif wines are often more bitter than vermouth but are
usually flavored with a smaller number of herbs and spices. See Latronico
(1947) on other flavored wines.

Garino-Canina (1934) gives the composition of two well-known aperitif
wines as follows:

	Byrrh	Dubonnet
Alcohol, volume %	18.1	16.2
Extract, g/100 ml	13.7	18.8
Total acid, g/100 ml	0.49	0.47
pH	3.30	3.42
Alkaloid, g/100 ml	0.005	0.095
Tannin, g/100 ml	0.12	0.15

Bitter-tasting aperitif wines containing quinine, and so labeled, are
made in Europe and South America, but have not proven popular in the

United States. For methods of determining the quinine, an alkaloid, see Garelik (1953), and Bonastre (1955). As much as 25 g of cinchona bark (the usual source of quinine) per gallon of wine has been recommended. Federal regulations limit them to not more than 83 mg/liter of total cinchona alkaloids in the finished beverage. Vanilla, angostura, and cinnamon are listed in some formulas. The finished wines are sweet and bitter and are served either "straight" or with soda or in certain cocktails.

Special Natural Wines

On September 2, 1958 a new type of wine was provided for—special natural (U.S. Bureau of Alcohol, Tobacco and Firearms 1976). These are products produced by the use of approved formulas with a natural wine base (including heavy-bodied blending wine). Natural herbs, spices, fruit juices, aromatics, essences, and other natural flavorings may be used in such quantities as to enable such products to be distinguished from any natural wine not so treated. Sugar or liquid sugar, water and caramel may be employed. Since sugar may not be used to produce a "California" wine they are designated as "American" wine.

These new types of wines had wide market acceptance, especially in the 1960's. They have been labeled with proprietary names, such as Thunderbird, Silver Satin, Golden Spur, Key Largo, Bali Hai, Spanada, and Eden Roc, among many. Not all the new types, however, have achieved lasting popularity. Several after a momentary popularity disappeared. A few gained consumer acceptance in some areas but not in others. Some of these wines are made with wine that is very light in color, but several are amber in color. The composition of three different brands of these wines is given earlier in this chapter (see p. 492).

These wine types are very different from traditional types. They are obviously intended to enlarge the basis of wine sales by attracting the nonwine drinking public. This seems to have been achieved as shown by the rapid increase in sales of special natural wines, much of which is now under 14% alcohol (Table 13.4). It is believed, hopefully, that they have increased consumption of the traditional nonflavored types.

Several flavor houses supply a variety of natural flavors for producing these types of wines.

REFERENCES[2]

AMERINE, M.A. 1973. A multi-language dictionary of vermouth ingredients. Riv. Ital. Essenze, Prof., Piante Offic., Aromi, Saponi, Cosmet., Aerosol 55 (8) 504-516.

---

[2]Titles have been translated only for nonwestern European languages.

AMERINE, M.A. 1974. Vermouth: An Annotated Bibliography. University of California, Division of Agricultural Sciences, Berkeley, Calif.

BALZAC, F. 1915. Le artemisie dei Vermouths e dei Génépis. Am. R. Accad. Agric. Torino 58, 279-303.

BENNET, H. 1935. The Chemical Formulary, Vol. II. D. Van Nostrand Co., New York.

BO, M.J. and FILICE, M.J. 1948. Gold medal sweet vermouth.Wines Vines 29 (8) 27-29.

BONASTRE, J. 1955. Evaluation de la quinine des quinquinas aperitifs par chromatographie sur papier. Ann. Fals Fraudes 48, 109-113.

BRÉVANS, J. DE. 1920. Fabrication des Liqueurs, 4th Edition. J.-B. Baillière et Fils, Paris.

COTONE, D.A. 1922. Vino Vermouth ed i Suoi Componenti. Casa Editrice F. Marescalchi, Casale Monferrato.

DOBER, W. 1927. Formulario para la Fabricación de Licores por Destilación y sin Destilación. Casa Editiorial Araluse, Barcelona.

FESSLER, J.H. 1959. Personal communication.

FESSLER, J.H. and JACOBY, O.F. 1949. Vermouth. Its production and future. Wines Vines 30 (12) 15-17.

GARELIK, A. 1953. Analisis de vinos quinados. Anales Nacl. Direc. Quím. 6 (11) 20-21.

GARINO-CANINA, E. 1934. Vini aperitivi francesi. Annuar. R. Staz. Enol. Sper. Asti 1, 223-233.

GRIEBEL, C. 1955. Gemahlene Wermutkräuter. Z. Lebensm. Unters. Forsch. 100, 270-274.

HOPKINS, A.A. 1921. The Scientific American Cyclopedia of Formulas. Scientific American Publishing Co., New York.

JACOBY, O.F. 1948. Developing the vermouth formula. Wines Vines 29 (4) 73-75.

JOSLYN, M.A. and AMERINE, M.A. 1964. Dessert, Appetizer and Related Flavored Wines. University of California, Division of Agricultural Sciences, Berkeley.

KASAKOVA, E. 1958. Preparing spices for the production of vermouth. (transl.) Izvest. Vysshikh. Ucheb. Zavadenii Tekhnol. 1, 109-112. (Chem. Abs. 53, 8532, 1959.)

LATRONICO, N. 1947. I Vini Medicinali, dalle Antiche Formule alle Preparazioni Moderne, 2nd Edition. Casa Editrice Bertuzzi, Milan.

LAZARUS, J.R. 1965. Final botanical bulletin. Wine Institute Bull. 1360-L, 1-8.

LUCKOW, C. 1937. Trübung in Wermut Bitter. Wein Rebe 19, 11-13.

MARESCALCHI, A. 1943. Manuale del Enologo e del Cantiniere. Casa Editrice Fratelli Marescalchi, Casale Monferrato.

MATTIROLO, O. 1915. Sulla coltivazione e sul valore delle "Artemisie" usate nella fabricazione dei Vermouths. Ann. R. Accad. Agric. Torino 58, 225-227.

MÉRAT, E., MARTIN, E., DURET, M. and VOGEL, J. 1976. Extraction et dosage par chromatographie de β-asarone et de α et β-thuyone dans les apéritifs. Mitt. Geb. Lebensmittelunters. Hyg. 67, 521-526.

MORINI, P. 1955. Le piante officinali nella industria dei liquori. Riv. Ital. Essenze Prof. 37, 16-19.

OTTAVIO, O. and GARINO-CANINA, E. 1930. Vini di Lusso, 8th Edition. Casa Editrice Fratelli Ottavi, Casale Monferrato.

PILONE, F.J. 1954. Production of vermouth. Am. J. Enol. 5, 30-46.

RIZZO, F. 1957. La Fabricazione del Vermouth. Edizione Agricole, Bologna.

SÉBASTIAN, V. 1909. Traité Pratique de la Préparation des Vins de Luxe. Coulet et Fils, Montpellier.

SICHEL, H.O. 1945. Vermouth. Its production and future. Wines Vines 26 (3) 22-25.

U.S. FOOD AND DRUG ADMINISTRATION. 1970. Food additives regulations. Washington, 21 Code of Federal Regulations, Section 121.1163.

U.S. BUREAU OF ALCOHOL, TOBACCO AND FIREARMS. 1976. Wine. Part 240 of Title 27, Code of Federal Regulations. Govt. Print. Off., Washington, D.C. [This is the most important U.S. document on wines.]

USSEGLIO-TOMASSET, L. 1966. La determinazione dell'α e β-Tujone nelle bevande alcoliche aromatizzate. Riv. Viticolt. Enol. (Conegliano) 19, 3-24.

VALAER, P. 1950. The Wines of the World. Abelard Press, New York.

VALVASSORI, S. 1954. Le piante officinalli nell'industria dei vermut e degli aperitivi. Riv. Ital. Essenze Prof. 36, 639-643.

WALTER, E. 1956. Wermut Wein. Carl Knoppke Grüner Verlag, Berlin.

WRIGHT, D. 1960. Factors affecting the color of dry vermouth. Am. J. Enol. Vitic. 11, 30-34.

14

Fruit Wines

Fruits and berries, as well as grapes, yield wines upon fermentation. Techniques for their production closely resemble those described in this book for the production of white and red grape wines. Differences arise from two facts. It is somewhat more difficult to extract the sugar and other soluble materials from the pulp of some fruits than it is from grapes, and the juices obtained from most of the fruits are lower in sugar content and higher in acids than is true for grapes. The first problem is dealt with by use of special equipment that more thoroughly chops or disintegrates the fruit or berries, followed by use of presses that extract the juices from the finely divided pulp. The second is solved by the addition of water to dilute the excess acid and of sugar to correct this deficiency.

In the United States, the production of fruit wines is primarily regulated by the Bureau of Alcohol, Tobacco and Firearms of the Treasury Department. Most of the regulations are summarized in Wine, Part 240 of Title 27—CFR, ATF P 5120.2 (12/74). Fundamentally, these rules permit the addition of water to dilute the excess acidity down to a level of 0.5 g/100 ml, of sugar to produce not more than 14% by volume of alcohol, and then of more sugar to sweeten the wine to a solids content of not more than 21% by weight. In no case is the volume constituted by the added water and sugar to exceed 35% of the final volume of the wine produced, except that for loganberries, currants and gooseberries this figure is increased to 60%. Yeast, yeast food, sulfur dioxide, and normal cellar practices are permitted. Fruit wines may be fortified provided spirits from the same kind of fruit are used.

Apples, pears, plums, cherries, currants (*Ribes* sp.) and the various types of berries are the most frequently used nongrape wine sources, although wine has been made from almost every type of fruit berry, herb, root and flower at some time or another. For general discussions see Baumann (1959), Charley (1953, 1954), Charley and Harrison (1939),

Cruess *et al.* (1935), Duerr and Schobinger (1976), Dupaigne (1959), Gachot (1955, 1957), Koch (1956), Kroemer and Krumholz (1932), Lüthi (1953), Mehlitz (1951), Paragul'gov *et al.* (1976A,B), Rokhlenko and Grebeshova (1977), Schanderl and Koch (1957), Valaer (1950A,B), Villforth (1954), Wallrauch (1975), Webb (1974), and Yang (1953).

CIDER AND APPLE WINE

In Great Britain and France the term "cider" (cidre) means apple wine, hard cider, or fermented apple juice, while in the United States it may designate either fermented or unfermented apple juice. In Germany it is *Apfelwein*. For general information see Arengo-Jones (1941), Barker (1911A,B, 1937), Bol'shakova and Belko (1976), Braskat and Quinn (1940), Charley (1937, 1953), Clague and Fellers (1936), Cruess and Celmer (1938), Czapski (1976), Davis (1933), Heatherbell (1976A,B), Martinez *et al.* (1958), Smock and Neubert (1950), Tschenn (1934), and Vecher *et al.* (1976).

Composition of Cider Apples

Table 14.1 illustrates the range in composition that has been observed in the composition of apples used for cider. Cider apples are higher in tannin. Special varieties are grown in France, Switzerland, and England for cider making, whereas in the United States, Germany, and Canada table varieties are usually employed.

TABLE 14.1. COMPOSITION OF APPLES USED FOR CIDER PRODUCTION

Variety	Region Grown	Sugar °Brix	%	Acid g/100 ml	Total Tannin g/100 ml	Source
Cider apples, avg 4 varieties	Normandy	17.5		0.39	0.26	Alwood (1903)
Cider apples, avg	England	13.7		0.27	0.32	Charley (1937)
St. Laurent[1]	Virginia		16.5	0.27	0.24	Caldwell (1928)
Bramlot[1]	Virginia		19.05	0.22	0.53	Caldwell (1928)
Omont[1]	Virginia		14.2	0.33	0.27	Caldwell (1928)
Bidan[1]	Virginia		14.9	0.14	0.20	Caldwell (1928)
Several varieties, mostly table, avg	Germany		14.4	0.73	0.07	Kroemer and Krumholz (1932)
Several varieties, mostly table, avg	Oregon		11.2	0.70	—	Yang and Wiegand (1949)
8 varieties, mostly table, 1933 and 1944, avg	New England		12.3	0.50	0.06	Clague and Fellers (1936)

[1]French cider apple varieties.

European Methods

Cider is made by storing the apples in bins for a few days to develop aroma then washing, sorting to remove rotten fruit, crushing and pressing in a rack and cloth press (Kroemer and Krumholz 1932; Charley 1937). Some crushed apples are not pressed at once but are allowed to stand for 3 to 24 hr to develop color and flavor. This maceration greatly improves the "pressability" of the crushed apples. Sulfur dioxide (50–100 mg/liter is added to the juice, it is cooled to 0° to 7.8°C (32° to 46°F) and settled. This practice is termed "keeving." The clear juice is fermented at 4.4° to 10°C (40° to 50°F).

Cidre marchand and *petite cidre* are made by adding water and sugar to the pomace for two more fermentations.

The cider is drawn off from the yeast lees and below the cap, "*chapeau brun*," when active fermentation terminates. It undergoes a slow secondary fermentation for several months in casks at about 4.4°C (40°F) following which it is racked and bottled. Residual sugar or malo-lactic fermentation generates some CO_2 in the bottle.

Pectic enzymes are often added to the juice to hasten and improve clearing of the cider during and after fermentation (Kertesz 1930; Kilbuck *et al.* 1949).

Pure yeasts are used in some fermentations. A malo-lactic fermentation sometimes occurs before the alcoholic fermentation is completed. The new wine may be stored under carbon dioxide.

German apples used for production of cider, according to Kroemer and Krumholz (1932), Schanderl and Koch (1957), and Wilhelm (1957), are, on the average, of lower sugar content and higher acidity than those of Normandy and England.

The apples are washed, sorted, and crushed and then pressed at once without maceration. Juice expressed from pears of high tannin content is sometimes added to apple juice deficient in tannin. If the acidity of the juice is below 0.6 g/100 ml Schanderl and Koch (1957) recommend the addition of lactic acid to increase the acidity to that level. They recommend the addition of potassium metabisulfite and advocate the use of selected yeast, such as Steinberg or Winningen. Often, the juice is centrifuged before fermentation to clarify it partially and remove much of the undesirable bacteria and wild yeasts.

Schanderl and Koch, and also Kroemer and Krumholz, state that a dessert apple wine is also made in Germany in one of two ways. The cider may be fortified with high proof brandy; or a cider of high alcohol content may be made by fermentation of sweetened, pasteurized juice to which is added about 20 g/hl of ammonium phosphate as a yeast food. A selected yeast of high alcohol-forming power is used. The sugar is not all added at once, but in three portions during fermentation.

Vogt (1977) in making apple and pear wine recommended washing and crushing the fruit, adding 50 ppm of sulfur dioxide and 10% water and pressing after several hours. The press juice is then sugared to the desired degree. Pure yeast cultures of cold-acclimated yeasts are recommended. Nitrogen, as ammonium chloride or phosphate, must be added. European apple wines contained 5.6 to 7.3% alcohol.

Charley and Harrison (1939) have described the usual procedure of making cider in England as follows: Washed apples are sorted to remove rotten fruit not previously separated from the sound fruit by flotation in water. The apples are grated or hammer milled and pressed at once in a rack and cloth hydraulic press.

Fermentation is allowed to proceed naturally in most plants to a specific gravity of 1.008 to 1.005. Racking from the yeast sediment and centrifugation slow down the fermentation. The cider is usually stored in concrete tanks lined with a suitable coating.

Before delivery to retail establishments the cider is usually sweetened by the addition of boiled cane or beet sugar syrup and sterilized by germ proof filtration.

If a naturally sweet hard cider is to be made the fermentation is allowed to proceed to a specific gravity of 1.025 to 1.030, approximately 5° to 7.5° Brix. It is filtered or centrifuged to arrest fermentation. The clarified cider is then stored in wooden casks or other suitable containers until needed for consumption when it is again filtered, carbonated and bottled.

Increasingly large quantities of surplus table and cooking apples are used in England for production of cider. Their juices ferment very rapidly. Charley and Harrison (1939) state that only cider varieties of apples should be used for making dry cider, as the dessert and cooking varieties give dry cider of harsh flavor. Considerable sparkling cider is also made by the Charmat process (p. 469).

United States Methods

Federal regulations define apple wine as "the product of the normal alcoholic fermentation of the juice of sound ripe apples, with or without the addition of cane, beet or glucose sugar for the purpose of perfecting the produce according to standards, but without the addition or abstraction of other substances, except as may occur in the usual cellar treatment." Although there is confusion in labeling today, eventually producers of hard cider and apple wine and the trade will probably establish standards of identity for hard cider and apple wine.

The apples used in California and elsewhere in the United States are those grown for table or culinary use. Of the varieties available in commercial quantities on the Pacific Coast, Winesap is one of the best in composition and fermentation characteristics. It is grown chiefly in the state of Washington. The Northern Spy, Rome Beauty, Gravenstein, Stayman Winesap, Yellow Newtown, McIntosh, Spitzenberg, Jonathan, Roxbury, and other varieties of pronounced flavor and medium acidity are satisfactory. In California, the Gravenstein is of excellent flavor and desirable acidity. It is available in midsummer to early fall. The Newtown (Yellow Newtown) is a late fall apple of excellent keeping quality and available in abundance. Its juice is rather mild in flavor and of medium acidity. It should be blended with a more flavorful and acid variety such as the Winesap.

The Delicious, now grown extensively in the Pacific Northwest, is of poor quality both for unfermented juice and for cider because of its low acidity. If it is used at all for cider its juice should be blended with that of a variety of higher acidity such as the Winesap or Northern Spy. It is common practice to mix two or more varieties for cider production.

Only fruit that is sound and free of rot and worm damage should be used for cider. The apples are thoroughly washed and then sorted. It is reported by apple juice producers that spray removal is no longer an important problem since other insecticdes have replaced lead arsenate for control of codling moth and most of these new agents disappear from the fruit before it is picked.

The washed and sorted sound apples are prepared for pressing by passage through a grater or hammer mill. The latter is now much the more common. The pressing of the hammer milled apples gives a higher yield of juice because of the more thorough grinding by the mill. The grated or hammer milled fruit is pressed in a rack and cloth press. Press cloths of nylon are stronger than cotton cloths and are more easily washed, more easily separated from the press cake, and more durable than cotton, though more costly.

In plants in which the juice goes directly from the press to the fermentors, sulfur dioxide is added to give about 100 to 125 ppm. If the juice is to be held overnight to permit settling and clearing with use of a pectic enzyme, somewhat more sulfur dioxide is used in order to delay fermentation. The sulfur dioxide also aids in preventing undue oxidation and browning and inhibits wild yeasts and bacteria. Spontaneous fermentation may begin during settling. Glucose is added so that after fermentation is completed the cider will have about 13% alcohol by volume. The juice is fermented rapidly. When fermentation is completed or has proceeded to the desired point, cane or beet sugar is added to give about 10° Brix. The cider is usually clarified with bentonite. It is then filtered, bottled and pasteurized. In most cases no pectic enzyme is employed. According to Fessler (1959), much hard cider is made from apple concentrate. The final product is darker in color and less fruity in flavor than that made from the fresh fruit. Apple essence can be added for flavor and excess color can be removed with decolorizing carbon.

Clouding due to excess copper or iron is seldom encountered today as most of the equipment used is of stainless steel, wood or plastic. If present in excess, iron and copper can be removed with Cufex or ion exchange as described in Chap. 6 and 15.

The effect of temperature on fermentation was found by Yang and Wiegand (1949) to be pronounced. Apple juice sweetened and fermented 5 days with champagne yeast at 24.4°, 30.0°, and 36.7°C (76°, 86°, and 98°F) contained 17.3, 14.95, and 6.2% alcohol by volume, indicating that the lowest of the three temperatures was the most favorable. Seven strains of wine yeast were compared in fermentation at 24.4°C (76°F); champagne yeast gave the best results. For information on the yeast flora of apples and ciders, see Pearce and Baker (1939) and Legakis (1961). Clark *et al.* (1954) found that the fermentation rate of apple juice varied more or less directly in proportion to the amount of yeast extract added.

Yang and Wiegand (1949) give the average composition of Pacific Northwest hard cider at the time of their report as: alcohol 12.8% by volume; Brix 4.6°; total acidity as malic, 0.41; volatile acid, 0.105; and total sulfur dioxide, 96 ppm. Analysis of three California 1959 hard ciders gave alcohol 11.10, 13.6, and 11.6%; 9.0°, 7.4°, and 7.0° Brix; total acidity as malic, 0.48, 0.47, and 0.35 g/100 ml; and volatile acidity, 0.045, 0.06, and 0.015 g/100 ml.

SPARKLING APPLE WINE

Sparkling apple wines are produced by carbonation in tank- or bottle-fermentation. Tressler *et al.* (1941) describe a tank process for apple wines and Atkinson *et al.* (1959) give an outline of the carbonation process. A clear juice is obtained by pectinase treatment and rough filtering. This is ameliorated to 16% solids with sucrose, and fermented at 25°C (77°F). At a refractometer reading of 8.9% soluble solids (in about 4 days) the wine is cooled to −1.7°C (29°F) to stop fermentation at approximately 5% alcohol. The cold wine is polish-filtered and carbonated at about 35 lb pressure. It is bottled and pasteurized.

Brown *et al.* (1959) report that the best apples for carbonated wine are those of firm ripe fruit used after a minimum storage period. Delicious blended with Jonathan made the best cider.

Recently, slightly sparkling apple and apple-pear wines have become popular. They have excellent fruit aroma, probably owing to addition of apple flavor essence in some cases.

WINES OF HIGHER ALCOHOL

Hard cider of high alcohol content can be made by a freezing process. Hard cider, made in conventional manner is filtered, frozen to a slushy consistency and the concentrated cider and ice crystals are then separated by draining by the Monti process. The final alcohol content is about 18—20% by volume. The aged concentrated hard cider is of pleasing flavor and suitable for use as a dessert wine. The ice crystals and concentrated hard cider could be separated also by basket centrifuge (Gore 1914), or the Linde-Krause method as described by Charley (1937) could be used. This latter process consists of freezing the product on the outside of a slowly revolving, refrigerated drum. Ice is removed from the drum by a scraper and the lower part of the drum dips into a tank of the product which becomes concentrated by freezing water on the drum. Modern heat-exchangers-chillers could be used.

WINES OTHER THAN APPLE

Pear Wine

In Europe, special varieties of pears of high tannin content are used for making perry, a fermented pear beverage.

Bartlett pears have been made into wine experimentally at the University of California as follows. The pears were grated in an orchard size apple grater and pressed in a rack and cloth press. The juice was of 14° Brix and approximately 0.25% acidity as malic. Sugar was added to increase the Brix to 21° and sufficient citric acid was then added to increase the total acidity to 0.5%; also about 100 ppm of sulfur dioxide and a starter of pure wine yeast were used. Fermentation to dryness was rapid. The wine was allowed to settle in glass containers, was racked and aged in glass with oak chips. It was clarified with bentonite after final racking. The final product was dry and fairly palatable. A pectic enzyme should be used as the wine is difficult to filter or fine. The dry wine could be sweetened and pasteurized or fortified and sweetened as with other fruit wines.

Berry Wines

Both table and dessert wines are made from various berries (Henry 1936; Osterwalder 1948). The methods described by Schanderl and Koch (1957) and Wilhelm (1957) for preparing both types of wine from red currants (*Ribes* sp.) will illustrate the customary procedures. The red currants have about 2.4% acid content, expressed as tartaric. Therefore, considerable dilution of the juice with water is necessary in order to produce a palatable wine. The juice has about 6% sugar. If a wine of 8% alcohol by volume is desired there is added to each liter of juice 2 liters of water and 345 g of sugar; if 10% alcohol is desired, 445 g of sugar are used. More water should not be used as the resulting wine will be too "dilute" in flavor. If a dessert wine of 16% alcohol is to be made, 1 liter of juice, 2 liters of water and 735 g of sugar are used; or 1 liter of juice, 1.4 liters of water and 570 g of sugar. Schanderl and Koch also give the proportions of the three materials to make dessert wines of other alcohol content.

In making both the table wine and the dessert wine, a starter of pure yeast is added. For rapid clarification of the wine, addition of a pectic enzyme is beneficial. The addition of 10 to 15 g of potassium bisulfite per hl (100 liters) is recommended. The directions given by Schanderl and Koch (1957) for other berry wines are similar to those for red currant wine. They suggest that only enough water be used to reduce the acidity to 0.8% as tartaric.

Fermentation is conducted with a starter of 2 to 5% by volume of a powerful wine yeast such as Steinberg. Cellar processing is conducted as outlined for apple cider. Berry wines should not be aged too long as they then lose color and flavor. Usually, they are sweetened to properly balance sugar and acidity and to "bring out" the berry flavor. Germ-proof filtration or pasteurization is recommended for the bottled berry table wines.

Yand and Wiegand (1949) give the average values shown in Table 14.2 for sugar and acid content of several fruits and berries used in Oregon for production of fruit wines.

TABLE 14.2. AVERAGE SUGAR AND ACID CONTENTS OF SEVERAL FRUITS USED IN WINE MAKING IN THE PACIFIC NORTHWEST[1]

Fruit	Total Sugar %	Total Acid %
Apple	11.2	0.70 as malic
Blackberry	7.2	1.20 as citric
Cherry	8.5	1.00 as malic
Currant	6.4	2.10 as citric
Loganberry	6.9	2.00 as citric
Plum	12.0	0.90 as malic
Raspberry	6.8	1.60 as citric

[1]Source of data: Yang and Wiegand (1949).

Yang (1955) recommended harvesting the fruit at optimum maturity. Since blackberries have higher pigment concentration toward the end of the season and this leads to pigment deposits in the bottle, harvest before full maturity may be desirable.

Stillman (1955) states that maturity, sugar and acid content, variety, and whether the fruit has been held in cold storage are factors. Fruit held in cold storage apparently produces lesser quality wine.

Yang and Wiegand (1949) have reported the analyses of Pacific Northwest fruit wines as shown in Table 14.3.

TABLE 14.3. TYPICAL COMPOSITION OF FRUIT WINES OF THE PACIFIC NORTH-WEST[1]

Wine	Alcohol %/vol	°Brix	Total Acid g/100 ml	Vol. Acid g/100 ml	Total SO₂ ppm
Apple	12.8	4.6	0.411	0.105	96
Blackberry	12.2	8.2	0.890	0.069	103
Cherry	12.3	6.8	0.534	0.102	113
Currant	13.0	9.1	1.000	0.051	87
Loganberry	12.6	8.0	0.870	0.074	64
Plum (fortified)	19.8	11.9	0.790	0.088	70
Raspberry	12.0	8.8	0.903	0.060	75

[1]Source of data: Yang and Wiegand (1949).

Yang *et al.* (1950), reporting on the effect of the use of a pectic enzyme at the rate of 1 lb per ton of fruit, have given the data presented in Table 14.4. The enzyme was added before fermentation.

TABLE 14.4. EFFECT OF PECTIC ENZYME ON YIELD OF JUICE[1] (GAL./TON)

Treatment	Loganberry	Blackberry	Currant	Concord Grape
Enzyme treated	195	200	193	182
Untreated	180	183	183	163
Percentage increase	7.69	8.5	5.18	10.44
Yield after amelioration:				
Enzyme treated	512	317	509	270
Untreated	475	300	480	224
Percentage increase	7.22	5.36	5.7	17.04

[1]Source of data: Yang *et al.* (1950).

Yang and Wiegand (1949) state that apple juice, plums, and cherries produced in the Pacific Northwest ferment satisfactorily without the addition of nitrogenous yeast food (urea or ammonium phosphate), but that such addition is necessary for rapid and complete fermentation of ameliorated (diluted and sweetened) berry juices. Their data on the effect of added urea are given in Table 14.5.

Addition of urea increased the rate markedly of blackberry, currant, loganberry, and raspberry juices. Apparently addition of 0.05% of urea was about as effective as 0.10%.

Yang (1959) states that in the Pacific Northwest berries are not usually crushed before fermentation; that fermentation lasts from 7 to 14 days depending on the temperature; about 100 ppm of sulfur dioxide or an equivalent amount of metabisulfite is added before fermentation; about ¼ of the total amount of sugar is added before fermentation and

TABLE 14.5. EFFECT OF ADDED UREA ON FERMENTATION OF VARIOUS JUICES AT 24.4°C (76°F) BY CHAMPAGNE YEAST[1]

% of Urea Added	Alcohol Volume Percent After 5 Days Fermentation						
	Apple	Blackberry	Cherry	Currant	Loganberry	Plum	Raspberry
0	17.00	5.90	16.60	7.90	9.20	14.20	8.70
0.05	17.10	8.30	16.55	10.25	12.50	14.00	12.50
0.10	17.30	8.80	16.45	10.70	13.00	13.80	12.70

[1]Source of data: Yang and Wiegand (1949).

the remainder during fermentation; pure yeast is used in most plants; that amelioration with water and sugar may be made before, during, or after fermentation; that the use of pectic enzymes is not universal but that they are used in some plants; and that the alcohol content of the new wine before final sweetening is 12–14% by volume. Addition of sugar after fermentation reduces the alcohol content about 1% owing to the dilution effect of the added sugar.

Cherry Wines

Schanderl and Koch (1957) recommend sour cherries in preference to sweet for making wine as the acidity of the latter is too low. A blend of the two or a blend of currant and a table variety of cherries may be used. In crushing the cherries, up to 10% of the pits may be broken in order to enhance the flavor of the wine. Hydrogen cyanide, from hydrolysis of amygdalin in the pits, has been discovered by Baumann and Gierschner (1974), Benk (1976), Misselhorn and Adam (1976), and Stadelmann (1976).

A cherry dessert wine rather than a table wine is recommended by Schanderl and Koch, who give the amounts of sugar required for each liter of juice plus a liter of water to give dessert wines of various alcohol contents ranging from 12 to 17%. For one of 16% alcohol the amount is 430 g to each liter of juice. The sugar is dissolved in water. Like berry wines, the cherry wine should not be aged very long. Sugar may be added before bottling to give the desired degree of sweetness. Germ-proof filtration or pasteurization may be used to preserve the bottled wine. The use of a small amount of potassium metabisulfite is advisable before fermentation. The use of a pectic enzyme to hasten and improve clarification is desirable.

Plum Wines

Schanderl and Koch (1957) recommend that to the crushed plums or sour prunes a liter of water be added for each pound of crushed fruit.

Sugar and a starter of yeast are added. The mixture is allowed to ferment for 8 to 10 days before pressing, as it is practically impossible to press the fruit before fermentation. Addition of a pectic enzyme before fermentation greatly facilitates pressing, increases the yield of juice and hastens clearing of the wine. Additional sugar may be added to the partially fermented juice; the amount will vary according to whether a table or a dessert wine is to be made. Aging, filtration, bottling, and preservation are similar to these operations for berry wines.

Pomegranate Wine

Pomegranate wine is made by pressing the whole fruit without preliminary crushing in order to avoid excessive astringency.

Cruess *et al.* (1935) have given the following directions based on pilot scale experiments. Add sugar to 22°−23° Brix and 2 lb of metabisulfite to each 1000 gal. of juice. Ferment with a starter of wine yeast. Age and finish in the same manner as red grape wine. Bottle pasteurize or sterile bottle to ensure stability if residual sugar is present.

Pineapple Wine

Apparently only small amounts of pineapple have been vinified for consumption as wine, although in Hawaii and the Philippines wine is made from pineapple waste for the production of distilled vinegar.

As the natural juice is of only 12°−15° Brix, the addition of sugar to give 22°−23° Brix is desirable in order to give a wine of 12−13% alcohol by volume. Such a wine can be sweetened and preserved by pasteurization as described earlier in this chapter for hard cider and berry wines. Also, the wine can be fortified and sweetened to give a dessert wine. Unfortunately, the pineapple flavor is not stable and oxidation occurs easily.

Wine from Oranges

A fortified sweet dessert orange wine has been made. The wine was dark amber in color and resembled angelica wine in composition. See Von Loesecke *et al.* (1936) for Florida experiments; Joslyn and Marsh (1934), Cruess (1914) and Cruess *et al.* (1935) for California experiments with orange wine.

Orange wines darken rapidly and develop a harsh, stale taste unless a fairly high level of sulfur dioxide is maintained. The fruit should be thoroughly ripe, but not over-ripe, as the wine then is likely to have a stale flavor. Although the juice can be extracted by crushing the fruit and pressing in a rack and cloth press or by use of a continuous screw press, the juice then contains so much essential oil from the peel that it ferments very slowly. The juice is best extracted by the usual juice equipment in which the oranges are cut in half by machine and reamed mechanically in a Brown or FMC juice extractor. However, a rotary juice extractor such as is used in Florida or a Citro-Mat extractor, both of which obtain the juice by pressure, can be used if the juice is centrifuged to remove most of the essential oil.

The oranges should be sorted to remove rotten and other unfit fruit. They should then be washed thoroughly. For efficient juice extraction the fruit should be graded into three sizes as the machines are usually built to work best on fruit of fairly uniform size.

To the fresh juice should be added about 150 ppm of sulfur dioxide or an equivalent amount of bisulfite or metabisulfite. Sugar dissolved in a small amount of juice should be added to increase the Brix degree to $22°-23°$, and a starter of wine yeast should be used. About 0.1% pectic enzyme should be added, as untreated orange wine does not clear satisfactorily and is difficult to filter.

Fermentation of orange juice is rapid, as it is an excellent culture medium for yeast. It should be fermented as previously described for apple juice and to dryness. Sugar may then be added to about $10°$ Brix; sulfur dioxide added to about 200 mg/liter of total sulfur dioxide, the wine filtered, and pasteurized.

Alternately the wine, after addition of sugar, may be fortified to 20% alcohol, aged, given an addition of sulfur dioxide as for the table wines, filtered and bottled without pasteurization. A small amount of terpeneless orange oil or orange extract may be added before filtration to impart an orange flavor.

Von Loesecke *et al.* (1936) made an orange cordial by distilling orange wine to give an orange brandy, adding sugar to the brandy and diluting with distilled water to about 33% alcohol content and about 37% sugar. A small amount of cold pressed orange oil was added; the cordial was then aged, and finally filtered before bottling.

Grapefruit Wine

Grapefruit may be used in the same manner as oranges for the production of table wine, dessert wine, and cordials. The wines are somewhat bitter. If the wine is too high in acidity, as is sometimes the case, a calculated amount of potassium carbonate may be added, or the calculated amount of calcium carbonate may be added and the mixture heated to $65.6°$ to $71.1°C$ ($150°$ to $160°F$) to hasten the reaction and to make the calcium citrate less soluble, filtering hot, and cooling. Ion-exchange treatment may also be used to reduce the acidity.

Wines of Tropical Fruits

Morales de Leon (1976) and Garcia *et al.* (1974) have discussed the characteristics of several tropical fruits and the wines made from them. Many subtropical and tropical fruits have low acidity and are difficult to make into attractive, stable wines. Since the flavors are "strange" to consumers in temperate regions, export markets are difficult to develop.

Wine from Dried Fruits

Dried figs and dates can be made into a fair wine as follows: to the dried, shredded fruit in a vat or open barrel, add 1.4-1.8 kg (3–4 lb) of boiling hot water to each pound of fruit or about 37.9 liters (10 gal.) to each 11.34 kg (25 lb) of fruit. The water should contain about 0.6% citric acid (about 0.23 kg per 37.9 liters or 0.5 lb per 10 gal.) Let cool, and then add about 150 ppm of sulfur dioxide. Add a starter of pure yeast.

As shredding or grinding the dried fruit before adding the water is difficult, a better procedure is as follows. Pass the fruit, with the proper amount of hot water, through a Rietz disintegrator and pump the resulting slurry of ground fruit and water through a cooler into a fermenting vat. Add the required acid (0.6% citric acid) and 100 to 150 ppm sulfur dioxide and pure yeast. Ferment until most of the sugar is fermented. Draw off the free-run, and bag filter the pomace, or press it in a rack and cloth press, adding, if needed, filter aid.

Analyze the wine for sugar and alcohol content. Add sufficient dextrose or sucrose to give, on complete fermentation, about 12% of alcohol. When fermentation is complete, treat as any other white table wine.

Raisins should be passed through raisin seeder rolls with fingers removed, to cut the raisins. From this point, handle in the same manner as previously described for figs and dates. Raisins contain about 60% sugar, hence somewhat less water than that recommended for figs and dates may be used. Another method is soaking the raisins in water until plump. They may then be crushed and pressed, as are fresh grapes. The cold water in which they are soaked should contain about 150 mg/liter of sulfur dioxide.

Dried apricots and peaches are not very satisfactory for making wine as they are too "solid" or "pulpy" and the extract too gummy.

HONEY WINE (MEAD)

Wine is made from honey in a manner similar to that used in making fruit wines (Morse *et al.* 1975). Mead is more or less a synonym for honey wine and dates back to prebiblical times.

Filipello and Marsh (1934) found that the addition of a nitrogenous yeast food to the diluted honey was necessary for successful fermentation and that phosphate was also very beneficial. A honey of mild flavor is recommended in preference to honeys of very strong flavor. The addition of acid was also found very desirable, as the nonacidified product is almost neutral in reaction.

On the basis of Filipello and Marsh's experiments as well as the instructions given by Wilhelm (1957) the following method is suggested for producing a dry table wine from honey: A sound honey of pleasing and rather mild flavor should be used. It is diluted with water to about 22° Brix. To each liter of diluted honey is added 5 g citric acid, 1.5 g diammonium monohydrogen phosphate [$(NH_4)_2HPO_4$], 1 g potassium bitartrate (cream of tartar) and 0.25 g each of magnesium chloride and calcium chloride. These can be dissolved in a small amount of the diluted honey by heating and stirring and this solution then added to and mixed with the main volume of diluted product. The addition of about 100 ppm of sulfur dioxide and a starter of 2−3% by volume of pure wine yeast is recommended. The starter can be grown in pasteurized diluted honey prepared as above or in pasteurized grape or other fruit juice. See Chap. 6 for directions for preparing yeast starters. During the final stages of fermentation, the cask or tank should be fitted with a fermentation bung in order to prevent acetification.

The new wine is allowed to settle for several weeks and is racked. Filter aid is added and the wine is filtered, aged a few months in completely filled, tightly sealed casks or tanks, racked, polish filtered, and bottled. It is suitable for use on the table.

It may be sweetened to 5° to 10° Brix by addition of honey or sugar, filtered and pasteurized or sterile bottled.

The sweetened wine may be fortified to 18−20% alcohol by addition of high proof brandy as outlined in the chapters on dessert wines. Another method of producing a fortified sweet honey wine consists of adding brandy to the partially fermented product.

REFERENCES[1]

ALWOOD, W.B. 1903. A study of cider making in France, Germany and England. U.S. Dept. Agric., Bur. Chem Bull. *71*.

ANON. 1965. France, Minist. de l'Agric., Statistique Agricole *1964*, 243.

ARENGO-JONES, R.W. 1941. The preparation of fermented ciders. Fruit Prod. J. *20*, 300-309, 321.

ATKINSON, F.E., BOWEN, J.F. and MACGREGOR, D.R. 1959. A rapid method for production of a sparkling apple wine. Food Technol. *13*, 673-675.

[1]Titles have been translated only for nonwestern European languages.

BARKER, B.T.B. 1911A. Processes of cider making. J. Bd. Agric. (London) *18*, 501-511.

BARKER, B.T.B. 1911B. The principles and practices of cider making. J. Inst. Brew. *17*, 425-441.

BARKER, B.T.B. 1937. Cider apple production. Great Britain Minist. Agric. Fisheries Bull. *104.*

BAUMANN, G. and GIERSCHNER, K. 1974. Studies on the technology of juice manufacture from sour cherries in relation to the storage of the product. Fluess. Obst. *41* (41) 123-129.

BAUMANN, J. 1959. Handbuch des Süssmosters. Eugen Ulmer, Stuttgart.

BENK, E., BERGMANN, R. and CUTKA, I. 1976. Quality control of sour cherry juices and beverages. Fluess. Obst. *43* (1) 17-18, 23.

BOL'SHAKOVA, E.I. and BELKO, G.F. 1976. Apple wine, by fermenting wine material, clarifying, fortifying, maturing and sugaring. U.S.S.R. 538,019.

BOWEN, J.F., MACGREGOR, D.R. and ATKINSON, F.E. 1959. Effect of variety and maturity on quality of apple wine. Food Technol. *13*, 676-679.

BRASKAT, N. and QUINN, H.A. 1940. Apple wine. Wine Rev. *8* (2) 6-9, 26-27.

CALDWELL, J.S. 1928. Chemical composition of American grown French cider apples. J. Agric. Res. *36*, 391-406.

CHARLEY, V.L.S. 1937. Notes on cider making practices in Europe. Long Ashton Res. Sta. Ann. Rep. *1937*, 160-170.

CHARLEY, V.L.S. 1953. The Cider Factory. Plant and Layout. Leonard Hill, London.

CHARLEY, V.L.S. 1954. Principles and Practices of Cider Making. Leonard Hill, London.

CHARLEY, V.L.S. and HARRISON, T.H. 1939. Fruit juices and related products. Imp. Bur. Hort. Plantation Crops, East Malling, Kent, Tech. Communication *11*, 1-104.

CLAGUE, J.A. and FELLERS, C.R. 1936. Apple cider and cider products. Mass. Agric. Expt. Sta. Bull. *336.*

CLARK, D.S., WALLACE, R.H. and DAVID, J.J. 1954. Factors affecting the fermentation of apple juice. Appl. Microbiol. *2*, 334-348.

CRUESS, W.V. 1914. Utilization of waste oranges. Calif. Agric. Exp. Stn. Bull. *244.*

CRUESS, W.V. and CELMER, R. 1938. Utilization of surplus apples. Fruit Prod. J. *17*, 325-356; *18*, 4, 43, 79.

CRUESS, W.V., MARSH, G.L. and MENDELS, S. 1935. Fruit wines. *Ibid. 14*, 295-298.

CRUESS, W.C. and MONTGOMERY, L.M. 1934. A study of cider fermentation. *Ibid. 14*, 107-109.

CZAPSKI, J. 1976. The influence of clarification, concentration and temperature on changes occurring during storage of concentrated apple juices. Acta Alimen. Polonica *2* (4) 273-286.

DAVIS, M.B. 1933. The manufacture of sweet and fermented cider by the closed cuvée method. Fruit Prod. J. *12*, 294-298.

DUERR, P. and SCHOBINGER, U. 1976. Use of enzymes in the preparation of fruit and vegetable drinks. Alimenta *15* (5) 143-149.

DUPAIGNE, P. 1959. L'Analyse des Jus de Fruits. Masson et Cie., Paris.

FESSLER, J.H. 1959. Personal communication.

FESSLER, J.H., PARSONS, J. and NASLEDOV, S. 1949. Sterile filtration. Proc. Am. Soc. Enol. 1949, 52-68. (*See also* Wines Vines *30* (6) 24; (9) 67 and Wine Rev. *17* (5) 14-16; (6) 9-11, 1949.)

FILIPELLO, F. and MARSH, G.L. 1934. Honey wine. Fruit Prod. J. *14*, 40-42, 61.

GACHOT, H. 1955. Manuel des Jus de Fruits, 2nd Edition. P. H. Heitz, Strasbourg.

GACHOT H. 1957. Dictionnaire Technique de l'Industrie des Jus de Fruits. Français-Anglais-Allemand. Fruit-Union Suisse, Zoug, Switzerland.

GARCIA, E. H., CAHANAP, A.C. and CABRERA, M.P. 1974. Organoleptic and chemical properties of Philippine fruit wines. Philipp. J. Plant Ind. *39* (1) 25-46.

GORE, H.C. 1914. Apple syrup and concentrated cider. U.S. Dept. Agric. Year Book *1914*, 233-245.

HEATHERBELL, D.A. 1976A. Haze and sediment formation from starch degradation products in apple wine and clarified apple juice. Confructa *21* (1-2) 36-42.

HEATHERBELL, D.A. 1976B. Haze and sediment formation in clarified apple juice and apple wine. II. The role of polyvalent cations, polyphenolics and proteins. Food Technol. N. Z. *11* (6) 17, 23.

HENRY, B.S. 1936. Studies of yeasts and the fermentation of fruits and berries of Washington. Univ. Washington Bull. Published by the Secretary of State, State of Washington.

JOSLYN, M.A. 1959. Private communication. Berkeley, Calif.

JOSLYN, M.A. and AMERINE, M.A. 1964. Dessert, Appetizer and Other Flavored Wines. University of California, Division of Agricultural Sciences, Berkeley.

JOSLYN, M.A. and MARSH, G.L. 1934. Suggestions for making orange wine. Fruit Prod. J. *13*, 307-315.

KERTESZ, Z.I. 1930. New method for enzymic clarification of unfermented apple juice. N.Y. Agric. Expt. Sta. Bull. *589*.

KILBUCK, J.H., NUSSENBAUM, F. and CRUESS, W.V. 1949. Pectic enzymes. Investigations on their use in wine making. Wines Vines *30* (8) 23-25.

KOCH, J. 1956. Neuzeitliche Erkentnisse auf dem Gebiet der Süssmostherstellung, 2nd Edition. Verlag Sigurd Horn, Frankfurt.

KROEMER, K. and KRUMHOLZ, G. 1932. Obst- und Beerenwein. Dr. Serger und Hempel, Braunschweig, Germany.

LEGAKIS, P.A. 1961. A Contribution to the Study of the Yeast Flora of

Apples and Apple Wine. Athens.

LÜTHI, H. 1953. Gärführung und Behandlung der Obstweine im Kleinbetrieb, 2nd Edition. Verlag Huber and Co., A. G. Frauenfeld.

MARTINEZ, D.V., CONTÉS, I.H. and MARQUEZ, J.G. 1958. Elaboración de sidra. Ensayos de fermentación usando enzymas pectolíficas y sulfuroso. Rev. Cienc. Appl. 63, 229-303.

MEHLITZ, A. 1951. Süssmost, Fachbuch der gewerbsmässigen Süssmoster-zeugnung, 7th Edition. Dr. Serger and Hempel, Braunschweig, Germany.

MISSELHORN, K. and ADAM, R. 1976. On the cyanide contents in stone fruit products. (transl.) Branntweinswirtschaft 116 (4) 49-50.

MORALES DE LEON, J.C. 1976. Tropical fruits. Characteristics and physico-chemical properties. Tecnol. Aliment. (Mexico City) 11 (5) 205-206, 208-212, 214-223.

MORSE, R.A., STEINKRAUS, K.H. and PATERSON, P.D. 1975. Wines from the Fermentation of Honey. Honey: A Comprehensive Survey. Eva Crane (Editor). Heinemann, London.

OSTERWALDER, A. 1948. Vom Mäuselgeschmack der Weine, Obst- und Beerenwein; eine Erwiderung. Schweiz. Z. Obst- Weinbau 57, 429-431.

PARAGUL'GOV, O.D., LINETSKAYA, A.E., GERMANOVA, L.M., FETIS-OVA, V.A. and ROZINA, L.I. 1976A. Determination of the bottle stability of fruit-berry wines. Vinodel. Vinograd. SSSR (6) 19-21.

PARAGUL'GOV, O.D., LINETSKAYA, A.E., GERMANOVA, L.M., FETIS-OVA, V.A., and ROZINA, L.I. 1976B. Clarification and stabilization of fruit-berry wine materials and wines. Vinodel. Vinograd. SSSR (4) 10-14.

PEARCE, B. and BAKER, P. 1939. The yeast flora of bottled ciders. J. Agric. Sci. 3, 55-79.

REITTERSMANN, R. 1952. Die Frucht-Liköre, mit besonderer Berücksichti-gung der Fruchtsaft- und Fruchtsirup-Herstellung, 2nd Edition. Carl Knoppke Grüner Verlag und Vertrieb, Berlin.

ROKHLENKO, S.G. and GREBESHOVA, R.N. 1977. Effect of the enzymatic treatment of fruit on the quality of fruit wine. Prikl. Biokhim. Mikrobiol. 13 (1) 112-117.

SCHANDERL, H. and KOCH, J. 1957. Die Fruchtweinbereitung. Eugen Ul-mer, Stuttgart.

SMOCK, R.M. and NEUBERT, A.M. 1950. Apples and Apple Products. Inter-science Publishers, New York and London.

STADELMANN, W. 1976. Content of hydrocyanic acid in stone fruit juices. Fluess. Obst. 43 (2) 45-47.

STILLMAN, J.S. 1955. Fruit and berry wine production in California. Am. J. Enol. 6, 32-35.

TSCHENN, C. 1934. Modern cider manufacture in France. Fruit Prod. J. 14, 111-113, 118.

TRESSLER, D.K., CELMER, R.F. and BEAVENS, E.A. 1941. Bulk fermentation process for sparkling cider. Ind. Eng. Chem. *33*, 1027-1032.

U.S. INTERNAL REVENUE SERVICE. 1955. Wine; Part 240 of Title 26 (1954). Code of Federal Regulations. U.S. Govt. Print. Office, Washington. (U.S. Treasury Dept. IRS Pub. *146.*)

VALAER, P.J. 1950A. Blackberry and other fruit wines, their methods of production and analysis. Alcohol Tax Unit, Bur. Intern. Revenue. Mimeo. Circ.

VALAER, P.J. 1950B. Wines of the World. Abelard Press, New York.

VECHER, A.S., YURCHENKO, L.A., VASIL'KEVICH, S.I., LEVITSKAYA, M.V. and SOKOLOVA, E.D. 1976. Reasons for acidity changes during apple juice fermentation. (transl.) Izv. Vyssh. Uchebn. Zaved., Pishch. Tekhnol. (5) 48-51.

VILLFORTH, F. 1954. Die Bereitung und Behandlung von Obstmost und Obstwein. Eugen Ulmer, Stuttgart.

VOGT, E. 1977. Der Wein, seine Bereitung, Behandlung und Untersuchung, 7th Edition. Verlag Eugen Ulmer, Stuttgart. (Revised)

VON LOESECKE, H.W., MOTTERN, H.H. and PULLEY, G.N. 1936. Wines, brandies and cordials from citrus fruits. Ind. Eng. Chem. *28*, 1224-1229.

WALLRAUCH, S. 1975. Adulteration of fruit juices, its identification and evaluation. Fluess. Obst. *42* (6) 255-229.

WEBB, A.D. 1974. Chemistry of Winemaking. Advances in Chemistry Series *137*. American Chemical Society, Washington, D.C.

WILHELM, C.F. 1957. Fruchtweine, Obst- und Beerenweine. Carl Knoppke Grüner Verlag, Berlin.

WINE INSTITUTE. 1971. Fruit and fruit speciality wine type specifications. Wine Institute, San Francisco. June 14.

YANG, H.Y. 1953. Fruit wines. Requisites for successful fermentation. J. Agric. Food Chem. *1*, 331-333.

YANG, H.Y. 1955. Selection of fruits and berries in wine production. Am. J. Enol. *6* (2) 32-35.

YANG, H.Y. 1959. Personal communication.

YANG, H.Y. and WIEGAND, E.H. 1949. Production of fruit wines in the Pacific Northwest. Fruit Prod. J. *29*, 8-12, 27, 29.

YANG, H.Y., THOMAS G.E. and WIEGAND, E.H. 1950. The application of pectic enzymes to berry and Concord wines. Wines Vines *31* (4) 77-78.

15

Nonbacterial Spoilage

In addition to spoilage by microorganisms, wines are subject to various types of clouding resulting from metallic contamination, protein precipitation or, occasionally, to oxidation of certain organic constituents. Crystalline deposits of cream of tartar or calcium tartrate may also occur. Haziness, cloudiness or a sediment indicate a defective wine to many consumers, although the affected wine may be fundamentally sound. However, a wine may be aged too long and it then exhibits breaking of the color, and deposition of a sediment, even though it is free of bacterial spoilage or excess metallic contamination.

NONMETALLIC DETERIORATION

In this section we shall consider nonmetallic conditions which favor darkening, primarily in white wines.

Darkening of Color

With age, wine in barrels or tanks darkens in color naturally or may change in color. One is not alarmed if old port or burgundy becomes slightly tawny in color. However, bottled white dry table wines of normal age should not be amber in color. Red table or dessert wines 3 to 5 years of age should be bright in tint and little color should have been deposited.

Berg has defined wine stability as the attainment of a state or condition such that the wine will not *for some definite period* exhibit undesirable physical or organoleptic changes. To give specific meaning to this definition, the duration of the stable condition, the undesirable changes, and the conditions to which the wine will be subjected should be specified. Stability is a relative term. The undesirable changes that denote instability (Berg and Akiyoshi 1956) are: (1) browning or darkening of the color, (2) haziness,[1] (3) cloudiness, (4) deposits, and (5)

---

[1]By haziness we mean a very slight cloudiness.

undesirable taste or odor. In this section we shall discuss the first item.

Amerine (1953) and Berg and Akiyoshi (1956) have discussed a number of factors of importance in the browning of white wines. An important one is temperature. The latter determined the rates of darkening at four temperatures by measuring the optical density of the wines. The rate of darkening increased as the temperature of storage increased. They obtained evidence that there are substances that react at different rates at low and at high temperatures. Variation in the proportions of these substances may account, they suggest, in part for the great variation in rate of increase of browning in different wines with rise in temperature. The oxygen supply was 600 ml/liter at the start of the test.

It is very probable that browning not due to oxidation also occurs. One such darkening reaction for sweet wines may be that between amino acids and hexose sugars (the Maillard reaction).

Berg and Akiyoshi (1956) state that varietal effect is the most important factor in the darkening of white wines and that other factors merely modify its influence. Wines of the varieties Emerald Riesling, Palomino, and Pinot blanc were found to darken especially easily. This observation has been verified by winery experience.

Enzymic Oxidation

Berg and Akiyoshi (1956) found that enzymic darkening of commercial white California wines is not important. Pasteurization of these wines at a high enough temperature to inactivate oxidase did not noticeably reduce the rate of browning. Both enzymic and nonenzymic browning are directly related to the flavonoid concentration in the wines (see Singleton 1969; Peri *et al.* 1971). However, the rapid browning of fresh grape juice is due to enzymic oxidation. Traverso-Rueda and Singleton (1973) found that bruising of grapes prior to juice separation greatly increases catecholase (polyphenoloxidase) activity in the musts.

In certain wine producing regions summer rains are frequent and, as a consequence, the fungus *Botrytis cinerea* often develops extensively on grapes and secretes a polyphenoloxidase. If not inactivated, it will, under proper conditions, cause browning of white wines. Occasionally, it has been observed that wines made from moldy California grapes in California are subject to oxidasic browning.

Oxidasic browning of wines made from botrytis-infected grapes can be prevented by heating the must or new wine to a high enough temperature for a sufficient time to inactivate the enzyme. It appears that 1 to 2 min at 82.2°C (180.0°F) would be sufficient. For the inactivating effect of sulfur dioxide see Chap. 6.

Berg and Akiyoshi (1956) found that California white wines that had been treated to destroy oxidase darkened more rapidly on exposure to air than the unheated—indicating that the heating had resulted in the production of precursors that materially increased the rate of browning. *This observation suggests that heating of white wines should be kept to the absolute minimum.*

Removal of Excess Color

Excess color can be removed by fining with casein or by use of activated carbon. Ibarra and Cruess (1948) and O'Neal *et al.* (1950) found casein fining a convenient and effective means of reducing the color of dark white wines. They reported casein to affect the flavor of the wine less than did the activated carbon used by them in comparative experiments. Special carbons may be used to remove excess color from wine as in the production of pale sherries and white ports, but legal restrictions must be taken into account. This treatment is discussed further in Chap. 9. Special ion exchange resins can also be used for this purpose.

De Villiers (1961) and Cantarelli (1962) recommended use of nylon paste to improve the color of white wines, to remove browning precursors, to increase resistance to browning, and to reduce anthocyanogen and tannin content. Fuller and Berg (1965) recommended nylon in preference to casein because of its greater protection against browning and absence of an adverse effect on wine quality. They emphasized the necessity for laboratory trials in view of Caputi and Peterson's finding (1965) that in some cases nylon treatment can increase browning. Nitrogen stripping, carbon dioxide blanketing, and addition of sulfur dioxide or sometimes of ascorbic acid all have their place in the handling of these wines as does the use of polyvinylpyrrolidone.

Other Factors in Browning

In Berg and Akiyoshi's experiments, addition of grape-seed tannin decreased the rate of browning, whereas synthetic tannic acid increased it. Small amounts of soluble copper and iron increased the rate of darkening, but their effect was additive rather than synergistic. Iron was a more active catalyst than copper in the presence of dissolved oxygen. That galacturonic acid can also be a factor in browning is evidenced by the study of Jayaraman and Van Buren (1971) who found the non-enzymatic rate of browning of galacturonic acid in model solutions was much faster than that of glucose.

Added citric acid at the rate of 2 g/liter (about 19 lb/1000 gal.) exerted

an inhibitory effect on browning because of its ability to form nonpig-
mented compounds with iron.

Darkening of sherry during heating is probably due to oxidation and
caramelization of sugars. Heitz *et al.* (1951) have made a study of the
changes that occur during the baking of sherry. See also p. 397.

Browning Stability Test

Singleton and Kramling (1976) developed the following test for predicting browning stability: mix 100 ml of wine with 1.0 g of dry bentonite, stopper it under nitrogen, and wait (with occasional shaking) for
at least 2 hr. Settle and centrifuge, then filter through a 0.45-micron
membrane filter enough to prepare 4 replicate test tubes (7 ml wine in
18 × 150-mm test tubes). Sparge 2 of the tubes thoroughly with N_2, and
the other 2 with O_2. Seal each tube with taped-down rubber stoppers or
tight screw caps as the sparging tip is removed. Hold at 55°C (131°F)
for 5 days and read at 420 nm. Wines with a tendency to brown have
higher readings, and generally the N_2 samples do not brown.

Protein Clouding

Protein clouding is mainly a problem of white wines. Where the pH of
the wine is near to the isoelectric point of the wine proteins, greater
precipitation will occur. This may also occur during blending. Fermentation results in precipitation of proteins, more of Koch's (1963) fraction
II than I. Lowering the pH of the must increases the precipitation
(Du Plessis 1964). Proteins are lost during aging. They can be removed
by heating or bentonite fining with the former removing more of fraction
I than II and the latter removing equal amounts of the two fractions. See
Kean and Marsh (1956A,B) and Koch and Sajak (1959). Wucherpfennig
and Frank (1967) found that bentonite-treated German musts produced
protein-stable wines.

Either heat treatments or the addition of protein precipitants is used
to test for protein instability. Heating tests correlate most closely with
the behavior of bottled wine. Berg and Akiyoshi (1961) stored wine at
48.9°C (120°F) for 4 days, room temperature for 1 day. A wine was
classified as stable if there was complete absence of haze or amorphous
deposit at all stages. Pocock and Rankine (1973) recommended heating
for 6 hr at 80°C (176°F). If no haze or deposit is present after cooling, the
wine is considered heat stable. Koch's test (1963) for successful removal
of protein was to add 5% of saturated ammonium sulfate to a sample of
the wine and heat at 45°C (113°F) for 9 hr. The sample was then placed
in water at 0.6°C (33.0°F) for 15 min. The wine was considered protein
stable if there was no precipitation. Berg and Akiyoshi (1961) added 1 ml

of 55% trichloroacetic acid to 10 ml of wine and heated in boiling water for 2 min. After cooling to room temperature, the amount of haze was determined in a Coleman Model 9 Nepho-Colorimeter. The Bentotest, a commercial phosphomolybdic acid protein precipitating procedure, was compared by Rankine and Pocock (1971) with heating 15 min at 70°C (158°F) and the trichloracetic acid precipitation method. The Bentotest was found somewhat more sensitive than the other two procedures. These quick tests can be used to disclose the obviously stable and unstable wines. The borderline cases can then be decided by the heat-cold test.

Moretti and Berg (1965) found four major protein fractions with one being much more heat labile than the others. Protein stability in wine is apparently a function of the ratio of the amount of this fraction to the combined amount of the other fractions.

METALLIC DETERIORATION

The more serious nonbacterial defects of wine are due to excess metals. See Amerine and Joslyn (1970) and Draper and Thompson (1955).

White Casse

The common form of casse in California wines is due to formation of a white precipitate or cloud of ferric phosphate. Blue casse is the result of precipitation of iron tannate, and is very rare in California.

Amerine and Joslyn (1970) pointed out that the formation of iron clouds in wine depends upon a number of factors: the concentration of iron, the nature of the predominant acid and its concentration, the pH value, the oxidation-reduction potential, the concentration of phosphates and the kind of tannin and its concentration.

Ribéreau-Gayon (1930, 1933) found that iron phosphate casse can only form in the range of pH 2.9 to 3.6. Marsh (1940) confirmed his findings with California wines. Many of our wines have pH values above 3.6 and hence are not subject to white casse. Iron is present in the ferrous (Fe^{++}) and ferric (Fe^{+++}) forms. Normally, the ferrous predominates over the ferric. On aeration, ferrous is converted to ferric and ferric phosphate may then form and cause clouding—if other conditions, such as pH value, etc, are favorable. The wine usually contains more than sufficient phosphate to form a haze or cloud with the iron, if other conditions are favorable.

Ribéreau-Gayon (1933) made an extensive study of the conditions under which iron casse forms. He studied the role of redox potential, pH value, state of oxidation of the iron, iron concentration, enzymes, and other factors. Even if the iron concentration is fairly high, casse will not form unless other conditions are proper. Iron forms complex ions with citrate ion in which form it no longer reacts as ferric or ferrous ion and, on that account, addition of citric acid to susceptible wines will usually prevent ferric phosphate casse. Amerine and Joslyn (1970) state that addition of 120 mg/liter (1 lb/1000 gal.) of citric acid is usually sufficient.

Blue casse occurs in white wines occasionally, but only after addition of tannin or tannic acid. In red wines it may result in a blue cloud and later a blue deposit. Amerine and Joslyn (1970) state that aeration may convert the ferrous to the ferric condition. If followed by fining and filtration this usually results in a clear, stable wine. Many California wines become brown and vapid in taste by such a treatment. The removal of iron and copper from wine by use of ferrocyanide or Cufex or by other methods is discussed in a later section in this chapter. For a general review of iron clouding see Berg (1953B).

Sources of Iron

Some wine makers have the impression that the natural iron content of grapes is sufficient to cause iron casse. However, research indicates that much (to most) of the excess iron present in grapes disappears during fermentation. Thoukis and Amerine (1956) found that 47.5 to 70% of the iron was lost from must during fermentation on a laboratory scale, and that most of this was bound by the yeast cells. Schanderl (1959) found a marked decrease in the iron content of German musts during fermentation; the yeast contained most of the iron that had disappeared from the must. Capt (1957) concluded that 8 mg/liter of iron was the critical concentration for Swiss wines to which no citric acid is added.

Vitagliano (1956) found that the iron content of wines of southern Italy stored in concrete tanks was six times that of wines stored in wood. Capt (1957) has stated that gelatin and isinglass used in fining may increase the iron content appreciably.

Excessive iron content in wine comes from the equipment rather than from the grapes. In the California industry, thanks to the widespread use of stainless steel and other corrosion-resistant materials, iron clouding is now rarely encountered.

Copper Casse

Occasionally, white wines containing sulfur dioxide and a small amount of dissolved copper, when stored in sealed bottles, develop a haze or cloud that eventually settles out as a reddish brown precipitate. The haziness or deposit occurs only in the absence of oxygen and ferric iron and redissolves readily upon exposure of the wine to air or upon addition of

hydrogen peroxide. Storage of the bottled wine in sunlight hastens formation of the cloudiness (copper casse).

Ribéreau-Gayon (1933, 1935) believed at one time that the cloud
consisted of cupric sulfide. The following reactions explain on this basis
the formation of copper casse:

(1) $Cu^{++} + RH \rightarrow Cu^{+} + R + H^{+}$
(2) $6Cu^{+} + 6H^{+} + SO_2 \rightarrow 6Cu^{++} + H_2S + 2H_2O$
(3) $Cu^{++} + H_2S \rightarrow CuS + 2H^{+}$
(4) CuS + electrolytes + colloids $\rightarrow$ flocculation
(5) $6RH + SO_2 = 6R + H_2S + 2H_2O$

On exposure to air or addition of hydrogen peroxide, he suggested that
the following reaction occurred: $CuS + 2O_2 \rightarrow CuSO_4$. He did not believe
that copper ions were directly involved in reduction of the sulfur dioxide
but that a reducing agent of unknown composition reduces cupric ions to
cuprous, and these, in turn, reduce sulfur dioxide to hydrogen sulfide.

Kean and Marsh (1956A) reported that copper casse is high in nitrogen
and low in sulfur content and that the nitrogen represents protein nitrogen rather than amino nitrogen, although the nitrogen content of
wines is principally in the form of amino acids. The protein content is low;
nevertheless, under California conditions there is sufficient to take part
in formation of copper casse. In one case, the protein content of a
sauterne wine was only 1 mg/liter, yet copper casse, with a sediment
containing 49.6% of protein, developed. The total nitrogen content of
this wine was 312 mg/liter. Joslyn and Lukton (1956) obtained similar
results.

Kean and Marsh confirmed by chromatographic technique that the
nitrogen of the copper casse cloud is proteinaceous or polypeptide in character. With synthetic wines containing a hydrolysate of lactalbumin of
low protein and high amino acid content, they found that sulfur dioxide
and copper were necessary for formation of a completely reversible cloud
(forming under reducing conditions and disappearing under oxidizing
conditions). No casse appeared when amino acids were the only source of
nitrogen. Sulfur dioxide always catalyzed clouding in sunlight. A completely irreversible cloud formed in the absence of copper and sulfur
dioxide and a partially reversible cloud formed if copper was present and
sulfur dioxide absent. They concluded that what is referred to as copper
casse is usually a combination of several "clouds," namely, protein-tan-
nin, copper-protein, and a copper-sulfur complex (probably copper sulfide).

Joslyn and Lukton (1956) concluded on the basis of X-ray data taken
on purified copper casse that both cuprous and cupric sulfide were pres-

ent. At that time there was some doubt as to whether the sulfur of the copper sulfide came from the reduction of sulfur dioxide or from cleavage of the disulfide bonds in protein. Peterson *et al.* (1958) used a sulfite containing radioactive sulfur and concluded that in light the copper complex is formed by reduction of sulfite with subsequent formation of insoluble cupric sulfide and the flocculation by protein. In the dark, some denaturation of protein by sulfite occurs, resulting in a copper-protein complex capable of yielding sulfate-S on oxidation.

It has long been known that wines vary greatly in their susceptibility to copper casse. The reasons for this variability are the complexing power of the wines and the kind and amount of proteins present.

Removal of Iron and Copper

Over 70 years ago, Möslinger found that excess iron in wine could be removed by addition of ferrocyanide. This treatment of wine is known as blue fining. It is in common use in Germany at present. It is not officially permitted in the United States.

Until recently, the use of ferroycanide was prohibited in France, but may now be used under specified conditions. Calcium phytate, sodium sulfide, and charcoal can be used in France in the treatment of wine under the control of designated chemists. Properly used, ferrocyanide removes not only excess iron but also copper and protein and does not adversely affect the flavor and bouquet of the wine.

Heide (1933) stated that a simple iron and copper determination cannot be used as a guide for the amount of potassium ferrocyanide required, for the reason that some of the ferrocyanide is used in precipitating organic colloids, including protein. He recommended that a series of practical tests be made with measured volumes of the wine and 0.5% ferrocyanide solution followed by measured volumes of tannin and gelatin solutions, allowing them to settle, filtering and testing for excess ferrocyanide by addition of dilute ferric potassium sulfate and a little hydrochloric acid. Any such test should be made on the wine immediately after removal of the sample from the storage tank, because in standing much of the ferrous iron may be oxidized to the ferric condition and be precipitated.

The complicated and not completely resolved chemistry of the reaction of ferrocyanide and iron has been studied by Bonastre (1959). Castino (1965) recommended adding 50 mg/liter of ascorbic acid to bring all the iron to the ferrous state and thus increase the efficiency of blue fining. The wine should have a pH of about 3.4 for best results.

An addition of ferrocyanide that will remove most of the iron usually removes all of the copper. Fessler (1952) has recommended that the copper be completely removed, although Lherme (1931–1932) has stated that Bordeaux wines can tolerate 0.5 mg/liter of copper and Amerine and Joslyn (1970) gave 0.3 mg/liter as the maximum tolerance for California wines. Marsh (1959A) suspects that European wines of very low protein content tolerate more copper than many California wines.

In 1951 and 1952, a test on the use of a new preparation known as the "Fessler compound" for removal of copper and iron from wine was made in six California wineries. Marsh (1952), who cooperated with the California Department of Public Health, and Fessler in conducting the experiments reported that over 3800 hl (100,000 gal.) of wine were treated. All of the copper was removed by the treatment, and although ten times the required amount of the Fessler compound was used experimentally no cyanogenetic residues were found by the Hubach test. Later, the Fessler compound was given the trade name of Cufex. As described by Fessler (1952), it is a mixture of salts that are brownish in color and disperse easily in wine. Marsh reports that it reacts instantly with the copper in the wine and settles quickly. He states that the lees or sediment is small in volume and that the flavor and bouquet of the wine are not damaged. The preparation is now sold in the form of a cream. It is included in the list of permissible chemicals for use in wine. It is also allowed by federal and state of California regulation agencies, but under the limitation that the treated wine shall contain no insoluble residue in excess of 1 mg/liter and no soluble residue; in other words, it must be used at the wine producer's risk. Nevertheless, it is in common use.

The usual test for residual cyanide in wine is the Hubach (1948) test (see pp. 700–701). When ferrocyanide or a special preparation such as Cufex has been used in wine to remove copper and iron, special care should be taken in order that all of the precipitate be removed from the wine by close filtration. Berg (1953A,B) has given precautions that should be observed. Among them are the following: Only clear wines should be treated. The treated wine should be allowed to stand overnight. In precoating the filter, use filtered wine or water. Care must be taken to remove all of the entrapped air from filter presses. Low pressure and a constant, medium flow rate should be maintained during filtration. This will require the use of a vari-speed drive pump. The filtration should be stopped when the pressure rises beyond 22.7 kg (50 lb). Add pink filteraid at such rate that a constant flow rate is maintained. After each filtration flush out with water all hoses, the filter, and other equipment used. Finally, flush out with a dilute alkali solution followed by water. Additional directions are given for handling screen and plate and frame filters in Berg's articles.

Phytates and phytic acid have been suggested for removal of iron and copper from wine. Joslyn et al. (1953) report that calcium phytate and phytic acid removed some of the iron from wine, but none of the copper. Auerbach and DeSoto (1955) have reported that Aferrin, principally magnesium phytate, removed up to 88% of the iron from dry white wine but none of the copper. As phytates react only with ferric iron, aeration must be used if an appreciable part of the iron is to be removed. Aeration followed by refrigeration and filtration has also been used for iron removal.

The sequestering effect of EDTA (ethylenediaminetetraacetate, also known as Versene and Sequestrene) has been studied. Joslyn and Lukton (1953) found that iron in wine is apparently tightly bound by Versene and no longer reacts with ferrocyanide or thiocyanate. In Joslyn and Lukton's experiments, Versene was effective in preventing copper casse in many, but not in all, cases.

To sum up: the copper content should preferentially be nil or at the most 0.3 mg/liter. The iron content should not be over 5 mg/liter though frequently no trouble is encountered up to 10 mg/liter. Citric acid is usually effective ensurance against iron clouding. Cufex is the best available material for copper and iron removal in this country.

Calcium Tartrate Instability

A troublesome cause of instability in California wines has been the deposition of calcium tartrate crystals after bottling. As Berg (1957) has stated, refrigeration as now used by commercial wineries for removal of excess tartrates by formation of potassium bitartrate and calcium tartrate crystals usually does not remove enough calcium tartrate to prevent later deposition on prolonged standing after bottling.

Amerine (1958), as well as other enologists, states that excess calcium gets into the wine from plastering (see p. 405), from storage or fermentation in concrete tanks, from filter pads, and from fining materials. Cambitzi (1947) observed that on long standing some of the dextro-rotatory tartaric acid of wines changes into the racemic form. The calcium salt of the racemic tartaric acid is soluble only to the extent of 30 mg/liter, whereas 230 mg/liter of the calcium salt of dextro-tartaric acid is soluble. Cambitzi (1947) states that at ordinary cellar temperature enough of the racemate is formed to exceed its solubility. Crawford (1951) observed calcium tartrate deposits in wines ranging from 50 to 120 mg/liter of calcium, crystallization taking from 4 to 7 months to become apparent.

The customary method of removal of excess calcium tartrate is by refrigeration of the wine to near its freezing point for a period of about two weeks. After refrigeration the wine is filtered cold to prevent redissolving of the crystals of tartrates. The wine maker hopes that the treated wine will remain stable insofar as subsequent deposition of tartrates is concerned, However, experience has shown that the treated wine on long standing in the bottle may show a deposit of calcium tartrate. Garoglio (1957), Kielhöfer (1957), Pecheur (1957), Dickinson and Stoneman (1958), Rankine (1955B), Schanderl (1957), and others have found that proper treatment of wine with cation resins lowers the calcium content below the level required for formation of crystalline deposits in bottled wine.

A predictive test for calcium tartrate stability in wine is based on determination of the concentration product (CP): CP = (mol/liter Ca) (mol/liter total tartrate) (% tartrate ion). This requires analyses for pH and the content of alcohol, calcium and tartrate. The percentage of the total tartrate in the form of the tartrate ion is found by referring to the table of percent tartrate ion calculated by Berg and Keefer (1958–1959).

In an effort to establish safe CP's, DeSoto and Yamada (1963) analyzed a number of commercially finished bottled table wine samples which had been stored for 22 to 27 months (whites) and 16 to 26 months (reds) at 16.7° to 25.6°C (62.0° to 78.0°F). All wines examined were completely free of crystalline deposits. Based on these tables, they recommended the following "safe" CP's: dry white—20.0×10^{-7}; dry red—40.0×10^{-7}. Using these CP's and the range of pH and tartrate values reported by Berg and Akiyoshi (1971), the maximum amounts of calcium that would assure stable table wines were calculated (Table 15.1). Again, using the data of DeSoto and Yamada (1963) and that of Berg and Akiyoshi (1971), the calculations were repeated for dessert wines (Table 15.2).

TABLE 15.1. MAXIMUM AMOUNTS OF CALCIUM THAT WOULD ASSURE STABLE TABLE WINES AT VARIOUS pH'S AND TARTRATE CONTENTS

Tartrate mg/liter	Dry White—CP: 20.0×10^{-7} 1130		3420	
pH	2.96	3.91	2.96	3.91
Calcium mg/liter	440	37	147	12
Tartrate mg/liter	Dry Red—CP: 40.0×10^{-7} 1250		3770	
pH	3.07	4.23	3.07	4.23
Calcium mg/liter	560	40	185	13

Source of data: Berg (1977).

Other Calcium Salt Instabilities

Crawford (1951) found the lack of correlation between the amount of calcium and the presence or absence of tartrate precipitation in sherry was due to the formation of calcium oxalate. Krug (1964) showed that

TABLE 15.2. MAXIMUM AMOUNTS OF CALCIUM THAT WOULD ASSURE STABLE DESSERT WINES AT VARIOUS pH'S AND TARTRATE CONTENTS

Tartrate mg/liter	Dry Sherry—CP: 90×10^{-8} 640		2050	
pH	2.93	4.11	2.93	4.11
Calcium mg/liter	564	25	176	8
Tartrate mg/liter	Cream Sherry—CP: 120×10^{-8} 710		1830	
pH	3.04	4.08	3.04	4.08
Calcium mg/liter	480	34	186	13
Tartrate mg/liter	Muscatel—CP: 250×10^{-8} 1020		1960	
pH	3.31	4.36	3.31	4.36
Calcium mg/liter	313	32	163	17
Tartrate mg/liter	Port—CP: 275×10^{-8} 880		1850	
pH	3.25	4.28	3.25	4.28
Calcium mg/liter	436	44	207	21

Source of data: Berg (1977).

oxalic acid forms stable complexes with heavy metals (iron, for example), thus preventing its precipitation as the calcium salt. However, with passage of time an increase in redox potential occurs causing the transformation of the stable ferrous oxalate to the unstable ferric oxalate. The release of oxalic acid from the latter salt permits it to combine with calcium and precipitate as calcium oxalate. Oxalic acid can be removed in early stages by fining with potassium ferrocyanide. In later stages the only possibility of removal is by addition of calcium. This treatment would usually require cation exchange to remove the excess calcium.

Kielhöfer and Würdig (1961) found calcium saccharate responsible for crystalline deposits in some German wines. Würdig (1977) also found the stereoisomer of saccharic acid, mucic acid, responsible as the calcium salt for some crystalline deposits in German wines. Both acids are believed to be produced in grapes infected with *Botrytis cinerea*. To prevent their precipitation in the bottle, they are precipitated prior to bottling by adding predetermined amounts of calcium. As in the treatment for removal of oxalic acid, this would usually require subsequent cation exchange.

Potassium Bitartrate Instability

Wine, when new, is supersaturated with potassium bitartrate, cream of tartar, and unless the excess is removed in some manner deposits of it are certain to form in the bottled wine. Although such crystallization does not constitute spoiling of the wine, the consumer is likely to consider it a serious defect.

The variables influencing tartrate stability have been studied in many laboratories (Berg 1957, 1960; Marsh 1959B). Among the factors which have been shown to be important are alcohol, acids, cations, anions, pH, pigments, and various complexing compounds. A detailed study of 34 white Bordeaux table wines by Peynaud *et al.* (1964) showed that sulfate was the most important factor in stability, other than potassium or tartrate. Pilone and Berg (1965) showed that the changes in potassium and tartrate content during storage or after ion-exchange or charcoal treatment could not be explained solely on the basis of a simple reaction between the two ions. In red wines, resolubilization of potassium acid tartrate occurred. This, they attributed to polyphenol-tartrate reactions. They also suggested potassium-colloidal pigment reactions. In white wines, solubilization of tartrates was attributed to the binding power of proteins for tartaric acid. Balakian and Berg (1968) reported that a grape-skin extract, containing both pigments and tannins and the usual assortment of other cations and anions, markedly increased the solubility of potassium bitartrate in both decolorized wines and model solutions. The extract remaining after dialysis was also effective in decolorized wine, though not in a model solution, suggesting the dialyzable electrolytes as required co-factors of the pigments. Berg *et al.* (1968) showed that the addition of 300 to 1200 mg/liter (2.5 to 10.0 lb/1000 gal.) of bentonite reduced the concentration product, CP, of dry white wines from 15 to 18% and dry red from 25 to 32%. As shown in Table 15.3, ion exchange can have a drastic effect on the tartrate holding ability of table wines, reducing the CP as much as 90%.

TABLE 15.3. AVERAGE EFFECT OF ION EXCHANGE ON CONCENTRATION PRODUCT

| | Percentage Decrease in CP from Control | |
% Exchanged	Dry White	Dry Red
25	17	21
50	39	38
75	66	70
100	93	89

Source of data: Berg *et al.* (1968).

A tartrate stabilization procedure commonly used in California involves first refrigeration followed, if necessary, by ion exchange. As the response of wines to refrigeration varies greatly, not only between types but even between wines of the same type, it is recommended that the wines be analyzed for potassium and tartrate contents at 0, 4 and 6 days of refrigeration. The decrease in CP values may then be used to determine if it is worthwhile to continue refrigerating. If the CP is still too high, ion exchange with the resin in the hydrogen form is used to the extent governed by taste considerations. If necessary, this can be followed by exchange with the resin in the sodium form.

While refrigeration or ion-exchange is used to achieve tartrate stability in the United States, metatartaric acid is widely used in France (see Ribéreau-Gayon and Peynaud 1960–1961). Its effect is not permanent and it is not recommended for use in this country.

Koch and Schiller (1964) found little effect of pH on the rate of crystallization of potassium acid tartrate. The tartrate concentration had less effect on rate of crystallization than the potassium content. Reduced temperature, of course, speeded up the precipitation rate but with a constant supersaturation the opposite was observed. Presence of magnesium, calcium, and ferrous iron speeded up crystallization, but sodium slowed it down. Seeding with potassium bitartrate crystals during refrigeration not only speeds up the precipitation rate but also markedly increases the amount precipitated.

Cold Stability Test

In a recent survey of table wine processing practices in California, Cooke and Berg (1971, 1973) found great variability in the cold test procedures. Wineries either stored samples at temperatures ranging from $-5.5°$ to $+4.4°C$ ($22.0°$ to $40.0°F$) for 1 to 14 days and observed cold and again after standing at room temperature for 1 day, or frozen solid overnight and observed after thawing. Complete absence of crystals at observation is required for the wines to be classified as cold stable. Because wines which have passed a cold test will occasionally precipitate tartrates in the bottle, the use of CP's is recommended instead of the cold test: CP = (mol/liter K) (mol/liter total tartrate) (% acid tartrate ion). This requires analyses for pH and the content of alcohol, potassium and tartrate. The percentage of the total tartrate in the form of the acid tartrate ion is found by referring to the table of percent acid tartrate ion calculated by Berg and Keefer (1958–1959).

What are safe CP levels? To answer this question Berg and Akiyoshi (1971) determined by refrigeration with and without added potassium bitartrate (KHT) the minimum CP values of nearly 1000 wines, ranging in age from 3 months to 10 years and in treatment from none to completely finished (Table 15.4). Using the dry white wines with added KHT as an example, of the 143 wines tested, the lowest CP found at $0°C$ ($32°F$) was 4.1. Therefore, if the winemaker wants to be sure that his dry white wines will not precipitate KHT when held at $0°C$ ($32°F$) the CP

TABLE 15.4. MINIMUM CONCENTRATION PRODUCT VALUES ATTAINED BY RE-FRIGERATION[1]

| Wine Type | $CP \times 10^5$ | | | | | |
| | With Added KHT | | | Without Added KHT | | |
	0°C	5°C	10°C	0°C	5°C	10°C
Dry white	4.1	6.3	10.3	9.4	14.6	23.6
Rosé	4.6	7.2	11.7	8.8	13.7	22.1
Dry red	7.7	12.6	20.4	17.6	27.3	44.2
White port	3.7	5.9	10.4	6.8	10.7	18.8
Muscatel	4.1	6.5	11.4	8.1	12.7	22.4
Port	5.1	8.3	14.6	10.6	16.6	29.3
Dry sherry	1.9	3.0	5.3	5.9	9.2	16.3
Medium sherry	2.5	3.9	6.9	7.6	11.9	21.0
Cream sherry	2.9	4.5	8.0	5.7	8.9	15.7

Source of data: Berg and Akiyoshi (1971).
[1]At 1.0°C (33.8°F) for 21 days.

value should not exceed 4.1, or 6.3 at 5°C (41°F), or 10.3 at 10°C (50°F). This table also shows that if the wines are not seeded, the CP values are about twice those of the seeded wines. However, these are not equilibrium values but, instead, are only a measure of what can be expected when unseeded wines are exposed to low temperatures for 21 days.

This table offers the winemaker several alternatives in selecting the CP values he wishes to attain in his wines. He may decide he wants to be absolutely certain his wines will be stable and thus select the minimum CP which can be obtained only by seeding the wine with KHT. Alternatively, he may select the values obtained with unseeded wines. Or, on the basis of his experience, he might decide to use values lying somewhere between those obtained with and without seeding. In addition, he must decide at what temperature he wants his wines to be stable. To aid him in making a decision, commercially finished wines were classified by the values in this table. This information is presented in Table 15.5.

Overall, it appears that the CP values obtained at 0°C (32°F) without added KHT are the lowest values deemed necessary for 81% of the wines with some wineries satisfied with higher CP's, and 100% would not require lower values than those obtained at 5°C (41°F) with added KHT. [Those at 0°C (32°F) with added KHT are over-ion-exchanged.]

Other Metals

Lead may be present in wines made from grapes that have been

TABLE 15.5. CLASSIFICATION OF COMMERCIALLY FINISHED WINES BY CP
VALUES

	With KHT	Both[1]	\multicolumn{3}{c}{Without KHT}		
Wine Type	0°-5°	5°-0°	0°-5°	5°-10°	>10°
Dry white	—	17.8	35.6	40.0	6.6
Rosé	—	—	45.8	50.0	4.2
Dry red	7.1	26.2	64.3	2.4	—
White port	7.1	27.3	54.5	18.2	—
Muscatel	6.7	13.3	66.7	13.3	—
Port	5.9	17.6	70.6	5.9	—
Dry sherry	—	6.2	56.3	37.5	—
Medium sherry	5.9	35.3	47.0	11.8	—
Cream sherry	—	—	42.9	42.9	14.2
Average[2]	2.8	16.0	53.7	24.7	2.8

Percentage Considered Stable at Indicated °C

Source of data: Berg and Akiyoshi (1971).
[1]5°C (31°F) with added KHT and 0°C (32°F) without added KHT. This range used because of overlaps or gaps with the
CP values at 10°C (50°F) with added KHT and 0°C (32°F) without KHT.
[2]Average of wine types.

sprayed with lead compounds, now rare. It may also get into the wine
from the lead foil capsule used on some bottles of wine, the lead mi-
grating through the cork into the wine (Ferré and Jaulmes 1948). The
legal limit in Germany is 0.35 mg/liter. Several European investigators
have found considerably more than this amount in samples of European
wines. Noble *et al.* (1976) reported from 0.07 to 0.14 mg/liter in representative wines from the San Joaquin Valley.

Lead sprays are not used in California on grape vines (see also Greenblau and Westhuyzen 1957; Rankine 1955A).

Insofar as the authors know, magnesium is not a cause of instability in
wines, as its salts are more soluble than those of calcium. The sodium
content of wines is of interest in connection with low sodium diets and in
the use of sodium ion-exchange resins. Excessive amounts may adversely
affect the flavor. Amerine (1958) has summarized the data on the sodium
content of wines of various wine producing regions as shown in Table
15.6. No reports of cloudiness due to excessive sodium have been published.

Amerine (1958) states that the normal tin content of wine is less than
one milligram per liter. Protein precipitation occurs when wine containing
tin is heated. (See also Kielhöfer and Aumann 1955.)

The zinc content of French wines made from grapes that have not been
sprayed with a zinc spray is low, less than 1 mg/liter, according to Ney
(1948). Amerine noted that much higher concentrations have been

TABLE 15.6. SODIUM CONTENT OF VARIOUS TYPES OF WINES

Region	Type	No. of Samples	Min. mg/liter	Max. mg/liter	Avg. mg/liter
Algeria	Table	8	51	162	118
California	Table	155	10	172	55
California	Dessert	104	15	253	71
France	Various	28	30	125	62
Germany	Table	187	5	43	15
Miscellaneous	Dessert	24	19	443	167
Portugal	Miscellaneous	33	30	87	58
Spain	Table	4	80	343	221
Switzerland	Table	11	23	65	41

Source of data: Amerine (1958).

reported by some European investigators. Noble *et al.* (1976) reported 0.26 to 1.99 mg/liter in California wines.

Zinc salts are poisonous, and wine should be free or nearly so of zinc.

Cadmium should not be used as a lining for wine containers since it is soluble and toxic.

Wines are naturally low in aluminum, but may dissolve it from aluminum equipment. If excessive amounts are dissolved, they may cause clouding, or the aluminum may reduce sulfur dioxide to hydrogen sulfide. Thaler and Mühlberger (1956) found a maximum of 1.52 and a minimum of 0.30 mg/liter of aluminum in 103 Swiss musts.

Eschnauer (1963) cautions against undue aluminum pick-up, clearly undesirable changes being caused by amounts of over 10 mg/liter. Aluminum haze is rare in California since equipment containing this metal is seldom used. In Australia, Rankine (1962) showed that a maximum of 5 mg/liter could be tolerated in dry white table and white dessert wines. The maximum haze occurred at pH 3.8.

Arsenic-containing insecticides in grape production may lead to public health problems. In some European countries, arsenical sprays are illegal and they are not recommended for use on grapes in California.

DETERMINATION OF CAUSES OF CLOUDING OR DEPOSITS

In many cases it is difficult to identify the cause of nonbacterial clouding or defects. The following key (partially adapted from Tanner and Vetsch 1956) should be helpful.

Group Classification by Microscopic Examination.—Group A is mostly crystals and group B is mostly amorphous.

	Group A		
	Potassium Bitartrate	Calcium Tartrate	Calcium Oxalate
		Screening Tests	
Silver mirror reaction	Positive	Positive	Negative
Flame color with magnesia rod without cobalt glass	—	Brick red flame	Brick red flame

Group A (*Continued*)		
Potassium Bitartrate	Calcium Tartrate	Calcium Oxalate
Flame color with magnesia rod with cobalt glass Red flame	—	—
Confirmatory Tests		
Microscopic appearance Prisms	Prisms	Small cubic crystals
Chilling		
pH 3.6 Crystals form	—	—
pH 6.0 —	Crystals form	—
Oxalic acid Crystals may form	Crystals always form	Crystals may form
Solubility of precipitate 0.492 g/100 ml H₂O at 20°C (68°F)	0.0322 g/100 ml H_2O at 20°C (68°F)	0.00067 g/100 ml H_2O at 12.8°C (55°F)
Chromatography of precipitate Positive	Positive	Negative

Group B
Subgroup Classification by Hydrochloric Acid Addition: With Group B-1 Turbidity Disappears and with Group B-2 Turbidity Remains

Group B-1

	Copper Sulfide	Copper-Proteinate	Ferric Phosphate
		Screening Tests	
Hydrogen peroxide	Turbidity disappears	Turbidity remains	Turbidity remains
Burning precipitate	Doesn't burn	Burns partly	Doesn't burn
Potassium ferrocyanide			
without HCl	Red coloration	Red coloration	No change
with HCl			Blue coloration
		Confirmatory Tests	
Sulfur demonstration	Positive	Usually positive	Negative
Flame color with magnesia rod without cobalt glass	Green	Green	—
Biuret test	Negative	Positive	Negative
Nitrogen demonstration	Negative	Positive	Negative
Copper test	Positive	Positive	Negative
Iron test	Negative	Negative	Positive

Group B-2		
	Protein	Protein-Tannate	Pigment-Tannin
		Screening Tests	
Conc. sulfuric with gentle warming	Carbonizes	Carbonizes—may become red	Red coloration later becoming dark red to black
Silver mirror reaction	Negative	May be positive	Positive
Nitrogen demonstration	Positive	May be positive	Negative
		Confirmatory Tests	
Biuret test	Positive	May be positive	Negative
Sulfur demonstration	Usually positive	May be positive	Negative

Centrifuge sufficient wine to give a few milliliters of sediment. Save centrifuged wine for additional tests. Wash sediment with 5–10 ml of 95% ethanol, re-centrifuge and decant.

Equipment and Reagents Required.—Centrifuge, centrifuge tubes, microscope, Bunsen burner, filter funnels, filter paper, sodium fusion tubes, standard test tubes and pipettes, cobalt glass 5 × 5 cm in size and 3 to 4 mm thick, magnesium oxide rods (copper free), stainless steel spatula and silver coin (grease free), Whatman No. 1 filter paper and small chromatography tube, cation exchange resin (IR-120 or Duolite C-3 regenerated with 5% hydrochloric acid and thoroughly washed with distilled water to remove all traces of hydrochloric acid), ferrous ammonium sulfate crystals, sodium metal (keep under kerosene; *do not* allow sodium to contact water), ethyl alcohol (95% by volume), concentrated sulfuric acid, hydrogen peroxide (30% and 3%), hydrochloric acid (concentrated and 10%), methyl alcohol, saturated oxalic acid solution, organic phase of *n*-butanol-formic acid-water (10:2:15 v/v/v), potassium ferrocyanide (0.5%), silver mirror reagent (keeps well if stored in a brown bottle, mix 50 ml *N*/10 silver nitrate solution with 5 ml 10% sodium hydroxide solution, add concentrated ammonium hydroxide drop by drop until silver hydroxide precipitate has dissolved, prevent the reagent from drying as there is danger of explosion when it is dry), biuret reagent (to 50 ml of 40% sodium hydroxide solution add 1% copper sulfate solution, drop by drop, with constant stirring, until the mixture assumes a deep blue color). This reagent is quite stable (if kept in a brown bottle), copper test reagents and iron test reagents for Marsh procedure, solution of 0.04% chlorophenol red in 95% alcohol with pH adjusted to 10, sodium hydroxide (50%), and pine shavings.

Group A

(1) Silver mirror reaction: Dissolve some of the precipitate in hot water in a test tube. Add three "kitchen knife tips" of cation exchange resin, shaking after each addition. Filter into a test tube, add 5 ml silver mirror reagent, and then heat lightly for 5 min over an open flame. The colloidal silver that is produced is deposited on the test tube walls forming a shining mirror. This is a positive test for both tartaric acid and tannins.

(2) Flame color with magnesia rod: Heat the end of a magnesia rod (magnesium oxide) red hot and dip for an instant into the wet precipitate. Heat again for a short time in the hot part of the Bunsen burner and again dip into the precipitate. Repeat this procedure until the magnesia rod is loaded. Then place the loaded end of the rod in the outer part of the flame. A brick red flame without the cobalt glass is a positive test for calcium. A beautiful rose flame looking through the cobalt glass is a positive test for potassium.

(3) Chilling: Adjust pH of the centrifuged wine with either concentrated hydrochloric acid or 50% sodium hydroxide solution and then chill in a test tube. Crystal formation at pH 3.6 is a positive test for potassium bitartrate. Crystal formation at pH 6.0 is a positive test for calcium tartrate.

(4) Oxalic acid: To centrifuged wine add oxalic acid. Crystal formation indicates presence of calcium. Confirmation is obtained by adding a few drops of concentrated sulfuric acid to precipitate which will dissolve. Then add excess methyl alcohol and heat gently—precipitate will reappear.

(5) Chromatography of precipitate: Dissolve precipitate in hot water—if not

soluble add concentrated hydrochloric acid. Run through a cation exchange column in the hydrogen form. Spot effluent (the equivalent of 0.04 to 0.05 ml of wine) on paper and develop with n-butanol-formic acid-water (10:2:15 v/v/v) using the organic phase (supernatant) as the developing solution. Dry paper at room temperature until odor of developing solution disappears. Spray paper with 0.04% chlorophenol red. Compare with known tartaric acid spot.

(6) If negative tests are obtained for tartaric and oxalic acids, the crystalline deposit can be checked for the presence of saccharic acid by means of the pyrrole reaction. Wash the crystalline deposit with water and alcohol and dry by suction. Put in 1 ml of water and add a little ammonia to dissolve. Evaporate a few drops to dryness. Place pine shavings moistened with hydrochloric acid over the deposit. Now heat. The rising fumes color the pine shavings an intense red violet if saccharic acid is present. Tartaric acid colors the pine shavings only a faint red.

Group B

(1) Add several ml of 10% hydrochloric acid to 20 ml of wine.

Group B-1

(1) Add a few drops of 30% hydrogen peroxide to 20 ml of wine. See table on p. 549 for interpretation of results.

(2) Burning precipitate: Place a small amount of precipitate on a fine, stainless steel spatula, and heat very carefully to complete dryness with a small luminous flame placed several centimeters from the material. Then bring spatula close to flame and continue to heat.

(3) Potassium ferrocyanide: Add several ml of 0.5% potassium ferrocyanide to 20 ml of wine. Red color development is a positive test for copper. Add several milliliters of 10% hydrochloric acid. Blue color development is a positive test for iron.

(4) Sulfur demonstration: Place sediment in a soft glass test tube (6 mm diameter × 7 cm length), add 1 drop of 30% hydrogen peroxide and carefully dry over a luminous flame. Dry a piece of sodium metal on blotting paper, cut sides to produce a piece about one cubic centimeter in size, and drop into the test tube. Using a wooden clamp, hold the test tube in a flame until the contents are completely charred, and then drop test tube into another tube containing 3 ml of water. The small test tube shatters and its contents are dissolved in the water. Place 1 to 2 drops of the liquid on a defatted silver coin. Formation of a black discoloration shows the presence of sulfur.

(5) Flame color with magnesia rod without cobalt glass: See (2) under Group A. A green flame is confirmation of the presence of copper.

(6) Biuret test: To the sediment in water add biuret reagent, a drop at a time with mixing, until the solution assumes a violet color. This is a positive test for protein.

(7) Nitrogen demonstration: Filter liquid left over from the sodium fusion (see

(4) under Group B-1). Add 3 small ferrous ammonium sulfate crystals, boil for a short time, cool, and add 1 ml of 10% hydrochloric acid. Blue coloration proves presence of nitrogen.

(8) Copper test: Determine copper content of the sediment using the Marsh procedure (see Chap. 19).

(9) Iron test: Determine iron content of the sediment using the Marsh procedure (see Chap. 19).

Group B-2

(1) Concentrated sulfuric with gentle warming: Add 1 ml of concentrated sulfuric acid to sediment and gently warm. Carbonization indicates the presence of protein. A red coloration later becoming dark-red to black is evidence of the presence of pigment and tannin.

(2) Silver mirror reaction: See (1) under Group A.

(3) Nitrogen demonstration: See (7) under Group B-1.

(4) Biuret test: See (6) under Group B-1.

(5) Sulfur demonstration : See (4) under Group B-1. Proteins usually give a positive reaction.

REFERENCES[1]

AMERINE, M.A. 1953. Influence of variety, maturity, and processing on clarity and stability of wines. Proc. Am. Soc. Enol. *1953*, 16-29.

AMERINE, M.A. 1958. Composition of wines. II. Inorganic constituents. Advan. Food Res. *8*, 133-225.

AMERINE, M.A. and JOSLYN, M.A. 1970. Table Wines: the Technology of Their Production in California, 2nd Edition. Univ. Calif. Press, Berkeley and Los Angeles.

AUERBACH, R.C. and DESOTO, R. 1955. Phytates for removal of metals in wine. Wine Inst. Tech. Advis. Committee, August 5, 1955.

BALAKIAN, S. and BERG, H.W. 1968. The role of polyphenols in the behavior of potassium bitartrate in red wines. Am. J. Enol. Vitic. *19*, 91-100.

BERG, H.W. 1953A. Special wine filtration procedures recommended for use following Cufex fining of wines. Wine Inst. Tech. Advis. Committee, July 30, 1953.

BERG, H.W. 1953B. Wine stabilization factors. Proc. Am. Soc. Enol. *1953*, 91-116.

BERG, H.W. 1957. Use of ion exchange resins for the stabilization of tartrates. Wine Inst. Tech. Advis. Committee, May 13, 1957.

BERG, H.W. 1960. Stabilization studies on Spanish sherry and on factors influencing KHT precipitation. Am. J. Enol. Vitic. *11*, 123-128.

BERG, H.W. 1977. Personal communication. Davis, Calif.

[1] Titles have been translated only for nonwestern European languages.

BERG, H.W. and AKIYOSHI, M. 1956. Some factors involved in browning of white wines. Am. J. Enol. 7, 1-8.

BERG, H.W. and AKIYOSHI, M. 1961. Determination of protein stability in wine. Am. J. Enol. Vitic. 12, 107-110.

BERG, H.W. and AKIYOSHI, M. 1971. The utility of bitartrate concentration-product values in wine processing. Ibid. 22, 127-134.

BERG, H.W., DESOTO, R. and AKIYOSHI, M. 1968. The effect of refrigeration, bentonite clarification and ion exchange on potassium behavior in wines. Ibid. 19, 208-212.

BERG, H.W. and KEEFER, R.M. 1958-1959. Analytical determination of tartrate stability in wine. Ibid. 9, 180-193; 10, 105-109.

BONASTRE, J. 1959. Contribution à l'étude des matières minérales dans les produits végétaux. Application au vin. Ann. Technol. Agric. 8, 377-446.

CAMBITZI, A. 1947. The formation of racemic calcium tartrate in wines. Analyst 72, 542-543.

CANTARELLI, C. 1962. I trattamenti con resine poliammidiche in enologia. Atti Accad. Ital. Vite Vino 14, 219-249.

CAPT, E. 1957. Un enquête sur la teneur en fer des vins de la suisse romande. Annuaire Agric. Suisse 58, 801-808.

CAPUTI, A., JR. and PETERSON, R. G. 1965. The browning problem in wines. Am. J. Enol. Vitic. 16, 9-13.

CASTINO, M. 1965. L'azione riducente dell'acido ascorbico nella demetallizzazione dei vini con ferrocianuro potassico. Ann. Accad. Ital. Vite Vino 17, 143-151.

COOKE, G.M. and BERG, H.W. 1971. Varietal table wine processing practices in California. II. Clarification, stabilization, bottling, and aging. Am. J. Enol. Vitic. 22, 178-183.

COOKE, G.M. and BERG, H.W. 1973. Table wine processing practices in the San Joaquin Valley. Ibid. 24, 153-158.

CRAWFORD, C. 1951. Calcium in dessert wine. Proc. Am. Soc. Enol. 1951, 76-79.

DESOTO, R.T. and YAMADA, H. 1963. Relationship of solubility products to long range tartrate stability. Am. J. Enol. Vitic. 14, 43-51.

DE VILLIERS, J.P. 1961. The control of browning of white table wines. Ibid. 12, 25-30.

DICKINSON, B.N. and STONEMAN, C.F. 1958. Stabilization of wines by ion exchange. Chemical Process Co., Mimeo. Circ., Redwood City, Calif.

DRAPER, W. and THOMPSON, J.L. 1955. Cloudiness in wines. Chem. Can. 78 (8) 35-38.

DU PLESSIS, C.S. 1964. The ion exchange treatment (H cycle) of white grape juice prior to fermentation. II. The effect upon wine quality. S. Afr. Agric. Sci. 7, 3-15.

ESCHNAUER, H. 1963. Aluminiumtrübungen im Wein. Vitis 4, 57-61.

FERRÉ, L. and JAULMES, P. 1948. Les capsules en étain plombifère, cause de la presence de plomb dans les vins. Compt. Rend. Acad. Agric. France *34*, 864-865.

FESSLER, J.H. 1952. Development of the Fessler compound. Wines Vines *33* (7) 15.

FULLER, W.L. and BERG, H.W. 1965. Treatment of white wine with nylon 66. Am. J. Enol. Vitic. *16*, 212-218.

GAROGLIO, P.G. 1957. Contributo Sperimentali allo Studio delle Possibili Applicazione Enologiche delle Resine Scambiatrici di Ioni. Inst. Ind. Agrarie, Università de Firenze, Florence.

GREENBLAU, N. and WESTHUYZEN, J.P. VAN DER. 1957. Lead contamination of wines, spirits, and foods. S. Afr. Ind. Chem. *11*, 150-153.

HEIDE, C. VON DER. 1933. Die Blauschönung. Wein Rebe *14*, 325-335, 348-359, 400-408; *15*, 5-19, 35-44.

HEITZ, J., ROESSLER, E.B., AMERINE, M.A., and BAKER, G.A. 1951. A study of certain factors affecting the composition of California sherry during baking. Food Res. *16*, 192-200.

HUBACH, C.E. 1948. Detection of cyanides and ferrocyanides in wines. Anal. Chem. *20*, 1115-1116.

IBARRA, M. and CRUESS, W.V. 1948. Observations on removal of excess color from wine. Wine Rev. *16* (6) 14-15.

JAYARAMAN, A. and VAN BUREN, J.P. 1971. Browning of galacturonic acid in a model system simulating fruit beverages and white wines. J. Agric. Food Chem. *20*, 122-124.

JOSLYN, M.A. and LUKTON, A. 1953. Prevention of copper and iron turbidities in wine. Hilgardia *22*, 451-533.

JOSLYN, M.A. and LUKTON, A. 1956. Mechanism of copper casse formation in white wines. I. Relation of changes in redox potential to copper casse. Food Res. *21*, 384-396.

JOSLYN, M.A., LUKTON, A. and CANE, A. 1953. The removal of excess copper and iron from wine. Food Technol. *7*, 20-29.

KEAN, C.E. and MARSH, G.L. 1956A. Investigation of copper complexes causing cloudiness in wines. I. Chemical composition. Food Res. *21*, 441-447.

KEAN, C.E. and MARSH, G.L. 1956B. Investigation of copper complexes causing cloudiness in wines. II. Bentonite treatment of wines. Food Technol. *10*, 355-359.

KIELHÖFER, E. 1957. Die Weinentsäuerung mittels Ionenaustaucher Vergleich zu der Entsäuerung mit kohlensäurem Kalk. Weinberg Keller *4*, 136-145.

KIELHÖFER, E. and AUMANN, H. 1955. Das Verhalten von Zinn gegenüber Wein. Mitt. Rebe Wein, Ser. A (Klosterneuburg) *5*, 127-135.

KIELHÖFER, E. and WÜRDIG, G. 1961. Kristalltrübungen in Wein durch das Kalzalz einer bisher unbekannten Säure des Weines. Deut. Wein-Ztg. *97*, 478-480.

KOCH, J. 1963. Protéines des vins blancs. Traitements des précipitations protéiques par chauffage et à l'aide de la bentonite. Ann. Technol. Agric. No. Hors Ser. I, *12*, 297-313.

KOCH, J. and SAJAK, E. 1959. A review and some studies on grape protein. Am. J. Enol. Vitic. *10*, 114-123.

KOCH, J. and SCHILLER, H. 1964. Kinetik der Kristallisation von Weinstein. Z. Lebensm.-Untersuch. Forsch. *124*, 180-183.

KRUG, K. 1964. Calcium-Ausscheidungen im Wein und ihre Verhinderung. Weinberg Keller *11*, 547-554.

LHERME, G. 1931-1932. La teneur en cuivre des vins de la Gironde (récolte 1931). Proc. Verb. Séan. Soc. Sci. Phys. Nat. Bordeaux *1931-32*, 119-121.

MARSH, G.L. 1940. Metals in wine. Wine Rev. *8* (9) 12-13; (10) 24-29.

MARSH, G.L. 1952. New compound ends metal clouding. A report on the Fessler compound. Wines Vines *33* (6) 19-21.

MARSH, G.L. 1959A. Personal communication. Davis, Calif.

MARSH, G.L. 1959B. Refrigeration in wine making. Am. Soc. Refrig. Eng. Data Book, Vol. I, Chap.10.

MORETTI, R.H. and BERG, H.W. 1965. Variability among wines to protein clouding. Am. J. Enol. Vitic. *16*, 69-78.

NEY, M. 1948. Dosage rapide du zinc. Ann. Fals. Fraudes *41*, 533-537.

NOBLE, A.C., ORR, B.H., COOK, W.B. and CAMPBELL, J.L. 1976. Trace element analysis of wine by proton-induced-X-ray fluorescence spectrometry (PIX). J. Agric. Food Chem. *24*, 532-535.

O'NEAL, R., MEIS, L. and CRUESS, W.V. 1950. Observations on the fining of wines with casein. Food Technol. *5*, 64-68.

PECHEUR, P. (Translated by H. C. Stollenwerk). 1957. Ion exchange in wines by percolation through continuous columns. Wine Inst. Tech. Advis. Committee, December 6, 1957.

PERI, C., POMPEI, C., MONTEDORO, G. and CANTARELLI, C. 1971. Maderization of white wines. I. Influence of pressing on the susceptibility of the grapes to oxidative browning. J. Sci. Food Agric. *22*, 24-28.

PETERSON, R.G., JOSLYN, M.A. and DURBIN, P.W. 1958. Mechanism of copper casse formation in white table wine. III. Source of the sulfur in the sediment. Food Res. *23*, 518-524.

PEYNAUD, E., GUIMBERTEAU, G. and BLOUIN, J. 1964. Die Löslich-keitsgleichgewichte von Kalzium und Kalium in Wein. Mitt. Rebe Wein, Ser. A (Klosterneuburg) *14*, 176-186.

PILONE, B. and BERG, H.W. 1965. Some factors affecting tartrate stability in wine. Am. J. Enol. Vitic. *16*, 195-211.

POCOCK, K.F. and RANKINE, B.C. 1973. Heat test for detecting protein instability in wine. Austr. Wine Brewing Spirit Rev. *91* (5) 42-43.

RANKINE, B.C, 1955A. Lead content of some Australian Wines. J. Sci. Food Agric. *6*, 576-579.

RANKINE, B.C. 1955B. Treatment of wine with ion-exchange resins. Austr. J. Appl. Sci. 6, 529-540.

RANKINE, B.C. 1962. Aluminum haze in wine. Austr. Wine Brewing Spirit Rev. 80 (9) 14, 16.

RANKINE, B.C. and POCOCK, K.F. 1971. A new method for detecting protein instability in white wines. Ibid. 89, 61.

RIBÉREAU-GAYON, J. 1930. La fer et le cuivre dans les vins blancs. Ann. Fals. Fraudes 23, 535-544.

RIBÉREAU-GAYON. J. 1933. Contribution à l'Étude des Oxydations et Réductions dans les Vins, 2nd Edition. Delmas, Bordeaux, France.

RIBÉREAU-GAYON, J. 1935. Le cuivre des moûts et des vins. Ann. Fals. Fraudes 28, 349-360.

RIBÉREAU-GAYON, J. and PEYNAUD, E. 1960-1961. Traité d'Oenologie, 2 Vol. Librairie Polytechnique Ch. Béranger, Paris.

SCHANDERL, H. 1959. Die Mikrobiologie des Mostes und des Weins. Eugen Ulmer, Stuttgart.

SCHANDERL, S. 1957. The use of cation exchange resins in the prevention of tartrate crystal precipitation after bottling of wine. Wine Inst. Tech. Advis. Committee, May 13, 1957.

SINGLETON, V.L. 1969. Browning of wines. Die Wynboer, (455) 13-14.

SINGLETON, V.L. and KRAMLING, T.E. 1976. Browning of white wines and an accelerated test for browning capacity. Am. J. Enol. Vitic. 27, 157-160.

TANNER, H. and VETSCH, U. 1956. How to characterize cloudiness in beverages. Ibid. 7, 145-146.

THALER, H. and MÜHLBERGER, F. H. 1956. Der Aluminum Gehalt von Pfälzer Traubenmost und Wein. Z. Lebensm.-Untersuch. Forsch. 103, 97-108.

THOUKIS, G. and AMERINE, M.A. 1956. The fate of copper and iron during fermentation of grape musts. Am. J. Enol. 7, 62-68.

TRAVERSO-RUEDA, S. and SINGLETON, V.L. 1973. Catecholase activity in grape juice and its implications in wine making. Am. J. Enol. Vitic. 24, 103-109.

VITAGLIANO, M. 1956. I constituenti minerali del vino. II. Il ferro. Ann. Sper. Agrar. (Rome) 10, 659-668.

WUCHERPFENNIG, K. and FRANK, I. 1967. Zur Frage der Eiweissstabilisierung von Wein durch eine Bentonitbehandlung des Mostes. Wein-Wissen. 22, 213-226.

WURDIG, G. 1977. Apparition de l'acide mucique dans le moût provenant de raisins attaques par le Botrytis. Bull. OIV 50 (551) 50-56.

16

Bacteria in Wine

The bacteria that can develop in wine are of two types in respect to their oxygen requirements. The acetic acid bacteria require oxygen for growth and acetification, whereas the lactic acid bacteria grow best under conditions of reduced oxygen content, that is, they are microaerophilic. In modern winery practice, the lactic acid bacteria are much more important during wine storage than the acetic bacteria. For general discussions see Castelli (1959), Cruess (1943), Dittrich (1977), Maestro Paló (1952), Niehaus (1930), Schanderl (1959), Vaughn (1955), Verona and Florenzano (1956).

At the end of the chapter, procedures are outlined for differentiation of the major groups of microbes (bacteria and yeast) found in spoiled wine.

ACETIC SPOILAGE

The acetic acid bacteria, that is to say the bacteria of the genus *Acetobacter,* are classified in Bergey's Manual (Buchanan and Gibbons 1974) together with the Gram-negative aerobic rods (and cocci)—but in with the genera of "uncertain affiliation." They are characterized by their strong ability to oxidize, at pH 4.5, ethanol to acetic acid and to oxidize the acetic acid further to carbon dioxide and water. Three species are now recognized: *A. aceti, A. pasteurianus* and *A. peroxydans,* each of which has been found in wine. In some of the older literature reference is made to isolation of other species, especially from grapes and must, which carry out the oxidation of ethanol only as far as acetic acid (e.g., *A. melanogenum, A. oxydans, A. roseum* and *A. suboxydans* (see Vaughn 1955). These organisms are now included in the genus *Gluconobacter* of the Pseudomonadaceae family. Vaughn (1955) indicated that these latter organisms are of little importance in the spoilage of California wines. *A. xylinum,* which is also often mentioned in the older literature (Vaughn 1955), is now accepted as a subspecies of *A. aceti.* Strains of *A. aceti* are generally used in commercial production of vinegar; however, Dupuy (1957B) makes a special point that the acetic acid bacteria flora of wines is different from that of vinegar.

The acetic acid bacteria are usually about 0.5 × 1.0 μm and are non-motile. They occur frequently in pairs or in chains, and may be surrounded by a zoögloeal sheath. Vaughn (1942) and others found that involution forms occur under certain conditions; these may be long filaments or other distorted forms.

Acetic bacteria that occur in fermented apple juice usually form a heavy, leathery film, called "vinegar mother," but in wines of 12–14% ethanol the vinegar bacteria are usually found as a thin gray surface film or found throughout the wine and without formation of typical "mother," probably because the strains which form "mother" cannot grow in this range of alcohol content.

Aside from oxygen, Dupuy (1957B) reported pH and percentage ethanol were the most important factors influencing the growth of *Acetobacter*. He found little growth at pH 3.2 or 13% ethanol. Sulfur dioxide was most effective as an antiseptic.

During Red Wine Fermentation

Acetification may occur in the pomace of the cap that forms on open vats of fermenting crushed red grapes, unless the pomace is punched down regularly, or the fermenting must is pumped over the cap frequently in small open tanks, or the tanks are covered and kept under an atmosphere of carbon dioxide. Air supply is usually adequate for vinegar bacteria to develop and to convert ethanol to acetic acid. Use of moderate amounts of sulfur dioxide, about 100 mg/liter, in the crushed grapes will usually minimize or prevent acetification. See especially Cruess (1912) and Quinn (1940).

During Muscat Fermentation

During the first few years following Repeal, considerable spoilage of muscat must occurred in the San Joaquin Valley of California during fermentation in periods of unusually hot weather. The grapes, frequently overripe or harvested late in the season, were crushed at 35°–38°C (95°–100°F), and the musts allowed to ferment naturally without use of sulfur dioxide or cooling. At such elevated temperatures the wine yeast is sluggish in growth and usually ceases multiplication at 40°–41°C (105°F). At this temperature some acetic and lactic bacteria are still active. It was thought at one time that lactic bacteria were the principal cause of spoilage, since they were observed in large numbers under the microscope in samples of the spoiled wine and grew abundantly in 40 liter (10 gal.) lots of muscat juice allowed to ferment naturally in the laboratory at 30°C (85°F). However, research by Vaughn (1938) proved that vinegar bacteria growing in association with the yeast were the chief cause of the observed spoilage. As the yeast produced ethanol, the bacteria oxidized it to acetic acid. When the population of acetic acid bacteria or the temperature rose sufficiently, yeast activity ceased and the bacteria then oxidized the glucose of the must to gluconic acid, $CH_2OH(CHOH)_4$-COOH, and some of the accumulated acetic acid to carbon dioxide and water. Therefore, both the volatile acid and the fixed acid rose. The spoiled must had a "sweet-sour" and usually an "odd" flavor, which is possibly an indication of the activity of certain lactic acid bacteria responsible for wine spoilage. Vaughn (1938) found acetic bacteria in this type of spoilage under winery conditons to be an unusual strain of *Acetobacter*.

During Storage

If wine of less thn 15% ethanol is stored in casks or tanks that are not completely filled and tightly sealed against entrance of air, the wine will often become vinegar sour. Prevention consists of keeping casks and tanks well filled and sealed at all times.

Flor Wine

Bobadilla (1943) recommended that wine to be used in the production of flor sherry in Spain contain at least 14.5% ethanol. Cruess (1937), however, found experimentally that acetification sometimes occurred rapidly in dry wine at 14.7% ethanol under California conditions and recommended that wine for flor sherry production be brought to 15.5% ethanol before inoculating with flor yeast. Vaughn (1955) states that the maximum ethanol tolerance of most acetic bacteria lies between 14 and 15%; but he also states that species and strains of *Acetobacter* exist which cannot develop at above 10% ethanol.

California Wines

Using the older nomenclature (see above), Vaughn (1955) encountered only two species of *Acetobacter* capable of causing acetification in California wines. These were *A. aceti* and *A. oxydans.* However, he frequently isolated *A. xylinum* from grapes and must and *A. melanogenum, A. suboxydans,* and *A. roseum* infrequently.

Pomace and Stuck Wines

Pomace rapidly acetifies after pressing and should be disposed of as quickly as possible. Also, it is an excellent breeding place for vinegar flies, drosophila, which carry vinegar bacteria from the pomace to fermenting crushed grapes or other exposed wine or must surfaces. At present, most wineries dispose of the pomace daily. Stuck wines are very susceptible to spoilage by vinegar bacteria if in partially filled tanks or casks. Addition of sulfur dioxide to maintain a level above 125 mg/liter and prompt refermentation of the stuck wine are recommended. (See Chap. 6 for further information on stuck wines.) Vinegar production is presented in Chap. 18.

Volatile Acidity

The volatile acid content of wine is a good indication of its soundness. Wines that are high in volatile acid usually smell vinegar-sour. The present California regulations provide that white table and dessert wines must not have a volatile acidity above 0.110 g/100 ml, calculated as acetic and exclusive of sulfur dioxide. The limit for red wines is 0.120 g/l00 ml. The federal limits are somewhat higher, namely, 0.120 and 0.140 respectively. The principal reaction in acetification is:

$$C_2H_5OH + O_2 \rightarrow CH_3COOH + H_2O$$

However, Peynaud (1936, 1937) has shown that much of the spoiled odor of vinegar-sour wines is due to ethyl acetate, an ester formed by acetic bacteria:

$$C_2H_5OH + CH_3COOH \rightarrow CH_3COOC_2H_5 + H_2O$$

Some vinegar bacteria produce more ethyl acetate than do others. In the case of rotten grapes, the ethyl acetate produced may be lost by evaporation prior to fermentation, whereas most of the acetic acid produced may carry through the fermentation and into the wine. These factors cause wines to have different ratios of acetic acid to ethyl acetate.

Vaughn (1955) states that acetic bacteria can oxidize glycerol, citric acid, malic acid, and tartaric acid *in vitro*, but there is no evidence that they attack these compounds in wine.

Deacetification

While the total acidity of a wine can be reduced by the addition of any permissible alkaline substance, the volatile acidity, acetic acid chiefly, is not reduced. If a wine slightly exceeds the legal limit in volatile acidity and is sound in other respects, it may be blended with wine of low volatile acidity. However, if the volatile acidity is very high, the wine may be only fit for distillation or for making into vinegar.

It was found by Pasteur (1864) and confirmed subsequently by Cruess (1948) and others that certain film yeasts (Spanish flor yeasts and French Chalon yeasts) can oxidize acetic acid in wine to carbon dioxide and water. Flor yeast has seldom been used commercially for this purpose.

SPOILAGE BY LACTIC ACID BACTERIA[1]

Not all lactic acid bacteria are necessarily spoilage bacteria. As early as 1900, Koch pointed out that many sound wines contain bacteria. In fact, modern enological practice often utilizes them; see Malo-lactic Fermentation, p. 565.

Both the appearance and flavor of the wine may be altered by lactic acid bacteria. When gently shaken in a test tube or bottle, the wine will have a silky-cloudy appearance. This characteristic of streaming of "silkiness," according to Amerine and Joslyn (1970), is caused by alignment of the rod bacteria in chains (not to be confused with silkiness caused by precipitated tartrates). A wine spoiled by lactic bacteria usually has a disagreeable smell, sometimes mousy, and a flocculent or pulverulent sediment. As Vaughn (1955) has pointed out, acetic acid bacteria also can produce a mousy smell in musts. Lactic bacteria can inhibit growth of *Saccharomyces cerevisiae*, possibly because they produce L-ornithine (Biodron 1969).

The most common acid-tolerant bacteria responsible for wine spoilage are those that produce lactic acid. Many different species of lactic acid bacteria have been found in wine, but by modern classification (Buchanan and Gibbons 1974) only the genera *Lactobacillus, Leuconostoc,* and *Pediococcus* are included. See Orla-Jensen (1919), Shimwell (1941), Snell (1946) and Wood *et al.* (1940) and references in section on Malolactic Fermentation, p. 565. Lüthi (1957) has emphasized that it may not be a single species which causes spoilage but several growing symbiotically.

Of the lactic acid bacteria, the rod forms, either heterolactic or homolactic (see next paragraph), are of the genus *Lactobacillus* of the Lactobacillaceae family (Gram-positive, asporogenous). The spherical or coccoid are the *Leuconostoc* (heterofermentative) and *Pediococcus* (homofermentative) of the Streptococcaceae family. The leuconostocs are

[1]The authors are greatly indebted to Prof. R. H. Vaughn for much of the information presented in this section.

sometimes elongated and thus may be confused with short heterofermentative lactobacilli (Garvie 1974).

Homofermentative Versus Heterofermentative Lactobacilli

The homofermentative lactic acid bacteria convert glucose chiefly to lactic acid without formation of appreciable amounts of carbon dioxide or acetic acid, whereas the heterofermentative species produce not only lactic acid from glucose but also carbon dioxide, acetic acid, ethanol, and glycerol. They also reduce considerable amounts of fructose to mannitol. Many strains of both species can ferment malic and citric acids in wine, although some strains seem to prefer malic acid. In accordance with modern bacterial nomenclature, the following homolactic species have been listed as isolated from wine: *L. acidophilus, L. casei, L. delbrueckii, L. leichmannii* and *L. plantarum*, and the heterolactic species *L. fermentum, L. brevis, L. buchneri, L. hilgardii* and *L. trichodes* (Kunkee 1967, 1974; Barre 1978). Some of these organisms are indeed difficult to study. Rogosa (1974) lists *L. hilgardii* and *L. trichodes* in Bergey's Manual (Buchanan and Gibbons 1974) with the "less well known" heterofermentative lactobacilli and as slower growing or "indifferent" toward most carbohydrates. Both of these latter species have been isolated only from wine (Douglas and Cruess 1936A; Vaughn *et al.* 1949). *L. trichodes* is discussed in more detail on p. 571−572. The isolation of *L. acidophilus,* or *L. acidophilus*-like bacteria (Barre 1978) is unusual, since these are thermophiles. These were isolated from fermenting must at 40°−43°C (104°−109°F) following thermovinification of must. Four other unusual thermophilic homofermentative lactobacilli were also isolated by Barre (1978).

Leuconostoc and Pediococcus

Like the heterofermentative rod-shaped lactobacilli, leuconostocs form lactic acid, acetic acid, carbon dioxide and ethanol from glucose and, in addition, form mannitol from fructose. According to Bergey's Manual (Garvie 1974), all heterolactic cocci capable of growth in wine (at low pH and in presence of 10% ethanol) are strains of *Leuconostoc oenos,* although other terminology is also being used (Peynaud and Domercq 1968; see also discussion by Pilone and Kunkee 1972). Some of these "cocci" are rather elongated, but would have a length no longer than twice the width. Elongated leuconostocs can be differentiated from short heterolactic lactobacilli isolated from wine by the inability of the former to produce ammonia from arginine (Garvie 1974). *Leuconostoc mesenteroides* is a spherical (coccal) species which can be an important producer of lactic acid in the fermentation of sauerkraut and pickles. It may cause ropiness in fruit wines containing sucrose because of the formation of dextrans (polysaccharides).

Little problem in identification of the homolactic cocci is found. They are always quite spherical. Of the pediococci, only the species *P. cerevisiae* and *P. pentosaceus* have been isolated from wine (see Kunkee 1967; Weiller and Radler 1970).

Historical

Pasteur (1873A) was one of the first to study the spoilage of wines which we now recognize as lactic acid bacterial spoilage in the period 1861 to 1870. He recognized four types of spoilage, namely: (1) acetification, (2) the spoilage known as *tourne* and *pousse*, (3) slimy wine spoilage, and (4) the bitterness disease *(amertume)* of wines. In the lactic spoilage, termed *pousse,* gas is formed and many enologists considered it separate and distinct from *tourne.* Pasteur, however, considered *pousse* merely a gassy type of *tourne.* At one time, enologists thought that each form of spoilage or bacterial transformation was caused by a specific organism and it was customary to speak of *tourne* (Nickles 1862) bacteria, *pousse* bacteria, *malo-lactic* bacteria, and *mannite* bacteria, whereas it is now recognized that each of these conditions can be produced by several species of bacteria. Pasteur and other early investigators were handicapped by having no means of making pure cultures. Koch's pure culture technique (1881) was soon widely applied by various microbiologists in the study of wine spoilage organisms. Vaughn suggested that the words *tourne, pousse* and others be used to designate wine conditions rather than the microorganisms concerned. There is still much confusion among enologists in respect to wine spoilage terminology, and we now feel these terms ought to be avoided. For example, one time, as a result of the research of Carles (1891), Gayon and Dubourg (1894, 1901) and Laborde (1904), mannitol production in wines by bacterial action on fructose was considered as due to the activity of a short rod bacterium termed by them *ferment mannitique* and thought to be quite distinct from the bacteria causing *tourne* or *pousse.* We now know that a considerable number of species of lactic acid bacteria are heterofermentative and form mannitol. *Lactobacillus brevis, L. hilgardii,* and others, as well as *Leuconostoc oenos,* form mannitol from fructose. The term mannitic bacteria *(ferment mannitique)* is no longer valid.

Although one still hears of bacterial spoilage of wines as "diseases," Vaughn (1955) rightfully objects to this usage since wine is inanimate. Spoilage is a more appropriate term.

The research of Müller-Thurgau and Osterwalder in Switzerland

(1912, 1918, 1919) did much to clarify the previously confused situation applying to the bacterial spoilage of wine. They made pure cultures of wine spoilage bacteria by Koch's methods and conducted well-planned and exhaustive studies of the pure cultures. For example, they recognized four species of bacteria capable of producing mannitol from fructose and, therefore, that the *ferment mannitique* of Gayon and Dubourg is only one of a group of heterofermentative lactobacilli that form mannitol from fructose. An important result of their investigations was the finding that malic acid is fermented by all sorts of lactic acid bacteria, and that enologists should not speak of the malo-lactic bacteria (p. 565) as a single species. Arena (1936) in Argentina confirmed much of the research of Müller-Thurgau and Osterwalder.

Lactic acid bacterial spoilage was very prevalent in California wineries during the first two years following repeal of the 18th Amendment. Because of the inexperience of the winemakers of that period, much wine was made without use of sulfur dioxide or cooling. This form of spoilage is now very rare in California wineries.

Tartrate Decomposition

Although several European investigators claimed that tartaric acid underwent decomposition in wine spoilage with production of propionic acid, Vaughn (1955) stated that this view is untenable because the lactic acid bacteria do not produce propionic acid from any of the major fermentable constituents of wine. In view of the research of Fornachon (1943), Fornachon *et al.* (1940, 1949), Olsen (1948) and Vaughn *et al.* (1949), in which only one strain of the bacteria ioslated from spoiled wine was able to decompose tartrates in wine or culture media, it would appear that, insofar as Californian and Australian conditions are concerned, tartrate decomposition is not a good criterion of spoilage. Berry and Vaughn (1952) did, however, obtain from spoiled red wine and from lees tartrate-fermenting cultures of *L. plantarum* which, after adaptation to ethanol, could be grown in wines enriched with yeast autolysate. The major end products of tartrate decomposition were lactic acid and carbon dioxide (Krumperman *et al.* 1953). See also Cruess (1935) and d'Estivaux (1935). Radler and Yannissis (1972) have reported the enzymatic pathway of catabolism of tartaric acid by some lactic acid bacteria, but this was found in whole cells only at pHs greater than that found in wine.

For other studies on the possibilities of lactic acid bacterial decomposition of tartrate in wine, see Arena (1936), Duclaux (1898–1901), Fornachon (1936, 1943, 1957), Ribéreau-Gayon (1938, 1946), Ribéreau-Gayon and Peynaud (1938), Sémichon (1905) and Vaughn (1955).

MALO-LACTIC FERMENTATION

Deacidification

A considerable portion of the fixed acidity of wine is due to malic acid. In cool wine producing regions, such as Switzerland, the Rheingau of Germany and certain sections of France, the wines may naturally be high in total acidity. In some cool regions, Germany, for example, the high acidity is usually reduced by chemical means, such as by the double salt (calcium malate-tartrate) deacidification procedure (Münz 1960; Kielhöfer and Würdig 1963, 1964). In other cool regions, it is customary to promote the growth of malo-lactic bacteria in the wine, which converts malic acid to lactic acid and carbon dioxide. The titratable acidity of the wine may be reduced as much as ⅓ by this fermentation. The resulting wine, particularly when new, is slightly sparkling (*pétillant*).

The bacteria which carry out the malo-lactic fermentation are certain strains of lactic acid bacteria (p. 562). Their most important attribute for the winemaker in cool regions is their deacidification capability. However, the malo-lactic fermentation is also prevalent in warm regions where the loss of acidity is not especially desirable. In these cases, the winemaker may wish to encourage the malo-lactic fermentation anyway because of the microbiological stability it renders, or because of a change in flavor which it may impart. These attributes of the bacteria are discussed in some detail below. For further reading, see Fell (1961), Peynaud and Domercq (1961), Radler (1966), Kunkee (1967), Rankine *et al.* (1970), Rankine (1972), Kunkee (1974), Morenzoni (1974), Carr *et al.* (1975), Ribéreau-Gayon *et al.* (1975), and Kunkee and Goswell (1977).

Many of the malo-lactic bacteria are extremely fastidious nutritionally and require special growth factors, of which some are known. The effect of various amino acids and vitamins (constituents of wine) on growth of selected organisms has been reported (Weiller and Radler 1972; Peynaud and Domercq 1968). Pantothenic acid derivatives, which have been isolated from tomato juice, serve as specially active growth factors for some malo-lactic bacteria (Amachi 1975; Yoshizumi 1975). Malic acid itself stimulates the growth rate of some malo-lactic bacteria. This phenomenon is discussed further below (p. 566).

Anecdotal observations, and some laboratory experiments, support the idea that the yeast strain used in the ethanolic fermentation has an important influence on the rate of the subsequent malo-lactic fermentation (Ribéreau-Gayon and Peynaud 1961; Milisavlejov 1964; Fornachon 1968; Lafon-Lafourcade 1973; Boidron 1969; Challinor and Rose 1954; Beelman *et al.* 1977).

The Malo-lactic Reaction

The presence of malic acid has been shown to stimulate the uptake of glucose by the bacteria. This occurs because the resulting increase in pH leads to increased growth (Radler 1958A). However, malic acid has also been shown to stimulate the initial growth rate of some strains of malo-lactic bacteria, independent of the change in pH (Pilone and Kunkee 1976; Pukrushpan 1976). This latter stimulation is unexpected. Although the malo-lactic reaction has been shown to be exergonic (Kunkee 1967)[2], the energy yield is low (−2 kcal/mole) (Pilone and Kunkee 1970), and apparently not biologically available (Pilone and Kunkee 1976). The pathway of the reaction has been shown to be a direct decarboxylation by a single malate carboxy lyase enzyme (Schütz and Radler 1973), with no formation of high energy phosphate or net change in redox potential of the coenzyme, nicotine adenine dinucleotide, involved. The role of malic acid in the stimulation of the growth rate seems to result from the formation of small amounts of hydrogen acceptors during the reaction (Morenzoni 1973; Kunkee 1975). Other workers have shown stimulation with certain hydrogen acceptors (Meyrath and Lüthi 1969; Stamer and Stoyla 1970). It is interesting to note that the optimal concentration for this malic stimulation is about that which is found in California musts—0.3% L-malic acid. For a description of the history of research on the malo-lactic reaction, including the work of Korkes et al. (1950) and Flesch and Holbach (1965), see Morenzoni (1974).

Bacteriological Stabilization

In many sections of California, and in other warm grape growing regions, the deacidification which accompanies the malo-lactic fermentation is not in itself desirable. Nevertheless, the fermentation is widespread in California. One reason for this is probably that it is often easier to encourage its occurrence than to prevent it. Once the fermentation is completed, the winemaker can consider the wine (if kept anaerobic) to be bacteriologically stable and can safely store it for further aging or can begin the finishing operations on wines to be marketed as young wines. The loss of acidity brought about by the fermentation can be adjusted by addition of organic acids, within legal limits. Because of price, citric acid and malic acid are often used. How-

---

[2]The reaction was first shown to be endothermic (Schanderl 1959), and then later shown also to be, at the same time, exergonic (Kunkee 1967).

ever, tartaric acid, because of its biological stability, is preferred, even though some of the added acid will be lost as potassium bitartrate. We have mentioned the widespread occurrence of the malo-lactic fermentation in California. Of the several studies on its incidence (Suverkrop and Tschelistcheff 1949; Vaughn and Tschelistcheff 1957; Amerine 1950; and Vaughn 1955), the most systematic survey (Ingraham and Cooke 1960) came with the development of a simplified paper chromatographic method for detection of the completion of the fermentation (e.g., Kunkee 1968, 1974). The survey of Ingraham and Cooke (1960) was of red wine normally stored for several years before being bottled. In this survey, it was revealed that a very high proportion (about 75%) of these wines had undergone malo-lactic fermentation. It is now generally considered that the highest quality of aged red wines in California have usually had malo-lactic fermentation. However, other surveys indicate that lesser red wines and also white wines have a high incidence of malo-lactic fermentation in California, also (Kunkee *et al.* 1965; Cooke and Berg 1973; Kunkee 1975). The encouragement of the fermentation in these latter wines, especially those to be marketed early, comes from the winemaker's desire for biological stability which the fermentation affords (in dry wines), as well as any flavor improvement which the fermentation might bring about.

It should be pointed out again that the malo-lactic fermentation is not a California phenomenon, but occurs worldwide in winery areas (Kunkee 1967).

Flavor Changes

It is generally considered that the end-products of the malo-lactic bacterial metabolism bring about a desirable increase in flavor complexity in the wine. French producers of the Bordeaux and Burgundy areas believe that the high quality of their red wines is due, in part, to malo-lactic fermentation. As indicated above, it is considered essential to lower the acidity of many very acid wines of northern Europe.

Any enhancement in flavor of wine resulting from malo-lactic fermentation is difficult to evaluate. Small increases in complexity of flavor have been suggested as being favorable (Singleton and Ough 1962). The established increase in volatile acidity or diacetyl production (Ribéreau-Gayon and Peynaud 1961; Kunkee *et al.* 1965; Pilone 1967; Rankine 1972; Rankine *et al.*1969) may contribute to this. In taste tests with wines fermented by various strains of malo-lactic bacteria, Pilone and Kunkee (1965) found the judges able to differentiate significantly between some of the wines, but the differences were small. Rankine

(1972) suggests that any taste differentiation arising from the malo-lactic fermentation comes only from the deacidification and diacetyl formation. Of course, high levels of diacetyl or other unpleasant end-products would be detrimental to the wine. Indeed, malo-lactic fermentation can also be considered a spoilage reaction. In the sensory experiment mentioned above (Pilone and Kunkee 1965), one pediococcus fermentation resulted in a wine with a very easily detectable off-character. Sometimes, sauerkraut or other fermented pickle-like flavors are formed. This seems to have led to the description of some malo-lactic wines having a "lactic taste" (Dittrich and Kerner 1964), not from lactic acid itself. This is one of the reasons why the fermentation has sometimes been discouraged, especially in delicate and light white wines. For example, German winemakers have avoided the malo-lactic fermentation for several years, although the difficulty in obtaining it consistently in their wines of low pH undoubtedly also played a role in this decision to avoid it.

Control of Malo-lactic Fermentation

Perhaps practical methods for absolute control of malo-lactic fermentation cannot be described at this time, but the following guidelines will assure a high rate of successful control [see Fornachon (1957) and Kunkee (1974) for greater details].

For *inhibition* of the fermentation, the winemaker should have the highest regard for sanitation in the winery, and to avoid the storage of this wine in wooden cooperage, especially if the cooperage has a history of storage of wine which has undergone malo-lactic fermentation. The new wine, in which the malo-lactic fermentation is to be prevented, should be removed from the yeast lees as soon as possible; rough filtered and/or fined, with a possible centrifugation before filtration; treated with sulfur dioxide (30 mg/liter free) and acidulating material to bring the pH to as close to pH 3.3 as possible without upsetting the flavor balance; and then maintained at a temperature at least below $16°-18°C$ ($61°-65°F$). Where legal, some winemakers employ addition of fumaric acid (0.03–0.05%). Used in connection with good winemaking practices, the fumaric acid addition seems to be an absolute deterrent to growth of malo-lactic bacteria in wine (Cofran and Meyer 1970; Kunkee 1974; Pilone 1975). Pasteurization of the wine, or sterile filtration, followed in either case by sterile bottling, is also a means of inhibition of malo-lactic fermentation.

To *encourage* the malo-lactic fermentation, the opposite procedure to that outlined above should be used. No treatment of the new wine ought to be made with regard to sulfur dioxide or acid addition, or with regard to filtration or fining. The wine should be left on the yeast lees for a longer time than usual. The temperature of the wine ought to be maintained at 18°−21°C (65°−70°F). Because these conditions are exactly the conditions which would promote yeast spoilage, especially *Brettanomyces* or *Dekkera* yeast (Chap. 4), this wine must be closely watched. To overcome the possibility of difficulty with yeast spoilage, it is helpful to inoculate the wine with a starter culture of malo-lactic bacteria. Beelman *et al.* (1977) have suggested that the most suitable organisms for that would be those isolated from wines of the region. Their results (Beelman *et al.* 1977) show more rapid fermentation with a *Leuconostoc oenos* strain isolated from a wine from the region as compared to others. Thus, one might wish to use *L. oenos* ML 34 in California (Kunkee 1967), *L. oenos* PSU1 in Pennsylvania (Beelman *et al.* 1977), *L. oenos* L181 in Australia (Rankine 1977) or a proprietary strain of *Lactobacillus* sp. for parts of France (Ardin 1972).

Very few malo-lactic cultures are commercially available in the form of starter cultures (see Kunkee 1974), but they can be prepared by some commercial winery laboratories on special order. As already mentioned, most of these bacteria are nutritionally fastidious and any quick, large-scale production of them for starter cultures has some practical limitations.

It has been suggested that characteristic malo-lactic microflora may be established in individual vineyard areas or even in wineries, in the same way that certain yeast strains are said to be established (Amerine and Singleton 1977). There is poor agreement to the actual origin of the malo-lactic bacteria in wineries. Almost every unbottled dry wine sample, red or white, examined by Ingraham *et al.* (1960) contained lactic acid bacteria capable of decomposing malic acid. However, essentially no lactic acid bacteria have been found on grape skins or in fresh must (Radler 1958B). Other alternative suggestions as to their origin have been discussed (Kunkee 1967, 1974). *If* a winery were noted for a characteristic indigenous malo-lactic fermentation, it might be desirable for the winery microbiologist to isolate the resident organisms, test them, and cultivate them for inoculation during the vintage.

In any case, it is suggested (Kunkee 1967) that the inoculation of the bacteria for inducing the malo-lactic fermentation be made during the middle of the ethanolic fermentation, before there is a possibility of build-up of too much bacterial end-product material (Barre 1972) and before the ethanol level, itself, becomes too high. It is our experience that it is extremely difficult to speed up a malo-lactic fermentation by inoculation with bacteria after the end of the ethanolic fermentation. Alternately, the malo-lactic fermentation in the wine-must may be started by addition of several percent of wine which has just completed malo-lactic fermentation or by storage of the wine in wooden cooperage which has been infected with a bacterial population from earlier (good) malo-lactic fermentation.

In spite of apparently favorable conditions, sometimes it is difficult to obtain a malo-lactic fermentation when it is desired. Some possible explanations for these failures can be presented: lack of essential nutrients in the wine for these fastidious bacteria (see Kunkee 1974); the inhibitory effect of bound sulfur dioxide (e.g., acetaldehyde-bisulfite) as well as free sulfur dioxide, the bound sulfur dioxide coming from sulfur dioxide additions for control of other reactions (Lafon-Lafourcade 1975); and from bacteriophage infection of the bacteria (Sozzi et al. 1976).

At the end of the malo-lactic fermentation, some of the finishing procedures should be begun: sulfur dioxide, acid and temperature adjustment. Some winemakers at this time carry out aeration, fining and high quality filtration (Kunkee 1974).

Further discussion of lactic acid bacteria is also found in Chap. 6, pp. 290–293.

Spoilage of Fortified Wines

In California, Australia and South Africa many of the fortified wines contain 19–20% ethanol and, therefore, bacteria that are able to grow in such wines must have an exceptionally high tolerance for ethanol. Fevrier (1926) isolated a long rod bacillus from South African wines of 20% ethanol content. It possessed high heat resistance, withstanding 80°C (176°F) for 15 min. Niehaus (1932) found a thread-like bacillus in South African wines that grew readily in wines containing 18% ethanol and formed mannitol from fructose. It was probably the same organism described by Fornachon et al. (1949) as L. trichodes (see p. 562).

Fornachon (1943) made an extensive study of the bacteria of spoiled Australian wines. The 110 strains investigated were all heterofermentative species. These were divided into five groups or types which seem to correspond to various lactobacilli listed on p. 562. He stated that the bacteria were widely distributed and probably occurred in all Australian wineries. Therefore, a wine which remains sound does so because it is not susceptible to bacterial attack. None of the strains was able to cause serious spoilage in wines which contained only traces of fermentable sugar. According to Fornachon, spoilage of Australian fortified wines is characterized by an increase in the volatile and fixed acidities and by production of mannitol and carbon dioxide.

All of Fornachon's cultures were sensitive to sulfur dioxide and failed to grow in wines containing 75–80 mg/liter total sulfur dioxide; at 100, the bacteria were killed. Growth was prevented at pH 3.6 or lower, and, thus, one means of control is acidification of the must or wine. He found, however, that acidification to pH 3.6 of wines of exceptionally high pH value often caused them to be too sour in taste. In the study of one type of his isolates, he found pasteurization at 70°C (158°F) for 60 sec killed the bacteria and 65°C (149°F) for 15 min was also effective. He emphasized the necessity of heating all portions of a given wine to pasteurizing temperature. The temperature of destruction certainly depends to a great extent on the ethanol content and pH value of the wine. Oak tannin and Merck's reagent tannin prevented growth of this type when 1 g/liter was added and only a trace of growth occurred when 0.5 g/liter was added.

During the early post-Repeal period in California, Cruess and Saywell (Amerine *et al.* 1972) received many samples of fortified wines of 18 to 20.5% ethanol containing a flocculent sediment which under the high power of the microscope appeared as a mass of tangled filaments, hence the name "hair bacillus" given it in the wineries and wine trade. It was also known as Fresno "mold" since the macroscopical appearance of the sediment is mold-like. Douglas and Cruess (1936B,C) reported briefly on this spoilage, finding it very susceptible to sulfur dioxide, as 50 mg/liter prevented its growth in sherry. Douglas and McClung (1937) described the organism and its culture characteristics.

Fornachon *et al.* (1949) have made an exhaustive study of this bacillus and have named it *Lactobacillus trichodes*, a new species (see Fig. 16.1). Unless autolysed yeast extract is added, it fails to grow in the customary

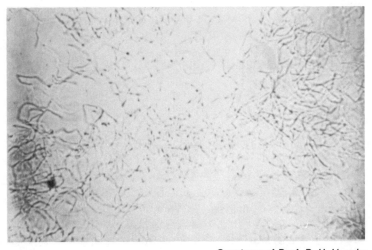

Courtesy of Prof. R. H. Vaughn

FIG. 16.1. *LACTOBACILLUS TRICHODES*

Not stained

laboratory culture media. Briefly, its cultural characteristics are as follows: Rods are 0.4 to 0.6 by 2 to 4 μm; they occur in pairs or chains with a marked tendency to grow into very long, thread-like chains and filaments. Acid is formed in glucose and fructose media, and sometimes a small amount is formed in sucrose and maltose media. It fails to attack arabinose, xylose, galactose, lactose, raffinose, glycerol, mannitol, malic acid, citric acid, and tartaric acid and is catalase-negative. Lactic acid, acetic acid, carbon dioxide, and ethanol are the chief products from glucose. In addition to these, mannitol is formed from fructose. It grows well at 20% ethanol and some strains grow at 21%.

Dupuy (1957A) isolated a new lactobacillus from a muscat dessert wine. It resembled one of Fornachon's isolates. The wines were gassy, of high viscosity (*graisseux*), high in ammonia, mannitol, and volatile acidity and contained no malic acid. The material causing the increased viscosity was a polyoside which gave on hydrolysis 90% reducing sugars. See Kayser and Manceau (1909) for an early report of this type of spoilage, which was prevalent at that time.

Until recently, *L. trichodes* was the only identified organism associated with the spoilage of fortified dessert wines in California. Gini (1959) and Gini and Vaughn (1962) have isolated members of the genera *Bacillus* and *Pediococcus* from experimentally-spoiled dessert wines. Six strains were recovered from spoiled dessert wines and 19 from winery production and storage equipment. The authors have not encountered spoilage of dessert wines by bacilli or pediococci.

At present, "California sherry" wines may legally contain a minimum of 17% ethanol, and thus are susceptible to the spoilages described above and should be handled accordingly.

For further information on bacterial spoilage of dessert wines, see Joslyn and Amerine (1964), Radler (1962) and Goswell and Kunkee (1977).

BITTER WINES

Bitterness in wines has been mentioned by several French investigators, including Pasteur (1873B), Duclaux (1898–1901), and Voisenet (1910, 1918). Voisenet, who ascribed the condition to bacterial action, thought the responsible organism was *Bacillus amaracrylus*. He found that it forms acrolein from glycerol. Vaughn (1955) states that it is identical to *B. polymyxa*, but that the exact cause of the bitter taste is not clear. Pasteur (1873) sterilized 100 bottles of red Burgundy wine and left a similar set unheated. All of the unheated samples became cloudy and finally bitter; all of the pasteurized samples remained clear and free of bitterness. Müller-Thurgau and Osterwalder (1918) suggested that the

TABLE 16.1. DETERMINATION OF CAUSES OF MICROBIAL SPOILAGE

	Yeast	Bacteria		
		Acetic Acid Bacteria	Bacilli	Lactic Acid Bacteria
Visual appearance	Fine haze or precipitate or film; wine may be gassy.	Gray film on surface.	Fine haze or precipitate or cloud when shaken.	Fine haze or precipitate or silky, streaming cloud when shaken. Wine may be dull.
Odor	Not characteristic.	Vinegary (acetic acid and ethyl acetate).	—	Wine may be slightly gassy. Sauerkraut or diacetyl character.
Microscopic appearance	Greater than 4–5 mµ.	Ellipsoidal or rods (involutionary forms may be present).	Less than 4–5 mµ. Rods.	Less than 4–5 mµ. Rods or cocci (like tangled mass of hair=*Lactobacillus trichodes*).
Growth on Basic medium[1]	+	+	+	+ (Ferments malate to lactate= malo-lactic bacteria.)
Basic medium + cycloheximide[2]	0 or +[3]	0 or +	0 or +	+
Catalase test[4]	—	+	+	—
Spore formation	0 or +	—	+	—
Calcium carbonate plates[5]	—	Clearing.	No clearing.	No clearing.

[1]Basic medium: The basic culture medium contains 2.0 g/100 ml of Bacto tryptone, 0.5 of Bacto peptone, 0.5 of Bacto yeast extract, 0.3 of glucose, 0.2 of lactose, 0.1 of liver extract (Wilson), 0.1 ml of 5% aqueous Tween 80, 100 ml of diluted and filtered tomato juice. To prepare tomato juice, dilute 4-fold with distilled water, filter through Whatman No. 1 paper using a Büchner funnel and Super Cel filter aid. To prepare the basic medium dissolve solid ingredients in diluted tomato juice by heating (avoid scorching by frequent agitation of the flask). When cool, adjust pH to 5.5 with concentrated hydrochloric acid, add 2 g agar/100 ml, and autoclave 15 min at 15 psig.

[2]"Acti-dione": 1 ml containing 10 mg of cycloheximide is added to each 100 ml of medium.

[3]Growth is presumptive evidence of *Brettanomyces* or *Dekkera* yeast (see Chap. 4 for confirmatory evidence).

[4]Basic medium with cycloheximide: Add a drop of 3% of fresh hydrogen peroxide to colonies. If gas is evolved the organism is catalase positive.

[5]Basic medium with cycloheximide minus the glucose and lactose and containing 2% calcium carbonate and 3% ethanol (the ethanol is added after the autoclaving). If acetic acid bacteria grow they will cause clearing of this cloudy medium around the colonies.

Source of data: Tanner and Vetsch (1956) and personal observations of authors.

bitter taste is due to compounds of tannin; the ethyl ester of gallic acid is intensely bitter. The authors have not encountered this spoilage of wine in California.

DETERMINATION OF CAUSES OF MICROBIAL SPOILAGE

It is outside the scope of this text to include all of the tests to determine which bacterium is involved; however, the procedures shown in Table 16.1 will differentiate the major groups including yeast (see Chap. 4 for further details on yeast). Microscopic examination is the first step in determination of whether the wine spoilage is microbiological or not, and, if microbiological, whether it results from yeast or bacteria. A special point must be made: for examination of bacteria in wine microscopically, a microscope with oil immersion and with phase contrast optics must be available. Generally speaking, a wine which has just undergone microbiological spoilage will contain a high concentration of cells (with "too many organisms to count" in a high magnification field: 90–100× objective). If only few cells are present, it may be helpful to centrifuge a sample of the wine and collect the pellet.

REFERENCES[3]

AMACHI, T. 1975. Chemical structure of a growth factor (TJF) and its physiological significance for malo-lactic bacteria. *In* Lactic Acid Bacteria in Beverages and Foods. J. H. Carr, C. V. Cutting and G. C. Whiting (Editors). Academic Press, London.

AMERINE, M.A. 1950. The acids of California grapes and wines. I. Lactic acid. Food Technol. *4*, 177-181.

AMERINE, M.A. and JOSLYN, M.A. 1970. Table Wines: The Technology of Their Production, 2nd Edition. University of California Press, Berkeley and Los Angeles.

AMERINE, M.A., BERG, H.W. and CRUESS, W.V. 1972. The Technology of Wine Making, 3rd Edition. AVI Publishing Co., Westport, Conn.

AMERINE, M.A. and SINGLETON, V.L. 1977. Wine: An Introduction, 2nd Edition. University of California Press, Berkeley.

ARDIN, F. 1972. Note sur l'utilisation pratique des levains de bactéries malolactiques. Rev. Fr. Oenol. (46) 66-68.

ARENA, A. 1936. Alteraciones bacterianas de vinos argentinos. Rev. Agric. Vet. (Buenos Aires) *8*, 155-320.

BARRE, P. 1972. Degradation des sucres par les bactéries lactiques du vin. Rev. Fr. Oenol. (45) 37-41.

---

[3]Titles have been translated only for nonwestern European languages.

BARRE, P. 1978. Identification of thermobacteria and homofermentative, thermophilic, pentose-utilizing lactobacilli from high temperature fermenting grape musts. J. Appl. Bacteriol. *44*, 125-129.

BEELMAN, R.B., GAVIN A., III and KEEN, R.M. 1977. A new strain of *Leuconostoc oenos* for induced malo-lactic fermentation in eastern wines. Am. J. Enol. Vitic. *28*, 159-165.

BERRY, J.M. and VAUGHN, R.H. 1952. Decomposition of tartrates by lactobacilli. Proc. Am. Soc. Enol. *1952*, 135-138.

BOBADILLA, G.F. DE. 1943. Aplicaciones industriales de las levaduras de flor. Agric. (Rev. Agropecuaria) *12* (133) 203-207.

BOIDRON, A.M. 1969. Étude de l'antagonisme entre les levures et les bactéries lactiques du vin. Conn. Vigne Vin *3*, 315-378.

BUCHANAN, R.E. and GIBBONS, N.E. 1974. Bergey's Manual of Determinative Bacteriology, 8th Edition. Williams & Wilkins Co., Baltimore.

CARLES, P. 1891. Sur la caractéristique des vins figue. Compt. Rend. *112*, 811-812.

CARR, J.G., CUTTING, C.V. and WHITING, G.C. 1975. Lactic Acid Bacteria in Beverages and Food. Academic Press, London.

CASTELLI, T. 1959. Introduzione alla Microbiologia Enologica. Tipografia Setti et Figlio, Milan.

CHALLINOR, S.W. and ROSE, A.H. 1954. Interrelationships between a yeast and a bacteria when growing together in defined medium. Nature *174*, 877-878.

COFRAN, D.R. and MEYER, B.J. 1970. The effect of fumaric acid on malolactic fermentation. Am. J. Enol. Vitic. *21*, 189-192.

COOKE, G.M. and BERG, H.W. 1973. Table wine processing practices in the San Joaquin Valley. Am. J. Enol. Vitic. *24*, 153-158.

CRUESS, W.V. 1912. Effect of sulfurous acid on fermentation organisms. Ind. Eng. Chem. *4*, 581-585.

CRUESS, W.V. 1935. Control of tourne. Fruit Prod. J. *14*, 359-360.

CRUESS, W.V. 1937. Observation of '36 season on volatile acid formation in muscat fermentations. Fruit Prod. J. *16*, 198-200, 219.

CRUESS, W.V. 1943. The role of micro-organisms and enzymes in wine making. Advan. Enzymol. *3*, 349-386.

CRUESS, W.V. 1948. Investigations of the flor sherry process. Calif. Agric. Exp. Stn. Bull. *710*.

DITTRICH, H.H. 1977. Mikrobiologie des Weines. Eugen Ulmer, Stuttgart.

DITTRICH, H.H. and KERNER, E. 1964. Diacetyl als Weinfehler. Ursache und Beseitigung. Wein-Wiss. *19*, 528-535.

DOUGLAS, H.C and CRUESS, W.V. 1936A. A lactobacillus from California wine: *Lactobacillus hilgardii*. Food Res. *1*, 113-119.

DOUGLAS, H.C. and CRUESS, W.V. 1936B. A note on the spoilage of sweet wine. Fruit Prod. J. *15*, 310.

DOUGLAS, H.C. and CRUESS, W.V. 1936C. Sweet wine treatment. Wine Rev. 6 (12) 9-10.

DOUGLAS, H.C. and MCCLUNG, L.S. 1937. Characteristics of an organism causing spoilage in fortified sweet wines. Food Res. 2, 471-475.

D'ESTIVAUX. 1935. Sur un développement intense du microbe de la tourne dans un milieu très alcoolique. Ann. Fals. Fraudes 28, 288-291.

DUCLAUX, E. 1898-1901. Traité de Microbiologie, Vol. 4. Masson, Paris.

DUPUY, P. 1957A. Une nouvelle altération bactérienne dans les vins de liqueur. Ann. Technol. Agric. 6, 93-102.

DUPUY, P. 1957B. Les facteurs du développement de l'acescence dans le vin. Ibid. 6, 391-407.

FELL, G. 1961. Étude sur la fermentation malolactique du vin et les possibilités de la provoquer par ensemencement. Land. Jahr. Schweiz 75, 249-264.

FEVRIER, F. 1926. A bacterial diesease of wine. J. Dept. Agric. Union S. Afr. 12, 120-122.

FLESCH, P. and HOLBACH, B. 1965. Zum Abbau der L-Äpfelsäure durch Milchsäurebakterien. I. Über die Malat-abbauenden Enzyme des Bakterium "L" unter besonderer Berücksichtigung der Oxalessigsäure Decarboxylase. Arch. Mikrobiol. 51, 401-413.

FORNACHON, J.C.M. 1936. A bacterium causing "disease" in fortified wines. Austr. J. Exp. Biol. Med. Sci. 14, 214-222.

FORNACHON, J.C.M. 1943. Bacterial Spoilage of Fortified Wines. Austr. Wine Board, Adelaide.

FORNACHON, J.C.M. 1957. The occurrence of malo-lactic fermentation in Australian wines. Austr. J. Appl. Sci. 8, 120-129.

FORNACHON, J.C.M. 1968. Influence of different yeasts on the growth of lactic acid bacteria in wine. J. Sci. Food Agric. 19, 374-378.

FORNACHON, J.C.M., DOUGLAS, H.C. and VAUGHN, R.H. 1940. The pH requirements of some heterofermentative species of Lactobacillus. J. Bacteriol. 40, 644-655.

FORNACHON, J.C.M., DOUGLAS, H.C. and VAUGHN, R.H. 1949. Lactobacillus trichodes nov. spec., a bacterium causing spoilage in appetizer and dessert wines. Hilgardia 19, 129-132.

GARVIE, E.I. 1974. Genus II. Leuconostoc van Tieghem 1878, 198, emend. mut. char. Hucker and Pederson 1930, 66. In Bergey's Manual of Determinative Bacteriology, 8th Edition. R. E. Buchanan and N. E. Gibbons (Editors). Williams & Wilkins Co., Baltimore.

GAYON, V. and DUBOURG, E. 1894. Sur les vins mannités. Ann. Inst. Pasteur 8, 108-116.

GAYON, V. and DUBOURG, E. 1901. Nouvelles recherches sur la ferment mannitique. Ibid. 15, 526-569.

GINI, B. 1959. Characteristics of some bacteria associated with the spoilage of dessert wines. M.A. Thesis, Univ. Calif., Davis.

GINI, B. and VAUGHN, R.H. 1962. Characteristics of some bacteria associated with spoilage of California dessert wines. Am. J. Enol. Vitic. *13*, 20-31.

GOSWELL, R.W. and KUNKEE, R.E. 1977. Fortified Wines. *In* Economic Microbiology, Vol. 1. A. H. Rose (Editor). Academic Press, London.

INGRAHAM, J.L. and COOKE, G.M. 1960. A survey of the incidence of the malo-lactic fermentation in California. Am. J. Enol. Vitic. *11*, 160-163.

INGRAHAM, J.L., VAUGHN, R.H. and COOKE, G.M. 1960. Studies on the malo-lactic organisms isolated from California wines. Am. J. Enol. Vitic. *11*, 1-4.

JOSLYN, M.A. and AMERINE, M.A. 1964. Dessert, Appetizer and Related Flavored Wines. University of California, Division of Agricultural Sciences, Berkeley.

KAYSER, E. and MANCEAU, E. 1909. Les Ferments de la Graisse des Vins. Henri Villers, Épernay.

KIELHÖFER, E. and WÜRDIG, G. 1963. Die Entsäuerung sehr säurer Traubenmoste durch Ausfällung der Weinsäure und Äpfelsäure als Kalkdoppelsalz. Dtsch. Wein. Zt. Wein Rebe *99*, 1022-1028.

KIELHÖFER, E. and WÜRDIG, G. 1964. Die Doppelsalzentsäuerung sehr säurer Traubenmoste. Wein-Wiss. *19*, 159-168.

KOCH, A. 1900. Ueber die Ursachen des Verschwindens der Säure bei Gärung und Lagerung des Weines. Weinbau Weinhandel *18*, 395-396, 407-408, 417-419.

KOCH, R. 1881. Zur Züchtung von pathogenen Mikro-organismen. Kaiserl. Gesundheitsampte *1*, 4-48.

KORKES, S., DEL CAMPELLO, A. and OCHOA, S. 1950. Biosynthesis of dicarboxylic acids by carbon dioxide fixation. IV. Isolation and properties of an adaptive "malic" enzyme from *Lactobacillus arabinosus*. J. Biol. Chem. *187*, 891-905.

KRUMPERMAN, P.H., BERRY, J.M. and VAUGHN, R.H. 1953. Utilization of tartrate by *Lactobacillus plantarum*. Bacteriol. Proc. *1953*, 24.

KUNKEE, R.E. 1967. Malo-lactic fermentation. Advan. Appl. Microbiol. *9*, 235-279.

KUNKEE, R.E. 1968. Simplified chromatographic procedure for detection of malo-lactic fermentation. Wines Vines *49* (3) 23-24.

KUNKEE, R.E. 1974. Malo-lactic fermentation and winemaking. *In* Chemistry of Winemaking. A. D. Webb (Editor). Advances in Chemistry Series, (137) American Chemical Society, Washington, D.C.

KUNKEE, R.E. 1975. A second enzymatic activity for decomposition of malic acid by malo-lactic bacteria. *In* Lactic Acid Bacteria in Beverages and Foods. J. G. Carr, C. V. Cutting and G. C. Whiting (Editors). Academic Press, London.

KUNKEE, R.E. and GOSWELL, R.W. 1977. Table Wine. *In* Economic Microbiology, Vol. 1. A. H. Rose (Editor). Academic Press, London.

KUNKEE, R.E., PILONE, G.J. and COMBS, R.E. 1965. The occurrence of malo-lactic fermentation in Southern California wines. Am. J. Enol. Vitic. *16*, 219-223.

LABORDE, J. 1904. Sur le ferment de la maladie des vins poussés et tournés. Compt. Rend. *138*, 228-231.

LAFON-LAFOURCADE, S. 1973. De la fermentation malolactique des vins: intéraction levures-bactéries. Conn. Vigne Vin *6*, 203-207.

LAFON-LAFOURCADE, S. 1975. Factors of the malo-lactic fermentation of wine. *In* Lactic Acid Bacteria in Beverages and Foods. J. G. Carr, C. V. Cutting and G. C. Whiting (Editors). Academic Press, London.

LÜTHI, H.R. 1957. Symbiotic problems relating to bacterial deterioration of wines. Am. J. Enol. Vitic. *8*, 176-181.

MAESTRO PALÓ, F. 1952. Defectos y Enfermedades de los Vinos. Tip. "La Académica," Zaragoza.

MEYRATH, J. and LÜTHI, H.R. 1969. On the metabolism of hexoses and pentoses by *Leuconostoc* isolated from wines and fruit juices. Lebensm. Wiss. Technol. *2*, 21-27.

MILISAVLEJOV, D. 1964. Méthodes d'isolément, de culture et de classification des bactéries malolactiques. Bull. Off. Intern. Vin. *37*, 374-384.

MORENZONI, R.A. 1973. A second enzymatic malic acid decomposing activity in *Leuconostoc oenos*. Ph.D. Thesis, University of California, Davis.

MORENZONI, R.A. 1974. The enzymology of malo-lactic fermentation. *In* Chemistry of Winemaking. A. D. Webb (Editor). Advances in Chemistry Series, (137) American Chemical Society, Washington, D.C.

MÜLLER-THURGAU, H. and OSTERWALDER, A. 1912. Die Bakterien im Wein und Obstwein und die dadurch verursachten Veränderungen. Zentr. Bakteriol. Parasitenk. Abt. II *36*, 129-338.

MÜLLER-THURGAU, H. and OSTERWALDER, A. 1918. Weitere Beiträge zur Kenntnis der Mannitbakterien im Wein. *Ibid. 48*, 1-35.

MÜLLER-THURGAU, H. and OSTERWALDER, A. 1919. Ueber die durch bakterien verursachte Zersetzung von Weinsäure und Glyzerin im Wein. Land. Jahr. Schweiz. *33*, 313-371.

MÜNZ, T. 1960. Die Bildung des Ca-Doppelsalzes der Wein- und Äpfelsäure, die Möglichkeiten Seiner Fällung durch $CaCO_3$ im Most. Weinberg Keller *7*, 239-247.

NICKLES, J. 1862. Sur le vin tourné. Compt. Rend. *54*, 1219-1220.

NIEHAUS, C.J. 1930. The principal South African Wine diseases. Farming S. Afr. *4*, 475-476, 521-522, 526.

NIEHAUS, C.J. 1932. Mannitic bacteria in South African sweet wines. Farming S. Afr. *4*, 443-444.

OLSEN, E. 1948. Studies of bacteria in Danish fruit wines. Antonie van Leeuwenhoek J. Microbiol. Serol. *14*, 1-28.

ORLA-JENSEN, S. 1919. The lactic acid bacteria. Kgl. Danske Videnskab. Selskabs. Skritter Naturvidenskab. Math. Afdel *5* (8) 81-196.

PASTEUR, L. 1864. Étude sur les vins. Compt. Rend. *58*, 142-150.

PASTEUR, L. 1873A. Études sur le Vin, 2nd Edition. F. Savy, Paris.

PASTEUR, L. 1873B. Étude sur le vinaigre et sur le vin. *In* Oeuvres de Pasteur. III. Masson et Cie., Paris. 1924.

PEYNAUD, E. 1936. L'acétate d'éthyl dans les vins atteints d'acescence. Ann. Ferment. *2*, 367-384.

PEYNAUD, E. 1937. Études sur les phénomènes d'estérification dans les vins. Rev. Viticult. *86*, 209-215, 227-231, 248-253, 299-301, 394-396, 420-423, 440-444, 472-475; *87*, 49-52, 113-116, 185-188, 242-249, 278-285, 297-301, 344-350, 362-364, 383-385.

PEYNAUD, E. and DOMERCQ, S. 1961. Études sur les bactéries lactiques des vins. Ann. Technol. Agric. *10*, 43-60.

PEYNAUD, E. and DOMERCQ, S. 1968. Étude de quatre cent souches de coques hétérolactiques isolés de vins. Ann. Inst. Pasteur-Lille *19*, 159-169.

PILONE, G.J. 1967. Effect of lactic acid on volatile acid determination of wine. Am. J. Enol. Vitic. *18*, 149-156.

PILONE, G.J. 1975. Control of malo-lactic fermentation in table wines by addition of fumaric acid. *In* Lactic Acid Bacteria in Beverages and Foods. J. G. Carr, C. V. Cutting and G. C. Whiting (Editors). Academic Press, London.

PILONE, G.J. and KUNKEE, R.E. 1965. Sensory characterization of wines fermented with several malo-lactic strains of bacteria. Am. J. Enol. Vitic. *16*, 224-230.

PILONE, G.J. and KUNKEE, R.E. 1970. Carbonic acid from decarboxylation by "malic" enzyme in lactic acid bacteria. J. Bacteriol. *103*, 404-409.

PILONE, G.J. and KUNKEE, R.E. 1972. Characterization and energetics of *Leuconostoc oenos* ML 34. Am. J. Enol. Vitic. *23*, 61-70.

PILONE, G.J. and KUNKEE, R.E. 1976. Stimulatory effect of malo-lactic fermentation on the growth rate of *Leuconostoc oenos.* Appl. Environ. Microbiol. *32*, 405-408.

PUKRUSHPAN, L. 1976. The role of L-malic acid in the metabolism of malo-lactic bacteria, Ph.D. Thesis, University of California, Davis.

QUINN, D.G. 1940. Sulfur dioxide: Its use in the winery. J. Dept. Agric. Victoria *38*, 200-204.

RADLER, F. 1958A. Untersuchung des biologischen Säureabbaus im Wein. III. Die Energiequelle der Äpfelsäure-abbauenden Bakterien. Arch. Mikrobiol. *31*, 224-230.

RADLER, F. 1958B. Untersuchung des biologischen Säureabbaus im Wein. II. Isolierung und Charakterisierung von Äpfelsäure-abbauenden Bakterien. Arch. Mikrobiol. *30*, 64-72.

RADLER, F. 1962. Über die Milchsäurebakterien des Weines und den biologischen Säureabbau. I. Systematik und chemische Grundlagen. Vitis *3*, 144-176.

RADLER, F. 1966. Die mikrobiologischen Grundlagen des Säureabbaus im

Wein. Zentr. Bakteriol. Parasitenk. Abt. II *120*, 237-287.

RADLER, F. and YANNISSIS, C. 1972. Weinsäureabbau bei Milchsäurebakterien. Arch. Mikrobiol. *82*, 219-239.

RANKINE, B.C. 1972. Influence of yeast strain and malo-lactic fermentation on composition and quality of table wines. Am. J. Enol. Vitic. *23*, 152-158.

RANKINE, B.C. 1977. Developments in malo-lactic fermentation of Australian red table wine. Am. J. Enol. Vitic. *28*, 27-33.

RANKINE, B.C., FORNACHON, J.C.M., and BRIDSON, D.A. 1969. Diacetyl in Australian dry red wines and its significance in wine quality. Vitis *8*, 129-134.

RANKINE, B.C., FORNACHON, J.C.M., BRIDSON, D.A. and CELLIER, K.M. 1970. Malo-lactic fermentation in Australian dry red wines. J. Sci. Food Agric. *21*, 471-476.

RIBÉREAU-GAYON, J. 1938. Les bactéries du vin et les transformations qu'elles produisent. Bull. Assoc. Chim. de Sucr. et de Distill. de France et des Colon. *55*, 601-656.

RIBÉREAU-GAYON, J. 1946. Sur la fermentation de l'acide malique dans les grands vins rouges. Bull. Off. Intern. Vin *19* (182) 26-29.

RIBÉREAU-GAYON, J., and PEYNAUD, E. 1938. Bilan de la fermentation malo-lactique. Ann. Ferment. *4*, 559-569.

RIBÉREAU-GAYON, J. and PEYNAUD, E. 1961. Traité d'OEnologie, Vol 2. Béranger, Paris.

RIBÉREAU-GAYON, J., PEYNAUD, E., RIBÉREAU-GAYON, P. and SUDRAUD, P. 1975. Traité d'OEnologie, Sciences et Techniques du Vin, Vol. 2. Dunod, Paris.

ROGOSA, M. 1974. *Genus I*. Lactobacillus *Beijerinck 1901, 212. Num. cons. Opin. 38, Jud. Comm. 1971, 104. In* Bergey's Manual of Determinative Bacteriology, 8th Edition. R.E. Buchanan and N.E. Gibbons (Editors). Williams & Wilkins Co., Baltimore.

SCHANDERL, H. 1959. Die Mikrobiologie des Mostes und Weines. Eugen Ulmer, Stuttgart.

SCHÜTZ, M., and RADLER, F. 1973. Das "Malatenzym" von *Lactobacillus plantarum* und *Leuconostoc mesenteroides*. Arch. Mikrobiol. *91*, 183-202.

SÉMICHON, L. 1905. Maladies des Vins. Librairie Coulet, Montpellier.

SHIMWELL, J.L. 1941. The lactic bacteria of beer. Wallerstein Lab. Commun. *4*, 41-48.

SINGLETON, V.L. and OUGH, C.S. 1962. Complexity of flavor and blending of wines. J. Food Sci. *27*, 189-196.

SNELL, E.E. 1946. The nutritional requirements of the lactic acid bacteria and their application to biochemical research. J. Bacteriol. *50*, 373-382.

SOZZI, T., MARET, R. and POULIN, J.M. 1976. Mise en évidence de bactériophages dans le vin. Experientia *32*, 568-569.

STAMER, J.R. and STOYLA, B.O. 1970. Growth stimulation in plant extracts for *Leuconostoc citrovorum*. Appl. Microbiol. *20*, 672-676.

SUVERKROP, B. and TCHELISTCHEFF, A. 1949. Malo-lactic fermentation in California wines. Wines Vines *30* (7) 19-23.

TANNER, H. and VETSCH, U. 1956. How to characterize cloudiness in beverages. Am. J. Enol. *7*, 145-146.

VAUGHN, R.H. 1938. Some effects of association and competition on *Acetobacter*. J. Bacteriol. *36*, 357-367.

VAUGHN, R.H. 1942. The acetic bacteria. Wallerstein Lab. Commun. *5*, 5-26.

VAUGHN, R.H. 1955. Bacterial spoilage of wines. Advan. Food Res. *6*, 67-108.

VAUGHN, R.H., DOUGLAS, H.C. and FORNACHON, J.C.M. 1949. The taxonomy of *Lactobacillus hilgardii* and related heterofermentative lactobacilli. Hilgardia *19*, 133-139.

VAUGHN, R.H. and TCHELISTCHEFF, A. 1957. Studies on the malic acid fermentation of California table wines. Am. J. Enol. *8*, 74-79.

VERONA, O. and FLORENZANO, G. 1956. Microbiologia Applicata all'Industria Enologica. Edizioni Agricole, Bologna.

VOISENET, E. 1910. Nouvelles recherches sur les vins amers et la fermentation acrylique de la glycérine. Compt. Rend. *151*, 518-520.

VOISENET, E. 1918. Sur une bactérie de l'eau végétant dans les vins amers capable de deshydrater la glycérine. Glycéro-réaction. Ann. Inst. Pasteur *32*, 476-510.

WEILLER, H.G. and RADLER, F. 1970. Milchsäurebakterien aus Wein und von Rebenblättern. Zentr. Bakteriol. Parasitenk. Abt. II. *124*, 707-732.

WEILLER, H.G. and RADLER, F. 1972. Vitamin- und Aminosäurebedarf von Milchsäurebakterien aus Wein und von Rebenblättern. Mitt. Klosterneuburg *22*, 4-18.

WOOD, H.G., GEIGER, C. and WERKMAN, C.H. 1940. Nutritive requirements of the heterofermentative lactic acid bacteria. Iowa State Coll. J. Sci. *14*, 367-378.

YOSHIZUMI, H. 1975. A malo-lactic bacterium and its growth factor. *In* Lactic Acid Bacteria in Beverages and Foods. J.G. Carr, C.V. Cutting and G.C. Whiting (Editors). Academic Press, London.

17

Brandy Production

Since at least the Middle Ages wine has been distilled to concentrate the alcohol to a higher percentage than occurred in the original wine.[1] These wine distillates have been called *aqua vini, eaux-de-vie, Weinbrand,* Cognac, *Branntwein, aquardiente, aquavit,* and in English-speaking countries, brandy. For general information on brandy, see Amerine and Winkler (1938), Büttner (1938), Chaminade (1930), Dujardin (1955), Hartmann (1955), Hirsch (1936), Joslyn and Amerine (1941), Pieper *et al.* (1977), Ricciardelli (1909), Rocques (1913), Stanciulescu *et al.* (1975), Suomalainen *et al.* (1968), U.S. Treasury Department (1977), Valaer (1939), Wüstenfeld and Haesler (1964), and Xandri (1958).

DEFINITIONS

In the United States, with which this book is primarily concerned, spirits distilled from wine are classified as follows (U.S.Treasury Department 1977):

Sec. 5.22. Standards of Identity. (d) Class 4: *brandy.*
"Brandy" is an alcoholic distillate from the fermented juice, mash, or wine of fruit, or from the residue thereof, produced at less than 190° proof in such manner that the distillate possesses the taste, aroma, and characteristics generally attributed to the product, and bottled at not less than 80° proof. Brandy, or mixtures thereof, not conforming to any of the standards in subparagraphs (1) through (8) of this paragraph shall be designated as "brandy," and such designation shall be immediately followed by a truthful and adequate statement of composition.

---

[1]The Chinese may have discovered distillation at a very early period according to Simmonds (1919). Needham (1954), however, doubts this. Alchemists were distilling wine in the 13th century and Shakespeare refers to it in Othello (Act II, Scene 3): "O thou invisible spirit of wine, if thou hast no name to be known by, let us call thee devil." See Egloff and Lowry (1929) for further information on ancient methods of distillation.

(1) "Fruit brandy" is brandy distilled solely from the fermented juice or mash of whole, sound, ripe fruit, or from standard grape, citrus, or other fruit wine, with or without the addition of not more than 20 percent by weight of the pomace of such juice or wine, or 30 percent by volume of the lees of such wine, or both (calculated prior to the addition of water to facilitate fermentation or distillation). Fruit brandy shall include mixtures of such brandy with not more than 30 percent (calculated on a proof gallon basis) of lees brandy. Fruit brandy, derived from grapes, shall be designated as "grape brandy" or "brandy," except that in the case of brandy (other than neutral brandy, pomace brandy, marc brandy or grappa brandy) distilled from the fermented juice, mash, or wine of grapes, or the residue thereof, which has been stored in oak containers for less than 2 years, the statement of class and type shall be immediately preceded, in the same size and kind of type, by the word "immature." Fruit brandy, other than grape brandy, derived from one variety of fruit, shall be designated by the word "brandy" qualified by the name of such fruit (for example "peach brandy"), except that "apple brandy" may be designated "applejack." Fruit brandy derived from more than one variety of fruit shall be designated as "fruit brandy" qualified by a truthful and adequate statement of composition.

(2) "Cognac," or "Cognac (grape) brandy," is grape brandy distilled in the Cognac region of France, which is entitled to be so designated by the laws and regulations of the French Government.

(3) "Dried fruit brandy" is brandy that conforms to the standard for fruit brandy except that it has been derived from sound, dried fruit, or from the standard wine of such fruit. Brandy derived from raisins, or from raisin wine, shall be designated as "raisin brandy." Other brandies shall be designated in the same manner as fruit brandy from the corresponding variety or varieties of fruit except that the name of the fruit shall be qualified by the word "dried."

(4) "Lees brandy" is brandy distilled from the lees of standard grape, citrus, or other fruit wine, and shall be designated as "lees brandy," qualified by the name of the fruit from which such lees are derived.

(5) "Pomace brandy," or "marc brandy," is brandy distilled from the skin and pulp of sound, ripe grapes, citrus or other fruit, after the withdrawal of the juice or wine therefrom, and shall be designated as "pomace brandy," or "marc brandy," qualifed by the name of the fruit from which derived. Grape pomace brandy may be designated as "grappa" or "grappa brandy."

(6) "Residue brandy" is brandy distilled wholly or in part from the fermented residue of fruit or wine, and shall be designated as "residue brandy" qualified by the name of the fruit from which derived. Brandy distilled wholly or in part from residue materials which conforms to any of the standards set forth in subparagraphs (1), (3), (4), and (5) of this paragraph may, regardless of such fact, be designated "residue brandy," but the use of such designation shall be conclusive, precluding any later change of designation.

(7) "Neutral brandy" is brandy produced at more than 170° proof and shall be designated in accordance with the standards in this paragraph, except that the designation shall be qualified by the word "neutral," for example, "neutral citrus residue brandy."

(8) "Substandard brandy" shall bear as a part of its designation the word "substandard," and shall include:

(i) Any brandy distilled from fermented juice, mash, or wine having a volatile acidity, calculated as acetic acid and exclusive of sulfur dioxide, in excess of 0.20 gram per 100 cubic centimeters (20°C.); measurements of volatile acidity shall be calculated exclusive of water added to facilitate distillation.

(ii) Any brandy which has been distilled from unsound, moldy, diseased, or decomposed juice, mash, wine, lees, pomace, or residue, or which shows in the finished product any taste, aroma, or characteristic associated with products distilled from such material.

(e) Class 5: *blended applejack.* "Blended applejack" (applejack—a blend) is a mixture which contains at least 20 percent of apple brandy (applejack) on a proof gallon basis, stored in oak containers for not less than 2 years, and not more than 80 percent of neutral spirits on a proof gallon basis if such mixture at the time of bottling is not less than 80° proof.

(i) Class 9: *flavored brandy, flavored gin, flavored rum, flavored vodka,* and *flavored whisky.* "Flavored brandy," "flavored gin," "flavored rum," "flavored vodka," and "flavored whisky" are brandy, gin, rum, vodka, and whisky, respectively, to which have been added natural flavoring materials, with or without the addition of sugar, and bottled at not less than 70° proof. The name of the predominant flavor shall appear as a part of the designation. If the finished product contains more than 2½ percent by volume of wine, the kinds and percentages by volume of wine must be stated as a part of the designation, except that a flavored brandy may contain an additional 12½ percent by volume of wine, without label disclosure, if the additional wine is derived from the particular fruit corresponding to the labeled flavor of the product.

(j) Class 10: *imitations.* Imitations shall bear, as a part of the designation thereof, the word "imitation" and shall include the following:

(1) Any class or type of distilled spirits to which has been added coloring or flavoring material of such nature as to cause the resultant product to stimulate any other class or type of distilled spirits;

(2) Any class or type of distilled spirits (other than distilled spirits required under Sec. 5.35 to bear a distinctive or fanciful name and a truthful and adequate statement of composition) to which has been added flavors considered to be artificial or imitation. In determining whether a flavor is artificial or imitation, recognition will be given to what is considered to be "good commercial practice" in the flavor manufacturing industry;

(3) Any class or type of distilled spirits (except cordials, liqueurs and specialties marketed under labels which do not indicate or imply, that a particular class or type of distilled spirits was used in the manufacture thereof) to which has been added any whisky essence, brandy essence, rum essence, or similar essence or extract which simulates or enhances, or is used by the trade or in the particular product to simulate or enhance, the characteristics of any class or type of distilled spirits; . . .

(k) Class 11: *geographical designation.* (1) Geographical names for distinctive types of distilled spirits (other than names found by the Director under subparagraph (2) of this paragraph to have become generic) shall not be applied to distilled spirits produced in any other place than the particular region indicated by the name, unless (i) in direct conjunction with the name there appears the word "type" or the word "American" or some other adjective indicating the true place of production, in lettering substantially as conspicuous as such name, and (ii) the distilled spirits to which the name is applied conform to the distilled spirits of that particular region. The following are examples of distinctive types of distilled spirits with geographical names that have not become generic: Eau de Vie Dantzig (Danziger Foldwasser), Ojen, Swedish punch. Geographical names for distinctive types of distilled spirits shall be used to designate only distilled spirits conforming to the standard of identity, if any, for such type specified in this section, or if no such standard is so specified, then in accordance with the trade understanding of that distinctive type.

(2) Only such geographic names for distilled spirits as the Director finds have by usage and common knowledge lost their geographical significance to such extent that they have become generic shall be deemed to have become generic. Examples are London dry gin, Geneva (Holland) gin.

(3) Geographical names that are not names for distinctive type of distilled spirits, and that have not become generic, shall not be applied to distilled spirits produced in any other place than the particular place or region indicated in the name. Examples are Cognac, Armagnac, Greek brandy, Pisco brandy, Jamaica rum, Puerto Rico rum, Demerara rum.

Sec. 5.23: Alteration of class and type.

(a) *Additions.* (1) The addition of any coloring, flavoring, or blending materials to any class and type of distilled spirits, except as otherwise provided in this section, alters the class and type thereof and the product shall be appropriately designated.

(2) There may be added to any class or type of distilled spirits, without changing the class or type thereof, (i) such harmless coloring, flavoring, or blending materials as are an essential component part of the particular class or type of distilled spirits to which added, and (ii) harmless coloring, flavoring, or blending materials such as caramel, straight malt or straight rye malt whiskies, fruit juices, sugar, or wine, which are not an essential component part of the particular distilled spirits to which added, but which are customarily employed therein in accordance with established trade usage, if such coloring, flavoring, or blending materials do not total more than 2½ percent by volume of the finished product.

(3) "harmless coloring, flavoring, and blending materials" shall not include (i) any material which would render the product to which it is added an imitation, or (ii) any material whatsoever in the case of neutral spirits or straight whisky, or (iii) any material, other than caramel and sugar, in the case of Cognac brandy.

(b) *Extractions.* The removal from any distilled spirits of any constituents to such an extent that the product does not possess the taste, aroma, and characteristics generally attributed to that class or type of distilled spirits alters the class and type thereof, and the product shall be appropriately redesignated. In addition, in the case of straight whisky the removal of more than 15 percent of the fixed acids, or volatile acids, or esters, or soluble solids, or higher alcohols, or more than 25 percent of the soluble color, shall be deemed to alter the class or type thereof.

(c) *Exceptions.* This section shall not be construed as in any manner modifying the standards of identity for cordials and liqueurs, flavored brandy, flavored gin, flavored rum, flavored vodka, and flavored whisky or as authorizing any product which is defined in Sec. 5.22(j), Class 10, as an imitation to be otherwise designated.

In practice, two types of spirits are prudced from wine or wine residue materials. Beverage brandy is distilled at 170° proof or lower from the fermented juice or mash of whole fruit; it is typically reduced to 102° to 130° proof for at least 2 years of aging in oak and further to 80° to 100° proof for bottling. "Wine spirits" (formerly called "fortifying brandy") includes all spirits eligible for addition to wines, and comprises three standards of identity for distillation: (a) neutral spirits (190° or more proof); (b) neutral brandy (171°−189° proof); and (c) brandy (170° proof or less but not less than 140° proof). For further information on legal restrictions see Chap. 20.

Ethanol Content

The ethanol (ethyl alcohol) concentration of distilled spirits is expressed differently in various countries. In Germany, percent alcohol by weight (g per 100 g) is used. In France, percent by volume (ml per 100 ml) at 15°C (59°F) is official. In other countries, percent by volume is most often determined at 15.56°C (60°F).

In England and the United States, proof is commonly used but the definition varies in the two countries. In the United States the official definition is: " 'proof' shall mean the ethyl alcohol content of a liquid at 60°F, stated as twice the percent ethyl alcohol by volume." In addition " 'proof spirits' shall mean that alcoholic liquor which contains 50 percent of ethyl alcohol by volume at 60°F and which has a specific gravity of 0.93418 in air at 60°F referred to water at 60°F as unity." From this, "proof gallon" is defined as "the alcohol equivalent of a United States gallon at 60°F, containing 50 percent of ethyl alcohol by volume." In England, proof is measured by Sike's alcohol hydrometer so that "proof spirit" contains 49.28 alcohol by weight or 57.10% by volume at 15.56°C (60°F). For alcohol percentages below "proof spirit" the proof is expressed as "under proof" and above 57.10% as "over proof."

The approximate alcoholic strength by different systems is summarized in Table 17.1. These values are not entirely interchangeable owing to the use of slightly different values for the specific gravity of alcohol and to varying calibration temperatures.

TABLE 17.1. ALCOHOL STRENGTHS BY DIFFERENT SYSTEMS

Italy, Austria, U.S.S.R., U.S.	United States	Great Britain	France, Belgium	Germany	Specific Gravity	Cartier[1]
Percent by Vol 15.56°C (60°F)	Proof 15.56°C (60°F)	Proof 15.56°C (60°F)	Percent by Vol 15°C (59°F)	Percent by Wt 15°C (59°F)	15.56°C (60°F)	15°C (59°F)
0.0	0.0	100 u.p.[2]	0.00	0.0	1.0000	10.03
5.0	10.0	91.3 u.p.	4.90	4.0	0.9928	10.97
10.0	20.0	82.5 u.p.	9.85	8.0	0.9866	11.82
15.0	30.0	73.8 u.p.	14.81	12.0	0.9810	12.57
20.0	40.0	65.1 u.p.	19.57	16.2	0.9759	13.25
30.0	60.0	47.6 u.p.	29.78	24.5	0.9653	14.73
40.0	80.0	30.0 u.p.	39.78	33.4	0.9517	16.66
50.0	100.0	12.3 u.p.	49.78	42.3	0.9342	19.25
57.1	114.2	Proof	56.80	49.1	0.9197	21.46
60.0	120.0	5.0 o.p.[3]	59.73	52.0	0.9133	22.46
70.0	140.0	22.5 o.p.	69.83	62.3	0.8899	26.26

Source of data: Office International de la Vigne et du Vin (1963).
[1]Now used only in Switzerland.
[2]Under proof.
[3]Over proof.

BRANDY TYPES

Brandy is produced from wine in many parts of France. Some of it is for industrial use. A small amount is used for fortifying dessert wines. That produced for beverage purposes may be divided into the following classes: Cognac, Armagnac, *eaux-de-vie*, and *eaux-de-vie de marc*. Brandy is also produced in most other wine-producing countries.

Cognac

This brandy can be produced in France only in the Departments of Charente and Charente Maritime (with a small acreage in Deux Sèvres and Dordogne). The right to the name is limited by law by the United States, Germany, Cuba, Denmark, Italy, Switzerland, etc., to brandy produced in this region of France. From 1933 to 1971 production of Cognac varied from about 0.7 million to 16 million gallons (as pure alcohol), averaging nearly 5 million, per year. Sales also vary from year to year as the figures for the years from 1933 to 1971 show (as gallons of pure alcohol):

	Minimum	Maximum	Average
France	342,408	1,617,949[1]	694,737
Export[2]	188,549[3]	7,046,529	2,415,800

Source of data: Lafon *et al.* (1973).
[1]Includes some W.W. II shipments to Germany.
[2]Includes shipments of wines fortified to 22% alcohol.
[3]Low values are for 1943−1944.

The vineyard acreage (204,436 in 1970, of which 94% was bearing) of the departments is subdivided into the districts of Grande Champagne 12.8%, Petite Champagne 13.9, Borderies 4.0, Fin Bois 36.2, Bons Bois 24.8, and Bois Ordinaires 8.3 (Fig. 17.1.). All are entitled to produce wine which, when distilled, may be labeled Cognac. The soils of these regions differ in their calcium carbonate content. The prices paid for wines or brandies from the first two districts are always higher than those of the others. Cognacs produced from these districts are also entitled to the appellation "fine champagne." Fine champagne is a blend of at least 50% Grande Champagne and Petite Champagne (Anon. 1978).

Courtesy of Goguet, Cognac

FIG. 17.1. HARVESTING SCENE IN COGNAC VINEYARD

The predominant variety is Saint Émilion (also called Trebbiano in Italy or Ugni blanc in the south of France) with lesser amounts of Colombar (called French Colombard in this country) and Folle Blanche. Because of its greater resistance to botrytis, Saint Émilion has gradually replaced Folle Blanche. Variety *per se* is usually not a critical factor in brandy quality. The cool climate of the region limits ripening so that the wines for distillation have a relatively low alcohol content. Lafon *et al.* (1973) found the alcohol varied from 6.1 to 12.0% with an average for the 34 years from 1936 to 1969 of 9.0. Between 1900 and 1920 the average was 7.9%.

The grapes are pressed immediately after crushing as fermentation on the skins produces less desirable wines for distillation. Moldy grapes constitute a difficult problem in certain years and, besides removing the fruit with more rot, special care in pressing, settling, etc., is taken in these seasons. Lafon *et al.* (1973) stress the following quality factors: no late vineyard sulfuring, no botrytis on the fruit, high must fixed acidity, clean fermentation (pure yeast cultures are not used), little or no sulfur dioxide, little press wine, low alcohol, removal of seeds and dry stems, low wine volatile acidity, and storage of the wine in the absence of air.

Distillation starts immediately after the vintage and continues until all the newly fermented wine is distilled. All authorities emphasize the use of wine which has been stored for as short a time as possible, and which must not be oxidized. Normally, only direct-fired pot stills of small capacity, not over 30 hl (792 gal.) are employed (p. 604). The new wine (with its lees, but with not more than 8% of added lees) is placed in the still and brought to boiling. The distillation continues until the vapor contains negligible alcohol. The distillation takes eight or more hours and the main distillate *(brouillis* or low wines) contains about 24 to 32% alcohol. A tails fraction may be separated. The still is then emptied, refilled with fresh wine (and, also, often with the "tails" of the previous distillation) and a second distillation made. A third distillation is also made. The three main distillates are finally combined and then redistilled. This last distillation takes longer than the original distillations—14 or more hours. About 1–2% heads are separated. The main distillate *(coeur)* averages 58 to 60% ethanol and cannot exceed 72%. A tails fraction *(seconde)* is also separated. Continuous tasting and use of an alcohol hydrometer are practiced to control the amount of each fraction. The heads and tails are recycled. Lafon *et al.* (1973) note that individual distillers modify the process in various details, particularly in years of moldy grapes. In some cases, the product of the second distillation is reduced to 26–28% with water and redistilled.

The new brandy is placed in new or reused Limousin or Tronçais oak casks of 275 to 350 liters (72 to 92 gal.) capacity. The oak wood is well dried before being made into casks. New casks are washed several times with water and once with brandy. Before too much tannin is extracted, the brandy is transferred to used casks or tanks. Brandy usually acquires its best quality by 15 to 20 years in the wood. In some cases, this improvement may continue to 40 or even 50 years, but not longer. Older brandies are kept in glass where the rate of aging is negligible.

The important production quality factors are the crus (region of production), method of double distillation and especially its careful execution, and the aging of the brandy in special oak casks. Hennig and Burkhardt (1962) reported a different chromatographic pattern in Cognac compared to German brandies, particularly of higher tannin content (especially of ellagic and gallic acids) and less caramel and sugar. Longer aging in oak containers appeared to be responsible for the differences. For further information on Cognac see Anon. (1947), Chaminade (1930), Delamain (1935), Hartmann (1955), Jackson (1928), Lafon *et al.* (1973), Layton (1968), Prioton (1929), Ravaz (1900), Ray (1974), and Suomalainen *et al.* (1968).

For formulas for making imitation cognac see Xandri (1958). None of these recipes produces an artificial cognac worthy of commercial production in our opinion. Nevertheless, there may be an opportunity for mildly flavored brandy in the hand of a skillful blender.

Armagnac

This brandy is produced in a delimited area in the southwest of France, mainly in the department of Gers. The western portion is called Bas-Armagnac, the central portion *Ténarèze*, and the eastern Haut-Armagnac. The products of these districts are not, however, distinguishable on a quality basis as are those of the Cognac sub-districts. Many Armagnac producers claim to find differences in the quality produced on the different soil types. The climate is cool and is influenced by the proximity of the Atlantic.

Phylloxera caused a change in the varieties planted in this region. The Saint Émilion, as in Cognac, is important. Folle Blanche (there called Picpoul or Piquepoult) has been nearly abandoned and a direct-producer hybrid, Baco 22A, is extensively planted because of its resistance to mildew and anthracnose. Some red grapes are used for wine for distilling. The composition of Armagnacs produced from three varieties has been studied by Flanzy and Jouret (1963) using gas chromatography. The brandy of Folle Blanche was richer in a wider range of esters than those of Saint Émilion or of Baco 22A. Sensory examination showed the Folle Blanche brandy had a better bouquet. No ethyl laurate was found, possibly due to the method of distillation used for Armagnac. They were unable to detect differences in the higher alcohol content of brandies made from the three varieties.

The new preheated wines are distilled in semicontinuous stills of special design, Verdier system (Fig. 17.2). The stripping column has only 5 or 6 plates. The heat is supplied by fire so that some destructive distillation

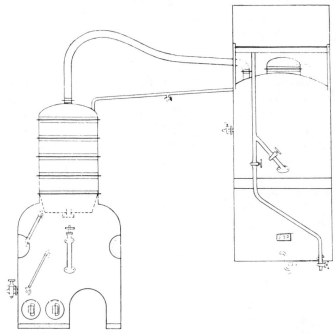

FIG. 17.2. ARMAGNAC–TYPE OF STILL

does occur. The proof of distillation is very low, not exceeding 126°. The brandy is aged in native Gascon oak casks of not over 110 gal. While some Armagnac brandy is aged for 20 or more years, much is sold after only 5 to 8 years' aging. Generally, Armagnac is drier to taste than Cognac and the odor less distinctive. See Gaubert (1946) and Flanzy and Lamazou-Betbeder (1938).

Other Regions

Many other *eaux-de-vie* are produced in France, particularly in the south where continuous stills are used. Pomace brandy (*eaux-de-vie de marc*) occasionally is made in Burgundy, Champagne, and elsewhere. Pot stills are used and the brandy is often aged in glass or paraffined barrels as it is nearly colorless. The aroma is very pungent and one must acquire a taste for it. Flanzy and Lamazou-Betbeder (1938) have shown that marc brandies are very high in their coefficient of nonalcohols (acid plus aldehyde plus ester plus higher alcohols), and especially in aldehydes (indicating that the pomace is not fresh).

Other Countries

Brandy is made in Australia, Bulgaria (Fig. 17.3), Germany (some from imported wine), Greece, Italy, Mexico, Peru, South Africa (Fig. 17.4), the Soviet Union, Spain and elsewhere. Limited amounts from Germany, Greece and Spain are exported to this country. Greek brandies are often sweet and some are flavored. Spanish brandy has the merit of being reasonably uniform (owing to the use of fractional blending systems, p. 407) but they also are often sweet, and the younger types are hot to the taste. Reinhard (1976) reports Greek brandies to be generally lower in 2-methyl-1-propanol and propanol than French or Italian brandies. Iso-amyl alcohol was about the same. The lower 2-methyl-1-propanol and propanol/isoamyl ratio may distinguish Greek and other brandies.

The Spanish brandy industry originated in the region of Jerez de la

Courtesy of Prof. N. Nedeltchev

FIG. 17.3. DISTILLERY IN LIASKOVETS, BULGARIA

Frontera according to Xandri (1958) and much Spanish brandy for local use or for export comes from this region. Some interesting brandies are also produced in the Montilla district south of Cordova. Details of the Spanish regulations are also given by Xandri (1958). Originally direct-fired pot stills were used but an Armagnac-type or continuous column still is now employed. Both new and used oak casks are used for aging. The commercial products vary from 5 to 25 years of age with 80° to 90° proof. Spain also uses wine spirits to produce anise-flavored liqueurs. Italian brandy is also imported into this country. Some appears to be flavored. Italian pomace brandy is called grappa.

We have tested good Soviet brandies, especially from Armenia and Moldavia, but some of their ordinary brandies are hot to the taste. They are producing a series of qualities of brandies (p. 49). The brandies from Mexico (and in Mexico) have not been of superior quality and some were flavored with "oil of cognac." Elena (1941) has given a description of the Argentinean brandy industry. Both pot and continuous stills are employed. She found that many of the products were then made with neutral alcohol and simply flavored and sold without aging.

South Africa has made a major effort to improve the quality of its brandy by use of pot stills and adequate aging (Fig. 17.4). The result is that the South African brandies have been of very pleasant character but are more neutral than those of Cognac. For a discussion of the aging of Australian brandies, see Kluczko (1978).

Courtesy of K.W.V.

FIG. 17.4. DISTILLERY IN SOUTH AFRICA

Note wine being delivered in tank trucks

Peru has long been a producer of brandy. At present these brandies can hardly be called quality products. Muscat and other wines are distilled and the brandy aged in paraffined containers. It does not, therefore, darken with aging. It is called pisco[2] and the samples we have tasted have been hot and hardly worthy of its nineteenth century reputation. Pisco punch, a long drink made with pisco brandy, was popular in California before Prohibition.

California

Brandy has been produced in this state since the Mission days. In the pre-Prohibition period a number of producers distilled wines to produce beverage brandy, some of which achieved a good reputation. Both pot and continuous stills were employed but aging was almost always in new 50 gal. American oak barrels. These were aged for 3 to 10 or 15 years. American regulations made blending difficult but some fairly distinctive types were produced. Grappa, or pomace brandy, was also produced in limited quantities.

Following Prohibition, the pot stills were gradually abandoned and at present nearly all California brandy is produced in continuous column stills. The crop control program of 1938 included compulsory distillation so that a very large amount of brandy was placed in barrels. These brandies were most useful to the industry during and after W.W. II when other alcoholic beverages were in short supply. Production of California brandy has continued to increase since the war. See Table 17.2 for beverage brandy and Table 17.3 for brandy and spirits for addition to wines.

The quality of some of the brandy produced immediately after Repeal was variable because of the poor quality of some of the distilling material used and also because of the erratic operation of some of the stills. At present, both California wine spirits and brandy are produced from wines of the Thompson Seedless, Emperor, and Tokay varieties. Quady and Guymon (1973) reported that wines of French Colombard produced brandies of more distinctive aroma but that those of Thompson Seedless were "significantly better." Late-harvested French Colombard produced wines whose distillates were of lesser quality compared to earlier harvesting. Time of harvest had little effect on distillate quality with Thompson Seedless. Onishi et al. (1978) prepared distillates of wines of Thompson

---

[2]From the Pisco Indians of the Ica Valley who made pottery which, when lined with beeswax, was used to store, age, and transport the brandy, according to Carranza (1939). The port of Pisco got its name from the brandy jars, not vice versa.

TABLE 17.2. BEVERAGE BRANDY PRODUCTION AND INVENTORY IN CALIFORNIA AND UNITED STATES (FIVE-YEAR MEANS OF FISCAL YEARS, JULY–JUNE, IN THOUSANDS OF PROOF GALLONS)

Year(s) July 1–June 30	Production California	U.S. Total	Inventory California[4,7]	U.S. Total[4,6,7]
1950–1955	3111[2]	3813[8]	7245[7]	13156[7,4]
1955–1960	4830[2]	7532[2]	8717[7]	15355[7,4]
1960–1965	6769[2]	9384[2]	13680[7]	21052[7,4]
1965–1970	14038[3]	16392[3]	27170[4]	37536[6,4]
1970–1975	11055[1]	11179[1]	29586[5]	40532[5,6]
1975–1976	14789[1]	14891[1]	32178[1]	45033[1]
1976–1977	15363[1]	15656[1]	34718[1]	48345[1]

Sources:
[1] Wine Institute Economic Research Report (WIERR) (1976) Part 1, Table 13 (excludes neutral brandy) and Wine Institute Bulletin 77-10.
[2] 1950–1963 data from Wine Institute Bulletin (WIB) 1318, Part 1, March 26, 1965. Segregation into beverage and nonbeverage estimated. Only beverage estimate is shown.
[3] 1963–1970 data from WIERR July 16, 1970, Table 10. Segregation into beverage and nonbeverage (neutral) not available. Almost entirely grape brandy mostly for use as beverage brandy.
[4] From Wine Institute Bulletins 967, 1137, 1201, 1310, 1399, 1435, 1540, 1592, 1644, 75-16 and 76-9. Includes all material reported as brandy but not material reported as spirits under 190° and spirits 190° and over which were produced from fruits. Segregation into beverage and neutral brandy not available prior to 1971.
[5] Beverage brandy only.
[6] Includes 22944 P.G. imported brandy in 1970. Includes 17250 P.G. imported brandy in 1969.
[7] Statistical Survey (1965). Segregation into beverage brandy and neutral brandy estimated prior to 1964. Only beverage estimate reported.
[8] 1950–1954 vs. total beverage production from W.I.B. 967. Beverage brandy total estimated.

TABLE 17.3. WITHDRAWALS OF BRANDY AND SPIRITS FOR ADDITION TO WINES; UNITED STATES[1] (FISCAL YEARS, JULY–JUNE, IN THOUSANDS OF PROOF GALLONS)

Year(s) July 1–June 30	Brandy	Spirits[2]	Total[3]
1965–70	1362	36233	37594
1970–71	1850	26267	28117
1971–72	2191	35704	37894
1972–73	1000	24419	25419
1973–74	1268	35850	37118
1974–75	312	34791	35103
1975–76	76	36443	36518
1976–77	70	36468	36539

[1] Wine Institute Bulletins 1486, 1540, 1592, 1644, 75-16, 76-9 and 77-10.
[2] Spirits include materials reported as "spirits under 190°" and "spirits 190° and over."
[3] Sum of components is not equal to U.S. total in all cases as a result of rounding of individual figures.

Seedless, Sauvignon blanc, Peverella and French Colombard in a small copper pot still operated in the "Charente" style (p. 591). There was little difference in the gas chromatograms. Sensory panels seemed to prefer French Colombard to Thompson Seedless. They conclude that for California brandies grape variety is of lesser importance than clean low-temperature fermentations, use of fresh wine of immature grapes, good distillation practice and proper aging.

While our bonded brandies and unflavored and flavored brandies are justifiably popular and have a distinctive quality in highballs there is need for development of a smoother brandy for consumption straight. Neutral sweet brandy is not the answer to this problem, in our opinion. (See Table 17.4 for U.S. brandy production and consumption data.)

TABLE 17.4. BEVERAGE BRANDY ENTERING DISTRIBUTION CHANNELS[1,2]
(IN THOUSANDS OF PROOF GALLONS)

Calendar Years	U.S. Produced	Imported	Total	Gallons per Adult Capita
1955–59	3139	1445	4584	0.050
1960–64	4584	1952	6536	0.068
1965–69	7379	2245	9624	0.096
1970–74	9921	2536	12457	0.098
1975[3]	9765	2574	12339	0.092
1976[3]	10654	3475	14129	0.103
1977[3,4]	10616	2815	13431	0.096

[1]Sources: Prepared by Wine Institute from reports of U.S. Treasury Department, Internal Revenue Service, and U.S. Department of Commerce, Bureau of the Census.
[2]For population of age 21 years and over.
[3]Calculated from bottled brandy entering distribution channels.

For general information on California and brandies other than French see Hannan and Blumberg (1976), Joslyn and Amerine (1941), Layton (1968), Stanciulescu *et al.* (1975), and Suomalainen *et al.* (1968).

COMPONENTS OF BRANDY

The chief constituent of brandy is, of course, ethanol. But many other volatile compounds are present in grapes or are formed during alcoholic fermentation of grape must (see Chap. 2 and 6). Since these distill with and are not completely separated from the alcohol during distillation they appear in larger or smaller amounts in the distillate. Other components are formed during aging or are extracted from the wood. Finally, some are added to beverage brandy during processing. For further data see Joslyn and Amerine (1964) and Marsh (1965).

Ethanol

Ethanol (ethyl alcohol), C_2H_5OH, is completely miscible with water and forms a constant boiling point mixture with it at 96.0% alcohol by weight (Horsley 1952). It is clear, colorless, inflammable liquid with a density of 0.7939 at 100% alcohol or at 200° proof. During aging of Cognac the ethanol content decreases from about 70 to 60% the first 12 years.

Other Alcohols

Grapes of high pectin content, particularly if moldy, may yield considerable methanol (methyl alcohol). A small amount may be present in the brandy, as methanol has physical properties similar to those of ethanol. Valaer (1939) reported traces to 0.188% (average 0.048) of methanol in 114 samples of California commercial brandy (average proof 103.4°). It is apt to be higher in the brandy if the pomace is present during distillation. Tolu (1962) reported 0.039 to 2.86% methanol (average 1.65) in 37 uncut Piedmont pomace brandies (average 63.5% alcohol). Fruit brandies are higher in methanol than grape brandies.

The fusel oil of brandy is made up of higher alcohols. Their total content is usually less than 0.3% but they constitute an important part of the flavor of brandies. In 31 California commercial brandy distillates (156°–169° proof) Guymon (1970) found 7.4 to 30.0 (mean 17.2) g/100 liters at 100° proof of n-propanol, 6.8 to 25.0 (mean 15.7) of isobutanol and 20.0 to 87.5 (mean 50.8) of combined amyls. sec-Butanol was found in 6 samples, 4 from one distillery, and was considered a negative quality indicator. Valaer reports that amyl alcohol is the principal higher alcohol in the California product. Extensive analysis of fusel oils from different varieties of grapes in California have been made by Webb et al. (1952) and Ikeda et al. (1956). Their analyses are summarized as follows (weight percent):

Component		Thompson Seedless	Emperor	Muscat of Alexandria	Mixed Varieties
1-Propanol	n-Propanol	0.66	5.14	1.07	4.1
2-Butanol	sec-Butanol	0.00[1]	0.40	0.00	4.9
2-Methyl-1-propanol	Isobutanol	6.52	9.77	5.20	18.3
1-Butanol	n-Butanol	0.95	0.55	0.65	1.9
2-Methyl-1-butanol	act-Amyl	15.31	14.00	15.02	9.6
3-Methyl-1-butanol	Isoamyl	67.89	61.38	72.73	54.0
1-Hexanol	n-Hexanol	1.40	1.14	1.49	1.5
2-Phenylethanol	β-Phenethyl	Trace	?[2]	Trace	0.0
Acetate ester		Trace	0.00	0.00	—
Residue (mainly esters)		7.25	7.61	3.85	5.6

[1]May have been removed during washing process.
[2]Distillation discontinued before boiling point of component.

The presence of 2-propanol in wine has been reported by Genevois and Lafon (1958) and others but it is apparently often absent. For a review of the origin and composition of fusel oils, see Brau (1957B), Genevois and Lafon (1957), Thoukis (1958), Ingraham and Guymon (1960), Baraud (1961), and Pfenninger (1963).

The composition of a fusel oil from the distillation of wine made from Muscat of Alexandria raisins was studied by Kepner and Webb (1961). They separated a fraction (15%) with a boiling range higher than 3-methyl-1-butanol. This fraction contained ethyl caprate (25%), ethyl laurate (13), ethyl caprylate (13), 2-phenethyl acetate (12), isoamyl caprate (4), ethyl palmitate (3), isoamyl laurate (3), ethyl pelargonate (2), isoamyl capryate (2), ethyl myristate (1.5) and small amounts of ethyl pentadecanoate, n-propyl caprylate, isobutyl caprylate, isoamyl caproate, act-amyl caprylate, act-amyl caprate, act-amyl laurate and traces of act-amyl caproate, acetic, caproic, caprylic, capric and isovaleric acids and 4% of 1-hexanol. Probably present were n-hexyl acetate, ethyl caproate, isobutyl caprate, ethyl heptanoate, isoamyl myristate, act-amyl myristate, isobutyric acid, heptanoic acid, pelargonic acid, a heptanoate ester and a pelargonate ester. Similar results on the esters and other compounds in Cognac are given by Baraud (1961).

Charro and Simal (1964) have also identified ethyl formate, acetaldehyde, acetal, ethyl acetate, methanol, 2-butanol, 1-propanol and 3-methyl-l-butanol in Spanish brandies. Pomace brandies were especially high in 1-propanol.

The total fusel oil of various brandies analyzed by Valaer (1939) was as follows (grams per hectoliter):

Source	Number of Samples	Proof	Minimum	Maximum	Average
California	114	103.7	14.1	250.0[1]	90.7
California	12	92.3[2]	14.1	77.4	48.5
Cognac	20	84.6	89.8	127.0	103.9
Armagnac	4	84.8	91.5	96.8	94.4
Greek	25	89.1	10.6	121.4	58.0

[1]One sample of 385 omitted.
[2]Apparent proof.

Riffart and Diemair (1944) found Cognacs generally higher in higher alcohols than other European brandies. Bikfalvi and Paszter (1977) also found better quality distillates had more higher alcohols, always contained 2-propanol (isopropanol), moderate amounts of 1-propanol (n-propanol), and 2-methyl-1-butanol (isoamyl) of about 100 mg/liter. If evaporation is taken into account, the higher alcohols do not increase during aging of Cognac according to Lafon et al. (1973). To reduce higher alcohol formation, Guymon (1972) recommended pressing the juice from the skins, less aeration of musts, use of clearer musts, lower fermentation temperatures (> 20°C, 68°F), and use of white grapes.

The fusel oils are of higher boiling points than ethanol and can be separated from it to a large degree during distillation. They tend to collect on certain plates of the distillation column (p. 621). While they are more toxic than ethanol, they are present in brandy in such low concentrations that they cause no danger to the health of the average brandy consumer.

Aldehydes

Aldehydes, chiefly acetaldehyde, are present in small amounts in brandy. Propanal, butyraldehyde, and heptanal have been reported. During distillation and aging some acetaldehyde is produced by the oxidation of ethanol. This reaction is hastened by charcoal or aeration. The aldehyde content of Cognacs increases slowly during aging. The free aldehyde content of Cognacs is reported by Procopio (1958) to be 38 to 112 mg/liter. The range for Italian brandies was 30 to 116. In 31 commercial brandy distillates (156°–169° proof) in California, Guymon (1970) reported 0.3 to 3.8 g/100 liters at 100° proof (mean 1.1) of aldehydes (as acetaldehyde). Ethanol and acetaldehyde react slowly to form acetal, a compound of rather pronounced odor. Lafon et al. (1973) found Cognacs to increase in acetal content to about 20 mg/liter although some contain much more. From the sensory point of view acetals are important because of their screening effect on the undesirable sensory effects of the parent carbonyls.

Furfural is mainly formed during distillation. The acetal in Cognacs varied from 26.5 to 77.5 mg/liter and in young Italian brandies, from 27 to 165, in old 18 to 112. The percentage of the total aldehyde that is combined varies generally from 17 to 28%. Lichev (1976) associated the vanilla flavor of Cognacs with their higher amount of aromatic and higher aldehydes. The aldehyde and furfural content of various brandies analyzed by Valaer (1939) were as follows (g/hl):

Source	Number of Samples	Proof	Aldehydes			Furfural		
			Minimum	Maximum	Average	Minimum	Maximum	Average
California	114	103.7	1.4	24.0	10.7	Trace	5.0[1]	1.7
California	12	92.3[2]	2.3	14.0	7.9	0.4	4.0	1.8
Cognac	20	84.6	6.3	14.0	8.6	1.0	3.0	1.3
Armagnac	4	84.8	8.7	9.5	9.1	0.6	1.0	0.7
Greek	25	89.1	4.0	23.6	13.8	Trace	2.4	1.0

[1]One sample with 48 omitted.
[2]Apparent proof.

Egorov and Borisova (1957) found eight or more aromatic aldehydes in Soviet brandy, including vanillin, coniferyl and syringyl aldehydes, and p-hydroxybenzaldehyde—all apparently from the oak containers. In authentic young Cognacs, Ronkainen et al. (1962) reported these plus isobutyraldehyde, isovaleraldehyde (or act-valeraldehyde), methylglyoxal and glyoxal. These are undoubtedly of importance to the character of the brandy. Guymon and Crowell (1968) found 7 to 13 mg/liter of vanillin, 11 to 21 mg of syringaldehyde and other aromatic compounds in alcoholic extracts of French and American oak wood. Joseph and Marche (1972) also reported coniferyl aldehyde, sinnaldehyde, scopoletine, aesculetin, umbelliferone, β-methylumbelliferone and scopoline in Cognacs aged in wood. Deibner *et al.* (1976) also found increasing aromatic aldehydes in Armagnacs during aging in the wood.

Pisarnitskii *et al.* (1977) found pentane-2-3-dione, acetoin, cyclopentane-1,2-dione, and 5-methylcyclopentane-1,2-dione in oak wood. These passed into the brandy during distillation and improved its aroma.

The acetals of acrolein (3,3-diethoxybutan-2-one) and of diacetyl (1,1, 3-triethoxy-propane) were found in wine distillates by Williams and Strauss (1975): 0−77 mg/liter and 0.25 mg/liter, respectively. When diluted, acid hydrolysis and release of the carbonyls occurred. Neither of the acetals had as much odor as their respective carbonyl.

Esters

During distillation and aging ethanol reacts with acids to form small amounts of esters such as ethyl acetate:

$$C_2H_5OH + CH_3COOH \rightleftarrows CH_3COOC_2H_5 + H_2O$$

Many other esters are also formed during fermentation, distillation, and aging (p. 598). If changes due to evaporation are taken into account, there is little change in total esters in Cognacs during about 12 years, according to Lafon *et al.* (1973). They are responsible for some of the flavor of brandy, the highly volatile esters being associated with the "Cognac" odor (Lichev 1976). Marche and Joseph (1975) found 124 esters in Cognacs.

Among the esters of brandy, ethyl acetate is the most common. Esters of propyl and butyl alcohols have also been reported and in small concentrations are not disagreeable.

In 31 commercial California brandy distillates (156° to 169° proof) Guymon (1970) reported 2.6 to 12.8 (mean 5.7) g/100 liters at 100° proof of total esters (as ethyl acetate). In 7 samples, caprylic (C_8), capric (C_{10}) and lauric (C_{12}) ethyl esters were 0.34, 0.76 and 0.74 g/100 ml at 100° proof respectively. Guymon and Crowell (1972) found the total ethyl esters present in unaged brandy decrease in amount during aging in the wood, particularly ethyl laurate and caprate. Williams (1975) found high concentrations of ethyl *n*-butyrate and ethyl *n*-valerate gave brandy an undesirable "lolly-like" odor. Valaer found amyl acetate in French but not in California brandy (see, however, p. 598). There is some evidence that during aging the volatile ester content increases at the expense of the nonvolatile. The ester content of brandies investigated by Valaer (1939) is summarized below (grams per hectoliter as ethyl acetate):

Source	Number of Samples	Proof	Minimum	Maximum	Average
California	114	103.7	20.2	18.4	68.9
California	12	92.3[1]	17.6	77.4[2]	48.5
Cognac	20	84.6	36.1	58.1	44.3
Armagnac	4	84.8	49.3	59.8	52.8
Greek	25	89.1	7.9	79.2	40.5

[1]Apparent proof.
[2]One sample with 374 omitted.

Other Constituents

Wine contains acetic and lactic acids and small amounts distill into the brandy—usually less than 100 mg/liter of 100° proof brandy. Guymon (1970) found 0.70, 0.59 and 0.24 g/100 liters at 100° proof of caprylic (C_8), capric (C_{10}) and lauric (C_{12}) free fatty acids in 7 California commercial brandy distillates. If spoiled wine is distilled, propionic and butyric acids may be found in the distillate. The total and volatile acid contents of various brandies analyzed by Valaer (1939) were as follows (grams per hectoliter as acetic):

Source	Number of Samples	Proof	Total Acid			Volatile Acid		
			Mini-mum	Maxi-mum	Aver-age	Mini-mum	Maxi-mum	Aver-age
California	114	103.7	4.8	101.0	54.8	4.8	88.0	42.9
California	12	92.3[1]	21.6	86.4	57.0	19.2	64.8	57.2
Cognac	20	84.6	26.4	110.4	51.5	21.0	72.0	34.2
Armagnac	4	84.8	62.4	67.2	64.0	37.8	45.6	41.9
Greek	25	89.1	21.6	103.2	51.9	6.0	70.8	33.8

[1]Apparent proof.

Brandy made from muscat wines often has considerable muscat aroma. Terpenes produce the flowery characteristic of certain brandies (Lichev 1976). When young wines are distilled they usually foam, owing partly to the rapid loss of carbon dioxide. The foam-producing compounds have not been identified (Amerine *et al.* 1942).

Sulfur dioxide, if present in the wine, will distill with the alcohol and be present in the brandy. High proof brandy which is high in sulfur dioxide will dissolve iron and other metals from pumps, pipe lines, and metal storage tanks; therefore, such brandy should not be stored in metal tanks. In oak, the sulfur dioxide oxidizes to sulfuric acid, an undesirable constitutent of beverage brandy. Therefore, it is desirable to control fermentation of must for distilling for beverage brandy by means other than by sulfur dioxide. By special venting of the still, much of the sulfur dioxide can be removed during distillation but the quality suffers.

Ammonia and various nitrogenous degradation products have been reported in distillates. Sulfur from dusts applied to the vines and grapes may be reduced to hydrogen sulfide during fermentation. This may react with alcohols to form mercaptans, compounds of very disagreeable (garlic or skunk) odors. Such wines should be treated before distilling or used only for the production of wine spirits for fortifying. Acrolein is highly toxic, is irritating to the eyes and nose and has a horseradish odor. Rosenthaler and Vegezzi (1955) reported small amounts in Swiss fruit brandies but seldom in brandy distilled from wine or pomace. The amount decreases but does not disappear in storage. It was completely removed by redistillation in a multicolumn still.

Occasionally, brandy has an excessive copper or iron content. Australian brandies contain 0.7 to 12 mg/liter of copper (average 3.4), according to Rankine (1961A). He reported that it can be removed from unaged brandy by treatment with cation-exchange (but not by anion-exchange).

Rankine (1961B) found 0.01 to 0.06 mg/liter of lead (average 0.029) in 37 Australian brandies. For a summary of the composition of many brandies, see Schreier et al. (1979).

Measures of Quality

A minimum nonalcohol content of 280 has been established in France for beverage brandy. The nonalcohol content is the sum of the acidity (as acetic), esters (as ethyl acetate), aldehydes (as acetaldehyde), higher alcohols (as isobutyl) and furfural—all as grams per hectoliter of 100% alcohol. Maltabar (1952) suggests the following standards for brandy: (a) a higher alcohol/ester ratio of two to one, (b) a nonalcohol content of not less than 300, (c) a high oxidation coefficient (amounts of acetal and aldehyde), and (d) a minimum amount of vanillin and coloring substances. Similar standards for Cognac were given by Rocques (1913).

De Vries (1958) determined the approximate amount of volatile minor constituents in spirits by measuring the absorption at 218 mμ. He also determined the fusel oil content. The results were divided as follows:

Group	Fusel Oil mg/100 ml	Absorption 218 mμ
1	≤ 0.30	≤ 0.050
2	$>0.30-\leq0.50$	$>0.050-\leq0.085$
3	$>0.50-\leq1.00$	$>0.085-\leq0.125$
4	>1.00	>0.125

A total of 719 samples were then divided into 2 quality groups by sensory tests. For the more neutral brandies there was a coefficient of correlation of 0.971 between the analytical and sensory data. For samples of high flavor the correlation was less but the overall correlation of the 719 samples was 0.870. See also Margerand and Thellier (1946).

DISTILLATION

As the temperature of a liquid is raised, the mean kinetic energy of its molecules increases and the number and velocity of the molecules escaping from the surface of the liquid become greater—thus increasing the vapor pressure. When the vapor pressure of the liquid equals that of the external (atmospheric) pressure on the liquid surface the liquid "boils." Different substances require varying degrees of heat to raise their temperature one degree, i.e., their specific heat varies—that of alcohol is only about 0.6 compared to water at 1.0. The heat required to change the substance from the liquid state to the vapor state is known as the heat of vaporization. It is approximately the same for substances of similar molecular weights.

In a mixture of gases the pressure exerted by each gas is independent of the pressures of the other gases (Dalton's law). The vapor pressure of a liquid is reduced in proportion to the mol percentage of the dissolved solute (Raoult's law). When the solute is nonvolatile the total pressure of the solvent is reduced; if volatile, the partial pressure of the solvent is lowered. Furthermore, the vapor pressure of the solute is proportional to the mol fraction of the solute in the solution (Henry's law).

The liquid-vapor system of ethanol and water follows the above laws and particularly the phase rule which states that for a given system the number of components (c) plus 2, minus the number of phases (P) is equal to the number of variables (V) which must be fixed for the system to be in equilibrium, without altering the original number of phases present. Pressure, temperature, and concentration are the variables. If two of the variables are specified the value of the third is fixed. Thus, in the usual distilling apparatus the pressure is constant and temperature and concentration are interdependent. At constant pressure there is a definite boiling temperature for each concentration of ethanol and water.

The vapor leaving a water-alcohol boiling mixture contains a higher percentage of ethanol than the original liquid. This is the basis for the separation of ethanol and water by fractional distillation. The nature of the mixture and the method of distillation also affect the degree of separation. Furthermore, binary mixtures may form maximum or minimum boiling point mixtures and thus prevent separation of the two components at lower or higher temperatures. The ethanol-water system has a minimum boiling point at 97.4% ethanol so that separation of the two components above a boiling point of 78.1°C (172.6°F) is impossible at atmospheric pressure. (At reduced pressures the ethanol content of the constant boiling point mixture is higher.)

The ratio between the percentage of ethanol in the vapor and that in the liquid is called the Sorel or k value. It varies according to the ethanolic strength of the liquid as shown in Table 17.5. For further discussion of distillation see Barron (1944), Forbes (1948), Gay (1935), Guymon (1949A), Hanson (1948), Hausbrand (1925), Horsley (1952), Kirschbaum (1960), Klimovskii and Stabnikov (1950), Lafon et al. (1973), McCabe and Smith (1967), Mariller (1948), Meloni (1952–1958), Monier-Williams (1922), Robinson and Gilliland (1950), Simmonds (1919), Van Winkle (1967), Villa (1946), Walker et al. (1937), Willkie and Prochaska (1943), Wüstenfeld and Haeseler (1964) and Young (1922).

Pot Stills

Originally, the wine was simply placed in a closed pot with an outlet line leading to a suitable vapor-condensing apparatus. Heat was applied and the ethanol concentration of the vapor at any given moment would be in equilibrium with the ethanol concentration of the liquid in the pot. Since the ethanol concentration of the liquid was gradually reduced the ethanol concentration of the vapor decreased correspondingly. Today, this simple system is employed only for Cognac (Fig. 17.5). A diagram of such a still is found in Fig. 17.6. Attention is called to the economy introduced by using the wine to be distilled to partially cool the vapors. This, of course, warms the wine and reduces the amount of heat required to bring it to the boiling point when heated in the pot. Some pot stills have simple or complex rectifying columns.

In the first (brouillis) distillation (Fig. 17.7) of Cognac (see p. 610) Lafon et al. (1973) find the nonalcohol components distill early in the distillation when the percentage of alcohol in the distillate is above 50%, except for the higher alcohols which continue to be carried over in appreciable amounts until the percentage of alcohol reaches about 30%. Furfural, however, only appears when the alcohol drops to about 40% and continues to distill down to 25%.

In the first distillation (brouillis), aldehydes distill first, then ethyl acetate, ethyl caprylate, ethyl caprate, and ethyl caproate; then ethyl laurate and ethyl lactate at the end of the distillation. The volatile acids, particularly acetic, distill throughout the distillation. Higher molecular weight fatty acids distill in the early stages as do the higher alcohols. Furfural is formed and distills throughout the distillation.

In the second distillation (bonne chauffe) the curves are similar but the product varies because of the separation of the three fractions. This is shown in Fig. 17.8. Note that the aldehydes are primarily in the heads, while the esters which are also found in the heads continue to pass over, particularly in the tails. The higher alcohols appear in the highest amounts in the heads and in rapidly decreasing amounts in the tails. In

TABLE 17.5. BOILING POINT AND COMPOSITION IN THE LIQUID AND VAPOR OF ETHANOL AND WATER MIXTURES

Percent Alcohol in Liquid by Weight %	Boiling Temperature			Percent Ethanol in Vapor by Weight				Ratio (k) of Ethanol Content of Vapor to That of the Liquid			
	Sorel and Groening °C	Gay °C	Internatl. Critical Tables °C	Sorel %	Groening %	Gay %	Internatl. Critical Tables %	Sorel Ratio	Groening Ratio	Gay Ratio	Internatl. Critical Tables Ratio
0	100.0	100.0	100.0	0.0	0.0	0.0	0.0	0.00	0.00	0.00	0.00
1	98.9	98.9	98.5	9.4	12.0	9.3	13.0	9.40	12.00	9.30	13.00
2	97.8	97.9	97.1	18.0	26.0	17.5	23.6	9.00	13.00	8.80	11.80
3	96.8	96.9	96.0	24.3	32.2	23.8	32.4	8.10	10.73	7.93	10.80
4	95.9	95.9	94.8	30.0	36.5	28.9	39.4	7.30	9.13	7.23	9.85
5	95.0	95.0	93.8	33.9	40.6	33.4	44.8	6.78	8.12	6.68	8.96
6	94.1	94.2	92.9	37.6	43.8	37.3	49.4	6.27	7.30	6.22	8.23
7	93.4	93.5	92.0	40.8	46.5	40.7	52.9	5.83	6.64	6.81	7.56
8	92.6	92.7	91.3	43.5	49.2	43.9	55.9	5.44	6.15	5.49	6.99
9	92.0	92.1	90.7	46.2	51.6	46.4	58.2	5.13	5.73	5.16	6.47
10	91.3	91.4	90.1	49.3	53.6	48.8	60.4	4.93	5.36	4.88	6.04
11	90.8	90.9	89.6	51.4	55.6	51.1	62.3	4.67	5.05	4.65	5.66
12	90.2	90.2	89.1	53.6	57.6	53.5	64.0	4.47	4.80	4.46	5.33
13	89.7	89.7	88.6	55.1	59.2	55.0	65.4	4.24	4.55	4.23	5.03
14	89.2	89.3	88.1	56.5	60.7	56.3	66.9	4.04	4.34	4.02	4.78
15	88.8	88.9	87.7	57.5	61.8	57.5	68.3	3.83	4.12	3.84	4.55
16	88.4	88.4	87.3	58.3	63.2	58.0	69.5	3.64	3.95	3.62	4.35
18	87.7	87.8	86.6	59.4	65.6	58.1	71.1	3.30	3.64	3.28	3.95
20	87.0	87.1	85.9	60.2	67.7	60.2	72.6	3.01	3.39	3.01	3.65
22	86.4	86.4	85.4	60.9	69.5	61.0	73.7	2.77	3.16	2.77	3.35
24	85.9	85.9	84.8	61.6	71.0	61.7	74.7	2.57	2.96	2.57	3.11
26	85.4	85.4	84.4	62.3	72.4	62.4	75.4	2.40	2.78	2.40	2.90
28	85.0	85.0	84.0	62.9	74.0	63.0	76.2	2.25	2.64	2.25	2.72
30	84.6	84.7	83.6	63.6	74.8	63.5	76.9	2.12	2.50	2.12	2.56
32	84.3	84.3	83.2	64.3	75.7	64.3	77.5	2.01	2.37	2.01	2.42
34	84.0	84.0	82.8	64.9	76.2	65.1	78.0	1.91	2.24	1.92	2.30
36	83.7	83.6	82.5	65.6	77.3	65.8	78.5	1.82	1.14	1.83	2.18
38	83.4	83.4	82.3	66.4	78.0	66.4	78.9	1.75	2.05	1.75	2.08

TABLE 17.5. (Continued)

Per cent Alcohol in Liquid by Weight %	Boiling Temperature			Percent Ethanol in Vapor by Weight				Ratio (k) of Ethanol Content of Vapor to That of the Liquid			
	Sorel and Groening °C	Gay °C	Internatl. Critical Tables °C	Sorel %	Groening %	Gay %	Internatl. Critical Tables %	Sorel Ratio	Groening Ratio	Gay Ratio	Internatl. Critical Tables Ratio
40	83.2	83.1	82.1	67.2	78.8	67.0	79.3	1.68	1.96	1.68	1.98
42	82.9	82.9	81.9	67.8	79.4	67.8	79.7	1.61	1.89	1.61	1.90
44	82.6	82.6	81.7	68.4	80.0	68.4	80.0	1.55	1.82	1.55	1.82
46	82.4	82.4	81.5	69.1	80.5	69.0	80.3	1.50	1.75	1.50	1.75
48	82.2	82.2	81.3	69.9	81.1	69.7	80.6	1.46	1.69	1.45	1.68
50	82.0	81.9	81.2	70.6	81.6	70.7	80.9	1.41	1.63	1.41	1.62
52	81.8	81.8	81.0	71.5	82.0	71.2	81.3	1.37	1.58	1.37	1.56
54	81.6	81.6	80.9	72.3	82.5	71.9	81.6	1.34	1.53	1.33	1.51
56	81.4	81.4	80.7	73.1	83.0	72.7	81.9	1.31	1.48	1.30	1.46
58	81.2	81.2	80.6	73.9	83.4	73.6	82.2	1.27	1.44	1.27	1.42
60	81.0	81.0	80.4	74.8	83.8	74.6	82.5	1.25	1.40	1.24	1.37
62	80.8	80.9	80.3	75.6	84.3	75.2	82.9	1.22	1.36	1.21	1.34
64	80.7	80.7	80.1	76.4	84.7	76.1	83.2	1.19	1.32	1.19	1.30
66	80.5	80.6	80.0	77.4	85.0	77.2	83.6	1.17	1.29	1.17	1.27
68	80.3	80.4	79.9	78.4	85.3	78.3	83.9	1.15	1.26	1.15	1.23
70	80.2	80.2	79.7	79.4	85.9	79.4	84.2	1.13	1.23	1.13	1.20
72	80.0	80.1	79.6	80.4	86.2	80.0	84.7	1.12	1.20	1.11	1.18
74	79.8	79.9	79.4	81.7	86.5	80.9	85.3	1.10	1.17	1.09	1.15
76	79.7	79.7	79.2	83.0	87.0	82.0	85.9	1.09	1.145	1.08	1.13
78	79.6	79.6	79.0	83.9	87.4	82.9	86.6	1.075	1.145	1.07	1.11
80	79.5	79.45	78.8	85.1	87.7	84.8	87.0	1.064	1.097	1.059	1.096
82	79.3	79.2	78.6	86.1	88.1	85.4	88.4	1.051	1.075	1.040	1.078
84	79.2	79.0	78.4	87.6	88.8	86.9	89.4	1.041	1.058	1.032	1.067
86	79.1	78.8	78.35	88.8	89.2	88.3	90.2	1.032	1.038	1.026	1.049
88	79.0	78.6	78.25	90.2	89.8	90.2	90.8	1.025	1.029	1.023	1.031
90	78.9	78.4	78.21	92.0	—	91.0	91.0	1.031	—	1.012	1.011
91.2	—	—	78.20	—	—	—	91.2	—	—	—	1.000
92	78.75	78.25	—	93.4	92.5	92.8	—	1.015	1.035	1.010	—

TABLE 17.5. (Continued)

Percent Alcohol in Liquid by Weight %	Boiling Temperature			Percent Ethanol in Vapor by Weight				Ratio (k) of Ethanol Content of Vapor to That of the Liquid			
	Sorel and Groening °C	Gay °C	Internatl. Critical Tables °C	Sorel %	Groening %	Gay %	Internatl. Critical Tables %	Sorel Ratio	Groening Ratio	Gay Ratio	Internatl. Critical Tables Ratio
93	78.7	78.20	—	94.0	—	94.0	—	1.012	—	1.010	—
94	78.7	78.18	—	94.8	—	94.8	—	1.008	—	1.003	—
95	78.65	78.16	—	93.6	—	93.4	—	1.008	—	1.002	—
95.57	—	78.15	—	—	—	95.57	—	—	—	1.000	—
96	78.6	—	—	98.1	—	—	—	1.002	—	—	—
96.8	78.5	—	—	99.8	96.8	—	—	1.000	1.000	—	—

Sources of data: Sorel, E., cited by Monier-Williams (1922); Groening, cited by Boullanger (1925); Gay (1935); and Keys, D.B. (1928).

Courtesy of Goguet, Cognac

FIG. 17.5. TYPICAL COGNAC DISTILLING SCENE

contrast, the amount of volatile acids in the distillate increases as the distillation continues. Furfural passes over in very small amounts throughout the second distillation. Rapid heating of the pot increases the rate of distillation of the volatile acids and esters up to 65% and may cause a secondary undesirable odor to appear in the tails. A slow distillation gives a higher quality product with less of the undesirable secondary odor. Redistillation of the tails results in lesser amounts of volatile acids and fewer volatile esters and improves the product. Removing more heads improves the brandy made from poor wine but reduces the quality of that made from good wine. When the wine is good, the odor of the tails is less undesirable than that of the heads.

According to Lafon *et al.* (1973) at least two procedures are now used in Cognac. In the first the *secondes* and tails from the second *(bonne*

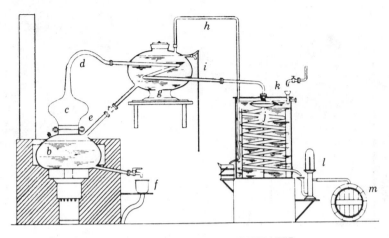

FIG. 17.6. DIAGRAM OF A POT STILL WITH PREHEATER

Pot *b*, preheater *g*, worm condenser *j*

chauffe) distillation are returned to the *brouillis*. In the second procedure the *secondes* and tails from the *bonne chauffe* are returned to the wine. Various modifications of these two procedures are also used.

Lafon *et al.* (1973) attribute an important role to the copper of the pot stills. Organic copper compounds of butyric, caproic, caprylic, capric, and lauric acids are apparently formed during heating and are distilled. These acids have a very disagreeable odor but the copper fixes these as their salts are insoluble. They found that products distilled in glass stills were less desirable than those distilled in copper stills. They recommend cleaning pot stills every eight days.

Lafon and Couillaud (1953) reported low copper in Cognacs, usually less than 3 mg/liter. Some copper is dissolved during distillation. Some of this is precipitated during aging, but, as the acidity increases during aging, there is a redissolution of copper from the precipitate. Young Cognacs contained 0.5 mg/liter while very old Cognacs had 3 to 4 mg/liter. With copper bottling equipment, copper pick-up may occur.

While the actual complexing of copper and phytate in brandy is not clear, Cordonnier (1954) found sodium phytate a useful means of removing copper from brandy, especially if calcium was present to ensure the formation of a calcium-copper phytate complex. When more than 6 mg/liter of copper were present, the efficiency of removal of copper was less.

Lafon *et al.* (1960) found normal Cognacs to have less than 0.2 mg/liter of lead. Old brandy and brandy stored in crystal bottles or in bottles

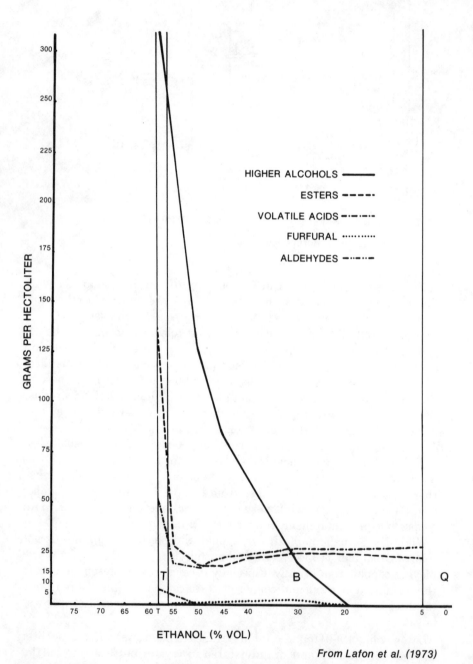

FIG. 17.7. DISTILLATION OF VARIOUS COMPONENTS DURING THE *BROUILLIS* DISTILLATION

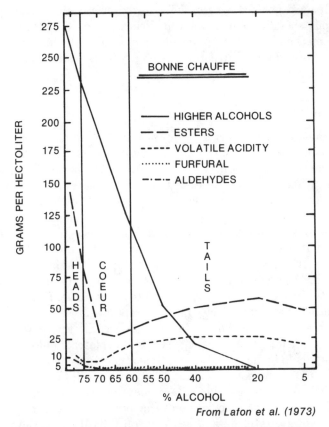

FIG. 17.8. DISTILLATION OF VARIOUS CONSTITUENTS DUR-
ING THE SECOND DISTILLATION

stored on their side with lead foil capsules were higher in lead, up to 1.2 mg/liter or more.

Guymon (1949A) found little analytical difference between pot- and column-distilled brandies from the same wine but noted that they were readily distinguishable by sensory testing. Maltabar (1971) believes the differences between continuous- and pot-distilled brandies is through the thermal load during distillation leading to newly-formed constituents in the pot-still products. He suggests a procedure for intensification in the formation of desirable compounds. Furthermore, it is unlikely that the slow pot still procedure would have survived in the Cognac region if it did not contribute to the character of the brandy.

When pot stills are used for producing grappa, either fresh or aged pomace may be used. Fresh pomace produces a less distinctive product but the odor of grappa from aged pomace is too strong for many consumers. If aged pomace is used the oxidized-acetic surface layer of the pomace pile should not be employed. Vegezzi *et al.* (1951) have shown that the methanol in pomace brandy may exceed the legal limit if the pomace is pressed too tightly. It is customary in California to redistill the pot-still product in a continuous still.

Column Stills

A continuous still is a sort of series of interconnected pot stills. Their continuous operation is more efficient than that of pot stills.

The modern column still (Fig. 17.9 and 17.10) is a cylindrical shell divided into sections by a series of plates. The plates are perforated or have openings covered by bubble caps (about 10% of their area is open) to allow passage of vapor. Nowadays, perforated or sieve plates are used in the lower stripping section of the column since they permit using distilling material with a higher percentage of suspended solids. Bubble cap plates with down pipes are used in the upper (rectifying) section of the column, although recent installations use valve or sieve trays.

The plates in the column are spaced 18 to 30 in. apart. If the plates are close together the vapor velocity must be kept low. If the vapor velocity is too great mechanical carryover of liquid will occur in the column. Barron (1944) recommends that, as a general rule, the plates should be spaced a distance apart in inches equal to ten times the vapor velocity in feet per second. Thus, for a vapor velocity of 2.4 ft per second the plates should be 24 in. apart. In practice, columns are operated at velocities 25 to 50% greater than this. For a calculation of the number of plates required and other principles of still design, see Hanson (1948). With sieve or perforated plates recent stills have 18 to 22 plates with 15- to 18-in. spacing.

Heat is supplied by a steam sparger at the bottom of the column. Down pipes between plates provide for return of liquid from one plate to another. The down pipes are located on opposite sides of the still for alternate plates so that the liquid passes across the plate before entering the next down pipe. The upper part of the down pipe extends above the plate so as to allow a liquid layer of 1 to 2 in. on the plate. The lower end of the down pipe is inserted in a cup on the lower plate to form a liquid seal.

Wine is introduced at some intermediate plate in the column. The ascending steam vapor prevents the liquid from falling through the perforations on the plate. There is a layer of liquid on each plate—the overflow passing to the next lower plate through the down pipe. The vapor leaving the boiling layer of liquid on the plate passes through perforations of the plate above and condenses in the liquid layer on that plate. Some of the liquid is evaporated by the heat released by the

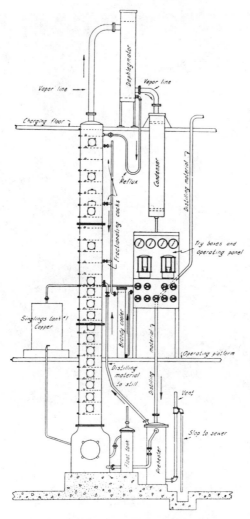

FIG. 17.9. DIAGRAM OF SIMPLE MODERN COL-
UMN STILL

condensation of the incoming vapor and passes on to the next higher
plate. Ethanol has a higher vapor pressure than water and thus evaporates from each plate more easily than water. The ethanol concentration thus increases from plate to plate. The ethanol concentration on
each plate of the stripping section remains essentially constant (once the
still is in balance) since it continuously receives a fresh feed supply from
the plate above.

To conserve heat, the hot dealcoholized liquid which accumulates at the

Courtesy of N. Nedeltchev

FIG. 17.10. COLUMN STILLS IN SUHINDOL, BUL-
GARIA

base of the still is discharged through a heat exchanger which warms the
incoming wine. Recent installations use thermocompressors to transfer
heat energy from the bottoms (stillage) to the entering steam. Some
columns, particularly the fractionating section, are insulated (lagged) to
avoid heat loss. Insulation is also useful with small columns to secure
better control.

Three different types of column stills are shown in Fig. 17.11. The
single column and double or split column stills may be operated either
with an overhead product or side draw. The column still with an aldehyde section is particularly useful in producing neutral fortifying spirits. Recently, some rather complicated stills have been built which produce a rather neutral product at below 170° proof. In one such case, a low
oils cut, about 20% of the brandy rate, is fed into a fusel oil concentrating
column to concentrate the alcohol in the low oils from approximately

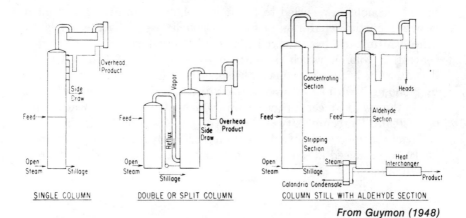

From Guymon (1948)

FIG. 17.11. VARIOUS TYPES OF COLUMN STILLS

130° to 190° proof. A fusel oil cut from this column is thus sufficiently concentrated to separate into oil and aqueous layers in a conventional fusel oil decanter (Fig. 17.12). The 190° proof alcohol (thus very low in

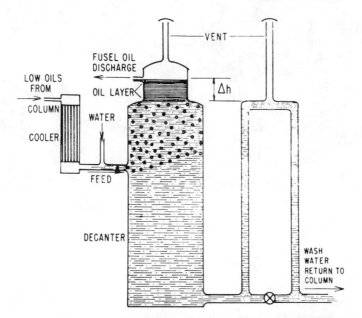

From Guymon (1958)

FIG. 17.12. SCHEMATIC ARRANGEMENT OF A FUSEL OIL DECANTER

higher alcohols) is recycled to the main column. Another arrangement effects a partial separation of higher alcohols, especially the amyls, by concentrating the brandy well above 170° proof in the primary concentrating column which permits some separation of fusel oil in its decanter; the brandy stream is subsequently reduced to 170° proof or less by blending it with a low proof stream drawn from an appropriate plate low in the heads concentrating column which, of necessity, is heated with open steam. The complexity of the control panel is indicated in Fig. 17.13. A Soviet continuous, double distillation for brandy production (Maslov *et al.* 1976) produced 26% ethanol from the first column and 66.4% from the second.

Courtesy of Mont La Salle Vineyards

FIG. 17.13. CONTROL PANEL FOR TWO 4–COLUMN STILLS

Condensers

Whatever system of distillation is employed, the ethanol-containing vapor must be condensed back to a liquid. Condensers serve two functions: conversion of vapor to liquid and cooling the resultant liquid to room temperature. The second step removes only a small amount of the total heat but requires greater condenser area since there is a slower heat transfer through cooling surfaces with liquids on both sides. The transfer of heat between liquid and vapor is by the film of stationary liquid on the water side and the film of stationary vapor on the vapor side. Vapor films are thinner; hence, heat transfer is more rapid for an apparatus condensing a vapor than for the same apparatus cooling a liquid. The heat transfer coefficient may be increased by increasing the velocity of the cooling water through the tubes or by using condensers of special design. Air-cooled condensers are used in some recent stills.

The vapor from the top of the column still passes through a dephlegmator and condenser. A portion of the vapor condenses in the first and is returned to the column as the reflux. The condenser may also return a reflux to the column and the remainder be taken off as heads. The actual product in this case is removed as a side stream from the upper plates in the column. Guymon (1948) has shown that a side stream take-off results in fewer esters and aldehydes in the product. This was true either for production of fortifying brandy at 186° to 189° proof or of beverage brandy at 164° to 167° proof. A modified still was designed by Williams et al. (1976) to reclaim ethanol from the heads fraction. The charge was diluted to 55/60% ethanol (v/v) to ensure hydrolysis of acetals. It is boiled under reflux at pH $\leq$ 2 with sparging by inert gas (CO_2 or N_2). The discharge vapors are vented under water and thence to the exterior of the still-house. When the acetaldehyde concentration in the charge is <200 mg/liter, it is adjusted to pH >10 with sodium hydroxide solution and the reflux continued 20 min. It is then distilled at over 95%. A recovery of 99% is reported. The reclaimed spirit is mixed 2:1 with wine spirits and used for fortification. Asmaev et al. (1976) used a sensor for controlling the withdrawal of the ester-aldehyde cut from continuous brandy stills.

Fusel Oil Removal

Separation of ethanol and water is not the only problem of distillation. Various desirable and undesirable congeners must be retained or removed—at least partially. Separation of the higher alcohols, particularly from wine spirits for fortifying, is an especially important problem. The higher alcohols (p. 599) are only slightly soluble in water. Their boiling points are higher than that of water but they have a high relative volatility with steam and are thus distilled upward in the column. As they reach plates of higher ethanol content they become soluble; their volatility is then normal and they tend to return down the column. The result is that they concentrate in the region of the still where the increase in alcohol percentage is greatest—at about 135° proof or at a boiling point of about 84°C (183°F) as can be seen in the data of Table 17.6.

The best recent data on the composition of plate samples are those of

TABLE 17.6.   ANALYSES OF CUTS FROM INDIVIDUAL PLATES OF A COLUMN STILL[1]

Plate	Initial Boiling Temp. °F	Proof Degrees	Acidity %	Extract mg/liter	Ash mg/liter	Esters mg/liter	Aldehydes[2] mg/liter	Furfural mg/liter	Higher Alcohols mg/liter
4	174.6	187.1	0.0024	26	14	422.4	17.6	Nil	440.0
7	175.4	183.5	0.0036	14	2	264.0	22.0	Trace	2,288.0
10	176.8	171.3	0.014	24	2	1,108.8	30.8	12.5	15,100.8
12	178.9	163.3	0.029	26	0	2,164.8	44.0	29.0	27,209.6
14	183.0	134.6	0.139	78	20	8,430.4	79.2	54.0	65,650.0
16	198.9	19.3	0.420	342	134	11,897.6	44.0	15.0	8,304.0
18	206.0	7.9	0.216	796	170	3,555.2	30.8	Trace	1,056.0
20	206.3	7.6	0.102	274	116	844.8	17.6	Trace	704.0
22	206.4	7.4	0.047	202	44	352.0	13.2	Trace	528.0
24	206.4	7.4	0.035	150	6	281.6	13.2	Trace	352.0
26	206.6	7.3	0.030	140	2	211.2	13.2	Nil	528.0
28	206.7	7.2	0.034	152	38	211.2	13.2	Nil	274.0
30	206.6	7.4	0.041	154	58	299.2	8.8	Nil	440.0
32	206.3	9.6	0.264	13,928	1944	211.2	8.8	Trace	352.0

[1]Source of data: Wilkins and Walling (1939).
[2]Includes furfural.

Guymon (1960). He showed that, to be meaningful, the distilling material must be normal, the column in balance, and the balance must not be upset by sampling. A 54-in. diameter commercial column was used. The higher alcohols concentrated on plates nearest in apparent proof to 135°. The observed plate temperature was 85°C (185°F). When the column is used to produce commercial brandy at 170° or less proof, the highest higher alcohol content on a plate was about 0.5%. This is due to the fact that much of the higher alcohols pass over into the product. He showed that higher alcohols cannot be separated by dilution with water and passage through a decanter if the proof of distillation is 170° or less. Some reduction in higher alcohols can occur when a "low oils" cut is made one or two plates below that used for product removal. Even when distilling at 185° to 190° proof not all the higher alcohols are removed. Isobutyl is the chief higher alcohol present in the product in such cases. When distilling at a high proof to obtain the most neutral brandy, Guymon recommended taking off the product as a side stream from a plate 5 to 10 plates from the top. This permits removal of low boiling point aldehydes and esters in a head cut.

In the distillation of fortifying brandy the concentration of fusel oil in the column is sufficient so that it exceeds its solubility at about 135° proof. It is possible to draw a fraction from this plate which will be very high in higher alcohols. Most continuous column stills now have fusel oil decanters (Fig. 17.12). In their simplest form, these consist of a try box into which the fusel oil is introduced at the top through a pipe. Inside this pipe is a smaller perforated water pipe. The water is thus intimately mixed with the incoming fusel oil. The mixture then flows through perforated screens and falls to the liquid surface in the try box.

Guymon (1958) presented complete data on the principles of separation of fusel oils (higher alcohols) during distillation. Dilution ratios of 2 to 2.7 would improve fusel oil recovery by decantation. He recommended that a minimum of four contiguous plates be connected to provide for drawing off of the fusel oils. Temperature indicators should be installed on one or more of these plates. Experience should then determine the best plates for fusel oil removal. Flow meters should be provided for the "low oils" cut and the dilution water lines.

A vertical draw-off pipe extends 12 in. from the bottom of the try box. It is completely enclosed in another tube which has an opening several inches below the top of the draw-off pipe. This allows continuous withdrawal of the water-alcohol mixture back to the still while maintaining a constant liquid level in the try box.

Fusel oil draw-off is accomplished through another vertical pipe which extends several inches above the water alcohol draw-off pipe. When visual observation shows a layer of fusel oil on top of the water-alcohol, water is then introduced through a third pipe and the liquid level raised so as to allow the fusel oil layer to flow out the fusel oil draw-off pipe.

In the production of beverage brandy, where the product has only about 160° proof, the plate with 135° proof is only one or two plates lower on the column than the plate with 160° proof. The higher ethanol content of the distillate is sufficiently high so that accumulation on the 135° proof plate sufficient to permit draw-off seldom, if ever, occurs. Reduction of the fusel oil content of the distillate is still possible if a fraction is taken from the appropriate plate and later redistilled.

Guymon (1949A) found little difference in composition of brandies distilled at 165° to 170° proof compared to 170° to 180° proof except a reduction of fusel oil in the latter. Since this is generally considered desirable he recommended that the maximum legal proof distillation for beverage brandy be raised from 170° to 180° proof. Brandies for aging should not have over 125 mg/100 ml (at 100° proof) of higher alcohols, in his opinion. However, more recently, Guymon (1975) recommended a proof of distillation for beverage brandy of 160° to 170° proof. If a low fusel oils cut (7 to 10% of the brandy flow rate) is taken, the fusel oil content will be reduced by about 5%. This may be important for brandies that are aged for a minimum time (2 years). If this cut is not taken the proof of distillation may be, in his opinion, as low as 140°–150° proof without reducing the quality of the aged brandy.

Aldehyde Removal

Removal of aldehydes is also desirable. This can be done by use of an aldehyde column. Guymon and Nakagiri (1955) and Guymon and Pool (1957) have shown that the most rational use of this high aldehyde product is by introducing it into rapidly fermenting musts where it is utilized for ethanol production. Guymon (1949A) recommended that brandies for aging contain no more than 3 mg/100 ml of aldehydes or 50 of esters.

Automatic Control

Most modern column stills have automatic controls so as to produce a uniform product. These consist of an actuating element or bulb which electrically or mechanically actuates a diaphragm valve. A continuous recorder is a part of the system. The usual controls include steam supply to the base of the stripping column, the feed, the product flow, and the flow of water to the dephlegmator.

Even when the manual control is employed, better uniformity in the product can be achieved by providing thermometers and temperature recorders. The thermometer bulb should be placed in the plates directly above the feed. Thermometers in the plate of product draw and a manometer or pressure gauge are also useful. Rotameters to indicate feed and product rates as well as reflux rate, heads and fusel oil fractions and water flow also help maintain control. Stillage testers are desirable to prevent loss of alcohol from the bottom of the still in the still slop.

Brau (1957A) has given a description of several different types of automatic control systems. He found quantity-control systems were inadequate since they are not capable of detecting and correcting changes in composition in the column. In his system (two column) a control system based on altering the rate of feed proved best. Other types of control are also employed. Use of automatic sampling and gas chromatographic analysis to continuously control aldehydes, esters, and higher alcohols in the distillate of pot stills was proposed by Nefedov (1976).

Periodically, stills must be cleaned to remove sediment. If wines containing sulfur dioxide are employed much corrosion may occur and the bubble caps or sieve plates eventually may not function properly.

Metzner Stills

A still (Fig. 17.14) to handle undisintegrated pomace has been introduced into the California industry (Metzner 1945). Basically this still

FIG. 17.14. METZNER STILL FOR POMACE

mechanically moves the pomace through several levels of the still and a moderate rectification occurs so that a product of about 20% ethanol is produced. This low wine is then diluted and redistilled in a regular column still. The recovery of ethanol from the pomace is nearly 100% and justifies the double distillation. Several modifications have been built. Another type of pomace dealcoholizing process involving use of a slight vacuum was proposed by Bachmann (1957). At present in California pressing, washing or disintegration of the pomace is used.

Vacuum Distillation

Flanzy and Lamazou-Betbeder (1938) found vacuum distillation produced an especially desirable brandy but with a coefficient of nonalcohols of below 280. Since French law requires beverage brandies to have a coefficient of at least 280 this eliminated them from the beverage brandy market, which they considered unfair. Guymon has made interesting and promising experiments with vacuum distillation at the Enology Laboratory at Davis, California. Large vacuum stills are, of course, expensive. Rakcsányi (1958) in Hungary has also made successful experiments with vacuum distillation. Lafon *et al.* (1973) found the process to produce too-neutral distillates for Cognac.

Fire and Explosion Hazards

The distillery premises should be of fireproof materials. Smoking or open fires, such as blow torches, should not be permitted near the still. Recently-emptied brandy barrels contain a highly explosive mixture of ethanol and air. A cigarette spark can cause an explosion of such barrels.

Distilling Material

Berti (1949) has emphasized the importance of using sound grapes for producing distilling material even for wine spirits for fortifying. He writes, "The use of moldy, partially fermented, and otherwise rotten grapes, cannot be excused . . . and we should prohibit the crushing of poor grapes by law, if necessary."

It is generally believed that wines of high total acidity produce the best beverage brandy. Maltabar (1952) harvested grapes at four stages of maturity and concluded that the best brandy was made from mature grapes. Soviet brandy experts believe that a higher alcohol/volatile ester ratio of 2 to 1 makes the best brandy. Wines from early-harvested grapes (14% sugar, 1.2% titratable acidity) produced brandies with ratios of 1.52 to 1.62 while wines of mature grapes (22–23% sugar, 0.5–0.6%

titratable acidity) produced brandies with ratios of 2.29 to 3.34. An experiment with the acidity modified would be desirable.

Berti (1949) recommended addition of 50 mg/liter of sulfur dioxide to the must. Certainly as little sulfur dioxide as possible should be used as is necessary to secure a clean fermentation. Sulfur dioxide distills over and produces brandy of high fixed acid and of reduced olfactory quality. Guymon (1974) recommends white varieties, clarified juice (to reduce fusel oil formation), no sulfur dioxide (unless grapes of poor quality), use of yeast strains that form relatively small quantities of fusel oil, fermentation at temperatures below 24°C (75°F) (also to reduce fusel oil production) and immediate distillation after fermentation.

Where pomace wash is used for distilling material, the alcohol content will be low and contamination and undesirable microorganism growth may occur. Early distillation should always be employed for such material. Wines of high volatile acidity produce poor brandy.

Generally, the best wines for distillation are clean white wines. It is believed that the best beverage brandy should be made only from wine. Pomace wash wines should be used for production of wine spirits for fortifying. Raisins and raisin seed wash water have also been used successfully. The raisins must be thoroughly soaked in water and may then be passed through a hammer mill to secure their complete disintegration. Pomace is also frequently ground in a hammer mill to secure complete disintegration of sugar-containing materials that have escaped solution and fermentation. Ground raisins or pomace material after fermentation must be kept constantly agitated. It is then pumped to special column stills which are capable of handling liquids with a high percentage of suspended solids. This type of distilling material should, of course, be used only for the production of wine spirits for fortifying.

Wine Spirits

"High proof," wine spirits or fortifying brandy is produced in California at 185° proof. This should give a neutral spirit but the data of Berti (1949) show that, at least at the time of his study, considerable variation in composition occurred (Table 17.7).

Pool and Heitz (1950) reported that, generally, fortifying brandies of high fusel oil (over 600 mg/liter), high aldehyde (over 200 mg/liter), and of poor sensory quality produced poor dessert wines. Guymon and Amerine (1952) confirmed this. Filipello (1951) reported a negative coefficient of correlation of $r = -0.480$ between fusel oil content and wine quality, but noted exceptions. Webb (1951) recommended neutral wine spirits for production of early-maturing dessert wines, but wine spirits for slower maturing wines should, he states, be produced from lower-proof brandy.

TABLE 17.7. COMPOSITION OF FORTIFYING BRANDY[1] (MG PER LITER)

Constituent	Number of Samples	Minimum	Maximum	Average
Fusel oil				
Colorimetric	42	84	2510[2]	572
AOAC	21	141	1038	270
Aldehyde	36	0	480	70
Esters	7	190	740	500
Total acidity	7	20	80	50
pH	6	3.3	6.6	—

[1]Source of data: Berti (1949).
[2]One sample of 6000 mg per liter omitted.

The quality of high proof alcohol is frequently determined by permanganate titration—the time required for decoloration of the permanganate being directly proportional to the quality. Tamburrini *et al.* (1955) showed that acids and aldehydes most affected the test. Esters and higher alcohols were of minor importance.

DISTILLERY SLOP DISPOSAL

The disposal of the dealcoholized solution from the still constitutes one of the major problems of the wine industry. This results from its high percentage of material in solution or suspension and the difficulty in decomposing this material. The oxygen requirements for its complete decomposition are very great. According to York (1958) and MacMillan *et al.* (1959) the BOD[3] may amount to 1500 to 5000 ppm for ordinary stillage and 7000 to 50,000 ppm for lees stillage—very high values indeed. For this reason the distillery slop may not be run into streams since it constitutes a hazard to fish. If it is run onto the land and is not speedily evaporated its decomposition results in volatile and obnoxious odors which constitute a public nuisance. Not only are the odors unpleasant for neighbors but they give a poor impression to prospective clients who visit the winery. Joslyn and Amerine strongly condemned this nuisance in 1941. Therefore, care must be taken if stillage is used for irrigation.

City Sewage

Many wineries are located in or near cities and can use the city sewage disposal system. This is satisfactory where the city system is large enough to handle this very seasonal input. Even where the city system can handle it, the disposal district may charge a special fee.

The alternative of building a sewage disposal plant for the exclusive use

[3]Biological oxygen demand.

of the winery has so far not been found economically feasible. However, city systems might find the distillery waste a more attractive product if more of the suspended material were removed. Several California wineries have tried flocculation and sedimentation systems but none have proven practicable.

Duval (1977) proposed a biological flocculation treatment for the lees discharged from the column. This process involves use of microorganisms. A modified sludge recycling procedure is used to produce a highly active sludge which is mixed with the distillery effluent. This is subjected to agitation and aeration. Within 48 hours the pH rises from 5.03 to 7.84, suspended matter increases and carbon dioxide content decreases. The final sludge is free of added chemicals and may be useful for animal feeds.

Field Disposal

This is the most common system presently used in California, and often the only feasible one. Where the winery is located in an area with plenty of sandy land for disposal of the distillery slop, it makes an admirable system, particularly when there is sufficient sunshine to assure rapid evaporation. Successful operation of this system requires ponds with dividing ridges not more than 1 ft high. Each pond should be large enough to hold, at a depth of not more than 6 in., the stillage output over a period of 24 hours. This requires an area of 1 acre for each 100,000 gal. The ponds are filled in succession, one each day. Thus, each pond is filling one day and drying six. After the ponds have been filled with stillage three or four times the soil, after thorough drying of the cake on the bottom of the ponds, is loosened with a disc.

Deep ponding should not be used as objectionable odors will be produced by gas-forming bacteria. Pretreatment before ponding is being used, usually by adding lime and settling or even centrifuging. For Cognac distillation residues, Magny et al. (1977) recommended centrifugation. The liquid had a COD of 44,000 mg O_2/liter. This was cooled to 20°C (68°F), enriched with ammonium phosphate [$(NH_4)H_2PO_4$] and inoculated with 3×10^6 cells/liter of Penicillium spinulosum. After 43 hours with aeration, the COD was reduced to 4000 mg O_2/liter. (This process is protected by a patent.)

AGING

Most distilled spirits intended for sale as a beverage, except grappa, pisco, vodka, and gin, are aged in wood following distillation. The improvement in the character and quality of the product is, of course, the reason for this aging process. The harsh burning taste and unpleasant odor of newly-distilled spirits are ameliorated by this aging and certain new and desirable odors and flavors develop from the aging. The following section is primarily on California and similar brandies.

Preparation for Aging

As it comes from the still at 170° proof, or less, the brandy is further diluted to about 110° or more for aging. Usually, burnt sugar or caramel syrup is added before the water for dilution. The usual amount of caramel is 4 oz per 50-gal. barrel. Only iron-free caramel which is completely soluble in 110°-proof brandy should be employed. Following dilution, the brandy is placed in weighed 50-gal. barrels—preferably new, according to most industry authorities (Fig. 17.15). However, some brandy has been aged in reused whiskey barrels. Brown (1938) recommends

Courtesy of Wine Institute

FIG. 17.15. BRANDY AGING IN OAK BARRELS IN CALIFORNIA WINERY

that dry oak be used in making the barrels as new oak has a higher moisture percentage and retards aging. The barrels are not treated before use as the soakage allowance would not be permitted. Teodorescu *et al.* (1958) recommended aging brandies in 130-gal. oak casks. Casks which had been used for storage of wine or brandy were preferred.

Changes During Aging

Dzhanpoladyan and Petrosyan (1957) believe the aging process begins with the extraction of phenolic compounds from the wood, followed by their oxidation by atmospheric oxygen to peroxides and participation of the peroxides in subsequent reactions. Lignin was shown to decrease during aging and it is considered to play an especially important role as vanillin is one of its oxidation products.

Petrosyan *et al.* (1976) found more free-radical products in aged brandies. Irradiation of wooden barrels with UV or γ-rays increased the oxidative reactions, enhanced maturation and gave higher free-radical products. Similar effects were found when the barrels were heated with oxygen for 12 days. Mndzhoyan *et al.* (1977) heat-treated the oak in an autoclave at 120°C (248°F) for 100 hours at 15 atm oxygen pressure. This reduced the cellulose and increased the lignin and aromatic aldehydes. Ethanol extracts of the treated wood were very high in aromatic aldehydes—comparable to 20 to 50-year-old brandy.

Onishi *et al.* (1977) compared new brandy and brandy aged in new and used American and French oak barrels. Acetate esters of isoamyl, n-hexyl, and β-phenethyl alcohols decreased during aging in oak barrels while ethyl caproate, caprylate, and caprate increased. Ethyl laurate did not change appreciably. Compounds derived partially or totally from oak—furfural, 5-methyl furfural, diethyl succinate and β-methyl-λ-octalactone *cis* and *trans*—were more abundant in brandies aged in American oak compared to French oak. Lesser amounts were found in brandies aged in reused barrels. De Smedt and Liddle (1978) found more 1,1'-diethoxypropan-2-one than the oak lactones.

Guymon (1949B) has classified the changes occurring during aging:

1. Physical
   a. Losses by evaporation or soaking.
   b. Changes due to concentration by evaporation or to dissolution of substances from the wood.
2. Chemical
   a. Oxidation of original or extracted constituents.
   b. Reaction between original and oxidation product or dissolved substances.

The factors which influence these changes were given as:

1. Initial composition—as affected by raw material, fermentation and distillation.
   a. Percentage of alcohol.
   b. Fixed acid content.
   c. Sulfur dioxide, hydrogen sulfide, etc.
2. Length of aging period
3. Cooperage
   a. Size and type: surface to volume ratio.
   b. Porosity and wood thickness.
   c. Composition of wood (dryness, tannin content, etc.).
   d. Condition: new or reused, pretreatment, etc.
4. Environment
   a. Temperature and variations in temperature.
   b. Relative humidity.
   c. Vapor pressure of alcohol in warehouse.
   d. Air circulation and replacement.
   e. Agitation.

The changes occurring in the brandy in a plain new barrel during a 4-year period were measured by Valaer (1939) and may be summarized as follows (except for proof, pH, and color, as grams per hectoliter, not calculated to proof; acidity as acetic, esters as ethyl acetate, fusel oil as a mixture of isoamyl and isobutyl alcohol, and aldehyde as acetaldehyde):

Age	Proof	pH	Total Acidity	Esters	Fusel Oil	Aldehyde	Furfural	Solids	Color in 0.5 Lovibond
0	100.3	5.35	8.4	40.5	79.2	2.0	0.5	66	2.5
1	102.8	3.96	62.4	58.1	85.3	7.9	1.4	172	10.0
2	103.4	3.93	69.6	59.8	88.9	7.8	1.4	194	10.5
3	104.6	3.91	76.8	66.6	102.0	9.8	2.0	214	—
4	105.1	3.90	79.2	71.3	104.3	11.2	2.0	230	13.5

Note the increase in acidity, esters, fusel oil, aldehyde, furfural, solids, and color. This results from the concentration effect of evaporation losses. The increase in the ethanol is due to the greater loss of water compared to ethanol under the low-humidity conditions in California warehouses (see p. 630). There are obviously some increases which result from chemical and physical changes. The increase in aldehydes and acids is probably largely chemical. The increase in acidity accounts for the decrease in pH. The increase in color and solids results from solution of substances from the wood. The changes when the brandy is stored in reused cooperage are much smaller (Guymon 1975).

Tolbert *et al.* (1943) found that brandy stored in small cooperage extracts more tannin than from large cooperage, even taking into account evaporation losses. However, more tannin is extracted per square centimeter of exposed surface from larger than from smaller containers.

High surface/volume ratios accelerate aging (as measured by compositional changes) but tend to give unbalanced brandies (owing to greater evaporation losses) according to Guymon (1975).

In new Bulgarian brandies the pH varied from 4.5 to 5.0. The heads were higher (6.2) than the tails (3.1). After aging in the wood the pH was 4.1 to 4.8, decreasing with time. The development of a "cognac" flavor was best at a lower pH, according to Lichev (1959). He also (1976) reported a rapid decrease in volatile esters. High boiling point esters, ethyl laurate and capronate, participate in bouquet production. Aldehydes, terpenes and octolactones were also important. Higher alcohols were significant quality factors in young brandies and Cognacs.

Old cognacs may develop a *rancio* odor. Lafon (1976) found this mainly due to lauric acid. Degradation products of lignin add to this odor. Also, peroxidases from molds on the exterior of the casks may react with fatty acids to increase the odor.

Petrosyan (1975) found more nitrogenous compounds in brandy stored in new barrels than in used barrels. The older the brandy the higher the total nitrogen, amino acid, higher alcohol and β-1-phenylethanol contents. The author postulates oxidative deamination during brandy maturation but without subsequent decarboxylation, thus preserving ketoacids.

Guymon and Crowell (1972) made extracts of American and French oak. The former had relatively high concentrations of diethyl succinate, 5-methyl furfural and β-methyl-λ-octalactone compared to the latter.

Guymon (1949A) has demonstrated that for proofs of distillation from 120° to 186° the changes in esters in the brandy during aging are essentially parallel. The distillation of wines high in volatile acids results in brandies of high ester content. Distillation of wines containing sulfur dioxide yields brandies of high fixed acid and high aldehyde content. They darken with age and have a characteristic and unpleasant odor. He also showed that the rate of increase of chemical substances and the percentage loss are proportionately larger for the smaller containers.

The best temperature and humidity of storage are not known. If the temperature is too high there will be excessive losses of alcohol. If too dry, there will be excessive losses of water and the proof of the brandy will rise. A cool (below 21.1°C, 70°F) and even temperature with moderate humidity seems best.

Guymon (1973) found that during aging the higher the tier level of the barrel in the warehouse, the greater the losses in wine gallons, the more the increase in proof and the higher the proof gallons (see Fig. 17.16). However, losses in actual ethanol were about the same irrespective of the tier of storage. Loss of ethanol is greater at higher humidity in storage

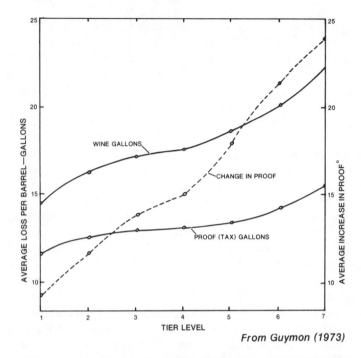

FIG. 17.16. BRANDY LOSSES AND INCREASE IN PROOF DURING 7.9 YEARS STORAGE AS AFFECTED BY TIER LEVEL FOR A FRESNO WAREHOUSE

than at lower. Guymon (1975) reported that French oak resulted in more extract (tannin, color and wood components) in a given period than American oak. A good correlation between extract content and the "smoothing" effect of aging could be made. However, the woody flavor is not appreciated by all consumers. He recommended 55% (110° proof) and warehouse temperatures of 12.8° to 18.3°C (55° to 65°F). Maximum extraction of solids and tannins occurs at 55% (Singleton and Draper 1961).

The government allows a certain loss from barrels for each period of storage. This increases from 1 proof gallon at 2 months' storage, 5 proof gallons at 18 months, 8 gallons at 36 months, and 13.0 at up to 80 months.

Rapid Aging

Various mechanical, physical, and chemical procedures have been used to age brandy more rapidly. Mechanical vibration (even by long ocean transport), variable temperatures, ultrasonics, adsorption, ion exchangers, ultraviolet and infrared have been tried (Singleton 1962). Ozone, peroxide, permanganate, electrolysis and metallic and biological catalyzers have also been used. Tolbert and Amerine (1943) reported improvements in certain brandies using activated charcoal, particularly in reducing excessive tannin. Dekov and Tsakov (1957) reported favorable effects of storing 140° proof brandy in 5-liter oak barrels for 15 days at temperatures which varied from 39° to 75°C (102.2° to 167°F). No statistical data were given. The best that can be said is that some of the results have been encouraging. The economics of the treatment and unprejudiced sensory examination of the products have not always been adequately considered. Further work could be profitably done.

The Soviet literature recommends using oak chips (treated with alkali or untreated) in the aging of brandy. Oxidation of tannin substances during aging was responsible for the darkening of color. Ethanolysis of lignin and hydrolysis of hemicellulose also occurs. Ethanolysis of lignin results after oxidation in formation of aldehydes of the vanillin type. Optimum results were secured by treating oak chips with $0.063-0.075\ N$ alkali at $10°-15.56°C$ ($50°-60°F$) for 2 days, according to Skurikhin (1960). He recommended keeping the brandy with the treated oak chips at $20°-25°C$ ($68°-77°F$) for 6 to 8 months with periodic introduction of oxygen (15−20 mg/liter). This was considered the equivalent of 3 to 5 years' aging in the wood. Lashki (1963) found that lack of oxygen during storage slowed the rate of aging but that too much oxygen resulted in loss of bouquet and the harmonious relation between components. Finished bottled brandy should contain no more than 3 to 5 mg oxygen per liter. The legal aspects would have to be clarified if such processes were used in the United States.

Heat treatment of young brandies for 20 days at $38°-40°C$ ($100.5°-104°F$) with or without oak chips (30 days) improved their sensory quality (higher volatile esters, aldehydes and furfural and less volatile higher alcohols) according to Abramov et al. (1976).

Semenenko and Ketrar (1977) reported less tannin, lignin and aromatic aldehydes in wines stored in used oak casks, compared to similar brandies in new oak casks. They suggested adding wood extracts to brandy at the beginning of aging and then holding in old wooden casks. This was to secure the advantage of some but not excessive amounts of lignin, tannin and aromatic aldehydes.

Otsuka and Imai (1964) reported extraction of syringic- and vanillin-like compounds as well as gallic acid from oak chips.

Pro and Etienne (1959) have shown that distilled spirits produced before 1954 can be dated with reasonable accuracy from their tritium contents. After 1954 the tritium content of the atmosphere was affected by hydrogen bomb explosions. Further, it is not possible to determine accurately the age of spirits which have been diluted with post-bomb water.

Removal from Storage

Brandy may be removed from storage at any time. If less than 4 years of age it may not be bottled in bond, that is, it may not be bottled at 100° proof with a revenue stamp giving the dates of distillation and bottling. Most brandies for sale are reduced to 80° proof with deionized or distilled water. Some are flavored to give them a distinctive character. This flavoring is, of course, the trade secret of each producer. It usually consists of some sweetening agent with a variety of flavoring materials added. We have not been impressed with the wine-flavored brandies that we have tasted. As a matter of fact, some of the flavored brandies are too sweet and too obviously treated for our taste. It would be preferable to limit treatment to caramel color and not over 1% sweetening.

When young brandies are cut they often throw a sediment of caramel or of oak extractives. Chilling to −4° to 6.7°C (20° to 25°F), settling at a low temperature for a day or two, and close filtration have been reported (p. 301) useful to prevent this sediment getting into the bottle.

Brandies of more than 4 years' age often, but not always, are simply cut to 100° proof, chilled, filtered, and bottled. During filtration the clarity may be controlled by a nephelometer operating at a 90° angle [for detecting colloidal haze according to Struck et al. (1976)]. They recommend a HIAC Model 305 particle counter for particles in the 2−5 μm range. Under present regulations, the tax is paid on the content of the containers as they are removed from storage and this need not be before the 20th year.

Rectification and Purification

If the brandy is purified or treated after distillation in any but the manner specified in the regulations, a special rectification tax must be paid and the treatment done in a separate building.

But, after approval of the Bureau of Alcohol, Tobacco and Firearms is secured, it is permissible to treat the brandy continuously during distillation by passing it through oak shavings, or treating with an oxidizing agent to improve flavor or to remove sulfur dioxide or other impurities.

Blending

Blending would be beneficial to uniformity of quality. Present regulations permit some blending under specified conditions. In other cases blending may be called rectification.

No experiments have been performed in this country with fractional blending systems for brandy but they have been successfully used for brandy in Spain. Extensive changes in the regulations would be necessary but it might make possible the production of more uniform and higher quality brandies than is possible under present regulations. The calculations for sherry (p. 407) could be applied to determine the average age of the product.

Lichev and Mitev (1976) used a linear mathematical method with a computer to make blends to the desired ethanol, total extract, tannin, lignin, vanillin, aldehydes, acetals, higher alcohols, esters, furfural, pH, and sensory quality. A linear program was used in four stages.

For sensory examination see pp. 666–672. Analytical procedures are given on pp. 702–706.

FRUIT BRANDY

Apple brandy or applejack was an important commercial product of colonial and 19th century America. At present there is a small production of apple brandy. Similar brandy produced in the Normandy district of France is sold as Calvados. The method of production has been described by Valaer (1939). The classic American process included a double pot-still distillation of the hard cider. In the first distillation a product of 60° proof was produced. This was then redistilled to 110°–130° proof with appropriate head and tail cuts. Continuous column stills are now often used. We find some American apple brandies to be aged for too short a period in the wood. Use fresh, mold-free, ripe apples, a clean fermentation, and distill after clarification. Only the juice should be fermented to keep the methanol content as low as possible. Distillation at reduced pressure (600 mm Hg) has been recommended as a means of reducing the methanol content (Kaladare et al. 1975).

The work of Margerand and Thellier (1946) suggests that chemical standards are necessary to prevent inferior Calvados reaching the market in France. These included amount of esters and higher alcohols and their ratio and sum, the ratio of total acidity to aldehydes and their sum.

There have been sporadic attempts to make pear, fig, plum, peach, and prune brandy in California. The use of waste fruit of poor quality usually dissipated any chance of success. For methods of preparing cherry, plum and other fruit brandies see Pieper et al. (1977) and Stanciulescu et al. (1975). There appears to be some commercial demand for small quantities of fruit brandies in California.

In 10 authentic laboratory brandies of stone fruits (sour and sweet cherry, damson plum, and apricot) Bandion et al. (1976) reported 0 to 6.4 mg of benzaldehyde per 100 ml of absolute ethanol and traces to 8.6 mg of hydrocyanic acid. In 12 commercial samples benzaldehyde ranged from traces to 13.4 and hydrocyanic acid from traces to about 10.

Bandion and Valenta (1976) have found λ-undecalactone is used in certain apricot liqueurs. Crowell and Guymon (1973) reported lower amounts of benzyl and 2-phenethyl alcohols, ethyl benzoate and eugenol in imported plum brandies compared to California laboratory products. The ethyl esters of the fatty acids were higher in the California product except ethyl lactate was higher in French quetsch and mirabelle and in Yugoslavian slivovitz. For analyses of pear brandies see Woidich *et al.* (1978).

The sensory examination of brandy is more difficult than that of wines because of their high ethanol content. Rocques (1913) recommends diluting the brandy with lukewarm water (*not* distilled), covering the glass with a watch glass, shaking, and then smelling. Four distinct observations may be made: the odor of the straight brandy, the odor of the diluted brandy, the taste of the straight brandy, and the taste of the diluted brandy. Also, the glass containing the straight brandy may be emptied and the odor observed after a few minutes.

For methods of analysis of brandy, see pp. 596–603.

REFERENCES[4]

ABRAMOV, S.A., NEFEDOV, M.P., BELOUSOV, V.N., GADZHIEV, G.R., BAGAEV, K.D. and ZYAZINA, E.A. 1976. Vliianie teplovoĭ obrabotki na kachestvo ordinarnykh kon'iakov. (Effect of heat treatment on the quality of ordinary brandies.) Vinodel. Vinograd. SSSR (7) 11–13.

AMERINE, M.A., MARTINI, L.P. and DEMATTEI, W. 1942. Foaming properties of wine, method and preliminary results. Ind. Eng. Chem. *34*, 152–157.

AMERINE. M.A. and WINKLER, A.J. 1938. Brandy. Wines Vines *19* (10) 1.

ANON. 1947. Cognac et Sa Region. Ses Grandes Eaux-de-Vie. Bordeaux et le Sud-Ouest. Éditions Delmas, Bordeaux.

ANON. 1978. Appellation d'origine contrôlée Petite Fine Champagne. Le Vrai Cognac *322*, 5.

ASMAEV, M.P., DOLGIKH, V.V. and PIĂBOV, A.I. 1976. Datchik raskhoda efiro-al'egidnoĭ frakt'sii kon'iachnykh apparatov nepreryvnogo deĭstviia. (Sensor for recording transition of the ester-aldehyde fraction through continuous distillation apparatus.) Vinodel. Vinograd. SSSR (2) 41–51.

BACHMANN, J.A. 1957. Pomace dealcoholizing process. Wine Inst., Tech. Advis. Committee, Dec. 6, 1957. This is covered by U.S. Pat. 2,690,019.

BANDION, F. and VALENTA, M. 1976. Zum Nachweis von λ-Undecalacton in Likören, Edelbranntweinen und Essenzen. Mitt. Rebe Wein- Obstbau Früchteverw. Klosterneuburg *26*, 43–50.

BANDION, F., VALENTA, M. and KAIN, W. 1976. Zur Beurteilung des Benzaldehydgehaltes in Steinobst-Edelbranntweinen und Steinobst-Früchlikören. Mitt. Rebe Wein- Obstbau Früchteverw. Klosterneuburg *26*, 131–138.

[4]Titles have been translated only for nonwestern European languages.

BARAUD, J. 1961. Étude quantitative, par chromatographie en phase vapeur, des alcools et esters de la fermentation alcoolique. Bull. Soc. Chim. France [5] *1961*, 1874–1877.

BARRON, H. 1944. Distillation of Alcohol. Joseph E. Seagram and Sons, Louisville, Kentucky.

BERTI, L.A. 1949. Problems of the production of distilling material and fortifying brandy. Proc. Wine Tech. Conf., Davis *1949*, 129–134.

BIKFALVI, I. and PASZTOR, L. 1977. Study of the components of distillates of wine using gas chromatography. (transl.) Sziszipar *25*, 96–100.

BOULLANGER, E. 1925. Distillerie Agricole et Industrielle, Vol. 2. Librairie J.-B. Baillière et Fils, Paris. (See pp. 8–9.)

BRAU, H.M. 1957A. Automatic Controls in Continuous Alcoholic Distillation. Univ. Puerto Rico, Agric. Exp. Stn., Río Piedras, Tech. Paper *18*.

BRAU, H.M. 1957B. Review of the Origin and Composition of Fusel Oil. *Ibid.* Tech. Paper *17*.

BROWN, E.M. 1938. The production of brandy. Wine Rev. *6* (12) 8–10, 34.

BÜTTNER, G. 1938. Branntweine. *In* Alkoholische Genussmittel. E. Bleyer (Editor). Julius Springer, Berlin.

CARRANZA, F. 1939. Licores de Peru. Bull. Soc. Quím. Peru *5*, 3–27.

CHAMINADE, R. 1930. La Production et le Commerce des Eaux-De-Vie de Vin. Librairie J.-B. Baillière et Fils, Paris.

CHARRO ARIAS, A. and SIMAL LOZANO, J. 1964. Application de la chromatographie en phase vapeur à l'analyse des eaux-de-vie espagnoles. IV Congrès d'Expertise Chimique, Athènes (Special No.) 375–390.

CORDONNIER, R. 1954. L'élimination du cuivre dans les eaux-de-vie par les phytates de calcium et de sodium. Ann. Technol. Agric. *3*, 179–191.

CROWELL, E.A. and GUYMON, J.F. 1973. Aroma constituents of plum brandy. Am. J. Enol. Vitic. *24*, 159–165.

DEIBNER, L., JOURET, C. and PUECH, J.-L. 1976. Substances phénoliques des eaux-de-vie d'Armagnac. I. La lignine d'extraction et les produits de sa degradation. Ind. Aliment. Agric. *93*, 401–414.

DEKOV, L., and TSAKOV, D. 1957. Thermal treatment of brandy. (transl.) Sadovod. Vinograd. Vinodel. Moldavii *12* (1) 45–57.

DELAMAIN, R. 1935. Histoire du Cognac. Librairie Stock, Paris.

DE SMEDT, P. and LIDDLE, P.A.P. 1978. Identification of 1,1'-diethoxypropan-2-one in spirits aged in wood. Am. J. Enol. Vitic. *29*, 286–288.

DE VRIES, M.J. 1958. Spektrofotometriese ontleding van wyspiritus. S. Afr. J. Agric. Sci. *1*, 195–202.

DUJARDIN, J. 1955. Recherches Retrospectives sur l'Art de la Distillation. Dujardin-Salleron, Paris.

DUVAL, P. 1977. Prétraitement des rejets. Rev. Cons. Aliment. Mod. *51*, 67–68.

DZHANPOLADYAN, L.M. and PETROSYAN, T.L. 1957. Okislitel'nye reaktsii pri sozrevanii kon'yachnykh spirtov. (Oxidation reactions during the aging of brandy.) Biokhim. Vinodeliya 5, 46−53.

EGLOFF, G. and LOWRY, C.D., JR. 1929. Distillation methods, ancient and modern. Ind. Eng. Chem. 21, 920−923.

EGOROV, I.A. and BORISOVA, N.B. 1957. Aromaticheskie al'degidy kon'yach-nogo spirta (The aromatic aldehydes of brandy). Biokhim. Vinodeliya 5, 27−37.

ELENA MARTINEZ, J. 1941. El Cognac, Consideraciones Sobre el Estado Actual de su Fabricación en el Pais. Imprenta de la Universidad, Buenos Aires.

FILIPELLO, F. 1951. Correlation of fortifying brandy with wine quality. Proc. Am. Soc. Enol. 1951, 154−156.

FLANZY, M. and JOURET, C. 1963. Contribution à l'étude des eaux-de-vie d'Armagnac par chromatographie en phase gazeuse. Ann. Technol. Agric. 12, 39−50.

FLANZY, M. and LAMAZOU-BETBEDER, M. 1938. Sur la composition des eaux-de-vie de la région languedocienne. Ibid. 1, 106−119.

FORBES, R.J. 1948. Short History of the Art of Distillation. E.J. Brill, Leiden.

GAUBERT, I. 1946. Armagnac, Terre Gasconne. Édition Havas, Paris.

GAY, M. 1935. Distillation et Rectification. Librairie J.-B. Baillière et Fils, Paris.

GENEVOIS, L. and LAFON, M. 1957. Origine des huiles de fusel dans la fermentation alcoolique. Chem. Ind. (Paris) 78, 323−326.

GENEVOIS, L., and LAFON, M. 1958. Dosage de l'isopropanol et du butanol secondaire dans les boissons fermenté. Chem. Anal. 40, 156−158.

GUYMON, J.F. 1948. Principles of still operation. Proc. Wine Tech. Conf., Davis 1948, 64−73.

GUYMON, J.F. 1949A. Composition of brandy, investigation of the influence of distillation practices upon the composition of brandies. Wines Vines 30 (10) 21−24.

GUYMON, J.F. 1949B. Factors effecting physical and chemical changes in beverage brandy during aging. Proc. Wine Tech. Conf., Davis 1949, 135−146.

GUYMON, J.F. 1958. Principles of fusel oil separation and decantation. Am. J. Enol. Vitic. 9, 64−73.

GUYMON, J.F. 1960. The composition of plate samples from distilling columns with particular reference to the distribution of higher alcohol. Ibid. 11, 105−112.

GUYMON, J.F. 1970. Composition of California commercial brandy distillates. Am. J. Enol. Vitic. 21, 61−69.

GUYMON, J.F. 1972. Higher alcohols in beverage brandy. Feasibility of control of levels. Wines Vines 53 (1) 37−40.

GUYMON, J.F. 1973. Influence of warehouse temperatures on the aging of California brandy. Wines Vines 54 (1) 36−38.

GUYMON, J.F. 1974. Chemical aspects of distilling wines into brandy. Advan. Chem. Ser. 137, 232−252.

GUYMON, J.F. 1975. An authority discusses the making of brandy. Wines Vines *56* (1) 38, 40.

GUYMON, J.F. and AMERINE, M.A. 1952. Tasting of experimental dessert wines produced with brandies of different qualities. Wines Vines *33* (9) 19.

GUYMON, J.F. and CROWELL, E.A. 1968. Separation of vanillin, syringaldehyde and other aromatic compounds in the extracts of French and American oak woods by brandy and aqueous alcohol solution. Qual. Plant. Material Veget. *12*, 320−333.

GUYMON, J.F. and CROWELL, E.A. 1972. GC-separated brandy components derived from French and American oaks. Am. J. Enol. Vitic. *23*, 114−120.

GUYMON, J.F. and NAKAGIRI, J.A. 1955. Utilization of heads addition to alcoholic fermentations. Am. J. Enol. Vitic. *6* (4) 12−25. *See also* Wines Vines *36* (10) 29−30, 33−34 and Am. J. Enol. Vitic. *8*, 68−73. 1957.

GUYMON, J.F. and POOL, A. 1957. Some results of processing heads by fermentation. *Ibid. 8*, 68−73.

HANNUN, H. and BLUMBERG, R.S. 1976. Brandies and Liqueurs of the World. Doubleday & Co., Garden City, N.Y.

HANSON, D.N. 1948. Principles of still design. Proc. Wine Tech. Conf., Davis *1948*, 46−63.

HARTMANN, G. 1955. Cognac, Armagnac, Weinbrand. Carl Knoppke Grüner Verlag und Vertrieb, Berlin.

HAUSBRAND, E. 1925. Principles and Practice of Industrial Distillation. John Wiley & Sons, New York.

HENNIG, K. and BURKHARDT, R. 1962. Chromatographische Trennung von Eichenholzauszügen und deren Nachweis in Weinbränden. Weinberg Keller *9*, 223−231.

HIRSCH, I. 1936. Manufacture of Whiskey, Brandy and Cordials. AVI Publishing Co., Westport, Conn.

HORSLEY, L.H. 1952. Azeotropic Data. American Chemical Society, Washington, D.C.

IKEDA, R.M., WEBB, A.D. and KEPNER, R.E. 1956. Comparative analysis of fusel oil from Thompson Seedless, Emperor, and Muscat of Alexandria wines. J. Agr. Food Chem. *4*, 355−363.

INGRAHAM, J.L. and GUYMON, J.E. 1960. The formation of aliphatic alcohols by mutant strains of *Saccharomyces cerevisiae*. Arch. Biochem. Biophys. *88*, 157−166.

JACKSON, G.H. 1928. The Medicinal Value of French Brandy. Thérien Frères, Montreal.

JOSEPH, E. and MARCHE, M. 1972. Contribution à l'étude du vieillissement du Cognac. Identification de la scopolétine, de l'aesculétine, de l'ombelliférone, de la β-méthylombelliférone, de l'aesculétine et de scopoline, hétérosides provenant de bois. Conn. Vigne Vin *6*, 273−330.

JOSLYN, M.A. and AMERINE, M.A. 1941. Commercial production of brandies. California Agric. Exp. Stn. Bull. *652*.

JOSLYN, M.A. and AMERINE, M.A. 1964. Dessert, Appetizer and Related Flavored Wines. University of California, Division of Agricultural Sciences, Berkeley.

KALADARE, G.A., ZINCHENKO, V.I., GORYA, G.IA., and MALTABAR, V. M. 1975. Production of spirits of low methanol content. (transl.) Sadovod. Vinograd. Vinodel. Moldav. *30* (3) 33–35.

KEPNER, R.E. and WEBB, A.D. 1961. Components of muscat raisin fusel oil. Am. J. Enol. Vitic. *12*, 159–174.

KEYS, D.B. 1928. Variation of boiling point with composition for liquid mixtures of volatile constituents. *In* International Critical Tables, Vol. 3. McGraw-Hill Book Co., New York.

KIRSCHBAUM, E. 1960. Destillier- und Rektifiziertechnik, 3rd Edition. Springer Verlag, Berlin.

KLIMOVSKIĬ, D.N. and STABNIKOV, V.N. 1950. Tekhnologiya Spirtovogo Proizvidstva. (Technology of Spirit Production.) Pishchepromizdat, Moscow.

KLUCZKO, A. 1978. Brandy maturation. Australian Wine Brew. Spirit Rev. *97* (10) 34–35.

LAFON, I. 1976. L'origine et la formation du rancio charentais dans les Cognacs vieux. Ann. Falsif. Expert. Chim. *69*, 315–318.

LAFON, J. and COUILLAUD, P. 1953. Sur la présence du cuivre dans les eaux-de-vie de Cognac. Ann. Technol. Agric. *1*, 41–50.

LAFON, J., COUILLAUD, P., CAUMEIL, M. and MARCHE, M. 1960. Teneur en plomb des eaux-de-vie de Cognac. *Ibid. 9*, 109–116.

LAFON, J., COUILLAUD, P. and GAYBELLILE, F. 1973. Le Cognac; Sa Distillation, 5th Edition. J.-B. Baillière et Fils, Paris.

LASHKI, A.D. 1963. Izmenenie sostavnykh komponentov spirtov raznykh vozrastov pri ikh vyderzhke. (Changes in the components of brandies of different ages.) Biokhim. Vinodeliya *7*, 173–188. *See also* Chem. Abst. *57*, 17203e (1962).

LAYTON, T.A. 1968. Cognac and Other Brandies. Harper Trade Journals, London.

LICHEV, V.I. 1959. The pH in wine brandy. (transl.) Nauch. Trud. Tekh. Inst. Vina. Vino. Promishlenosti *3*, 155–166.

LICHEV, V.I. 1976. Ergebnesse von Untersuchungen über die Bukettbildung bei Weinbranden. Mitt. Rebe Wein- Obstbau Früchteverw. Klosterneuburg *26*, 139–148. *See also* Lozarstvo Vinarstvo *25*, 26–36 (1976).

LICHEV, V.I. and MITEV, D. 1976. Use of mathematical methods and a computer for production of brandy blends. (transl.) Vinodel. Vinograd. SSSR (2) 33–37. *See also* Lozarstvo Vinarstvo *25* (2) 29–39.

MCCABE, W.L. and SMITH, J.C. 1967. Unit Operations in Chemical Engineering, 2nd Edition. McGraw-Hill Book Co., New York.

MACMILLAN, J.D., YORK, G.K. and VAUGHN, R.H. 1959. B.O.D. vs C.O.D. methods of determining brandy stillage purification. Am. J. Enol. Vitic. *10*, 199–205.

MAGNY, J., MONTANT, C., RAYNAUD, P., GONTIER, C. and DARDENNE,

J. 1977. Treating the Distillation Residues from White Wine Production. Ger. Offen. 2,630,680. U.S. Pat. Application 593,983, July 8, 1975. Chem. Abst. *86*, 87690.

MALTABAR, V.M. 1952. Ovliyanii khimicheskogo sostava vinomaterialov na kachestvo kon'yachnykh spirtov. (The effect of chemical composition of raw wine materials on the quality of brandy.) Vinodel. Vinograd. SSSR *12* (6) 22–26.

MALTABAR, V.M. 1971. Intensivierung des Prozesses der Neubildung flüchtiger Komponenten bei der Destillation von Wein für Weindestillat. Branntweinwirt. *111*, 89.

MARCHE, M. and JOSEPH, E. 1975. Étude théorique sur le cognac, sa composition et son vieillissement. Rev. Franç. Oenol. (57) 1–108.

MARGERAND, P. and THELLIER, R. 1946. Introduction à l'étude analytique et organoleptiques des eaux-de-vie. Rev. Viticult. *92*, 387–392.

MARILLER, C. 1948. Manuel du Distillateur, 3rd Edition. J.-B. Baillière, Paris.

MARSH, G..L. 1965. Composition of brandy. Fruit Prod. J. *15*, 42–43.

MASLOV, V.A., LINKE, O.E. and STABNIKOV, V.N. 1976. Gorizontal'naia isparitel'naia ustanovka neprereyvnogo leïstviia dlia polucheniia kon'iachnogo spirta. (Continuous action horizontal evaporator for the production of brandy.) Vinodel. Vinograd. SSSR (8) 45–47.

MELONI, G. 1952–1958. L'Industria dell'Alcole. Editore Ulrico Hoepli, Milan. (3 vol.) Vol. 1—Alcolometria. (1952); Vol. 2—Processi e Impianti di Produzione e Trasformazione. Le Materie Prime—Le Acquaviti. (1953); Vol. 3—Processi e Impianti de Produzione e Trasformazione. Spiriti, Alcole Assoluto, Alcoli Sintetici. (1958).

METZNER, E.K. 1945. Grape pomace. A source of alcohol and tartrates. Chem. Met. Eng. *52* (10) 102–103.

MNDZHOYAN, E.I., NALBANDIAN, R.M., AKHNAZARIAN and SAAKIAN, A.S. 1977. New way of treating oak for brandy production. Dokl. Akad. Nauk Arm. SSR *65*, 46–51.

MONIER-WILLIAMS, G.W. 1922. Power Alcohol. Frowde and Hodder and Stoughton, London.

NEEDHAM, J. 1954. Science and Civilization in China, Vol. 1. University Press, Cambridge.

NEFEDOV. M.P. 1976. Use of a chromatograph in the production of brandy. (transl.). Sadovod. Vinograd. Vinodel. Moldav. *31* (4) 24–26. See also Ibid. *31* (7) 27–29.

ONISHI, M., CROWELL, E.A. and GUYMON, J.F. 1978. Comparative composition of brandies from Thompson Seedless and three white-wine grape varieties. Am. J. Enol. Vitic. *29*, 54–59.

ONISHI, M., GUYMON, J.F. and CROWELL, E.A. 1977. Changes in some volatile constituents of brandy during aging. Am. J. Enol. Vitic. *28*, 152–158.

OTSUKA, K. and IMAI, S. 1964. Studies on the mechanism of aging of distilled spirits. I. On phenolic compounds from oak wooden chips. Agric. Biol. Chem. *28*, 356–362.

PETROSYAN, T.I. 1975. Azot v kon'iake. (Nitrogen in brandy.) Voprosy Biokhimii Vinograda Vina *8*, 404−406.

PETROSYAN, T.I., DZHANPOLADIAN, L.M. and BEILERIAN, N.M. 1976. Electron paramagnetic resonance study of oxidative processes during the aging of brandy. (transl.) Vinodel. Vinograd. SSSR (4) 24−26. Chem. Abst. *85*, 141279.

PFENNINGER, H. 1963. Gaschromatographische Untersuchungen von Fuselölen aus verschiedenen Gärprodukten. III. Ergebnisse der gaschromatographischen Untersuchung von Fuselölen aus verschiedenen Gärprodukten. Z. Lebensm.-Untersuch. -Forsch. *120*, 117−126.

PIEPER, H.J., BRUCHMANN, E.E. and KOEB, E. 1977. Technologie der Obstbrennerei. Eugen Ulmer, Stuttgart.

PISARNITSKII, A.F., EGOFAROVA, R.K. and EGOROV, I.A. 1977. Dicarbonyl substances of oakwood and brandies. (transl.) Prikl. Biokhim. Microbiol. *13*, 194−198. Chem. Abst. *86*, 187607.

POOL, A. and HEITZ, J.E. 1950. Correlation of fortifying brandy with wine quality. Proc. Am. Soc. Enol. *1950*, 101−109.

PRIOTON, H. 1929. La Culture de la Vigne dans les Charentes et la Production du Cognac. Librairie J.-B. Baillière et Fils, Paris.

PRO, M.-J. and ETIENNE, A.D. 1959. Dating distilled spirits. J. Assoc. Offic. Agric. Chem. *42*, 386−392.

PROCOPIO, M. 1958. Studio sulle acqueviti di vino aldeidi e acetati. Riv. Viticolt. Enol. (Conegliano) *11*, 253−260.

QUADY, A.K. and GUYMON, J.F. 1973. Relation of maturity, acidity and growing region of Thompson Seedless and French Colombard grapes to wine aroma and quality of brandy distillate. Am. J. Enol. Vitic. *24*, 166−175.

RAKCSÁNYI, L. 1958. Égetett szeszesitalok készitése vákuumlepárlással. (Production of brandy by vacuum distillation.) Kisérlet. Közlem *52*, 31−77.

RANKINE, B.C. 1961A. Factors influencing uptake of copper from brandy by ion-exchange resins. J. Sci. Food Agric. *12*, 188−194.

RANKINE, B.C. 1961B. Lead content of Australian brandies. *Ibid.* *12*, 194−196.

RAVAZ, L. 1900. Le Pays du Cognac. Louis Coquemard, Angoulême.

RAY, C. 1974. Cognac. Stern and Day, Briarcliff Manor, N.Y.

REINHARD, C. 1976. Ueber Gaschromatographische Untersuchungen in alkoholischen Erzeugnissen. VIII. Zur Beurteilung griechischer Brennweine und Rohbrände aus Wein. Weinwirtschaft (Mainz) *112*, 172−174.

RICCIARDELLI, N. 1909. I Cognacs Italiani. Libreria Editrice Concetto Battiato di Francisco Battiato, Catania.

RIFFART, H. and DIEMAIR, W. 1944. Beitrag zur Untersuchung von Brennwein. Z. Lebensm.-Untersuch. -Forsch. *87*, 61−64.

ROBINSON, C.S. and GILLILAND, E.R. 1950. The Elements of Fractional Distillation. McGraw-Hill Book Co., New York.

ROCQUES, X. 1913. Eaux-De-Vie. Librairie Polytechnique Ch. Béranger, Paris.

RONKAINEN, P., SALO, T. and SUOMALAINEN, H. 1962. Carbonylverbindungen der Weindestillate und deren Veränderungen im Verlaufe der Reifeprozesse. Z. Lebensm.-Untersuch. -Forsch. *117*, 281−289.

ROSENTHALER, L. and VEGEZZI, G. 1955. Acrolein in Spirituosen. *Ibid.* *102*, 117−123.

SCHREIER, P., DRAWERT, F. and WINKLER, F. ·1979. Composition of neutral volatile constituents in grape brandies. J. Agric. Food. Chem. *27*, 365−372.

SEMENENKO, N.T. and KETRAR, P.M. 1977. Evaluation of 3−5-year-old brandies. (transl.) Vinodel. Vinograd. SSSR (6) 20−22.

SIMMONDS, C. 1919. Alcohol, Its Production, Properties, Chemistry, and Industrial Applications. Macmillan and Co., London.

SINGLETON, V.L. 1962. Aging of wines and other spiritous products, acceleration by physical treatments. Hilgardia *32*, 319−392.

SINGLETON, V.L. and DRAPER, D.E. 1961. Wood chips and wine treatment; the nature of aqueous alcohol extracts. Am. J. Enol. Vitic. *12*, 152−158.

SKURIKHIN, I.M. 1960. Khimizm protsessov sozrevaniya kon'yachnykh spiritov v emalirovannykh tsisternakh. (Chemical processes of treating brandy in metal tanks.) Trudy Konferentsii po Biokhimii Vinodeliya *1960*, 179−190.

SOREL, E. 1899. Distillation et Rectification Industrielle. G. Carré et Cie., Paris.

STANCIULESCU, G., RUSNAC, D. and BORTES, G. 1975. Tehnolgia Distilatelor Alcoolice din Fructe şi Vin. Ceres, Bucharest.

STRUNK, D.H., TIMMEL, B.M. and ANDREASEN, A.A. 1976. Clarity evaluation of distilled alcoholic products with particle counter. J. Assoc. Off. Anal. Chem. *59*, 671−674.

SUOMALAINEN, H., KAUPPILLO, O., NYKÄNEN, L. and PELTONEN, R.J. 1968. Branntweine. Handbuch Lebensmittelchem. 7, 496−653.

TAMBURRINI, V., PALLADINI, F. and DARD, E. 1955. Caratteristiche di alcoli buon gusto del commercio e considerazioni sul saggio merceologico di resistenza al permanganante in relazioni alle loro impurezze. Riv. Viticolt. Enol. (Conegliano) *8*, 53−65.

TEODORESCU, S.C., ILIESCU, L.V. and IONESCU, A.I. 1958. Evolution de la composition chimique des eaux-de-vie au cours du vieillissement. Anal. Inst. Cercet. Agron. *26*, 115−140.

THOUKIS, G. 1958. The mechanism of isoamyl alcohol formation using tracer techniques. Am. J. Enol. *9*, 161−167.

TOLBERT, N.E. and AMERINE, M.A. 1943. Charcoal treatment of brandies. Ind. Eng. Chem. *35*, 1078−1082.

TOLBERT, N.E., AMERINE, M.A. and GUYMON, J.F. 1943. Studies with brandy. II. Tannin. Food Res. *8*, 231−236.

TOLU LIBERO, A. 1962. Il metanolo nelle acqueviti di vinaccia. Ann. Fac. Sci. Agric. Univ. Torino *1*, 199−202.

U.S. TREASURY DEPARTMENT. 1977. Code of Federal Regulations Title 27. Alcohol, Tobacco Products and Firearms. Subchapter A, Part 5. Labeling and Advertising of Distilled Spirits; Subchapter M, Part 170, Miscellaneous Regulations Relating to Liquor, Part 186. Gauging Manual, Part 194, Liquor Dealers, Part 196, Stills, Part 201, Distilled Spirits Plants. *Note:* These regulations were formerly codified as 26 CFR.

VALAER, P. 1939. Brandy. Ind. Eng. Chem. *31*, 339–353.

VAN WINKLE, M. 1967. Distillation. McGraw-Hill Book Co., New York.

VEGEZZI, G., HALLER, P. and WANGER, O. 1951. Le problème de l'eau-de-vie de marc de raisin. Mitt. Gebiete Lebensm. Hyg. *42*, 316–341.

VILLA, Q. 1946. Elementi di Calcolo sulla Distillazione Frazionata. Editore Ulrico Hoepli, Milano.

WALKER, W.H., LEWIS, W.K., MCADAMS, H.H. and GILLILAND, E.R. 1937. Principles of Chemical Engineering, 3rd Edition. McGraw-Hill Book Co., New York.

WEBB, A.D. 1951. Flavor factors in fortifying brandy. Proc. Am. Soc. Enol. *1951*, 148–153.

WEBB, A.D., KEPNER, R.E. and IKEDA, R.M. 1952. Composition of a typical grape brandy fusel oil. Anal. Chem. *24*, 1944–1949.

WILKINS, E.A. and WALLING, M.E. 1939. Quality brandy through controlled distillation. Wine. Rev. *7* (9) 7–9, 27.

WILLIAMS, P.J. 1975. Aspects of brandy and fortifying spirit research. Austr. Wine Brew. Spirit Rev. *93* (10) 38, 40.

WILLIAMS, P.J. and STRAUSS, C.R. 1976. 3-3-Diethoxybutan-2-one and 1, 1,3-triethoxy-propane: acetals in spirits distilled from *Vitis vinifera* grape wines. J. Sci. Food Agric. *26*, 1127–1136.

WILLIAMS, P.J., STRAUSS, C.B. and HARDY, W.D. 1976. A modified still for the treatment of grape wine distillation heads. Austr. Wine Brew. Spirit Rev. *94* (12) 14–15.

WILLKIE, H.G. and PROCHASKA, J.A. 1943. Fundamentals of Distillery Practice. Joseph E. Seagram and Sons, Louisville, Ky.

WINE INSTITUTE (San Francisco). Bulletins *967, 1137, 1201, 1310, 1318, 1399, 1435, 1486, 1540, 1592, 1644, 75-16, 76-9, 77-10.*

WINE INSTITUTE (San Francisco). 1970. Economic Research Report *1976.*

WINE INSTITUTE (San Francisco). 1965. Statistical Survey.

WOIDICH, H., PFANNHAUSER, W. and EBERHARDT, R. 1978. Untersuchungen von Aromastoffen aus Williamskirnen-Branntwein mittels Kapillarchromatographie und Massenspektrometrie. Mitt. Hoeheren Bundeslehr-Versuchsans. Wein- Obstbau (Klosterneuburg) *28*, 112–118.

WÜSTENFELD, H. and HAESELER, G. 1964. Trinkbranntweine und Liköre. Verlag Paul Parey, Berlin.

XANDRI TAGÜENA, J.M. 1958. Elaboración de Aguardientes Simples, Compuestos y Licores. Salvat Editores, S.A., Barcelona.

YORK, G.K. 1958. Winery waste disposal. Wine Inst. Tech. Adv. Committee, May 26, 1958.

YOUNG, S. 1922. Distillation Principles and Practices. Macmillan Co., London and New York.

18

Winery By–Products

The most recent evaluation of by-product recovery potential from winery wastes is that of Rice (1976). He listed tartrates, grape seed oil and tannin, and stock feed and fertilizer from pomace. Other possible by-products are absorption carbons and pigments.

The production of wine vinegar, concentrate and grape juice will also be discussed, since from the winery's standpoint they are by-products rather than primary products.

TARTRATES

Tartrates occur naturally in winery pomace, still slops from brandy distillation, in the lees that settle in wine tanks, and in the argols that separate on the walls and bottoms of wine storage tanks.

Recovery of Tartrate from Pomace

This involves storage of the pomace, extraction of tartrate from the pomace, and precipitation of the tartrate as calcium tartrate.

As it is usually not practicable to extract tartrate from the pomace as rapidly as it accumulates, it is stored until processed. To prevent destruction of tartrates by mold growth the pomace must be stored anaerobically. By removing all stems and compacting the pomace well, growth occurs only in the outer 15 to 20 cm (6 to 8 in.) of the pomace pile.

The tartrate may be extracted from the pomace with cold or hot water or a cold acid solution using either batch or continuous extraction. See Marsh and Guadagni (1942) for detailed procedures used in both cold acid extraction and hot water extraction without the use of acid (see also Marsh 1943).

Marsh points out that no single calcium compound such as lime, $Ca(OH)_2$, or calcium carbonate, $CaCO_3$, will precipitate more than 50% of the tartrate. However, a combination of salts, such as calcium chloride and neutralization with calcium hydroxide, will give nearly complete precipitation. Marsh (1942) and Marsh and Guadagni (1942) give the method for calculating the required amounts of the two reagents.

After precipitation the supernatant liquid is racked off and discarded. The precipitate is resuspended in water by pumping, and settled in order to remove impurities of low specific gravity. This is repeated one or more times. The addition of 200 mg/liter of sulfur dioxide to the wash water is recommended in order to prevent bacterial spoilage during washing. The compacted tartrate is then dried to below 5% moisture content to prevent spoilage by microorganisms (see Vaughn and Marsh 1943).

Recovery of Tartrates from Still Slops

Precipitation of calcium tartrate can be made before or after distillation. Precipitation after distillation is preferred because a purer tartrate is obtained as settling is better. Also there is less danger of spoilage by microorganisms.

The slop from the still should be cooled to below 50°C (122°F), allowed to settle, and racked before precipitating as calcium tartrate.

In California during W.W. II, because of the interruption of imports, calcium tartrate was made from the tartrate and tartaric acid occurring in pomace and stillage. At the present time, 1979, the recovery of tartrates from pomace and stillage has practically ceased, owing to the resumption of imports of tartrates. Tartrates are still recovered commercially in Europe (see Aries 1957).

Tartrates from Lees

The lees which settle in storage tanks after fermentation or fortification are rich in cream of tartar. The usual practice is to dilute the lees with about an equal volume of water, distill to recover alcohol, settle hot to get rid of most of the suspended matter, cool and then precipitate as calcium tartrate.

Argols

The "wine stone" that forms on the walls and floors of wine tanks is almost pure cream of tartar. "Wine stone" adheres tightly to the walls of the tank. It is dissolved by applying strong sodium hydroxide solution to the surface. Soluble Rochelle salt, $NaKC_4H_4O_6$, is formed.

The solution can be acidified to pH 3.5 with hydrochloric acid, which converts the salt to cream of tartar and sodium bitartrate. The cream of tartar then crystallizes out. The remaining tartrate is precipitated as calcium tartrate.

OIL AND TANNIN FROM GRAPE SEEDS

Oil

Recovery of oil from grape seeds involves drying of the pomace, separation of the seeds, and extraction of oil from the seeds.

The pomace is dried in rotary, direct gas-fired drum driers and the seeds separated by threshing and sieving. The oil may be extracted either by pressing the seeds, or by grinding the seeds and then extracting the oil with solvents (see Kinsella 1974).

Grape seed oil is characterized by a very high content of linoleic acid which is considered the essential fatty acid for man. In this respect, grape seed oil is similar to safflower and somewhat superior to corn, soybean and cottonseed oils. It can be safely used as an edible oil and its composition makes it very desirable for inclusion in diets designed to lower serum cholesterol. See Kinsella (1974) for composition.

Despite its advantages as an edible oil, the production of other oils has made the use of grape seeds for oil recovery economically unattractive in the United States. However, wine grape seed oil is still made commercially in Europe (see Aries 1957).

Tannin

In France and Italy, tannin is extracted from grape seeds for use in winemaking. It is not recovered in the United States as the use of dark brown-colored grape seed tannin is not legal, and the leather industry uses little vegetable tannin.

CARBON FROM POMACE

Walter and Sherman (1975) suspended grape and apple pomace in 25—40% sulfuric acid and then pyrolyzed the charred material at a low temperature to yield charcoals. They reported that both materials would appear to be excellent sources of low-ash carbons whose extensive porosity could be used to advantage in absorption operations.

USE OF POMACE FOR STOCK FEED

Several large wineries and others have dehydrated winery pomace to low moisture content and ground it for use in feeding livestock, particularly dairy cows. The principal defect of winery pomace for use as stock feed is its very high crude fiber content, largely the indigestible hulls of the seeds. An additional factor in the poor feed value of seeded pomace is the tannin content which ties up protein. Therefore, it cannot be fed safely as the sole feed, but at best as a supplemental feed. One dairyman mixed it with bran in preparing a wet mash.

The analysis on the tags attached to bags of one producer's dried ground pomace was: crude protein not less than 11.08%; crude fat not less than 6%; crude fiber not over 40%; and crude ash not over 8%.

Other crude fiber determinations reported by commercial chemists showed an apparent crude fiber content below 30%. Six dried pomace samples for dessert wineries of the Lodi area showed moisture contents from 2.6 to 8.1%; ash, 4.7 to 8.1%; oil, 3.7 to 6.4%; crude protein, 11 to 12.7%; crude fiber 31.3 to 40.9%; reducing sugars 0.40 to 1.4%; and 7.4 to 7.9% "starch" (on acid hydrolysis). Sixteen other samples showed crude fiber of 26.2 to 38.8% and oil 3.3 to 7.4%, the averages being oil 4.52% and crude fiber 34.02%. The composition of 160 samples of dehydrated grape pomace meal[1] ranged from 3.26 to 9.59% in moisture content, 5.01 to 9.64% in ash content, 12.05 to 14.88% in protein content, 5.63 to 8.97% in fat content and 17.74 to 34.99% in fiber content. The averages were: moisture, 5.10%; ash, 6.42%; protein, 13.45%; fat, 7.35%; and fiber, 26.94%. Analyses[1] of four samples of washed, dried seeds gave an average crude fiber content of 53%.

Sémichon (1907) in France called attention to the value of grape pomace as a stock feed. The French considered the dried pomace of about the same feeding value as meadow hay; but experiments by Folger (1940) indicated that it is no better than good quality wheat straw in feeding value. Nevertheless, several dairymen have mixed the ground dried pomace with molasses and used it as a supplementary feed (see Latreto 1953).

Rotary, direct-fired drum driers are used for drying the pomace. The usual drum resembles a cement kiln and is about 1.67 to 2.22 m (6.0 to 8.0 ft) in diameter and about 16.7 to 19.6 m (60.0 to 70.0 ft) long. It is inclined, the pomace entry port being at the higher end and exit port at the lower. A gas or crude oil burner throws a generous flame into the upper end of the drier and a large fan draws a blast of air that mixes with the products of combustion and carries the spent gases and moisture vapor out the cooler end of the drier. The wet pomace drops into the hot air and combustion gases zone at the furnace end of the tunnel; the

---

[1]Data furnished by the Roma Wine Co., Fresno, California.

estimated temperature at this point is above 535°C (1000°F). Evaporation is very rapid and cools the pomace, preventing much scorching, although some skins dry instantly and then scorch.

The bone-dry pomace passes through a hammer mill which grinds it to a meal. The meal may or may not then be admixed continuously and mechanically with a small amount of molasses to improve its palatability and carbohydrate content.

The dried, ground pomace must be low in moisture (preferably not over 6%), otherwise it will be subject to spoilage. On the basis of 63% moisture content—the average for samples analyzed in 1938 and 1939—a ton of fresh pomace would yield about 350 kg (775 lb) of dried pomace of 5% moisture content· a ton of pomace of 50% moisture would yield about 478 kg (1050 lb) of dry pomace of 5% moisture. Agostini (1964) reported pomace may be improved as a cattle feed if lime is added to raise the pH.

USE OF POMACE AND STILLAGE AS FERTILIZERS

Jacob and Proebsting (1937) found that winery pomace has about the same ultimate fertilizing value as barnyard manure, although it becomes available more slowly. They reported 1.5−2.5% nitrogen, about 0.5% phosphorus and 1.5−2.5% potassium on a dry-weight basis. It also improves the physical texture of heavy soils. Pirrone (1958) preferred composting before spreading.

They found that very heavy applications of still slops created a temporary toxic condition in the soil, sometimes killing plants. Seepage along the hard pan from a settling basin has killed vines at a considerable distance from the basin. Evidently, toxic substances are formed during early stages of decomposition. That the toxicity is temporary is shown by the fact that after old slop settling basins have dried and stood several months, growth of grass and weeds in the basin is very luxuriant during the ensuing spring. Probably if the slops were put through a sewage treating system, such as a trickle filter, and were limed to recover tartrate before sewage treatment, the effluent would be useful and safe in irrigation if not applied in excessive amounts.

PIGMENTS FROM POMACE

With the banning of Red Dye No. 2 and the expected banning of Red Dye No. 40 by the United States Food and Drug Administration there is great interest by the food industry in finding a new source of coloring materials for foods. This warrants consideration of the utilization of grape pigments as replacements for these dyes.

Legal Definition of Grape Skin Extract

Under the Federal Food, Drug and Cosmetic Act (Anon. 1966A), grape skin extract is defined as a purplish-red liquid prepared by the aqueous extraction (steeping) of the fresh deseeded marc remaining after grapes have been pressed to produce grape juice or wine. The extract is concentrated by vacuum evaporation. Diluents suitable in color additive mixtures for coloring foods may be added. It must comply with the following specifications: Pb, not more than 10 mg/liter; As, 1; pesticide residues, not more than permitted in or on grapes. It may be used without certification for coloring still and carbonated drinks and ades, beverage bases, and alcoholic beverages.

Extraction of Pigments

According to Philip (1975) the classical method of pigment extraction involves extraction with a low boiling alcohol (ethanol or methanol) containing a mineral acid (usually HCl), solvent removal, and purification of the pigments by ion-exchange chromatography. The mineral acid present in the extract is objectionable due to the low pH when added to foods or beverages and ion-exchange purification is slow and costly. These objections were overcome in a new process developed by Philip (1974).

In this process, the pomace was dried in a vacuum oven to below 10% moisture level, and extracted 3 times with methanol containing 1% tartaric acid. Some 85 to 90% of the total tartaric acid was neutralized with 40% KOH solution, the extracts cooled to 15°C (59°F) and the precipitated cream of tartar filtered off. The methanol was removed from the filtrate by vacuum evaporation and the concentrate cooled to 10°−15°C (50°−59°F) and again filtered. The pomace can also be dehydrated with methanol (1 liter/kg) instead of oven drying.

Palamidas and Markovis (1975) compared extraction with boiling water and a cold 500 mg/liter SO_2 water solution. The skins were separated and ground twice in a mill with successive portions of extractant, and the macerate removed from the liquid by filtration. The filtrates were concentrated in a flash evaporator at 50°C (122°F), and the suspended material removed by centrifugation at 30,000 × G. There was no appreciable difference in yield between the two solvents. However, the pigment extracted with the SO_2 solution was much more stable.

Morawe and Glandorf (1965) extracted pigment from red wine lees by adsorbing on Duolite S-30 resin, desorbing with alcohol, filtering, and then evaporating the filtrate to dryness.

Bernou et al. (1976) devised still another procedure for recovering pigment from pomace extracts. They added 80 g/liter (670 lb/1000 gal.) of talc to the extract, stirred for 5 min, removed the talc by centrifuging and washed with water. The pigments were eluted with water:ethanol (1:1) containing 50 g/liter (420 lb/1000 gal.) of tartaric acid, and the talc removed by centrifuging. The used talc can be recycled, and the tartaric acid recovered by addition of KOH, concentrating, and cooling the solution.

DISPOSAL OF DISTILLERY SLOPS AND STEMS

The disposal of distillery slops is a serious problem compared with the disposal of stems.

Distillery Slops

Where suitable land is available, the disposal of distillery slops by intermittent irrigation is the preferred method. See Chap. 6 for a detailed discussion. Marsh and Vaughn (1944) propose recovery of tartrates from the still slops to make the waste more satisfactory for disposal on land. Schroeder *et al.* (1973) report that biological treatment of stillage is possible, but is dependent upon pretreatment for solids removal. It is an alternative to intermittent irrigation but should be considered only if land disposal is not possible.

Stems

The utilization and disposal of stems have been discussed previously (see p. 258).

Amerine and Bailey (1960) found the reducing sugar content of the main stem of the cluster to be 0.08 to 0.70 g per 100 g while that in the side stems varied from 0.15 to 0.40 g. Sucrose in the main stem fluctuated from 0.04 to 1.4 g per 100 g and from 0.12 to 0.197 in the side stems. Starch in the main stem amounted to 2.37 to 7.09 g and from 1.94 to 5.20 in the branches. Their results indicate that appreciable amounts of fermentable carbohydrate can be recovered from the stems.

Schreffler (1954) has reported on a method of handling waste stems from a large winery by which distilling material is obtained and a previous cost of disposal of $75 to $100 a day avoided. The stems are disintegrated in a Rietz hammer mill. Water is added automatically during disintegration. The ground stems are drained and the resulting liquid is used in extracting pomace for distilling material. An average of 16.3 proof gallons of brandy was obtained per ton of stems; or about 0.5 proof gallon per ton of grapes crushed.

WINE VINEGAR

Considerable wine vinegar is made in California. One large plant was devoted solely to this product and several wineries and vinegar plants make moderate amounts of vinegar from wine. Red wine vinegar is more in demand than the white.

If table wine is exposed to the air, various species of acetic bacteria develop and convert the alcohol into acetic acid; that is, they cause acetification. As defined in the Food, Drug and Cosmetic Act, grape vinegar or wine vinegar is made by the alcoholic and subsequent acetous (acetic) fermentation of the juice of grapes and at 20°C (68°F) must contain more than 1 g of grape solids, more than 0.13 g of grape ash and at least 4 g of acetic acid per 100 ml. Vinegar made from diluted distilled alcohol from any source, such as brandy made from wine, must be called spirit vinegar or distilled vinegar. The vinegar bacteria have been described in Chap. 16 and by Vaughn (1942).

Slow Methods of Acetification

Acetification is an oxidation process, essentially according to the reaction:

$$C_2H_5OH + O_2 \rightarrow CH_3COOH + H_2O$$

There are three general methods of vinegar making or acetification in commercial use, namely, the slow process, the generator and the submerged culture tank process. For more detailed discussion see Carpentieri (1947), Maestro (1952), Mitchell (1926), and Pacottet and Guitonneau (1926).

In the slow process, barrels of wine are left partially filled with the bung open until the wine changes to vinegar of its own accord. An abundant supply of air is necessary. The bunghole should be plugged with cotton or covered with fine screen to exclude vinegar flies. If the wine becomes covered with a film yeast, acetification may be very slow and much alcohol wasted by the film yeast. If the alcohol content of the wine is too high, acetification will also be slow. Lactic bacteria may then develop and damage the flavor of the vinegar.

A better slow process is that known as the "Orleans" system. The barrels are filled about ¾ full and holes are bored in both ends of the barrel slightly above the surface of the liquid. The bunghole is left open and all openings are screened. The wine should be diluted to 10% alcohol if necessary. To the wine is added from ¼ to ⅕ its volume of new wine vinegar to serve as an inoculum and to raise the acetic acid content sufficiently to prevent the growth of film yeast. A temperature of 21.1°

to 29.4°C (70.0° to 85.0°F) should be maintained. Acetification will usually be complete within three months. Then, ¼ to ⅓ of the vinegar is drawn off and replaced with wine of about 10% alcohol. Normally, thereafter from ¼ to ⅓ of the contents of the barrels may be drawn off and replaced with wine 3 or 4 times a year. The Orleans process results in aging as well as acetification and therefore usually produces a vinegar of superior flavor and general quality.

Generator Process

The rate of acetification is proportional to the oxygen supply. Therefore, if the surface-to-volume ratio is increased the rate is correspondingly increased. The generator process makes use of this principle. The "old style" vinegar generator consists of a cylindrical wooden tank, 122 to 152 cm (48 to 60 in.) in diameter and about 9.1 to 12.8 m (10.0 to 14.0 ft) in height, divided into 3 compartments. The central compartment occupies most of the volume and is filled with beechwood shavings, pieces of coke, corn cobs, rattan, or other suitable material. The uppermost compartment has a perforated head over which the incoming wine is distributed by a tilting trough or by sprinkler head. The lowermost compartment is a receiving chamber for the acetified liquid.

The wine trickles slowly downward over the filling material on which the vinegar bacteria develop. Usually, an equal volume of vinegar is added to the wine before it enters the generator. One passage through the generator will then usually complete the acetification. The generator operates more satisfactorily on such a mixture than on wine only.

The modern vinegar generator is usually of the recirculating type. It consists of a much larger tank than the old style generator. The bottom compartment is large and may hold several thousand gallons of wine or other vinegar stock. The liquid is delivered by pump from the lower compartment to the sprinkling device in the uppermost compartment. The liquid trickles downward over the coke or shavings into the lower compartment from which it is pumped continuously to the distributor. Acetification is rapid. When it is completed a fresh lot of wine replaces about ⅔ of that in the generator. Some cooling of the liquid is usually necessary as the acetification is an exothermic reaction. In this generator, and in the old style generators as well, considerable alcohol is lost by evaporation, by oxidation to carbon dioxide and water and by utilization by the bacteria for growth.

Tank Process

Vinegar making by the submerged acetification process is now coming into commercial use. It has been described by Joslyn (1955). In this method air in the form of very fine bubbles is passed through the vinegar stock (wine in this instance). Vinegar bacteria growing in the liquid conduct rapid acetification. The process is efficient and rapid; but the bacteria must be in contact with the air bubbles *continuously,* as they die rapidly if the air supply is cut off. There is very little loss of alcohol. Several California wineries have vinegar generators of this type.

Aging

Freshly-made vinegar is often harsh in taste and odor. On aging for several months in well-filled barrels or tanks it becomes more mellow in flavor. Aging is, in part, due to the formation of esters.

Vinegar is often clarified by fining, in much the same manner as wine. Bentonite is the usual clarifying agent, although casein or gelatin plus tannin can also be used. If the vinegar is reasonably clear, filtration alone may be sufficient. The filter should be made of stainless steel, or hard rubber, or other material that will not be attacked by the acetic acid (see Chap. 7). Considerable clouding of vinegar because of excess copper or iron content has occurred. Fining with "Cufex" or other agent may be necessary in such cases as described in Chap. 6 and 15.

Vinegar is usually given a final polishing filtration to render it brilliantly clear. It may be flash-pasteurized and bottled hot to kill vinegar bacteria and thus prevent their growth and clouding of the bottled product. Addition of about 150 mg/liter of sulfur dioxide at the time of bottling may be made instead of pasteurization. For further information see Cruess (1958), Joslyn (1955), Mitchell (1926), Saywell (1934), or Smock and Neubert (1950).

GRAPE CONCENTRATE

While the principal use for grape concentrate in California has been to sweeten dessert wines, there is now a good demand for concentrate of high quality for other purposes. It is used for blending with other concentrates, particularly frozen pack Concord grape, and orange, and other frozen concentrates. These may be processed into jellies, beverages, bakery products, etc. For data on the European industry see Mensio (1929).

Discontinuous Process

In making a white concentrate the free-run fresh juice should be treated overnight with a pectic enzyme as described in Chap. 6, filtered and concentrated in a modern, low-temperature vacuum concentrator. A small amount, about 125 mg/liter of sulfur dioxide should be added to the crushed grapes in order to prevent undue browning of the juice. With high acid grapes, some favor detartrating with calcium carbonate prior to concentration. Clarification by fining with bentonite is also practiced.

To make a red juice for concentrate, the crushed and stemmed grapes are heated to about 60°C (140°F) but not above 62.8°C (145.0°F) because of damage to flavor at higher temperatures. Heating can be done in large stainless steel kettles as in the making of Concord juice in the eastern United States, or may be done in lined or stainless metallic tanks by continuously drawing off the free-run juice, heating it in a continuous-type pasteurizer, such as the plate type pasteurizer used for wine pasteurization, and recirculating the heated juice over the crushed grapes. This is continued until the crushed grapes and juice reach 60°C (140°F). The free-run is drawn off and the grapes pressed in a basket, bladder, or rack-and-cloth press. The juices may be mixed and should then be cooled by water-cooled plates or tubes to near room temperature. The juice may be treated overnight with a pectic enzyme and filtered. Pectic enzyme treatment greatly facilitates filtration of the juice and prevents jelling of the concentrate. Bentonite fining is also recommended. In most cases the pomace is not pressed but is used for making distilling material.

Continuous Process

A continuous method of extraction of juice and color from red grapes in commercial use in a California winery has been described by Nury (1957). The stemmed, crushed grapes are pumped continuously through a heat exchanger in which they are heated for a short time (about 2 min) to 87.8° to 93.3°C (190.0° to 200.0°F). They then pass through a second heat exchanger in which they are cooled to about 37.8°C (100.0°F). A solution of pectic enzyme is added continuously to the stream of cooled must. The juice is allowed to drain from the skins and seeds in special tanks and is then screened to remove suspended materials (fines). The drained pomace is pressed in a continuous press. The juice may then be filtered or clarified if a clear concentrate is desired. Nury reports that concentrate made by this procedure is much superior in color and flavor to that made from juice extracted by the discontinuous heat extraction process. Berg (1950) and Berg and Marsh (1950) have also described a similar procedure for extraction of color and juice from grapes for the production of red wine.

Cream of tartar slowly separates from grape concentrate and its removal is a difficult problem. Consequently, the excess should be removed before concentration by cooling the juice to near its freezing point, storing it at or below 0°C (32°F) for about 2 weeks and filtering it cold. Even this treatment does not remove all of the cream of tartar that will become excess upon concentration. Following the refrigeration, treatment with a cation exchange resin in the sodium form is necessary.

The clear stabilized juice is now ready for concentration by vacuum pan. In order to prevent heat damage, a low temperature and high vacuum should be used during concentration. A stainless steel vacuum pan (Fig. 18.1, 18.2 and 18.3) with a continuous outside heating unit is preferred. The juice is flash-heated and enters the vacuum pan as a spray as the pan is under very high vacuum. The juice and concentrate are not above 48.9°C (120.0°F) in the pan, usually at about 48.3°C (110.0°F). All metal equipment that comes in contact with the juice should be of corrosion-resistant metal or alloy.

Types of Concentrators

Orange juice is concentrated in Florida and California in vacuum concentrating units of two types at temperatures of 15.6°C (60.0°F) and lower. In one type the concentrator is of triple effect, falling film design. Water at 32.2°C (90.0°F) is used as the heating medium in the first effect. Water vapor from the first effect heats the second effect and vapor from it heats the third effect. The water used in heating drops to 26.7°C (80.0°F) in the first effect, after which it is returned to the jacket of the compressor used in compressing the vapor of the refrigerant, Freon. The liquefied Freon is used to cool water to 2.8°C (37.0°F) for use in the barometric condenser of the vacuum pan. The vacuum in the first effect is 73.98 cm (29.13 in.), in the second 74.78 cm (29.44 in.) and in the third 75.29 cm (29.64 in.). The temperature of the final orange concentrate is about 10°C (50°F). This is known as the Kelly-Howard or Carrier-Howard concentrator. It has been known for some time that grape concentrates produced at temperatures of below 37.8°C (100.0°F) have a fresh grape flavor and a greenish color. Matalas et al. (1965A) compared 3 concentrates produced at 20.6° to 21.7°C (69.0° to 71.0°F), 33.3°C (92.0°F) and 55.6°C (132.0°F). They found that the initial color of the product was proportional to the temperature.

In another type of vacuum concentrator, ammonia is used as the heating medium. It is a multistage type and is a single effect in operation; that is, all units of the concentrator are under the same degree of vacuum. The three stages are heated by warm ammonia gas direct from a compressor. The ammonia gas or vapor gives up its heat of condensation to the three boiling chambers in which the juice is being concentrated. Juice at room temperature flows under high vacuum into stage 1 and concentrate is pumped continuously from stage 3 at about 10°C (50°F). The liquefied ammonia is used to cool and condense the water vapor from the juice and is, in turn, vaporized. It then goes to a compressor and is

Courtesy of Valley Foundry and Machine Works, Inc.

FIG. 18.1. SIXTY–INCH DIAMETER STAINLESS STEEL VAC-
UUM PAN WITH STEAM JET VACUUM PUMP AND BARO-
METRIC CONDENSER

compressed. From the compressor it flows at 40.6°C (105.0°F) to begin
the cycle again. A two-stage steam ejector removes uncondensable gases
and maintains a very high vacuum in the concentrator. Multiple-effect
evaporating equipment has been used by the sugar industry for a number
of years. Nowlin (1963) has calculated that triple-effect evaporators
would not be economical for the seasonal operations of the grape industry. However, double-effect installations appear economical. He estimated savings of about $5000 per season for a 1900 liter/hr (500 gal./hr)
capacity evaporator (see Beisel 1954), Cruess (1958), Heid (1943) and
Heid and Kelly (1953) for further description of these two types of low
temperature vacuum concentrators. See also Cross and Gemmill (1948),
Kelly (1949), and Walker and Patterson (1955).

The degree of concentration will depend upon whether the grape con-

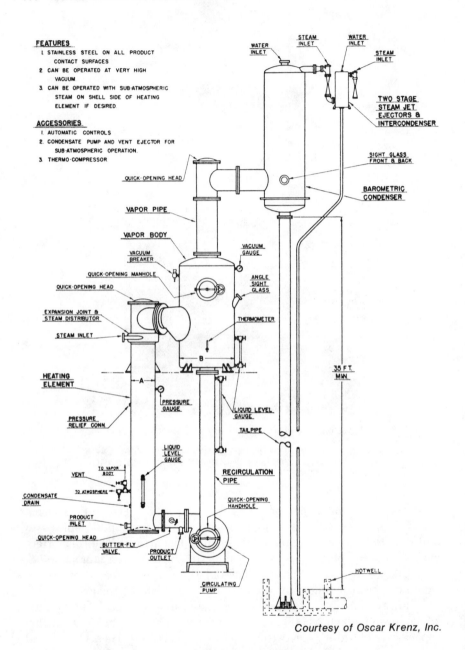

FEATURES
1. STAINLESS STEEL ON ALL PRODUCT CONTACT SURFACES
2. CAN BE OPERATED AT VERY HIGH VACUUM
3. CAN BE OPERATED WITH SUB-ATMOSPHERIC STEAM ON SHELL SIDE OF HEATING ELEMENT IF DESIRED.

ACCESSORIES
1. AUTOMATIC CONTROLS
2. CONDENSATE PUMP AND VENT EJECTOR FOR SUB-ATMOSPHERIC OPERATION.
3. THERMO-COMPRESSOR

Courtesy of Oscar Krenz, Inc.

FIG. 18.2. MODERN FORCED CIRCULATION CONCENTRATOR

Courtesy of Vie-Del Grape Products Co.

FIG. 18.3. CONTINUOUS VACUUM CONCENTRATOR

centrate is to be used soon or is to be stored for several months. If it is to be used within a few weeks it may be concentrated to only 68° Brix; if it is to be held at room temperature for several months it may be concentrated to 72° to 74° Brix to prevent or minimize damage by fermentation. However, at concentrations above 68° Brix there is serious danger of crystallization of dextrose (grape sugar) which may become so extensive as to convert the concentrate into a solid or pasty mass.

Konlechner and Haushofer (1959) were apparently the first to point out that quality concentrates must be stored at low temperatures of 0°C (32°F) for 60°–70° Brix concentrate and at –5°C (23°F) for 40°–65° Brix concentrate. Matalas *et al.* (1965B) also reported undesirable darkening of color when concentrate was stored at 30°C (86°F). The effect was greater the higher the temperature used for concentrating. The harmful effect was reflected in poorer quality wines produced from such reconstituted concentrates. They recommended storage of high quality concentrate at or near 0°C (32°F).

Dimotaki-Kourakou and Kandilis (1964) added 1.5–2.5% of concentrate to flour and successfully made bread from it.

Flavor Recovery

In concentrating under vacuum, the juice boils and most of the volatile flavor constituents are lost unless special methods are used for their recovery. In several California fruit concentrate plants, the vapor from the vacuum pan is fractionally condensed, the most volatile fraction being at a very low temperature. This fraction containing most of the volatile flavor constituents may be added back to the concentrate.

Another method described by Milleville (1944) consists in momentarily flash heating the juice to above its boiling point in a closed system and then passing it in the form of a spray into a chamber in which it flash boils and is cooled quickly to below the heat-damage temperature. About 30% of the juice is vaporized. The vapor is fractionally condensed in such a manner that most of the volatile flavor constituents are held in a distillate equal to only about 1/150 of the volume of the original juice. The cooled juice, now stripped of its volatile constituents, is concentrated in a low temperature vacuum pan. The concentrated volatile constituents fraction may be blended with the concentrated juice. It may be blended with Concord grape concentrate, the blend diluted to 50°−52° Brix and preserved by freezing. For use as a beverage, 1 part of the concentrate by volume is mixed with 3 parts of water. For household use, the concentrate of 50°−52° Brix is packed in 170-g (6-oz) cans.

Plate type evaporators and essence recovery systems are now available. They are reported to be more economical in their use of steam. Other advantages of the plate type evaporator are the rapid start-up (compared to traditional tubular calandria), their adjustable capacity (by adding or removing plates), ease of shutdown and cleaning, and low liquid hold-up.

Recovery of the methyl anthranilate in grape concentrate production is more difficult since this ester is not very volatile. It is necessary to strip 25 to 30% of the incoming juice even to attain 50% recovery. In the traditional tubular calandria the essence-bearing vapors from the first effect are concentrated in a vapor feed column. With the plate type evaporators, the unit is arranged as a triple-effect evaporator. The first effect evaporates about 25% of the incoming juice and thus acts as a stripping evaporator. The available heat of the vapor is recovered as the vapor condenses in the steam chest of the second effect. The weak essence condensate is then fed to the liquid feed column. For a description of a highly versatile unit, see Anon. (1966B).

For shipment to jelly makers or other large users, the concentrate of 68° to 74° Brix may be packed in enamel-lined 13.6-kg (30-lb) tins or in plastic lined metal drums. There is a growing demand for red grape concentrate for blending with Concord grape concentrate and for use in fruit punch syrup blends. Some interest is also reported in the use of grape concentrate for home wine making.

Use of Raisins

Occasionally in Europe, especially in years of short crops, raisins may be used to produce wines. While the general chemical characteristics of these wines appear normal, they usually have a distinct caramel odor and, unless especially treated, a darker color. For the use of raisins to produce syrups see Musco *et al.* (1954).

JUICES

While most fruit juices are considered primary products rather than by-products, some fruit wine producers and some vinegar factories also make unfermented fruit juices. At least one large winery in California produces unfermented grape juice commercially. See Cruess (1958) or Tressler and Joslyn (1954), for further information. European methods are described by Mehlitz (1951), Koch (1950, 1951), and Baumann and Schliessmann (1960).

Grape Juice

While Concord *(Vitis labrusca)* is used almost exclusively for making grape juice in this country, various varieties of *V. vinifera* are used in Europe. Certain direct-producing hybrids gave higher quality grape juice than that of Chasselas doré or Müller-Thurgau in the study of Huglin and Schwartz (1960). The best hybrids were Kuhlman 191-1, Landot 244, and Seyve-Villard 5276.

The grape juice industry of France depends to a large extent on desulfiting *muté* (highly sulfited grape juice). Flanzy and André (1959) constructed a continuous vacuum desulfiter operating at 44.4°C (112.0°F). If grape juice undergoes some fermentation, the aldehyde-bisulfite complex will be formed. This compound distills unchanged, according to Deibner and Benard (1954–1955).

Red grape juice can be made by crushing and stemming, followed by heating the crushed grapes to 60.0° to 65.6°C (140.0° to 150.0°F) to extract the color; refrigerating and filtering followed by treatment with a sodium cation exchange resin to prevent separation of tartrates in the bottled product; treatment with a pectic enzyme overnight; filtering; flash pasteurizing to 85.0° to 87.8°C (185.0° to 190.0°F); bottling hot; and sealing and cooling the bottled product in sprays of water. Most plants, however, still rely upon removal of excess cream of tartar and calcium tartrate by storage of the juice under refrigeration for several months. The refrigerating followed by ion exchange method is much less costly and much more effective.

Commercial pectolytic enzyme preparations sometimes are helpful in fruit and grape juice clarification and in the clarity of the wines but the results usually cannot be correlated with the methyl esterase (PE) or polygalacturonase (PG, whether of the endo- or exo-type) content of the enzyme, according to Joslyn *et al.* (1952), Berg (1959), and Marteau *et al.* (1963). The latter also found no direct correlation between speed of clarification and amount of methanol produced. Natural clarification of grape juices appears to be limited by their low endo-PG activity. The commercial preparations, on the other hand, appear to have a large excess of endo-PG activity and their efficiency seems limited by their PE activity.

Flanzy and André (1959) have studied the problem of desulfitation of *muté* to produce grape juice or for concentration. To reduce the sulfur dioxide to 100 mg/liter, a vacuum of 200 mm of mercury and a temperature of at least 50°C (122°F) was necessary. At greater vacuum more sulfur dioxide can be removed. More sulfur dioxide is, of course, removed at a low pH than at a high.

Kern (1964) showed that grape juices have a greater tendency to form hydroxymethylfurfural (hmf) than those of apples, oranges or black currants. Flash pasteurization at 87.2°C (189.0°F) for 2 min produces only traces of hmf. He set the level for quality reduction at 100 mg/liter. To produce this amount, grape juice had to be heated at 95°C (203°F) for 2½ hours. However, a sensory difference is produced by heating for 30 min, even though only 4 mg/liter is produced in this period. He believes that undesirable sensory differences are due to chemical changes induced by hmf or by changes in other components. In Kern's work with fruit juice (apple?), fermentation removed the hydroxymethylfurfural (hmf). No hmf was found in fresh grapes by Flanzy and Collon (1962B). It was found in grape juices heated at 80°C (176°F) for more than 5 min, in desulfited grape juice that had been stored 3 years, and in grape concentrate. Flanzy and Collon (1962A) consider the presence of hmf in grape juice to be evidence of poor handling techniques. Probably other compounds are also present.

The efficiency of pressure versus vacuum filtration of grape juice was studied by Harris (1964) but the latter is less versatile. He showed that pressure filtration is more costly, but, if used during the period when a winery is not using its pressure filtration equipment for wines, might be more desirable. He recommended enzyme treatment and relatively high temperature pressure filtration. The original paper should be consulted for details since his data admittedly apply to only a single grape juice under specified plant conditions. Costs of grape juice filtration appear to be about 1¢ per 3.8 liters (1 gal.). Garoglio and Stella (1964) also found DEPC useful in preparing nonfermentable grape juice. The technique was to filter and then add 25.0 mg/liter (3.4 oz/1000 gal.) of sulfur dioxide and 500 to 1000 mg/liter (4.2 to 8.4 lb/1000 gal.) of DEPC. In our opinion 500 mg/liter (4.2 lb/1000 gal.) of DEPC is an excessively high level for grape juice.

Berry Juices

Berry juices have been prepared by coarsely crushing, heating to 79.4° to 82.2°C (175.0° to 180.0°F) to extract the color; pressing hot; cooling; treatment with a pectic enzyme overnight; filtering; adding water and sugar in such proportions that a palatable beverage is obtained; flash pasteurizing and bottling or canning as described for apple and grape juices. Loganberries, Youngberries, sour varieties of blackberries, and red currants give very attractive beverages.

In European countries, particularly in Germany, Switzerland, Holland, and England, the Boehi (also called the Seitz-Boehi) cold process is used, particularly for apple juice. The juice is usually depectinized with a pectic enzyme and filtered brilliantly clear. It is then chilled, heavily charged with carbon dioxide and preserved by carbon dioxide and refrigeration in glass-lined steel tanks until it is to be bottled. It is then filtered through sterile germ-proof filter pads under aseptic conditions into sterile bottles and the bottles sealed with sterile closures. No heating is employed. Preservation in the bottle depends on removal of all yeast and mold cells by germ-proof filtration. Usually the bottled product is carbonated.

At present the best apple juices are produced by use of aroma concentrates and by flash pasteurization of the clear juice according to Wucherpfennig and Bretthauer (1964). Storage of opalescent juice, sterile filtration without enzyme inactivation and storage under carbon dioxide pressure (Boehi-process) are less satisfactory. See Tressler and Joslyn (1954) or Mehlitz (1951) for details.

REFERENCES[2]

AGOSTINI, A. 1964. Utilization of by-products of vines and wines. Wynboer *32* (395) 13–16.

AMERINE, M.A. and BAILEY, C. 1960. Carbohydrate content of various parts of the grape cluster. Am. J. Enol. Vitic. *10,* 196–198.

ANON. 1966A. Color additives. Grape skin extract (enocianina). Fed. Regist. *31,* 4784.

---

[2]Titles have been translated only for nonwestern European languages.

ANON. 1966B. Grape and apple processing. Food Technol. *20*, 49.

ARIES, R.S. 1957. Tartrates. *In* Encyclopedia of Chemistry. G.L. Clark (Editor). Reinhold Publishing Co., New York.

BAUMANN, J. and SCHLIESSMANN, C. 1960. Gärunglose Obst- und Beerenverwertung. Gesundheitswerte und Herstellung von Obst-, Beeren- und Traubensüssmosten. Eugen Ulmer, Stuttgart.

BEISEL, C.G. 1954. Vacuum concentration of fruit and vegetable juices. *In* The Chemistry and Technology of Fruit and Vegetable Production. D.K. Tressler and M.A. Joslyn (Editors). AVI Publishing Co., Westport, Conn.

BERG, H.W. 1950. Heat treatment of musts. Wines Vines *36* (6) 24—26.

BERG, H.W. 1959. The effect of several fungal pectic enzyme preparations on grape musts and wines. Am. J. Enol. Vitic. *10*, 130—134.

BERG, H.W. and MARSH, G.L. 1950. Heat treatment of musts. Wines Vines *31* (7) 23—24; (8) 29—30.

BERNOU, J., BOURZEIX, M., TOUZEL, M., DU BREIL DE PONTBRIAND, P. and HERIDA, H. 1976. Nouveau procédé d'extraction des vins destinés à la distillation, des piquettes, des extraits de marcs et d'autres extraits végétaux. Ann. Fals. Expert. Chim. *69* (738) 153—163.

CARPENTIERI, F. 1947. L'Aceto, 7th Edition. Ottavi, Casale Monferrato.

CROSS, J.A. and GEMMILL, A.V. 1948. Revolutionary evaporator raises quality and lowers costs. Food Ind. *20*, 1421—1423.

CRUESS, W.V. 1958. Commercial Fruit and Vegetable Products, 4th Edition. McGraw-Hill Book Co., New York.

DEIBNER, L. and BENARD, P. 1954—1955. Recherches sur la séparation de l'acide acétaldéhyde sulfureux contenu dans les boissons alcooliques. Ind. Agric. Aliment. (Paris) *71*, 973—978; *72*, 13—18.

DIMOTAKI-KOURAKOU, V. and KANDILIS, J. 1964. Méthode de constation de l'emploi du moût de raisin concentré dans la panification de la farine de blé. IV Congrès d'Expertise Chimique, Athènes (Special No.) 411—416.

FLANZY, M. and ANDRÉ, P. 1959. Désulfitation des jus de raisin. Ann. Technol. Agric. *8*, 171—192.

FLANZY, M. and COLLON, Y. 1962A. Sur la présence de l'hydroxyméthylfurfural dans certains jus de raisin. *Ibid. 11*, 227—233.

FLANZY, M. and COLLON, Y. 1962B. Sur l'origine de l'hydroxyméthylfurfural de certains jus de raisin. *Ibid. 11*, 271—273.

FOLGER, A.H. 1940. The digestibility of ground prunes, winery pomace, avocado meal, asparagus butts, and fenugreek meal. Calif. Agric. Exp. Stn. Bull. *635.*

GAROGLIO, P.G. and STELLA, C. 1964. Recerche sull'impiego in enologia dell'estere dietilico dell'acido pirocarbonico (DEPC). Riv. Viticolt. Enol. (Conegliano) *17*, 422—453.

HARRIS, M.B. 1964. Grape juice clarification by filtration. Am. J. Enol. Vitic. *15*, 54—62.

HEID, J.L. 1943. Concentrating citrus juices by the vacuum method. Food Ind. *15*, 7—8.

WINERY BY-PRODUCTS 663

HEID, J.L. and KELLY, E.J. 1953. The concentration and dehydration of citrus juices. Canner *116* (5) 9–13; (6) 13–15.

HUGLIN, P. and SCHWARTZ, J. 1960. Essai d'obtention et de dégustation de jus de raisin à partir d'hybrides-producteurs. Ann. Technol. Agric. *9,* 53–65.

JACOB, H.E. and PROEBSTING, E.L. 1937. Grape pomace as a vineyard and orchard fertilizer. Wine Vines *18* (10) 22–23.

JOSLYN, M.A. 1955. Vinegar. In Encyclopedia of Technology, Vol. 14. Interscience Publisher, New York.

JOSLYN, M.A., MIST, S. and LAMBERT, E. 1952. The clarification of apple juice by fungal pectic enzyme preparations. Food Technol. *6,* 133–139.

KELLY, E.J. 1949. New low-temperature evaporator doubles plant production. Food Ind. *21,* 1386–1389.

KERN, A. 1964. Die Bedeutung des Hydroxymethylfurfurols als Qualitätsmerkmal für Fruchtsäfte und Konzentrate. Intern. Fruchtsaft-Union, Berichte wissensch.-techn. Kommission *5,* 203–214.

KINSELLA, J.E. 1974. Grapeseed oil: a rich source of linoleic acid. Food Technol. *28,* 58–60.

KOCH, J. 1950. Über die Herstellung von Süssmost nach dem Böhi-Verfahren. Ind. Obst-Gemüseverwert. *35,* 248–251.

KOCH, J. 1951. Neuzeitliche Erkenntnisse auf dem Gebiet der Süssmostherstellung. Joh. Wagner & Söhne, Frankfurt/Main.

KONLECHNER, H. and HAUSHOFER, H. 1959. Konzentrieren von Traubenmost. Mitt. Rebe. Wein, Ser. A (Klosterneuburg) *9,* 161–217.

LATRETO, R. 1953. New method of developing fertilizer and compost values in winery pomace. Wine Inst. Tech. Advis. Committee, Mar. 9, 1953.

MAESTRO PALÓ, F. 1952. Vinagre, 2nd Edition. Semper, Zaragoza.

MARSH, G.L. 1942. Method of determining tartrate and calculations of the amounts of precipitants required for its recovery. Wine Institute, San Francisco. Mimeo Circ.

MARSH, G.L. 1943. Recovery of tartrates from winery wastes. Proc. Inst. Food Technol. *1943,* 183–195.

MARSH, G.L. and GUADAGNI, D. 1942. Extraction and recovery of tartrates from pomace of table wines. Excerpts from a report to Wine Institute, San Francisco.

MARSH, G.L. and VAUGHN, R.H. 1944. Slop disposal system based on tartrate recovery. Wines Vines *25* (6) 15–19.

MARTEAU, G., SCHEUR, J. and OLIVIERI, C. 1963. Le rôle des enzymes pectolytiques du raisin ou de préparations commerciales dans le processus de la clarification des jus. Ann. Technol. Agric. *12,* 155–176.

MATALAS, L., MARSH, G.L. and OUGH, C.S. 1965A. The effect of concentration conditions and storage temperatures on grape juice concentrate. Am. J. Enol. Vitic. *16,* 129–135.

MATALAS, L., MARSH, G.L. and OUGH, C.S. 1965B. The use of reconstituted grape concentrate for dry table wine production. *Ibid. 16,* 136–143.

MEHLITZ, A. 1951. Süssmost, Fachbuch der gewerbsmässigen Süssmoster-zuegung. Drs. Serger and Hempel, Braunschweig, Germany.

MENSIO, C. 1929. I Mosti Concentrati. Fratelli Ottavi, Casale Monferrato.

MILLEVILLE, H.P. 1944. Recovery of natural apple flavors. Fruit Prod. J. 24, 48–51.

MITCHELL, C.A. 1926. Vinegar, Its Manufacture and Examination, 2nd Edition. Chas. Griffin and Co., London.

MORAWE, H.G. and GLANDORF, K. 1965. Natürliche natürlicher Farbstoff aus Rotwein oder Rotwein-Bodensatz für Färben von Lebensmittel und Lebensmittel-Zusatzen. German Pat. 1,190,313. April 1.

MUSCO, D., YANASE, K. and LEE, L.J. 1954. Results of University of California studies on quality of syrups made from low-grade raisins. Food Packer 35 (12) 27–35.

NOWLIN, R.L. 1963. The economics of multiple-effect evaporation for production of grape juice concentrate. Am. J. Enol. Vitic. 14, 80–85.

NURY, M.S. 1957. Continuous color and juice extraction of grapes. Wine Inst. Tech. Advis. Committee, Dec. 6, 1957.

PACOTTET, P. and GUITTONNEAU, L. 1926. Eaux-de-Vie et Vinaigres. J.-B. Baillière et Fils, Paris.

PALAMIDAS, N. and MARKOVIS, P. 1975. Stability of anthocyanin in a carbonated beverage. J. Food Sci. 40, 1047–1049.

PHILIP, T. 1974. An anthocyanin recovery system from grape wastes. J. Food Sci. 39, 859.

PHILIP, T. 1975. Utilization of plant pigments as food colorants. Food Prod. Dev. 9, 50–56.

PIRRONE, A.F. 1958. Composting of pomace piles. Wine Inst. Tech. Advis. Commmittee, May 26, 1958.

RICE, A.C. 1976. Solid waste generation and by-product recovery potential from winery residues. Am. J. Enol. Vitic. 27, 21–26.

SAYWELL, L.G. 1934. Clarification of vinegar. Ind. Eng. Chem. 26, 981–982.

SÉMICHON, L. 1907. Dried grape marc as a feed for farm animals. Compt. Rend. Cong. Soc. Aliment. Ration. Betail. 12, 144–150.

SCHREFFLER, C. 1954. Recovery of sugar from grape stems. Wine Inst. Tech. Advis. Committee, Dec. 3, 1954.

SCHROEDER, E.D., REARDON, D.J., MATTEOLI, R. and HOVEY, W.H. 1973. Biological treatment of winery stillage. Rept. Wine Inst. Tech. Advis. Committee, San Francisco.

SMOCK, R.M. and NEUBERT, A.M. 1950. Apples and Apple Products. Interscience Publishers, New York and London.

TRESSLER, D.K. and JOSLYN, M.A. 1954. Fruit and Vegetable Juice Production. AVI Publishing Co., Westport, Conn.

VAUGHN, R.H. 1942. The acetic bacteria. Wallerstein Lab. Commun. 5, 5–27.

VAUGHN, R.H. and MARSH, G.L. 1943. Bacterial decomposition of crude calcium tartrate during the process of recovery from grape residues. J. Bacteriol. *45*, 35—36.

WALKER, L.H. and PATTERSON, D.C. 1955. A laboratory fruit-essence recovery unit. Food Technol. *9*, 87—90.

WALTER, R.H. and SHERMAN, R.M. 1975. Grape and apple pomace charcoal. J. Agric. Food Chem. *23*, 1218.

WUCHERPFENNIG, K. and BRETTHAUER, G. 1964. Beitrag zur Veränderung in Apfelsäften während der Lagerung. Intern. Fruchtsaft-Union, Berichte wissensch.-techn. Kommission *5*, 105—130.

19

Evaluation of Wines and Brandies

Examination of wines in the laboratory is a necessary and regular practice in all wineries and must include sensory evaluation, microscopical examination, fining tests, and determination of ethanol, total titratable and volatile acidity, sugar, extract, tannin, sulfur dioxide, depth of color, etc. These observations and analyses may be made for one or more of the following and other purposes: to ascertain a wine's soundness, to check the sensory quality of wines to be bought or to be sold, to aid in blending, to ascertain the completeness of the fermentation, and to guide the wine maker in ameliorating a wine.

SENSORY EXAMINATION

This is an important and often critical operation. Every winery must have at least one person who is responsible for collecting and evaluating the sensory examination made by individuals or panels. The panel of judges should have keen palates, discriminating judgments, and know wine types. They should know the desired and characteristic aroma and bouquet of the types of wine which the winery produces. Familiarity with European types is often of little value to California producers. The climatic conditions, varieties, and processes used here are different. Resemblance between wine types of different regions is often minimal (even when produced from the same varieties). This does not mean that California producers may not profitably evaluate European types. But they *should* develop their own standards of identity and quality. These may or may not resemble European wine types (see Chap. 1).

Troost (1965) stressed three objectives of sensory evaluation: (1) to care for the wines at the winery, (2) to evaluate quality, and (3) to satisfy governmental food regulations. In the first and last cases, chemical analysis should be used to supplement the sensory data. With qualified personnel no difficult problems should arise. In the second case, problems arise when wines of different regions or seasons are compared. Psychological factors influence tasters, particularly information as to source or price. Analytical data are of limited value because wines with the same analysis may have very different tastes and odors. As Troost notes, quality and market success are not necessarily related. In the third case (not used in this country), the tasters are asked to judge the relative merit of a group of wines in relation to normal conditions. Is the wine deserving of a "Spätlese"? Is the year a bad, good or excellent one? Analytical data are useful in reaching a decision, particularly for abnormal wines.

Sensory examination may be for several purposes: (a) to classify the wine as to type (as established by winery policy and practicability), (b) to detect incipient microbial activity, (c) to evaluate the desirability or undesirability of constituents such as sugar, tannin, total acidity, (d) to suggest necessary cellar treatment, (e) to decide whether the wine is "bottle ripe," and (f) to establish the quality of the wine.

Successful tasters should have good sense of differentiation of color, odor and flavor, and, as well, a good memory for these wine characteristics. The results of Filipello (1957) as summarized by Filipello and Berg (1959) demonstrated that experienced judges were significantly better in wine quality evaluations than inexperienced judges.

Tasting should be done in a clean, neat, well-lighted room free of pronounced odors or distracting sounds.

Glasses

For general evaluation an 8 to 10 oz tulip-shaped thin-walled glass is best. Special glasses with narrow openings are useful for judging aroma and bouquet but the tulip-shaped glass is generally sufficient. For brandies snifters are sometimes useful.

Appearance

The appearance of a wine will often tell the experienced judge much about its condition. White wines with a brown hue are usually oxidized and overaged in odor, or so low in sulfur dioxide that oxidation has occurred. Or, a brown color in a white wine may mean great age; or, in a Madeira, normal color.

A silky, "wavy" sheen in a hazy or cloudy white or red dry wine accompanied by a characteristic odor is unmistakable evidence of bacterial spoilage.

High acid red wine will have a bright red color. The depth of color is important. The age of red wine is indicated by the tint; the older the wine the more the red color shifts toward the brown or brownish red. Old port is likely to be tawny in color, young port red or purplish red. Angelica and muscatel should be light gold or gold-amber in color; Madeira is light amber to brown. Chablis and Riesling should be pale yellow, sauterne more yellow. Sherry may range from very pale to a dark amber, depending on type (see pp. 146−147).

Ough and Berg (1959) showed that extremely small differences in color, as determined from tristimulus data, could be differentiated by their panel. A fluorescent light (Sylvania, 40 watt, cool white standard with white reflector) was significantly better for identifying small differences compared to daylight or incandescent light. Orange tints were especially disliked under fluorescent light. Ough and Amerine (1970) found both untrained student judges and highly trained judges had similar wine color preference.

Odor

After visual inspection, the bouquet and aroma of the wine are noted. The age of the wine greatly affects the bouquet. Even a slight vinegar or lactic souring can be detected. Excess sulfur dioxide or hydrogen sulfide can be easily recognized.

Certain varieties of grapes impart characteristic aromas to wine: among the vinifera varieties, e.g., muscat, Cabernet, Sémillon, Sauvignon blanc, White Riesling, and Zinfandel; and among the labrusca-type varieties, Catawba, Delaware and Concord. Tasters should distinguish between bouquet and aroma. Bouquet is the odor developed in aging. Aroma is the odor derived from the fresh grapes and products of fermentation.

Taste

Following olfactory examination one proceeds to the evaluation of the taste. The four aspects of taste are sour, sweet, salty, and bitter. Astringency is a tactile sensation. All are important but the salty taste is seldom encountered. The acid taste is essential, particularly for table wines. Low acidity gives wines a flat or insipid taste. Sweetness is critical for sweet table and dessert wines and for some sparkling wines. Red wines have some bitter taste. The goal is a slight but not persistent bitterness and a balanced astringency. Pangborn et al. (1964), using 12 highly trained judges, showed that increasing acidity interfered with sweetness perception and intensity. Caffeine reduced response to sweetness but bitterness perception was slightly enhanced by sucrose.

Flavor

Flavor is the "in mouth" bouquet and aroma, though taste may play a role. To some, this is the "over-all" impression of the wine. It is completed by the aftertaste—the sensory impressions which linger on the palate after the wine is swallowed.

The sensory evaluation may be supplemented by chemical analysis, especially if the evaluation is of importance in connection with cellar treatment or purchase or sale of wine. Wine evaluation and subsequent checking with the analysis improve the judge's ability to detect incipient spoilage. It is advisable to judge the same wines on several different dates in a blind testing of several wines each time. By keeping notes and comparing them, skill and confidence are increased. Wines for such comparisons cannot be kept in a refrigerator since they will change when stored in less than full containers. For such comparisons all tasting conditions should be standardized.

Difference Tasting

It is often desirable to determine if a sensory difference exists between two wines. If the difference is a *known* chemical difference the paired test is usually used. In this test the taster is presented coded glasses containing the two wines. A panel (or an individual) successfully differentiating the two wines a certain number of times establishes the probability of difference between the wines (Table 19.1).

TABLE 19.1. SIGNIFICANCE IN PAIRED TASTE TESTS[1] $(p=\frac{1}{2})$

Number of Tasters or Tastings	Minimum Correct Judgments to Establish Significant Differentiation (One-tailed Test) Probability Level[2]			Minimum Agreeing Judgments Necessary to Establish Significant Preference (Two-tailed Test) Probability Level[2]		
	0.05	0.01	0.001	0.05	0.01	0.001
7	7	7	—	7	—	—
8	7	8	—	8	8	—
9	8	9	—	8	9	—
10	9	10	10	9	10	11
11	9	10	11	10	11	11
12	10	11	12	10	11	12
13	10	12	13	11	12	13
14	11	12	13	12	13	14
15	12	13	14	12	13	14
16	12	14	15	13	14	15
17	13	14	16	13	15	16
18	13	15	16	14	15	17
19	14	15	17	15	16	17
20	15	16	18	15	17	18
21	15	17	18	16	17	19
22	16	17	19	17	18	19
23	16	18	20	17	19	20
24	17	19	20	18	19	21

TABLE 19.1. *(Continued)*

Number of Tasters or Tastings	Minimum Correct Judgments to Establish Significant Differentiation (One-tailed Test)			Minimum Agreeing Judgments Necessary to Establish Significant Preference (Two-tailed Test)		
	Probability Level[2]			Probability Level[2]		
	0.05	0.01	0.001	0.05	0.01	0.001
25	18	19	21	18	20	21
30	20	22	24	21	23	25
35	23	25	27	24	26	28
40	26	28	31	27	29	31
45	29	31	34	30	32	34
50	32	34	37	33	35	37
60	37	40	43	39	41	44
70	43	46	49	44	47	50
80	48	51	55	50	52	56
90	54	57	61	55	58	61
100	59	63	66	61	64	67

[1]Source of data: Amerine and Roessler (1976).
[2]$p=0.05$ indicates that the odds are only 1 in 20 that this result is due to chance; $p=0.01$ indicates a chance of only 1 in 100; and $p=0.001$, 1 in 1000.

Where the difference is a qualitative one, a triangular test is commonly used. In this the two wines are poured into three coded glasses—one into two glasses and one into the third. If the wines are A and B, six orders of presentation are possible: AAB, ABA, BAA, BBA, BAB, ABB. A panel (or an individual) identifying the odd glass a certain percentage of the time establishes a certain probability of a difference between the wines (Table 19.2). For further information see Amerine *et al.* (1965) and Amerine and Roessler (1976).

TABLE 19.2. SIGNIFICANCE IN TRIANGULAR TASTE TESTS[1]

Number of Judges or Judgments	Minimum Correct Judgments to Establish Significant Differentiation ($p=\frac{1}{3}$)			Number of Judges or Judgments	Minimum Correct Judgments to Establish Significant Differentiation ($p=\frac{1}{3}$)		
	Probability Level				Probability Level		
	0.05	0.01	0.001		0.05	0.01	0.001
5	4	5	5	21	12	13	15
6	5	6	6	22	12	14	15
7	5	6	7	23	13	14	16
8	6	7	8	24	13	14	16
9	6	7	8	25	13	15	17
10	7	8	9	30	16	17	19
11	7	8	9	35	18	19	21
12	8	9	10	40	20	22	24
13	8	9	10	45	22	24	26
14	9	10	11	50	24	26	28
15	9	10	12	60	28	30	33
16	10	11	12	70	32	34	37
17	10	11	13	80	35	38	41
18	10	12	13	90	39	42	45
19	11	12	14	100	43	46	49
20	11	13	14	200	80	84	89

[1]Source of data: Roessler *et al.* (1948).

Scoring Wines Numerically

It is customary to assign a numerical score to each wine tested in many situations. With experience and practice, it is possible to assign a fairly accurate score, after noting the appearance, bouquet and aroma, and the flavor of the wine. A score card such as the following may be used:

Characteristic	Weight
Appearance	2
Color (depth and tint and appropriateness, for type)	2
Aroma and bouquet	4
Volatile acidity	2
Total acidity	2
Sweetness	1
Body	1
Flavor	2
Bitterness	1
Astringency	1
Over-all impression	2
	20

Ratings: Superior (17—20); standard (13—16); below standard (9—12); unacceptable or spoiled (1—8).

Admittedly, this is an arbitrary score card, but it will aid in distinguishing wines of different quality. When several wines are scored by the same taster a number of times or by the various tasters, it is possible to determine the probability that the average scores differ significantly from each other. See Amerine and Roessler (1976) or Amerine et al. (1965) for the appropriate statistical procedures. Score cards should not have more than 20 steps and 10 is often sufficient. With a 20-step scale, wines of 13 or more points may be considered commercially acceptable and with 17 points or over to constitute a quality product. For an evaluation of the extended use of this system, see Ough and Winton (1976). They show excellent response with a trained panel. Some deviation from normal distribution results with untrained tasters. This has little significance on the usual statistical analysis of the score card data.

Hedonic and Flavor Profile

Another procedure for differentiating wines is the use of attitude rating scales such as hedonic score cards. The judge rates the wine on a scale of pleasantness or unpleasantness. A typical seven-step scale is:

1. Like very much
2. Like moderately
3. Like slightly
4. Neither like nor dislike
5. Dislike slightly
6. Dislike moderately
7. Dislike very much

The steps can then be converted to scores, 1 to 7, and averaged and the averages treated statistically. For modifications of this see Amerine *et al.* (1965) and Amerine and Roessler (1976).

A descriptive system using panels has found commercial use for a number of food products. It has not yet been applied in its original form to wines but the descriptive score cards are similar in intent. See Amerine and Roessler (1976) for a score card with suggested descriptive words. Rank-order procedures (Amerine *et al.* 1965) were praised by Paul (1967) when the ranking was made on specified characteristics.

Frequency of Tasting

One thorough sensory examination by a panel is worth several superficial evaluations. Normally, a testing every six months is sufficient. Previous results should not be available to the panel before or during testing. Discussions after the results have been recorded are often useful. The room should be quiet and individual tasting booths are desirable for critical work. The panel members should be given time off from their regular duties and motivation by praise or extra compensation is valuable. The paper by Amerine and Ough (1964) is a good reference source for a sensory panel operation.

MICROSCOPICAL EXAMINATION

Microscopical examination will usually indicate whether or not fermenting must or wine contains viable spoilage organisms.

Musts

Usually no microscopical examination is made of fermenting musts unless a fermentation sticks or unless the volatile acidity of the new wines is high. If the volatile acidity of the newly-fermented wines is running abnormally high, microscopical examination of the musts is advisable. A sample of the must from a vat or tank may be taken by sterile bottle. A drop or two of the liquid is placed on a clean microscope slide. A clean cover glass is placed on this drop of liquid and pressed down gently. The slide is placed under the high dry power of the microscope and the material between the cover glass and slide is brought into focus. See pp. 569–574 for identification of the cause of the spoilage.

In a properly operated fermentation cellar, the fermenting musts and new wines should be relatively free of spoilage microorganisms. Most of them are very sensitive to sulfur dioxide, and maintenance of as little as 100 mg/liter of sulfur dioxide during fermentation will prevent their development. There is no excuse for their presence in excessive numbers.

Examination of Yeast Starters

Some wineries grow starters from pure dry yeast in sterilized must or in must treated with sulfur dioxide and use the starter for inoculating crushed grapes or white musts (p. 268). In order to make certain that the starter is relatively free of contamination with *Acetobacter* sp., *Kloeckera* sp., *Pichia* sp., lactobacilli, etc., the starter should be examined microscopically. Examination will indicate whether or not the starter is relatively free of these or other undesirable organisms. Because wine yeast strains usually cannot be differentiated by microscopic examination, it will not show whether the original pure wine yeast culture consists of a single desired strain.

Wines

Microscopical examination of table wines is made at regular intervals, usually every six months and fortified wines at least once a year. If the wine is heavily infected with bacteria, these can be seen by merely mounting a drop of the wine on a slide and examining it under the high dry power of the microscope. Usually, it is necessary to place a few milliliters of the wine in a centrifuge tube and centrifuge it for several minutes. A clinical centrifuge is satisfactory. The supernatant liquid is poured off and a drop of the sediment is mounted on a slide and examined. If preferred, the drop may be dried and stained as follows:

Place a drop of the sediment on a slide. Pass the slide quickly above a small flame of a Bunsen burner in such manner that the liquid is evaporated but the dry material is not scorched. The slide should be heated only sufficiently so that it can be barely borne on the palm of the hand. When the sample is dry, apply a drop of dilute methylene blue or carbon fuchsin bacterial stain, prepared as described in any laboratory manual of bacteriology. Hold the slide well above the flame a few seconds to heat the stain to steaming. Let stand a minute. Pour off the stain. Rinse the slide under a tap of cold water. Dry the slide well above the flame and examine under the high dry objective of the microscope or under oil immersion.

This procedure will sometimes show the presence of lactic bacteria before they have noticeably injured the wine. The use of phase-contrast optics avoids the need to stain. For use of the microscope in the wine laboratory see Castelli (1969).

CHEMICAL ANALYSIS OF WINES

While sensory tests are indispensable, chemical analyses are equally important. For some purposes they are paramount.

For general instructions on wine analyses, see AOAC (1975), Amerine and Ough (1979), Franck and Junge (1970), Franck (1973), Mori (1975), Anon. (1962–1976), Joslyn (1970), Vogt and Bieber (1970), and Beythien and Diemair (1963).

Hydrometers

Hydrometers are used to measure the soluble solids content of grape musts, the alcohol content of the wine distillate, the apparent sugar content of fortified dessert wines, and for other purposes. Those used in American wineries are of three types: Brix hydrometers (Fig. 19.1) which indicate dissolved solids expressed as grams of sucrose in 100 g of solution; alcohol hydrometers, which are calibrated directly in percentage of alcohol; and specific gravity hydrometers. The last-named is sometimes used in determining alcohol content of wine distillates.

A hydrometer consists of a hollow cylindrical glass bulb weighted at the lower end with shot or mercury and attached to a long, narrow stem containing a graduated scale. The hydrometer sinks in a liquid until the weight of the displaced liquid equals the weight of the hydrometer. Thus, it sinks further in a liquid of low density than in one of high density. The Brix and Balling hydrometers are identical in respect to the meaning of degrees Brix or degrees Balling; thus, a pure sucrose solution containing 20 g sucrose/100 g solution will read 20° Brix or 20° Balling. Both read 0° in distilled water at the temperature of calibration.

All hydrometers measure specific gravity. Specific gravity of liquids may be explained as follows: Water at standard temperature has by definition a specific gravity of 1.000. Sugar solutions are heavier (of greater specific gravity) than water whereas ethanol solutions are lighter (of lower specific gravity) than water. Density and specific gravity, inso-

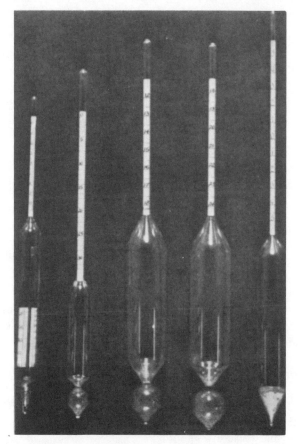

FIG. 19.1. HYDROMETERS FOR WINERY USE

From left to right: 0° to 8° Brix with enclosed
thermometer, 0° to 30°, 12° to 18°, 18° to 24°, −5° to +5°

far as wines and musts are concerned, are more or less synonymous. Specific gravity is the ratio of the mass of a specified volume of liquid to the mass of the same volume of water at a specified temperature (usually 20°C). It has no units of measure. Density is expressed in wt/vol units and for water is the weight of 1 ml at 4°C. The variation between the specific gravity and density of water is only a couple of parts per 1000.

If the weight of a measured volume of liquid is known, its specific gravity can be calculated from the formula $S = W/V$, where S is the specific gravity, W the weight of the liquid, and V its volume. Once the specific gravity of a must is known, its Brix degree can be found from tables (see Table 19.3). Similarly, mixtures of pure ethanol and water vary in specific gravity with the ethanol content (see Table 19.4).

TABLE 19.3.   SPECIFIC GRAVITY CORRESPONDING TO READINGS OF THE BRIX HYDROMETER[1]

Brix Degrees	Specific Gravity	Brix Degrees	Specific Gravity	Brix Degrees	Specific Gravity
0.00	1.0000	10.0	1.03925	20.0	1.082104
1.00	1.00318	11.0	1.043395	21.0	1.086567
2.00	1.00708	12.0	1.04757	22.0	1.091058
3.00	1.011007	13.0	1.051781	23.0	1.095582
4.00	1.01496	14.0	1.05602	24.0	1.100138
5.00	1.019935	15.0	1.06029	25.0	1.104729
6.00	1.02294	16.0	1.064589		
7.00	1.02697	17.0	1.068923		
8.00	1.03104	18.0	1.073286		
9.00	1.035127	19.0	1.07768		

[1]Source of data: U.S. Treasury Dept., Bureau of Alcohol, Tobacco and Firearms Division (1976).

Temperature affects the specific gravity; hence it must be determined simultaneously. Temperature correction tables are available in books on food analysis, such as the Methods of Analysis of the AOAC (1975). See also Tables 19.5 and 19.6. See Jaulmes and Brun (1967) for details on temperature and volume corrections.

To measure °Brix by hydrometer pour the sample of must or wine into a hydrometer cylinder, which may be of glass, metal or plastic, about 1.5 in. in diameter and about 15 in. high. In filling the cylinder tilt it to an angle of about 45 degrees and pour the liquid down the side of the cylinder in order that froth and bubbles do not form. Bubbles clinging to the hydrometer cause serious error. Insert the hydrometer and twirl it gently with the fingers to disengage bubbles and to assure a proper resting point. Excess gassiness will cause hydrometers to sink lower than is correct causing false low readings.

When the hydrometer comes to rest, read the indicated degree Brix at the bottom of the meniscus, that is, at the general level of the surface of the liquid, not at the top of the meniscus. The meniscus is the surface of the liquid that climbs up the stem of the hydrometer because of surface tension. The difference between the top of the meniscus and the general surface can result in an appreciable error. Insert a thermometer into the liquid and note the temperature. Also note from the printing on the hydrometer its temperature of calibration. By means of Table 19.5 or 19.6 make the necessary addition to the observed reading for temperatures above calibration and subtract if the temperature is below. The table can be used even if the hydrometer is calibrated for different standard temperature than that of the table, 20°C (68°F), as the following examples show.

Example 1.—For a hydrometer calibrated at 20°C (68°F) the observed

TABLE 19.4. PROOF, PERCENT ALCOHOL BY VOLUME AND BY WEIGHT,
AND SPECIFIC GRAVITY AT 60°F

Proof	Alcohol Percent by Vol.	Alcohol Percent by wt.	Alcohol g/100 ml	Specific Gravity[1]
0.0	0.00	0.00	0.00	1.00000
1.0	0.50	0.40	0.40	0.99923
2.0	1.00	0.79	0.79	0.99849
3.0	1.50	1.19	1.19	0.99775
4.0	2.00	1.59	1.59	0.99701
5.0	2.50	1.99	1.98	0.99629
6.0	3.00	2.39	2.38	0.99557
7.0	3.50	2.80	2.78	0.99487
8.0	4.00	3.20	3.18	0.99417
9.0	4.50	3.60	3.58	0.99349
10.0	5.00	4.00	3.97	0.99281
11.0	5.50	4.40	4.37	0.99215
12.0	6.00	4.80	4.76	0.99149
13.0	6.50	5.21	5.16	0.99085
14.0	7.00	5.61	5.56	0.99021
15.0	7.50	6.02	5.96	0.98959
16.0	8.00	6.42	6.35	0.98897
17.0	8.50	6.83	6.75	0.98837
18.0	9.00	7.23	7.14	0.98777
19.0	9.50	7.64	7.54	0.98719
20.0	10.00	8.04	7.93	0.98660
21.0	10.50	8.45	8.33	0.98603
22.0	11.00	8.86	8.73	0.98546
23.0	11.50	9.27	9.13	0.98491
24.0	12.00	9.67	9.52	0.98435
25.0	12.50	10.08	9.92	0.98381
26.0	13.00	10.49	10.31	0.98326
27.0	13.50	10.90	10.71	0.98273
28.0	14.00	11.31	11.11	0.98219
29.0	14.50	11.72	11.51	0.98167
30.0	15.00	12.13	11.90	0.98114
31.0	15.50	12.54	12.30	0.98063
32.0	16.00	12.95	12.69	0.98011
33.0	16.50	13.37	13.09	0.97960
34.0	17.00	13.78	13.49	0.97909
35.0	17.50	14.19	13.89	0.97859
36.0	18.00	14.60	14.28	0.97808
37.0	18.50	15.02	14.68	0.97758
38.0	19.00	15.43	15.08	0.97708
39.0	19.50	15.84	15.47	0.97658
40.0	20.00	16.26	15.87	0.97608
41.0	20.50	16.67	16.26	0.97558
42.0	21.00	17.09	16.66	0.97507
43.0	21.50	17.51	17.06	0.97457
44.0	22.00	17.92	17.46	0.97406
45.0	22.50	18.34	17.86	0.97355

Source of data: Hodgman (1964).
[1]Referred to water at the same temp. Multiply by 0.99808 to convert to specific gravity referred to water at 4°C.

Brix was 21.3° at a temperature of 25°C (77°F). The necessary correction is found as follows: the nearest degree Brix is 20° in the table. Follow down the 20° Brix column to 25°C (77°F) and note the correction, which is 0.34. Then 21.3 + 0.3 = 21.6° Brix. Interpolation between intermediate °Brix and temperatures may be made for even more exact corrections.

TABLE 19.5. CORRECTIONS FOR BRIX HYDROMETERS[1] CALIBRATED AT 20°C (68°F)

Temperature of Solution		Observed Percentage of Sugar						
		0	5	10	15	20	25	30
Below Calibration °C	°F			Subtract				
15	59.0	0.20	0.22	0.24	0.26	0.28	0.30	0.32
15.56	60.0	0.18	0.20	0.22	0.24	0.26	0.28	0.29
16	60.8	0.17	0.18	0.20	0.22	0.23	0.25	0.26
17	62.6	0.13	0.14	0.15	0.16	0.18	0.19	0.20
18	64.4	0.09	0.10	0.11	0.12	0.13	0.13	0.14
19	66.2	0.05	0.05	0.06	0.06	0.06	0.07	0.07
Above Calibration				Add				
21	69.8	0.04	0.05	0.06	0.06	0.07	0.07	0.07
22	71.6	0.10	0.10	0.11	0.12	0.13	0.14	0.14
23	73.4	0.16	0.16	0.17	0.17	0.20	0.21	0.21
24	75.2	0.21	0.22	0.23	0.24	0.27	0.28	0.29
25	77.0	0.27	0.28	0.30	0.31	0.34	0.35	0.36
26	78.8	0.33	0.34	0.36	0.37	0.40	0.42	0.44
27	80.6	0.40	0.41	0.42	0.44	0.48	0.52	0.52
28	82.4	0.46	0.47	0.49	0.51	0.56	0.58	0.60
29	84.2	0.54	0.55	0.56	0.59	0.63	0.66	0.68
30	86.0	0.61	0.62	0.63	0.66	0.71	0.73	0.76
35	95.0	0.99	1.01	1.02	1.06	1.13	1.16	1.18

[1]Source of data: AOAC (1975).

TABLE 19.6. CORRECTIONS FOR HYDROMETERS IN DESSERT WINES AT 20 PERCENT ALCOHOL[1]

Temperature		Observed °Brix					
°C	°F	0	2.5	5.0	10.0	12.5	15.0
				Subtract			
15	59.0	0.43	0.46	0.49	0.53	0.55	0.57
16	60.8	0.34	0.35	0.39	0.41	0.43	0.44
17	62.6	0.26	0.27	0.27	0.29	0.30	0.31
18	64.4	0.17	0.17	0.19	0.21	0.23	0.25
19	66.2	0.09	0.09	0.09	0.09	0.10	0.11
20	68.0			Add			
21	69.8	0.08	0.08	0.08	0.08	0.09	0.10
22	71.6	0.20	0.17	0.19	0.21	0.23	0.25
23	73.4	0.25	0.27	0.29	0.29	0.30	0.31
24	75.2	0.35	0.37	0.39	0.41	0.43	0.44
25	77.0	0.43	0.45	0.49	0.49	0.51	0.54

[1]Source of data: Jaulmes (1951).

Example 2.—If the hydrometer is calibrated for 15.6°C (60°F) and the observed temperature is 26.1°C (79°F), then subtract 15.6° from 26.1° and 10.5°C is the temperature correction. Then 20°C, the standard temperature of the table, plus 10.5°C, 20° + 10.5°C = 30.5°C and the correction will be the same for your hydrometer as it would for a 20°C standard hydrometer read at 30.5°C. Table 19.5 does not show 30.5°C, the nearest value being 30°C. Each 1°C in the table causes about 0.072° Brix change. Then the correction is 0.71° + (0.072° × ½) = 0.75° Brix; and the corrected Brix degree is 21.3° + 0.75° = 22.05° Brix. The hydrometer value is rounded off to the nearest 0.1°. The same result is obtained using °F.

Extrapolation can be made for temperatures slightly off the table and interpolation for temperatures between those given in the table.

Table 19.3 will be found useful in showing the relation between specific gravity and degree Brix. This table is also useful in determining the dealcoholized extract content of wines.

The refractometer is also used for determination of approximate sugar content (Arnold 1957). The sugar values determined do not agree with the true values and a correction table and a temperature correction are needed. In the United States, the refractometer is checked against a standard sugar solution and adjusted accordingly.

Soluble solids measurements by hydrometer on grape musts are influenced by the presence of solid materials. Cooke (1964) showed the hydrometer readings of unfiltered musts were 0.4° to 0.7° Brix higher than those of the refractometer. An empirical correction of the refractometric readings is needed because the refractive index of glucose and fructose is less than that of sucrose upon which the refractometer scale is based. This correction amounts to +0.3 for Brix readings of 15.0° to 15.5°, +0.4 for Brix readings of 15.6° to 20.2°, +0.5 for Brix readings of 20.3° to 24.7° and +0.6 for Brix readings of 24.8° to 29.3°.

Acidity

The total titratable acidity, volatile acidity, and pH of musts and wines are important in their rational handling. All wineries should have facilities for their rapid and accurate determination. For legal purposes and to follow changes during the malo-lactic fermentation the fixed acidity may be useful. A measure of the individual fixed acids, particularly tartaric, malic and lactic, is occasionally desirable.

The determination of the tartrate content by precipitation of potassium bitartrate was first used by Pasteur. Rebelein (1973) modified the vanadate procedure for determining total tartrate. The method is rapid and satisfactory for control analysis. For research measurements the wine or must should be ion-exchanged and the tartaric fraction separated from the interfering malic acid (Hill and Caputi 1970).

There are numerous procedures for the determination of malic acid in musts and wines. Peynaud and Blouin (1965) compared five procedures (chemical, chromatographic, enzymatic, manometric, and microbiological). They recommend the microbiological procedure of Peynaud and Lafon-Lafourcade (1965). The enzymatic method of Mayer and Busch

(1963) appears more precise; however, the report of Poux (1969) that L-malate dehydrogenase has some effect on tartaric acid casts doubt on this procedure. For details see Amerine and Ough (1979).

The titratable acidity is commonly measured in the United States by a potentiometric titration to a given pH, usually 8.2. Titrimeters or automatic titrimeters are also useful.

The standard method, without using a pH meter, is to place 200 ml of boiling distilled water into a 500-ml Erlenmeyer flask; add 1 ml of a 1 g/100 ml phenolphthalein indicator solution (1 g phenolphthalein dissolved in 80 ml ethanol and 20 ml water) and titrate with approximately 0.1 N sodium hydroxide solution to a faint but definite pink color. Using a volumetric 5-ml pipette, place a portion of the must or wine into the boiled neutralized solution. Again titrate to a distinct faint endpoint with the standardized sodium hydroxide.

When the pH meter is used to detect the endpoint, titrate to pH 8.2 after the solution has cooled to room temperature.

The total titratable acidity is expressed as tartaric acid:

$$\text{Tartaric acid, g/100 ml} = \frac{(V)(N)(75)(100)}{(1000)(v)}$$

where V = volume of sodium hydroxide solution used for the titration, in milliliters
       N = normality of the sodium hydroxide solution
       v = sample volume, in milliliters

The standardized sodium hydroxide should be restandardized at monthly intervals with an acceptable standard, such as potassium acid phthalate.

Volatile Acidity

The volatile acidity is a measure of the soundness of fermentation of a new wine and the keeping quality of older wines. An appreciable rise in the volatile acidity in a wine during storage indicates bacterial spoilage and usually the wine needs immediate pasteurization, or addition of 100 to 150 mg/liter of sulfur dioxide or both. Small amounts of acetic acid are formed in normal alcoholic fermentation but sound, new wine should show less than 0.04 g/100 ml of volatile acidity and a sound aged wine less than 0.07. The present California legal maximum limits of volatile acidity are 0.110 g/100 ml for white wines and 0.120 g for red wines, exclusive of sulfur dioxide. If sorbic acid is present in the wine it will distill and must be accounted for. Caputi and Slinkard (1975) did an

AOAC collaborative study on the UV and on the colorimetric method of determining sorbic acid in wine. Either of these official methods is adequate to determine sorbic acid in wine. One gram of sorbic acid is equivalent to 0.536 g acetic acid. Pilone *et al.* (1972) found the addition of mercuric oxide to the wine prior to distillation would bind the sulfur dioxide and prevent it from distilling over and interfering with the volatile acid determination.

A Cash distillation still (Fig. 19.2) or an equivalent still, a supply of cooling water, 10-ml volumetric pipette, 250-ml wide-mouth Erlenmeyer flask, 10- or 25-ml burette, and standardized sodium hydroxide are needed. The still is charged with water, the heat source turned on and 10 ml of wine pipetted into the distilling chamber. Add 1 ml of a 1 g/100 ml solution of red mercuric oxide (dissolve 1 g HgO in 90 ml of water and 10 ml sulfuric acid) to the distilling chamber. Distill 100 ml into a 250-ml Erlenmeyer flask. Titrate to a distinct faintly pink endpoint after the addition of 1 ml phenolphthalein solution. Normality of the standardized sodium hydroxide should be between 0.01 and 0.05 N.

The volatile acid is expressed as acetic acid:

$$\text{Acetic acid, g/100 ml} \quad = \quad \frac{(V)\,(N)\,(60)\,(100)}{(1000)\,(v)}$$

where   V = volume of sodium hydroxide used for the titration, in milliliters
   N = normality of the sodium hydroxide solution
   v = sample volume, in milliliters

The official AOAC method calls for 25 ml of wine and a 300 ml distillate.

Fixed Acidity and pH

The total titratable acidity less the volatile is called the fixed acidity. While there is some difficulty in expressing each exactly, the term has utility in indicating changes in the nonvolatile acid components. Since the titratable acidity is usually expressed as tartaric acid, it is necessary to convert the volatile acidity (as acetic) to its equivalent as tartaric before making the subtraction. The volatile acidity × 1.25 will make the conversion.

The pH should be determined by a pH meter. The directions accompanying the meter should be followed carefully. A saturated solution of potassium acid tartrate, pH 3.57 at 20°C (68°F), is used for standardization.

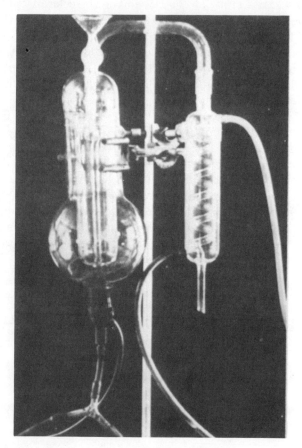

FIG. 19.2. CASH VOLATILE ACID APPARATUS

Note electrical heating coil

Ethanol

Ethanol can be determined by ebullioscope, by means of the specific gravity of the distillate from a measured volume of wine, or by chemical means by dichromate oxidation of the distillate from a measured volume of wine.

The ebullioscope method is based on the change in the boiling point of mixtures of water and alcohol. Many of the ebullioscopes in use in foreign wineries are of the Dujardin-Salleron type (Fig. 19.3). They are nickel-plated copper and consist of a small boiling chamber, a standard Celsius

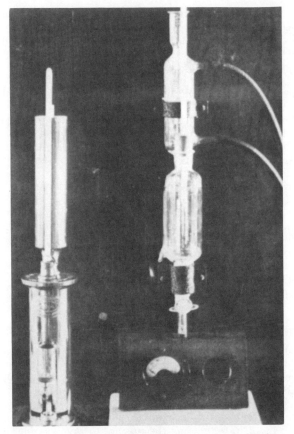

FIG. 19.3. METAL AND GLASS EBULLIOSCOPES

Note rheostat for control of rate of heating with the
latter

thermometer, the bulb of which is inserted into the boiling chamber, a
metal reflux condenser, a small alcohol lamp, a measuring cyclinder and a
special slide rule that has a special adjustable scale showing the relation
between boiling point and alcohol content of the sample. Similar in-
struments are produced in the United States.

In using the ebullioscope for dry table wine proceed as follows:

Place 25 ml of distilled water in the previously rinsed boiling chamber. Insert
the thermometer. Screw the reflux condenser in place but do not fill with water.
Fill the alcohol lamp with 95% denatured alcohol or use a micro gas burner. Light
the burner and place it under the boiling spout of the ebullioscope. Heat the
water to boiling and continue boiling with steam escaping from the empty

condenser until the height of the mercury column in the thermometer remains constant. In California wine making areas this will usually be about 100°C (212°F). Set the slide rule so that 0.0% alcohol is opposite this temperature. The boiling point of water should be rerun once or twice per day, especially if the barometric pressure is changing rapidly.

Empty the ebullioscope and rinse it with a few milliliters of the wine sample. Discard the rinsings and with a cylinder measure 50 ml of the wine sample into the boiling chamber. Insert the thermometer and screw the reflux condenser in place. Fill the latter with cold water. Light the alcohol lamp (or gas burner) and place it below the boiling chamber. Heat until the boiling point on the thermometer becomes constant. Read the temperature. Remove the flame. On the slide rule, read off the percent of alcohol opposite the observed boiling point of the wine. There may be two alcohol scales on the slide rule; use the one which is labeled for wine. When used with precision the ebullioscope should give values within 0.25% above or below the true percent alcohol content. With fermenting musts or sweet wines, it is customary to accurately dilute the sample in a volumetric flask so that the extract content is 5% or less. The results must then be multiplied by the appropriate dilution factor.

More accurate results for alcohol are obtained by distilling the wine and using the distillate in the ebullioscope. An accuracy of ±0.15% is possible by this procedure. The alcohol scale on the slide rule is used in this case.

In using the ebullioscope for wines of low alcohol content care should be taken that the condenser has adequate cooling capacity.

To determine the alcohol by hydrometry proceed as follows:

Set up a small distilling apparatus consisting of a 500-ml or 800-ml round bottom Kjeldahl flask and connect it to a vertical condenser, both attached to a heavy ring stand. Place a gas burner or electric hot plate beneath the flask. Place a 200-ml volumetric flask under the outlet of the condenser.

Fill a volumetric flask with the wine and bring it to temperature and volume. Then pour the contents of the flask into the distilling flask and rinse the flask 3 times with 15 ml of water, adding the rinsings to the distilling flask. Use this volumetric flask to receive the distillate. If the wine is high in volatile acidity (above 0.10 g/100 ml), neutralize the wine with N sodium hydroxide to a pH of 7. Start cold water flowing through condenser. Heat the sample to boiling and boil until about 96−98 ml of distillate collects in the volumetric flask. Using distilled water, bring the contents of the flask to volume at the original temperature of the wine. Then bring the contents of the flask to a temperature as near to that of the calibration temperature of the alcohol hydrometer as possible—usually 15.6°C (60°F).

Transfer the distillate to a hydrometer cylinder and insert a clean dry alcohol hydrometer. Read the indicated alcohol content very quickly, yet accurately, before the liquid can change appreciably in temperature. Also take its temperature. Make a correction by use of the temperature correction in Table 19.7.

For slightly more accurate results one may use a pycnometer. A pycnometer is a small (50 ml, usually), thin-walled bottle fitted with ground glass stopper and accurate thermometer. For a rapid technique for use of the pycnometer see Jaulmes and Brun (1963). The procedure is based on accurately measuring the temperature of the pycnometer (made from specified glass) rather than bringing the pycnometer and its contents to a specified temperature. They prefer a pycnometer of Pyrex glass and a thermometer calibrated to read to 0.02°C. The corrected tables were also published by Jaulmes and Brun (1967).

TABLE 19.7. CORRECTIONS OF ALCOHOL HYDROMETERS CALIBRATED AT 15.6°C (60°F) IN PERCENT BY VOLUME OF ALCOHOL,[1] WHEN USED AT TEMPERATURES ABOVE OR BELOW 15.6°C

To or from the Observed

Ob-served Alcohol Content	Add at			Subtract at														
	13.8°C 57°F	14.4°C 58°F	15.0°C 59°F	16.1°C 61°F	16.7°C 62°F	17.2°C 63°F	17.8°C 64°F	18.3°C 65°F	18.9°C 66°F	19.4°C 67°F	20.0°C 68°F	20.6°C 69°F	21.1°C 70°F	22.2°C 72°F	23.3°C 74°F	24.4°C 76°F	25.6°C 78°F	26.7°C 80°F
%	%	%	%	%	%	%	%	%	%	%	%	%	%	%	%	%	%	%
1	0.14	0.10	0.05	0.05	0.10	0.16	0.22	0.28	0.34	0.41	0.48	0.55	0.62	0.77	0.93	—	—	—
2	0.14	0.10	0.05	0.05	0.11	0.17	0.23	0.29	0.35	0.42	0.48	0.56	0.63	0.78	0.94	1.10	1.28	1.46
3	0.14	0.10	0.05	0.06	0.12	0.18	0.24	0.30	0.36	0.43	0.52	0.57	0.64	0.80	0.96	1.13	1.31	1.50
4	0.14	0.10	0.05	0.06	0.12	0.19	0.25	0.32	0.38	0.45	0.52	0.59	0.67	0.83	1.00	1.17	1.35	1.54
5	0.15	0.11	0.05	0.07	0.13	0.20	0.26	0.33	0.40	0.47	0.54	0.62	0.70	0.86	1.03	1.21	1.40	1.60
6	0.17	0.11	0.06	0.07	0.14	0.20	0.27	0.34	0.42	0.50	0.57	0.66	0.74	0.90	1.09	1.27	1.46	1.66
7	0.18	0.12	0.06	0.07	0.14	0.21	0.29	0.36	0.44	0.52	0.60	0.68	0.77	0.94	1.13	1.32	1.52	1.73
8	0.19	0.13	0.06	0.08	0.16	0.23	0.31	0.39	0.47	0.55	0.64	0.73	0.81	0.99	1.18	1.38	1.59	1.80
9	0.21	0.14	0.07	0.08	0.16	0.24	0.32	0.41	0.50	0.58	0.67	0.76	0.86	1.04	1.25	1.46	1.67	1.89
10	0.23	0.16	0.08	0.08	0.17	0.25	0.34	0.43	0.52	0.61	0.71	0.80	0.90	1.10	1.32	1.54	1.76	1.99
11	0.25	0.16	0.08	0.09	0.18	0.27	0.37	0.46	0.56	0.65	0.75	0.85	0.96	1.16	1.39	1.61	1.84	2.09
12	0.27	0.18	0.09	0.10	0.20	0.29	0.39	0.49	0.59	0.70	0.80	0.91	1.02	1.23	1.46	1.70	1.94	2.20
13	0.29	0.19	0.10	0.10	0.21	0.31	0.42	0.52	0.63	0.74	0.85	0.97	1.08	1.31	1.55	1.80	2.05	2.31
14	0.32	0.21	0.11	0.11	0.22	0.32	0.44	0.55	0.66	0.78	0.91	1.02	1.14	1.39	1.65	1.91	2.17	2.44
15	0.35	0.23	0.12	0.12	0.24	0.35	0.48	0.60	0.71	0.84	0.97	1.10	1.23	1.50	1.76	2.03	2.30	2.58
16	0.37	0.24	0.12	0.13	0.26	0.38	0.52	0.65	0.77	0.90	1.03	1.17	1.31	1.60	1.88	2.16	2.44	2.72
17	0.40	0.26	0.13	0.14	0.27	0.41	0.54	0.68	0.82	0.96	1.10	1.25	1.40	1.70	1.99	2.28	2.58	2.87
18	0.44	0.29	0.14	0.14	0.29	0.44	0.58	0.73	0.88	1.03	1.18	1.33	1.49	1.80	2.10	2.41	2.72	3.02
19	0.47	0.32	0.16	0.15	0.30	0.46	0.62	0.78	0.94	1.10	1.26	1.42	1.58	1.90	2.22	2.54	2.86	3.17
20	0.51	0.34	0.17	0.16	0.32	0.49	0.66	0.82	0.98	1.15	1.33	1.48	1.65	2.00	2.32	2.65	2.98	3.33
21	0.53	0.35	0.18	0.17	0.34	0.51	0.68	0.85	1.02	1.20	1.38	1.54	1.72	2.06	2.41	2.76	3.10	3.45
22	0.56	0.38	0.19	0.17	0.36	0.53	0.71	0.90	1.07	1.25	1.44	1.61	1.78	2.13	2.48	2.84	3.20	3.56
23	0.58	0.40	0.20	0.18	0.37	0.55	0.74	0.92	1.11	1.30	1.49	1.66	1.84	2.20	2.56	2.93	3.30	3.67
24	0.60	0.40	0.20	0.18	0.38	0.56	0.77	0.96	1.16	1.35	1.54	1.72	1.91	2.27	2.65	3.03	3.40	3.78

[1]Source of data: U.S. Internal Revenue Service (1970B).

Weigh the pycnometer when dry and empty, using an analytical balance and weigh to 0.1 mg. Fill with distilled water a degree or two below the standard temperature, usually 15.6°C (60°F). Insert the thermometer. Bring the contents to exactly the standard temperature—in this example 15.6°C. Wipe the pycnometer dry with a soft cloth and put the ground glass cover of the overflow tube in place. Weigh again very accurately. These two weighings need be done only once for a given pycnometer. Thereafter one need only weigh the pycnometer filled with the alcoholic distillate of a wine sample.

Now empty the pycnometer. Prepare the wine distillate as indicated above, taking care to bring the contents to volume at the same temperature as used for the original wine. Rinse the pycnometer with a little of the distillate. Cool the distillate in the pycnometer to a little below the standard temperature. Insert and seat the thermometer. Allow the contents to warm up to exactly the standard temperature—in this example 15.6°C (60°F). Wipe the pycnometer dry with a clean soft cloth. Put the overflow tube's cap in place and weigh accurately.

Then calculate specific gravity of distillate as follows:

$$\frac{\text{Wt of pycnometer with distillate} - \text{wt of empty pycnometer}}{\text{Wt of pycnometer with water} - \text{wt of empty pycnometer}}$$
$$= \text{specific gravity of distillate}$$

From a standard alcohol table for 15.6°C (60°F) (or from Table 19.4) find the corresponding alcohol content. The alcohol of wines is always expressed in volume percentage (ml of alcohol per 100 ml of sample). To transform it to g/100 ml, multiply it by density of absolute alcohol, 0.7931.

The alcohol content of the distillate can also be determined chemically by oxidizing an aliquot with a known volume of standard dichromate solution and titrating the excess dichromate with standard ferrous ammonium sulfate. This method requires experience in chemical analysis. Those who wish to use the method should consult Caputi and Wright (1969), Caputi (1970), and Amerine and Ough (1979). Careful attention must be paid to the details of the reaction.

Zimmerman (1963) reported that dichromate results were 0.24% higher in alcohol than the results of densimetric procedures. Dichromate and pycnometric results were identical. This result he showed to be fortuitous because of a compensation of errors (due to a highly volatile component other than alcohol which is eliminated by aerating the fresh distillates). The volatile acidity and sulfur dioxide depress the pycnometer and hydrometer results but have little influence on the dichromate results. About 40% of the remaining difference between pycnometer and dichromate results appears to be due to a substance which depresses the pycnometer results but does not affect those of the dichromate procedure. Zimmermann argues that the dichromate results more accurately reflect the true alcohol content of the wine. This may be true under very precise laboratory controls.

The automatic determination of ethanol using equipment which distills the wine, reacts the distillate with dichromate, reads the change in absorbance, and prints out the ethanol concentration is not difficult. See Sarris *et al.* (1969) and Lidzey *et al.* (1971).

Extract of Dealcoholized Sample

The extract of a wine is the alcohol-free soluble solids and is made up mainly of tartaric, malic, lactic, and succinic acids, glycerol, tannin, protein, and other nitrogenous compounds, and sugar. In low acid (high pH) wines there may be considerable neutral potassium tartrate. In sweet wines sugar predominates over the other constituents.

There are several methods of determining extract. One simple procedure is to take the Brix degree of the dealcoholized sample, from the alcohol determination, which has been brought to the original volume and temperature. A hydrometer graduated in 0.1° Brix is used. Or, if no such residue is available, pipette 100 ml of wine into a 250-ml beaker. Evaporate on a hot plate or steam bath to 20 ml or slightly less, taking care to prevent splattering or burning. Transfer to a 100-ml volumetric flask. Cool the flask and sample in cold water to the temperature of calibration of the flask. Bring to volume with distilled water and mix well. Pour into a hydrometer cylinder and float a Brix hydrometer in it. Hydrometers calibrated for ±5° Brix or 0°−8° or 8°−16° are used. Note the temperature and make the appropriate correction according to Table 19.5. The reading will be in g/100 g. Multiply by the specific gravity to report in terms of g/100 ml. The extract should then be reported as "soluble solids by hydrometer."

The extract may also be approximately determined by calculation from the alcohol content and specific gravity of the wine as follows:

Determine the specific gravity of the wine by an accurate specific gravity hydrometer, a Westphal balance, or an accurate Brix hydrometer and convert this reading to specific gravity from Table 19.3. This must be done at the standard temperature of the hydrometer, usually 15.6°C (60°F). Determine the alcohol content by any of the methods previously described and find the corresponding specific gravity of an alcohol solution of this alcohol content from the table of alcohol percent and specific gravity (see Table 19.4). Subtract the specific gravity of the alcohol from the specific gravity of the wine; add 1 for the specific gravity of water and the result will be the specific gravity of the alcohol-free wine.

Convert this specific gravity to Brix from Table 19.3. This will be the extract content of the wine in g/100 g. Multiply by the specific gravity to get the extract in terms of g/100 ml.

The percentage of soluble solids of musts and dealcoholized wines may also be determined by the Abbé refractometer.

Reducing Sugars

For a sweet dessert wine it is rarely necessary to determine the sugar content chemically since the Brix degree of the wine or the extract determination is usually sufficient. The sugar content of dry table wines is very important since it indicates if fermentation is complete. For dry sherries the sugar content determined chemically is also often of legal importance. There are many methods of determining sugar in beverages and foods. Glucose and fructose reduce the cupric copper of copper salts in heated alkaline solution to cuprous copper. The cuprous copper separates as red cuprous oxide. The amount formed is proportional to the amount of sugar present. Practically all sugar determinations in the winery are made by one of the approved volumetric methods. The Lane and Eynon method (described below) is convenient and satisfactory.

Have on hand a 50-ml burette, glass filter funnel about 3 in. in diameter, filter paper of rapid filtering quality about 6 to 8 in. in diameter, several 250- or 300-ml Pyrex Erlenmeyer flasks, a wooden flask tongs to hold the Erlenmeyer flask during titration, a burette stand and clamp, tripod and wire gauze on which to heat the flask, two 50-ml pipettes, two 25-ml pipettes, a 10-ml pipette, a 100-ml volumetric flask, a 500-ml volumetric flask, and a Bunsen burner.

The following solutions and reagents are needed: decolorizing charcoal such as Darco, Norit, or Nuchar; infusorial earth filter aid such as Hyflo Super-Cel; Fehling's copper sulfate solution, made by dissolving 34.639 g of copper sulfate ($CuSO_4 \cdot 5H_2O$) in distilled water and diluting to 500 ml in a volumetric flask; Fehling's alkaline tartrate solution, made by dissolving 173 g of Rochelle salts (sodium potassium tartrate) and 50 g of CP sodium hydroxide (free of carbonate) in distilled water and diluting to 500 ml and then filtering if necessary; methylene blue solution, made by dissolving 1 g of methylene blue in water and diluting to 100 ml; standard glucose solution made by dissolving exactly 0.500 g of reagent ACS anhydrous glucose in 100 ml of distilled water. The solution is not stable and must be made up fresh as required. Saturated neutral lead acetate (dissolve 20 g in 100 ml water) and glacial acetic acid are also required.

Prepare the wine sample as follows: to 50 ml of the wine in an Erlenmeyer flask add 2 or 3 teaspoonfuls of decolorizing charcoal and reduce to about 20 ml volume by boiling. Cool and add 3 ml saturated lead acetate and several drops of glacial acetic acid, a teaspoon of Hyflo Super-Cel, or similar filter aid, and shake. Bring to 100 ml in a volumetric flask. Filter through a folded filter paper in a glass funnel. If the filtrate contains charcoal, filter a second time. The filtrate should be water-white and clear. This treatment removes acids, proteins, tannin, coloring matter, and certain other copper-reducing substances. Add 0.4 g of sodium oxalate crystals to precipitate the excess lead.

Standardize the Soxhlet solution as follows: using a separate pipette for each solution, pipette 50 ml of Fehling's copper sulfate solution and 50 ml of the alkaline tartrate into an Erlenmeyer flask and mix well. It should be clear and deep blue. Pipette 10 ml of the mixed Fehling solution into a narrow-mouth, 250-ml Erlenmeyer flask. Add 40 ml of distilled water. Fill a burette with the standard 0.5 g/100 ml glucose solution. Place the flask on a wire gauze on a tripod. Take a burette reading. Add 4 to 5 ml of 0.5 g/100 ml glucose solution from the burette. Heat the flask to boiling. Boil 15 to 20 sec, shake the flask with tongs to avoid bumping. Now add 2 to 3 ml more of glucose solution. Again boil 15 to 20 sec. Add about 5 to 6 drops of the methylene blue indicator. Keep the liquid in the flask boiling and slowly add from the burette 0.5 g/100 ml glucose solution, boiling 3 to 4 sec after each addition, until one drop changes the color from blue to a full brick red.

Repeat this titration adding about 90% of the necessary glucose solution immediately. After the solution boils, titrate to the endpoint as above. It must not take longer than 2 min after the solution begins to boil, after the first addition of glucose solution, until the endpoint is reached. This gives the glucose equivalent of the Fehling solution.

Place in another Erlenmeyer flask 10 ml of the mixed solution, 40 ml of distilled water, and 10 ml by pipette of decolorized wine. Boil 20 to 30 sec. Add methylene blue indicator. Then add dropwise from the burette, standard glucose solution, boiling a few seconds after each addition until one drop bleaches the blue color to a full red color. If the 10 ml of wine "uses up" the 10 ml of Fehling solution as shown by complete disappearance of all the blue color before adding any glucose, then the wine must be diluted before use. Try a portion of the decolorized wine in a volumetric flask with distilled water until the repeat titration using 10 ml of this diluted wine takes a significant amount of glucose solution.

With sweet wines, first dilute the wine to below 0.50 g/100 ml sugar, preferably to about 0.25 to 0.30 g/100 ml by means of an accurate pipette and volumetric flask. For muscatel, port, and angelica this is a dilution of about 25:1 or of 10 ml diluted to 250 ml with distilled water. Then decolorize this diluted material and proceed as with the dry wine. Multiply the final result by the dilution factor, in this case 25. For the drier sherries dilution of 10:1 will usually be sufficient.

The reducing sugar is calculated as glucose (g/100 ml):

$$\text{Reducing sugar, g/100 ml} = \frac{(A-B)(0.005)(100)}{v}$$

where   A = volume of 0.5 g/100 ml glucose solution used to titrate
           Soxhlet reagent, in milliliters
        B = volume of 0.5 g/100 ml glucose used to titrate wine sample,
           in milliliters
        v = volume of wine in the final aliquot, in milliliters

Robirds and Rossi (1966) pointed out that the Lane-Eynon method does not account for all of the fructose present in grape juice, and accounts for only about 96% of the total sugars. They recommended the Luff-Schoorl copper reagent. The difference between the methods is negligible for solutions of low sugar content but for musts it is appreciable. For wineries which calculate winery efficiency from must sugar analysis it will be worthwhile to use the Luff-Schoorl reagent or to correct the values obtained by the Lane-Eynon procedure.

Brix-Alcohol-Extract Chart

In Fig. 19.4 is given a chart by which one can readily find the approximate extract of a wine if its alcohol content and Brix degree are known; of it the extract and alcohol are known, the approximate Brix degree can be found. Also the sugar content of sweet dessert wines can be roughly estimated by first finding the extract content from the chart and then, for white dessert wines, subtracting 2.0 from the extract and for port, subtracting 2.5. The remainder is the approximate sugar content.

Determination of Sulfur Dioxide

Distillation.—The keeping quality of low alcohol wines is partially dependent on their sulfur dioxide content. That of white dry table wines should not fall below 15−20 mg/liter free sulfur dioxide and of fortified wines below 75 total mg/liter during storage in tanks or casks. Another reason for accurate determination of the sulfur dioxide content is the legal maximum for both total and free in many countries and states (p. 742). Total sulfur dioxide may be determined either by the distillation method or by the Ripper method. The distillation method outlined below is the more accurate.

The following equipment is needed: an 800-ml or 600-ml Kjeldahl distillation flask, Liebig condenser with rubber tubing connections, ring stand and clamps to hold the flask and condenser, Kjeldahl distillation trap, 500-ml Erlenmeyer flask to receive the distillate, 50-ml burette, 5- and 50-ml pipettes, piece of glass tubing attached to end of condenser to deliver the distillate into the iodine solution in the Erlenmeyer flask, a gas flame or electric heater and ring to hold the flask above the burner. The following reagents are needed: concentrated hydrochloric acid, 0.1 N iodine solution. 0.1 N thiosulfate solution, saturated solution of sodium bicarbonate, and 1 g/100 ml freshly-made starch solution, made by boiling 1 g of corn starch in water and diluting to 100 ml. The 0.1 N iodine and thiosulfate can be purchased from any chemical supply house, or can be made up as directed in any text book on quantitative chemical analysis. The iodine solution is made by dissolving 12.70 g of reagent ACS iodine and 25 g of reagent ACS potassium iodide in a little distilled water and diluting to 1000 ml in a volumetric flask. It must always be standardized just before use. Thiosulfate should be restandardized every few months.
Proceed as follows: pipette 50 ml of wine and 200 ml of distilled water into the distillation flask and 25 ml of iodine and 25 ml of water into the 500-ml Erlenmeyer flask. Mark this flask at 200 ml. Place the latter beneath the outlet of the condenser with the outlet tube dipping into the solution. In order to avoid loss of iodine it is desirable to set the Erlenmeyer flask in a large beaker or small

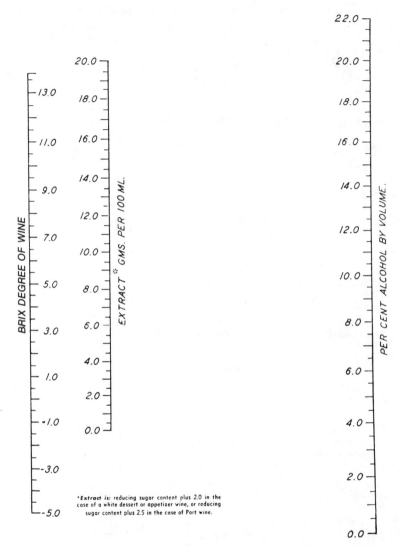

*Extract is: reducing sugar content plus 2.0 in the case of a white dessert or appetizer wine, or reducing sugar content plus 2.5 in the case of Port wine.

Prepared by G.L. Marsh for Wine Institute

FIG. 19.4. NOMOGRAPH BETWEEN BRIX OF WINE, EXTRACT, AND ALCOHOL PERCENT OF DESSERT WINES

To use, lay ruler connecting the two known values and then read off the value of the unknown

pan containing ice water and ice.

Pipette 10 ml of the bicarbonate solution and 5 ml of the concentrated hydrochloric acid into the 50 ml of wine in the distillation flask and connect the flask to the condenser. Start water flowing through condenser jacket. Heat the distillation flask and wine with a gas burner or electric heater to boiling and distill 150 ml of the sample into the iodine solution in about 45 min. Remove the iodine flask; rinse off the delivery tube with water.

Add 0.1 N thiosulfate from the burette to the iodine solution until the color fades to a light yellow. Then add 5 ml of starch indicator solution and continue the titration until the color just changes from blue to colorless.

The result is given as total sulfur dioxide (mg/liter):

$$\text{Total sulfur dioxide, mg/liter} = \frac{(V_1 N_1 - V_2 N_2)(32)(1000)}{v}$$

where V_1 = volume of iodine solution added, in milliliters
N_1 = normality of the iodine solution
V_2 = volume of the thiosulfate solution used for the back-titration, in milliliters
N_2 = normality of the thiosulfate solution
v = volume of the wine sample, in milliliters

Ripper Method for Total Sulfur Dioxide.—This is a volumetric method based on direct titration of the sulfur dioxide in the wine after hydrolysis of the combined sulfur dioxide by strong alkali. It is not as accurate as the distillation method previously described but is more rapid.

The following apparatus is needed: 10-, 25-, and 50-ml pipettes, one 50-ml burette, and one 30-ml Erlenmeyer flask; and the following reagents: 10 g/100 ml sodium hydroxide solution, dilute sulfuric acid consisting of 100 ml of concentrated sulfuric acid added to 300 ml of distilled water, freshly made 0.02 N iodine solution made by diluting 0.1 N iodine 5:1 as needed, 1 g/100 ml starch solution made by boiling 1 g of starch in 100 ml of water 3 min, and 0.1 N thiosulfate solution.

Proceed as follows: check the normality of the 0.02 N iodine solution by pipetting 25 ml into 50 ml of distilled water in a 300-ml Erlenmeyer flask. Add 10 ml of the dilute sulfuric acid and a few drops of starch solution. From a burette add standardized 0.1 N thiosulfate until one drop finally destroys the blue color. The normality of the iodine solution is then obtained by the following calculation: (ml thiosulfate × N thiosulfate)/25 = normality of iodine. For example, suppose 4.9 ml of thiosulfate were used. Then (4.9 × 0.10)/25 = 0.49/25 = 0.0196 N.

Now pipette 20 ml of the wine into a 300-ml Erlenmeyer flask. Add 25 ml of 10 g/100 ml sodium hydroxide. Mix, stopper, and allow to stand 15 min. Then add 10 ml of the dilute sulfuric acid solution and 5 ml of starch indicator solution. Titrate immediately to a permanent blue color with the 0.02 N iodine.

The result is calculated as total sulfur dioxide (mg/liter):

$$\text{Total sulfur dioxide, mg/liter} \ = \ \frac{(V)\,(N)\,(32)\,(1000)}{v}$$

where   V = volume of iodine solution used for the titration, in milliliters
       N = normality of the iodine solution
       v = volume of the wine sample, in milliliters

Ripper Method for Free Sulfur Dioxide.—It is the free sulfur dioxide that one tastes in a freshly-sulfured wine or in a heavily-sulfured older sauterne. However, during aging in the cask or bottle much of the free sulfur dioxide is fixed and is much less perceptible.

To 50 ml of wine add 10 ml of 3:1 sulfuric acid (the 1 volume of sulfuric to 3 of water used in the total sulfur dioxide determination; 3:1 by weight is about equal to 4:1 by volume for sulfuric acid solutions). Quickly add a few drops of starch indicator and titrate to the first persistent blue color with 0.02 N iodine.

The free sulfur dioxide is calculated in a manner similar to the total.

Total Phenols

The phenol content of wine is of importance because it affects the flavor, color, and stability of many wines. The recommended method for must and wine analysis is the Folin-Ciocalteu procedure. Singleton and Rossi (1965) optimized the conditions of use. The use of lithium salts, instead of sodium, prevents problems of precipitation that occurred with the Folin-Denis reagent. The method has been adapted for use with the AutoAnalyser by Slinkard and Singleton (1977).

Phenol.—The method of Singleton and Rossi is given below:

Prepare the Folin-Ciocalteu reagent by dissolving 25 g of sodium molybdate, $Na_2MoO_4 \cdot 2H_2O$, and 100 g of sodium tungstate, $Na_2WO_4 \cdot 2H_2O$ in 700 ml of water in a 2-liter, round bottom flask. Add 100 ml of concentrated hydrochloric acid and 50 ml of 85% phosphoric acid. Connect a reflux condenser, add some glass beads, and reflux for 10 hr. Rinse the condenser and add 150 g of lithium monohydrate and a few drops of bromine and boil for 15 min in a hood. Cool the light yellow solution, place in a liter volumetric flask and bring to volume. Filter into and store in an amber bottle.
Prepare a 20 g/100 ml sodium carbonate solution (200 g $NaCO_3$ in 1 liter of water).
Dissolve 0.500 g of dry gallic acid in water and bring to 100 ml in volumetric flask.
A calibration curve is prepared by pipetting 0-, 1-, 2-, 3-, 5-, and 10-ml aliquots of the gallic acid standard into 100-ml flasks. Bring to volume with water. The

concentration in these flasks, as gallic acid equivalents, is 0, 50, 100, 150, 250, and 500 mg/liter. Pipette 1 ml of each of these solutions into separate 100-ml flasks; add 60 ml of water, mix and 5 ml of the Folin-Ciocalteu reagent. Mix; add after 30 sec and before 8 min 15 ml of the 20 g/100 ml sodium carbonate; mix; and bring the flasks to volume with water. After about 2 hr at 23.9°C (75°F) determine the absorbance at 765 nm against a water blank. Make a plot of absorbance against concentration.

For white wines, pipette 1 ml of the wine into a 100-ml volumetric flask; for a red wine dilute the wine accurately 1:10 and pipette 1 ml of this diluted sample; then proceed as with the standards for both.

Color

A number of inherent shortcomings exist in the currently-used method for the determination of color in white wines. Work by Little (1971A,B) and Little and Simms (1971) culminated in the development of a simple device which gave results that corresponded to the intensity of white wine color as perceived visually far more closely than the single wavelength Lovibond procedure, now in government regulations. In addition, it is much less subject to error from haze or suspended particulate matter. A collaborative study by Wildenradt and Caputi (1976) led to its adoption by AOAC. Additional work presented at the 1976 AOAC Meeting (Wildenradt and Stafford 1976) showed that its use was also applicable to determination of color of white grape juice. Recently, the use of other colorimeters, if properly operated, has been suggested as adequate or equal to the one-purpose colorimeter.

Color assay is of importance in blending and standardizing wine types. The tint and depth of color of red wines are difficult to measure accurately, except with spectrophotometric equipment. However, it now appears that such procedures are necessary for color standardization in large wineries according to papers by Crawford et al. (1958) and Amerine et al. (1959). Abridged colorimeters give data which are only satisfactory for approximate color standardization.

Eagerman et al. (1974) compared 13 different color scales used to measure beverages. None of these scales proved satisfactory for dark-colored liquids.

A simple method involves the use of a photoelectric colorimeter equipped with three tristimulus filters. By making one transmission measurement with each filter, it is possible to specify a color in the same numerical values obtained with a spectrophotometer.

Sudraud (1958) stresses the fact that the brilliance and dominant wavelength are the two most important factors in the specification of color of red wines. He recommends, therefore, specifying the color of red wines by the ratio of the optical density at 420/520 nm and the sum of the optical densities at 420 and 520 nm.

Pataky (1965) has emphasized the importance of pH in the spectrophotometric determination of anthocyans. He recommended a pH of 0.8 and establishment of the pH by pH meter rather than with buffers.

Berg (1963) presented data indicating the presence of two types of pigments: one pH-responsive and the other nonresponsive to pH change. This would invalidate spectrophotometric measurement at a given pH as a means of determination of anthocyans in wine.

The wine maker is chiefly interested in making blends that will match the color of previous blends. The simplest procedure, then, is to take a sample of a previous blend that he has set aside for the purpose, and fill a test tube or small bottle with it, then from the cellar obtain samples of the wines he proposes to use in the new blend. Next measure and blend various amounts of each and compare with his standard blend until a match is obtained.

A major drawback to the above method for matching blends is that the reference samples change in color with time. Spectrophotometric determination of color provides a permanent standard, but requires a number of measurements and a rather lengthy calculation. To simplify color matching of blends, Berg *et al.* (1964) developed charts from which, for values of the respective trichromatic coefficients for two wines, the dominant wavelength of luminous-transmittance differences necessary for discrimination are read directly.

Aldehydes

A measure of the aldehyde content of sherries is of value to the wine maker and is sometimes of importance for other types of wine. It is even more important in brandies than in sherries.

This is essentially the direct bisulfite procedure of Jaulmes and Espezel (1935) as modified by Guymon and Crowell (1963). See Amerine and Ough (1979).

The equipment and reagents required include 10- and 50-ml pipettes, 1-liter Erlenmeyer flask (marked at 370 ml), 500-ml Kjeldahl flask, 500-ml graduated cylinder, capillary tubes or boiling chips, condenser, delivery tube, source of heat, 10- or 25-ml burette, saturated borax ($Na_2B_4O_7 \cdot H_2O$), 0.2 g/100 ml starch indicator solution, 0.1 N iodine, 0.050 N iodine, and solutions A, B, C, and D. Solution A is made by mixing 15 g potassium metabisulfite, $K_2S_2O_5$, 70 ml concentrated hydrochloric acid and diluting to 1000 ml with water; solution B by dissolving 200 g trisodium phosphate ($Na_3PO_4 \cdot 12H_2O$) and 4.5 g disodium ethylenediamine tetraacetate (EDTA) in water and diluting to 1000 ml; solution C by diluting 250 ml concentrated hydrochloric acid to 1000 ml with water; and solution D by mixing 100 g boric acid, H_3BO_3, with 170 g sodium hydroxide and diluting to 1000 ml with water.

Pipette 50 ml of wine into the Kjeldahl flask, add 50 ml of the saturated solution of borax, boiling chips and connect to condenser. Add 300 ml of boiled water and 10 ml each of solution A and solution B to the Erlenmeyer flask. Use calcium chloride tube as an adapter and set so that it just dips into this solution. Distill 50 ml into the Erlenmeyer flask, stopper, swirl to mix and let stand 15 min. Add 10 ml solution C and 10 ml of starch solution, swirl to mix and add 0.1 N iodine to just destroy the excess bisulfite and bring the solution to a light blue endpoint. Add 10 ml solution D and titrate liberated bisulfite ion with 0.050 N iodine solution to the same light blue endpoint with continuous swirling.

The results are given as acetaldehyde (mg/liter):

$$\text{Acetaldehyde, mg/liter} = \frac{(V)(N)(22)(1000)}{v}$$

where V = volume of iodine used in the final titration, in milliliters
   N = normality of the iodine used in the final titration
   v = volume of the sample, in milliliters

The above procedure determines only free aldehydes. For table wines (12% alcohol), the amount of aldehyde present as acetal is negligible. For dessert wines (20% alcohol), and essentially free of bisulfite, the amount of acetal present usually amounts to only 2–3% of the free aldehyde.

Iron Determination

Marsh and Nobusada (1938) gave the following method of determining the iron content of wines:

Pipette 2 ml of wine into 25 × 150 mm Pyrex test tubes previously marked at 10 ml. Evaporate to dryness, cool, and add 1 ml of concentrated sulfuric acid. Heat over a flame under a hood with care until the contents of the tube are completely liquefied. Allow to cool, and then add 0.5 ml of 70 g/100 ml perchloric acid. Heat *continuously* until partial clarification has occurred, set aside to cool, and then add 0.5 ml of perchloric acid. Continue the digestion until the sample is clear and *until all the excess perchloric acid has been evaporated off.* At this stage set the tubes aside to cool. *Caution:* the digestion should be conducted behind a shatterproof glass, because perchloric acid occasionally explodes during heating.
Add 2 ml of distilled water and a small piece (0.5 sq cm) of Congo red paper. Then add 1 ml of 10 g/100 ml aqueous solution of hydroxylamine hydrochloride and 1 ml of 0.1 g/100 ml solution of o-phenanthroline in 50% alcohol. Titrate to the color change (blue to a light red) of the Congo red paper with concentrated ammonium hydroxide and set aside to cool. Make to 10 ml with distilled water for spectrophotometric reading at 490 nm.
The standard iron solution of 1 g/liter is prepared as follows: weigh out 7.022 g of ferrous ammonium sulfate; dissolve it in 500 ml of distilled water to which 5 ml of concentrated hydrochloric acid has been added. Transfer to a liter volumetric flask and make to volume with distilled water.

Prepare from this standard stock solution a series of solutions containing known concentrations (0 to 15 mg/liter). Run these solutions through the preceding procedure for the unknown, using all the reagents and following directions closely. Prepare a standard curve.

Copper Determination

Copper sometimes causes clouding of white table wines and when the clouding of such wines occurs it is important to know whether or not it is due to traces of copper and, if due to copper, how much copper is present in order that the proper amount of Cufex or other permissible precipitant can be used. Caputi and Ueda (1967) found that the copper in wine could be determined directly by an atomic absorption using the proper burner. This is the method of choice; however, corrections for sugar and ethanol are required. The colorimetric method of Marsh is recommended if an atomic absorption unit is not available. The Marsh method is as follows (see Amerine and Ough 1979):

Pipette 10 ml of wine into a 25 × 150 mm Pyrex test tube. Add 1 ml of hydrochloric-citric acid reagent, shake, and then add 2 ml of 5 N ammonium hydroxide (333 ml/liter concentrated ammonium hydroxide), and again shake. Then add 1 ml of a 1 g/100 ml aqueous solution of sodium diethyldithiocarbamate, shake and set aside for a minute or so before adding 10 ml of amyl acetate. Follow with 5 ml of absolute methyl alcohol.

Shake the test tube vigorously for at least 30 sec. Set aside and allow the two phases to separate. Draw off the aqueous phase with a Pasteur pipette. Then dry the organic phase by adding anhydrous sodium sulfate, powdered, from the tip of a spatula and shaking, adding only a sufficient amount to accomplish the purpose. It should be added while holding the tube at an angle and at the same time rotating the tube for the purpose of drying the moisture film adhering to the walls. Filter the dried organic phase to clean dry test tubes and read with a spectrophotometer at 435 nm against a set of standards or to the colorimeter tubes of the Duboscq or any photoelectric colorimeter.

The absolute methyl alcohol which is added to the reaction mixture serves two purposes. It reduces the tendency of the two phases to emulsify. More important is its second purpose. Without methyl alcohol, the color intensity of the extracted colored solution was dependent upon the pH value (maximum 8.0 to 8.5) of the aqueous phase. With methyl alcohol present the pH value of the aqueous phase can vary over rather wide limits with no effect on the color intensity.

Standard copper solution for this procedure is best prepared from Merck copper metal (reagent quality) so as to contain 0.50 mg of copper per milliliter. Solutions for the preparation of the series of standards are prepared by pipetting 1, 2, 3, 4, 5, 6, 8, and 10 ml of the above stock solution into separate liter volumetric flasks, adding 150 ml of 95% ethyl alcohol and making each up to volume with distilled water. These solutions then contain 0.5, 1.0, 1.5, 2.0, 2.5, 3.0, 4.0 and 5.0 mg/ liter of copper, respectively.

Pipette 10 ml of each solution into separate 25 × 150 mm test tubes and proceed as directed for the unknown. The solutions so obtained can be used to establish standard curves.

Ester Determination

Joslyn and Amerine (1941) state that the ester content of wine can be determined by the method generally used for brandy and whisky.

Volatile esters are measured accurately and rapidly by reduction with hydroxylamine after which a colored complex with ferric ion is formed. The method of Libraty (1961) has proved useful. The method is an official AOAC procedure for brandy but has not been collaboratively studied in wine.

Redistill reagent grade ethyl acetate. Take a fore-cut of 5%, then collect the desired amount from the next 20% (if at exact boiling point of ethyl acetate). Dissove 1 g of the ethyl acetate in 1 liter of water. Pipette 2.5, 5.0, 7.5, and 10.0 ml of this stock solution into 100-ml flasks and bring to volume with water. This results in standard solutions of 25, 50, 75, and 100 mg/liter as ethyl acetate. Pipette 3 ml of each of the standard solutions into 15-ml capacity test tubes, add 2 ml of 2 M hydroxylamine hydrochloride (13.9 g dissolved in 100 ml of water), add 2 ml of 3.5 N sodium hydroxide (140 g dissolved in 1 liter of water), and stopper with a neoprene closure, mix and allow to stand for 10 min. Add 2 ml of a 4 N hydrochloric acid (330 ml of concentrated acid diluted to 1 liter with water), add 2 ml of ferric chloride reagent (10 g of $FeCl_3 \cdot 6H_2O$ dissolved in and brought to 100 ml with 0.1 N HCl), and stopper and mix. The solutions are read directly at 510 nm in a spectrophotometer. A standard curve is made. Wine samples are first distilled.

Pipette exactly 200 ml of wine (or brandy) and about 35 ml of water into a 500-ml distillation flask. Distill slowly nearly 200 ml into a 200-ml volumetric flask. The receiving tube from the condenser should reach well into the receiving flask. The receiving flask should be immersed in an ice bath. Bring the distillate to volume at the temperature of calibration.

From the distillate, brought to volume, a 3-ml sample is taken and treated as with the standards. The value of the ethyl acetate for the wine is determined from the standard curve.

Hydroxymethylfurfural

When sugars such as fructose are heated in acid solution they may be dehydrated and yield hydroxymethylfurfural. Its presence is thus a good test of heat treatment of dessert wines. Grape concentrate as usually produced is also high in this substance. The quantitative Winkler's method is outlined by Amerine and Ough (1979). Fiehe's solution is used for its semiquantitative measurement. The procedure is that of Amerine (1948).

Needed are 2- and 10-ml pipettes, 125-ml separatory funnels, 100-ml evaporating dish, 30% hydrochloric acid, freshly-prepared Fiehe's solution (0.1 g resorcinol in 10 ml of concentrated hydrochloric acid), freshly purified anhydrous ether (prepared by washing the ether twice with water, once with cleaning solution, again with water, and then with 10 g/100 ml sodium hydroxide, finally with water, and filter through ashless filter paper).

Pipette 10 ml of wine and 10 ml of the ether into a 125-ml separatory funnel. Shake, allow the layers to separate and draw off the wine into another funnel. Add 10 ml more ether to the wine and shake. Discard the wine and combine the two ether extracts in the evaporating dish. Allow the ether to evaporate at room temperature. Wash down the sides of the dish with 5 ml of the hydrochloric acid; add 2 ml of Fiehe's solution. The presence of hydroxymethylfurfural is indicated by a slight pink color. Greater concentrations will give a full red color. A rough estimate of the amount is made from trace to +, ++, and +++.

Carbon Dioxide

Since the enactment of Public Law 85-859 (85th Congress, H.R. 7125, Sept. 2, 1958) which classifies wines containing a certain maximum amount of carbon dioxide as still wines, an accurate method for determining carbon dioxide is obviously important. The present method of choice is one developed by Caputi *et al.* (1970) and Caputi (1971). This method is simple and does not require sophisticated equipment other than a good pH meter. The procedure is as follows:

Chill one bottle of the wine to be analyzed to about 0°C (32°F). A second bottle is opened and completely degassed by applying a vacuum (28 torr), with agitation, for at least 2 min. This is the blank. Pipette 10 ml of this wine into a 150-ml beaker containing 40 ml of water and a magnetic stirrer bar. Adjust the pH to 10−11 with 50% w/w sodium hydroxide. The addition of 3 drops of carbonic anhydrase solution at a concentration of 1 mg/ml at this time is optional if the rate of titration is not exceptionally rapid. Stir with a magnetic stirrer and adjust the pH to 8.6 with standardized sulfuric acid (about 0.0700 N). Then titrate from pH 8.6 to 4.0 using the standard sulfuric acid. This second titration value is that for the blank.

The cooled bottle (750 ml) is carefully opened without agitation and 7 ml of 50% w/w sodium hydroxide is added. The cap is put back on the bottle and it is gently but thoroughly mixed. Pipette a 10-ml sample and proceed as with the blank.

The result is calculated as carbon dioxide, mg/100 ml:

$$CO_2, mg/100\,ml \quad = \quad \frac{(A-B)\,(N)\,(44)\,(100)}{v}$$

where   A = volume of sulfuric acid used for sample titration, in milliliters

B = volume of sulfuric acid used for blank titration, in milliliters

N = normality of the sulfuric acid

v = volume of sample used, in milliliters

Modified Hubach Test for Residual Cyanide

The apparatus (Fig. 19.5) consists of an aeration tube, condenser, and glass flanges for the test tube, assembled in that order. It is of importance that all connections be made airtight so that the only possible path for air is into the liquid in the aeration tube, and out by way of the condenser, and through the test paper held in the flanges. Side leaks of air markedly reduce the sensitivity of the test.

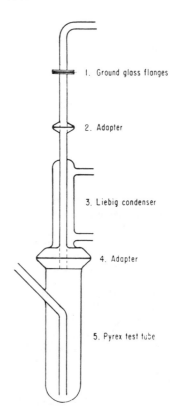

1. Ground glass flanges

2. Adapter

3. Liebig condenser

4. Adapter

5. Pyrex test tube

FIG. 19.5. MODIFIED HUBACH APPARATUS FOR CYANIDE AND FERROCYANIDE

Immerse a sheet of Whatman No. 50 filter paper in a solution of ferrous sulfate (5 g $FeSO_4 \cdot 7H_2O$ and 1 drop of 1:1 sulfuric acid in 50 ml of water) for 5 min. Remove the filter paper from the solution, suspend it by means of a clamp and allow it to dry in the air. When dry, immerse the paper in alcoholic sodium hydroxide solution (10 ml saturated sodium hydroxide solution made to 100 ml with 95% ethyl alcohol). When the paper is thoroughly wet in the alcoholic sodium hydroxide solution, remove and again allow to air dry. The paper should have a light green or a light tan color. The paper is now ready for use. Cut into circles or squares to fit the flange. The paper should be stored in a cool dark place in a tightly-closed amber bottle containing calcium chloride.

To prepare the wine sample for testing, neutralize 20 ml of the wine with 6 N sodium hydroxide solution and add one drop in excess. Evaporate over a steam bath to 5 ml to remove alcohol. To test the wine for cyanides, scrub the apparatus with air until dry and place the test paper between the flanges and tighten the flanges securely. Turn on the water to the condenser. Wash the evaporated wine sample into the test tube through the aeration tube with 10 ml of water and acidify with several drops of 1:1 sulfuric acid solution. Dilute to approximately 20 ml with distilled water. Add 10 mg of cuprous chloride to the solution in the aeration tube. Quantities in excess of 15 mg must be avoided. Turn on the vacuum and connect the test tube to the condenser. Add 1 ml of the sulfuric acid solution through the air inlet tube and draw air through the solution. Adjust the rate of flow so that air just ceases to bubble through the solution and begins to form a continuous stream. Immerse the test tube in a beaker of hot water to just above the sample liquid level. (The water temperature must not be below 80° or exceed 90°C). Aerate the sample for 10 min. Remove the test paper and place it in a 1:3 hydrochloric acid solution in a clean, white evaporating dish. Leave the paper in the dish until white. The appearance of a blue stain in the center of the test paper indicates the presence of cyanide or of a soluble or insoluble ferro- or ferricyanide compound. A little as 0.05 to 0.1 mg/liter of hydrogen cyanide or its equivalent in the ferro- or ferricyanide will give a positive test. It is recommended that a blank be run after each positive test. Test papers showing faint or questionable stains should be confirmed by two or more checks.[1] See Edge (1958), Gettler and Goldbaum (1947) and Hubach (1948).

Other Determinations

Modern winery operation may require a knowledge of metals other than copper and iron, especially of calcium, potassium and sodium.

Jouret and Poux (1961A) reported that simply diluting wines 1:25 or 1:50 made it possible to determine potassium directly in the flame photometer with an error of ±3% in the usual wine and ±5% in the most unfavorable case. They especially did not recommend ashing as there was often a loss, apparently due to volatilization, during ashing. The chief interference is from sulfates and phosphates. For determining sodium by flame photometry, Jouret and Poux (1961B) recommend diluting 1:10 or 1:25. Both sulfates and phosphate cause low sodium results so they recommend adding 0.01 to 0.3 meq/liter of sodium to the diluted samples. In using flame photometry for potassium, sodium and calcium in fruit juices, Ditz (1965) emphasized the importance of preparing the standard curves containing normal amounts of the other cations as well as sugar and citric acid. Because of the severe inhibitory effect of phosphate on calcium emissivity (Dean 1960), it is essential that phosphate be added to both the standard solutions and wine samples if reliable results

---

[1]The assistance of Prof. George Marsh and Mr. Min Akiyoshi in preparing this section is gratefully acknowledged.

are to be obtained. Lactate ion also inhibits calcium emissivity. See also Amerine and Ough (1979), Amerine and Joslyn (1970), Amerine and Kishaba (1952), Amerine *et al.* (1953), Diemair and Gundermann (1959), Jaulmes (1951), Pro and Mathers (1954), and Ribéreau-Gayon *et al.* (1972). Semi-micro methods for metals are given by Bonastre (1959).

Atomic absorption spectrophotometry is now the preferred method for determining cations. Bergner and Lang (1971) give precise directions for determining iron, copper, zinc, manganese, and cadmium by this procedure.

It is invaluable to be able to determine sources of oxidation in the wine making and bottling processes. The use of a Clarke-type membrane electrode is well suited for this. Ough and Amerine (1959) demonstrated its excellent function in wine. Care must be taken in obtaining samples to exclude air and not to inadvertently sparge out the existing oxygen in the samples. Most of the present units are temperature compensated. In-line units are also available for continuous operation.

There are many new techniques and methods being developed and applied to wines. Among these are a rapid gas chromatographic analysis of organic acids (Modi *et al.* 1976), optical rotation assay of mannitol and sorbitol (Dokladalova and Upton 1973), rapid thin-layer separation and identification of 2,3-butanediols and glycerol (Savage and Wagstaffe 1973), gas-liquid determination of methyl anthranilate (Nelson *et al.* 1976), and separation and determination of organic acids, carbohydrates, and amino acids in wine (Drawert *et al.* 1976).

BRANDY

Because of their high alcohol content accurate analyses of brandies are more difficult to attain than with wine. The high coefficient of cubical expansion may introduce volumetric errors. Ethanol itself may interfere in the reaction or modify the endpoint. The procedures given here generally follow those of the Association of Official Analytical Chemists (AOAC 1975). For a method of determining esters, see p. 699. See also Guymon (1976) and Soumalainen *et al.* (1968).

Apparent Proof

Float an appropriate hydrometer in the brandy. The usual hydrometers used by government agents are for 80° to 100° proof, 100° to 140°, 130° to 170°, or 160° to 206°. These are calibrated in 0.5% subdivisions at 15.6°C (60°F). It is possible to estimate to 0.1°. Measure the temperature and make the appropriate correction from Table 19.8.

Schoeneman (1959) has shown that distilled spirits can be proofed more

TABLE 19.8. APPROXIMATE TEMPERATURE CORRECTION TABLE FOR ALCOHOL HYDROMETERS[1] (HYDROMETER CALIBRATED AT 15.6°C, 60°F)

Proof Reading	Average Correction per °F			
	51°−59°F	61°−70°F	71°−80°F	81°−90°F
	Add	Subtract	Subtract	Subtract
10	0.08	0.13	0.16	0.19
20	0.12	0.16	0.20	0.23
30	0.20	0.23	0.25	0.26
40	0.29	0.30	0.30	0.30
50	0.37	0.35	0.35	0.35
60	0.42	0.39	0.38	0.38
70	0.41	0.40	0.41	0.41
80	0.40	0.40	0.41	0.41
90	0.38	0.39	0.39	0.40
100	0.37	0.38	0.38	0.39
110	0.36	0.36	0.37	0.38
120	0.34	0.35	0.36	0.36
130	0.33	0.34	0.35	0.35
140	0.32	0.33	0.34	0.34
150	0.31	0.32	0.32	0.33
160	0.29	0.31	0.31	0.32
170	0.28	0.29	0.29	0.30
180	0.25	0.26	0.27	0.28
190	0.21	0.22	0.24	0.25
200	—	0.17	0.18	0.20

[1]Source of data: U.S. Internal Revenue Service (1970A).

accurately at room temperature. If it is necessary to proof spirits at a temperature different from room temperature, the temperature gradient between the spirits and the room should not be greater than 5.5°C (10°F). Schoeneman recommends in proofing operations that the hydrometer, thermometer, cylinder, and sample should be allowed to come to room temperature. Then after the first set of hydrometer and thermometer readings, the analyst should remove and dry the hydrometer, re-invert the cylinder and contents (with thermometer left in place) several times to again bring about complete thermal equilibrium throughout the system, re-temper the hydrometer, dry the stem, and again take readings.

Legal equipment and methods and techniques are fully described by U.S. Internal Revenue Service (1970B).

True Proof

An approximation of the true proof can be obtained by correcting the apparent proof for the effect of the extract. Determine the extract as indicated on p. 705 and for every 100 mg of extract per 100 ml add 0.4° proof. This procedure is applicable to brandies containing not more than 600 mg of extract per 100 ml.

The pycnometer procedure requires a water bath, an accurate analytical balance, and a distillation apparatus. Fill a 100-ml glass-stoppered volumetric flask, and bring to 15.6°C (60°F) or 20°C (68°F) in the water bath. Correct to the exact volume and transfer to a 500-ml distillation flask. Rinse 3 times using a total of 25 ml of water. Place the volumetric flask so that the adapter just extends into the bulb. Surround the volumetric flask with ice. Distill about 96 ml in not less than 30 or more than 60 min. Rinse off the adapter. The water at the outlet of the condenser should not be more than 25°C (77°F). Place in the water bath and bring to volume and temperature (after mixing). Use a filter paper to dry the neck of the volumetric flask. Dry the outside and weigh. The volumetric flask should previously have been weighed dry and empty and filled with water at 15.6°C (60°F) or 20°C (68°F). The specific gravity in air equals weight of sample divided by the weight of water. The alcohol percentage at 15.6°C (60°F) corresponding to the specific gravity is given in Table 19.9. A more complete table is given by the Association of Official Analytical Chemists (AOAC 1975).

TABLE 19.9. PERCENTAGES BY VOLUME AT 15.6°C (60°F) CORRESPONDING TO SPECIFIC GRAVITIES AT VARIOUS TEMPERATURES[1]

Apparent Specific Gravity	15.6°C (60°F)	20°C (68°F)	Apparent Specific Gravity	15.6°C (60°F)	20°C (68°F)
0.9532	39.04	37.69	0.9389	47.52	46.18
0.9525	39.49	38.14	0.9380	48.00	46.67
0.9517	40.01	38.65	0.9371	48.48	47.15
0.9509	40.52	39.16	0.9361	49.01	47.68
0.9501	41.02	39.67	0.9351	49.52	48.21
0.9493	41.52	40.16	0.9341	50.04	48.73
0.9485	42.01	40.65	0.9332	50.50	49.19
0.9477	42.49	41.14	0.9322	51.01	49.70
0.9468	43.04	41.68	0.9312	51.51	50.21
0.9460	43.51	42.15	0.9302	52.01	50.71
0.9451	44.04	42.60	0.9292	52.51	51.21
0.9443	44.50	43.15	0.9282	53.00	51.70
0.9434	45.02	43.67	0.9272	53.50	52.20
0.9425	45.53	44.18	0.9261	54.03	52.74
0.9416	46.04	44.69	0.9251	54.52	53.22
0.9408	46.48	45.14	0.9241	55.00	53.71
0.9398	47.03	45.69			

[1]Source of data: AOAC (1975).

The true proof can also be obtained on the distillate by the use of the proper hydrometer or with the immersion refractometer.

Extract

Clean a platinum crucible or a porcelain evaporating dish and dry at 110°C (230°F). Cool in a desiccator and weigh. Transfer the residue from the alcohol determination to the crucible or dish. Rinse out 3 times with a total of 25 ml of 50% alcohol. (Of course, the original brandy may also be used as the sample.) Evaporate nearly to dryness on a steam bath, then heat 30 min in a drying oven at 100°C (212°F). Cool in a desiccator and weigh.

Acidity

Neutralize about 250 ml of boiled distilled water in a large porcelain evaporating dish. Use 2 ml of 1 g/100 ml phenolphthalein in neutral alcohol as an indicator. Now add 25 ml of brandy and titrate with 0.1 N sodium hydroxide using a 10-ml burette calibrated in 0.05 ml. With aged brandies the endpoint is more to an orange rather than pink. Calculate the titratable acidity as acetic (mg/100 ml):

$$(N \times \text{ml sodium hydroxide} \times 60 \times 100/25)$$

The fixed acidity is determined by evaporation of 25 or 50 ml of brandy in a platinum or porcelain dish to dryness on a steam bath. Then dry in an oven for 30 min at 100°C. Dissolve the residue with several portions (25 to 50 ml in all) of neutral alcohol (of about the same proof as the sample) and transfer to a large porcelain dish. Add 250 ml of boiled, distilled, neutralized water. Titrate with 0.1 N sodium hydroxide and calculate as above.

The volatile acidity is obtained by the difference between the total and fixed acidities. For problems in the determination of the pH and total acidity of brandy, see Koch et al. (1965).

Fusel Oil

The procedure is that of Guymon and Nakagiri (1952). Dissolve 0.05 g of p-dimethylaminobenzaldehyde in 100 ml concentrated sulfuric acid. (Prepare daily.) Prepare fusel oil standards by mixing 4 volumes of isoamyl alcohol and 1 volume of isobutyl alcohol. (The alcohols should be redistilled and a middle cut used for the standards.) Then weigh 1.0 g of this mixture and dilute to 1000 ml with water. Finally, pipette 0, 5, 10, 25, 35 ml of this solution into 100-ml volumetric flasks, add 7 ml of 95% neutral ethanol, and dilute to volume with water.

The distillate from the ester or alcohol determinations (p. 699, 705) may be used for fusel oil analysis following an appropriate dilution, generally 1:5.

Pipette 1 ml samples of standards and diluted brandy distillates into 25 × 150 mm Pyrex test tubes and place in an ice bath. With the bottom of the test tube submerged in the ice water, add 20 ml of ice-cold p-dimethylaminobenzaldehyde in sulfuric acid with a free-flowing pipette. Care should be taken to agitate the contents of the tube as the first few milliliters are run in. Mix and keep in the ice bath until all samples are prepared. Cover the tops of all the tubes with aluminum foil. Transfer the tubes to a boiling water bath for 20 min. After 20 min return the tubes to the ice bath for 3 to 5 min. Finally, bring the contents of the tubes to room temperature and determine the transmittancy in a colorimeter at 530 nm against concentrated sulfuric acid. Read the fusel oil content from a standard curve of concentration versus transmittancy as fusel oil, mg/100 ml.

This colorimetric procedure measures "total fusel oil" as combined isobutyl, active amyl, and isoamyl alcohols. Normal propyl alcohol, the other important fusel oil alcohol, does not respond to the color reagent. Two gas chromatographic procedures are given by the AOAC (1975). Using a gas chromatographic liquid substrate of 2% (w/w), 1,2,6-hexanetriol and 2% (w/w) glycerol, all 4 fusel oils may be separated and quantified. Secondary butyl alcohol, if present, is not resolved from n-propanol. For details using other liquid substrates see Kahn and Blessinger (1972), Brunelle (1967), and Burgett (1974).

Aldehydes

The reagents are the same as those given under aldehyde determination in wines on p. 696.

To 300 ml of boiled distilled water, add 10 ml of solution A and 50 ml of brandy distillate of about 50% alcohol content. Stopper, mix, and allow to stand 15 min. Add 10 ml of solution B, mix, and let stand another 15 min. Then, add 10 ml of solution C, 10 ml of starch solution, mix, and titrate to a faint blue endpoint with ca. 0.1 N iodine solution. Now add 10 ml of solution D and titrate to the same blue endpoint with 0.05 N iodine. Total aldehydes as acetaldehyde, mg/100 ml, equal ml iodine $\times$ N $\times$ 22.4 $\times$ 100/ml sample. This procedure gives total aldehyde.

For free aldehydes see procedure on p. 696. Also see Guymon and Crowell (1963).

Furfural

The furfural content of wine is of minor importance and is seldom determined. However, it is of importance in the analysis of brandy and is given here for those who may wish to assay the furfural content of brandy. The following procedure is that of Schoeneman (1961).

Pipette 25 ml brandy into the Cash volatile acid still and steam distill until 200 ml are collected. If a haze is present in the distillate add a known volume of alcohol. Determine absorbance at 277 nm.

Prepare standard solutions from redistilled furfural containing 0, 1, 2, 3, 4, and 5 mg/liter of furfural. Determine absorbance of the solutions and plot a curve, concentration versus absorbance. Compare test solution to the standard curve and correct, if necessary, for the added alcohol.

An aliquot of the distillate prepared for the ester determination may be used for this procedure. (If this is the case, distill the last 50 ml at maximum rate to be sure all the furfural is distilled.) Dilute 10 to 20 ml of this distillate to 50 ml with 50% alcohol in a large test tube. Also dilute 0.5, 1, 2, 3, and 4 ml of the dilute furfural standard with 50% alcohol to 50 ml in large test tubes. Add 2 ml of colorless aniline and 0.5 ml of hydrochloric acid (sp gr 1.125) to all the tubes. Mix and leave in a water bath at about 15°C for 15 min. Compare the color in the unknown with that of the standards, either directly or with one of the knowns in a color comparator. A photoelectric color comparator may be used advantageously.

REFERENCES[2]

United States

AMERINE, M.A. 1948. Hydroxymethylfurfural in California wines. Food Res. *13*, 264−269.

AMERINE, M.A. and JOSLYN, M.A. 1970. Table Wines: The Technology of Their Production, 2nd Edition. University of California Press, Berkeley, Los Angeles.

AMERINE, M.A. and KISHABA, T.T. 1952. Use of the flame photometer for determining the sodium, potassium and calcium content of wine. Proc. Am. Soc. Enol. *1952*, 77−86.

AMERINE, M.A. and OUGH, C.S. 1964. The sensory evaluation of California wines. Lab. Pract. *13*, 712−717.

AMERINE, M.A. and OUGH, C.S. 1979. Wine and Must Analysis, 2nd Edition. John Wiley & Sons, New York.

AMERINE, M.A., OUGH, C.S. and BAILEY, C.B. 1959. Color values of California wines. Food Technol. *13*, 170−175.

AMERINE, M.A., PANGBORN, R.M. and ROESSLER, E.B. 1965. Principles of Sensory Evaluation of Food. Academic Press, New York.

AMERINE, M.A. and ROESSLER, E.B. 1976. Wines: Their Sensory Evaluation. W.H. Freeman and Co., San Francisco.

AMERINE, M.A., THOUKIS, G. and VIDAL-BARRAQUER MARFÁ, R. 1953. Further data on the sodium content of wines. Proc. Am. Soc. Enol. *1953*, 157−166.

ANON. 1962−1976. Recueil des Méthodes Internationales d'Analyses des Vins. Office International de la Vigne et du Vin, Paris.

ARNOLD, A. 1957. Beiträge zur refraktometrischen Methode der Mostgewichtsbestimmung. Vitis *1*, 109−120.

AOAC. 1975. Official Methods of Analysis of the Association of Official Analytical Chemists, 12th Edition. Washington, D.C.

BERG, H.W. 1963. Stabilisation des anthocyannes. Comportement de la couleur dans les vins rouges. Ann. Technol. Agric. *12*, numéro hors-série (1) 247−261.

BERG, H.W., OUGH, C.S. and CHICHESTER, C.O. 1964. The prediction of perceptibility of luminous-transmittance and dominant wave-length differences among red wines by spectrophotometric measurements. J. Food Sci. *29*, 661−667.

BERGNER, K.G. and LANG, B. 1971. Zur Bestimmung von Eisen, Kupfer, Zink, Mangan und Cadmium in Traubenmost und Wein mit Hilfe der Atomabsorptionsspektrophotometrie. Deut. Lebensm.-Rundsch. *67*, 121−124.

BEYTHIEN, A. and DIEMAIR, W. 1963. Laboratoriumsbuch für den Lebensmittelchemiker, 8th Edition. Verlag von Theodor Steinkopff, Dresden und Leipsig. (The German AOAC for wines, brandy, etc. Later editions should be consulted.)

---

[2]Titles have been translated only for nonwestern European languages.

BONASTRE, J. 1959. Contribution à l'étude des matières minérales dans les produits végétaux application au vin. Ann. Technol. Agric. 8, 377–446.

BRUNELLE, R.L. 1967. Evaluation of gas-liquid chromatography for the quantitative determination of fusel oils in distilled spirits. J. Assoc. Off. Anal. Chem. 50, 322–329.

BURGETT, C.A. 1974. Automated system for the gas-liquid chromatographic determination of acetaldehyde, ethyl acetate, and fusel oils in alcoholic beverages. J. Assoc. Off. Anal. Chem. 57, 1176–1179.

CAPUTI, A., JR. 1970. Determination of ethanol in wine by chemical oxidation: 1969 studies. J. Assoc. Off. Anal. Chem. 53, 11–12.

CAPUTI, A., JR. 1971. Determination of carbon dioxide in wine. J. Assoc. Off. Anal. Chem. 54, 782–784.

CAPUTI, A., JR. and SLINKARD, K. 1975. Collaborative study of the determination of sorbic acid. J. Assoc. Off. Anal. Chem. 58, 133–135.

CAPUTI, A., JR. and UEDA, M. 1967. The determination of copper and iron in wine by absorption spectrophotometry. Am. J. Enol. Vitic. 18, 66–70.

CAPUTI, A., JR., UEDA, M., WALTER, P. and BROWN, T. 1970. Titrimetric determination of carbon dioxide in wine. Am. J. Enol. Vitic. 21, 140–144.

CAPUTI, A., JR. and WRIGHT, D. 1969. Collaborative study of the determination of ethanol in wine by chemical oxidation. J. Assoc. Off. Anal. Chem. 52, 85–88.

CASTELLI, T. 1969. Il Vino al Microscopio. L. Scialpi, Rome.

COOKE, G.M. 1964. Effect of grape pulp upon soluble solids determinations. Am. J. Enol. Vitic. 15, 11–16.

CRAWFORD, C., BOUTHILET, R.J. and CAPUTI, A., JR. 1958. Color standards for white wines. Am. J. Enol. 9, 194–201.

DEAN, J.A. 1960. Flame Photometry. McGraw-Hill Book Co., New York.

DIEMAIR, W. and GUNDERMANN, E. 1959. Zur Kalium und Natriumbestimmung in Wein. Z. Lebensm.-Untersuch. -Forsch. 109, 469–474.

DITZ, E. 1965. Contribution au dosage des jus de fruits. Détermination du phosphore, du potassium, du sodium et du calcium. Ann. Technol. Agric. 14, 67–78.

DOKLADALOVA, J. and UPTON, R.P. 1973. Optical rotation assay for determination of sorbitol in the presence of mannitol and sugars. J. Assoc. Off. Anal. Chem. 56, 1382–1387.

DRAWERT, F., LESSING, V. and LEUPOLD, G. 1976. Gruppentrennung von organischen Säuren, Kohlenhydraten und Aminosäuren mit Ionenaustauschern und quantitative gas-chromatographische Bestimmung der Einzelsubstanzen. Chromatographia 9, 373–379.

EAGERMAN, B.A., CLYDESDALE, F.M. and FRANCIS, F.G. 1974. Comparison of color scales for dark colored beverages. J. Food Sci. 38, 1051–1059.

EDGE, R.A. 1958. The detection of cyanides and ferrocyanides in wines. S. Afr. J. Agric. Sci. 1, 337.

FILIPELLO, F. 1957. Organoleptic wine-quality evaluation. II. Performance of judges. Food Technol. *11*, 51–53.

FILIPELLO, F. and BERG, H.W. 1959. The present status of consumer tests on wine. Am. J. Enol. Vitic. *10*, 8–12.

FRANCK, R. 1973. Weinanalytik, Teil C, 2. Erganzungslieferung, Oktober 1973 von R. Franck und Ch. Junge. C. Heymanns Verlag, Köln.

FRANCK, R. and JUNGE, C. 1970. Weinanalytik. Untersuchung von Wein und ähnlichen alkoholischen Erzeugnissen sowie von Früchtsäften. Carl Heymanns Verlag, Köln.

GETTLER, A.O. and GOLDBAUM, L. 1947. Detection and estimation of microquantities of cyanide. Anal. Chem. *19*, 270–271.

GUYMON, J.F. 1976. Analytical Procedures for Brandy. Department of Viticulture and Enology, Univ. California, Davis.

GUYMON, J.F. and CROWELL, E.A. 1963. Determination of aldehydes in wines and spirits by the direct bisulfite method. J. Assoc. Off. Anal. Chem. *46*, 276–284.

GUYMON, J.F. and NAKAGIRI, J. 1952. Methods for the determinations of fusel oil. Proc. Am. Soc. Enol. *1952*, 117–134.

GUYMON, J.F. and NAKAGIRI, J. 1957. The bisulfite determination of free and combined aldehydes in distilled spirits. J. Assoc. Off. Agric. Chem. *40*, 561–575.

HILL, G. and CAPUTI, A., JR. 1970. Colorimetric determination of tartaric acid in wine. Am. J. Enol. Vitic. *21*, 153–161.

HODGMAN, C.D. 1964. Handbook of Chemistry and Physics, 45th Edition. Chemical Rubber Co., Cleveland. (See latest edition.)

HUBACH, C.E. 1948. Detection of cyanides and ferrocyanides in wines. Anal. Chem. *20*, 1115–1116.

JAULMES, P. 1951. Analyse des Vins, 2nd Edition. Librairie Coulet, Dubois et Poulain, Montpellier.

JAULMES, P. and BRUN, S. 1963. La mesure pycnometrique de la masse volumique de la densité et du degré alcoolique des vins. Ann. Fals. Expert. Chim. *56*, 129–142.

JAULMES, P. and BRUN, S. 1967. Table alcoolmetrique internationale O.I.V. Tables d'emploi usuel et de corrections de temperature. Ann. Fals. Expert. Chim. *60*, 101–145.

JAULMES, P. and ESPEZEL, P. 1935. Le dosage de l'acetaldehyde dans les vins et les spiritueux. *Ibid. 28*, 325–335.

JOSLYN, M.A. 1970. Methods in Food Analysis: Physical, Chemical, and Instrumental Methods of Analysis. Academic Press, New York.

JOSLYN, M.A. and AMERINE, M.A. 1941. Commercial production of brandy. Calif. Agric. Exp. Stn. Bull. *652*.

JOURET, C. and POUX, C. 1961A. Étude d'une technique de dosage du potassium par spectrophotométrie de flamme dans les vins et les moûts. Ann. Technol. Agric. *10*, 351–359.

JOURET, C. and POUX, C. 1961B. Note sur les teneurs en potassium, sodium et chlore des vignes des terrains salés. *Ibid. 10,* 369–374.

KAHN, J.H. and BLESSINGER, E.T. 1972. Collaborative study of the quantitative gas-liquid chromatographic determination of fusel oil and other components in whiskey. J. Assoc. Off. Anal. Chem. *55,* 549–556.

KOCH, J., HESS, D. and SCHILLER, H. 1965. Zur Analytik von Weinbrand. I. Bestimmung des pH-Wertes und der Gesamtsäure. Z. Lebensm.-Untersuch. -Forsch. *126,* 275–281.

LIBRATY, V. 1961. Ester determinations and their application to wine. M.S. Thesis. University of California, Davis.

LIDZEY, R.G., SAWYER, R. and STOCKWELL, P.B. 1971. Improvements relating to the automatic determination of alcohol in beers and wine, using a distillation technique. Lab. Pract. *20,* 213–216.

LITTLE, A. 1971A. The color of white wine. I. A review and critical analysis of the Lovibond unit specification. Am. J. Enol. Vitic. *22,* 138–143.

LITTLE, A. 1971B. The color of white wine. II. Evaluation by trans-reflectometry. *Ibid. 22,* 144–149.

LITTLE, A. and SIMMS, R.J. 1971. The color of white wine. III. The design, fabrication, and testing of a new instrument for evaluating white wine color. *Ibid. 22,* 203–209.

MARSH, G.L. and NOBUSADA, K. 1938. Iron determination methods. Wine Rev. *6* (9) 20–21.

MAYER, K. and BUSCH, I. 1963. Über eine enzymatische Äpfelsäurebes-timmung in Wein und Traubensaft. Mitt. Geb. Lebensmittelunters. Hyg. *45,* 60–65.

MODI, G., GUERRINI, M. and SIMIANI, G. 1976. Sul contenuto di acidi fissi liberi in alcuni vini nazionali. Boll. Chim. Unione Ital. Lab. Prov. *27,* 183–189.

MORI, L. 1975. Metodi Razionali di Analisi nella Moderna Tecnica Enologica, 3rd Edition. Editore Luigi Scialpi, Rome.

NELSON, R.R., ACREE, T.E., LEE, C.Y. and BUTTS, R.M. 1976. Gas-liquid chromatographic determination of methyl anthranilate in wine. J. Assoc. Off. Anal. Chem. *59,* 1387–1389.

OUGH, C.S. and AMERINE, M.A. 1959. Dissolved oxygen determination in wine. Food Res. *24,* 744–748.

OUGH, C.S. and AMERINE, M.A. 1970. Effect of subjects' sex, experience, and training on their red wine color-preference patterns. Percept. Mot. Skills *30,* 395–398.

OUGH, C.S. and BERG, H.W. 1959. Studies on various light sources concerning the evaluation and differentiation of red wine color. Am. J. Enol. Vitic. *10,* 159–163.

OUGH, C.S. and WINTON, W.A. 1976. An evaluation of the Davis wine-score card and individual expert panel members. Am. J. Enol. Vitic. *27,* 136–144.

PANGBORN, R.M., OUGH, C.S. and CHRISP, R.B. 1964. Taste inter-relationship of sucrose, tartaric acid, and caffeine in white table wine. Am. J. Enol. Vitic. *15,* 154–161.

PATAKY, M.B. 1965. Sur les particularités du dosage spectrophotométrique des anthocyannes. Ann. Technol. Agric. *14*, 79—85.

PAUL, F. 1967. Die "Rangziffern-Methode," ein einfache Möglichkeit für den organoleptischen Vergleich zweier oder mehrerer Proben. Mitt. Rebe Wein Obstbau Früchteverw. (Klosterneuburg) *17*, 280—288.

PEYNAUD, E. and BLOUIN, J. 1965. Comparaison de quelques méthodes de dosage de l'acide L-malique. Ann. Technol. Agric. *14*, 61—66.

PEYNAUD, E. and LAFON-LAFOURCADE, S. 1965. Étude d'un dosage simple de l'acide malique appliqué aux vins à l'aide de *Schizosaccharomyces pombe. Ibid. 14*, 49—59.

PILONE, G.J., RANKINE, B.C. and HATCHER, C.J. 1972. Evaluation of an improved method for measuring volatile acid in wine. Austr. Wine, Brewing Spirit Rev. *91*, 62—64, 66.

POUX, C. 1969. Dosage enzymatique de l'acide L(−) malique. Ann. Technol. Agric. *18*, 359—366

PRO, M.J. and MATHERS, A.P. 1954. Metallic elements in wine by flame photometry. J. Assoc. Off. Agric. Chem. *37*, 945—960.

REBELEIN, H. 1973. Verfahren zur genauen serien mässigen Bestimmung der Wein- und Milchsäure in Wein und ähnlichen Getränken. Chem. Mikrobiolog. Technol. Lebensm. *2*, 33—38.

RIBÉREAU-GAYON, J., PEYNAUD, E., SUDRAUD, P. and RIBÉREAU-GAYON, P. 1972. Traité d'Oenologie. Sciences et Techniques du Vin, Vol. I—Analyse et Contrôle des Vins. Dunod, Paris.

ROBIRDS, F.M. and ROSSI, E.A., JR. 1966. Non-sugar solids in various varieties of California grapes. Am. J. Enol. Vitic. *17*, 31—37.

ROESSLER, E.B., WARREN, J. and GUYMON, J.F. 1948. Significance in triangular taste tests. Food Res. *13*, 503—505.

SARRIS, J., MORFAUX, J.N., DUPUY, P. and HERTZOG, D. 1969. Détermination automatique du degré alcoolique du vin. Ind. Alim. Agric. *86*, 1241—1246.

SAVAGE, R.I. and WAGSTAFFE, P.J. 1973. Une methode rapide de detection du glycerol et du butane-2:3-diol dans les produits de fermentation alcoolique. Ann. Fals. Expert. Chim. *66*, 246—249.

SCHOENEMAN, R.L. 1959. Report on distilled spirits. J. Assoc. Off. Agric. Chem. *42*, 327—329.

SCHOENEMAN, R.L. 1961. Determination of furfural in distilled spirits. J. Assoc. Off. Anal. Chem. *44*, 392—394.

SINGLETON, V.L. and ROSSI, J.A., JR. 1965. Colorimetry of total phenolics with phosphomolybdic-phosphotungstic acid reagents. Am. J. Enol. Vitic. *16*, 144—158.

SLINKARD, K. and SINGLETON, V.L. 1977. Total phenol analysis: automation and comparison with manual methods. *Ibid. 28*, 49—55.

SOUMALAINEN, H., KAUPPILA, O.A.P., NYKÄNEN, L. and PEETONEN, R.J. 1968. Branntweine. *In* Alkoholische Genussmittel. W. Diemar (Editor). Springer Verlag, Berlin. (See p. 496—653.)

SUDRAUD, P. 1958. Interpretation des courbes d'absorption des vins rouges. Ann. Technol. Agric. 7, 203−208.

TROOST, T. 1965. Unter welchen Voraussetzungen lässt eine organoleptische Weinprüfung in Zusammenspiel mit einer Weinanalyse ein Höchstmass an Zuverlässigkeit erwarten? Deut. Weinbau 20, 262−264.

U.S. INTERNAL REVENUE SERVICE. 1970A. Title 26, Part 240.531. Code of Federal Regulations. U.S. Govt. Print. Office, Washington, D.C.

U.S. INTERNAL REVENUE SERVICE. 197?B. Gauging Manual Embracing Instructions and Tables for Determining the Quantity of Distilled Spirits by Proof and Weight. U.S. Govt. Pring Office, Washington, D.C. (U.S. Treasury Dept., IRS Publ. 455).

U.S. TREASURY DEPT., BUREAU OF ALCOHOL, TOBACCO AND FIREARMS DIVISION. 1976. Title 27, Part 240. Code of the Federal Regulations. U.S. Govt. Print. Office, Washington, D.C.

VOGT, E. and BIEBER, H. 1970. Weinchemie und Weinanalyse, 3rd Edition. Verlag Eugen Ulmer, Stuttgart.

WILDENRADT, H.L. and CAPUTI, A., JR. 1976. Collaborative study of the determination of color in white wine. J. Assoc. Off. Anal. Chem. 59, 777−779.

WILDENRADT, H.L. and STAFFORD, P. 1977. Determination of color in white wine and white juice using the white wine colorimeter. J. Assoc. Off. Anal. Chem. 60, 739−740.

ZIMMERMANN, H.W. 1963. Studies on the dichromate method of alcohol determination. Am. J. Enol. Vitic. 14, 205−213.

OTHER COUNTRIES[3]

France

ANON. 1963. Textes d'intérêt général, répression des fraudes. Méthodes officielles d'analyses des vins et des moûts (Arrêté du 24 juin 1963). Journaux Officiels, Paris.

RIBÉREAU-GAYON, J., PEYNAUD, E., SUDRAUD, P. and RIBÉREAU-GAYON, P. 1972. Analyse et Contrôle des Vins. Dunod, Paris. (Not official.)

Germany

BEYTHIEN, A. and DIEMAIR, W. 1963. Laboratoriumsbuch für den Lebensmittelchemiker, 8th Edition. Verlag von Theodor Steinkopff, Dresden und Leipsig. The German AOAC for wines, brandy, etc. (Later editions should be consulted.)

---

[3]These are official or semi-official procedures.

FRANCK, R. and JUNGE, C. 1970. Weinanalytik. Untersuchung von Wein und ähnlichen alkoholischen Erzeugnissen sowie von Fruchsäften nach der allgemeinen Verwaltungsvorschrift und den Vorschriften des Internationalen Amtes für Rebe und Wein. Verlag Carl Heymanns, Köln. (Not official.)

HENNIG, K. and JAKOB, L. 1973. Untersuchungenmethoden für Wein und ähnliche Getränke. E. Ulmer, Stuttgart. (Not official.)

HESS, D. and KOPPE, F. 1968. Wein II: Weinanalytik. *In* Alkoholische Genussmittel. W. Diemar (Editor). Springer Verlag, Berlin. (See p. 311−495.)

International

OFFICE INTERNATIONAL DE LA VIGNE ET DU VIN, PARIS. 1960−1977. Recueil des Méthodes Internationales d'Analyse des Vins. (Loose leaf, up-dated periodically.)

Italy

ANON. 1958. Metodi Ufficiali Analisi per Materie che Interassano l'Agricoltura. II (part I). Mosti, Vini, Birre, Aceti, Sostanze Tartariche, Materie Tanniche. Librerie dello Stato, Rome.

MORI, L. 1967. Metodi Razionali di Analisi Nella Moderna Tecnica Enologica, 2nd Edition. L. Scialpi, Rome. (Not official.)

Portugal

ANON. 1963. Métodos Oficiais para a Análise de Vinhos, Vinagres e Azeites. Ministério do Comércio, Indústria e Agricultura, Direccão Geral de Accão Social Agrária, Lisbon.

Romania

TÂRDEA, C. 1971. Metode de Arťaliză și Control Tehnologie al Vinurilor. "Ceres," Bucharest.

Soviet Union

AGABAL'IANTS, G.G. 1969. Khimiko-tekhnologicheskii Kontrol Vinodeliia. (Chemical-technical Control of Wines.) Pischepromizdat, Moscow. (Not official.)

Spain

ANON. 1956. Analisis de Vinos. Metodos Oficiales para los Laboratorios Dependientes del Ministerio de Agricultura. Ministerio de Agricultura, Madrid.

GODED Y MUR, A. 1964. Técnicas Modernas Aplicadas al Análisis de los Vinos. Editorial Dossat, Madrid.

Switzerland

SCHWEIZ. VEREIN ANALYTISCHER CHEMIKER. 1937. Schweizerisches
Lebensmittel Buch, 4th Edition. Zimmermann & Cie, Berne (wines p. 287–
310).

20

Legal Restrictions on Wine Making

Assyrian records indicate legal controls on wine making are several thousand years old. The regulations were made to prevent adulteration. To prevent dilution of wine in the Middle Ages, taverns were forbidden to have water. Similar objectives are found in the laws of many countries. During Roman and later times wines became a source of revenue. Various legal restrictions prevented wines from being diluted or otherwise reduced in quality with consequent loss in sales and reduction in the state's revenue. In Italy, a law of August 4, 1954, provides a fine for use of prohibited nongrape products in wine making. This aspect is inherent in many of the regulations of the U.S. Bureau of Alcohol, Tobacco and Firearms (hereafter abbreviated BATF). The importance of this is indicated by the large volume of alcoholic beverages sold in this country (Table 20.1). The federal revenue from the sale of alcoholic beverages amounted to 5.3 billion dollars in fiscal year 1976: wine 0.2 billion, beer 1.4 billion and distilled spirits 3.8 billion.

Another concept, particularly in England, was that alcoholic beverages were a luxury product and should be taxed to produce additional revenue for the state. This idea is very much in evidence in modern British and American taxes on alcoholic beverages and is not absent from the tax structure of other countries. In the 19th and 20th centuries, taxes also took on a puritanical aspect as a means of controlling alcoholism or of securing conformity in behavior.

In the late 19th century, public health regulations of foods began and many of these were applied to wines. This aspect of legal control is still being developed. Wiley's (1906) tour to Europe specifically considered the public health aspects of wine and brandy production.

Where a certain region has developed a desirable reputation for the quality of its wines, the growers may attempt to prevent other areas from using the geographical appellation for their wines. Many countries, particularly France, thus protect their most famous regional wine names.

715

TABLE 20.1. UNITED STATES PER CAPITA CONSUMPTION OF ALCOHOLIC BEVERAGES (In thousands for totals)

Calendar Years Average	Population[1]	All Wine	Per Capita	Malt Beverages[2]	Per Capita	Distilled Spirits[3]	Per Capita
1900–1904	79,127	—	0.38	—	17.32	—	1.39
1905–1909	87,057	—	0.46	—	19.96	—	1.47
1910–1914	95,590	—	0.52	—	20.77	—	1.48
1915–1919	102,699	—	0.54	—	15.62	—	1.19
1935–1939	128,967	63,285	0.49	1,519,521	11.78	121,738	0.94
1940–1944	133,225	100,121	0.75	1,971,855	14.80	161,121	1.21
1945–1949	142,148	117,162	0.82	2,555,883	17.98	188,665	1.33
1950–1954	155,977	137,493	0.88	2,589,912	16.60	190,321	1.22
1955–1959	171,126	151,593	0.89	2,621,886	15.32	213,558	1.25
1960–1964	185,778	172,922	0.93	2,839,867	15.29	252,978	1.36
1965–1969	197,875	206,707	1.04	3,329,714	16.80	326,738	1.65
1970–1974	207,901	321,247	1.55	4,087,702	19.66	392,172	1.89
1975	213,032	368,029	1.73	4,599,352	21.59	422,609	1.98
1976	214,669	376,389	1.75	4,672,652	21.77	425,891	1.98
1977	216,332	400,348	1.85	4,905,626	22.68	432,565	2.00

Source: Private communications, Wine Institute (1959, 1966, 1971, 1977).
[1] Population 1955–1977, inclusive, from Bureau of the Census, U.S. Department of Commerce.
[2] Data for 1955–1977, inclusive, from U.S. Brewers Association, Inc. See Annual Statistical Review of Distilled Spirits Industry.
[3] Data for 1955–1977, inclusive, from the Distilled Spirits Council of the United States. See Annual Statistical Review of Distilled Spirits Industry.

Restrictions may also be placed on the producers as to varieties, production, minimum alcohol in addition to the geographical origin of the wine (p. 5). An attempt to establish a regional appellation was the California law protecting the name "Central Coast Counties Dry Wine." The wines of this region have a reputation for quality but the name has not been used, probably because it does not represent a distinctive type. Is this why varietal appellations have achieved public recognition to a much greater extent than regional appellations in California? Recent amendments to federal regulations (U.S. BATF 1978B) provide new regulations on geographical appellations.

The 21st Amendment to the U.S. Constitution repealed the 18th (Prohibition) Amendment and control of alcoholic beverages was returned to the states. The states have enacted 50 diverse legal and tax structures under which wines may be made, shipped or sold. Although wine can be legally made or sold in all states, there are areas which by local option laws are dry or which seriously obstruct the sale of wine.

Only the most important California and federal regulations can be reviewed. The laws are often changed and further changes in the regulations can be anticipated. For those who wish to go into wine production in this country in the future we recommend that they consult the local regulatory agencies as well as the nearest regional office of the Bureau of Alcohol, Tobacco and Firearms. Regional offices are located in Atlanta, Chicago, Cincinnati, Dallas, New York, Philadelphia, and San Francisco. The head office is in Washington, D.C. For its members, the legal staff of the Wine Institute in San Francisco is a valuable source of information and advice. There are a number of consultants who specialize in wine regulations. Seff (1979) discussed U.S. wine laws.

WINES—FEDERAL

The statutory basis of the federal regulations relating to the production of distilled spirits, wine, and beer is United States Internal Revenue Code of 1954, as amended, Subtitle E, Chapter 51, Title 26, United States Code 5001 *et seq.*; see U.S. Laws (1954, 1958, 1965). Similarly, regulations relating to the advertising of wine and distilled spirits and related matters are based on the Federal Alcohol Administration Act of 1935, as amended, 49 Stat. 977; see U.S. Federal Alcohol Administration (1937), U.S. BATF (1976C,D,E, 1978B), and Udell (1968).

Definitions

Our intention here is to indicate the major provisions of state and federal regulations. In the United States:

Grape wine must contain not less than 7 nor over 24% alcohol. Grape wine is defined (U.S. BATF 1976C) as "wine produced by the normal alcoholic fermentation of the juice of sound, ripe grapes (including restored or unrestored pure condensed grape must), with or without the addition, after fermentation, of pure condensed grape must, and with or without added fortifying grape spirits or alcohol, but without other addition or abstraction except as may occur in cellar treatment: *Provided,* That the product may be ameliorated before, during or after fermentation by either of the following methods:

(i) By adding, separately or in combination, dry sugar, or such an amount of sugar and water solution as will not increase the volume of the resulting product more than 35%; but in no event shall any product so ameliorated have an alcohol content, derived by fermentation, of more than 13% by volume, or a natural acid content, if water has been added, of less than 5 parts per thousand, or a total solids content of more than 22 g per 100 cc.

(ii) By adding, separately or in combination, not more than 20% by weight of dry sugar, or not more than 10% by weight of water.

(iii) In the case of domestic wine, in accordance with section 5383 of the Internal Revenue Code.

The maximum volatile acidity, calculated as acetic acid and exclusive of sulphur dioxide, shall not be, for natural red wine, more than 0.14 g, and for other grape wine, more than 0.12 g, per 100 cc (20°C). Grape wine deriving its characteristic color or lack of color from the presence or absence of the red coloring matter of the skins, juice, or pulp of grapes may be designated as "red wine," "pink (or rose) wine," "amber wine," or "white wine" as the case may be. Any grape wine containing no added grape brandy or alcohol may be further designated as "natural."

(2) "Table wine" is grape wine having an alcoholic content not in excess of 14% by volume. Such wine may also be designated as "light wine," "red table wine," etc., as the case may be.

(3) "Dessert wine" is grape wine having an alcoholic content in excess of 14% but not in excess of 24% by volume. Dessert wine having the taste, aroma and characteristics generally attributed to sherry and an alcoholic content, derived in part from added grape brandy or alcohol, of not less than 17% by volume, may be designated as "sherry." Dessert wines having the taste, aroma and characteristics generally attributed to angelica, madeira, muscatel and port and an alcoholic content, derived in part from added grape brandy or alcohol, of not less than 18% by volume, may be designated as "angelica," "madeira," "muscatel," or "port" respectively. Dessert wines having the taste, aroma, and characteristics generally attributed to any of the above products and an alcoholic content, derived in part from added grape brandy or alcohol, in excess of 14% by volume but, in the case of sherry, less than 17%, or, in other cases, less than 18% by volume, may be designated as "light sherry," "light angelica," "light madeira," "light muscatel" or "light port," respectively."

The definition in the wine making section of the Code of Federal Regulations (U.S. BATF 1976L) differs somewhat. It defines natural grape wine as:

the product of the juice of sound, ripe grapes, made with cellar treatment authorized by this part and having a total solids content subject to limitations stated in this subpart, but the total solids content of the wine shall in no case exceed 21% by weight.

In the production of natural grape wine without the use of sugar, no materials may be added to the juice or crushed grapes at the time of starting fermentation, except:

(a) Water to reduce the juice to not less than 22° (Brix) of total solids;

(b) Yeast, or yeast cultures grown in grape juice, to any extent desired; or

(c) Yeast foods, sterilizing agents, or other fermentation adjuncts under the provisions of subpart zz of this part.

Natural grape wine is not quite the same in eastern states and California. Under California climatic conditions grapes almost always ripen sufficiently to produce 10% or more ethanol and the acid content of the juice is rarely excessive. The opposite conditions prevail in many grapes grown in eastern states. Regulations generally permit use of a minimum amount of water at the time of crushing to flush equipment if the density of the juice is not reduced below 22° Brix or by more than 1° but do not permit addition of sugar *per se.*

Outside California, on the other hand, dry sugar or a sugar-water solution is commonly added: the latter when the acid content of the grape juice is high. The volume of ameliorating material (sugar and water) may not exceed 35% of the total volume. Water, dry sugar or invert sugar solutions are used. This amelioration must not reduce the acidity of the finished wine below 0.5% (calculated as tartaric acid). The same limitations apply to natural fruit wines. The pertinent regulations regarding amelioration (U.S. BATF 1976L) are as follows:

Sec. 5383. Amelioration and Sweetening Limitations for Natural Grape Wines.

(a) SWEETENING OF GRAPE WINES.—Any natural grape wine may be sweetened after fermentation and before taxpayment with pure dry sugar or liquid sugar if the total solids content of the finished wine does not exceed 12% of the weight of the wine and the alcoholic content of the finished wine after sweetening is not more than 14% by volume; except that the use under this subsection of liquid sugar shall be limited so that the resultant volume will not exceed the volume which could result from the maximum authorized use of pure dry sugar only.

(b) HIGH ACID WINES.—

(1) AMELIORATION.—Before, during, and after fermentation ameliorating materials consisting of pure dry sugar or liquid sugar, water, or a combination of sugar and water, may be added to natural grape wines of a winemaker's own production when such wines are made from juice having a natural fixed acid content of more than five parts per thousand (calculated before fermentation and as tartaric acid). Ameliorating material so added shall not reduce the natural fixed acid content of the juice to less than five parts per thousand, nor exceed 35% of the volume of juice (calculated exclusive of pulp), and ameliorating material combined.

(2) SWEETENING.—Any wine produced under this subsection may be sweetened by the producer thereof, after amelioration and fermentation, with pure dry

sugar or liquid sugar if the total solids content of the finished wine does not exceed (A) 17% by weight if the alcoholic content is more than 14% by volume, or (B) 21% by weight if the alcoholic content is not more than 14% by volume. The use under this paragraph of liquid sugar shall be limited to cases where the resultant volume does not exceed the volume which could result from the maximum authorized use of pure dry sugar only.

(3) WINE SPIRITS.—Wine spirits may be added (whether or not wine spirits were previously added) to wine produced under this subsection only if the wine contains not more than 14% of alcohol by volume derived from fermentation.

Citrus and fruit wines are similarly defined; only the definitions for fruit wine will be given (U.S. BATF 1976C):

(i) "Fruit wine" is wine (other than grape wine or citrus wine) produced by the normal alcoholic fermentation of the juice of sound, ripe fruit (including restored or unrestored pure condensed fruit must), with or without the addition, after fermentation, of pure condensed fruit must, and with or without added fruit brandy or alcohol, but without other addition or abstraction except as may occur in cellar treatment: *Provided,* That a domestic product may be ameliorated or sweetened in accordance with the provisions of section 5384 of the Internal Revenue Code and any product other than domestic may be ameliorated before, during, or after fermentation by adding, separately or in combination, dry sugar, or such an amount of sugar and water solution as will increase the volume of the resulting product, in the case of wines produced from loganberries, currants, or gooseberries, having a normal acidity of 20 parts or more per thousand, not more than 60%, and in the case of other fruit wines, not more than 35%, but in no event shall any product so ameliorated have an alcoholic content, derived by fermentation, of more than 13% by volume, or a natural acid content, if water has been added, of less than 5 parts per thousand, or a total solids content of more than 22 g per 100 cc.

(ii) The maximum volatile acidity, calculated as acetic acid and exclusive of sulphur dioxide, shall not be, for natural fruit wine, more than 0.14 g and for other fruit wine, more than 0.12 g, per 100 cc (20°C).

(iii) Any fruit wine containing no added brandy or alcohol may be further designated as "natural."

(2) "Berry wine" is fruit wine produced from berries.

(3) "Fruit table wine" or "berry table wine" is fruit or berry wine having an alcoholic content not in excess of 14% by volume. Such wine may also be designated "light fruit wine," or "light berry wine."

(4) "Fruit dessert wine" or "berry dessert wine" is fruit or berry wine having an alcoholic content in excess of 14% but not in excess of 24% by volume.

(5) Fruit wine derived wholly (except for sugar, water, or added alcohol) from one kind of fruit shall be designated by the word "wine" qualified by the name of such fruit, e.g., "peach wine," "blackberry wine." Fruit wine not derived wholly from one kind of fruit shall be designated as "fruit wine" or "berry wine," as the case may be, qualified by a truthful and adequate statement of composition appearing in direct conjunction therewith. Fruit wines which are derived wholly (except for sugar, water, or added alcohol) from apples or pears may be designated "cider" and "perry," respectively, and shall be so designated if lacking in vinous taste, aroma, and characteristics. Fruit wine rendered effervescent by carbon dioxide resulting solely from the secondary fermentation of the wine

within a closed container, tank, or bottle shall be further designated as "sparkling"; and fruit wine rendered effervescent by carbon dioxide otherwise derived shall be further designated as "carbonated."

The definition in U.S. BATF (1976L) or U.S. Laws (1954) for fruit wine differs from that of U.S. Federal Alcohol Administration (1937). Fruit wine is not specified as a fermented product and an upper limit of 21% by weight of total solids is imposed.

Other types of wine which are provided for are "light" wine (alcohol not over 14%), "natural" wine (wine spirits may be added), raisin wine, retsina wine, sake (rice wine), etc.

The definition of vermouth is as follows (U.S. BATF 1976C):

"Vermouth" is a type of aperitif wine compounded from grape wine, having the taste, aroma, and characteristics generally attributed to vermouth, and shall be so designated.

Not less than 80% of the volume of the finished product must be natural wine.

"Special natural wine" is defined in Section 5386 of the Internal Revenue Code (U.S. Laws 1954) as follows:

(a) In General.—Special natural wines are the products made, pursuant to a formula approved under this section, from a base of natural wine (including heavy-bodied blending wine) exclusively, with the addition, before, during or after fermentation, of natural herbs, spices, fruit juices, aromatics, essences, and other natural flavorings in such quantities or proportions as to enable such products to be distinguished from any natural wine not so treated, and with or without carbon dioxide naturally or artificially added, and with or without the addition, separately or in combination, of pure dry sugar or a solution of pure dry sugar and water, or caramel. No added wine spirits or alcohol or other spirits shall be used in any wine under this section except as may be contained in the natural wine (including heavy-bodied blending wine) used as a base, or except as may be necessary in the production of approved essences or similar approved flavorings. The Brix degree of any solution of pure dry sugar and water used may be limited by regulations prescribed by the Secretary or his delegate in accordance with good commercial practice.
(b) Cellar Treatment.—Special natural wines may be cellar treated under the provisions of section 5382 (a) and (c).

A formula giving a complete list of the ingredients (Form 698-Supplemental) must be filed and the process of production stated in detail.

In addition to federal regulations, wines made in California must comply with state regulations. Though federal regulations authorize the production of natural grape wine with the use of sugar, Section 17010 (a) of the California Standards of Identity and Quality for Wine (Title 17,

Chap. 5, Sub-Chap. 2 of the California Administrative Code) expressly forbids the use of sugar (see State of California 1970). This section thus prohibits the production of special natural wines sweetened with sugar. However, Section 17010 (a) (2) permits the use of sugar in the production of carbonated and special natural wines, and Section 17010 (a) (1) permits the use of sugar in the production of sparkling wine (where sugar or liquid sugar may be used only in the traditional secondary fermentation and dosage) if produced in accordance with a formula approved by BATF.

Sugar, sugar-water solutions and liquid sugar would be permissible components of the essence used in producing special natural wines in the volume indicated in the approved formula.

Other types of wine defined in U.S. BATF (1976L) include high-fermentation, heavy-bodied blending, Spanish-type blending, distilling material, and spoiled wine, and specially sweetened natural wine. High fermentation wine is a wine made within the restrictions for natural wines (see U.S. BATF (1976L) paragraphs 240.483 and 240.365 or 240.405), except that the alcohol content after complete fermentation or complete fermentation and sweetening is more than 14% and that wine spirits may not be added. "High fermentation wine is not a natural wine or a standard[1] wine" but it may be produced, stored, and handled on standard wine premises.

Heavy-bodied blending wine and Spanish-type blending wines fall under similar regulatory provisions—they are not to be sold as beverage wine. The former has a total solids in excess of 21%. The latter is made with caramelized grape concentrate. These wines are used by whisky and other blenders whose products need their sugar, flavor or color.

Distilling material is wine produced without sugar, but unlimited water can be employed. Lees, filter wash, unmarketable special natural wine (under conditions specified in Section 240.632 of U.S. BATF (1976L) and other wine residues may be used as distilling material. They are reported as wine on Form 702 (p. 740) but can only be used for distilling purposes.

Vinegar stock permits use of water, either at the time of fermentation, or preferably, after fermentation is completed. If water is added the wine is transferred to the vinegar stock inventory. Spoiled wine is standard wine which has become substandard. Wines of over a certain percentage volatile acidity fall in this class. Sections 240.545 through 240.550 (U.S. BATF 1976L or U.S. Laws 1954) contain a provision for "experimental" wine. This permits scientific institutions and colleges of learning to produce and receive wine with a minimum of forms, bonds, etc., free of

---

[1]Standard wine includes natural wine, specially sweetened natural wine, special natural wine, and standard agricultural wine.

tax for experimental or research purposes, but not for consumption or sale.

Effervescent wines are provided for: artificially carbonated and fermented. The former are seldom produced at present. Both types of wine are limited to 14% ethanol. The producer of effervescent wine must submit a detailed statement of the process to be employed to BATF on Form 698-Supplemental. For fermented effervescent wines this must include a description of the tank or bottle process used. The specific type definitions are given in U.S. BATF (1976C). Champagne is defined as a "sparkling light wine which derives its effervescence solely from secondary fermentation of the wine within containers of not greater than one gallon capacity and which possesses the taste, aroma and other characteristics attributed to champagne as made in the Champagne district of France." Sparkling wines made in larger containers but otherwise conforming to the above standard must be designated as "sparkling wine" and may, in addition, be designated as "champagne-style," "champagne type," "American champagne bulk process," "Charmat process," etc.

The regulations (U.S. Federal Alcohol Administration 1937; U.S. BATF 1978B) also define grape-type (varietal) wines—the varietal name may be used as the type designation of a grape wine if the wine derives its predominant taste, aroma, and characteristics, and at least 75% (51% until 1983) of its volume from that variety of grape, except for native American varieties and hybrids thereof which require only 51% and for other exceptions specifically made by the Director of BATF. An explanatory statement as to the significance of the varietal appellation is permitted on the label. For example:

Beginning in 1983 the names of 2 or 3 grape varieties may be used as the type designation if: (1) All of the grapes used to make the wine are of the labeled varieties; (2) the percentage of the wine derived from each variety is shown on the label (with a tolerance of ±2%); (3) if labeled with a multicounty appellation, the percentage of the wine derived from each variety from each county is shown on the label; and (4) if labeled with a multistate appellation, the percentage of the wine derived from each variety from each state is shown on the label (U.S. BATF 1978B).

Foreign appellations of origin frequently limit the varieties permitted; they seldom specify a single variety. An appellation of origin for a "Médoc," therefore, does not guarantee that it be made wholly from Cabernet Sauvignon, though it may. Varietal labels on imported wines need to be made more specific.

These regulations also define generic, semigeneric and nongeneric designations of geographical origin. Vermouth and sake are considered generic appellations. Semigeneric names listed in the regulations include angelica,[2] burgundy, claret,[3] chablis, champagne, chianti, malaga, marsala, madeira, moselle, port, rhine wine (syn. hock), sauterne, haut sauterne, sherry, and tokay.[4] In using these for any except the region where the name originated, the proper geographical origin must be stated: thus "American," "New York," or "California" port.

The new regulations (U.S. BATF 1978B) on geographical appellations of origin are somewhat complicated and are cited here:

(a) *Definition.* (1) *American wine.* An American appellation of origin is: (i) the United States; (ii) a State; (iii) two or no more than three States which are all contiguous; (iv) a county (which must be identified with the word "county," in the same size of type, and in letters as conspicuous as the name of the county); (v) two or no more than three counties in the same States; or (vi) a viticultural area (as defined in paragraph (e) of this section).

(2) *Imported wine.* An appellation of origin for imported wine is: (i) a county; (ii) a state, province, territory, or similar political subdivision of a country equivalent to a state or county; or (iii) a viticultural area.

(b) *Qualification.* (1) *American wine.* An American wine is entitled to an appellation of origin other than a multicounty or multistate appellation, or a viticultural area, if (i) at least 75% of the wine is derived from fruit or agricultural products grown in the appellation area indicated; (ii) it has been fully finished (except for cellar treatment pursuant to 4.22(c), and blending which does not result in an alteration of class or type under 4.22(b)) in the United States, if labeled "American"; or, if labeled with a State appellation, within the labeled State or an adjacent State; or if labeled with a county appellation, within the State in which the labeled county is located; and (iii) it conforms to the laws and regulations of the named appellation area governing the composition, method of manufacture, and designation of wines made in such place.

(2) *Imported wine.* An imported wine is entitled to an appellation of origin other than a viticultural area if: (i) at least 75% of the wine is derived from fruit or agricultural products grown in the area indicated by the appellation of origin; and (ii) the wine conforms to the requirements of the foreign laws and regulations governing the composition, method of production, and designation of wines made in such country, province, etc., as appropriate.

(c) *Multicounty appellations.* An appellation of origin comprising two or no more than three counties in the same State may be used if all of the grapes were grown in the counties indicated, and the percentage of the wine derived from grapes grown in each county is shown on the label, with a tolerance of ±2%.

(d) *Multistate appellation.* An appellation of origin comprising two or no more than three States which are all contiguous may be used, if: (1) all of the grapes were grown in the States indicated, and the percentage of the wine derived from grapes grown in each State is shown on the label, with a tolerance of ±2%; (2) it has been fully finished (except for cellar treatment pursuant to

---

[2]An error as the type is of California origin and has no geographical significance as far as we can determine.
[3]Also an error. Claret is not used in France as a geographical appellation. In England, claret is commonly used as a type name for the red wines from Bordeaux.
[4]The spellings and capitalization are not as in the regulations but conform to good practice.

4.22(c), and blending which does not result in an alteration of class or type under 4.22(b) in one of the labeled appellation States; (3) it conforms to the laws and regulations governing the composition, method of manufacture, and designation of wines in all the States listed in the appellation.

(e) *Viticultural area.* (1) *Definition.* (i) *American wine.* A delimited grape growing region distinguishable by geographical features, the boundaries of which have been recognized and defined in part 9 of this chapter.

(ii) *Imported wine.* A delimited place or region (other than an appellation defined in paragraphs (a)(2)(i) or (ii)) the boundaries of which have been recognized and defined by the country of origin for use on labels of wine available for home consumption.

(2) *Establishment of American viticultural areas.* Petitions for establishment of American viticultural areas may be made to the director by any interested party, pursuant to the provisions of 71.41(c) of this title. The petition may be in the form of a letter, and should contain the following information: (i) evidence that the name of the viticultural area is locally and/or nationally known as referring to the area specified in the application; (ii) historical or current evidence that the boundaries of the viticultural area are as specified in the application; (iii) evidence relating to the geographical features (climate, soil, elevation, physical features, etc.) which distinguish the viticultural features of the proposed area from surrounding areas; (iv) the specific boundaries of the viticultural area, based on features which can be found on U.S. Geological Survey (U.S.G.S.) maps of the largest applicable scale; and (v) a copy of the appropriate U.S.G.S. map with the boundaries prominently marked.

(3) *Requirements for use.* A wine may be labeled with a viticultural area appellation if: (i) the appellation has been approved under part 9 of this title or by the appropriate foreign government; (ii) not less than 85% of the wine is derived from grapes grown within the boundaries of the viticultural area; (iii) in the case of American wine, it has been fully finished within the State, or one of the States, within which the labeled viticultural area is located (except for cellar treatment pursuant to 4.22(c), and blending which does not result in an alteration of class or type under 4.22(b); and (iv) it conforms to the laws and regulations of all the States contained in the viticultural area.

The term "estate bottled" has been used with various interpretations by American and foreign producers. The new regulations provide:

Estate bottled (not mandatory before January 1, 1983).

(a) *Conditions for use.* The term "Estate bottled" may be used by a bottling winery on a wine label only if the wine is labeled with a viticultural area appellation of origin and the bottling winery: (1) is located in the labeled viticultural area; (2) grew all of the grapes used to make the wine on land owned or controlled by the winery within the boundaries of the labeled viticultural area; (3) crushed the grapes, fermented the resulting must, and finished, aged, and bottled the wine in a continuous process (the wine at no time having left the premises of the bottling winery).

(b) *Special rule for cooperatives.* Grapes grown by members of a cooperative bottling winery are considered grown by the bottling winery.

(c) *Definition of "Controlled."* For purposes of this section, "Controlled by" refers to property on which the bottling winery has the legal right to perform, and does perform, all of the acts common to viticulture under the terms of a lease or similar agreement of at least 3 years duration.

(d) *Use of other terms.* No term other than "Estate bottled" may be used on a label to indicate combined growing and bottling conditions.

Obviously, this is more restrictive than present practices and its complete impact on the practices of the American wine industry is not yet clear.

Regulations also concern the use of terms such as "Late Harvest" (U.S. BATF 1978A):

In accordance with the requirements of 27 CFR 4.38(f), the Bureau will approve the use of the terms "Late Harvest" and "Late Picked" and acceptable variations thereof, for appearance on labels for grape wine, provided the amount of sugar contained in the grapes at the time of harvest and the amount of residual sugar in the finished wine are accurately stated on a front or back label for the product. The amount of sugar may be stated in degrees Brix, percent by weight, per 100 ml or grams per liter, but must be stated in the same kind of measure for both the sugar content of the juice and the residual sugar content of the finished wine. When degrees Brix are used, the provisions of 27 CFR 240.972 through 240.975 apply.

The terms "Botrytis Infected," "Pourriture Noble" and other synonyms for infection by the botrytis cinerea mold will be acceptable on labels for wine made from grapes which have been infected with the mold, provided the labels bear the statements of sugar content as required for "Late Harvest" and "Late Picked" wines.

The term "Ice Wine" may appear on labels for wine made from grapes which have been partially frozen on the vine, provided the labels bear the statements of sugar content as required above for "Late Harvest" and "Late Picked" wines.

Except for vintage wine, harvest or picking dates may not be stated on labels since such dates would have little meaning due to variations of growing locations, grape varieties, and climatic conditions, and could likely mislead the consumer into believing the wine is vintage wine.

Permits, Notices, Bonds, etc.

To establish a bonded wine cellar application for a basic permit (under the Federal Alcohol Administration Act and the regulations pursuant thereto in Part 1, Title 27 of the Code of Federal Regulatons) is made. See U.S. Internal Revenue Service (1977).

BATF Form 698 must be filed in triplicate with the appropriate regional regulatory administrator to operate the winery. The operating name, ownership, location of and description of premises and equipment, etc., is required in Form 698. A bond for winery operation is filed on BATF Form 700 and in addition on Form 2053 for payment of taxes by return. Various other kinds of bonds may be required and detailed provisions for termination of bond, etc., are given in U.S. BATF (1976L) or U.S. Laws (1954). An accurate plot of the premises in a specific form is prescribed. When changes in ownership, location, etc., are made, certain specific reports are required.

The regulations (U.S. Federal Alcohol Administration 1937; U.S. BATF 1976L) provide in substance that before a vintage date can be used on a label, there must be an appropriate appellation of origin. Further, 95% of the wine must be produced from grapes gathered in the same calendar year and in the same viticultural area. The 5% leeway is for topping. Foreign vintage wines need only be labeled and produced in accordance with the laws and regulation of the country of origin but this fact must be attested to by a certificate issued by a duly authorized official of the country of origin of the wine. Foreign regulations, at least of certain countries, often appear to be less restrictive than those of this country.

Construction and Equipment

Bonded wine cellars must be located, constructed and equipped in accordance with pertinent federal regulations, subject to approval by the regional regulatory administrator. The intent of the regulations is that the wines' potential revenue must be protected and that the wines not be difficult to inspect by authorized personnel. A government office for the exclusive use of BATF officers must be provided. However, small wineries usually simply designate the winery office or laboratory as the official office for government personnel. A government cabinet for safeguarding government seals, keys, etc., is necessary.

Tanks must be arranged to permit ready examination. The capacity of all tanks and other containers on a bonded winery premise must be accurately determined and marked, including capacity per inch of depth for tanks of uniform dimensions or for each inch of depth for tanks of irregular dimensions. Subpart XX of U.S. BATF (1976L) or U.S. Laws (1954) gives rules for determining capacity. The tanks must be marked with permanent serial number and the capacity in wine gallons. Tanks of uniform dimensions will also be marked as noted above with the capacity per inch of depth. Also, it must be marked to indicate its current use, i.e., "Fermenting Tank" or "Fermenter," "Intermediate Storage Tank," "Wine Spirits Addition Tank," etc. Abbreviations are permitted and the use signs may be changed. Some tanks have to be permanently marked to show their use—"Vermouth Processing Tank," "Grape Concentrate Storage Tank," etc. Containers of 60-gal. capacity or less need not have a permanent serial number but their capacity must be given. Wine spirits storage tanks have to be of metal and the tanks must be provided with facilities for locking or other secure fastening or sealing. They must also have floats or other devices to indicate actual contents.

Finally, the proprietor must provide at his own expense a measuring rod or steel tape, scales, and measures for weighing materials received or used in the production of wine (except that when used immediately upon receipt a shipper's weight or public weighmaster certificate may be accepted). When wine or wine spirits are tax paid by weight a set of 50-lb cast iron test weights conforming to Class C requirements of the National Bureau of Standards will be needed. The weights may not be required when an accurate scale is provided.

Production

Many of the restrictions in production have been considered in the definition of the various types of wines. The process of adding wine spirits is so important that it deserves special comment. The proprietor must advise the regional regulatory administrator of the intent to use wine spirits. An ATF officer no longer must be present.

The wine to be fortified is placed in approved tanks. The volume and alcohol content of the wine and of the wine spirits to be added are accurately determined. Form 275 of the BATF is prepared in triplicate and one copy delivered to a government officer. The wine spirits must be gauged and Form 2629 completed and attached to Form 275.

Following addition of wine spirits, the wine maker thoroughly agitates the mixture and following stirring takes three pint samples—two for the government officer. The other is immediately tested for alcohol and the percentage entered on Form 275. The alcohol content must not exceed 24%. The total volume is entered on Form 702.

Concentrate or fresh grape juice may be fortified in the manner just described.

Baking of wine is permitted on bonded wine cellar premises. A record must be maintained showing the serial number of the tank, the date the wine was placed in the tank, the quantity, the alcohol content of the wine, and the dates when baking started and was completed, as well as the date on which the wine was removed from the tank and the quantity and alcohol content of the baked wine. In case baking is done in barrels, the records may be maintained on the basis of groups of barrels. Sun baking is permitted provided the area is secure and on bonded premises.

Flor sherry producers have special permission to add wine spirits at two different times. Producers of Spanish type and flor sherry may also add calcium sulfate (gypsum) providing the finished wine contains no more than 2 g of gypsum[5] per liter of wine.

At present the primary restriction on the use of grape concentrate in producing natural grape wine is that the finished wine contain not more than 21%, by weight, of total solids. Fruit concentrates of the same kind of fruit may be used for natural fruit wines in the same way.

Storage and Finishing

Wine may be stored on the bonded premises in tanks, casks, barrels, cased or uncased bottles, or in any other approved containers. If fermenting or storage tanks previously used for one class of wine are to be used for wine of another class they must be carefully cleaned to avoid contamination. The regulations specifically call attention to the necessity of cleaning or treating tanks which have contained special natural wine before using for another wine. They could also have noted the necessity of thorough cleaning of tanks used for vermouth and of the necessity of removing tartrates before placing fruit wines in the tanks.

The materials which may be used in normal cellar practices are specified—subpart ZZ of part 240 of 27 Code of Federal Regulations (U.S. BATF 1976L)—as follows:

Material	Use	Reference or Limitations[6]
Acetic acid	To correct natural deficiencies in grape wine.	The use of acetic acid shall not exceed 0.4 gal. of the equivalent of 100% pure acetic acid per 1000 gal. of grape wine, and such acid shall not be added in a solution of less than 50% strength. Acetic acid in finished red grape wine shall not exceed 0.14 g per 100 cc or 0.12 g per 100 cc in other finished grape wine. §240.364. 21 CFR 121.101(d)(8).
Actiferm (Roviferm)	Fermentation adjunct.	The amount used shall not exceed 2 lb per 1000 gal. of wine. GRAS.
Activated carbon	To assist precipitation during fermentation.	§§ 240.361, 240.366, 240.401, 240.405. GRAS.
	To clarify and purify wine.	GRAS.[7]
	To remove excess color in white wine.	§ 240.527. GRAS.[7]
Aferrin	To reduce trace metals from wine.	No insoluble or soluble residue in excess of 1 ppm shall remain in the finished wine, and the basic character of the wine shall not

[5]Undoubtedly an error. Should be potassium sulfate.
[6]See Section 240.1051 (U.S. BATF 1976L).
[7]GRAS means "generally recognized as safe."

Material	Use	Reference or Limitations[6]
		be changed by such treatment. GRAS.
AMA special gelatin solution	To clarify wine.	GRAS.[7]
Amber By F and/or[8] Amberex 1003	Yeast nutrient in fermentation of grape and fruit wine.	GRAS[7]
Antifoam "A"; Antifoam AF emulsion; Antifoam C	Defoaming agent in production of wine.	The residual silicone content in the wine shall not exceed 10 ppm. 21 CFR 121.1099.
Ascorbic acid; isoascorbic acid (erythorbic acid)	To prevent darkening of color and deterioration of flavor in wines and wine materials, and the overoxidation of vermouth and other wines.	May be added to fruit, grapes, berries, and other materials used in wine production, to the juice of such materials, or to the wine, within limitations which do not alter the class or type of the wine. Its use need not be shown on labels. 21 CFR 121.101(d)(2).
Atmos 300	Antifoaming agent.	No soluble residue in excess of 25 ppm shall remain in the finished wine. GRAS.[7]
Bentonite (Wyoming Clay)	To clarify wine.	21 CFR 121.101(d)(8).
Bentonite compound (Bentonite, activated carbon, copper sulfate)	To clarify and stabilize wine.	Copper added in the form of copper sulfate shall not exceed 0.5 ppm of copper with a residual level not in excess of 0.2 ppm of copper. GRAS.[7]
Bentonite slurry	To clarify wine.	Not more than 2 gal. of water shall be added to each pound of Bentonite used. The total quantity of water shall not exceed 1% of the volume of wine treated. GRAS[7]
Bone charcoal	To clarify wine.	GRAS.[7]
Calcium carbonate	To reduce the excess natural acids in high acid wine.	The natural or fixed acids shall not be reduced below five parts per 1000. 21 CFR 121.101(d)(8).
Calcium sulfate (gypsum)	Production of Spanish type or flor sherry wine.	§ 240.385. Finished wine shall not contain more than 2 g of calcium [potassium?] sulfate per 1000 ml of wine. GRAS.[7]
Carbon	To clarify and purify wine.	GRAS.[7]
Carbon dioxide, CO_2	To stabilize and pre-	§§ 240.531 through 240.535. 21

[8]BATF Ruling 77-29.

Material	Use	Reference or Limitations[6]
	serve wine. To maintain counter-pressure during the transfer of finished sparkling wines.	CFR 121.101(d)(8).
Casein	To clarify wine.	GRAS.[7]
Citric acid	To increase the acidity of wine.	§§ 240.364, 240.404. 21 CFR 121.101(d)(8).
	To stabilize grape wine.	§§ 240.526, 240.539. 21 CFR 121.101(d)(8).
Combustion product gas	To maintain pressure during filtering and bottling of sparkling wines.	The carbon dioxide content of the combustion gas shall not exceed 1%. 21 CFR 121.1060.
	To stabilize wine and prevent oxidation in still wines.	§ 240.531. 21 CFR 121.1060.
Compressed air	Aeration of sherry wine.	The use of compressed air shall not cause changes in the wine other than those occurring during the usual storage in wooden cooperage over a period of time. GRAS.[7]
Copper sulfate	To clarify and stabilize grape and fruit wine.[8]	Copper added in the form of copper sulfate shall not exceed 0.5 ppm of copper with a residual level not in excess of 0.2 ppm of copper. GRAS.[7]
Cufex	To remove trace metal from wine.	No insoluble or soluble residue in excess of 1 ppm shall remain in finished wine. Basic character of wine shall not be changed by such treatment. GRAS.[7]
Defoaming agents (polyoxyethylene-40-monostearate and silicon dioxide) (sorbic acid, carboxy methyl cellulose, dimethyl polysiloxane, polyoxyethylene (40) monostearate, and sorbitan monostearate)	Defoaming agent	Defoaming agents which are 100% active may be used in amounts not exceeding 0.15 lb per 1000 gal. of wine. Defoaming agents which are 30% active may be used in amounts not exceeding 0.5 lb per 1000 gal. of wine. Silicon dioxide shall be completely removed by filtration. 21 CFR 121.1099, 121.101(d)(2), 121.101(d)(8).
Eggs (albumen or yolks)	To clarify wine.	GRAS.[7]
Freon C-318 (octafluorocyclobutane)	Propellant in aerosol containers of vermouth.	Only a minute amount of the gas shall remain in the dispensed vermouth. 21 CFR 121.1065.

Material	Use	Reference or Limitations[6]
Fulgur (aluminum silicate and albumin)	To clarify wine.	The amount used shall not exceed 6.6 lb per 1000 gal. of wine. GRAS.[7]
Fumaric acid	To stabilize grape wine and to correct natural deficiencies in grape and fruit wine.	The amount used shall not exceed 25 lb per 1000 gal. of wine. The fumaric acid content of the finished wine shall not exceed 0.3%. §§ 240.364, 240.404. 21 CFR 121.1130.
Gelatin	To clarify wine.	GRAS.[7]
Granular cork	For treatment of wine.	The amount used shall not exceed 10 lb per 1000 gal. of wine. GRAS.[7]
Gum arabic	To clarify and stabilize wine.	The amount used shall not exceed 2 lb per 1000 gal. of wine. 21 CFR 121.101(d) (7).
Gypsum (see calcium sulfate)		
Hydrogen peroxide	To reduce aldehydes in distilling material.	The amount used shall not exceed 200 ppm. GRAS.[7]
	To facilitate secondary fermentation in production of sparkling wine.	The amount used shall not exceed 3 ppm. The finished product shall not contain any hydrogen peroxide. GRAS.[7]
Ion exchange resins	Treatment of wine.	Anion, cation, and non-ionic resins, except those anionic resins in the mineral acid state, may be used in batch or continuous column processes as total or partial treatment of wine, provided that after complete treatment:
		1. The basic character of the wine has not been altered.
		2. The color of the wine has not been reduced to less than that normally contained in such wine.
		3. The inorganic anions in the wine have not been increased by more than 10 mg per liter.
		4. The metallic cation concentration in the wine has not been reduced to less than 300 mg per liter.
		5. The natural or fixed acid in grape wine has not been reduced below 4 parts per

Material	Use	Reference or Limitations[6]
		thousand for red table wines, 3 parts per thousand for white table wines, or 2.5 parts per thousand for all other grape wines; and the natural or fixed acid in wine, other than grape wine, has not been reduced below 4.0 parts per thousand.
		6. The pH of the wine has not been reduced below pH 3 nor increased above pH 4.5.
		7. The resins used have not imparted to the wine any material or characteristic (incidental to the resin treatment) which may be prohibited under any other section of the regulations in this part.
		Conditioning and/or regenerating agents consisting of water, fruit acids common to the wine being treated, and inorganic acids, salts and/or bases may be employed, provided the conditioned or regenerated resin is rinsed with water until the resin and container are essentially free from unreacted (excess) conditioning or regenerating agents prior to the introduction of the wine. Tartaric acid may not be used in treating wines other than grape. 21 CFR 121.1148.
Isinglass	To clarify wine.	GRAS.[7]
Koldone[8]	A fining agent for cold stabilization and/or acid reduction.	The amount used shall not exceed 30 lb per 1000 gal. of wine. If prepared for use in a water slurry, the total amount of water used may not exceed 1% of the wine treated nor exceed 2 gal. of water per 1 lb of Koldone when 5 lb or less of Koldone is used.
Lactic acid	To stabilize wine and correct natural defi-	§§ 240.364, 240.404, 240.526. 21 CFR 121.101(d)(8).

Material	Use	Reference or Limitations[6]
	ciencies in wine.	
Malic acid	To increase acidity of wine.	§§ 240.364, 240.404. 21 CFR 121.101(d)(8).
Milk powder[8]	A fining agent in the clarification of wine.	The amount used shall not exceed 3 lb per 1000 gal. of wine.
Mineral oil	On surface of wine in storage tanks to prevent the access of air to the wine.	The oil shall not remain in the finished wine when marketed. 21 CFR 121.1146.
Nitrogen gas	To maintain pressure during filtering and bottling of sparkling wine. To prevent oxidation of wine.	The gas shall not remain in sparkling or still wine. 21 CFR 121.101(d)(8).
Oak chips (charred)	To treat Spanish type blending sherry.	The finished product, after addition of oak chips, shall have the flavor and color of Spanish type blending sherry commonly obtained by storage of sherry wine in properly treated used charred oak whisky barrels. GRAS.[7]
Oak chips (uncharred and untreated)	To treat wines.	21 CFR 121.1163.
Oak chip sawdust (uncharred and untreated)	To treat wines.	21 CFR 121.1163.
Oxygen	In baking or maturing wine.	May be used provided it does not cause changes in the wine other than those occurring during the usual storage in wooden cooperage over a period of time. Application must be filed. GRAS.[7]
Pectolytic enzymes	To clarify and stabilize wine, and to facilitate separation of the juice from the fruit.	The pectolytic enzymes shall be derived from non-toxic strains of *Aspergillus niger*. 21 CFR Part 121. GRAS.[7]
Phosphates	Yeast food in distilling material and wine production, and to start secondary fermentation in manufacturing champagne and sparkling wines.	As a yeast food in distilling material, the amount shall not exceed 10 lb per 1000 gal. In wine production, the amount shall not exceed 1.7 lb per 1000 gal. In manufacturing champagne and sparkling wines, a small quantity only shall be used. 21 CFR 121.101(d)(8).
Polyvinylpolypyrrolidone (PVPP)	To clarify and stabilize wine.	The amount used shall not exceed 6 lb per 1000 gal. of wine.

Material	Use	Reference or Limitations[6]
		Material shall be removed during filtration. 21 CFR 121.1110.
Polyvinylpyrrolidone (PVP)	To clarify wine.	The residual level of PVP in the finished wine will not exceed 60 ppm.
Potassium metabisulphite	Sterilizing and preserving wine.	The sulphur [dioxide?] content of the finished wine shall not exceed the limits prescribed in 27 CFR Part 4. 21 CFR 121.101(d)(2).
Potassium salt of sorbic acid	As a sterilizing and preservative agent and to inhibit mold growth and secondary fermentations.	Not more than 0.1% of sorbic acid or salts thereof shall be used in wine or in materials for the production of wine. 21 CFR 121.101(d)(2).
Promine-D	To clarify and stabilize wine.	The amount used shall not exceed 1.5 lb per 1000 gal. of wine. Water used in process shall not exceed 0.5% of wine treated. GRAS.[7]
Protovac PV-7916	To clarify wine.	The amount used shall not exceed 2 lb per 1000 gal. of wine. GRAS.[7]
Roviferm (see Actiferm)		
Sodium bisulfite	As a sterilizing or preserving agent.	§ 240.523. 21 CFR 121.101(d)(2).
Sodium carbonate	To reduce excess natural acidity in wine.	Natural or fixed acids shall not be reduced below 5 parts per thousand. §240.523. 21 CFR 121.101(d)(8).
Sodium caseinate	To clarify wine.	§ 240.523. 21 CFR 121.101(d)(8).
Sodium isoascorbate[8] (sodium erythorbate)	Antioxidant	The amount used must be within the general limitations of 27 CFR 240.524.
Sodium metabisulphite	Sterilizing and preserving wine.	§ 240.523. 21 CFR 121.101(d)(2).
Sodium salt of sorbic acid	As a sterilizing and preservative agent and to inhibit mold growth and secondary fermentations.	Not more than 0.1% of the sorbic acid or salts thereof shall be used in wine or in materials for the production of wine. 21 CFR 121.101(d)(2).
Sorbic acid	As a sterilizing and preservative agent and to inhibit mold growth and secondary fermentations.	Not more than 0.1% of the sorbic acid or salts thereof shall be used in wine or in materials for the production of wine. 21 CFR 121.101(d)(2).

Material	Use	Reference or Limitations[6]
Sparkolloid No. 1	To clarify wine.	GRAS.[7]
Sparkolloid No. 2	To clarify wine.	GRAS.[7]
Sulphur dioxide	Sterilizing and preserving wine.	§ 240.523, 27 CFR Part 4. 21 CFR 121.101(d)(2).
Sulfuric acid	To effect a favorable yeast development in distilling material.	§ 240.486. 21 CFR 121.101(d)(8).
Takamine cellulase 4000	To clarify wine.	The amount used shall not exceed 5 lb per 1000 gal. of wine. The enzymes shall be derived from non-toxic strains of *Aspergillus niger.* GRAS.[7]
Tannin	Clarifying grape wine.	§ 240.525. GRAS.[7]
Tansul clays Nos. 7, 710, and 711	To clarify wine.	The amount used shall not exceed 10 lb per 1000 gal. of wine. GRAS.[7]
Tartaric acid	To increase acidity of grape wine.	§ 240.364. 21 CFR 121.101(d)(8).
Uni-Loid Type 43B (pure USP agar agar and standard supercel)	To clarify and stabilize wine.	The amount used shall not exceed 2 lb per 1000 gal. of wine. GRAS.[7]
Urea	To facilitate fermentation of wine.	The amount used shall not exceed 2 lb per 1000 gal. of wine. GRAS.[7]
Veltol (maltol)	As a stabilizing and smoothing agent.	The amount used shall not exceed 250 ppm. 21 CFR 121.1164.
Wine clarifier (containing pure USP agar agar and standard supercel)	To clarify wine.	The amount used shall not exceed 2 lb per 1000 gal. of wine. GRAS.[7]
Wine clarifier (Clarivine B) (containing locust bean gum, carragheen, alginate, bentonite, agar agar, and diatomaceous earth)	To clarify wine.	The amount used shall not exceed 2 lb per 1000 gal. of wine. GRAS.[7]
Yeastex	To facilitate fermentation.	The amount used shall not exceed 2 lb per 1000 gal. of wine. GRAS.[7]
Yeastex 61	To facilitate fermentation.	The amount used shall not exceed 2 lb per 1000 gal. of wine. GRAS.[7]

Citric acid is limited to 5.8 lb per 1000 gal. of wine for the purpose of stabilization. In another section, this and tartaric or malic acid may be employed to correct natural deficiencies, providing the finished wine does not exceed 0.8% fixed acid (calculated as tartaric). Obviously, the latter section is much more liberal and is the one under which the wineries operate.

Lactic acid may be used under the limitations imposed by Sections 240.364, 240.404 and 240.526, 27CFR to correct natural deficiencies and to stabilize. Section 240.1051, 27CFR (U.S. BATF 1976L) permits the addition of not over 25 lb of fumaric acid per 1000 gal. of wine to correct natural deficiencies provided it constitutes not over 0.3% by weight of the finished wine. Under Section 240.1015, 27CFR acetic acid may be used to correct natural deficiencies, provided the addition does not exceed 0.4 gal. of 100% acetic acid per 1000 gal. of wine, and provided the acetic acid is not added in a solution of less than 50%. The acetic acid content may not exceed 0.14 g per 100 cc in red wine or 0.12 g per 100 cc in all other finished grape wines.

In using tannin, finished white wines shall not contain more than 0.08 g of tannin per 100 ml after clarification and red wines more than 0.3. Only tannins which do not color the wines may be used.

Filter aids such as inert fibers, pulps, earths, or similar materials can be used without limit provided they do not alter the character of the wine. With regard to sulfur dioxide, Section 4.22 of U.S. BATF (1976C) limits the total sulfur dioxide in the finished wine to not more than 350 mg/ liter. Records need not be maintained for the use of inert fining agents, oxygen, filter aids or sulfur dioxide.

The removal of excessive color from white wines is provided for but treated and untreated samples of the wine and of the activated carbon or other material used must be submitted to the assistant regional commissioner. A written statement of the reasons for desiring to treat the wine, the quantity, kind or type of wine to be treated, the kind and quantity of the material to be used, and the proposed process must be submitted.

If the chemical analysis of the samples shows that the proposed treatment will remove only the excess color and will not remove any of the usual natural color or other characteristics of the wine the assistant regional commissioner will authorize the treatment of the wine in question. If the chemical analysis shows that the proposed treatment will remove the natural characteristics of the wine the regional regulatory administrator will disapprove the application. A separate application with representative samples must be submitted for each lot of wine it is desired to treat.

Obviously, this regulation is subject to interpretation of "usual natural color or other characteristics." A minimum color level of 0.6 Lovibond reading is presently specified. This is to be changed to 95% transmittance per AOAC method 11.B01 (Wildenradt and Caputi 1976). Up to 9 lb of charcoal per 1000 gal. is permitted without submitting samples.

For additional information on permitted additives and treatments in other countries, see Paronetto (1963), Cerutti (1963) and Office International de la Vigne et du Vin (1975). The latter also gives the tolerance limits for impurities in permitted additives.

Containers for Removal

Wine may be removed from bond in casks, barrels, kegs, tanks, tank trucks, railroad tank cars, tank ships, barges, deep tanks of vessels, in cases (when bottled) of any legal size, in uncased demijohns (or bottles) of 2-gal. or more capacity, and by pipeline. Movement of wine between noncontiguous portions of a bonded wine cellar is not considered a removal of wine. Serial numbers must be used on all containers used for removal except on cases which may be marked with the date of fill in lieu of a serial number. There are detailed provisions for certain other exceptions. Requirements for masks, labels, and tags and for their destruction are also given.

The alcohol content must be stated in all cases and must definitely show the taxable grade of the wine. The liter content is also required. In the case of bottles, they must be filled as nearly as possible to conform to the amount shown on the label or blown in the bottle.

Labeling Bottled Wine

The label must show: (a) the brand name; (b) the name and address of the bottler, or the name, registry number, and state where the premises of the bottler are located; (c) the kind of wine (class and type); (d) the alcohol content by volume (except "Table" or "Light Wine" may be so designated in lieu of alcohol content); and (e) the net contents of the bottle, unless legibly blown into the bottle. If there is no brand name, the name of the bottler may take the place of a brand name. A certificate of label approval (BATF Form 1649) must be obtained for all bottled wines for distribution or sale in interstate or foreign commerce. Relabeling is possible when approval is requested.

As of January 1, 1980 wines can only be bottled in metric size containers of 100, 187, 375 and 750 ml or 1, 1.5 or 3 liters. Wines may be bottled in containers of more than 3 liters and up to 18 liters, if they are filled and labeled in even liter quantities. Up to 3 liters, these correspond roughly to the previous 3 oz, 2/5 pt, 4/5 pt, 4/5 qt, 1 qt, 2/5 gallon and 4/5 gallon containers, respectively.

Tax Payment

The tax on wine is to be determined at the time of removal from bonded wine cellar premises (or transfer to a tax paid room on the premises) for consumption or sale. The tax is paid with BATF Form 2050 which is filed semimonthly at prescribed times. Considerable penalties are provided for failure to pay the tax or to file the return at the time required.

The present federal taxes are: (a) on still wine containing not more than 14% alcohol by volume, 17¢ per wine gallon; (b) on still wine containing more than 14% and not exceeding 21%, 67¢; (c) on still wine containing more than 21% and not exceeding 24%, $2.25; (d) on champagne and other sparkling wine, $3.40; and (e) on artificially carbonated wine, $2.40.

Records and Reports

The basic form is the monthly Form 702 which reports all bonded wine cellar operations. Instructions for filling in this form are given on the form or issued with it. The necessary information to properly complete this form is obtained from wine cellar records.

Form 2050 is used when wine subject to tax is removed from a bonded wine cellar. Provision for reporting previous errors is made. Form 2052 is used to prepay the tax. Form 702-C is a detailed report made on the inventory of a bonded wine cellar at the close of business on June 30 and December 31 of each year. Forms 275 and 2629 are used when wine spirits are used in the production of wine. Form 2056 is a record of still wine made with excess water. Form 2057 gives the details of the production of effervescent wine. Form 2058 does the same for special natural wines. Form 2621 is a record of bottled wine received in or removed from bond.

Records must be kept of sugar received and used, of other materials received and used, of wines eligible for varietal or vintage designations, of acids used, of wine baked, etc. All prescribed returns, reports and records must be retained for a period of 3 years (or up to 3 years longer if the assistant regional commissioner so requires). Records must be kept at the bonded wine cellar and be available for inspection by BATF officers at any reasonable hour.

Miscellaneous

The addition to and retention in still wines of small amounts of carbon dioxide has been permitted since 1974. The maximum is 0.392 g per 100 ml of wine with a tolerance of 0.009 based on good commercial practices.

Notice of intention to add carbon dioxide is required, with information on the equipment and process to be employed and the kinds of wine to be treated. Penalties are provided for misrepresenting this as sparkling wine.

In 1959, Treasury Decision No. 6395 redefined the term "own production" so that addition of wine spirits, amelioration, or both could be done at one or several bonded wineries affiliated or owned or controlled by the same proprietor located within a state. The Treasury Decision also provided for increase in the amount of amelioration permitted with fruit wines of 23° to 25° Brix. In 1970, Treasury Decision No. 7031 amended the regulations to permit the addition of grape wine spirits to natural grape wine in a bonded cellar, the proprietor of which produces natural wine by fermentation, and which is located in the same state as the bonded wine cellar where the natural wine was produced. Invert sugar or liquid sugar of not less than 60° Brix may be used in amelioration of the juice or wine produced from fruit other than grapes, and in special natural wine.

Finally, unmerchantable wine may be returned to bond so as to recover the tax. This applies to United States or foreign wine.

Federal law formerly permitted a United States resident returning from a trip abroad to bring in not over one wine gallon of alcoholic beverages duty free, if for his own use and not intended for sale. In 1965, this was reduced to one quart.

The term "unfortified" on labels for wine is prohibited (U.S. Internal Revenue Service 1977). For regulations on vinegar, procedures, tax-paid bottling rooms, gauging, and volatile fruit-flavor concentrates, see U.S. BATF (1976F,G,I,K).

Food and Drug Administration

Under the Food Additives Amendment of 1958 substances which are presently added to wine may also come to the attention of the Food and Drug Administration.

CALIFORNIA—WINES

The main California regulations are in Title 17 of the California Administrative Code, section 17000–17116. They have been published in a special pamphlet hereafter referred to as California (1970). These regulations apply primarily to California but they may also apply in states or countries which provide for recognition of local regulations. Further regulations may be found in the California Alcohol Beverage Control Act effective September, 11, 1957 (State of California 1976).

Definitions

The present California (1970) standards of identity and quality for wine produced in California or elsewhere are as follows:

(a) The standards herein established are minimum standards for wine of the several classes and types defined.

(b) *Prohibited Wine.* Wine derived from raisins, dried grapes, dried berries, and other dried fruit, and imitation or substandard wine, shall not be produced, imported, or sold in this state except for distillation into wine spirits or for industrial or nonbeverage purposes.

(c) *Cellar Treatment.* Cellar treatment shall conform to the methods and materials authorized for treatment of wine by the Bureau of Alcohol, Tobacco and Firearms as well as the California Pure Foods Act and the Federal Food, Drug, and Cosmetic Act and the regulations adopted thereunder. In case of conflict between Federal and State laws or regulations, the California law or regulation shall take precedence.

(d) *Appellations of Origin.* Wines of any defined class or type, which are labeled or advertised under an appellation of origin such as "Spanish," "New York," "Ohio," "Finger Lakes," "California," etc., shall meet the requirements of the standards herein prescribed applicable to such wines and shall, in addition, contain the minimum percentage of alcohol and conform as to composition in all other respects with all standards of identity, quality and purity applicable to wines of such classes, or types marketed for consumption in the place or region of origin.

For wines produced in California the following provisions apply:

(a) *Sugar Use.* No sugar, or material containing sugar, other than pure condensed grape must, and no water in excess of the minimum amount necessary to facilitate normal fermentation, may be used in the production or cellar treatment of any grape wine except:

(1) In the production of sparkling wine (where sugar or liquid sugar may only be used in the traditional secondary fermentation and dosage),

(2) Carbonated and special natural wine; provided, however, that sparkling and carbonated wine or the residuum thereof may be reconverted into still wine, and such wine and special natural wine or the residuum thereof may be distilled into wine spirits if the unfermented sugar has not been refermented.

(3) Natural grape wine produced outside of the State of California with the use of sugar pursuant to applicable federal regulations may be blended with grape wine produced in California pursuant to these regulations only for the purpose of producing sparkling wine and carbonated wine. The resultant blend shall not be entitled to the appellation of origin "California" or any geographical subdivision thereof.

(b) *Sweetness Limitation.* (1) The Brix saccharometer test, using a saccharometer calibrated at 20°C and made in the presence of the alcohol content provided herein shall be:

(A) Not less than 5.5 degrees for Angelica, Muscatel, Port and White Port.

(B) Not less than 3.5 degrees for Tokay (as a dessert wine).

(2) The reducing sugar content (per 100 ml at 20°C and calculated as dextrose [i.e., glucose] for sherries shall be as follows:

	Minimum	Maximum
Dry Sherry	0.0	2.5
Sherry	2.5	4.0
Sweet, Golden, Cream or Mellow Sherry	4.0	

(c) *Fixed Acidity.* The minimum titratable fixed acidity per 100 ml at 20°C for grape wine (except wine used solely for blending, medicinal or industrial purposes) calculated as tartaric acid, shall be as follows:

Red table wine	0.4 g
White table wine	0.3 g
All other wine	0.25 g

The maximum volatile acidity, calculated as acetic acid and exclusive of sulfur dioxide, is 0.12 g per 100 cc[9] for red table wines and 0.11 g for other wines. The California limit for sulfur dioxide is 350 mg/liter.

For wines bearing the appellation of origin "California" or of any geographical subdivision thereof the following limitations apply:

(1) 100% of its volume is derived from fruit grown and juice therefrom fermented within the State of California, and

(2) It has been fully produced and finished within the State of California, and

(3) It conforms to the requirements of these regulations; provided, that no wine shall be entitled to an appellation of origin in violation of Section 25236 or Section 25237 of the California Alcoholic Beverage Control Act."

Vintage wines must be produced from 95% of grapes grown in the year and identified on the label.

The California definitions for vermouth, champagne, champagne-style or champagne-bulk process, carbonated wines, berry, citrus and fruit wines generally follow federal regulations and will not be repeated here.

California regulations limit cellar treatment but do provide for use of neutral potassium tartrate or calcium carbonate, acidifying agents such as tartaric acid "produced from grapes," or commercial malic or citric acid, sulfur dioxide "where required to ensure the soundness and stability of the wine, and blending processes and treatments, such as electrolysis, where desirable or necessary to improve the quality of the finished product." No definitions of what constitutes improvement are given. In fact, the following paragraph specifically recognizes that new processes may be recognized as proper. Monochloroacetic acid or other chemical preservatives, except sulfur dioxide and its compounds, may not be used in wines in this state. However, sorbic acid and sorbates are permitted.

[9]cc not ml are specified.

Labeling

The California regulations do not differ fundamentally from the federal rules except insofar as the definitions above are concerned, including the fact that federal label approval is required. There is one curious permissive section: blends of foreign and United States wines require reference to the exact percentage of foreign wine. So far as we know this blending privilege has not been utilized.

Labeling may not be false or misleading, it may not disparage competitor's products (surely difficult to avoid), may not be indecent or obscene, may not imply municipal, state or federal approval of the product (even if licenses, registry numbers or permits are required, all of which do imply approval of the respective agencies), may not carry a statement, design, device, a representation relative to the armed forces or the flag, may not imply fortification (an ostrich-like requirement) and may not imply that the wine is old if it is not.

California regulations prohibit sale of wines which bear labels with:

(1) A type or brand designation which implies mixtures of wines for which standards of identity have been established in this Article:

(2) A type or brand designation which resembles an established wine type name such as Angelica, Madeira, Marsala, Muscatel, Port, Tokay, White Port, Sherry, Sauterne, Claret, Burgundy, etc.

If the wine is sold in distinctive containers the following limitation applies:

The sale of wine in containers which have blown, branded, or burned therein the name or other distinguishing mark of any person engaged in business as a wine grower, wine blender, importer, rectifier, or bottler, or any person different from the person whose name is required to appear on the brand label, is hereby prohibited.

Miscellaneous Requirements.—Advertising not in conformity to regulations is prohibited. Prohibited statements on labels may likewise not be used in advertising. Brands may not be confused in advertising.

Wine growers may supply display materials to retailers with certain specified exceptions and limitations (State of California 1976). The intent of the restrictions is to prevent giving retailers premiums, gifts, or free goods.

Wineries are subject to all the requirements of the Health and Safety Code, the Food Sanitation Act, and all rules and regulations prescribed in the California (1970) regulations. Furthermore these specifically state that "all containers, pipelines and other equipment of whatever description shall be thoroughly cleansed in conformity with established sanitary practices for foodstuffs and beverages, before such containers, pipelines and other equipment are used for, or in any other manner come into contact with, wine." This section of the California Administrative Code is, of course, admirable.

Finally, producers, bottlers, wholesalers and retailers of wine are required to furnish samples for analyses and the wine may be seized and disposed of if in violation of these regulations.

Permits and Notices

Various licenses are *annually* required by the Alcoholic Beverage Control Act (State of California 1976): wine growers or wine blenders, 5000 gal. or less, $22.00, over 5000 to 20,000, $44.00, over 20,000 to 100,000, $82.50, over 100,000 to 200,000, $110.00, over 200,000 to 1,000,000, $165.00, and for each 1,000,000 gallons or fraction thereof over 1,000,000, $110.00; wine rectifiers, $276.00; wine brokers, $56.00; beer and wine importers, no fee; beer and wine wholesalers, $56.00; retail package off-sale beer and wine, $24.00; on-sale beer and wine, for public premises, $168.00; on-sale beer and wine, for trains and airplanes, $16.00, on-sale beer and wine, for boat, $56.00, etc. General license fees will be given under brandy (pp. 752–753).

Applications for license must be on prescribed forms which require certain information on ownership and location. If the applicant has been convicted of a felony it may be grounds for denial of his application.

Wine growers and retailers have the privilege of selling wine and brandy to consumers without any limitation per sale for consumption off the premises. A California wine grower's license is issued to those who have obtained a permit to operate a winery or bonded wine cellar under Bureau of Alcohol, Tobacco and Firearms regulations.

Taxes

The taxes on wines are given in the California Alcoholic Beverage Tax Law (State of California 1975). On still wines of not over 14% alcohol (by volume), the tax is 1¢ per wine gallon. For still wines over 14% it is 2¢ per gallon. On all types of sparkling wine, it is 30¢ per gallon; but on sparkling hard cider it is 2¢.

OTHER STATES

The rules and regulations of other states generally closely follow those of the federal government, particularly the permission to use sugar for amelioration of musts and wines. Mention should be made of the limitation of alcohol in Michigan to 16% unless sold in state stores. This regulation is an anachronism in modern wine practice and obviously works hardships on non-Michigan producers of dessert wines.

For general introduction to the state regulations see Anon. (1941) and Distilled Spirits Institute (1977). More than 25 years ago the Wine Institute (1950) suggested uniform wine regulations for all states. In spite of this, many variations in laws and regulations exist among the states.

BRANDY—FEDERAL

The basic federal regulations are contained in U.S. Bureau of Alcohol, Tobacco and Firearms (1976D,H,J). Federal liquor laws have been summarized by Udell (1968).

Definitions

Legal definitions of distiller, distillers, distillery premises, heads, and tails, etc., are given in U.S. Laws (1954), and U.S. BATF (1976J). Proof means the ethyl alcohol content of a liquid at 15.6°C (60°F), stated as twice the percentage of ethyl alcohol by volume. Proof gallon means the alcoholic equivalent of a U.S. gallon at 15.6°C (60°F) containing 50% ethyl alcohol by volume. Proof spirits means an alcoholic liquor which contains 50% ethyl alcohol by volume at 15.6°C and which has a specific gravity of 0.7939 at 15.6°C referred to water at 15.6°C as unity. Wine spirits means brandy, as later defined, distilled at 140° proof or more and not reduced with water from distillation proof and neutral spirits distilled at 190° proof or over.

Brandy as such is defined as spirits distilled at less than 190° proof. If distilled at not over 170° proof solely from wine with a volatile acidity of less than 0.20 g per 100 ml (exclusive of sulfur dioxide) and with not more than 20% by weight of pomace or 30% of lees is classed as fruit brandy. Depending on the raw material, it may be labeled as "grape brandy" or "brandy," "peach brandy," "apple brandy," etc. If more than one fruit is used it must be labeled "fruit brandy . . . % grapes and . . . % blackberries" or as appropriate.

Dried fruit brandy, raisin brandy, dried peach, apple, etc., brandy, lees brandy, pomace brandy (which may also be labeled as marc brandy, grape brandy, or grappa), residue brandy, etc., are also defined in the regulations.

If distilled at 190° proof or over, the spirits are known as "neutral spirits—fruit—grape" (or other fruit if appropriate).

Location and Construction

Distilled spirits plants may not be located in a dwelling house, on board a vessel or boat, on premises where beer, wines, or vinegar are produced, or where sugars or syrups are refined or where any other business is carried on—with certain specified exceptions.

The distillery buildings must be securely constructed and must be completely separated from contiguous buildings not on distillery premises, again, subject to stated exceptions. There are provisions for foundations, floors, walls, roofs, doors, windows, shutters, skylights, ventilators, drains, etc. Many distilleries are now located outside of buildings but must be secured by fencing of a specified nature.

A brandy deposit room was formerly provided for unless all the brandy is removed from the distillery during the regular working hours of the same day on which it is drawn from the receiving tanks. All the doors of the brandy deposit room were provided with locks. This is no longer needed since spirits may now be left in the receiving tanks if the tanks are indicated on the plat as being used for this purpose. A filled-package room and a fermenting room may be required in certain cases.

A government office is obligatory, except that the government office on contiguous premises may be used (see p. 728). A government cabinet is also necessary.

A conspicuous sign, not less than 3 in. in height of lettering, must be placed outside and in front of the distillery indicating the name of the distiller, the distilled spirits plant number (fruit distillery), and the character of the business, or businesses, conducted on its premises.

Equipment

Where brandy or heads or tails are drawn into packages for tax payment at the distillery, the distiller must provide suitable and accurate scales. Weighing tanks of a specific design and construction are also required where brandy is received from a distillery by pipeline. Test weights are required—again, unless they are provided on contiguous premises (p. 729). However, volumetric methods of measurement are now permitted and are used more often than weighing. Locks on furnace doors, and steam and fuel lines must be provided for. Distilling material measuring and storage tanks are required. In some cases fermentors and washwater receiving tanks are required.

Stills must be of substantial construction and must have a clear space of 1 ft around them. Locks are necessary. The doubler or worm tanks must be elevated not less than 1 ft from the floor.

All tanks used as receptacles for brandy between the outlet of the first condenser or worm and the receiving tanks must be constructed of metal unless enclosed within a securely constructed room equipped for locking with a government lock. All tanks must be constructed with a suitable measuring device. Where such tanks are of irregular dimensions, a table showing capacity of the tank for each inch of depth is needed. The tanks must be clearly labeled as to use, serial number and capacity in gallons. Distilled water tanks need not be equipped with locks. The "heads and tails" tanks must be labeled with serial number and the capacity in gallons.

Try boxes must be provided to permit reading the proof and temperature of the brandy. These too must be equipped with a government lock.

Singlings tanks may be used and sumps or chargers into which they may be run—again, the inlets, outlets, and other openings must be provided for closing and securing with government locks. Receiving tanks of a size so that the receiving and singling tanks can hold a three days run are needed when the distillery is of such a size as to require frequent attendance of a storekeeper-gauger. Otherwise, the receiving tanks should be large enough so that a visit of an internal revenue officer more than twice a month to gauge the brandy is not needed.

The pipelines must be painted blue for the conveyance of spirits (green for denaturants or denatured spirits). These colors may not be used for any other pipelines. Different colors for other pipelines may be required.

Documents

To establish a distilled spirits plant, application for registration notice and for the basic distiller's permit is made on BATF Form 2607 to the regional regulatory administrator. If the operation is not covered by a Federal Alcohol Administration basic permit, an operating permit is necessary. The lot or tract of land on which the distillery is situated is described on BATF Form 2607. The continuity of the distillery premises must be unbroken, except that the premises may be divided by a public street or highway. The buildings and rooms must be accurately described. The estimated maximum number of proof gallons of brandy that will be distilled in 15 days, or are in transit to the premises, must be stated. This estimated maximum volume is to be based on maximum capacity of the stills and the use of maximum alcoholic strength of the distilling material. Likewise, the maximum volume of each kind of material intended for distilling each day must be stated.

Technical provisions concerning ownership, alternating ownerships, bonds, certificate of title, corporate documents, changes in ownership, list of stockholders, power of attorney, registry of still, plat and plans, changes in premises or equipment in construction or use, and statement of process are also given in the regulations. Special note should be made of the detailed requirements concerning the plat and plans. These include very specific drawings at specified scales, definition of contiguous premises, floor plans, elevational flow diagrams, etc.

Following filing of BATF Form 2607 and receipt of notice, plat, plans, bond (Form 2601), and consent (Form 1602), the regional regulatory administrator will assign an inspector to examine the premises, buildings, apparatus and equipment to determine whether they conform with the proprietor's description. Corrections may be made during the inspection. The regional regulatory administrator will also ascertain whether an individual firm, partnership, corporation controlling or actively participating in the business has been convicted of, or has compromised, any fraudulent noncompliance with any provision of any law of the United States relating to internal revenue or customs taxation of distilled spirits, wines, or fermented malt liquors or of any felony in the same connection.

If all documents are in order and the inspector's report is favorable a notice of registry is issued and a distilled spirits plant number is assigned.

Operation

To commence operations, the proprietor files BATF Form 2610 with the regional regulatory administrator specifying the date. Storekeeper-gaugers are assigned at the start of operations but normally are not on constant duty. The government agents remove and apply locks as required.

Materials received for distillation are entered on Form 2730. This form requires that the volume and alcohol content of the distilling material be known. If water is added to permit more economical distillation, the volume and alcohol percentage are determined after addition of the water. The government inspector may verify the accuracy from time to time. An approved ebullioscope is used for the alcohol determination, though other procedures may be approved. No chemicals or other materials, such as essences, flavors, coloring matter, etc., which are volatile and would remain incorporated in the brandy may be added to the distilling material. Tracer amounts of rare nontoxic metals may be added.

The regulations provide that the process of distillation must be a continuous one, i.e., that the brandy passes through continuous, closed stills, pipes, and vessels from the time the vapors rise in the first still until the finished brandy is deposited in the receiving tanks. However, during this process the distiller may carry the product through as many distilling operations as he may desire. The collection of heads and tails for the purpose of redistillation is not considered a break in the continuity of the distilling process.

On written application, chemicals separated during distillation may be removed as the proprietor wishes and the regional regulatory administrator permits. Chemicals separated during distillation may be refermented or added to the distilling material.

Distilled water and carbon dioxide may be produced on distillery premises. Redistillation is possible on approval of application. BATF Form 236 is used following approval. Burnt sugar or caramel, not containing any substantial quantity of sugar, may be added but this must be done prior to the time the brandy is gauged for removal from the distillery.

Tax-free samples of unfinished brandies in limited but reasonable amounts may be removed by the operator. They may be used only for sensory and laboratory analysis. The regulations impose limitations on this privilege.

Other Regulations

Brandy may be removed to Internal Revenue bonded warehouses—usually for aging in wooden containers as beverage brandy, to bonded wine cellars for fortification, or for exportation. Very detailed regulations on gauging for removal (BATF Forms 2629 and 2630) are given. If to be used in the winery for fortification of wine, Form 257 is used. Only spirits of 140° proof or over may be used in wine production.

The tax on all brandy becomes attached to brandy as soon as it is produced but may not be paid until removed from bond. It is a first lien on distilled spirits. The present tax is $10.50 per proof gallon. Taxes are determined when spirits are withdrawn from bond. They are paid by return on BATF Form 2521 if prepaid and on Form 2522 if deferred.

Formerly, there were several provisions whereby treating or handling brandy in a certain way resulted in payment of a rectification tax. At present, few if any California brandies are subject to a rectification tax (U.S. Laws 1965, see Action 805, Subsection k).

If operations are to be suspended for 30 days or more or if operations are to be resumed, BATF Form 2610 is filed. Provision for locking furnace doors, etc., is made.

The basic record of distillery operations is BATF Form 2730. This is filled in daily and is kept at the distillery as a permanent record. One copy is forwarded to the regional regulatory administrator monthly. Form 2629 is used for the storekeeper-gaugers reports for the quantity of brandy produced. When tax-paid distilled spirits are received, stored or sold in bulk, Forms 338 or 2731 are used. These are semiannual and monthly reports. A list of the forms and records is given in U.S. Laws (1954) and U.S. BATF (1971).

Experimental or research operations to produce and treat brandy at scientific institutions or colleges of learning are provided for (U.S. BATF 1976J).

The product is tax-free if not removed from the premises.

STATE REGULATIONS

A summary of state laws and regulations relating to distilled spirit has been made by the Distilled Spirits Institute (1977). This study reveals how illogical and restrictive many state rules are. They range from preventing sale of miniatures (or imposing excessive taxes on them), to forbidding advertising in Sunday newspapers. The 18 monopoly states (where liquor is bought and sold mainly through a government agency) are usually the least favorable to the sale of alcoholic beverages, though Georgia, which is not a monopoly state, has its share of unusual laws affecting alcoholic beverages.

California

There are several definitions and regulations affecting brandy production in this state; State of California (1970, 1976) contain the main provisions.

Federal definitions for brandy produced in California (1970) apply in this state.

The California Alcoholic Beverage Control Act (State of California 1976) also imposes certain restrictions on brandy sale. The producer is known as a brandy manufacturer. The annual license fees are as follows: brandy manufacturer, $168.00; still, $12.00; rectifier, $276.00; brandy importer, no fee; distilled spirits or brandy wholesalers, $276.00; retail package off-sale general, $200.00; on-sale general, $580.00 in cities of 40,000 population or over; $412.00 for cities of 20,000 to 40,000; and $360.00 (for all other localities); on-sale general license for seasonal (per quarter), $145.00, $103.00, and $90.00 (for cities as above), etc.

Restrictions in issuing licenses for on-sale of brandy are as for wine in California (p. 744). Distilled spirits sold at retail must be sold at fair trade and at the prices posted.

The Alcoholic Beverage Tax Law of California (State of California 1976), gives the detailed provisions for collecting this tax. A surety bond is prescribed equivalent to twice the estimated monthly tax. The excise tax is $2.00 per wine gallon for distilled spirits of 100° proof or less. The tax is due monthly. Brandy for fortification is not so taxed.

REFERENCES[10]

United States Regulations

ANON. 1941. State Liquor Legislation. Prepared by the Marketing Laws Survey. U.S. Govt. Print. Office, Washington, D.C.

CARR, J.D. 1960. A survey of American wine laws. Food, Drug Cosmetic Law *16*, 335–360.

CERUTTI, G. 1963. Manuale Degli Additivi Alimentari. Et/As Kompass, Milan.

DISTILLED SPIRITS INSTITUTE. 1977. Summary of State Laws and Regulations Related to Distilled Spirits, 17th Edition. Distilled Spirits Institute, Washington, D.C. (See also later editions.)

PARONETTO, L. 1963. Ausiliari Fisici Chimici Biologici in Enologia. Enostampa Editrice, Verona.

PEYSER, J. 1974. The law and the California wine industry. Regional Oral History Office, Bancroft Library, Berkeley.

SEFF, J.M. 1979. An introduction to federal wine laws and regulations. Vinifera Wine Growers J. *6* (2) 65-79.

STATE OF CALIFORNIA. 1970. Regulations Establishing Standards of Identity, Quality, Purity, Sanitation, Labeling, and Advertising of Wine. California Administrative Code, Title 17, Chap. 5, Article 14, Sections 17000–17116. California State Printing Office, Sacramento. (Amended periodically.)

STATE OF CALIFORNIA. 1971. California Excise Tax Laws, Part 14. Revenue and Taxation Code. California State Print. Office, Sacramento.

STATE OF CALIFORNIA. 1976. Deerings California Codes, Sections 23,000 to 25,762. Alcoholic Beverages, Business and Professions Code, Division 9, Bancroft-Whitney Company, San Francisco.

UDELL, G.G. 1968. Liquor Laws. U.S. Govt. Print. Office, Washington, D.C.

U.S. BUREAU OF ALCOHOL, TOBACCO AND FIREARMS. 1971. Public Use Forms. U.S. Internal Revenue Service Publ. *480.*

U.S. BUREAU OF ALCOHOL, TOBACCO AND FIREARMS. 1976A. Nonindustrial Use of Distilled Spirits and Wines. Part 2 of Title 27, Code of Federal Regulations. Govt. Print. Off., Washington, D.C.

U.S. BUREAU OF ALCOHOL, TOBACCO AND FIREARMS. 1976C. Labeling and Advertising of Wine. Part 4 of Title 27, Code of Federal Regulations. Govt. Print. Off., Washington, D.C. Amended in the Federal Register of May 9, 1978 regarding standards of fill. See also 1978A,B.

U.S. BUREAU OF ALCOHOL, TOBACCO AND FIREARMS. 1976D. Labeling and Advertising of Distilled Spirits. Part 5 of Title 27, Code of Federal Regulations. Govt. Print. Off., Washington, D.C.

U.S. BUREAU OF ALCOHOL, TOBACCO AND FIREARMS. 1976E. Inducements Furnished to Retailers. Part 6 of Title 27, Code of Federal Regulations, Govt. Print. Off., Washington, D.C.

U.S. BUREAU OF ALCOHOL, TOBACCO AND FIREARMS. 1976F. Production of Volatile Fruit-Flavor Concentrates. Part 18 of Title 27, Code of Federal Regulations. Govt. Print. Off., Washington, D.C.

U.S. BUREAU OF ALCOHOL, TOBACCO AND FIREARMS. 1976G. Gauging Manual. Part 186 of Title 27, Code of Federal Regulations. Govt. Print. Off., Washington, D.C.

U.S. BUREAU OF ALCOHOL, TOBACCO AND FIREARMS. 1976H. Liquor Dealers. Part 194 of Title 27, Code of Federal Regulations. Govt. Print. Off., Washington, D.C.

U.S. BUREAU OF ALCOHOL, TOBACCO AND FIREARMS. 1976I. Production of Vinegar by the Vaporizing Process. Part 195 of Title 27, Code of Federal Regulations. Govt. Print. Off., Washington, D.C.

U.S. BUREAU OF ALCOHOL, TOBACCO AND FIREARMS. 1976J. Distilled Spirits Plants. Part 201 of Title 27, Code of Federal Regulations. Govt. Print. Off., Washington, D.C.

U.S. BUREAU OF ALCOHOL, TOBACCO AND FIREARMS. 1976K. Tax-paid Wine Bottling Houses. Part 231 of Title 27, Code of Federal Regulations. Govt. Print. Off., Washington, D.C.

U.S. BUREAU OF ALCOHOL, TOBACCO AND FIREARMS. 1976L. Wine. Part 240 of Title 27, Code of Federal Regulations. Govt. Print. Off., Washington, D.C. [This is the most important U.S. document on wines.]

U.S. BUREAU OF ALCOHOL, TOBACCO AND FIREARMS. 1978A. Use of Descriptive Terms on Wine Labels. Ind. Circ. 78-5. April 21, 1978.

U.S. BUREAU OF ALCOHOL, TOBACCO AND FIREARMS. 1978B. Labeling and Advertising of Wine. Appellation of origin, grape type designations, etc. Federal Register 43, 37672—37678. Aug. 23, 1978.

U.S. FEDERAL ALCOHOL ADMINISTRATION. 1937. Federal Alcohol Administration Act of 1935, as Amended, 49 Stat. 977. Govt. Print. Off., Washington, D.C.

U.S. INTERNAL REVENUE SERVICE. 1977. Statement of Procedural Rules. Part 601 of Subpart C (includes Distilled Spirits, Wines, and Beer) of Title 26, Code of Federal Regulations. Govt. Print. Off., Washington, D.C.

U.S. LAWS. 1954. Internal Revenue Code of 1954, as amended. Title 26, United States Code 1, Sub-title E, Chap. 51. Washington, D.C.

U.S. LAWS. 1958. Excise Tax Technical Changes Act of 1958, Public Law 85-859, 85th Congress, H.R. 7125, Sept. 2. Washington, D.C.

U.S. LAWS. 1965. Excise Tax Reduction Act of 1965. Public Law 89-44. Title VIII. Miscellaneous structural changes, p. 26. (This amends the Internal Revenue Code of 1954, paragraph 23, 370A).

WILDENRADT, H.L. and CAPUTI, A., JR. 1976. Collaborative study of the determination of color in white wines. J. Assoc. Off. Anal. Chem. 59, 777—780.

WILEY, H.W. 1906. Foreign Trade Practices in the Manufacture and Exportation of Alcoholic Beverages and Canned Goods. Govt. Print. Off., Washington, D.C. (U.S. Dep. Agric., Bureau Chem. Bull. 102).

WINE INSTITUTE. 1950. Uniform Wine Regulations. Wine Institute, San Francisco. August 14, 1950.

OTHER COUNTRIES

General

No attempt will be made here to discuss the legal restrictions on wine and brandy production of foreign countries. Those of France and Germany, for example, are very voluminous. A few suggestions for research in this field are given in the following references.

BAMES, E. 1938. Ausländische Gesetzgebung über Alkoholische Genussmittel. *In* Alkoholische Genussmittel. E. Bleyer (Editor). Julius Springer, Berlin. pp. 760–797.

BARY, H. DE. 1971. Eigenartendes Europaischen Weine, 14th Edition. Orion-Heinreiter-Verlag, Heusenstamm.

CAVIGLIA, P., NIEDERBACHER, A. and ROMEO, D. 1977. Codice Comunitario Vitivinicola. Unione Italiana Vini, Milan.

EUROPEAN ECONOMIC COMMUNITY. 1977. Nouvelles dispositions relatives aux pratiques et traitements oenologiques. Jr. Off. (France) *20* (187) 10.

FOOD AND AGRICULTURE ORGANIZATION. 1952–date. Food and Agricultural Legislation. Rome. (4 times a year.)

OFFICE INTERNATIONAL DE LA VIGNE ET DU VIN. 1975. Mémento de l'O.I.V. Édition de 1975. Paris. This and preceding editions (some entitled Annuaire) have excellent summaries of the legislation of many countries. The monthly Bulletin of this organization should also be consulted for current information. See also its Codex oenologique internationale 1964, 1971, 2 vol.

France

ANON. 1970. Code du Vin et Textes Viti-Vinicoles Français et Communautaires. Edition de "La Journée Vinicole," Montpellier.

BLANCHET, B. 1962. Code au Vin et Textes Viti-Vinicoles. (New Edition.) Édition de "La Journée Vinicole," Montpellier.

DÉAGE, P. and MAGNET, M. 1959. Le Vin et le Droit, 2nd Edition. Éditions de "La Journée Vinicole," Montpellier.

PISANI, R. 1977. Le Vin en France à l'Heure de l'Europe. "La Journée Vinicole," Montpellier. (Includes European Common Market.)

QUITTANSON, C., CIAIS, A. and VANHOUTTE, R. 1970. La Protection des Appellation d'Origine des Vins et Eaux-de-Vie. "La Journée Vinicole," Montpellier.

VIVEZ, J. 1964. Legislation et Réglementation au Vin. J. Delmas, Paris.

Germany and Austria

ANON. 1960. Allgemeine Verwaltungsworschrift für die Untersuchungen für Wein und ahnlichen alkoholischen Erzeugnissen sowie Fruchsäften. Bonn. (Legal methods for wine analyses.) Bundesanzeiger (86) vom 5 Mai 1960.

ANON. 1969. Das neue deutsche Weingesetz. Gesetz über Wein, Dessert-wein, Schaumwein, weinhaltige Getränke und Branntwein aus Wein. Zeitschriftenverlag Bilz. und Fraund, Wiesbaden.

BERGNER, K.G. 1968. Hinweise für die lebensmittelrechtliche Beurteilung. *In* Alkoholische Genussmittel. W. Diemar (Editor). Springer-Verlag, Berlin. (See p. 720—728.)

BÜRKLIN, A. 1934. Rechtliche Probleme in Weingeschäft. J. Kruse & Söhne, Bruchsal in Baden.

GALLOIS, H. 1954. Handelsbräuche und allgemeine Verkehrssitte im Deutschen Weinhandel. D. Meininger, Neustadt a.d. Weinstrasse.

GOLDSCHMIDT, E. 1951. Deutschlands Weinbauorte und Weinbergslagen, 6th Edition. Verlag der Deutschen Wein-Zeitung, Mainz. (See pp. 4—14.)

HIERONIMI, H. 1958. Weingesetz, 2nd Edition. Verlag C.H. Beck, Munich and Berlin. Ergänzungsband. 1967.

HIERONIMI, H. 1959. Lebensmittelgesetz, 2nd Edition. Verlag C.H. Beck, Munich and Berlin.

HOLTHÖFER, H. 1938A. Deutsche Gesetzbung über Branntwein. *In* Alkoholische Genussmittel. E. Bleyer (Editor). Julius Springer, Berlin. (See pp. 719—759.)

HOLTHÖFER, H. 1938B. Deutsche Gesetzebung über Wein. *In* Alkoholische Genussmittel. E. Bleyer (Editor). Julius Springer, Berlin.

HOLTHÖFER, H., JUCKENACK, A. and NÜSE, K.-H. 1959. Das Lebensmittelgesetz und sonstiges Deutsches Lebensmittelrecht. I. Carl Heymanns Verlag, Berlin-Köln.

HOLTHÖFER, H. and NÜSE, K.-H. 1959. Das Weingesetz, 2nd Edition. Carl Heymanns Verlag, Berlin-Köln. Ergänzungsband. 1967.

JESIONEK, U., and BRUSTBAUER,, K. 1972. Das oesterreiche Weingesetz und seine praktische Anwendung. Juridica Verlag, Vienna.

KOCH, H.-J. 1970. Das Weingesetz. Verlag Daniel Meininger, Neustadt a.d. Weinstrasse.

REINER, H. 1957. Die Bestimmugen über Spirituosen und Fruchtsäfte im Sinnes des Oesterreichischen Lebensmittelbuches, 2nd Edition. Verlag Hans Mally, Vienna.

RENZ, F. and NEURNANN, H. 1969. Dan neue Weinrecht. Weingesetz 1969 und Zugehoriger Rechtsaoff. Ulmer, Stuttgart.

WEHLING, H.G. 1971. Die politische Willensbildung auf dem Gebiet des Weinwirtschaft. A. Kümmerle, Göppnigen. (Lobbyists and the law.)

Italy

ABALDO, G. 1971. La Carta Guiridica dei Vini a Denominazione di Origine Controllata. L. di G. Pirola, Milan.

ANON. 1976. Codice del Vino, 5th Edition. Editore L. Scialpi. Rome.

CAVIGLIA, P. 1970. La Legge sul Vino e sua Applicazione. Instituto Editoriale Brera, Milan.

CAVIGLIA, P. 1972. La Legislazione Vinicola. Instituto Editoriale Brera, Milan.

SCIALPI, L. 1961. Codice del Vino. Legislazione, Guirisprudenza Circolari e Risoluzione Ministeriali, 2nd Edition. Luigi Scialpi Editore, Rome.

SCIALPI, L. 1965. Agenda Vinicola, 2nd Edition. Luigi Scialpi Editore, Rome. (Also contains much statistical information).

Soviet Union

BASHKANSKII, I.Z. 1969. Postavka Produktsii Vmodel'cheskoi Promyshlennosti "Kartia Moldoveniaskie," Kishinev.

Spain

ANON. 1933. Estatuto del Vino, 2nd Edition. Grafica Administrativa, Madrid.

ANON. 1955. Reglamento del Impuesto sobre el Alcohol Aprobado por Decreto de 22 de Octubre de 1954, Madrid.

LEYTE MARRERO, J. 1960. El Estatuto del Vino y Legislación Complementaria Posterior; su Interpretación Práctica. Roel, La Coruña.

Index

Espumante, 456
Essence, 493, 504, 506, 510, 721–722
Est! Est!! Est!!!, 27
Estate bottled, 725–726
Ester, 109–110, 197, 219–220, 290–291,
    424–425, 488, 597, 600
  acetate, 597
  acid, 219, 239
  determination of, 220, 698
  distillation of, 604, 608, 610–611, 617–
    619, 621
  during aging, 219, 291, 600
  ethyl, 291
  -forming yeasts, 169, 174, 219
  in brandy, 590, 592, 600–601, 620, 624,
    628–629, 631, 633
  loss, 488
  methyl, 291
  suggested limit, 220
Esterase, 109, 219
Esterification, 219–220, 291
Ethanethiol, 236, 471
Ethanol, Balling-extract chart, 690–691
  boiling point of, 603–607
  definition of, 596
  determination of, 64, 277, 320, 375, 394,
    589, 674–679, 748
  distillation of, 604, 610–617, 621,
    See also Distillation
  effect on color extraction, 367, 438
  effect on color reaction, 377
  effect on sucrose threshold, 225
  effect on tartrate stability, 542, 544
  effects on acid thresholds, 223
  effects on bacteria, molds and fermenta-
    tion, 154, 292, 559–562, 570–572
  -ester ratio in brandy, 622–623
  fermentation of, 174, 194
  formation, 167–168, 171–172, 176, 186–
    189, 194, 196
  -glycerol ratio, 215
  hydrometry, 674
  in brandy, 583, 586–587, 596, 599, 631
  in fruit and berry wines, 516–521
  in grapes, 84, 96, 109–111
  in herbs, 494, 499
  in sherry, 406, 409–410, 417–418, 420–
    425
  in wine (dessert), 25, 31, 33, 45, 55, 145,
    492, 516
  in wine (sparkling), 14–15, 89, 457–458
  in wine (special natural), 492
  in wine (special natural and vermouth),
    140, 459, 491, 494, 496, 503–
    508, 510–511, 718, 720
  in wine (table), 6, 8, 11, 18, 24–25, 27, 32,
    47, 55, 58, 111, 119, 142–143, 524,
    718

increase during aging, 32, 414, 589, 720
limits, 5, 140, 142–143, 145–146, 152,
    212–213, 459, 718, 720
loss, 192, 208–209, 290, 397, 488, 629
systems of expressing, 586
tolerance of film yeasts, 185, 195–196,
    413
toxicity, 598
yield, 27, 187–188, 190–195, 209, 373
See also Fortifying brandy, Legal restric-
    tions, and Proof
Ethanolyses, 631
2-Ethoxyhexa-3,5-diene, 207, 267
Ethyl, acetate, 91, 109, 173–174, 219–220,
    289, 424, 573, 597–598, 600–601,
    604
  acid succinate, 425
  benzoate, 634
  butyrate, 109, 600
  caprate, 597, 600, 604, 627
  caproate, 111, 424, 598, 604, 627
  capronate, 629
  caprylate, 424, 598, 627
  carbonate, 207
  2-carboxyfuranoate, 109
  disulfide, 236
  esters, 111
  formate, 598
  heptanoate, 598
  hexanoate, 109
  isobutyrate, 424
  isopropionate, 109
  lactate, 424, 604
  laurate, 109, 291, 590, 598, 600, 604, 627,
    629
  linoleate, 477
  mercaptan, 235–236
  2-methylbutyrate, 109
  3-methylbutyrate, 109
  myristate, 598
  palmitate, 598
  pelargonate, 598
  pentadeconate, 598
  phenethyl acetate, 109
  propionate, 109
  succinate, 223, 425
  valerate, 600
Ethylene oxide, 206
Ethylenediaminetetraacetate. See EDTA
4-Ethylguaiacol, 230
4-Ethylphenol, 230
1-Ethyl-1-propanol. See 3-Pentanol
Eugenol, 230, 634
Europe, 1–2, 118, 121, 452, 510
  berry wines in, 520–523
  statistics on, 3
European centaury, 494–495, 497, 499–
    500, 504–505, 507–508, 510

for sulfate, 235
for vermouth, 493–494, 503, 506, 508–511
for volatile and special natural acidity, 560, 718, 720, 729, 737, 742
French, 5, 8, 234
German, 20
in Italy, 25
materials approved, 370, 729–736
on blue fining, 539
on geographically-named wines, 8, 20, 36, 724–725
on ion exchange, 302, 732–733
on labeling, 327, 723–727
on use of charcoal, 534
on use of herbs, 493–494
on use of tannin, 645
on varietal wines, 723
on vintage dating, 459, 727
permits, 726–727
production, 728–729
records and reports, 739
storage and finishing, 729–738
See also California laws, Food and drug agencies, Internal Revenue Service, Labeling, and Taxation
Lemon, balm, 495, 497, 505, 507
juice, 152, 510
verbena, 497
Lesser Cardamom. *See* Cardamom
Lessivage system, 373
Leucine, 98, 100, 227–228
+ isoleucine, 476–477
Leucoanthocyanin, 85, 102, 106
Leucodelphinidin, 102, 106
Leuconostoc sp., 292–293, 372, 561–563
mesenteroides, 265–266, 292
oenos, 268, 562–563, 569
Levulose. *See* Fructose
Licorice, 506
Light, effect of, 107, 115–116, 120, 295, 322, 538–539
Light, sweet muscat, 149, 718
Lignin, 627, 631, 633
Lime, 285, 341, 344, 644–647
Limonene, 110
Limousin oak, 589
Linaloöl, 109–110
Linden, 498
Linoleic acid, 645
Lipomyces sp., 157
Liqueurs, 584, 593, 634
Lithium, 237
Livermore, 114, 118, 148
Ljutomer, 47
Lodderomyces sp., 157
Lode, 116, 118

Loganberry, 520–521, 661, 720. *See also* Berry wine
Loire, 17–18, 452
Lovibond color, 442, 509, 694, 737
Lumiflavine, 101
Lungmoss, 494, 498–499
Lungwort, 494–495, 498–499, 508
lichen, 495, 498
Luxembourg, 3
Lysine, 97–100, 227–228, 476–477

Maccabeo, 54
Mace. *See* Nutmeg and mace
Macération carbonique, 373, 377
Mâconnais, 6
Madeira, 40–41, 121, 219, 221, 287, 391, 432, 447, 667
in the U.S., 145, 447, 718, 743
Magarach, 48
Magnesium, 19, 112, 117, 200, 222, 237, 545, 547
effect on tartrate precipitation, 545
in fermentation, 526
phytate, 319, 541
removal, 301, 304
Maidenhair fern, 498
Maillard reaction, 533
Malaga, wine, 31, 219, 432
in the U.S., 145, 150, 447, 724
Malathion, 334
Malbec, 9, 57–58, 101
Malic acid and malates, 9, 81, 96, 111, 116, 221, 237, 292, 572
addition, 734, 736, 742
and *Botrytis*, 78, 160
and malo-lactic fermentation, 10, 223, 237, 371, 417, 454, 565–570
carboxy lyase, 566
determination, 679–680
enzyme, 566
fermentation by yeasts, 173, 262
intracellular fermentation of, 373
of wines, 9, 112, 239
oxidation of, 560
pK's of, 222
relative sourness, 222–223
threshold, 222
Malic enzymes, 566
Malmsey, 41
Malo-lactic fermentation, 199, 205–206, 223–224, 291–293, 359, 363, 369, 371, 452, 454, 463, 565–570, 679
and alcoholic fermentation, 270

of distillation, 604, 608, 610–611, 614–
620, 626, 629, 633, 749
Propanal. *See* Propionaldehyde
1-Propanol. *See* n-Propyl alcohol
2-Propanol. *See* Isopropyl alcohol
Propionaldehyde, 424, 599
Propionic acid, 111, 197, 220, 291, 564, 601
iso-Propyl acetate, 109
n-Propyl acetate, 109
  alcohol, 109, 163, 213–215, 592, 597–598
  caprylate, 598
Prosek, 417
Proteins, 97–99, 112, 227–228, 535, 547
  and copper casse, 538–539
  during fermentation, 198–199, 201
  during ripening, 82
  from fining agents, 314
  precipitation, 532, 535–536, 539, 549
  removal, 316, 319, 338, 398, 535, 539
  -tannin, 230, 538, 549
  tests for excess, 535–536
  use for metal removal, 539
Protocathechuic acid, 104–105, 230
Protovac, 735
Provence, 18
Prune. *See* Plum
Pruning, 33, 122
Pteroylglutamic acid, 107, 229
Pulp, 78–79
Pumping over, 364–365, 367, 370, 372,
  393, 400, 416, 434, 445, 504, 558
Pumps and pumping, 295–296, 601
  centrifugal, 296, 308
  cleaning, 337, 363
  gear and rotary, 296
  impeller pump, 297
  lead from, 237
  must, 258, 363
  oxidation from, 289–290
  piston, 296
  vacuum, 296
Punching down, 367
PVPP, 318, 387, 734–735
Pycnometer, 684, 703–704
Pyrethrin, 332, 334, 336
Pyridoxine, 107–108, 199, 229, 304
Pyroglutamic acid, 112
Pyrophosphatase, 201
Pyroracemic acid, 100
Pyrrolidone carboxylic acid, 96
Pyruvate kinase, 189
Pyruvic acid, 188–189, 199, 204, 222
P.X., 404

Quality, 191, 210–211, 232
Quality control, 328
Quassia, 494–495, 498–499, 505, 507–508
Quaternary ammonium compounds, 236,
  339, 341
Quercetin, 100, 102, 104–105, 112, 231
Quercetrin, 112
Quetsch, 634
Quinic acid, 104, 111
Quinine, 494, 510–511
  fungus, 496, 499, 505, 507
Quinoid anhydrobase chromophores, 337
Quinones, 233

99R (rootstock), 121
Raboso Piave, 101
Racemization, 187, 223
Racking, 15, 19, 33, 36, 237, 286, 314, 318,
  370–372, 375, 385, 387, 443, 458,
  463–465, 489
  aeration by, 233–234, 267, 290, 374
  and yeast, 176
  early, 294, 387, 487, 567
  of sherry, 33–34, 393, 398, 406–408
Radiation, ionization, effect of, 295
Raffinose, 572
Rainfall, effect of, 43, 52, 57, 61, 79, 85, 91,
  113, 120–122, 332–333, 382, 434
Raisining and raisins, 26–27, 33, 83, 87,
  113, 118, 121–122, 125, 192, 219,
  433, 444
  brandy, 487, 583, 745
  distilling material, 623
  for wine, 583, 659, 721
  wine from, 526, 583, 623, 721
Rakia, 45
Rancio, 18, 31, 629
Raspberry, 508, 520–521
Ratios, enological, 90
Rats, 335–336
Rayas, 406–407
Rectification, 632, 749
Red Dye No. 2, No. 40, 267
Red Pinot, 150
Red spider, 85
Red Veltliner, 125
Redox-potential. *See* Oxidation-reduction
  potential
Reduced musts, 28, 35, 447

Other AVI Books

A GUIDE TO THE SELECTION, COMBINATION AND
COOKING OF FOODS Volume 1   *Rietz*

ALCOHOL AND THE DIET
Roe

BASIC FOOD MICROBIOLOGY
Banwart

BEVERAGES: CARBONATED AND NONCARBONATED
Woodroof and Phillips

COFFEE TECHNOLOGY
Sivetz and Desrosier

FOOD AND BEVERAGE MYCOLOGY
Beuchat

FOOD COLORIMETRY: THEORY AND APPLICATIONS
Francis and Clydesdale

FOOD MICROBIOLOGY: PUBLIC HEALTH AND
SPOILAGE ASPECTS   *deFigueiredo and Splittstoesser*

FRUIT AND VEGETABLE JUICE PROCESSING TECHNOLOGY
2nd Edition   *Tressler and Joslyn*

FUNDAMENTALS OF FOOD FREEZING
Desrosier and Tressler

MENU PLANNING
2nd Edition   *Eckstein*

MICROBIOLOGY OF FOOD FERMENTATIONS
2nd Edition   *Pederson*

NON-ALCOHOLIC FOOD SERVICE BEVERAGE HANDBOOK
2nd Edition   *Thorner and Herzberg*

RIETZ MASTER FOOD GUIDE
Desrosier

TECHNOLOGY OF FOOD PRESERVATION
4th Edition   *Desrosier and Desrosier*